T0310679

Handbook of Research on the Societal Impact of Digital Media

Barbara Guzzetti
Arizona State University, USA

Mellinee Lesley
Texas Tech University, USA

A volume in the Advances in Media,
Entertainment, and the Arts (AMEA) Book Series

Information Science
REFERENCE
An Imprint of IGI Global

Managing Director:	Lindsay Johnston
Managing Editor:	Keith Greenberg
Director of Intellectual Property & Contracts:	Jan Travers
Acquisitions Editor:	Kayla Wolfe
Production Editor:	Christina Henning
Development Editor:	Erin O'Dea
Typesetter:	Amanda Smith; Kaitlyn Kulp
Cover Design:	Jason Mull

Published in the United States of America by
Information Science Reference (an imprint of IGI Global)
701 E. Chocolate Avenue
Hershey PA, USA 17033
Tel: 717-533-8845
Fax: 717-533-8661
E-mail: cust@igi-global.com
Web site: http://www.igi-global.com

Library of Congress Cataloging-in-Publication Data

Handbook of research on the societal impact of digital media / Barbara Guzzetti and Mellinee Lesley, editors.
     pages cm
  Includes bibliographical references and index.
   ISBN 978-1-4666-8310-5 (hardcover) -- ISBN 978-1-4666-8311-2 (ebook) 1. Information society. 2. Digital media--Social aspects. 3. Information technology--Social aspects. 4. Educational innovations. I. Guzzetti, Barbara J. II. Lesley, Mellinee, 1965-
   HM851.H34836 2016
   302.23'1--dc23
                              2015019888

This book is published in the IGI Global book series Advances in Media, Entertainment, and the Arts (AMEA) (ISSN: Pending; eISSN: pending)

British Cataloguing in Publication Data
A Cataloguing in Publication record for this book is available from the British Library.

All work contributed to this book is new, previously-unpublished material. The views expressed in this book are those of the authors, but not necessarily of the publisher.

For electronic access to this publication, please contact: eresources@igi-global.com.

Advances in Media, Entertainment, and the Arts (AMEA) Book Series

Giuseppe Amoruso
Politecnico di Milano, Italy

ISSN: Pending
EISSN: pending

MISSION

Throughout time, technical and artistic cultures have integrated creative expression and innovation into industrial and craft processes. Art, entertainment and the media have provided means for societal self-expression and for economic and technical growth through creative processes.

The **Advances in Media, Entertainment, and the Arts (AMEA)** book series aims to explore current academic research in the field of artistic and design methodologies, applied arts, music, film, television, and news industries, as well as popular culture. Encompassing titles which focus on the latest research surrounding different design areas, services and strategies for communication and social innovation, cultural heritage, digital and print media, journalism, data visualization, gaming, design representation, television and film, as well as both the fine applied and performing arts, the AMEA book series is ideally suited for researchers, students, cultural theorists, and media professionals.

COVERAGE

- Environmental Design
- Blogging & Journalism
- Popular Culture
- Fine Arts
- Print Media
- Digital Media
- Digital Heritage
- Communication Design
- Sports & Entertainment
- Applied Arts

IGI Global is currently accepting manuscripts for publication within this series. To submit a proposal for a volume in this series, please contact our Acquisition Editors at Acquisitions@igi-global.com or visit: http://www.igi-global.com/publish/.

Titles in this Series

For a list of additional titles in this series, please visit: www.igi-global.com

Handbook of Research on Digital Media and Creative Technologies
Dew Harrison (University of Wolverhampton, UK)
Information Science Reference • copyright 2015 • 554pp • H/C (ISBN: 9781466682054) • US $310.00 (our price)

Handbook of Research on the Impact of Culture and Society on the Entertainment Industry
R. Gulay Ozturk (İstanbul Commerce University, Turkey)
Information Science Reference • copyright 2014 • 737pp • H/C (ISBN: 9781466661905) • US $345.00 (our price)

www.igi-global.com

701 E. Chocolate Ave., Hershey, PA 17033
Order online at www.igi-global.com or call 717-533-8845 x100
To place a standing order for titles released in this series, contact: cust@igi-global.com
Mon-Fri 8:00 am - 5:00 pm (est) or fax 24 hours a day 717-533-8661

Dedication

We dedicate this book to the scholars who contributed to this volume and to all researchers who are engaged in examining the impact of new media on the shared phenomenon of contemporary human life.

List of Contributors

Table of Contents

Section 1
Overview of Digital Media in Society

Section 3
Issues Associated with Digital Media

Detailed Table of Contents

Section 1
Overview of Digital Media in Society

Donna E. Alvermann, University of Georgia, USA
Crystal L. Beach, University of Georgia, USA
George L. Boggs, Florida State University, USA

The purpose of this integrative review of theory and research is to assess the economic impact of digital media in ways that are unreached by instrumental means of measuring economic activity. Specifically, we use three overarching arguments identified from a review of the literature that broadly defines the economic force of digital media content in contemporary society. We contextualize those arguments in terms of current issues in the field and gaps in the research base before concluding with a discussion of the implications of what we learned for education, civic engagement, social practice, and policy.

Patricia Dickenson, National University, USA
Martin T. Hall, Charles Sturt University, Australia
Jennifer Courduff, Azusa Pacific University, USA

The evolution of the web has transformed the way persons communicate and interact with each other, and has reformed institutional operations in various sectors. Examining these changes through the theoretical framework Connectivism, provides a detailed analysis of how the web impacts individuals' context within communities as well as the larger society. This chapter examines the evolution of the web and the characteristics of various iterations of the web. A discussion on the emergence of participatory media and other participatory processes provides insight as to how the web influences personal and professional interactions. Research on how the web has changed cultural contexts as well as systems such as education, governments and businesses is shared and analyzed to identify gaps and provide direction for future research.

Chapter 3

In this chapter I consider contemporary global conditions pointing to what some scholars term "a global risk society" where digital media and Cosmopolitan Critical Literacy offer a counterpoint to human rights, health, climate, and terrorist threats. By examining current research in global youth communication across nation-state boundaries via the Internet, existing research suggests that tapping into digital media literacy and critical media literacy will be crucial for developing an informed and critical citizenry. At present, studies of transnational youth navigating old and new affiliations across national borders are in their infancy. Nevertheless, the existing research holds promise for developing global world citizens who can realize an ethos of cosmopolitan, critical citizenship through the affordances of digital media.

Situated in the context of the role digital technology plays in the lives of young children in today's society, this chapter is comprised of four sections examining children's thinking involving digital spaces. First, a succinct overview of current research will be presented, focusing on emergent themes regarding young children navigating digital spaces and their im/material thinking. Following this is an examination of the issues raised from this research. This section highlights disparate access to technology and children's construction of identity in digital spaces. The next section presents the gaps in current research and the final section of this chapter focuses on implications for literacy practice, policy, and research.

In our digital society, the ability to communicate has irrevocably changed. The purpose of this chapter is to provide a glimpse into the impact of digital media on society, specifically digital communication. This glimpse is framed in terms of four characteristics of digital communication: product/ion, semiotic, public, and transitory. Issues are examined that relate to the democratization and monopolization of communication, who has access, the persistent Spiral of Silence, privacy, cyber bullying, identity theft, the ethereal being captured, as well as education and new literacies. Methodological gaps are noted in the research corpus and suggestions are proposed regarding the need for timeliness, support for a comprehensive span of research paradigms, and representation of a full range of populations. Finally, implications and recommendations are explored for civic engagement, commerce, education, and policy.

Chapter 6
Julie A. Delello, The University of Texas at Tyler, USA
Rochell R. McWhorter, The University of Texas at Tyler, USA

This chapter examines how new visual literacies allow students to create meaning and develop competencies needed for the 21st century. Today's generation is continually exposed to visual and digital media. Through empirical work, this chapter highlights how emerging visual technologies such as big data, infographics, digital badges, electronic portfolios (ePortfolios), visual social media, and augmented reality are facilitating the development of technology-related skills required for students in academics and in the workforce. Each visual technology platform will be examined for their usefulness in promoting engagement, subject-matter knowledge, and collaborative learning outside the traditional classroom approach.

Chapter 7
Jessica R. Olin, Wesley College, USA

Both academic and public libraries have, since the inception of the internet and the world wide web, experienced a seismic level of change when compared to the past. The impacts of such specific issues as social media, open access, and the digital divide, and how they change both the short and long term operations and planning for libraries, are considered here through the lens of recent research on these topics. Some attention is also given to gaps in the current research and recommendations are made for further study. Particular attention is given to ways in which these issues overlap for academic and public libraries.

Chapter 8
George L. Boggs, Florida State University, USA

Digitization by computers, like steam power and internal combustion, is widely recognized as a pervasive, disruptive engine powering new ways of living and affecting all aspects of economic life. Research on its economic impact cannot be entirely disentangled from powerful cultural stories connecting technological, educational, and economic progress. As cracks appear in the narratives of constant progress through technology, science, civilization, and economic prosperity, research on the economic impact of digital media develops nuance. This review of literature examines a wide range of perspectives on the economic impact of digital media as a basis for suggesting areas of further research and implications for education, civic, engagement, and policy.

Chapter 9
Terry Cottrell, University of St. Francis, USA

The proliferation of the use of digital media for learning and instruction continues to be investigated and pondered as the advance of a broad range of technologies eclipses currently available traditional text and face-to-face learning modalities for K-12 and higher education instruction. Digital media's affect on educational processes and delivery, an analysis of existing research reviewing whether digital media is benefitting educational outcomes in instruction and learning, and recommendations for the future are the primary goals of this chapter. Investigation into each of the aforementioned topics separately reveals an intersection that is far from being maturely assessed. The topic of digital media affecting how people learn will elicit further research as education continues to call for an increased focus on high outcomes while also increasing the adoption of digital media resources for the transmission and acquisition of knowledge.

Section 2
New Digital Media Practices and Implications for Education, Society, Politics, and Economics

The purpose of this chapter is to provide an overview of current literature on video game making and modding (modification). The chapter describes key game making tools and educational programs that incorporate game making, to promote student outcomes ranging from media literacy to the development of computational thinking and greater interest in computer science. This is followed by a discussion of empirical literature on game making and modding as fan practices, and an overview of new game making tools and communities that are blurring the lines between educational, professional, and fan-driven game making practices. Lastly, the chapter addresses key issues, directions for future research, and recommendations for policy and practice.

The recent emergence of digital creativity that extends beyond the screen and into the physical world, engendering new forms of creative production, has transformed educational and professional fields. From AT&T's bio-tracking clothing to Lady Gaga's smart-hydraulic "Living Dress," e-textiles infuse fashion with electronics to produce unique and aesthetic effects using new conductive materials, including thread, yarn, paint, and fabrics woven from copper, silver, or other highly conductive fibers. This chapter outlines both the educational and societal implications of these new materials in the field of e-textile creation like consumer-ready e-textile toolkits, high-profile displays of imaginative e-textile creations and an increasing body of Do-It-Yourself (DIY) literature on e-textile design that have emerged in the past decade. It also looks at ways in which e-textiles are transforming new solutions to old and persistent problems of underrepresentation of women and minorities in STEM fields and providing a vehicle in which to rethink teaching and learning in these disciplines.

Chapter 12
Virtual Worlds and Online Videogames for Children and Young People: Promises and Challenges 291
Guy Merchant, Sheffield Hallam University, UK

Online virtual worlds and games provide opportunities for new kinds of interaction, and new forms of play and learning, and they are becoming a common feature in the lives of many children and young people. This chapter explores the issues that this sort of virtual play raises for researchers and educators, and the main themes that have emerged through empirical investigation. I focus on children and young people within the age range covered by compulsory schooling, providing illustrative examples of virtual environments that promote play and learning as a way of underlining some key areas of interest. Drawing on work from a range of theoretical and disciplinary perspectives the chapter emphasises how these environments have much in common with other imagined worlds and suggests that looking at the ways in which the virtual is embedded in everyday contexts for meaning making provides an important direction for future research.

Chapter 13
Digital Storytelling 317
Alan Davis, University of Colorado – Denver, USA
Leslie Foley, Grand Canyon University, USA

Digital storytelling, especially in the form of short personally-narrated stories first pioneered by the Center for Digital Storytelling in Berkeley in 1993, is a practice that has now expanded throughout English speaking countries and Western Europe, and has a smaller but growing presence in the developing world. This review examines the origins of the practice and early dissemination, and its current uses in community-based storytelling, education, and by cultural institutions. Research regarding the impacts and benefits of digital storytelling and relationships between storytelling, cognition and identity, and mediating technologies are examined. Current issues in the field, including issues of voice, ownership, power relationships, and dissemination are considered, along with possible future directions for research and implications for social practice and policy.

Chapter 14
Use of Apps and Devices for Fostering Mobile Learning of Literacy Practices 343
Richard Beach, University of Minnesota, USA
Jill Castek, Portland State University, USA

Given the increased use of apps and mobile devices in the classroom, this chapter reviews research on secondary and college students' uses of educational apps employed with mobile devices in the classroom supporting mobile learning (m-learning). It focuses on research analyses of m-learning activities fostered through ubiquity/authenticity, portability, and personalization/adaptivity of apps and mobile devices fostering collaboration/interactivity, multimodality, and shared productivity. These practices serve to enhance information search and acquisition, reading digital texts, formulating and sharing responses to texts, shared productivity, and language learning. While there is some research documenting how m-learning serves to foster these literacy practices, there remains a need for further research on how effective design of m-learning activities supports literacy learning, as well as how larger economic and policy issues shape or impede effective m-learning.

Chapter 15

This chapter presents the unique case of deviantART.com – a popular social networking and image-sharing platform for artists. The chapter introduces and describes the platform, its history, and some of the features the platform offers. It forwards a brief summation of current research, outlines issues emerging from that research, explores the strength and weaknesses of that research, and discusses some of the many difficulties related to researching the platform and its members. The chapter includes a discussion of "creativity" and the economically centric rhetoric and misconceptions latent in hyped popular discourse surrounding the rise of a "creative economy." A discussion of educational issues from an art education perspective is also included in the chapter, which concludes with a presentation of larger social and policy issues related to deviantART.com.

Chapter 16

This chapter describes how children and youth are using digital media to address inequity in their schools, communities, and in society. The chapter begins with a review of the historical and cultural roots of children making digital media for the social good, and situates the approach in the context of other civic and community-based movements. The next section focuses on the range of ways that children and youth are making digital media, including who is participating, and the social and institutional factors involved. The next sections describe the benefits for the participants and for society, as well as the barriers to broader participation. Two case studies highlight key strategies for engaging marginalized youth in making digital media for the social good, and ways to expand the popularity of this approach. The chapter concludes with suggestions for future research, and the broader implications for education, civic engagement, social practice and policy.

Chapter 17

Appification represents the rapid movement of digital tools and media from a Web-based platform to mobile apps. While appification makes the former Web-based tools and apps more accessible, and improves users' quality of life, it also undermines traditional literacy skills and practices associated with print literacies. After defining appification and presenting examples, the chapter explores how appification impacts literacy in the broader society and critiques how schools, via standards, are adapting to the broader appification. Apps and appification play a significant role in changing globally what is meant by literacy. Yet, in the US, schools and educational policy are not keeping up with the rapid transition. Although schools are increasingly embracing the idea of apps and portable devices like tablets, there is little systematic connection between using the new technologies in schools and improving literacy required to be proficient in the app-o-verse.

Chapter 18

Melanie Kittrell Hundley, Vanderbilt University, USA
Teri Holbrook, Georgia State University, USA

Dennis Baron (1999) writes about the impact of digital technology on literacy practices and thus is a good exemplar for considering how communication technologies are changing the ways in which stories are told. In this chapter, we argue that young adult literature authors and readers are currently in what Baron terms an inventive stage as they devise new ways of producing storied texts. Young adult authors, aware of their readers as avid, exploring, and savvy tech users, experiment with text formats to appeal to readers growing up in a digital "participatory culture" (Jenkins, Purushotma, Weigel, Clinton & Robins, 2009). In a cultural climate where the very notion of what constitutes a book is changing, our chapter responds to Baron's (2009) claim that readers and writers are in the process of "[learning] to trust a new technology and the new and strange sorts of texts that it produces" (p. x).

Chapter 19

Katina Zammit, Western Sydney University, Australia

As people, of all ages, take advantage of the opportunities offered by Web 2.0 to be active participants in the process of knowledge building, they become publishers and producers of knowledge not simply consumers of information. In this chapter I will draw upon Bruns and Humphrey's (2007) concept of produsage and the four capacities of produsers as a frame through which to consider the use of wikis for collaborative writing and the social construction of meaning in an online environment. In presenting an overview of the literature on wikis in educational, work and interest-group (affinity spaces) contexts, the issues and gaps, connections will be made between these two concepts and other complementary ideas. While the chapter focuses, primarily, on wiki usage in educational contexts commentary is also included on wikis in workplace environments and for interest-groups (affinity spaces).

Chapter 20

Gloria E. Jacobs, Portland State University, USA

This chapter contains an examination of the research into texting and instant messaging. Instant messaging and texting are shown to be powerful technologies for maintaining relationships, building identities, and functioning within an information based society. The author raises questions about the implications of these social practices for those individuals who remain on the digital margins. The chapter provides an overview of the research, including a brief history of the technology and a theoretical framing of the terms used to discuss the phenomenon. A discussion of who uses instant messaging and why, and what the research has found regarding the conventions of use associated with instant messaging and texting follows. The chapter ends with a discussion of the current issues in the field, locates gaps in the research, and identifies implications and recommendations for education, civic engagement, social practice, and policy.

Section 3
Issues Associated with Digital Media

Chapter 21

Deirdre M. Kelly, University of British Columbia, Canada
Chrissie Arnold, University of British Columbia, Canada

The chapter considers cyberbullying in relation to Internet safety, concentrating on recent, high quality empirical studies. The review discusses conventional debates over how to define cyberbullying, arguing to limit the term to repeated, electronically-mediated incidents involving intention to harm and a power imbalance between bully and victim. It also takes note of the critical perspective that cyberbullying—through its generic and individualistic framing—deflects attention from the racism, sexism, ableism, and heterosexism that can motivate or exacerbate the problem of such bullying. The review concludes that: (a) cyberbullying, rigorously defined, is a phenomenon that is less pervasive and dire than widely believed; and (b) cyber-aggression and online harassment are more prevalent, yet understudied. Fueled by various societal inequalities, these latter forms of online abuse require urgent public attention. The chapter's recommendations are informed by a view of young people as apprentice citizens, who learn democratic participation by practicing it.

Chapter 22

Eliane Rubinstein-Avila, University of Arizona, USA
Aurora Sartori, University of Arizona, USA

This chapter explores access to, and engagement with, digital media by United States' (U.S.) by nonmainstream populations. Framing the issue from a sociotechnical standpoint, the authors explore how engagement with digital media is shaped by socioeconomic status (taking into account confounding factors, such as race and ethnicity, and social and geographical ecologies). The authors highlight studies that focus on the robust digital practices with which nonmainstream populations already engage, and to which they contribute. One example is how some black Twitter users engage in signifyin'–a culturally specific linguistic practice—as a means of performing racial identity online. The authors also problematize concepts such as the new digital divide and digital exclusion, and finally, reiterate that a universal roll-out of high speed broadband alone will not necessarily lead to further engagement with digital media for ALL populations. In fact, the authors claim that providing more or faster access is likely not enough to prevent the entrenchment of a global digital underclass.

Chapter 23

Judith M. Dunkerly-Bean, Old Dominion University, USA
Helen Crompton, Old Dominion University, USA

In this chapter the authors review the fairly recent advances in combating illiteracy around the globe through the use of e-readers and mobile phones most recently in the Worldreader program and the United Nations Educational Scientific and Cultural Organization (UNESCO) mobile phone reading initiatives. Situated in human rights and utilizing the lens of transnational feminist discourse which addresses globalization and the hegemonic, monolithic portrayals of "third world" women as passive and in need of the global North's intervention, the authors explore the ways in which the use of digital media provides increased access to books, and other texts and applications in both English and native languages for people in developing countries. However, while advances in combating illiteracy through the use of e-readers, mobile phones and other mobile learning initiatives are promising, the tensions and power imbalances of digital literacies, which resources are available by whom, for whom and why, must also be examined.

Chapter 24

In light of many recent Internet-led revolutions, the Internet and its tools of social media have been heralded as instrumental in facilitating the uprisings. This chapter provides a close examination of the social media role in grass roots political and social change movements. The chapter discusses the ways activists have used social media tools for organizing and generating awareness of political mobilization and the characteristics of social networking that can be harnessed in a particular cultural and historical context to achieve collective political actions. The chapter also discusses long-established theories of communication to explain how social networking tools became appealing to the activists in these Internet-led movements. The chapter will look at various Internet-led political movements around the globe to demonstrate the enormous potential of social networking tools to facilitate and expedite political mobilization.

Chapter 25

Using Performance Theory as an explanatory basis, this essay explicates the performance of gender in social media beginning with the gendered history of digital technologies and an articulation of the social media venues' unique affordances for gender performance. Then, the chapter reviews the scientific research examining gendered online behavior in social media noting opportunities for enacting traditional sex role stereotypes and thus socializing others to do so as well as opportunities to enact equality and thus disseminating calls for liberation and increased equality between the sexes in all aspects of social life. Facebook, blogs, and online games are examined in detail as exemplars of specific social media cites of gender performance.

Foreword

This handbook engages with a wide range of disciplines, with a focus on the very different ways in which digital media have impacted on far reaching societal changes. It has a particular focus on social justice, education and the concerns of children and young people. The editors have assembled a broad range of authors, who write from very different epistemological and ontological standpoints, yet the handbook is able to weave together these perspectives to create a much broader perspective on the impact of digital media on everyday life. Collectively, the chapters provide situated perspectives on subjects such as alternative art websites, children as digital meaning makers, mobile learning, visual literacies, children's meaning making across material and (im)material worlds, video game making, texting, digital storytelling, e-textiles, Apps, Wikis and video games, set in the context of a changing communicational landscape, the shaping by late capitalism of the way that the digital is positioned and constructed, cyberbullying, pressing issues of privacy and intellectual freedom, gender, activism and deep divides across the planet in relation to access to resources and power.

Within the chapters, fault lines across different spaces and places are profiled, for example, between the world of 'high art' and the 'vernacular' in the chapter describing 'Dangerously Deviant' art, or between 'developed' and 'developing' nations in the chapter on 'Exploring the Digital Divide'. These fault lines also can be located within epistemological standpoints, as authors probe the various ways in which digital and social media tools have both emancipated, and also been tools of oppression for young people in particular. This account of the digital divide is nuanced, and authors in this handbook recognize that research has not yet adequately looked at everyday digital practices in low income/ethnic minority communities. Changing knowledge practices have also necessitated changing methodological approaches, as the democratization of knowledge enabled by digital media has made research into these forms more collaborative, participatory and co-constructed. The field has become both more complex and more transparent. By raising these debates the editors have done the field a service in enabling wider understandings of the social impact of digital media to be articulated in one volume.

In my own work I have also explored young people's meaning making practices across and between the landscape of the digital, but also, more specifically, within the everyday (Pahl 2014). I have also explored how young people's text-making can offer glimpses of their vision of the future (Pahl 2012). More recently, I have linked this work to an epistemology of 'radical hope', drawing on the work of Levitas (2013), Facer (2011) and Pink (2012) in thinking through how futures research can sensitize us to ways of knowing that de-stabilize established understandings of what is possible within digital cultural spaces. I would like to draw on this field because I think it has much to say about the topic of this handbook. I am particularly interested in visions of hope and utopia, as a methodology (Levitas 2013). Through this lens, I explore what these visions of better imagined futures have to offer scholarship within digital media.

One of my key arguments here is that hope resides in the everyday. Through ordinary interactions and shifts in practice, small changes can begin. The everyday is a field of practice that continues to remain under-explored within literacy and digital media research. As a space of practice and though moments of sensuous enchantment (Bennett 2010) the everyday both de-centers conventional ways of knowing and thinking but is also a site for radical hope. Here, I explore the methodological consequences of this way of thinking. I then tie these ideas back in with the writing presented in this volume, so that their work can be read in a context of a scholarship that is lively, hopeful and always on the move, much as the young people are as they traverse digital worlds in new configurations, settings and ways of being.

Thinking about futures is itself a field that has become more mainstream in contemporary sociology (Levitas 2013, Facer 2011). Here I also draw on the philosophy of continental philosopher Ernst Bloch, most particularly in his three volume treatise 'The Principle of Hope'. (1995 [1959]). These thinkers have offered the concept of radical hope – a moment when the present can be a site to radically re-imagine the future, as a site of immanent possibility and radical action. As Facer (2016, in preparation) articulates, radical novelty offers a way of acknowledging that our visions of the future might be more than we think they are. She argues for a 'pedagogy of the present' which focuses on the present as a space to play with futures and open up potential. Here, I engage with some of the key ideas emerging from this handbook, with this lens in mind.

Futures' thinking, as a field, has been linked to the world of digital media, initially providing a language of how digital technologies are futures orientated. The refrain from initial adopters of ICT's was a discourse of, 'this is going to change how things are' which was very much bound up with a technological determinism. Harnessed to these views was the work of Lankshear and Knobel (2006) and others who offered a compelling vision of new literacies that engaged with a trope of the 'wise child', able to navigate online spaces more successfully than the helpless, de-skilled adult. However, more recently, Selwyn (2011) and Facer (2011) have warned that the digital does not always mean better. Their version of futures thinking is not only an exercise in thinking differently, it is a practical way of looking at the everyday through an alternative lens, and seeing within the 'now' the immanent forms of possibility contained within everyday structures. Much of what emerges in the everyday is unexpected and contains immanent possibility within it. This could be conceptualized as the 'not yet' from the work of Ernst Bloch (Daniel and Moylan 1997). Meaning making by children and young people falls into this category of the 'not yet' as new ways of doing things emerge almost continually, and especially within digital media. For example, new and emerging communicational media are almost continually being found and written about, and the list of digital forms grows longer, as this volume attests. These immanent forms are themselves important sites of possibility and hope.

Many of these chapters articulate a steady march of diversification of new technologies, further spreading into everyday life, schooling and civic engagement arenas. The authors trace, carefully and hopefully, ways in which children and young people engage with new media in diverse ways. For example in 'New and Strange Sort of Texts' the authors trace a path from the early adoption of hypertext to seeing hypertext as transformational technology to a more rhizomic and unboundaried account of how young adult readers have engaged with texts in non-linear and complex ways. These kinds of blurring and multi authoring practices are described in many chapters. For example, Di Cesare, Harwood and Rowsell in their chapter on 'Mapping children's im/material thinking in a digital world' describe how digital spaces contain immanent affordances for play, experimentation and emergent practices that enable new identity formations to surface, as avatars become tools of 'as if' possible worlds. Reclaiming digital spaces is a powerful way in which digital media can be harnessed to the social good, as Denner and Martinez explore in their chapter on 'Children and Youth Making Digital Media for the Social Good'. The potential for digital media in fostering civic engagement and local as well as global activism is articulated with a series of examples where by young people have engaged with 'DIY media' to re-configure what is possible within digital spaces. These moments of change are enabled through increased access to programming skills and participatory media that offers youth a platform for their voices to be heard equitably and across global and local spaces.

In these chapters, it is clear that an account of digital media that is congruent with existing cultural concerns and strengths of young people is essential. What this therefore necessitates is a kind of nuanced attentiveness to the present moment, recognizing that a rhetoric of the deterministic march of technology is something that can be easily disrupted by the 'darkness of the lived moment' (Bloch 1995). Selwyn (2011) guards against a sense of false hope when thinking about the potential of digital media to iron out inequalities of the present. This handbook likewise traverses a wide ground and is not afraid to confront the darker and more complex digital worlds of everyday life. For example, in the chapter on cyberbullying and internet safety, the process of mapping this terrain alerts us to the entwined nature of on-line and offline identities, but also alerts the reader to a nuanced understandings of how digital media can amplify existing vulnerabilities. Recent concerns about Twitter trolls and the clear campaigning of the Everyday Sexism website (http://everydaysexism.com/) have alerted researchers to the way in which digital platforms can act as coercive and sometimes extremely harmful sites of harassment and bullying. The interface with the law is also explored in the chapter on the Leveson inquiry which provides a useful perspective on the ethics of press regulation. These very public debates draw on present concerns about whose voice counts, where and how, and draws us into a wider framework of regulation that is both protective, and in some cases, could also be restrictive.

What this necessitates is a vision that recognizes the fault lines across the many worlds that digital technologies evoke. Many of the chapters describe the ability of digital technologies, or ICT's to open up new opportunities for civic engagement. Twitter in particular has been valorized in its role in the Occupy movement and protests across the world. At the same time, concerns about trolling and extreme sexism on Twitter continue to be strongly voiced within the media. However, the potential for everyday creativity, engaged and cosmopolitan engages of ideas across local and global spaces, and experimentation and vernacular creativity is also a feature of digital media as articulated so eloquently in this handbook. The handbook celebrates sites of possibility (Hill and Vasudevan 2008) where children and young people are engaging in processes of re-making and re-visioning their worlds through creatively engaging with digital spaces. Sliding between and within these spaces are ordinary citizens living their everyday lives in particular trajectories and settings. These lives are subject to the materiality of the digital – mobile phones fall and shatter, people spill tea on lap tops, run out of money for mobile phone contracts, and are living in and between instructions of how to do things, meanwhile, eating, sleeping and learning. Digital stuff pervades these worlds, but also is apprehended in more complex ways than can be initially understood by the research community. Unless studies are embedded and truly ethnographic, we can only apprehend at second hand some of these experiences young people are having, particularly within communities not immediately accessible to the research community of the university.

In the field of education, the New London Group (1996) articulated a new pedagogical vision, focused on situated practice, overt instruction, critical framing and transformed practice. This offered a vision for literacy education that incorporated critical literacies pedagogy together with a multimodal framework that considered design as part of the process. As a modernist vision of progress, it was widely cited, and for many years after, this was the touchstone of a pedagogical moment whereby young people were urged to create and reflect critically on texts. However, as this handbook shows, meaning making through digital media is both more complex, more wide, more deep and more dangerous than these visions allowed. Young people are engaging in complex and risky work through and within digital spaces, and this is precipitating a re-thinking of what it means to make texts and engage with them online. At the same time, slowly, scholarship in the field of the post human and the new materialism has encroached on settled conceptualizations of what 'the digital' might mean. Work by Bennett (2010) has challenged the way in which settled understandings of the relationships between matter and the body have emerged. Instead, a dialogic relationship between the making of texts, together with an appreciation of the importance of the body in space has led to new forms of understanding of how digital forms are apprehended based on concepts of emergence and entanglement (Ingold 2011).

Leander and Boldt (2013) have articulated a new understanding of how young people engage bodily with digital stuff. Rather than apprehension being linear, purposeful and directed, they recognize everyday engagement with the digital as being entangled, with youth moving across material and immaterial worlds with ease, thereby providing a challenge for researchers who then have to come to terms with these blurred realities. Researchers instead have to move beyond the boundaries of the social, the material and the immaterial, and recognize the constant oscillation that takes place between these different worlds in everyday life. The present becomes the urgent space of practice where research needs to concentrate itself more powerfully. Tracing the flows of power and mapping the geometrics across the spaces of home, school and public places becomes a new and exciting task in the field of digital research.

The consequence of this new recognition of the processes of coming to know what it is like to live within and around digital stuff is that methodological tools need to be more complex and more nuanced. The potential for big data tools, and existing affordances such as Twitter to harvest data, for example, on the riots in the UK, has been described by researchers such as Farida Vis (Procter, Vis and Voss 2013). However at the same time, the lived experience of new technologies still needs teasing out with small and disturbing moments in classrooms, homes and communities recorded in interaction with more spatial mapping technologies. Equally, sensory ethnographies of the digital might include feelings, emotion, touch and smell in new ways (Pink 2009).

The role of the imagination in constructing better possible futures and spaces of hope and possibility is critical in the process of re-visioning digital technologies. While the present is a key site for research, many of the chapters in this handbook point to the role of the digital in both education and civic engagement. The digital as a site for democratic engagement and as a place where culture can create alternative spaces of practice, through art and imaginative engagement with model forms, is critical here. This new space of radical openness requires new tools of engagement. Within the handbook many of these are mentioned, for example relational cosmopolitanism, interdisciplinary, participatory and dialogic spaces of enquiry. Co-production is a way of acknowledging the contested and distributed nature of knowledge (Pahl and Pool 2015). The practice of 'not knowing' might become as important as the practice of 'knowing' (Vasudevan 2011). In many of the chapters, beginnings of things were accidental or part of wider activist agendas. This requires a conceptual framework that is distributed, and understands communicative practices to be a meshwork drawn from a complex of multimodal semiotic resources. Acknowledging the deep complexity of everyday life sometimes means that methodologies derived from one mode only, such as interviews, are inadequate for apprehending what is going on here. As Law (2004) said, methods and even more methods' practices, construct the reality they purport to investigate.

Investigations also do not need to be made by those who define themselves as researchers. The knowledge that is building up of the ways in which digital stuff is used within communities is broken down in terms of who accesses knowledge and who can understand and grasp the significance of these new ways of knowing. The role of schooling has therefore come into question, from early critiques by Lankshear and Knobel (2006), to more recent critiques by Facer (2011) of the ways in which schools adopt conservative models of possibility in relation to new technologies. However, sites of possibility have opened up, through movements to create critical literacies in classrooms and out of school spaces across the globe (Morrell 2008, Stornaiuolo 2015). This then opens up a new question, which is what is the role of schools when children are learning in very different ways in out of school sites? The concept of learning needs to be allowed to be permeable, and 'third spaces' of blended learning in and out of classroom spaces can be opened up (Davies and Pahl 2007). This creates a layered engagement with digital stuff, with complex lines of engagement traced across diffuse spaces. Researching digital daily life might involve recording a tapestry of these engagements, over time and space.

Within and beyond these spaces lies a challenge to consider the role of the imagination in realizing new digital spaces of possibility. This process requires 'pluralistic tools' that can grasp the ways of knowing and practices that are slippery evasive and not linked to dominant paradigms of literacy and language within schooling. The range and multiplicity of approaches in this handbook attests to this complex task. Issues of voice, agency and power begin to press upon the utopian visions of the internet as a space for everyone. The boundaries where things happen continue to move, so that the panoptic visions of policymakers continue to be eluded by the muddled logic of everyday practices and the slippage outside the observed world where things happen unobserved and out of site. What is known continues to resist a naming that is settled and historically agreed. The process of producing space then becomes further contested (Leander and Sheehy 2004). Space that the imagination seeks to change is emergent, contingent on everyday life. As stuff comes from stuff, we cannot predict these uncertain, messy moments of transformation. This site of uncertainty is radically different in feeling from the settled accounts of the march of technological innovation. In this handbook it is possible to glimpse the unstable present within a diverse and compelling collection of ideas and articulations of the interrelationship between the digital and the social.

Kate Pahl
University of Sheffied, UK

REFERENCES

Bennett, J. (2010). *Vibrant matter*. Duke University Press.

Bloch, E. (1995). *The principle of hope* (Vol. 1). Cambridge, MA: MIT Press. (Original work published 1959)

Daniel, J. O., & Moylan, T. (Eds.). (1997). *Not yet: Reconsidering Ernst Bloch*. London: Verso.

Davies, J., & Pahl, K. (2007). Blending voices, blending learning: Lessons in pedagogy from a post-16 classroom. In E. Bearne & J. Marsh (Eds.), *Closing the gap: Literacy and social inclusion*. Stoke on Trent, UK: Trentham Press Ltd.

Facer, K. (2011). *Learning futures: Technology, education and social change*. London: Routledge.

Facer, K. (2016). Using the future in education: Creating space for openness, hope and novelty. In Leeds & Noddings (Eds.), Palgrave international handbook of alternative education. Palgrave Macmillan.

Hill, M. L., & Vasudevan, L. (Eds.). (2008). *Media, learning and sites of possibility*. New York: Teachers College Press.

Ingold, T. (2011). *Being alive: Essays on movement, knowledge and description*. London: Routledge.

Lankshear, C., & Knobel, M. (2006). *New literacies: Everyday practices and class-room learning* (2nd ed.). Maidenhead, UK: McGraw Hill/Open University Press.

Law, J. (2004). *After method: Mess in social science research*. London: Taylor and Francis.

Leander, K., & Boldt, G. (2013). Rereading "a pedagogy of multiliteracies": Bodies, texts and emergence. *Journal of Literacy Research*, *45*(1), 22–46. doi:10.1177/1086296X12468587

Leander, K., & Sheehy, M. (Eds.). (2004). *Spatializing literacy research and practice*. New York: Berg.

Levitas, R. (2013). *Utopia as method: The imaginary reconstitution of society*. Basingstoke, UK: Palgrave MacMillan. doi:10.1057/9781137314253

Morrell, E. (2008). *Critical literacy and urban youth: Pedagogies of access, dissent and liberation*. London: Routledge.

Pahl, K. (2012). Time and space as a resource for meaning-making by children and young people in home and community settings. *Global Studies of Childhood*, *2*(3), 201–216. doi:10.2304/gsch.2012.2.3.201

Pahl, K. (2014). *Materializing literacies in communities: The uses of literacy revisited*. London: Bloomsbury.

Pahl, K., & Pool, S. (2015). The role of art in the age of mechanical co-production. In D. O'Brien & P. Mathews (Eds.), *After urban regeneration*. Bristol, MA: Policy Press.

Pink, S. (2009). *Doing sensory ethnography*. London: Sage.

Pink, S. (2012). *Situating everyday life*. London: Sage.

Procter, R., Vis, F., & Voss, A. (2013). Reading the riots on Twitter: Methodological innovation for the analysis of big data. *International Journal of Social Research Methodology*, *16*(3), 197–214. doi:10.1080/13645579.2013.774172

Selwyn, N. (2011). *Education and technology: Key issues and debates*. London: Continuum.

Stornaiuolo, A. (2015). The arts of worldmaking: Multimodality, creativity and cosmopolitanism. In J. Rowsell & K. Pahl (Eds.), *The Routledge handbook of literacy studies*. London: Routledge.

The New London Group. (1996). A pedagogy of multiliteracies: Designing social futures. *Harvard Educational Review*, *66*(1).

Vasudevan, L. (2011). An invitation to unknowing. *Teachers College Record*, *113*(6), 1154–1174.

Preface

CRAFTING REFLECTIONS ON THE PAST, PRESENT, AND FUTURE OF DIGITAL MEDIA

Impetus for the Text: Looking Back and Moving Forward

With the advent of Web 2.0 technologies launched in the mid-90s, a century later isn't it about time to reflect on how digital media has, is, and will be influencing daily life? In considering this possibility, we asked ourselves - how have digital media impacted education and advanced social and civic engagement in a global society? This became the guiding question that we as editors asked ourselves as we conceived this book and selected the authors of its 26 chapters who could best address the question. We believed that due to the rapidly evolving, nuanced, and often unpredictable nature of digital media, it was time to assess the impact of digital media on society from a variety of perspectives.

Our reasons for attempting to provide answers to our question were both professional and personal ones. On a personal level, we both have been amazed by and entrenched in the flurry of new digital media that has changed how we communicate with our friends, colleagues, and family; how we engage in social and political life; and even how we go about our recreational pursuits of reading and watching television or movies! It seems digital media has been seeping into every aspect of our lives from the clothing and accessories that we wear, like handbags with cell-phone pockets that accommodate "being wired" to the Apps on Smartphones that allow us to perform daily functions, like track our calories, find the cheapest gas price, evaluate the safety of products, check in for a flight, exercise, and stay constantly in touch with one another.

On a professional level, digital media has changed how we each teach our classes; how we conduct our research; and what topics we take up in our lines of inquiry. For example, Mellinee has investigated how the National Aeronautics and Space Administration (NASA) uses Twitter to educate the lay public about science (Lesley, 2014). Barbara has examined how middle-school and high-school teachers can use interactive sites in the virtual world of Second Life for teaching their disciplines (Guzzetti & Stockrocki, 2013). As members of the Baby Boomer generation, these are research topics that we never would have fathomed as we began our careers as literacy researchers and academicians in higher education. We are reminded that we both are "digital migrants" (Prensky, 2001) who did not grow up with digital media, but who as adults have embraced it and benefited from it in both our personal and professional lives.

Content of the Chapters: Providing Directions and Perspectives

This attention to generation became an important consideration in designing this edited text and in selecting its authors. Today's young people are commonly referred to as "millennials" and "digital natives" (Prensky, 2001) having grown up with digital media. Youth spend nearly eight hours a day interacting with these media (Rideout, Foehr & Robbins, 2010). They are more likely to be "produsers" (Bruns, 2007) or those who are both users and producers of digital media than their parents or grandparents. Certainly, they will have the most influence on the future of new digital media as they will be designing the new technologies that we cannot even begin to imagine now.

Therefore, several chapters in this book focus on youth and digital media and the resulting implications for education and society - both now and in the future. For example, through case studies, Jill Denner and Jacob Martinez describe how children and youth make digital media to address inequities in their schools, communities, and societies; how they go about doing so; and the benefits to them and to society, as well as the barriers they face in their endeavors. Denner and Martinez argue media production is not neutral and suggest ways digital media can be used by youth as a platform for social justice. Richard Beach and Jill Castek examine how Apps and mobile devices are used by high school and college students for learning in formal and informal settings and the larger policy issues that impact mobile or m-learning. Beach and Castek note much more research is needed to address the usefulness of m-learning applications for various purposes and populations of users (e.g., individuals with special needs). Terry Cottrell focuses on digital multimedia for learning in higher education settings and the extension of this learning to broader society and work contexts. In his chapter, Cottrell questions whether digital media benefits educational outcomes. Dane Marco Di Cesare, Debra Harwood, and Jennifer Rowsell describe how children's thinking through/with digital worlds is impacting how they learn and approach the learning environment. They describe the changing nature of texts and how they are stored and accessed with the advent of new digital media. Di Cesare, Harwood and Rowsell also examine the ways children construct identities in digital spaces. Contributing to this theme, David O'Brien and Megan McDonald Vandeventer discuss the nature of digital texts and the "Applification" of textbooks. They also examine the "affordances" of apps and consider the implications of the prevalence of apps in educational settings and broader society. Melanie Hundley and Teri Holbrook examine digital and multimedia texts and how these hybrid texts have changed the ways in which youth and adults read books and young adult novels in a more active and interactive way due to digital media. Hundley and Holbrook also posit that such texts point to a new kind of reader who visibly participates in the process of constructing meaning with a text thus blurring the lines between author and reader. Jessica Olin describes the impact of digital media on university and public libraries and how information is archived and obtained. Olin discusses issues surrounding the use of social media and open access in library settings and how such phenomenon changes the short and long term operations and planning of libraries.

Additional chapters focus on the creation, production, and consumption of new kinds of texts. Katina Zammit examines how wikis have fostered collective and cooperative writing and changed how texts are co-constructed in ways that support the 21st century skill of collaboration. Zammit also examines wikis from the standpoint of knowledge management. Alan Davis and Leslie Foley undertake a discussion of digital storytelling or telling personal narratives through digital images, sound, and words. They examine the ways digital media shapes, voice, power relations, ownership and dissemination in storytelling. Julie Delello and Rachel McWhorter highlight how emerging visual technologies, including big data, infographics, digital badges, electronic portfolios (ePortfolios), visual social media, and augmented reality are facilitating the development of technology-related skills required for academics and the workforce. Delello and McWhorter examine the ways in which visual platforms promote engagement, subject-matter knowledge, and collaborative learning.

Providing a broader historical picture, Patricia Dickenson, Martin Hall, and Jennifer Courduff trace the evolution of Web 2.0 technologies. Their chapter examines the development of the Web and its various iterations while discussing how the emergence of participatory media influences personal and professional interactions, as well as education, governments, and businesses. Other chapter authors take up specific participatory digital media of Web 2.0, highlighting the new 21st century skills and abilities they foster. This section includes chapters on how digital media has changed the ways in which people live and communicate, including a chapter by Guy Merchant describing how individuals create alternative lives within virtual worlds. Merchant also examines the extent to which the virtual is embedded in everyday activities. Similarly, Gloria Jacobs examines texting and Instant Messaging and explores the implications of such synchronous forms of communication for marginalized individuals. Elizabeth Hayes Gee and Kelly Tran explain how creating and modding video games fosters 21st century design thinking. Gee and Tran offer an overview of new game making tools and describe ways game making blurs the lines between educational, professional, and fan-driven goals.

Brian Jones' chapter illustrates how art is created, shared, and critiqued in online spaces. Jones includes a discussion of the construct of "creativity" and the economically centric rhetoric and misconceptions latent in popular discourse surrounding the rise of a "creative economy." Expanding on the notion of digital media for creativity, Kylie Peppler provides insights into digital design through e-textiles and wearable technologies. Her discussion extends to how avocations like crafting incorporate digital media to facilitate their production. Co-authors Elizabeth Baker, Arwa Alfayez, Christy Dalton, Renee Smith McInnish, Rebecca Schwerdtfeger, and Mojtaba Khajeloo discuss digital communication through social media, such as YouTube, Twitter and Wikipedia and describe the indications that the democratization of communication is in peril. As part of this discussion, they examine the monopolization of communication and a "persistent spiral of silence."

Other chapter authors focus on the germane issues that surround the take up of these digital media. Lynn Webb and Nicholas Temple describe gender equality and gender stereotyping in online spaces and call for liberation and increased equality between the sexes. In particular, they look at social media as sites for enacting gender equity. Deirdre Kelly and Chrissy Arnold describe instances of cyberbullying and how Internet safety is still a concern for many, suggesting important guidelines for interventions. Kelly and Arnold argue for rigorous definitions of cyberbulling and a greater understanding of online harassment. They also caution that youth experience online digital spaces as apprentice citizens and form views about democratic participation in these sites. Eliane Rubinstein Avila and Aurora Sartori draw attention to how nonmainstream populations access and engage with digital media and trouble notions of "the digital divide." In particular, Rubinstein Avila and Sartori examine ways individuals perform racial identity online. In her chapter, Shelfai Virkar raises questions about the distributive impact of digital technologies and the social and political dynamics of digital technologies as tools for furthering global economic, social, and political development. Virkar asks, "Is the promise of ICT's illusory?" and examines the gap between great optimism and reality of digital media in international contexts. Thomas Bean cites the need for a critical literacy approach to digital media, arguing that a global risk society overlaps with a need to develop an astute global citizenry able to collaborate and solve social problems, including war, climate change, racism, sexism, and identity theft. Further, Bean notes such transnationalism collapses geopolitical boundaries and necessitates the infusion of cosmopolitanism with globalization.

Another set of authors address wider social economic and political issues surrounding digital media in a global society. Donna Alvermann, Crystal Beach, and George Boggs characterize digital media and discuss how these media disrupt traditional meaning making and identify the economic force of digital media content in contemporary society. Alvermann, Beach and Boggs also note the inequalities in economic opportunities in digital media "space." George Boggs discusses how digital media affects the economy in a global society. He also discusses the significant changes to ways humans provide for their needs through digital media. Amir Manzoor describes social media for promoting grassroots political movements and social change on an international level. Manzoor's chapter looks at the enormous potential of social networking tools to facilitate political mobilization. Judith Dunkerly and Helen Crompton identify the role of digital media in promoting global citizenship and human rights for women and girls. Through a lens of transmational feminist discourse, Dunkerly and Crompton examine advances in combatting illiteracy through mobile learning.

Focal Areas: Offering Insights into Digital Media, Issues, and Contextualization

These diverse topics that touch on digital media reflect three main areas of focus. The first focal area these authors explore is examining digital media that allow for content creation and interaction with Web 2.0 technologies. These chapters focus on such topics as creating video games; residing in virtual worlds; and creating, sharing, and reviewing art in online spaces. The second area authors explore encompasses the issues that surround these new digital media, particularly in terms of access and use. These chapters address how gender and diversity impact access to and use of digital media. The final area that these chapters reflect is how digital media have evolved and are situated within a larger society and a global economy. These chapters explore the economic significance of digital media in a global society and the political and social conditions that impact their adoption.

Structure and Format: Fostering Accessibility and Readability

Despite the diversity in this broad range of topics surrounding digital media that that reflect these focal areas, each chapter of this text follows the same format and structure. Following the Abstracts, each chapter begins with an introductory overview of the topic. The bulk of the chapter then follows with a succinct summary of the current and relevant research on the topic. Chapter authors also identify related issues raised by their reviews of the research on their topics. In doing so, these scholars identify gaps in the extant research and provide directions for future inquiries. Each chapter concludes with implications for education, policy, and civic and social engagement. Some of the chapters also include a list of additional readings to provide further information about topics presented in the chapters.

Several format features were designed to make these chapters and their structures readily accessible and comprehensible. Key terms or jargon are defined within the context in which they are used, as well as in a brief glossary following each chapter. Search terms are provided proceeding each chapter to make the chapter topics readily apparent to readers. Biographies of the chapter authors, including their institutional affiliations, are included to document their expertise and to provide readers with a glimpse into these scholars' backgrounds and perspectives on their topics.

Intentions and Acknowledgements: Continuing the Dialogue

It is our hope that readers of this volume will continue to explore these topics – perhaps by contacting these authors - to carry on the discussion of the impact of digital media on a global society; to solicit advice or direction for future inquires; or to satisfy personal curiosities. These scholars who have contributed to this book deserve our acknowledgement and recognition for a thorough yet succinct presentation of pressing topics, issues, and perspectives on the impact of digital media on myriad aspects of daily life. We also wish to thank our editorial board members who contributed their expertise to help these scholars refine their chapters by checking for currency of citations and references, breadth and depth of content, and readability of their writing style and format.

We anticipate that the readers of this volume will have their own perspectives and expertise they bring with them to reading this text. We would welcome any comments and questions from readers. Our hope is to both advance and continue the dialogue we have begun here; we have included our email addresses below to facilitate that interaction. We hope you will find this volume useful as a resource and reference guide to exploring both new and familiar topics surrounding the impact of digital media on a changing and global society. In particular, we hope this volume helps to illuminate not only the present status of digital media in modern life (e.g., education, politics, civic engagement, social practices), but also compels readers to consider the possibilities digital media hold for mobilizing greater equity in the world. We hope this book serves you well in traversing our digital world.

Barbara Guzzetti
Arizona State University, USA

Mellinee Lesley
Texas Tech University, USA
March 2015

REFERENCES

Bruns, A. (2007). Produsage: Towards a broader framework for user led content creation. In *Creativity & Cognition: Proceedings of the Sixth ACM SIGCHI Conference on Creativity & Cognition*. Washington, DC: ACM.

Guzzetti, B. J., & Stokrocki, M. (2013). Reflections on teaching and learning in virtual worlds. *E-Learning and Digital Media*, *10*(3), 243–260. doi:10.2304/elea.2013.10.3.242

Lesley, M. (2014). "Spacecraft reveals recent geological activity on the moon": Exploring the features of NASA Twitter posts and their potential to engage adolescents. *Journal of Adolescent & Adult Literacy*, *57*(5), 377–385. doi:10.1002/jaal.258

Prensky, M. (2001). Digital natives, digital immigrants. *On the Horizon*, *9*(5), 1–6. doi:10.1108/10748120110424816

Rideout, V. J., Foehr, U. G., & Roberts, D. F. (2012). *Generation M2: Media in the lives of 18 year olds*. Menlo Park, CA: The Kaiser Family Foundation.

Section 1
Overview of Digital Media in Society

Chapter 1
What Does Digital Media Allow Us to "Do" to One Another?
Economic Significance of Content and Connection

Donna E. Alvermann
University of Georgia, USA

Crystal L. Beach
University of Georgia, USA

George L. Boggs
Florida State University, USA

ABSTRACT

The purpose of this integrative review of theory and research is to assess the economic impact of digital media in ways that are unreached by instrumental means of measuring economic activity. Specifically, we use three overarching arguments identified from a review of the literature that broadly defines the economic force of digital media content in contemporary society. We contextualize those arguments in terms of current issues in the field and gaps in the research base before concluding with a discussion of the implications of what we learned for education, civic engagement, social practice, and policy.

INTRODUCTION

The purpose of this chapter is to interpret the economic significance of digital media through three general arguments about digital communication in contemporary society. Understanding linkages between digital media and social networks enables a view of economic significance driven by digital media's potential to shape human life. In the rapidly shifting digital world, moving beyond explicitly financial or monetary measures of economic activity shifts emphasis away from reactive analysis of completed sales toward proactive understanding of change and exchange as a core feature of human culture. Such a view helps interpret tensions in education surrounding literacy. It affords analysis

DOI: 10.4018/978-1-4666-8310-5.ch001

of changes in human communication readily, but not yet fully, commodified economically. Such a perspective, we argue, is necessary for productive thinking about literacy as a social practice, literacy education, civic engagement, and policy.

SUCCINCT OVERVIEW OF THE RESEARCH

We begin with an integrative review of theory and research on the role of digital media in contemporary society's global economy. Definitions of *digital media*, *contemporary society*, and *global economy* are best formulated as systems within systems. For example, in Nick Couldry's (2012) *Media, Society, World: Social Theory and Digital Practice*, he lays the foundation for a new sociology of digital media as a means of dealing with the complexities of living in a 21st century media-saturated world that extends beyond the social to include the economics of production and consumption. Amid unceasing calls for education, policy, social practice, and civic engagement to "keep up" with digital media, Couldry asks a moral question that holds a key, we argue, to understanding the nested economic impact of systems within systems. What does digital media allow us to "do" to one another?

The term *digital media* defies attempts to reach consensus on its meaning. We review literature on the construction of digital media as content (print and nonprint) that has been digitized and thus potentially ready for dissemination on the Internet. We echo the insistence from various fields of research on digital media that digital media content is a kind of tip of the iceberg for the ways digital media is reorganizing and managing our actual and metaphorical households and villages. Starting with content serves as a starting point for discussing digital media's broader impact on our lives in the broad sense that Couldry intends.

Below, we pursue three arguments we identified from a review of the literature that broadly define the economic force of digital media content in contemporary society. We then contextualize the arguments about digital media content in terms of relevant social, political, and economic factors that mediate the production of digital content. This approach makes it possible to assess economic impact of digital media in ways that are unreached by instrumental means of measuring economic activity (e.g., Boggs, this volume; Chambers, 2013). We seek to capture the essence of how digital media affects the "management of the household or village" (Author C's interpretation of etymology of *Greek oikonomia*).

Argument #1

Digital media in a contemporary society—one that requires a global marketplace to satisfy daily needs—is multimodal (i.e., composed of images, sounds, and bodily performances, as well as oral and written language).

One result of the breakdown between formal and informal learning (Dabbagh & Kitsantas, 2012; Hull, Stornaiuolo, & Sterpont, 2013) is the opening up of spaces in which users explore new online ways of participating and communicating specifically in multimodal ways—ways that require collaboration, production, and dissemination of one's own digital texts as opposed to mere consumption of such. Media production has always been multimodal, but digital media makes multimodality a core feature of interactions with economic potential.

However, digital media *content* and digital media *space* suggest quite different economic possibilities. On the Internet, digital content generated by users, such as a Facebook post, could change nothing or everything, and it seems impossible to predict. However, the social *space* created via

Facebook has far more stable, predictable, *tradable* economic value. The newsworthy buying and selling of social media pillars and startups is only one part of the picture. Innumerable businesses make calculated investments about the potential for their enterprises to succeed through merger into digital spaces produced by other vendors.

These developments are not insignificant. They represent a major disruptive innovation in the production of social space. Lefebvre (1992), in Geography, proposed that a place like a city or a rural area at a particular time was a social construction, a kind of script guiding behavior in service of a set of controlling interests. The rapid production and valuation of distinctive online spaces underline digital media's role as a socially produced economic space.

How many downloads per dollar investment? How much traffic is generated by a slicker website? How do customers relate to new products through online video, live chat, and so forth versus traditional print and telephone support? How many purchases per ten new followers? How many additional reservations per dollar spent for online services? These questions resemble those of the shopkeeper or farmer, yet they are following, according to Lefebvre (1992), an overarching ideological and economic script. The distinction between content and space points up the economic importance of digital spaces as socially constructed tools that alter day-to-day activities, job creation, and balance sheets.

Moreover, the situations elicited above largely rely on existing spaces that attract investment. Online *learning* spaces represent a different but equally important multimodal digital media environment where, again, digital content by no means indicates economic impact. In the case of Wikipedia, for instance, donations purchase server space and employ editors, but the economic impact of readily available information cannot be quantified. Yet it is unquestionably greater than the economic footprint of the web encyclopedia organization. Online learning spaces marshal-

ling experts' knowledge resources daily shape economically significant choices worldwide, from when to plant corn and beans to projected trading values of those commodities. Networks of various kinds have formed to define formal and informal research agendas for their particular areas of expertise. However, these networks that connect digital media content and digital media spaces participate in complex economies beyond the traditional buying, selling, and distribution of goods and services. The economic impact, then, is a matter of potentiating connection.

Online learning communities spanning the early grades through higher education (Ito, Gutierrez, Livingstone, Penuel, Rhodes, Salen et al., 2013) have used "connected learning" to evoke this sense of potentiality. A report of the work (http://dmlhub.net/sites/default/files/ConnectedLearning_report.pdf) presents the concept:

It advocates for broadened access to learning that is socially embedded, interest-driven, and oriented toward educational, economic, or political opportunity. Connected learning is realized when a young person is able to pursue a personal interest or passion with the support of friends and caring adults, and is in turn able to link this learning and interest to academic achievement, career success or civic engagement. This model is based on evidence that the most resilient, adaptive, and effective learning involves individual interest as well as social support to overcome adversity and provide recognition. (p. 2)

The nine case studies detailed in the report demonstrate how the connected learning framework addresses our interest in knitting together education, civic engagement (both local and global), social practice, and policy.

Numerous research projects confirm Ito et al.'s orientation toward choice and cultural relevance in the expansion of digital media as an economically meaningful part of life (e.g., Kleine, 2010; Mansell, 2001; Selwyn, 2004). In sum, then, digital media is crucially multimodal, both in terms of digitized content as well as in the social interactions it mediates: the production of new social spaces and the facilitation of learning for economically significant action.

Argument #2

Given all the frenetic activity associated with online broadly-defined text productions, virtual collaborations, and novice dissemination efforts, a savvy consumer will make decisions about what digital content is worthy of attention and what is not.

Nearly two decades ago, an economist named Michael Goldhaber (1997) predicted that the *economics of attention* increasingly important in the global age, as a glut of information, news, and entertainment flooded communication pathways. He rested his economics of attention on the commonly accepted notion that a resource that is in short supply will be in high demand. The scarce resource, for Goldhaber, was human attention.

Attention economy is not a *laissez faire* theory of digital media that gives market dynamics responsibility for producing quality. Instead, scarcity of attention guides the designs of digital spaces, efforts to regulate access to certain kinds of information deemed "spam" or antisocial, policies that protect intellectual property, and campaigns to grant or increase access to digital media. Each of the above areas assumes the economic importance of interwoven online and less-connected aspects of our lives. Garnering and controlling attention via digital media is an important part of altering economic behavior, especially, but also political and personal as well.

The attention economy helps explain why digital media is an unstable constellation of ever-changing platforms. The quest for high ranks in search engine results illustrates how attention economy drives the continual refinement of information delivery on the web. Again, the eco-nomic impact of attaining high rank on Google has obvious yet hardly quantifiable impact. More importantly, the development of new opportunities for interacting digitally results in fundamental changes in human interactions, driven indirectly by quests to stay on top of search engine rankings, earn privileged status in a mobile app store, or otherwise justify investors' risk.

Argument #3

The role of digital media in contemporary society's global economy is reflected in the speed with which memes—e.g., phrases, images, videos, sound effects, songs and the like are copied and spread rapidly by Internet users—typically without regard for whether the message or intended meaning is clear or not.

With few exceptions, digital media content readily accommodates strategic re-use. Internet memes express digital media's affordance for sharing and re-combination. However, they expose a serious vulnerability of discussing digital media as content only, since the importance of memes rests in their strategic use and popularity (i.e., social elements), and their power (i.e., political and ideological elements). Online strategic sharing of excerpted information for new users' purposes underscores the weakness of a content-oriented assessment of digital media's work upon us. Economically, the meme stands for digital media's capacity to blend the human and nonhuman elements of geographically, politically, and even temporally disparate groups or divided people otherwise enjoying fellowship. The production of new households or villages manifested in massively or locally popular memes displays the economic muscle of digital media as it works upon us.

A common critique of digital media's apparent disregard for accuracy in communicating messages online is harbored in memes that go viral. For example, in a 2002 TED talk, Dan Dennett, a philosopher and cognitive scientist, unleashed a barrage of ideas that led to 1,266,365 views as of October 26, 2014 about why memes are dangerous and in need of monitoring (www.ted.com/talks/dan_dennett_on_dangerous_memes?language=en). Briefly, Dennett argued that a meme is often misused, even abused, with each repetition of an idea that a meme comes to represents. To prevent a meme from being caricatured by people intent on turning a benign idea into a variant idea that is dangerous when spread by individuals bent on serving their own needs or causes, Dennett claims we must be ever vigilant. He likens a meme to a virus, giving Richard Dawkins (1976) credit for that term, which spreads and becomes toxic to those who have no immunity to it. Here, Dennett is speaking of cultural memes—ideas tolerated in one community but viewed as abhorrent in another community.

For example, the well-known meme featuring Don Draper from the television show *Mad Men* has gone viral with the saying, "They say a woman's work is never done. Maybe that's why they get paid less" (Gallagher, 2014). Here, we see a message being spread online that depicts the reality that women are paid less than men in the work force today. Yet, the premise behind *Mad Men* is to actually bring those issues of injustice to light (Gallagher, 2014).

For purposes of illustrating Argument #3, we used Dennett's TED talk on dangerous memes as the impetus for mining a substantive body of critical media research (Meehan, 2002; Smythe, 2006). Key to interpreting that literature is a knowledge of how the feminist political economist Eileen Meehan's (2002) research shifted an earlier focus on large-scale, impersonal media corporations and their shaping of cultural commodities and media markets to a focus on women who worked in the media industries. Meehan argued that despite what pleasures a viewer outside the commodity market, which at that time equated to white, 18-34 year-old heterosexual males, television was an agent of oppression. Expanding on Meehan's earlier claim, we see a parallel in some video games' digitized

content that results in online harassment of women http://www.democracynow.org/2014/10/20/women_are_being_driven_offline_feminist). The market potential of such misogynist online video games demonstrates the economic muscle of digital media as it works to transform women into mere commodities.

CURRENT ISSUES IN THE FIELD

The purpose of this section is to describe the linkages between the three more general arguments already identified and the specific relationships of power that embed themselves in those arguments. We begin with an observation that occurred to us as we read broadly in the literature on digital media: that is, technology today creates an exciting terrain for society to create in ways it has been unable to do before now. People with access to the Internet are able to navigate the digital mediasphere with relative ease despite an abundance of information that comes at them from every angle and at all times. It is an incessant display of affordances that individuals before the 21st century could not have imagined, except perhaps in a science fiction film that provided viewers with a glimpse into all that could be connected in a world of touch screens and other digital devices.

Yet, the freedom such affordances provide in terms of communication channels, especially those with nontraditional ways of communicating, makes digital media content and digital media spaces compete for the user's attention. For example, what "app" on a phone will help us create that perfect touch to our photo? Which "hashtag" on a social media site, such as Twitter, will most quickly reach a group of like-minded folks to let them know a new song has just been released? What can we add to our online profile to draw people to our page? These questions point to an overall bigger issue, namely, how, and more importantly, *why* does one have time to interact with most, or even some, of the digital media available today? Furthermore, if digital media is multimodal, readily available, and participatory how do the consumers and producers impact the spaces in which they are connected through the digital media? While there are no easy or simple answers to these questions, slicing it into smaller bits, such as the three sub-issues examined next, is as good a starting point as any.

Digital Media's Challenge to Traditional Print Literacy Practices

Multimodality refers to forms of communication that extend beyond print only. Briefly, multimodality views "representation, communication, and interaction as something more than language" (Jewitt, 2011, p. 1). As noted previously in this chapter, boundaries between formal and informal learning are being broken down (Dabbagh & Kitsantas, 2012; Hull, Stornaiuolo, & Sterpont, 2013), and our society is taking a more connected approach to its interactions (Ito et al., 2013). The problem, however, is that multimodality challenges traditional print-based literacy practices and not all parents, researchers, administrators, teachers, and teacher educators like the changes they see occurring. For example, high-stakes testing remains on the radar and continues to draw heated debates. Standardized tests come in for their share of critique largely because they traditionally privilege print-based reading and writing skills at a time when many young literacy learners with high-speed Internet access are using multiple modes of communication and digital media (e.g., still and moving images, sounds, gestures, and live performances) to interact with others within both local and global spaces. Thus, the disconnects in learning that can develop when traditional literacy practices meet technology-rich, multimodal ways of perceiving are quite stark and create challenges on all fronts (Leu, Kinzer, Coiro, Castek, & Henry, 2013).

Due to "changing relationships to truth and authority—in which knowledge is no longer certain or stable" (Jewitt, 2001, p. 3), we now are experiencing "mediated interactions" in which knowledge is consumed, produced, and disseminated in a variety of complex ways all of which impact the economic capital within the digital sphere. To limit our understanding of these (social) complexities would be to act as if "social, cultural, and historical conditions of societies" were not interconnected at all (Jewitt, 2011, p. 5). In other words, while multimodality has "emerged from linguistic theories" (Jewitt, 2011, p. 6) and pulls from a traditional foundation, it allows us a certain flexibility to engage with and question what constitutes a text. Furthermore, multimodality helps us see why and how people become authors of texts, how texts are read within situations, and how we can analyze these mediated texts, as well as the responses that they produce outside of the traditional definition of print-based language only.

When we look beyond the traditional definition of language, we start to see how a variety of "modes" facilitate varieties of participation in digital media environments. Kress (2011) defines a mode as "a socially shaped and culturally given resource for making meaning" (p. 54). For example, youth use media that is "converged around multifunctional screens that integrate voice and text communication, image and video, games, photography, music, television, print, and apps" (Ito et al., p. 28). These user-friendly tools train us for a new economy in which digital media allows and requires us to connect to others in ways that extend beyond *meanings* into new forms of formal and informal economic activity.

Thus, as our contemporary society becomes more globally connected through digital interactions, literacy practices shift. In these digital media spaces, it becomes possible to be used by our literacies even as we use them for our own purposes (Brandt & Clinton, 2002). For this reason, efforts to expand literacy practices of students become entangled in economic imperatives of forging connections among local and global communities.

This entanglement works upon literacy education in multiple directions. Teachers may be using digital media to help prepare students to engage with the literacy practices that allow them to participate in the global economy through connected learning opportunities (Ito et al., 2013), but regional or national political and economic interests—represented by departments of education, educational textbook publishers, and curriculum and assessment developers, to name a few—work to standardize outcomes of formal schooling that do not necessarily focus upon those opportunities. Testing demands, financial commitments to curriculum developers, and the politics of education can stifle the difficult work of building authentic classroom connections with local and global communities. As a result, many classrooms still privilege print-based language uses over digital media.

As Ito et al. (2013) suggest, it is not that society should abandon traditional literacy skills, but instead it should focus on "diversifying and multiplying entry points and pathways to opportunity and meaningful participation in society" (p. 34). Students' literacy futures, identities, and opportunities as productive consumers and producers within society today collide with efforts of a strong central government to safeguard existing economic commitments to the teaching profession, manufacturing, publishing industries, higher education, and other economic dynamos of bygone years.

By allowing our definitions of texts and their meanings to encompass multimodality through digital media, we allow students more opportunities to use language in ways that value their experiences, knowledge sets, beliefs, and learning spaces. Furthermore, this expansion of the traditional definitions that privilege print-only texts leaves room for innovative projects such as the Europeana Space Project (http://www.europeana-space.eu).

This project focuses on creating "new opportunities for employment and economic growth within the creative industries sector based on Europe's rich digital cultural resources." Thus, its strength lies in its ability to use available digital media in ways that incorporates multimodal "language" to prepare students to be effective members in a global society. At the same time, the development of new literacies among students position them to be exploited by the potentially adverse economic conditions of the new work order (Gee, Hull, & Lankshear, 1996). Under its terms, the buzzwords of the new economy—democratic, horizontal organization and collaboration—mask economic directions that preserve status quo and maintain traditional boundaries of wealth and power.

In order to communicate effectively within the global landscape, we build "language toolboxes" to help us understand how messages are represented in a variety of formats and what they are supposed to mean to others and to ourselves (Ivarsson, Linderoth, & Säljö, 2011, p. 203). Within the economic sphere, advertisers want consumers to use their toolboxes to embed every part of their company's message into their daily lives. Ivarsson, Linderoth, and Säljö (2011) believe that "representations serve as resources for communicating and meaning making, and they are essential to all human practices including perception, remembering, and thinking and other psychological activities" (p. 201). For this reason, the "mediated action," or the process of integrating the producer's message into our daily lives, is always important to keep in mind (Ivarsson, Linderoth, & Säljö, 2011, p. 211) when we are trying to understand the space in which a text's content develops its economic impact for its audience.

When we consider digital media content here, we see that if the content is taken up by a company's consumers, then this consumption is the driving force behind all of the mediated actions that re-delivers the message in a variety of multimodal formats. Using the Internet as an example, we know that websites are feeding us unique content (through words, images, videos, and the like) that we potentially consider in our own lives. This process of expanding the Internet to become a means of navigating, thinking, speaking, and living is an attempt to foster at once an individual's own representation and a conduit for vast new domains of economic participation. Thus, with the proliferation of potential for asserting meaning comes immeasurable "traffic," or a volume of digital media activity on which its economic power rests. And, if more immeasurable traffic is present, then one must begin to question if consumers are duped, or, in fact, quite savvy with the digital media with which they work.

Media Dupes or Savvy Consumers?

Prior to the 1970s when Stuart Hall's (1973) work in what came to be called "cultural studies" made its mark in intellectual debates, media audiences were viewed as mere dupes of popular culture and mass communication. Though not digitized at the time, media producers' content was thought to represent the way people were positioned in the world and their inability to do little to counteract such representation. Hall, who was then Professor of Sociology in England's Open University, downplayed the role of media content and its influence on viewers' meaning-making abilities. Hall contended that images do not have stable meanings, and that producers' intentions at the time of creation do not guarantee that audiences will take up such meanings. It would be a mistake to characterize Hall as believing that media nearly five decades ago, and especially contemporary digital media, have no real and significant social, political, and economic effects on the world. He realized fully the influence of content and its intersection with powerful forces in society, especially in relation to what gets represented in the media. However, we contend that only with Latour's (2007) work on reassembling the social so that it accounts for nonhuman actants—a term

that Latour (2007) used to denote an entity whether human or nonhuman that modifies the actions of another entity (e.g., pouring vinegar on baking soda)—has it become possible to trace associations "between things that are not themselves social" (p. 5). Latour boldly separated his work from postmodernism's attempt to deconstruct grand narratives that have long held people to hegemonic practices, which harm rather than advance their freedoms. In Latour's words, "Dispersion, destruction, and deconstruction are not the goals to be achieved but what needs to be overcome" (p. 11). Proponents of new materialism who have incorporated much of Latour's work continue to redefine the role of nonhuman actants. Most recently, posthumanist philosophers (e.g., Braidotti, 2013) and New Materialist scholars such as political theorist Jane Bennett (2010) use Latour's (2007) and Deleuze and Guattari's (1987) concept of assemblages—ad hoc groupings of human and nonhuman elements—to argue that agency is not strictly a human capacity. In Bennett's (2010) words, the material elements in an assemblage, "while they include humans and their (social, legal, linguistic) constructions, also include some very active and powerful nonhuman actants: electrons, trees, wind, fire, electromagnetic fields" (p. 24). To this list of nonhuman actants, we would add digital media.

Just as Latour and the posthumanist movement have sought to even the playing field that was central to Hall's (1973) concern about representation and the media, so too have education researchers worked to demonstrate the interface between human and nonhuman actants. For example, Bigum, Knobel, Lankshear, and Rowan's (2003) research illustrates how digital media content and space exacerbate tensions that exist between the highly regulated economics of attention inside schools as contrasted with the relatively deregulated economics of attention outside schools, particularly in situations where mass media and new communication technologies dominate.

Specifically, Bigum and his co-researchers studied a group of Grade 9 boys who attended a rural school with Internet access in northern Australia's eastern coast. Their participants were initially viewed as "disadvantaged" in terms of "the lads' 'inability' to carry out the kinds of literacy based activities regarded as mainstream for Grade 9 English" (p. 103). Inside their school's regulated curriculum, the Grade 9 boys attracted negative, even punitive, attention—the kind that often resulted in instruction that merely re-inscribed the boys' sense of failure. However, when Bigum et al. intervened with a project that involved the boys in constructing a website on motorcycles—an interest that stemmed from a previous project in which they created a motorcycle magazine—the "disadvantaged" lads were positioned as experts in an area that attracted positive attention from their peers and supervising teacher.

This role reversal (going from "disadvantaged" to expert) demonstrates digital media's mediating effects on traditional ways of thinking of defining "failure" and its supposed fixed or permanent place in education discourse. We submit that with digital media as a player, so-called failure is an idea that teachers and students might jointly challenge in their effort to engage with learning on their own terms. In doing so, they might also find reasons to discard previous negative evaluations of student performance.

Digital Media's Disruption of Traditional Meaning Making

Researchers working within contemporary digital media culture, especially in the realm of social media, have reported numerous instances in which the *effect* of people's interactions is more important than the content or meaning derived from those interactions (Varis & Blommaert, 2015). An earlier recognition of this phenomenon is attributed to Vincent Miller (2008), a sociologist and social researcher who noted that in the digital age, "We are seeing how in many ways the Internet has become as much about interaction with others as it has about accessing information" (p. 398). Anyone who participates in Facebook and Twitter is well aware of how memes (or signs that go viral, such as the Don Draper meme discussed earlier) are more characteristic of networks involving human and nonhuman entities than they are of communities in which social interaction is not dependent on the internet.

Particularly in the digital world, relying on the disruption of meaning as a motivating factor in producing and consuming media content is complicated by issues of fair use and the marketplace, especially when transformative remixing is involved. Joyce Valenza (2009), a school library media specialist in a suburban Philadelphia high school, explained *transformativeness* this way:

When a user of copyrighted materials adds value to, or repurposes materials for a use different from that for which it was originally intended, it will likely be considered transformative use; it will also likely be considered fair use. Fair use embraces the modifying of existing media content, placing it in new context.

Examples of transformativeness might include: using campaign video in a lesson exploring media strategies or rhetoric, using music videos to explore such themes as urban violence, using commercial advertisements to explore messages relating to body image or the various different ways beer makers sell beer, remixing a popular song to create a new artistic expression. (Valenza, 2009, para. 6 and 7).

Legal backing for Valenza's interpretation of transformativeness grew out of a study conducted by Aufderheide and Jaszi (2008) at the Center for Social Media in Washington, DC, in which the researchers concluded that a "significant set of creative practices is potentially both legal and at risk of curtailment by currently discussed ways to control online piracy and theft of copyrighted works" (Executive Summary, para. 2).

Using copyrighted material to make something new—what noted media scholar Renee Hobbs (2010) calls *repurposing*—is still a gray area in the field of legal studies due to recurring battles over pirated content. As a result, researchers who want to study the use of digital media for creative purposes have increasingly turned to nonprofit organizations such as Creative Commons (CC) (www.creativecommons. org) for guidance in how to share content legally. A study by Alvermann, Beach, and Johnson (2014) is a case in point. The co-researchers designed a public website, Becoming 3lectric (www.becoming3lectric.com), for the purpose of studying the degree to which remixing digital content would push the boundaries of authorial intent and ownership. They settled on a CC license that met their university's requirements for studying and protecting human subjects. As a result, contributors to Becoming3lectric are legally able to collaborate, repurpose, and share their remixes while retaining their choice of options. For instance, contributors may not want to allow any commercial repurposing of their work, but still allow others to build upon that work if they are credited for it. Or, they may opt to upload their work without granting others any remixing privileges or the right to analyze their work.

With its various licenses for working flexibly and responsibly with digital texts, CC helps people forge new ways of disseminating multimodal content that might otherwise be impossible. Furthermore, as Suthersanen (2007) has pointed out, "Nowadays…do-it-yourself tools, including the CC licensing regime, empower and enable individual authors of literary and musical works to retain more control over their work" (p. 60). Theoretically, CC has flattened the global marketplace in terms of who can participate, as well as what kinds of knowledge count.

GAPS IN THE RESEARCH

Two major topics in the literature on the role of digital media in contemporary society's global economy for which little research has been generated are these: inequality in economic opportunity and the general fallout from untapped digital spaces and connections.

Inequality in Economic Opportunity

Speaking at the American Educational Research Association's tenth annual *Brown v. Board of Education* lecture, Gary Orfield (2014), Distinguished Research Professor of Education, Law, Political Science, and Urban Planning at the University of California, Los Angeles called for a new civil rights agenda. Specifically, Orfield argued that while the United States continues to celebrate Martin Luther King, Jr. and other civil rights leaders, as a nation it currently is failing to focus on the rights that are being lost. He specifically called attention to the fact that close to 60 years after *Brown v. Board of Education*, 40% of Black and Latino/a students are in what he described as "intensely segregated schools . . . with about twice the poverty concentration of the schools of Whites and Asians" (p. 273). To further complicate attitudes of low expectations for children in poverty schools in which advanced intellectual work is viewed as being beyond their reach, all too often scarce digital technologies are used for basic skill and drill activities.

Echoing Orfield's grim observation, Ito and her colleagues (2013) described what they perceive as a downward trend in equal opportunity for society's least well off students: Over much of our nation's history, expanding educational opportunity has been, in fact and in perception, a key element in the 'rising tide that lifts all boats.' [Currently], after thirty years of steadily rising economic inequality in the United States, that tide is now running out, and our educational system may be doing more to perpetuate and even to increase inequality than to expand economic opportunity" (p. 13).

In their discussion, Ito et al. (2013) point to educational institutions as places that cater to only a certain group of students despite the fact that the economy and work force have become increasingly competitive and limited even for job seekers with a college degree. They draw from their pool of data to argue that educational institutions offer programs with alternative career paths to meet an increasingly diverse applicant pool. And, as previously discussed, they recommend that institutions "expand and diversify meaningful life options and pathways available to young people" or else they will be "reinforcing an educational system that only serves the interests of elites, breeding a culture of competition for scarce opportunities (Ito et al., 2013, p. 14).

In sum, claiming that currently a majority of institutions' responses to the need for equality in economic opportunity is unacceptable, Ito and her colleagues (2013) call for an increased awareness of how "in a world of global interconnections and rapid change, effective learning is lifelong and integrated into the real world of work, civic engagement, and social participation" (p. 14). For this awareness to grow and become second nature to society's way of thinking about inequality, a major shift in how we define *opportunity* must first occur.

A study funded by the William T. Grant Foundation (Carter & Reardon, 2014) is a starting point. This report begins to fill a gap in the research literature on the role of digital media in contemporary society because it lays out a strategic research agenda, which if heeded, could produce more than simply advocating for social justice and access to high-speed internet. Briefly, Carter and Reardon (2014) strategize a research program that would have researchers focus on the following questions: a) how do unequal opportunities occur insidiously over time, b) what social

processes preserve inequality, c) which strategies can reduce the consequences of social inequality, and d) what mechanisms are at work that make the distribution of inequality taken for granted?

Fallout from Untapped Digital Spaces and Connections

Digital media content is reorganizing and managing numerous aspects of our lives on a daily basis as Couldry (2012) contends. However, less often studied and reported in the research literature on adolescents' out-of-school uses of digital media is the point that interactions between human and nonhuman actants have valuable economic potential. School-age young people's preferences for producing and learning with multimodal texts that combine moving and still images, sounds, performances, icons, symbols, and the like suggests that their ways of telling, listening, viewing, and thinking in out-of-school digital environments have potential for informing both their in-school identities as learners and hence the trajectories they will follow after graduation (Alvermann, 2010; Ito, Horst, Bittani, boyd, Herr-Stephenson, Lange et al., 2008; McClenaghan & Doecke, 2010; Rennie & Patterson, 2010; Skinner & Hagood, 2008; Thomas, 2007; Walsh, 2008).

Yet it is generally the case that the work of students who self-identify as users and producers of multimodal digital texts on their own terms and time is rarely visible to teachers. Alvermann (2011) linked this phenomenon to other research that suggested four barriers to teachers becoming aware of what their students are producing online in after-school hours. Briefly, she relied on two key tenets to analyze research findings on young people's out-of-school use of digital media. The first is that today's youth interact with each other and the web in ways that rely on collective meaning making, which Jenkins (2006b) describes as a condition in which "none of us can know everything; each of us knows something; and we can put the pieces together if we pool our resources and combine our skills" (p. 4). The second tenet is that literacy is a social practice (Gee, 1990; Street, 1993) and thus implicated in social reasons for getting things done (Barton, Hamilton, & Ivanic, 2000), whether for social, ideological, or economic gain. Experiencing social connectedness while engaging collectively in online literacy practices affords a sense of belonging and an opportunity to identify with others who have similar interests but may vary in their skills and access to material resources.

Among the numerous findings that Alvermann (2011) reported are several that point to barriers, which if overcome, could open spaces for more freely exchanging information, motivations, and accomplishments. The first of these was the prevailing assumption that multimodal digital content distracts. A second barrier consisted of socially constructed artificial dichotomies between in-and-out-of school learning (e.g., schools must be held accountable for covering a set curriculum whereas after-school online learning is just for fun). Third, the results of some studies Alvermann (2011) analyzed suggested that professional development efforts aimed at building teachers' awareness of the role of digital media in their students' lives fall flat when attempts at mediated action result in short-lived interventions that rely more on talking the talk than walking the walk. Finally, a fourth and all-encompassing barrier was the mistaken assumption that age-old tensions between institutional authority and youth identity politics could be easily resolved. When schools and adults are positioned as experts on all topics and students (novices) on few or none, the potential for in-school learning to capitalize on the digital literacy skills, interests, and competencies that youth are free to explore, trade, and expand on in online spaces.

IMPLICATIONS FOR EDUCATION, CIVIC ENGAGEMENT, SOCIAL PRACTICE AND POLICY

Here, our purpose is to highlight the implications of this chapter's integrative review of theory and research on the role of digital media in contemporary society's global economy. Specifically, we address implications for education, civic engagement (global and local), social practice, and policy. In doing this, we draw from each of the three arguments in Section 1 of the chapter that play out in overlapping ways through supporting evidence (Section 2) or lack thereof (Section 3) to inform this last section on implications.

Education

With the increasing focus on new literacy practices and digital media within classrooms today, there is not a question of *why* we should study digital media in contemporary society today, but *how* we should and can study its implications for the global economy. When preparing students with the skills they will need to be productive members of the global economy, we know that we are currently preparing them for jobs that have yet to be created with skills that may become outdated. Teachers, and by extension educational researchers take on moral responsibility for the ways in which we position children to have their skills exploited economically.

Nonetheless, as previously discussed, "multiple forms of literacy have been named in the literature including information literacy, visual literacy, computer or digital literacy, and media literacy, but there is considerable overlap between these forms" (Considine, Horton, and Moorman, 2009, p. 471-472). The problem is not how these multiple forms of literacy overlap, but instead, how we begin to help today's students navigate these overlaps to better understand their role in contemporary economies.

When we take a "critical" approach to how media and culture are impacting classrooms, we bring an "understanding of ideology, power, and domination" to help students explore "how power, media, and information are linked" (Kellner & Share, 2007, p. 8). For these reasons, there is an increasing need for today's students to actively and critically consume and produce in both the classroom and their lives outside of school, too. With the expectation of their increased engagement comes responsibility to help students ask, as we have in this chapter, what should digital media be able to do to us?

For example, Jocson's (2010) study that noted the need for "critical multiculturalism" (p. 78) is important to consider when we think about the "dialogical relationship between consumption and production and what it means for youth who actively engage various media forms" (p. 79). In fact, as we know, "many young people are not just consuming cultural media but also producing and distributing their own" (Jocson, 2010, p. 80). For Jocson, her qualitative research focus on the process, product, and practice (p. 80) helped her understand the students' poetry through her critical multicultural lens. She notes that "to understand the poem is to understand the actual production" (Jocson, 2010, p. 84) and that "youth are active consumers as well as knowledge producers who with support from others are able to participate in a democratic order and confront social inequities in their lives" (Jocson, 2010, p. 86). The process she describes here and the outcome ties back to the role reversal that demonstrates digital media's mediating effects that allow students be the experts in spaces that extend beyond the classroom walls.

Economically, the technological changes encapsulated by the term digital media signals the possibility for classrooms to move out of a perpetual "research and development" existence. Students can create in a variety of ways that extends beyond classroom walls or the pages of a book. Their posts can go viral, earn money, shape policy, solve meaningful problems, and attract all manner of attention. Instead of focusing on how to keep these mediated intersections of multimodal digital media and print-only language uses from occurring in schools, we should be actively invite them in by "creating school discourse that is not separate and distinct from the blurred discourses of our lives outside of school" (Alvermann & Hagood, 2000, p. 203). When we keep the doors open to the possibilities of digital media and literacy, we create opportunities for all to be valued in and out of school, both now and in the future.

We continue to see that "young people are tirelessly editing and remixing multimodal content they find online to share with others, using new tools to show and tell, and rewriting their social identities in an effort to become who they say they are" (Alvermann, 2008, p. 8). In other words, today's students' literacy practices are both narrative as well as connective especially as these texts become more social.

For this reason, the social nature of literacy practices today gives all of us a new way to think and connect with those around us. In fact, literacy is not just limited to the "local" realm either, such as the classroom. Literacy infiltrates, disjoints, and displaces local life (Brandt and Clinton, 2002, p. 343). It is never just the local impacting literacy practices, but instead the transaction that takes place within that moment: the consumption and production of media with the tools to disseminate "new" information in a "new" way created by the consumer, which invites new literacy forms that essentially connect everyone everywhere.

However, what do these new literacy forms mean in regards to today's classrooms? Because we are placed in social situations that "call for critical approaches that make us aware of how [the] media construct meanings, influence and educate audiences, and impose their messages and values" (Kellner & Share, 2007, p. 8), we need to help students move past the obvious meanings and work on a deeper level with the texts in front of them. And, because these mediated, "new" texts are constantly changing in form, it is important for them to understand why and how those changes are being made, including how different formats impact our reading of those texts.

Typically, the "critical component of media literacy must transform literacy education into an exploration of the role of language and communication media in order to define relationships of power and domination that are ultimately deeply embedded in ideological notions" (Kellner & Share, 2000, p. 8). For this reason, students need to see how authors of multimodal messages are consuming (including billboards, music videos, newspaper articles, and novels to name a few) and positioning them as consumers with many mediated messages.

In addition, by helping students to understand how they are already being positioned in the real world by their critical productions (e.g. blog posts, tweets, lyrical raps), we can help many students see connections between their in and out of school literacy practices. "We live in and move in a material world; the things in it—objects, visual representations, machines, and tools—take part in our dramas of meanings as well" (Gee, 2012, p. 185). Thus, students "dramas of meanings" are created in all that they do; yet, the need to help them navigate those many connections and meanings continues to be critical since they are already consuming, producing, and sharing digital media on their own.

Civic Engagement

The production of new social spaces engenders new forms and avenues of civic engagement. Numerous large-scale social movements on every continent underscore the role of social media in landmark social protests. Part of educating students, then, is helping them understand how to manipulate digital media, through which they may be working on a daily basis, to serve civic engagement purposes.

Jones (2011) emphasizes the fact that these communication spaces, or sites of display, become "social occasions in which particular configurations of modes and media coverage in a particular time and space in order to make particular social actions possible" (p. 114). Of course, "the problem with examining sites of display outside of the context of their use by 'watchers' to perform particular social practices is that what people can do with different sites of display alters radically in different contexts" (Jones, 2011, p. 114). Thus, every site of display, or composition space, changes depending on who is viewing it, from what angle it is being viewed, and how it is positioned and embedded within other sites of displays before it may be repurposed within the digital sphere.

In other words, sites of displays are where the reader/viewer actively participates and makes meaning of the constructed text, emphasizing a symbiotic relationship between social practices and itself (Jones, 2011, p. 116). Because sites of display involve social practices, they do become a form of social interaction, where the viewer can become a part of the action by creating her or his own meanings, and social identity/identities as well.

When we think about the attention economy and schools as sites of display, we recognize the restrictive norms for language use that represent the antithesis of the flexible stance needed for civic engagement. Language use within schools traditionally focuses on what is deemed as a "success" (such as writing a five paragraph persuasive essay) versus what is deemed as a "failure" (such as devaluing that same essay created through a video narrative). If schools devalue students' language by restricting them from creating and sharing information in meaningful ways, then students' attention will be spent on what matters to them and what gives them the most social capital, or power, within society. Thus, it's not about the highest score on a test; it's about how many new followers one gets on Twitter thanks to a strategic tweet at just the right time, for example.

Within contemporary society, we all navigate a text-mediated world in which time, space, identity, and meanings are intricately connected. By using these components as tools, we can create digital texts that accommodate the amount of time we have while moving from one place to another and sharing within a public or private digital space. For this reason, it is increasingly important to understand that "meanings are made across time, across space, in and through matter" (Lemke, 2011, p. 143). However, as educators and researchers, we cannot be afraid of this mediated world and must focus on working towards a common goal of considering how both local and global civic engagements are impacted by these mediated meanings.

"Grassroots social movements, nongovernmental organizations (NGOs), scientists, activists, governments, and some businesses resist IP [intellectual property] with a range of tactics, both inside and outside the policy world, in local, national, and international venues" (Schweidler & Costanza-Chock, in-press, p. 4). Regarding digital media, this point suggests that meanings and knowledge are privileged and guarded closely by those organizations/powers in charge. Yet, if our goal is to unlock the potential of digital media, we must work towards ways of using what we learn from social practices that have the potential to inform policy.

Social Practice

Studies that focus on digitally mediated actions in 21st century learning environments (whether formal or informal) share a common characteristic: "irreducible tension between cultural tools, on the one hand, and agents' active uses of them, on the other" (Wertsch, 1998, pp. 518-525). This is the case even when tools are redefined to reflect Latour's (2007) thinking on human and nonhu-

man actants. Regardless of whether those actions are socially distributed or directed at individuals, networked digital media technologies ensure that social practices associated with online production, distribution, and consumption are partially dependent on one's audience—whether approving or even disapproving audiences (de Castell & Jenson, 2004).

This factor plus a growing awareness in the field of education that it is the quality rather than the quantity of attention that matters have influenced researchers to focus on young people's penchant for curating online texts that have potential for later remixing. In studying the social practices around remixed texts, for example, Ian O'Byrne and Greg McVerry (in press) found consistent evidence in support of contemporary's youth's movement away from individualistic consumption of commercially prepared texts toward an ethos of collaboration in producing their own socially constructed texts. Yet, as O'Byrne (2014) also reported, there is a general disregard among youthful online curators for applying critical literacy skills as part of their social practices in remixing.

Mellinee Lesley (2012) found a similar disregard for social practices that involve critical thinking. In her study, technically savvy adolescent girl writers did not automatically apply their knowledge and experiences in ways that reflected sophisticated critical thinking skills. For the girls to be able to apply those skills, Lesley argued, it would require a teacher's investment in instruction on how to frame critical literacy in socially relevant spaces that fostered online text production, distribution, and consumption. Moreover, Lesley contended, without a critical framing of such texts, the girls in her three-year ethnography were likely to find it difficult, if not impossible, to resist the dominant ideologies coming at them on all sides. Succumbing to a loss of voice or personal agency on the part of her participants in *Invisible Girls* was not a finding that Lesley viewed as helpful or even tolerable.

The centrality of pedagogy in mediating people's online social practices was a key finding in Korina Jocson's (2015) design-based action research project. In choosing to theorize through a new media literacies perspective the cultural production of digital texts and use of DIY tools, Jocson learned that the undergraduate and graduate students enrolled in her semester-long teacher education course needed her to intervene at various points in order for them to grasp the importance of developing an ethos of collaboration, participation, and distributed expertise in online text production. This finding has direct implications for working with youth who have not experienced, or at least do not indicate, an awareness of the need to use critical literacy in socially constructed online spaces.

Policy

Privileging language over other modes of communication is common in education as well as in civic and social practices in which digital media plays a role, at least in part because of centuries of print publishers' careful management of intellectual property rights. As technology has made other modes of communication as replicable and able to be distributed as print, concomitant expansion of digital media and its economic significance has major ramifications for policy. Vast national and international economies possess inertia that digital development, education, and intellectual property policy must balance against the need to prepare for uncertain but certainly different economic futures. The decade of economic engines "too big to fail" and educational reform efforts that thwart their own mission (Au, 2011) sound somber notes for U.S. and international policymakers.

Efforts within industry to promote forward thinking in terms of literacy education have gained considerable credibility (e.g., Partnership for 21st century skills), but the underlying economic narratives are lost here and there in patriotic and altruistic abstractions. On the other hand, the real potential for learning and doing through acquisition of literacies in digital media environments has local economic importance beyond preparing a nation's workforce or ending poverty.

Building on Lanham's (2001) work that critiqued the linguistic bias in traditional text production, de Castell and Jenson concluded ". . . new multimodal technologies of representation… actually consolidate, extend, and improve upon [one's] literate capabilities" (p. 392). Yet who has access to these technologies is a perennial issue for social justice researchers in their attempt to influence policy makers. Digital media's role in influencing how content is distributed via the marketing of social capital through clicks, likes, views, followers, and shares (Terranova, 2012) is not inconsequential.

As discussed earlier, the role of digital media content is reflected in the speed with which memes (images, videos, sound effects, songs and the like) are spread rapidly by Internet users, and typically without regard for whether message is clear or not. This phenomenon, coupled with the breakdown of distinctions between real-world and virtual experiences, which Voithofer (2005) called attention to nearly a decade ago, are associated with the human-computer interface that most of us (including policy makers) take for granted today. However, more mundane observations (mundane, that is, to people outside the field of education) are those that stake out a future for researchers entering the professions 10 or 15 years hence. What do we mean by this? Here, we're referring to a Pew Internet Report published in 2012 that concluded for most teachers and students alike, "research" means "Googling" or relying on Wikipedia for their information. Reacting to this observation, some teachers we know (as well as those participating in the Pew Report) admit that for their students "doing research" has shifted from a relatively slow process requiring various levels of inquiry to a "hurry-and-get-it-over" one-step process that consists of selecting bare-minimum information to complete an assignment. Whether those in policy-making positions are aware of this development is up for speculation.

Beyond the speed and superficial processing of information today is an ongoing discussion in the academy "about the nature of the participatory democratic utopia and participatory culture and how groups take (or do not take) advantage of the affordances new and emerging media" (Jenkins & Carpentier, 2013, p. 265). In the article cited here, media critic Henry Jenkins concedes that he has contributed to the utopian nature of participatory culture by failing to make distinctions between descriptive and normative language such that all too often we are lured into believing our participation is something more than superficial—something that can lead to our empowerment, when it cannot because the groups who are in control of "that something" are not about to relinquish their power over it.

Ending on a more positive note, we would call attention to Michael Dezuanni's (2014) four-year study in a primary school in Queensland, Australia, and its implications for policy makers worldwide. Dezuanni, a Senior Lecturer of Film and Media Curriculum in the Faculty at Queensland University of Technology, uses Latour's (2007) actor-network theory to focus on young learners' material practices and how those developed over time. Specifically, he uses a building-block metaphor to capture how the children he studies deploy technology and media concepts to participate materially in digital-networked culture not unlike that of older students.

That the children in Dezuanni's research are part of a larger participatory culture should not be lost on those who are responsible for policies governing the ever-changing requirements of copyright law for media literacy education. In point of fact, he and his colleagues (Dezuanni, Kapitzke, & Iyer, 2010) argue that copyright literacy be required for preservice teachers who will be charged with helping young people participate successfully in digital learning networks that have economic significance for both media content and connections.

CONCLUSION

In summary, digital media's economic impact is a bit like winning the lottery. There are many changes that are easily anticipated. One can count how many relations ask for a cut, how much each one expects. However, there's really no way to quantify far more important and economically significant shifts. People relate differently. Everyday actions take on economic significance in ways that may only be recognized in hindsight.

In our chapter, we have steered away from the hundreds of studies commissioned and carried out around the world that counted up the money that changed hands as a result of digital media, the increased tax revenue collected as a result of broadband penetration in a region, and the per capita income comparisons between technological haves and have nots. Instead, we have attempted to listen and understand the economics of digital media in a way that provokes much needed conversation among researchers.

Too often, economic questions are boiled down too far as we question whether some enterprises are worth the risk. The stakes are far too high—and the changes to education, policy, civic engagement, and social practice too far reaching—merely to rate digital media's gains and losses. Instead, two outcomes are most needed: first, that we think about what we are doing to ourselves by means of digital media; and second, we begin to inquire into the economic meaning of the conveniences we love, the challenges we endure, and the discoveries we make.

REFERENCES

Alvermann, D. E. (2008). Why bother theorizing about adolescents' online literacies for classroom practice and research? *Journal of Adolescent & Adult Literacy*, *52*(1), 8–19. doi:10.1598/JAAL.52.1.2

Alvermann, D. E. (Ed.). (2010). *Adolescents' online literacies: Connecting classrooms, digital media, & popular culture*. New York, NY: Peter Lang.

Alvermann, D. E. (2011). Moving on, keeping pace: Youth's literate identities and multimodal digital texts. In S. Abrams & J. Rowsell (Eds.), *Rethinking identity and literacy education in the 21st century. National Society for the Study of Education Yearbook* (Vol. 110, part I (pp. 109–128). New York, NY: Columbia University, Teachers College.

Alvermann, D. E., Beach, C. L., & Johnson, J. (2014). *Becoming 3lectric*. Retrieved from www.becoming3lectric.com

Alvermann, D. E., & Hagood, M. C. (2000). Critical media literacy: Research, theory, and practice in 'new times'. *The Journal of Educational Research*, *93*(3), 193–205. doi:10.1080/00220670009598707

Au, W. (2011). Teaching under the new Taylorism: High-stakes testing and the standardization of the 21st century curriculum. *Journal of Curriculum Studies*, *43*(1), 25–45. doi:10.1080/00220272.2010.521261

Aufderheide, P., & Jaszi, P. (2008). *Recut, reframe, recycle: Quoting copyrighted material in user-generated video*. Washington, DC: American University, Center for Social Media, School of Communication.

Barton, D., Hamilton, M., & Ivanic, R. (Eds.). (2000). *Situated literacies: Reading and writing in context*. London: Routledge.

Bennett, J. (2010). *Vibrant matter*. Durham, NC: Duke University Press.

Bigum, C., Knobel, M., Lankshear, C., & Rowan, L. (2003). Literacy, technology and the economics of attention. *L1-Educational Studies in Language and Literature*, *3*(1/2), 95–122. doi:10.1023/A:1024588324175

Braidotti, R. (2013). *The posthuman*. Cambridge, UK: Polity.

Brandt, D., & Clinton, K. (2002). Limits of the local: Expanding perspectives on literacy as a social practice. *Journal of Literacy Research*, *34*(3), 337–356. doi:10.1207/s15548430jlr3403_4

Carter, P.L., & Reardon, S.F. (2014, September). *Inequality matters*. Palo Alto, CA: Stanford University.

Chambers, J. (2013). Foreword. In B. Bilbao-Osorio, S. Dutta, & B. lanvin (Eds.), The global information technology report, 2013 (pp. ix-x). Academic Press.

Considine, D., Horton, J., & Moorman, G. (2009). Teaching and reaching the millennial generation through media literacy. *Journal of Adolescent & Adult Literacy*, *52*(6), 471–472. doi:10.1598/JAAL.52.6.2

Couldry, N. (2012). *Media, society, world: Social theory and digital media practice*. Cambridge, UK: Polity Press.

Creative Commons. (n.d.). *Creative commons*. Retrieved from https://creativecommons.org

Dabbagh, N., & Kitsantas, A. (2012). Personal learning environments, social media, and self-regulated learning: A natural formula for connecting formal and informal learning. *The Internet and Higher Education*, *15*(1), 3–8. doi:10.1016/j.iheduc.2011.06.002

Dawkins, R. (1976). *The selfish gene*. New York, NY: Oxford University Press.

de Castell, S., & Jenson, J. (2004). Paying attention to attention: New economies for learning. *Educational Theory, 54*(4), 381–397. doi:10.1111/j.0013-2004.2004.00026.x

Deleuze, G., & Guattari, F. (1987). *A thousand plateaus*. Minneapolis, MN: University of Minnesota Press.

Dennett, D. (2002). Dangerous memes. *TED*. Retrieved from http://www.ted.com/talks/dan_dennett_on_dangerous_memes?language=en

Dezuanni, M. (2014). The building blocks of digital media literacy: Socio-material participation and the production of media knowledge. *Journal of Curriculum Studies*. doi:10.1080/00220272.2014.966152

Dezuanni, M., Kapitzke, C., & Iyer, R. (2010). Copyright, digital media literacies and preservice teacher education. *Digital Culture & Education, 2*(2), 230–245.

Gallagher, B. (2014). 10 sexist memes we should probably stop using. *Complex*. Retrieved from http://www.complex.com/pop-culture/2014/02/sexist-memes-we-should-probably-stop-using/

Gee, J. P. (1990). *Social linguistics and and literacies: Ideology in discourses*. London: Falmer.

Gee, J. P. (2012). *Social linguistics and literacies: Ideology in discourses* (4th ed.). New York, NY: Routledge.

Gee, J. P., Hull, G., & Lankshear, C. (1996). *The new work order: Behind the language of the new capitalism*. Boulder, CO: Westview.

Goldhaber, M. H. (1997). The attention economy and the net. *First Monday, 2*(4). doi:10.5210/fm.v2i4.519

Hall, S. (1973). *Encoding and decoding in the television discourse*. Birmingham, UK: Centre for Contemporary Cultural Studies.

Hobbs, R. (2010). *Copyright clarity: How fair use supports digital learning*. Thousand Oaks, CA: Corwin.

Hull, G., Stornaiuolo, A., & Sterpont, L. (2013). Imagined readers and hospitable texts: Global youths connect online. In D. E. Alvermann, N. J. Unrau, & R. B. Ruddell (Eds.), *Theoretical models and processes of reading* (6th ed.; pp. 1208–1240). Newark, DE: International Reading Association. doi:10.1598/0710.44

Ito, M., Gutiérrez, K., Livingstone, S., Penuel, B., Rhodes, B., Salen, K., & Watkins, S. C. et al. (2013). *Connected Learning: An agenda for research and design*. Irvine, CA: Digital Media and Learning Research Hub.

Ito, M., Horst, H., Bittanti, M., boyd, d., Herr-Stephenson, B., Lange, P. G., et al. (2008, November). *Living and learning with new media: Summary of findings from the Digital Youth Project*. (Funded by The John D. and Catherine T. MacArthur Foundation). Boston: The MIT Press.

Ivarsson, J., Linderoth, J., & Säljö, R. (2011). Representations in practices: A socio-cultural approach to multimodality in reasoning. In C. Jewitt (Ed.), *The Routledge handbook of multimodal analysis* (pp. 201–212). New York, NY: Routledge.

Jenkins, H., & Carpentier, N. (2013). Theorizing participatory intensities: A conversation about participation and politics. *Convergence (London), 19*(3), 265–286. doi:10.1177/1354856513482090

Jewitt, C. (2011). Introduction: Handbook rationale, scope and structure. In C. Jewitt (Ed.), *The Routledge handbook of multimodal analysis* (pp. 1–7). New York, NY: Routledge.

Jocson, K. M. (2010). Youth writing across media: A note about the what and the how. In S. J. Miller & D. E. Kirkland (Eds.), *Change matters: Critical essays on moving social justice research from theory to policy* (pp. 77–87). New York, NY: Peter Lang.

Jocson, K. M. (2015). New media literacies as social action: The centrality of pedagogy in the politics of knowledge production. *Curriculum Inquiry, 45*(1), 30–51.

Jones, R. H. (2011). Technology and sites of display. In C. Jewitt (Ed.), *The Routledge handbook of multimodal analysis* (pp. 114–126). New York, NY: Routledge.

Kear, K., Chetwynd, F., & Jefferis, H. (2014). Social presence in online learning communities: The role of personal profiles. *Research in Learning Technology, 22*(0). doi:10.3402/rlt.v22.19710

Kellner, D., & Share, J. (2007). Critical media literacy, democracy, and the reconstruction of education. In D. Macedo & S. R. Steinberg (Eds.), *Media literacy: A reader* (pp. 3–23). New York, NY: Peter Lang Publishing, Inc.

Kleine, D. (2010). ICT4What? Using the choice framework to operationalise the capability approach to development. In *Proceedings of the IEEE/ACM International Conference on Information Technology and Development 2009*. Retrieved from http://ieeexplore.ieee.org/xpl/login.jsp?tp=&arnumber=5426717&url=http%3A%2F%2Fieeexplore.ieee.org%2Fxpls%2Fabs_all.jsp%3Farnumber%3D5426717

Kress, G. (1997). *Literacy, identity and futures. Before writing: Rethinking the paths to literacy* (pp. 1–17). New York, NY: Routledge.

Kress, G. (2011). What is mode? In C. Jewitt (Ed.), *The Routledge handbook of multimodal analysis* (pp. 54–67). New York, NY: Routledge.

Lanham, R. A. (2001). What's next for text? *Education Communication and Information, 1*(2). Retrieved from http://www.open.ac.uk/eci/lanham/femoset.html

Latour, B. (2007). *Reassembling the social: An introduction to actor-network theory*. Oxford: Oxford University Press.

Lefebvre, H. (1992). *The production of space*. New York, NY: Wiley-Blackwell.

Lemke, J. (2011). Mulimodality, identity, and time. In C. Jewitt (Ed.), *The Routledge handbook of multimodal analysis* (pp. 140–150). New York, NY: Routledge.

Lesley, M. (2012). *Invisible girls: At risk adolescent girls' writing within and beyond school*. New York, NY: Peter Lang.

Leu, D. J., Kinzer, C. K., Coiro, J., Castek, J., & Henry, L. A. (2013). New literacies: A dual-level theory of the changing nature of literacy, instruction, and assessment. In D. E. Alvermann, N. J. Unrau, & R. B. Ruddell (Eds.), *Theoretical models and processes of reading* (6th ed.; pp. 1150–1181). Newark, DE: International Reading Association. doi:10.1598/0710.42

Mansell, R. (2001). Digital opportunities and the missing link for developing countries. *Oxford Review of Economic Policy, 17*(2), 282–295. doi:10.1093/oxrep/17.2.282

McClenaghan, D., & Doecke, B. (2010). Resources for meaning-making in the secondary English classroom. In D. R. Cole & D. L. Pullen (Eds.), *Multiliteracies in motion: Current theory and practice* (pp. 224–238). New York, NY: Routledge.

Meehan, E. R. (2002). Gendering the commodity audience: Critical media research, feminism, and political economy. In E. R. Meehan & E. Riordan (Eds.), *Sex and money: Feminism and political economy in the media* (pp. 209–222). Minneapolis, MN: University of Minnesota Press.

Miller, V. (2008). New media, networking and phatic culture. *Convergence (London), 14*(4), 387–400. doi:10.1177/1354856508094659

O'Byrne, W. I. (2014). Empowering learners in the reader/writer nature of digital information space. *Journal of Adolescent & Adult Literacy, 58*(2), 102–104. doi:10.1002/jaal.337

O'Byrne, W. I., & McVerry, J. G. (in press). Online Research and Media Skills: An instructional model to support students as they search and sift online informational text. In T. Rasinsky, K. Pytash, & R. Ferdig (Eds.), Comprehension of informational texts. Academic Press.

Orfield, G. (2014). Tenth annual *Brown* lecture in education research: A new civil rights agenda for American education. *Educational Researcher*, *43*(6), 273–292. doi:10.3102/0013189X14547874

Pooley, J. (2014, February). Interview with Nick Couldry. *New books in media & communication*. Retrieved from http://newbooksincommunications.com/2013/02/04/nick-couldry-media-society-world-social-theory-and-digital-media-practice-polity-press-2012/

Project Overview. (n.d.). *Europeana Space Project*. Retrieved from http://www.europeana-space.eu

Rennie, J., & Patterson, A. (2010). Young Australians reading in a digital world. In D. R. Cole & D. L. Pullen (Eds.), *Multiliteracies in motion: Current theory and practice* (pp. 207–223). New York, NY: Routledge.

Rushkoff, D. (2014). *Present shock*. New York, NY: Penguin Group.

Schweidler, C., & Costanza-Chock, S. (in press). Common cause: Global resistance to intellectual property rights. In D. Kidd, C. Rodriguez, & L. Stein (Eds.), Making our media: Mapping global initiatives toward a democratic public sphere. Creskill, NJ: Hampton Press. Retrieved from https://www.academia.edu/8297101/COMMON_CAUSE_GLOBAL_RESISTANCE_TO_INTELLECTUAL_PROPERTY_RIGHTS

Selwyn, N. (2004). Reconsidering political and popular understandings of the digital divide. *New Media & Society*, *6*(3), 341–362. doi:10.1177/1461444804042519

Skinner, E. N., & Hagood, M. C. (2008). Developing literate identities with English language learners through digital storytelling. *The Reading Matrix*, *8*(2), 12–38. Retrieved from http://www.readingmatrix.com/articles/skinner_hagood/article.pdf

Smythe, D. W. (2006). On the audience commodity and its work. In M. G. Durham & D. M. Kellner (Eds.), *Media and culture: Key works* (revised edition; pp. 230–256). Oxford, UK: Blackwell Publishers.

Street, B. V. (1993). *Cross-cultural approaches to literacy*. Cambridge, UK: Cambridge University Press.

Suthersanen, U. (2007). Creative commons – The other way? *Learned Publishing*, *20*(1), 59–68. doi:10.1087/095315107779490616

Terranova, T. (2012). Attention, economy and the brain. *Culture Machine, 13*, 1-19. http://www.culturemachine.net/index.php/cm/article/view/465/484

Thomas, A. (2007). *Youth online: Identity and literacy in the digital age*. New York, NY: Peter Lang.

Valenza, J. (2008, April 1). Fair use and transformativeness: It may shake your world. *School Library Journal*. Retrieved from http://blogs.slj.com/neverendingsearch/2008/04/01/fair-use-and-transformativeness-it-may-shake-your-world/

Varis, P., & Blommaert, J. (2015). Conviviality and collectives on social media: Virality, memes and new social structures. (Paper #108). Blommaert & Varis. Retrieved from http://www.tilburguniversity.edu/upload/83490ca9-659d-49a0-97db-ff1f8978062b_TPCS_108_Varis-Blommaert.pdf

Voithofer, R. (2005). Designing new media education research: The materiality of data, representation, and dissemination. *Educational Researcher*, *34*(9), 3–14. doi:10.3102/0013189X034009003

Walsh, M. (2008). Worlds have collided and modes have merged: Classroom evidence of changed literacy practices. *Literacy*, *42*(2), 101–108. doi:10.1111/j.1741-4369.2008.00495.x

Wertsch, J. V. (1998). Mediated action. In W. Bechtel & G. Graham (Eds.), *Companion to cognitive science* (pp. 518–525). Malden, MA: Blackwell.

ADDITIONAL READING

Alvermann, D. E., & Heron, A. H. (2001). Literacy identity work: Playing to learn with popular media. *Journal of Adolescent & Adult Literacy*, *45*, 118–122.

Alvermann, D. E., Marshall, J. D., McLean, C. A., Huddleston, A. P., Joaquin, J., & Bishop, J. (2012). Adolescents' web-based literacies, identity construction, and skill development. *Literacy Research and Instruction*, *51*(3), 179–195. doi:10.1080/19388071.2010.523135

Basu, D., & Vasudevan, R. (2011). Technology, distribution and the rate of profit in the US economy: Understanding the current crisis. Retrieved from http://people.umass.edu/dbasu/BasuVasudevanCrisis0811.pdf

Beer, D. (2013). *Popular culture and new media: The politics of circulation*. London: Palgrave Macmillan. doi:10.1057/9781137270061

Fields, D. A., Grimes, S. M., Magnifico, A., Lammers, J. C., Gomez, K., & Curwood, J. S. (2013). What's next in studying online social networking? Future research directions for creative, DIY-based sites. Proceedings of the Annual Conference 9.0 of Games + Learning + Society, University of Wisconsin-Madison.

Friesen, N., Gourlay, L., & Oliver, M. (2014). Scholarship and literacies in a digital age. [no page numbers given.]. *Research in Learning Technology*, 21.

Hall, R. (2013). Educational technology and the enclosure of academic labour inside public higher education. *Journal for Critical Education Policy Studies*, *11*(3), 52–82.

Hill, M., & Vasudevan, L. (Eds.). (2007). *Media, learning, and sites of possibility*. New York: Peter Lang.

Hobbs, R. (2010). *Digital and media literacy: A plan of action*. Washington, DC: The Aspen Institute, Communications and Society Program.

Holland, D., Lachicotte, W., Skinner, D., & Cain, C. (2001). *Identity and agency in cultural worlds*. Cambridge, MA: Harvard University Press.

Ito, M., Horst, H., Bittanti, M., & Boyd, D. (Eds.). (2010). *Hanging out, messing around, geeking out: Kids living and learning with new media*. Cambridge, MA: MIT Press.

Jappe, A. (2014). Towards a history of the critique of value. *Capitalism, Nature, Socialism*, *25*(2), 25–37. doi:10.1080/10455752.2014.906820

Jenkins, E. S. (2014). The modes of visual rhetoric: Circulating memes as expressions. *The Quarterly Journal of Speech*, *100*(4), 442–466. doi:10.1080/00335630.2014.989258

Knobel, M., & Lankshear, C. (2007). Online memes, affinities, and cultural production. In C. Lankshear, M. Knobel, C. Bignum, & M. Peters (Eds.), *A New Literacies Sampler* (pp. 199–227). New York, NY: Peter Lang.

Lapavitsas, C. (2010). Financialisation and capitalist accumulation: Structural accounts of the crisis of 2007-9. *Research on Money and Finance*, Discussion paper no.16. Retrieved from http://bit.ly/1l0cdwA

McLean, C. (2010). A space called home: An immigrant adolescent's digital literacy practices. *Journal of Adolescent & Adult Literacy, 54*(1), 13–22. doi:10.1598/JAAL.54.1.2

Radomska, M. (2013). Posthumanist pedagogies: Toward an ethics of the non/living. *Journal of Curriculum and Pedagogy, 10*(1), 28–31. doi:10.1080/15505170.2013.789999

Robinson, W. I. (2004). *A theory of global capitalism: Production, class, and state in a transnational world.* Baltimore, MA: John Hopkins University Press.

Shifman, L. (2013). *Memes in digital culture.* Cambridge, MA: MIT Press.

U.S. Department of Commerce. (2014). *Exploring the digital nation: Embracing the mobile internet.* Washington, DC: U.S. Department of Commerce, National Telecommunications and Information Administration.

KEY TERMS AND DEFINITIONS

Actant: A term used to denote an entity whether human or nonhuman that modifies the actions of another entity (e.g., pouring vinegar on baking soda).

Agency: A human's capacity to make choices; typically contrasted to natural forces or nonhuman elements.

Digital Media: A term given to the tools for communicating that involve conversion into machine-readable formats within human networks.

Economy: Production, distribution, and consumption of goods and services by agents, at times involving intermediaries for exchange known as money.

Global Economy: Combinations of the economies of countries *or* economic interactions that cross geopolitical boundaries overland, by air, by sea, and virtually.

Memes: Phrases, images, videos, sound effects, songs, etc. that are copied and spread rapidly by Internet users—typically without regard for whether the message or intended meaning is clear or not.

Modality: The vehicle/way in which meaning is made through text, speech, or gestures.

Mode: A resource through which people communicate that are socially and culturally determined.

Multimodality: Refers to multiple forms of communication that include language but do not privilege it over other modes such as still and moving images, sounds, gestures, icons, and performances.

New Materialists: 21st century scholars who claim that agency is not strictly a human capacity.

Transformativeness: The state of having been repurposed by a user of copyrighted materials to make them more amenable to fair use criteria.

Chapter 2
Moving beyond the Basics:
The Evolution of Web 2.0 Tools from Preview to Participate

Patricia Dickenson
National University, USA

Martin T. Hall
Charles Sturt University, Australia

Jennifer Courduff
Azusa Pacific University, USA

ABSTRACT

The evolution of the web has transformed the way persons communicate and interact with each other, and has reformed institutional operations in various sectors. Examining these changes through the theoretical framework Connectivism, provides a detailed analysis of how the web impacts individuals' context within communities as well as the larger society. This chapter examines the evolution of the web and the characteristics of various iterations of the web. A discussion on the emergence of participatory media and other participatory processes provides insight as to how the web influences personal and professional interactions. Research on how the web has changed cultural contexts as well as systems such as education, governments and businesses is shared and analyzed to identify gaps and provide direction for future research.

SUCCINCT OVERVIEW OF THE RESEARCH

Technology has revolutionized the way we communicate, send and receive information. It has changed the way businesses sell goods and operate services by creating a means for exchanges to take place at any time and any place with the power of the Internet, or World Wide Web (Fang, 1997). For the purposes of this chapter, the terms World Wide Web and the web will be used interchangeably with the assumption that the terms refer to access to and interaction with information and resources that are online. Emerging technological tools such as Smartphones and tablet computers may have the power to change how we work, learn, and

DOI: 10.4018/978-1-4666-8310-5.ch002

stay connected in our personal and professional lives. With the power of the web, synchronous discussion, educational course delivery, and other professional training options now reach beyond traditional face-to-face models. This continual access and connectivity phenomenon provides users with the ability to stay connected no matter where they are. But has this movement to digitize our lives been driven solely by the Internet, or has the influx of Web 2.0 tools created a more socially connected web to engage users as active participants? This chapter examines the evolutions of Web 2.0 tools and technology and explores the influence of social and political perspectives in the evolution of participatory media.

Learning in a Digitally Connected World through the Theoretical Lens of Connectivism

The ability for users to interact, share ideas, and create content is at the heart of Web 2.0. Many believe the emergence of Web 2.0 tools has flipped the script from previewing web-based content to participating in it. Through the availability of Web 2.0 tools, people are able to do more than simply consume information - they are able to produce information and make it available and accessible to the world. This phenomenon is changing the very basics of communications. According to O'Reilly (2006), "The Internet for the first time gives us many-to-many and few-to-few communications. This has vast implications for the former audience and for the producers of news because the difference between the two are becoming harder to distinguish" (p. 26) . In this quote, O'Reilly is referring to *the former* as the population at large or the *many-to-many*. The implication is that the *few,* in this case, newscasters, no longer have control over dissemination of information. Rather, dissemination is now available from the masses to the masses (many-to-many). The World Wide Web is no longer simply a read-only platform through which the user accesses and consumes information.

Rather, it is an enhanced system with capability to not only access information, but also contribute to it. This read-write capability is available for all who choose to participate. This is also evidenced by changes in education. Social networking tools such as blogs, wikis, and other online collaborative resources have changed approaches to teaching to being more learner-driven. The student now takes charge of his or her own learning and uses Web 2.0 tools to make deep connections between what is known and what is to be known.

Examining the transformation of the web through the lens of a theoretical framework provides insight as to how changes may impact social, personal, and political contexts. The framework of Connectivitism (Siemens, 2006) focuses on emerging individual and group knowledge through access to information online. One concept clearly delineated by Connectivism is the idea that the depth and degree to which we understand is directly related to the learner connecting to and exchanging information within the larger community. Siemens posits that the exchange of information begins with the clustering of similar ideas of interest that allow for interaction, sharing, and thinking together. Connectivism understands the powerful influence that culture, intelligence, perspective, and individual difference plays in any learning process. Connectivism assumes the continually changing nature of information in the 21st century. Knowledge is not static; it changes as quickly as information is updated to reflect culture, perspective, and individual experience (Bruner, 1987; Brown, 2002; Christensen, 2008; Gardner, 2006; Siemens, 2006). In knowing, we weave a "...bricolage of cognition, emotion, intuition, information, consumption, doubt, and belief" (Siemens, 2006, p. 59).

Traditional views of knowing are product-based rather than process-based. Product-based knowledge is knowing about things and knowing how to do things. These container-views assume a knowledge-in, product-out philosophy and align with behaviorist theories that humans can be trained through a process of rewards and consequences known as conditioning (Driscoll, 2004). On the other hand, process-based views extend knowledge beyond what one knows to what one does with that knowledge. For example, in product-based knowledge, a person knows how to do something. In process-based knowledge, not only does that person know how to do something, but he or she also knows how to apply what is known to a larger context. He or she understand how to navigate within a community, find information through connections with others, and how to transform my thoughts into new knowledge that successfully contributes what other people know. The essential purpose of process-based knowledge is to learn to live more deeply. Process-based knowing occurs over a lifetime and aligns with Bruner's cognitive view that learning is not only about gaining knowledge but also adding to it. It further aligns with Dewey's constructivist views that learning is built on communication, experiences, and ideas (Driscoll, 2004). Connectivism is a process-based emerging theory (Siemens, 2005) that redefines how humans acquire, store, and share knowledge in the digital age. The overarching assumptions of Connectivism are:

1. Intention to bring the most current information to the knowledge base.
2. Ability to make connections between fields, ideas, and concepts including refocusing on information and perspectives that are intentionally ignored.
3. Selection of learning focus and accurate determination of meaning within incoming information through a realistic lens.
4. Diversity of human opinions: the viewpoints of others allow us to see a unified whole.
5. Connection made between information sources called nodes: the connections allow the transfer of information and ideas resulting accurate / original knowledge.
6. Generation and storage by non-human, technological resources.

7. Emerging and extended knowledge is maintained through connectedness to individuals and groups.
8. Emerging knowledge is more important than current knowledge because knowing is based on perspective and situatedness; relying only on current knowledge stagnates and suppresses creativity, diversity, and free thought.

Connectivism suggests the process of acquiring, applying and storing knowledge involves the flow of information and interactivity between individuals and groups. In effect, knowledge is acquired along a continuum that is constantly reassessed through feedback loops of new information. Examining current trends and emerging technology through the lens of Connectivism has the potential to not only capture how information is shared, managed, and created using online technologies but also examine the ways in which social media mediates interaction among people and groups.

The Evolution of the World Wide Web

The World Wide Web, or the web, has progressed from sole use of personal computers to the ubiquitous use of hand-held devices and most recently wearable technology. In 1989, Tim Berners-Lee proposed having a global space in which any information that could be accessible by a network is identified by one Universal Document Identifier (Berners-Lee & Fischetti, 1999). Berners-Lee's ideas were visionary and influenced the way the web is used and viewed.

Many persons use the terms Internet and the web interchangeably. However, the two are not exclusively the same (Patel, 2013). The Internet is an architectural design of a meta-network, where many networks communicate through common communication protocols (Carpenter, 1996). The design of the Internet is portrayed through its name - inter-networking. On the other hand, the

World Wide Web is an information library where documents are connected to other documents in a matrix through links. This allows users to search for and access information which is stored in the matrix. While the web and the Internet are different, the web is seen as the most important part of the Internet. Researchers refer to the web as a techno-social system which encourages interaction and participation (Fuchs, Hofkirchner, Schafranek, Raffl, Sandoval, & Bichler, 2010; Patel, 2013). The concept of a techno-social system means that the web, as it is used today, cannot be described without connections being made to human and social interactions. Thus exploring the use of web tools and social media through a Connectivism lens lends itself to a greater understanding of how current trends and emerging technology shapes knowledge.

The first iteration of the web, or Web 1.0, was known as read-only web. Websites were used to store information that could be accessed by anyone at any point in time. There was a heavy emphasis on owning information, and sharing that information in an expository tranmissionist way. Websites were static and mono-directional and were akin to electronic brochures used to offer services for sale via the web. The type of web tools associated with this developmental stage of *the* web encouraged little or no participation from the audience.

Today, many of our interactions are guided by Web 2.0 technologies, with much talk about the development of Web 3.0 and buzz words about Web 4.0 (Aghaei, Nematbakhsh, & Farsani, 2012). The vision behind the initial development of the web was to provide a space where persons communicated through the sharing of information (Berners-Lee & Fischetti, 1999). While it is difficult to make a technical comparison between Web 1.0 and Web 2.0, due to the fact that Web 2.0 operates on the same substrate as Web 1.0, there are some fundamental differences between them (Cormode & Krishnamurthy, 2008).

Web 2.0, which is also known as "the wisdom web, people centric web, participative web, and read-write web" (Aghaei, Nematbakhsh, & Farsani, 2012, p. 3), was conceptualized in a brainstorming meeting between MediaLiveInternational and Tim O'Reilly. Web pioneers, Dale Dougherty, and Tim O'Reilly acknowledged the contributions and importance of the web, but recognized it was time for a call to action that would signify a turning point for Web 1.0. In 2006 Tim O'Reilly defining Web 2.0 stated,

Web 2.0 is the business revolution in the computer industry caused by the move to the Internet as platform, and an attempt to understand the rules for success on that new platform. Chief among those rules is this: Build applications that harness network effects to get better the more people use them (O'Reiley, 2006).

Web 2.0 is bi-directional, it is interactive, including opportunities to both read and write content and share information via several mediums. Additionally, Web 2.0 provides platforms for the user to build applications on the web instead of users building applications on their personal desktop. For example, using Google tools one can create a website, blog, spreadsheet, video, presentation, survey, and more. Participants are actively involved with more interactivity and with less control (Aghaei, Nematbakhsh, & Farsani, 2012). Examples of Web 2.0 sites include Facebook, Wikispaces, Twitter, and Youtube (See Table 1 for the description of other webtools). There is a strong social component, including user profiles, social networking, business networking, and other user generated content through various mediums. "Web 2.0 is mostly a social revolution in the use of Web technologies, a paradigm shift from the Web as a publishing medium" (Lassila & Hendler, 2007).

Table 1. Common Web 2.0 Tools and Technologies

Blogs (Weblogs)	Synonymous for a personal website for all that requires no high level of ICT knowledge to run. It is argued that the most important characteristics of weblogs is to have a permanent Universal Resource Locater (URL) by which contents are allowed to be disseminated permanently with a permission for others to be in collaboration (Stephens, 2011).
Wikis	Types of software allowing the users to form a new web page or make additional changes in already present ones. As clearly understood from the definition, wikis can be edited, designed or shared by any one at any specific time. Traunmüller (2010, 78) defines wikis as "knowledge collections built by collaborative edition".
Social Media	Types of websites which aim to make people get in touch with each other through sharing personal or any other information with permitted peers. "The users of social networking sites are registered users who are allowed to interact with other users for social or professional purposes" (Wigand, 2010, 169).
RSS Technologies	The dissemination of information based on subscription. Wigand (2010, 169) describes really simple syndication's aim as "RSS feeds are generally used for updating blogs, news headlines, or podcasts to users".
Social Tagging	Synonymous with collaborative indexing. Social tagging is a process through which "users add metadata in the form of keywords to shared content" (Golder and Huberman, 2006, 198).
Visual Share	The transmission of visual images via Web 2.0 technologies. Wigand (2010, 169) states that YouTube is the leading site in terms of video share. Flickr can be exemplified as the dissemination of photos over web.

Source: Gil-Garcia & Criado, 2013, p. 10

One of the affordances of Web 2.0 technologies, and is believed to become increasingly ubiquitous with the developing Web 3.0 movement, is the increased use of portable devices with greater access to cloud based sites. This will realize more cross-devices and platform sharing of content. These affordances will impact mobility, portability, interactivity, collaboration and will result in shared productivity.

Important distinctions between Web 1.0 and Web 2.0 include the static nature of Web 1.0. For example, one might see frequent or infrequent updates of website content in Web 1.0 sites, while Web 2.0 offers dynamic live sites that are continuously updated from multiple sources. In Web 1.0, the creators of content are few and users are simply content consumers. Conversely, Web 2.0 includes many content creators to ensure that information is shared democratically (Kaplan & Haenlein, 2010). Web 1.0 sites are hierarchical in structure, while Web 2.0 sites are a part of the integrated network. These distinctions can be classified as technological (coding that allow users to interface with each other), structural (site design, organization and function), and sociological (operating within friend and professional circles and with other like-minded individuals). Scripting and presentation technologies allow for user interaction, structural creativity (purpose and layout of the site), and sociological connections (notions of friends and groups) (Cormode & Krishnamurthy, 2008).

Web 2.0 tools aim to achieve portalization when encouraging users to repeatedly return to websites by providing options that meet their needs. Portalization is the idea that once a person is on a site that he/she does not have to leave. Users are able to access VoIP services, email, RSS feeds, and can communicate with friends and other persons within professional circles. There have been numerous studies that examined Web 2.0 tools and how these tools differed from Web 1.0 tools. Given the fact that many users of Web 2.0 tools still access Web 1.0 sites, research must be conducted that will seek to answer a range of questions regarding specific reasons relating to use. For example, acknowledging the fact that users access sites for various reasons, studies that group participants by areas of interest and other classifications will enable comparative analyses of functionality and design of Web 1.0 and Web 2.0 sites.

Although Web 1.0 sites are still very relevant, with more than half a billion users of Web 2.0 sites still accessing Web 1.0 sites (Cormode & Krishnamurthy, 2008), the evolution of web tools has transitioned the end-user from consumers of information to creators and participants in information development and sharing. This has given rise to participatory journalism/media or social media.

Social media refers to the social relations among and between people. It is the way in which they construct, reconstruct, and exchange information. Social media is defined as a cluster of web-based tools which build on the development of Web 2.0 technology (Kaplan & Haenlein, 2010). One of the most popular types of social media is Facebook. Facebook connects users through their profile page. A profile page is a web page that has a dynamic interface for the user to add content such as video, pictures, text as well as information from other sites. By the end of 2013, Facebook boasted 1.23 billion monthly active users worldwide, adding 170 million in just one year. According to Facebook, 757 million users log on to Facebook daily as of December 31 2013. Although persons have tried to classify social media into different types (Kaplan & Haenlein, 2010), many argue the lines between different types of social media are blurred (Shi, Rui, & Whinston, 2014).

Web 3.0 is the third generation of the web, and the focus is on delivering a web experience that is personalized by being responsive to the end-users needs and interests.

Every interaction on the web is used as data to learn more about the user. Personal information, search history, and web application use, can reveal one's interests, likes, and daily activities. This iteration of the web experience is widely referred to as the semantic web or the intelligent web. The term, Web 3.0 was coined by John Markoff (2006) and was the brainchild of Tim Berners-Lee. Metadata is used to produce information that could be accessed, analyzed, and disseminated by software agents (Morris, 2011). For example, "mobile phones will be equipped with an appropriate interface to arrange a lunch date with a business partner, automatically negotiating an adequate time by accessing both calendars" (Wahlster & Dengel, 2006, p. 20). This ability for Web 3.0 to become machine readers and writers are the types of processes will be the foundation of the semantic web (McEneaney, 2011). This phase of the Web, explained through the theoretical framework of Connectionism, is technologically advanced where users are not only reading what is on the Web, but where the Web is also reading users.

A symbiotic relationship between humans and machines was the motive behind Web 4.0. Although Web 4.0 is still developing, the idea is that we will be able to communicate with computers in a reciprocal way. The version of the web is also called the read-write execution concurrency web. Concurrency refers a collection of systems where several computations are being executed in a simultaneous fashion with the potential for interaction across computations. "Web 4.0 achieves a critical mass of participation in online networks that deliver global transparency, governance, distribution, participation, collaboration in industry, political and social networks and other key community endeavors" (Cake, n.d.).

Intelligent machines will be able to read what is on the web and respond by executing actions. These machines are expected to be as powerful as the human brain. Global transparency will be achieved since it is expected that mass participation will be achieved in online spaces. Table 2 outlines the distinguishing characteristics of the different versions of the web. There is no real idea of how Web 4.0 will be defined, but four key distinguishing features were provided in the following table.

The Emergence of Participatory Media

Participatory media, participatory journalism or new media as it is sometimes referred to, is defined as information that is gathered, exam-

Table 2. Distinctions in the Various Iterations of the World Wide Web

Distinguishing Features	Web 1.0	Web 2.0	Web 3.0	Web 4.0
Name	The World Wide Web	The Social Web	The Semantic Web	The Symbiotic Web/The Ubiquitous Web
End-user Function	Read-only	Read-write features	Read-write and execute/Portable Personal Web	Read-write execution concurrency Web
Connectivity	Connects Information	Connects People	Connects Knowledge	Connects People and Knowledge in a Symbiotic relationship
Mass Communicative Processes	One to many	Many to Many	Semantic many to semantic many	Many to one and one to many
Directionality of Information Flow	Web is unidirectional	Web is bidirectional	Highly interactive leading to AI (Artificial Intelligence)	
User Interface	Homepages	Follksonomies/ Social Tagging	Smart-web	
Creators/Consumers of Content	Content creator	Content creator and consumer of content	Data driven; Highly personalized end user experience	
Drivers of Information Flow	Companies Publish Content	People Publish Content	Applications and Platforms are built so that services and other special content are published and shared	
Information Management	Content Management System	Wikis, Blogs, Online Journals	Semantic Wikis, Semantic Blogs, Semantic Online Journals	
Contacts	Address books	Social networks	Semantic social networks	

ined, added to or altered, and shared through the participation of audiences. Since the evolution of the web, participatory media has been linked to social networking, tags, Wikis, blogs and other online forums, and the sharing of various media content in several formats. "Generations of people have changed their perception of and participation in the web, and have accepted the web as a communication medium" (Vossen & Hagemann, 2007, p. 41).

Although the evolution of Web 2.0 tools provided a strong platform for participatory media, popularising it and catapulting its use making it a ubiquitous part of everyday life, participatory journalism existed in various forms throughout history (Ekström, Jülich, Lundgren, & Wisselgren, 2012; Carpentier, 2009; Carpentier, 2011). One form is the collection of essays, letters and drawings published in the early 1940s in protest to the Nazi regime (Křížková, Kotouč, & Ornest, 1999 as cited in Carpentier, 2011). Other examples include the forwarding of chain letters and the forwarding of emails. In the latter examples, users were passive contributors to content; however, their active participation was necessary to maintain the flow of information from one participant to the other.

The evolution of Web 2.0 tools has increased the ability of people from different countries and cultures to connect and work together across miles. This participatory culture (Jenkins, 2009) – one in which people use Web 2.0 to collaborate for work and for play is evidenced clearly through the popularization of massive online multiplayer games. Participatory culture is also exploding in the education world. Massive Open Online Courses (MOOCs) have been developed free to the public by many colleges and universities. Most recently, there is a body of new work on the *spreadability* of digital texts and the subsequent influence on longevity of texts and the shift to readers becoming responsible for the spread of information (Jenkins, Ford, & Green, 2013).

According to Rushkoff (1994), Greg Ruggiero is credited as being the first person to publicly use the term 'participatory media'. Subsequently, the phrase has been popularized by various researchers and media journalists. This omnipresent phenomenon whereby users are voicing their opinions and are more involved in the production of news and entertainment has been precipitated by online technologies. Through personal blogs and other narratives, members of the media are now ordinary citizens. It is likely that participatory media might take on new forms given the rise of different iterations on the web, although it is not clear how these might look. While emerging forms of participatory media will be heavily influenced by the iterations of the web, the evolution of participatory media will also be shaped by larger sociological and political structures. Participatory media will shape and change many of the systems and processes that we are accustom today. It has and will continue to have an effect on education and educational institutions, governments, political processes and other forms of political engagements, and culture within societies. The subsequent sections explore how participatory media has shaped education, government and politics, businesses, and culture.

CURRENT ISSUES IN THE FIELD RAISED BY THESE STUDIES

Exploring the Application of Web 2.0 Technologies in the Context of Culture

According to Chen and Zhang (2010), "the compression of time and space, due to the convergence of new media and globalization, has shrunk the world into a much smaller interactive field" (p. 14). The platforms that exist connect people from all over the world. Persons can communicate from one corner of the globe to the opposite corner in real-time. This inevitably brings communities and societies together, causing persons from different cultural contexts to interact with each other on a range of issues and interests within the 'virtual village square'. Not only has the evolution of the web and its participatory nature encouraged interaction between cultures, but it has also had an impact on cultures.

Due to the emergence of the participatory web, there is much more interaction between cultures, and persons are increasingly becoming more connected through online interaction via social media sites. Some persons are of the view that social media thwarts traditional human interaction and therefore does not encourage any real connection (Kraut, Patterson, Lundmark, Kiesler, Mukophadhyay, & Scherlis, 1998). This creates a paradoxical view of connectedness in this online space. An external analysis of online interactions may view the process as unsocial. On the other hand, those who remain connected to their friends, family, and other persons of similar likes and interests might be more receptive to this type of ubiquitous interaction. It seems that on many fronts social media draws persons and cultures closer, while at the same time distancing them.

In light of the above, the implications that this may have on a person's psychological well-being should be considered. It is clear that a strong social presence will exist; however, this might result in reduced real life human interactions and could diminish the value of traditional social interaction. The quality of relationships that persons have with each other significantly contribute to psychological well-being (Umberson, Chen, House, Hopkins, & Slaten, 1996). This becomes a concern since "it is possible that many of the social relationships persons maintain online are less substantial and sustaining than relationships that people have in their actual lives" (Kraut, Kiesler, Mukhopadhyay, Scherlis, & Patterson, 1998, p. 21). Nevertheless, there is a need for research on how relationships are shaped and sustained as a result of social media and how this might impact psychological well-being.

Some persons suggest time spent engaging in online participatory activities may not only reduce real life interaction, as suggested above, but detract from other valuable activities such as reading (Kraut, Kiesler, Mukhopadhyay, Scherlis, & Patterson, 1998). In the opinion of Rose (2011), social media is not replacing other activities and is having a positive impact on culture. He argues that web 2.0 technologies do not replace other important activities but fills the spaces between those activities. Research must then explore how online use is negotiated with other salient activities. Cultural as well as gender and age differences may exist therefore a robust body of research is needed to explore how participatory media effects people from diverse backgrounds and ethnicities.

One of the impacts of participatory media is a more connected and informed society due to increased access to information. Persons have been able to engage on issues relating to the Obama Health Care initiative, terrorists attacks on September 11, 2001, and the capture of Saddam Hussein, and were able to contribute opinions on these widely shared areas of concern. These issues went viral across the Internet and were viewed by millions of persons around the globe. However, this open access to information begs several questions to be answered. Is access to all

types of information beneficial to communities? How legitimate is the information that is received? Should persons be concerned about their privacy due to increased access? What happens to the information after we die?

While increased access to information results in a more informed culture, the disadvantage might be the sharing of illicit information. The content of these messages could be quite graphic, and in some cases may include gut-wrenching images of murder victims or sexual activity. Although the potential impact is not known, continuous engagement of this type of information could desensitize persons to violence and crime, and could eventually become problematic. Evidence of new ways of petitioning, and fundraising, achieved all through social media, is testimony to the reach, level of access, and effect that participatory media has achieved.

Of course increased access to information means access to information that could be altered due to participatory mechanisms. As discussed above, traditional means of sharing information was one to many formats which were characteristic of mass communication principles. Now citizens create and share content and are part of the media. However, the reliability of the information shared is a point requiring debate. One of the pillars of social media is trust. It is through trust that connections are made and information is shared. However, enough processes are not in place to verify the validity and trustworthiness of information shared, especially information highly sensationalized to increase the number of shares and social tags. Social media scams are becoming increasingly common and may result in viruses, credit card fraud, and stealing of identity. Lopez (2014) reports common social media scams may seem harmless and even reports other friends or colleagues liking a page or an app, but once installed this can open the door to personal information being shared and used. In 2008, the Guardian reported 1.8 million users of the Yahoo chat services were spied on through the webcams that were turned on during their chat session (Lopez, 2014). Another research gap is presented here. The credibility of information that is shared via social media must be examined.

On the one hand where access to incorrect information may be undesirable, lack of access or inequitable access could equally be as problematic (Jenkins, 2009). The evolution of the web has changed how news agencies operate. Many newspapers have gone fully online and are sharing the news in that space through participatory means. As a result, there is a reduction in the use of the other means of communication. Participatory media has provided greater access to information for persons living in rural, regional and urban areas, and in developed and developing countries. However, if persons decide not to access Web 2.0 sites due to skill or preference, they may be excluded from information that is shared if the information is not also shared via traditional means. There are some cultures where some social media sites have been censored. This means that some types of information will fail to reach non-users, and creates issues of equity and access to information, an issue for some cultures more than others (Gomez, 2013; Jenkins, 2009).

Social media has been able to speed up the flow of information, outpacing traditional news outlets. While increased access to information is beneficial, studies have shown that there might be privacy issues (Omand, Bartlett, & Miller, 2012; Privacy Rights Clearinghouse, 2012; Sánchez Abril, Levin, & Del Riego, 2012; Shin, 2010). Persons upload their life story to social media sites and that information is available for anyone to read if it is not protected. Even where privacy settings prevent some persons from accessing intimate and sensitive information, data is still collected by the sites and is used to gain insights into users for a range of reasons such as profiling, targeted marketing, and research and development.

Another concern linked to privacy issues is the digital footprint that remains online. The evolution of web technologies has realized an era where persons engage in virtual realities and second life games through the creation of avatars. The information that is uploaded remains online until it is removed. As a matter of fact, "based on the information [that is provided] online, users expose themselves to various physical and cyber risks, and make it extremely easy for third parties to create digital dossiers of their behavior" (Gross & Acquisti, 2005, p. 10). This has a cultural impact on members of the digital community as more and more companies are being developed to make arrangements for digital death and afterlife.

Exploring the Application of Web 2.0 Technologies in the Context of Business

In 2006, Harvard business professor Andrew McAfee coined the term Enterprise 2.0 to describe the use of emergent Web 2.0 technologies for companies to collaborate, share, and organize information with their customers, employees, and suppliers. Internal and external communication moved from one-way transmission approaches to highly interactive practices that include social media such as Facebook and Twitter and corporate blogging sites to share information and promote a Connectivist culture. Common internal practices of social media tools include searching for information on an internal blog using tags, uploading and sharing documents, presentations and other files on a web-based platform for others to use, share and edit. Video conferencing and instant messaging with other employees, companies and even customers are also common Web 2.0 practices. According to Hinchcliffe (2007), Enterprise 2.0 technologies explore this aspect by empowering collaboration and knowledge sharing between workers. These practices will contribute to a less hierarchical and more transparent organization. Overwhelmingly business managers perceived these emerging tools to be relevant and useful today especially in the area of marketing, innovation, operations and leadership (Kiron et al., 2012).

According to a recent Harvard Business Review survey (2010), 79% of companies are either using or planning to use social media. Of those who have adopted social media practices, 87% use social media to promote their brand, product, and other services. This finding suggests most companies use social media in a one-way transmission approach without fully capitalizing on the information that can be retrieved from customers sharing ideas, trends, and reviews of their products. Although the use of social media may be common for many large companies, in small businesses the adoption of social media is moving at a much slower pace. According to a recent survey of small business owners (Yodle, 2013) about 34% use technology for customer relationship management and only 14% use these tools for acquisition marketing. It is unclear why small business owners are reluctant to use social media as a tool for marketing and customer relations; however, small businesses are also behind the times when it comes to adopting other technology tools as well. Less than half of all small business owners have a website (49%) or use technology for other common practices such as accounting (51%) or appointment booking and scheduling (39%). Research is needed to understand why small business owners lag behind their corporate counterparts, but also what support is needed so that small businesses can use technological tools to support and grow their business.

Social media can influence a company's reputation both in a positive and negative light. This can impact their political and business decisions which can result in success or failure. For example in 2014, Virgin Airlines launched a social media campaign asking their customers to sign online petitions and make supportive posts to Facebook and Twitter. The campaign was launched in an effort to beat out their competition for additional gates at a popular Texas airport. The airline also publicized a commitment to donate to local schools in an effort to enhance their reputation. Their social media campaign worked. According to Kim Nash (2014), companies are using social media to "rehabilitate corporate reputations, uncover ideas for breakthrough products and figure out what competitors are up to." Nash also believes that the future of social media includes analyzing the behaviors of not only customers, but competitors as well, to increase market share. However, social media can take a toll on a company's reputation when unfavorable news hits the public eye and this can have negative repercussions for years to come. What once was considered private information between a company and their customers can impact the choices and decisions of future consumers and have a severe impact. In 2013, a major security breach at Target, a popular retailer in the United States, not only cost the company 61 million in response to the breach (Riley, et al., 2014), but much more as their reputation in terms of trust with their customers quickly eroded. Future research should examine how reputations are impacted as a result of social media campaigns. Whether or not companies decide to embrace social media, it is important to explore how this impacts a company's reputation and customer base. The use and misuse of business Web 2.0 technologies must be explored to understand the scope and significance of these emerging tools.

Exploring the Application of Web 2.0 Technologies in the Context of e-Government: The Case of Governments (Institutions) and Politics (Ideologies)

Although studies and perceptions of social media in government and politics are not consistent, the application of Web 2.0 tools to government and politics is emerging. For example, some studies suggest that government agencies are about two years behind Web 2.0 philosophy, values, and culture. Government websites continue to function under a Web 1.0 philosophy where information is presented as static text. Existing literature posits that there is a scarcity of the use of social media tools on both local and federal government websites, and the mentality of control over information remains the status quo (Macnamara 2010, Karkin, 2013). Interestingly, the 2008 elections revealed higher levels of use of social media tools among candidates. Most notably was the emergence of *politics 2.0* brought about by candidates' use of social media resources such blogs and wikis to provide a means of interacting directly with the people (Chen, Chiang, & Storey, 2012). As Web 3.0 tools emerge and become mainstream, social networking sites have become an important arena for politics. They are a resource for political news, information, finding similar minded issue-oriented people, and a tool for voter outreach in run-up to elections.

Conversely, there is a body of literature that suggests a more proactive approach of government in support of social media. The Obama campaign and subsequent presidency have supported the use of social media for direct government interaction with the people. Bertot, Jaeger, Munson, & Glaisyer, (2010) list a number of opportunities for public engagement in the governmental process. These include public engagement and opportunities to voice individual opinions in the policy-making process, the co-production, design, and deliverance of government services, and *crowdsourcing* - a process through which public innovation and talent is tapped in order to develop solutions to large-scale public issues. This high level of societal interaction is evidence of the power of Connectivism in supporting shared knowledge for the betterment of society. Government agencies also use social media as a means of disseminating information and services electronically. As such, a greater cross section of the population is able to access information, apply for, and receive support services than any time in history. Current and emerging legislation on equitable access and use of social media for government services includes a focus on three goals: (1) physical access to technology resources for all peoples,

(2) equitable access to technology resources for persons with disabilities and language barriers, (3) a minimum standard for information and civics literacy in support of basic understanding in how to use social media to access and understand government processes and policies.

While the support of social media in government exists and is expanding, there are challenges within the process. One emerging challenge is truth within opportunity to voice public opinion of the political process. Although social media has the power to create a platform to discuss a variety of topics and share divergent opinions, when it comes to political issues research suggests social media users are less willing to speak up about political issues if they feel their opinion is not widely shared. (Hampton, et al., 2013). In fact, Hampton and colleagues found that about 86% of participants were willing to have an in-person discussion about political issues but just 42% were willing to post about a political topic online. There are other challenges within the integration of social media uniformly within the system. Bertot, Jaeger, and Hansen (2010) suggest that while the government has clearly defined processes for online privacy, security, and access, many of the policies contain vague application to social media, and some do not include social media at all. Processes for governing and governance, while well defined, do not include application to social media. Moreover, there is limited research on the impact of social media on campaign financing and spending of funds. Many have already called on government agencies to provide greater access to information, and greater support in understanding and using the information to gain access to services, and to gain a voice in the political process. Although research has shown that this affects how these organizations operate, there must be more research that investigates whether government use and control of social media increases accountability for the betterment of the economy and society at large.

The Evolution of Web Tools and Participatory Media on Education

In the K-12 classroom, policy and curriculum reform not only influence the kinds of technology to which teachers have access, but also the instructional choices they make. In higher education, this can drive how teacher education programs prepare new teachers to utilize technology in the classroom. The quantity and quality of pre-service teachers technology experiences in teacher education programs have been found to be a critical factor that influences new teachers adoption of technology (Agyei & Voogt, 2011; Drent & Meelissen, 2008). In recent years, technology education has gone through significant change and revision. The introductory technology course has gone through a particularly dynamic era, with nearly half of all topics appearing as recent as 2010. Of particular note among the new topics are SMART Boards and Web 2.0 technologies such as Blogs, Wikis, and Professional and Social Networking Sites (Betrus, 2010). Over the last twenty years the curriculum for technology has advanced as a result of standards, new initiatives, and an emphasis on teaching design (Welty, 2003).

The National Council for Accreditation of Teacher Education (NCATE) emphasized the use of technology for teacher education by developing the National Education Technology Standards for Teachers (2008) which requires teachers to use technology in their classroom and design learning environments and experiences that support teaching, learning, and curricula. In addition, the Obama administration's educational technology plan "Transforming America Education: Learning Powered by Technology" (2010) calls for the application of technology throughout the entire education system as a means to improve student learning. Most recently in the United States, the Common Core State Standards Initiative (2014) outlines what a student should know and be able to do by the end of each grade and strives to weave technology use throughout the content standards

rather than treat technology as a separate strand of content. Despite the acceptance among school policies and political entities there are a multitude of challenges to integrating technology into teacher education programs and the classroom including; access and availability to equipment, limitations in funding, training and technical and instructional support (Duhaney 2001).

Advocates of technology such as the International Society for Technology in Education (ISTE) and Consortium for School Networking (COSN) believe emerging technologies have the capacity to impact teaching and learning and to transform education. Further these organizations contend technology holds the potential to deliver instruction in a way that will engage students and customize learning at the students' pace, rather than at a pace set by the teacher. Unlike past innovations where technology was used to supplement instruction in a one-to-one learning environment, technology is central to learning, self-paced, and student-centered. However, in his book *Oversold & Underused* (2001), Larry Cuban argues that not much has changed in terms of instruction despite the proliferation of technology in the classroom. Cuban outlines levels of technology integration including: entry, adoption, adaptation, appropriation and invention based on the work by Sandholtz, Ringstaff & Dwyer (1997). Cuban's research found most schools remain in the "adoption" level - a traditional approach to instruction with some explanation on how to use computers and very few teachers reach the 'intervention' level where project-based and interdisciplinary approaches to instruction are seamlessly integrated with technology.

Although Cuban's research is somewhat outdated it is important to note that technology adoption does not always mean technology application. A recent Speak Up survey (2014) reported 20% of high school students in a traditional learning environment use digital tools like blogging and just 10% reported creating digital books or magazines. The use of digital tools was more common among students in virtual schools with 32% blogging and 27% creating digital books. These findings suggest that despite technology proliferation there are still low levels of technology application happening in the classroom.

Conversely, more than 60% of teachers in the Speak Up survey reported that their classroom included a blended learning model that includes online content and curriculum to support student learning. This style of instruction mirrors more traditional approaches to teaching with knowledge being transmitted through the use of online course content such as synchronous discussion boards, video presentation, and lecture style material. In this approach, the teacher reinforces product-based knowledge in which there is an assumption that knowledge is transmitted and humans can be trained through a process of rewards and consequences known as conditioning (Driscoll, 2004). Although technology is influencing how teachers present material, not much has changed in the role of the student as consumers of content rather than producers. The majority of the more than 300,000 students surveyed in the Project Tomorrow report (2014) indicate they would like their classroom environment to replicate the way they are using digital tools outside of school to support greater communication and collaboration. Findings from this study suggest that the classroom environment does not mirror how students are using technology in their personal lives.

Studies on the impact of social media on education and the way students participate in educational spaces also exist; however, these studies produced mixed results (Fewkes & McCabe, 2012; Gao, Luo, & Zhang, 2012; Kist, 2013; Lennon, 2012; Moran, Seaman, & Tinti-Kane, 2011; Sherer & Shea, 2011). Social media use is more prominent in educators' personal lives but not when it comes to connecting with students. A recent survey found only 17% of K-12 teachers encourage their students to connect with them via social media and only 18% integrate it in the classroom (Burden, 2013). Although middle and high school students report that they believe the academic experience would be more engag-

ing if they could use these tools in the classroom (DeGennaro, 2008; Spires, Lee, Turner, & Johnson, 2008), research has yet to reveal that most teachers tend to do so (Speak Up, 2014). When it comes to the impact of social media in the classroom, most research have focused primarily on universities, community colleges, or other institutions of higher learning rather than on K-12 education (Anderson, 2012; Boulos & Wheeler, 2008; Cain & Fox, 2009; Covington, Petherbridge, & Warren 2009; Fascher-Herro, 2010; Gouseti, 2010; Granitz & Koerning, 2011; Hartman, Brown, Bonk, Boston, & Stringer, 2010; Oliver, 2011).

Universities and colleges use social media for similar purposes to businesses. A research study conducted by the University of Massachusetts Dartmouth (2008) found that 100% of surveyed universities and colleges are using social media but mostly as a tool for recruitment, admission, and promoting campus activities. Social media provides a platform for students to interact with the university; student generated content on a social media site can create a personality of the school and increase usage to the site (Pidaparthy, 2011).

When it comes to teaching and instruction in higher education, the Babson report (2013) found instructors were more likely to require students to create content for blogs and wikis rather than read or just comment on another user's blog. Faculty in the areas of Humanities and Arts, Professional and Applied Sciences and the Social Sciences were more likely to report using social media for teaching purposes than those in Natural Sciences or Mathematics and Computer Sciences (Seaman & Tinti-Kane, 2013).

GAPS IN THE EXTANT RESEARCH AND DIRECTIONS FOR FUTURE RESEARCH

Participatory culture has been able to connect and increase interaction between and among cultures. Although this is a given, the impact of this on culture has not been explored empirically. There needs to be a cross-cultural study that examines the impact of the participatory nature on unique civilizations and on how or whether the impact is negotiated with age and gender. Additionally, the impact that participatory media has on psychological well-being must be explored using experimental longitudinal designs. Studies have shown that persons spend a large portion of their time on social media, which prohibits them from spending time doing other valuable activities. Nevertheless, how social media affects psychological or physical well-being is not clearly articulated and therefore warrants further investigation. Equally as important is the type of relationships which are forged and maintained as a result of social media. Studies on the quality of these relationships and their enduring nature would contribute significantly to understanding social virtual connectivity within this connected space. Moreover, whether the types of information shared desensitize participants is also a much-needed area of research. Major gains have been made in eye tracking research and could be used here to respond to this question. The results could make inferences regarding crime and violence within societies. A major area of concern and an identified research gap is the trustworthiness of the information that is created and shared. This is an important question and the results could encourage or discourage further use of social media tools. Furthermore, the fact that third parties, such as employers, marketing agencies, and other social media users have been accessing social media sites to gain information about members is common knowledge. Information stored on the site is archived and remains there even after the user account has been deactivated. However, there has not been empirical research on the extent to which social media encroaches on a person's privacy or the effect that this encroachment might have on either professional or personal engagements.

Is It Too Good to Be True: Issues in Education

Current research on the way technology influences teaching and learning is limited not only in scope but also in function. Research needs to go beyond the traditional survey on attitudes and perceptions and extend into the impact of technology innovations on students' motivation, engagement, and achievement. Further, universities need to build partnerships with K-12 schools to fill the research gap and support new and tenured teachers with successful ways to implement a variety of technologies in their classroom. Shifting instructional ideologies from a teacher-centered approach to one that is student-centered will require student access to technology and the Internet on a regular basis, as well as professional development on the variety of web tools and applications across the discipline. This will enable students to be more than just consumers but producers of technology and facilitate the use of technology as a means for student participation. Research clearly indicates that children are using technology in their personal lives but not accessing it in meaningful ways in the classroom. According to the Pew Research Internet Project (2013), 95% of teens are online and 81% use social networking sites such as Facebook and Twitter. Guidelines are needed to not only address effective uses of social media but also prevent cyber bullying. Concerns about the integrity of student work as well as privacy concerns are among the top reasons to prevent the use of social media in teaching (Seaman, & Tinti-Kane, 2013). Future research should examine effective ways to prevent cyber bullying in the classroom and maintain student privacy. Web tools and technologies should be developed to support teachers in monitoring social media. The evolution of Web 3.0 may be supportive in the role of tagging key words or phrases that would alert teachers or prohibit students from posting online. The evolutionary nature of the Web begs the question of whether we reshape educational practices to match the evolution of the Web or whether we repurpose new Web technologies in an effort to fit educational contexts (Bennett, Bishop, Dalgarno, Waycott, & Kennedy, 2012). Whatever the question, there will be a need for further research on the types of learning interactions that will be mediated by new iterations of the Web.

RECOMMENDATIONS AND IMPLICATIONS FOR EDUCATION, CIVIC ENGAGEMENT, SOCIAL PRACTICE, AND POLICY

According to the New Media Consortium "Relationships are ultimately the lifeblood of social media" (p.8). Social media would not exist if personal relationships were not part of connecting users and their lives. Research studies relating to social media have been conducted on the level of use (Nielsen, 2012), with some asserting that it is the primary means of communication for many persons (Harris, 2008) and therefore has become a ubiquitous part of everyday life. However what draws us to social media can have positive and negative effects depending on the frequency of use and personal dispositions of the end-user. As producers and consumers of digital content, self-regulation is key to maintaining homeostasis. In some circles persons are known as *social media junkies* and several research studies have confirmed its addictiveness (Cabral, 2008; Ottalini, 2010). Research has found that spending a lot of time on Facebook is correlated with both high levels of feeling connected to other people and with high levels of disconnection (Sheldon, 2011). Paul, Baker, and Cochran (2012) assert that social media affects one's ability to concentrate, and Kaplan and Haenlein (2010) have shown that more use of social media results in higher levels of cyber bullying. In essence, what might

be considered acceptable use for one user may have negative implications for another. Education is needed to bring awareness to the potential addictive nature of social media and the Internet. Moreover, resources and tools are needed to self-assess one's use and find alternative ways to stay connected without the use of social media in a digitally connected world.

People in their personal and professional lives have embraced Web 2.0 and the emerging Web 3.0. However, the impact of such a shift has yet to be fully understood or examined. Rosen (2011) found both positive and negative impacts on children who use social media. Daily use of social media can make children more prone to psychological disorders such as anxiety, depression, and other antisocial behaviors. On a more positive note, teens have been found to develop empathy and help others, and more introverted teens learn how to socialize. Rosen encouraged parents to spend more time listening to their teens and less time talking. He suggested talking to teens about appropriate use of social media and to learn about online trends and websites that children and teens are using.

Although the interactivity supported by Web 2.0 and 3.0 are dominant forces in the way people communicate, there is still a lag in sectors such as public relations media, government, and education. Perhaps it is the permanent nature of digitizing thoughts, beliefs, and opinions that makes social media unappealing to people in those professions. There has been a considerable amount of backlash for those in public roles when social media portrays them participating in activities or making statements that others may deem unacceptable. Instances of viewing social media pages as a precursor to hiring new teachers as well as a motivator for firing teachers (Simpson, 2014) may seem acceptable to some, but unconstitutional to others. Due process is needed to establish the fair use and misuse of social media in one's professional and personal life. New laws and policies will need to be erected to address discrimination as a result of social media. Regulations may also come into play to support equity in access to social media communities and practices. For example, social media sites such as LinkedIn may prevent individuals from career opportunities and advancement if they are not part of particular group. Recommendations for government include:

1. A shift away from top-down management approaches in government, public relations, and policy development.
2. A perspective shift that embraces the philosophy, values, and culture of Web 2.0 and beyond.
3. Focus on collaborative dissemination of information and shared responsibility for truth in media.
4. Robust opportunities for interaction on government and policy development systems including websites, social media, and other emerging technologies.

In the field of education, change in the instructional practices of teachers will only occur if there is more than just technical know-how and accessibility. Teachers also need clear and explicit practices for successfully integrating technology into teaching and learning. They also need strategies for partnering with parents about the use of digital tools and social media. Creating a digital community requires more than an understanding of digital tools but explicit guidelines in terms of the dialogue that would govern social practices. To be a producer of content requires one to know what is acceptable, and what is unacceptable educationally and culturally. This can be a challenge to students who often lack the filter to monitor their thinking or understand the long-term effects of posting online. Recommendations for education include:

1. High levels of support for the use of social media in education - focus on preparing students to use Web 2.0 and future iterations to attain, examine, and synthesize information in order to make sense of the world and of truth within it.
2. Devise a plan for implementation and management of technology resources, including Web. 2.0 and 3.0 tools.
3. The use of social media as a tool for student access to content, especially students with disabilities.
4. Parent support and training on the effective use of social media, monitoring children's access and communicating with children about their social media use and activity.

In a critical analysis study, Macnamara (2010) proposes that in public relations companies, "practice lags behind public relations theory" (p.1). He suggested that public relations abandon current practices of communication through static text such as newsletters, interview, and even news conferences. He further suggests that the interactive two-way communication and relationship building capabilities of Web 2.0" (p.1) be utilized to enter conversations online, correct inaccurate information, defend criticisms, and move to a more blogger/social media mentality. This paradigm shift can be applied to education, civic engagement, social practice, and policymakers alike. However embracing such a shift requires more than just access to technological tools and redefining practices, but a shift in the mindset that have been part of peoples' routines for quite some time. Such transformation can only occur if actualized by all sectors of the global community – including policy makers, educators, industrialists, leaders of human resources, and all others who contribute not only to the global society, but also the smaller microcosms in remote communities. Indeed, the shift to full participation in the web will require a village-like mentality that requires the voices of all to share their struggles, achievements, and experiences. This is a global community that is digitally connected.

REFERENCES

Aghaei, S., Nematbakhsh, M. A., & Farsani, H. K. (2012). Evolution of the world wide web: From Web 1.0 to Web 4.0. *International Journal of Web & Semantic Technology*, *3*(1), 1–10. doi:10.5121/ijwest.2012.3101

Bennett, S., Bishop, A., Dalgarno, B., Waycott, J., & Kennedy, G. (2012). Implementing Web 2.0 technologies in higher education: A collective case study. *Computers & Education*, *59*(2), 524–534. doi:10.1016/j.compedu.2011.12.022

Berners-Lee, T., & Fischetti, M. (1999). *Weaving the Web: The original design and ultimate destiny of the World Wide Web by its inventor.* San Francisco: Harper San Francisco.

Bertot, J. C., Jaeger, P. T., Munson, S., & Glaisyer, T. (2010). Engaging the public in open government: The policy and government application of social media technology for government transparency. *IEEE Computer*, *43*(11), 53–59. doi:10.1109/MC.2010.325

Brown, J., & Duguid, P. (2002). *The social life of information.* New York: Harvard Business School Press.

Bruner, J. (1986). *Actual minds, possible worlds.* MA: The President and Fellows of Harvard College.

Burden, T. (2013). K-12 Teachers Uncertain about how to connect with student and parents via social media. *Business Wire*. Retrieved from http://www.businesswire.com/news/home/20140114005604/en/K-12-Teachers-Uncertain-Connect-Students-Parents-Social#.VB-tqC5dVUO

Cabral, J. (2008). Is generation Y addicted to social media? *The Future of Children*, *18*, 125.

Cake, M. (n.d.). *Web 1.0, Web 2.0, Web 3.0 and Web 4.0 explained.* Retrieved from http://www.wisdomnetworks.im/economic-development/internet-evolution

Carpenter, B. E. (1996). *Architectural principles of the Internet.* Retrieved from http://www.rfc-editor.org/rfc/rfc1958.txt

Carpentier, N. (2009). Participation is not enough: The conditions of possibility of mediated participatory practices. *European Journal of Communication*, *24*(4), 407–420. doi:10.1177/0267323109345682

Carpentier, N. (Ed.). (2011). *Media and participation: A site of ideological-democratic struggle.* Intellect Books.

Chen, G. M., & Zhang, K. (2010). New media and cultural identity in the global society. In R. Taiwo (Ed.), *Handbook of Research on Discourse Behavior and Digital Communication: Language Structures and Social Interaction* (pp. 801–815). Hershey, PA: Idea Group Inc. doi:10.4018/978-1-61520-773-2.ch051

Chen, H., Chiang, R., & Storey, V. C. (2012). Business intelligence and analytics: From big data to big impact. *Management Information Systems Quarterly*, *4*(36), 1165–1188.

Christensen, C. M. (2008). *Disruptive diplomas: The future of education.* New York: McGraw Hill.

Cormode, G., & Krishnamurthy, B. (2008). Key differences between Web 1.0 and Web 2.0. *First Monday*, *13*(6). doi:10.5210/fm.v13i6.2125

DeGennaro, D. (2008). Learning designs: An analysis of youth-initiated technology use. *Journal of Research on Technology in Education*, *41*(1), 1–20. doi:10.1080/15391523.2008.10782520

Dewey, J. (1938). *Experience and education*. New York: Simon & Schuster.

Driscoll, M. (2005). *Psychology of learning for instruction* (3rd ed.). Boston: Pearson Education.

Ekström, A., Jülich, S., Lundgren, F., & Wisselgren, P. (Eds.). (2012). *History of participatory media: Politics and publics, 1750–2000*. Routledge.

Fang, I. (1997). *A history of mass communication: Six information revolutions*. Boston: Focal Press.

Fewkes, A. M., & McCabe, M. (2012). Facebook: Learning tool or distraction? *Journal of Digital Learning in Teacher Education*, *28*(3), 92–98.

Fuchs, C., Hofkirchner, W., Schafranek, M., Raffl, C., Sandoval, M., & Bichler, R. (2010). Theoretical foundations of the web: Cognition, communication, and co-operation. Towards an understanding of Web 1.0, 2.0, 3.0. *Future Internet*, *2*(1), 1–59. doi:10.3390/fi2010041

Gao, F., Luo, T., & Zhang, K. (2012). Tweeting for learning: A critical analysis of research on microblogging in education published in 2008–2011. *British Journal of Educational Technology*, *43*(5), 783–801. doi:10.1111/j.1467-8535.2012.01357.x

Gardner, H. (n.d.). *Changing minds: The art and science of changing our own and other people's minds*. Boston: Harvard Business School Press.

Gillmor, D. (2006). *We the media: Grassroots journalism by the people, for the people*. O'Reilly Media, Inc.

Harris, K. (2008). Using social networking sites as student engagement tools. *Diverse Issues in Higher Education*, *25*(18), 4.

Holdings, N. (2012). *State of social media: The social media report*. The Nielsen Company. Retrieved from http://www.nielsen.com/content/dam/corporate/us/en/reports- downloads/20 1 2-Reports/The-Social-Media-Report-2012.pdf

Jenkins, H. (2009). *Confronting the challenges of participatory culture: Media education for the 21st century*. MIT Press.

Jenkins, H., Ford, S., & Green, J. (2013). *Spreadable media: Creating value and meaning in a networked culture*. New York: NYU Press.

Johnson, L., Adams Becker, S., Estrada, V., & Freeman, A. (2014). NMC Horizon Report: 2014 Higher Education Edition. Austin, TX: The New Media Consortium. Retrieved from http://redarchive.nmc.org/publications/2014-horizon-report-higher-ed

Kaplan, A. M., & Haenlein, M. (2010). Users of the world, unite! The challenges and opportunities of Social Media. *Business Horizons*, *53*(1), 59–68.

Karkin, N. (2013). Web 2.0 Tools for Public Participation through Government Websites. In Gestion y Politica Publica Electronic, 309-332.

Kiss, J. (2014). Facebook's 10th birthday: from college dorm to 1.23 billion users. *The Guardian. com* Retrieved from: http://www.theguardian.com/technology/2014/feb/04/facebook-10-years-mark-zuckerberg

Kist, W. (2013). Class, get ready to tweet: Social media in the classroom. *Our Children: The National PTA Magazine*, *38*(3), 10–11.

Kraut, R., Kiesler, S., Mukhopadhyay, T., Scherlis, W., & Patterson, M. (1998). Social Impact of the Internet: What Does It Mean? *Communications of the ACM*, *41*(12), 21–22. doi:10.1145/290133.290140

Kraut, R., Patterson, M., Lundmark, V., Kiesler, S., Mukophadhyay, T., & Scherlis, W. (1998). Internet paradox: A social technology that reduces social involvement and psychological well-being? *The American Psychologist*, *53*(9), 1017–1031. doi:10.1037/0003-066X.53.9.1017 PMID:9841579

Lassila, O., & Hendler, J. (2007). Embracing Web 3.0. *IEEE Internet Computing, 11*(3), 90–93. doi:10.1109/MIC.2007.52

Lennon, R. G. (2012). Bring your own device (BYOD) with cloud 4 education. In *Proceedings of the 3rd annual conference on Systems, programming, and applications: software for humanity* (pp. 171-180). ACM. doi:10.1145/2384716.2384771

Macnamara, J. (2010). Public communication practices in the Web 2.0-3.0 mediascape: The case for PRevolution. *Prism, 7*(3). Retrieved from http://www.prismjournal.org

Markoff, J. (2006). Entrepreneurs see a web guided by common sense. *New York Times, 12.*

McEneaney, J. E. (2011). Web 3.0, litbots, and TP-WSGWTAU. *Journal of Adolescent & Adult Literacy, 54*(5), 376–378. doi:10.1598/JAAL.54.5.8

Moran, M., Seaman, J., & Tinti-Kane, H. (2011). *Teaching, learning, and sharing: How today's higher education faculty use social media.* Babson Survey Research Group.

Morris, R. D. (2011). Web 3.0: Implications for Online Learning. *Techtrends: Linking Research & Practice To Improve Learning, 55*(1), 42–46. doi:10.1007/s11528-011-0469-9

O'Reilly, T. (2005). *What is Web 2.0: Design patterns and business models for the next generation of software.* Academic Press.

O'Reilly, T. (2006). *Web 2.0 compact definition: Trying again.* Retrieved from http://radar.oreilly.com/2006/12/web-20-compact-definition-tryi.html

Omand, D., Bartlett, J., & Miller, C. (2012). Introducing social media intelligence (SOCMINT). *Intelligence and National Security, 27*(6), 801–823. doi:10.1080/02684527.2012.716965

Ottalini, D. (2010). Students Addicted to Social Media-New UM Study. *University of Maryland Newsdesk.* Retrieved from http://www.newsdesk.umd.edu/undergradexp/release.cfm

Patel, K. (2013). Incremental journey for world wide web: Introduced with web 1.0 to recent web 5.0 - A survey paper. *International Journal of Advanced Research in Computer Science and Software Engineering, 3*(10), 410–417.

Paul, J. A., Baker, H. M., & Cochran, J. D. (2012). Effect of online social networking on student academic performance. *Computers in Human Behavior, 28*(6), 2117–2127. doi:10.1016/j.chb.2012.06.016

Pew Research Internet Project. (2013). *Internet and American Life Teen-Parent Survey.* Retrieved from http://www.pewinternet.org/2013/05/21/part-1-teens-and-social-media-use/

Pidaparthy, U. (2011). *How colleges use, misuse social media to reach students.* Retrieved from: http://www.cnn.com/2011/10/20/tech/social-media/universities-social-media/

Privacy Rights Clearinghouse. (2012). *Fact sheet 35: Social Networking Privacy: How to be Safe, Secure and Social.* Retrieved from https://www.privacyrights.org/social-networking-privacy-how-be-safe-secure-and-social

Review, H. B. (2010). *The New Conversation: Taking Social Media from Talk to Action.* Retrieved from: http://www.sas.com/resources/whitepaper/wp_23348.pdf

Ricardo, G. (2014). When you do not have a computer: Public-access computing in developing countries. *Information Technology for Development, 20*(3), 274-291, doi:10.1080/02681102.2012.751573

Rose, J. (2011). How social media is having a positive impact on culture. *Mashable*. Retrieved from http://mashable.com/2011/02/23/social-media-culture/

Rosen, L. (2011). *Social Networking's Good and Bad Impact on Kids*. American Psychological Association. Retrieved from http://www.apa.org/news/press/releases/2011/08/social-kids.aspx

Rushkoff, D. (1994). *Media virus!: Hidden agendas in popular culture*. New York: Ballantine Books.

Sánchez Abril, P., Levin, A., & Del Riego, A. (2012). Blurred boundaries: Social media privacy and the twenty firstcentury employee. *American Business Law Journal*, *49*(1), 63–124. doi:10.1111/j.1744-1714.2011.01127.x

Seaman, J., & Tinti-Kane, H. (2013). *Social Media for Teaching and Learning*. Boston, Ma: Pearson Learning Solutions and Babson Survey Research Group.

Sheldon, K. M., Abad, N., & Hinsch, C. (2011). A two-process view of Facebook use and relatedness need-satisfaction: Disconnection drives use, and connection rewards it. *Journal of Personality and Social Psychology*, *100*(4), 766–775. doi:10.1037/a0022407 PMID:21280967

Sherer, P., & Shea, T. (2011). Using online video to support student learning and engagement. *College Teaching*, *59*(2), 56–59. doi:10.1080/87567555.2010.511313

Shi, Z., Rui, H., & Whinston, A. B. (2014). Content sharing in a social broadcasting environment: Evidence from twitter. *Management Information Systems Quarterly*, *38*(1), 123–142.

Shin, D. H. (2010). The effects of trust, security and privacy in social networking: A security-based approach to understand the pattern of adoption. *Interacting with Computers*, *22*(5), 428–438. doi:10.1016/j.intcom.2010.05.001

Siemens, G. (2006). *Knowing knowledge*. Lulu.com.

Siemens, G. (2008, January 29). ELI podcast: Connectivism. *Educause Connect*.

Speak Up Report. (2014). *Trends in Digital Learning: Students' views on Innovative Classroom Models*. Retrieved from: http://www.tomorrow.org/speakup/2014_OnlineLearningReport.html

Spires, H. A., Lee, J. K., Turner, K. A., & Johnson, J. (2008). Having our say: Middle grade student perspectives on school, technologies, and academic engagement. *Journal of Research on Technology in Education*, *40*(4), 497–515. doi:10.1080/15391523.2008.10782518

Umberson, D., Chen, M. D., House, J. S., Hopkins, K., & Slaten, E. (1996). The effect of social relationships on psychological well-being: Are men and women really so different? *American Sociological Review*, *61*(5), 837–857. doi:10.2307/2096456

Vossen, G., & Hagemann, S. (2007). *From Version 1.0 to Version 2.0: A brief history of the web*, No 4, ERCIS Working Papers. Westfälsche Wilhelms-Universität Münster (WWU) - European Research Center for Information Systems (ERCIS). Retrieved from http://EconPapers.repec.org/RePEc:zbw:ercisw:4

Vygotsky, L. S., & Cole, M. (1978). *Mind in society: The development of higher psychological processes*. Cambridge, MA: Harvard University Press.

Wahlster, W., & Dengel, A. (2006). Web 3.0: Convergence of web 2.0 and the semantic web. In Technology radar (Vol. 2). German Research Center for Artificial Intelligence (DFKI).

Wenger, E. (1998). *Communities of practice: learning, meaning, and identity*. New York, NY: Cambridge University Press. doi:10.1017/CBO9780511803932

Yodle. (2013). *Yodle's First Annual Small Business Sentiment Survey*. Retrieved from http://www.yodle.net/files/smb-sentiment-report.pdf

KEY TERMS AND DEFINITIONS

Connectivism: The idea that the depth and degree to which we understand is directly related to the learner connecting to and exchanging information within the larger community.

Metadata: Data that is used to produce information that could be accessed, analyzed, and disseminated by software agents (Morris, 2011).

Participatory Media: Media where the user can share their opinions and voice involved in the production of news and entertainment has been precipitated by online technologies.

Portalization: With the use of Web 2.0 tools users can repeatedly return to websites that provide options to meet all their needs such as blogging, email, RSS feeds, etc.

Social Media: Refers to a group of web-based tools that allow people to construct, reconstruct, and exchange information.

Web 2.0: This iteration of the web is bi-directional, it is interactive, including opportunities to both read and write content and share information via several mediums. It provides platforms for the user to build applications on the web instead of users building applications on their personal desktop.

Web 3.0: It is the third generation of the web, and the focus is on delivering a web experience that is personalized by being responsive to the end-users needs and interests. Collects data based on the end-users web activity.

Chapter 3
Digital Media and Cosmopolitan Critical Literacy:
Research and Practice

Thomas W. Bean
Old Dominion University, USA

ABSTRACT

In this chapter I consider contemporary global conditions pointing to what some scholars term "a global risk society" where digital media and Cosmopolitan Critical Literacy offer a counterpoint to human rights, health, climate, and terrorist threats. By examining current research in global youth communication across nation-state boundaries via the Internet, existing research suggests that tapping into digital media literacy and critical media literacy will be crucial for developing an informed and critical citizenry. At present, studies of transnational youth navigating old and new affiliations across national borders are in their infancy. Nevertheless, the existing research holds promise for developing global world citizens who can realize an ethos of cosmopolitan, critical citizenship through the affordances of digital media.

INTRODUCTION

Digital media permeate nearly all aspects of our lives from the connectedness of our families and communities through cell phones, tablets, computers at home, on the road, in the kitchen, and at work. The present chapter considers the impact of digital media and Cosmopolitan Critical Literacy (CCL) (Dunkerly-Bean, Bean, & Alnajjar, 2014) on the development of an astute citizenry capable of critiquing public policies, human rights, and elements of a "risk society" (Beck & Sznaider, 2010; Delanty, 2006). I begin by providing an

overview of ongoing scholarly work aimed at defining the interplay of the three elements (risk society, digital media, and CCL) by first considering what it means to live in a global, risk society (see Figure 1).

Following this section, critical literacy is considered along with an expanded notion of cosmopolitan theory and Cosmopolitan Critical Literacy (CCL). Critical literacy is often confused with its older sibling, critical reading, making it imperative that the very different stances underpinning critical reading and critical literacy are clearly defined (Cervetti, Pardales, & Damico, 2001; Stevens &

DOI: 10.4018/978-1-4666-8310-5.ch003

Figure 1. Risk Society, Digital Media, Critical Cosmopolitan Literacy, Research & Practice

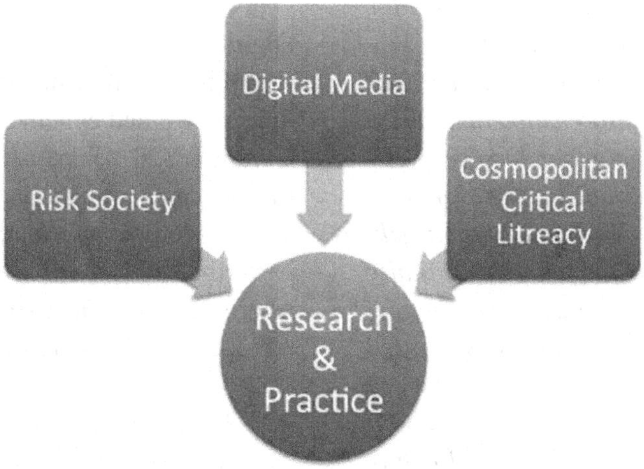

Bean, 2007). Research incorporating these elements and digital media is reviewed with an eye toward how this work might guide our practice in a global context.

In essence, I argue that a global risk society overlaps with a need to develop an astute global citizenry able to collaborate and solve serious problems including war, climate change, racism, sexism, identity theft, and a host of other issues facing the planet. Figure 1 shows the three major elements considered in this chapter.

BACKGROUND

Defining a Global Risk Society

Globalization involves the increasingly fluid and borderless movement of people, ideas, information, and capital that position the global and local as mutually interdependent (Beck & Sznaider, 2010). In this environment the Internet affords an increasingly connected, transnational youth culture (Hull & Stornaiulo, 2010). This increasingly interconnected world society supports positive elements in the form of cultural exchange, as well as negative dimensions including terrorism, disease, and climate change (Trepanier & Habib,

2011) Sociologist Ulrich Beck (2012) argues that our successes and hubris in harnessing nuclear energy, developing advanced weaponry, and producing global warming place us at risk. Beck and other European scholars (Strydom, 2002) note that we now live in a global "risk society" where it will be crucial to develop an informed, critical citizenry. Because of the increasingly powerful Internet, individuals and groups of citizens can examine, deconstruct, and critique geopolitical and local policies.

To get a sense of how profound a change in communication technologies the Internet is, consider that every two years computer power doubles, rendering our cell phones more powerful than all of NASA when it placed two men on the moon in 1969 (Kaku, 2014).

Machio Kaku is a professor of theoretical physics at the City College and City University of New York. He is the co-founder of string theory and conducted interviews with over 166 prominent scientists to explore the future of Artificial Intelligence (AI), the Internet, expert systems, robotics, and new directions in brain research. In the 1900's, the differences in our current lives and those of our ancestors' lives are even more profound. Kaku notes:

To appreciate how technology reduces, rather than accentuates, societal fault lines, consider the lives of our ancestors around 1900. Life expectancy in the United States back then was forty-nine years. Many children died in infancy. Communicating with a neighbor involved yelling out the window. The mail was delivered by horse, if it came at all. Medicine was largely snake oil. The only treatments that actually worked were amputations (without anesthetics) and morphine to deaden the pain. Food rotted within days. Plumbing was nonexistent. Disease was a constant threat. And the economy could support only a handful of the rich and a tiny middle class. (p. 321)

Yet there are places on the planet that look very much like the description in Dr. Kaku's account of life in the United States during the 1900's. South African scholar Hilary Janks (2014) notes that while wealthier countries promote citizens' access to and use of Internet technologies, poorer countries may suffer from high illiteracy rates, and absence of flush toilets, and hunger. Thus, the notion of a risk society applies both on a local, village level in developing countries and on a global level. The essential difference is the degree to which parts of the globe are creating entirely new cities that are avoiding the creaking wired infrastructure of our own urban areas. For example, China and India have embraced wireless technologies and the Internet "to leapfrog past other, more developed nations that have laboriously wired their cities" (Kaku, p. 321).

Despite the escalation of wireless technology around the globe, a digital divide will likely continue to plague isolated and unplugged areas of the planet. Nevertheless, for many youth, digital media are second nature vehicles to keep up with pop culture, gaming, political issues, and families scattered around the globe through voluntary and involuntary diasporas. The point here is that this is complex terrain, a kind of disparate moving target of haves and have-nots.

Defining Digital Media

Digital media scholars struggle to generate a straightforward definition of the field, largely due to its robust and ephemeral nature. For example, Golumbia (2014) noted that: "The field of digital media can be arguably understood to be so wide as to encompass virtually everything" (p. 54). Nevertheless, Golumbia listed the following characteristics in an effort to define, and momentarily "freeze" this dynamic field:

- Digital media are *nonlinear*. That is, the temporal order of texts are largely fluid with authors able to collaborate and easily add to pre-existing texts. In addition, this nonlinearity is a characteristic of e-book readers and bookmarking websites.
- Digital media embrace and capitalize on *multimedia*. Texts can be embellished with elements that go beyond the written word to include hyperlinks and URL's that let the reader branch to multiple sites for additional information on a topic.
- Digital media supports *collaboration* across distant boundaries through the use of applications like Dropbox and others where multiple authors can confer on a project.

In addition to these characteristics, digital media are highly portable, easily archived and preserved electronically. A host of studies exploring multimodal forms in diverse fields including advertising images and angles, green corporate marketing, digital home design and decoration, and computer animation suggest that this is a rich field for research (O'Halloran & Smith, 2011). For example, a German researcher explored the impact of popular social networking sites including Facebook to evaluate the impact of representational qualities (Esenlauer, 2011). Something as seemingly simple as a profile page and adding friends on Facebook may engender a variety of responses in viewers based on the positioning of one's profile. For example, the direct gaze where a potential "friend" is looking directly into the camera is an image that demands an action on the part of the viewer. By contrast, a more neutral profile photo where a person depicted in a grainy image is balancing on a sidewalk curb with his back to the viewer is more innocuous. Esenlauer found that despite the predetermined linguistic profile categories on Facebook, personal images serve to modulate these templates, allowing for personal expression and varying how a viewer is likely to respond. Thus, multimodal images in social network sites, advertisements, and contemporary design methods call for analysis and critique.

The implications these characteristics hold for developing informed citizens able to navigate and critique this unwieldy and vast collection of information are huge. For example, early on, noted new literacies scholar Gunther Kress (2003) observed that the nonlinearity and idiosyncratic nature of reading in digital environments poses new challenges for functioning as literate citizens. For example, paying attention to visual clues to meaning including salience, color, spatial configurations, font changes, and other nonlinear elements constitutes new demands on readers and what it means to be literate.

Multimodal scholars note that studies in this area now cut across a wide array of fields (O'Halloran & Smith, 2011) including personal publishing and design issues (e.g. FaceBook), education, business, advertising, home design, and discipline specific applications (e.g. biology, history, mathematics). O'Halloran and Smith argue that in the 21st Century we are moving away from the age of the disciplines toward technology uses devoted to problem solving applications that are interdisciplinary (e.g. climate change).

In addition, the ability to successfully engage in multimodal composing has already moved well beyond writing the linear print-based texts of the past century (Miller & McVee, 2012). Design issues predominate now and are crucial for active

civic, personal, and workplace activities. For example, the creation of visually appealing flyers, signs, social network pages, and videos revolve around design decisions about color, size, font, spacing, white space, movement, music, and other media. Aesthetics become ever more important in creating appealing and attractive digital media (Miller & McVee, 2012).

To gain a sense of what these new digital literacy demands might mean for careers by the year 2025, the *Pew Research Center Report* (2014) charted jobs that could be eliminated in the not too distant future. The list centered on jobs that are repetitive, rote, and easily automated, including:

- Proofreaders,
- Motion-picture projectionists,
- Meter readers,
- Butchers and meat cutters,
- Secretaries and stenographers,
- Payroll and timekeeping clerks,
- Bank tellers
- File clerks,
- Cashiers,
- Typists,
- Bookkeepers and accounting clerks.

In contrast, careers least likely to be eliminated generally involve significant educational preparation and the ability to navigate and use digital media and technology. These positions include:

- Teachers,
- Foresters and conservation scientists,
- Engineers,
- Software designers,
- Artists,
- Archivists and curators,
- Airline pilots and navigators,
- Actors, directors, and producers.

Similarly, the International Society for Technology Education (ITSE) (2007) standards for students proposes that 21st Century professions call for creativity and innovation, communication and collaboration, research and information fluency, critical thinking, problem solving, decision making, and digital citizenship.

In essence, the dispositions and skills needed for today and into tomorrow call for a critical citizenry able to cull through a vast array of digital media material and able to critique both local and global geopolitical risks. To get a sense of the ways in which globalization and cosmopolitanism interact, I turn briefly to recent work in these areas and compare the two views, noting that both conceptions of society are in flux, and, to a great extent, interdependent.

The term, "cosmopolitanism" has a long and contested history. Dating from the Greek kosmopolites, it refers to citizens of the world (Harper, Bean, & Dunkerly, 2010).

Indeed, theorists Beck and Sznaider (2010) argue that:

Cosmopolitanization thus includes the proliferation of multiple cultures (as with cuisines from around the world), the growth of many transnational forms of life, the emergence of various non-state political actors (from Amnesty International to the World Trade Organization), the paradoxical emergence of global protest movements, the hesitant formation of multi-national states (like the European Union) etc. There is simply no way of turning the clock back to a world of sovereign nation states and national societies. (p. 390)

The philosopher, Kwame Anthony Appiah (2006) takes a more critical view of the term "globalization," contending that this moniker has shape shifted from a global marketing strategy to a macroeconomic notion that is largely meaningless. Rather, Appiah sees two major strands of cosmopolitanism:

- The belief that we have obligations to others on the planet beyond our families and members of a shared citizenship, and,
- The belief that we should take seriously the value of human life generally, as well as particular human lives

Acknowledging the pitfalls of cosmopolitanism where cultural imperialists ride into town with their own new order akin to any colonizing entity, Appiah argues for human variety. "A tenable cosmopolitanism tempers a respect for difference with a respect for actual human beings" (p. 113).

The impact of globalization introduces both positive elements for some people (e.g. economic growth) while simultaneously reducing opportunities for others experiencing terrorism, disease, and the effects of climate change. Globalization may reduce geographic isolation from each other through the exchange of ideas, commodities, people, culture, and institutions through a worldwide economy (Trepanier & Habib, 2011). The process of globalization may diminish the sovereignty of the state with a greater interdependence of global citizens across geopolitical landscapes. Thus contemporary postmodern cosmopolitanism offers a philosophical position that invites social difference and values social justice (Appiah, 2006; Trepanier, 2011). Nevertheless, as Trepanier notes, no single school of thought is adequate for defining the various permutations of cosmopolitanism but it offers a way to address some of the complex issues that globalization entails. For example, given the ease with which digital images can be doctored and used as a vehicle for misinformation and propaganda, media scholars argue that the time is ripe for schools and society to embrace critical literacy theories and practices (Lim, Nekmat, & Nahar, 2011).

COSMOPOLITAN CRITICAL LITERACY

In the following section I introduce the notion of Cosmopolitan Critical Literacy (CCL) and situate this concept within critical media literacy. Subsequent sections provide an overview of relevant research and future research directions.

Defining Cosmopolitan Critical Literacy

Critical Literacy

At its most basic level, critical literacy can be defined as an emancipatory endeavor centered on interrogating issues of power, representation, and marginalization (Stevens & Bean, 2007). Its genesis is related to critical social theory and the Frankfurt School (Habermas, 1975) where scholars undertook an interdisciplinary, neo-Marxist critique of society that supported a strong interest in social justice (Borsheim-Black, Macaluso, & Petrone, 2014).

To get a sense of critical literacy as a stance it is helpful to distinguish this position from critical thinking. South African scholar, Hilary Janks (2010) notes that unlike critical thinking or critical reading with its emphasis on textual analysis, critical literacy is centered on deconstructing a message in terms of how it positions the reader or viewer, who benefits from the message, and who is disenfranchised or silenced by the message.

Applying this stance to digital literacies is crucial as the Internet is an open access network where virtually anyone can step on board and publish whatever they want (Leu, Kinzer, Coiro, Castek, & Henry, 2013). The potential for political, economic, and ideological posturing is significant and calls for readers to be critical consumers of virtual texts.

Critical Media Literacy

Critical literacy practices are increasingly applied to digital media under the banner of Critical Media Literacy (Hobbs, 2007; Morrell, Duenas, Garcia, & Lopez, 2013). Growing out of diverse disciplines in the 1990's including literary theory, cultural studies, film studies, semiotics, media studies and other disciplines, critical media literacy centers on the following precepts (Hobbs, 2007):

- All media represent constructions.
- Media messages are shaped by semiotic signs and design conventions.
- Media messages are imbued with particular values and points of view.
- People are likely to interpret the same media message differently.
- Media messages are typically constructed to advance profit and/or power.

Thus, Critical Media Literacy centers on critiquing how diverse people are portrayed and positioned in digital media including films, advertisements, video games, songs, popular culture, Facebook, YouTube, and other social media sites (Stevens & Bean, 2007). Questions aimed at guiding their critique may include:

- What is represented?
- Who is the intended audience?
- Who stands to benefit from the use of this media?
- Who is left out, marginalized, or silenced in this media?
- How are you positioned as a viewer of this media?

For example, one of the activities I do with my graduate students in a New Literacies class involves critiquing the popular Kenny Chesney song, "The Boys of Fall" (Chesney, 2010) chronicling high school football players. In particular, students note who is left out of this picture. Students who are not football players but may do more non-mainstream sports like swimming, tennis, and golf, as well as a host of others including handicapped student athletes, girls, the school band members, and so on.

Thus, digital media including music, YouTube advertisement clips, cartoons, video games, and other Internet content offer available sites where critical media literacy can be used to deconstruct and reconstruct ideological messages. For example, African American ballet dancer Misty Copeland, a ballerina with the prestigious American Ballet Theater is featured in an Under Armour advertisement that juxtaposes her stunning dance performance with the background voice of a teenage girl reading aloud from one of Misty Copeland's actual Ballet school rejection letters (YouTube, 2014). The letter reads: "Thank you for your application to our Ballet Academy. Unfortunately, you have not been accepted. You have the wrong body type for ballet. And, at 13 you are too old to be considered."

This advertisement has garnered over four million viewers worldwide. The ad provides a powerful counterpoint to Under Armour's male football oriented ads and is aimed at empowering women to move past perceived barriers to career choices. Thus, digital critical media literacy can serve to expose discriminatory positions and help reconstruct who has agency, voice, and possible futures.

Cosmopolitan Critical Literacy

While both critical literacy and critical media literacy undoubtedly help create a discerning questioning stance on the part of a reader, these practices remain tied to nation state standards rather than global issues (Bean, & Dunkerly-Bean, in press). Youth are living at the nexus of the local and global. They are the generation that currently studies in educational settings that are striving to become relevant amidst high stakes assessments that often narrow the curriculum to what Australian scholar Allan Luke (2013) calls "first wave" literacy. In contrast, a "second wave" curriculum would address local and global problems impinging on students' lives including water quality, immigration, and other pressing issues.

As I noted earlier, the term, "cosmopolitan" has a long and contested history. Diogenes, a Greek philosopher in the 4th century BCE, used the term to make known his political allegiance to the world (Harper, Bean, & Dunkerly, 2010; Trepanier & Habib, 2011). In the eighteenth century, cosmopolitanism has been associated with Kant's (1795/1972) notions of "Perpetual Peace," and more recently with globalization and mass migrations across various borders that call for intercultural communication (Hansen, 2014).

Although critical literacy and critical media literacy address and critique instances of social inequality and injustice, a cosmopolitan stance focuses on human rights and the reverberations of actions in one part of the world on other areas around the globe (Bean & Dunkerly-Bean, in press). Digital media connect the local and the global in ways that reveal injustices, sometimes in stark ways with respect to war, civil unrest, immigration, and the distant outfall from pollution in one part of the planet on disparate areas thousands of miles away from the original site of the problem. Indeed, critical literacy scholars like Hilary Jenks (2010) argue that critical literacy must be agile enough to address local and global issues. Cosmopolitan Critical Literacy (CCL) moves youth conversations into a larger sphere where they may find common ground centered on basic human rights issues (Dunkerly-Bean, Bean, & Alnajjar, 2014).

The succinct overview of research that follows encompasses the interrelated forms of critical literacy, critical media literacy, and CCL with a focus on refereed studies published in major journals, books, and book chapters. Additional criteria applied to the selection of particular studies centered on research involving digital media and transnational youth at both local, United States settings (e.g. Morrell et al., 2013), as well as globally situated contexts (e.g. Hull & Stornaiulo, 2014) where intercultural communication is considered (Sorrells, 2013).

Overview of Current Research

Social networks can serve to bridge vast distances, as well as ethnic and cultural differences. As cosmopolitan theorist David Hansen (2014) notes:

Education is a transformative experience of becoming aware of one's skills or lack thereof, of grasping their significance or their triviality, of discovering (often with surprise) that knowledge is a many-sided concept, or experience than merely having information. (p. 10)

When youth communicate across national and international boundaries via the Internet, they begin to find common ground around human rights issues and collaborate to generate solutions to problems. For example, in a study using a social media site called Space2Cre8, youth from the United States, South Africa, India, and Norway carried on a three-year collaboration (Hull & Stornaiulo, 2010; 2014). Embracing cosmopolitan practices, they created and shared digital stories, digital music, stop animation videos, digitized artwork, and critical dialogues about their everyday lives and diverse cultures. Their dialogues discussed human rights issues encompassing discrimination, school stresses, and poverty. For example, when the Norwegian students created a movie on drug and alcohol abuse, one of the students in the United States site resonated with this issue. He lived with parents who regularly got drunk and beat him and his siblings. Although this is a challenging situation, the U. S. student was able to discuss something hidden with a peer

thousands of miles away, potentially reducing some of the isolation and despair accompanying their daily lives.

In a follow-up analysis of the Space2Cre8 data, 13 young women from Locknow, India and 12 young men and women from New York City rallied around a video developed by the India students aimed at halting domestic violence against women in their community (Hull & Stornaiulo, 2014). When the video was completed, the India students shared it with the New York City students and this inspired the New York City group to create a 6-minute video showing gang violence and being "jumped into" a street gang. The India students were mystified as to why anyone would elect to join a street gang and urged the New York City students to develop a community action group aimed at resisting gang intimidation.

Thus, the transformative power of digital media afforded these students an opportunity to critique their respective worlds as well as the worlds of others, ultimately proposing and creating solutions to gang violence, drug and alcohol abuse, and other problems. Over the three years, Hull and Stornaiulo (2014) noted: "Participants gradually become more reflexive, achieving enough distance from themselves to move closer to distant others" (p. 25).

Other transnational studies of youth maintaining contact with their homelands and balancing the stresses of being a new student in the United States, suggest that digital media play an important role in quelling some of the anxiety that youth experience in a new social setting. For example, in a case study of a 10th grade girl from Trinidad, Cheryl McClean (2010) investigated how Zeek was able to adopt her digital world as a virtual home while she transitioned into a new high school in the United States. Zeek was able to preserve her Trinidad identity by using her home dialect, "Trini" to communicate with friends back in Trinidad, Tobago. In contrast, in her new high school students mocked her dialect and made her feel self-conscious. The Internet provided a way to maintain her native language while simultaneously taking up the more homogenized, and at times stressful American school setting where students made fun of her.

Clearly, if Zeek were in a school setting that adopted cosmopolitanism with its emphasis on funds of knowledge the Other brings to a new setting, there would at least be potential for what sociologist Elijah Anderson (2011) terms the cosmopolitan "canopy." Although not specifically encompassing digital media, Anderson chronicles urban Philadelphia where people gather across social difference in diners as a counterpoint to views of the Other in a city where de facto segregation is the norm. Similarly, educational philosopher David Hansen (2008) sees a cosmopolitan disposition as "a sustained readiness to learn from the new and different while being heedful of the known and familiar" (p. 289). It is not hard to reconstruct Zeek's experiences that might have been quite different in a high school where her Trinidad-based funds of knowledge were respected and valued. Indeed, the lens of cosmopolitan critical literacy (CCL) suggests that it might well be possible to find ways to reconstitute and reduce educational anxiety and stress for transnational learners trying to bridge homeland and immigration to another country, in this case, the United States.

In another study of two sisters whose family voluntarily immigrated to the United States, McClean's (2013) qualitative case study illustrated the pressure to assimilate in both language and dress. The girls, Sade age 17 and Kai, 14 attended school in a metropolitan city in the south. Both used digital technology and online social networks to maintain membership in various affinity groups and take up new identities in the U. S. context. They produced content on their blogs, podcasts, and iMovies. Digital media afforded a means to bridge the gap between the social mores of their native and adopted homes.

In McClean's (2013) interviews with Sade, she noted that the girls in her school mocked her style of dress and tried to pick fights with her. In her native Jamaica, Sade wore uniforms to school and now, in the United States, she felt compelled to assimilate and change her style of dress to conform to the normative pressures of her classmates. Indeed, her Facebook profile shifted to indicate that she shopped at fashionable stores like Nordstrom. In essence, Sade's U. S. classmates did little to embrace and appreciate social difference and learn from the Other.

In contrast, Kai elected a different approach to enculturation in the new U. S. setting. She resisted her female classmates' criticism of how she talked (with a Jamaican intonation pattern), by using her digital literacy prowess to create a blog site for diverse youth. This site offered Kai and other diverse bloggers a space to share multiple points of view and world-views, as well as open discussion with local and global audiences regarding racism and other hot button topics for youth.

In addition, Kai resisted dominant ways of naming race (e.g. African American) by proclaiming she was part of the "human race" (p. 70). McClean noted that: "Digital literacies became the multimodal approach through which the girls resisted and re-presented traditional definitions of who they were as girls, racial/ethnic, and immigrants" (p. 71). Although Kai was not invited by her classmates to share her cultural experiences in Jamaica, her blog site provided a forum for these conversations with other youth locally and globally.

In a related study, Skerrett (2012) conducted a case study of Vanessa, a 15-year old Mexican girl who immigrated to the United States but continued to participate in life in Mexico where her father remained to run a business. Vanessa successfully navigated and used Internet social media to traverse online permeable borders. Skerrett completed detailed in and out of school observations, field notes, and artifact analysis. Vanessa kept a diary to chronicle her life in the United States. In addition, she sent regular text messages to her friends in Mexico. Vanessa code shifted from Spanish to English in her communications and she was comfortable enough to take up a transnational, cosmopolitan perspective. She embraced African American vernacular and hip-hop dance. Unlike Zeek who struggled with homesickness and deeply missed her Trinidad friends, Vanessa managed to use her social media savvy to ease the transition to the United States.

Despite the promising trends in these studies, Skerrett (2012) cautioned that studies of transnational youth constitute an underrepresented research area within digital literacies. Nevertheless, the existing body of research suggests that transnational youth have much to teach us about intercultural understanding and the unique skills and dispositions afforded by this nomadic lifestyle. Vanessa, accustomed to very few reading and writing resources in her native Mexico, enthusiastically read books recommended by her teachers. Similar to a cosmopolitan disposition, Skerrett concluded that transnational proficiencies "include multilingual repertoires and consciousness, cultural flexibility, a sense of global citizenship, and nomadic awareness" (p. 388). Thus, in this study the potential for cosmopolitan literacy was realized and exemplified by Venessa's online and school based communication where she took up art and dance, in particular learning about African American dialect and hip hop. In essence Vanessa managed to border cross dimensions of race, ethnicity, culture, and language.

Cosmopolitan Critical Literacy (CCL) was the theoretical foundation for a year-long study exploring middle grade students' multiple identities as global and local citizens creating a short film on the challenges of immigrants and refugees (Dunkerly-Bean, Bean, & Alnajjar, 2014). Students wrote and acted out scenes following their reading of global young adult literature (Bean,

Dunkerly-Bean, & Harper, 2014), multimedia texts, YouTube video clip simulations, and other selections related to immigration, citizenship education, and human rights.

The study was located in a diverse urban international charter school offering afternoon electives by student choice. Nine middle grade students were involved in this global elective entitled: Project *iFLICK*, an acronym for *Integrating Film and Literature for Intercultural Knowledge*. Students had access to a global/international array of young adult literature provided by the researchers. In addition, students also explored Internet sites including Youth for Human Rights as it could be accessed at www.youthforhumanrights.org.

The charter school where this study took place had few material resources. There were no computers, a functioning library, Smart Boards, or other digital media. Thus, the researchers supplied laptops and their smartphones and iPads so that students could create a short iMovie on Article Fourteen of the Universal Declaration of Human Rights. This article states: "Everyone has the right to seek and to enjoy in other countries asylum from persecution." This human right resonated with these students as their personal experiences as Latina/o and the immediate experiences of their families centered on issues related to immigration. The short digital movie entitled: *Asylum: Seeking a Safe Place to Live* may be viewed at: https://www.youthtube.com/watch?v=Qgo7P-f5ba4.

The students' film was set in the year 3033 where war breaks out in a fictional poverty-stricken country called Chinaka. The war was related to a long- standing rivalry between the Jermians and the Evins over a Romeo and Juliette like scenario between two young lovers. The two groups clash violently and a young Jermian named "Ydoc" is killed. A group of refugees decide to flee war-torn Chinaka for the peaceful and prosperous country of Niwaka. They confront government corruption when the ruler of Niwaka bribes their guide for information on the refugees before he decides to close the border to prevent their passing into his country. Only after the intercession of the human rights minded (female) Vice President, does the president give in and grant asylum to the refugees.

It is important to note that the film features a blend of serious, tragic scenes interspersed with comedic elements. Although students drew from their readings of print and multimedia texts where poverty, war, oppression, and deportation where daily events, they gave the film their own creative spin.

Findings from this study revealed that students' understanding of the global and local elements at play became more complex, and at times contradictory to immigrants assimilating into a new culture. The film served as a way to deconstruct and critique the status quo of immigration while questioning exclusionary policies, bribery, and corruption. In the tradition of Cosmopolitan Critical Literacy (CCL), these students learned how to deconstruct a local reality in their lives, along with thinking about how, through a forced diaspora from their native counties, they could reconstruct a better life in their new homeland.

Consistent with the intent of CCL to move from deconstruction to advocacy and reconstruction, scholars in social studies have created a model based on "relational cosmopolitanism" (Baildon & Damico, 2011; Damico & Baildon, 2013). This research points to the interdependence of people across the globe as they attempt to manage pollution and other risk society problems that span national boundaries. These researchers see a profound need for interdisciplinary digital collaboration to address global risk factors including: climate change, pollution, disease, war, terrorism, financial crisis, public health, and poverty.

Toward that end, Baildon and Damico (2011) created the *Critical Web Reader*: http://cwr.indiana.edu/ to help learners engage critically with digital, web-based texts. This work has resulted in a number of research publications including those in international settings and offers users a powerful template to organize competing texts on various topics, many specific to social studies content.

Other researchers focus on issues of civic engagement and democracy for disenfranchised populations. For example, Ernest Morrell and colleagues engage youth in regularly filming, editing, producing, and distributing high quality digital videos that take up challenging issues including gang violence, immigration, animal cruelty, tagging, budget cuts and other topics (Morrell, Duenas, Garcia, & Lopez, 2013).

These researchers argue that we need to view critical media literacy as a core literacy practice and as a civic tool in the pursuit of democracy. For example, in Ms. Garcia's 9th and 10th grade English class, students created a one minute public service announcement on Arizona's SB1070 which allowed law enforcement to require identification papers proving citizenship for anyone suspected of being an undocumented immigrant. The actors in the video were harassed when they tried to purchase sodas in a convenience store, despite armbands identifying their "legal" status. By writing and producing this counterpoint video these students were able to challenge an untenable position and transform their thoughts into action using digital media. Indeed, this form of communication is rapidly surpassing print based, formal school approaches to civic engagement.

In a study that examined 90 youth civic engagement web sites in terms of the affordances for political action these sites provided, researchers Bennett, Freelon, and Wells, (2010) found that:

Young social media users are increasingly comfortable with replacing old gatekeepers such as journalists, teachers, and officials with crowd-sourced information flows developed through information aggregation technologies, (e.g. Google news) wikis, (e.g. Wikipedia), trusted friends networks, (e.g. Facebook, LinkedIn, Move On) and recommendation engines (e.g. Amazon, iTunes. (p. 397)

In their analysis of the 90 sites they observed, Bennett et al. used a two level taxonomy to name the impact of these sites. At the lowest level of impact, "Dutiful Citizenship" (p. 397) characterized civic engagements as a matter of nation state duty and obligation., with print-based government, newscast, and policy discussions at the center of this model. In contrast, they termed advocacy models as "Actualizing Citizenship" (p. 397) because they were more likely to rely on digital media and social action networks. These participatory cultures are potentially powerful sites for political involvement and organization because of the following five characteristics (Bennett, et al., 2010, p. 401):

1. Low barriers to artistic expression and civic engagement.
2. Support for creating and sharing one's creations with others.
3. Informal mentorship with experienced users helping novices.
4. The feeling that members contributions to the greater good matter.
5. A feeling of belonging and social connection to one another.

Examples of digital media embracing these dispositions include (Bennett, et al., 2010).

- Streaming online video content that is political in nature (e.g. immigration reform videos on YouTube.
- International coalitions that are able to avoid censorship.
- Civic gaming where youth can learn and practice civic engagement.
- Virtual summer camps for discussing issues via *Second Life* (e.g. World Without Oil).

Although these characteristics and examples of the potential digital media holds for youth civic engagement, in the analysis of 90 of North America's most visited civic engagement sites (e.g. TakingIT Global), the researchers found that only 23 percent of online only sites offered participants opportunities to join public and take action projects with only 9 percent providing actual take action possibilities (Bennett, et al., 2010). The researchers noted that the online sites often mirrored the age-old school emphasis on the Dutiful Citizen model of civic engagement (i.e. vote, be a law abiding citizen). Thus, in this study of 90 popular online sites for citizenship, the affordances and potential impact of digital media on social action was quite limited.

Reconceptualizing the extant research on digital media considered through the lens of Cosmopolitan Critical Literacy (CCL), with its potential to disrupt and problematize narrow interpretations of youth, it may be possible to use digital media to improve intercultural communication. For example, in McClean's (2010) study of Zeek, her Trinidad roots were mocked in her new high school but she was able to cope by talking with her friends in Trinidad using her preferred dialect, "Trini."

Similarly, McClean's (2013) study of Sade and Kai from Jamaica found that, although they were mocked by their respective classmates and reacted to this exclusion in different ways, digital literacies offered a space, at least in Kai's approach, to resist and comment on racist attitudes. The unfortunate missing element was a cosmopolitan disposition that invited dialogue around social and cultural difference. Zeek's Trinidad roots and Sade and Kai's Jamaican homeland could offer United States classmates a larger look at the world versus an insular, isolationist stance.

In Skerrett's (2012) study, Vanessa maintained her connection to her homeland, Mexico via the Internet. While Vanessa also assimilated cultural practices taken up in her new school (e.g. dance and hip hop), she would have much to offer in terms of transnational funds of knowledge and intercultural communication. Sorrells (2013) notes that: Intercultural communication is an embodied experience" (p. 51). Social difference is marked by language, dialects, nonverbal gestures, register, eye contact, clothes and other embodied elements in face-to-face contact or via media images.

The use of digital media exemplified by the Asylum research study considered earlier (Dunkerly-Bean, Bean, & Alnajjar, 2014), represents citizen media or participatory media aimed at challenging a political position through "culture jamming" (Sorrells, 2013). Culture jamming is a form of remixing visual and textual elements to challenge taken-for-granted notions advanced in advertising and other media (e.g. fast food ads), by creating counterpoint or alternative versions this material (Knobel & Lankshear, 2014).

Given that one out of every 35 people in the world reside outside their home country; it seems imperative to develop a more cosmopolitan perspective in schools and community settings. Figure 2 offers a useful framework for examining the current issues raised in the studies reviewed.

In the studies considered, youth were engaged in forming new identities and imagined futures, very much in the spirit of cosmopolitan

Figure 2. Creating Cosmopolitan Critical Literacy Spaces

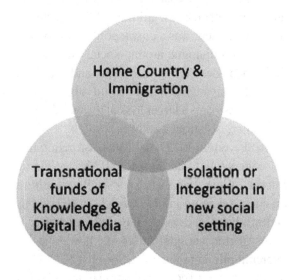

critical literacy (CCL). Delanty (2006) argued that: "Cosmopolitanism concerns processes of self-transformation in which new cultural forms take shape and where new spaces of discourse open up leading to a transformation in the social world" (p. 44). While this is an optimistic view of the effects of globalization, I want to apply the ideas in Figure 2 to an analysis of extant studies of youth in fluid, transnational spaces like those inhabited by Zeek and Venessa.

SOLUTIONS AND RECOMMENDATIONS

Although focusing on studies that highlight the tensions that exist between a United States nation-state based school curriculum and students' transnational funds of knowledge may seem overly narrow, Williamson (2013) noted that: The curriculum is a microcosm of the wider society outside school" (p. 2).

The reality of living in a risk society (Beck & Sznaider, 2010) suggests that our current school curriculum may be out of alignment with the need to develop a creative, astute citizenry able to address challenging global issues (Williamson, 2013). In a series of case studies located internationally (e.g. New Basics in Australia), Williamson found that:

The visions for the future of society imagined by the various prototypical examples of the curriculum of the future all challenge the idea that a single, central, and official version of the curriculum is possible. Instead, they promote a much more centrifugal and decentralized vision of schooling. Centrifugal schooling, as the collective name given to the prototype curriculum projects, represents an emergent and unofficial vision of the curriculum of the future—a style of thought for the curriculum of the digital age. (p. 121)

Toward that end critical media literacy (Hobbs, 2007) and Cosmopolitan Critical Literacy (Dunkerly-Bean, et al., 2014) take on particular importance in the transnational flows of people and ideas via the Internet. Research reviewed earlier in the chapter reveals the transformative power of digital media. For example, the three-year international collaborative project, Space2cre8 (Hull & Stornaiulo, 2014) engaged youth from the United States, Africa, India, and Norway in media projects on discrimination, poverty, and other topics. Students' intercultural communication barriers were reduced as the project progressed over time. Thus integration rather than isolation in disparate locales of the globe was a positive outcome for the youth involved in this international project.

In contrast, McClean's (2010) study of Zeek and her difficult transition to a United States high school showed the pain of isolation when U. S. students mocked her Trinidad dialect. Digital media helped preserve her identity by providing a space where she could communicate with her homeland friends using "Trini" and maintaining her home identity even a she attempted to negotiate her new transnational identity. Sade and Kai in McClean's (3013) study of these Jamaican immigrant students revealed their very different ways of coping with having their culture and language mocked by classmates. While Sade assimilated by changing her style of dress to conform to her classmates' norms, Kai resisted peer pressure by using her digital literacies to create a blog site aimed at discussing transnational issues.

Skerrett's (2012) study of Vanessa's navigation of her new home in the United States after moving from Mexico revealed her approach to integrating into the new culture through expressive dance and hip-hop, as well as embracing African-American vernacular. She was able to maintain contact with her family in Mexico via digital media while taking up a new identity in American teen culture. However, it is less clear that Vanessa's culture and language were seen as transnational funds of knowledge. Rather, she seemed to do what many

immigrant families have done for ages, assimilate the mainstream cultural mores while trying to maintain her native culture as well.

In the middle school iFLICK asylum study, the researchers found students' understanding of the global and local elements at play became more complex, and at times contradictory to immigrants assimilating into a new culture (Dunkerly-Bean, Bean, & Alnajjar, in press). Writing and acting in the short iMovie film "Asylum" served as a way to deconstruct and critique the status quo of immigration while questioning exclusionary policies, bribery, and corruption. In the tradition of Cosmopolitan Critical Literacy (CCL), the students in this study learned how to deconstruct a local reality in their lives, along with thinking about how, through a forced diaspora from their native counties, they could reconstruct a better life in their new homeland. Thus, their transnational funds of knowledge were respected and invited into the global period where they felt welcomed.

Baildon and Damico's (2011) software aimed at critiquing issues offers a useful tool for critical literacy practices. Similarly, the production of counterpoint high quality videos provided students in various classrooms a vehicle for the critique of immigration policies and a host of other important issues (Morrell, et al., 2013).

Although each of these studies show promise for engaging youth in political critique and potential action projects aimed at transforming social injustices across a range of issues, research by Bennett et al. (2010) shows that the majority of citizenship education is mired in older models of the "Dutiful Citizen."

In their analysis of 90 of North America's most visited civic engagement sites (e.g. TakingIT Global), the researchers found that only 23 percent of online only sites offered participants opportunities to join public advocacy projects with only 9 percent providing actual take action possibilities.

The main issue raised by these studies suggests that intercultural communication and capitalizing on transnational youth's global experiences will be a long-term journey with starts and stops along the way (Hansen, 2014). As Hansen noted in a themed issue on cosmopolitanism in *Curriculum Inquiry*, "People necessarily speak from who or what they have become up to that moment. Their prejudices or presumptions take from through the course of socialization and life experience" (p.9). At times when I have offered a graduate diversity and literacy seminar, this has become readily apparent. That is, the ideals and dispositions of cosmopolitanism go well beyond merely respecting difference. This positioning means one is able to walk in the Other's shoes and see multiple perspectives expressed in transnational encounters like those of Zeek, Vanessa, and the students in the Asylum production. This is not easy work or easy scholarship and research. As Hull and Stornaiuolo, 2014) concluded:

Yet, we are still a distance away for knowing how to foster a cosmopolitan citizenry, being yet at the beginning of imagining conceptions of imagining conceptions of education, schools, and curricula that produce the globally alert, linguistically versatile, ethically turned, and geographically nimble, or individuals able to converse, understand, identify, and act, not locally but beyond. (p. 40)

With that caveat in mind, I turn to a consideration of the gaps in the extant research and possible directions for future study.

FUTURE RESEARCH DIRECTIONS

It seems to me that the most glaring gap in the existing research on digital media and CCL relates to exemplar settings (e.g. classrooms) where youth from diverse transnational settings have a chance to share their unique funds of knowledge rather than simply assimilate. Although the concept of funds of knowledge is certainly not new (Moll, 1992), we have very few examples of classrooms

and other sites where students are, in the best sense of cosmopolitanism, seeing their diverse cultural mores and artifacts acknowledged (Jimenez, Smith, & Teague, 2009).

These researchers noted that: "We believe that the act of embracing and implementing transnational and community literacies is one way for teachers to begin to build productive relationships with students who are English Language Learners" (p. 16). For example, barrio neighborhoods in Nashville where their exploration occurred often feature advertisements for a host of instrumental tasks such as transmitting funds to Mexico, China, and Nigeria. Additional documents explain how to open a banking account in Spanish, as well as informational material on how to apply for a mortgage. These researchers compiled a collection of over 30 digital photos of these "texts" that could be used in the classroom.

In addition, the researchers took photos of foods (e.g. tomatillos) that might not be known outside the local context. Learning the cultural history of these foods would help all students appreciate the diversity in their classrooms and the powerful funds of knowledge students bring from their home countries. Digital media including YouTube clips can be used to further orient students to far flung villages in their home countries, whether in Mexico or elsewhere.

In the Luis Moll (1992) account, Tucson's Latino community possessed a wealth of knowledge about agriculture, mining, economics, household management, science, medicine, folk medicine, ranching, mechanics, carpentry, masonry, electrical wiring, biology and math. Working with teachers to revamp lessons so that students' diverse funds of knowledge were included meant developing units on building and construction where students read, researched, and finally created model buildings. Enroute to this culminating project, students were learning the language of construction as they created streets, parks, and other buildings.

Moll (1992) listed a number of key questions aimed at evaluating the degree to which a school site takes up a multicultural, cosmopolitan curriculum likely to engage transnational students:

1. How well does a school link student learning to families and communities?
2. Have teachers had professional development to learn how they can incorporate their students' unique funds of knowledge?
3. In what way do teachers use students' informal language as a way to bridge to the curriculum (e.g. dialects, hip hop, and so on)?

Given the studies I reviewed in this chapter, there is a pressing need for new studies that explore how these changes might create a cosmopolitan canopy (Anderson, 2011) and a two-way exchange of cultural resources. At present, studies suggest that transnational students assimilate as best they can, or outright resist the hegemonic, conformist pressures to leave their native ways behind. Thus, in this light, even the questions posed by Moll may be too restrictive. A CCL perspective would marshal students' questioning stance to critique policies that limit their voice and agency. Rather, a study aimed at creating the kind of interchange across global boundaries in the fashion of Hull and Stornaiulo's Space2Cre8 (2010/2014) would help the field further understand the potential for moving beyond cultural communication toward intercultural communication.

Other areas within the digital media realm that need further study include how youth might go about critiquing global risk issues (e.g. immigration and human rights). The study where students created a film on Asylum (Dunkerly-Bean, Bean, & Alnajjar, 2014) provides an example of a promising research direction. Additional studies that cut close to home for students (e.g. discrimination, bullying, sexual harassment, cyberbullying, and so on) are hot button topics in many school districts and amenable to CCL practices.

Cross cultural civic engagement studies where youth reach out to tutor younger students in literacy offer yet another venue for intercultural communication and research. For example a study exploring an afterschool program in Los Angeles sought to reduce the digital divide for students of poverty (Felt, Vartabedian, Literat, & Mehta, 2012). Because schools often block social media sites that have the potential for participatory cultures where there are few impediments to creativity, artistic expression, and civic engagement, the researchers sought to change this situation. They noted that participatory cultures are characterized by (p. 214):

*   Creative original works;
*   Circulating in knowledge exchange by disseminating products across networks;
*   Collaborative efforts aimed at problem solving or community engagement;
*   Connecting with affinity groups around a common interest.

In this study, set in a high density Pico Union Latino area of Los Angeles where 84 percent of the students were Latino and low income with 50 percent ELL, students had access to a state-of-the art digital media lab, archive, and community center focused on social justice and digital media. Eight participants (6 male and 2 female) age 15 participated. As the 15-week program progressed, these students became more adept at working with digital cameras, video composition, and numerous sites and applications (e.g. YouTube). Their school was located on the site of the former Ambassador Hotel where Robert F. Kennedy was assassinated in 1968. Students developed a video production entitled "This is my L.A." that was presented to a large audience of family members, administrators, teachers, researchers, and peers. The project reviewed existing schools in their community with an eye toward successful elements and social barriers needing improvement. At the close of the project, students earned Digital Citizenship Certificates.

CONCLUSION

At this relatively early stage of extant research at the intersection of CCL and digital media, this body of work points to needed changes in how curriculum can become responsive to transnational and immigrant youth, as well as how digital media can be instrumental in this transformation. As Ben Williamson argued based on international case studies of curriculum designs (e.g. New Basics in Australia):

A very cosmopolitan vision of curriculum is required. Cosmopolitanism represents the sharing of values on a global scale that transcend local and parochial interests. Such concerns are linked to the diversity of multiculturalism, changes in traditional family structure and everyday life; to the expansion of notions of community and civic participation, powered by digital media, and its effect on the individual's capacity for belonging; as well as to global economic and political forces. (p .90)

Thus, digital media and cosmopolitan critical literacy hold great promise for transforming the lives of youth. As the youth in the studies reviewed for this chapter demonstrate, it is no small accomplishment to immigrate from one's home country and its familiar culture and language to a new land, a new school, a new neighborhood that may, or may not be welcoming. Clearly, one of the ways these youth bridged barriers to active participation as citizens in a new land was through digital media and related practices. Indeed, to be literate now and in the future implies that one can manage a fairly lengthy set of competencies that alter the once lauded basic skills related to reading and understanding print based texts. New Literacies competencies include (Simsek & Simsek, 2013, p. 129):

- *Sharing* via communal bookmarking, photo/video sharing, social networks, writer's workshops, fanfiction
- *Thinking* via blogs, podcasts, online discussion forums
- *Co-creating* through wikis, collaborative file creation, mashups, collective media creation, collaborative social change communities

In addition to these competencies, contemporary citizens must be able to navigate multimodal material that includes visual, aural, and media based content while respecting social difference in viewpoints and multiple perspectives (Simsek & Simsek, 2013). While embracing this vision it is important to keep in mind that, as Hansen (2014) noted, we are in the very early stages of fieldwork aimed at placing cosmopolitanism practices, and CCL on the ground. The studies I reviewed in this chapter suggest that alternative and more inclusive curriculum designs that tap local and global funds of knowledge hold the potential to create citizens who respect each other and are able to use digital media successfully to transform theirs and others' life trajectories.

REFERENCES

Anderson, E. (2011). *The cosmopolitan canopy: Race and identity in everyday life.* New York: W. W. Norton & Company.

Appiah, K. A. (2006). *Cosmopolitanism: Ethics in a world of strangers.* New York: W. W. Norton.

Baildon, M., & Damico, J. S. (2011). *Social studies as new literacies in a global society: Relational cosmopolitanism in the classroom.* New York: Routledge.

Bean, T. W., & Dunkerly-Bean, J. (in press). Expanding conceptions of adolescent literacy research and practice: Cosmopolitan theory in educational contexts. *Australian Journal of Language and Literacy*.

Bean, T. W., Dunkerly-Bean, J., & Harper, H. J. (2014). *Teaching young adult literature*. Thousand Oaks, CA: SAGE.

Beck, U. (2012). *World at risk*. Cambridge, UK: Polity Press.

Beck, U., & Sznaider, N. (2010). Unpacking cosmopolitanism and the social sciences: A research agenda. *The British Journal of Sociology, 61*(1), 381–403. doi:10.1111/j.1468-4446.2009.01250.x PMID:20092506

Bennett, W. L., Freelon, D., & Wells, C. (2010). Changing citizen identity and the rise of a participatory media culture. In L. R. Sherrod, J. Torney-Purta, & C. A. Flanagan (Eds.), *Handbook of research on civic engagement in youth* (pp. 393–423). Hoboken, JH: John Wiley & Sons. doi:10.1002/9780470767603.ch15

Borsheim-Black, C., Macaluso, M., & Petrone, R. (2014). Critical literature pedagogy: Teaching canonical literature for critical literacy. *Journal of Adolescent & Adult Literacy, 58*(2), 123–133. doi:10.1002/jaal.323

Cervetti, G., Pardales, M. J., & Damico, J. (2001, April). A tale of differences: Comparing the traditions, perspectives, and educational goals of critical reading and critical literacy. *Reading Online, 4*(9). Retrieved from http://www.reading.org/articles/art_index.asp?HREF=/articles/cervetti/ index.html

Chesney, K. (2010). *Boys of Fall-CMA Awards 2010-HD Quality*. Available from YouTube.

Copeland, M. (2014). *New Under Armour ad featuring Misty Copeland promotes female empowerment*. Available from YouTube: www.youtube.com/watch?v=52tc3STY3fc

Damico, J. S., & Baldwin, M. (2013). Content literacy for the 21st Century: Evacuation, elevation, and relational cosmopolitan in the classroom. *Journal of Adolescent & Adult Literacy, 55*(3), 232–243. doi:10.1002/JAAL.00028

Delanty, G. (2006). The cosmopolitan imagination: Critical cosmopolitanism and social theory. *The British Journal of Sociology, 5*(1), 25–47. doi:10.1111/j.1468-4446.2006.00092.x PMID:16506995

Dunkerly-Bean, J. M., Bean, T., & Alnajjar, K. (2014). Seeking asylum: Adolescents explore the crossroads of human rights education and cosmopolitan critical literacy. *Journal of Adolescent & Adult Literacy, 58*(3), 230–241. doi:10.1002/jaal.349

Esenlauer, V. J. (2011). Multimodality and social actions in 'personal publishing' text: From the German 'Poetry Album' to Web 2.0 'Social Network Sites. In K. L. O' Halloran & B. A. Smith (Eds.), *Multimodal studies: Exploring issues and domains* (pp. 131–152). New York: Routledge.

Felt, L. J., Vartabedian, V., Literat, I., & Mehta, R. (2012). Explore locally, excel digitally: A participatory learning after school program for engaging citizenship on and offline. *Journal of Media Literacy Education, 4*(3), 213–228.

Golumbia, D. (2014). Characteristics of digital media. In M. L. Ryan, L. Emerson, & B. J. Robertson (Eds.), *The John Hopkins guide to digital media*. Baltimore, MD: John Hopkins University Press.

Habermas, J. (1975). *Legitimation crisis*. London, England: Beacon Press.

Hansen, D. T. (2008). Curriculum and the idea of cosmopolitan inheritance. *Journal of Curriculum Studies*, *40*(3), 289–312. doi:10.1080/00220270802036643

Hansen, D. T. (2014). Theme issue: Cosmopolitanism as cultural creativity: New modes of educational practice in globalizing times. *Curriculum Inquiry*, *44*(1), 1–14. doi:10.1111/curi.12039

Harper, H., Bean, T. W., & Dunkerly, J. (2010). Cosmopolitanism, globalization, and the field of adolescent literacy. *Canadian and International Education. Education Canadienne et Internationale*, *39*(3), 1–13.

Hobbs, R. (2007). *Reading the media: Media literacy in high school English*. New York: Teachers College Press.

Hull, G. A., & Stornaiulo, A. (2010). Literate arts in a global world: Reframing social networking as a cosmopolitan practice. *Journal of Adolescent & Adult Literacy*, *54*(2), 85-97.

Hull, G. A., & Stornaiulo, A. (2014). Cosmopolitan literacies, social networks, and "proper distance": Striving to understand in a global world. *Curriculum Inquiry*, *44*(1), 15–44. doi:10.1111/curi.12035

International Society for Technology in Education. (2007). *ISTE Standards for students*. Available at: http://www.iste.org

Janks, H. (2010). *Literacy and power*. New York: Routledge.

Janks, H. (2014). *Doing critical literacy*. New York: Routledge.

Jimenez, R., Smith, P., & Teague, L. (2009). Transnational and community literacies for teachers. *Journal of Adolescent & Adult Literacy*, *53*(1), 16–28. doi:10.1598/JAAL.53.1.2

Kaku, M. (2014). *The future of the mind*. New York: Doubleday.

Kant, I. (1972). *Perpetual peace: A philosophical essay, translation M. Campbell Smith*. New York: Garland.

Knobel, M., & Lankshear, C. (2014). Studying New Literacies. *Journal of Adolescent & Adult Literacy*, *58*(2), 97–101. doi:10.1002/jaal.314

Kress, G. (2003). *Literacy in the new media age*. New York: Routledge. doi:10.4324/9780203164754

Leu, D. J., Kinzer, C. K., Coiro, J., Castek, J., & Henry, L. A. (2013). New literacies: A dual-level theory of the changing nature of literacy instruction, and Assessment. In D. E. Alvermann, J. J. Unrau, & R. R. Ruddell (Eds.), *Theoretical models and processes of reading* (6th ed., pp. 1150–1181). Newark, DE: International Reading Association. doi:10.1598/0710.42

Lim, S. S., Nekmat, E., & Nahar, S. N. (2011). The implications of multimodality For media literacy. In K. L. O'Halloran & B. A. Smith (Eds.), *Multimodal studies: Exploring issues and domains* (pp. 167–183). New York: Routledge.

Luke, A. (2013). *Second wave change*. Available at: www.youtube.com/watch?v-RgciQLj-57k7

McClean, C. (2010). A space called home: An immigrant adolescent's digital literacy practices. *Journal of Adolescent & Adult Literacy*, *54*(1), 13–22. doi:10.1598/JAAL.54.1.2

McClean, C. (2013). Literacies, identities, and gender: Reframing girls in digital Worlds. In B. J. Guzzetti & T. W. Bean (Eds.), *Adolescent literacies and the gendered self: (Re)constructing identities through multimodal literacy practices* (pp. 64–73). New York: Routledge.

Miller, S. M., & McVee, M. B. (2012). Multimodal composing: The essential 21st Century literacy. In S. M. Miller & M. B. McVee (Eds.), *Multimodal composing in classrooms: Learning and teaching for the digital world* (pp. 1–12). New York: Routledge.

Moll, L., Amanti, C., Neff, D., & Gonzalez, N. (1992). Funds of knowledge for teaching: Using a qualitative approach to Connect homes and classrooms. *Theory into Practice*, *3*(2), 132–141. doi:10.1080/00405849209543534

Morrell, E., Duenas, R., Garcia, V., & Lopez, J. (2013). *Critical media pedagogy: Teaching for achievement in city schools*. New York: Teachers College Press.

O'Halloran, K. L., & Smith, B. A. (2011). Multimodal studies. In K. L. O'Halloran & B. A. Smith (Eds.), *Multimodal studies: Exploring issues and domains* (pp. 1–13). New York: Routledge.

Pew Research Center. (2014, August). *Digital life in 2025: AI, robotics, and the future of jobs*. Available: http://www.pewinternet.org/2014/08/06/futureofjobs/

Simsek, E., & Simsek, A. (2013). New literacies and digital citizenship. *Contemporary Educational Technology*, *4*(2), 126–137.

Skerrett, A. (2012). Language and literacies in translocation: Experiences and perspectives of a transnational youth. *Journal of Literacy Research*, *44*(4), 364–395. doi:10.1177/1086296X12459511

Sorrells, K. (2013). *Intercultural communication: Globalization and social justice*. Thousand Oaks, CA: SAGE.

Stevens, L. P., & Bean, T. W. (2007). *Critical literacy: Context, research, and practice in the K-12 classroom*. Thousand Oaks, CA: SAGE.

Strydom, P. (2002). *Risk, environment and society: Ongoing debates, current issues, and future prospects*. Buckingham, UK: Open University Press.

Trepanier, L. (2011). The postmodern condition of cosmopolitanism. In L. Trepanier & K. M. Habib (Eds.), *Cosmopolitanism in the age of globalization: citizens without states* (pp. 211–227). Lexington, KY: The University of Kentucky Press.

Trepanier, L., & Habib, K. M. (2011). Introduction. In L. Trepanier & K. M. Habib (Eds.), *Cosmopolitanism in the age of globalization: citizens without states* (pp. 1–10). Lexington, KY: The University of Kentucky Press.

Williamson, B. (2013). *The future of the curriculum: School knowledge in the digital age*. Cambridge, MA: The MIT Press.

KEY TERMS AND DEFINITIONS

Cosmopolitanism: At times a contested term referring to the framing of self and other in relation to the world rather than a nation-state, and a concomitant ethical obligation to others beyond local and national borders and citizenry.

Critical Literacy: An emancipatory endeavor centered on interrogating issues of power, representation, and marginalization. Who is acknowledged and who is silenced in a text becomes crucial, along with the understanding that no text is neutral.

Cosmopolitan Critical Literacy: This framework moves beyond nation-state boundaries and interests to critically address a host of global human rights issues (e.g. immigration) via digital media as a vehicle for discussion and transformation.

Critical Media Literacy: Critiques how diverse people are portrayed and positioned in digital media including films, advertisements, video games, songs, popular culture, and social media sites.

Globalization: The increasingly fluid and borderless movement of people, ideas, information, and capital that position the global and local as mutually interdependent.

Digital Media: Digital Media is a highly dynamic category that includes multimodal elements (e.g. visual images and sound). Digital Media are portable, searchable, and able to be digitally preserved.

Risk Society: Globalization, while at times treated as an economic element, renders nations interdependent such that events in one part of the globe spill over into other parts, sometimes with dire consequences (e.g. terrorism, climate change, pollution, involuntary diasporas, economic problems).

Transnationalism: The increasing diversity of people immigrating voluntarily and involuntarily to new home countries argues for an appreciation of cosmopolitan cultural funds of knowledge that values social difference in languages and cultural beliefs.

APPENDIX

ADDITIONAL READING

Digital Resources

The following web-based digital resources are provided to guide Cosmopolitan Critical Literacy discussion of many of the global risk society issues explored in this chapter. As this is an evolving area of study, the list is not meant to be exhaustive.

Canadian Museum for Human Rights

Established in 2014 in Winnipeg, Manitoba, Canada this resource includes a website offering a virtual exploration of the museum at:

http://museumforhumanrights.ca

Centre for Human Rights and Civic Engagement

Developed by St. Patrick's College in Dublin, Ireland the following two websites include global exemplars of human rights education in the classroom.

http://www.spd.dcu.ie/site/chrce/index.shtml
http://www.hrea.org/pubs/Compendium.pdf

Choices Program

Sponsored by Brown University, this virtual collection engages youth with international issues and discussion.

www.choices.edu

Research by Columbia Teachers College scholar Earnest Morrell in urban settings with African-American youth engaged in multimedia critique of issues can be found at:

http://earnestmorrell.com

Me to We and *Free the Children* features a wealth of examples aimed at interesting students in issues of global civic engagement.

http://www.metowe.com/speakers-bureau/view-all-speakers/craig-kielburger
http://www.freethechildren.com/about-us/our-story/

United Nations Children's Emergency Fund

This well-known resource includes issues lessons on global issues.

Youth for Human Rights

Video clips running 1 to 2 minutes are centered on specific human rights and offer a rich resource for discussion.

www.youthforhumanrights.org

Chapter 4

It *Is* Real Colouring?
Mapping Children's Im/Material Thinking in a Digital World

Dane Marco Di Cesare
University at Buffalo, USA

Debra Harwood
Brock University, Canada

Jennifer Rowsell
Brock University, Canada

ABSTRACT

Situated in the context of the role digital technology plays in the lives of young children in today's society, this chapter is comprised of four sections examining children's thinking involving digital spaces. First, a succinct overview of current research will be presented, focusing on emergent themes regarding young children navigating digital spaces and their im/material thinking. Following this is an examination of the issues raised from this research. This section highlights disparate access to technology and children's construction of identity in digital spaces. The next section presents the gaps in current research and the final section of this chapter focuses on implications for literacy practice, policy, and research.

INTRODUCTION

Media and literature often polarize the debate regarding the benefits and downfalls of exposing young children to digital worlds (Cordes & Miller, 2000). Parents and educators alike worry if exposure to digital worlds at a young age is dangerous for a child and counters healthy child development. Adults often romanticize childhood and a protectionist type of attitude has traditionally prevailed within the field of early childhood education (Robinson & Diaz, 2005). As part of a larger ethnographic study of integrating iPads into early childhood educational contexts, we asked parents a series of survey questions related to children's access and use of digital worlds in the home environment (for a discussion of research methods see Harwood, forthcoming). Additionally, we also inquired about parents' personal beliefs related to play, literacy, education, and the digital world.

DOI: 10.4018/978-1-4666-8310-5.ch004

Overall, the 24 parents who responded to the survey demonstrated a cautious attitude toward the idea of integrating iPads into early educational contexts, favoring ideas of using technology only for clear educational aims with well-defined time limits. In response to one of our questions, how much time in your child's kindergarten program should be dedicated to 'new technologies' (e.g., tablet), a parent stated:

Not a major portion…It is more important that a child should be taught about all the aspects of life like learning to co-operate, adjust with peers, how to cope with failure as well as how to behave when you win. Be competitive in a positive manner. All these endless character formations can never be learnt with the use of 'new technologies'. Making a child concentrate on new technologies would make him more a techie and robotic. I see many kids who do not talk or play with others but spend all their time in front of a computer or iPad. This should be discouraged. So, it is very important that children should be taught new technologies and should spend some time with it, without [sacrificing] other major activities.

The crux of the debate appears to be fuelled by a general lack of understanding and information about how children's thinking *through/with* digital worlds is impacting how they learn and approach the learning environment. Yet, digital spaces are increasing at a rapid rate (Burke, 2010; Lim & Clark, 2010), and young children are immersed in the world of digital media (Rideout, Vandewater, & Wartella, 2003). One only has to make a quick stop at a local toy store to realize that children's play and learning has extended into these digital spaces. Toy store offerings include such items as the Fisher-Price® Laugh & Learn Apptivity™ Storybook Reader. This 'baby' aged intended toy offers parents a book-like case to house their digital device and the capability to interact with applications that focus on early literacy. And although in this chapter we are not advocating for either side of the debate regarding the age of appropriateness for introducing children to the digital world, what is apparent is that digital worlds are as much a part of a child's early experiences as other traditional types of play (e.g., lego, sand/water play, doll play). And as these digital spaces continue to evolve and expand, how they affect children's thinking and learning in these converged spaces have become key questions for society (Burke, 2010; Marsh, 2007). Collectively, in this paper, we use the terms *digital spaces* and *digital worlds* interchangeably to refer to and encompass digital technologies and media, digital toys and games, and virtual spaces that children occupy. The chapter is broken up into four parts, which examine children's im/material thinking: the first section presents a succinct overview of the research; the second section examines the issues raised in relation to the existing research; in the third section, several gaps in the existing research are discussed; the fourth and final section draws out the implications of such research for literacy practice, policy and research.

SUCCINCT OVERVIEW OF THE RESEARCH

This section will review current research with young children involving the intersection of literacy and digital spaces in relation to children's im/material thinking. The research reviewed in this section involves how children construct identity and meaning, make complex compositional choices, form and forge collaborative spaces, as well as navigate and create within digital spaces. Additionally, research concerning crossing the im/material boundaries between the physical and digital, as well as children's virtual worlds is also presented.

Im/Material Thinking

Within the discussion that follows, we refer to Burnett's (2014) concept of im/materialities. The construct of im/materialities can be thought of as "those things that are materially absent or intangible but central to meaning-making: associations, memories, feelings and imaginings as well as all the events and processes that have led up to the production of the things that are physically present" (Burnett et al., 2014, p. 125). Burnett emphasizes that the materialities, the physical aspects of meaning-making (i.e., the concrete artifacts), are equally important to understanding how the relationship and amalgam of the material and immaterial impact literacy learning. It is the *relationship* between the immaterial and material of digital worlds that seems most significant in challenging 'reductivist' models of literacy (Burnett, in press).

Constructing Identity

In digital spaces, interaction and identity take on layered and varied roles. Drawing on extant research, scholars like Merchant (2003) explored communication and identity through computer-mediated communication between children/researcher via email. This research illuminated the varied identities and relationships fostered by digital communication. Additionally, Burnett, Dickinson, Myers, and Merchant (2006) noted that a variety of relationships emerge as children from different settings engaged in online collaboration to construct PowerPoint presentations. These interactions were influenced by audience awareness and prior task experience. Labbo, Eakle, and Montero (2002) explored multimodal meaning making to give children agency and to develop their identities and voices. One of the children re-imagined herself as a writer, another child gained control of her learning. In both cases, the children developed their voices and identity. Digital spaces often not only afford the opportunity to construct an avatar (an image representing the identity of the user), but encourage it (Merchant, 2011). Marsh (2011) found children used both literacy and multimodal practices to construct identities when developing their penguin avatar in Club Penguin. Additionally, digital spaces, such as Club Penguin, also afford users a capacity to modify their spaces to suit their identity, personality, and needs (Marsh, 2011). For example, users of Club Penguin can design their own igloos with furniture and varied designs (Marsh, 2011; 2014). This is also apparent in other spaces, such as web pages, blogs, or even on the devices themselves. Tablet owners can choose wallpapers and backgrounds to personalize their devices, and the home pages of blogs or other web spaces can be reconfigured and personalised (Merchant, 2011). Children's offline selves often inform their identities in these spaces and a relationship exists between who they are as a person offline and how they construct their online identity (Marsh, 2011; Merchant, 2011).

Digital Media and Bricolage

While exploring emergent identity in digital spaces, research has also found children capable of making critical choices in composing. Wohlwend (2009) found children were selective in choosing particular modes best suited to represent their intended meanings. In digital spaces, children have a wider variety of modes to choose from in creating their meanings. In making these deliberate choices, they demonstrate critical engagement, drawing from online and offline sources. Literacy practices are being transformed, facilitating learner centered and collaborative practices (Wohlwend, 2009). When children compose with digital video, they do so collaboratively, with the participants taking on a series of roles in producing a shared text (Husbye, Buchholz, Coggin, Powell, & Wohlwend, 2012). In these texts, children may produce original pieces or remix images, sound, and text to create new, modified compositions. Marsh (2006) explored the filmmaking process by three and four year old children. The children showed evidence of critical engagement throughout the process, making deliberate choices in regard to props, settings, characters, and soundtracks. Children used both new and existing material, remixing their original content with familiar songs or images. Knobel and Lankshear (2008) identify remixing information as exponential; with each new mix having the potential for a series of new and future remixes.

Forming and Forging Collaborative Spaces

Burnett et al. (2006) purport new technology provides children with opportunities to explore literacy in a broader context. Further, these contexts offer new types of relationships and communication to emerge and expand. Burnett (2014) found when children engaged in online collaboration in the classroom with their peers, they had the ability to augment this collaboration with communication in physical spaces. Students were able to clarify information presented in digital spaces, a unique affordance when collaboration can traverse the line between the digital and physical (Burnett, Merchant, Pahl, Rowsell, 2014). Additionally, the process of digital reading and composing may outline spaces in ways that challenge conventional literacy routines in schools; boundaries are mutable and may shift at any given moment (Burnett, 2011). With a shift in boundaries, new opportunities for meaning making emerge and though purposes and audience may vary, classroom boundaries may blur as children interact in larger, global media landscapes (Burnett, 2011).

Collapsing Boundaries between Online/Offline Worlds

In new media, the lines between reading and writing are often blurred; affording children opportunities to both read and produce text in digital environments (Burnett & Merchant, 2011;

Merchant, 2007). With text unbound from the physical page, it becomes more complex and layered, collaborative and multi-voiced, blending the roles of the reader and the writer. Web pages and blogs can be authored by multiple persons, updated, edited, and layered with connections to other pages through the use of hyperlinks (Burnett & Merchant, 2011). These pages often allow users to comment directly on the page, providing the opportunity to write and contribute to text they have just read. Pelletier, Reeve, and Halewood (2006) explored how kindergarten children engaged with and interacted in a collaborative photo journal website. The children were highly motivated to post images to the site, as well as add comments and engage in conversations with others (Pelletier et al., 2006). Their roles as producer/consumer shifted and blurred as they engaged with the site. Meaning making in digital spaces allows for collaboration from multiple parties, either sharing the same physical location or across space and time online.

As children navigate the im/material, the boundaries between the digital and physical are also quite blurred. Research observing young children's technology use, though limited in quantity, has often found this a common practice. O'Mara and Laidlaw (2011) observed children participating in an im/material tea party. The children operated in the digital world, engaging with the Toca Tea Party app, and transitioned to the physical world, with plastic teapots, cups, and a blanket. The children shifted between these two worlds seamlessly, engaging in dramatic play that spanned two realms. Burnett et al. (2014) identify how common classroom tasks, such as students writing on a smartboard, illustrate how children navigate the im/material. "As children take their turns to access the [smartboard] programme, they must both navigate the material world to avoid bumping into one another and deploy the whiteboard tools to navigate the virtual world. In doing so, they appear to *believe* in both worlds" (Burnett et al., 2014, p. 5). Conversations and attention too must traverse the im/material line between digital and physical spaces. Danby et al. (2013) explored conversational activity surrounding iPad/iPhone use in the home environment. Talk, engagement, and attention moved in, between, and through digital and physical spaces.

Like the boundaries between the digital and physical worlds, children often change, organize, or create space to situate the im/material. By pushing these boundaries, children challenge typical literacy routines with regard to changes to space (Burnett, 2014). While there may be pre-established expectations for operating digital and physical spaces alike set in the classroom context, the boundaries in digital spaces were not often kept in tact (Burnett, 2014). In the classroom, children organize and create space with their devices. They can open laptops to face others, inviting them into their digital spaces, or establish privacy by turning their laptops to create walls. They can cradle their iPad, making it a solitary experience, or place it in front of them openly, inviting others to collaborate, play, and participate. These shifts are often based upon the emergent and shifting needs of both the child and the classroom context (Burnett, 2014).

Virtual Worlds

Children's virtual worlds both inform and are informed by offline spaces. Offline interaction can be traced back into online, digital worlds (Marsh, 2014; Marsh, 2010). In studies observing patterns of behaviour, interaction, and literacy in the virtual world of *Club Penguin*, children navigated various spaces and maintained appropriate practices for constructing social order; this order was shaped by their offline experiences (Marsh 2010; 2014). Consequently, the offline and online worlds could not be treated as detached entities. Additionally, children's literacy activities were informed by offline practices, tools, and routines; children perceived the intent of sending postcards

to other avatars as the same as sending postcards in the physical world (Marsh, 2010; 2014). While the offline world informs and is informed by the online world, there are still distinct differences between the two. Marsh (2014) identified the construction of friendships as one of these differences. The children exhibited different criteria for forming friendships including the evaluation of screen names.

Virtual worlds also represent another space for children to engage in literacy practices and for a variety of purposes. These worlds may share common purposes for literacy in offline environments (Marsh, 2014). Though reading can occur on and offline, children reported the reading activities that they engaged in during virtual world reading sessions were pleasurable, contrasting their opinion the same activities in offline environments (Marsh, 2014).

Converged Spaces for Playing and Learning

A generally accepted notion in society is that young children learn through play (Gonzalez-Mena, 2005). The importance of providing young children with 'real' and natural materials is part of the developmentally appropriate discourse that has shaped and continues to influence the field of early childhood education and much of parents' thinking. However, the nature of children's play has undergone some dramatic shifts in the 21st Century. Deriving from Prensky's (2001) description of college age students, we do think of the 5-year-old child in terms of being a 'digital native'. And although a preschooler might require guidance or support from an adult in using a digital medium or application (Plowman & Stephen, 2007), we use the term 'digital native' here to refer to an individual born into a world of digital technologies and a 'native speaker' of the "digital language of computers, video games and the Internet" (Prensky, 2001, p. 3). The pervasive nature of this digital world is well represented in children's playthings. As authors Lim and Clark (2010) note, everything from Barbie, Lego, Play-Doh, Little People, Pokemon, Power Rangers, and Sesame Street action figures "has an online presence in the form of websites with interactive games, smartphone apps or full-fledged virtual worlds boasting of multiple environments, activity genres and levels of play" (p. 4). Wohlwend too (in Press) examines how "media flows into every aspect of children's daily lives and circulate a range of identity-shaping messages through franchises of commercial products" (p. 153). In addition to Wohlwend's work, other scholars such as Willett, Burn, Bishop, Richards, and Marsh (2013) remark that the incorporation of new media within children's play can be viewed as a positive. In Willett and colleagues' ethnographic study of children's play on schoolyard playgrounds in the UK, they found that children used elements of new media within their games, representing a type of "hybrid/intertextual forms of media-referenced play" (p. 41).

Similarly, some of our research notes taken while observing children at play (Fieldnotes, 02/11 p. 2) demonstrates how youngsters move seamlessly between and within the concrete and digital world creating *hybrid/intertexual* spaces for literacy play. Informed by the work of other scholars (Duff, 2003; Kristeva, 1980; Shegar & Weninger, 2010), our notion of hybrid/intertexual spaces refer to the range of socio-cultural texts (e.g., popular culture), everyday dialogue (Bakhtin, 1981), artifacts, and experiences children actively draw upon to make meaning; including oral, aural, pictorial, written, digital, and bodily-kinesthetic experiences. Children draw upon these texts in this hybrid/intertexual space to create an mélange of literary play experiences and outputs. And as Kristeva (1980) originally explained "any text is constructed of a mosaic of quotations; any text is the absorption and transformation of another" (p. 66). Children's need to express their thoughts and intentions appear to govern their choice of mode, and often multiple modes appear to better meet their need of expressing these often complex thoughts and play behaviours.

In the house dramatic play center, 4 kindergarten age children were playing a type of cooking game. They found the Grandma's Kitchen app (on the tablet) and started playing it too. They were watching the videos in the app and then making the food in their pretend play (that was pictured in the app). For example, the video showed cracking eggs and the children were pretending to break eggs for baking. When the app said, "give Grandma a kiss", one of the children actually kissed the tablet!

As the children played this 'baking game' they drifted back and forth between the app and concrete toys (Figures 1 and 2). Children would take information from the app and trial that knowledge with concrete toys. Similarly, play themes that had started within the concrete world (e.g., baking a cake) would be enhanced and extended using the app's content (e.g., using measuring spoons for ingredients). The children then blended this converged experience and knowledge to write a menu with a stylus pen on the tablet. Could the children have achieved their play aims with either the concrete toys or the tablet? We argue that the "converged" world of the children's play offered greater and more dynamic opportunities to combine and develop multifarious skills.

Scholars such as Marsh (2010) and Plowman, McPake, and Stephen (2010) also support the notion that the traditional boundary between 'real' and 'virtual' play has eroded. The title of our chapter alludes to this idea that children tend not to differentiate between what was "real" versus what was "virtual". The inspiration for the title of our chapter was drawn from a conversation between a researcher and a kindergarten child. The child was coloring with a stylus on a tablet and the researcher commented, "That's just like real coloring" to which the child matter-of-factly

Figure 1. Children use a tablet to explore and extend "baking theme" play

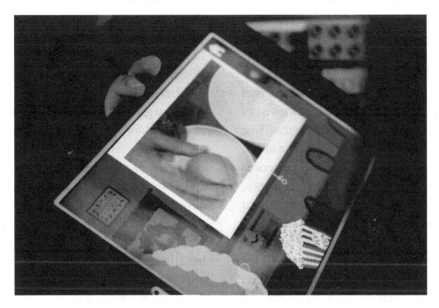

stated, "It is real coloring". To the child's way of thinking, a picture colored on the ipad or with paper and crayons were the same, both equally valid in representing her thinking and needs. And as Marsh (2010) has suggested in her discussion of virtual worlds, perhaps viewing children's experiences as existing along a "continuum in which children's online and offline experiences merge" (p. 25) more accurately reflects children's realities.

Lim and Clarke's (2010) conceptualization of the virtual world as a 'third space' for play (with family and schooling being the other two spaces) helps underscore the discussion here on the benefits of blurring the boundaries of play. 'Third

Figure 2. Children use play materials in support of play theme

space' scholars suggest that new knowledge and discourses emerge from the blending and merging of understanding and experiences from a child's home, community, and peer network with the more formalized learning encountered in schooling (Levy, 2008; Moje et al., 2004). In the digital world, 'third space' thinking can be conceived of as the intersections created by online and offline play experiences. As other researchers can attest, young children draw from a range of experiences (e.g., popular culture, television, computer games, play) and incorporate these within more formalized contexts for learning (Levy, 2008; Marsh, 1999). In our own study, we observed several examples of this 'third space' emerging in children's play and creative texts involving themes centered on the Disney movie Frozen™ (Rowsell & Harwood, in press). Lim and Clark (2010) posit that these types of abilities, that is children traversing the various platforms (including digital mediums), allows for a convergence of play on four levels; the convergence of social spheres, a convergence of play spaces and playthings, a convergence of cultures, and a convergence of learning experiences (p. 6).

Convergence of Social Spheres

A consistent discussion point within the research on children's virtual spaces is related to how the virtual world offers opportunities for children to enhance and expand their social interactions. For example, Burke's (2010) study of children's identities within Club Penguin, found that children who were not regular playmates were able to extend their relationships and play together outside of the classroom within the virtual space. In Black's (2010) research of the virtual world of WebKinz World she cites the benefits of virtual play as providing an opportunity to immerse children in literacy rich environments that are academically oriented and allows for some experimentation with identity. On the cautionary side, Black and other researchers (Grimes & Shade, 2005) discuss the 'consumerist' nature of virtual worlds like WebKinz, the ethics of immersive child-targeted advertising often incumbent with these sites, and Internet safety. Additionally, Black (2010) brands WebKinz as grounded in a 'physical-industrial mindset' where "often technology is employed in ways that reproduce conventional forms of literacy in a digital format, rather than in ways that leverage the technical components in concert with the ethos of new digital literacies" (p. 20). Yet, what appears obvious is that children's social spheres have expanded beyond just the immediate face-to-face interactions in the classroom or playground. Thus, the digital world holds both the promise of benefits and caution and care in understanding the impact of this social convergence on children's development and learning.

Evidence of children experimenting with identity, and forming and reforming new social relationships was observed in our observational study of digital play. Some of the most interesting observations focused on children's discussions of gender spurned on by choices made when creating avatars within varied applications. The digital world appeared to invite experimentation with what in the concrete world was considered

Figure 3. Avatar created by Kindergarten-aged boy

clearly for 'boys' or only for 'girls'. And although the children clearly categorized their avatar's based on their own gender (i.e., they labeled their avatars a boy or girl based on their own gender), the choice of clothing, features, and accessories was much more experimental in nature (Figure 3). The digital world affords for a range of tools allowing children to represent their identities in a low-risk environment for experimentation. Potentially, the converged play spaces can provide new avenues to explore social spheres and question social understandings of such things as 'boy' and 'girl' stereotypes that are often present within concrete playthings.

Convergence of Play Things and Spaces

Figures 1 and 2 helped to present this idea of a convergence of play things and spaces (Lim & Clark, 2010). Here, Edwards' (2013) work is helpful in extending the definition of play by considering the post-industrial context upon which children now play, that is an intersection of multiple platforms. She suggests what is most significant is "a conceptualization of play that acknowledges the meaning-making processes associated with children's play experiences in relation to both traditional and converged play" (p. 13). Edward's stance helps counter opponents of converged play who often criticize the limited and constrained nature of converged play and the potential negative effects of digital and media-based experiences on child development and imagination (Karpov, 2005; Singer & Singer, 2005). Perhaps, a converged play definition appears to align more closely with the experiences of how children play in the 'real world'. The children and families interviewed in Edwards' (2013) study stated that both types of play (traditional and converged) fostered opportunities for "children to create 'webs of meaning' that were personally relevant to their lives" (p. 23). Moreover, the study found that the

converged play experiences helped to inform the children's pretend and role-play. Additionally, parents acted as important supporters of play, providing both traditional opportunities (e.g., adding materials or acting as co-players) and intertextualised opportunities (e.g., Toy Story game on a Nintendo DS) to help extend their child's play. Thus, the relationship between traditional play and converged play appears to be very significant in the lives of children (Marsh, 2005, 2006, 2010; McPake, Plowman, & Stephen, 2013; Plowman et al., 2010; Plowman, Stevenson, Stephen, & McPake, 2012).

Similarly, Plowman and her colleagues' (2012) case study research focused on 3 and 4 year old children's experiences with technology in their homes in the United Kingdom (and how family practices influence children's encounters with technology). This body of research also helps to challenge the dichotomy between 'real' versus 'converged' play. The researchers found that all the children in their study had experienced a wide range of technologies prior to entering formal schooling. Additionally, the young children were also exposed to and encountered a diverse range of traditional toys (e.g., props for pretend play, puzzles and jigsaws, soft toys and dolls, cars, farms, construction kits, musical instruments, books, art and craft materials, and educational games). Children's play preferences tended to be highly contextualized and largely dependent on family values as opposed to what was available for play. For example, children were not necessarily drawn to technology in households characterized by a lot of technology. And like other researchers (Marsh, 2005), Plowman and her colleagues found that the children's lives were well balanced.

Convergence of Culture

A convergence of culture is the third notion discussed by Lim and Clark (2010). Here, the authors presuppose that the digital platform can act as a space for experimentation and identity construction related to one's culture, peer culture, and media culture. It is helpful here to examine how children can move in and out of varied platforms while experiencing the same characters or theme of play. Elsewhere (Rowsell & Harwood, in press) we have discussed young children's capabilities to experiment with their roles as a producer, consumer, and inventor in relation to mixing and remixing Disney's Frozen media texts. This convergence of media culture was fostered and achieved through a union of both traditional and digital literacy modes. As one of our other young research participants helped illuminate, children often experiment with their own identities. In a 5-year-old boy's experimentation with the theme of the children's book, *The Wrong Side of the Bed* (Keller, 1992), he recreated the story using the story maker app on an ipad, embedding digital photos of him in the story in varied physical positions and text. Equally interesting, this young digital author did not perceive himself as competent in more traditional literacy modes (i.e., story construction with pen and paper and a teacher assigned topic). In our examples, the digital world afforded children an opportunity to transcend the different modalities in their (literacy) play. Poignantly, Edwards' (2010) stresses how the digital world represents the "conceptual tools of this generation, of these twenty-first century children and how these tools [are] working to define their development in new ways" (p. 266). And as children continue to negotiate between the converged and traditional, perhaps even more sophisticated play and learning will emerge.

Convergence of Learning Experiences

The digital world offers opportunities for a convergence of learning experiences with multiple modes (text, visual, aural) as well as diverse learning processes (viewing, doing, experimenting, problem solving, dramatizing, collaborating, etc.) (Lim & Clark, 2010). There is a growing body of literature on the educational implications of the convergence of the digital world in relation to older children and youth's learning and being (Buckingham & Willett, 2006; Carrington & Robinson, 2009; Itō, 2009). However, little is known of the younger child's experiences. The older school aged child's learning experiences both inside and outside the classroom will often include a myriad of traditional and converged spaces. Social media sites such as Facebook, Twitter, and Instagram have been utilized in the teaching and learning process for a myriad of subjects for older students and undergraduates (Bell, 2013; Daher, 2014; McKenzie, 2014; Metz, 2014) but thus far the educational use of social media sites with younger children is not widely evidenced. However, in Jenkins' report (Jenkins & MacArthur Foundation, 2006) he notes that a myriad of skill development is possible within new media sites. In discussion of the skills needed beyond traditional literacy, Jenkins (Jenkins & MacArthur Foundation, 2006) cites the need for additional talents to be fostered in the 21st Century learner, the list of skills includes:

1. **Play:** The ability to experiment with one's surroundings in the course of problem-solving;
2. **Simulation:** The ability to interpret and construct dynamic models of real world processes;
3. **Performance:** The ability to adopt alternative identities for the purpose of improvisation and discovery;
4. **Appropriation:** The ability to meaningfully sample and remix media content;
5. **Multi-Tasking:** The ability to scan one's environment and shift focus onto salient details on an ad hoc basis;
6. **Distributed Cognition:** The ability to interact meaningfully with tools that expand our mental capacities;
7. **Collective Intelligence:** The ability to pool knowledge and compare notes with others towards a common goal;

8. **Judgment:** The ability to evaluate the reliability and credibility of different information sources;

9. **Transmedia Navigation:** The ability to deal with the flow of stories and information across multiple modalities;

10. **Networking:** The ability to search for, synthesize, and disseminate information;

11. **Negotiation:** The ability to travel across diverse communities, discerning and respecting multiple perspectives, and grasping and following alternative sets of norms (pp. 22-53).

In our research, many of these skills were evidenced within the context of one of our examples of a group of kindergarten children's interest in an emerging inquiry related to movies and movie making. Over the course of several weeks, the children explored ideas such as what makes a 'great' movie, how to make a movie theatre in their class, and the elements and processes to create a digital movie. As part of their initial plan, the children collected information and resources and collaboratively built the 'movie star theatre' (Figure 4). Movies were discussed, dramatized, and deconstructed over the course of the next several weeks. We also witnessed transmedia navigation as children turned story scripts into filmed projects, complete with titles, music, drama, and complex negotiations among the director/filmographer, and actors (Figure 5).

What is apparent is that children capably negotiate these converged spaces in a myriad of beneficial ways utilizing a complex set of skills and experiences. This one example signals the im/materialities thinking (Burnett, in press) that framed our earlier discussion. The material aspects of the children's literacy play included both traditional (e.g., children, posters, texts, pen, paper, cardboard) and digital artifacts (e.g., movie maker, ipad, YouTube). And equally important to the literacy play were the *associations*, *memories*, *feelings and imaginings* (Burnett, in press) that the children experienced through the series of events and processes that unfolded in relation to the movie making inquiry.

Figure 4. The beginning construction of the 'Movie Star Theatre'

Figure 5. Children construct a digital movie

CURRENT ISSUES IN THE FIELD

With movement in and out of physical spaces like sand or water play and then into immaterial, digital spaces such as *Grandma's Kitchen* or *Toca Band*, children have naturalized movements and knowledge practices that are quite different from more traditional notions of literacy within early years contexts. These naturalized movements are often problematic for educators and curricula that are based on more rigid and universal ideals of literacy learning. Universal ideals of children's learning and development can be limiting in that the child's own agency and capabilities are not often recognized nor the social contexts within which they learn (Donaldson, 1978). Understanding the concept of *digital worlds as being material* is challenging within early childhood education given the historical predominance of developmentalist thinking. Yet, challenging the dominant discourse of psychological criteria upon which early childhood curriculum was founded is not a new idea (Spodek & National Association for the

Education of Young Children, 1977). However, by redefining ideals and by viewing digital spaces as a creative process filled with culture production where children construct designs with concrete features such as colours and animations, an expanded perspective of play and literacy learning can be realized. Children, when viewed as active agents in social-cultural processes (Ryan & Grieshaber, 2005; Whitty & Iannacci, 2009), can then be included in the "public domains of active citizenry" (Robinson & Diaz, 2005, p. 6) which we argue includes digital worlds. Scholars such as Burnett (2014) and Wohlwend (2014; 2007) have created a language for these knowledge practices that can be helpful to fine-tune and nuance our understandings about contemporary play spaces.

There are several contemporary issues concerning digital worlds that are receiving attention. One area is the issue of disparate access to technologies and the affordances that technologies can offer, escalating a separation of the haves and have-nots. Differential access to technologies can be experienced in different ways, such as not having the Internet at home, or, slower wireless in homes. Furthermore, technologies like tablets and iPads are expensive commodities for many families – those children who have them have a greater facility with them than those who do not have them. Attention needs to be paid to how these dynamics manifest themselves in schools, and particularly how people not situated in the most privileged conditions engage in digital knowledge practices (Prinsloo and Rowsell, 2012). Taking an im/material lens on communication and digital literacy practices allows researchers and educators to witness movements across physical spaces, artifacts, and pedagogic objects and contrast them with how children engage and think through digital and media-driven texts. Perhaps there can be frameworks or practices put in place to compensate for the gap in access.

Yet another contemporary issue related to this chapter and to larger issues concerning digital and media worlds is identity performance. As children move within learning spaces from conventional creative play with puppets and dress-ups to 21st century versions of creative play using apps and producing stories out of media texts, they are performing and shaping their identities. We have highlighted several researchers in the chapter who are engaged in this type of research and it will be an increasingly important topic as educators transform their teaching practices to speak more to 21st century forms of communication.

GAPS IN THE EXTANT RESEARCH AND FUTURE RESEARCH

Looking back at early research on virtual worlds shows that digital environments were often positioned as separate from physical, offline spaces. All things virtual were cast as places for researchers to visit, in which worlds were created and people behaved differently from how they did in their physically grounded 'real' lives (Burnett et al., 2014). However, a burgeoning body of research from scholars such as Burke, Marsh, and Wohlwend suggests that children's literacy experiences involve a convergence of the digital and concrete. Yet, understanding how these experiences *converge* and the impact on children's learning is still not readily understood.

Burnett talks about moving *inside* of digital worlds. In our research exploring how young children move within digital worlds and physical spaces, there is far more blurring between the lines – that is, digital worlds are a part of their everyday, lived experiences and not separate. However, understanding, conceptualizing, and researching literacy from this type of rhizomatic lens (Deleuze & Guattari, 1987) is challenging. Each event, player, transition, context, and relationship must be examined and understood from an im/material perspective. In our research studies we too have observed instances of children's literacy play that appeared to have no end and no beginning with "multiple entryways and exits and its own lines of flight" (Deleuze & Guattari 1987, p. 21). The nature of the children's literacy play often combined, collapsed, and merged their digital worlds with their concrete experiences in a collaborative, negotiated dance. And given this level of interconnectedness, fluidity, and complexity of the digital and concrete (the im/material), research from a *'connective'* ethnographic framing will be needed in future studies (Hine 2000; Leander & McKim 2003).

There is yet another often hidden dimension of digital worlds that is currently under-researched. Few studies thus far have critically examined literacy work in early childhood contexts where immaterial concepts and realities such as race, socio-economics, and belief systems are embedded in play. More typically, these particularities are opaque next to more dominant and well-researched early childhood ideologies such as inquiry, phonemic awareness, and reading fluency (Kuby, 2013). Instead, in the chapter, we have promoted a view of digital play as what Lewis describes as 'social acts' (Lewis,

2001), where digital literacy practices are not neutral acts but rather tied to identity-shaping, power and the production of knowledge. More research is needed to examine the liminal spaces between digital and non-digital texts.

IMPLICATIONS FOR EDUCATION, CIVIC ENGAGEMENT, SOCIAL PRACTICE, AND POLICY

As early educational contexts have often demonstrated reluctance in allowing new technologies a place in the classroom (Wohlwend, 2008), research exploring young children's engagement and play in digital spaces offers a promising implication for these contexts to make space for im/material movement. Knobel and Lankshear (2014) recommend educators immerse themselves in digital spaces, to experience firsthand how full engagement in digital spaces and new literacies environments feels. Additionally, since children may be more adept at navigating the digital realm, educators should allow them the opportunity to lead and demonstrate this knowledge. As Wohlwend (2008) indicated, even when children are required to leave their technology at the classroom door, they find spaces to bring these technologies into their play through paper crafted devices and imagination. In this way, they demonstrate the importance that the digital world plays on their lives.

Implications for Education

Digital spaces in educational contexts are shaped by firewalls, bandwidth, and other related factors (Burnett, 2014). As such, spontaneous opportunities and activities requiring Internet use are bound by these factors. Rather than accepting defeat, educators can proactively design workflows around these barriers. This can contribute to a shift in focus, moving from being defeated by barriers to focusing on cultivating productive

environments to engage within and around digital spaces (Burnett, 2014). Consequently, classrooms devoid of digital spaces are in need of restructuring.

Restructuring Classrooms

Restructuring classrooms to include digital spaces and access to new technology provides young children with engaging new literacy opportunities. These restructured environments recognize and support the mutability of spaces, allowing children's experiences and perspectives to alter these spatial boundaries (Burnett, 2014). Allowing digital spaces may help educators understand the natural movement children engage in when traversing the im/material line in addition to how engagement in digital spaces shape and can be shaped by offline experiences. Educators should allow these digital spaces to shift as children engage in im/material experiences, capitalizing on children's new experiences (Burnett et al., 2014). Additionally, with a wide range of online experiences available in digitally enhanced classrooms, children have opportunities to extend communication to authentic audiences (Merchant, 2007). These restructured classrooms can build a sense of community, fostering collaboration, creativity, and experimentation (Burnett, 2014).

Critical Engagement

Educators should consider how new, digital technology is provided/presented, the role it plays in early writing activities, and developing approaches for critical digital literacy (Burnett, 2010). Digital literacy involves new possibilities and methods for text production and expression and gives children voice and agency in composing. Additional possibilities include exploration and evaluation of new, interactive and multimodal forms of text, digital and multimodal storytelling (Marsh 2006), and literacy opportunities in virtual worlds (Marsh 2010; 2014). Digital storytelling and multimodal texts provide children with opportunities to demonstrate critical engagement skills through the decision-making processes involved in creating said texts (Marsh, 2006). Furthermore, educators can capitalize on children's' interest in virtual worlds as these worlds often provide highly engaging opportunities for reading and writing (Marsh, 2010; 2014). Husbye et al. (2012) recommend a play-based media literacies curriculum as it provides an avenue for new digital learning spaces around played text. Consequently, early years educators should support and extend these opportunities for supporting critical engagement (Marsh, 2006).

New Affordances for Assessment

Digital spaces also bring new affordances for assessment; opportunities for immediate, peer, and ongoing feedback. One such benefit of immediate feedback is it corrects student misunderstandings and misconceptions right after they are made. Digital spaces offer places for students to provide feedback to one another, either in real time or asynchronously. Additionally, ongoing feedback allows students to have their performance evaluated as they learn and hone their skills. These methods of feedback are linked to deep learning (Knobel & Lankshear, 2014). Consequently, using digital spaces has meaningful implications for how educators assess their students (Knobel & Lankshear, 2014).

Implications for Civic Engagement

The role of the digital technologies in civic engagement was clearly evidenced with the recent 'Umbrella Revolution' in Hong Kong. The protestors and news agencies kept the world abreast of the pro-democracy movement as it unfolded by utilizing live video streaming, blogs, and twitter feeds. However, young children are often

overlooked and disregarded when it comes to thinking about civic engagement. Yet, in many respects children possess all the necessary traits for civic engagement and social action, that is the ability to think divergently, imaginative and inventive as well as being able to represent the voices of many (Kirsch, 2014). Researchers such as Kelly (2008), Montgomery (2014), and Ruane, Kavanagh, and Waldren (2010) discuss the need for civic engagement and critical engagement to occur early in life. As children enter preschool having absorbed the biases and prejudices of their families, peers, and the media, the need for global justice/civic engagement education is crucial to support these children in becoming well informed global citizens (Ruane, Kavanagh, & Waldren, 2010). In their study, Ruane, Kavanagh, and Waldren (2010) found children drew on previous experience to understand issues and identify similarities and differences between their own experiences and that of others. Some children in the study were already aware of the wider world, understood as the context being outside of their home country (Ireland). There was also significant evidence that children began to form stereotypical ideas of Africa in relation to poverty based upon influence from the media, home setting, or school.) And as Montgomery (2014) noted, digital devices have "the potential to be empowering and offers neomillennials the opportunity for democratic communication and participation in virtual spaces that traverse geographical boundaries" (p. 199).

Often educators are uncomfortable with the idea of engaging young children in thinking and sharing ideas about sensitive topics. Nonetheless, young children have demonstrated incredible insight and understanding about complex issues such as global warming, animal welfare in zoos, and fiscal constraints often expressing a desire to effect real change (Ruane, Kavanagh, & Waldren, 2010; Vasquez, 2010). Montgomery (2014) conducted research with grade 3 children and explored the ways in which technology (i.e., podcasts) could be used to support and promote democratic ideals.

The podcasts covered a range of topics including "issues of gender, race, and class, covering such topics as child labour, women's suffrage, slavery, and American Indian boarding schools" (p. 207). Montgomery found that not only did the children benefit from their new knowledge of these varied social justice issues, but also the digital platform enabled connections beyond the classroom's four walls. And although research with young children like that of Vasquez's (2010) and Montgomery (2014) is still uncommon, it is encouraging to see examples of how technology can be utilized for greater civic engagement with young children. Berson (2006) noted:

Fusing the power of technology and democratic ideals opens opportunities for greater access to information and offers a medium for people to be heard and to express their voice with dissemination to the masses through digital tools, such as blogs, podcasts, and wikis. (p. vii)

Implications for Research and Policymakers

With often varied intent and purposes of technology in research, Burnett (2010) calls for categorization of research involving technology, offering technology as a deliverer of literacy, technology as a site for interaction around texts, and technology as a medium for meaning making as categories for which to divide research. While divisions of technology are not new, as new technology emerges and spaces are redefined and reconfigured, examination and refinement of these categories is necessary (Burnett, 2010). Without this, the potential of diverse ways new technology contributes to literacy can be lost when research is masked by broad, all-encompassing titles such as "technology use" (Burnett, 2010). Consequently, use of specific categories should be used in empirical research involving technology.

Mapping New Digital Possibilities in Research

There are many avenues for new research involving digital technology and literacy. With mobile technology particularly pervasive in today's culture, examination of how these new technologies have been incorporated into existing and evolving practices should continue to be explored in research (Merchant, 2012). Many studies explore technology use through teacher-led tasks, and though this line of research is valuable and should continue (Merchant, 2012), studies examining children's agency when problem solving and navigating digital spaces and new technology is still underexplored (Burnett, 2010; Merchant, 2003). Research mapping the possibilities and potential of digital literacy is also warranted (Merchant, 2011), and research tends to focus on the effectiveness within currently existing models (Burnett, 2010).

Research on digital spaces and technology tends to focus on either classroom or home contexts. What is lacking, and therefore warranted, is research linking the interplay of digital spaces and technology between these environments (Burnett, 2010). This line of research can inform educational practices and develop a deeper understanding of the relationship between explorations of digital spaces across contexts. Additionally, inherent to digital spaces is the openness and interconnectedness they afford, accessible across time and space, unconfined and open to multiple settings and contexts. As texts take up residence in digital spaces, new opportunities emerge for exploring consumption, collaboration, and interaction (Burnett, 2011). Social media spaces, interactive literacy websites (e.g. starfall.com), and virtual worlds offer opportunities to interact, collaborate, and engage in literacy in digital environments. Continued exploration of how children engage in literacy practices in these contexts is warranted (Marsh, 2010, 2014; Merchant, 2007).

Policy Developments

Research on multimodal and digital literacy supports the reexamination of current educational policy to make space for play in schools (Husbye et al., 2012; Wohlwend, 2008). There are many opportunities for play using new technology in either digital or im/material spaces. Play can emerge in creating multimodal texts, collaborative storytelling, producing media, and exploring virtual worlds and spaces (Husbye et al., 2012; Wohlwend, 2008). Additionally, Merchant (2012) indicates policy developments need to address the transformation power of literacy in digital environments, with learner centered and collaborative practices to be adopted in curriculum and pedagogy. Writing is transformed in digital spaces in terms of form, process, and interaction; writing in the 21st century is not confined to paper. As such, digital and multimodal texts should be developed in the classroom to prepare children for today's digitally infused world. As professionals adept at navigating digital environments with multimodal skills are becoming increasingly more vital to today's society, it is important to allow these practices a place in curriculum (Merchant, 2012).

Stepping back from extant research and our own observations for the research study that we are conducting across five early years contexts (Rowsell & Harwood, in press), children's knowledge practices and imaginings through physical play objects and apps on tablets display a myriad of approaches. The point is that there is a difference between a sand table and *Grandma's Kitchen* that point to different forms of meaning making and children today have naturalized these interpretative processes, but we have yet to actually harness our teaching, policy, and pedagogy to the potential and generative qualities of im/material thinking.

CONCLUSION

Research featured in the chapter approaches digital worlds from a multimodal framework. Multimodality starts from an assumption that communication and meaning making occur in multiple modes that can be visual in one instance and then embodied, written and immersive in the next instance and designs are built around these modes. Modes have certain affords and constraints and they can work together in powerful, symbiotic and contrastive ways. What is more, modes mediate tangible, physical features such as the choice of particular fonts, colours, animated features in designs as well as more intangible features such as aesthetic preferences and sensibilities on the look, feel and associations of designs that children discern and make as they design and produce in virtual spaces. A theory of multimodality allows for ideas to be represented visually as well as in writing and there are rich examples of multimodal meaning in research. What is a newer approach that captures a more dispersed, rhizomatic picture of children's meaning making accounts for im/material thinking and actions that are enacted when young children play in virtual and non-virtual spaces.

Framing children's meaning making as a fluid, naturalized movement from physical worlds that early childhood educators have acknowledged and celebrated for some time such as the classic sand table to newer versions of meaning making in virtual worlds such as in Club Penguin where children decorate igloos needs to be embedded in early childhood policy and conceptions of early learning. Im/materiality, as a possible framing of these physical and virtual movements and mobilities, acknowledges both concrete, physical worlds as well as more amorphous concepts like associations and connections, emotions, thoughts as well as aesthetic sensibilities that are in prominent display when children design virtual worlds are part of the fabric of early learning, yet they are relatively absent in contemporary accounts of early childhood learning. In our view, the notion of im/material thinking and design practices captures well what Leander and Boldt describe in their article as the contemporary "unruly ways" and the "and … and … and relations" (Leander & Boldt, 2013, p. 41) of children's meaning making which transpire when they move across digital and non-digital domains of practice and thinking. In the chapter, we foregrounded current research that accounts for this line of inquiry as well as drawing out data excerpts from our ethnographic study of children engaging in im/material forms of thinking and learning in early childhood contexts.

REFERENCES

Bakhtin, M. M. (1981). *The dialogic imagination* (M. Holquist, Ed., M. Holquist & C. Emerson, Trans.). Austin, TX: University of Texas Press.

Bell, M. A. (2013). Picture this! Using Instagram with students. *Internet@Schools, 20*(4), 23–25.

Berson, M. (2006). Enhancing democracy with technology in the social studies. *The International Journal of Social Education, 21*(1), vii–viii.

Black, R. W. (2010). The language of Webkinz: Early childhood literacy in an online virtual world. [DCE]. *Digital Culture & Education, 2*(1), 7–24.

Buckingham, D., & Willett, R. (2006). *Digital generations: Children, young people, and the new media*. Mahwah, NJ: Lawrence Erlbaum Associates.

Burke, A. (2010). Children's construction of identity in virtual play worlds–a classroom perspective. *Language and Literature, 15*(1), 58–73.

Burnett, C. (2010). Technology and literacy in early childhood educational settings: A review of research. *Journal of Early Childhood Literacy, 10*(3), 247–270. doi:10.1177/1468798410372154

Burnett, C. (2011). Pre-service teachers' digital literacy practices: Exploring contingency in identity and digital literacy in and out of educational contexts. *Language and Education, 25*(5), 433–449. doi:10.1080/09500782.2011.584347

Burnett, C. (2014). Investigating pupils' interactions around digital texts: A spatial perspective on the "classroom-ness" of digital literacy practices in schools. *Educational Review, 66*(2), 192–209. doi:10.1080/00131911.2013.768959

Burnett, C. (in press). (Im)materializing literacies. In J. Rowsell & K. Pahl (Eds.), *The Routledge Handbook of Literacy Studies*. London, UK: Routledge.

Burnett, C., Dickinson, P., Myers, J., & Merchant, G. (2006). Digital connections: Transforming literacy in the primary school. *Cambridge Journal of Education, 36*(1), 11–29. doi:10.1080/03057640500491120

Burnett, C., & Merchant, G. (2011). Is there a space for critical literacy in the context of social media? *English Teaching, 10*(1), 41–57.

Burnett, C., Merchant, G., Pahl, K., & Rowsell, J. (2014). The (Im)materiality of literacy: The significance of subjectivity to new literacies research. *Discourse (Abingdon), 35*(1), 90–103. doi:10.1080/01596306.2012.739469

Carrington, V., & Robinson, M. (2009). *Digital literacies: Social learning and classroom practices*. Los Angeles: SAGE Publications. doi:10.4135/9781446288238

Cordes, C., & Miller, E. (2000). *Fool's Gold: A critical look at computers in childhood (Report)*. College Park, MD: Alliance for Childhood.

Daher, W. (2014). Students' adoption of social networks as environments for learning and teaching: The case of the Facebook. *International Journal of Emerging Technologies in Learning, 9*(4), 16–24. doi:10.3991/ijet.v9i8.3722

Danby, S., Davidson, C., Theobald, M., Scriven, B., Cobb-Moore, C., & Houen, S. ... Thorpe, K. (2013). Talk in activity during young children's use of digital technologies at home. *Australian Journal of Communication, 40*(2). Retrieved from http://www.austjourcomm.org/index.php/ajc/article/view/4

Deleuze, G., & Guattari, F. (1987). *A thousand plateaus: Capitalism and schizophrenia.* Minneapolis, MN: University of Minneapolis Press.

Donaldson, M. C. (1978). *Children's minds.* New York, NY: Norton.

Duff, P. A. (2003). Intertextuality and hybrid discourses: The infusion of pop culture in educational discourse. *Linguistics and Education, 14*(3-4), 231–276. doi:10.1016/j.linged.2004.02.005

Edwards, S. (2010). "Numberjacks are on their way": A cultural historical reflection on contemporary society and the early childhood curriculum. *Pedagogy, Culture & Society, 18*(3), 261–272. doi:10.1080/14681366.2010.504649

Edwards, S. (2013). Post-industrial play: Understanding the relationship between traditional and converged forms of play in the early years. In *Children's virtual worlds: Culture, learning and participation* (pp. 10–25). New York, NY: Peter Lang Publishing.

Gonzalez-Mena, J. (2005). *Foundations of early childhood education: Teaching children in a diverse society.* Boston, MA: McGraw-Hill.

Grimes, S. M., & Shade, L. R. (2005). Neopian economics of play: Children's cyberpets and online communities as immersive advertising in NeoPets.com. *International Journal of Media & Cultural Politics, 1*(2), 181–198. doi:10.1386/macp.1.2.181/1

Harwood, D. (2015). Crayons & iPads: Children's meaning making in the digital world. *An Leanbh Óg (The Young Child) Journal, 9*(1), 107-120.

Hine, C. (2000). *Virtual ethnography.* London, UK: Sage.

Husbye, N. E., Buchholz, B., Coggin, L., Powell, C. W., & Wohlwend, K. E. (2012). Critical lessons and playful literacies: Digital media in PK–2 classrooms. *Language Arts, 90*(2), 82–92.

Itō, M. (2009). *Hanging out, messing around, and geeking out: Kids living and learning with new.* Cambridge, MA: MIT Press.

Jenkins, H., & MacArthur Foundation. (2006). *Confronting the challenges of participatory culture: Media education for the 21st Century. An occasional paper on digital media and learning.* Chicago, IL: MacArthur Foundation.

Karpov, Y. V. (2005). *The Neo-Vygotskian approach to child development.* New York, NY: Cambridge University Press. doi:10.1017/CBO9781316036532

Keller, W. E. (1992). *The wrong side of the bed.* Bel Air, CA: Children's Universe.

Kelly, D. C. (2008). Civic readiness: Preparing toddlers and young children for civic education and sustained engagement. *National Civic Review, 97*(4), 55–59. doi:10.1002/ncr.234

Kirsch, G. E. (2014). Creating vision of reality: A rhetoric of response, engagement, and social action. *Journal of Rhetoric, Culture, &. Politics*, *34*(1-2). Retrieved from http://www.jaconline-journal.com/archives/vol34.1.html

Knobel, M., & Lankshear, C. (2008). Remix: The art and craft of endless hybridization. *Journal of Adolescent & Adult Literacy*, *52*(1), 22–33. doi:10.1598/JAAL.52.1.3

Knobel, M., & Lankshear, C. (2014). Studying new literacies. *Journal of Adolescent & Adult Literacy*, *58*(2), 97–101. doi:10.1002/jaal.314

Kuby, C. R. (2013). *Critical literacy in the early childhood classroom: Unpacking histories, unlearning privilege*. New York, NY: Teachers College Press.

Labbo, L. D., Eakle, A. J., & Montero, M. K. (2002). Digital language experience approach: Using digital photographs and software as a language experience approach innovation. *Reading Online*, *5*(8), 24–43.

Leander, K., & Boldt, G. (2013). Rereading "A pedagogy of multiliteracies" bodies, texts, and emergence. *Journal of Literacy Research*, *45*(1), 22–46. doi:10.1177/1086296X12468587

Leander, K. M., & McKim, K. K. (2003). Tracing the everyday 'sitings' of adolescents on the internet: A strategic adaptation of ethnography across online and offline spaces. *Education Communication and Information*, *3*(2), 211–240. doi:10.1080/14636310303140

Levy, R. (2008). "Third Spaces" are interesting places: Applying "Third Space Theory" to nursery-aged children's constructions of themselves as Readers. *Journal of Early Childhood Literacy*, *8*(1), 43–66. doi:10.1177/1468798407087161

Lewis, C. (2001). *Literacy practices as social acts: Power, status, and cultural norms in the classroom*. New York, NY: Routledge.

Lim, S. S., & Clark, L. S. (2010). Virtual worlds as a site of convergence for children's play. *Journal for Virtual Worlds*, *3*(2), 3–19.

Marsh, J. (1999). Batman and Batwoman go to school: Popular culture in the literacy curriculum. *International Journal of Early Years Education*, *7*(2), 117–131. doi:10.1080/09669769990070201

Marsh, J. (2005). *Popular culture, new media and digital literacy in early childhood*. New York, NY: Routledge Falmer. doi:10.4324/9780203420324

Marsh, J. (2006). Emergent media literacy: Digital animation in early childhood. *Language and Education*, *20*(6), 493–506. doi:10.2167/le660.0

Marsh, J. (2007). Digital childhoods, digital classrooms: The teaching and learning of literacy in a new media age. In B. Dwyer, G. Shiel, Reading Association of Ireland, & Conference (Eds.), Literacy at the crossroads: Moving forward, looking back (pp. 36–50). Dublin, Ireland: Reading Association of Ireland.

Marsh, J. (2010). Young children's play in online virtual worlds. *Journal of Early Childhood Research*, *8*(1), 23–39. doi:10.1177/1476718X09345406

Marsh, J. (2011). Young children's literacy practices in a virtual world: Establishing an online interaction order. *Reading Research Quarterly*, *46*(2), 101–118. doi:10.1598/RRQ.46.2.1

Marsh, J. (2014). Purposes for literacy in children's use of the online virtual world Club Penguin: Literacy purposes in virtual worlds. *Journal of Research in Reading*, *37*(2), 179–195. doi:10.1111/j.1467-9817.2012.01530.x

McKenzie, B. A. (2014). Teaching Twitter: Re-enacting the Paris commune and the Battle of Stalingrad. *The History Teacher, 47*(3), 355–372.

McPake, J., Plowman, L., & Stephen, C. (2013). Pre-school children creating and communicating with digital technologies in the home. *British Journal of Educational Technology, 44*(3), 421–431. doi:10.1111/j.1467-8535.2012.01323.x

Merchant, G. (2003). E-mail me your thoughts: Digital communication and narrative writing. *Reading, 37*(3), 104–110.

Merchant, G. (2007). Writing the future in the digital age. *Literacy, 41*(3), 118–128. doi:10.1111/j.1467-9345.2007.00469.x

Merchant, G. (2011). Unravelling the social network: Theory and research. *Learning, Media and Technology, 37*, 1, 4–19.

Merchant, G. (2012). Mobile practices in everyday life: Popular digital technologies and schooling revisited: Mobile practices in everyday life. *British Journal of Educational Technology, 43*(5), 770–782. doi:10.1111/j.1467-8535.2012.01352.x

Metz, S. (2014). New tools-new possibilities. *Science Teacher (Normal, Ill.)*, (3): 10.

Moje, E. B., Ciechanowski, K. M. I., Kramer, K., Ellis, L., Carrillo, R., & Collazo, T. (2004). Working toward third space in content area literacy: An examination of everyday funds of knowledge and discourse. *Reading Research Quarterly, 39*(1), 38–70. doi:10.1598/RRQ.39.1.4

Montgomery, S. E. (2014). Critical Democracy Through Digital Media Production in a Third-Grade Classroom. *Theory and Research in Social Education, 42*(2), 197–227. doi:10.1080/009331 04.2014.908755

O'Mara, J., & Laidlaw, L. (2011). Living in the iWorld: Two literacy researchers reflect on the changing texts and literacy practices of childhood. *English Teaching, 10*(4), 149–159.

Pelletier, J., Reeve, R., & Halewood, C. (2006). Young children's knowledge building and literacy development through Knowledge Forum®. *Early Education and Development, 17*(3), 323–346. doi:10.1207/s15566935eed1703_2

Plowman, L., McPake, J., & Stephen, C. (2010). The technologisation of childhood? Young children and technology in the home. *Children & Society, 24*(1), 63–74. doi:10.1111/j.1099-0860.2008.00180.x

Plowman, L., & Stephen, C. (2007). Guided interaction in pre-school settings. *Journal of Computer Assisted Learning, 23*(1), 14–26. doi:10.1111/j.1365-2729.2007.00194.x

Plowman, L., Stevenson, O., Stephen, C., & McPake, J. (2012). Preschool children's learning with technology at home. *Computers & Education, 59*(1), 30–37. doi:10.1016/j.compedu.2011.11.014

Prensky, M. (2001). Digital natives, digital immigrants part 1. *On the Horizon, 9*(5), 1–6. doi:10.1108/10748120110424816

Prinsloo, M., & Rowsell, J. (2012). Introduction to special issue on Digital literacies as placed resources in the globalised periphery. *Language and Education, 26*(4), 271–277. doi:10.1080/09 500782.2012.691511

Rideout, V. J., Vandewater, E. A., & Wartella, E. A. (2003). Zero to Six: Electronic media in the lives of infants, toddlers, and preschoolers. Menlo Park, CA: Henry J. Kaiser Family Foundation. Retrieved from http://www.kff.org/entmedia/3378.cfm

Robinson, K., & Diaz, C. J. (2005). *Diversity and difference in early childhood education: Issues for theory and practice.* Columbus, OH: Open University Press.

Rowsell, J., & Harwood, D. (in press). Let it Go. In *Exploring the image of the child as a producer, consumer, and inventor* (Special Edition). Theory into Practice Journal.

Ruane, B., Kavanagh, A., & Waldron, F. (2010). *Young children's engagement with issues of global justice: A report by the Centre for Human Rights and Citizenship Education.* Retrieved from http://www.spd.dcu.ie/site/chrce/documents/Trocaire-CHCREreport.pdf

Ryan, S., & Grieshaber, S. (2005). *Practical transformations and transformational practices: Globalization, postmodernism, and early childhood education.* Oxford, UK: Elsevier JAI.

Shegar, C., & Weninger, C. (2010). Intertextuality in preschoolers' engagement with popular culture: Implications for literacy development. *Language & Education: An International Journal, 24*(5), 431–447. doi:10.1080/09500782.2010.486861

Singer, D. G., & Singer, J. L. (2005). *Imagination and play in the electronic age.* Cambridge, MA: Harvard University Press. doi:10.4159/9780674043695

Spodek B, National Association for the Education of Young Children. (1977). *Teaching practices: Reexamining assumptions* [e-book]. Available from: ERIC, Ipswich, MA. Accessed December 10, 2014.

Vasquez, V. (2010). *Getting beyond "I like the book": Creating space for critical literacy in K–6 classrooms* (2nd ed.). Newark, DE: International Reading Association.

Whitty, P., & Iannacci, L. (Eds.). (2009). *Early childhood curricula: Reconceptualist perspectives.* Calgary, AB: Detselig.

Willett, R., Burn, A. C., Bishop, J., Richards, C., & Marsh, J. (2013). *Children, media and playground cultures: Ethnographic studies of school playtimes.* New York, NY: Palgrave Macmillan. doi:10.1057/9781137318077

Wohlwend, K. (2008). Play as a literacy of possibilities: Expanding meanings in practices, materials, and spaces. *Language Arts, 86*(2), 127–136.

Wohlwend, K. (in press). Making, remaking, and reimagining the everyday: Play, creativity and popular media. In J. Rowsell & K. Pahl (Eds.), *The Routledge Handbook of Literacy Studies.* London, UK: Routledge.

Wohlwend, K. E. (2007). Friendship meeting or blocking circle? Identities in the laminated spaces of a playground conflict. *Contemporary Issues in Early Childhood, 8*(1), 73–88. doi:10.2304/ciec.2007.8.1.73

Wohlwend, K. E. (2009). Early adopters: Playing new literacies and pretending new technologies in print-centric classrooms. *Journal of Early Childhood Literacy, 9*(2), 117–140. doi:10.1177/1468798409105583

ADDITIONAL READING

Berson, I. R., & Berson, M. J. (2010). *High-tech tots: Childhood in a digital world.* IAP. Retrieved from https://books.google.ca/books?hl=en&lr=&id=OvMMk0Cj57MC&oi=fnd&pg=PR7&dq=early+childhood+digital+worlds+virtual+worlds&ots=Y9gNhARGyQ&sig=Jolqbg1Z6h_6bPioHUsvzdjwUaU

Beschorner, B., & Hutchison, A. (2013). iPads as a literacy teaching tool in early childhood. *International Journal of Education in Mathematics. Science and Technology, 1*(1), 16–24.

Black, R. W. (2010). The language of Webkinz: Early childhood literacy in an online virtual world. *Digital Culture & Education*, 2(1), 7–24.

Blackwell, C. K., Lauricella, A. R., & Wartella, E. (2014). Factors influencing digital technology use in early childhood education. *Computers & Education*, 77, 82–90. doi:10.1016/j.compedu.2014.04.013

Blackwell, C. K., Lauricella, A. R., Wartella, E., Robb, M., & Schomburg, R. (2013). Adoption and use of technology in early education: The interplay of extrinsic barriers and teacher attitudes. *Computers & Education*, 69, 310–319. doi:10.1016/j.compedu.2013.07.024

Couse, L. J., & Chen, D. W. (2010). A tablet computer for young children? Exploring its viability for early childhood education. *Journal of Research on Technology in Education*, 43(1), 75–96. doi:10.1080/15391523.2010.10782562

Dautenhahn, K. (1998). Story-telling in virtual environments. In *ECAI'98 Workshop on Intelligent Virtual Environments, Brighton, UK*. Citeseer. Retrieved from http://citeseerx.ist.psu.edu/viewdoc/download?doi=10.1.1.54.976&rep=rep1&type=pdf

Davidson, C. (2009). Young children's engagement with digital texts and literacies in the home: Pressing matters for the teaching of english in the early years of schooling. *English Teaching*, 8(3), 36–54.

Dickey, M. D. (2011). The pragmatics of virtual worlds for K-12 educators: Investigating the affordances and constraints of Active Worlds and Second Life with K-12 in-service teachers. *Educational Technology Research and Development*, 59(1), 1–20. doi:10.1007/s11423-010-9163-4

Edwards, S. (2013). Digital play in the early years: A contextual response to the problem of integrating technologies and play-based pedagogies in the early childhood curriculum. *European Early Childhood Education Research Journal*, 21(2), 199–212. doi:10.1080/1350293X.2013.789190

Falloon, G. (2013). Young students using iPads: App design and content influences on their learning pathways. *Computers & Education*, 68, 505–521. doi:10.1016/j.compedu.2013.06.006

Geist, E. A. (2012). A qualitative examination of two year-olds interaction with tablet based interactive technology. *Journal of Instructional Psychology*, 39(1), 26.

Henderson, S., & Yeow, J. (2012). iPad in education: A case study of iPad adoption and use in a primary school. In *System Science (HICSS), 2012 45th Hawaii International Conference on* (pp. 78–87). IEEE. Retrieved from http://ieeexplore.ieee.org/xpls/abs_all.jsp?arnumber=6148617

Hutchison, A., Beschorner, B., & Schmidt-Crawford, D. (2012). Exploring the use of the iPad for literacy learning. *The Reading Teacher*, 66(1), 15–23. doi:10.1002/TRTR.01090

Marsh, J. (2008). Out-of-school play in online virtual worlds and the implications for literacy learning. *Centre for Studies in Literacy, Policy and Learning Cultures, University of South Australia*. Retrieved from http://w3.unisa.edu.au/eds/documents/JackieMarsh.pdf

Marsh, J. (2011). Young children's literacy practices in a virtual world: Establishing an online interaction order. *Reading Research Quarterly*, 46(2), 101–118. doi:10.1598/RRQ.46.2.1

Merchant, G. (2007). Writing the future in the digital age. *Literacy*, 41(3), 118–128. doi:10.1111/j.1467-9345.2007.00469.x

Merchant, G. (2010). 3D virtual worlds as environments for literacy learning. *Educational Research*, 52(2), 135–150. doi:10.1080/001318 81.2010.482739

Neumann, M. M. (2014). An examination of touch screen tablets and emergent literacy in Australian pre-school children. *Australian Journal of Education*, 0004944114523368.

Neumann, M. M., & Neumann, D. L. (2014). Touch screen tablets and emergent literacy. *Early Childhood Education Journal*, 42(4), 231–239. doi:10.1007/s10643-013-0608-3

Northrop, L., & Killeen, E. (2013). A framework for using iPads to build early literacy skills. *The Reading Teacher*, 66(7), 531–537. doi:10.1002/TRTR.1155

Pegrum, M., Howitt, C., & Striepe, M. (2013). Learning to take the tablet: How pre-service teachers use iPads to facilitate their learning. *Australasian Journal of Educational Technology*, 29(4).

Plowman, L., & McPake, J. (2013). Seven myths about young children and technology. *Childhood Education*, 89(1), 27–33. doi:10.1080/00094056 .2013.757490

Sandvik, M. (2012). Digital practices in the kindergarten. *Nordic Journal of Digital Literacy*, 7(3), 152–154.

Shifflet, R., Toledo, C., & Mattoon, C. (2012). Touch tablet surprises: A preschool teacher's story. *Young Children*, 67(3), 36–41.

Verenikina, I., & Kervin, L. (2011). iPads, digital play and pre-schoolers. *He Kupu*, 2(5), 4–19.

Wohlwend, K. (2010). A is for avatar: Young children in literacy 2.0 worlds and literacy 1.0 schools. *Language Arts*, 88(2), 144–152.

Yelland, N. (1999). Technology as play. *Early Childhood Education Journal*, 26(4), 217–220. doi:10.1023/A:1022907505087

KEY TERMS AND DEFINITIONS

Digital Spaces: The term 'digital spaces' refers to what is displayed on the screen of a digital device (e.g. laptops, computers, tablets, or smartphones). What can be displayed in digital spaces is vast and diverse, and can take countless forms. The home screen of the device, applications (or apps), movies, photos, and website all occupy digital space.

Hybrid/Intertexual Spaces: Refers to the range of socio-cultural texts (e.g., popular culture), everyday dialogue, artifacts, and experiences children actively draw upon to make meaning; including oral, aural, pictorial, written, digital, and bodily-kinesthetic experiences. Children draw upon these texts in this hybrid/intertexual space to create an mélange of literary play experiences and outputs.

Im/Materiality: Refers to the intangible aspects that are central to meaning-making, such as associations, memories, feelings and imaginings as well as all the events and processes that have led up to the production of the things that are physically present.

Multimodality: Multimodality is a theory of communication. It refers to an artifact or product comprised of multiple modes (e.g. textual, aural, visual). Multimodal artifacts can be "read" using multiple senses.

Semiotics: This field involves the study of signs and symbols in communicative behavior, focusing on how meaning is created. Semiotics also involves discerning how meaning is communicated.

Third Space: 'Third space' can be defined as the intersection where new knowledge and discourses emerge from the blending and merger of understanding and experiences from a child's home, community, and peer network with the more formalized learning encountered in schooling. In the digital world, 'third space' thinking can be conceived of as the intersections created by online and offline play experiences.

Virtual Worlds: Virtual worlds (e.g. Club Penguin, Webkinz, Minecraft) are environments or worlds housed in a pre-defined digital space, typically on a particular website or within an application. These worlds typically require a user to select or create an avatar to represent him/herself and this avatar is then used to explore the world. Virtual worlds can be hosted in either online or offline environments and allow users to interact with non-playable characters and/or other users via their selected avatar.

Chapter 5
The Irrevocable Alteration of Communication:
A Glimpse into the Societal Impact of Digital Media

Elizabeth (Betsy) A. Baker
University of Missouri, USA

Arwa Alfayez
University of Missouri, USA

Christy Dalton
University of Missouri, USA

Renee Smith McInnish
University of Missouri, USA

Rebecca Schwerdtfeger
University of Missouri, USA

Mojtaba Khajeloo
University of Missouri, USA

ABSTRACT

In our digital society, the ability to communicate has irrevocably changed. The purpose of this chapter is to provide a glimpse into the impact of digital media on society, specifically digital communication. This glimpse is framed in terms of four characteristics of digital communication: product/ion, semiotic, public, and transitory. Issues are examined that relate to the democratization and monopolization of communication, who has access, the persistent Spiral of Silence, privacy, cyber bullying, identity theft, the ethereal being captured, as well as education and new literacies. Methodological gaps are noted in the research corpus and suggestions are proposed regarding the need for timeliness, support for a comprehensive span of research paradigms, and representation of a full range of populations. Finally, implications and recommendations are explored for civic engagement, commerce, education, and policy.

INTRODUCTION

Communication is core to human existence. Throughout time and civilizations, humans consistently created varied forms of communication.

Ancient civilizations created cave drawings, petroglyphs, pictograms, cuneiform, hieroglyphs, and alphabets. More recently, civilizations created newspapers, magazines, telephones, and radio. The ability to share ideas, emotions, desires, and

DOI: 10.4018/978-1-4666-8310-5.ch005

plans, to mention a few reasons we communicate, is the essence of the human experience. The purpose of this chapter is to discuss the societal impact of digital media on communication. We view society, digital media, and communication as dynamic entities that are inextricably intertwined and continually impact one another. Therefore, we examine both the impact of society and digital media on communication as well as the impact of digital communication on society. To manage this broad and varied topic our discussion is framed in terms of four characteristics of digital communication: product/ion, semiotic, public, and transitory (Baker, 2001). We define and illuminate each characteristic by exploring research related to exemplars. Issues emerge regarding the democratization and monopolization of communication, access to digital communication, persistent Spiral of Silence, online ethics and safety, ethereal captured while privacy is compromised, and education. Methodological gaps are evident in the extant research corpus. Implications are discussed and recommendations are made for local and global civic engagement, commerce, education and policy. We acknowledge that other frameworks, constructs, and exemplars can be used to understand digital communication. Our goal is not to provide a comprehensive or conclusive discussion of digital communication but to provide fodder for grappling with this timely and emerging topic.

IMPACT OF DIGITAL MEDIA ON COMMUNICATION

Production Nature of Digital Communication

Production is defined as "the process of making something" while product is defined as "something that is the result of a process" ("Production", n.d., para. 1; "Product", n.d., para. 1). By definition, written communication culminates as a product.

Up through the first millennium mankind created varied written products including pictographs, hieroglyphs, letters, and scrolls. In 1999, the Biography channel broadcasted a countdown of the most influential people of the second millennium. This countdown included such notables as Newton, Darwin, and Einstein. Among these notables, they concluded the most influential person of the second millennium was Gutenberg. Arguably, one reason Gutenberg was given this distinction is that the printing press made it easier to transform communication into products that, in turn, could be widely disseminated. Communication has always been shaped by the technology at hand (Hartman, Morsink, & Zheng, 2010; Leu, 2006; Leu & Kinzer, 2000). With the advent of digital media, it is argued that we are witnessing a comparably significant, and likely more significant, even unprecedented development in the history of communication (D. Hartman, personal communication, August 17, 2012).

In her analysis of the ontology of literacy, Baker (2010a, 2013b) argued that the ability to transform communication into products is significant because products can travel through time and space. Written communication can defy the laws of physics. Authors and readers can become time travelers who explore historical times and geographical locations that are beyond their physical limitations. Because Socrates' words were written down we can read his thoughts--even though we live in a different time and place. The product/ion nature of written communication allows authors and audiences to travel through time and space. In our digital era, this travel is not only instantaneous but also global. Each day 182.9 billion emails are sent (Radicati, 2013), 55 million Facebook statuses are updated (Facebook Statistics, 2014), and 1,400 hours of YouTube video are uploaded (YouTube, n.d., para. 3). The instantiation of communication as products defies physical limitations to time and space by affording global dissemination within seconds. The mitigation of production means that anyone with a digital device and Internet access can produce a message that is instantly available worldwide. Publishers are no longer the gatekeepers of producing and disseminating written communication. The proliferation of blogs, FaceBook, Twitter, citizen journalism, self-publishing, and eBooks exemplifies the product/ion nature of digital communication.

- **Blogs:** Blogs, "originally a space for narrating personal life stories" (Harrison, 2014, p. 337) are often used to create traffic for business endeavors, incite political action, and teach audience members interested in affinity content (e.g., parenting and cooking). For example, blogs written by ordinary people whose purpose is to share private information among an affinity group, such as individuals struggling with infertility, now "play an important role in public and political negotiations of fertility issues" (Harrison, 2014, p. 338). Drawing a similar comparison to blogging and foreign policy, Hestres (2008) asserted, "blogs have evolved into more than alternative media outlets: they have become vehicles for online organizing and activism for ordinary individuals who care about foreign policy and are willing to take action to influence it" (p. 1). Endorsed with sponsored advertising, bloggers have the opportunity to communicate with a polished and professional appearance. In 2014, one blog platform, WordPress, boasted 75.5 million blogs that had 409 million views and 60.5 million posts each month (Digital Marketing Ramblings, 2014b). Blogs, produced with the specific intent to inform, educate, and persuade audience members across the globe, are a tool accessible to any unskilled person. What was once a casual conversation between like-minded individuals, or a nicely designed tri-fold brochure for local distribution, has become an opportunity to influence the masses by creating a polished blog that is official in appearance.

- **Facebook and Twitter:** Beyond blogs, platforms such as Facebook (launched in 2004) and Twitter (launched in 2006), contribute to the unskilled person's ability to produce professional-grade communication. In a 2013 survey of 1,802 Internet users, Duggan and Brenner (2013) found 16% used Twitter while, ranking the highest, 67% used Facebook. The ability to produce written communication on these platforms, at face value, might not seem to yield global impact. Originally designed to connect users with families and friends, the possible applications of these platforms has evolved to include audience solicitation and audience retention methods which provide publishers, skilled and unskilled alike, with a forum to sell ideas, products, and entire belief systems to a global audience. The statistics indicate that the public is taking advantage of available platforms to publish their ideas.

- **Self-Publishing and eBooks:** In 2000, Mace (2010) deemed eBooks as "failed" for the following reasons: not enough eBooks, cost, cumbersome hardware, nascent digital periodicals, and poor marketing. Mace noted that "at least six eBook reader devices [were] on the market or in preparation" (para. 2) with estimates of seven million devices to be sold in 2011, by 2015 over 10 percent of the publishing market will be eBooks, and by 2030 over 90 percent will be eBooks. The increase in eBook production provides greater variety and choice for consumers and illuminates challenges for self-publishers. Aside from the few that skyrocketed to fame, the majority of self-publishers engage in time-consuming activities to build a fan base and create awareness of their offering in a market ripe with choices. Social media endeavors and exclusive content offerings are two of the ploys that authors use. One such author, Rachel Abbott, reported spending 12 hours a day just to build her profile (Carolan & Evain, 2013). Self-publishers are not discouraged by these statistics. It seems the allure of production is more compelling than roadblocks to monetary gain. Baverstock and Steinitz (2013) found that self-publishers have two fundamental motives: desire for control and pure love of writing.

Semiotic Nature of Digital Communication

Since the advent of the alphabet, written communication has been predominantly verbocentric (Reinking, 1998). That is to say, written communication has historically been dominated by the use of words. While printed newspapers, magazines, and books include non-verbocentric information such as illustrations, photographs, and charts, written communication has been overwhelmingly dependent on words. With the advent of digital media, written communication is increasingly semiotic. Semiotics is the study of sign systems (Peirce, 1991). The alphabet is merely one of a myriad of sign systems we use daily. For example, we communicate with body language. A smile, smirk, cold stare, and frown communicate volumes. We communicate with paintings, sculpture, and music. Baker (2001) noted that digital communication increasingly mimics face-to-face communication by allowing authors to compose multimedia products. The popularity of incorporating audio, photos, and video in digital communications demonstrates the semiotic nature of digital communication.

- **Popularity of Audio, Photo, and Video:** Podcasts, Pinterest, and YouTube are less verbocentric than print media because they allow authors to capture auditory and visual communication. Podcasts are an example of audio-based digital communication. Podcasts are defined as, "a program (as of music or talk) made available in digital format for automatic download over the Internet"

("Podcast," n.d., para. 1). The term podcast was coined by technology writer, Ben Hammersly, who made an off-hand comment about names for online radio (Sterne, Morris, Baker, & Freire, 2008). Podcasts were first made popular by the introduction of the iPod. Free software such as Audacity, launched in 2002, made the production of professional-grade audio ubiquitous (Sterne, Morris, Baker, & Freire, 2008).

In 2010, the top three podcasts were categorized as general, music, and technology; education came in 8th and news 14th (Olmstead, Mitchell, & Rosentstiel, 2011). In 2004, Duke University provided Apple iPods to all incoming freshmen so they could download podcasts with schedule information as well as lectures (Flanagan & Calandra, 2005). From 2009 to 2010 Olmstead, Mitchell, and Rosenstiel (2011) noted a 28% growth in podcast production; nonetheless only 45% of Americans knew what a podcast was. In 2014, Wolf found that podcasts were on the rise and posits this is due to "continued smartphone growth, better podcast apps and the explosion in great content, [as well as] dedicated podcast fans" (para. 1). The product/ion and semiotic nature of digital communication are unmistakable; digital communication that emulates a full range of *semiotic* sign systems appears to increase as technology enables both authors and audience to *produce*, disseminate and access digital semiotic communication.

Pinterest is an example of photo-based digital communication. Pinterest is a social network where photos are "pinned" to a virtual board. These pins are linked to websites of origin. Authors share pins and re-pin photos on other authors' boards. The basic function is to allow users to collect, organize, and share pins (Han et al., 2014). The pins are organized on the boards by tastes and interests. Pinterest was launched in 2010 and by 2014 had 70 million users who had created more than 750 million boards with over 30 billion individual pins

(Digital Marketing Rambling Statistics, 2014a; See also Smith, 2014a). In addition, 54 million new pins are added each day (Bercovici, 2014). To emphasize the popularity of photo-based digital communication, it has been said, "Facebook is selling the past and Twitter the present, Pinterest is offering the future" (Bercovici, 2014, para. 9). Users access Pinterest with computers as well as mobile devices with 52% using smartphones as the primary device to pin photos (Smith, 2014b). Each board, each pin, is a photo that is posted to communicate ideas, thoughts, and possibilities. These statistics are staggering and underscore the semiotic nature of digital communication.

YouTube is an example of video-based digital communication. YouTube, since its inception in 2005, has transformed daily life into a global production, capitalizing on the semiotic nature of communication. Anyone with a digital camera, a smart-device, or a computer, can become authors of video-based communication. Prior to YouTube, there were other online video websites that did not succeed. Shareyourworld.com, launched in 1997, was one of the first video-sharing websites. Then came Singfish in 2000, which was acquired by Thompson Multimedia. Blinkx, founded in 2004, offered a video search engine. These forums did not flourish, but the power of video-based digital communication did. In 2005, Google Video as well as Yahoo! Video began as video search engines that allowed people to search the web for videos (Soukup, 2014). Meanwhile, in 2005 Chad Hurley, Steve Chen, and Jawed Karim founded YouTube as a way to post and share video. Google bought YouTube in 2006 with expectations that the website would grow (Strangelove, 2010). YouTube was transformed from a repository of videos to "becoming a force that is investing in content creation" (YouTube & News, 2012).

By 2010, 150 million videos were posted to YouTube each week (Strangelove, 2010). In 2011, YouTube was viewed for the one-trillionth time. By 2014, YouTube had one billion users who uploaded 100 hours of video per minute, posted 150 million videos per week, and watched six billion hours each month (Smith, 2014c). According to Purcell (2013), 72% of adult Internet users have watched a video on a video-sharing site like YouTube, 56% have watched videos online, and 36% have downloaded video files to a phone or computer so they can watch at a later time. Four features are credited for the success of YouTube: video recommendations, email links that enable video sharing, comments, and an embedded video player (Gannes, 2006). It also offers social networking features (Soukup, 2014). Given its magnitude, Strangelove stated that YouTube showcases the lives of people around the world, from videos providing intimate details of indiscretion, to American presidential primaries, to soldiers documenting their lives and killings in Iraq (Strangelove, 2010). These statistics indicate that what was once the purveyance of face-to-face communication has migrated to digital communication.

Vine is an example of the semiotic nature of digital communication that, similar to YouTube, embraces video. Vine is designed for smartphone users and allows them to create six-second videos and then embed these videos in text messages, Facebook, and Twitter (M. Miller, 2013). Vine launched in 2012. In 2013, Twitter bought Vine, which quickly attained 40 million users (Fiegerman, 2013). By late 2014 over one billion Vine loops were played each day (Crook, 2014).

- **Ubiquity of Capturing the Ethereal:** An important aspect of the semiotic nature of digital communication is the ubiquity of capturing the ethereal. Ethereal refers to, "lacking material substance" ("Ethereal," n.d., para. 2). With the ability to record audio, photo, and video with Internet-connected mobile devices the ethereal is readily captured and shared, worldwide. Before the ubiquity of such digital devices, conversations, actions, and settings were fleeting—they lacked substance, they were ethereal. Now, surveillance videos assist with crime detection (e.g., Boston Marathon bombing), street witnesses capture police brutality (e.g., Arab Spring), and on a lighter note, cat owners capture the antics of their pets.

In 2012, Google developed Google Glass; a pair of glasses intended to provide seamless online access. Users see an Internet screen in the upper right side of one lens. Among other things, they can capture covert videos and photos and instantly share them online. Honan (2013) conducted an informal study of Glass by wearing them throughout most of 2013. He wore them to identify their usefulness—but instead found consistent derision and increased animosity by those around him. He became known as the "Glasshole." Even his wife was willing to let him video record the birth of their child with a traditional video camera—but not with Glass. While there are reports that Google Glass is being abandoned, wearable technology is in its infancy and will likely become less obvious and a social norm. As it does, the capturing and sharing of the ethereal will become increasingly normal.

British surveillance cameras demonstrate the pervasive ability to capture the ethereal. Schlosberg and Ozer (2007) described Britain's response to the bombing of London in the 1990s by the Irish Republican Army. By 1994, 79 British cities installed surveillance cameras for their central districts. By 1998, up to 75% of Britain's crime prevention budget was spent on cameras. The result was that by 2004, Britain installed over four million surveillance cameras in approximately 500 British towns. By 2006, the average person in London was captured on video 300 times per day.

Google Glass and the British video surveillance system are two examples of how the ethereal is readily captured and shared. Consider the sheer number of audio, photo, and video postings made to social networks. Users post conversations, actions, and settings that were formerly ethereal. The ethereal has become a product—and these products are readily distributed.

Public Nature of Digital Communication

Public is defined as "exposed to general view" ("Public," n.d., para. 2). There is a plethora of digital communication that is public. Consider web sites, blogs, and social networks. These digital communications, pending privacy settings, are public. Anyone with Internet access can view these digital forms of communication. Ten billion "ALS ice bucket challenge" views on Facebook alone during the summer of 2014 (Smith, 2014d) is evidence of the speed at which digital communication is crafted, distributed, and received, internationally. Due to the breadth of this topic, in this section we focus on a particular phenomenon related to the Public nature of digital communication: collective intelligence. Wooley, Chabris, Pentland, Hashmi, and Malone (2010) contended that just as individuals have intelligence, so do groups. The Center for Collective Intelligence at MIT examines how people and computers can work together "more intelligently than any person, group, or computer has ever done before" (2014, para. 2). While collective intelligence is as old as society and exhibited by most forms of life (Malone & Bernstein, in press), due to the public nature of digital communication, we are on the precipice of something previously unattainable. We can formulate collaborative communities that span the globe to generate intelligence that previously lacked coordination and the power generated through think-tank contributions on a global scale (Weiss, 2005). Some examples include Wikipedia, Arab Spring, Kickstarter, online product reviews, HapMap, Uber, World of Warcraft, and Coursera. These examples represent the following types of collective intelligence: knowledge, political action, funding, commerce, medicine, crowdsourcing, entertainment, and education. A closer examination of citizen journalism, Massive Multiplayer Online Games (MMOGs), Massive Open Online Classes (MOOCs), and Arab Spring reveals the public nature of digital communication.

- **Citizen Journalism:** Glaser (2006) described citizen journalism as,

People without professional journalism training [using] the tools of modern technology and the global distribution of the Internet to create, augment or fact-check media on their own or in collaboration with others.... The average citizen can now make news and distribute it globally, an act that was once the province of established journalists and media companies.... One of the main concepts behind citizen journalism is that mainstream media reporters and producers are not the exclusive center of knowledge on a subject — the audience knows more collectively than the reporter alone. (Para. 1, 2, 3)

Citizen journalism has become a modern vehicle for communication of events, both in the realm of serious news writing as well as entertainment. Howe (2008) stated that in order to keep costs and profits in balance, news reporting is outsourced to "a large, undefined group of people via an open call, generally over the Internet" (p. 47). Several platforms support the organized dissemination of news via citizen journalists. Huffington Post and BuzzFeed are among the most popular with BuzzFeed staffing 170 writers, including reputable award-winning writers. Mitchell (2014) reported that in 2012 there was a 6.4% decline in newspaper jobs while in 2014 there were more than 5,000 full-time professional jobs for online journalists at approximately 500 digital news outlets.

Photojournalism by citizens is also on the rise. According to Pew Research Center's Journalism Project Staff (2012), during the week following the 2011 tsunami in Japan, videos of the disaster, mostly recorded by eyewitnesses, were watched more than 96 million times. Another example of citizen journalism is evident in the dissemination of photographs by American soldiers, wherein soldiers capture their daily activities and observations, and share them with the world via email and other platforms (Sontag, 2004).

- **MMOGs:** Massively Multiplayer Online Games (MMOGs) are an example of collective intelligence. MMOGs "are highly graphical two-or three-D video games played online, allowing individuals, through their self-created digital characters or 'avatars,' to interact not only with the gaming software (the designed environment of the game and the computer-controlled characters within it) but with *other players'* avatars as well" (Steinkuehler, 2007, p. 298). MMOGs are an example of collective intelligence because players around the world are able to perform acts of "intelligence" that are qualitatively different and enhanced over what they would accomplish as individuals. Users form teams or organizations that cooperate together in order to win virtual battles or accomplish virtual tasks. Typically, team members are familiar with each other only in these online environments. Online voice communication and a shared online interface allows users to play concurrently. Users are able to interact and work in real time to organize activities in the games (Ruiz, 2013).

According to Wiess (2006), this mode of sharing is increasingly growing and affecting the mindset of the present and future generations. Collective intelligence for these generations has become the norm. Flew and Humphreys (2005) argued that "interactivity" in the online game environment and the continual dialogue between consumers and game designers, who are active in videogames as groups or associations, frequently collaborate to accomplish their goals (see also Lévy & Bononno, 1998). Jenkins (2006) suggested, "collective intelligence can be seen as an alternative source of media power" (para. 6). Because of their collective intelligence, the participatory cultures that emerge between media companies, game producers, and users show a central change in the nature of media production and consumption. Gosney (2005) examined

Alternate Reality Gaming and described it as an "across-media game that deliberately blurs the line between the in-game and out-of-game experiences" (p. 2). Actions occur outside the game reality and extend into players' lives. This genre of gaming requires an exceptional level of collaboration and collective intelligence to solve mysteries posed within the game.

Banks (2003), a cultural theorist and online community developer, studied the influence of online fan communities in the invention of Trainz (a series of 3D train simulator computer games). He claimed that its commercial success was primarily due to "the formation and growth of an active and vibrant online fan community that would both actively promote the product and create content extensions and additions to the game software" (p. 11). The fans' collective intelligence enabled improvement and promotion of the game.

- **Massive Open Online Classes (MOOCs):** Massive Open Online Courses (MOOCs) are an example of collective expertise. MOOCs have open registration, publicly shared curriculum, open-ended outcomes, and are commonly free (McAuley, Stewart, Siemens, & Cormier, 2010). MOOCs incorporate social networking, available online resources, and are assisted by leading experts in the field of study. More importantly, MOOCs engage students according to their personal learning goals, background knowledge and skills, and mutual interests. The collective knowledge created by participants generates a whole that is greater than the sum of its parts. "It is, in many ways, a microcosm of a nation" (McAuley, Stewart, Siemens, & Cormier, 2010, p. 54). MOOCs work best when people bond on the basis of their lives, interests, and understandings of their worlds. MOOCs create a collaborative and interactive experience for those who would otherwise not have the opportunity to get an elite education.

Coursera is a MOOC identified as a "social entrepreneurship company that partners with many top universities across the globe to offer free courses online for anyone to take" (Audsley, Fernando, Maxson, Robinson & Varney, 2013, p. 137). Its purpose is to educate millions of people around the world by offering courses on numerous topics from privileged universities such as Stanford, Princeton, the University of Michigan, and the University of Pennsylvania. Professors have the ability to teach 30,000 or more students at once due to an instructional platform reinforced by vigorous computing power and complex infrastructure (Audsley et al., 2013). Anyone in the world with Internet access has the capability to obtain a self-paced education. Coursera purposely encourages digital communication between students. For example, students work together through discussion boards and virtual study rooms. Al Filreis, professor at the University of Pennsylvania, is fascinated by the ways in which the students interact on the discussion boards. "Coursera is building a system like Yelp that will let these students value each other's comments; the most valued and respected will rise to the top" (Henn, 2012). Filreis noted that within just one Coursera class, he is able to teach more students than he ever has throughout his career (Borup, West, & Graham, 2012). MOOCs focus on collective intelligence over individual intelligence, participation over publishing, breadth of expertise over concentrated expertise, and collaboration over individual authorship (Stewart, 2013).

- **Arab Spring:** The Arab Spring is another example of collective intelligence. It represented a new kind of revolution; a "Revolution 2.0" as Ghonim (2012) called it. The ability to orchestrate efforts reverberated throughout the world. Conventional forms of civil disobedience were transformed by the capabilities of digital communication. Howard and colleagues (2011) suggested that social media is commonly used for political conversations. The demographic group in the Arab Spring was "young, urban, relatively well-educated individuals, and many of whom were women" (p. 2). Social networks were used to coordinate efforts and recruit participants. In a Facebook-based survey, Salem and Mourtada (2011) found that nine out of ten Egyptians and Tunisians reported that they used social networks to heighten awareness and arrange protests. During the Arab Spring, the use of social media doubled (Huang, 2011). Although the Arab Spring occurred for many reasons, collective intelligence is recognized as pivotal in efforts to advocate for democratic revolution (Rheingold, 2007).

In addition, news media contributed to the collective by forming an almost symbiotic relationship with people reporting from the front lines. This relationship allowed participants to effectively raise awareness of the more violent actions of the ruling governments against their citizens. This awareness reached international news sources that promoted their cause with unprecedented velocity. This type of dissemination informed citizens throughout the world and facilitated the organization of protests. Before and throughout the revolutions, these people worked on social media to put pressure on their governments. Governments also recognized the power of opposition movements armed with social media. Tunisia officials tried to block social media sites and arrested people who used social media to spread negative news about the government (Howard et al., 2011). While these efforts stalled and disrupted digital communication, the collective was tech-savvy and gained assistance from hackers and skilled computer programmers who were able to close online government services and offer protesters alternatives to censored access. Information that had been localized was instantly made public. Aided by the power of collective intelligence,

young Arab people overcame what was thought to be insurmountable barriers and made their plight known. Government forces were unable to stop the movement. Internet controls were transcended by the ingenuity of the collective. A local issue became a worldwide concern through digital communication of text, image, and video.

Transitory Nature of Digital Communication

Baker (2001) argued that digital sources and compositions are in continual flux; they are transitory. Transitory is defined as "tending to pass away: not persistent" ("Transitory," n.d., para. 1). In the morning, you might read an article in the digital version of USA Today®—then when you share it with someone the same afternoon it may be updated; it may no longer be the same article. The same is true of postings made to social media, YouTube, eBooks, retail sites, and the list continues. Digital media is readily revisable making it perpetually transitory. Karlsson (2012) referred to digital communication as liquid, dynamic, and fluid. Others referred to the ephemeral nature of digital communication (Metz, 2013). Analyses of wikis, Snapchat, online news, and video production demonstrate the transitory nature of digital communication.

- **Wikis:** Wikis are an example of the transitory nature of digital communication because users can update them—at any moment. Unlike print media, that is stable, wikis are transitory. WikiWikiWeb, created in 1995 by Ward Cunningham, is credited with being the first wiki ("WikiWikiWeb," n.d.). "The term 'wiki' comes from the Hawaiian word "wee kee wee kee" which means, "fast" (Shu & Yu-Hao, 2011). As the Hawaiian name implies, wikis are quickly and easily modified; they are transitory. Wikis allow multiple people to make changes instantaneously.

Wikipedia, established in 2001, is the most widely used wiki (Rand, 2010). According to Rand, the English version of Wikipedia receives 8,291,487 views per hour, which equals nearly 200 million views per day—in English alone. Any registered user can revise Wikipedia (Rand, 2010). Due to the openness of revisions, Wikipedia maintains administrative oversight of these revisions. At the time of this writing, Wikipedia had active editors in 285 languages that contributed to 31,000,000 articles ("Wikipedia: About," n.d.). "Every day, hundreds of thousands of visitors from around the world collectively make tens of thousands of edits and create thousands of new articles to augment the knowledge held by the Wikipedia encyclopedia" ("Wikipedia: About," n.d., para. 4). The English edition is the largest with 4,641,658 articles ("Wikipedia: About," n.d.). "Wikipedia is among the most prolific collaborative authoring projects ever sustained in an online environment" (Bryant, Forte, & Bruckman, 2005, p. 1).

Wikipedia's accessibility (Bryant, Forte, & Bruckman, 2005) makes it easy for the 23,051,284 registered users of the English version ("Wikipedia: About", n.d.) to edit and contribute new information. Unlike printed encyclopedias, authors do not have to worry about size constraints (Rand, 2010). Rainie and Tancer (2007) contended that Americans' reliance on search engines and the prevalence of Wikipedia sources on those search engines, have contributed to the growth and popularity of Wikipedia. Google's algorithm is interested in the number of links a site has. The vast number of links within Wikipedia, which also links readers to other Wikipedia articles, is a contributing factor for its popularity in search engines (Rainie & Tancer, 2007).

- **Snapchat:** App users have become interested in a type of social media that claims to erase their digital communication within a timeframe they specify. What was available a few seconds ago (10 seconds is the maximum amount of time that Snapchat postings can be viewed) has now vanished ("Support," n.d.). Snapchat has 100 million monthly active users who send over 700 million Snaps and view over 1 billion Stories per day (Wong, 2014). These numbers have doubled since the third quarter of 2013 when 350 million Snaps were sent (Duggan, 2013). MacMillan (2013) reported that rival apps are available in China and Japan. There is fascination with digital communication that disappears as soon as it is viewed. Users appear to value the transitory nature of digital communication.

- **Online News:** Online news has entered the transitory arena, although it did not begin this way. Originally, it was much like print news with the exception that it was online (Karlsson, 2012). Online and offline news were comparably static. In his examination of online media, Karlsson found that this is no longer true of all online news sources. He stated, "Online news has the ability to rework or delete incorrect stories or facts swiftly and without notice" (Karlsson, 2012, p. 390). Karlsson studied four different Swedish news sites. He monitored 15 stories on these sites for a period of three months. He manually captured what the sites published every 10 minutes. He continued to watch a story until that it had not been updated for three hours. He then revisited the story three more times over the next 24 hours to see if any additional changes had occurred. While Karlsson's work focused on Swedish news sites, which are subsidized and therefore may have the resources to revise more frequently than others, this work demonstrates the transitory nature of digital news. He found that not only were the online articles changing via internal updates but also external updates. Three of the four sites encouraged citizen journalism by asking viewers to send in pictures, videos, and other information. He found news reports were updated between three to nine times with stories commonly updated eight times.

- **Video Production:** If we purchase a DVD, we know that the movie we purchased will be the same each time we play it. However, digital video files can be manipulated quite easily. In his book *Rewire,* Zuckerman (2013) gave the example of the film *Desert Warrior* created by Sam Bacile in the summer of 2011. The script was poorly written and ridiculed by the actors. When the trailer was published on YouTube in 2012, the actors' lines had been overdubbed and the title had been changed to *The Innocence of Muslims.* At this point, it became clear why the filmmaker was indifferent to the quality of the script. He had a different agenda. "The actors now delivered lines about the Prophet Muhammad, portraying the Prophet as a sex-obsessed, violent pedophile" (Zuckerman, 2013, p. 31). According to one of the actors, Tim Dax, those who were hired for their roles thought they were starring in a film about ancient warriors. Dax thought he was hired to play the role of the Biblical character, Samson (Gould, 2012). Unbeknownst to the actors, the director re-created the film for his own purposes. The transitory nature of digital video surprised the actors but fulfilled the purposes of the filmmaker.

Summary

In this section, we explored digital communication in terms of the following characteristics: product/ion-oriented, semiotic, public, and transitory. We highlighted exemplars for each characteristic (see Table 1). We want to point out that these exemplars, while used to illustrate specific characteristics, in reality exemplify multiple characteristics. For example, while Facebook mitigates challenges to production it is simultaneously semiotic, public, and transitory. While Wikipedia mitigates challenges to revising encyclopedia entries (transitory) it is simultaneously product/ion-oriented, semiotic, and a perfect example of collective intelligence

Table 1. Exemplars used to Illustrate Characteristics of Digital Communication

Production Exemplars	• Blogs • Facebook • Twitter • eBooks
Semiotic Exemplars	• Podcasts • Pinterest • YouTube • Vine • Surveillance cameras • Google Glass
Public Exemplars	• Citizen journalism • MMOGs • MOOCs • Arab Spring
Transitory Exemplars	• Wikipedia • Snapchat • Online news • Video production

(public). In a sense, the fact that these exemplars can be used to illustrate multiple characteristics reiterates our point: digital communication is product/ion-oriented, semiotic, public, and transitory.

CURRENT ISSUES

A range of issues emerges in a world with blogs, eBooks, podcasts, Pinterest, YouTube, Vine, Google Glass, surveillance cameras, collective intelligence, wikis, Snapchat, and ubiquitous video production. It is argued that digital communication, while being democratized is simultaneously being monopolized. In addition, there are issues related to access, the persistence of the Spiral of Silence, ethical violations and safety, the ethereal being captured while privacy is compromised, and the preparedness of education.

Democratization and Monopolization of Communication

It has been argued that digital media fosters the democratization of communication (Boler, 2010; Howard & Hussain, 2011). The ability to capture the ethereal, record previously fleeting moments of conversations and actions, and produce a message that no longer requires gatekeeper approval for dissemination, is lauded as providing voice to the masses. The aforementioned discussions of citizen journalism, self-publishing, YouTube, FaceBook, Twitter, Google Glass, MMOGs, MMOCs, Arab Spring, and Wikipedia all lend themselves to the democratization of communication. The bottleneck, formerly held by gatekeepers who maintained access to audience, has been opened. Anyone with an Internet-ready digital device can *produce* a *semiotic* message and make it available to the *public*.

There are, however, indications that the democratization of communication is in peril. There is concern that the masses rely too heavily on a few providers (Greenwald, 2014). Currently, Facebook with 1.2 billion active users, Twitter with 300 million active users (comparable to the U.S. population), Google with 3.5 billion searches each day, and YouTube with over 4.2 billion video streams each day (YouTube Statistics), outpace their rivals. Given limited conduits for digital communication raises serious issues. While the popular providers of digital communication will come and go, concern for the monopolization of communication remains anytime few providers control access to digital communication. "We are nearing the point where an idea banished by Twitter, Facebook, and Google all but vanishes from public discourse entirely" (Greenwald, 2014). McChesney (2013) argued that capitalism is turning the Internet against democracy and noted, "that what is emerging veers toward a classic definition of fascism: the state and large corporations working hand in hand to promote corporate interests, and a state preoccupied with militarism, secrecy, propaganda, and surveillance" (p. 171).

Access to Digital Communication

The monopolization of communication raises issues of access. For some, access is a matter of availability. For others it is an issue of government control. In terms of availability, Wang (2013) found that more people own cell phones than have access to functioning toilets. Specifically, nearly 6 billion of the estimated 7 billion people in the world have access to mobile phones while only 4.5 billion have access to properly functioning toilets. In 2014, Mobithinking reported that there were 6.9 billion mobile cellular subscriptions with broadband subscriptions expected to reach 2.3 billion in 2014 (Sanou, 2014). This data indicated that the Internet, on average, appeared to be accessible. However, government control remains a concern.

Because organizers used social media to plan the 2009 Ürümqi riots in China, the government shut down access to Facebook (Kirkland, 2014). With pressure from international businesses, in 2013, the Chinese government reopened access—but only within 17 miles of Shanghai. Since the 2009 shut down, the Chinese government has taken an active role in monitoring online communication. The Chinese government deletes posts and blocks access to websites (Kirkland, 2014). Bradsher and Mozur (2014) pointed out that Chinese Internet censorship causes economic problems for companies that export out of China. In 2014, Google decided to encrypt users' searches. The Chinese government responded by blocking access to Google (Bradsher & Mozur, 2014). The Google blockade made it difficult for businesses to place ads and collaborate via Google Drive.

In addition to China's efforts to censor and deny access to digital communication, there are other dictatorial governments that actively monitor Internet communication, censor digital communication, shut down access to primary providers (e.g., Twitter, Facebook, and Google), and shut down Internet access (see Table 2). Nonetheless, citizens in these countries find ways to get around bans via proxy servers, virtual private networks (VPNs), and anonymous browsers (Bennett, 2014). Digital communication is so vital that citizens around the world strive to gain access.

Table 2. Countries That Have Limited Access to Social Media*

Country	Facebook	Twitter	YouTube
Bangladesh	Government monitors for inappropriate posts. In 2010, it was shut down for an entire week.		
China	Banned except for a 17 square mile zone of Shanghai	Banned	Banned
Cuba	Internet is difficult and costly to access with slow download speeds. The only place that the Internet can be accessed is in Internet cafes.	Internet is difficult and costly to access with slow download speeds. The only place that the Internet can be accessed is in Internet cafes.	Internet is difficult and costly to access with slow download speeds. The only place that the Internet can be accessed is in Internet cafes.
Egypt	For several days in 2011, several social media sites were blocked due to the fact that people were trying to overthrow the regime of President Hosni Mubarak.	For several days in 2011, several social media sites were blocked due to the fact that people were trying to overthrow the regime of President Hosni Mubarak.	For several days in 2011, several social media sites were blocked due to the fact that people were trying to overthrow the regime of President Hosni Mubarak.
Iran	Banned except for government officials.	Banned except for government officials.	Banned
Mauritius	Blocked for a day in 2007 due to someone making a fake account pretending to be the current prime minister.		
North Korea	Banned Foreign visitors can access the Internet via a new 3G network.	Banned Foreign visitors can access the Internet via a new 3G network.	Banned Foreign visitors can access the Internet via a new 3G network.
Pakistan	Blocked for two weeks in 2010 due to blasphemous content about the prophet Muhammad. Continues to be monitored for such actions.	Allowed	In discussion with Google about the possibility of allowing it.
Syria	Blocked from 2007 to 2011 as the government feared Israeli infiltration.		
Turkey	Allowed	Allowed However, it was blocked for two weeks in March 2014 ahead of the government elections.	Banned since March 2014
Vietnam	Although, it is not banned, many people who live there state difficulty being able to get on. In 2009, it is reported that for a week no one could access the social media site. What can be said on the social media sites is limited by Decree 72, which was put into place September 2013. Prohibits news being shared on social media sites.	Allowed What can be said on the social media sites is limited by Decree 72, which was put into place September 2013. Prohibits news being shared on social media sites.	Allowed What can be said on the social media sites is limited by Decree 72, which was put into place September 2013. Prohibits news being shared on social media sites.

*Data from Bennett (2014) and Kirkland (2014)

Persistent Spiral of Silence

The Spiral of Silence (Noelle-Neumann 1974, 1993) is the phenomenon in which people do not talk about topics that are not popular or will not be well received. "A major insight into human behavior from pre-Internet era studies of communication is the tendency of people not to speak up about policy issues in public... when they believe their own point of view is not widely shared" (Hampton et al., 2014, para. 1). Hampton and colleagues wondered if Facebook and Twitter had changed the culture of talk and empowered people to speak despite the Spiral of Silence. In a survey of 1,801 adults, they found that the pre-Internet Spiral of Silence phenomenon persists in the Internet era. They asked participants if they would be willing to discuss the Snowden issue (an American computer professional who leaked classified information from the National Security Agency). Eighty-six percent of respondents said that they would discuss it in person, while only 42% said they would share information on the issue via Facebook or Twitter. The survey results indicate that one's audience, similar to the pre-digital era, influence self-censorship. According to Hampton and colleagues, "In both personal settings and online settings, people were more willing to share their views if they thought their audience agreed with them" (para. 7). For the vast majority of authors, a like-minded audience remains key to choosing whether to produce and disseminate digital communication.

In an era in which digital communication is readily available to the masses, the Spiral of Silence raises concern regarding the voices being heard. There is an issue regarding the variety of information being communicated through digital media. It also follows that, if there is not an audience for a particular viewpoint, then it may not get communicated, despite the digital tools at our disposal. Wikipedia may be an example. The English version offers more than double the selection of the next largest edition, Swedish (Wikipedia, 2014). This creates an imbalance of power, or at the very least, presence, in this digital space.

Ethics and Safety

- **Privacy Settings:** Based on the growth trajectory of social media, it appears that such services will persist into the foreseen future and remain a conduit of digital communication for millions of people. The popularity of these services raises issues of ethics and safety. Wasike (2013) explained that when information is public, there are limited guarantees of privacy. Even if the information is deleted from the author's account, the information may have been copied and shared. Thus, the information persists. Vander Veer (2008) found that 25% of social media consumers cannot locate the security settings offered by social media services and are therefore left to the mercy of default settings. Flatow (2008) found that control of privacy has limited benefits to the users by noting that too many options confuse the users who then make poor choices. For example, he describes how consumers use their self-designated "friends" to guarantee privacy, and this can make users' information more accessible than if they are presented with fewer, but easier-to-understand options. Lenhart and Madden (2007) found that only 66% of teenagers use the privacy settings to reduce access to their profiles. Regardless of an increasing awareness of the importance of their "digital footprint," tracking personal information left behind by social media communication, only 3% of social media users check their online presence regularly (Madden, Fox, Smith, & Vitak, 2007). Acquisti and Gross (2005) found that many users have misconceptions about the privacy of their communications.

- **Cyber Bullying:** The two-edged nature of digital communication, balancing between opportunities and risks, reveals an emerging societal issue recognized as cyber bullying (Walrave & Heirman, 2011). Electronic bullying, online bullying, and cyber bullying are new means of bullying. These types of bullying are defined as harassment using technology such as social websites, email, chat rooms, mobile phone texting and cameras, picture messages, IM (instant messages), and/or blogs (Miller & Hufstedler, 2009;

Beale & Hall, 2007). Studies confirmed that cyber bullying is a widespread and a serious problem. Mishna, Khoury-Kassabri, Gadalla, and Daciuk (2012) found that over 30% of students had personally experienced cyber bullying, either as victims or offenders; within a three month period, one in four (25.7%) stated that they were involved in cyber bullying as both a bully and a victim. Adams (2010) found that around 20% of students said they had been cyber bullied. Meanwhile, in a survey of 62 adolescents, Wong-Lo and Bullock (2011) found that 90% of the participants had experienced cyber bullying either as victims or as bystanders. The outcomes of cyber bullying can be serious. Brown, Jackson, and Cassidy (2006) reported indications that victims struggle with suicide, eating disorders, and in extreme cases homicide. Victims of cyber bullying can show "consequences ranging from low self-esteem, anxiety, anger, depression, school absenteeism, poor grades, an increased tendency to violate against others, to youth suicide" (p. 16). Cyber bullying "can contribute independently to psychological distress" (Mitchell, Finkelhor, Wolak, Ybarra & Turner, 2010, p. 132).

- **Identity Theft:** Reznik (2012) described two types of identity theft. The more common type happens when a perpetrator builds a fabricated profile of the victim and then uses that identity for online communications. The second type happens when the perpetrator steals a victim's password or gets access to a victim's social media account and subsequently impersonates the victim by using that account. Rainie and colleagues (2013) found that 55% of Internet users ages 18-29 have experienced at least one of these types of identity theft problems, compared with 42% of those ages 30-49, 30% of those ages 50-64 and 24% of those ages 65 and older.

Ethereal Captured while Privacy Compromised

In the not too distant past, people told strangers only basic information about themselves. But, nowadays, revealing names and place of birth as well as other information like the names of favorite books, movies, first pets, etc. is a common practice. People share this information without much concern. On social media, people share not only basic information but also narrate their lives through photos, videos and comments. This information has become fodder for such companies as Google, Microsoft, and Facebook. They use this information to create user profiles, which in turn allows them to provide personalized advertisements. Microsoft, for example, identified women with risk of postpartum depression through mining online conversations, and Facebook studied how parents and kids interact (Jayson, 2014). What was once private has become public. What was once ethereal has been captured and distributed worldwide.

In a world where we capture and document what was once ethereal, privacy issues are not just limited to social media; video surveillance raises issues. Kelly (2013) explained that facial recognition software…

… Identifies objects by shape, size and color. It can read license plates and recognize cars. When it comes to people, it can detect their gender, approximate age, mood and other demographic information. Using multiple cameras, it can track their patterns and some behaviors. It automatically zooms in on any person's face and identifies them based on things like the distance between their eyes or the shape of their nose. (Para. 15)

When cameras with facial recognition software are linked to the same database, it becomes possible to track people. It becomes possible to single out a person who has attended multiple political protests at different places (Kelly, 2013). The ability to capture what was formerly ethereal raises issues of privacy.

Given that the ethereal can be captured and made public, the European Union has actively sought and formulated regulations known as the "Right to be Forgotten." The concept is that people have the right to control their online identities. Instead of misleading, erroneous, and negative information being replicated and persistently available online, individuals should have the right to erase such information. The primary strategy for this erasure is to eliminate information from Google searches. In other words, regulations require Google to censor its search results. It is argued that international laws of censorship sets precedent for additional forms of online censorship thus stepping over "a first amendment red line" (Scheer, 2014, para. 1). To facilitate the Right to be Forgotten, others call for the breakup of Google (Shapiro & Meyer, 2014).

Education, New Literacies, and Digital Communication

The ability to proficiently communicate with digital media is an active research agenda among the literacy research community. Leu and colleagues investigated the literacy skills required to skillfully find, synthesize, and report findings from Internet-based queries (e.g., Leu et al., in press; Leu et al., 2011). Gee and colleagues examined the literacy skills involved in gaming (e.g., Gee, 2007; 2010). Others examined the literacy skills required to proficiently communicate with various digital formats such as fan fiction (Black, 2008; Chandler-Olcott & Mahar, 2003; Thomas, 2007), multimedia (Mayer, 2008; Stein, 2008; Wyatt-Smith & Elkins, 2008), synchronous chats (Baker, Vogler & Schallert, 2014), voice recognition (Baker, 2012, 2013c, 2014), and zines (Guzzetti, 2010). There is research that examined the blurred lines between digital authors and digital audience (Baker, Rozendal, & Whitenack, 2000), ways to

support comprehension of digital texts (Proctor, Dalton, Grisham, 2007), embodied literacies (Fleckenstein, 2003; Leander & Boldt, 2013; M. Miller, 2013), as well as theoretical groundwork of reading and writing with technology (Baker, 2010b; Leu & Kinzer, 2003). These and others contended that the ability to communicate with digital media requires literacies that previously did not exist. These literacies are known as New Literacies (Baker, 2010b; Coiro, Knobel, Lankshear, & Leu, 2008).

Despite significant investment in technology, schools struggle to incorporate these digital and informational literacy skills into the curriculum (Leu et al., 2013). In 2011, Hutchison and Reinking conducted a national survey of U.S. teachers to examine their perceptions of how well they support students' development of new literacies and digital communication. They found that the research being done has had relatively little infiltration into classrooms. In an analysis of elementary classroom web sites, Baker (2007a, 2007b) found woefully lackluster opportunities for students to learn and use either traditional or new literacies and therefore proposed strategies for making a match between technologies and classrooms (Baker, 2003). Some teachers do not know how to use technology tools. Some mistake the transfer of curriculum from print to pixel as inherently equivalent (Hartman, Morsink, & Zheng, 2010). Others feel constrained by high-stakes tests that focus on traditional instead of new literacies (Hobbs, 2010). Legislation that was intended to "leave no child behind" has had the opposite effect. Those struggling to pass the high-stakes tests are required to practice for the test and therefore do not have time to learn new literacies (which are not on the test) (Baker & Dooley, 2010; Baker, Schmidt, & Whitmore, 2011; Leu, 2006).

Some may argue that students do not need to be taught how to effectively communicate with digital devices. After all, they are digital natives (Prensky, 2001) who have spent their entire lives communicating digitally. They have extensive out of school experiences with video, social networking, gaming, and texting (Alvermann, Hutchins & De-Blasio, 2012; Zickuhr, 2010). Surprisingly, research indicates that even digital natives know relatively little about digital communication (Bennet, Maton, & Kervin, 2008; Leu, 2006). Rather, K-16 students tend to be proficient communicators with the few platforms they use with their peers. This leaves them woefully unprepared for the digital communication required in the workplace (Mikulecky, 2010). Students struggle to find, critically evaluate, and read online information (Forzani & Burlingame, 2012; Graham & Metaxas, 2003; Kuiper & Volman, 2008). "Rather than seeing the web as a neutral source of 'information,' students need to be asking questions about the sources of that information, the interests of its producers and how it represents the world" (Buckingham, 2007, p. 113).

As part of the standards movement, the United States has moved from No Child Left Behind (2002) legislation to the Common Core State Standards (CCSS) which specify learning goals for the end of each K-12 grade. Several of these goals support the use of new literacies in the classroom. For example, Writing Anchor Standard 6 states, "Use technology, including the Internet, to produce and publish writing and to interact and collaborate with others" (CCSS, 2012, p. 43). Writing Anchor Standard 8 states, "Gather relevant information from multiple print and digital sources, assess the credibility and accuracy of each source, and integrate the information while avoiding plagiarism" (p. 44). These CCSS require students to develop the ability to participate in complex digital communication tasks that involve multiple steps and skills that emulate the real world. These standards expect teachers to think in new ways about how to evaluate and teach students to proficiently communicate digitally (Drew, 2013; Leu et al., 2013). While these standards draw some attention to new literacies they lack specificity. It is uncertain how educational policies, curricula, and pedagogy will make the necessary shifts to prepare children to be proficient digital communicators.

METHODOLOGICAL GAPS AND FUTURE RESEARCH

Given the transitory nature of digital communication, there is a wide range of topics emerging for which relatively little is known. Instead of discussing these topical gaps, that quickly emerge and fade, in this section we focus on something more fundamental: we focus on methodological gaps. As we explored research regarding the societal impact of digital media on communication, we noted that the research methods themselves had the following gaps: timeliness, paradigm, and population.

Timeliness Gaps

Traditionally, it takes three to five years for research to be conceived, conducted, and reported in peer-reviewed journals. The impact of digital media on communication outpaces conventional research cycles. By the time research is published it may provide insights into bygone digital communications. The current process of scholarship fails to keep pace with a world in which 100 hours of video was uploaded to YouTube in the last 60 seconds (YouTube, n.d.). Each of these videos provided semiotic illuminations that impact who we are, what we favor, and how we choose to communicate in and about our world. The information we receive from research studies can be stymied by being out of date before they are published. We refer to this phenomenon as a timeliness gap.

News reporters provide up-to-date information about digital communication. Many news outlets have sections dedicated to technology. Other news outlets specialize solely in the societal impact of technology (e.g., CNET, Wired). There are daily reports of the impact of online bullying, government censorship, the use of Twitter, Facebook, YouTube, and such to influence politics and instigate revolution. While trusted news reporters research their stories, their research methods do not meet the robust criteria required by scientific research. Thus, while trusted news outlets provide timely information, they lack systematic and scientific research methods.

Paradigm Gaps

Kuhn (1970) argued that the history of science is a history of scientific paradigms that coalesce around concepts of ontology, epistemology, and methodology (Hatch, 2002). Different paradigms have "fundamentally different beliefs systems concerning how the world is ordered" (Hatch, 2002, p. 11). In this sense, Hatch described five research paradigms: positivist, postpositivist, constructivist, critical/feminist, and poststructuralist. Each paradigm defines reality differently and therefore enacts research differently. Positivists define reality in objective terms and therefore collect and analyze objective statistical data. Such data can be quickly generated and analyzed by software. Internet sites such as Pew Research, Expanded Ramblings, and KISSmetrics provide information about who, what, and how many people use various forms of digital communication. Herein, positivistic studies are poised to address the aforementioned timeliness gap. While valuable, positivistic research only one of many paradigms.

Postpositivists are described as those who view reality as complex and "due to limitations of human inquiry… [view reality as] approximated but never fully apprehended" (Hatch, 2002, p. 14). Research therefore can merely provide approximations of reality. Constructivists define reality in terms of the users. Research therefore involves labor-intensive examination of individual cognition and is commonly situated within social norms. Critical/feminists define reality in terms of power structures and focus on who is being empowered and disempowered. Such research also requires labor-intensive analysis of social norms. Finally, poststructuralists say there is no inherent reality. While positivistic and non-positivistic paradigms derive insights from both quantitative and qualitative data it is common for non-positivistic paradigms

to employ qualitative research methods that require prolonged, in-situ data collection and analyses that are inordinately labor-intensive such as those used to grounded theory, conduct ethnography, case study, phenomenology, and naturalistic inquiry. Herein lies a conundrum: On one hand, research that seeks to understand the societal impact of digital media on communication is threatened by lack of timeliness; on the other hand, there is a need for the research corpus to represent a full range of paradigmatic insights. Positivistic insights can be timely—but represent only one of many views of reality. Non-positivistic research can reveal a range of valued insights—but commonly require extensive labor-intensive work with findings that emerge over time.

Population Gaps

Another noteworthy methodological gap is *who* is represented in the research corpus. We contend that digital communication permeates digital cultures and therefore impacts users from birth to death. However, the majority of studies we found were skewed toward 18-45 year olds. While there were studies that focused on preschool and elementary children as well as adults over 45, the vast majority focused on the 18-45 year old population. A population gap creates a skewed understanding of digital communication. For example, the research corpus about MMOGs focuses on adolescent gamers and therefore creates a misconception that gamers are a youth subculture. An entire volume of the *Journal of Adolescence, Vol. 21*(1), was dedicated to the damaging effects of video games on adolescent gamers. Yee (2006) pointed out that research reiterates the stereotype that gamers are both adolescent and that gaming has damaging effects. Griffiths, Davies and Chappell (2003) noted, "the image of a typical gamer is seen as socially negative and remains firmly within a youth subculture" (p. 81). Population gaps leave us relatively uninformed of digital communication among large pools of the population.

Future Directions for Research Methodologies

Given insights into research gaps, we offer suggestions for future research. Our suggestions are limited by our own research methods. Specifically, we sought to glean research that revealed understanding of the product/ion, semiotic, public, and transitory nature of digital communication. So, while we posit that research gaps in timeliness, paradigm, and population appear to be significant, we base this on our review of research as it pertained to our framework. We recommend that both meta-analyses and metasyntheses (S. Miller, 2013; Sandelowski & Barroso, 2007) of research that investigates digital communication be conducted to dis/confirm the following recommendations we make for future directions of research methodologies.

Timeliness is currently addressed by statistical reports and trusted news outlets. As stated, statistical reports ignore insights offered by multiple paradigms and news reports lack scientific rigor. We advocate for continued statistical reports as well as concerted efforts to support non-positivistic research. Federal and foundation funding for grounded theory, ethnographies, case studies, phenomenologies, naturalistic inquiry, and other non-positivistic work is necessary if we are to ascertain an informed understanding of digital communication. Given the plethora of news reports, one such effort could be an on-going systematic content analysis of these reports that focuses on social interactions and the nature of digital cultures as well as varied non-positivistic constructs. Open access and online journals may mitigate challenges to timeliness by decreasing the time it takes to disseminate research. Population gaps need to be addressed by all research paradigms. We recommend statistical as well as qualitative analysis of all age groups. While our work indicated a population gap as it relates to age we recommend a systematic analysis of whether

a range of populations related to gender, race, class, sexuality and disability, are included in the research corpus.

IMPLICATIONS AND RECOMMENDATIONS

The title of this chapter is, *The Irrevocable Alteration of Communication: A Glimpse into the Societal Impact of Digital Media.* Some may argue that digital media has had little impact on the alteration of communication. After all, communication has always had a production component (e.g., cave drawings, cuneiform, alphabets), included semiotic sign systems (e.g., body language, illustrations, photos), for an audience/the public, and been edited and revised (transitory). What is irrevocably altered? Isn't digital communication simply non-digital communication—just in digital form? At the beginning of this chapter, we stated that communication is fundamental to human existence. Linguists argue that humans communicate to satisfy physical, emotional and social needs as well as to learn about one's milieu, be creative, and convey facts (Halliday, 1977). Our exploration of the nature of digital communication reveals that the *reasons* humans communicate remain unaltered, while the *ability* to communicate appears to have been profoundly altered. A brief discussion of implications and recommendations for local and global civic engagement, commerce, education, and policy brings to light a sample of alterations in our ability to communicate.

Civic Engagement

Civic engagement is dependent on communication. To be civically engaged, local and global citizens must ascertain issues relevant to the public. Citizens engage in face-to-face conversations with their friends and neighbors, read local newspapers, and attend local city council meetings. In the past, geographic restrictions limited citizens' abilities to have these conversations with those across the state, country, and globe. In our digital world, what was once limited to local civic engagement can be instantaneously distributed and accessed regardless of geographic location. Whether by real-time interactive video feeds (e.g., Skype) or by following hashtags, digital communication mitigates challenges to geographic limitations. Hackers and skilled programmers were civically engaged in the Arab Spring regardless of their geographic location. Their participation subverted government attempts to shut down communication and facilitated open access for local protestors to organize and communicate with one another as well as with the world. The ability to *produce* a *semiotic* message that can be made *public* and instantaneously distributed worldwide has irrevocably changed how citizens engage in local and global civic action. The digital *collective* appears to be qualitatively different from previous forms of civic engagement. It will be interesting to see how the nature of digital communications continues to impact the civic engagement of citizens and in turn impact our societies.

Commerce

The *public* nature of digital communication appears to have an irrevocable impact on commerce. Consumers share evaluations of products and services. Before purchasing a toy, book, or car, consumers read previous consumers' ratings and decide whether to buy the product and from whom to make the purchase. Using smartphones, consumers scan bar codes to attain price comparisons. Is the baby food in your cart offered elsewhere at a better price? You no longer have to drive around town to find out. Just check prices from multiple merchants on your smart phone. It remains to be seen if this collective intelligence favors monopolies that can sell at cheaper prices. Some may be concerned that Amazon and Alibaba are too big. The purpose of this chapter is not to

parse economic philosophies. However, we would be remiss if we did not highlight the significant impact that digital communication is having on commerce.

In 1999, DiNucci popularized the term, Web 2.0. He argued that a paradigm shift had occurred on the Internet. Early web sites were dispensary. Users could explore retail shops and local grocery store web sites to see what was on sale. In the late 1990s this changed. Web sites became interactive. Users could respond to web sites. They could post comments. They could join social networks. In the case of wikis, they could become co-authors. In 2006, Markoff argued that the Web morphed again. Specifically, in Web 1.0 and Web 2.0 iterations, the user reads the web. In Web 3.0 iterations, the web reads the user. Cookies, algorithms, and artificial intelligence are used to personalize what users receive as they explore the Internet. Web 3.0 has implications for many areas of our lives, but we highlight it here for the implications it has for commerce. Information on the Internet is immense. Users want to find what they are looking for. Web 3.0 attempts to understand users and sift through the myriad of information online to provide them with what they seek. This includes giving users advertisements that pertain to their interests. Users are more likely to pay attention to ads that feature goods and services they want. On the other hand, Web 3.0 has implications for who is empowered to discern search results: the Web or the users? Similar to shifts in civic engagement, it will be interesting to see where commerce goes in an increasingly interconnected, digitally communicative world.

Education

Digital communication requires heightened awareness of new communication skills, demands an understanding of new pedagogies, and provides new opportunities for learners. Studies indicate that the ability to read offline has no correlation to the ability to read online (see Current Issues:

Education, new literacies, and digital communication). In this chapter we discussed a range of technologies (e.g., blogs, Twitter, Facebook, YouTube). Each technology requires specialized communication skills. Each technology has specialized affordances. For example, for a parent to communicate with a child to determine if he is ready to be picked up from soccer requires an understanding of the affordances of text messaging versus email, social media, and the like. Baker (2013a) proposed that these affordances can be readily integrated into classrooms as new genres. Every teacher teaches genre (e.g., Baker & Monte-Sano, 2012; Baker & Shanahan, 2012). Every teacher can teach new genres. There are new communication skills required to proficiently read digital texts as well as compose digital texts. Too often, it is assumed that digital natives will pick up on these skills. Yet, we do not make this assumption regarding print natives. Why would we make this assumption about digital literacies? Policymakers, principals, parents, teachers, and the public need to be made aware of the need to teach K-16 students how to effectively communicate in our digital world. We recommend a heightened awareness of this need. Otherwise, we are in danger of preparing our children for the 1950s instead of the 2050s (Baker, Pearson, Rozendal, 2010).

Similarly, there are new pedagogies. There is a need to recognize that classrooms that integrate technology as well as online education are not merely digitized versions of traditional classrooms. There is a need to recognize the existence and harness the affordances of new pedagogies. We recommend extensive support for teachers. In his seminal sociological study of teachers, Lortie (1975) found that teachers teach the way they were taught. In other words, pedagogy is a social practice. Teachers emulate those who taught them. Herein lies the dilemma: the pedagogies of yesteryear are insufficient for today. Concerted efforts must be made to heighten awareness as well as support teachers as they prepare children

to be active citizens who can effectively compete in a global, digital market. We recommend that professional development, advanced degrees, pedagogical coaching, any and every innovative and effective support be given to teachers as they face this exciting and challenging time. High stakes tests appear to exacerbate this effort by threatening teachers who neglect to teach to the test (Baker & Dooley, 2010; Baker & Pacheco, 2011; Baker, Schmidt, & Whitmore, 2011). We recommend professional support as teachers surmount and master these cultural shifts.

Meanwhile, digital communication is opening doors previously unavailable educational opportunities. MOOCs, online universities and university courses, as well as online K-12 schools and K-12 courses are increasingly available. Students are no longer limited by their inabilities to travel to schools, pay for schools, or find time for schools. Education is available to those with Internet access, MOOCs and a myriad of educational information are available for free (e.g., Khan Academy), and many are asynchronous which allows students to participate at times that fit their family and work schedules. Critics warn that MOOCs simply disseminate information, which should not be confused with an education and are driven by profit not pedagogy (Mazoue, 2013; Rees, 2013). It remains to be seen whether MOOCs and other online K-12 courses are forces for democratization or economic exploitation.

Policy

We advocate for policies that support digital communication. This includes continued efforts to protect users from online exploitation. Identity theft, privacy, and cyber bullying are just a few examples of the need for policies that keep online users safe. In addition, we advocate for access. At the time of this writing, net neutrality and corresponding policies are being debated. While these policies are politicized, we advocate for policies that protect access. Digital communication is central to civic engagement, commerce, education, entertainment and more. Policies should support efforts to communicate. Finally, policies need to support research. Funding for multiple paradigms that investigate digital communication among a broad spectrum of the population in a timely fashion is needed.

FINAL THOUGHTS

This chapter provided a glimpse into the impact of digital media on society, specifically digital communication. We framed this glimpse in terms of four characteristics of digital communication: product/ion, semiotic, public, and transitory. To explicate the nature of digital communication we highlighted a few exemplars of each characteristic. These exemplars included blogs, Facebook, Twitter, eBooks, podcasts, Pinterest, YouTube, Vine, surveillance cameras, Google Glass, citizen journalism, MMOGs, MOOCs, Arab Spring, wikis, Snapchat, online news, and video production. We discussed issues related to the democratization and monopolization of communication, who has access, the persistent Spiral of Silence, privacy, cyber bullying, identity theft, the ethereal being captured, as well as education and new literacies. We explored methodological gaps in the research corpus and made recommendations regarding the need for timeliness, support for a comprehensive span of research paradigms, and representation of a full range of populations. Finally, we discussed implications and recommendations for civic engagement, commerce, education, and policy.

Our attempt to understand the nature of digital communication was ambitious. This chapter is characterized as a mere glimpse. Given the breakneck pace by which varied instantiations of communication technologies rise and fall, this glimpse will quickly become an historical record--a snapshot in time. The impact of digital communication on society is evolutionary. It is our hope that this chapter, in concert with this

volume, contributes to the national and international dialog that seeks to understand the impact of digital media on society.

REFERENCES

Acquisti, A., & Gross, R. (2005, November). *Information revelation and privacy in online social networks*. Paper presented in the ACM Workshop on Privacy in the Electronic Society, Alexandria, VA.

Adams, C. (2010). Cyberbullying: How to make it stop. *Instructor, 120*(2), 44–49.

Alvermann, D., Hutchins, R. J., & DeBlasio, R. (2012). Adolescents' engagement with Web 2.0 and social media: Research, theory, and practice. *Research in the Schools, 19*(1), 33–44.

Audsley, S., Fernando, K., Maxson, B., Robinson, B., & Varney, K. (2013). An examination of Coursera as an information environment: Does Coursera fulfill its mission to provide open education to all? *The Serials Librarian: From the Printed Page to the Digital Age, 65*(2), 136–166. doi:10.1080/0361526X.2013.781979

Baker, E. A. (2001). The nature of literacy in a technology rich classroom. *Reading Research and Instruction, 40*(3), 153–179.

Baker, E. A. (2003). Integrating literacy and technology: Making a match between software and classroom. *Reading & Writing Quarterly, 19*(2), 193–197. doi:10.1080/10573560308221

Baker, E. A. (2007a). Elementary classroom web sites: Support for literacy within and beyond the classroom. *Journal of Literacy Research, 39*(1), 1–38.

Baker, E. A. (2007b). Support for new literacies, cultural expectations, and pedagogy: Potential and features for classroom web sites. *New England Reading Association Journal, 43*(2), 56–62.

Baker, E. A. (2010a). New literacies, new insights: An exploration of traditional and new perspectives. In E. A. Baker (Ed.), *The new literacies: Multiple perspectives on research and practice* (pp. 285–311). New York: Guilford Press.

Baker, E. A. (Ed.). (2010b). *The new literacies: Multiple perspectives on research and practice.* New York: Guilford Press.

Baker, E. A. (2012, November). *Dragons, iPads, and literacy, O-My: Examining the feasibility of voice recognition apps in a first-grade classroom.* Paper presented at the meeting of the Literacy Research Association, San Diego, CA.

Baker, E. A. (2013a, October). *That was then: Definitions, explorations, and prognostications of literacies.* Paper presented at the meeting of the Kentucky Reading Association, Lexington, KY.

Baker, E. A. (2013b, April). *Traversing time and space: An ontological analysis of traditional and new literacies.* Paper presented at the meeting of Digital Classics Association, Buffalo, NY.

Baker, E. A. (2013c, December). *Voice recognition apps: A systems theory exploration of grapho-semantic awareness.* Paper presented at the meeting of the Literacy Research Association, Dallas, TX.

Baker, E. A. (2014, December). *Siri got it wrong!: Dialogic negotiations among first-grade authors using voice recognition to compose.* Paper presented at the meeting of the Literacy Research Association, Marco Island, FL.

Baker, E. A., & Dooley, C. (2010, March 1). Teaching language arts in a high stakes era. *Voice of Literacy* [Podcast]. Retrieved from http://voiceofliteracy.org

Baker, E. A., & Monte-Sano, C. (2012, October 1). Writing prompts that help adolescents think as historians. *Voice of Literacy* [Podcast]. Retrieved from http://voiceofliteracy.org

Baker, E. A., & Pacheco, M. (2011, January 3). How elementary bilingual literacy teachers negotiate policy with students' needs. *Voice of Literacy* [Podcast]. Retrieved from http://voiceofliteracy.org

Baker, E. A., Pearson, P. D., & Rozendal, M. S. (2010). Theoretical perspectives and literacy studies: An exploration of roles and insights. In E. A. Baker (Ed.), *The new literacies: Multiple perspectives on research and practice* (pp. 1–22). New York: Guilford Press.

Baker, E. A., Rozendal, M., & Whitenack, J. (2000). Audience awareness in a technology rich elementary classroom. *Journal of Literacy Research, 32*(3), 395–419. doi:10.1080/10862960009548086

Baker, E. A., Schmidt, R., & Whitmore, K. (2011, January 17). The language of struggle in search of hope for teachers. *Voice of Literacy* [Podcast]. Retrieved from http://voiceofliteracy.org

Baker, E. A., & Shanahan, C. (2012, January 16). Gleaning insights from historians, mathematicians, and chemists about how they read within their disciplines. *Voice of Literacy* [Podcast]. Retrieved from http://voiceofliteracy.org

Baker, E. A., Vogler, J., & Schallert, D. (2014, January 20). The democratization of classrooms: Examining online discussions. *Voice of Literacy* [Podcast]. Retrieved from http://voiceofliteracy.org

Banks, J. (2003, May). *Negotiating participatory culture in the new media environment: Auran and the Trainz online community an (im)possible relation.* Paper presented in *Digital Arts Conference*, Melbourne.

Baverstock, A., & Steinitz, J. (2013). Who are the self-publishers? *Learned Publishing, 26*(3), 211–223. doi:10.1087/20130310

Beale, A. V., & Hall, K. R. (2007). Cyberbullying: What school administrators (and parents) can do. *The Clearing House: A Journal of Educational Strategies, Issues and Ideas, 81*(1), 8–1. doi:10.3200/TCHS.81.1.8-12

Bennet, S., Maton, K., & Kervin, L. (2008). The 'digital natives': A critical review of the evidence. *British Journal of Educational Technology, 39*(5), 775–786. doi:10.1111/j.1467-8535.2007.00793.x

Bennett, S. (2014, August, 4). North Korea, Iran, China, Pakistan, Turkey - countries who block social media. *Mediabistro*. Retrieved from http://www.mediabistro.com/alltwitter/countries-social-media-banned_b59035

Bercovici, J. (2014). Inside Pinterest: The coming ad colossus that could dwarf Twitter and Facebook. *Forbes, 194*(6), 70–82. Retrieved from http://www.forbes.com/sites/jeffbercovici/2014/10/15/inside-pinterest-the-coming-ad-colossus-that-could-dwarf-twitter-and-facebook/

Black, R. W. (2008). *Adolescents and online fan fiction*. New York: Peter Lang.

Boler, M. (Ed.). (2010). *Digital media and democracy*. Cambridge, MA: MIT Press.

Borup, J., West, R. E., & Graham, C. R. (2012). Improving online social presence through asynchronous video. *The Internet and Higher Education, 15*(3), 195–203. doi:10.1016/j.iheduc.2011.11.001

Bradsher, K., & Mozur, P. (2014, September 21). China clamps down on web, pinching companies like Google. *New York Times*. Retrieved from http://www.nytimes.com/2014/09/22/business/international/china-clamps-down-on-web-pinching-companies-like-google.html?_r=0

Brown, K., Jackson, M., & Cassidy, W. (2006). Cyber-bullying: Developing policy to direct responses that are equitable and effective in addressing this special form of bullying. *Canadian Journal of Educational Administration and Policy, 57*, 1–36.

Bryant, S. L., Forte, A., & Bruckman, A. (2005). Becoming Wikipedian: Transformation of participation in a collaborative online encyclopedia. In *Proceedings of the 2005 International ACM/SIGGROUP Conference on Supporting Group Work* (pp. 1-10). ACM. Retrieved from http://dl.acm.org/citation.cfm?id=1099205

Buckingham, D. (2007). Media education goes digital: An introduction. *Learning, Media and Technology, 32*(2), 111–119. doi:10.1080/17439880701343006

Carolan, S., & Evain, C. (2013). Self-publishing: Opportunities and threats in a new age of mass culture. *Publishing Research Quarterly, 29*(4), 285–300. doi:10.1007/s12109-013-9326-3

Center for Collective Intelligence. (2014). MIT. Retrieved October 20, 2014 from http://cci.mit.edu/

Chandler-Olcott, K., & Mahar, D. (2003). Adolescents' *anime*-inspired "fanfictions": An exploration of multiliteracies. *Journal of Adolescent & Adult Literacy, 46*, 556–566.

Coiro, J., Knobel, M., Lankshear, C., & Leu, D. J. (Eds.). (2008). *Handbook of research on new literacies*. New York: Taylor and Francis Group.

Common Core State Standards Initiative. (2012). *Common Core State Standards Initiative: Preparing America's students for college and career*. Retrieved from http://www.corestandards.org

Crook, J. (2014). Vine finally lets you import video from your camera roll. *TechCrunch*. Retrieved from http://techcrunch.com/2014/08/20/with-a-billion-loops-every-day-vine-finally-lets-users-import-video-from-their-camera/

Digital Marketing Ramblings. (2014). *DMR directory of social network, app and digital stats: WordPress stats and facts*. Retrieved from http://expandedramblings.com/index.php/business-directory/?listing=wordpress&wpbdp_sort=field-10

DiNucci, D. (1999). Fragmented Future. *Print, 53*(4), 32.

Drew, S. (2013). Open up the ceiling on the common core state standards: Preparing students for 21st-century literacy-now. *Journal of Adolescent & Adult Literacy, 56*(4), 321–330. doi:10.1002/JAAL.00145

Duggan, M. (2013, October 28). Photos and video sharing grow online. *Pew Internet Research Project*. Retrieved from http://www.pewinternet.org/fact-sheets/social-networking-fact-sheet/

Duggan, M., & Brenner, J. (2013, February 14). The demographics of social media users - 2012. *Pew Research Center*. Retrieved from www.pewinternet.org/2013/02/14/the-demographics-of-social-media-users-2012

Ethereal. (n.d.). In *Merriam-Webster.com*. Retrieved from http://www.merriam-webster.com/dictionary/ethereal

Facebook Statistics. (2014). *KISSmetrics*. Retrieved from blog.kissmetrics.com/facebook-statistics

Fiegerman, S. (2013, August 20). Vine tops 40 million users. *Mashable*. Retrieved from http://mashable.com/2013/08/20/vine-40-million-registered-users/

Flanagan, B., & Calandra, B. (2005). Podcasting in the classroom. *Learning and Leading with Technology*, 20–25.

Flatow, I. (2008, March 21). *Web privacy concerns prompt Facebook changes* [Talk show]. Retrieved from http://www.highbeam.com/doc/1P1-150730298.html

Fleckenstein, K. S. (2003). *Embodied literacies: Imageword and a poetics of teaching*. Carbondale: Southern Illinois University Press.

Flew, T., & Humphreys, S. (2005). Games: Technology, industry, culture. In *New media: An introduction* (pp. 101–114). South Melbourne: Oxford University Press.

Forzani, E., & Burlingame, C. (2012, December). *Evaluating representative state samples of seventh-grade students' ability to critically evaluate online information*. Paper presented at the annual meeting of the Literacy Research Association, San Diego, CA.

Gannes, L. (2006, October 26). Jawed Karim: How YouTube took off. *Gigaom*. Retrieved from https://gigaom.com/2006/10/26/jawed-karim-how-youtube-took-off/

Gee, J. P. (2007). *What video games have to teach us about learning and literacy* (2nd ed.). New York: MacMillan.

Gee, J. P. (2010). A situated sociocultural approach to literacy and technology. In E. A. Baker (Ed.), *The new literacies: Multiple perspectives on research and practice* (pp. 165–193). New York: Guilford Press.

Ghonim, W. (2012). *Revolution 2.0: The power of the people is greater than the people in power: A memoir*. New York: Houghton Mifflin Harcourt.

Glaser, M. (2006, September 27). Your guide to citizen journalism. *Mediashift*. Retrieved from http://www.pbs.org/mediashift/2006/09/your-guide-to-citizen-journalism270/

Gosney, J. W. (2005). *Beyond reality: A guide to alternate reality gaming*. Boston, MA: Course Technology Press.

Gould, J. E. (2012, September 13). *Actor Tim Dax on Sam Bacile and "Innocence of Muslims"*. Retrieved from http://nation.time.com/2012/09/13/the-making-of-innocence-of-muslims-one-actors-story/

Graham, L., & Metaxas, P. T. (2003). Of course it's true: I saw it on the Internet! *Communications of the ACM, 46*(5), 71–75. doi:10.1145/769800.769804

Greenwald, G. (2014). Should Twitter, Facebook, and Google executives be the arbiters of what we see and read? *The Intercept*. Retrieved from https://firstlook.org/theintercept/2014/08/21/twitter-facebook-executives-arbiters-see-read/

Griffiths, M., Davies, M., & Chappell, D. (2003). Breaking the stereotype: The case of online gaming. *Cyberpsychology & Behavior, 6*(1), 81–91. doi:10.1089/109493103321167992 PMID:12650566

Guzzetti, B. J. (2010). Feminist perspectives on the new literacies. In E. A. Baker (Ed.), *The new literacies: Multiple perspectives on research and practice* (pp. 242–264). New York: Guilford Press.

Halliday, M. A. K. (1977). *Learning how to mean: Explorations in the development of language*. New York: Elsevier.

Hampton, K., Rainie, L., Lu, W., Dwyer, M., Shin, I., & Purcell, K. (2014). Social Media and the 'Spiral of Silence'. *Pew Internet Research Project*. Retrieved from http://www.pewinternet.org/files/2014/08/PI_Social-networks-and-debate_082614.pdf

Han, J., Choi, D., Chun, B., Kwon, T., Kim, H., & Choi, Y. (2014). Collecting, organizing, and sharing pins in Pinterest: Interest-driven or social-driven? *Performance Evaluation Review, 42*(1), 15–27. doi:10.1145/2637364.2591996

Harrison, K. (2014). Online negotiations of infertility: Knowledge production in (in)fertility [Blog post]. *Convergence (London), 20*(3), 337–351. doi:10.1177/1354856514531400

Hartman, D. K., Morsink, P. M., & Zheng, J. (2010). From print to pixels: The evolution of cognitive conceptions of reading comprehension. In E. A. Baker (Ed.), *The new literacies: Multiple perspectives on research and practice* (pp. 131–164). New York: Guilford Press.

Hatch, J. A. (2002). *Doing qualitative research in education settings*. Albany, NY: State University of New York Press.

Henn, S. (2012, April 18). From Silicon Valley, a new approach to education. *National Public Radio*. Retrieved from http://www.npr.org/blogs/alltechconsidered/2012/04/18/150846845/from-silicon-valley-a-new-approach-to-education

Hestres, L. (2008, March). *The blogs of war: Online activism, agenda setting and the Iraq war*. Paper presented at the meeting of the International Studies Association, San Francisco, CA.

Hobbs, R. (2010). *Digital and media literacy: A plan of action. A white paper on the digital and media literacy recommendations of the Knight Commission on the information needs of communities in a democracy*. Washington, DC: The Aspen Institute, Communications and Society Program.

Honan, M. (2013, December 30). I, Glasshole: My year with Google Glass. *Wired*. Retrieved from http://www.wired.com/2013/12/glasshole/

Howard, P., & Hussain, M. M. (2011). The upheavals in Egypt and Tunisia: The role of digital media. *Journal of Democracy, 22*(3), 35–48. doi:10.1353/jod.2011.0041

Howard, P. N., Duffy, A., Freelon, D., Hussain, M., Mari, W., & Mazaid, M. (2011). Opening closed regimes: What was the role of social media during the Arab Spring? *Project on Information Technology Political Islam,* 1-30.

Howe, J. (2008). *Crowdsourcing: How the power of the crowd is driving the future of business.* Great Britain: Business Books.

Huang, C. (2011). Facebook and Twitter key to Arab Spring uprisings: Report. *The National UAE.* Retrieved from http://www.thenational.ae/news/uae-news/facebook-and-twitter-key-to-arab-spring-uprisings-report#ixzz3GMtr6Mwa

Hutchison, A., & Reinking, D. (2011). Teachers' perceptions of integrating information and communication technologies into literacy instruction: A national survey in the United States. *Reading Research Quarterly, 46*(4), 312–333.

Jayson, S. (2014, March 12). Social media research raises privacy and ethics issues. *USA Today.* Retrieved November 7, 2014, from http://www.usatoday.com/story/news/nation/2014/03/08/data-online-behavior-research/5781447/

Jenkins, H. (2006, June 19). *Welcome to Convergence Culture* [Blog post]. Retrieved from http://henryjenkins.org/2006/06/welcome_to_convergence_culture.html

Karlsson, M. (2012). Charting the liquidity of online news moving towards a method for content analysis of online news. *International Communication Gazette, 74*(4), 385–402. doi:10.1177/1748048512439823

Kelly, H. (2013, April 26). *After Boston: The pros and cons of surveillance cameras.* Retrieved from http://www.cnn.com/2013/04/26/tech/innovation/security-cameras-boston-bombings/

Kirkland, A. (2014, February 4). *10 countries where Facebook has been banned.* Retrieved from http://www.indexoncensorship.org/2014/02/10-countries-facebook-banned/

Kuiper, E., & Volman, M. (2008). The Web as a source of information for students in K–12 education. In J. Coiro, M. Knobel, C. Lankshear, & D. Leu (Eds.), *Handbook of research on new literacies* (pp. 241–246). Mahwah, NJ: Lawrence Erlbaum.

Leander, K. M., & Boldt, G. (2013). Rereading "A pedagogy of multiliteracies": Texts, identities, and futures. *Journal of Literacy Research, 45*(1), 22–46. doi:10.1177/1086296X12468587

Lenhart, A., & Madden, M. (2007). Teens, privacy & online social networks: How teens manage their online identities and personal information in the age of MySpace. *Pew Internet Research Project.* Retrieved from http://www.pewinternet.org/2007/04/18/teens-privacy-and-online-social-networks/

Leu, D. J. (2006). New literacies, reading research, and the challenges of change: A deictic perspective. In J. V. Hoffman, D. L. Schallert, C. M. Fairbanks, J. Worthy, & B. Maloch (Eds.), *Fifty-fifth National Reading Conference Yearbook* (pp. 1-20). Oak Creek, WI: National Reading Conference.

Leu, D. J., Forzani, E., Burlingame, C., Kulikowich, J., Sedransk, N., Coiro, J., & Kennedy, C. (2013). The new literacies of online research and comprehension: Assessing and preparing students for the 21st century with Common Core State Standards. In S. B. Neuman & L. B. Gambrell (Eds.), *Quality Reading Instruction in the Age of Common Core Standards* (pp. 219–236). Newark, DE: International Reading Association. doi:10.1598/0496.16

Leu, D. J., Forzani, E., Rhoads, C., Maykel, C., Kennedy, C., & Timbrell, N. (in press). The new literacies of online research and comprehension: Rethinking the reading achievement gap. *Reading Research Quarterly*.

Leu, D. J. Jr, & Kinzer, C. K. (2000). The convergence of literacy instruction and networked technologies for information and communication. *Reading Research Quarterly*, *35*(1), 108–127. doi:10.1598/RRQ.35.1.8

Leu, D. J., & Kinzer, C. K. (2003). Toward a theoretical framework of new literacies on the Internet: Central principles. In J. C. Richards & M. C. McKenna (Eds.), *Integrating multiple literacies in K-8 classrooms: Cases, commentaries, and practical applications* (pp. 18–37). Mahwah, NJ: Lawrence Erlbaum Associates, Publishers.

Leu, D.J., McVerry, J.G., O'Byrne, W. I., Kiili, C., Zawilinski, L. Everett-Cacopardo, H., Kennedy, C., & Forzani, E. (2011). The new literacies of online reading comprehension: Expanding the literacy and learning curriculum. *Journal of Adolescent and Adult Literacy, 55*(1), 5-14. International Reading Association. doi:10.1598/JAAL.55.1.1

Lévy, P., & Bononno, R. (1998). *Becoming virtual: reality in the digital age*. Da Capo Press, Incorporated.

Lortie, D. C. (1975). *Schoolteacher: A sociological study*. Chicago: University of Chicago.

Mace, M. (2010, March 19). Why e-books failed in 2000, and what it means for 2010. *Business Insider*. Retrieved from www.businessinsider.com/why-ebooks-failed-in-2000-and-what-it-means-for-2010-2010

MacMillan, D. (2013, November 20). *Snapchat CEO: 70% of users are women* [Blog post]. Retrieved from http://blogs.wsj.com/digits/2013/11/20/snapchat-ceo-says-70-of-users-are-women/

Madden, M., Fox, S., Smith, A., & Vitak, J. (2007). Digital footprints: Online identity management and search in the age of transparency. *Pew Internet Research Project*. Retrieved from http://www.pewinternet.org/files/old-media/Files/Reports/2007/PIP_Digital_Footprints.pdf.pdf

Malone, T. W., & Bernstein, M. S. (in press). Introduction. In *Collective intelligence handbook*. Boston: MIT Press. Retrieved from https://docs.google.com/document/d/1CRVN8uxa_g8i3oL-RfVxhsltWNZ_ZMwoI-pl5IosG9VU/edit?pli=1

Markoff, J. (2006, November 12). Entrepreneurs see a web guided by common sense. *New York Times*. Retrieved from http://www.nytimes.com/2006/11/12/business/12web.html?pagewanted=all&_r=0

Mayer, R. E. (2008). Multimedia literacy. In J. Coiro, M. Knobel, C. Lankshear, & D. J. Leu (Eds.), *Handbook of research on new literacies* (pp. 359–376). New York: Taylor and Francis Group.

Mazoue, J. G. (2013). Five myths about MOOCs. *Educause Review Online*. Retrieved from http://www.educause.edu/ero/article/five-myths-about-moocs

McAuley, A., Stewart, B., Siemens, G., & Cormier, D. (2010). *The MOOC model for digital practice*. Retrieved from https://oerknowledgecloud.org/sites/oerknowledgecloud.org/files/MOOC_Final_0.pdf

McChesney, R. W. (2013). *Digital disconnect: How capitalism is turning the Internet against democracy*. New York: New Press.

Metz, R. (2013). Now you see it, now you don't: Disappearing messages are everywhere. *MIT Technology Review*. Retrieved from http://www.technologyreview.com/news/513006/now-you-see-it-now-you-dont-disappearing-messages-are-everywhere/

Mikulecky, L. (2010). An examination of workplace literacy research from new literacies and sociocultural perspectives. In E. A. Baker (Ed.), *The new literacies: Multiple perspectives on research and practice* (pp. 217–241). New York: Guilford Press.

Miller, J. D., & Hufstedler, S. M. (2009, Jun 28). *Cyberbullying knows no borders.* Paper presented at the Annual Conference of the Australian Teacher Education Association, Albury.

Miller, M. (2013). *Sams teach yourself Vine in 10 minutes.* Indianapolis, IN: Sams.

Miller, S. M. (2013). A research metasynthesis on digital video composing in classrooms: An evidence-based framework toward a pedagogy for embodied learning. *Journal of Literacy Research, 45*(4), 386–430. doi:10.1177/1086296X13504867

Mishna, F., Khoury-Kassabri, M., Gadalla, T., & Daciuk, J. (2012). Risk factors for involvement in cyber bullying: Victims, bullies and bully–victims. *Children and Youth Services Review, 34*(1), 63–70. doi:10.1016/j.childyouth.2011.08.032

Mitchell, A. (2014, March 26) *State of the news media 2014.* Retrieved from www.journalism.org/packages/state-of-the-news-media-2014

Mitchell, K. J., Finkelhor, D., Wolak, J., Ybarra, M. L., & Turner, H. (2010). Youth Internet victimization in a broader victimization context. *The Journal of Adolescent Health, 48*(2), 128–134. doi:10.1016/j.jadohealth.2010.06.009 PMID:21257110

No, C. L. B. (2002). (NCLB) Act of 2001, Pub. L. No. 107-110, § 115. *Stat,* 1425.

Noelle-Neumann, E. (1974). The spiral of silence: A theory of public opinion. *Journal of Communication, 24*(2), 43–51. doi:10.1111/j.1460-2466.1974.tb00367.x

Noelle-Neumann, E. (1993). *The Spiral of Silence: Public Opinion - Our Social Skin.* Chicago, IL: University of Chicago Press.

Olmstead, K., Mitchell, A., & Rosenstiel, T. (2011). *Audio: By the numbers* [Report]. Retrieved from http://stateofthemedia.org/2011/audio-essay/data-page/

Peirce, C. S. (1991). *Peirce on signs: Writings on semiotic.* Chapel Hill, NC: University of North Carolina Press.

Pew Research Center's Journalism Project Staff. (2012, July 16). YouTube and news: A new kind of visual news. *Pew Research Journalism Project.* Retrieved from http://www.journalism.org/2012/07/16/youtube-news/

Podcast. (n.d.). In *Merriam-Webster.com.* Retrieved from http://www.merriam-webster.com/dictionary/podcasts

Prensky, M. (2001). Digital natives, digital immigrants. *On the Horizon, 9*(5), 1–6. doi:10.1108/10748120110424816

Proctor, C. P., Dalton, B., & Grisham, D. L. (2007). Scaffolding English language learners and struggling readers in a universal literacy environments with embedded strategy instruction and vocabulary support. *Journal of Literacy Research, 39*(1), 71–93.

Production. (n.d.). In *Merriam-Webster.com.* Retrieved from http://www.merriam-webster.com/dictionary/production

Public. (n.d.). In *Merriam-Webster.com.* Retrieved from http://www.merriam-webster.com/dictionary/public

Purcell, K. (2013, October 10). Online video 2013. *Pew Internet Research Project.* Retrieved from www.pewinternet.org/2013/10/10/online-video-2013

Radicati, S. (2013). Email statistics report, 2009-2013. The Radicati Group, Inc.

Rainie, L., Kiesler, S., Kang, R., Madden, M., Duggan, M., Brown, S., & Dabbish, L. (2013). Anonymity, privacy, and security online. *Pew Internet Research Project*. Retrieved from http://www.pewinternet.org/2013/09/05/anonymity-privacy-and-security-online/

Rainie, L., & Tancer, B. (2007, April 24). Wikipedia users. *Pew Internet Research Project*. Retrieved from http://www.pewinternet.org/2007/04/24/wikipedia-users/

Rand, A. C. (2010). Mediating at the student-Wikipedia intersection. *Journal of Literacy Administration*, *507*(7-8), 923–932. doi:10.1080/01930826.2010.488994

Rees, J. (2013). The MOOC racket: Widespread online-only higher ed will be disastrous for students—and most professors. *Slate*. Retrieved from http://www.slate.com/articles/technology/future_tense/2013/07/moocs_could_be_disastrous_for_students_and_professors.html

Reinking, D. (1998). Synthesizing technological transformations of literacy in a post typographic world. In D. Reinking, M. C. McKenna, L. D. Labbo, & R. Kieffer (Eds.), *Handbook of literacy and technology: Technological transformations in a post-typographic world* (pp. xi–xxx). Mahwah, NJ: Erlbaum.

Reznik, M. (2012). Identity theft on social networking sites: Developing issues of Internet impersonation. *Touro Law Review*, *29*, 455.

Rheingold, H. (2007). *Smart mobs: The next social revolution*. Basic books.

Ruiz, J. (2013, December 14). *The cloud and the crowd: Distributed cognition and collective intelligence*. [Blog Post]. Retrieved from https://blogs.commons.georgetown.edu/cctp-797-fall2013/archives/699

Salem, F., & Mourtada, R. (2011). Civil movements: The impact of Facebook and Twitter. *The Arab Social Media Report*, *1*(2), 1.

Sandelowski, M., & Barroso, J. (2007). *Handbook for synthesizing qualitative research*. New York, NY: Springer.

Sanou, B. (2014). ICT facts and figures. *WORLD (Oakland, Calif.)*, *2014*.

Scheer, P. (2014, December 17). EU bureaucrats want to dictate what content Americans can view on U.S.-based websites. *Huffington Post*. Retrieved from http://www.huffingtonpost.com/peter-scheer/eu-bureaucrats-want-to-di_b_6342762.html

Schlosberg, M., & Ozer, N. (2007, August 1). *Under the watchful eye: The proliferation of video surveillance systems in California*. Retrieved from http://www.aclunc.org/publications/under-watchful-eye-proliferation-video-surveillance-systems-california

Shapiro, A., & Meyer, D. (2014, November 28). A closer look at EU Parliament's vote to break up Google. In NPR (Producer), *All Things Considered*. Retrieved from http://www.npr.org/2014/11/28/367244283/a-closer-look-at-eu-parliaments-vote-to-break-up-google

Shu, W., & Yu-Hao, C. (2011). The behavior of wiki users. *Social Behavior and Personality*, *39*(6), 851–864. doi:10.2224/sbp.2011.39.6.851

Smith, C. (2014a, October 7). By the numbers: 140 amazing Pinterest statistics. *Digital Marketing Ramblings*. Retrieved from http://expandedramblings.com/index.php/pinterest-stats/5/

Smith, C. (2014b, July 24). *Newsflash: Pinterest is very popular on phones (new and updated stats)* (Rep.). *Digital Marketing Ramblings*. Retrieved from http://expandedramblings.com/index.php/new-updated-pinterest-stats-2/

Smith, C. (2014c, October 1). By the numbers: 60 amazing YouTube statistics. *Digital Marketing Ramblings*. Retrieved from http://expandedramblings.com/index.php/youtube-statistics/

Smith, C. (2014d, October 6). How much time do users spend on Facebook each day? (New and updated Facebook stats). *Digital Marketing Ramblings*. Retrieved from http://expandedramblings.com/index.php/much-time-users-spend-facebook-day-new-updated-facebook-stats/

Sontag, S. (2004, May 22). Regarding the torture of others. *New York Times*. Retrieved from http://www.nytimes.com/2004/05/23/magazine/regarding-the-torture-of-others.html

Soukup, P. A. (2014). Looking at, with, and through YouTube. *Communication Research Trends*, *33*(3), 3–34.

Stein, P. (2008). Multimodal instructional practices. In J. Coiro, M. Knobel, C. Lankshear, & D. J. Leu (Eds.), *Handbook of research on new literacies* (pp. 871–898). New York: Taylor and Francis Group.

Steinkuehler, C. (2007). Massively multiplayer online gaming as a constellation of literacy practices. *E-learning*, *4*(3), 297–318. doi:10.2304/elea.2007.4.3.297

Sterne, J., Morris, J., Baker, M. B., & Freire, A. M. (2008). The politics of podcasting. *The Fibreculture Journal*, *13*.

Stewart, B. (2013). Massiveness + openness = new literacies of participation? *MERLOT Journal of Online Learning and Teaching*, *9*(2), 228–238.

Strangelove, M. (2010). *Watching YouTube: Extraordinary videos by ordinary people*. Toronto: University of Toronto Press.

Support. (n.d.). In *Snapchat.com*. Retrieved from https://support.snapchat.com/ca/snaps

Thomas, A. (2007). Blurring and breaking through the boundaries of narrative, literacy, and identity in adolescent fan fiction. In M. Knobel & C. Lankshear (Eds.), *A new literacies sampler* (pp. 137–166). NY: Peter Lang.

Transitory. (n.d.). In *Merriam-Webster.com*. Retrieved from http://www.merriam-webster.com/dictionary/transitory

Vander Veer, E. A. (2008). *Facebook: The missing manual*. Sebastopol, CA: O'Reilly Media.

Walrave, M., & Heirman, W. (2011). Cyberbullying: Predicting victimization and perpetration. *Children & Society*, *25*(1), 59–72. doi:10.1111/j.1099-0860.2009.00260.x

Wang, Y. (2013, March 25). *More people have cell phones than toilets, U.N. study shows*. Retrieved from http://newsfeed.time.com/2013/03/25/more-people-have-cell-phones-than-toilets-u-n-study-shows/

Wasike, J. (2013). Social media ethical issues: Role of a librarian. *Library Hi Tech News*, *30*(1), 8–16. doi:10.1108/07419051311320922

Weiss, A. (2005). The power of collective intelligence. *Networker*, *9*(3), 16–23. doi:10.1145/1086762.1086763

Wikipedia About. (n.d.). In *Wikipedia.org*. Retrieved November 7, 2014 from http://en.wikipedia.org/wiki/Wikipedia:About

WikiWikiWeb. (n.d.). In *Wikipedia.org*. Retrieved November 3, 2014 from http://en.wikipedia.org/wiki/WikiWikiWeb

Wolf, M. (2014, January 3). Four predictions about podcasting for 2014. *Forbes*. Retrieved from http://www.forbes.com/sites/michaelwolf/2014/01/03/4-predictions-about-podcasting-for-2014/

Wong, K. (2014, October 22). Why marketers should put Snapchat on their home screen. *Forbes*. Retrieved from http://www.forbes.com/sites/kylewong/2014/10/22/why-marketers-should-put-snapchat-on-their-homescreen/

Wong-Lo, M., & Bullock, L. M. (2011). Digital aggression: Cyberworld meets school bullies. *Preventing School Failure*, *55*(2), 64–70. doi:10.1080/1045988X.2011.539429

Wooley, A. W., Chabris, C. F., Pentland, A., Hashmi, N., & Malone, T. W. (2010). Evidence for a collective intelligence factor in the performance of human groups. *Science*, *330*(6004), 686–688. doi:10.1126/science.1193147 PMID:20929725

Wyatt-Smith, C., & Elkins, J. (2008). Multimodal reading and comprehension in online environments. In J. Coiro, M. Knobel, C. Lankshear, & D. J. Leu (Eds.), *Handbook of research on new literacies* (pp. 899–940). New York: Taylor and Francis Group.

Yee, N. (2006). The demographics, motivations and derived experiences of users of massively-multiuser online graphical environments. *Presence (Cambridge, Mass.)*, *15*(3), 309–329. doi:10.1162/pres.15.3.309

YouTube. (n.d.). *Statistics*. Retrieved October 29, 2014 from https://www.youtube.com/yt/press/statistics.html

YouTube & News. (2012, July 16) Retrieved from http://www.journalism.org/2012/07/16/youtube-news/

Zickuhr, K. (2010, December 16). Generations 2010. *Pew Internet Research Project*. Retrieved from http://www.pewinternet.org/~/media//Files/Reports/2010/PIP_Generations_and_Tech10

Zuckerman, E. (2013). *Rewire*. New York: W. W. Norton & Company.

KEY TERMS AND DEFINITIONS

Collective Intelligence: Collective intelligence is the phenomenon that emerges when large pools of individuals share, collaborate, and compete thus formulating intelligence that was unattainable by individuals. Examples include collective political action, collective funding, collective medicine, and collective reviews.

Ethereal Captured: Ethereal captured is the phenomenon whereby conversations, actions, and settings that lack substance are electronically captured. When the ethereal is captured, what lacked substance (e.g. conversations, actions, settings) is instantiated and becomes available for replay and dissemination.

New Genres: New genres refer to categories of digital communication that provide unique affordances. Examples include text messages, email, and social networks. Text messages have communication affordances dissimilar to email or social networks.

New Literacies: New literacies refer to the abilities needed to communicate with digital media in ways that were non-existent in a pre-digital era. Examples include the abilities to find online information, use hyperlinks, and compose multimedia texts.

New Pedagogies: New pedagogies refer to the abilities needed to teach with digital media in ways that were impractical or non-existent in a pre-digital era. Focus is placed on the affordances of technology to support learning that were impractical or non-existent in pre-digital era. Examples include using social media to foster the development of a community of learners, asynchronous conversations with a worldwide group of learners and experts to forge collective intelligence, and situating learners in authentic settings via virtual reality.

Spiral of Silence: Spiral of Silence is the phenomenon in which people do not talk about topics that are perceived as unpopular or anticipated to be ill received.

Transitory: Transitory is the characteristic of being fleeting, temporary; something that lasts a short time.

Verbocentric: Verbocentric refers to phenomena that are dominated by words. Examples include oral language and alphabetic print media.

Web 3.0: Term coined in 2006 by John Markoff of the *New York Times* to characterize a paradigm shift in the evolution of the Web from dispensary (Web 1.0) to interactive (Web 2.0) to reciprocal (Web 3.0) whereby instead of users reading the Web, as done with Web 1.0 and 2.0, the Web also reads the users. Examples include cookies, algorithms, and artificial intelligence that personalizes what users receive as they explore the Internet.

Chapter 6
New Visual Literacies and Competencies for Education and the Workplace

Julie A. Delello
The University of Texas at Tyler, USA

Rochell R. McWhorter
The University of Texas at Tyler, USA

ABSTRACT

This chapter examines how new visual literacies allow students to create meaning and develop competencies needed for the 21st century. Today's generation is continually exposed to visual and digital media. Through empirical work, this chapter highlights how emerging visual technologies such as big data, infographics, digital badges, electronic portfolios (ePortfolios), visual social media, and augmented reality are facilitating the development of technology-related skills required for students in academics and in the workforce. Each visual technology platform will be examined for their usefulness in promoting engagement, subject-matter knowledge, and collaborative learning outside the traditional classroom approach.

INTRODUCTION

The design of visual information is not a new concept. Historically, humans have been utilizing images to communicate with each other for thousands of years. From pictograms on cave walls to Egyptian hieroglyphics to modern day data visualizations, humans have utilized graphic depictions as a representation of information (Krum, 2013). In fact, visual information is one of the most effective forms of communication for humans (Beegel, 2014; HP, 2004) more

than 80% of learning takes place visually when compared to what's read in text alone. We are a society barraged with images through advertising, television, and the Internet. According to Lester (2013), "Something is happening. We are becoming a visually mediated society. For many, an understanding of the world is being accomplished, not through reading words, but by reading images" (p. 423). Thus, the use of visual imagery is significantly changing what it means to be literate in the 21ˢᵗ century (Hattwig, Bussert, Medaille, &, Burgess, 2011).

DOI: 10.4018/978-1-4666-8310-5.ch006

Figure 1. Tsunami Hazard Sign to denote a tsunami evacuation area
Image in Public Domain. Source: http://commons.wikimedia. org/wiki/File:TsunamiHazardSign.svg

Visual literacy is the ability to ascertain and use images. According to The Association of College and Research Libraries, *visual literacy* is a group of skills that "enables an individual to effectively find, interpret, evaluate, use, and create images and visual media" (Hattwig, et. al. 2011, para. 2). Visual literacy is the combination of both images and text. And, "although visual perception seems to precede any textual explanations, the combination of images, media, and new technologies will require students to be multi-literate" (Delello & McWhorter, 2013, p. 2).

For example, to the uninformed tourist, a road sign (See Figure 1) may not be recognizable as a hazard but certainly may make the difference between safety and loss of life. By being visually literate as to the meaning of the road sign (entering a tsunami-prone area), the traveler will be able to more readily adhere to natural and man-made warnings should a tsunami be of imminent danger. According to Lester (2013), street signs that indicate dangerous conditions are icons that represent a safety issue requiring acute visual literacy skills to insure the safety of the individual and possibly others in the vicinity.

The traditional notion of literacy in the form of reading and writing is expanding as new technologies become available. In fact, Leu, Kinzer, Coiro, & Cammack (2004) reported that the definition of literacy is a moving target, changing at a pace never

before experienced due to the prolific growth of information communication technologies (ICTs) and the demands of society. The world as we know it is influenced by both images and technology. And, we will need visual and technological literacies to understand and process the volumes of data in this age of information (Burmark, 2002).

Overview of the Research

Pritchard and O'Hara (2009) suggested that "in addition to being able to communicate in oral and written form, to be considered truly literate, one must be able to think critically, reason logically, and use technology" (p. 15). This view is reinforced by the International Reading Association (2002) in its position on literacy and technology, which stated: "Traditional definitions of reading, writing, and viewing, and traditional definitions of best-practice instruction—derived from a long tradition of book and other print media—will be insufficient" (p. 2). Additionally, these new forms of literacy will "fuse visual literacy with innovative forms of technology and digital communications" (Delello & McWhorter, 2013, p. 369). Visual literacy, also known as visual competencies, allows students to function in an increasingly digital and visual workplace through the use of computer applications to share images, presentations, and understand data from images. All of which will require students "to learn to communicate with visual language, to become skilled at information visualization presentation, and to master the tools of visual knowledge" (Marcum, 2002, p. 201). Each of these factors must be considered to connect to the digital learner of today.

We must also consider the need for the development of student visual competencies, which are not always aligned with that of academia or faculty (Hattwig, et. al, 2011). Also, a review of the literature reveals new visual technologies are not generally integrated into higher education. *Visual technology* is defined as "any form of apparatus designed either to be looked at or to enhance natural vision, from oil paintings to television and the Internet" (Mirzoeff, 1998, p. 3). Visual technologies include those such as *visual social media* (Pinterest, Facebook; Delello & McWhorter, 2013; Delello, McWhorter, & Camp, in press), *virtual reality platforms* (QR codes, augmented reality; virtual worlds; Ausburn & Ausburn, 2014; Mancuso, Chlup & McWhorter, 2010; Perey, 2011), and the *use of graphics* (infographics; big data visualizations; Krum, 2013). Also, Delello & McWhorter (2013) recommended that additional research be conducted to examine the value of instructing students in visual platforms, examining both the student as well as the employer perspective. One such example is a pilot study of pre-service teachers in their development of visual literacy for themselves then the application of these skills to the K-12 classroom with documented success (Fattal, 2012).

The proliferation of the Internet has created a highly competitive marketplace where businesses are constantly challenged to attract customers leading to a content-driven culture (Alexander & Parsehian, 2014) necessitating visual literacy skills (Moritz, 2014). The following sections of this chapter will discuss how visual literacy will reshape our educational practices and better prepare students for working in the 21st century. Topics include the use emerging digital media including big data, infographics, digital badges, electronic portfolios, visual social media, and augmented reality. Additionally, each section provides a broad overview of the implications that the arrival of such media has created for education and the workforce.

Big Data

The term *big data* represents an enormous array of information from both traditional and digital sources produced and consumed on a daily basis. IBM (2014) described the term big data as information being produced by every digital process and social media exchange transmitted by

Figure 2. The Complexity of Big Data

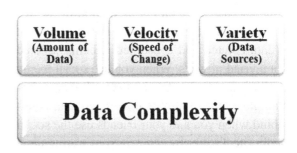

systems, sensors and mobile devices: "Big data is arriving from multiple sources at an alarming velocity, volume and variety (see Figure 2). To extract meaningful value from big data, you need optimal processing power, analytics capabilities and skills" (IBM, 2014, para. 1).

In order to understand where the alarming velocity, volume, and variety of data come from, consider the video titled *Did You Know 2014,* a derivative of the original video *Shift Happens* (Rose, Fisch, & McLeod, 2011):

More than 150 million people will be born in 2014...they will be born into a data economy... never has data been so important. Never has technology been so focused on the access of data. We are currently preparing students for jobs that don't exist...using technologies that haven't been invented...in order to solve problems that we don't even know are problems yet. We are in the age of visual data. More than 4,000 books are published every day. It is estimated that a week's worth of The New York Times, contains more information than a person was likely to come across in a lifetime in the 18th Century. 3.5 zetabytes (3.5 x 10^{21}) of unique information will be created worldwide this year. That is more than in the previous 5,000 years. The amount of technology information is doubling every two years.

The amount of digital data generated is staggering—according to IBM, 90% of data that existed in the world in 2013 was created in the prior two years (Petronzio, 2013). Further, although the video estimates are only a prediction of the advancement of our global society, the daily amount of data created and consumed is being utilized in a myriad of ways. When you use social media like Twitter, you leave behind a trail of data. For example, you can look at how much data is left behind when you and your friends use the social media site Twitter by entering your username at the following Website: http://www.cartridgesave. co.uk/printeffect/ .

From improving health care and advancing education to creating an efficient economy, big data is shifting the current way we do business (Cukier & Viktor Mayer-Schonberger, 2013). For example, in higher education, The WICHE Cooperative for Educational Technologies along with several colleges and universities produced the Predictive Analytics Reporting Framework which housed over 3 million pieces of data from student records (Fain, 2012). This data aided institutions in identifying which student variables (demographics, course type, course load) might impact student performance and retention. Likewise, IBM and the Wroclaw University Library created the largest digital archive of data consisting of approximately 800,000 pages (300 terabytes) of mediaeval European manuscripts, books, and old maps rarely seen in public (PR, 2013). According to Ramirez (2011), "the identification, collection and preservation of digital data created as a result of research is an important issue, particularly because the sharing and reuse of raw research outputs offer great potential for subsequent recombination, analysis, insight and discovery" (p. 21). Overall, a vast amount of data is being produced in education which has the potential to provide valuable information to schools in terms of overall student outcomes.

Big data is likewise influencing industry. Intel (2013) noted that big data is "creating unprecedented opportunities for businesses to achieve deeper, faster insights that can strengthen decision making, improve customer experience, and accelerate the pace of innovation" (p. 3). For example, institutions in the private and public healthcare sector are using new operating models relying on big data and advanced analytics to provide fully digitized networks and services (Biesdorf & Niedermann, 2014; IBM, 2014). According to Schmarzo (2013), advanced analytics for transforming vital business processes include: *procurement* (identifying suppliers), *product development* (insights to speed development processes), *manufacturing* (identifying quality problems), *distribution* (derive optimal inventory and supply chain activities), *marketing* (optimizing marketing mix), *pricing* (perishable goods price optimization), *store operations* (inventory level predictions), and *human resources* (identify characteristics for star employees).

For the average person, a large concept like "big data" might be confusing; however, on the personal level, big data is quite useful. For instance, the end user (the individual) benefits when companies utilize big data analysis such as the added convenience when airlines improve their arrival time estimates (Brynjolfsson & McAfee, 2012) or when companies make helpful purchase suggestions on websites such as Amazon or Netflix based on purchases by millions of their customers who had a similar taste in products (Harvard Magazine, 2014).

There is a connection between big data and visual literacy. Data, according to Tufte (2001), can be communicated through words, numbers, and pictures. In fact, Tufte acknowledged that well-designed images or graphical displays are the most effective and powerful way to describe large sets of numbers. Biller, Gorlenko, and McColgin (2014) indicated that designing and understanding "data visualization" is the new literacy… by using visuals to communicate vast amounts of data, we are better able to see the big picture, recognize patterns, and make comparisons.

Infographics

According to Gareth Cook, Pulitzer Prize-winning science journalist and series editor of the *Best American Infographics,* we are in an "era of big data, a time when information moves faster than ever, and infographics provide us with quick, often influential bursts of insight and knowledge" (Cook, 2013). Infographic is an abbreviation for "information graphics." In other words, an infographic is a visual representation of data (see Figure 3). Once used only by art directors and in print publications, the term infographic, according to Krum (2013), has evolved into a new definition of graphic design that merges data visualizations, text, illustrations, and images together for the purposes informing, entertaining, or persuading an audience. Therefore, an infographic is a type of picture that blends data with design to communicate messages (Smiciklas, 2012).

An infographic helps users visualize the "big picture" of an idea that might otherwise be difficult to understand and facilitate new ways of thinking when linked with particular topics. Tufte (2001) stated that "Graphics reveal data" [by focusing] "the viewer's attention to the sense and substance of the data" (p. 91). Infographics are a powerful and fascinating way to see and understand the world around us (Jackson, 2014).

Using Infographics in Education

The shift to visual communication is having an impact on education (Delello & McWhorter, 2013) whereas infographics are becoming an important teaching tool. Mark Smiciklas (2012), author of *The Power of Infographics: Using Pictures to Communicate and Connect with Your Audiences* contends that "infographics combine data with design to enable visual learning. This communication process helps deliver complex information in a way that is more quickly and easily understood" (p. 4). When infographics are used in the classroom, students are fully engaged not only in

carrying out the research for classroom projects but also in presenting the result of their research to their peers (see Figure 4).

Davidson (2014) found that when students used and created infographics, they made a deeper connection to the content than with text or PowerPoint presentations. Infographics became a tool to help her students identify and exhibit important information contributing to higher order thinking skills. Furthermore, research has shown that "the use of well-designed visual representations can replace cognitive calculations with simple perceptual inferences and improve comprehension, memory, and decision making" (Heer, Bostock, & Ogievetsky, 2010, p. 59). Also, it was suggested through the creation of infographics, students learn several literacy goals including:

- Learning appropriate methods for filtering information to find credible sources;
- Learning how to locate copyright-free pictures or how to take their own in order to illustrate a point; and
- Learning how to sort through data and interpret what they found and to decide what they could use to provide evidence for their claims (Davidson, 2014, p. 37).

Students learn and remember best through visual images, not through written text or spoken words (Burmark, 2002; Kostelnick & Roberts, 2010; Medina, 2014). Infographics use color, images, and text to visually convey a snapshot of information that students can begin to deconstruct and understand (Kimmel, 2013). Infographics, according to Lamb and Johnson (2014), can become an invitation to inquiry. These graphical depictions of data connect students to complex sets of information, while building their representational competence and 21st century literacy skills (Lamb, Polman, Newman, & Smith, 2014).

Figure 3. Home Gardening Infographic
2011 Copyright Mother Nature Network (MNN.com) and Russell McLendon. Used with permission for print publication.

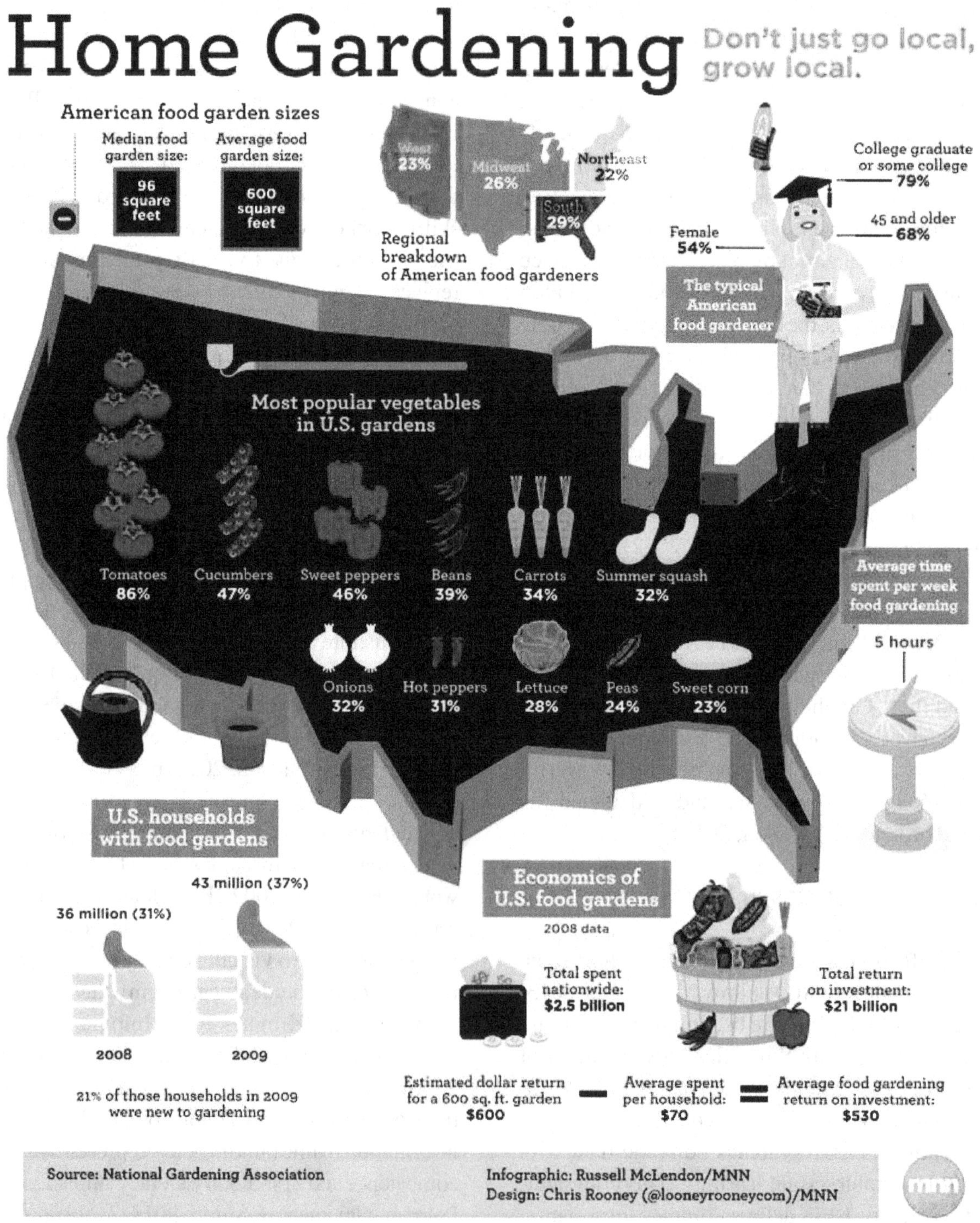

Home Gardening Don't just go local, grow local.

American food garden sizes

Median food garden size:
96 square feet

Average food garden size:
600 square feet

West **23%**
Midwest **26%**
Northeast **22%**
South **29%**

Regional breakdown of American food gardeners

The typical American food gardener

Female **54%**
College graduate or some college **79%**
45 and older **68%**

Most popular vegetables in U.S. gardens

Tomatoes **86%**
Cucumbers **47%**
Sweet peppers **46%**
Beans **39%**
Carrots **34%**
Summer squash **32%**

Onions **32%**
Hot peppers **31%**
Lettuce **28%**
Peas **24%**
Sweet corn **23%**

Average time spent per week food gardening

5 hours

U.S. households with food gardens

36 million (31%)
2008

43 million (37%)
2009

21% of those households in 2009 were new to gardening

Economics of U.S. food gardens

2008 data

Total spent nationwide: **$2.5 billion**

Total return on investment: **$21 billion**

Estimated dollar return for a 600 sq. ft. garden **$600** — Average spent per household: **$70** = Average food gardening return on investment: **$530**

Source: National Gardening Association

Infographic: Russell McLendon/MNN
Design: Chris Rooney (@looneyrooneycom)/MNN

Figure 4. Student Infographic Created for a Kindergarten Science Lesson
Copyright 2014 Sherry Spraggins. Used with Permission.

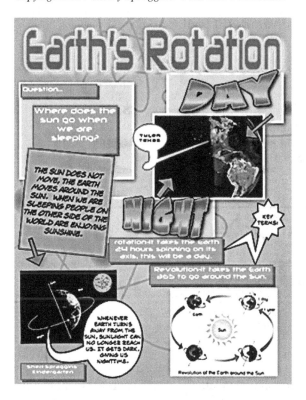

Using Infographics in the Workplace

Organizations have begun utilizing infographics for numerous reasons. According to Lankow, Crooks and Ritchie (2012), the primary reason that infographics have found popularity in business is due to the increased use of these visuals in online marketing campaigns. Further, speaking to business professionals, Lewis (2013) remarked that infographics are "a highly engaging method for presenting content to your target audience" (para. 5). Also, Business Wire (2013) added that infographics are a way for brands to demonstrate "value with their audiences in simple shareable format- they represent a chance to extend the reach of a marketing message" (para. 2) that is accomplished through the sharing of content that

connects the brand with relevant issues. Thus, organizations will need to discern how an infographic might be advantageous to advance their mission.

In addition to the use of infographics for marketing, organizations also utilize infographics for *data visualization* which has been defined as "the study of the visual representation of data" (Mashable, 2013, para. 1). Data visualization can be very useful in understanding complex data. For instance, in the case of NASA (2013), an infographic was designed to depict and explain the seven-minute time period for the entry, descent, and landing phases of the land rover named Curiosity to travel to the Mars surface. Also, the National Oceanic and Atmospheric Administration (NOAA) utilize infographics for data visualization such as hurricanes, ocean debris, and marine life (NOAA.gov, 2014). See Figure 5 that illustrates the 25-year recovery of the Alaskan ecosystem following the 1989 Exxon Valdez Oil Spill.

The Huffington Post recently published an article of why businesses should be using infographics. Among the reasons cited in the article was the notion that when an infographic utilizes appropriate design, layout, and content it can "provide the serious return on investment (ROI) that every business owner desires" (Long, 2013, para. 4). Further, as infographics are considered a tool for engaging others in usable content, a well-designed infographic often results in sharing it on relevant websites and Google now gives credit for those content creators that inspire "natural link building" (para. 3) and Google increases their website ranking accordingly. The digital literacies utilized in creating infographics should also be a concern of business educators at the university level. For instance, Toth (2013) discussed the value of teaching infographics in business courses at the university level and remarked that infographics are a way to teach business communication skills such as "presenting information clearly and succinctly, targeting audiences, defining

Figure 5. Infographic depicting the timeline of recovery from the 1989 Exxon Valdez Oil Spill
Created by NOAA (2014). Used with Permission.

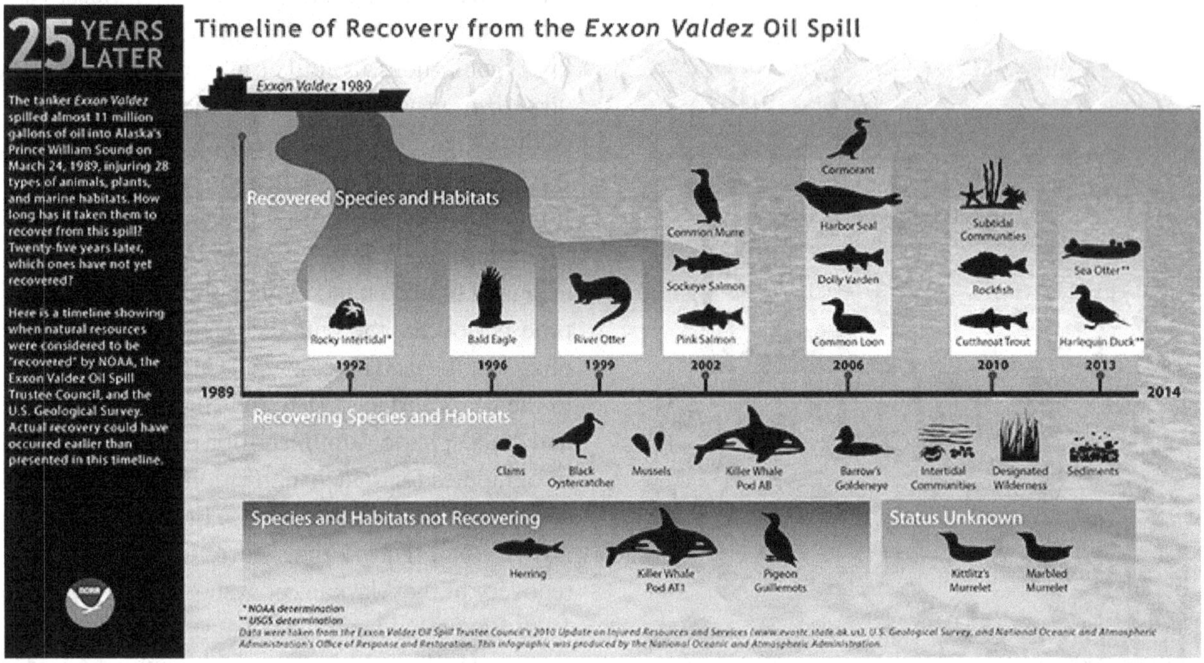

clear purposes, developing ethos, understanding document design principles, using persuasion techniques, effectively branding, and conducting and summarizing research" (p. 451) prior to students' entry into the workforce.

Digital Badges

Digital badges are gaining traction in education and the workforce. Digital badges are a visual record of one's accomplishments linked to metadata (Waters, 2013). More than a static visual image, the digital badge is a system of micro-credentials including who earned the badge, who issued the badge, the date the badge was awarded, and the purpose of the badge. Like the familiar merit badge earned by the Boy Scouts and Girl Scouts of America, to earn a digital badge, the recipient must show or demonstrate knowledge in a particular area. Digital badges may also be part of an *open badges infrastructure* (OBI), where a badge may

contain metadata for sharing across social media such as Twitter, Facebook, or LinkedIn (Mozilla, 2014). Such metadata allows for the documentation of the issuer of the badge and details about how it was earned (Carey, 2012).

In K-16 schools, badges are being considered as a means to help students set long-term goals and recognize skills such as leadership and collaboration. For example, Purdue nursing professors are awarding badges to students who showcase skills in the safety and quality of patient care (Purdue, 2014). Also, high school students can take online courses like those offered at Purdue and showcase their badges on college applications (Carey, 2012). According to a recent report by U.S. News and World Report, digital badges have the potential to replace the traditional college diploma (O'Shaughnessy, 2011). For example, massively open online courses (MOOCs) are now integrating badges into learning management systems such as those used by the Kahn Academy. This may create

Figure 6. Dallas Museum of Art (DMA) Digital Badges for Patron Engagement.
Copyright 2014 DMA. Used with Permission.

a disruptive innovation to the current system of higher education replacing or enhancing outdated, traditional ways of measuring and communicating students' skills and knowledge (Nilsson, 2014). Christensen (2008) defined a disruptive innovation as "an innovation that makes a complicated and expensive product simpler and cheaper and thereby attracts a new set of customers" (p. 43). And, United States Secretary of Education Arne Duncan remarked, "Badges can help speed the shift from credentials that simply measure seat time, to ones that more accurately measure competency" (USDE, 2011, para. 13). The use of digital badges shows promise for demonstrating student competencies across education.

Digital badges are not limited to the classroom. For example, badges can document skills such as "computer programming, social media, and even leadership can be proven with a digital badge" (Harven, 2014). They are also being used in non-profits to increase connections with patron. For example, to engage patrons in its collection and expand its role in the cultural life of the region, the Dallas Museum of Art (DMA) launched a new membership model. Moving away from the transaction-based model of traditional museum membership, the Friends model is designed to build long-term engagement with visitors providing "benefits that accrue based on active participation…a key component of the program is a digital tracking system developed by the DMA to better understand visitors' needs and interests,

based on the accumulation of voluntarily provided data" (DMA, 2014, para. 2). Thus, the DMA returned to free admission and also offered a free digital badge program to engage and incentivize patrons in museum activities. Each badge has its own criteria for rewarding various levels of involvement. See Figure 6 for an illustration of several badges available.

Also, the Badge Alliance and the Digital Youth Network partnered with 100 organizations in 2013 to give more than 100,000 children across the greater Chicago area opportunities to learn and earn digital badges. The Cities of Learning initiative has provided youth opportunities to access informal learning experiences such as museums, libraries, and parks for little to no cost. By participating in these experiences, youth may earn badges to showcase their learning. According to Cities of Learning (2014),

Badges level the playing field by highlighting opportunities where any youth can pursue an interest, either online and in the community; by helping create pathways for deepening knowledge and skills; and by connecting youth to encouraging peers and mentors who can help make their dreams come true (para. 15).

According to the Chicago Art Department (CAD), "badges are a new idea to recognize the learning that happens anywhere and share it in the places that matter" (2013, para. 1). The CAD created a useful introductory video titled "What is a badge?" found at: https://www.youtube.com/watch?v=HgLLq7ybDtc#t=125

A recent study by The McKinsey Center for Government reported that the International Labor Organization estimated that 75 million youth are unemployed and at the same time while 40% of employers said that many of the vacancies were due to a lack of skills (Mourshed, Farrell, & Barton, 2012). Further, Everhart (2014) remarked " to prepare their students for the workforce, higher education institutions are beginning to define and issue badges that represent valuable job skills that are in high demand by employers" (para. 8). Also, organizations are currently using digital badge platforms to recognize employee milestones, welcome new hires (Basno, 2014), and as a means to verify continued professional development (University of Illinois, 2014).

Foster (2013) reported that digital badges can supplement a personal resume providing proof to the future employer of an individual's specific skills. "By leveraging interest-driven learning and recognizing skills and competencies wherever they are acquired, badges can illuminate unique and personalized pathways to job, career and civic success" (Reconnect Learning, 2014, para. 1).

Digital badges are rooted in video gaming (Antin & Churchill, 2011) that keeps users playing until they advance to the next level. According to Kapp (2012), the mechanics of game playing includes: "levels, earning badges, point systems, scores, and time constraints" (p. 11). Further, Kapp reported that most games have reward structures and there are two viewpoints on using badges in gaming: (1) make it easy to earn at the beginning of game playing so that a player gets hooked; and, (2) do not use easy badges for sake of reward but should be related to activities that are rewarding themselves. These views should be examined when digital badges are being considered (Buckingham, 2014).

Gibson, Ostashewski, Flintoff, Grant and Knight (2013) noted that digital badges have ap-

peared to any degree in texts of scholarly literature since 2010 likely due to the lag between research to the time allowed for publication. Recently, Vah Seliskar (2014) reported that a variety of companies offer badges to motivate learners in the classroom to:

- Foster deeper learning of course material, as the badges are content driven, specific to the course goals and content;
- Create practical ways for students to learn in the classroom, and to share what they have learned in a public forum if they so choose, such as through Mozilla's open badging platform, or through a class blog, class website, class wiki or another social networking tool; and
- Add an element of fun to the classroom, as students are encouraged to compete against their class (Vah Seliskar, 2014, para. 3). Various platforms offering badges are depicted in Table 1.

Table 1. Resources for Digital Badges for Learning

Company and URL	Description of Resource
Edmodo.com	"A full, social learning platform with over 35 million users. With so many teachers and students already on board, it is worth mentioning that badges are integrated into this platform" (ShakeupLearning.com, 2014, para. 4)
Credly.com	"Allows teachers to create badges, upload their own designs, and give credit through their platform. This easy-to-use application is available as a web version, iOS app, and has an open API to allow integration with other platforms" ShakeupLearning.com, 2014, para. 3).
Openbadges.org	"Mozilla Open Badges are NOT proprietary like most systems. This means that any teacher can create and issue badges that do not have to be tied to a certain platform" (ShakeupLearning.com, 2014, para. 5).

Displaying of badges in a social media encourages performance among peers and recognition of past achievements. Antin and Churchill (2011) noted that "Badges challenge users to meet the mark that is set for them. Goal setting is known to be an effective motivator...Also, badges advertise one's achievements and communicate one's past accomplishments without explicit bragging. More difficult achievements may be assumed to lead to greater status" (p. 3). Therefore, performance can be enhanced through the use of digital badges displayed online.

Electronic Portfolios

Historically, portfolios have been used for a variety of purposes including the showcasing of written or creative work in the fields of history, music, and art. According to the Merriam-Webster (2014) dictionary, the word portfolio is derived from the 18th century Italian word *portafogli* which stems from the Latin word *portare,* which means to carry and *foglio*, meaning sheet of paper. Corbett and Higgins (2006) defined a portfolio as a "balanced collection of holdings related to one person such as financial assesses, job responsibilities, artistic works, and accomplishments... the portfolio represents the whole—it represents what you have or have done as an expression of who you are" (p. 4). It was not until the 1980s that portfolios shifted from a paper-based approach to a digital or electronic platform (ePortfolio) and not until the early 1990s that this shift was recognized in higher education research (Lorenzo & Ittelson, 2005). Lorenzo and Ittelson (2005) described an ePortfolio as "a digitalized collection of artifacts, resources, and accomplishments that represent an individual, group, or institution" (p. 2). Over the last century, ePortfolios have utilized powerful multimedia, whereby students are able to combine visual images, graphics, and sound along with text to demonstrate their achievements (Abrams, 2009). Furthermore, ePortfolios can be shared across a plethora of Web 2.0 platforms such as blogs and social networks (Barrett, 2011).

Like traditional portfolios, ePortfolios have been frequently used in education as a means of assessment, evaluation, and accreditation. In fact, the 2013 Educause Center for Analysis and Research (ECAR) reported that over half of higher education students surveyed used e-portfolios in at least one course in the past year (Dahlstrom, Walker, & Dziuban, 2013). In examining how students perceive the use of ePortfolios, recent research has confirmed that if "students see value for the potential usage of their ePortfolio, they will spend time learning the tool and building the final product" (McWhorter, Delello, Roberts, Raisor, & Fowler, 2013, p. 277). Also, Delello (2013) found that when students were allowed to have ownership in the choices of styles, backgrounds, colors, and visual images within the ePortfolio, they were more engaged in learning (see Figure 7). Cohn and Hibbits (2004) noted that ePortfolios may be "The show-and-tell of the millennium" (para. 1). Thus, the ePortfolio used in education can be a valuable asset when implemented with adequate communication, clear expectations, training, and support as important considerations before the implementation of ePortfolios across higher education (McWhorter, et. al, 2013).

LinkedIn as ePortfolio

The value of ePortfolios can also be seen in their usefulness for improving expertise and building community in professional settings (McWhorter & Bennett, 2012). One web-based platform that has been utilized by business professionals is LinkedIn (linkedin.com) and ranked in 2014 as the third most used social media site (Rollandi, 2014). Although traditionally used by employees as a professional social networking site, it can also be useful as an ePortfolio. For instance, LinkedIn allows users to share their work and accomplishments, connect with colleagues, receive endorsements for their business skills, and receive online recommendations that show in their profile from others on LinkedIn such as former employers, customers,

Figure 7. Example of Student ePortfolio.
Created by Katie Westberry. Used with Permission.

and colleagues (McWhorter, Johnson, Roberts, Delello & Hall, 2014).

In addition, LinkedIn offers a user the opportunity to add their professional Twitter.com URL to their profile as well as up to three URLs for other websites such as a professional blog (i.e. Wordpress.com), web-based repository of their work (i.e. Pathbrite.com, Academia.com, or ResearchGate.net) and their business page if they are self-employed or have a dedicated page at the employer's site. The authenticity of skills and work history is also elevated when a worker highlights their skills online (McWhorter, et al., 2013).

For many employees, presentations are part of their professional work and facilitate dissemination of their projects, ideas and research. Since

LinkedIn.com recently acquired SlideShare.net, the leading online website where professionals can upload and share their presentations, word processing documents and PDF documents (slide-share.net), workers can easily distribute their work through their LinkedIn profile to showcase their competencies and build or extend their professional brand (Loof, 2014).

Professional Portfolio

In a recent survey by the Hart Research Associates (2013), 83% of employers stated that a portfolio which showcased a student's knowledge and understanding of key skills would be beneficial in evaluating potential candidates. Further, this is substantiated by a recent national survey of nonprofit and business leaders who felt that an ePortfolio would be useful to ensure job applicants have the "knowledge and skills they need to succeed in their company or organization" (Association of American Colleges and Universities, 2013, para. 12). Venable (2013) noted that employers are interested in online career portfolios that focus on "accomplishments, applied practice, and demonstration of skill" (para. 4) and recommended that students choose *artifacts* (assignments or projects that demonstrate skills) wisely and should include their best work such as presentations, images, and video. Scivicque (2013) described several occasions that a professional portfolio can be very useful. A job interview is an appropriate time to consider "having a portfolio on hand [that] contributes to your professional image" (para. 3). Also, performance reviews, salary negotiations, and promotions are other instances a professional portfolio can be crucial for examining resumes, letters of recommendation, work samples and other accomplishments.

Micro-Credentialing International Study through Digital Badges and ePortfolios

The delivery of education is changing as access to learning opportunities through the Internet include informal learning, online professional development, and massively open online courses (MOOC's) where each is playing a part in the non-traditional learning of college-aged students. According to Middleton (2013), in the case of International students who spend the majority of their time at the institution granting the degree, the use of *micro-credentials* such as digital badges and ePortfolios that document learning over a short term are a possible solution for gaining evidence of learning experiences who travel home for the summer. Oftentimes, undergraduate and graduate international students travel home for the summer and have access to "unique educational opportunities of excellence that augment, without

disrupting, the curricular trajectory of their home educational institution" (para. 6) where the students are able to gain cross-disciplinary work at their home institution during the summer that still complements their primary degree focus. In this case, the utilization of alternative credentials may be warranted if their home institution "has yet to develop particular areas of excellence" (para. 5) that is transferable to the student's degree program.

Proliferation of Mobile Devices

According to Cisco (2014), mobile data traffic in 2013 grew over 81 percent since 2012 which they noted was about 18 times the amount of the entire global Internet traffic in 2000 with smartphones accounting for 77 percent of that growth. They predicted that "by end of 2014, the number of mobile-connected devices will exceed the number of people on earth, and by 2018 there will be nearly 1.4 mobile devices per capita" (para. 20) with smartphones creating about 70 percent of the mobile data traffic by 2018.

Easy access to electronic books (eBooks), movies, games, television, and information take place through mobile applications "apps". For example, Apple, creator of mobile iOS devices such as the iPad, iPhone, and iPod, distributed more than 1 million mobile apps worldwide including over 260,000 games and entertainment apps (Apple, 2015). And, Google (2013) offers Android, an open-source mobile software platform, which offers 600,000 apps and 5 million eBook titles. These "apps" provide easy access to text, visual images, the visualization of data, and the creation of images (Moline, 2011).

Mobile Devices in Education

Livingston (2004) described a mobile tool as "a device small enough to fit comfortably into a purse, pocket or holster, so you can continually keep it with you at all times" (p. 47). According to Shuler (2009), one of the fastest growing segments of mobile technology users in the U.S. are children under the age of 12. In fact, the use of mobile devices by school age students is on the rise with a recent survey noting that 58% of students regularly use a laptop-type device regularly (2-3 times a week), 29% a digital tablet, 30% a smartphone, and 7% a hybrid computer/tablet device (Herold, 2014).

As technology evolves, twenty-first century students are expected to utilize emerging technologies as learning tools (Kazlauskas & Robinson, 2012). This digital revolution is the beginning of the next generation of wireless technology presenting a unique opportunity to create learning experiences which create personal meaning and engage the learner. In fact, Hartnell-Young and Vetere (2008) reported that the use of mobile apps allowed students to capture and edit videos and photographs, communicate through social media apps, and download information from the Internet, personalizing learning. And with more schools moving to "bring your own devices" (BYOD), perhaps, as Bjerede and Bondip (2012) stated, these "technology-rich environments, with personal devices for all students, tailored to their preferences, and the freedom for every child to discover and develop and own her learning is a powerfully effective model for the future of education" (p. 21). Thus, students are able to utilize mobile devices for research tools, taking visual notes, accessing eBooks, and connecting to experts at a distance (Lepi, 2014).

Mobile Devices and the Workplace

According to Hackett (2014), consumers are driving technology adoption by "purchasing cutting-edge technology on their own dime for their own use, forcing companies to react to the reality that their employees often have better technology at their disposal at home than they have at work" (para. 1). With the rise of the smartphone and digital tablets, employees are bringing their own devices (BYOD) to the workplace (IBM, 2012).

One of the key benefits of BYOD is employee productivity due to the familiarity and speed of access to information.

Visual Social Media

Social Media platforms are the new evolution of digital and visual communication in the 21st century. The most popular social media platforms share visual messages rather than traditional text alone (Delello & McWhorter, 2013). A variety of emerging online social networks allow individuals to create and share digital stories of their life through images and sound (see Table 2). For instance, Facebook created a new Paper application in 2014 to allow users to share visual stories using high resolution photo images and distraction free templates (EducatorsTechnology.com, 2014). Pinterest allows the user to pin or save images or links to a visual bulletin board from a website. These images represent a repertoire of favorite things where an imaged pinned is "worth a thousand words."

We live in a world where visual images are also instantaneous and convenient. For many users, social media postings will be composed of images, videos, or microvideos, which are ephemeral, lasting only seconds before disappearing. Temporary videos like those posted on social media platforms such as Vine are "little windows into the people, settings, ideas and objects that make up your life" (in Vine, 2014, p. 6). And, these images and minuscule videos may be the next generation of social media applications to appear in education (Borovoy, 2013) and across the workplace (Hebberd, 2013).

These next-generation visual social platforms create communities of practice (CoP) through the sharing of knowledge and information across visual Web 2.0 platforms. For example, a recent study of education and business students who used Pinterest as part of a classroom assignment noted that the visual images allowed them to share ideas and create new knowledge through social

Table 2. Comparison of Visual Social Networking Platforms

Name	URL	Description
Facebook	www.facebook.com	• Launched in 2004 • Social networking Website • Users may create a personal profile, exchange, messages, photos, videos, and links. • Ability to search for people, find friends • No chatroom • New Paper application in 2014 • Over 1 billion users world-wide
Pinterest	www.pinterest.com	• Launched in 2009 • Visual scrapbook or pinboard • Facebook and Twitter association • Allows user to "pin" images from websites • Upload to a board via the "Pin It" button • Third most popular social network
Snapchat	https://www.snapchat.com/	• Launched in 2011 • Photo messaging application • Allows user to draw color images on photos or videos • Chatting feature • Videos may be up to 10 seconds and viewed only once • Images may be shared for 1-10 seconds • Cannot be shared to outside social media • Estimated 700 million photos and videos sent daily
Instagram	www.instagram.com	• Launched in 2010 • Mobile phone application allows users to share text, images, and video • Allows user to color/tint images with choice of 20 filters • Works across Twitter, Facebook, Tumbler, and Flickr • Hyperlapse feature allows short time-lapsed videos • Videos may be up to 15 seconds
Vine	https://vine.co/	• More than 150 million users • Launched 2013 by Twitter • Video sharing platform • Users may create and share videos up to 6 seconds • Videos may be shared across Twitter and Facebook • Allows users to find and follow others • Built in camera options (filters, flash settings) • Application in 17 languages • 100 million visitors per month

interactions. Also, students were able to identify professional practices for the work environment while helping to further their careers (Delello & McWhorter, 2014).

Social Media in Organizations

Nonprofit organizations have found value in connecting with potential donors through social media. Dixon and Keyes (2013) found in their research that social media has disrupted traditional donor-engagement models. New types of donor behavior are enhanced by digital communications including social media, e-newsletters, and other automated digital channels. Making connections with nonprofits through social media is important to a number of Americans implying that if nonprofits are not utilizing the power of social media, they are not leveraging their power to impact society as well as their sustainability. Also, many for-profit businesses have noticed that customers like to share experiences they have with products and services through online channels and social media and the researchers found that the ideal customer may be an irregular purchaser but is the most valuable customer because they post ratings and reviews that in turn will influence many more potential buyers.

Another idea spreading in organizations is the use of short spurts of visual content in the form of video posted to social media. For example, one of the latest trends is the use of short videos for visual content strategy. Time-lapse videos are becoming more mainstream now that there are apps that support their creation and their playback; in the past, time-lapse videos have depended upon holding the camera or smartphone still while filming but the new Hyperlapse platform from Instagram has built-in technology for stabilization allowing for moving, hand-held time lapses (Woollaston & Prigg, 2014). And, according to Moritz (2014), Instagram's Hyperlapse application "app" has encouraged businesses to create short videos with the cinema-like look and feel of time-lapse video but without the expensive equipment. See the "Biker Lapse" video at http://vimeo.com/104788899. Five brands that are already using this new video format including Whole Foods Market, Hubspot, Lauren Bath Photography, Tesla Motors, and Southwest Airlines.

Augmented Reality

The term Augmented Reality (AR) is the overlaying of computer-generated content such as video, graphics, text, sound, or global positioning system (GPS) data onto real-world images captured by devices such as smartphones, tablets, and hi-tech glasses (See Thomas, 2014). The term AR was first coined by former Boeing researcher Tom Caudell to describe head-mounted displays for the assembly of aircraft wires (Sawers, 2011). Today, examples of AR have wide-spread applications ranging from interactive gaming to wearable technologies. One such example of AR is the computer-enhanced replay of a sporting event that superimposes lines, arrows or other data onto a digital video image (Honey & Milnes, 2013).

AR has been posited as a facilitator of visual literacy. For example, Marques, Costello, & Azevedo (2014) pointed out that AR facilitates visual

literacy and understanding in informal learning environments such as museums. Typically, in museums, there is a large amount of text which may not be understood by visitors who do not speak the native language; AR allows the visitor to extract meanings from the AR representations, in turn, increases visitor engagment. In another study, Delello (2014) reported that AR not only increased student engagement in elementary classrooms but also held students' attention longer than traditional teaching methods.

Wearable Technology

A major technology trend in the workplace is wearable technology (CNET.com). Spence (2013) predicted that 2014 would be the year of wearable technology (wearables) that includes devices such as smart wristwatches (enabled for emailing, watching videos, making calls), health and fitness wearables (enabled for monitoring heart, blood pressure). Other wearable devices include Google Glasses (features of a smart phone but worn like glasses) and smart rings (enabled for messaging, music and camera features) (Meister, 2014).

DeFranco (2014) found that utilizing a smartwatch is much less intrusive in the workplace as emails from VIP clients can be directed to your wrist during a lengthy business meeting rather than choosing to miss an important email or appearing rude to your colleagues by routinely checking a smartphone. Also, software applications are getting on board with wearables. For instance, Evernote.com, the notetaking and archiving software company, is joining the wearables market and releasing its app for "Android Wear, and its big goal is to build a handy personal assistant who relieves you from mundane tasks like rifling through your pile of digital notes for information" (Zambelich, 2014, para. 4).

The likely users of the first wave of employees to use wearables in the workplace are mobile workers who use their bodies and hands. In addition, healthcare is seen as one field where smartwatches can be very beneficial, "these are work environ-

Figure 8. Healthcare worker utilizes wearable technology.
Copyright 2014 Accenture. Used with permission

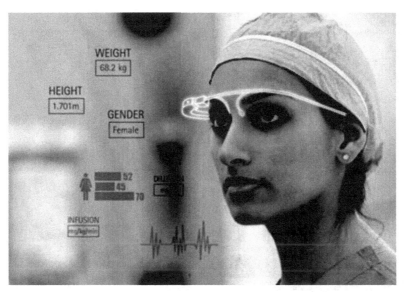

ments where 'handsfree' has a different meaning… communication remains possible…[and] you can be alerted to how far a team member or necessary piece of equipment may be without needing to take yourself away from the task at hand" (DeFranco, 2014, para. 6). See Figure 8 for a depiction of a healthcare worker utilizing wearable technology.

Using AR in Education

There are numerous examples of how schools are implementing AR into classrooms. For example, The Heritage Elementary School in Texas grew the world's first augmented garden to bring technology and nature together in an innovative way (Aurasma, 2013a). Pérez-López and Contero (2013) used a combination of oral explanations, AR models, and animations of anatomical structures with 4th graders. Their research showed a significant increase in student interest, motivation, and knowledge. Other studies have found similar results. For example, Yuen, Yaoyuneyong, and Johnson's (2011) study showed that through the use of books and games, knowledge retention improved if the content was delivered using AR.

Also, when AR platforms such as Aurasma (www. aurasma.com) were used with children diagnosed with Autism spectrum disorders (ASD), students were able to recognize how a particular device such as the telephone works, increasing independence from their parents (May, 2013).

According to colAR creator Adrian Clark, numerous studies have been done on the effect of adding AR technology to a book improving "recall of information in the children who use it because it's so engaging, and decreases the reading comprehension gap between high and low level readers so children who struggled with reading retain the information that is being portrayed" (University of Canterbury, 2012, para. 6). BooksARalive (2013) proposed that by adding 3D AR into their print-based, illustrated stories, reading would become more "interesting, entertaining, and fun" (para. 17) (see Figure 9). The use of augmented books has the potential to improve literacy through the combination of both text and interactive visual representations.

AR applications may also enhance the curriculum standards. For example, the Common Core State Standards (CCSS) English Language

Figure 9. BooksARalive
Copyright 2013. Used with permission

Arts (ELA)-Literacy Speaking and Listening Strand (6.5) require multimedia components (e.g., graphics, images, music, sound) and visual displays to be included in the learning environment (National Governors Association Center for Best Practices [NGA Center] & Council of Chief State School Officers [CCSSO], 2010). According to Coiro, Karchmer, and Walpole (2009), when selected carefully to fulfill logical, authentic, and individualized educational goals, technologies for literacy and learning have shown to have considerable potential. Furthermore, according to Jongedijk (2013), AR may allow the user to construct meaning that may not be possible to see by natural means.

Augmented Reality has been posited as a learning tool in higher education. Researchers examined 25 studies and found that healthcare education is one area that could benefit from the use of AR as prototypes could be developed to use AR where "virtual learning experiences could be embedded in a real physical context" (Zhu, Hadagar, Masiello & Zary, 2014, para. 1). Another area that shows promise for the use of AR in higher education is the field of engineering. For instance, Liarokapis

and Anderson (2010) found that AR is useful in making complex concepts in mechanical engineering much more easily comprehended by students. AR is also showing up in college literature such as a college prospectus that allows a potential student to view short video clips of current and former students (McWhorter, 2012). Also, AR applications have created opportunities for students to utilize simulated practice examinations (Noll & von Jan, 2013) and allowed physicians to view anatomical structures prior to surgeries (Mesko, 2013).

CURRENT ISSUES IN THE FIELD RAISED BY THESE STUDIES

Traditional literacy, the ability to read and write, has taken on new meanings in the 21st century. Today, to be truly literate, one must be equipped with technological knowledge to contend with the fast-paced society in which we live. As we develop newer conceptions of literacy, Thoman and Joles (2004) remind us that literacy is more than words on a piece of paper. Literacy also includes the "powerful images and sounds of our multi-media culture" (p. 1).

The topic of visual literacy has been studied extensively in recent years. From education to the workplace, each of the examples presented in this chapter illustrate that digital and visual forms of literacy enhance communication and the sharing of information. Also, within these examples, the use of visual Web 2.0 tools show support for use as a means of classroom motivation and student engagement. Although the benefits for using new visual technologies are evident, the research suggests that, many times, there are unintended consequences to be considered for using such tools including privacy issues, distractions, limited technology access, ever changing digital platforms, and the need for a better trained workforce.

Privacy Issues

The integration of new visual and digital tools into education or the workforce may pose a possible threat to individual privacy and blur the boundaries between our personal and our professional lives. The social nature of digital media and technologies (e.g. Facebook, Pinterest), leave behind a digital footprint. According to Common Sense Media (2014), a digital footprint is all of the online information intentionally or unintentionally posted by a person or others. Kiss (2014) noted, "Each of us chooses what we present to the outside world…. every tweet, every Facebook posting, every Flickr upload is part of reinforcing the image we want people to see" (para. 4). And, according to a Pew Media Report, the more content we contribute to the Web, "the more we are not only findable, but also knowable" (Madden, Fox, Smith, Vitak, 2007, p. i). In reality, many of the popular social networks such as Facebook, Twitter, and Pinterest are already capturing data to create a comprehensive profile of the metadata from their end users (Sherman, 2014).

Part of this chapter examines the use of digital badges and visual ePortfolios as a means to showcase evidence of lifelong learning achievements. Badges are linked to metadata and may be shared across social media sites. In addition, ePortfolios may contain large amounts of personal information. Furthermore, the use of technologies such as AR may also bring unanticipated computer security and privacy risks. For example, companies like USAA, an insurance company, have already chosen to ban wearables due to concerns over the privacy of employees and customers (Meister, 2014). Smartwatches and other wearables are concerning because they are "another device IT has to secure….and expand official security measures to protect against data leaks when wearables are connected to the corporate network" (O'Neill, 2014).

Likewise, digital face recognition combined with geo-location data could reveal who you are and where you are. For example, the new application TwittaRound combines Twitter, AR technology, and the iPhone's compass to pinpoint your exact location as you tweet (Perez, 2009). All of these examples raise concerns as to how best to use new media while protecting the privacy of individuals in the classroom and in the workforce.

Distractedness

As students come to class socially connected and networked to their devices, new visual technologies may be viewed as a distraction by many educators. According to a Pew Research Center Study, teachers reported that although today's students are savvier with media, they are "less literate and more distracted than previous generations" (Purcell, Rainie, Heaps, Buchanan, Friedrich, Jacklin, Chen, & Zickuhr, 2012, p. 60). McCoy (2013) noted that there is reason to believe that digital devices interfere with learning. In a recent study, McCoy (2013) showed that in a typical college classroom, students used their mobile devices an average of 10.9 times day to text, send emails, and use social media sites. The consensus from 70% of classroom teachers surveyed by Common Sense Media (2012) is that digital media interferes with the attention span of students, negatively affecting student learning.

In addition to privacy concerns, new wearable devices may also cause distractions in the workplace as employees try to multitask between work and non-work activity (Donston-Miller, 2014). According to MIT, the distractibility accompanying wearables is of real concern, "it's a great myth that people can multi-task without any loss in the quality of their work... just-in-time information provided by wearable computers seems wonderful...but we lose engagement with the real world" (Norman, 2013, para. 6). Thus, instructors must utilize and enforce policies that minimize distractions in the classroom while still building necessary visual literacy skills.

Lack of Access and Acceptance

Recently, a White House (2013) report titled *Four Years of Broadband Growth* reported the findings on U.S. access to the Internet. The report revealed that at least 81% of Americans have mobile wireless access and almost 91% have wired Internet access. Yet, these statistics may not depict the total picture. The study revealed that although 72% percent of U.S. households had broadband coverage, participants who did not complete high school (35%), had incomes below $25,000 per year (43%), lived in rural areas (58%), or were Hispanic (56%) or African American (55%) were less likely to have access to the Internet thus underscoring that differences to access still exist among racial and economic lines.

A recent Pew research study noted that disparities also exist within the classroom due to the socioeconomic status of the students (Purcell, Heaps, Buchanan & Friedrich, 2013). For example, in low-income schools, over half of teachers reported a lack of resources among students to access digital technologies. And, in the White House (2013) report, it was noted that "While broadband access has improved considerably in recent years, broadband infrastructure in America's K-12 schools and local libraries has lagged far behind...the average school has about the same connectivity as an average American home" (p. 22) only with 200 times more users. Burmark (2002) noted that we must recognize that children born into poverty are even more affected by visual imagery than those who are more advantaged. For these children, an absence of books in the household does not mean there is a shortage of television.

Infrastructure is not only vital to education but also to industry as the world now depends on technology for everything from banking to global communication. However, many developing countries lack infrastructure needed to support technology use. For example, USAID (2012) reported that in developing countries, only 20 percent of people have access to the Internet. In addition, when industry looks at adding devices such as wearables, they need to consider if their current WiFi connectivity can support additional devices on their network as well as the battery consumption of such devices (O'Neill, 2014).

In 2001, Mark Prensky termed the generation of students born into a technologically connected world *Digital Natives*. These Millennial students are always connected and according to Prensky "are used to the instantaneity of hypertext, downloaded music, phones in their pockets, a library on their laptops, beamed messages and instant messaging" (p. 2). In fact, Pew research reported that most teens (90%) are online and almost 80% use social networks to connect with one another (Lenhart, Madden, Smith, Purcell, Zichuhr, & Raine, 2011). And, although research has shown that social networking websites such as Facebook are popular among students, they are not widely accepted by faculty (Dogoriti & Pange, 2014; Roblyer, McDaniel, Webb, Herman & Witty, 2010).

For many students, access to mobile devices and technology ends at the classroom door. Some faculty see technology as a source of stress (Lynch, Altschuler, & McClure, 2002) while others lack the skills necessary to integrate such innovative applications and tools into the classroom (Gu, Zhu, & Guo, 2012). Jukes, McCain, and Crockett (2010) remarked that the "majority of teachers who have incorporated new media into their instruction have largely grafted the new tools onto an old approach to teaching" (p. 122). In a recent study by Marzilli, Delello, Marmion, McWhorter, Roberts, and Marzilli (2014), PowerPoint and video technology were the most favored approaches for faculty to illustrate concepts to students. Furthermore, Levine (2004) stated that the lack of technology use may stem from the "organizational culture where they work" (p. 1). In addition, even though over half of students have access at home or other public spaces to mobile devices, according to a recent survey by Pearson, only one in six students in the United States attend a school where a mobile device is provided to them. As student mobile usage is outpacing school technology programs, the question of both access to technology and worldwide competition is evident.

The health effects of digital devices on school children are unknown. For this reason, the Department of Health in the United Kingdom (UK) has launched the largest study of mobile phone effects on children's brains to determine if the devices have an effect on childhood development (Arthur, 2014). Dr. Mireille Toledano, who is leading the health study, remarked that "by assessing the children in year seven and again in year nine we will be able to see how their cognitive abilities develop in relation to changing use of mobile phones and other wireless technologies" (para. 10).

Also, when teaching new media such as AR, instructors are likely to find it very challenging with a steep learning curve for both themselves and their students. For example, faculty members have also reported difficulty finding time to learn to integrate visuals into classrooms (Metros & Woolsey, 2006; Purcell, et. al, 2013). And for those that do, their methods may be discounted by colleagues, possibly even seen as frivolous (Metros & Woolsey, 2006). In order to ensure that students become visually literate, teachers must feel competent to teach with new media and feel supported to take risks in using it.

Employers may be hesitant to allow social media in the workplace. For instance, the U.S. Equal Employment Opportunity Commission (EEOC) issued a press release that saying that "the increasing use of social media in the 21st century workplace presents new opportunities as well as questions and concerns… [requiring examination of] the employment context and what impact it may have on the laws we enforce and on our mission to stop and remedy discriminatory practices in the workplace" (EEOC, 2014, para. 2). Thus, employers must find common ground for what is acceptable and what is not in the workplace in regards to social media usage; therefore, decisions should be made context-specific on where and when it is appropriate.

Constant Evolution

Technology is progressing at a rapid speed and educators and employers are constantly faced with ever-expanding options. According to Dembo and Bellow (2013), there is a "sea of sites that are constantly in flux" which create an "environment where people are constantly searching for the next great thing" (p. 77). These advances present many significant opportunities but also pose major challenges in both the classroom and the workforce.

Consider how technology has evolved in over the last thirty years. In the early 80s, many of us grew up without access to a single computer in our homes or schools. There were 3,054 Internet service providers in 1996 and by 2000, 15.79 billion Web connections had been made (WGBH, 1998). However, in 2001, only 20% of U.S. households had access to the Internet (U.S. Department of Commerce, 2002). In 2013, over half a billion (526 million) mobile devices and connections were created (Cisco, 2013).

Social media wasn't the way we communicated with one another until My Space was brought forth in 2003, followed by Facebook in 2004, YouTube in 2005, and Twitter in 2006 (Delello & McWhorter, 2013). Additionally, traditional text based social media platforms shifted to image based platforms as platforms such as Pinterest (2009), Instagram (2010), and Snap Chat (2012) emerged. Anderson, Boyles, and Rainie (2012) noted that "Cloud-based computing, digitalized textbooks, mobile connectivity, high-quality streaming video, and "just in time" information gathering" (p. 2) will drive the future of education. Furthermore, Massive Open Online Courses (MOOCs) and flipped classroom models will, according to The New Media Consortium, change the nature of how we currently educate students (Johnson, Adams Becker, Estrada, & Freeman, 2014). The NMC predicts that the future of education may include intuitive electrovibration technology to allow students to go beyond just "seeing" but actually "feeling" the content they are learning. According to Jukes, et al. (2010), the evolution of digital media will have an impact upon the way we teach and the way students learn.

The Need for a Trained Workforce

Data visualization tools such as charts, maps, infographics, and interactive images will help illustrate large sets of data and complex information. According to Yale University professor Edward Tufte (2001), graphics are instruments for thinking about quantitative information and often the most effective way to make large sets of data coherent is to look at pictures of those numbers. Davenport (2013) remarked that, "data is worthless if not effectively communicated" (para. 1). Intel (2013) suggested that turning this data into something meaningful is much more difficult as businesses struggle to know how to store, analyze, and interpret the enormous amounts of information.

The sheer volume of information collected will require a new set of visual skills which includes seeing the meaning and significance in vast amounts of data and effectively sharing it with others (Davies, Fidler, & Gorbis, 2011). Additionally, the capacity to collect and analyze the vast amounts data will require new computational literacies, both financial and technical and "at all levels of society, people will increasingly have to turn data and information into usable computational forms in order to understand it at all" (Berry, 2011, p. 15). Thus, higher educators who are preparing students for the workforce should be seeking ways to weave these new visual skills into their curriculum.

IMPLICATIONS AND RECOMMENDATIONS FOR EDUCATION, CIVIC ENGAGEMENT (GLOBAL AND LOCAL), SOCIAL PRACTICE, AND POLICY

The use of visual technologies has implications across education and industry. The development of new visual media will change the nature of education in that educators will need to find more efficient methods to let students communicate with one another in meaningful and relevant ways.

There are several reasons cited in the literature as to why visuals should be incorporated into teaching and learning. Rambe (2012) noted that technological innovations such as the use of social media "necessitate the provision of authentic learning resources; embedding learning in engaging, multimedia environments; supporting individualized learning processes, and equipping learners with powerful tools for knowledge exchange and collaboration" (p. 132). Furthermore, the use of visuals connects students to the digital world they live in making learning relevant (Delello, 2014). Students will also need to develop 21st century skills needed to compete in the workforce. These include computational thinking skills and the ability to produce visually stimulating content using new forms of media (Davies, et. al., 2011).

Roussos, Johnson, Moher, Leigh, Vasilakis, and Barnes (1999) remarked that one of the most important purposes of an educational environment is to promote social interaction among users located in the same physical space. Holum and Gahala (2001) noted that besides basic literacy skills, "technology skills for communicating, investigating, accessing and using information, computing, thinking critically about messages inherent in new media, and understanding and evaluating data" are needed (para. 3). New visual media may be another disruptive innovation that changes the way traditional education has always been done.

However, as Sosa (2009) noted, not only must students be aware of visuals, they must also be provided the appropriate tools for the products they are creating. Pat Skorkowsky, Superintendent of the 5th largest school district in the U.S. stated: "Policies that restrict cell phone use, social media or other emerging technologies may have made sense at one time, but it's getting harder to justify keeping these powerful tools out of students' hands" (in Krueger, 2014, para. 26). However, for this to work, it will be critical that policies and guidelines (e.g. social media, BYOD) be developed across education and in the workplace to protect both students and employees. But, integrating new and innovative technologies into classrooms will only succeed when educators spend time learning how to use such tools and applications (Delello & McWhorter, 2013). Mishra and Koehler (2006) suggested using the Technological Pedagogical Content Knowledge (TPACK) framework as a means to assess and execute effective technology integration in specific educational settings. Also, to improve teaching and learning with technology, The International Society for Technology in Education (ISTE) has developed educational technology standards for students, teachers and administrators (ISTE, 2008).

Higher education will need also to consider creating programs to fill the shortage of employees that will be needed for organizations to make effective use of such information. This will include the recruitment and retention of students in science, math, technology, and engineering (STEM) fields. Gartner (2012) predicted that in the field of Big Data, more than 4.4 million technology jobs will be created by 2015. Morris (2013) reported that "three specialty fields will emerge soon: technologists, who write the algorithms and code to transverse the large amounts of data; statisticians and quantification experts; and artist-explorers, creative people who can navigate content and find something others don't see" (para. 8). To address these shortages, institutions of higher education will need to prepare graduates for these positions including providing adequate curriculum and training programs. Davies, et al. (2011) noted that "A workforce strategy for sustaining business goals should be one of the most critical outcomes of human resource professionals and should involve collaborating with universities to address lifelong learning and skill requirements" (p. 13). Continued professional development on the use of new technologies should be a requirement for teachers and employees in both education and in industry.

Recommendations for both mobile and wearable technologies in the workplace include the creation of company policies for or against such devices. For instance, the organization should control the environment and have policies defining the work-related information that can be accessed from an employee's devices, what apps are utilized to access organizational information, and what devices the IT department will support to avoid pitfalls of BYOD (Chie, 2014). Likewise, policies for wearables should be created to circumvent difficulties later. According to Zetlin (2014), when formulating policies, leaders should consider such things as *detection* (the company knowing when they are being worn), *security* (wearables can pose security risks for networks), and *privacy* (when and where wearables can be worn).

GAPS IN THE EXTANT RESEARCH AND DIRECTIONS FOR FUTURE RESEARCH

We live in an age of information, constantly surrounded by visual images. According to Kellner (2008), it is evident that multimedia visual imagery is essential to our culture; wherein, visual technology is connected to the communication needs of the current generation. Through the implementation of visually-enhanced experiences, students become active participants in authentic learning.

Brumberger (2011) concluded that we must "teach our students to be visually literate, just as we teach them to be verbally literate" (p. 46). Likewise, Jukes, McCain, and Crockett (2010), we must not only teach students visually, we must allow them to be producers of visual information. "Instruction in visual literacy will better prepare students for the dynamic and constantly changing online world they will inevitably be communicating through" (Riesland, 2010, para. 10). However, according to Gabriel, Campbell, Wiebe, MacDonald, and McAuley (2012), many of the innovative uses of technology have not yet emerged in the typical classroom. And, for the classrooms that have integrated new media, this technological expansion seems to have mixed results. Kazlauskas and Robinson (2012) wrote, "The caricature of the 21st century student as an avid consumer of any and all technology does not necessarily transfer to the learning environment" (p. 328). Many times, when schools integrate new technologies, it takes place in pockets, "pushed ahead by an innovative teacher, a passionate researcher, a risky developer, or an inspired parent (Shuler, 2009, p. 15) rather than integrated across the curriculum. More research is needed on valid measures of learning using new visual and digital technologies.

Furthermore, mobile learning is a relatively new phenomenon and the theoretical basis is currently under development (Kearney, Schucka,

Burden & Aubusson, 2012). According to Schuler (2009), there is no widely accepted learning theory for mobile technologies, thus "hampering the effective assessment, pedagogy, and design of new applications for learning" (p. 6). Part of the reason for this is that technologies are rapidly changing and little time has been given to developing theoretical constructs which respond adequately to the day-to-day needs of schools (Lapointe & Linder-Vanberschot, 2012). While research in this area is still in its infancy, it will serve as an essential foundation in determining the effectiveness of new visual literacies.

The workplace is changing as well. Preparation for today's world requires that students find information rapidly, an essential element for their future careers. Access to technology has transcended global barriers that once existed resulting "in images easily travelling across cultural, political, economic, and language barriers, but whether or not they are interpreted by particular viewing audiences in the manner that was intended by their creators is another matter" (Gibson & Owens, 2009, p. 10). Also, empirical research into the use of emerging technologies in the workplace is lagging behind practice (McWhorter, 2010) and scholarly inquiry is needed to discover best practices into visual literacy and competencies.

Finally, the world has shifted from a read-only environment to one where visual images are reshaping our world. From photographs, to television, video and the World Wide Web, people learn, create, and exchange information through images. Jukes, et al. (2010) reminds us that "A new way of communicating is rapidly emerging, one that incorporates visual components along with words to convey messages more effectively for people operating in the fast-paced, time-starved modern personal and professional environment" (p. 118). In order to be truly literate in today's digital world, the ability to utilize emerging visual technologies will be necessary in both education and the workforce.

REFERENCES

Abrams, A. (2009). *The portfolio builder 2 for PowerPoint*: *Templates for creating digital portfolios with PowerPoint*. Retrieved from http://www.arnieabrams.net/portfolio/Chapter1-%20 PB_overview.pdf

Alexander, J., & Parsehian, S. (2014). Content-driven commerce: Differentiating and driving sales with content in commerce. *FitForCommerce*. Retrieved from http://www.fitforcommerce.com/ whitepaper-signup-weblinc-content-driven-commerce.html

Anderson, J. Q., Boyles, J. L., & Rainie, L. (2012, July 27). *The future impact of the Internet on higher education: Experts expect more-efficient collaborative environments and new grading schemes; they worry about massive online courses, the shift away from on-campus life*. Retrieved from http://pewinternet.org/~/media//Files/Reports/2012/ PIP_Future_of_Higher_Ed.pdf

Antin, J., & Churchill, E. F. (2011). Badges in social media: A psychological perspective. *Gamification Research Network*. Retrieved from http://gamification-research.org/wp-content/ uploads/2011/04/03-Antin-Churchill.pdf

Apple. (2015). *Get your game face on*. Retrieved from http://www.apple.com/ipod-touch/from-the-app-store/

Arthur, C. (2014). UK launches largest study of mobile phone effects on children's brains. *The Guardian*. Retrieved from http://www. theguardian.com/technology/2014/may/20/uk-launches-largest-study-of-mobile-phone-effects-on-childrens-brains

Association of American Colleges and Universities (AACU). (2013). *It takes more than a major: Employer priorities for college learning and student success: Overview and key findings*. Retrieved from http://www.aacu.org/leap/presidentstrust/ compact/2013SurveySummary

Association of College and Research Libraries. (2011). *ACRL visual literacy competency standards for higher education*. Retrieved from http:// www.ala.org/acrl/standards/visualliteracy

Aurasma. (2013a). *About Us*. Retrieved from http://www.aurasma.com/about-us/

Ausburn, L. J., & Ausburn, F. B. (2014). Technical perspectives on theory in screen-based virtual reality environments: Leading from the future in VHRD. *Advances in Developing Human Resources*, *16*(3), 371–390. doi:10.1177/1523422314532125

Barrett, H. (2011). *Balancing the two faces of ePortfolios*. Retrieved from http://electronicportfolios.org/balance/balancingarticle2.pdf

Basno. (2014). *Create digital badges that recognize employee milestones*. Retrieved from http:// basno.com/employers

Beegel, J. (2014). *Infographics for Dummies*. Hoboken, NJ: John Wiley & Sons, Inc.

Berry, D. M. (2011). The computational turn: Thinking about the digital humanities. *Culture Machine*, *12*, 1–22.

Biller, G., Gorlenko, L., & McColgin, D. (2014, Nov.). *Data visualization: The new literacy*. The Artefact Group. Retrieved from http://www. artefactgroup.com/content/data-visualization-the-new-literacy/

Bjerede, M., & Bondi, T. (2012). Learning is personal: Stories of android tablet use in the 5th grade. *Learning Untethered*. Retrieved from http:// www.learninguntethered.com/?p=24

Biesdorf, S., & Niedermann, F. (2014, July). *Healthcare's digital future*. McKinsey & Company. Retrieved from http://www.mckinsey.com/ insights/health_systems_and_services/healthcares_digital_future

Bleed, R. (2005). Visual literacy in higher education. *ELI Explorations*, 1-11. Retrieved from http://net.educause.edu/ir/library/pdf/ELI4001.pdf

Bloomberg, T. V. (2014). *Wearable technology seen as biggest trend in 2014*. [video]. Retrieved from http://www.bloomberg.com/video/wearable-technology-seen-as-biggest-trend-in-2014-xsbl35YaToS8p2PQZ2551Q.htmlhttp://www.bloomberg.com/video/wearable-technology-seen-as-biggest-trend-in-2014-xsbl35YaToS8p-2PQZ2551Q.html

BooksARalive. (2013). *Posts: Augmented reality books*. Retrieved from http://www.booksaralive.com/

Borovoy, A. (2013). *Five-Minute film festival: Vine and Instagram video in the classroom*. Edutopia. Retrieved from http://www.edutopia.org/blog/film-festival-vine-instagram-video-education

Brumberger, E. (2011). Visual Literacy and the digital native: An examination of the millennial learner. *Journal of Visual Literacy*, *30*(1), 19–46.

Brynjolfsson, E., & McAfee, A. (2012). Big data's management revolution. *Harvard Business Review*. Retrieved from https://hbr.org/2012/09/big-datas-management-revolutio

Buckhingham, J. (2014). Open digital badges for the uninitiated. *Teaching English as a Second Language, 18*(1). Retrieved from http://tesl-ej.org/pdf/ej69/int.pdf

Burmark, L. (2002). *Visual literacy. Learn to see, see to learn*. Alexandria, VA: ASCD.

Carey, K. (2012). Show me your badge. *The New York Times*. Retrieved from http://www.nytimes.com/2012/11/04/education/edlife/show-me-your-badge.html?_r=0

Chicago Art Department. (2013). *What is a badge?* Retrieved from https://www.youtube.com/watch?v=HgLLq7ybDtc#t=125

Chie, D. (2014). The perils and pitfalls of BYOD in your workplace. Retrieved from Christensen, C. (2008). Disruptive innovation and catalytic change in higher education. *Forum for the Future of Higher Education,* 43-46. Retrieved from http://www.paloaltostaffingtech.com/news-insights/thought-leadership/the-perils-and-pitfalls-of-byod-in-your-workplace/http://net.educause.edu/ir/library/pdf/ff0810s.pdf

Cisco. (2013). *Cisco visual networking index: Forecast and methodology, 2013–2018*. Retrieved from http://www.cisco.com/c/en/us/solutions/collateral/service-provider/ip-ngn-ip-next-generation-network/white_paper_c11-481360.html

Cisco. (2014). *Cisco visual networking index: Global mobile data traffic forecast update, 2013-2018*. Retrieved from http://www.cisco.com/c/en/us/solutions/collateral/service-provider/visual-networking-index-vni/white_paper_c11-520862.html

Cities of Learning. (2014). *One summer, more than 100,000 badges and a movement is born*. Retrieved from http://citiesoflearning.org/learn/

CNET.com. (2014). *Wearable tech*. CNET. Retrieved from http://www.cnet.com/topics/wearable-tech/

Cohn, E. R., & Hibbits, B. (2004). Beyond the electronic portfolio: A lifetime personal web space. *Educause Review Online*. Retrieved from http://www.educause.edu/ero/article/beyond-electronic-portfolio-lifetime-personal-web-space

Coiro, J., Karchmer, R. A., & Walpole, S. (2009). *Critically evaluating educational technologies for literacy learning*. Retrieved from newliteracies.uconn.edu/coiro/handbookeval.pdf

Cook, G. (2013). *The best American infographics*. New York: Houghton Mifflin Harcourt.

Common Sense Media. (2012). *Children, teens, and entertainment media: The view from the classroom.* Retrieved from https://www.common-sensemedia.org/research/children-teens-and-entertainment-media-the-view-from-the-classroom

Common Sense Media. (2014). *Trillion dollar footprint.* Retrieved from https://www.common-sensemedia.org/educators/lesson/trillion-dollar-footprint-6-8

Corbett, D., & Higgins, R. (2006). *Portfolio life: The new path to work, purpose, and passion after 50.* Jossey-Bass.

Cukier, K., & Mayer-Schonberger, V. (2013). *Big data: a revolution that will transform how we live, work, and think.* Houghton Mifflin Harcourt.

Dahlstrom, E., Walker, J. D., & Dziuban, C. (2013). ECAR study of undergraduate students and information technology, 2013. Louisville, CO: Educause Center for Analysis and Research. Retrieved from https://net.educause.edu/ir/library/pdf/ERS1302/ERS1302.pdf

Dallas Museum of Art. (2014). *Dallas Museum of Art partners with Grace Museum in Abilene, TX to expand friends membership program.* Retrieved from http://www.dm-art.org/press-release/dallas-museum-art-partners-grace-museum-abilene-tx-expand-friends-membership-program

Davenport, T. (2013). *Data is worthless if you don't communicate it.* Harvard Business Review. Retrieved from http://blogs.hbr.org/2013/06/data-is-worthless-if-you-dont/

Davidson, R. (2014). Using infographics in the science classroom. *Science Teacher (Normal, Ill.)*, *81*(3), 34–39. doi:10.2505/4/tst14_081_03_34

Davies, A., Fidler, D., & Gorbis, M. (2011). *Future work skills 2020. Institute for the Future for University of Phoenix Research Institute.* Retrieved from http://www.iftf.org/uploads/media/SR-1382A_UPRI_future_work_skills_sm.pdf

DeFranco, M. (2014). Don't be rude, adopt wearables at your workplace. *Forbes.* Retrieved from http://www.forbes.com/sites/michaeldefranco/2014/08/05/dont-be-rude-adopt-wearables-at-your-workplace/

Delello, J. A. (2013, May). *Case study: Students digitally archive newly minted classroom management skills.* Pathbrite Inc. Retrieved from http://partner.pearson.com/sites/default/files/UTT%20Case%20Study%20EDU_v2.pdf

Delello, J. A. (2014). Insights from pre-service teachers using science-based augmented reality. *Journal of Computers in Education*, *1*(4), 295–311. doi:10.1007/s40692-014-0021-y

Delello, J. A., & McWhorter, R. R. (2013). New visual social media for the higher education classroom. In G. Mallia (Ed.), *The Social Classroom: Integrating Social Network Use in Education.* Hershey, PA: IGI Global.

Delello, J. A., & McWhorter, R. R. (2014, August). Creating virtual communities of practice with the visual social media platform Pinterest. *International Journal of Social Media and Interactive Learning Environments*, *2*(3), 216. doi:10.1504/IJSMILE.2014.064205

Delello, J. A., McWhorter, R. R., & Camp, K. (2014). Social media as a classroom learning tool. *International Journal on E-Learning.*

Dembo, S., & Bellow, A. (2013). *Untangling the web.* Thousand Oaks, CA: Corwin Press.

Dixon, J., & Keyes, D. (2013). The permanent disruption of social media. *Stanford Social Innovation Review.* Retrieved from http://www.ssireview.org/articles/entry/the_permanent_disruption_of_social_media

Dogoriti, E., & Pange, J. (2014). Considerations for online English language learning: the use of Facebook in formal and informal settings in higher education. In G. Mallia (Ed.), *The Social Classroom: Integrating Social Network Use in Education.* Hershey, PA: IGI Global. doi:10.4018/978-1-4666-4904-0.ch008

Donston-Miller, D. (2014). Workplace wearables: The pros and cons for businesses. *Techpage One.* Retrieved from http://techpageone.dell.com/technology/workplace-wearables-the-pros-and-cons-for-businesses/#.VDUkHvldW1g

EducatorsTechnology.com. (2014). *Facebook has just released a new iPad app called Paper.* Retrieved from http://www.educatorstechnology.com/2014/02/facebook-has-just-released-new-ipad-app.html

EEOC. (2014). Social media is part of today's workplace but its use may raise employment discrimination concerns. *U.S. Equal Employment Opportunity Commission.* Retrieved from http://www.eeoc.gov/eeoc/newsroom/release/3-12-14.cfm

Esteves, J. (2014). *Did You Know? 2014.* Retrieved from http://www.youtube.com/watch?v=XrJjfDUzD7M

Everhart, D. (2014). *Badges: Bridging the gap between higher ed and the workforce.* Retrieved from http://blog.blackboard.com/badges-bridging-gap-higher-ed-workforce

Facebook. (2014). *Introducing paper.* Retrieved from https://www.facebook.com/paper

Fain, P. (2012). Big data's arrival. *Inside higher ed.* Retrieved from https://www.insidehighered.com/news/2012/02/01/using-big-data-predict-online-student-success

Fattal, L. F. (2012). What does amazing look like? Illustrator studies in pre-service teacher education. *Journal of Visual Literacy, 31*(2), 17–22.

Foster, J. C. (2013). The promise of digital badges. *Techniques: Connecting Education & Careers, 88*(8), 30.

Gabriel, M. A., Campbell, B., Wiebe, S., MacDonald, R., & McAuley, A. (2012). The role of digital technologies in learning: Expectations of first year university students. *Canadian Journal of Learning & Technology, 38*(1), 1–18.

Gartner. (2012). *Gartner says big data creates big jobs: 4.4 million IT jobs globally to support big data by 2015.* Retrieved from http://www.gartner.com/newsroom/id/2207915

Gu, X., Zhu, Y., & Guo, X. (2013). Meeting the "digital natives": Understanding the acceptance of technology in classrooms. *Journal of Educational Technology & Society, 16*(1), 392–402.

Gibson, M., & Owens, K. (2009). The importance of critically examining what it now means to be visually literate. In *Conference Proceedings from Power 2 Empowerment: Critical Literacy in Visual Culture.* Dallas, TX: Academic Press.

Google. (2013). *Celebrating Google Play's first birthday.* Retrieved from http://googleblog.blogspot.com/2013/03/celebrating-google-plays-first-birthday.html

Greenhow, C. (2008). Commentary: Connecting formal and informal learning in the age of participatory media: A response to Bull et al. *Contemporary Issues in Technology & Teacher Education, 8*(3). Retrieved from http://www.citejournal.org/vol8/iss3/editorial/article1.cfm

Hackett, R. (2014). Showdown at the B.Y.O.D. corral. *Fortune.* Retrieved from http://fortune.com/2014/07/24/bring-your-own-device-byod-enterprise-showdown/

Hartnell-Young, E., & Vetere, F. (2008). A means of personalizing learning: Incorporating old and new literacies in the curriculum with mobile phones. *Curriculum Journal, 19*(4), 283–292. doi:10.1080/09585170802509872

Hart Research Associates. (2013). *It takes more than a major: Employer priorities for college learning and student success.* Retrieved from http://www.aacu.org/leap/documents/2013_EmployerSurvey.pdf

Magazine, H. (2014). *Why 'Big Data'is a big deal.* Retrieved from http://harvardmag.com/pdf/2014/03-pdfs/0314-30.pdf

Harven, M. (2014). Digital badges gain traction in higher education. *EdTech Times.* Retrieved from http://edtechtimes.com/2014/03/28/digital-badges-gain-traction-higher-education/

Hattwig, D., Burgess, J., Bussert, K., & Medaille, A. (2011). *ACRL Visual Literacy Competency Standards for Higher Education.* Retrieved from http://www.ala.org/acrl/standards/visualliteracy

Hebberd, L. (2013). *How to recruit using Instagram [5 simple steps].* Retrieved from http://theundercoverrecruiter.com/how-to-recruit-using-instagram-in-5-simple-steps/

Heer, J., Bostock, M., & Ogievetsky, V. (2010). A tour through the visualization zoo. *Communications of the ACM, 53*(6), 59–67. doi:10.1145/1743546.1743567

Herold, B. (2014). Student mobile device usage outpacing school tech programs, survey finds. *Education Week.* Retrieved from http://blogs.edweek.org/edweek/DigitalEducation/2014/09/student_mobile_device_usage_survey_pearson.html

Hewlett-Packard Development Company. (2004). *The power of visual communication.* Retrieved from http://www.hp.com/large/ipg/assets/bus-solutions/power-of-visual-communication.pdf

HITLabNZ. (2013). *colAR.* Retrieved from http://www.hitlabnz.org/index.php/products/colar

Honey, S., & Milnes, K. (2013). The augmented reality America's cup: Augmented reality is making sailboat racing a thrilling spectator sport. *IEEE Spectrum.* Retrieved from http://spectrum.ieee.org/consumer-electronics/audiovideo/the-augmented-reality-americas-cup

IBM. (2012). *The flexible workplace: Unlocking value in the 'bring your own device' era.* Retrieved from http://www-01.ibm.com/common/ssi/cgi-bin/ssialias?infotype=SA&subtype=WH&htmlfid=ENW03010USEN

IBM. (2014). *Big data.* Retrieved from http://www.ibm.com/big-data/us/en/

Intel. (2013). *Big data visualization: Turning big data into big insights. The rise of visualization-based data discovery tools.* Retrieved from http://www.intel.com/content/dam/www/public/us/en/documents/white-papers/big-data-visualization-turning-big-data-into-big-insights.pdf

International Reading Association (IRA). (2002). *Integrating literacy and technology in the curriculum: A position statement.* Newark, DE: International Reading Association.

International Society for Technology in Education (ISTE). (2008). *ISTE standards.* Retrieved from http://www.iste.org/standards

Jackson, A. (2014). *Beautiful science: Picturing data, inspiring insight at the British Library.* Retrieved from http://blogs.nature.com/ofschemesandmemes/2014/02/20/beautiful-science-picturing-data-inspiring-insight-at-the-british-library

Johnson, L., Adams Becker, S., Estrada, V., & Freeman, A. (2014). *NMC horizon report: 2014 K-12 edition*. Austin, TX: The New Media Consortium.

Jongedijk, L. (2013). Definition and key information on AR. *Trends in EdTech: Augmented Reality*. Retrieved from http://augreality.pbworks.com/w/page/9469035/Definition%20and%20key%20information%20on%20AR

Jukes, I., McCain, T., & Crockett, L. (2010). Understanding the digital generation. 21st Century Project.

Kapp, K. M. (2012). *The gamification of learning and instruction: Game-based methods and strategies for training and education*. San Francisco, CA: John Wiley & Sons, Inc.

Kazlauskas, A., & Robinson, K. (2012). Podcasts are not for everyone. *British Journal of Educational Technology*, *43*(2), 321–330. doi:10.1111/j.1467-8535.2010.01164.x

Kearney, M., Schuck, S., Burden, K., & Aubusson, P. (2012). Viewing mobile learning from a pedagogical perspective. *Research in Learning Technology*, *20*(1), 1–17.

Kellner, D. (2008). Critical perspectives on visual imagery in media and cyberculture. *Journal of Visual Literacy*, *22*(1), 81–90.

Kimmel, S. (2013). Graphic information visualizing STEM with elementary school students. *Knowledge Quest*, *41*(3), 36–41.

Kiss, J. (2014). Twitter is changing how we interact with the world. *The Guardian*. Retrieved from http://www.theguardian.com/technology/pda/2010/aug/02/twitter

Kostelnick, C., & Roberts, D. (2010). *Designing visual language: Strategies for professional communicators* (2nd ed.). Boston, MA: Allyn & Bacon.

Krueger, N. (2014, July). *3 barriers to innovation education leaders must address*. ISTE. Retrieved from http://www.iste.org/explore/ArticleDetail?articleid=98

Krum, R. (2013). *Cool infographics: Effective communication with data visualization and design*. Indianapolis, IN: Wiley.

Lamb, A., & Johnson, L. (2014). Infographics part 1: Invitations to inquiry. *Teacher Librarian*, *42*(4), 54–58.

Lamb, G., Polman, J., Newman, A., & Smith, C. (2014). Science news infographics: Teaching students to gather, interpret, and present information graphically. *Science Teacher (Normal, Ill.)*, 25–30.

Lankow, J., Crooks, R., & Ritchie, J. (2012). *Infographics: The power of visual storytelling*. Hoboken: Wiley.

Lapointe, D. K., & Linder-Vanberschot, J. A. (2012). *International research: Responding to global needs. In Trends and Issues in Distance Education: International Perspectives* (2nd ed.; pp. 5–22). Charlotte, NC: Information Age Publishing.

Lenhart, A., Madden, M., Smith, A., Purcell, K., Zichuhr, K., & Raine, L. 2011. *Teens, kindness and cruelty on social network sites*. Pew Research Internet Project. Retrieved from http://www.pewinternet.org/2011/11/09/teens-kindness-and-cruelty-on-social-network-sites/

Lepi, K. (2014). 10 ways to use mobile devices in the classroom. *Edudemic*. Retrieved from http://www.edudemic.com/mobile-devices-in-the-classroom-2/

Lester, P. (2013). *Visual communication: Images with messages*. Independence, KY: Cengage Learning.

Leu, D. J. Jr, Kinzer, C. K., Coiro, J., & Cammack, D. (2004). Toward a theory of new literacies emerging from the Internet and other ICT. In R. B. Ruddell & N. Unrau (Eds.), *Theoretical Models and Processes of Reading* (5th ed.; pp. 1568–1611). Newark, DE: International Reading Association.

Lewis, K. (2013). Infographics: All the rage, but a must-do for your business? *Forbes.* Retrieved from http://www.forbes.com/sites/kernlewis/2013/08/30/infographics-all-the-rage-but-a-must-do-for-your-business/

Levine, J. (2004). Faculty adoption of instructional technologies: Organizational and personal perspectives. In C. Crawford et al. (Eds.), *Proceedings of Society for Information Technology and Teacher Education International Conference 2004* (pp. 1595-1598). Chesapeake, VA: AACE.

Liarokapis, F., & Anderson, E. F. (2010). Using augmented reality as a medium to assist teaching in higher education. In *Proceedings of the 31st Annual Conference of the European Association for Computer Graphics* (Eurographics 2010). Eurographics Association.

Livingston, A. A. (2004). Smartphones and other mobile devices: The Swiss Army Knives of the 21st Century. *EDUCAUSE Quarterly*, 2746–2752.

Long, J. (2013). Why your business should be using infographics. *Huffington Post.* Retrieved from http://www.huffingtonpost.com/jonathan-long/why-your-business-should-_b_4192309.html

Lorenzo, G., & Ittelson, J. (2005). An overview of ePortfolios. Boulder, CO: EDUCAUSE Learning Initiative. Retrieved from www.educause.edu/ir/library/pdf/ELI3001.pdf

Lynch, D., Altschuler, G. C., & McClure, P. (2002). Professors should embrace technology in courses... and colleges must create technology plans. *The Chronicle of Higher Education*, 48(19), B15.

Madden, M., Fox, S., Smith, A., & Vitak, J. (2007). *Digital footprints: Online identity management and search in the age of transparency.* Washington, DC: Pew Internet & American Life Project.

Mancuso, D. S., Chlup, D. T., & McWhorter, R. R. (2010). A study of adult learning in a virtual world. *Advances in Developing Human Resources*, 12(6), 681–699. doi:10.1177/1523422310395368

Marcum, J. W. (2002). Beyond visual culture: The challenge of visual ecology. *Libraries and the Academy*, 2(2), 189–206. doi:10.1353/pla.2002.0038

Marques, D., Costello, R., & Azevedo, J. (2013). *Augmented reality facilitating visual literacy for engagement with science in museums.* Paper presented at Electronic Visualisation and the Arts (EVA 2013), London, UK.

Marzilli, C., Delello, J. A., Marmion, S., McWhorter, R. R., Brown, P., & Marzilli, T. S. (2014). Faculty attitudes towards integrating technology and innovation. *International Journal on Integrating Technology in Education*, 3(1), 1–20. doi:10.5121/ijite.2014.3101

Mashable. (2013). *Data visualization.* Retrieved from http://mashable.com/category/data-visualization

May, P. (2013). *Apps for helping autistic kids socially and academically.* San Jose Mercury News. Retrieved from http://www.aurasma.com/education/aurasma-listed-among-apps-for-helping-autistic-kids-socially-and-academically/

McCoy, B. (2013). Digital distraction in the classroom: Student classroom use of digital devices for non-class-related purposes. *Journal of Media Education.* Retrieved from http://en.calameo.com/read/000091789af53ca4e647f

McDermott, R., & Archibald, D. (2010, March). Harnessing Your Staff's Informal Networks. *Harvard Business Review*, *88*(3), 82–89. PMID:20402051

McWhorter, R. R. (2010). Exploring the emergence of virtual human resource development. *Advances in Developing Human Resources*, *12*(6), 623–631. doi:10.1177/1523422310395367

McWhorter, R. R. (2012). *Augmented reality for virtual HRD*. Retrieved from http://virtualhrd. wordpress.com/2012/01/18/augmented-reality-for-virtual-hrd/

McWhorter, R. R., & Bennett, E. E. (2012). *Facilitating transition from higher education to the workforce: A literature review of ePortfolios as virtual human resource development*. Paper presented at the Academy of Human Resource Development International Conference, Denver, CO.

McWhorter, R. R., Delello, J. A., Roberts, P. B., Raisor, C. M., & Fowler, D. A. (2013). A cross-case analysis of the use of web-based eportfolios in higher education. *Journal of Information Technology Education: Innovations in Practice*, *12*, 253–286. Retrieved from http://www.jite. org/documents/Vol12/JITEv12IIPp253-286Mc-Whorter1238.pdf

Medina, J. (2014). *Brain rules: 12 principles for surviving and thriving at work, home, and school*. Seattle, WA: Pear Press.

Meister, J. (2014). The wearable era is here: Implications for the future workplace. *Forbes*. Retrieved from http://www.forbes.com/sites/ jeannemeister/2014/06/16/the-wearable-era-is-here-implications-for-the-future-workplace/

Merriam-Webster. (2014). *Portfolio*. Retrieved from http://www.merriam-webster.com/dictionary/portfolio

Mesko, B. (2013). *Augmented reality in operating rooms soon! Science roll*. Retrieved from http:// scienceroll.com/2013/08/22/augmented-reality-in-operating-rooms-soon/

Metros, S. E., & Woolsey, K. (2006, May/June). Visual literacy: An institutional imperative. *EDU-CAUSE Review*, *41*(3), 80–81.

Middleton, C. (2013). *Certificates, badges, and portfolios: International education and micro-credentialing*. UT Global Initiative, The University of Texas at Austin. Retrieved from http://sites. utexas.edu/utgi/2013/11/certificates-badges-and-portfolios-international-education-and-mico-credentialing/

Mirzoeff, N. (1998). What is visual culture? In N. Mirzoeff (Ed.), *The visual culture reader* (pp. 3–13). London: Routledge.

Mishra, P., & Koehler, M. J. (2006). Technological pedagogical content knowledge: A Framework for teacher knowledge. *Teachers College Record*, *108*(6), 1017–1054. doi:10.1111/j.1467-9620.2006.00684.x

Moline, S. (2011). I see what you mean: Visual Literacy K-8 (2nd ed.). Portland, ME: Stenhouse Publishers

Moritz, D. (2014). *5 brands shaking up visual content strategy with Hyperlapse*. Retrieved from http://sociallysorted.com.au/visual-content-strategy-hyperlapse/

Morris, C. (2013). *The sexiest job of the 21st century: Data analyst*. Retrieved from http://www. cnbc.com/id/100792215# Mourshed

Farrell, D., & Barton, D. (2012). *Education to employment: Designing a system that works*. Retrieved from http://mckinseyonsociety.com/ downloads/reports/Education/Education-to-Employment_FINAL.pdf

Mozilla. (2014). *Open badges.* Retrieved from http://openbadges.org/display/

NASA.gov. (2013). *Curiosity – 7 minutes of terror.* NASA Jet Propulsion Laboratory. Retrieved from http://www.jpl.nasa.gov/infographics/infographic.view.php?id=10776

National Governors Association Center for Best Practices & Council of Chief State School Officers. (2010). Common Core State Standards for English language arts and literacy in history/social studies, science, and technical subjects. Washington, DC: Author.

Nilsson, B. (2014). *Digital badges are clearing the final hurdles for disruption. Extreme networks viewpoints.* Retrieved from http://www.extremenetworks.com/digital-badges-are-clearing-the-final-hurdles-for-disruption/

NOAA.gov. (2014). *Timeline of recovery from the Exxon Valdez oil spill.* Retrieved from http://response.restoration.noaa.gov/oil-and-chemical-spills/significant-incidents/exxon-valdez-oil-spill/timeline-ecological-recovery-infographic.html

Norman, D. (2013). The paradox of wearable technologies. *MIT Technology Review.* Retrieved from http://www.technologyreview.com/news/517346/the-paradox-of-wearable-technologies/

O'Shaughnessy, L. (2011). *Digital badges could significantly impact higher education.* Retrieved from http://www.usnews.com/education/blogs/the-college-solution/2011/10/04/digital-badges-could-significantly-impact-higher-education

Perey, C. (2011). Print and publishing and the future of augmented reality. *Information Services & Use, 31*(1/2), 31–38. doi:10.3233/ISU-2011-0625

Perez, S. (2009). Hot, hot, hot! A Twitter augmented reality app for iPhone. *Readwrite.* Retrieved from http://readwrite.com/2009/07/08/a_twitter_augmented_reality_app_for_iphone

Pérez-López, D., & Contero, M. (2013). Delivering educational multimedia contents through an augmented reality application: A case study on its impact on knowledge acquisition and retention. *Turkish Online Journal of Educational Technology, 12*(4), 19–28.

Petronzio, M. (2013). 10 fascinating data visualization projects. *Mashable.* Retrieved from Retrieved from http://mashable.com/2013/03/05/data-visualization-projects/

Prensky, M. (2001, December). Digital natives digital immigrants, part II: Do they really think differently? *On The Horizon NCB University Press, 9*(6).

Purcell, K., Heaps, A., Buchanan, J., & Friedrich, L. (n.d.). *How teachers are using technology at home and in their classrooms.* Pew Research Center Report. Retrieved from http://www.pewinternet.org/files/old-media//Files/Reports/2013/PIP_TeachersandTechnologywithmethodology_PDF.pdf

Purcell, K., Rainie, L., Heaps, A., Buchanan, J., Friedrich, L., Jacklin, A., & Zickuhr, K. (2012). *How teens do research in the digital world.* Pew Research Center's Internet & American Life Project.

Purdue University. (2014). *Nursing faculty and students implement Passport badges to measure learning, achievement.* Retrieved from http://www.itap.purdue.edu/newsroom/news/140417_passport_nursing.html

PR Newswire. (2013, July 31). Wroclaw University Library turns to IBM big data solution to preserve European heritage, open digital archives to the world. *PR Newswire US.* Retrieved from http://www.prnewswire.com/news-releases/wroclaw-university-library-turns-to-ibm-big-data-solution-to-preserve-european-heritage-open-digital-archives-to-the-world-217739731.html

Pritchard, R., & O'Hara, S. (2009). Vocabulary development in the science classroom: Using hypermedia authoring to support English learners. *The Tapestry Journal, 1*, 15–29.

USAID. (2012). *Infrastructure.* Retrieved from http://www.usaid.gov/what-we-do/economic-growth-and-trade/infrastructure

Ramirez, M. L. (2011). Whose role is it anyway? A library practitioner's appraisal of the digital data deluge. *Bulletin of the American Society for Information Science and Technology, 37*(5), 21–23. doi:10.1002/bult.2011.1720370508

Rambe, P. (2012). Constructive disruptions for effective collaborative learning: Navigating the affordances of social media for meaningful engagement. *The Electronic Journal of e-Learning, 10*(1), 132-146.

Riesland, E. (2010). Visual literacy and the classroom. *New Horizons for Learning.* Retrieved from http://education.jhu.edu/PD/newhorizons/strategies/topics/literacy/articles/visual-literacy-and-the-classroom

Learning, R. (2014). *Why badges?* Retrieved from http://www.reconnectlearning.org/#whybadges

Rich, M. (2008). *Literacy debate: Online, R U really reading?* The New York Times Online. Retrieved from http://www.nytimes.com/2008/07/27/books/27reading.html

Roblyer, M. D., McDaniel, M., Webb, M., Herman, J., & Witty, J. V. (2010). Findings on Facebook in higher education: A comparison of college faculty and student uses and perceptions of social networking sites. *The Internet and Higher Education, 13*(3), 134–140. doi:10.1016/j.iheduc.2010.03.002

Rose, D., Fisch, K., & McLeod, S. (2011). *Did you know: Shift happens.* Retrieved from https://www.youtube.com/watch?v=F9WDtQ4Ujn8

Roussos, M., Johnson, A., Moher, T., Leigh, J., Vasilakis, C., & Barnes, C. (1999). Learning and building together in an immersive virtual world. *Presence (Cambridge, Mass.), 8*(3), 247–263. doi:10.1162/105474699566215

Sawers, P. (2011). *Augmented reality: The past, present and future.* Retrieved from http://thenextweb.com/insider/2011/07/03/augmented-reality-the-past-present-and-future/

Schmarzo, B. (2013). *Big data: Understanding how data powers big business.* Hoboken: Wiley.

Scivicque, C. (2013). *Why you (yes, you) need a professional portfolio.* Retrieved from https://www.themuse.com/advice/why-you-yes-you-need-a-professional-portfolio

ShakeUpLearning.com. (2014). *5 awesome resources for badges in the classroom.* Retrieved from http://www.shakeuplearning.com/blog/5-awesome-resources-for-badges-in-the-classroom#sthash.2b9wVKTI.ZEgy8y1v.dpbs

Sherman, C. (2014). What's the big deal about big data? *Online Searcher, 38*(2), 10–16.

Shuler, C. (2009). *Pockets of Potential: Using Mobile Technologies to Promote Children's Learning.* New York: The Joan Ganz Cooney Center at Sesame Workshop.

Smiciklas, M. (2012). *The power of infographics: Using pictures to communicate and connect with your audience.* Indianapolis, IN: Pearson Education, Inc.

Sosa, T. (2009). Visual literacy: The missing piece of your technology integration course. *TechTrends, 53*(2), 55–58. doi:10.1007/s11528-009-0270-1

Spence, E. (2014). 2014 will be the year of wearable technology. *Forbes.* Retrieved from http://www.forbes.com/sites/ewanspence/2013/11/02/2014-will-be-the-year-of-wearable-technology/

Thomas, D. (2014). Augmented reality gives physical world a virtual dimension. *BBC News*. Retrieved from http://www.bbc.com/news/business-28399343

Thoman, E., & Jolls, T. (2004). Media literacy: A national priority for a changing world. *The American Behavioral Scientist*, *48*(1), 18–29. doi:10.1177/0002764204267246

Toth, C. (2013). Revisiting a genre: Teaching infographics in business and professional communication courses. *Business Communication Quarterly*, *76*(4), 446–457. doi:10.1177/1080569913506253

Tufte, E. (2001). *Visual display of quantitative information*. Cheshire, CT: Graphics Press.

University of Canterbury. (2012). *New technology brings children's drawings alive*. Retrieved from http://www.comsdev.canterbury.ac.nz/rss/news/index.php?feed=news&articleId=455

University of Illinois. (2014). *Badges at Illinois*. Retrieved from http://news.badges.illinois.edu/

U.S. Department of Commerce. (2002). *A nation online: How Americans are expanding their use of the Internet*. Retrieved from http://www.ntia.doc.gov/legacy/ntiahome/dn/anationonline2.pdf

USDE. (2011). *Digital badges for learning*. Retrieved from http://www.ed.gov/news/speeches/digital-badges-learning

Vah Seliskar, H. (2014). *Using badges in the classroom to motivate learning*. Retrieved from http://www.facultyfocus.com/articles/teaching-with-technology-articles/using-badges-classroom-motivate-learning/

Venable, M. (2013). *The power of the online career portfolio*. Retrieved from http://www.onlinecollege.org/2013/08/05/the-power-of-a-career-portfolio/

Vine. (2014). *Embed vine posts*. [Web log comment]. Retrieved from http://blog.vine.co/page/6

Waters, J. K. (2013). Digital badges. *The Journal*, *40*(5), 14.

WGBH. (1998). *A science odyssey: The Internet gives rise to the World Wide Web 1992*. PBS. Retrieved from http://www.pbs.org/wgbh/aso/databank/entries/dt92ww.html

White House. (2013). *Four years of broadband growth*. Washington, DC: Office of Science and Technology Policy & The National Economic Council.

Woollaston, V., & Prigg, M. (2014). Rise of the #selfielapse: Instagram adds a new feature to its Hyperlapse app that lets users film themselves more easily. *MailOne*. Retrieved from http://www.dailymail.co.uk/sciencetech/article-2770554/Rise-selfielapse-Instagram-adds-new-feature-Hyperlapse-app-lets-users-film-easily.html

Yuen, S., Yaoyuneyong, G., & Johnson, E. (2011). Augmented reality: An overview and five directions for AR in education. *Journal of Educational Technology Development and Exchange*, *4*(1), 119–140.

Zambelich, A. (2014). Evernote's savvy plan to join the wearables race. *Wired*. Retrieved from http://www.wired.com/2014/07/evernotes-savvy-plan-to-join-the-wearables-race/

Zetlin, M. (2014). Five things to consider when creating a wearables policy. *CIO*. Retrieved from http://www.cio.com/article/2369944/consumer-technology/five-things-to-consider-when-creating-a-wearables-policy.html

Zhu, E., Hadadgar, A., Masiello, I., & Zary, N. (2014). *Augmented reality in healthcare education: An integrative review. PeerJ*. doi:10.7717/peerj.469

KEY TERMS AND DEFINITIONS

Augmented Reality: Augmented reality (AR) is an emerging technology blending physical objects with virtual reality.

Big Data: Large or complex datasets that are too difficult to easily analyze with traditional processes including the utilization of predictive analysis for decision making.

Digital Badge: A graphic representation of an individual's accomplishment, interest or demonstrated skill.

Digital Literacy: The capability to use digital technologies to read, write, interpret, and apply knowledge.

Electronic Portfolios: A digital collection of a variety of artifacts that can be shared with others.

Infographics: Information graphics that are visual representations of data or information.

Personal Branding: The process whereby an individual communicates their core attributes across multiple platforms.

Social Media: A digital tool or platform that allows users to communicate and share interests with others.

Visual Literacy: The ability to create, understand, and communicate through the use of visual images.

Visual Social Media: The sharing of images through digital platforms or social media tools.

Chapter 7
Libraries and Digital Media

Jessica R. Olin
Wesley College, USA

ABSTRACT

Both academic and public libraries have, since the inception of the internet and the world wide web, experienced a seismic level of change when compared to the past. The impacts of such specific issues as social media, open access, and the digital divide, and how they change both the short and long term operations and planning for libraries, are considered here through the lens of recent research on these topics. Some attention is also given to gaps in the current research and recommendations are made for further study. Particular attention is given to ways in which these issues overlap for academic and public libraries.

INTRODUCTION

When confronted with a topic like this, it can boggle the mind a bit. Much like contemplating the idea of infinity, the possible permutations of the impact of digital media on academic and public libraries are endless. Regardless, this topic is an undercurrent of the daily lives of most (if not all) librarians, not just those working at public and academic libraries. To be honest, this topic could possibly be turned into a series of dissertations and an encyclopedia. Rather than try to tackle all of the literature about all the different ways in which digital media impacts public and academic libraries, this chapter focuses on three major areas that are, in the opinion of the author, the most broad reaching and have resulted in sea-level changes across the board. Because of the limita-

tions of space and time, much has been left out that could potentially be very important. Further, this chapter examines only a small cross-section of the research being done in these areas and is in no way meant to be exhaustive.

The specific topics under the umbrella of "digital media" that are presented within this chapter are: social media, the interplay of open access / digital repositories / proprietary databases, and the digital divide. In each section, the reader will find an introductory overview of the topic, including definitions; a consideration of the research being done on that topic as it relates to public libraries and then academic libraries; and finally, an overview of areas needing more research - both as suggested by the authors of the studies and articles presented and as identified by the author of this chapter.

DOI: 10.4018/978-1-4666-8310-5.ch007

Please note that any gaps in materials considered in this chapter are based upon access to said materials. This is not intended to be either an exhaustive consideration of the research in any area or a historical perspective about the evolution of the interplay of libraries, both academic and public, and these digital media.

SOCIAL MEDIA

Succinct Overview of the Research

Social media are an inescapable part of much of modern culture, and as a result they are very much a part of the lives of the communities most public and academic libraries serve. This means social media are necessarily a part of those same libraries. While definitions vary, most people agree that social media are an expression of Web 2.0, a somewhat misleading term that captures those places on the internet where the content is cooperatively created by the users and the owners of websites. Social media, as an extension of that, are applications and websites where the purpose of the cooperative creation is primarily "social" in nature. This, therefore, describes everything from the (mostly) anonymous conversations being held on some applications known only by a few that exist almost exclusively between and among smartphone users to the web, and identity based discussions on platforms that are broadly known and available pretty much worldwide. While libraries exist or are at least discussed in every permutation of social media, from Yik Yak (an anonymous social networking application that has conversations structured around the physical location of the users) to Facebook (an almost ubiquitous social network), the research relating social networks to libraries is much less extensive. Further, so much of what has been written is opinion based (described as "best practices" which, many times, comes down to "lots of people do it this way, so we think everyone should do it this

way") so, even when it is peer reviewed, it is not necessarily helpful research. Much of the actual research that has been done in this area is capturing a baseline and assessing the "lay of the land" for libraries and social media. That kind of research is important, but we need to move beyond that to learn how to best serve our constituents with these powerful tools. Thankfully, some of what was reviewed in preparation for this chapter is moving in that direction.

Current Issues in the Field Raised by These Studies

Please note: in this and subsequent sections, current issues are presented through the lens of a more detailed examination of the research.

Public

As was stated previously, most of the available literature about the intersection of social media and libraries is more about how libraries are using these tools than about active research which tries to find research-based strategies for effective use. (It is important to note that much work has been done on the role of social media for e-government, a lot of which touches on, but is not exclusively about, public libraries.)

One such study, "Social Media Practices and Support in U.S. Public Libraries and School Library Media Centers," looks at the different ways that public and school libraries use these tools and how their policies influence those efforts (Magee, Naughton, O'Gan, Forte, & Agosto, 2012). This study is broad in aspect, based on the researchers using stratified sampling to select both 750 public libraries and 750 school libraries. Their response rate was somewhat disheartening, with only ~18% of public libraries completing the surveys and ~5% of school media centers, but the study's authors were still able to draw a couple of conclusions from what they have gained so far. Unsurprisingly, it is clear from their data that the most commonly used social media outlet - both for school and for public libraries - is Facebook (p. 29). However, it seems that the response of intended audiences is lackluster with regards to Facebook and is more robust when outreach is targeted through more traditional outlets like library websites (p.29). Another unsurprising finding of this study is that public libraries are far more likely to go beyond Facebook with their efforts, extending to image sharing sites (such as Flickr), video hosting sites (YouTube, Vimeo), social bookmarking (Delicious), and beyond.

A marketing survey conducted in 2012 by *Library Journal*, a library oriented periodical with a broad readership, which was then interpreted by Nancy Dowd, saw similar results (2013). The title of her piece alone is enough to give the reader a solid idea: "Social Media: Libraries Are Posting, but Is Anybody Listening?" Dowd puts it succinctly by saying, "According to *Library Journal's* Survey on Public Library Marketing Methods and Best Practices, 86 percent of libraries said they were using social media" (2). Despite the overwhelming majority of the 471 libraries saying that they do make use, at least somewhat, of social networks, those same respondents were less than satisfied with the results of their efforts - with only 59% saying that their marketing efforts are only "somewhat successful" (*Library Journal*, p. 7).

Academic

Much more of the focused research that is readily available considers the impact of social media on academic libraries as opposed to public. (This was not unexpected, as academic librarians frequently have publication expectations for continued employment, whereas this kind of restriction is pretty much unheard of for public librarians.

One interesting study that was encountered, "Impact of Web 2.0 Technologies on Academic Libraries: A Survey of ARL Libraries," focused on the impressions of academic librarians have

about social media (Mahmood & Richardson, 2011). All Association of Research Libraries (ARL) members, minus Canadian members and libraries not connected to academic institutions, were all contacted and a total of 67 responded. While there are trends to be spotted - such as Really Simple Syndication (RSS), blogs, and social networking sites being the most common tools used and virtual environments being used only rarely - use of these tools seemed to track more closely to the librarians exposure to the tools than to any sense of efficacy (p. 516). There is no doubt that ARL librarians have a high opinion of social media and other Web 2.0 tools; the authors point out that respondents "believe that such tools were essential for the twenty-first century library" (p. 516). One statement from the study's authors stands out as representative of much of what has been said about the topic: "With the basic philosophy of interacting with users, libraries use Web 2.0 tools in various ways" (p. 514).

Another study that diverges from the typical mode just a bit is "Social Media, Academic Research and the Role of University Libraries" (Nicholas, Watkinson, & Rowlands, 2011). This article presents the results of focus group discussions about the role an academic library plays in an emerging model of academic research that depends on researchers using social media as part of their process". Inspired by research into this new mode which showed that "social media are beginning to have a significant impact on scholarly communication and, in particular, on many aspects of the research process" (p. 1), the authors wanted to find out what role librarians could/did play in this kind of research. Rather than the central role academic librarians have played in the past, the studied seemed to indicate that librarians were seen as consumers of research instead of partners or producers. Even in the focus groups where librarians and libraries were explicitly mentioned by those conducting the research, librarians were perceived as an afterthought to participants. "The role of the library in the new social media environment came up only after prompting on the part of the facilitators" (p. 1). One quote from participants that was shared in this article stands out as indicative of faculty attitudes towards librarians: " 'The library is a building. Google has world-wide [*sic*] reach'" (p. 2). This particular study was fairly disheartening in its conclusions. It points back to the typical use academic librarians have for social networking, that of marketing and outreach, seems the one to which even the faculty at our institutions have relegated us.

A paper presented at the 2012 Annual Conference of the Canadian Association for Information Science (CAIS), similar to the ARL study discussed above, shares conclusions drawn from a survey of the use of social media by Ontario university libraries (Collins). In "Social Media Use By Ontario Universities: Challenges and Ethical Considerations," gives a longitudinal perspective of the growth of use of Web 2.0 tools over the course of fourteen months. The three main takeaways are not surprising in light of other studies on this topic: there was a slow increase in adoption rates that was mostly focused on the increased use of tools that were already being employed - especially by libraries in the Southwestern portion of the area being studied; there was a broad diversity of methods and content being shared via these tools; and very few libraries employed the platforms to do more than advertise to their constituents (Collins, 2012). The conclusion drawn by the author echoes the trend seen elsewhere: "The present study shows that while Ontario university libraries are adopting social media tools, they may not have a clear vision of how to integrate these tools into the overall goals of the library," (p. 5).

In a follow up study, Collins and co-author Quan-Haase, added another year's worth of data to expand their examination of social media use in the same academic libraries (2013). While this study's findings mostly echoed those of the previous paper, such as "the adoption of [social media] by Ontario university libraries remains largely

slow in overall growth," (p. 62) there were a few interesting tidbits that merit its inclusion here. While, in general, the researchers found that the more active a library's use of specific platforms, the more followers/"likes" they earned, YouTube was an outlier (p. 57). However, even a year later, most university libraries in Ontario seemed to be using Web 2.0 as a means for advertising and pushing information than as a venue for sustained conversations with their communities.

Broader Studies

Additionally, work has been done that does not neatly fall within the public or academic library category, but that still has bearing on where things stand between social networking and these sectors. Most interestingly, there are a number of articles available that present models and metrics that libraries can use to judge the success of their social media efforts.

One such article is "A SWOT Analysis for Social Media in Libraries," (Fernandez, 2009). SWOT (Strengths, Weaknesses, Opportunities, Threats) is a tool most frequently used in industries far removed from libraries, such as independent business ventures. However, it can and should be used more broadly because, as Fernandez suggests, "cultivating user loyalty is just as important as building library collections," (p. 37). Fernandez does enumerate what he sees as the aspects of social networking that fall into each of the listed categories, but what is more interesting is where his tool has gone since then. This short article has been cited 29 times according to a Google Scholar search, and has informed many social media strategies - not just for library related publications.

Another suggestion for adopting business venture tools for the assessment of social media in libraries was part of "ROI. Measuring the Social Media Return on Investment in a Library," by Romero (2011). One of the author's main conclusions, "Opening a new channel of communication with users on the internet is a challenge for libraries that can be optimized with the development of a strategy for the use of social media. The library should make an effort to manage these resources efficiently and obtain the largest possible return on their use," (p. 151), seems to have resonated well considering Google Scholar shows 21 citations for this piece.

One final business venture tool that has been suggested as having application within libraries has intriguing possibilities, but does not seem to have been taken up by the broader library science community yet. "A Proposed Scale for Measuring the Quality of Social Media SErvices: An E-S-QUAL Approach," (Kim & Nitecki, 2014) talks about applying the E-S-QUAL tool, which is designed to "survey instrument used to assess electronic service quality" (IGI Global, 1988-2015), to library electronic services with a special focus on social media. This publication reads more as a proof-of-concept piece than actual research, but the ideas are intriguing.

Gaps in the Extant Research and Directions for Future Research

Others have noted the gaps in the literature with libraries and social media. In a piece published in late 2011, "Asking the right Questions: A Critique of Facebook, Social Media, and Libraries," Bodnar and Doshi pointed out "the limitations we see in current conversations, practices, and writings about Facebook and other social networking sites in order to uncover and suggest questions and directions" (p. 103) where there needs to be further work. They call for attention to how the use of these tools fits into the daily routines and workflow of those charged with maintaining online library presences. Bodnar and Doshi also point out the lack of library science literature that covers the "design assumptions of… social networking sites" (p. 105) and how those designs work for or against the efforts of librarians - a call with which the author of this chapter agrees, especially considering how some of the bigger players in the field, like

Twitter and Facebook, seem to constantly change their algorithms (generally, the way the computer program underlying the interface presents results) in ways to confound those who have no or limited money to spend promoting their posts.

As was mentioned in the calls for further research in some of the articles reviewed here, especially by Collins and Quan-Haase (2013), "aspects of user privacy and social media have been minimally addressed within the literature," (p. 52). While it has been broadly reported that there are people in the communities served by libraries that have a much more lax approach to their online privacy, librarians have traditionally been highly protective of that same information - even going so far as to change the way we handle user information in response to the Patriot Act and other similar legislation. There clearly needs to be more research here.

Most of what was read in preparation for this chapter focused on one type of library over another, academic or public, and there is a need to compare across library types. Although it is not a commonly discussed fact, there is much crossover in the populations served by different kinds of libraries. It would be interesting to find how the social media expectations communities have for public libraries intersect and diverge. Finally, more attention has been paid to the use of social media in the libraries of the United States, and if nothing else it would be nice to see a comparison across different English speaking nations.

While it is true that the reviewed research was not exhaustive nor necessarily representative of all that has been done, it is still clear that the approach to the study of the impact of social media on academic and public libraries has been dictated more by interest and convenience than by any sort of organized agenda. It is hard to construct a narrative of the work without feeling pulled in multiple directions at once, which is unfortunate because there is rich data available and plenty of room to come up with a more unified perspective on the impact of social media on academic and public libraries.

Implications and Recommendations

Beyond the obvious need for extensive further research, there is one other implication that becomes apparent the more one reads the research: librarians need to learn to use more than Facebook and Twitter. Use and regard for the different tools both seem to correlate with awareness, and if members of library communities are already using these tools, it seems important for librarians to follow suit.

OPEN ACCESS / DIGITAL REPOSITORIES

Succinct Overview of the Research

The interplay of the impact of proprietary databases, the open access (OA) movement, and digital repositories is hard to parse into separate pieces. Traditional publishing models, where the publisher owns the copyright for the materials, has long been supported by the tenure requirements at many academic institutions. Traditional publishing pricing models, embodied in those same proprietary databases, are getting to the point where they cannot be sustained. Many academic libraries - and even public libraries - have started to cut ties with the database providers. There is increased interest in the OA model of publishing, where published materials are constantly and freely available to anyone. There are downsides to this model: the money has to come from somewhere, and that can mean the researcher and/or their employer pays to publish; and a sizeable proportion of the top tiered publications are still on the traditional model. One final wrinkle is the role of digital repositories in the publication game. Digital repositories, sometimes called digital libraries, are traditionally just focused collections of digital items organized much like physical items are organized in a brick-and-mortar library. However, for libraries, the idea has come to mean

providing "open, online access to the products of... research and scholarship, to preserve these works for future generations, [and] to promote new models of scholarly communication" (University of Texas Libraries, n.d.).

The vast majority of research that is available about these topics, which boil down to the idea of who gets to provide access to the products of research and culture and who has to pay, has been done with a focus on academia. It is important to note, however, that this is a growing area of concern for public libraries and public library consortia, as even larger cooperative institutions are being priced out of the market.

Current Issues in the Field Raised by These Studies

In the interests of representing the multifaceted nature of this issue, the author of this chapter has included what is essentially an opinion piece that is more biased than normal: "The Shifting Sands of Open Access Publishing, a Publisher's View," by Regazzi (2004). While it is slightly out of date, these thoughts have been echoed again and again both in the publishing record and in more informal venues. This article invokes the spectre of scientific fraud, alludes to the sometimes exorbitant prices charged by some open access outlets (interestingly, those outlets seem to be predominantly supported by the same publishers with ties to the sought after top-tier traditionally published journals, such as Springer), and the frequently disproven idea of "publishers in partnership with librarians already [providing] near universal access to STM literature" (p. 279). Despite the bias, it is important to note that there is some truth to this article. Of special importance to the present discussion is how Regazzi describes OA. He says "the significance of Open Access, its financial model, and its very definition is almost changing on an ongoing basis" (p. 279). There seems to be a disrespect for the movement implied in his writing.

Not too long after Regazzi's piece was published, a similarly themed although differently toned piece was published in *College and Research Libraries* (which is, it is interesting to note, a top tiered journal of library science literature that is completely open access). "New Roles for a Changing Environment: Implications of Open Access for Libraries," by Schmidt, Sennyey, and Carstens (2005) agrees on the changeable nature of OA but from a place of support. The authors of this piece took the existing research about OA and suggested three possible outcomes. The first possibility they shared was that the OA movement could "fizzle out", mostly due to the perceived lack of impact and prestige of OA journals; the second suggestion had OA movement becoming such a success that traditional publishing models died away; and the third suggestion, a mixed model of OA and traditional publishing, is the one the authors say "is likely to endure" (p. 409). Interestingly, the prediction in which they placed the most faith closely reflects the state of things currently. While this piece presents supposition based on minimal research, it is important here because it points to a role librarians need to play in this aspect of the impact of digital media: that of serving our communities well in open access adoption and support. "Although identifying high-quality open-access resources is critically important, these resources will not be useful to patrons unless libraries communicate their existence and usefulness... "(p. 411). This and other evolving methods of scholarly communication, especially in light of the Obama administration's commitment to expand access to the results of government funded research (Stebbins, 2013), are deeply important to the work that all librarians do.

Some encouraging research that was encountered while preparing for this review examined the usability (meaning "How effectively, efficiently and satisfactorily a user can interact with a user interface" (usability.gov) and usefulness (according to the authors, whether or not resources "constitute valuable tools for the completion of users' tasks"

(Tsakonas & Papatheodorou, 2008, p. 1237) the interfaces of open access digital libraries really are. "Exploring Usefulness and Usability in the Evaluation of Open Access Digital Libraries," by Tsakonas & Papatheodorou takes as its premise the fact that OA is supposed to serve the needs of the user, and checks to see if these repositories are doing their jobs. While their work was fairly circumscribed, looking at a very specific and limited group of interfaces, the importance of this research piece is not in its results but in its implications for further work. The idea that the content or even making sure that the communities libraries serve are aware of the content of digital libraries is, indeed, highly important. However, what use will OA serve if the constituencies being served by digital libraries cannot even find the materials?

Another concern that has been considered is the rate of buy-in from faculty, especially science faculty who were at the forefront of this movement. According to "Open Access to the Scientific Journal Literature: Situation 2009" (Björk et al., 2009), there are encouraging numbers but still a lot of room for improvement. The researchers examined a large sample of science periodicals published in a specific timeframe to determine what portion, if any, were open access. While the numbers were fairly skewed in favor of traditionally published content (only 20.4% of the articles examined were available freely on the web), the authors still seemed heartened by the results. This study was a follow up to one from three years prior in which a much smaller sample had 19.4% OA articles. This is not enough for libraries to give up the subscription proprietary databases, but it is encouraging.

On the librarian/libraries side of this topic are digital and institutional repositories (DRs and IRs). Loosely defined, digital repositories are the back end of the publicly facing digital libraries. And one of the biggest problems facing librarians is getting content for the repository. One piece of research in this area is "Understanding Faculty to Improve Content Recruitment for Institutional Repositories," by Foster and Gibbons (2005). This anthropological study of faculty research and writing looked at a cross-section of faculty across a spectrum of departments from social science, hard sciences, and humanities. Unlike what many librarians may expect, the key finding from this study is actually unsurprising: "what faculty members and university researchers want [from digital repositories is a tool that will help them] to do their research, read and write about it, share it with others, and keep up in their field," (p. 3). Especially for faculty who are already comfortable with digital tools, this makes so much sense. Librarians tend to think of preservation of and access to research, but so many of the faculty academic librarians support have the creation of new research as their primary focus. "These faculty… are in desperate need of an authoring system to assist with document versioning, collaborative authoring, and centralized document access from any computer at any location" (p. 5). One further problem uncovered by these researchers is that the very vocabulary librarians use has become a barrier to faculty participation. For them, the idea of DRs "implies that the system is designed to support and achieve the needs and goals of the institution, not necessarily those of the individual" (p. 5). The language surrounding digital repositories has not change and the role that they play - of a place where completed research is deposited - is also still the same.

A subsequent publication, "Reducing Psychological Resistance to Digital Repositories," by Quinn (2010), follows up on the work of Foster and Gibbons. The very first sentence in this article sums up, perfectly, the exact problem facing all librarians involved with digital repositories: "The potential value of digital repositories is dependent on the cooperation of scholars to deposit their work" (p. 67). Quinn gives important background information on the psychology of resistance, then moves on to specific research based suggestions for future practices. Quinn covers ideas such as

"priming and imaging" (giving potential partners mental images, in detail, of the outcomes of the prospective partnership, as opposed to just telling them how it could be helpful), "identification and liking" (helping potential partners feel like they have a lot in common with the people already involved with the project), "perceived consensus and social modeling" (goes beyond identification to establishing behaviors as social norms), "redefinition, consistency, and depersonalization" (reframing the idea as a positive instead of a negative), "narrative, timing, and anticipation" (telling the story as opposed to presenting the argument), and "options, comparisons, and guarantees" (presenting options and establishing the ideal as the first, but then something more reasonable as the second). These suggestions might be a tad unconventional, but it is obvious that digital repositories have not been as successful as they could be and a lot of that is tied to faculty resistance.

Gaps in the Extant Research and Directions for Future Research

The research that was reviewed in preparation for writing this chapter barely scratched the surface of what is available, but even with that caveat in mind, there are some clear gaps in the literature. One very obvious piece that should be addressed is the relative lack of research into the interplay between public libraries and the open access movement. While it's true that academic libraries have differences in their core missions from those of public libraries, the impact of subscription database costs is still a huge factor regardless of library type. Another area that needs examining is effective practices for making communities and patrons aware of these resources (although it must be said that librarians have difficulties making sure their communities know about anything beyond the traditional resource of books). It is also crucial that libraries, across the board, build upon the work of Tsakonas and Papatheodorou as discussed above. Comparison of usability, usefulness, and accessibility of multiple different standard interfaces used for digital repositories and other open access platforms, with attention paid to the literature of human computer interaction, could be key to the future success of these efforts. While the literature of open access has much about the makeup of science research available, there seems to be a need to examine what kinds of research is available in other fields such as social science and literary criticism - particularly fields that are of broader interest and therefore overlap with the interests of the communities served with public libraries. Finally, something studying the effectiveness of the techniques suggested by the Quinn article is also clearly needed. Finally, a follow up to the work of Foster and Gibbons that takes into account the fact that tools for online collaboration exist now, such as Google Drive and Dropbox, seems needed.

Implications and Recommendations

More than anything else, there is a clear need for outreach to public libraries. The kinds of resources represented by the open access movement are more pertinent to the needs of the communities served by academic libraries, but as has been stated: the costs of providing access to digital materials is growing faster than the budgets of all libraries.

DIGITAL DIVIDE

Succinct Overview of the Research

So much has been written on the topic of the digital divide that it is difficult to know where to start, even with respects to how this phenomenon impacts academic and public libraries. Scholars don't even agree on a basic definition of the term and it has become a lightning rod of sorts for discussions of inequity all around the world. Further, to truly capture the impact of the digital

divide on libraries, you have to consider each and every possible definition that has been put forward (although this chapter will follow in the footsteps of other publications and stick to general categories of definitions).

One helpful resource for understanding these distinctions is "Conceptualizing and Testing a Social Cognitive Model of the Digital Divide" by Wei, Teo, Chan, and Tan (2011). This piece delineates different definitions have for this term. First, there is how "digital divide" can refer to "both hardware access as well as use of software;" second, "inequality of IT capability;" and third, "the 'digital outcome divide,' which arises due to the" other aspects already described (Dewan & Riggins, 2005, qtd. in Wei, Teo, Chan, and Tan, 2011, p. 171). All three of these definitions have bearing on public and academic libraries, although some are better covered in the research literature than others.

Current Issues in the Field Raised by These Studies

Public

The digital divide has been of concern to librarians almost as long as the World Wide Web has existed. As far back as 2001, in an article titled "The Impact of the Internet on the Public Library: Current Status and Signs for the Future" and written by Jörgensen, D'Elia, Woelfel, and Rodger, relayed the results of a national telephone survey into the impact of the internet on public libraries and their use. While this article does cover a lot of other permutations of the early results of this then new phenomenon, the authors found something unexpected. While they did find some evidence of the access divide in some of their respondents, it was not as clear cut as one might expect. Even in 2001, "In their consumption of information, these [results] point out somewhat of an 'informational divide' rather than a 'digital divide'" (p. 317).

In "Bridging the Digital Divide Through e-Governance: A Proposal for Africa's Libraries and Information Centers," by Mutula, it is made clear that librarians beyond North America are impacted by the digital divide (2005). Much as it does in North America, the digital divide plays out in a variety of ways in Africa: bandwidth issues are especially problematic. There are also cultural implications, such as "the under-utilisation of existing… infrastructures due to poor policies or unnecessary restrictions" (p. 596). With other problems, such as e-governance being very hit-or-miss, it is clear that public libraries in the United States have a lot more in common with those in Africa than one might expect.

Another piece, one that actually shaped how this chapter talks about the digital divide, "Who's Responsible for the Digital Divide? Public Perceptions and Policy Implications," was written in 2011 by Epstein, Nisbet, and Gillespie. While not exclusively about libraries, in this piece, the authors clearly delineate the different ways in which this term has been defined and used in policy and discourse. The E-rate program (a government mandated discount for schools and public libraries as part of telecommunication infrastructure) has bearing especially. The authors discuss the discourse around access versus disparity of skills, bringing numerous library related documents into the mix. Epstein et al. spend time looking at what has been written about who is responsible for bridging that divide (institutions or individuals?). Then finally, they discuss the results of their study which asked survey respondents to declare who is responsible for bridging the digital divide, and the survey changed the framing of the question to see what impact that change would have on their results. As might be expected within the framework of a nationally representative study, ideas about responsibility changed depending on many factors such as the political affiliation of the person taking the survey, but different attributions for responsibility also had a significant impact on the way questions were answered. Clearly this should

be taken into consideration when framing our discussions with the communities libraries serve.

And yet, even with access to the internet available at local libraries, sometimes that is not enough according to a study done by Collins, Yoon, Rockoff, Nocenti, and Bakken: "Digital Divide and Information Needs for Improving Family Support Among the Poor and Underserved" (2014). In this article, the researchers discussed what they learned from looking at how low income families and individuals are not won over to using the internet access provided by public libraries. The kinds of services study participants want to use, such as Google Voice or other low-cost online communication options, are not conducive to a public library atmosphere: "private internet is expensive and public internet is inconvenient… [and] social media are not private enough" (p. 5). This points to a disheartening idea: that, even when we bridge the access divide, the problems of the digital divide do not disappear.

Another aspect of the digital divide that is frequently left out of the conversation is the way it intersects with problems of gender. In "Gendered Space: The Digital Divide Between Male and Female Users in Internet Public Access Sites" (Dixon et al., 2014), the authors look library and government policies concerning the digital divide and the provision of public access, but then go on to examine how it has evolved to be a gendered problem. "In-depth interviews revealed that both sexes saw public access as the the least desirable place to use the Internet, but discourses around libraries differed" (p. 991). Some of the difference can be tied back to socialization and how the respondents were exposed to technology (or lack thereof) as children. There is also a strong tie between computer anxiety and library anxiety, which can also be tied to gender differences. The findings of this study showed that, with one minor exception, men used public access computers at significantly higher rates than women - even when age and ethnicity were taken into account. Dixon et al.'s findings echoed those of Collins, Yoon,

Rockoff, Nocenti, and Bakken (discussed above) in that their respondents saw the public library as internet access of last resort.

Of even more importance, in some ways, is the distinction between urban and suburban public libraries and those serving rural communities. In "Rural Public Libraries and Digital Inclusion: Issues and Challenges," Real, Bertot, and Jaeger seem to suggest that, though the data is being collected, not much has been done with statistics gathered about the work and roles of rural public libraries (2014). The authors took a small portion of what has been gathered, and tried to draw some conclusions from it. Of particular interest was the 2012 Public Library Funding and Technology Access Survey (PLFTAS). One of the more interesting, although not surprising, findings that the authors shared is that "70.3% of rural libraries are the only free Internet and computer terminal access providers in their service communities, compared to 40.6% of urban and 60.0% of suburban libraries" (#6 from their resource list, as cited in Real, Bertot, and Jaeger, 2014, p. 9). This is exacerbated in other ways. Rural libraries also lag behind with regards to important online resources such as employment assistance and government service access. Funding is, once again unsurprisingly, the main cause of these deficits. "A lack of funding and resources affect not only rural public libraries, but also rural public *librarians*," [emphasis in original article] (p. 16). This plays out not only with the number of staff, but the qualifications of the employees at rural libraries - many of whom not only do not have the master's degree in the field (Master of Library Science or Master of Library and Information Science, traditionally), but also some who only have a bachelor's degree or even only a high school diploma.

Another piece that considers rural communities is "Standing on a Corner: The Access Gap in Rural Communities," written in 2014 by Harlan. Just like the article above, this piece has some startling statistics. Citing another study (Beede & Neville, 2013), Harlan shared that "only 39.7 percent of rural homes have access to broadband via cable, and 7.5 percent have access via optical fiber" (p. 38). The rest of her article focused on the day to day of school librarians. While not written about public libraries, Harlan's examination of the participation gap (when individuals only have access to the internet during school and public library hours and therefore cannot participate in online culture to the level at which people with constant access can participate) has bearing on all libraries. She suggests a number of interventions, such as loaning digital devices to patrons to give them access even while the school is closed.

Academic

One recent study, while it does not specifically address the impact of the digital divide on academic library services, needs to be discussed: the *Ithaka S+R US Library Survey 2013* by Long and Schonfeld. One of the changes we have seen in recent years in higher education is increasing numbers of college returners and a similarly increasing number of first generation college students. Some has been written about providing academic library services to these groups, but nobody seems to be specifically addressing the role that an access gap or a skills gap (hallmarks of the digital divide) would have on the level of support and service a library can/should provide to first generation and college returners. While the Ithaka S+R piece, a survey of academic library top administrators across the country, does not specifically address the digital divide, it does mention repeatedly that the majority of respondents do not feel that they have "a well-developed strategy for serving the changing needs of users" (p. 6). These same academic libraries report an increasing dependence on digital formats - books and periodicals, and an increasing role in the online education efforts of their parent institutions. The two factors of increased reliance on digital tools and a lack of agile plans point to a possible downfall.

Like with public libraries, these issues are not exclusive to academic libraries in the United States. The problems of distance learners are fairly universal actually, as is made clear in Oladokun's piece, "The Information Environment of Distance Learners: A Literature Review" (2014). Oladokun points out that there are consistent library needs among those engaged in distance education: materials and facilities, information services, and user services. The author makes an important point, however, when he says "While there is preponderance of literature on the information behaviour and/or environment of distance learners from advanced countries of the world, there seems to be a dearth of studies on this subject in Africa," (p. 306). What does exist, as described by Oladokun, is scattershot and definitely older than one would hope considering the importance of this subject to academic libraries in Africa. The digital divide between and even within countries on that continent is so stark that distance students are sometimes forced to rely on mass media or even their friends and colleagues as information sources (p. 308). That an article published in 2014 in a peer reviewed journal has no sources that were published later than the mid-2000s is indicative of a great need for research.

Another region outside the United States is represented in the literature is India. "Higher Education and the Digital Divide," by Intekhab Alam (2011) looks specifically at the role that the Indian government, the Ministry of Human Resource Development especially, plays in the attempts to bridge the digital divide within higher education. While Alam's examination of the specific initiatives is important, more interesting for the purposes of this chapter is his discussion of the challenges being faced in India higher education circles. The article presents two levels of the divide that have become familiar through the current examination of the impact of digital media on libraries: the divide between those who do and do not have access to resources online, and the divide between those who do and do not have

the skills to take advantage of the resources they find there (p. 138-139). The examination shared in this piece might leave the reader feeling a bit skeptical, but the author does point to how the efforts, at the least, are encouraging.

Gaps in the Extant Research and Directions for Future Research

With as much as has been written about libraries and the digital divide, this is an area that needs more attention than the other two topics considered above combined. There is still so much we need to know, especially when one considers the different ways to consider the idea of "digital divide." For instance, it is clear that gender feeds into the way digital divides can play out, but it seems only to have been discussed in regards to public libraries. It would be interesting to know if there are gendered responses to library access and internet access in academic libraries, especially at schools with high proportions of students from low socioeconomic status backgrounds and/or first generation college students. Another area that could be further examined, in regards to the gendered aspects of digital divide, would be to follow up on the Dixon et al. article, but in a broader context, since that piece was very geographically prescribed.

One particularly intriguing piece of research was the examination of the the 2012 Public Library Funding and Technology Access Survey (PLFTAS). It seems a ready opportunity, and a necessary area for research, to look at what prior years and subsequent years of PLFTAS have to say to find longitudinal trends. Further, how do the PLFTAS compare to other measures taken to measure rural/public libraries? How do the PLFTAS data compare to similar measures for academic libraries, such as the NCES Library Statistics Program materials?

Another obvious area for further research is a follow up on all the research reviewed in Oladokun article. Even better would be to fill the gap with research across the board in Africa or even around the globe that looks at the way the digital divide impacts the way academic libraries serve the needs of distance students.

One of the most surprising gaps in the research literature is the relative lack in examining how the digital divide impacts how academic libraries support the members of their communities, even those who are attending the brick-and-mortar campuses. The skills gap alone merits serious examination.

Implications and Recommendations

More than anything else, the most apparent implication of the research on the digital divide is the need for proper framing of the issue. If a simple change in the way an issue is presented can sway public perception so much, it is clear that libraries and librarians need to be careful and consistent with their language so as to best influence those with responsibility for funding.

CONCLUSION

The most surprising thing about the research that was considered for this chapter is the scattered approach that has been taken to three clearly important aspects of digital media as it impacts libraries. There is obviously interest in these areas, since the research exists, but not in any kind of organized way. While it would be nice to be able to pen a concise and neat narrative about the evolving responses of public and academic libraries to the demands of social networking, open access, and the digital divide, it does not seem possible. While there was one surprising gap in the research, that of the impact of the digital divide on academic libraries in the United States, most of the uncoordinated approach is understandable. Like many service industries, libraries are predominantly underfunded and therefore understaffed and overworked. Research and interpretation of data beyond what is seen here might be slow in coming - especially from those most needing the research to help guide professional practice. Yes,

it needs to be better and libraries have got a lot of research to do, but it is still encouraging because there are clear directions we can take.

REFERENCES

Alam, I. (2011). Higher education and digital divide in India. *Journal of Library and Information Science*, *1*(2), 133–139.

Björk, B., Welling, P., Laakso, M., Majlender, P., Hedlund, T., & Guðnason, G. (2010). Open access to the scientific journal literature: Situation 2009. *PLoS ONE*, *5*(6), e11273. doi:10.1371/journal.pone.0011273 PMID:20585653

Bodnar, J., & Doshi, A. (2011). Asking the right questions: A critique of Facebook, social media, and libraries. *Public Services Quarterly,* *7*(3-4), 37-41. doi: 101.1080/15228959.2011.623594

Collins, G. (2012). *Social media use by Ontario university libraries: Challenges and ethical considerations.* Paper presented at the Annual Conference of CAIS. Retrieved from http://www.cais-acsi.ca/proceedings/2012/caisacsi2012_submission_117.pdf

Collins, G, & Quan-Haase. (2014). Are social media ubiquitous in academic libraries? A longitudinal study of adoption and usage patterns. *Journal of Web Librarianship,* *8*(1), 48-68. doi: 10.1.1080/19322909.2014.873663

Collins, S. A., Yoon, S., Rockoff, M. L., Nocenti, D., & Bakken, S. (2014). Digital divide and information needs for improving family support among the poor and underserved. *Health Informatics Journal*, 1–11. PMID:24935213

Dixon, , Correa, T., Straubhaar, J., Covarrubias, L., Graber, D., Spence, J., & Rojas, V. (2014). Gendered space: The digital divide between male and female users in internet public access sites. *Journal of Computer-Mediated Communication*, *19*(4), 991–1009. doi:10.1111/jcc4.12088

Dowd, N. (2013). Social media: Libraries are posting, but Is anyone listening? *Library Journal.* Retrieved from http://lj.libraryjournal.com/2013/05/marketing/social-media-libraries-are-posting-but-is-anyone-listening/#_

Epstein, D., Nisbet, E. C., & Gillespie, T. (2011). Who's responsible for the digital divide? Public perceptions and policy implications. *The Information Society*, *27*(2), 92–194. doi:10.1080/01972243.2011.548695

Fernandez, J. (2009). A SWOT analysis for social media in libraries. *Online, 33*(5), 35-37. Retrieved from http://search.proquest.com/docview/199913917?accountid=45950

Foster, N. F., & Gibbons, S. (2005). Understanding faculty to improve content recruitment for institutional repositories. *D-Lib Magazine, 11*(1). doi:10.1045/january2005-foster

IGI Global. (2015). *Qhat is E-S-QUAL.* IGI Global. Retrieved from http://www.igi-global.com/dictionary/e-s-qual/8910

Harlan, M. A. (2014). Standing on a corner. *Teacher Librarian*, *42*(1), 38–42. Retrieved from http://search.proquest.com/docview/1610735348?accountid=45950

Jörgensen, C., D'Elia, G., Woelfel, J., & Rodger, E. J. (2001). The impact of the internet on the public library: Current status and signs for the future. In *Proceedings of the Annual Conference of CAIS*. Academic Press.

Kim, H. M., & Nitecki, D. A. (2014). *A proposed scale for measuring the quality of social media services: An E-S-QUAL approach.* Paper presented at ASIST 2014. Retrieved from https://www.asis.org/asist2014/proceedings/submissions/posters/250poster.pdf

Library Journal. (2012). *Public library marketing: Methods and best practices.* Retrieved from: https://s3.amazonaws.com/WebVault/PublicLibraryMarketingRpt2013.pdf

Long, M. P., & Schonfeld, R. C. (2014). *Ithaka S+R US Library Survey 2013*. Retrieved from http://sr.ithaka.org/research-publications/ithaka-sr-us-library-survey-2013

Magee, R. M., Naughton, R., O'Gan, P., Forte, A., & Agosto, D. E. (2012). *Social media practices and support in U.S. public libraries and school library media centers.* Paper presented at ASIST 2012. Retrieved from https://www.asis.org/asist2012/proceedings/Submissions/334.pdf

Mahmood, K., & Richardson, J. V. Jr. (2011). Impact of web 2.0 technologies on academic libraries: A survey of ARL libraries. *The Electronic Library*, *31*(4), 508–520. doi:10.1108/EL-04-2011-0068

Mutula, S. M. (2005). Bridging the digital divide through e-governance: A proposal for Africa's libraries and information centres. *The Electronic Library*, *23*(5), 592–602. doi:10.1108/02640470510631308

Nicholas, D, Watkinson, A., Rowlands, I., & Jubb, M. (2011). Social media, academic research and the role of university libraries. *Journal of Academic Librarianship, 27*(5), 373-375. doi:10.1.1016/j.acalib.2011.06.023

Oladokun, O. (2014). The information environment of distance learners: A literature review. *Creative Education, 5*(5), 303-317. Retrieved from http://search.proquest.com/docview/1518671480?accountid=45950

Quinn, B. (2010). Reducing psychological resistance to digital repositories. *Information Technology and Libraries, 29*(2), 67-75. Retrieved from http://search.proquest.com/docview/325047755?accountid=45950

Ramsey & Vecchione. (n.d.). Retrieved from http://scholarworks.boisestate.edu/cgi/viewcontent.cgi?article=1101&context=lib_facpubs

Real, B., Bertot, J. C., & Jaeger, P. T. (2014). Rural public libraries and digital inclusion: Issues and challenges. *Information Technology and Libraries, 33*(1), 6-24. Retrieved from http://search.proquest.com/docview/1512388143?accountid=45950

Regazzi, J. The shifting sands of open access publishing, a publisher's view. *Serials Review, 30*(4), 275-280. doi:.10.1016/j.serrev.2004.09.010

Romero, N. L. (2011). ROI. measuring the social media return on investment in a library. *The Bottom Line, 24*(2), 145–151. doi:10.1108/08880451111169223

Schmidt, K. D., Sennyey, P., & Carstens, T. V. (2005). New roles for a changing environment: Implications of open access for libraries. *College & Research Libraries, 66*(5), 407–416. doi:10.5860/crl.66.5.407

Stebbins, M. (n.d.). *Expanding public access to the results of federally funded research.* Retrieved from http://www.whitehouse.gov/blog/2013/02/22/expanding-public-access-results-federally-funded-research

Tsakonas, G., & Papatheodorou, C. (2007). Exploring usefulness and usability in the evaluation of open access digital libraries. *Information Processing and Management: An International Journal, 44*(2), 1234–1250.

University of Texas Libraries. (n.d.). *Digital repository.* Retrieved from http://repositories.lib.utexas.edu/

usability.gov. (n.d.). Retrieved from http://www.usability.gov/what-and-why/glossary/u/index.html

Wei, K. K., Teo, H. H., Chan, H. C., & Tan, B. C. Y. (2011). Conceptualizing and testing a social cognitive model of the digital divide. *Information Systems Research, 22*(1), 170–187. doi:10.1287/isre.1090.0273

KEY TERMS AND DEFINITIONS

ARL: Association of Research Libraries, a nonprofit organization comprised of the largest research libraries both in the United States and Canada.

College Returner: An individual who attended college in the past and took a semester or more off before going back.

Digital Repositories: Collections of digital objects, such as documents or photographs, organized and typically made available through a web interface.

NCES: National Center for Educational Statistics, the United States Department of Education department responsible for gathering pertinent statistics.

Open Access: Scholarly works available with unlimited access and unlimited reuse.

ROI: Return on Investment.

Web 2.0: Websites that are built on collaborative sharing and building principles.

Chapter 8
Economic Impact of Digital Media:
Growing Nuance, Critique, and Direction for Education Research

George L. Boggs
Florida State University, USA

ABSTRACT

Digitization by computers, like steam power and internal combustion, is widely recognized as a pervasive, disruptive engine powering new ways of living and affecting all aspects of economic life. Research on its economic impact cannot be entirely disentangled from powerful cultural stories connecting technological, educational, and economic progress. As cracks appear in the narratives of constant progress through technology, science, civilization, and economic prosperity, research on the economic impact of digital media develops nuance. This review of literature examines a wide range of perspectives on the economic impact of digital media as a basis for suggesting areas of further research and implications for education, civic, engagement, and policy.

INTRODUCTION

The breadth and depth of research on the economics of digital media point to a view shared across academic disciplines and governments that the production of machine-readable information is affecting how humans provide for their needs (Dobson & Willinsky, 2009); in other words, digital media is affecting the economy. "The economy" is often an opaque package of ideology, often exchanged without acknowledgement of which economy, whose economy, what parts matter, and why. The combination of ubiquity and lack of clarity in lay political and educational discourse about the economy complicates efforts to conduct and share research. Equally challenging is researching and discussing the set of materials, texts, and social practices that make up digital media. Assessing the relation between economies and digital media(s) often involves unpacking cultural myths or overarching stories linking the two.

DOI: 10.4018/978-1-4666-8310-5.ch008

Digitization by computers, like steam power and internal combustion, is widely recognized as a pervasive, disruptive engine powering new ways of living (Carlsson, 2004; McQuivey, 2013). Economic growth and, therefore, digital media access are routinely equated with national or global stability (e.g., European Commission, 2014; Yu, 2002). Economic prosperity is often absolutely linked to digital literacy (e.g., Graff, 1979, 2011). These master narratives answer research questions so forcefully that it can be difficult to imagine disconfirmation. However, as cracks appear in the narratives of constant progress through technology, science, civilization, and economic prosperity, research on the economic impact of digital media develops nuance. Under emerging conditions of economic research across numerous academic fields, poverty is less likely to be viewed as a condition of privation to be alleviated by the actions of fiscally and politically powerful groups. Digital media is less likely to be viewed as a static set of tools to be 'rolled out' for others to access. Large-scale formal governing bodies are less likely to be viewed as unproblematic benefactors of struggling villages, regions, and countries.

Powerful stories, old and new, continue to inform research and discussion of the economic impact of digital media. These stories express belief in or suspicion of intrinsic benefits of market economics, global commerce, and privatization. They consequently shape digital media education, policy, and research. As a result, readers approaching the topic of digital media and the economy are likely to encounter a fragmented array of studies verifying and contesting causal links between digital media phenomena and economic life (e.g., Atkinson & McKay, 2007; Brynjolfsson & McAfee, 2012). Projects offer heterogeneous policy recommendations and reports for governments, corporations, and development and educational organizations, whose fragmented missions call for concerted action to steer economic development through digital media education, access, and use.

In order to review the literature comprehensively, digital media is defined broadly to encompass broadband networks, the physically wired infrastructure that supports them, information and communication technologies (henceforth, ICTs) that they support, and the merging of social and economic life into these digital spaces.

WHAT IS A SUCCINCT OVERVIEW OF THE RESEARCH?

Economic Impact of Digital Media in the New Economy

Prior to the Great Recession, research across multiple fields pointed to an emerging "New Economy" explicitly driven by machine-readable information as a "General Purpose Technology" comparable to steam power and the internal combustion engine (Carlsson, 2004). Two studies of the decade prior to the economic downturn found Broadband infrastructure and ICTs to affect national economic growth in Europe (Czernich, Falck, Kretschmer, & Woessmann, 2011; Vu, 2011). The New Economy was shown to depend fundamentally on digital media for increasing productivity, making markets more efficient, improving the quality of goods and services, and creating new or innovative products (Atkinson & McKay, 2007). This influence was "not likely to run out of gas anytime soon and should power robust growth [globally]." These studies before and after the Great Recession provided empirical backing for the "growth" imperative seemingly intrinsic to the Internet and cellular phone technology. In many cases, research explicitly claimed that the "lion's share" of economic growth belonged to digital media (p. 1).

After an initial boom and bust of dot-com industry had passed, yet before the financial crises of the mid-2000s, digital media's true believers trumpeted the narrative linking digital media with economic growth (Litan & Rivlin, 2001).

179

Research teams carried these growth imperatives into international development settings (Galperin & Rojas, 2013), where technological and market determinism would fix a temporary digital, and therefore economic, divide (Guillen & Suarez, 2005). Skeptics questioned the effect of the Internet on productivity (Gordon, 2000) or connected the dot-com bubble with exaggerated projections regarding the Internet's economic impact (Gadrey 2003). Many more studies, however, strongly correlated changes in Gross Domestic Product with a region or country's degree of access to broadband technology or Internet Communication Tools in order to argue that they drive growth (Chambers, 2013).

The widespread view that digital media was linked fundamentally with economic prosperity spurred attention to the problem of a digital divide reinforcing traditional economic access issues. Digital divides were defined as unequal access to information and communication technologies based on wealth (Mun-Cho & Jong-Kil, 2001). Research on access to digital media in rural North America and Europe, and in numerous regions outside comparatively wealthy cities and countries worldwide was predicated on the assumption that lack of access to digital media was a serious threat to economic and political security, while access to digital media represented an opportunity to "leapfrog" historical developmental obstacles (Dunn, 2013; Faye, 2000). The digital divide has become an important part of research on the economic impact of digital media: It has developed over time, and it demonstrates characteristics of combining factors, zooming in, and critically reflecting found in research not geared toward the digital divide in particular.

Questioning simple causal connections between economic growth and digital media on the basis on historical productivity paradoxes, technology-rich environments have not always demonstrated increased output (Eliasson, Johansson, & Taymaz, 2004; Solow, 1987). Such studies suggest a category of research on the economics of digital media in which scholars have argued that realizing economic opportunities digitally depends upon organization of multiple factors, not just the existence of or access to digital tools. Chambers (2013), for instance, questions the ability to isolate ICTs' impact in the presence of other major factors like recession and war, plus rapid technological changes make longitudinal studies difficult. He notes a shift in research from measuring access to measuring particular economic effects of ICTs in specific developing regions that impede simple comparisons. Among the most important additional factors that may have been overlooked in early projections of the Internet's economic power are social practices and cultural norms that shape how Internet Communication Tools are used.

Another category of research follows in the wake of the global economic downturn beginning in 2007, embracing a mixed picture of economic effects of digital media. Zooming in on particular economic effects allows research to account for economic recession and constriction of markets whose across-the-board growth had previously been used to point up the advantages of digitization before 2007. In this category, the recognition remains that economies are more flexible and adaptable when networked digitally, yet growth claims are more modest (Kim, Park, Kim, & Hwang, 2013). Brynjolfsson and McAfee's report (2012) argued that digital media drives growth despite many signs of economic calamity such as collapse of job sectors and persistent unemployment. Destruction in the New Economy, they argued, makes room for innovative combinations, new products, and new markets, but research increasingly acknowledges that economic benefits may be fragmented:

Technological progress does not automatically benefit everyone in a society. In particular, incomes have become more uneven, as have employment opportunities. . . . The problem is that our skills and institutions have not kept up with the rapid changes in technology (p. 2).

While grand narratives of technology-driven economic growth are still being produced that tout the 'natural' connection between digital media and the economy, a great deal of research has zoomed in to see particular effects.

Research on the economic impact of digital media is *combining* digital media with other factors to understand a more complex economic significance, on one hand. On the other, *zooming in* on smaller scale economic questions, much research seeks a less coherent, but more accurate assessment of digital media's impact. A third major research development involves reflecting critically on the epistemological, political, and social consequences of digital media. Thus, in addition to combining digital media with other factors and zooming in for finer-grained analysis of economic effects, critically reflective research adds further nuance to the economic impact once attributed to digital media by noting the way economic research on literacy, media, and digital access plays into powerful cultural myths. These myths, such research argues, affect global, national, and regional media and educational policies, and they underwrite the massive financial commitments driving universal broadband access and literacy campaigns. Decentering literacy in relation to economics may be essential for making appropriate recommendations for education and digital media policy.

Combining. As early as 1993, studies combined digital media with changing business choices in order to measure an impact (Clemons, Reddi, & Rowe, 1993). But more recent research suggests that oscillations between social and material digital worlds have inadequately characterized the "blurred realities" of life in digital worlds. Moving beyond binaries requires recognition of the complex existence of digital media in the economy (Ettlinger, 2008).

The human and economic networking potential of digital media are closely intertwined, and research on the combined economic and political effects of digitization has shown that authoritarian regimes only withstand the economic and political pressure of digital networks at great cost (Kalathil & Boas, 2003). Related research examined governments' ability to filter available entertainment and found that perceptions of domestic versus foreign entertainment quality played a major role (Cheng, Feng, Koehler, & Marston, 2010). A related study drew similar conclusions by comparatively examining legal and illegal digital content downloading occurring during and after a corporation pulled popular content (Danaher, Danasobhon, Smith, & Telang, 2010). Other studies have examined the intersection of digital media, intellectual property, and government intervention: Chambers (2013) correlated vibrant intellectual property rights policy in European countries with large scale economic growth; MacQueen (2007) sought explicitly to balance the goals of economic growth with copyright protection; Van den Bulck (2014) addressed the pressure on governments to develop new regulatory frameworks to respond to rapidly changing industrial boundaries, such as between media producers and media outlets.

Research on the regulatory responsibilities of government foreshadow new possibilities for "completely digital entrepreneurship" (Asghari & Gedeon, 2010), which takes advantage of protected markets and reduces or eliminates overhead costs. The New Economy thus involves integrating the changing rules of business with responsive government policies (Oh & Larson, 2013).

Digital media spending, on the other hand represents a significant corruption problem. The increase in pork-barrel or preferential government spending on digital media projects prompted research on the messy combination of digital media expansion and undemocratic political processes (Thierer, Crews, & Pearson, 2002). In contrast to the free market goals of the former research project, Bennett and Segerberg (2011) examined how the digital forces enabling globalization also afforded forms of democratic protest and collective action.

Zooming in. Researchers zoom in past grand narratives of economic growth to test digital media's impact more accurately. The degree of mobile phone penetration was correlated with increased Gross Domestic Product (Gruber & Koutroumpis, 2011). Convergence of media devices (Alam & Prasad, 2007), convergence of databases (Janowicz & Hitzler, 2012), and cloud computing (Chambers 2013) have all been evaluated discretely in terms of their economic impact.

Zysman (2010) connected the growth of digital media with service sector expansion in US and global job markets. Much research has clustered around music, film, and entertainment industries as areas susceptible to massive change through digitization. Some have questioned whether digitization and reduced opportunity costs in producing and distributing films will loosen Hollywood's hold on the film industry (De Vinck & Lindmark, 2014; Zhu, 2001). Similar shifts in power were examined in the music industry from large US-based labels to digital community networks (Hughes & Lang, 2003). By contrast, Lee (2009) called into question the liberating possibilities of digital media in view of the complex and still-powerful industrial dynamics too easily overlooked by studies overemphasizing democratizing possibilities of digital media. Other research in this vein has recognized local synergy between university communities and arts and culture clusters (Breznitz & Noonan, 2013), where digital media is argued to play a central role in multiplying the economic impact of local resources. Similarly Morgan (2013) showed that creative media industries could have regionally significant economic impact despite their longstanding marginalization prior to the emergence of a new digital economy.

Possibilities for economic growth through new and reduced-cost outlets for digital cultural content produce economic challenges for existing outlets (Maggiolino, Montagnini, & Nuccio, 2014) in the transition away from brick-and-mortar shops (Waelbroeck, 2013). Booksellers online offer advantages for customers that translate to

increased economic activity (Brynolfsson, Hu, & Smith 2003), and consumer-generated content is integrated into their business models (Ghose, 2011). The business developing around the distribution of digital content vary widely, yet the configurations and ownership of digital and non-digital content providers, such as with ebook and print text markets, themselves have measurable economic impact (Jiang & Katsamakas, 2010). At the same time, retailers' internal marketing strategies vary in terms of the way they make use of available digital information about their intended or actual clients (Ziliani & Bellini, 2003).

Critically reflecting. Historians Graff (1979, 2010, 2011) and Trigger (1976) have discussed ahistorical yet culturally important post-Enlightenment liberal social theories that tie literacy and schooling to socioeconomic development. Graff's interrogation of "literacy myths" continues to inform contemporary researchers questioning the autonomous relationship between techno-literacy and sustained economic development. Trigger (1976) used evidence from prehistoric civilizations to argue that literacy is not required to support highly complex economies, even if literacy developed to support complex economies in the Middle East. Katz & Stern (2008) argue that growth promises tied to education in the New Economy ring hollow, providing many medium-low wage jobs requiring no college degree, outsourcing many jobs, and rewarding a tiny percentage of college graduates who reap outsized rewards.

Katz and Stern's (2008) argument about college education touches on the changing value of specialized knowledge and knowledge in general in the "New Economy." Brynjolfsson and McAfee (2012) connect the economic impact of digital media with the educational need to focus on "soft skills" like leadership, team building, and creative thinking. The Partnership for 21st Century Skills (2011) represents core academic knowledge as a "base" for "21st century skills" implementation." The incorporation of educational recommendations manifests the shift in emphasis away from efficiency and cost saving as the main advantages to networked computing and communication. Researchers increasingly recognized the potential of digital media to affect every aspect of economic life, with a "multiplier effect" (Katz, 2010). Carlsson (2004), Geyer-Schulz, Neumann, Heitmann, and Stroborn (2004), and Maull and Mulligan (2014) locate the salient feature of digital media in its capacity to convert of information to knowledge. The economic and sociopolitical consequences of datafication or "metadata" are only beginning to be realized and studied.

Chambers (2013) claims that entire functions of society (e.g., education, health, security, privacy) are being rethought as they are being translated for exchange through digital media. Accompanying this translation is a shift toward "digital epistemologies" (Lankshear, 2007), where sweeping changes in individual and community life through digital media affects what counts as knowledge. The New Economy represents a structural shift toward "networked information" (Benkler, 2006, p. 3). Because the use of digital infrastructure for networks has been enclosed economically, laws of supply and demand apply to this process of translation. To understand the human consequences of an economic metric for digitizing information electronically, Foray and Lundvall (2009) argued that the economic importance of digitizing information disrupts traditional boundaries between codified and tacit knowledge, with consequences for the social organization of institutions. Zysman, et al (2010) echoed these claims and added that digital media affects how economic value is created: "When activities are formalized and codified, they become computable. Processes with clearly defined rules for their execution can be unbundled, recombined, and automated" (p. 8).

McChesney (1999) argued that, when it comes to the relation between economics and digital media, "the market has assumed mythological status," where "all must pledge allegiance" (p. 137). In an age in which knowledge must have market value to be digitized, Carrette (2007) warned that, despite decades of critical inquiry into the role of media in shaping human thought and behavior, markets for digitized information are increasingly controlling human thought. Gee (2007) agrees, attributing the view of digital media to neo-liberal myths that lasting good is only produced by markets. "Only markets ensure quality," says Gee, to explain a relation among economics, digital media, and human knowledge. Knowledge only counts when it has survived the test of the commodification of knowledge digitally.

Critically reflective research notes the importance of powerful cultural myths at work when people make sense of changes in communication, economy, and knowledge. Selfe (1999) saw the promise of technology as a savior as a uniquely American phenomenon, now being exported globally. Warnick (2001) characterized this view as a form of economic manifest destiny; Berland (2000) found techno-evolutionism at work in the view that technology was a key factor in realizing human potential for freedom, democracy, culture, intelligence, and progress (p. 243). *The new work order* (Gee, Hull, & Lankshear, 1996) argues that changes ascribed to the new economy parrot neoliberal myths of market driven progress, which actually spell increased inequality and oppression for the world's workers despite promises of great work satisfaction, autonomy, and teamwork. Other social criticisms of the rise of digital media (Carrington & Luke, 1997; Luke, 2008) draw on complex concepts of class, lifestyle, and capital found in the work of Bourdieu (1993). Brandt and Clinton (2002) argued that the notion of using literacy to manipulate one's environment overlooks a crucial economic feature of literacy, that using literacy means being used by literacy as well for potentially economic purposes beyond the view of researchers and participants. Similarly, court decisions and other structural factors play a role in the preservation of cultural myths about literacy and media use (Prendergast, 2009).

Critical media literacy has the goal of exposing economic underpinnings of digital media. Cultural messages about economic life and literacy are important (Luke, Iyer, & Doherty, 2011). One study noted the effects of neocolonial literacy education in parts of southeast Asia, where "The dominant characterization of the landless peasantry in Bangladesh and elsewhere in Asia is of illiteracy" (Maddox, 2001, p. 137). Another criticized the literacy education agendas sponsored by the World Bank and UNESCO as neocolonial in nature, that is, positioning the less developed regions for a new wave of economic exploitation through digital media.

Such critiques pave the way for new ways of looking at the economic significance of digital media. Ethnographic perspectives of digital media experiences are useful in considering more nuanced economic situations (Coleman, 2010). Case studies undermined the link between economic development and digital media use among low literacy adult workers in Australia (Black & Yasukawa, 2011).

As powerful cultural stories about markets, technology, literacy, and continue to be positioned as reasons to embrace digital media's positive econiomic effects on human life, more and more studies are published questioning the links and the stories that contextualize them. At the same time, the World Bank, United Nations Educational, Scientific and Cultural Organization, and transnational development organizations profit fantastically from "over-promising" (Heeks, 2010) and "overselling" (Kenny, 2001) digital media's or other utility infrastructure potential for economic impact. Still, research on economic impact of digital media continues to draw quite explicitly on problematic myths. The Deputy Secretary-General of the UN made literacy, and even "informatics" prerequisites for "a healthy, just, and prosperous world," (Frechette, 2003 cited in Rutsch, 2003, p. n.p.; Frechette, 1999). The urgency of the "Literacy Decade" represents the intersection of multiple narratives of progress

outlined above, but it focuses on the question of a digital divide ostensibly intensifying inequalities between former colonial powers of the Global North, comprising Europe, North America, and parts of Asia, and the formerly colonized regions of the Global South, comprising wealthy regions in Asia, Africa, and South America.

DIGITAL DIVIDE

Research on the Digital Divide flows out of concerns that the ostensibly vast benefits of the New Economy will not be realized apart from access to the Internet. Recent research has therefore either forwarded or confronted the philosophy and policy reinforcing the view that digital media holds a key to development in rural areas of the Global North and both rural and urban regions in the Global South. The World Bank funded research that purported to isolate access as the controlling factor in economic growth in poor countries (Dasgupta, Lall, & Wheeler, 2001), in spite of numerous studies arguing for an approach to increasing access that accounts for social practices shaping use (Warschauer, 2002). Compaine (2000) argued that decreasing cost of use and increasing ease of use would further isolate access alone as the key determiner of economic development through digital media. Bolt & Crawford (2000) neatly equated the economic *have-nots* with information *have-nots*. These research projects bear the marks of a global economy flexing its muscles, yet, even after the economic downturn of 2007, UNESCO-backed research by Katz (2010) still assumed economic growth as the norm despite numerous indicators otherwise. Katz' research supported the view that systematic, that is, top-down, internet access policy was a key global development priority. Global broadband access was recommended as a core step in alleviating the inequalities of the digital divide (Williams, 2013). A study reaching from the end of the dot-com crisis to before the economic downturn correlated broadband access with a broad set of economic growth factors (Lehr, 2005). Similarly, Mainardi (2013) connected Internet Communication Tools, "and specifically digitization," with the assumed need for countries to effectively compete as economic engines: Digital media is a "fundamental driver of economic growth" that holds the key to "the potential development and maintenance of absolute advantage" (p. vii). Despite the nationalistic zeal inherent in this research funded by Booz & Company, Mainardi's report identifies specific economic impact of digital media despite "continued sluggishness" of "financial crisis" (p. vii). Finally, the report's top down approach to development frames governments as chiefly responsible for building digital infrastructure, since increased digitization beyond basic broadband access produces increasing economic returns on digital infrastructure investment. This top-down view echoes in the pursuit of an inclusive information society (Guerrieri, Bentivegna, & Elgar, 2011).

Digital divide research does not unanimously endorse the top down approach to responding to the digital divide. Projects designed to increase access alone have been critiqued for their inefficiency. Heeks (2010) characterized projects designed to boost economies through networking centers as "heavy overpromising followed by noticeable under-delivery" (p. 629). One review of research (Chambers, 2013) found that economic growth in many regions that had *progressed* along the digitization spectrum had stagnated or even retreated. Recognizing the complexities of economic and cultural life in the Global South and in rural areas of the Global North has resulted, as it did with economic research not geared toward the digital divide, in projects that combine digital media with other factors and zoom in on more discrete economic effects.

Combining. Mansell (2001) found institutional foundations to be important coordinating factors for predicting growth from ICT use through uptake of digital media in business. That study argued

that the notion of leapfrogging, by which ICTs enable overcoming developmental obstacles, must move beyond one-dimensional views of access to technology. The same author argued in a later study that ICTs had to be deployed in ways that afforded people making authentic choices about their own lives. Access alone is not enough (Selwyn, 2004). In spite of massive fiscal and political support for global broadband initiatives, a study of a rural broadband access program showed no economic growth (LaRose, Strover, Gregg, & Straubhaar, 2011). Far from denying the economic impact of digital media, research in this vein echoes the view that

ICTs alone cannot improve peoples' lives; the use of ICTs needs to occur within broader strategies that are tailored to make the most use of these tools and techniques in order to reap their potential benefits for human development (Hamel, 2010, p. 59).

Responding to critiques of top-down approaches, much research on the digital divide has oriented on participatory design and implementation of ICTs. When "conceived and accommodated in locally meaningful ways," argued Maive & McGrath (2010), ICTs "can provide a platform for advancing development agendas in ways that are sustainable in the longer term" (p.2). Perhaps the most important combining effort in this vein of research is the recognition that the notion of a digital divide as distinct from issues of poverty is a fallacy. A study by Blake and Quiros (2012) following reviews of digital divide research (van Dijk, 2006; Wersch, 2009) attempted to address numerous reductionist tendencies both in looking at economic impact of digital media and discussing the nature of poverty.

Using a complex view of poverty (Alkire & Foster, 2009) and more grassroots action approach, Blake and Quiros (2012) recommend recasting poverty in terms of capability goals rather than privation, thereby supporting locally relevant strategies for integrated digital media. They argued that community participation was essential to the design of effective responses to the digital divide, and that "efforts aimed at bridging the digital divide therefore need to be refocused as strategies to address the multiple divides within which poverty has been fostered" (p. 8). Research in this vein invests local communities with agency for digital innovation around their own needs. Contrasting with the agenda of developing universal Internet and broadband policies, von Braun (2010) argues that the perceptions of the target population, rather than the supposed power of the new tools, are of paramount importance if development through digital media is to occur.

Language and gender play a role as well (O'Byrne, 2011; Looker & Thiessen, 2003; Bryson, Petrina, Braundy, & de Castell, 2003), as does race, and class (Mossberger, Tolbert, & Stansbury, 2003).

Combining environmental sustainability and economic issues has resulted in critical comparisons of environmental with economic impact (Cox, May, Kroder, & Franklin (2010). Other studies of environmental economic impact include assessment of "green broadband" (Valley Vision, 2012), energy consumption (Alonso, Hamdoun, Mangeni, & Dwivedi, 2013). At the same time, ICTs are enabling intensive environmental measurement, too, with complicated economic results, where economic growth depends upon public response to environemtnal sustainability imperatives regarding city water quality (Sitzenfrei & Rauch (2011), watersheds (Mishra, 2011), and urban sprawl (Shalaby, Ali, & Gad, 2012). These studies concur on the need for "technology that is suitable for the environmental, cultural and economic conditions in which the technology is intended to be used" (van Reijswoud, 2009, p.3).

Many concerned with a digital divide view education as a natural factor to be combined with economic growth (Borovoy & Cronin, 2011/2014). The combination of economic change and digital media has resulted in numerous rec-

ommendations for major educational changes to accommodate new digital literacies (Leu, 2000). Complex changes in the New Economy are said to underwrite a "transdisciplinary" approach to education (Lélé & Norgaard, 2005; Mollinga, 2010) that values academic specializations as it moves among them and to require "transliteracy," or the ability to respect norms of multiple communication environments (Selfe, 1999). At the same time, digital media is also supporting the creation of digital content for schools and digital tools for writing assessment, and educational technology is increasingly recognized as a site of struggle as academic labor is valued through its technological availability, distribution, and marketability (Hall, 2013). An emerging concern merges environmental stability with education. Gomes (2011) made the connection: "If education and development make an irreducible binomial and that development must be sustainable, then we need an education for sustainability" (p. 205).

Zooming in. Challenges to top-down, access-oriented, government-sponsored digital media development projects come from research that zooms in on specific economic effects. One critique rests on the notion that economic projections are made based on what might be possible through digital media when research does not strongly support the idea that economically beneficial activities will form a significant portion of internet use. One study found that digital media available in the home is a vehicle for reaching a region's elite, with poorer consumers' behaviors remaining largely unchanged (Reich, 1992]). Kenny (2011) criticizes the overzealous aims of UNESCO's Broadband Commission for Digital Development and their policy brief *Broadband inclusion for all.* Kenny skeptically cited universalist claims in the report: "international estimates suggest that for every 10 per cent increase in broadband penetration we can expect an average of 1.3 per cent additional growth in national gross domestic product" (cited in Kenny, 2011, p. 1). The critique pointed to numerous areas in which claims linking digital media access to economic growth rested on dubious assumptions, and that the actual margins of growth attributable to digital media rollout are very small.

In the report, partially titled "Overselling broadband," Kenny reveals a suspicion that the large scale of the recommended projects will disproportionately benefit those who will handle the development contracts, rather than a country's taxpayers. The author concludes by zooming in on numerous finer-grained approaches to supporting economic development through broadband rollout:

This is not to say that nothing can or should be done by policymakers to speed broadband rollout in the developing world. McKinsey [& Co. (2009)] estimates that a combination of adding to available spectrum for mobile broadband, encouraging infrastructure- and spectrum-sharing, reducing coverage obligation, reducing competition, and eliminating spectrum fees could reduce wireless broadband costs by as much as 75 percent. If one is less sanguine about the impact of reduced competition and prefer to see spectrum rights auctioned rather than given away, the impact of the remaining measures could still surpass a 50 percent cost reduction. This suggests there are powerful tools that governments could use prior to diverting scarce revenues towards broadband subsidies.

Zooming in on the digital divide led to inquiry into the significance of digital money in Uruguay (Cassoni & Ramada, 2012). Digitized geographies in Europe are consistently presented as domains of economic growth and impact (Mossberger, Tolbert, & Franco, 2012; Misuraca & Broster, 2010). Technological infrastructure is often isolated and its effects studied on particular regions: US states (Lloyd; Hohlfield, 2008), US rural versus urban areas (Whitacre, Gallardo, & Strover (2014), and sub-regions of Africa (Fuchs & Horak, 2006). Research also zooms in on the technological de-

vices themselves. Mobile phones in India (Moz & Tanz) were shown to benefit higher status groups most and marginalized groups least. Varian (2006) saw considerable potential for emerging low cost laptop manufacturing. Brazil's low cost laptop computer program was evaluated (Amiel, 2006, less favorably by Warschauer, 2003).

Critically reflective. The notion that rural regions in the Global North and areas in the Global South can overcome development obstacles through acquisition and use of digital media has been called into question from a range of perspectives for its many assumptions about development, literacy, technology, and globalization (Fuchs & Horak, 2006). Most obvious is the ahistorical assumption that ICT and broadband development funded by outside investors might differ in their economic intent and effect from well-documented exploitive colonial and neocolonial policies. A study conducted in Egypt cautioned against an ahistorical reading of changes in global communication and that digital divide research risked recapitulating the great literacy divide (Warschauer (2002), in which modes of communication were equated with the intelligence and civilization. Providing similar historical context for research in the Global South, others have argued that the digital divide masks exploitive economic imperatives driving outside investment in digital media. The Digital slavery, it is argued, results from bridging the digital divide, where

... the claim that our personal data and electronic interactions are owned by others is tantamount to accepting that we, as digital beings, can be owned by others. ... With ownership comes the right to use, trade and dispose. Existing legislation such as data protection is concerned with the legitimate use of data items. It does not consider data items to be the organs of a digital being and so is not concerned with the welfare of digital beings protecting them against servitude and slavery" (Rogerson & Rogerson, 2007, p. 1).

Further developing the historical critique, Ogunsola (2005) noted that leapfrogging the industrial stage of development is not a straight-forward move for most countries because past economic struggles have resulted in "tighter imperialist control of the continent" by lender countries, the International Monetary Fund, and the World Bank (n.p.).

Alzouma (2005) argued that advocates for development in the Global South assume that help must come from outside, and that ICT and broadband policies magically invest technology with power to solve entrenched human problems. The digital divide is itself a problem not likely to be eliminated, even if widespread access occurs (Lopez-Sintas, Filimon, & Garcia-Alvarez, 2012), confirming findings in a study of school and home ICT use nearly a decade before (Sunderland-Smith, Snyder, & Angus, 2003). Researchers have also questioned the environmental consequences of e-waste in the Global South, which already receives much of the world's electronic waste (Bjorn, Vanden Eynde, Viaene 2013).

WHAT ARE THE CURRENT ISSUES IN THE FIELD RAISED BY THESE STUDIES?

Educational policy is being affected globally by recognition that digital media and economic growth are entangled, if not always causally linked in an absolute sense. Research intended to inform corporate, industrial, economic, and educational speaks with many voices, without clear consensus. A lack of consensus does not mean a lack of important issues, however. On the contrary, research on economic impact in general and the divide in particular raises an important collage of issues, which provide an increasingly variegated or fragmented backdrop for action. That backdrop was once monochromatic: ICTs and broadband boost GDP, suggest the need to rethink education around watershed changes in human interaction, and demand heavy investment in less-development regions around the world. In the monochrome, social practices mattered less than material technological access, income alone defined poverty, and technology was environmentally clean and politically neutral. The evolution of the digital divide debate, the effects of the economic downturn on attitudes toward global economic progress, increasing attention to global climate change, as well as persistent critical reflections on cultural myths of technology and literacy have given researchers a far more diverse palette. Irreconcilable views among large-scale global anti-poverty groups (Denny, 2011) illustrate how colors may clash.

There is widespread agreement, however, that divisions between digital content, digital infrastructure, and digital practices are not easy to maintain. Digital media are widely regarded as critical elements of 21st century economic growth across scales and stakeholder groups, and the existence of a meaningful digital divide is widely confirmed, but current efforts seek more nuanced approaches that attend to digital media practices—the combination of digital media with cultural, material, and economically oriented practices. Additionally, studies have combined economic growth goals with questions of environmental sustainability in the recognition that limited resources, changing living conditions, and reliance on nonrenewable resources cannot be separated ultimately from digital media, despite the myth of clean technology. Studies have raised similar concerns about the role of digital in globalization, and the need to balance complex national and international interests with equally complex local and regional situations. The balance imperative stems from efforts to place the trendy in context.

The issue of balance and responding to rapid technological change is particularly important for literacy education and research. On one hand, notions of education and economic access as fundamental rights have placed schools on the education technology bandwagon. The technology imperative flows from the seeming urgency of technological and economic change: Schools must act as a stopgap bridge across the digital divide; teachers can hardly integrate enough current technology; and technology is well suited to schooling, because it so efficiently packages and distributes information, because students like learning with new technology, or because its use trains students entering the global workforce. Economic research on digital media potentially offers important balance to the view that schools must bridge the digital divide through digital literacy, as Brandt & Clinton (2002) argued, since the user-friendliness of digital media is, illusory. Digital media, via literacy, uses us. Other economic research on digital copyright, piracy, and intellectual property raises similar concerns about the elision of technology access with education: Ownership of digital media and the ontological status of digitized personal information does not square well with human rights arguments about digital media access or the school as its conduit.

On the other hand, documentation of specific, varied, and conditional economic impact of digital media is important in literacy research, where monochromatic notions of economic change have limited engagement with the particularities of growth sectors, malleable ICTs, economic meaning-making, and environmental impact such e-waste. These issues present significant opportunities to integrate economic particularities, questions, and problems where only grand narratives existed before. Among the most important issues raised by current research is confirmation of existing concerns about automation, outsourcing, and workforce development. The review of literature reflects a shift from nationally and internationally scaled economic impact studies (even though such studies continue to be produced) to more narrowly defined industrial, local, and personal economic effects of digital media. As the picture of economic impact of digitization comes to life, critical reflection upon techno-evolutionary myths continues to be crucial for literacy research.

Educational policies conceived on the basis of the older pre-Recession grand narratives can be revised to support local concerns and practices where they have been ignored or effaced in monochromatic narratives of globalization and national competitiveness.

At the same time, it must be recognized that the issues to which literacy education and research should respond are themselves fragmented. The digital divide, for instance, is hailed as an opportunity for reducing inequality through leapfrogging the glacial process of industrialization in the Global South, yet the too comfortable relationship of development corporations and World Bank or International Monetary Fund confirm fears that the digital divide really refers to neocolonial economic opportunity to expand markets in capitalism's last gasps as human, market, and environmental resources are exhausted. The issue of digital literacy as a set of practices embedded in the cultural life of particular groups (Lankshear, 2007) has been challenged similarly for its naïveté about how global economic forces are exploiting educational imperatives for profit. This issue further raises the questions about 21st century work, knowledge work, and the new work order. Research on digital media's economic impact has not produced a coherent picture of the 21st century worker, but has instead raised questions about "high" and "low" economic roads that preserve familiar class divisions, albeit overlaid with new literacies, new jobs, and new means of building elite social networks. The issue of workforce development in response to digitally mediated changes in the New Economy depends absolutely on economic impact research, and current research in the wake of the Great Recession is suggesting a more varied picture of digitized work.

Research suggests that monochromatic picture of economic growth driven by digital media depend on myths of autonomous or exogenous effects of digital literacy. The gaps in the logic that literacy *has* positive economic consequences are filled in (or papered over) by cultural stories linking high-status technologies with social status, progress, morality, and more. Research on the economic impact of digital media, while diverging in terms of critical and uncritical orientations toward these stories, point together to the importance of underlying literacy myths in shaping local, regional, national, and global policy. Graff (2011) points out that the core issue is not the expulsion of the stories so commonly told about literacy and economic development, but a need to gain some control over them and direct them.

The idea of using cultural myths about literacy strategically raises the important issue that little effort has been given to understanding economic factors affecting literacy outside the work of critical theorists of literacy (e.g., Gee, Hull, & Schultz, 2007; McLaren, 1998; Rose, 2010). Even with these broad critiques, knowledge of the relation between real schooling practices and local economic history is "pitifully thin" (Rose, 2014, para. 4).

Separating economic from literacy and cognition issues has been an explicit goal of a branch of literacy studies most apt to tackle the problem of linking literacy and economic life beyond the grand myths (see Scribner & Cole, 1981, introduction). Literature published in media studies, by contrast, has maintained a robust critical agenda linking economic goals with digital tools and literacy. So now, the research points up the issue of synchronizing the government, business, and philanthropic economic imperatives with local economic and educational settings, of working across scales, in other words. So far, the synchronization process has been trapped by the politics and economics of scale that produced it: National and transnational governing bodies, in partnership with large national and transnational corporations, have sought to reform educational practices to produce a workforce for the new millennium. But understandings of the nature of literacies constrained by national and transnational scales decreasingly answer to issues raised in the literature. One important feature of this synchronization and scale

problem is the failure to reconcile reform goals internally. Indeed, Au (2011) argued that reforms in assessment, driven by digital economies of scale and enabling new forms and levels of teacher, student, and curriculum surveillance, cannot be reconciled with curricular reform goals developed around the notion of disciplinary literacy practices and problem solving. In this study, the economic concept of alienation from work has been realized in the context of the educational reform for the digital age.

Alienation, poverty, and environmental consciousness are issues raised in the literature that demand reconceptualization for designing instruction and educational research. The digital divide debate presses the issue that definitions of poverty have implications for the kinds of economic activity and growth that can be projected upon a research site. Theories of poverty based on capabilities, agency, and freedom rather than "lack" have significant advantages in terms of predicting the way digital technologies may affect lived conditions. Although no consensus exists, digital divide research raises the issue of transdisciplinary approaches to questions of digital media development among underrepresented populations, which may significantly shape kinds of positions on digital literacy and technology integration in schools. A potential explosive conclusion from this research is that teachers, administrators, and educational researchers, as important stakeholders in the digital divide discussion, should or could cultivate transdisciplinary knowledge of digital media. Such knowledge would mean a holistic approach to questions of poverty, technology, literacy, and economics informed and clarified by disciplinary concepts (Mollinga, 2010).

The idea that education professionals should approach the digital divide or other questions of digital media and the economy holistically is an obviously tall order, yet it underlines a persistent problem raised in the literature, that a mythical relationship between economy and digital media has stunted or stood in the way of applied problem-solving about the needs of teaching practitioners, studies, and communities (Brown & Grant, 2010). But this issue applies to educational research as well, where "overly utopian and zealous belief in the role that ICTs play in development" is accompanied by a "lack of linkage" between ICT and poverty alleviation (Blake & Quiros, 2012, p. 3).

Finally, the literature confirms the issue in literacy research and schooling that instrumental and technocentric approaches to digital media should give way to pluralistic and participatory models "determined locally, according to local choices" (Chapman & Slaymaker, 2002, p. 25). In other words, schools, teachers, families, and researchers need pluralistic tools for connecting digital media, literacy, and economic life, for understanding poverty in the digital age, digital participation, possibilities for meaningful change, and possibilities for digital exploitation (Schimmel, 2009). All too familiar in literacy research, this review of literature underscores the problem of deficit models driving acquisition of digital tools and participation in digital spaces. In a review of digital divide literature, Vaughan (2011) distinguished "ICT programs which demonstrably and explicitly contribute to community well-being aspirations through the contribution they make to capabilities" as "being sustained by communities," while a lack of such meaningful connections result in failed programs and waste (p. 7). Lack of consciousness about the development goals being incorporated in contemporary education are specifically implicated in such indictments of digital media development programs (Maye and McGrath 2010). This tension between top down and bottom up or grassroots digital media acquisition represents a crucial issue present in the literature (Harris, 2004), where functionalist rationales, "What is and what can be achieved" meet moral challenges, "What should be done and how should we do it?" (Unwin, 2009, p.33). Further, participatory development efforts, should they be conceived and deployed in schools may still "hide or widen existing divides," hence a need

for balance between meaningful participation and "reinforcement of existing power hierarchies and exclusionary practices" (Grimshaw & Gudza, 2010, p.10; Blake & Quiros, 2012). The question has been raised by combining factors and zooming in on particulars, as well as by critically reflecting upon the stories told about literacy, technology, and growth: Whose economy matters, and why?

WHAT ARE THE GAPS IN THE EXTANT RESEARCH AND DIRECTIONS FOR FUTURE RESEARCH?

Position statements on digital media education pay scant attention to the economic significance of literacy, digital media, and adolescent digital media practices. References to economic impact rarely go deeper than mere mention of economic significance. Educational reform initiatives seeking to restructure schooling in Asia, Europe, and North America treat the New Economy as a form of progress for those who remain competitive (Asia-Pacific Economic Cooperation, 2014; Common Core State Standards Initiative, 2014). The idea of a set of "skills and competencies young people will be required to have in order to be effective workers and citizens" (Ananiadou & Claro, 2009) masks the diversity of use, meaning, and real economic significance of informational capitalism (Castells, 2010). It also reinforces a monochromatic view of the economic and political meaning of digital media. The idea of global skills for global competition (Partnership for 21st century skills, 2013; (US Chamber of Commerce Foundation, n.d.) justifies large scale co-option of education. In the US, many are crying foul, but widespread resistance across stakeholder groups to national and state standards initiatives has challenged almost everything about educational reform except its simplistic economic promises. In Florida, a leader in educational reform, the Career and professional Education Act (2013) is intended, to "lash our education system to the knowledge-based economy" (Florida Senate, President Office, 2013).

The literature does not univocally support the competition imperative. Global competition has resulted in significant job losses and even whole job sectors in the US and elsewhere. Other factors not related to the skill of the workforce shape economic life, and yet a persistent gap exists between research on the economics of digitization and narratives of educational reform, "which subsume educational attainment and social justice inside agendas for commodification, marketisation, employability and enclosure" (Hall, Atkins, & Fraser, 2014, p. 2).

The major gap has consequences for research on teaching and learning, since economics-minded research currently consists of recommendations based on the imaginary 21st century worker: her team spirit, critical thinking ability, ability to communicate, and adapt. Research has not yet connected what is known about economic impact of digital media with teaching. Instead, teaching is being connected with reductive literacy myths as proxies for knowledge about how digital media is integrated into economic life at multiple levels. Although popular and useful for guiding instruction away from more didactic, fact-based approaches, crosswalks that help teachers, families, and policy makers think between schooling and economics are much needed.

As research begins to responds to this gap, existing literature emphasizes the importance of participatory models of economic impact research that combine material and social dimensions of digital media, carefully evaluate how and why economic impact matters, and critically reflect upon potentially exploitive relationships. While international development fields increasingly embrace these characteristics of economic impact research, as markers of quality inquiry, they delineate a gap in digital media and literacy research attributable to longstanding disciplinary boundaries. The "funds of knowledge" project

and approach (Gonzalez, Moll, & Amanti, 2005) illustrate the troubled past of integrating literacy participation, economic considerations, and exploitation. In that landmark study, local economic structures and struggles were centrally important to researchers, who understood the precariousness of immigrant Latino economic participation and recognized the false promises of a literacy myth, in which poor kids could change their economic future by doing well in school. They observed the profound disconnect between vanishing funds of labor knowledge and alienating and evanescent labor opportunities. And yet the implication of their research and the heart of the funds of knowledge approach is to ignore the economic well-being of actual communities in favor of leveraging what funds are left for school success. In the end, the literacy myth won out against less coherent and perhaps less palatable alternatives. Scribner's concern that her predecessor Luria's (1976) interests in literacy, conceptual, and economic development together were too broad has, in a way, come home to roost. Sociocultural and cultural-historical literacy research is theoretically equipped to engage the economic question, to do so locally and beyond, and to do so in a way that attends to human experience.

Critical media literacy has contributed significantly to the discussion of economic impact of digital media, yet economic critique is less robust and distributed less across the field compared with other critical platforms. In some cases, economic critiques may even make it more difficult to interpret the economic impact of digital media for purposes of education, particularly when research implicitly and explicitly positions people as proactive or empowered *consumers*. Framing people as consumers participates in neoliberal systems of social change, in which markets, supported vigorously by strong states, become exclusive arbiters of human experience.

Economic research on the social impact of digital media seeks to refine educational and government policies regarding literacy education and digital media infrastructure. Efforts to link digital media with dramatic changes in the domestic and global economy, along with critiques of those efforts, are warranted in the wake of the most political and economic developments. Among the most relevant phenomena to economics and digital media are the global recession, state collapse in the Middle East, independence movements worldwide, surveillance practices tied to economic activity, and digitally-mediated antisocial behavior. Besides the gaps in research created by ongoing change, even structural change, in economic, political, and technological structures, there is need for focused attention on combined effects of digital media and state control of the Internet. Existing hierarchical structures (e.g., coding language, ownership of wired infrastructure, and data providers) by which digital content are produced are not absolute. Studying the economic impact of different regulatory and commercialization models is needed. In education, the push to digitize instruction has only just begun to be analyzed (Hall, Atkins, & Fraser, 2014). The enclosure of economic labor through educational technology represents a significant area for future research, given current imperatives to create and distribute digital records of scholarship, instruction, and student work.

These areas for additional research share an emphasis on the production of digital social space and educational responses. It is difficult to overestimate the significance, politically, economically, educationally, and civically, of digital media and digitization in the contemporary production of space. Because that production is regulated politically, economically, socially, and culturally, the politics of space as outlined by Lefebvre (1992) can be a way to interpret the meaning of new arrangements of space (Butler, 2012; Elden, 2004). In sum, the production of new forms of social space represents a crucial area for research relating economic life and digital media. However, issues of scale are everywhere in research on economic impact of digital media, and recogniz-

ing scale as a political and ideological construct (Delaney & Leitner, 1997) in defining problems and opportunities with digital media can lead to awareness of whose interests are likely to receive attention. Scale is an important yet unrealized tool for interpreting the significance of digital media development in educational research, too, although arguments drawing on the political and economic significance of scale are rare. Acknowledging scale and the production of social space as political and economic questions can be useful in suggesting alternatives to existing economic imperatives for digital media access and education (McKenzie, 2012).

WHAT ARE THE RECOMMENDATIONS/ IMPLICATIONS FOR EDUCATION, CIVIC ENGAGEMENT (GLOBAL AND LOCAL), SOCIAL PRACTICE, AND POLICY?

Research on digital ecologies, digital economies, and their interlocking systems of knowledge and value should continue to demand better articulation of the economic significance of digital media. Despite generations of glib projections of economic growth, a "triple crunch" of financial crisis, climate change, and energy production (Wallis, 2008, para. 1) threatens almost every possible conception of economic life. Far from constructing a crisis narrative to motivate an unmeasured response, the message of the economic triple crunch should tell literacy and civic education that there is real, possible, meaningful work to be done for which existing conceptions of cultural relevance and equality are inadequate.

Education

Better articulation of the economic significance of digital media in education cannot remain, as it is now, "pitifully thin" (Rose, 2014, para. 4), if educational goals of preparing people for personal, civic, and economic life are to ring true. This current situation is especially precarious given drastic economic changes and erosion of myths of permanent economic progress. At the same time the politicization of educational reform threatens to move the discussion out of the realm of academic argument into demagoguery. Still, current pressure on education to respond to economic needs signals a crucial opportunity, to incorporate economics as a feature of culture in culturally responsive pedagogy (Ladson-Billings, 1995). Slavish acceptance of monochrome cartoons of digitally driven economic progress should give way, as has much research outside the field of education, to a kaleidoscope in which multiple economic histories, theories of technology, and literacy pedagogies apply.

A shift away from a mythical, linear, and large-scale view of economic change in the digital economy depends upon dynamic rather than static views of culture. Cultural and economic responsiveness in pedagogy depend upon participatory research that frames problems of poverty, access, and practice in terms of capabilities and goals rather than privation.

For academic disciplines and teaching in particular, working between economic imperatives and instructional design is crucial. Research has not yet attempted to connect the dots between literacy instruction and economic impact, hence reliance on the literacy myth to fill in the gap (Graff, 2011). Rather than only exposing the myth, Graff recommends using it strategically to foster the development of literacies among researchers, teachers, and students that resist racism, classism, and violence inherent in the hollow promises of literacy for economic gain (Stuckey, 1990).

Civic Engagement

Research on the economic significance of digital media is growing more critical of techno-centric, exogenous solutions to digital divides across mul-tiple scales from the classroom and neighborhood to continents. This shift toward participation and fragmentation coincides with increased recognition that the promises of global, digitally-networked economies require careful consideration, especially regarding the scale of prosperity and the social, civic, and environmental consequences. Global economic change, regional political change, and environmental sustainability issues will continue to decenter literacy and technology from their prominent, yet mythical, role in safeguarding economic success. In civic life, as with education, such decentering sets the stage for exciting new research on the role of digital communication tools in economic development, which plays a dominant role in formal, national and international political arrangements. Changes projected for schools, teachers, students, families, and literacy research place these stakeholders in important positions of civic agency, with the likely outcome of increased accountability of government, philanthropic, and other agencies to this nuanced picture of economic aspects of digital media.

Managing the myths of literacy education and economic life requires critical civic consciousness. The development of critical digital literacies (Author and Colleague, 2014) by teachers and others produce digital media communication and spaces less as domains for consumption and more as boundary spaces in which alternative political and economic agency and arrangements may be explored. Thus the New Economy and its neoliberal underpinnings evoke responses constructed through new literacies (New London Group, 1996), and the new civics (Zuckerman, 2014). The "new" in the economy, literacy, and civics has less to do with time and more to do with space, participation, and multiple possibilities.

Social Practice

Everyday life is being digitized in ways that constantly defy the imagination. Musicians, news outlets, and artists thrive on virtual attention and approval. Digitized smiley faces and thumbs-up stand in for physical gestures. The "on demand" economy brings three dimensional printing, dry cleaners, restaurants, chauffeurs, programmers, and writers to our doors, promising to destabilize and reorganize the above and many other service and industrial sectors. In many ways, these innovations represent significant economic enclosures shaping social practice. Enclosure is an important economic concept of particular relevance as social life merges into digital spaces.

Enclosure refers to conversion of a thing, such as food or a word, from one economic status to another. An individual might enclose land formerly shared freely among neighbors, for instance, in order to convert the resource into personal wealth more efficiently. Digital media works the same way upon social practices. Social media platforms enclose everyday speech, emoticons enclose human gesture, and so on through music sharing tools, stock market trading aids, online instruction, and so forth.

The idea is that information is only digitized if it has value, if the process of digitization creates a stream of revenue for the parties responsible for the digital programming and infrastructure. Meetings once held in spaces occupied by a single business may allow third party companies to facilitate digital audio and/or videoconferences for which they will be compensated. So one or more brokers of digital media may enclose communication at work that was already monetized through wage labor. For contemporary work, such conveniences may be welcome, but what about indigenous knowledge encoded in unknown languages? Information and practical wisdom specific to particular places, such as highly sensitive ecological zones, is unlikely to be preserved digitally if current investors are not able to envision a timely return on investment. By the same token, the economic factor acts as a mediating influence on the information itself, not only acting as a gatekeeper for information, but inevitably changing it. This reordering knowledge (Author, 2011; Carrette, 2007) obviously shapes

social practices as well. Online recipes are a familiar example. Their accessibility and variety change how people cook, think about cooking, interact with elders, and value existing compendia of cultural knowledge. And they exist as economic ventures with very few exceptions.

Digital enclosure is important because, in addition to the economic conversion of hypothetically monetized information and practice, the practices change as they are translated. Cyber-bullying and human sex trafficking are troubling examples of how the translation of social practices into digital spaces brings about new challenges for law enforcement, families, and communities. Further, economic and political fallout from high profile instances of computer hacking and executions point to digital media as a potential catalyst for antisocial behaviors.

Policy

Much research on digital media and economics is explicitly oriented toward shaping Internet and digital media policy at the state, national, and multinational level. As research tends toward finer grained and more cautious analysis of digital media's effect on economic growth, policymakers continue to grapple with contradictory imperatives from established and new economic interests. The thrust of recommendations is to invest in telecommunication expansion, but questions and concerns in the research are proliferating. Intellectual property protection and enforcement have been serious concerns for policymakers for years. Imperatives of growth and copyright protection are seldom in agreement, however.

Contemporary developments in research directed at policy makers stress the importance of nuanced views of digital media access, poverty, and digital media use. Implications for educational policy include adjustment away from cherished literacy goals accompanied by myths of economic attainment to more adaptive views of literacy and economic opportunity.

The "triple crunch" of energy cost, financial instability, and climate change (Wallis, 2008) place educational and other policy makers in a precarious position. Established economic interests who profit from core factors in global insecurity make progressive policy development difficult. A particularly poignant conflict of interest in this context has to do with workforce development as a matter of local, regional, national, and international policy. The idea of developing a workforce for as yet unknown occupations (Frey & Osborne, 2013) tests the resolve of policymakers who are simultaneously asked to help businesses succeed in increasingly difficult and competitive circumstances. The result is a policy trap, where forward thinking becomes the only solution to decreasing profit margins in existing economic arrangements but established economic interests must be protected by increasingly outdated policy.

REFERENCES

Alam, M., & Prasad, N. R. (2007). Convergence transforms digital home: Techno-economic impact. *Wireless Personal Communications*, *44*(1), 75–93. doi:10.1007/s11277-007-9380-2

Alkire, S., & Foster, J. (2009). Counting and multidimensional poverty measurement. *Oxford Poverty & Human Development Initiative (OPHI)*. Retrieved from http://www.ophi.org.uk/wp-content/uploads/OPHI-wp32.pdf

Alzouma, G. (2005). Myths of digital technologies in Africa: Leapfrogging development? *Global Media and Communication*, *1*(3), 339–356. doi:10.1177/1742766505058128

Amiel, T. (2006). Mistaking computers for technology: Technology literacy and the digital divide. *Association for the Advancement of Computing in Education*, *14*(3), 235-256. Retrieved from http://www.editlib.org/p/6155/

Ananiadou, K., & Claro, M. (2009). 21st century skills and competences for new millennium learners in OECD countries. *OECD Education Working Papers*, *41*, 1-34. Retrieved from http://www.oecd.org/officialdocuments/publicdisplaydocumentpdf/?cote=EDU/WKP(2009)20&doclanguage=en

Asghari, R., & Gedeon, S. (2010). Significance and impact of Internet on the entrepreneurial process: E-entrepreneurship and completely digital entrepreneurship. In A. Kakouris (Ed.), Proceedings of the 5th European Conference on Innovation and Entrepreneurship (pp. 70–76). Reading, UK: Academic Publishing Limited. Retrieved from http://academic-conferences.org/pdfs/ECIE10-abstract%20booklet.pdf

Asia-Pacific Economic Cooperation. (2014). *Human resources working group: 21st century competencies*. Retrieved from http://hrd.apec.org/index.php/21st_Century_Competencies

Atkinson, R. D., & McKay, A. S. (2007, March). *Digital prosperity: Understanding the economic benefits of the information technology revolution*. Retrieved from http://www.itif.org/files/digital_prosperity.pdf

Au, W. (2011). Teaching under the new Taylorism: High-stakes testing and the standardization of the 21st century curriculum. *Journal of Curriculum Studies*, *43*(1), 25–45. doi:10.1080/00220272.2010.521261

Benkler, Y. (2006). The wealth of networks: How social production transforms markets and freedom. New Haven, CT: Yale University Press. Retrieved from http://www.benkler.org/Benkler_Wealth_Of_Networks.pdf

Bennett, W. L., & Segerberg, A. (2011). Digital media and the personalization of collective action: Social technology and the organization of protests against the global economic crisis. *Information Communication and Society*, *14*(6), 770–799. doi:10.1080/1369118X.2011.579141

Berland, J. (2000). Cultural technologies and the "evolution" of technological cultures. In A. Herman & T. Swiss (Eds.), *The world wide web and contemporary cultural theory* (pp. 235–258). New York, NY: Routledge.

Black, S. R., & Yasukawa, K. (2011). A tale of two councils: Alternative discourses on the 'literacy crisis' in Australian workplaces. *International Journal of Training Research, 9*(3), 218–233. doi:10.5172/ijtr.9.3.218

Blake, A., & Quiros, M. (2012). Boundary objects to guide sustainable technology-supported participatory development for poverty alleviation in the context of digital divides. *Electronic Journal of Information Systems in Developing Countries, 51*(1), 1-25. Retrieved from http://www.academia.edu/5632559/Boundary_Objects_to_Guide_Sustainable_Technology-Supported_Participatory_Development_for_Poverty_Alleviation_in_the_Context_of_Digital_Divides

Bolt, D., & Crawford, R. (2000). *Digital divide: Computers and our children's future.* York: TV Books.

Borovoy, A. E., & Cronin, A. (2011, November). *Resources for understanding the common core state standards | Edutopia.* Retrieved October 2014, from http://www.edutopia.org/common-core-state-standards-resources

Bourdieu, P., & Johnson, R. (1993). *The field of cultural production: Essays on art and literature.* New York: Columbia University Press.

Brandt, D., & Clinton, K. (2002). Limits of the local: Expanding perspectives on literacy as a social practice. *Journal of Literacy Research, 34*(3), 337–356. doi:10.1207/s15548430jlr3403_4

Breznitz, S. M., & Noonan, D. S. (2013, June). *Arts districts, universities, and the rise of digital media.* Retrieved from http://scholarworks.iupui.edu/bitstream/handle/1805/3567/breznitz-2013-arts.pdf?sequence=1

Brown, A. E., & Grant, G. (2010). Highlighting the duality of the ICT and development research Agenda. *Information Technology for Development, 16*(2), 96–111. doi:10.1080/02681101003687793

Brynjolfsson, E., Hu, Y. J., & Smith, M. D. (2003). Consumer surplus in the digital economy: Estimating the value of increased product variety at online booksellers. *Management Science.* Retrieved from http://papers.ssrn.com/sol3/papers.cfm?abstract_id=400940

Brynjolfsson, E., & McAfee, A. (2012). *Race against the machine: How the digital revolution is accelerating innovation, driving productivity, and irreversibly transforming employment and the economy.* Lexington, MA: Digital Frontier Press.

Bryson, M., Petrina, S., Braundy, M., & de Castell, S. (2003). Conditions for Success?: Gender in technology-intensive courses in British Columbia secondary schools. *Canadian Journal of Science, Mathematics, and Technology Education, 3*(2), 185–193. doi:10.1080/14926150309556559

Butler, C. (2004). *Henri Lefebvre: Spatial politics, everyday life, and the right to the city.* New York, NY: Routledge.

Carlsson, B. (2004). The digital economy: What is new and what is not? *Structural Change and Economic Dynamics, 15*(3), 245–264. doi:10.1016/j.strueco.2004.02.001

Carrington, V., & Luke, A. (1997). Literacy and Bourdieu's sociological theory: A reframing. *Language and Education, 11*(2), 96–112. doi:10.1080/09500789708666721

Cassoni, A. & Ramada, C. (2012). *Digital money and its impact on local economic variables: The case of Uruguay.* Academic Press.

Castells, M. (2010). The rise of the Fourth World: Informational capitalism, poverty, and social exclusion. In *End of millennium* (2nd ed.; Vol. 3, pp. 3–49). Oxford, UK: Wiley-Blackwell; doi:10.1002/9781444323436.ch2

Chambers, J. (2013). Foreword. In B. Bilbao-Osorio, S. Dutta, & B. lanvin (Eds.), The global information technology report (pp. ix-x). Academic Press.

Chapman, R. B., Slaymaker, T., & Overseas Development Institute. (2002). *ICTs and rural development: Review of the literature, current interventions and opportunities for action.* London: ODI. Retrieved from http://www.odi.org/sites/odi.org.uk/files/odi-assets/publications-opinion-files/2670.pdf

Clemons, E., Reddi, S., & Row, M. (1993). The impact of information technology on the organization of economic activity: The move to the middle hypothesis. *Journal of Management Information Systems*, (10): 9–35.

Coleman, E. G. (2010). Ethnographic approaches to digital media. *Annual Review of Anthropology*, *39*(1), 487–505. doi:10.1146/annurev.anthro.012809.104945

Common Core State Standards Initiative. (2014). *Myths vs facts*. Retrieved from http://www.corestandards.org/about-the-standards/myths-vs-facts/

Compaine, B. M. (2001). *Re-examining the digital divide* (130). Retrieved from Research Affiliate, Internet and Telecoms Convergence Consortium, MIT. Retrieved from http://digital.mit.edu/research/papers/130%20Compaine,%20Digital%20Divide.pdf

Cox, V. K., May, R. C., Kroder, S. L., & Franklin, G. M. (2010). Following the paper trail: Measuring the economic and environmental impact of digital content delivery. *Technological Developments in Networking. Education and Automation*, *37-41*. doi:10.1007/978-90-481-9151-2_7

Cumps, B., Vanden Eynde, O., & Viaene, S. (2013). Impact of e-waste on the operating model of a "close the digital divide" organisation. *ECIS 2013 Completed Research, 71*. Retrieved from http://aisel.aisnet.org/cgi/viewcontent.cgi?article=1294&context=ecis2013_cr

Czernich, N., Falck, O., Kretschmer, T., & Woessmann, L. (2011). Broadband Infrastructure and Economic Growth. *The Economic Journal*, *121*(552), 505–532. doi:10.1111/j.1468-0297.2011.02420.x

Danaher, B., Dhanasobhon, S., Smith, M. D., & Telang, R. (2010). Converting pirates without cannibalizing purchasers: The impact of digital distribution on physical sales and internet piracy. *Marketing Science*. Retrieved from http://www.heinz.cmu.edu/~rtelang/ms_nbc.pdf

Dasgupta, S., Lall, S., & Wheeler, D. (2001). Policy reform, economic growth, and the digital divide: An econometric analysis. *The World Bank Development Research Group Infrastructure and Environment, 2567*, 1-18. Retrieved from http://books.google.com/books?id=4v-04WJ4UBEC&pg=PP2&dq=Dasgupta,+Lall,+%26+Wheeler,+2001&hl=en&sa=X&ei=etBSVOrON8ergwTqiYOIBQ&ved=0CB0Q6AEwAA#v=onepage&q=Dasgupta%2C%20Lall%2C%20%26%20Wheeler%2C%202001&f=false

De Vinck, S., & Lindmark, S. (2014). *Innovation in the film sector: What lessons from the past tell us about Hollywood's digital future–and what that means for Europe.* Cheltenham, UK: Edward Elgar Publishing.

Delaney, D., & Leitner, H. (1997). The political construction of scale. *Political Geography*, *16*(2), 93–97. doi:10.1016/S0962-6298(96)00045-5

Dobson, T., & Willinsky, J. (2009). Digital literacy. In D. Olson & N. Torrance (Eds.), *Cambridge Handbook on Literacy*. Cambridge, UK: Cambridge University Press. doi:10.1017/CBO9780511609664.017

Dunn, H. S. (2010). Information literacy and the digital divide: Challenging e-exclusion in the Global South. In E. Ferro, Y. Dwivedi, J. Gil-Garcia, & M. Williams (Eds.), *Handbook of Research on Overcoming Digital Divides: Constructing an Equitable and Competitive Information Society* (pp. 326–344). Hershey, PA: Information Science Reference; doi:10.4018/978-1-60566-699-0.ch018

Elden, S. (2004). *Understanding Henri Lefebvre: Theory and the possible*. London: Continuum.

Eliasson, G., Johansson, D., & Taymaz, E. (2004, September). Simulating the new economy. *Structural Change and Economic Dynamics*, *15*(3), 289–314. doi:10.1016/j.strueco.2004.01.002

Ettlinger, N. (2008). The predicament of firms in the new and old economies: A critical inquiry into traditional binaries in the study of the space-economy. *Progress in Human Geography*, *32*(1), 45–69. doi:10.1177/0309132507083506

European Commission. (2014). *Economic stability and growth*. Retrieved from http://ec.europa.eu/economy_finance/euro/why/stability_growth/index_en.htm

Faye, M. (2000). *Developing national information and communication infrastructure: Policies and plans in Africa*. Paper presented at the Nigeria NICI Workshop.

Florida Senate, President Office. (2013). *Senators and business leaders discuss expanding career and professional education initiatives* [press release]. Retrieved from http://www.flsenate.gov/Media/PressReleases/Show/1392

Foray, D., & Lundvall, B.-A. (1996). The knowledge-based economy: From the economics of knowledge to the learning economy. In Organization for Economic Co-operation and Development (Ed.), Employment and growth in the knowledge-based economy (pp. 11-32). Paris: OECD.

Frey, C. B., & Osborne, M. A. (2013). *The future of employment: How susceptible are jobs to computerization?* Retrieved from http://www.futuretech.ox.ac.uk/sites/futuretech.ox.ac.uk/files/The_Future_of_Employment_OMS_Working_Paper_1.pdf

Fuchs, C., & Horak, E. (2006). Informational capitalism and the digital divide in Africa. *Masaryk University Journal of Law and Technology*, 11-32. Retrieved from https://mujlt.law.muni.cz/storage/1205244869_sb_s02-fuchs.pdf

Fukuda-Parr, S. (2003). The Human development paradigm: Operationalizing Sen's ideas on capabilities. *Feminist Economics*, *9*(2), 301–317. doi:10.1080/1354570022000077980

Gadrey, J. (2003). *New economy, new myth*. London: Routledge.

Galperin, H., & Rojas, F. (2011). Broadband policies in Latin America and the Caribbean. In V. Jordán, H. Galperin, & W. Peres (Eds.), Fast-tracking the digital revolution: Broadband for Latin America and the Caribbean. Santiago, Chile: United Nations. Retrieved from http://repositorio.cepal.org/bitstream/handle/11362/35351/S2011329_en.pdf?sequence=1

Gee, J., Hull, G., & Lankshear, C. (1996). *The new work order*. Bouler, CO: Westview Press.

Gee, J. P. (2007). *Social linguistics and literacies: Ideology in Discourses*. New York, NY: Taylor & Francis.

Geyer-Schulz, A., Neumann, A., Heitmann, A., & Stroborn, K. (2004). *Strategic positioning options for scientific libraries in markets of scientific and technical information: The economic impact of digitization*. Retrieved from https://journals.tdl.org/jodi/index.php/jodi/article/view/101/100

Gomes, L. F. (2011). Digital literacy and sustainability: The *vozes que ecoam* project. In M. L. Soares & L. Petarnella (Eds.), *Schooling for sustainable development in South America: Policies, actions and educational experiences* (pp. 205–217). Dordrecht, Netherlands: Springer. doi:10.1007/978-94-007-1754-1_13

González, N., Moll, L. C., & Amanti, C. (2005). *Funds of knowledge: Theorizing practice in households, communities, and classrooms*. Mahwah, NJ: L. Erlbaum Associates.

Gordon, R. J. (2000, August). *NBER Working Paper Series: Does the "New Economy" measure up to the great inventions of the past?* Retrieved from http://www.nber.org/papers/w7833.pdf

Graff, H. J. (1979). *The literacy myth: Literacy and social structure in the nineteenth century city*. New York, NY: Academic Press.

Graff, H. J. (2011). *Literacy myths, legacies, & lessons: New studies on literacy*. New Brunswick, NJ: Transaction Publishers.

Grimshaw, D. J., & Gudza, L. D. (2010). Local voices enhance knowledge uptake: Sharing local content in local voices. *Electronic Journal of Information Systems in Developing Countries*, *40*, 1–12.

Gruber, H., & Koutroumpis, P. (2011). Mobile telecommunications and the impact on economic development. *Economic Policy*, *26*(67), 387–426. http://onlinelibrary.wiley.com/doi/10.1111/j.1468-0327.2011.00266.x/abstract doi:10.1111/j.1468-0327.2011.00266.x

Grunfeld, H. (2011). *The contribution of information and communication technologies for development (ICT4D) projects to capabilities, empowerment and sustainability: a case study of iREACH in Cambodia* (Doctoral dissertation, Victoria University, Melbourne, Australia). Retrieved from http://vuir.vu.edu.au/19359/

Guerrieri, P., & Bentivegna, S. (2011). *The economic impact of digital technologies: Measuring inclusion and diffusion in Europe* (E. Elgar, Ed.). Cheltenham, UK: Edward Elgar Publishing. doi:10.4337/9780857935236

Guillen, M. F., & Suarez, S. L. (2005). Explaining the global digital divide: Economic, political and sociological drivers of cross-national Internet use. *Social Forces*, *84*(2), 681–708. doi:10.1353/sof.2006.0015

Hall, R. (2013). Educational technology and the enclosure of academic labour inside public higher education. *Journal for Critical Education Policy Studies*, *11*(3), 52–82. Retrieved from http://www.jceps.com/wp-content/uploads/PDFs/11-3-03.pdf

Hall, R., Atkins, L., & Fraser, J. (2014). Defining a self-evaluation digital literacy framework for secondary educators: The DigiLit Leicester project. *The Journal of the Association for Learning Technology*, 22(21440). Retrieved from https://www.dora.dmu.ac.uk/handle/2086/9892

Hamdoun, A., Mangeni, S., & Dwivedi, Y. K. (2013). Insights into sustainable energy-capacity trends towards bridging the digital divide a perspective of the need for green broadband communications in Sub Saharan Africa. In *Proceedings of International Conference on Computing, Electrical and Electronics Engineering (ICCEEE)* (pp. 459-463). ICCEEE. doi:10.1109/ICCEEE.2013.6633982

Hamel, J. Y. (2010). *ICT4D and the human development and capabilities approach: The potentials of information and communication technology.* Human development research paper 2010/37, UNDP. Retrieved from http://hdr.undp.org/sites/default/files/hdrp_2010_37.pdf

Harris, R. W., & United Nations Development Programme. (2004). *Information and communication technologies for poverty alleviation.* Kuala Lumpur: United Nations Development Programme's Asia-Pacific Development Information Programme. Retrieved from http://en.wikibooks.org/wiki/Information_and_Communication_Technologies_for_Poverty_Alleviation

Heeks, R. (2010). Do information and communication technologies (ICTs) contribute to development? *Journal of International Development*, 22(5), 625–640. doi:10.1002/jid.1716

Herman, A. (1999). So much for the magic of technology and the free market: The world wide web and the corporate media system. In A. Herman (Ed:), *The World Wide Web and contemporary cultural theory: Magic, metaphor, power.* New York, NY: Routledge.

Hughes, J., & Lang, K. R. (2003). If I had a song: The culture of digital community networks and its impact on the music industry. *International Journal on Media Management*, 5(3), 180–189. doi:10.1080/14241270309390033

Janowicz, K., & Hitzler, P. (2012): The digital earth as knowledge engine. *Semantic Web Journal*, 3(3), 213-221. Retrieved from http://geog.ucsb.edu/~jano/Semantics_Digital_Earth2012.pdf

Jiang, Y., & Katsamakas, E. (2010). Impact of e-book technology: Ownership and market asymmetries in digital transformation. *Electronic Commerce Research and Applications*, 9(5), 386–399. doi:10.1016/j.elerap.2010.06.003

Kalathil, S., & Boas, T. C. (2003). *Open networks, closed regimes: The impact of the Internet on authoritarian rule.* Washington, DC: Carnegie Endowment for International Peace.

Katz, M. B., & Stern, M. J. (2008). *One nation divisible: What America was and what it is becoming.* New York, NY: Russell Sage Foundation.

Katz, R. (2010). *The impact of broadband on the economy: research to date and policy issues.* International Telecommunication Union (ITU) GSR 2010 Discussion Paper.

Kenny, C. (2011, December). *Overselling broadband: A critique of the recommendations of the broadband commission for digital development.* Retrieved from http://www.cgdev.org/files/1425798_file_Kenny_overselling_broadband_FINAL.pdf

Kenny, R. (2001). Teaching, learning, and communicating in the digital age. In *Proceedings of Selected research and Development [and] Practice Papers Presented at the National Convention of the Association for Educational Communications and Technology.* Academic Press.

Kim, T.-Y., Park, J., Kim, E., & Hwang, J. (2011). *The faster-accelerating digital economy*. TEMEP Discussion Papers 201173. Seoul National University. Technology Management, Economics, and Policy Program (TEMEP). Retrieved from https://ideas.repec.org/p/snv/dp2009/201173.html

Kivunike, F. N., Ekenberg, L., Danielson, M., & Tusubira, F. F. (2009). Investigating perception of the role of ICTs towards the quality of life of people in rural communities in Uganda. In *Proceedings of the 10th International Conference on Social Implications of Computers in Developing Countries*. Dubai School of Government. Retrieved from http://www.ifip.dsg.ae/Docs/FinalPDF/Full%20 Papers/ifip_55_%20Kivunike,%20ekenberg%20 and%20danielson.pdf

Kleine, D. (2010). ICT4What? Using the choice framework to operationalise the capability approach to development. In *Proceedings of the IEEE/ACM International Conference on Information Technology and Development 2009*. Retrieved from http://ieeexplore.ieee.org/xpl/login. jsp?tp=&arnumber=5426717&url=http%3A% 2F%2Fieeexplore.ieee.org%2Fxpls%2Fabs_all. jsp%3Farnumber%3D5426717

Ladson-Billings, G. (1995). Toward a theory of culturally relevant pedagogy. *American Educational Research Journal*, *32*(3), 465–491. doi:10.3102/00028312032003465

LaRose, R., Strover, S., Gregg, J., & Straubhaar, J. (2011). The impact of rural broadband development: Lessons from a natural field experiment. *Government Information Quarterly*, *28*(1), 91–100. doi:10.1016/j.giq.2009.12.013

Lee, J. (2009). Contesting the digital economy and culture: Digital technologies and the transformation of popular music in Korea. *Inter-Asia Cultural Studies*, *10*(4), 489–506. doi:10.1080/14649370903166143

Lefebvre, H. (1992). *The production of space*. New York, NY: Wiley-Blackwell.

Lehr, W. H., & Osorio, C. A. (2005, December). Measuring broadband's economic impact. *Broadband Properties*, 12-24. Retrieved from http://www.broadbandproperties.com/2005issues/dec05issues/Measuring%20Broadband%20Eco%20 Impact,%20Lehr,%20Gilett,%20Sirbu.pdf

Lele, S., & Norgaard, R. B. (2005). Practicing interdisciplinarity. *Bioscience*, *55*(11), 967–975. doi:10.1641/0006-3568(2005)055[0967:PI]2.0.CO;2

Leu, D. J., Jr. (2000). Literacy and technology: Deictic consequences for literacy education in an Information Age. In M. L. Kamil, P. Mosenthal, P. D. Pearson, & R. Barr (Eds.), Handbook of Reading Research (Vol. 3). Mahway, NJ: Erlbaum. Retrieved from http://www.sp.uconn.edu/~djleu/ Handbook.html

Leys, C. (2006). The rise and fall of development theory. In M. Edelman & A. Haugerud (Eds.), *The anthropology of development and globalization: From classical political economy to contemporary neoliberalism* (pp. 109–125). Blackwell Anthologies in Social and Cultural Anthropology.

Litan, R., & Rivlin, A. M. (2001). Projecting the economic impact of the Internet. *The American Economic Review*, *91*(2), 313–317. doi:10.1257/ aer.91.2.313

Looker, D. E., & Thiessen, V. (2003). Beyond the digital divide in Canadian schools: From access to competency in the use of information technology. *Social Science Computer Review*, *21*(4), 475–490. doi:10.1177/0894439303256536

López-Sintas, J., Filimon, N., & García Álvarez, M. E. (2012). A social theory of Internet uses based on consumption scale and linkage needs. *Social Science Computer Review*, *30*(1), 108–129. doi:10.1177/0894439310390611

Luke, A. (2008). Using Bourdieu to make policy: mobilizing community capital and literacy. In J. Albright & A. Luke (Eds.), *Pierre Bourdieu and literacy education*. New York, NY: Taylor & Francis.

Luke, A., Iyer, R., & Doherty, C. (2011). Literacy education in the context of globalisation. In D. Lapp & D. Fisher (Eds.), Handbook of Research on Teaching of English Language Arts (3rd ed.). New York: Routledge. Retrieved from http://eprints.qut.edu.au/31587/2/31587.pdf

Luria, A. R. (1976). *Cognitive development, its cultural and social foundations*. Cambridge, MA: Harvard University Press.

Maddox. (2001). Literacy and the Market: The economic uses of literacy among the peasantry in northwest Bangladesh. In B. V. Street (Ed.), *Literacy and development: Ethnographic perspectives*. New York, NY: Psychology.

Maggiolino, M., Montagnini, M. L., & Nuccio, M. (2014). Cultural content in the digital arena: toward the hybridization of legal and business models. *Organizational Aesthetics, 3*(1), 42-64. Retrieved from http://digitalcommons.wpi.edu/oa/vol3/iss1/6/

Mainardi, C. (2013). Foreword. In B. Bilbao-Osorio, S. Dutta, & B. Lanvin (Eds.), The global information technology report 2013: Growth and jobs in a hyperconnected world (p. vii). Geneva, Switzerland: World Economic Forum. Retrieved from http://www.gov.mu/portal/sites/indicators/files/WEF_GITR_Report_2013.pdf

Maiye, A., & McGrath, K. (2010). ICTs and sustainable development: A capability perspective. *AMCIS 2010 Proceedings, 541*. Retrieved from http://aisel.aisnet.org/amcis2010/541

Mansell, R. (2001). Digital opportunities and the missing link for developing countries. *Oxford Review of Economic Policy, 17*(2), 282–295. doi:10.1093/oxrep/17.2.282

Maull, R., Godsiff, P., & Mulligan, C. E. (2014). The impact of datafication on service systems. *47th Hawaii International Conference on System Sciences (HICSS)*. Retrieved from http://www.computer.org/csdl/proceedings/hicss/2014/2504/00/2504b193-abs.html

McKenzie, M. (2012). Education for y'all: Global neoliberalism and the case for a politics of scale in sustainability education policy. *Policy Futures in Education, 10*(2), 165–177. doi:10.2304/pfie.2012.10.2.165

McKinsey & Co. (2009). *Mobile broadband for the masses: Regulatory levers to make it happen*. Ney York, NY: McKinsey & Co.

McQuivey, J. (2013). *Digital disruption: Unleashing the next wave of innovation*. New York, NY: Amazon.

Misuraca, G., Broster, D., Centeno, C., Punie, Y., Lampathaki, F., Charalabidis, Y., & Bicking, M. (2010). *Envisioning digital Europe 2030: Scenarios for ICT in future governance and policy modelling*. Luxembourg: Publications Office. doi:10.1145/1930321.1930392

Moe, H., & Van den Bulck, H. (2014). *Some Snowden, a lettuce bikini and grumpy cat? Searching for public service media outside the boundaries of the institution*. Retrieved from Paper for the 2014 RIPE Conference website: http://ripeat.org/wp-content/uploads/tdomf/3693/Moe%20&%20Van%20den%20Bulck%20RIPE%20paper%202014.pdf

Mossberger, K., Tolbert, C. J., & Franko, W. W. (2013). *Digital cities: The Internet and the geography of opportunity*. Academic Press.

Mossberger, K., Tolbert, C. J., & Stansbury, M. (2003). *Virtual inequality: Beyond the digital divide*. Washington, DC: Georgetown University Press.

Mun-cho, K., & Jong-Kil, K. (2001). Digital divide: conceptual discussions and prospect. In W. Kim, T. Wang Ling, Y.J. Lee & S.S. Park (Eds.), *The human society and the Internet: Internet related socio-economic Issues, First International Conference, Seoul, Korea: Proceedings*. New York, NY: Springer.

New London Group. (1996). A pedagogy of multiliteracies: Designing social futures. *Harvard Educational Review, 66*(1), 60–92. doi:10.17763/haer.66.1.17370n67v22j160u

O'Byrne, C. (2011). Get the girls online: Why Wales needs a gendered strategy to tackle digital exclusion. *Women in Society, 1*, 61–66.

Ogunsola, L. A. (2005). Information and communication technologies and the effects of globalization: twenty-first century "digital slavery" for developing countries-- myth or reality? *Electronic Journal of Academic and Special Libranianship, 6*(1-2). Retrieved from http://southernlibrarianship.icaap.org/content/v06n01/ogunsola_l01.htm

Oh, M., & Larson, J. F. (2011). *Digital development in Korea: Building an information society*. London, UK: Routledge.

Reich, R. (1992). *The work of nations*. New York, NY: Vintage Books.

Rogerson, S., & Rogerson, A. (2007). ETHIcol. *IMIS Journal, 17*(5), 1-3. Retrieved from http://www.ccsr.cse.dmu.ac.uk/resources/general/ethicol/Ecv17no5.pdf

Rose, M. (2014). *Public education under siege*. Retrieved from http://mikerosebooks.com/Public-Education-Under-S.html

Rutsch, H. (2003). Literacy as freedom. *UN Chronicle, 40*(2). Retrieved from https://www.questia.com/magazine/1G1-105657543/literacy-as-freedom

Schimmel, J. (2009). Development as Happiness: The Subjective Perception of Happiness and UNDP Analysis of Poverty, Wealth and Development. *Journal of Happiness Studies, 10*(1), 93–111. doi:10.1007/s10902-007-9063-4

Selfe, C. L. (1999). *Technology and literacy in the twenty-first century: The importance of paying attention*. Carbondale, IL: Southern Illinois University Press.

Selwyn, N. (2004). Reconsidering political and popular understandings of the digital divide. *New Media & Society, 6*(3), 341–362. doi:10.1177/1461444804042519

Shalaby, A. A., Ali, R. R., & Gad, A. (2012). Urban sprawl impact assessment on the agricultural land in Egypt using remote sensing and GIS: A case study, Qalubiya Governorate. *Journal of Land Use Science, 7*(3), 261–273. doi:10.1080/1747423X.2011.562928

Sitzenfrei, R., Kleidorfer, M., Meister, M., Burger, G., Urich, C., Mair, M., & Rauch, W. (2014). Scientific computing in urban water management. In G. Hofstetter (Ed.), *Computational engineering* (pp. 173–193). Switzerland: Springer International Publishing.

Solow, R. (1987, July 12). We'd better watch out. *New York Times Book Review*, p. 36. Retrieved from http://www.standupeconomist.com/pdf/misc/solow-computer-productivity.pdf

21. *st Century Skills Map*. (2011, March). Retrieved from https://www.actfl.org/sites/default/files/pdfs/21stCenturySkillsMap/p21_worldlanguagesmap.pdf

Star, S. L., & Griesemer, J. R. (1989). Institutional Ecology, `Translations' and Boundary Objects: Amateurs and Professionals in Berkeley's Museum of Vertebrate Zoology. *Social Studies of Science, 19*(3), 387–420. doi:10.1177/030631289019003001

Stuckey, E. (1990). *The violence of literacy*. New York, NY: Heinemann.

Sutherland-Smith, W., Snyder, I., & Angus, L. (2003). The digital divide: Differences in computer use between home and school in low socio-economic households. *Educational Studies in Language and Literature, 3*(1/2), 5–19. doi:10.1023/A:1024523503078

Thierer, A. D., Crews, C. W., Jr., & Pearson, T. (2002, October). *Birth of the digital New Deal: An inventory of high-tech pork-barrel spending.* Retrieved from http://www.cato.org/publications/policy-analysis/birth-digital-new-deal-inventory-hightech-porkbarrel-spending

Trigger, B. (1976). *Nubia under the pharaohs*. London, UK: Thames and Hudson.

UNCTAD. (2010). *Information economy report 2010: ICTs, Enterprises and Poverty Alleviation.* Technical Report. United Nations Conference on Trade and Development (UNCTAD). Retrieved from http://unctad.org/en/docs/ier2010_embargo2010_en.pdf

UNDP. (2010). *Human Development Report 2010 —20th Anniversary Edition: The Real Wealth of Nations: Pathways to Human Development.* Technical report. United Nations Development Programme (UNDP). Retrieved from http://hdr.undp.org/sites/default/files/reports/270/hdr_2010_en_complete_reprint.pdf

Unwin, P. T. (2009). *ICT4D: Information and communication technology for development.* Cambridge, UK: Cambridge University Press.

US Chamber of Commerce Foundation. (n.d.). *Center for education and workforce.* Retrieved from http://www.uschamberfoundation.org/center-education-and-workforce

van Dijk, J. A. (2006). Digital divide research, achievements and shortcomings. *Poetics, 34*(4-5), 221–235. doi:10.1016/j.poetic.2006.05.004

Varian, H. R. (2006). A plug for the unplugged $100 laptop computer for developing nations. *New York Times: Business.* Retrieved from http://www.nytimes.com/2006/02/09/business/09scene.html

Vaughan, D. (2011). The importance of capabilities in the sustainability of information and communications technology programs: The case of remote Indigenous Australian communities. *Ethics and Information Technology, 13*(2), 131–150. doi:10.1007/s10676-011-9269-3

Vision, V. (2012, March). *Broadband as a green strategy: Promising best practices to achieve positive environmental and economic benefits through accelerated broadband deployment and adoption.* Retrieved from http://valleyvision.org/sites/files/pdf/bbgreen_policy_brief_final_printer_withdate.pdf

Von Braun, J. (2010). ICT for the poor at large scale: Innovative connections to markets and services. In A. Picot & J. Lorenz (Eds.), *ICT for the next five billion people: Information and communication for sustainable development* (pp. 3–14). Heidelberg, Germany: Springer. doi:10.1007/978-3-642-12225-5_2

Vu, K. M. (2011). ICT as a source of economic growth in the information age: Empirical evidence from the 1996–2005 period. *Telecommunications Policy, 35*(4), 357–372. doi:10.1016/j.telpol.2011.02.008

Waelbroeck, P. (2013). Digital music: Economic perspectives. In R. Towse & C. Handke (Eds.), *Handbook of the digital creative economy.* Retrieved from http://papers.ssrn.com/sol3/papers.cfm?abstract_id=2249690

Waelde, C., & MacQueen, H. L. (2007). *Intellectual property: The many faces of the public domain.* Cheltenham, UK: Edward Elgar. doi:10.4337/9781847205582

Wallis, S. (2008). *Triple crunch: Joined-up solutions to financial chaos, oil decline and climate change to transform the economy.* Retrieved from new economics foundation website: http://b.3cdn. net/nefoundation/91cd89d66b0d556628_stm-6bqsxi.pdf

Warnick, B. (2002). *Critical literacy in a digital era: Technology, rhetoric, and the public interest.* Mahwah, NJ: Lawrence Erlbaum Associates.

Warschauer, M. (2003). *Technology and Social Inclusion: Rethinking the Digital Divide.* Cambridge, MA: The MIT Press.

Whitacre, B., Gallardo, R., & Strover, S. (2014). Does rural broadband impact jobs and income? Evidence from spatial and first-differenced regressions. *The Annals of Regional Science, 53*(3), 649–670. doi:10.1007/s00168-014-0637-x

Williams, S. (2013). *Fiber broadband: A foundation for social and economic growth.* Retrieved from http://www3.weforum.org/docs/GITR/2013/GITR_Chapter1.5_2013.pdf

Yu, P. K. (2002). *Terrorism and the global digital divide: Why bridging the divide is even more important after September 11.* Retrieved from http://writ.news.findlaw.com/commentary/20020211_yu.html

Ziliani, C., & Bellini, S. (2003). From loyalty cards to micro-marketing strategies: Where is Europe's retail industry heading? *Journal of Targeting, Measurement and Analysis for Marketing, 12*(3), 281-289. Retrieved from http://www.palgrave-journals.com/jt/journal/v12/n3/pdf/5740115a.pdf

Zuckerman, E. (2014), New media, new civics? *Policy & Internet, 6*(2), 151–168. Retrieved from http://onlinelibrary.wiley.com/doi/10.1002/1944-2866.POI360/abstract

Zysman, J., Feldman, S., Murray, J., Nielsen, N. C., & Kushida, K. E. (2010). Services with everything: The ICT-enabled digital transformation of services. *BRIE Working Paper, 187a.* Retrieved from http://brie.berkeley.edu/publications/WP_187a%20Services...%20revised%20 6.16.11.pdf

KEY TERMS AND DEFINITIONS

Digital Divide: A term patterned after 'achievement gaps' among demographic groups, digital divides refer to different outcomes for learning and economic participation based on access to information and communication technologies.

Digital Media: In contrast to analog media, which involve inscription with ink, carving, and the like, digital media use electronic switches to encode information. Programming involves arranging thousands of electronic switches to produce, receive, and exchange data. Digital media includes the physical hardware used in the encoding process, the digital "content" itself, and the mediating software.

Enclosure: A term in economic and agricultural history referring to the termination of shared rights (to land, especially) in favor of an owner, who subsequently uses a resource exclusively. The expansion of economic markets often involves changes in the way a natural or social resource is treated. Because digital spaces serve economic purposes, exchanges among users occurring there can involve economic enclosure. Social media provides numerous examples, in which creators of a networking site own and profit from the everyday communication of users.

Global North/South: Terms that denote the generic geographic, historical, economic, educational, and political division between North and South. North America, Europe, and developed parts of East Asia disproportionately control global resources. Disparities of wealth, housing, education, digital media access and numerous other factors underscore the power and privilege enjoyed by the Global North, while the Global South, home to the majority of natural resources and population, is excluded.

Knowledge Economy: A term denoting an economic shift toward knowledge as a chief commodity. A knowledge economy, unlike agriculture- or labor-intensive economies, places emphasis on expertise and other forms of human capital as opposed to material products. As nonrenewable resources dwindle, economic advantage shifts toward knowledge products—innovation and reorganization of existing frameworks.

Literacy Myth: Coined by educational historian Harvey Graff, literacy myths fuse the ability to read and write with economic and even moral progress. Graff and others, such as Stuckey (1990), argue that myths of economic progress through literacy obscure and oversimplify economic and political factors affecting prosperity, especially with regards to populations placed at risk because of race, socioeconomic status, and/or gender.

Neocolonialism: A term referring pejoratively to the economic influence of capitalism, especially in the form of foreign investment and market expansion, on developing countries. Neocolonialism refers to new means (i.e., business, free trade) to reach familiar ends (i.e., exploitation of developing regions, political influence) without direct military force.

Neoliberalism: A term that refers pejoratively to the tendency of governments in developed regions to use their resources to support privatization, free trade, and reduction of economic regulation.

New Economy: A term referring to the shift from the manufacturing-based economy to a service economy.

Chapter 9
Digital Media Affecting Society:
Instruction and Learning

Terry Cottrell
University of St. Francis, USA

ABSTRACT

The proliferation of the use of digital media for learning and instruction continues to be investigated and pondered as the advance of a broad range of technologies eclipses currently available traditional text and face-to-face learning modalities for K-12 and higher education instruction. Digital media's affect on educational processes and delivery, an analysis of existing research reviewing whether digital media is benefitting educational outcomes in instruction and learning, and recommendations for the future are the primary goals of this chapter. Investigation into each of the aforementioned topics separately reveals an intersection that is far from being maturely assessed. The topic of digital media affecting how people learn will elicit further research as education continues to call for an increased focus on high outcomes while also increasing the adoption of digital media resources for the transmission and acquisition of knowledge.

INTRODUCTION

The proliferation of the use of digital media resources in the field of education continues to be investigated and pondered as the advance of a broad range of technologies eclipses currently available traditional text and face-to-face learning modalities for K-12 and higher education instruction in the public and private spheres. Digital media's effect on educational processes and delivery, an analysis of existing research reviewing whether digital media is benefitting educational outcomes in instruction and learning, and recommendations

for the future are the primary goals of this chapter. Investigation into each of the aforementioned topics separately reveals an intersection that is far from being maturely assessed. Adoption of digital media for instruction is rising, and is predicted to grow indefinitely. The topic of digital media affecting how people learn will elicit further research as education continues to call for an increased focus on high outcomes while also increasing the adoption of multimedia resources for the transmission and acquisition of knowledge. Implications for the future are mixed with hope for positive progress, and suspicion that digital

DOI: 10.4018/978-1-4666-8310-5.ch009

media will make all areas of education less of an engaging enterprise and more of a commodity to be consumed.

The creation of instructional digital media by learners, not just its consumption, is another aspect of sweeping change throughout society that deserves investigation. Learners of all types continually create evidence of their learning outcomes in the form of media—papers, projects, presentations, and group reports. Written, text-based, forms of communication no longer hold the appeal they once had in a world filled with digital media. Students can (and often do) create digital video at the push of a button on a daily basis. They learn visual literacy techniques that increase their abilities to create info graphics and web pages that combine multiple elements of digital media together in the hopes of generating more engagement by audiences of all types. Teachers and professors alike are beginning to understand that communication through the written word is no longer the only essential skill to instill in their learners. The ability to work well with digital media software and hardware is increasingly becoming undebatable as an essential learning outcome.

Finally, some researchers make the assertion that digital media does not affect essential outcomes like reading, writing, mathematics, critical thinking (CT), problem-solving abilities (PSA) and other types of learning goals set in schools at any level. It can be argued that if digital media produce similar learning results in comparison to other forms of media, then the best choice for instructors is the cheapest and most-easily-acquired form of media available. Professor Anthony Grafton of Princeton University explains that all aspects of any medium's elements, including art and binding (as with plain text sources), create an environment that affects knowledge consumption and cognitive processing abilities (Prpick, Redel, & Grafton, 2011). For some, it is not safe to assume that digital media bears any different affect on users than a non-digital form of the same mate-

rial. For others, there is certainly an effect to be observed throughout society by the wide spread use of digital media. Mayer and Moreno (2003) propose that individuals process pictorial and verbal information differently in their minds, thereby establishing digital media's affect on the mind as something separate from text-based materials. The problem of cognitive overload can stifle learning, the researchers explain, as more information can be presented through digital media than can be presented through text-based materials. In the context of instruction and learning, is access and consumption of digital media (with its ability to present many different types of information to a consumer all at once) ultimately a negative or positive effect of the influence of technology throughout the greater society? Strategic planning and focused utilization may be the best way to integrate digital media in the educational arena in order to maximize positive effects.

BACKGROUND

Digital Media, Cognitive Load, and Cognitive Learning Theory

Cognitive theories related to the effects of digital and multimedia on learning and instruction include research into the visual and verbal channels for information processing and knowledge acquisition combined with the argument that these two channels are not unlimited in their abilities to gauge phenomena and cause heavy loads to weigh on cognition (Mayer & Moreno, 1998b). These cognitive load theories include three types of memory stores: (a) sensory memory, (b) working (sometimes called short-term) memory, and (c) long-term memory. Sensory memory captures the text and visuals in their most exact form, as well as auditory sounds, for a very limited amount of time. Working memory takes the sensory memory and allows for manipulation where the raw material from the sensory memory can be made into a model that includes spatial representations. For example, if a person hears the word "cat" they tend to immediately imagine a picture of one instead of an image of a bird. Long-term memory is deep storage where retrieval into working memory is problematic and unreliable at times for a variety of reasons (Mayer, 2005a).

Digital multimedia learning theory is consistent with learning design theories like cognitive load theory (Alasraj, Freeman & Chandler, 2013; Plass, Moreno & Brunken, 2010; Sweller, 1999; 2011), and the integrated model of text and picture comprehension presented by Schnotz and Bannert (2003). Schnotz and Bannert's (2003) model includes a structure mapping hypothesis which states that in order for visual materials like digital media to aid in learning they must be integrated well with corresponding textual information where it has been found that "interactions of . . . graphics, and text seem to be the key determinant of comprehension and performance in learning from [digital media]" (Rinck, 2008, p. 186). Each of the aforementioned theories lead to the sense that multiple channels (e.g., visual, verbal) working in concert together play a key role affecting memory and information processing in the minds of any type of learner at any age range (Mayer, 2005a). After starting with their initial proposition, the researchers develop their theory by explaining that there are limits to what people can mentally process when learning. The problem of cognitive overload brought on by digital media can stifle learning as more information can be presented through digital media materials than can be presented through text-based materials. Herein lies the need for their exploratory study eventually leading to nine suggestions for reducing the load that media can place on learners' minds. Mayer and Moreno (2003) provide definitions for their core concepts. They explain that they define media-based learning as "learning from words and pictures, and . . . 'multimedia instruction' as presenting words and pictures that are intended to foster learning" (p. 43). After providing these

definitions, the researchers begin to link them directly to common education outcomes like science, technology, engineering and mathematics (STEM), CT and PSA.

Since digital media is generally developed to facilitate increased learning in a more efficient manner, Mayer and Moreno (2003) provide ways to mediate the damage that can be done by overload of information through digital media consumption. An example of digital media damage is found by Wolf (2007) reporting that screen reading quickens the brain's senses and lessens the cognitive ability to "deep read." Calls for a "slow-reading" movement juxtaposed against the fast-paced nature of digital media use this type of research to support claims that digital media is detrimental to learning (Rosenwald, 2014). Mayer and Moreno (2003) use familiar terms when they argue that they define "meaningful learning" as deep "understanding of . . . material, which includes attending to important aspects . ., mentally organizing . . . into a coherent cognitive structure, and integrating . . .with relevant existing knowledge" (p. 43). This is where the clear connection to the investigators' research into digital media and learning outcomes can be found. They expand their connection between the mind and media processing by explaining that there are three channels for processing in the mind when it encounters images, text, and sound together as an information resource. Mayer and Moreno (2003) identify a

[1)] Dual channel [where] humans possess separate information processing channels for verbal and visual material, [2)] Limited capacity [where] there is only a limited amount of processing capacity available in the verbal and visual channels, [and 3)] Active processing [where] learning requires substantial cognitive processing in the verbal and visual channels. (p. 44)

These aforementioned channels provide a framework for the identification of five major ways in which overload can block learning and instructional outcomes. The scenarios include periods when only the visual or audio channel are taxed individually, times when both are overloaded, times when one or both channels are overloaded by essential and non-essential information, periods when one or both channels are overloaded by information that is presented in a poor manner, and finally times when the learner holds the wrong information in one channel and not the other.

Schema Theory and Mental Models

Concepts on schema became influential in the fields of cognitive psychology and education in the 1970s, and inspired learning and instruction research with picture and text processing, and in the world of television viewing (Krauskopf, Zahn & Hesse, 2012; Hayles, 2012; Seel, 2008). Schemas encompass organized collections of information with how pieces of information relate to one another. Schema Theory works under the understanding that human knowledge is collected in the human mind under such schema. Schemas can be modified, reassembled, and then integrated with other schema containing new and different pieces of knowledge (Hansen, 2012; Alessi & Trollip, 2001). Mental models are dynamic and active representations of knowledge that serve to make what is invisible visible, help to create analogies between what is known and not known, or integrate pieces of coherence with unexplained phenomena (Seel, 2008). Mental models can be created in the minds of learners by the use of schema and other elements. These models can be helped by text, pictures, and video—combinations of which are what is now known as digital media (Block, 2014; Buckingham & Willet, 2013; Clark & Feldon, 2005; Hegarty & Just, 1993; Sharp, Bransford, Goldman, Risko, Kinzer & Vye, 1995; Shrock, 1994). Images alone have the vast ability to help students make sense of things they have not witnessed first-hand. Combine images with text and audio for simulation, or other forms of digital

media, and instructors find the job of transmitting knowledge much more enhanced and learners are enticed to explore educational or entertainment content more deeply (Bull & Kozak, 2014; Dunleavy & Dede, 2014; Flew, 2014; Gold, 2012; Goldman, Pea, Barron & Derry, 2014; Schwartz & Heiser, 2006; Hayles, 2012; Tyner, 2014; Van Dusen, 2014).

The application of schema and their accompanying schemata allows the brain to map what the senses perceive in a mental model. Images in the schema and spatial relations that structure the images are mapped to semantic understanding through digital media in ways different from traditional text or audio of the past. This means that mapping is a process that aids in mental model development from images, text, and other media sources, and also helps an individual evaluate the model that was in his or her mind before interacting with the media itself (Rouet, Lowe, & Schnotz, 2008). Mapping is part of the process of critically segregating information for better understanding and eventual decision making desired with the development of learning outcomes. When learners are asked to take a test, or make decisions, they are essentially being asked to map schema in their minds to form mental models that allow for the finding of the "right" answer to a particular question. Digital media creates fundamentally different mental models in the minds of learners in educational environments leading to potentially worse or better outcomes depending on the subject matter combined with media delivery type (viz., audio, video, multimedia, etc.)

Clark and Kozma on Digital Media's Impact on Learning and Instruction

Richard Clark (1994) makes the assertion that media does not affect critical thinking (CT) skills, problem-solving abilities or other types of learning goals set in schools. Clark states that the true essence of all "media research question[s] is [that they are part of many] similarly confounded questions in educational research" (p. 27). In Clark's mind, media research is subordinate to instructional design research, because it is the design of instruction that influences learning regardless of media used. Digital media, therefore according to Clark, has no affect on society in terms of instruction and learning. The media does not matter, and if replicable media produce similar learning results, then the best choice for instructors is the cheapest and most-easily-acquired form of media available at any given point in time. Robert Kozma (1994a) responds by reframing the concern of media influencing learning from a design science (R. Glaser, 1976; Simon, 1996) perspective rather than from a natural science point of view that seeks to explain human cognitive interaction with the world not created by humans. Kozma explains that educational technology using elements like digital media is a design science deserving critique and analysis observed from relationships between human-created tools and other humans completely separate from the natural world. He offers a response to Clark that asserts that both instructional methods and elements like digital media "influence learning and they frequently do it by influencing each other . . . methods take advantage of a medium's capabilities in well-designed instruction . . . One cannot simply replace one medium with another in a design and hold everything else constant, as Clark . . . suggests" (1994b, p. 11). Both Clark and Kozma provide a review of the literature to support their claims about the effects of digital and multimedia on education. Kozma, however, provides a quantitative data analysis from a study using his 4M:Chem software that allows students to see the results of their chemistry-related course activities. Kozma's research shows that both the instructional methods used and the digital elements affected overall student learning outcomes. He then asks how this phenomenon is possible.

Kozma claims that learning is assessed not so much by the instructor or through the methods used, but by looking at learning "as it happens

and [collecting] data on the ways students interact with the system as they learn" (1994b, p. 12). This view is similar to Mitra's (2007) idea that learning occurs through the theory that education is a self-organizing process. In order to find answers, Kozma conducts a separate study and describes how five students from his first experiment participate in a second experiment where they demonstrate how they learned from 4M:Chem. The students show significant abilities to form inferences about particular chemical events through viewing video sequences in the software. This is the combination of media/medium and instructional method affecting learning outcomes consistent with the hypotheses Kozma desires to see. He concludes, refuting Clark's 'replaceability challenge' by stating, "If two [media] treatments yield a similar outcome it does not mean that they resulted from the same cause . . . [and the outcome] does not identify what that cause is . . . if you want to know what causes learning, you have to look at it as it occurs" (1994b, p. 13).

CURRENT ISSUES

Much debate on digital media replacing traditional media information resources in the field of education, along with the resulting effect on learning outcomes, is found in the literature. Comparisons of digital media's affects on learning outcomes can be generalizable only to a certain degree due the fundamental differences between outcomes like science, technology, engineering and math (STEM), language comprehension, CT, problem-solving ability (PSA), and more obtuse outcomes like moral judgment, and psychological/physiological behaviors. Of the extant studies available to-date, most carry mixed results of the basic learning effects of digital over traditional physical resources.

Digital Media Content vs. Traditional Instruction Content: "Mindtools" and Digital Media Affecting Learning Outcomes

Jonassen, Carr, and Yueh (1998) identified early forms of web-based digital media under a term they call "mindtools" describing how digital media computer applications challenge outcome skills by requiring students to think deeply about what they are seeing and hearing on a screen instead of merely accepting the premise that rote absorption is the primary educational goal. In their descriptive meta-analysis of different digital media tools, the researchers connect these various forms of media to educational outcomes such as: (a) interpretation, (b) inferences, (c) manipulation, (d) semantic organization, (e) linguistic evaluation, (f) visualization, (g) prediction, (h) elimination, and (i) inference. They ask, "Why do Mindtools work, that is, why do they engage learners in critical, higher-order thinking about content?" (Jonassen et al., 1998, p. 12). What the researchers assert here is that, in fact, individuals who are challenged in their learning environments (classroom location, materials, access to information/date, etc.) through any sort of combinations of input other than one (e.g., visual alone or audio alone or print text alone) are the individuals who wind up thinking the most about the content contained therein. If this maxim is true, digital media where individuals can both see and hear, or read and hear, or even see, hear, read, speak, and manipulate will engage outcomes more than their counterparts using traditional learning tools (like text alone) and techniques (e.g., lecture). Jonassen et al. (1998) also determine that individuals using "mindtools" as early forms of digital media are capable of more critical thought through ideas that would not be present without the actual use of the tool first. This coincides with the basic idea of learning-tool scaffolding as the genesis for all human innovation: The development of electricity, for example, leads humans toward critical inquiry into the powering of all sorts of

tools, like radios, which leads humans to the idea of mass communication over long distances which eventually begins the CT behind the creation of the idea of the internet.

Jonassen et al. (1998) contend that ultimately digital media-type tools are direct descendants of constructivist thinking about learning and education derived from earlier education pioneers like John Dewey (1897; 1909; 1916; 1933). The researchers note that digital media extends the capability of computers to move beyond simple presentation by "engaging learners in reflective, critical thinking about the ideas they are studying" (Jonassen et al., 1998, p. 15). Under this model, computer digital media information is another powerful partner in the learning process. It is not a merely upgraded and advanced way of storing information for reading and memorization, or for reference.

Mills and Exley (2014) studied a similar outcomes in K-12 students aged 8 to 10 years. A digital writing classroom was used as the environment where the research question centered on the time used by students to create text in a digital media environment. The study was conducted over 40 school weeks. Dialogue about writing in the digital classroom was the main method of analysis. The dialogue was recorded digitally and then coded. The results showed that digital media used as a format for writing gave a more explicit time frame for the K-12 students. Writing with physical paper and pen did not carry the same structure in the minds of the learners. More thoughts and content generation occurred in the digital environment. An overall assessment of the quality of the writing, however, was not assessed.

Liao (1999) conducted a comprehensive meta-analysis of over 45 studies conducted between 1986 and 1998 investigating the role of hypermedia on student achievement in many areas. The vast majority of this media research is heavily focused on subject-specific areas (e.g., historical facts, practical mathematics, language assimilation) instead of more over-arching concerns like ethics, intelligence, emotional response, or CT. What was found was the extant research on digital media's influence into student achievement shows mixed results. If no instructor intervenes (via live instruction, video, chat, etc.), digital media provides a larger effect on student outcomes. With the introduction of instructor interaction, however, text and other forms of traditional information sources become more effective at positively impacting outcomes (Okutsu, DeLaurentis, Brophy & Lambert 2013).

Stoney and Oliver (1999) found that learning outcomes can be enhanced, and more strategically focused upon, by adding digital media to learning environments. The researchers tested their hypothesis by means of one instructional unit inserted into one collegiate finance course focused on accounting. The design of the study called for the replacement of one of the traditional face-to-face instruction days with an equivalent digital media unit accessed by students during a time of their own choosing. The subject of the intervening treatment was a simple stock price valuation simulation where students had to decide how to pick stocks to increase the profits of a simulated portfolio. Eight students were separated into four groups for analysis of their discussions produced during and after engagement with the digital media treatment. The researchers analyzed and coded student activity looking for evidence of time spent utilizing the digital media content juxtaposed against time spent engaged in discussion rooted in the outcomes for the course. The cognitive activities of the students were grouped into two sub-groups: low-order activity and high-order activity. Low-order activity was defined by the researchers as discussion requiring little to no decision-making, cognitive engagement, or problem-solving effort (Stoney & Oliver, 1998; Stoney & Oliver, 1999). High-order activities were described as being any combination of discussion related to: prediction, strategy, contemplation of new and pre-existing knowledge, consideration of belief and evidence, eliminating falsities, and deducing uncertainties.

The findings of the study showed marked learning outcomes increases due to interaction with the digital media unit. All students were required to discuss and make decisions based on the content of the digital media content regardless of how much time was actually spent with the treatment. The evidence related to outcomes advancement was shown through analysis revealing that the more time students spent with the digital media, the more students exhibited higher-order skills. The particular media used in this study was not created by the course instructor or by anyone at the same university. The treatment materials were created by an outside firm specializing in the particular subject fields of business finance and accounting.

Alexander (2014) investigated increases in student engagement through the use of digital historical images to be integrated into presentations for K-12 students. The research cites disengagement research calling for more teacher effort as a primary reason for the attempts at using digital media to bridge the gap between what K-12 want to pay attention to during their leisure time and what they are challenged to focus on in school. Using the Technological Pedagogical Content Knowledge Framework (TPACK) framework, the students were analyzed on the interplay between their teacher's content, technology knowledge and instructional methods (Mishra & Koehler, 2006). Using two sixth-grade history classes, Alexander found that time devoted to the assignment at-hand increased dramatically using digital media. The students reported enjoying the assignment task much more than the teachers enjoyed designing it. The use of digital media was more burdensome to the teachers due to unfamiliarity with the technology and perceived learning curve. The outcomes received from the students, however, justified the integration of digital media within the class.

Thomas, Coppola, and Thomas (2001) questioned whether elements found in online classrooms (including digital media) had a demonstrable effect on learning outcomes. Their study was wide-ranging, mostly including the effect of learning management system (LMS) integration on outcomes. Included in their study was a measure for digital media's affect by way of on-demand video of course content. The study used a standardized assessment for CT in a pre and posttest design method on three different sections (three different instructors) of the same master's degree-level information systems course. The ages of the participants were between 20 and 29. The instructor was not the creator of all of the content for any of the courses. One class was conducted in a traditional face-to-face class format, one was conducted totally online via an LMS (Blackboard©), and one was conducted face-to-face with electronic treatments including on-demand video. The researchers define the third type of treatment of electronic classroom as "an interactive multimedia electronic classroom networked to the Internet and housing a video/ audio/ keyboard/ mouse broadcast-on-demand system" (Coppola & Thomas, 2000, para. 45). 20 to 40 students per course served as participants for the study.

This investigation found that the third digital media treatment section of the MBA course did show increased mean scores improving (11.00 pretest to 14.28 posttest) on the CT test over the Blackboard course. Posttest CT scores from the Blackboard course were actually lower (11.28 to 10.32) pretest to posttest. Final grades, however, were highest for the traditional face-to-face course. No analysis of teaching style was conducted during this study. A perceptions questionnaire was given at the end of the study asking participants to rate how they felt their method of instruction helped with their acquisition of CT skills. As with the final grade reports, the students in the face-to-face class were the most likely to report that they perceived their learning skills had improved most without technological assistance of any kind. At the end of the study, the researchers mention the need to extend their research to cover the same course taught by the same instructor to better control for pedagogical methods concerns.

Cavalier and Weber (2002) explored the effect of digital media on the learning outcome of moral decision-making through the use of a one-factor three-level experiment where students were surveyed after one group studied the case of burn victim Dax Cowart with only text materials, one group with only a 1-hour VHS documentary, and a third group only with an interactive digital media program created by a third-party vendor. The study was replicated the following year with three different sets of students as participants and using new graders different from the first study. The groups in both years ranged in sample sizes of 21 up to 38 undergraduate philosophy students. The students enrolled in the courses as a requirement for their major. The results of the experiment showed that performance in (a) understanding the complex perspectives and positions of the case, and (b) analyzing the case with respect to its morally relevant details was higher in the groups who were affected only by the interactive digital media program during the first year of testing. Statistically significant differences were not observed, however, in the study's second year. Aside from mixed results in both study periods, other problems with this study arise when considering the quality of the learning materials given to participants, and the fact that the materials were produced by three distinct creators.

Redsell, Collier, Garrud, Evans, and Cawood (2003) conducted a stratified cluster randomized controlled trial of bedwetting children (n=270) undergoing psychological treatment at 15 different nurse-led clinics for their condition. The students viewed and compared bedwetting mediation information in digital multimedia format with text that was mirrored word-for-word in content. The digital media learning materials contained an interactive assessment component not present in the text. The researchers' study showed no significant difference between the two information sources' ability to impact the learning outcomes (e.g., time to dry and remaining dry) of medical information for a specific condition post completion of the study and six months after completion.

Kumta, Tsang, and Hung (2003) used 163 final-year medical students in a study aimed at directly gauging the effects of digital media instructional materials on learning outcomes in an orthopedic surgery context. The study was randomized using a control and experimental group. The researchers begin their narrative with a fundamental problem of education and outcomes where the observable world is filled with so many information sources. This fact makes it difficult to distinguish between what sources will help solve problems and which will not. The researchers say lecture-based curricula are too commonplace, antiquated, and conventional, and therefore "not well-designed to develop . . . analytical thinking and problem-solving skills" (para. 1), because of inundation of information. Digital media sources, the researchers attest, can mediate this problem. The stakes are higher with medical students, because lack of proper cognitive skills can mean patient harm. The researchers find that their small study with web-based tutorial sources "led students through a thinking pathway that facilitated the development of higher cognitive skills such as analysis, application, and evaluation" (para. 18).

The researchers split their participants into 11 groups of 15 students who all attended a 3-week module on orthopedics throughout the span of their final year in medical school. Next, the researchers randomly assigned each group to a Study or Control group. A multiple-choice pretest was given to all participants before the experiment began. The Study group was exposed to a web-based clinical case simulation (CCS) program designed by the researchers, but tested by existing orthopedic surgeons, to foster logical thinking abilities in the students. They were not given any other lecture-based or digital teaching materials. The Control group was given a standard lecture-based curriculum supported by text materials and optional tutoring. At the end of 3-week module, both sets of students were tested on their knowledge and CT abilities in the arena of orthopedics. The researchers note there was no significant difference between the results of the Control and Study group on the pretest. There was a statistically significant difference on the final test at the end of the 3-week module with the Study group scoring higher than the Control. The researchers note that their study was small and limited. But they give commentary to their findings by suggesting their research demonstrates that "well-designed web-based tutorials stimulate students to think and . . . complement . . . teaching resources . . . foster[ing] better clinical and critical thinking skills in medical students, without subjecting them to an information overload" (para. 23).

Barlett and Strough (2003) conducted a 3-semester-long study where samples (25 min/61 max) of undergraduates in seven different Social Psychology courses taught by six different instructors each term were given one of three different methods of instruction: (a) traditional lecture, (b) traditional lecture with course guide, and (c) digital media with course guide. While the digital media in this study was, in fact, created by the same instructor in some of the courses, the products were not the same due to the inclusion of so many different instructors used in the study. Final grades in the course were the primary measure used to gauge the impact and effectiveness of the instructional method and information source used in each case. The final results showed that it was the course guide, not the delivery of traditional lecture or digital media, which improved final grades. The researchers note that redesigning their study so that "a comparison of traditional and multimedia formats when neither is accompanied by a course guide would be useful in understanding the unique contribution of multimedia formats" (p. 337).

Sheldon and DeNardo (2005) sought further explanation on the difference between how digital media video affected educational outcomes in prospective freshman and upper-level pre-service music education majors. The researchers' study design included two groups (n = 116 prospective freshmen) and (n = 130 upper-level) music education majors. Each participant was shown a digital video of a particular musical interaction from two earlier studies (Sheldon & DeNardo, 2004). The researchers describe the 20-minute media treatment as,

The . . . examples consisted of music in special education interactions . . . with mainstreamed groups and people who were mentally retarded, had cerebral palsy, were hearing-impaired, learning disabled, geriatric, abandoned, or were juvenile delinquents; music education interactions . . . with general, instrumental, or choral groups at the elementary, middle school, and high school levels; and professional, formal music performances . . . that included a piano concerto with both full orchestra and soloist shown and a violin solo accompanied by piano with only the violinist shown. (p. 7)

Each of the aforementioned segments in the treatment was displayed for one minute followed by two seconds of blank screen. The participants were required to watch the presentation, not speak to one another, and simply write down as many observations as they could describing each segment. Assessment by the researchers was made according to two criteria: factual and inferential content of the participants' written observations.

The final results were, like other studies, somewhat mixed. It was hypothesized that the upper-level student would score higher as their experience level would correlate more to what they saw through the digital media treatment. While this was most often the case, it was not always the case. In some instances, the prospective freshmen demonstrated more understanding about the segments they saw on screen. One-way ANOVA was used to compare scores. Post hoc analysis on certain demographic data connected to each participant (viz., GPA, class rank and ACT score) did show consistent correlations. Higher values in these measures equated to higher levels of learning regardless of student status.

Montgomery (2014) used K-12 students in a third-grade classroom as subjects for a study on critical democracy engagement through the production of digital media. Educational outcomes for students of all types mostly commonly come in the form of written text (digital or physical). This study explored the use of digital audio (viz., podcasting) as an outcome demonstrating students willingness to criticize aspects of government. The research found that the third-grade students in the study were much more willing to research governmental issues related to democracy, because of the need to create their podcast assignments. Consistent with Jonassen's (2014) assertion of digital media as mindtools for learning and productivity, the students output and engagement was positively impacted by digital media being incorporated into their learning and instructional environment. The students were using the digital media as mindtool "technology [that represents] what they know versus learning from technology as in traditional tutorial or drill and practice sessions" (Marra, 2013, p. 266). Students were not only more willing to share their views, because of the digital media, but they were also more willing to read and study their given topics because of the introduction of digital media requirements into their classroom experience.

Gerjets, Scheiter, and Schuh (2008) worked with 80 (48 female, 32 male) undergraduate students at a traditional German university. These students were presented with three complex word problems to be solved in an online digital media environment. A navigation bar was always present with the problems to be solved. The navigation bar contained links with information related to solving the problem at hand. Students had the ability to self-select how many links, and which links, they wanted to use to help solve the problem. They could not look at the information contained in the links while attempting to solve the problem. Students could only use this aspect of the digital media environment before attempting a solution.

An added value question was included with each "tip" given via the links that asked the students if they felt the information they received was helpful. The researchers say the dependent variables for their study were "problem-solving performance for the three . . . problems, time spent on studying example pages, and mean time spent per example retrieved [from the hyperlinks]" (p. 82). The results of this experiment found a significant difference in solution performance between genders, but not between how many tips were used via the media links. The only other significant factor found was with students who reported low prior knowledge of the problem material before interacting with the media links. As hypothesized by the researchers, the experiment suggests that digital media link prompting for "cognitive processing might result in a better problem-solving performance, particularly for learners with low prior knowledge" (p. 83).

In a second experiment, the researchers used 31 German high school students (14 female, 17 male) in the ninth grade. The students worked in a computer mediated course (CMC) environment where they worked on algebra problems. Each student was given an 11-item pretest that gauged their prior understanding of algebra concepts before beginning work on the main problems. The concept of "pre-knowledge" in the work of Gerjets et al. (2008) is an essential component for the overall understanding of deep-thinking toward problem solving using digital media. The ninth grade students in this study were first given examples of algebraic concepts in scenarios typically not emphasizing mathematics, viz., biology, chemistry, and politics. They were required to simply read and study the concepts in this first phase of the experiment. They were allowed use their web browser's forward and backward buttons to help guide their cognitive processing of the material during this phase. It was the second phase of the experiment that required the students to solve 21 algebraic problems. The researchers note they were interested in differential effectiveness and therefore "a second independent variable

was manipulated within the transfer distance of the 21 test problems that learners had to solve subsequent to the learning phase" (p. 86). The actual learner's solution performance on the 21 questions in the test phase was the dependent measure for the study. Ultimately, the researchers find that the ability to use digital media to view and interact with seemingly unrelated content in the same context of an intended problem (viz., algebraic equation problem solving) will positively affect a learner's ability to solve targeted related problems. The researchers find interactive media comparison tools "help learners to abstract . . . [and] compare examples that share the same cover stories across problem categories facilitat[ing] later problem-solving performance" (p. 87).

Kingsley and Boone (2008) conducted a quasi-experimental, pretest/posttest design study on the effects of digital media as an augmentation to the existing text and lecture content of a middle school American history class. The researchers compared pre and posttest scores for the students in control and experimental groups using a two-tailed *t*-test (unequal variance), because single-tailed *t*-tests are not as sensitive to unknown changes in the direction of mean test scores. Like the Barlett and Strough (2003) study, Kingsley and Boone (2008) used multiple sections of classes taught by multiple instructors (four, all female in total) for a total of 184 participants (93 aggregate in the experimental treatment group, 91 aggregate for control groups). The researchers in this case, however, conducted their research by pulling participants from three different schools. They also used digital media created by a different vendor from the text material used in the subject course sections. Gender, age, and experience level of the instructors studied were noted in descriptions of this experiment, but not studied in-depth. The results of the study showed a significant difference between the control and experimental groups with the experimental displaying 12.2% higher scores on the posttest assessment of their knowledge of American history subjects. In this particular study, the addition of digital media improved students' ability to meet the requirements of a standardized assessment based on NCLB guidelines for middle school student knowledge about American history. Whether or not the digital media provided more, better or clearer information as compared to the traditional instruction experienced by the control group was not discussed or studied by the researchers. The digital media was added to traditional instruction, in this case, not set up as a substitution for traditional instruction or instructional course materials like texts or print articles.

Following Kingsley and Boone's study, Smith (2012) investigated a similar aspect of digital media used for instruction and learning on K-12 students in an Algebra class. The media was used as a complete replacement for the instructor in the case of this study. Seeking to answer the question of whether or not digital media can make a physical instructor irrelevant to K-12 students, the researcher found interesting results. Students in the study had higher levels of self-regulation and lowers levels of intimidation through the use of digital media. A very large number of the students (ninety-three percent) preferred the teacher's "digital media presence" over their physical presence. The researcher indicates that, in the very least, digital media takes some of the pressure off the learning experience by depersonalizing aspects of instructional interchanges between teachers and learners.

Xu, Oh, and Teo (2009) conducted a one-factorial experiment with randomly assigned participants in two groups at a 1:1 gender ratio. The study tested the differential effects of text and digital media advertising on mobile consumers' perception and behavior. Forty-one males and 41 females were recruited from a large university to received simulated advertisements on their mobile devices in text or digital media format depending on their vicinity to a particular vendor in a simulated mall. The researchers found that digital media advertising information improved a viewer's attitude toward a product and signifi-

cantly increased the intention to buy vs. text-based advertising. Their study also showed that digital media was more of an irritation, but provided more information and entertainment value over text.

Serra and Dunlosky (2010) conducted a digital media study on undergraduate students at Kent State University. Two groups (n=40 for each) were initially studied with a third later added at the end of the research. The study participants either read 500 words (digitally displayed) on how storms develop, or they viewed similar, decreased amounts of text with images added to explicate the same content. The third group in the study examined showed no significant change in learning using text only versus digital media, while the original two groups did. All three groups also believed they would learn more through the use of digital media. The researchers provide commentary cautioning the overuse of digital media, as this heuristic did not always show improved learning, even if learners come to believe it is always a superior learning information source over text. They cite this as a reason for future research linking learning belief with learning format and outcomes performance.

Starbek, Erjavec, and Peklaj (2010) conducted a quasi-experimental pretest/posttest study on 3rd and 4th grade students to gauge overall content acquisition in a course module centered on genetics. The researchers used four comparable groups where the first group (n=112) received instruction only via lecture, the second (n=124) only by reading a text, the third group (n=115) only through two short computer animations, and the fourth (n=117) only through images combined with text on a screen. Their study showed evidence that digital media was a better instructional tool over text for the specific material to be acquired—the understanding of a single dynamic process. The researchers call for additional research to be performed due to the type of understanding the students were required to learn. The researchers say their study is ultimately not indicative of digital media's learning effects toward learning facts, data or other types of knowledge. This study's finding is a consistent precursor to what Hwang, Chu, Lin & Tsai (2011) found in their K-12 study involving fifth-graders in another science course centered on instruction involving the differentiating different species of butterfields. Their study used digital media as a mindtool which also successfully increased students' abilities to understand and learn the required material.

Chuang and Ku (2011) conducted a study comparing Chinese-language learning materials in combined text and image form against the same material presented only in images combined with digital audio narration. Their study resulted in mixed findings where the control group of undergraduate students (text with images, n=33) did not significantly differ from the experimental group (n=33) of undergraduate students in terms of posttest and delayed posttest performance on language learning assessment. There was a significant difference, however, found between the two individual test occasions. The overall results directly contradict Mayer's (2001) modality principle which suggests that text combined with images on the screen is a superior form of information acquisition over images combined with narration, because the mind working on both the visual and nonvisual channel (in tandem) devotes less time to each, thereby reducing learning potential.

Serin (2011) studied the effects of digital media on student ability to use information to make inferences and solve particular problems. The researcher's method included 26 fifth-grade students in a control group and 26 in an experimental group from a single school. In the study, the participants learned about general information on the Earth, the Sun and the Moon. Serin (2011) used a mixed design (pre and posttest) study to assess the impact of digital media created by the researcher and presented to the experimental group students three hours per week for three weeks. The control group did not have the media treatment added to their lessons for the three weeks during the study. The results of the study showed a statistically significant increase in problem-solving outcomes for learners receiving digital media treatment.

Serin, Bulut Serin, and Sayg (2010) used a self-created tool for their assessment of learning outcomes, and a general content-based assessment on the subject matter of the "Earth, Sun and Moon" to collect data from the participants in the study. Cronbach's (1951) Alpha for the self-created tool was reported at .85 with a KR-20 reliability level at .72. The contents of the digital media were also created by the researcher, and included some level of interactivity beyond simply watching, listening or reading in combination on a screen. The results of this study showed mean scores on the self-created tool to be significantly higher for the experimental group. Equivalencies of the groups were assessed by way of initial *t*-tests. Kolmogorov-Simirnov Z was used to determine normal distribution of the scores. The efficacy of the process of the experiment was assessed using ANCOVA. The researcher concludes with a general call for similar studies in different disciplines (and at different education levels) to be carried out using the same pre/posttest design with digital media content used as an experimental treatment.

Recently, Kayaoglu, Dag Akbas, and Ozturk (2011) used an achievement test to assess the impact of digital animation versus print text in two undergraduate English-language learning courses. Pretests were given to the control (n=22) and experimental (n=17) groups showing equivalent abilities before the introduction of the two different forms of learning materials. The researchers created both material types. The results of the study showed increased assessment scores on the posttest for the experimental group given only digital media animation as a means for learning English. Anecdotal opinion on learning via animation versus text was also collected from the participants and teachers, indicating that they were more excited to learn language via animations. The researchers caution, however, that excitement and statistically significantly higher posttest scores are not a justification to replace print text with digital media completely in all cases, because there was ultimately no difference between the groups in terms of overall increase in achievement. The students in both groups increased their performance on English language assessment at the end of the testing phase. In the end, both text and digital media each work to increase overall language performance.

IMPLICATIONS, POLICY AND PRACTICE

Universal Design, Self-Organizing Education, and Digital Media

Universal Design for Learning (UDL) is potentially the most provocative process design change for instruction and learning born in the 21st century. UDL attempts to account for educational theories that support there is no one-size-fits-all approach to learning appropriate for students in any setting (NYC Department of Education, 2014). Before the advent of digital media, education was delivered solely in either face-to-face environments supplemented by drawn visual aids, static images and print books, or remotely through printed material. In some cases, radio and television signals were used for instruction as well, but this market was relatively small and insignificant in comparison to massive commercial market for broadcasting radio wave signals (Saettler, 2004). Due to the advent of digital media for learning, UDL is unleashed allowing for more modalities of learning a single subject which, in theory, will benefit more students in terms of learning outcomes and efficiency.

Digital media development, deployment and adoption has started a trend where once there were only a few modalities supported and endorsed for learning to now all options, permutations and learning scenarios being supplanted by a great many ways to learn. The "many" modalities are almost entirely digital in nature today due to the introduction of the World Wide Web in 1995 (Segal, 1995). The World Wide Web allowed the mass distribution of digitized text via HTML, and

from that point forward, learning and instruction have never been the same. Once it was considered wonderful and democratizing for the masses to be able to read because of the Gutenberg's Printing Press (Gray, 1999). The Printing Press spread human knowledge quicker and more efficiently than any other technology prior. The masses, in this case, were required to find and purchase printed text once they were taught and encouraged to read. Still, this was a much slower process for knowledge acquisition and understanding than what occurred through the proliferation of digital print.

Textbooks used for education, and even the revered *Encyclopaedia Britannica*, have now succumbed to digital text (Sollisch, 2012). More and more students each day are finding digital text content they can use for educational purposes at the touch of a keystroke. Students, parents, educators and even some librarians ask, "Why purchase, read, and especially, be burdened with carrying print books when you can get the same content online through a digital device?" Due to physical sizes and weight, and the assumption that digital text content will always be cheaper than traditional print content, formers supporters of physical text content are running away from this format in favor of e-text. Even some librarians themselves are endorsing the elimination of print books from libraries. In the K-12 environment, boards and administrators take this scenario one step farther by eliminating print materials and school libraries entirely. Double-digit year-over-year decreases in school library funding are now common. Connecting the notion of literacy to libraries has also been dropped from the strategy of the U.S. Department of Education through its voluntary elimination of the $20 million Literacy Through School Libraries grant (Siu-Runyan, 2011).

The textbook in digital format is still in jeopardy due to the "many" digital audio, video and multimedia content options. Students in today's digital media environment have numerous choices for entertainment to occupy their minds throughout a day's time. These "many" choices compete with educational resources for the consciousness of learners. Digital media, as an influencer of the process of education, comes from the inherent form of the technology. Educational content, as well as un-related entertainment content, all are now delivered in the same form. These media are simple files sitting on interconnected servers in cyberspace only distinguishable by file extensions (e.g., .mp3, .mp4, .m4a, .png, .jpg, .js., .flv., etc.) and file size. Before the internet, digital content sat resident on digital media—memory cards/sticks, CDs/DVDs, disk drives. The digital media still needed a physical form in order to be consumed by a learner in the similar fashion that books used to be the media needed for the printed word. Instruction today is guided toward the discovery and the linking of digital media content directly to learners' media devices (tablets, computers, and smartphones). The form of the digital media is no longer a going concern influencing the process of instruction and learning (Gikas & Grant, 2013; Keskin & Metcalf, 2011; Wu, Wu, Chen, Kao, Lin & Huang, 2012).

Digital Media and the "Self-Organizing" Educational Process

In 1999, Sugata Mitra facilitated the installation of a computer terminal in an open area of a slum in New Delhi, India. This experiment, eventually known as the Hole-In-The-Wall experiment, resulted in a number of surprising educational outcomes (Orvis, 2006). Children in the New Delhi slum were encouraged to interact with the computer terminal in their neighborhood. Through their uninterrupted and unfacilitated interaction, the children were able to show the ability to learn through interactive digital media delivered via the internet through the terminal. Calling this development, Minimally Invasive Education (MIE), Mitra (2009) and his colleagues show more evidence of interactive digital media's ability to massively affect education without the need for human intervention. Through the installation of

21 additional internet computer stations, MIE allowed the children in the New Dehli slum to accomplish the following:

- Learn English to communicate—with no prior knowledge of the language,
- Not need to be "taught" how to use a computer and digital media; the media "taught" and self-empowered the children to learn on their own,
- Create their own media through drawing images on the computer screen,
- Increase STEM-based scores at their home schools,
- Modify their own social interaction\skills because of the ability to remotely see and hear (digital media) about other people and places (Mitra, 2007; Mitra, 2009).

The Hole-In-The-Wall project was expanded to Cambodia in 2004 after the results of the 1999 efforts worked against the original hypotheses that learning without a teacher through the internet, combined with large language barriers, was nearly impossible. Through MIE, Dr. Mitra seeks to explain that the internet delivering interactive digital media has the power to change the landscape of education as it is has been known since the educational methods were first inspired by Horace Mann (1848) and John Dewey (1897) in America in the 19th Century preceded by British Education developed in the 12th Century. Interactive digital media's ability to enable students is unprecedented, understudied and still in early development. Mitra (2007) also conducted another experiment where 32 children in groups of four working with the internet and digital media together on one station, and not on their own with their own computer, showed equal learning outcomes compared to children with a physical teacher over longer term breaks (two months between pre and post tests) with the non-teacher connected children interacting together with digital media above working alone with digital media.

Mitra and his team's research lead to an argument that education in itself is a self-organizing system where instruction is the vehicle (executed in his experiments entirely via interactive digital media) that can be experienced in a solo or group setting like traveling in a bus can be experienced as a rider or as a passenger with many participants resulting in differing outcomes depending on their role as driver or rider. Learning in this case, therefore, is a phenomenon that emerges from the self-organizing system enabled entirely by interactive digital media. There are limitations, however, to replacing physical teachers and physical media with digital equivalents. Perhaps these limitations are only found in the amount of access learners have to content online. Regardless, in settings where access to quality physical teachers and classroom mediators is limited, interactive digital media can be an acceptable (and perhaps preferred) replacement vehicle in the Self-Organizing Learning Environment (SOLE) that education is argued to be in the 21st Century (Mitra & Dangwal, 2010).

Learning environments that were previously only face-to-face for both K-12 learners and higher education students are seeing interactive digital media as an information source threatening to completely replace all three of the following learning methods: (a) asynchronous chat, (b) printed textual readings, and (c) face-to-face lectures (Kurzweil, 2005; Masten & Plowman, 2003; Thompson, 2011; Talbert, 2013; Vinge, 1993). Beyond the advantages given to learners via MIE, interactive digital media provides many advantages, including "the liberty to proceed or recede allow[ing] self-pacing [and] an immeasurable interconnectivity to information in a variety of possible combinations, sequences, and mixture of resources which shape . . . higher-order thinking" (Teoh & Neo, 2007, p. 28). Interactive digital media is also a very attractive information paradigm when compared to asynchronous chat via text, printed textual readings, and lecture, because it provides a combination of movement and sound that many find as a superior source

of entertainment. Entertainment methods and educational methods, however, are not always in parallel in their ability to demonstrate high outputs of happiness on par with learning outcomes. The problem is that there is not enough good data on the impact of digital on outcomes in K-12 and higher education to warrant replacing these older information formats entirely. Furthermore, while educators everywhere are becoming more unified in their calls for more consistency in outcome skill development, there debates on assessment that may never end.

It is understood that higher education, for example, desires an overall increase in the areas of STEM and CT. No generally agreed upon assessments for STEM and CT outcomes exist, however, and this situation combined with the fact that there is not enough data on the impact of replacing older information formats (viz., text, imagery, chat) with digital media shows a potentially dangerous convergence implying interactions yet to be maturely assessed when targeting a variety of educational outcomes (Cottrell, 2014). While Mitra's experiments may show equivalent outcomes for some STEM learning objectives in K-12 learners via the use of digital media, assessing something like English grammar skills of his New Dehli learners may very well show little improvement over a traditional one-term, face-to-face English as a Second Language (ESL) course.

FUTURE RESEARCH DIRECTIONS

David Wiley (2013) explains that digital media tools like Open Educational Resources (OERs) have been found to be better at increasing educational outcomes versus traditional texts. Wiley also cites an extensive research project from Nature comparing the quality of content from Wikipedia to peer-reviewed, for-purchase traditional text materials, viz., Encyclopaedia Britannica (Giles, 2005). The parity in the number of errors in like-minded content sections of the various information sources tested demonstrates the power to be found in digital media educational resources, some of which allow free access to material commonly used by students toward their learning outcomes. Britannica responded to Nature's research with a comprehensive negation of all results (Encyclopaedia Britannica, 2006). Similar to the Clark (1994) and Kozma (1994a: 1994b) debate 20 years ago, Nature has returned with another response, providing access to its research data and methodology and leaving room for future debate. What is undeniable is that learners want open digital content, and will use it as proliferation increases. It is also important for teachers, parents, school administrators and educational researchers to accept that students will augment instructor-created (or approved) digital content with random content they find on their own. This may skew research efforts in the future as researchers lose less and less of a sense of which digital media (approved or unapproved) is helping/hurting students' learning outcomes. If educational digital media content from anywhere (and hosted everywhere) is increasingly becoming impactful toward learning objectives, further research is warranted before wholesale adoption begins.

Google's Potential Edge in Transforming Instruction and Learning

Perhaps the single greatest concern in regards to digital media's potential affects on education throughout society is Google, Inc.—specifically in the form of one of its most popular subsidiaries, YouTube. While scientists and researchers debate the form, function and impact on outcomes of digital media in the learning ecosphere, Google has been slowly allowing for the creation of the worlds largest and most free educational institution (albeit devoid of an organized curriculum). Combining Google search and Google Scholar with YouTube gives an individual the power to learn more from digital media than ever before.

The convenience of educational and instructional content to be found on YouTube, for many users, trumps that of any traditional school or training center. If an individual wants to learn how to change the brake pads on their vehicle, YouTube will potentially be able to store digital media content related to a users' exact year, make and model of vehicle teaching him or her how to perform a specific action over and over again. If users want to know which version of a particular mobile device is most durable, YouTube can contain hundreds of digital media recording durability tests for one particular mobile device adding to potentially thousands of hours of video on every mobile device every made.

Siva Vaidhyanathan's (2012) book, *The Googlization of Everything*, offers a clear warning about the disruption Google and its subsidiaries can enact onto society at large. In addition to Google Search dominating individuals' ideas of what search engines are, and YouTube providing a dominant instructional digital video platform, Google has entered the educational hardware ecosphere with its very low cost and low-priced Chrome books for student access to its web browsing software and open productivity suite, Google Docs. In an educational environment where "dollars-per-student-spent" on technology equates to quality education at the same time that taxation for funding education is viewed by some as an abuse of civil rights (Rodriguez, 2014), Google can circumvent the notion that more money technology is better not through empirical research on learning outcomes, by providing completely integrated content, hardware, software, operating systems, mobile connectivity and remote broadcasting (through Chromecast) a very low price point. Essentially, Google is building the structure for the world's largest database of instructional information, digital text, video and audio media, and delivery hardware and software at a fraction of the cost to a user versus any traditional learning environment. And, many of their digital media offerings connect students to information for free.

The bulk of the future of educational digital media may already be in the hands of one corporation that does not declare itself to be a school of any type. Large-scale efforts to offer MOOCs (massively open online classes), whose basis for existence is the presentation of digital media to learners in a free (or nearly-free format), are already supported by long-standing, well-capitalized traditional brick-and-mortar institutions. Coursera is partnered with over 75 American traditional institutions of higher-education including Ivy League universities and large state institutions like the University of Virginia. They also are partnered with some of the largest universities from over 25 other countries (Coursera, 2014). A rival, EdX, offers courses from traditional higher education powerhouses MIT, Harvard, the University of Texas and others. They boast 200+ individual courses, 400+ faculty and 100,000+ online certificates granted so far (EdX, 2014). What, however, about the total amount of digital media needed to deliver this educational experience? The amount of raw educational content from these leading MOOC institutions, which comes solely in the form of digital media, pales in comparison to what can be found on Google servers today. All Google needs to do is begin charging for their services, and the ease of acquisition of their educational content can yield a sizable profit, or none at all; they are at their leisure to begin operations as an educational institution with a varied and diffuse instruction base. Essentially, Google may already be the largest educational institution on earth—all due to the advent of digital media throughout society. The company already has the search tool needed to aggregate their content into instructional, and even curricular, modules of their own.

Regardless of the source of the content, future work should explore what digital media is doing inside the minds of learners as it is presented to students in conjunction with text and other material types as the future of routine adoption of digital media-capable, cheap, lightweight, and mobile devices continues to supplant the traditional physically printed word (Hu, 2011; Hurdle, 2011; Schaffhauser, 2011). Studies that seek to indicate that a mixture of material types yields the best educational outcomes may become more necessary as ADA requirements, the long-standing impact and debate of Multiple Intelligences Theory (Gardner, 1985), and the newest addition of Universal Design for Learning (Orkwis & McLane, 1998; Gargiulo & Metcalf, 2012) impact all levels of education. The presentation of the same material in a variety of different formats (involving different or the same authors) could be found to hinder certain outcomes and improve others. Determinations on which outcomes are preferred in certain educational environments are a perplexing problem necessitating future research.

CONCLUSION

Throughout this chapter, a review of literature and concerns related to digital media's effects on society within the context of learning and instruction has been presented. The prevailing finding is that digital media is being created and consumed at ever-increasing rates, yet the outcomes in the minds of learners affected by digital media are not easy to predict or always moving in the desired direction. It is known that people are using digital media each day to gain knowledge, understand concepts and learn new ways of seeing the world around them. Digital media provides an unprecedented opportunity for the whole of society to instantly access instructional content to learn more concepts than any set of humans in recorded history.

Instructional and learning outcomes and digital media continue to be pressing issues for educators seeking strategies to improve the educational experiences of students. The need for increased accountability within the formal educational atmosphere also shows no sign of abating. As digital media takes over as the dominant form of classroom information source, assessment of its impact deserves attention. Challenges persist in linking learning outcomes and objectives to the influence of digital media in the classroom as K-12 and higher education advances through the remainder of the century. Historically, literacy—a goal achieved through engagement with the reading and creation of physical text—has been one of the chief concerns of education. As literacy has become more of a virtual guarantee (Central Intelligence Agency, 2012) for students in developed nations like the United States and Western Europe, more focused learning outcomes like STEM, CT and PSA take center stage. Learners can read and write text, but what can they do with what they have learned and how do they explain what they deduce, feel, believe, and know? Digital media will impact these outcomes as it presents information to and interacts with the cognitive ability of all learners. Finding how well the interaction is accomplishing educational outcome targets is now the necessary research goal.

Discussion between researches like Clark (1994) and Kozma (1994a), rooted in foundational assertions like Marshall McLuhan's (1964) "the medium is the message", provides some of the main catalysts for the need for future research. Kozma's refutation of Clark's replaceability challenge ultimately wins the going forward, because all digital media are truly not equal, and therefore, reaction and observed learning outcomes will never be equal across seemingly replaceable digital media types. Digital media types contain their own distinctive educational traits and will produce unique learning outcomes, if students under their influence can demonstrate what they assimilate as they learn. Mayer's (2001; 2005a, 2005) research into media and cognitive load give caution to instructors to assess effectiveness of media instead of adopting a "more is best" approach to the inundation of student minds with as many types of digital media as possible.

All digital media objects are increasing rapidly in development and deployment in all types of educational environments, because of their perceived benefits and efforts to conserve time. Importantly for research considerations, however, is that digital media research shows many mixed results on the impact of this popular and popularly easy-to-use and create medium on learning outcomes. Foundational research like Azevedo, Moos, Greene, Winters, and Cromley (2008), Mayer and Moreno (2003), Stoney and Oliver (1999), Thomas et al. (2001), Starbek et al. (2010), and Sullivan-Mann, Perron, and Fellner (2009), followed more recently by Kayaoglu et al. (2011), Serin (2011), Smith (2012), Marra (2013), Rodriguez (2014), Alexander (2014), and others described in this chapter and found in additional readings, give direction on how to conduct digital media versus traditional learning resource impact assessment studies in a variety of educational settings targeting many different instructional outcome goals. The limited amount of comprehensive research focused on the impact of digital media on learning and instruction is ironic considering (a) the sheer number of students using digital materials today, (b) the large number of digital media objects being created each hour, (c) the assumptions about their benefits to knowledge acquisition, and (d) the high degree of self-efficacy students feel about their engagement with digital media in learning environments despite mixed results on actual outcomes performance. Overall, finding solutions to the problems of cognitive overload combined with access to digital media material and determining what these media do to learners' brains in terms of outcomes serve as major influences for future research needs, as well as future strategic planning about digital media object distribution to students.

Teachers and instructional designers aspiring to design and use digital media that includes educational content that is convenient for a mass audience, entertaining to multiple senses, and potentially absorbed very quickly (versus traditional text-driven content) will find insight from exploring the research found in this chapter, and from any future replicating research going forward. As popular as digital media may be, educators today are potentially faced with many difficult choices regarding the use and popularity of digital media over older information formats (Broussard, 2014; Flood, 2012; Kurzweil, 2005; Vinge, 1993). While this chapter has reviewed the historically substantiating literature, the importance of text-based materials to learning is evident over hundreds of years of tradition since the time of the invention of the printing press. It cannot be ignored, however, that digital media changes the educational landscape in a way that is often initially perceived as a universal benefit containing few, if any, potentially negative learning consequences. Why would students not want to learn via a method that combines text with audio, video, and/or images? Why would this medium not be the best option in all cases for learning? Students do, in fact, a) believe that they are learning more through content-equivalent digital media, b) enjoy not being required to purchase a non-digital materials, and c) look forward higher outcomes for themselves after taking courses using digital media. The literature shows that perceived higher outcomes through digital media, however, are not always realized. Individual learners are viewing their educational experiences with digital media as a benefit before actually knowing how well or poorly they perform on examinations within courses or on their final grades.

Pursuing the questions found in this chapter will impact various types of educational leaders and policy makers as they struggle to meet the challenge of the mass adoption of digital media content for learning. Institutions can use questions like these as strategic markers for conversations regarding directions for the advancement of their own student learning goals and objectives. Regardless, the need for further research on the topic of digital media affecting society through learning and instruction is clear. Better understanding of how to either decrease the damage done to educational outcomes by digital media, or how to better integrate the positive cognitive benefits of traditional learning information materials into digital media, is a goal that will benefit students in the future.

REFERENCES

Alasraj, A., Freeman, M., & Chandler, P. (2013). Optimising layered integrated instructional design through the application of cognitive load theory. *Toulouse: Proceedings from the 6th International Cognitive Load Theory Conference.*

Alessi, S. M., & Trollip, S. R. (2001). *Multimedia for learning: Methods and development.* Needham Heights, MA: Pearson.

Alexander, C. (2014). Student-created digital media and engagement in middle school history. *Computers in the Schools*, *31*(3), 154–172. doi:10.1080/07380569.2014.932652

Azevedo, R., Moos, D., Greene, J., Winters, F., & Cromley, J. (2008). Why is externally-facilitated regulated learning more effective than self-regulated learning with hypermedia? *Educational Technology Research and Development*, *56*(1), 45–72. doi:10.1007/s11423-007-9067-0

Barlett, R. M., & Strough, J. (2003). Multimedia versus traditional course instruction in introductory Social Psychology. *Teaching of Psychology*, *30*(4), 335–338. doi:10.1207/S15328023TOP3004_07

Block, B. (2014). *The visual story: creating the visual structure of film, TV and digital media.* CRC Press.

Broussard, M. (2014). *Why e-books are banned in my digital journalism class.* Retrieved from http://www.newrepublic.com/article/116309/data-journalim-professor-wont-assign-e-books-heres-why

Buckingham, D., & Willett, R. (Eds.). (2013). *Digital generations: Children, young people, and the new media.* Routledge.

Bull, J. G., & Kozak, R. A. (2014). Comparative life cycle assessments: The case of paper and digital media. *Environmental Impact Assessment Review*, *45*, 10–18. doi:10.1016/j.eiar.2013.10.001

Cavalier, R., & Weber, K. (2002). Learning, media, and the case of Dax Cowart: A comparison of text, film, and interactive multimedia. *Interactive Learning Environments, 10*(3), 243–262. doi:10.1076/ilee.10.3.243.8763

Central Intelligence Agency (CIA). (2012). *CIA—The world fact book: United States.* Retrieved from https://www.cia.gov/library/publications/the-world-factbook/geos/us.html

Chuang, H., & Ku, H. (2011). The effect of computer-based multimedia instruction with Chinese character recognition. *Educational Media International, 48*(1), 27–41. doi:10.1080/09523987.2011.549676

Clark, R. E. (1994). Media will never influence learning. *Educational Technology Research and Development, 42*(2), 21–29. doi:10.1007/BF02299088

Clark, R. E., & Feldon, D. F. (2005). Five common but questionable principles of multimedia learning. In R. E. Mayer (Ed.), *The Cambridge handbook of multimedia learning* (pp. 97–116). New York, NY: Cambridge University Press. doi:10.1017/CBO9780511816819.007

Cottrell, T. (2014). *An assessment of the effect of multimedia on critical thinking outcomes. (Doctoral dissertation).* Retrieved from Dissertations & Theses: A&I. (AAT 3624781).

Coursera. (2014). *About Us.* Retrieved September 2 from https://www.coursera.org/about/partners

Cronbach, L. J. (1951). Coefficient alpha and the internal structure of tests. *Psychometrika, 16*(3), 297–334. doi:10.1007/BF02310555

Dewey, J. (1897). My pedagogic creed. *The School Journal, 54*(3), 7780.

Dewey, J. (1909). *How we think.* Boston, MA: D.C. Heath.

Dewey, J. (1916). *Democracy and education: An introduction to the philosophy of education.* New York, NY: MacMillan.

Dewey, J. (1933). *How we think* (rev. ed.). Boston, MA: D.C. Heath.

Dunleavy, M., & Dede, C. (2014). Augmented reality teaching and learning. In *Handbook of research on educational communications and technology* (pp. 735–745). NY: Springer. doi:10.1007/978-1-4614-3185-5_59

EdX. (2014). *Schools and Partners.* Retrieved from https://www.edx.org/schools-partners

Encyclopædia Britannica, Inc. (EBI). (2006). *Fatally flawed: Refuting the recent study on encyclopedic accuracy by the journal Nature.* Retrieved from http://corporate.britannica.com/britannica_nature_response.pdf

Flew, T. (2014). *Fast Times at Virtual U: Digital Media, Markets and the Future of Higher Education in the West Report.* Retrieved from http://184.168.109.199:8080/xmlui/bitstream/handle/123456789/2244/EJ577677.pdf?sequence=1

Flood, A. (2012). *Enhanced ebooks are bad for children finds American study.* Retrieved from http://www.theguardian.com/books/2012/jun/07/enhanced-ebooks-bad-for-children

Gardner, H. (1985). *Frames of mind: The theory of multiple intelligences.* New York, NY: Basic Books.

Gargiulo, R., & Metcalf, D. (2012). *Teaching in today's inclusive classrooms: A universal design for learning approach.* Cengage Learning.

Gerjets, P., Scheiter, K., & Schuh, J. (2008). Information comparisons in example-based hypermedia environments: Supporting learners with processing prompts and an interactive comparison tool. *Educational Technology Research and Development*, *56*(1), 73–92. doi:10.1007/s11423-007-9068-z

Gikas, J., & Grant, M. M. (2013). Mobile computing devices in higher education: Student perspectives on learning with cellphones, smartphones & social media. *The Internet and Higher Education*, *19*, 18–26. doi:10.1016/j.iheduc.2013.06.002

Giles, J. (2005). *Special report: Internet encyclopaedias go head to head*. Retrieved from http://www.nature.com/nature/journal/v438/n7070/full/438900a.html

Glaser, R. (1976). Components of a psychology of instruction: Toward a science of design. *Review of Educational Research*, *46*(1), 29–39. doi:10.3102/00346543046001001

Gold, M. K. (Ed.). (2012). *Debates in the digital humanities*. Minneapolis: U of Minnesota Press.

Goldman, R., Pea, R., Barron, B., & Derry, S. J. (Eds.). (2014). *Video research in the learning sciences*. NY: Routledge.

Gray, P. (1999). *Johann Gutenberg (c. 1395-1468)*. Retrieved August 16 from http://content.time.com/time/magazine/article/0,9171,36527,00.html

Hansen, M. B. (2012). *Bodies in code: Interfaces with digital media*. NY: Routledge.

Hayles, N. K. (2012). *How we think: Digital media and contemporary technogenesis*. Chicago: University of Chicago Press. doi:10.7208/chicago/9780226321370.001.0001

Hegarty, M., & Just, M. A. (1993). Constructing mental models from text and diagrams. *Journal of Memory and Language*, *32*(6), 717–742. doi:10.1006/jmla.1993.1036

Hu, W. (2011). *Math that moves: Schools embrace the iPad*. Retrieved from http://www.nytimes.com/2011/01/05/education/05tablets.html?pagewanted=all&_r=0

Hurdle, P. (2011). *Hello iPad. Goodbye textbooks?* Retrieved from http://www.mmaglobal.org/publications/ProceedingsArchive/2011_FALL_MMA.pdf#page=51

Hwang, G. J., Chu, H. C., Lin, Y. S., & Tsai, C. C. (2011). A knowledge acquisition approach to developing Mindtools for organizing and sharing differentiating knowledge in a ubiquitous learning environment. *Computers & Education*, *57*(1), 1368–1377. doi:10.1016/j.compedu.2010.12.013

Jonassen, D. H. (2014). *Mindtools (Productivity and Learning)*. NY: Springer. doi:10.1007/978-94-007-6165-0_57-1

Jonassen, D. H., Carr, C., & Yueh, S. P. (1998). Computers as Mindtools for engaging learners in critical thinking. *TechTrends*, *43*(2), 24–32. doi:10.1007/BF02818172

Kayaoglu, M., Dag Akbas, R., & Ozturk, Z. (2011). A Small Scale Experimental Study: Using Animations to Learn Vocabulary. *Turkish Online Journal of Educational Technology*, *10*(2), 24–30.

Keskin, N. O., & Metcalf, D. (2011). The current perspectives, theories and practices of mobile learning. *Turkish Online Journal of Educational Technology-TOJET*, *10*(2), 202–208.

Kingsley, K. V., & Boone, R. (2008). Effects of multimedia software on achievement of middle school students in an American history class. *Journal of Research on Technology in Education*, *41*(2), 203–221. doi:10.1080/15391523.2008.10782529

Kozma, R. (1994a). Will media influence learning: Reframing the debate. *Educational Technology Research and Development*, *42*(2), 7–19. doi:10.1007/BF02299087

Kozma, R. (1994b). A reply: Media and methods. *Educational Technology Research and Development*, *42*(3), 11–14. doi:10.1007/BF02298091

Krauskopf, K., Zahn, C., & Hesse, F. W. (2012). Leveraging the affordances of Youtube: The role of pedagogical knowledge and mental models of technology functions for lesson planning with technology. *Computers & Education*, *58*(4), 1194–1206. doi:10.1016/j.compedu.2011.12.010

Kumta, S. M., Tsang, P. L., & Hung, L. K. (2003). Fostering critical thinking skills through a web-based tutorial programme for final year medical student: A randomized control study. *Journal of Educational Multimedia and Hypermedia*, *12*(3), 267–273.

Kurzweil, R. (2005). *The singularity is near: When humans transcend biology*. New York, NY: Viking Adult.

Liao, Y.-K. C. (1999). Effects of hypermedia on students' achievement: A meta-analysis. *Journal of Educational Multimedia and Hypermedia*, *8*(3), 255–277.

Mann, H. (1848). *Annual report of the Board of Education together with the annual report of the Secretary of the Board* (Vol. 12). Boston, MA: Massachusetts Board of Education.

Marra, R. (2013). Mindtools in online education enabling meaningful learning. In Learning, Problem Solving, and Mind Tools: Essays in Honor of David H. Jonassen (pp. 260-277). Routledge.

Masten, D., & Plowman, T. M. P. (2003). *Digital ethnography: the next wave in understanding the consumer experience*. Retrieved from http://www.dmi.org/dmi/html/interests/research/03142MAS75.pdf

Mayer, R. E. (2001). *Multi-media learning*. Cambridge, MA: Cambridge University Press. doi:10.1017/CBO9781139164603

Mayer, R. E. (2005a). Cognitive theory of multimedia learning. In R. E. Mayer (Ed.), *The Cambridge handbook of multimedia learning* (pp. 31–48). New York, NY: Cambridge University Press. doi:10.1017/CBO9780511816819.004

Mayer, R. E. (2005b). Introduction to multimedia learning. In R. E. Mayer (Ed.), *The Cambridge handbook of multimedia learning* (pp. 1–18). New York, NY: Cambridge University Press. doi:10.1017/CBO9780511816819.002

Mayer, R. E., & Moreno, R. (1998a). *A cognitive theory of multimedia learning: Implications for design principles*. Retrieved from http://www.unm.edu/~moreno/PDFS/chi.pdf

Mayer, R. E., & Moreno, R. (1998b). A split-attention effect in multimedia learning: Evidence for dual processing systems in working memory. *Educational Psychology*, *90*(2), 312–320. doi:10.1037/0022-0663.90.2.312

Mayer, R. E., & Moreno, R. (2003). Nine ways to reduce cognitive load in multimedia learning. *Educational Psychologist*, *38*(1), 43–52. doi:10.1207/S15326985EP3801_6

McLuhan, M. (1964). *Understanding media*. New York, NY: McGraw-Hill.

Mills, K. A., & Exley, B. (2014). Time, space, and text in the elementary school digital writing classroom. *Written Communication*, 1–35.

Mishra, P., & Koehler, M. (2006). Technological pedagogical content knowledge: A framework for teacher knowledge. *Teachers College Record*, *108*(6), 1017–1054. doi:10.1111/j.1467-9620.2006.00684.x

Mitra, S. (2007). *Kids can teach themselves*. Retrieved August 22 from http://www.ted.com/talks/sugata_mitra_shows_how_kids_teach_themselves

Mitra, S. (2009). Case study: The hole in the wall, or minimally invasive education representations and imagery in learning. In P. T. H. Unwin (Ed.), *ICT4D: Information and communication technology for development* (p. 390). New York, NY: Cambridge University Press.

Mitra, S., & Dangwal, R. (2010). Limits to self-organising systems of learning—the Kalikuppam experiment. *British Journal of Educational Technology, 41*(5), 672–688. doi:10.1111/j.1467-8535.2010.01077.x

Montgomery, S. E. (2014). Critical Democracy through digital media production in a third-grade classroom. *Theory and Research in Social Education, 42*(2), 197–227. doi:10.1080/00933104.2014.908755

NYC Department of Education. (2014). *Universal design for learning*. Retrieved August 15 from http://schools.nyc.gov/Academics/CommonCoreLibrary/ProfessionalLearning/UDL/default.htm

Okutsu, M., DeLaurentis, D., Brophy, S., & Lambert, J. (2013). Teaching an aerospace engineering design course via virtual worlds: A comparative assessment of learning outcomes. *Computers & Education, 60*(1), 288–298. doi:10.1016/j.compedu.2012.07.012

Orkwis, R., & McLane, K. (1998). *A curriculum every student can use: Design principles for student access. ERIC/OSEP Topical Brief No. ED423654*. Reston, VA: ERIC/OSEP Special Project.

Orvis, P. (2006). *A 'hole in the wall' helps educate India*. Retrieved August 24 from http://www.csmonitor.com/2006/0601/p13s02-legn.html

Plass, J. L., Moreno, R., & Brünken, R. (Eds.). (2010). *Cognitive load theory*. Cambridge University Press. doi:10.1017/CBO9780511844744

Prpick, S., & Redel, D. (Interviewer) & Grafton, A. (Interviewee). (2011). *Closing the book*. [Interview audio file]. Retrieved from CBC Ideas Web site: http://www.cbc.ca/ideas/episodes/2011/01/31/closing-the-book/

Redsell, S. A., Collier, J. J., Garrud, P. P., Evans, J. C., & Cawood, C. C. (2003). Multimedia versus written information for nocturnal enuresis education: A cluster randomized controlled trial. *Child: Care, Health and Development, 29*(2), 121–129. doi:10.1046/j.1365-2214.2003.00321.x PMID:12603357

Rinck, M. (2008). The interaction of verbal and pictorial information in comprehension and memory. In J.-F. Rouet, R. Lowe, & W. Schnotz (Eds.), *Understanding multimedia documents* (pp. 185–202). New York, NY: Springer. doi:10.1007/978-0-387-73337-1_10

Rodriguez, J. (2014). *Stop fighting constitutional school funding*. Retrieved September 2 from http://krwg.org/post/rodriguez-stop-fighting-constitutional-school-funding

Rosenwald, M. (2014). *Serious reading takes a hit from online scanning and skimming, researchers say*. Retrieved September 1 from http://www.washingtonpost.com/local/serious-reading-takes-a-hit-from-online-scanning-and-skimming-researchers-say/2014/04/06/088028d2-b5d2-11e3-b899-20667de76985_story.html

Rouet, J.-F., Lowe, R., & Schnotz, W. (2008). *Understanding multimedia documents*. New York, Springer. doi:10.1007/978-0-387-73337-1

Saettler, P. (2004). *The evolution of American educational technology*. Greenwich, CT: Information Age.

Schaffhauser, D. (2011). *Is the iPad ready to replace the printed textbook?* Retrieved from http://campustechnology.com/articles/2011/06/15/is-the-ipad-ready-to-replace-the-printed-textbook.aspx

Schnotz, W., & Bannert, M. (2003). Construction and interface in learning from multiple representation. *Learning and Instruction, 13*(2), 141–156. doi:10.1016/S0959-4752(02)00017-8

Schwartz, D. L., & Heiser, J. (2006). Spatial representations and imagery in learning. In R. K. Sawyer (Ed.), *The Cambridge handbook of the learning sciences* (pp. 283–298). New York, NY: Cambridge University Press.

Seel, N. M. (2008). Empirical perspectives on memory and motivation. In J. M. Spector, M. D. Merrill, J. van Merrienboer, & M. P. Driscoll (Eds.), *Handbook of research on educational communications and technology* (pp. 39–54). New York, NY: Routledge.

Segal, B. (1995). *A short history of internet protocols at CERN*. Retrieved August 15 from http://ben.home.cern.ch/ben/TCPHIST.html

Serin, O. (2011). The effects of computer based-instruction on the achievement and problem-solving skills of science and technology students. *TOJET: The Turkish Online Journal of Educational Technology, 10*(1), 183–202.

Serin, O., Bulut Serin, N., & Sayg, G. (2010). Developing problem solving inventory for children at the level of primary education (PSIC). *Elementary Education Online, 9*(2), 446–458.

Serra, M. J., & Dunlosky, J. (2010). Metacomprehension judgments reflect the belief that diagrams improve learning from text. *Memory (Hove, England), 18*(7), 698–711. doi:10.1080/09658211.2010.506441 PMID:20730677

Sharp, D. L. M., Bransford, J. D., Goldman, S. R., Risko, V. J., Kinzer, C. K., & Vye, N. J. (1995). Dynamic visual support for story comprehension and mental model building by young, at-risk children. *Educational Technology Research and Development, 43*(4), 25–40. doi:10.1007/BF02300489

Sheldon, D. A., & DeNardo, G. (2004). Comparing prospective freshman and pre-service music education majors' observations of music interactions. *Journal of Music Teacher Education, 14*(1), 39–44. doi:10.1177/10570837040140010108

Sheldon, D. A., & DeNardo, G. (2005). Comparisons of higher-order thinking skills among prospective freshmen and upper-level pre-service music education majors. *Journal of Research in Music Education, 53*(1), 40–50. doi:10.1177/002242940505300104

Shrock, S. (1994). The media influence debate: Read the fine print, but don't lose sight of the big picture. *Educational Technology Research and Development, 42*(2), 49–53. doi:10.1007/BF02299092

Simon, H. (1996). *The sciences of the artificial* (3rd ed.). Cambridge, MA: MIT Press.

Siu-Runyan, Y. (2011). *Public and school libraries in decline: When we need them*. Retrieved August 17 from http://www.ncte.org/library/NCTEFiles/Resources/Journals/CC/0211-sep2011/CC0211Presidents.pdf

Smith, J. G. (2012). *Screen-capture instructional technology: A cognitive tool for blended learning*. (Doctoral dissertation). Saint Mary's College of California.

Sollisch, J. (2012). *On the death of Encyclopaedia Britannica: All authoritarian regimes eventually fall*. Retrieved August 16 from http://www.csmonitor.com/Commentary/Opinion/2012/0322/On-the-death-of-Encyclopaedia-Britannica-All-authoritarian-regimes-eventually-fall

Starbek, P. P., Erjavec, M., & Peklaj, C. C. (2010). Teaching genetics with multimedia results in better acquisition of knowledge and improvement in comprehension. *Journal of Computer Assisted Learning, 26*(3), 214–224. doi:10.1111/j.1365-2729.2009.00344.x

Stoney, S., & Oliver, R. (1998). Interactive multimedia for adult learners: Can learning be fun? *Journal of Interactive Learning Research*, *9*(1), 55–82.

Stoney, S., & Oliver, R. (1999). Can higher order thinking and cognitive engagement be enhanced with multimedia? *Interactive Multimedia Electronic Journal of Computer-Enhanced Learning*, *1*(2). Retrieved from http://imej.wfu.edu/articles/1999/2/07/index.asp

Sullivan-Mann, J., Perron, C. A., & Fellner, A. N. (2009). The effects of simulation on nursing students' critical thinking scores: A quantitative study. *Journal of Nurse Midwifery and Women's Health*, *9*(2), 111–116.

Sweller, J. (1999). *Instructional design in technical areas*. ACER Press.

Sweller, J. (2011). Cognitive load theory. *The Psychology of Learning and Motivation: Cognition in Education*, *55*, 37-76.

Talbert, R. (2013). *Khan Academy Redux*. Retrieved from http://chronicle.com/blognetwork/castingoutnines/2013/02/05/khan-academy-redux/

Teoh, B. S., & Neo, T.-K. (2007). Interactive multimedia learning: Students' attitudes and learning impact in an animation course. *The Turkish Online Journal of Educational Technology*, *6*(4), 28–37.

Thomas, J., Coppola, J., & Thomas, B. (2001). The effect of technology integration and critical thinking skills in a graduate introductory information systems course. In *Proceedings of the Information Systems Education (ISECON) Conference*. Chicago: AITP Foundation for Information Technology Education.

Thompson, C. (2011). *How Khan Academy is changing the rules of education*. Retrieved from http://southasiainstitute.harvard.edu/website/wp-content/uploads/2012/08/Wired_2011-8-HowKhanAcademyIsChangingtheRulesofEducation.pdf

Tyner, K. (2014). *Literacy in a digital world: Teaching and learning in the age of information*. NY: Routledge.

Vaidhyanathan, S. (2012). *The Googlization of everything:(and why we should worry)*. Univ of California Press.

Van Dusen, G. C. (2014). Digital Dilemma: Issues of Access, Cost, and Quality in Media-Enhanced and Distance Education. ASHE-ERIC Higher Education Report, 27(5).

Vinge, V. (1993). *The coming technological singularity: How to survive in the post-human era*. Retrieved from http://www.aleph.se/Trans/Global/Singularity/sing.html

Wiley, D. (2013). *On quality and OER*. Retrieved from http://opencontent.org/blog/archives/2947

Wolf, M. (2014). *Proust and the squid: The story and science of the reading brain*. HarperCollins.

Wu, W. H., Wu, Y. C. J., Chen, C. Y., Kao, H. Y., Lin, C. H., & Huang, S. H. (2012). Review of trends from mobile learning studies: A meta-analysis. *Computers & Education*, *59*(2), 817–827. doi:10.1016/j.compedu.2012.03.016

Xu, H., Oh, L., & Teo, H. (2009). Perceived effectiveness of text vs. multimedia location-based advertising messaging. *International Journal of Mobile Communications*, *7*(2), 154–177. doi:10.1504/IJMC.2009.022440

ADDITIONAL READING

Ahn, J. (2011). Digital divides and social network sites: Which students participate in social media? *Journal of Educational Computing Research, 45*(2), 147–163. doi:10.2190/EC.45.2.b

Beetham, H., & Sharpe, R. (Eds.). (2013). *Rethinking pedagogy for a digital age: Designing for 21st century learning.* Routledge.

Bennett, W. L. (Ed.). (2008). *Civic life online: Learning how digital media can engage youth.* Mit Press.

Billings, D. M., & Halstead, J. A. (2013). *Teaching in nursing: A guide for faculty.* Elsevier Health Sciences.

Blake, R. J. (2013). *Brave new digital classroom: Technology and foreign language learning.* Georgetown University Press.

Chen, B., & Bryer, T. (2012). Investigating instructional strategies for using social media in formal and informal learning. *The International Review of Research in Open and Distributed Learning, 13*(1), 87–104.

Dabbagh, N., & Kitsantas, A. (2012). Personal Learning Environments, social media, and self-regulated learning: A natural formula for connecting formal and informal learning. *The Internet and Higher Education, 15*(1), 3–8. doi:10.1016/j.iheduc.2011.06.002

Dahlgren, P. (Ed.). (2013). *Young citizens and new media: Learning for democratic participation.* Routledge.

Dimitrova, D. V., Shehata, A., Strömbäck, J., & Nord, L. W. (2011). The effects of digital media on political knowledge and participation in election campaigns: Evidence from panel data. *Communication Research,* 0093650211426004.

Donohue, C. (Ed.). (2014). *Technology and Digital Media in the Early Years: Tools for Teaching and Learning.* Routledge.

Fromme, J. (2012). Digital Games and Media Education in the Classroom: Exploring Concepts, Practices, and Constraints. In Computer Games and New Media Cultures (pp. 647-663). Springer Netherlands.

Fuller, B., Lizárraga, J., & Gray, J. (2015). *Digital media and Latino families–New channels for learning, parenting, and local organizing.* New York: The Joan Ganz Cooney Center at Sesame Workshop.

Gee, J. P. (2012, October). The old and the new in the new digital literacies. [). Taylor & Francis Group.]. *The Educational Forum, 76*(4), 418–420. doi:10.1080/00131725.2012.708622

Goldman, R., Pea, R., Barron, B., & Derry, S. J. (Eds.). (2014). *Video research in the learning sciences.* Routledge.

Guernsey, L., Levine, M., Chiong, C., & Severns, M. (2012). *Pioneering literacy in the digital wild west: Empowering parents and educators.* Washington, DC: Campaign for Grade-Level Reading.

Herro, D., King, E., Liu, K., Boyer, D. M., & Owens, C. (2013, March). Building Comprehensive Digital Media and Learning Programs with Teachers. In *Society for Information Technology & Teacher Education International Conference* (Vol. 2013, No. 1, pp. 1336-1340).

Hobbs, R. (2013). Improvization and strategic risk-taking in informal learning with digital media literacy. *Learning, Media and Technology, 38*(2), 182–197. doi:10.1080/17439884.2013.756517

Kahne, J., Lee, N. J., & Feezell, J. T. (2012). Digital media literacy education and online civic and political participation. *International Journal of Communication, 6,* 24.

Lankshear, C., Peters, M., & Knobel, M. (2013). Information, knowledge and learning. *Distributed learning: Social and cultural approaches to practice*, 16.

Mizuko, I., Gutiérrez, K., Livingstone, S., Penuel, B., Rhodes, J., Salen, K., & Watkins, S. C. (2013). *Connected learning: An agenda for research and design*. Digital Media and Learning Research Hub.

Moran, M., Seaman, J., & Tinti-Kane, H. (2011). *Teaching, Learning, and Sharing: How Today's Higher Education Faculty Use Social Media*. Babson Survey Research Group.

Nixon, H., & Hateley, E. (2013). Books, Toys, and Tablets: Playing and Learning in the Age of Digital Media. International Handbook of Research on Children's Literacy, Learning, and Culture, 28-41.

O'Keeffe, G. S., & Clarke-Pearson, K. (2011). The impact of social media on children, adolescents, and families. *Pediatrics*, *127*(4), 800–804. doi:10.1542/peds.2011-0054 PMID:21444588

Petko, D. (2012). Teachers' pedagogical beliefs and their use of digital media in classrooms: Sharpening the focus of the 'will, skill, tool' model and integrating teachers' constructivist orientations. *Computers & Education*, *58*(4), 1351–1359. doi:10.1016/j.compedu.2011.12.013

Robb, M., Takeuchi, L., & Kotler, J. (2011). Always connected: The new digital media habits of young children. Joan Ganz Cooney Center at Sesame Workshop.

Seaman, J., & Tinti-Kane, H. (2013). *Social media for teaching and learning*. Pearson Learning Systems.

Squire, K. (2011). Video Games and Learning: Teaching and Participatory Culture in the Digital Age. Technology, Education--Connections (the TEC Series). Teachers College Press. 1234 Amsterdam Avenue, New York, NY 10027.

Steinkuehler, C., Squire, K., & Barab, S. (Eds.). (2012). *Games, learning, and society: Learning and meaning in the digital age*. Cambridge University Press. doi:10.1017/CBO9781139031127

Su, T., Ma, P., Deng, S., Li, D., & Huang, H. (2014). Student-Centered Course Development of Digital Media Technology. In *Software Engineering Education for a Global E-Service Economy* (pp. 141–146). Springer International Publishing. doi:10.1007/978-3-319-04217-6_17

Takeuchi, L., & Stevens, R. (2011). *The new coviewing: Designing for learning through joint media engagement*. New York, NY: The Joan Ganz Cooney Center at Sesame Workshop.

Thomas, D., & Brown, J. S. (2011). *A new culture of learning: Cultivating the imagination for a world of constant change* (Vol. 219). Lexington, KY: CreateSpace.

Thomas, M., Reinders, H., & Warschauer, M. (2013). Contemporary computer-assisted language learning: The role of digital media and incremental change. *Contemporary computer-assisted language learning*, 30-47.

Thomas, M., & Thomas, H. (2012). Using new social media and Web 2.0 technologies in business school teaching and learning. *Journal of Management Development*, *31*(4), 358–367. doi:10.1108/02621711211219013

Velasco, H. F., Cabral, C. Z., Pinheiro, P. P., Rita de Cassia, S. A., Vitola, L. S., da Costa, M. R., & Amantéa, S. L. (2014). Use of digital media for the education of health professionals in the treatment of childhood asthma. *Jornal de Pediatria*. PMID:25431855

Warschauer, M. (2012). Learning in the Cloud: How (and Why) to Transform Schools with Digital Media. *Learning, 16*(3).

KEY TERMS AND DEFINITIONS

Digital Media: Any single item or set of items combining text with audio, video, or images for the purpose of conveying information leading to meaning in the mind of a user.

Education: The transfer of understanding, skills and/or knowledge from one source to another.

Instruction: The process of delivering education from one source to another.

Learning: The demonstration of understanding acquired through various aspects of educational experience.

Mental Model: Active and dynamic representations of knowledge that visualize the invisible by creating analogies between what is known and not known.

P-20: Pre-school through traditional undergraduate education in the United States.

Schema: Organized collections of information containing understanding of how each individual piece in the collection relates to one another.

Traditional Media: Any single item or set of items only relying upon physical form for the conveyance of information leading to meaning in the mind of a user.

Section 2
New Digital Media Practices and Implications for Education, Society, Politics, and Economics

Chapter 10
Video Game Making and Modding

Elisabeth R. Gee
Arizona State University, USA

Kelly M. Tran
Arizona State University, USA

ABSTRACT

The purpose of this chapter is to provide an overview of current literature on video game making and modding (modification). The chapter describes key game making tools and educational programs that incorporate game making, to promote student outcomes ranging from media literacy to the development of computational thinking and greater interest in computer science. This is followed by a discussion of empirical literature on game making and modding as fan practices, and an overview of new game making tools and communities that are blurring the lines between educational, professional, and fan-driven game making practices. Lastly, the chapter addresses key issues, directions for future research, and recommendations for policy and practice.

INTRODUCTION

Video games have existed almost since the creation of computer technology, and these games have grown rapidly in popularity, diversity, and sophistication along with the growing pervasiveness of computing. Video game, as an all-encompassing term, in this chapter refers to all types of digital games, ranging from simple, single player puzzle games to complex multiplayer games involving thousands of players. Currently more than half of all households in the United States own one or more game consoles, almost all children and teens report playing video games, and even the majority of adults, both women and men, play games at least occasionally (Lenhart, Jones, & MacGill, 2008). Games can be played on almost any digital platform, and mobile games, played on phones and tablets, have made gaming increasingly pervasive. The economic impact of gaming is huge: the Entertainment Software Association (2013) estimated that Americans spent more than $21 billion dollars on video games, hardware, and accessories in 2013 alone. The social impact of video gaming is enormous as well, ranging from gaming's significance as a means of socialization

DOI: 10.4018/978-1-4666-8310-5.ch010

(millions of players, for example, play games together online or face-to-face), its impact on popular culture in general (as an example, note the pervasiveness of the *Angry Birds* product line) to the growing interest in the use of games and gamification as tools for education, health promotion, scientific research, and a host of other "serious" purposes (ibid).

Academic interest in video gaming has exploded over the last couple of decades, and scholars have approached the study of gaming from fields as diverse as cognitive psychology, medicine, economics, sociology, law, computer science, and education. Much of this scholarship has focused on video game *play*; that is, who plays what kinds of games, how playing games affects cognitive, emotional, social or physiological capacities or dispositions, the dynamics of social interactions associated with game play, and so forth. A more limited amount of scholarly attention, primarily in education, has been devoted to *making* games as a practice associated with gaming and as an activity in its own right. Making video games encompasses all aspects of creating a game, from the more technical aspects of writing software code or graphic design to the more conceptual tasks of identifying engaging game goals, actions, and themes. As we will describe below, game making has been popularized through the availability of simplified game design tools that can be readily used by aspiring game makers of all ages and backgrounds. Scholarship on game making tends to take one of two directions. One line of investigation has focused on understanding game making, or in particular game modification (modding) as a fan practice. (This is in contrast to research on game design as a professional practice, of which there are surprisingly few studies; Khaled & Ingram, 2012). Video game modding, and to some extent, game making, is a popular leisure pursuit among game players, and there are many fan communities devoted to sharing game mods, advice, tutorials, and tools. The second line of work focuses on the use of game making, or less frequently, game

modding, as an educational strategy. Video game making has been increasingly adopted in K-12 educational settings, both in school and in after-school programs, as a means of introducing young people to programming, computational thinking, or other skills and dispositions. Research, often in the form of evaluative studies, has explored the outcomes and less frequently, the process of game design, in such settings. Video game design courses and programs have proliferated in post-secondary education over the last decade. These are primarily professional preparation programs (preparing students for jobs in the game design industry) and studies of such programs will be excluded from our chapter.

In this chapter we will review and discuss key literature on video game making and modding in both of these contexts. While there is great interest in game making and modding as fan practices and as educational approaches, the empirical literature on these topics is relatively sparse. In addition, the tools and practices associated with game making and modding are quite varied, which makes it difficult to draw conclusions about what students might learn from making games in school, or how participation in game modding communities might require particular forms of knowledge or skill. In addition, the lines between making and modding games and other forms of interactive media are often blurred in practice as well as in research. We will argue that such diversity of tools and practices and artifacts is valuable, in providing multiple gateways into game making and modding and potentially into broader forms of productive digital practices and communities. However, we also discuss the need for educators to make stronger connections between classroom-based programs involving game making/modding and informal fan communities devoted to game modding/making. We also call for more attention to the value of *game* making and modding; that is, understanding how games are a particularly powerful focus for the development of particular forms of knowledge and skill, and their potential as a focal point for communities and affinity spaces that support the engagement of participants as producers, not just consumers, of digital media.

In the next section, we review the academic literature on game making and modding in formal and informal educational settings, and in the context of fan communities. As noted above, game making and modding takes many forms, and can include:

1. The use of existing commercial games (or game "engines") to create new, stand alone games. These are often called "total game conversions" or just "mods" (modifications). A famous example is the computer game *Counter Strike*, which was a total conversion of the existing game *Half-Life*.
2. The use of software tools to modify existing games by creating an "add-on" or new content that changes a part of an existing game. Examples include the extensive amount of player-generated content, such as new building blocks, tools, and even game maps, created for the widely popular game *Minecraft*.
3. The use of other software to make new games. This includes software created specifically for game design, such as *GameMaker* and *GameStar Mechanic*, as well as software designed for a wider range of applications but adopted for game design, such as *Scratch*.

As Buckingham and Burn (2007) point out, games problematize any clear distinction between production and consumption of digital media (p. 330). "Sandbox" games, like *The Sims* or *Minecraft*, provide players with considerable freedom and tools to design objects or environments, while still other games often give players a more limited ability to customize features of their avatar or edit game maps or levels. What "counts" as game making or modding is a question that we struggled with as we wrote the chapter and that we will return to in the concluding sections.

KEY LITERATURE ON VIDEO GAME MAKING AND MODDING

The use of game making in education, particularly K-12, has become increasingly popular over the last decade, corresponding with the more general interest in using video games for learning. Gee's (2007) analysis of how video games support complex forms of learning, first published in 2003, prompted significant scholarly attention to video games in education and related fields. At the same time, game making and modding as a fan pursuit has also become more visible and widespread, encouraged by the incorporation of game modding tools into commercial games and the growth of online fan communities devoted to sharing knowledge and strategies for game modding. While many of these fan communities are devoted to mods of an existing commercial game, recently game designers have created tools and websites for more general game making. Some are designed only for entertainment, while others seem oriented towards attracting both pure fans as well as educators.

In the next section, we will start by reviewing current tools, programs, and research on game making in educational settings, both formal and informal.

Game Making in Educational Settings

Video game making has been adopted as an instructional strategy in afterschool programs, and to a lesser extent in school, for a variety of purposes. One of the original and still primary reasons for using game making was to help young people develop basic programming skills, and more broadly, computational fluencies, by giving them a goal — creating a game — that was assumed to be more motivating than traditional programming lessons. Making games has been assumed to be an appealing focus for youth typically underrepresented in computer science classes, including girls. Making games has been used to a lesser extent to help students develop other abilities, such as creativity or teamwork skills. Another popular purpose for game making is as a means of helping children learn or acquire deeper understanding of content in domains such as math or science, by asking children to create "educational" games that incorporate the content to be mastered (Burke & Kafai, 2014). Most recently, game making has been incorporated into broader efforts to promote digital literacies, DIY media production, and design thinking through, for example, the Maker Movement and the implementation of maker spaces in schools and community-based settings (Peppler, 2013).

While widespread interest in game making is a relatively recent phenomenon, the concept of children learning through the design, rather than solely the use of computer-based tools, has roots in Seymour Papert's cutting edge work in the 1960s and 1970s at MIT. Papert was an early advocate of the idea that computer technologies could be used to leverage radical change in the educational system, and his ideas about how children could use computers as tools for learning and for enhancing creativity laid the foundation for a number of game design tools and approaches that are prominent today (see www.papert.org for an overview of Papert's ideas and publications). In 1968, Papert and colleagues developed Logo, the first programming language designed expressly for use by children (Bliktein, 2013). Later with his student at the time, Idit Harel, Papert developed the principles of constructionism, a theory of learning and instruction that emphasizes a view of learning as the active construction of knowledge, combined with the idea that such knowledge construction is best facilitated when learners are engaged in the process of creating something, whether that be a tangible object like a robot, or something less tangible, like a computer program or a theory about the world (Papert & Harel, 1991). Yasmin Kafai, a student of Papert and Harel, conducted one of the first studies of the use of game design

for learning (Kafai, 1995). Kafai, who was interested in game design as a particular instantiation of constructionism, studied a group of fourth grade students who created games using Logo, to teach fractions to younger students. Both Harel and Kafai have continued this line of work; Harel as the creator of Globaloria, and Kafai as a collaborator on the creation of *Scratch*, a more recent software tool based on constructionist principles. Both are described in more detail in subsequent sections. Next, we look more closely at a few popular and representative tools used for making games.

Tools for Game Making

Game making rather than modding of existing games tends to be emphasized in educational settings, possibly because of the availability of game making tools and curricula designed specifically for education. A plethora of tools are available and have been used for making games in education (see Table 1 for a list of tools discussed in this section; for a more extensive list, see Burke and Kafai, 2014). Indeed, a challenge for educators is choosing an appropriate game making tool as well as identifying or developing an appropriate curriculum or set of learning activities. The tools used for game making vary considerably in the extent to which they are intended for game design in particular versus for production of a wide range of interactive media, and in the kind of technical and design skills required for or developed through their use.

Burke and Kafai (2014), drawing on the work of Resnick and Silverman (2005), propose a set of four criteria for evaluating game making tools: the ideal tool should have low floors, high ceilings, and wide walls, along a criterion they add, "new windows." The first three criteria were proposed for media construction kits in general, and assume that construction tools should be intuitive and accessible for new users (low floors), offer features that allow more experienced users to create increasingly complex and sophisticated construc-

Table 1. Popular Game Making Tools

Site		Platform	Export	Education Support?	Target Audience
Scratch	http://scratch.mit.edu/	Browser-based	Hosted on site	ScratchEd online community for educators	Educators, parents, informal learners (8-16 years old)
Gamestar Mechanic	https://gamestarmechanic.com/	Browser-based and stand-alone program)	Hosted on Site	Special features and pricing for educators	Educators, parents, informal learners (7-14 years old)
Kodu	http://www.kodugamelab.com/	Stand-alone program	File, can be with Kodu	Free classroom kit available with lesson plans	Informal learners (8 years and up), educators
MissionMaker	http://www.immersiveeducation.eu/index.php/missionmakerm	Stand-alone program	File, can be opened with MissionMaker	Teacher Support Packs with lesson plans	Educators
AgentSheets+ AgentCubes	http://www.agentsheets.com/	Stand-alone program	Hosted on Site	Curriculum Available	Educators

tions (high ceilings), and permit the creation of a wide range of products that reflect users' interests and creativity (wide walls). "New windows" refers to the accessibility of communities of media producers, or in this case, game makers, that can "open windows" in terms of providing guidance, support, and act as a receptive audience for user-created content. These criteria, particularly low floors and wide walls, might help explain why modding entertainment games is less frequently adopted as an educational strategy than game making (using software designed specifically for educational purposes). While some entertainment games offer relatively easy-to-use design tools, many require modders to master more sophisticated tools, as well as have prior knowledge of the game and its existing attributes. In addition, modding an existing game obviously will appeal primarily to users who already have an interest in that game.

Tools commonly used for game making in educational settings also vary considerably in the extent to which they reflect the above features. The desired attributes of a game making tool depends in part on the goals of the educational program or activity; and as we will discuss below, different features lend themselves to the achievement of certain goals more than others. As an illustration, below we describe three game making tools with quite different features and affordances for game design and learning: *Scratch, Gamestar Mechanic,* and *Kodu/Project Spark.*

- **Scratch:** *Scratch* (Resnick et al., 2009), initially created in 2003, is a software tool developed by Mitch Resnick and colleagues at the MIT Media Lab as a project for the Lifelong Kindergarten group. It is targeted to ages 8 to 16, and intended for use across a variety of formal and informal contexts. *Scratch* was not created just for game design, and can be used for a variety of creative projects, such as stories, videos, music projects, and so on.

Scratch is available as both a desktop and browser-based drag-and-drop programming interface. The user is presented with a box into which he or she can drag sprites. Sprites represent the characters and objects of the game. The user is also presented with two columns. The player drags blocks, which represent lines of code from the column on the left and drops them into the column on the right to add them to the program. These blocks say things like "move 10 steps" or "play sound." The blocks snap together in order to form more complex sentences ("when space pressed, turn 15 degrees").

The user can apply this code to sprites, and in this way can program multiple characters or objects. *Scratch* comes with a library of sprites and sound effects which makes it easy to create projects without having to create or find these assets. In this way, *Scratch* emphasizes ease of use so that creativity is the main focus. Once a user is done with a project, it can be uploaded to the site for other users to try out. Each project on the site has a 'see inside' button where users can access the code of any project and see how it was made, and even create a 'remix', which is a new project based on another user's existing project.

- **Gamestar Mechanic:** *Gamestar Mechanic* (Salen, 2007) is both a tool and a game. It is targeted to 4th to 9th grade students, and is intended to teach the basic principles of game design. It was created by the independent game company GameLab (now defunct), through a unique (at the time) collaboration with James Gee and other faculty at the University of Wisconsin-Madison and with support from the MacArthur Foundation. The software is currently distributed by E-Line Media, who offers an educational package so schools or teachers can purchase it for students. It is intended for use in formal and informal contexts, and runs online in a browser.

Gamestar Mechanic has a distinctive gameplay mode that positions players as apprentice "game mechanics" who are introduced to principles of game design as they play, repair and modify various games. For example, players have to fix broken game levels, which are flawed in some way. In fixing these flaws, students learn about what makes a game fun and playable. Players unlock sprites and unlock actions that they can use while making their own games in the workshop mode of the game, where players can design their own games and share them with other players.

The workshop mode is a drag and drop visual interface. Because the emphasis here is on design, not programming, and *Gamestar Mechanic* is intended only for creating games, game creation is made as simple as possible to allow students to focus on the design of their games and employ the principles which they have learned throughout the gameplay. Students can then upload their games to the *Gamestar Mechanic* website and receive feedback from other players in the broader community.

- **Kodu/Project Spark:** *Kodu Game Lab* (Fowler & Cusack, 2011) was developed by Microsoft's FUSE labs. It is available for the Xbox 360 as well as the PC. *Kodu* is intended for use by educators as well as by fans, and a Kodu Classroom Kit with lesson plans and other resources is available at the *Kodu* Community Site (http://www.kodugamelab.com/resources/). A distinctive feature is the 3D world's ability to respond dynamically to the user's inputs. The user can edit levels with a built-in terrain editor, making it easy to design levels and environments.

Programming in *Kodu* consists of arranging blocks of code to form a "sentence." When the blocks are put in order horizontally, they form a sentence of high-level code (i.e., "when keyboard (space) is pressed, do (shoot)"). Every object the user places in the game environment can be associated with a number of these sentences. Because the world is 3D and the blocks contain preset actions like "'move", "shoot", and "jump", users can easily create a variety of familiar game genres, such as shooting games or racing games.

Project Spark, newly released in October 2014, has been described as a "game maker" game based on *Kodu*. It allows players to create a wide variety of games, as well as movies and other sorts of digital experiences. Gameplay in *Project Spark* consists of playing through levels and completing challenges which introduce the player to various features of the software that allow her or him to modify the game itself or to create new games. Community is also important in *Project Spark*, and players can create and share tutorials and challenges, as well as discuss the games and game making, on the official website (http://www.projectspark.com/). Unlike *Kodu*, this game primarily was designed for entertainment and informal use among fans. It is available for Xbox 360, Xbox One, and Windows 8.

From these descriptions, we can identify several different points of comparison across these and similar tools used for game making. First, tools vary in the extent to which they are intended for game design in particular, versus other goals. *Scratch* is a tool intended to allow users to create many different forms of digital media, depending on their own interests; game making is thus conceptualized as one of many forms of "creative computing" and pathways into participatory culture (Peppler & Kafai, 2010). While *Kodu* and *Project Spark* can be used to create digital media beyond games, they are explicitly promoted as game design tools; for example, Project Spark is described as ". . . the ultimate digital sandbox where you can create the kinds of games you've always dreamed of" (from the Project Spark website). The *Kodu* language was designed specifically for game development, with basic elements derived from gaming scenarios. Similarly, *Gamestar Mechanic* is described as a way to "learn game design and make your own games." A second point of comparison is the extent to which the tool or software emphasizes programming or coding, such as *Scratch* and *Kodu*, versus a higher level design interface, such as that found in *Gamestar Mechanic*. Presumably,

the ability to code is linked to greater flexibility in the tool's potential applications. A third point of comparison is how game making is positioned in relation to game play. In *Gamestar Mechanic*, players play and at times, "fix" a variety of games as an important aspect of learning about potential game designs and features. Similarly, in *Kodu* and *Project Spark* in particular, game making is closely linked to game play. *Project Spark* is advertised as a game, or set of games, with appeal in their own right, as well as a game making tool. In contrast, while *Scratch* users can upload and play each others' games, there is no attempt to engage potential game makers through game play, nor is game play overtly recruited as a means of introducing design concepts.

Few game making tools of any sort have been studied extensively; typically game making software developed by academics has been the focus of most research. There have been almost no studies that compare the relative strengths and limitations of different game making tools for similar purposes and with similar populations. Instead, research on game making in educational settings tends to consist of either (a) studies of game making in the context of a specific program or curriculum, or (b) single studies of a particular implementation of game making, with the goal of generating general principles or findings about game making. Given the considerable diversity among game making tools, how they can be used, the students who might use them, and the educational settings in which they might be used, we found studies of single implementations to have limited utility. Instead, in the following section we will discuss several more substantive examples of game making programs or curricula and summarize some key empirical findings or research reports related to each. We begin with a discussion of two efforts that grew directly out of the early work by Papert and his colleagues at MIT. The first, Globaloria, was established by Idit Harel, and is a combination of game design courses, tools, and community resources based on principles of constructionism. The second is a line of research and educational efforts using *Scratch* as a game making tool. We next describe two projects that represent contrasting visions of how game making might be tied to larger educational goals and curricula. The first, the Making Games Project, locates games and game making in the context of media literacy education. The second, Scalable Game Design, has the goal of making computer science education more appealing and accessible to a wider range of students. We conclude this section with a discussion of two related projects led by game designers, and informed by a view of game design as a means of cultivating broader ways of thinking about and designing complex systems. First we discuss empirical studies of *Gamestar Mechanic* as a tool for fostering systems thinking, and then we move to a brief discussion of the Institute of Play and how game design has inspired its broader educational agenda.

Globaloria: Game Making and "21st Century Skills"

Globaloria was launched in 2006 by Idit Harel, an educational technology entrepreneur and advocate of constructionism. As we noted above, Harel completed her PhD at MIT with Seymour Papert, studying the outcomes of engaging children in the use of the Logo programming tool to create software tools for learning math. Globaloria is based on constructionist principles, that include learners' production of a meaningful, computational public artifact (e.g., a game), created and shared in a reflective workshop environment of peer and expert-guided scaffolding (Caperton, 2012). Currently, Globaloria consists of a digital learning platform and online game design courses that can be used by schools or after school programs. Students learn to use "real world" software tools such as Flash and ActionScript, based on the assumption that this is more relevant and useful than having students learn a simplified programming language. Students are typically expected

to construct educational games on STEM content such as math or biology, with the goal of enhancing their STEM content knowledge as well as digital literacies and other skills. Harel and her collaborators identified what they call "six contemporary learning abilities (CLAs)" that form the guiding framework for the educational activities and learning objectives of Globaloria. These are quite broad; for example the first CLA is "Invention, progression and completion of an original project idea (educational game or simulation system)" (Caperton, 2012, p. 24). The overall instructional approach is one of guided discovery, in which students work together in teams on design projects, supported by teachers, peers, and resources on the online learning platform (networking, playing each other's games). The students' learning platform wikis are also connected to the school-learning platform so that they are able to find and access help from the lessons and tutorials, as well as communicate with each other.

According to program documents, Globaloria has been implemented in over 180 schools in 14 states. A variety of studies have been conducted on the program's impact on both students and teachers (the program has a significant professional development component). Most of these studies have been evaluation reports, available through the World Wide Workshop site (http://worldwideworkshop.org/reports). In general, data collected on student outcomes indicate improved cognitive skills, enhanced self-efficacy with technology, and increased student achievement on math, science and social studies assessments (Reynolds, 2010; Reynolds & Caperton, 2009; Worldwide Workshop, n.d.). It is difficult to identify with confidence what student outcomes are due to engagement in game design in particular as opposed to, more broadly, the overall constructionist educational approach. Few of the existing studies of Globaloria have examined the game design process in particular, or the games that participants create. One exception is a recent study by Games (2013), who examined the evolution of 30 students' computational thinking skills as reflected in changes in their language use, design strategies, and game artifact production. Findings are detailed and nuanced; in general, Games found many examples of how students' computational thinking skills were evident. He notes that there was a concerted effort to shift the instructional approach used by teachers from instructionist to constructionist (for example, by reducing presentation of information and allowing students to engage in more iterative game development) which resulted in more diverse, engaging and thoughtful games.

Scratch and Open-Ended Design

As of Fall 2014, the *Scratch* website reported more than 4.3 million registered users, and more than 6.8 million shared projects. While there is no definitive accounting of how many teachers have used *Scratch* in educational settings, ScratchEd site for educators had more 7500 members at this time. A relatively large number of studies have examined the use of *Scratch* in various educational settings, as well as the dynamics of the online *Scratch* community, where participants share their creations (see http://scratch.mit.edu/info/research/). Here we discuss only the small set of studies focused on game making using *Scratch*.

One group of related studies drew on data from the use of *Scratch* in a Computer Clubhouse in South Los Angeles. The Clubhouse was a community space serving high-poverty youth, from the ages of 8-18 years old, although most participants were 10-14 years old. In the Clubhouse, participants could try out a variety of different technology tools, *Scratch* among them (Kafai & Peppler, 2012*)*. Using *Scratch* became the leading design activity, and game making with *Scratch* became the focus of one line of research about the Clubhouse. The researchers were interested in users' development of broad technical and creative fluencies, a focus somewhat different than in other game making studies. For analysis,

the authors collected the students' games, all of which were stored on the central server. The games were coded by features of the game genre (e.g., puzzle game) reflected in the game's design, and individual games were used as case studies.

Throughout the course of the project, these researchers found that students gained game design expertise over time (Kafai & Peppler, 2012) and that the Clubhouse was a unique environment in which to study the development of this expertise. Informal communities usually face the issue of shifting membership, but this more formal setting allowed the authors to study participants over a span of time. Peppler and Kafai (2010) also found that participants developed a mix of creative and technical fluencies that the authors describe as "gaming fluencies." Gaming fluencies relate not just to game design, but technology design more broadly.

Another primary interest of the researchers was how people become participants in game design culture, particularly those who might be traditionally unwelcome in video game culture and in the industry, such as women and racial minorities. The researchers were studying urban youth and English language learners and they observed the ways in which the Clubhouse attendees became participants in the gaming culture of the club. Participating in game making activities such as these might serve as a pathway into participation in gaming communities (Peppler & Kafai, 2007).

Other studies based on *Scratch* generally have focused on outcomes other than programming, with one exception. Adams and Webster (2012) studied middle schoolers in a programming camp, who were allowed to create a video game or music video in *Scratch*, or a storytelling project in another tool, *Alice*. The authors found that students who created game projects in *Scratch* used more complex code than students who made other kinds of media projects.

There also has been research on the use of *Scratch* in formal educational settings. Ke (2014) investigated how students engaged with math content and mathematical thinking while using *Scratch*. Ke found that students did engage with with math, but they were more interested in storytelling and world building. Feng and Chen (2014) used *Scratch* as a way to study the instructional elements of goal specificity and scaffolding. In this study, the focus was not on *Scratch* itself but on how its use could support the study of instructional elements.

Overall, the studies on *Scratch* and in particular the Clubhouse series of studies focused more on creativity than research on other gaming tools. Because *Scratch* is a tool which can be used to create a multitude of games and media projects, it appears to serve a variety of research interests and purposes.

The Making Games Project and Media Literacy

The Making Games project was a collaboration between London Knowledge Lab researchers at the University of London's Institute of Education and a software development company, Immersive Education Ltd. At the time of the project's inception, there was a perceived dearth of game making tools for children, and the project had four goals: (a) to produce a user-friendly game authoring tool in a 3D environment; (b) to develop a model of game literacy; (c) to develop a pedagogic model for teaching such literacies; and (d) to develop a design model involving users as co-designers (Pelletier, 2007). The project was guided by a view of game design as an approach to media literacy, with the assumption that games should be considered a cultural medium in their own right, and included in school media literacy curricula. Similar to approaches to critical media literacy with film or literature, a second assumption was that media literacy education should involve not only critical analysis of existing texts but also enabling students to create their own. Thus, the project emphasized the potential of game making

as a form of creative cultural expression in its own right and as a means of developing students' critical understanding of the medium.

Making Games was funded from 2003 to 2006 by the British government, and involved working with Year 8 students (approximately age 12) and teachers at two secondary schools, one with a predominantly middle-class white student population and the other with a primarily black African-Caribbean student profile. More than 100 students and a dozen teachers participated in the project as a whole, though the researchers worked most intensively with two small groups of students and two teachers. The game design software was iteratively designed, through a process that included interviews and activities with the students, and a study of game artifacts and design processes in English and Media Studies classroom lessons, after-school club meetings, and students' homes. In addition to informing the development of the software tool, the data analyses were used to support the development of course curricula and activities, as well as to elaborate a theoretical framework of game literacy (Pelletier, 2007).

The findings of the project have been discussed in a number of articles and chapters, as well as in several technical reports (e.g., Buckingham & Burn, 2007; Burn & Pelletier, 2011; Pelletier, 2007; Pelletier, Burn & Buckingham, 2010). The software, *MissionMaker*, is an authoring tool for 3-D puzzle and adventure games (see Table 1 for more details). Users create 3D worlds from assets such as locations, characters, objects, triggers (which trigger an action), and media such as sound and images. Externally created assets also can be imported into the 3D world, allowing for considerable customization. Users construct events and interactions using a rule editor and a dialogue editor. As Pelletier (2007) notes, "designing games with *MissionMaker* consists primarily of organizing relations between assets rather than having to produce the assets themselves" (p. 20).

Many of the published papers on the Making Games project focus on developing the model of game literacy and illustrating it through close analyses of participants' games and design processes (Buckingham & Burn, 2007; Burn & Buckingham, 2007). The researchers drew on earlier models of media literacy, as well as social semiotic and multimodal theories of textual design, along with ideas from play, game and narrative theory. They propose three dimensions of game literacy, common to media literacy more broadly: cultural, critical, and creative (Buckingham & Burn, 2007). These aspects of game literacy are intertwined, and many of the analyses indicated how students' experiences of varied game cultures as well as their engagement with popular culture more broadly informed their approach to game design and their critical stance towards games. Findings that influenced the design of educational activities in the project included the children's experience of games as part of cross-media franchises (e.g., Harry Potter), suggesting the need to account for how media fandom more broadly served as a resource for participants' understandings and game design choices. Very few children had an understanding of or language to describe game design principles.

The final curriculum resources include a Media Studies Teacher Support Pack with 16 activities that take students from a basic introduction to game elements through planning a launch event for a class-designed *Missionmaker* game. Another product is a Games, Game Engines and Design course with a somewhat more technical focus. Emphasis is placed on both introducing students to game elements such as rules and economies, as well as to narrative elements, such as character types, with the goal of helping students learn how both systems might work together in a game. Some aspects of a game production process are simulated in the course activities, including the creation of a collective game design proposal, paired work on levels of the collective game, and play-testing.

One issue that arose during the project concerned the nature of creativity in student-designed games. Fostering creativity is a common goal in media production activities of all sorts in formal education, and yet as Pelletier, Burns and Buckingham (2010) point out, what constitutes creativity in such activities is contested, particularly in relation to students' reappropriation of elements from popular culture in their own productions (Banaji, Burn, & Buckingham, 2010). The researchers identify a variety of ways that commercial games, media, and fan practices served as a resource for students' game designs and game play. However, perhaps due to the considerable freedom students had in designing their games, the games were not necessarily playable, readily understood, or appreciated except by an audience familiar with the pop cultural references and fandom that inspired them. The researchers raise thought-provoking questions about the evaluation of students' game designs. Is a "good" game necessarily one that conforms to widely understood design conventions? How can educators encourage students to draw on their own insider knowledge of pop culture and then penalize them if the resulting game experience is incomprehensible to outsiders, including the teacher, or perhaps not even a game?

Scalable Game Design and Computer Science Education

Scalable Game Design is a "low threshold, high ceiling game design curriculum" (Repenning, Webb & Ioannidou, 2010, p. 267) intended to teach computer science concepts and enhance students' interest in computer science. The current project and instructional approach (Scalable Game Design launched in 2008) grew out of two decades of work by Alexander Repenning and his colleagues at the University of Colorado-Boulder on the educational use of visual, agent-based game and simulation authoring environments. Currently, Scalable Game Design utilizes two software tools, *AgentSheets*, a 2D authoring environment, and *AgentCubes*, a 3D environment, that are intended to allow users to create playable games in a relatively short amount of time, bypassing the time-consuming process of learning a programming language such as Java, (Basawapatna, Koh & Repenning, 2010). *AgentSheets* (currently in its fourth version) allows users to create simple "agents" using a built-in drawing tool, assign behaviors to those agents by connecting actions and conditions using a drag and drop interface, and then construct game levels. *AgentCubes* allows users to start with 2D images and game elements and move to 3D designs, in an approach they call "gentle slope 3D."

Scalable Game Design (SGD) was conceived as a computational thinking curriculum for middle school, and is based on the concepts of flow and the zone of proximal development (Repenning & Ioannidou, 2008).). A key assumption is that students will be more motivated if they are engaged immediately in concrete projects (i.e., game design) and are introduced to programming in a way that keeps them challenged but not frustrated. SGD resources include detailed tutorials, instructional videos, lesson plans, rubrics for assessing completed games, an arcade where users can share their projects, and videos. The tutorials and lesson plans introduce users to the design of simple arcade, puzzle, and maze type games in familiar forms such as Frogger and Pacman and move to increasingly sophisticated 3D game design projects. The lesson plans emphasize the use of guided discovery rather than direct instruction. For example, teachers are encouraged to let students solve problems on their own or in small groups with minimal scaffolding from the teacher, with the goal of helping students understand that programming is a process of trial and error. However, the tutorials and lesson plans seem rather lock-step in specifying the types of games, game features, and skills that students should develop as they progress through the curriculum. Perhaps not surprisingly, one challenge has been moving teachers from direct instruction to a more guided

discovery approach (Koh, Repenning, Nickerson, Endo, & Motter, 2013). Notably, the use of guided discovery seemed to be particularly effective in enhancing the interest of girls in taking future game design courses (Webb, Repenning, & Koh, 2012).

Repenning argues that Scalable Game Design has the potential for far greater impact because it has been incorporated into school curricula rather than adopted primarily in after-school programs alone. While SGD is intended for use in middle school computer science education, its tools and approach have been used from elementary through high school; current figures indicate that from 2009-2013 more than 13,000 students participated in a Scalable Design course or activities, in 15 states and 3 countries beyond the USA. Girls made up about 45% of all students and 48% of the students were from underrepresented groups (2013 Research Report, 2013). These proportions are significantly higher than typical after-school programs, presumably because in-school programs are more accessible or meet curriculum requirements.

A large number of papers (see http://sgd.cs.colorado.edu/wiki/Publications) have described the rationale for features of the *AgentSheets* and *AgentCubes* tools and the Scalable Game design process. Empirical studies have examined student outcomes of participation in SGD activities, such as motivation to study game design in the future, interest in computer science and understanding of computer science, with generally positive results (Webb, Repenning, & Koh, 2012). One distinctive focus of research on SGD has been the assessment of what Repenning and colleagues call "computational thinking patterns" (Koh, Nickerson, Basawapatna & Repenning, 2014). Simply put, a computational thinking pattern (CTP) is an abstract concept that describes a set of actions or interactions that are commonly found in games or other computer applications. Examples of CTPs include one agent tracking another agent, one agent absorbing another agent, and one agent creating another agent. For example, the pattern

"Generate" refers to one agent creating a stream or series of other agents that move away, such as a gun shooting bullets, cars racing out of a tunnel, or rain falling from a cloud. Participants upload completed games and simulations to the SGD Arcade, where the games are scored by an automated tool that examines the programmed rules of these student-created artifacts to identify these higher level patterns and how they compare to the tutorial implementation of the game. Although the originality and the design of the game are part of teacher grading of student-created games, CTP assessment measures only programming skills.

The SGD model clearly reflects the use of game making to provide motivation for students to learn programming. The tools and lesson plans scaffold students' acquisition of programming skills and concepts; little attention to given to other learning goals, such as fostering design knowledge. The SGD website for teachers includes a "scope and sequence" document referring to the International Society for Technology in Education standards potentially achieved through SGD, including broader abilities such as creativity and innovation, collaboration, and digital citizenship, but these have not been the focus of much published research or assessment (for one exception, see Bennett, Koh, & Repenning, 2013). In addition, there has been little research on the process of game making, in terms of studying classroom implementation or students' design choices. For such a focus, we now turn to research on *Gamestar Mechanic*.

Gamestar Mechanic and Systems Thinking

The research around *Gamestar Mechanic* comes primarily from the dissertations and related articles of two graduate students who worked on the project (Games 2010; Torres 2009). Although both of these authors focus on *Gamestar Mechanic* (GSM) and the ways in which it can foster design thinking, the two authors have different foci regarding the benefits of designing with GSM.

Games (2008; 2010) focused on the potential of GSM to facilitate the development of language and literacy skills. He was interested in how participants learned to use game design language. Games characterized the sociotechnical practices and ways of thinking that students developed while creating games in the classroom. He proposed a framework for analyzing and assessing learning in the context of game production as a function of the acquisition of key constructs central to the discourse of professional game designers.

The framework portrays increasing sophistication in this discourse as a function of the degree to which learners' decisions, language, and tool use reflected a growing understanding of games as sociotechnical systems. This understanding is demonstrated through an awareness of (a) the affordances of the software code, materials, assets and tools available to them in creating games, (b) the abstractions necessary for an idealized player to play a game with these materials (e.g. rules, mechanics, goals and so on), and (c) the probable ways in which real players would interpret and understand these materials and abstractions during play. Games found that participants were able to learn and appropriate the Discourse of game designers in their learning and literacy skills. He also found that students, including those who did not have a strong academic background, demonstrated success in thinking strategically and manipulating systems. He called for further research on and development of game-based learning environments.

Torres (2009) was more concerned with the concept of systems thinking, and GSM's ability to foster this type of thinking. He contrasted a traditional school-based approach to learning with the theory of situated cognition, which he used to investigate learning in the study. He proposed four systems thinking sub-skills through which to frame the assessments and research program in the study. These skills were (a) understanding of systems dynamics: understanding that multiple (i.e., dynamic) relationships exist within a system, (b) understanding of feedback dynamics (i.e. reinforcing and balancing feedback loops): understanding that reinforcing and balancing feedback loops inform and can continually modify the workings of a system, (c) understanding the quality of relationships within a system: understanding when a system is working or not working at optimal levels, and (d) homological understanding: understanding that similar system dynamics can exist in other systems that may appear to be entirely different different. Torres found that 5 out of 6 participants showed gains in systemic reasoning, and suggested that GSM may serve to facilitate the development of systems thinking skills. Torres called for further research on game-based learning, as well as the the adoption of a situated learning perspective in schools and educational policy more broadly.

Finally, a recent guide to using *Gamestar Mechanic* for educators (Tekinbas, Salen, Gresalfi, Peppler, & Santo, 2014) describes how to implement the game in classrooms, with the goal of promoting systems thinking. The authors of this book (the first author, Katie Salen Tekinbas, was co-lead designer of the original version of *Gamestar Mechanic*) explain the importance of systems thinking and how GSM can be used to facilitate the development of systems thinking. The book provides a series of design challenges that introduce games, systems, and GSM. These challenges involve both classroom activities and activities within GSM. There are discussions and activities before and after the actual design activities, intended to foster thinking about systems and design. This book only uses the "workshop" mode of the game, not the single player "quest" which teaches players the fundamentals of game design. Overall, this book provides an explanation for how an educator can go about implementing GSM and introduce the core concepts of game design to a class.

The Institute of Play and Design-Inspired Learning

The Institute of Play describes itself as not-for-profit design studio that creates "learning experiences rooted in the principles of game design—experiences that simulate real world problems, and require dynamic, well-rounded solutions" (Institute of Play, 2015a). While the Institute's work does not focus exclusively or even primarily on the use of game making for learning, we include it here because the Institute's efforts represent perhaps one of the most radical ways of using games and game making as a means of transforming education. The Institute was founded in 2007 by Katie Salen Tekinbas and a group of game designers in New York City. The Institute's first project was the creation of a public school in New York City, called Quest to Learn, and they have since launched a second school in Chicago, both with financial support from the MacArthur Foundation and other organizations. These schools are based on the assumption that current approaches to education are out-dated, alienating, and do not inspire young people with the desire to learn that is necessary for them to meet the challenges of a rapidly changing society (Salen Tekinbaş, Torres, Wolozin, Rufo-Tepper, & Shapiro, 2010). In a design document for the initial school, Salen Tekinbaş and others (ibid) describe how the school's philosophy and approach to learning draws on features of games, play and game design. In this approach, game design becomes both inspiration and more concretely, one of multiple ways that students are engaged in creating and understanding complex systems throughout the curricula.

Other Institute activities that utilize game making in particular include *Gamekit* (http://beta. gamek.it/), a website currently in development that offers moderated game design challenges for teens, *TeacherQuest,* a professional development program that introduces teachers to game-based learning and trains them to create non-digital games for use in their classrooms, and *Mobile-Quest*, a week-long summer camp for new sixth graders that introduces game design for mobile platforms (Institute of Play, 2015b).

To date, there is little data available on the process or outcomes of the Institute's varied educational efforts involving game design or other game-based activities. In an early study, Shute and Torres (2011) found that students in Quest to Learn demonstrated significant improvement in systems thinking and time management, though not in team work skills, over just six months. Overall, students' standardized test scores and attendance at Quest to Learn compare favorably to those in other NYC schools (Institute of Play, 2015a). Overall, the Institute's philosophy and educational efforts may be the best example to date of Papert's original ideas for reforming school through engaging young people in design-based activities. The Institute's work encompasses the design of games in all forms, not just digital games, serving as an important reminder that the potential educational value of game design transcends any technological features.

Gaming Making and Modding among Fans

Game making outside of educational settings often takes the form of modding existing games designed for entertainment, typically as an extension of game play. Players have modded games practically since the first computer games were created (Unger, 2012), and game modding has grown in diversity and sophistication along with games themselves. As we noted previously, game modding can range from creating new content within the structure of an existing game to using a game engine to create an entirely new game experience. Some commercial game designers encourage game modding by releasing software

tools that allow players to modify game content; in addition, players have created their own modding tools. Fans share such tools, tutorials and completed mods, as well as discuss modding, through online fan communities, some devoted exclusively to sharing knowledge and strategies for game modding. As one example, Mod Data-Base (www.moddb.com) was launched in 2002 with the goal of serving as a clearinghouse of sorts for all types of game mods, add-ons, and user-generated content. As of November 2014, the site had more than 36,000 files available and more than 130 million downloads. ModDB is organized by game platform, and in addition to game content, has videos, news, tutorials, groups, and forums, among other features. The site also has a page with some basic information about mods for newcomers ("Anyone who complains 'nothing good in life is free' needs to be shown a few mods"), including a discussion of the "mod-friendliness" of various games.

A variety of tools available for game making, often with supportive online communities, are used independently by fans. *Scratch* and *Gamestar Mechanic*, for example, while designed with educational goals, also are used informally by players outside of any educational setting. Other tools are designed for players with more professional aspirations, such as *GameMaker* (https://www.yoyogames.com/studio). Blurring the lines still further, *Little Big Planet* is a game primarily designed for entertainment in which players can not only play the game, but also create their own games with its level editor (Rafalow & Tekinbas, 2014).

While there have been numerous studies of game-related fan practices and communities in general, scholarly discussions or empirical studies of game modding and making outside of educational settings are relatively few. Most research focuses on modding practices and modders in relation to online communities, rather than, for example, studying individual game modders. In this section, we discuss key ideas from the limited scholarly literature on the topic, and then will briefly identify some of the new game making tools that are available online, which have yet to be studied.

Scholarship on Game Modding

Scholarly work on fan game modding has focused on several key topics. One focus has been identifying and categorizing the various practices that might be associated with game making or modding "in the wild." Another focus has been understanding the game modders themselves, including creating demographic profiles and identifying motivations for engaging in modding practices. One issue is how definitions of what counts as modding contributes to different perceptions of who is and isn't engaged in modding; in particular, the underrepresentation of women in many examinations of modding practices. A third major focus has been on the social contexts of modding, including the nature and ethos of modding communities or affinity spaces, as well as the collaborative processes and forms of teaching and learning involved in modding. We briefly discuss each topic below.

Identifying Modding Practices

One challenge confronting researchers is the great diversity in the kinds of practices associated with game modding, as we noted above. There have been a few attempts to categorize mods, typically based on their scope and complexity. Sotamaa (2010), in a study of the game *Operation Flashpoint*, identified three major types of modding practices: the creation of missions, add-ons, and mods. Unger (2012) offers perhaps the most detailed discussion to date of issues related to classifying game mods. He proposes a general typology of game modding practices that included mutators/tweaks, add-ons, mods, and total conversions. Unger also proposes a means of analyzing mods by differentiating among "layers" of games that

might be modded, including the narrative, audible, visual, interface, and rule system layers. These and other analytic frameworks tend to emphasize the technical features of mods as a basis for analysis. As Unger suggests, mods may be understood in more qualitative terms, by identifying the extent to which mods change the nature of game play or narrative. Game mods might be characterized as an adjustment to the game, as an extension of game play or story, or as invention of a new story or form of game play (p. 519).

Who Mods and Why

The sheer number of game mods and the size of game modding communities might suggest that game modding is a widespread practice, but the proportion of game players who also mod is relatively small (Hayes, 2008). Given the distributed nature of game modding across different games and game communities, obtaining representative data about demographics, motivations, or other attributes of modders is understandably difficult, if not impossible. Several small exploratory studies have investigated the attributes of game modders in modding communities using non-representative samples. For example, Sotamaa (2010) collected information from 23 participants in the OFP modding forum along with 6 members of a local OFP modding team; Poor (201) distributed a questionnaire across a variety of game sites and modding forums, yielding 111 respondents; Owens (2011) collected survey data from 83 participants in the RPG Maker online community. Even these small scale studies make it clear, as Sotamaa (2010, p 239) wrote, "there is no such thing as an average computer game modder." Respondents in these studies ranged from high school age to senior citizens, and their levels of educational attainment were equally as diverse, though some college completion seemed predominant. Women comprised a very small percentage of modders in these studies, however, mirroring the low percentages of women in the professional game design industry (for more extensive discussion of gender issues in gaming and the game industry, see Kafai, Heeter, Denner, & Sun, 2008).

Participants in these studies report varied motivations for modding. Sotaama, for example, identified five major motivations that are similar to the findings of other studies: (a) playing, or improving game play, (b) hacking, or understanding and manipulating the game code, (c) researching, or gathering information about content relevant to the game mod, (d) artistic expression, and (e) cooperation with other modders. He also found that a number of modders hoped to use their experience as a stepping stone to employment in the game design industry, though the competition for such positions is considerable (also see Postigo, 2007).

Wirman (2014) argues that the association of modding with a "discourse of hackerism" (p. 79) has led to the marginalization or exclusion of certain practices from what counts as modding. This discourse places an emphasis on modding as a primarily technical activity that gives modders higher status based on their technological sophistication, in particular compared to "mere" players. This type of modding also carries the aura of a certain degree of illicitness, as modders operate outside the normal boundaries of what game developers intended. She contrasts this with the general ethos of *The Sims* modding communities, in which practices like graphics-focused "skinning" (changing the appearance of objects or people) are popular and valued, yet do not alter the underlying game code, and are encouraged by the game company. Wirman claims that the exclusion of skinning and similar practices from most discussions of modding, as well as the association of modding with first person shooter games, devalues the participation of women modders in games like *The Sims*, and contributes to a larger discourse that values a limited range of "intellectual" skills and knowledge in gaming. As an example, Gee and Hayes (2009) propose that "soft modding" skills, such as translating a book into a game or understanding how to engage players,

should be given just as much value as technical modding skills, though they also are typically overlooked in discussions of modding.

Very little attention has been given to how this discourse of hackerism might marginalize or be unappealing to particular groups of male gamers. Betsy DiSalvo and her colleagues' research into the orientations of African-American adolescent boys towards games and game modding is one exception. These boys tended to engage in social and competitive game play, and equated digital games with "real life" sports, where rules were not to be violated. Game modding and the hacker ideology conflicted with their views of sportsmanship and how the boys used competitive game play to increase their social status among their peers (DiSalvo, Crowley, & Norwood, 2008; DiSalvo & Bruckman, 2010).

Modding Community and Culture

The culture and community aspects of modding have been examined from different perspectives. Complex modding projects can require collaboration among a team of contributors, who have expertise in different areas, such as animation, scripting, interface design, and modeling, and some studies have examined this collaborative process (e.g., Steinkuehler & Johnson, 2009). Sotamaa (2010) found that although modding team members are formally assigned to different roles, their actual engagement with modding tasks is fluid, with members assisting each other on different aspects of a mod as needed. Collaboration also takes place through modding forums, where mod makers may ask for technical advice or share beta versions for debugging. Popular mods and modders can develop a fan base of their own, with fans even making requests for new design features (ibid).

Given the often communal nature of mod development, ownership and intellectual property rights have become topics of interest to researchers. Many mod communities actively promote an open source model, in which mods are made available freely for use by the community at large (Sotamaa, 2010; Unger, 2012). While requiring payment for mods is often frowned upon in mod communities, modders may request donations for mods that require considerable time and effort to produce. However, ownership of mods, or more specifically attribution rights, can be strictly enforced in these communities (Kow & Nardi, 2010).

Tensions can arise between modders and game design companies. Modding is both encouraged and viewed as subversive by game companies, and choices made by the game developer can greatly affect the ''moddability'' of a game. From one point of view, modding is a form of unpaid labor that benefits game companies by extending a game's playability and keeping fans engaged. From another perspective, modding might be viewed as an effort to hack the game rules, cheat or otherwise disrupt the game experience, or as an infringement of IP rights if copyrighted art or graphics are modified or "stolen." Game companies deal with this issue in two primary ways (Kow and Nardi, 2010): (a) through restrictions on the software platform or alternatively, by providing modding tools or development kits that allow players to make modifications while implicitly controlling what can be produced (Unger, 2012), and (b) through legal enforcement, spelling out the terms and conditions of game content use in legal documents such as end-user license agreements. Typically these documents give companies ownership rights to any user-created content uploaded to a game site or online game, and the right to restrict distribution they consider inappropriate or in violation of copyright agreements.

There has been little study of how modders and companies mutually negotiate their potentially competing interests: corporate profits on the one hand and a perceived common good on the other. In one analysis, Kow and Nardi (2010) discuss a conflict between the *World of Warcraft* modding community and Blizzard Entertainment that highlighted, for them, the negative repercussions

of a company's use of legal mandates — in this case, banning modders from seeking donations or charging players for use of a mod — on modders' commitment to modding and to their sense of ownership over their creations. They suggest that companies can control, for example, the use of mods with undesirable effects, by changes in the game software:

This way, the evolution of mods and the software changes are a concrete form of negotiation, in programming terms, between the company and the modders, as each develops code that suggests a new path forward to the other. Mutually exclusive values in different concrete situations can thus, in a way, be reconciled, without the need for one to succumb to the other (n.p.).

While this is an appealing proposition, there is little evidence to support one strategy over another.

How the culture of game modding communities supports mutual teaching and learning has also received some attention from scholars. Gee and Hayes (2010; 2012) describe features of game-based affinity spaces that seem to promote inclusive forms of learning, using examples from a modding community devoted to *The Sims*. They also identify affinity spaces that support elitist forms of participation and knowledge construction (reflecting the discourse of hackerism described by Wirman). While these features are not exclusive to modding sites, they do suggest how such spaces might be organized around different ethos of participation and mentorship of newcomers. Researchers have applied various forms of discourse analysis to understand how modders collectively build knowledge about modding practices and tools, as well as about broader issues related to games and their content. Hayes and Lee (2012), for example, analyzed a *Sims* modding forum to understand how participants learn the "language" of modding, a crucial step in newcomers' ability to request appropriate help and to experienced members' ability to provide assistance. Owens (2010), in a close analysis of a forum thread devoted to modding *Civilization III*, illustrates how participants' desire to increase the historical accuracy of the game led them to complex discussions of the role of science and technology in society.

New Game Making Tools and Communities

In recent years, a number of new tools have emerged which blur the line between informal and formal game making further. These tools, targeted toward non-programmers, allow individuals and game studios to easily design games. Some allow users to export their games to stores such as the iOS App Store or the Android Market. Other host the games on their sites. Additionally, many offer support for teachers and educational licensing.

There is currently little empirical research on the impact of these tools, perhaps because they have not yet been widely adopted in formal educational settings. Regardless, we believe that these tools and their respective communities represent an important new direction for game making, both formal and informal. Table 2 lists these tools and provides a brief summary of each tool's features.

KEY ISSUES

Game making as an educational strategy takes many different forms and is informed by a wide range of assumptions about the value of game making for achieving various educational goals. While such diversity makes it difficult to generalize about the benefits of game making or the "best" approaches, it also provides multiple pathways

Table 2. New Game Making Tools

	Site	Platform	Export	Education Support?	Target Audience
GameSalad Creator	http://gamesalad.com/	Stand-alone Program	iOS, Android, HTML5	A curriculum and education licenses are offered for purchase	Commercial game developers
Stenycl	http://www.stencyl.com/	Stand-alone program	iOS, Android, Flash	Free curriculum, no license fee	Commercial game developers
Flow Lab	http://flowlab.io/	Browser-based	Hosted on site, iOS	Teacher license available, no curriculum offered	Informal learners, classrooms
Gamefroot	http://gamefroot.com/	Browser-based	Hosted on site, HTML5	Free and open source curriculum, student blogging platform in development, no license fees	Commercial game developers, informal learners, teachers
Sploder	http://www.sploder.com/	Browser-based	Hosted on site	None, but the site is focused on young learners	Children and adolescents
Construct 2	https://www.scirra.com/construct2	Stand-alone program	Web, Standalone Mac or PC Applications, iOS or Android (need additional support)	Education licence fees, no curriculum	Commercial game developers, informal learners, classrooms

into the use of games, that can engage different kinds of learners and can be adapted to the needs of a particular situation. However, our review of existing approaches also suggests some gaps or omissions in how the value and practices of game making have been conceptualized.

One ongoing issue, identified in a previous review by the first author (Hayes & Games, 2008) is the extent to which game design is viewed as a valuable set of skills and perspectives in its own right, as opposed to a means to another end, for example to introduce students to programming. Of the programs and software we reviewed, only *Gamestar Mechanic* gave particular emphasis to scaffolding players' understanding of basic game elements and how they work together to create fun and satisfying game play experiences. Eric Zimmerman (2009), one of the co-creators of *Gamestar Mechanic*, argued that game design is a form of literacy, that is, "the ability to understand and create specific kinds of meanings" (p. 24). This gaming literacy, according to Zimmerman, consists of a distinctive set of cognitive, social, and creative skills that involve the ability to engage with *systems* of all sorts (human as well as technical), a *play*ful approach to interacting with and reinventing these systems, and the ability to *design* meaningful experiences. Burn and Buckingham (2007) also propose a definition of game literacy, while Peppler and Kafai (2010) describe "gaming fluency," though both of these conceptions are somewhat more narrow. The utility of these conceptions has yet to be established, and perhaps proposing yet another type of "literacy" is not the best way to establish the distinctive nature of game design. Still, further developing an understanding of the distinctive nature of game design as a practice or set of practices seems worthwhile.

A more holistic view of game design might help to draw attention to the creative, artistic, and social aspects of game making that tend to be underemphasized in current educational approaches to game making. The recent push in the United States and other countries to make coding a "basic skill" for all students has given even greater priority to the use of game making as an introduction to programming. This narrow focus limits potential conceptions of both game design and programming; game design is equated with writing code, and programming is associated with a form of digital media that may not appeal to all potential learners.

Another issue that became apparent in our review of existing game making tools is how these tools embody particular values and goals for game design, both opening up and closing down opportunities for different sorts of designs and for creativity in the design process, as well as promoting particular forms of computational and design thinking. While in theory, Kafai and Peppler's "wide walls" principle for a design tool seems optimal, it may be that a tool with greater restrictions on what users can do may be more appropriate for beginning game designers, or for particular goals. It might be just as fruitful to find ways to help novice game makers move from tool to tool, following a sort of trajectory based on their interests and experience. In fact, many game making programs focused on programming have the ultimate goal of encouraging learners to move from a more simplified game programming tool to the use of a standard programming language. As we will note below, we have little knowledge of whether or how learners actually make this transition.

The notion of a learning trajectory is clear in many educational game making programs, though only to a point. Several have curricula that take users through a process of mastering basic tools and skills and then on to increasingly sophisticated projects. However, it's not necessarily clear what paths the learner might take at the end of the curricula. These possible paths should go beyond the potential to use a different tool, and might involve taking on new roles and identities in relation to game making or beyond. This is one area where educators might both learn from and connect to broader game making or modding communities.

In most online modding communities, participants have the opportunity, if they choose, to develop expertise and achieve social recognition in a variety of ways. For example, a participant can specialize in a particular aspect of modding, like 3D modeling or interface design, she or he can write tutorials or take leadership roles in forums, or manage modding teams. In many educational approaches to game making, there is an emphasis on taking students through a common set of learning experiences, with little opportunity for specialization. This reflects in part the constraints of school settings, where a shared curriculum is required, as well as the typical focus on using game making to develop other skills that presumably will primarily help students be more successful in their future academic experiences.

A pertinent issue here concerns the relationship of these formal as well as informal game making and modding practices to the professional practices of game designers in industry, as well as to postsecondary game design courses and programs. For example, there may be potential benefits from aligning educational game making activities in K-12 with professional design practices. This might include using "real" tools, such as Globaloria's use of Flash rather than a simplified programming tool, or having students work in design teams. But such alignment might also be aimed at helping students adopt the "epistemic frame" (Shaffer, 2006) of game designers. An epistemic frame is a particular set of values, practices, and ways of thinking associated with a professional community, in this case game designers. Shaffer suggests that a focus on epistemic frames might be the most effective way to help students develop ways of thinking that persist beyond a particular learning experience; the goal is not to teach students about a particular profession as much as give them the experience of developing expertise within a community of practice. *Gamestar Mechanic* as a curriculum is the most closely aligned with this approach, with its emphasis on introducing learners to the language of game design and to some key design practices.

We find the apparent lack of intersections among game modding communities and educational game making to be a concern, though perhaps understandable. While the growing emphasis on cultivating online communities associated with educational game making tools, such as *Scratch* (Burke and Kafai, 2014) is a recognition of the value of bringing makers together to share their knowledge and games, educators stand to learn quite a bit more from how game modding communities have organized themselves as spaces for teaching and learning (Gee and Hayes, 2012).

Of course, game modding communities are not ideal models, and have problems of their own. One of the more prominent issues is that of inclusiveness, both in terms of who participates and in terms of what sort of skills and designs are valued. Up to recently, the most prominent modders and modding communities have been heavily dominated by white men, and have overvalued technical prowess. The growing number of game making or modding tools available for popular use is already giving a wider audience the tools to participate in game making, though even communities tied to widely appealing games with level editors like *Little Big Planet* seem to have, for example, small proportions of female modders (Rafalow & Tekinbas, 2014). Educational game making programs in afterschool contexts also tend to attract a far larger proportion of boys than girls (Webb, Repenning, & Koh, 2012). The reasons for these ongoing disparities are complex, involving both perceptions of games and game modding, and features of particular communities that are overtly or implicitly exclusive, but they merit further attention.

GAPS IN THE LITERATURE AND DIRECTIONS FOR FUTURE RESEARCH

Throughout the chapter, we have noted gaps in the scholarly literature and opportunities for further research on game making and game modding. Here we will summarize a few of the more prominent or pressing areas for investigation. But first, we point out the challenges facing researchers in this area, and indeed in any research on digital media. The biggest challenge is how rapidly game making tools are evolving, reflecting both the evolution of computer technology as well as the evolution of games and game platforms. Tools and programs come and go rapidly; many of the game making tools and programs currently available were not in existence a decade ago, and if they were, their features have been modified considerably. The rise in popularity of gaming on mobile devices like cell phones and tablets makes it likely that game design for apps will become much more common; a number of the new tools listed in Table 2 emphasize mobile game creation. In addition, each of the major game consoles has or will have game making software. We already discussed *Project Spark* for the Xbox One; in 2014 *GameMaker: Studio* was released for the Playstation4 and Nintendo plans to release *Mario Maker* for the Wii U in 2015. While these tools and others offer new opportunities for research, a challenge for researchers is identifying core questions and topics that transcend the features of individual tools.

There is a similar flux in game modding communities; communities can expand, shrink or disappear in proportion to the popularity of particular games. As we noted above, there are some long-lasting game communities, but these communities themselves are organic and evolving. While this poses a challenge, we also can see an opportunity, for little research has investigated how these communities change (for exceptions, see Lammers, 2011; Lee, 2012).

In general, we were surprised by the apparent lack of empirical studies of game making or modding beyond the classroom. There is a larger body of research on the dynamics of game fan communities, in which game modding is sometimes mentioned, and game modding also appears in some discussions of young people's out-of-school digital media practices more broadly (e.g., Ito et al., 2009). Building on this literature, we think there are several approaches to the study of informal game modding that are necessary and useful. First are descriptive studies devoted specifically to game modding practices and communities. We need studies of a much wider range of games and communities, to identify common elements as well as differences. A second approach is to focus on the modders themselves and build a better understanding of the role of modding in the context of their lives and broader trajectories of engagement with digital media (see, for example, Gee & Hayes, 2010; Rafalow & Tekinbas, 2014). A third approach is to locate game modding in the larger context of game play, devoting more attention, for example, to understanding how modding might be prompted by particular kinds of play, or even how the boundaries of play and modding are becoming intentionally blurred, in games like *Little Big Planet* or *Gamestar Mechanic*. How do play and modding mutually inform each other, and each make a contribution to what users gain from the experience? How do deliberate attempts on the part of game publishers to encourage game making, by providing level editors or modding tools, both encourage wider participation and potentially limit what users can do and create? The hacker ethos that pervaded earlier modding communities is hard to sustain when modding is simplified and officially sanctioned. How such tools encourage new forms of culture and community around modding is an empirical question worthy of investigation.

In addition to more descriptive studies, ethnographic interventions, carefully designed, might be implemented in fan communities as a means of identifying ways to promote learning, enhance participation, or promote new ways of collaboration and communication. While the thought of researchers "intervening" in fan communities might seem inappropriate or unethical, we draw on ideas of intervention that inform community art installations, where artists identify issues and ideas from intensive studies of local communities, and then create artwork that is intended to communicate these ideas and issues back to the community, with the goal of prompting new perspectives, dialogue, and community-driven change (Mounajjed, Peng, & Walker, 2007).

In the context of educational game making, we see several overarching needs or opportunities for future scholarship. Longer term studies of the impact of participation in game making programs are sorely needed. While many such programs have goals such as increasing the likelihood that participants will enroll in computer science courses, be more successful in STEM courses in general, or continue to engage in design practices in out-of-school contexts, few studies have followed students after the conclusion of a class or program. We also have little comparative data about the affordances and appeal of different tools for different purposes and populations, comparison of the outcomes of different game making programs, or comparisons of game making vs other forms of digital media production as a means of student learning. Lastly, Burke & Kafai (2014) argue for the importance of online communities and sharing knowledge as key to successful game making experiences for kids: "the really important tool is, in fact, the community" (p. 703). The growing number of communities designed to support the use of specific game making tools offer opportunities for in-depth study of particular communities as they develop, as well as comparisons across these communities.

RECOMMENDATIONS FOR POLICY AND PRACTICE

At the broadest level, game making and modding are just one aspect of the larger landscape of productive practices made possible or enhanced by digital media. The wide availability of accessible and digital tools, combined with the growth of networked communities that provide information, support, and a receptive audience for user-created media such as games and game mods, can allow increasing numbers of people to become producers as well as consumers of digital media. Ideally, these experiences will enable more people to find satisfaction, purpose, and recognition in an increasingly economically and politically divided society. And just perhaps, they might better equip people to take action to confront larger social issues (Lenhart et al., 2008)

On a more immediate level, we propose several key recommendations for the future. First, we emphasize the need for a broad conception of game making as a set of practices that are far more than technical in nature. Drawing on Zimmerman (2009), game making ultimately is about creating meaningful experiences, and requires an understanding of people, not simply code. We do not do justice to the potential - and reality - of game making if it becomes co-opted by educators as yet another way to lure young people into programming. While game literacy may or may not be a viable organizing concept for education, an awareness of the aesthetic, social, and even political aspects of game making will open up new perspectives on the potential role and impact of game making in school and beyond.

Second, while it's not yet clear how game making might best be incorporated into education, we do see a need for a good deal more innovation, combined with more critical assessments of what game making can accomplish. The use of digital game making in schools, for example, is still quite new and not at all widespread. In fact, we do not know if game making, at least in its current form, really belongs in school, at least on a large scale, given the pressure to direct it towards narrow curricular goals. We fear that game making may follow the route of a myriad of other educational innovations that are received with enthusiasm, saddled with high expectations, and ultimately are left behind in a search for the next way to "fix" deeply rooted educational problems. The Institute of Play's model of design-driven learning across the curriculum, as represented in the Quest Schools, is promising, but whether this model can be implemented on a large scale remains to be seen.

However, we do see game making and modding as one way into a broader effort to leverage what we are learning about out-of-school digital media practices to reconceptualize the role of such media in education. Decades of research have shown that the ways that new technologies are incorporated into schools tend to reproduce existing inequities; disadvantaged kids are given digital skill-and-drill curricula, while already advantaged kids use more advanced technologies that permit their development of more sophisticated skills and knowledge. It was heartening to see examples of game making programs that tried to break that mold. However, as we stated above, unless kids have access to trajectories of learning that go beyond a single class or the confines of a classroom, the impact will be small. Another thing is also clear: game making will have little impact unless more attention is given to introducing teachers to the importance of the skills and practices associated with *design* (and other productive practices) and to ways that they can utilize strategies such as game making to foster these skills among their students.

Lastly, and beyond schools, we are excited by the continued effort of the game industry to provide tools that may enable more players to be game designers as well. While such efforts can be viewed cynically as a way to sell more games, and potentially to take advantage of the "unpaid labor" of player communities, players have a tendency to resist constraints imposed on them by a game or by developers. In a popular though controversial book and TED talk, game designer Jane McGonigal (2011) argues that playing games, or the habits of mind that playing games develops, can help us more productively confront the global problems that threaten our society. While she mentions making games as particularly useful for developing creativity, we feel she does not do justice to the additional power of game design as a potential model for the forms of systems thinking, collective intelligence, and sociotechnical knowledge that we need to address these problems. Making games won't save the world, but perhaps it is one way to cultivate people who can.

REFERENCES

Adams, J. C., & Webster, A. R. (2012). What do students learn about programming from game, music video, and storytelling projects? In *Proceedings of the 43rd ACM Technical Symposium on Computer Science Education* (pp. 643–648). New York, NY: ACM. doi:10.1145/2157136.2157319

Banaji, S., Burn, A., & Buckingham, D. (2010). *The rhetorics of creativity: A literature review* (2nd ed.). London: Creativity, Culture and Education.

Basawapatna, A. R., Koh, K. H., & Repenning, A. (2010). Using scalable game design to teach computer science from middle school to graduate school. In *Proceedings from The Fifteenth Annual Conference on Innovation and Technology in Computer Science Education* (pp. 224-228). New York, NY: ACM. doi:10.1145/1822090.1822154

Bennett, V. E., Koh, K., & Repenning, A. (2013). Computing creativity: Divergence in computational thinking. In *Proceedings from The 44th ACM Technical Symposium on Computer Science Education* (pp. 359–364). New York, NY: ACM. doi:10.1145/2445196.2445302

Blikstein, P. (2013). *Seymour Papert's legacy: Thinking about learning, and learning about thinking*. Retrieved from https://tltl.stanford.edu/content/seymour-papert-s-legacy-thinking-about-learning-and-learning-about-thinking

Buckingham, D., & Burn, A. (2007). Game-literacy in theory and practice. *Journal of Educational Multimedia and Hypermedia, 16*, 323–349.

Burke, Q., & Kafai, Y. B. (2014). Decade of game making for learning: From tools to communities. In M. C. Angelides & H. Aguis (Eds.), *Handbook of digital games* (pp. 689–709). New York: Wiley-IEEE Press. doi:10.1002/9781118796443.ch26

Burn, A. (2008). The case of Rebellion: Researching multimodal texts. In J. Coiro, M. Knobel, C. Lankshear, & D. J. Leu (Eds.), *Handbook of research on new literacies* (pp. 149–177). London: Taylor & Francis.

Burn, A., & Buckingham, D. (2007). Towards game-literacy: Creative game authoring in English and Media classrooms. *English Drama Media, 7*, 40–46.

Burn, A., & Pelletier, C. (2011). Case study on the impact of the Making Games Project. London: Institute of Education, University of London. Retrieved from http://www.ioe.ac.uk/research_expertise/ioe_rd_a4_mgames_0511.pdf

Caperton, I. H. (2012). Toward a theory of game-media literacy: Playing and building as reading and writing. *The Journal of Media Literacy, 59*, 18–27.

Dekhane, S., & Xu, X. (2012). Engaging students in computing using Gamesalad: A pilot study. *Journal of Computing Sciences in Colleges, 28*, 117–123.

DiSalvo, B., & Bruckman, A. (2010). Race and gender in play practices: Young African American males. In *Proceedings of the Fifth International Conference on the Foundations of Digital Games* (pp. 56–63). New York, NY: ACM. doi:10.1145/1822348.1822356

DiSalvo, B. J., Crowley, K., & Norwood, R. (2008). Learning in context: Digital games and young black men. *Games and Culture, 3*(2), 131–141. doi:10.1177/1555412008314130

Entertainment Software Association. (2014). *2013 Industry facts*. Retrieved from http://www.theesa.com/facts/

Feng, C., & Chen, M. (2014). The effects of goal specificity and scaffolding on programming performance and self-regulation in game design. *British Journal of Educational Technology, 45*(2), 285–302. doi:10.1111/bjet.12022

Fowler, A., & Cusack, B. (2011). Kodu game lab: improving the motivation for learning programming concepts. In *Proceedings of the 6th International Conference on Foundations of Digital Games* (pp. 238–240). New York: ACM. doi:10.1145/2159365.2159398

Fristoe, T., Denner, J., MacLaurin, M., Mateas, M., & Wardrip-Fruin, N. (2011). Say it with systems: Expanding Kodu's expressive power through gender-inclusive mechanics. In *Proceedings from The 6th International Conference on Foundations of Digital Games* (pp. 227–234). New York, NY: ACM. doi:10.1145/2159365.2159396

Games, A. (2010). Bug or feature: The role of Gamestar Mechanic's material dialog on the metacognitive game design strategies of players. *E-Learning and Digital Media, 7*(1), 49–66. doi:10.2304/elea.2010.7.1.49

Games, A. (2013, March). *Understanding the evolution of adolescents' computational thinking skills within the Globaloria educational game design environment*. Retrieved from Globaloria_ComputationalThinkingSkills_Games_Mar2013.pdf

Games, I. A. (2009). *21st century language and literacy in Gamestar Mechanic: Middle school students' appropriation through play of the discourse of computer game designers* (Doctoral dissertation). Retrieved from ProQuest Dissertations and Theses. (3384100)

Games, I. A. (2010). Gamestar mechanic: Learning a designer mindset through communicational competence with the language of games. *Learning, Media and Technology, 35*(1), 31–52. doi:10.1080/17439880903567774

Gee, J., & Hayes, E. (2010). *Women as gamers: The Sims and 21st century learning*. New York: Palgrave Macmillan.

Gee, J. P. (2007). *What videogames have to teach us about learning and literacy* (2nd ed.). New York, NY: Palgrave Macmillan.

Gee, J. P., & Hayes, E. (2012). Passionate affinity groups. In C. Steinkuehler, K. Squire, & S. Barab (Eds.), *Games, learning, and society: Learning and meaning in the digital age* (pp. 129–153). London: Cambridge University Press. doi:10.1017/CBO9781139031127.015

Gee, J. P., & Hayes, E. R. (2009). "No quitting without saving after bad events": Gaming paradigms and learning in *The Sims. International Journal of Learning and Media, 1*(3), 1–17. doi:10.1162/ijlm_a_00024

Harel, I., & Papert, S. (Eds.). (1991). *Constructionism*. New York, NY: Ablex Publishing.

Hayes, E., & Lee, Y. (2012). Specialist language acquisition and trajectories of IT learning in a Sims fan site. In E. Hayes & S. Duncan (Eds.), *Learning in video game affinity spaces* (pp. 186–211). New York: Peter Lang.

Hayes, E. R. (2008). Game content creation and IT proficiency: An exploratory study. *Computers & Education, 5*(1), 97–108. doi:10.1016/j.compedu.2007.04.002

Hayes, E. R., & Games, I. A. (2008). Making computer games and design thinking: A review of current software and strategies. *Games and Culture, 3*(3-4), 309–332. doi:10.1177/1555412008317312

Howland, K., & Good, J. (2015). Learning to communicate computationally with Flip: A bi-modal programming language for game creation. *Computers & Education, 80*, 224–240. doi:10.1016/j.compedu.2014.08.014

Institute of Play. (2015a). *Institute of Play*. Retrieved January 15, 2015 from http://www.instituteofplay.org/about/

Institute of Play. (2015b). *Featured work*. Retrieved January 15, 2015 from http://www.instituteofplay.org/work/

Ito, M., Baumer, S., Bittanti, M., Boyd, D., Cody, R., Herr, B., … Tripp, L. (2009). Hanging out, messing around, geeking out: Living and learning with new media. Cambridge, MA: MIT Press.

Kafai, Y. B. (1995). *Minds in play: Computer game design as a context for children's learning*. Mahwah, NJ: Lawrence Erlbaum.

Kafai, Y. B., Heeter, C., Denner, J., & Sun, J. Y. (Eds.). (2008). *Beyond Barbie and Mortal Kombat: New perspectives on gender and gaming*. Boston: MIT Press.

Kafai, Y. B., & Peppler, K. (2012). Developing gaming fluencies with Scratch: Realizing game design as an artistic process. In C. Steinkuehler, K. Squire, & S. Barab (Eds.), *Games, learning, and society: Learning and meaning in the digital age* (pp. 355–380). New York, NY: Cambridge University Press. doi:10.1017/CBO9781139031127.026

Ke, F. (2014). An implementation of design-based learning through creating educational computer games: A case study on mathematics learning during design and computing. *Computers & Education, 73*, 26–39. doi:10.1016/j.compedu.2013.12.010

Khaled, R., & Ingram, G. (2012). Tales from the front lines of a large-scale serious game project. In *Proceedings from CHI '12: SIGCHI Conference on Human Factors in Computing Systems* (pp. 69–78). New York, NY: ACM. doi:10.1145/2207676.2207688

Koh, K. H., Nickerson, H., Basawapatna, A., & Repenning, A. (2014). Early validation of computational thinking pattern analysis. In *Proceedings from 2014 Conference on Innovation & Technology in Computer Science Education*. New York, NY: ACM. doi:10.1145/2591708.2591724

Koh, K. H., Repenning, A., Nickerson, H., Endo, Y., & Motter, P. (2013). Will It stick?: Exploring the sustainability of computational thinking education through game design. In *Proceedings from The 44th ACM Technical Symposium on Computer Science Education* (pp. 597–602). New York, NY: ACM. doi:10.1145/2445196.2445372

Kow, Y. M., & Nardi, B. (2010). Who owns the mods? *First Monday, 15*(5). doi:10.5210/fm.v15i5.2971

Lammers, J. C. (2011). *The hangout was serious business: Exploring literacies and learning in an online Sims fan fiction community* (Doctoral dissertation). Retrieved from ProQuest Dissertations and Theses. (3453240)

Lee, Y. (2012). *Learning and literacy in an online gaming community: Examples of participatory practices in a Sims affinity space* (Doctoral dissertation). Retrieved from ProQuest Dissertations and Theses. (3505612)

Lenhart, A., Jones, S., & MacGill, A. (2008). Adults and video games. Washington, DC: Pew Research Center. Retrieved from http://www.pewinternet.org/2008/12/07/adults-and-video-games/

Li, Q. (2010). Digital game building: Learning in a participatory culture. *Educational Research, 52*(4), 427–443. doi:10.1080/00131881.2010.524752

McGonigal, J. (2011). *Reality is broken: Why games make us better and how they can change the world.* New York: The Penguin Press.

Mounajjed, N., Peng, C., & Walker, S. (2007). Ethnographic interventions: A strategy and experiments in mapping sociospatial practice. *Human Technology, 3*(1), 68–97. doi:10.17011/ht/urn.200771

O'Donnell, C. (2013). Wither Mario Factory? The role of tools in constructing (co)creative possibilities on video game consoles. *Games and Culture, 8*(3), 161–180. doi:10.1177/1555412013493132

Owens, T. (2010). Modding the history of science: Values at play in modder discussions of Sid Meier's *Civilization. Simulation & Gaming, 42*(4), 481–495. doi:10.1177/1046878110366277

Owens, T. (2011). Social videogame creation: Lessons from RPG Maker. *On the Horizon, 19*(1), 52–61. doi:10.1108/10748121111107708

Papert, S. (1981). *Mindstorms: Children, computers, and powerful ideas.* New York, NY: Basic Books.

Papert, S., & Harel, I. (1991). Situating constructionism. In I. Harel & S. Papert (Eds.), *Constructionism* (pp. 1–11). Norwood, NJ: Ablex Publishing Corporation.

Pelletier, C. (2007). *Making games: Developing games authoring software for educational and creative use: Full research report* (ESRC End of Award Report No. RES-328-25-0001). Swindon: ESRC.

Pelletier, C., Burn, A., & Buckingham, D. (2010). Game design as textual poaching: Media literacy, creativity and game-making. *E-Learning and Digital Media*, *7*(1), 90–107. doi:10.2304/elea.2010.7.1.90

Peppler, K. (2013). *New opportunities for interest-driven arts learning in a digital age*. New York: The Wallace Foundation. Retrieved from http://www.wallacefoundation.org/knowledge-center/arts-education/key-research/Pages/New-Opportunities-for-Interest-Driven-Arts-Learning-in-a-Digital-Age.aspx

Peppler, K., Warschauer, M., & Diazgranados, A. (2010). Game critics: Exploring the role of critique in game-design literacies. *E-Learning and Digital Media*, *7*(1), 35–48. doi:10.2304/elea.2010.7.1.35

Peppler, K. A., & Kafai, Y. B. (2007). *What videogame making can teach us about literacy and learning: Alternative pathways into participatory culture*. Paper presented at the 2007 Meeting of Digital Games Research Association, Tokyo, Japan.

Peppler, K. A., & Kafai, Y. B. (2010). Gaming fluencies: Pathways into participatory culture in a community design studio. *International Journal of Learning and Media*, *1*, 45–58. doi:10.1162/ijlm_a_00032

Perrone, C., Repenning, A., & Clark, D. (1996). WebQuest: Using WWW and interactive simulation games in the classroom. *First Monday*, *1*(5). doi:10.5210/fm.v1i5.493

Pinkett, R. (2000). *Bridging the digital divide: Sociocultural constructionism and an asset-based approach to community technology and community building*. Paper presented at the 81st Annual Meeting of the American Educational Research Association, New Orleans, LA.

Poor, N. (2014). Computer game modders' motivations and sense of community: A mixed-methods approach. *New Media & Society*, *16*(8), 1249–1267. doi:10.1177/1461444813504266

Postigo, H. (2007). Of mods and modders: Chasing down the value of fan-based digital game modifications. *Games and Culture*, *2*(4), 300–313. doi:10.1177/1555412007307955

Rafalow, M., & Tekinbas, K. (2014). Welcome to Sackboy Planet: Connected learning among LittleBigPlanet 2 players. Irvine, CA: Digital Media and Learning Research Hub. Retrieved from www.dmlhub.net/publications

Repenning, A., & Ioannidou, A. (2008). Broadening participation through scalable game design. In *Proceedings of the 39th SIGCSE Technical Symposium on Computer Science Education* (pp. 305–309). New York, NY: ACM. doi:10.1145/1352135.1352242

Repenning, A., Webb, D., & Ioannidou, A. (2010). Scalable game design and the development of a checklist for getting computational thinking into public schools. In *Proceedings of the 41st ACM technical symposium on computer science education* (pp. 265–269). New York: ACM Press. doi:10.1145/1734263.1734357

Repenning, A., Webb, D. C., Brand, C., Gluck, F., Grover, R., Miller, S., & Song, M. (2014). Beyond Minecraft: Facilitating computational thinking through modeling and programming in 3D. *IEEE Computer Graphics and Applications*, *34*(3), 68–71. doi:10.1109/MCG.2014.46 PMID:24808170

2013. *Research Snapshot.* (2013). Retrieved January 9, 2015, from the Scalable Game Design Wiki: http://sgd.cs.colorado.edu/wiki/2013_Research_Snapshot

Resnick, M., Maloney, J., Monroy-Hernández, A., Rusk, N., Eastmond, E., Brennan, K., & Kafai, Y. et al. (2009). Scratch: Programming for all. *Communications of the ACM, 52*(11), 60–67. doi:10.1145/1592761.1592779

Resnick, M., & Silverman, B. (2005). *Some reflections on designing construction kits for kids.* Paper presented at the International Conference for Interaction Design and Children, Boulder, CO. doi:10.1145/1109540.1109556

Reynolds, R. (2010). Changes in middle school students' six contemporary learning abilities (6-CLAs) through project-based design of web-games and social media use. In A. Grove (Ed.), *Proceedings of the American Society for Information Science and Technology* (*Vol. 47*). Academic Press.

Reynolds, R., & Caperton, I. H. (2009). *The emergence of six contemporary learning abilities (6-CLAs) in middle school, high school and community college students as they design web-games and use project-based social media in Globaloria.* Paper presented at the Annual Conference of the American Educational Research Association, San Diego, CA. Retrieved from http://worldwideworkshop.org/pdfs/Globaloria-EmergencofSixCLAs.pdf

Salen, K. (2007). Gaming literacies: A game design study in action. *Journal of Educational Multimedia and Hypermedia, 16*, 301–322.

Salen Tekinbaş, K., Torres, R., Wolozin, L., Rufo-Tepper, R., & Shapiro, A. (2010). *Quest to Learn: Developing the school for digital kids.* Cambridge, MA: MIT Press.

Shute, V. J., Ventura, M., & Torres, R. (2013). Formative evaluation of students at Quest to Learn. *International Journal of Learning and Media, 4*(1), 55–69. doi:10.1162/IJLM_a_00087

Sotamaa, O. (2010). When the game is not enough: Motivations and practices among computer game modding culture. *Games and Culture, 5*(3), 239–255. doi:10.1177/1555412009359765

Steinkuehler, C., & Johnson, B. Z. (2009). Computational literacy in online games: The social life of a mod. *International Journal of Gaming and Computer-Mediated Simulations, 1*(1), 53–65. doi:10.4018/jgcms.2009010104

Tekinbaş, K. S., Gresalfi, M., Peppler, K. A., & Santo, R. (2014). *Gaming the system: Designing with Gamestar Mechanic.* Cambridge, MA: MIT Press.

Torres, R. J. (2009). *Learning on a 21st century platform: Gamestar Mechanic as a means to game design and systems-thinking skills within a nodal ecology* (Doctoral dissertation). Retrieved from ProQuest Dissertations and Theses. (3361988)

Unger, A. (2012). Modding as part of game culture. In J. Fromme & A. Unger (Eds.), *Computer games and new media cultures* (pp. 509–523). Doetinchem, Netherlands: Springer Netherlands. doi:10.1007/978-94-007-2777-9_32

Vos, N., van der Meijden, H., & Denessen, E. (2011). Effects of constructing versus playing an educational game on student motivation and deep learning strategy use. *Computers & Education, 56*(1), 127–137. doi:10.1016/j.compedu.2010.08.013

Webb, D. C., Repenning, A., & Koh, K. H. (2012). Toward an emergent theory of broadening participation in computer science education. In *Proceedings of the ACM Special Interest Group on Computer Science Education Conference* (pp. 173–178). New York: ACM. doi:10.1145/2157136.2157191

Wirman, H. (2014). Gender and identity in game-modifying communities. *Simulation & Gaming*, *45*(1), 70–92. doi:10.1177/1046878113519572

Workshop, W. (n.d.). *The results are in: Globaloria improves teaching and learning across the country.* Retrieved from http://globaloria.com/docs/Globaloria_Research_Overview.pdf

Wu, M. L., & Richards, K. (2011). Facilitating computational thinking through game design. In M. Chang, W.-Y. Hwang, M.-P. Chen, & W. Müller (Eds.), *Edutainment technologies. Educational games and virtual reality/augmented reality applications* (pp. 220–227). New York: Springer Berlin Heidelberg.

Zimmerman, E. (2009). Game design as a model for literacy in the twenty-first century. In B. Perron & M. J. P. Wolf (Eds.), *The video game theory reader 2* (pp. 23–32). New York, NY: Taylor & Francis.

KEY TERMS AND DEFINITIONS

Affinity Space: A virtual or physical location where groups of people come together because of a shared interest or engagement in a common activity.

Computational Thinking: A set of thought processes and problem-solving abilities, such as pattern recognition and abstraction, that are foundational to computer science.

Constructionism: A theory of learning based on the premise that knowledge is actively constructed and that learning is enhanced when people are creating tangible objects in the world.

Design Thinking: An approach to creating new and innovative ideas and products by drawing on an understanding of people, the possibilities of technologies, and design methodologies.

Game Design: Creating goals, actions, rules and other components of a game.

Gamification: The use of game features, such as badges, quests, or storylines, in non-game situations, to increase motivation and engagement.

Hacker: Someone who exploits weaknesses in computer programs.

Modding: Altering the program code of a video game to change its interface, operation or appearance.

Systems Thinking: A perspective and approach to problem-solving that emphasizes understanding the world in terms of dynamic systems, the interrelationships among elements of systems, and how systems influence each other.

Chapter 11
A Review of E-Textiles in Education and Society

Kylie Peppler
Indiana University, USA

ABSTRACT

The recent emergence of digital creativity that extends beyond the screen and into the physical world, engendering new forms of creative production, has transformed educational and professional fields. From AT&T's bio-tracking clothing to Lady Gaga's smart-hydraulic "Living Dress," e-textiles infuse fashion with electronics to produce unique and aesthetic effects using new conductive materials, including thread, yarn, paint, and fabrics woven from copper, silver, or other highly conductive fibers. This chapter outlines both the educational and societal implications of these new materials in the field of e-textile creation like consumer-ready e-textile toolkits, high-profile displays of imaginative e-textile creations and an increasing body of Do-It-Yourself (DIY) literature on e-textile design that have emerged in the past decade. It also looks at ways in which e-textiles are transforming new solutions to old and persistent problems of underrepresentation of women and minorities in STEM fields and providing a vehicle in which to rethink teaching and learning in these disciplines.

INTRODUCTION

Recent years have marked the emergence of digital creativity that extends beyond the screen and into the physical world, engendering new forms of creative production that are transforming educational and professional fields. This trend is exemplified with particular gusto in the rise of e-textiles: fabric artifacts that include embedded computers and other electronics. From AT&T's bio-tracking clothing to Lady Gaga's smart-hydraulic "Living Dress," e-textiles infuse fashion with electronics

to produce unique and aesthetic effects using new conductive materials, including thread, yarn, paint, and fabrics woven from copper, silver, or other highly conductive fibers (Buechley, Peppler, Eisenberg & Kafai, 2013).

While computing and textiles have a longstanding—though rarely acknowledged—relationship, the domain of e-textiles historically has been considered a highly specialized niche area of design. However, changing the possibilities and perceptions of a broader field of e-textile creation are new sets of consumer-ready e-textile toolkits

DOI: 10.4018/978-1-4666-8310-5.ch011

(Buechley, Elumeze, & Eisenberg, 2006; Reichel et al., 2006), high-profile displays of imaginative e-textile creations (e.g., Chalayan, 2011) and an increasing body of Do-It-Yourself (DIY) literature on e-textile design (Lewis & Lin, 2008; Pakhchyan, 2008; Eng, 2009) that have emerged in the past decade.

This chapter outlines both the educational and societal implications of these new materials, including how e-textiles are transforming the ways in which we re-envision new solutions to old and persistent problems of underrepresentation of women and minorities in science, technology, engineering, and mathematics (STEM) fields as well as enable us to radically rethink teaching and learning in these disciplines.

BACKGROUND: E-TEXTILES IN PRACTICE

E-textile projects can range from computationally enhanced articles of clothing to home furnishings to architecture, underscoring through tacit or explicit means how computing can be soft, colorful, approachable, and beautiful. E-textile artifacts can range from the whimsical (for example, dresses that expand in circumference when personal space is encroached upon, traditional embroideries that glow and sing) to the mission-critical (for example, smart military uniforms, sportswear that monitors health indicators, portable medical devices). Examples below help to situate e-textiles for those unfamiliar with this emerging domain.

- **Wearable Workout Buddy:** A knitted arm band embedded with a circular sensor and wireless transmitter detects whether its wearer's arm is bent or straight. This band communicates via Bluetooth with an application running on an Android phone, which keeps a running tally of the repetitions—a useful aid to workout sessions that involve push-ups, pull-ups, or other upper

body exercises (Kaufmann & Buechley, 2010). Circular sensors are nicely suited to a range of wearable applications since tubular structures make up the sleeves, torsos, and legs of garments.

- **Music-Improvisation Dance Costume:** A collaboration between multiple artists and software designers resulted in the development of a computationally enhanced dance costume and accompanying musical environment (Lindsay, 2013). The dance costume is augmented with a microcontroller, a wireless transmitter, and various sensors that detect and transmit the movements of the dancer to a laptop, which then converts dance data to sound parameters in MAX/MSP, a programming language for interactive music and multimedia. The e-textiles facilitate interactivity between dancers' movements and the music that accompanies their dancing, transforming the power dynamic between composer and choreographer by putting the power of live musical improvisation in the hands (bodies) of dancers. Like the development of a traditional instrument, designing a dance costume to facilitate musical improvisation requires careful cross-disciplinary consideration of its functional components as well as its expressive capabilities; sensors have to track the most communicative motions of the dancers, the music controls have to be sensitive to the gestures onstage but conspicuous enough so as to ensure the audience know what movements elicit which kinds of sounds, and the costumes have to withstand duress from stretching, heat, and perspiration.

- **Fairytale Fashion:** To promote science and technology learning through fashion design, a fashion collection was created using technology to make "magical" clothing that functions in real life (Eng, 2013). The resulting e-textile designs employ various combinations of motion-controlled electroluminescent (EL) wire, moving biomimetic deployable structures, audio-controlled twinkling, and inflation. The electroluminescent motion-controlled garments, inspired by bioluminescent sea creatures, are made from silk chiffon edged in EL wire to have the same motion as jellyfish. The EL wire is powered by custom accelerometer-controlled drivers paired with an Arduino Duemilanove encased in a 3D printed housing. As the wearer walks, the garment flows and illuminates in reaction to their movements. Similarly, twinkle garments sparkle in reaction to sound, particularly the wearer's voice. LEDs, hand-embroidered to the garments, light up to create the twinkling effect.

- **Embedding Knitting Patterns in Knitted Objects:** Despite associations with antiquated traditions, knitting communities are often hotbeds of innovative approaches to high-tech textile production. Blending traditional craft with modern science, the "Know-It-All Bag" is a knitting bag embedded with a programmable microcontroller and 10 LEDs that express a series of knit stitches in light patterns (Craig, 2013). The programmable patterns help knitters to keep track of their stitching pattern while presenting an interpretation of knitting as software engineering.
- **Haute Couture Meets High Tech:** Bringing together experts from diverse fields such as microelectronics, wireless communication, embroidery, fashion design, and interaction design, the "Climate Dress" is an interactive dress that reacts to CO2 changes in the nearby surroundings (Diffus Design, 2013). Using several microcontrollers and a CO2 sensor, the dress responds to the CO2 concentration in the air by producing diverse light patterns with over a hundred LEDs—varying from

slow light pulsations to hectic flashes. The Climate Dress is a statement that, through an aesthetic representation of environmental data, contributes to the ongoing debate about environmental issues.

Though the applications of e-textiles are varied, virtually all projects are unified in their incongruity, their unique combination of surprisingly disparate elements and construction practices. These juxtapositions serve as an invitation—for expertise across physical and digital domains to coalesce and spark new connections, for newcomers to engage in unfamiliar modes of production, as well as for upending stereotypes of who constructs technology and for what (and whom) they are designed.

E-Textiles as the Intersection of Coding, Crafting, and Circuitry Construction

E-textile designs involve the multiple disciplines of computer science, engineering, and the arts as designers engage in the three intersecting domains of coding, crafting, and circuitry (Kafai, Fields, & Searle, 2012; Peppler, 2013). However, despite sharing many common roots with robotic constructions (whose appearance is often secondary—if considered at all—to their ability to execute a task), e-textile artifacts are frequently conceived of as aesthetically compelling designs with electronically enhanced capabilities.

As a backbone to nearly any project at the intersection of physical and digital media, computer programming or "coding" is essential to more interactive forms of e-textile design (Peppler, 2010). However, e-textile designers are less concerned with coding efficiency valued in computer science and engineering—i.e., having as few lines of codes as possible—than with the aesthetics of the design, aiming to achieve a particular artistic effect. For example, what feelings do LEDs sewn into a fabric induce in a viewer when they are programmed to glimmer softly as opposed to blink rapidly? Coding can take on many forms in e-textile projects, ranging from text-based coding environments, like Arduino (Banzi, 2008), to more novice-friendly graphical programming block environments, like Modkit (Baafi & Millner, 2011).

In addition to coding, when e-textile designers create new works, they must make educated guesses about what material to use or craft with in their designs. In most cases, novices to e-textiles do not fully understand the energy-transfer capabilities of physical objects and have difficulty distinguishing conductive from insulating materials. For example, even adult designers will incorrectly hypothesize that oil-based clay will be conductive (as they consider it to be "wet" [Peppler, Sharpe & Glosson, 2013]). Designers also often have to envision novel uses for existing materials (for example, glass beads to insulate the conductive thread, a zipper on a hoodie to act as a switch in the circuit, or a patch of conductive fabric as a capacitor) or turn to new materials such as conductive yarn, paint, or thread. Coming up with new uses for mundane materials, or understanding the physical properties of unfamiliar materials, can take considerable trial and error. Novice designers who forget about the material properties of thick, metallic-conductive thread and use it for decorative stitching as well as to sew their electronic circuits will unintentionally create shorts in the circuitry.

Creating e-textiles requires a firm understanding of electronic circuitry, yet even simple circuits can pose a challenge to new designers. For example, balancing the number of LEDs that can be lit by a 3V battery, accounting for Ohm's law, and wiring components in series and in parallel are all considerations that affect even the most basic e-textile construction (Peppler, Salen-Tekinbaş, Gresalfi, & Santo, 2014). New materials also offer unique possibilities in electronic designs—for example, the natural resistance of conductive thread can be used instead of a traditional resistor or in place of a commercially available dimmer switch (i.e., the longer the thread, the greater the resistance in the circuit, and the shorter the thread, the less

resistance in the circuit, which will cause the light to grow brighter). Much innovation in e-textile designs comes from creating textile analogues of traditional electronic components: soft speakers from magnets and conductive thread, switches from conductive beads, and so on (Perner-Wilson & Buechley, 2013).

By merging sewing and electronics practices, e-textiles meaningfully combine two sets of gendered practices and expectations associated with craft and electronic materials. Drawing upon mediated discourse theory, each set of e-textiles practices and materials is situated in a *nexus of practice* (Scollon, 2001), a set of social practices and artifacts tacitly-shared and valued among members in a cultural group. Each cultural practice—with related tools and materials—carries distinct expectations for whom and what constitutes experts and expertise. For example, skillful sewing with needles and fabric signals expertise in crafting or fashion cultures, while successful construction of a working circuit signals expertise in electrical engineering or STEM learning communities. Additionally, these practices signal femininities and masculinities in gendered communities of practice (Connell & Messerschmidt, 2005; Paechter, 2003) through histories of sewing (Beaudry, 2006) for girls and electronics for boys (Foster, 1995a/1995b) along with their contemporary traces in expectations for female consumers of craft kits and fashion and for male consumers of video games and robotics. This new nexus of e-textiles practice has implications for both participation and learning over time.

Textiles + Electronics: A Symbiotic History

Contemporary e-textiles represent a unique juxtaposition of high-tech (for example, sensors, electronics and code) and low-tech (i.e., traditional crafting) materials. Despite the chasm implied by these diverse materials, high-tech computing has a long and intimate relationship with crafting practice, arcing back to the development of the Jacquard loom in the early 1800s. The Jacquard loom—the first "programmed" mechanical device—enabled the user to feed customizable reels of punched paper into the loom that would result in the weaving of specific patterns. These looms, in turn, inspired the design of the first machine, Babbage's Analytical Engine (Essinger, 2007).

Similarly, the integration of electronics and textiles has rich historical precedents. The best electrical conductors, metals, have been incorporated into textiles for over a thousand years (Fisch, 1996; Harris, 1993). From armor to decorative clothing to wall hangings, metal of various sizes has been sewn into clothing for a variety of aesthetic and functional purposes. Cultures around the world have long celebrated the work of artisans, some of the earliest pioneers of metal-textile integration, who embroidered fine fabrics with threads wrapped in fine metal foils like gold and silver (Chung, 2005; Digby, 1964). By the late 1800s, engineers were imbuing electrical novelty into the design of electricity-enhanced clothing and jewelry, such as illuminated and/or motorized necklaces, hats, broaches, and costumes (Marvin, 1990; Gere & Rudoe, 2010).

Worldwide fascination with space exploration in the 1960s sparked an invigorated interest in the relationship between technology and apparel. The Museum of Contemporary Craft in New York City encapsulated this trend with a groundbreaking exhibition in 1968 that featured astronauts' space suits along with clothing that could inflate and deflate, light up, and heat and cool itself (Smith, 1968). Diana Dew, a designer who created an entire line of electronic fashion, including electro-luminescent party dresses and belts that could sound alarm sirens, was particularly noteworthy figure in this era.

The 1990s saw another leap forward in the advancement of textile-electronic interaction, led by two different research groups at MIT. One team, led by researchers Steve Mann, Thad Starner, and Sandy Pentland, coined the term "wearable computers," which referred to traditional computer hardware that could attach to and be carried on the body (Starner, 2002). A second team, led by Maggie Orth, integrated far-reaching perspectives ranging from medical applications to toy design to fashion to car manufacturing into the exploration of how computationally enhanced electronics could be gracefully integrated into clothing and made relevant across industry verticals (Post & Orth, 1997; Orth, Post, & Cooper, 1998; Post et al., 2000). This later approach represented a notable shift in the concept of e-textiles with its equal focus on material design and technological innovation, an honoring of both engineering and traditional craft lineages.

Since these initial investigations, a small but growing community of scientists and engineers in materials science, electrical engineering, and health sciences, along with a handful of pioneers in art and design, has been exploring e-textiles (e.g., Post et al., 2000; Marculescu et al., 2003; Pacelli et al., 2006; Papadopoulos, 2007). The field remained highly specialized and inaccessible until the recent introduction of e-textile construction kits (Buechley, 2006; Buechley et al., 2008), which made the previously prohibitively complex domain accessible to educators, hobbyist DIYers, and youth designers.

The Design and Democratization of E-Textile Construction Kits

Today, the market for consumer-ready e-textile design toolkits is wide and ever-expanding. Though there are several such kits worthy of attention, this chapter focuses on the design and development of four compelling examples: the *LilyPad Arduino* (Buechley, Elumeze, & Eisenberg, 2006), *i*CATch* (Ngai, Chan & Ng, 2013), *Schemer* (Elumeze, 2013), and *"a kit of no parts"* (Perner-Wilson & Buechley, 2013). Each of these kits takes a strikingly different approach to the blending of crafts, coding and electronic circuitry construction inherent in e-textile design (Peppler, 2013).

In 2008, an open-source design appeared on Instructables.com featuring a jacket with turn signals that could be illuminated by the bike rider (Instructables.com, 2008). The signals were powered by a LilyPad Arduino kit (or simply "LilyPad"), the first e-textiles toolkit created for a consumer market (Buechley & Eisenberg, 2009; Buechley, 2006). Designed by MIT Professor Leah Buechley, the LilyPad Arduino was conceived in a similar fashion as the Lego Mindstorms (LEGO) kit for robotics, requiring a basic understanding of programming and electronics, but allowed people to build interactive fashion instead of robots. The kit features a small, programmable computer—a variation of the popular Arduino microcontroller (Banzi, 2008) called the LilyPad Simple Board—in addition to LED lights, switches, motors, and sensors. The kit's custom electronics are recognizable by their colorful and round designs as well as the large sewable petals. The electronic pieces can then be stitched together with conductive thread to create soft, interactive devices, such as electronically enhanced t-shirts, electronic cuffs, and solar-powered backpacks (Peppler, Gresalfi, Salen Tekinbaş, & Santo, 2014).

The LilyPad was designed to overcome two substantive challenges facing consumer-ready e-textiles projects. The first was the redesign of everyday electronics to make them both sewable and washable. This included material substitutions so that, for example, the two legs found on a typical LED could be replaced with flat, sewable holes that could be easily stitched into clothing. The second challenge was the development of a sewable microcontroller—and an accompanying easy-to-use programming language—so that even young learners could code complex interactivity into their creations. The resulting wearable computer was handmade out of circular pieces of fabric where designers could literally sew through the fabric of the computer to create a connection rather than snapping or soldering connections. The LilyPad board was named because of its resemblance to a flower, with sewable petals arranged around a central computing device (Buechley, 2013). In response to growing consumer demand, Buechley teamed up with SparkFun Electronics to transform the textile circuit board into a small, thin metal circle with 22 sew-holes around its circumference while maintaining the flower-like layout. With its dual emphasis on sewing and programming, the LilyPad enables the construction of highly customizable projects, making it popular with designers, engineers, artists, and educators alike.

The LilyPad Arduino, though immensely popular in today's landscape, represents one of many approaches to combining textiles and electronics. Another kit, i*CATch, designed by Grace Ngai and colleagues, emphasizes the computational ideas and processes in e-textiles creation (Ngai et al., 2010). Users of this kit employ snap-on electronic modules that attach to pre-made garments, like vests and t-shirts. The garments contain lengths of a special tape that carry electrical signals from one place to another. The kit is designed so that novices can be freed from the arduous task of designing and sewing electrical connections, and focus instead on defining the behavior of their constructions using a visual programming environment. Analyses of novices' projects in workshops indicate that i*CATch successfully facilitates the creation of computationally complex projects and encourages iterative experimentation and trial-and-error learning, as well as collaborative learning (Ngai, Chan, & Ng, 2013). For example, Ngai and colleagues noticed children reusing code from introductory tasks in their final projects, and the complexity of their projects also increased from task to task because of the affordances of the i*CATch designs.

Taking a different approach to programming e-textile construction kits, Schemer (Elumeze, 2013) is a set of sewable electronic modules similarly constructed to the LilyPad designs but offering more versatile approaches to programming. For instance, designers can compile code for their e-textile creations using a screen-based application, as well as create them physically by drawing pictures, tapping musical notes and melodies, scanning barcodes printed on various surfaces like paper, cloth, or walls, or by using a range of colored pieces of felt, paper, and cloth. These "physical programs" are then uploaded to a wearable computer wirelessly by waving Schemer constructions across the surface so that a light sensor can read the program or playing a tune that can be heard by a sound sensor and interpreted by Schemer. This kit presents a glimpse into an exciting future of tangible programming, where people will not need to shift their focus from their physical environment to onscreen devices in order to code and reprogram their devices.

Hannah Perner-Wilson and Leah Buechley further explore the relationships between construction kits and raw materials in their "kit of no parts" (2013), a kit notable for its lack of prefabricated electronic components. In their place, electronic components can be constructed out of raw crafting materials like conductive and non-conductive thread, fabric, yarn, and beads. Over the course of several years, Perner-Wilson and Buechley designed, developed, and tested their sensor library consisting of four basic categories: tilt sensors, stroke sensors, stretch sensors, and pressure/bend sensors. The "stroke sensor," by way of example, is a soft carpet-like fabric that can detect when it is touched. When the tufts of conductive yarn or thread are stroked or compressed, the threads brush against one another, thus decreasing the resistance between the two strips of conductive fabric and sensing touch. This kit encourages the repurposing of everyday and low-cost materials in e-textile designs, affording novel opportunities for personalization and learning. Because every element of a sensor is made by hand, designers achieve a rich understanding of basic electronic and sensing principles. Moreover, completed designs exhibit a functional transparency that supports understanding—all of the functional elements of the sensors remain visible in the finished artifacts (Perner-Wilson & Buechley, 2013; Kafai & Peppler, 2014).

The kits showcased here represent a variety of ways to engage with the tensions between mixing textiles and electronics, each emphasizing different intellectual, cultural, and aesthetic affordances that exist at this intersection. For example, the LilyPad Arduino and a "kit of no parts" introduce tools that emphasize traditional crafts and make visible electrical connections, while i*CATch works primarily to deepen computational experiences by lowering barriers to entry by minimizing craft and electronic activities and concealing and abstracting electrical connections. Schemer sits on the opposite end of the spectrum in its approach to programming that takes computation to the physical world, providing a provocative alternative to the screen-based programming environments used by LilyPad Arduino and i*CATch. The "kit of no parts," by contrast, stresses the kinds of material creativity possible without the addition of computation. This tension is present even in the language used by the designers themselves; where most designers use "electronic textiles" to refer to their projects, the i*CATch creators prefer "wearable computers" when describing their approach to e-textile designs.

Taken together, this collection of e-textile construction kits begins to illustrate the broad and diverse potential of e-textiles, which can be used to explore ideas in a range of fields including design, art, computer science, and engineering, and the unique affordances of each of these different kits help support different educational approaches.

E-Textiles in Education

While new e-textile construction kits offer an exciting new range of tools and materials, novice educators and students need a set of compelling sample projects, new guiding pedagogies and workshop models, and clear ties to the existing education system (for example, to the Common Core State Standards and/or the Next Generation Science Standards) in order for e-textiles to be used in educational settings. Speaking to the gap between the first encounter with e-textiles and initial design ideas, Maggie Orth reports that the general public tends to view e-textiles as "magic" and is unable to imagine what could be realistically designed with these new tools and materials:

To the general public electronic textiles seem fantastic. I have never forgotten the doctor who asked me, "Can you make a coat that will detect how my patients will react to chemotherapy?"

"What technology do you use now?" I responded.

"There is none," he said. This man of science hoped that electronic textiles might do something that no existing 1000 lb. piece of commercial lab equipment could do. He thought electronic textiles might be magic (Orth, 2013, p. 201).

This speaks to the general challenge that new tools and materials confront as they are first being adopted by the broader public but particularly as we seek to excite the imaginations of young children and inspire them to create working prototypes with e-textiles.

Seeking to help populate the collective imagination and lower barriers to getting started with e-textile creation, a series of DIY books on e-textiles have been published over the last decade (Lewis & Lin, 2008; Pakhchyan, 2008; Eng, 2009; Buechley & Qiu, 2013). In addition, the authors have also co-designed new curricular toolkits along with leading national educators from the National Writing Project to help bridge the gap between e-textile activities and creating an educational curriculum (Peppler, Gresalfi, Salen Tekinbaş, & Santo, 2014; Peppler, Salen Tekinbaş, Gresalfi, & Santo, 2014). The *Interconnections* curricular toolkit, for example, supports a design-based approach to learning about ways that e-textiles aligns with current Common Core and Next Generation Science Standards while still being relevant to youth interests in fashion, storytelling, and puppetry (ibid.). The series teaches design and systems thinking concepts and skills in the context of e-textiles and includes four design challenges or learning projects in each volume.

Consequently, given the new tools and supporting materials now available, as well as the general push for more hands-on making in educational settings spurred on by the larger Maker Movement (Peppler & Bender, 2013; Dougherty, 2013; Anderson, 2012; Kafai, Fields, & Searle, 2014; Kafai, et al, 2013, 2014), the use of e-textiles is rapidly expanding in educational contexts. This can be seen in workshops and applications ranging from early childhood science classrooms (Peppler & Danish, 2013) to out-of-school fine arts programs (Peppler, Sharpe, & Glosson, 2013) to college engineering courses (Eisenberg, Eisenberg, & Huang, 2013). Across these settings, e-textiles represent opportunities to revisit misperceptions perpetuated by traditional tools and materials or to spark creative exploration at the intersection of two or more domains.

Opportunities to learn with e-textiles can extend to students considered too young to design with thread and electronic components. For instance, I have worked with learning scientist Joshua Danish on the creation of computationally enhanced puppets that engage children in complex systems learning via participatory simulation (Peppler & Danish, 2013). Using bee puppets embedded with sensors, students become a bee in search of honey. E-textile sensors embedded in the puppets keep track of nectar collected while children forage for more nectar before returning to a computationally enhanced "hive." Such embodied participatory simulations turn e-textiles into prototyping tools that educators can use to design and customize their own simulations in a variety of content areas. This takes e-textiles into the realm of augmented learning and moves that genre of educational technology past tablets and smartphones into other softer forms.

In more advanced grade levels, educators have introduced e-textile design to promote deeper learning and connections across disciplines. For example, there are few opportunities for youth to learn about computing and engineering in high school classes, especially ones that introduce computing with non-traditional materials. Many efforts have focused on game design or robotics activities that are popular with boys but limited in appeal to girls. In response, Yasmin Kafai, Deborah Fields, and Kristin Searle introduced e-textiles to high school youth in a series of workshops designed to examine how youth forge connections across crafting, engineering, and computing in the process of e-textiles creation (Kafai, Fields, & Searle, 2012). The researchers discovered that designing across disciplines promoted transparency of learning across stages of their projects—the designers would reflect upon and rethink how to code their programs as they stitched their circuits, and vice versa.

Other learning settings have explored the affordances of body sensing and other aspects of physical computing in youth sports and theater projects (Schelhowe et al, 2013). Using a construction kit called EduWear, researchers Heidi Schelhowe, Eva-Sophie Katterfeldt, Nadine Dittert, and Milena Reichel used e-textiles to help youth keep track of and learn from their body movements in sports. Similarly, a multidisciplinary team of artists, fashion designers, and computer programmers studying at Indiana University used a similar method of body sensors and wireless transmitters in a contemporary dance performance that facilitated multiple levels of interactivity between dancers, costumes, and the environment (Lindsay, 2013).

E-textiles have been used more broadly in fine arts classrooms to examine how students reconcile the tensions between artistic expression and developing technical skillsets in a new domain, pushing the boundaries of traditional digital and visual arts education (Peppler, Sharpe, & Glosson, 2013). In such settings, young artists transform formerly static objects into interactive canvases, as well as extend opportunities for artists to work their way into computing as they explore

new languages and materials. By contrast, Mike Eisenberg, Ann Eisenberg, and Yingdan Huang have shown how e-textiles can be used in engineering courses to develop complex projects and ideas at the college level and beyond (2013). In higher education, e-textiles not only bring new materials to think with (Papert, 1980) but also have been shown to challenge students' thinking about their disciplines.

E-Textiles in Society

E-textiles play an important role in the national landscape, particularly in helping to bridge traditional gendered divides between high- and low-tech fields and interests. While the last decade has seen a resurgence in vibrant Do-It-Yourself (DIY) communities in a range of disciplines, including electronics and textiles (Kuznetsov & Paulos, 2010; Levine & Heimerl, 2008; Frauenfelder, 2010), there continues to be a split in the kinds of online communities frequented by men and women (Buechley, Jacobs, & Mako Hill, 2013). For example, technology-driven DIY communities—such as popular electronics blogs like Hack-a-day (over 700,000 unique visitors per month), Gizmodo (approximately 5.8 million visitors), and MAKE (more than 100,000 visitors)—attract predominantly male members (ibid.). Meanwhile, there has been a resurgence of interest in crafts within a number of notable online communities. Burda Style, a site that allows people to share and remix sewing patterns, is accessed monthly by around 350,000. Ravelry.com enables people to share knitting patterns and projects and is visited by over 700,000 unique individuals each month. Lookbook.nu, a site where users share photos of themselves dressed in their favorite outfits, draws over 800,000 visitors a month. Across these communities, women make up the majority of participants, with current estimates that cite approximately 70% of each of these communities as being women (ibid.). While these are just a sampling of online DIY communities, they generally demonstrate that the electronics and textile DIY communities have a sharp gender divide with textile and crafts dominated by women and electronics communities by men.

These larger trends in online DIY communities also mirror the persistently lopsided gender makeup of computer and information science programs in US universities and colleges, suggesting that the gender gap in computing education is still obstinately wide and has been getting progressively worse since the 1980s (Weaver & Prey, 2013). Yet despite several national initiatives to diversify participation in STEM fields, the underlying culture of computing education remains relatively stagnant, with curriculum, tools, and materials that continue to emphasize areas historically aligned more closely with male interests than women's (Margolis & Fisher, 2003).

Within this larger landscape, the field of e-textiles offers a notable exception. The capacity for e-textiles to diversify participation and pull more women into high-tech making and online communities, was first documented by Leah Buechley and Benjamin Mako Hill (2010), who discovered that e-textiles were arguably becoming the first-ever female-dominated computing industry. While males created the majority of traditional Arduino projects posted on Vimeo, YouTube, Flickr, and other sites (85% vs. about 1% by female designers), women created most of the e-textile projects created with the LilyPad Arduino projects (65% vs. about 25% male designers). What is striking about this comparison is that both types of projects share the same microprocessor and are programmed in the same language. Researchers posit that the resulting gender discrepancy could be due to some combination of the tools and materials used, the construction practices employed, and the nature of the products.

Further, e-textiles demonstrate a great deal of promise for transforming classroom practice in similar ways to transforming the DIY landscape. For example, a series of e-textile design experi-

ments in middle school settings were conducted and the gender dynamics and participation patterns of girls and boys were observed (Peppler, 2013; Buccholz, Shively, Peppler, & Wohlwend, 2014). From videotaped observations of subjects working in mixed-gender pairs, the authors found that both boys and girls equally engaged in e-textile activity, as evidenced by body language, gaze, talk-on-task, and other indicators, but girls tended to play a greater leadership role. Furthermore, the projects were positioned in front of the girls 81% of the time; the girls also spent 58% of the time directing activity, troubleshooting, and deciding next steps and made only 39% of the requests for help from teachers and peers. Moreover, this early leadership was predictive of having more sophisticated command of the technology in subsequent projects, requiring less troubleshooting, time, and assistance from others. Upon further analyses, the authors also found that pairs determined who would take the lead on the activity based on the practice (and its gendered history) that they were to engage, with girls placed in the leadership role when it was time to sew or craft and boys placed in a leadership role when it was time to test or solder the connections (ibid). This division of labor was consistent but not negotiated within the groups, even when the boys had more prior experience and were more proficient in sewing than the girls.

Taken together, these studies suggest e-textiles can impact the computing culture in both "the wild" and in the classroom. This can be largely attributed to e-textiles being a unique nexus of three distinct and historically gendered practices: crafting, coding, and circuitry (Peppler, 2013). Each cultural practice—with related tools and materials—carries distinct expectations for whom and what constitutes experts and expertise. For example, skillful sewing with needles and fabric signals expertise in crafting or fashion cultures, while successful construction of a working circuit signals expertise in electrical engineering or STEM learning communities (ibid).

E-Textiles: Promoting Transparency and Improving Learning Outcomes

Within this landscape, current research suggests that e-textiles are not only effective tools for broadening participation in computing, but might also offer greater transparency into STEM disciplinary content (Kafai & Peppler, 2014). Most of today's technology designs intentionally hide or make invisible what makes them work. Think of the iPhone or iPad, for example. While consumers love these devices for their ease of use, users are encouraged to consult an expert for assistance—even changing the battery. While this type of "invisibility" into the inner workings of the device can aid consumption, especially for the novice user, we need to think critically about the kind of learning that is enabled and circumvented in these types of experiences, especially as we begin to rethink schooling in the 21st century. What are youth learning about new technologies in these types of interactions? And, more importantly, what are they not learning that is critical to high-quality educational experiences, and how can we better design for high-quality learning and engagement?

Consequently, Buechley and others argue that—particularly for educational purposes—we need to privilege "visibility" or transparency as more beneficial in promoting understanding and high-quality learning (Buechley, 2010; Kafai, & Peppler, 2014). Moreover, e-textiles present particularly compelling examples of high-quality and transparent learning tools in that they make technology visible for the learner. For example, the uninsulated threads allow for shorts that are oftentimes prevented with our typical electronics toolkits, where we might snap circuits together with alligator clips or other similar devices. While these types of kits may be useful for helping the learner to meet the goal (i.e., illuminating a light bulb), the same designs that allow for easy entry and a high probability of success also appear to be detrimental to conceptual engagement, circumventing high-quality learning experiences.

Over the past few decades, traditional circuitry construction kits have been failing young learners, as they are arriving at college without an understanding of the big ideas important to electronics and computing (for a review, see Peppler & Glosson, 2013a as well as Maloney et al., 2008). Fortunately, contemporary electronics and computing is rife with new tools and materials that are spurring shifts in the ways we interact with technology, presenting opportunities for us to reshape learning and participation. To offer a compelling (but not an isolated) example, I have explored how this type of visibility in e-textiles is particularly suitable for engaging learners in high-quality conceptual engagement in circuitry (Peppler & Glosson, 2013a, 2013b; Peppler, 2014), which will be further presented below. Similar types of explorations into the role of conceptual understanding of coding and crafting are warranted and have been explored by Kafai and colleagues (Kafai, Fields, & Searle, 2013).

Transparency, E-Textiles, and Conceptual Understanding of Circuits

Central to our understanding of learning is the relationship between various tools and technologies and the structuring of disciplinary subject matter. Papert, for example, invited closer investigation of the specific tools we have available (i.e., "objects to think with") as they highly impact our ontological perspectives (1980). Emerging empirical research exists to inform our understanding of how our tools and materials shape learning and participation across this emerging technological landscape.

For instance, conceptual understanding of electrical circuitry is foundational to later engagement in many fields, including physics, engineering, and computer science, and is part of a broader investigation of energy within the physical sciences in the National Science Standards. Research over the years, however, has consistently shown how students have misconceptions about circuitry concepts and procedural knowledge stemming from the tools and materials used in classroom learning experiences. Andersson and Karrqvist (1979), for example, showed how 15-year-olds had difficulty understanding how the light bulb worked due to the invisibility of the two terminals of the bulb (i.e., it's unclear how the light bulb truly connects to the battery source). The same "invisibility factor" applies to light sockets, and some types of batteries. In further probing for misconceptions among undergraduates enrolled in introductory physics and engineering courses, Fredette and Lockhead (1980) concluded that schools needed to be more explicit in helping students understand how all elements of a circuit require voltage to pass through an IN and an OUT terminal in early physics education.

Leveraging new materials to inform youths' understanding of electronics is especially apt given the historical prevalence of youths' conceptual misunderstandings of simple circuitry (Evans, 1978; Thiberghien & Delacorte, 1976). In sum, students need in-depth understanding of the anatomy of each component in a circuit—an electrical power source, a load, and some wire to connect them in the most basic configuration—as well as fundamental concepts of how these components interact with each other; namely current flow (Osborne, 1981; Osborne, 1983; Shipstone, 1984), battery polarity (Osborne et al., 1991), and circuit connections (Osborne, 1983; Shepardson & Moje, 1994; Asoko, 1996), further defined below:

- *Current flow* is traditionally defined as a current (i.e., flow) around a circuit (i.e., following one of the simple circuit current models) (Osborne, 1981).
- *Polarity* is used when discussing connections, when the proper battery terminals are connected to the proper LED terminals in a simple circuit. It was defined in the 1991

Electricity report as "the necessity for any circuit to have two connections to a device and an electrical power source" (Osborne et al., 1981, p. 43).

- *Connection* refers to the joining of electrical parts to form a working circuit, thus lighting the bulb (Osborne, 1983; Osborne et al., 1981; Shepardson & Moje, 1994).

In prior work (Peppler & Glosson, 2013a), youth engagement in a 20-hour e-textile activities, involving the sewing of electronics into fabric-based materials using conductive thread, had shown gains in their ability to diagram working circuits, as well as specific circuitry concepts like current flow, connections, and polarity. While it's clear that e-textiles can contribute to conceptual learning about circuitry, it is unclear whether e-textiles can outperform traditional or other new circuitry toolkits that are on the market today. Further, it is unclear how long youth needed to engage the materials before walking away with this understanding. Further study should attempt to examine both a comparative view of the commercially available tools and materials as well as to determine whether any significant gains in understanding can be made in a much smaller timescale.

Circuit Diagrams: Assessing Learning

Historically, knowledge of circuits is usually assessed through circuit diagrams (Osborne, 1983). Students are tasked with diagraming a sample circuit with the materials used to create it—in most cases, this includes a 9V battery, a small light bulb, and wiring—and then indicate the direction of current flow. However, such assessments are historically tightly tied to the tools that are used in the learning experience, meaning that circuit diagrams consist of the same types of tools and materials used in the hands-on learning. Consequently, new assessments need to reflect the new materials when we move from using traditional electric circuit drawings that use light bulbs and batteries to draw upon pieces from the LilyPad e-textiles sewing kit (for example, a battery holder, LED, and switch), which the learner would be using in e-textile workshops.

In our recent study of conceptual understanding of circuitry after e-textile experience, youth were asked to use a set of LilyPad part stickers marked with clear positive and negative terminals to create a functioning circuit by drawing lines between the appropriate terminals. This assessment tests their knowledge of basic circuitry, specifically whether youth could create an overall working circuit, but more specifically, whether they understood three core concepts: current flow (i.e., completed circular paths with no redundancy or shorts), connections (i.e., completed lines successfully connecting one component to another and attention paid to the particular points of conductivity), and polarity (i.e., being mindful that the battery and LED have a positive side and a negative side).

In this work, we found that even those students with prior experience constructing simple circuits could not translate this understanding to the new materials. However, after creating with e-textile materials, we found that students significantly increased their understanding of key circuitry concepts (Peppler & Glosson, 2013a). Results demonstrated that students were able to diagram a working circuit considerably better in post-assessments than in pre-assessments. In addition, the students significantly increased their knowledge of current flow ($p < .05$), circuit polarity or directionality ($p < .05$), and connection ($p < .05$)—concepts even college undergraduates in introductory physics and engineering courses have persistent misunderstandings about (Fredette & Lochhead, 1980). Taken together, this work suggests e-textiles as a compelling case for transparency in the learning process.

New vs. Existing "Clubhouses"

Collectively, this body of research raises several key issues in the field. The first issue pertains to the endgame of introducing, or even replacing, traditional toolkits with new tools and materials in STEM, arts, and other classrooms. Specifically, what do e-textiles represent for the current and future issue of gender in computing? Despite the calls in recent decades to address the shrinking pipeline of underrepresented groups in engineering and computing professions, these fields remain male dominated. E-textiles signify an entirely different approach to diversifying these fields and what people can produce in them. This stands in stark contrast to prior endeavors to make monolithically gendered STEM cultures more accessible to women, as highlighted in Margolis and Fisher's groundbreaking study, "Unlocking the Clubhouse" (Margolis & Fisher, 2001; Fisher & Margolis, 2002). Instead of trying to fit people into existing cultures, current research on e-textiles provides us with a glimpse of what a "new clubhouse" may look like—one where decorative, feminine or otherwise "non-robotics" forms of engineering are not only encouraged but are poised to disrupt what we know about and who participates in STEM careers in the 21st century. In this view, the pipeline challenge of gender participation in STEM exists not because STEM cultures are unfairly exclusive but because they're limited in intellectual and cultural breadth. Some of the most revealing research in diversity has found that women and other minorities don't join communities, not because they are intimidated or unqualified but rather because they're simply uninterested (Weinberger, 2004). This is where the concept of e-textiles as a nexus of gendered practice shows promise as an attractive pathway to the rich intellectual possibilities of computation, engineering, craft, and design. This serves to benefit not only women and other underrepresented populations in STEM, but for the technical and cultural growth of the disciplines, themselves, re-contextualized by new tools and reenvisioned by new participants.

Feminist vs. Feminine Technologies

Implied in the current research is a cautious optimism that such women's participation in STEM may result in more widespread appreciation for the relevance, complexity, and importance of traditionally female-dominated pursuits. However, another key tension in this work pertains to the relationship between contemporary women and traditional "women's skills," like crafting and sewing. A number of women in academia and STEM fields, for example, see such skills as reinforcements of exhausted stereotypes and see them as retrogressions in the quest for greater respect from the broader STEM community. Bardzell speaks to this tension in her distinction between "feminine" and "feminist" technology (Bardzell, 2010, 2013; Layne et al., 2010). The latter describes explicit and intentional integration of feminist theory (and goals) with human-computer interaction research and practice. Feminist technologies include "tools and knowledge that enhance women's ability to develop, expand, and express their capacity" (Layne et al., 2010) while feminine technologies are "technologies associated with women by virtue of their biology" (McGaw, 2003, 1996, cited in Layne et al., 2010). Because of their complicated history and diverse applications, e-textiles can be both feminine technology and feminist technology, depending on the context of use; inasmuch as e-textiles enable designers to develop and expand embodied interactive experiences or generate strategies to increase the participation of historically marginalized users, they can be understood as feminist technologies.

WHAT ARE THE GAPS IN THE EXTANT RESEARCH AND DIRECTION FOR FUTURE RESEARCH?

The studies above suggest that we need to better understand a wider range of tools and materials (for example, those toolkits that are more masculine and/or gender neutral have yet to be systematically investigated). Early pilot data suggests that on tools and materials that are seen as tools for boys, boys will take the lead, reversing the patterns seen with e-textiles. This signals a call for additional research exploring the vast range of materials and tools being utilized within the educational spaces in order to better understand how cultural expectations materialize as mediated actions and authorize particular tool uses and tool users. More research is also needed to better understand the specific design features that are associated with gendered histories of tool use so that we might better be able to design tools in the future.

Similarly, there are some noticeable limitations of the early studies on transparency in learning. They have not yet revealed the specific design features that support learning, a comparative sense of whether e-textiles are more efficacious than other toolkits for learning about circuitry and computing more broadly, and whether the improved understanding of circuits is retained over time (i.e., does this new training impact long-term learning outcomes?), among other emergent questions in this line of inquiry. Seeking to address some of the prior limitations, we have currently developed new assessments to test for transfer of conceptual understanding to a broader range of electronic toolkits (testing for near and far transfer) (Peppler et al., 2015). However, there is also a need for a similar set of assessments to be developed to test for understanding of code or computation necessary in e-textile construction toolkits and how this might be transferred to other languages, tools, and materials.

In addition to the gaps in the prior research outlined above, there are four main gaps in the existing research and practice: (1) There is a gap in understanding of how to bridge DIY e-textile culture and classroom practice— though there are a number of emerging sites that are using e-textiles in schools and even across whole school districts. More research is needed on the efficacy of e-textile integration in schools as pathways into learning. (2) While there is an abundance of anecdotal evidence, there is no research on the long-term impact of e-textiles for learning and participation and there is subsequently a need for longitudinal studies that track the impact of early e-textiles design opportunities on subsequent careers, identities, and interests. (3) There is a need for more research on the intersection of the physical and the digital world. How does this translation between the physical and the digital support learning? What are the key challenges and what needs to be understood by today's youth? Lastly, (4) how can we use the set of emerging design principles outlined above to look at our existing classroom toolkits as well as envision new materials to support learning that is more open to expressive, iterative, and production-centered ways of participating in the classroom?

Implications for Learning

E-textiles serve to highlight that tools fundamentally change the way one relates to disciplinary content and that moving to a new set of tools makes visible concepts that otherwise may have been invisible to the learner. Such a shift is evident in the prior research, especially, where youths' conceptual understandings of current flow, connections and battery polarity were challenged and revised upon the move from designing circuits using traditional toolkits to fabricating them using e-textile materials.

In some ways, the additional challenges posed by the e-textile materials (for example, the sewing and other fine motor activities) themselves, are compensated by the deeper relationships to content that can be forged through troubleshooting. In contrast to this is the relative simplicity of more traditional tools for teaching introductory circuitry; though perhaps quicker to prototype with (for example, insulated wires, simplified design of bulbs vs. LED components, etc.), these toolkits unnecessarily limit the number and variety of mistakes that can be made in circuit construction. This may explain why prior research has repeatedly shown the limitation of these materials for providing deep insights into how connections, polarity, and current flow work. By contrast, the use of the LilyPad Arduino toolkit allows for more diverse ways for youth to "short" or "break" their circuit, creating manifold opportunities for discussion and questioning of misconceptions. What results is a deeper conceptual understanding through the mistakes and reasoning to fix those mistakes providing opportunities to fix those lingering conceptual misconceptions.

This constitutes a larger rationale for rethinking educational toolkits to support learning in other domains as well. Arguably, the most effective toolkits for educational settings allow learners to make a large number of mistakes (i.e., are more expressive) and should do less to scaffold the learning process. Underpinning this approach is a fundamental view that learning happens best when toolkits afford a sense of transparency by providing opportunities for concretizing knowledge through tinkering with the materials. This "revaluation of the concrete" (Turkle & Papert, 1992) is an epistemological stance towards knowledge—the relationships that learners build with knowledge and pathways that facilitate such knowledge construction.

There are also other reasons to consider the addition of e-textile toolkits in education. Given the recent emergence of national standards in science education that explicitly task educators to organize and present core content with many different emphases and perspectives in order to develop curricula that appeals to *all* students, "regardless of age, gender, cultural or ethnic background, disabilities, aspirations, or interest and motivation in science" (National Research Council of the National Academies, 2011, p. 2), now is an especially apt time to rethink the scope of what tools for scientific inquiry are included in the classroom so as to best support the diverse interests and experiences of youth, especially those in populations that science education in the United States has traditionally failed to engage—namely, women and students of color. E-textiles, as one example of a new domain to support science and engineering practices, has already demonstrated its capacity in the professional realm to invite and sustain participation from women (Buechley & Mako Hill, 2010). Thus, the emergence of e-textiles as a magnet for creative engineering from traditionally underrepresented groups represents the impact that a richer range of materials in early science education can have on the demographics and perspectives of the next generation of STEM professionals.

In contrast to theorizing that gender disparities evident particularly in STEM fields demonstrate an inherent "lack" in girls (i.e., girls *lack* the skills, interest, or confidence necessary to participate equitably with male counterparts), we should be reconceptualizing these disparities by looking at tacit expectations for cultural practices and social actors that are concretized through historical uses of tools, materials, and gendered communities of practice (Paechter, 2003; Buccholz, Shively, Peppler, & Wohlwend, 2014). Rather than viewing gender as a static identity marker that defines participation in electronics and computing projects, research is demonstrating that histories of materials, tools, and practices influenced which member of the dyads was implicitly granted hands-on access. In this case of e-textiles, the replacement of the traditional circuitry toolkit with new materials and tools like needles, fabric, and conductive thread ruptured traditional gender scripts around electronics and computing. In turn, girls take on leadership roles in completing highly complex electronics projects by engaging in practices historically embedded within communities of practice with gendered histories.

Implications for Participation

To date, efforts to draw more female youth into STEM-related pathways and experiences have largely revolved around two major efforts: (a) keeping male and female youth/children separated in STEM-related classes or clubs (e.g., Khoja, Wainwright, Brosing, & Barlow, 2012; Marcu et al., 2010) and (b) encouraging female youth/children to play with "boys'" toys and tools (i.e., toys and tools with masculinized identity markers; e.g., Clegg, 2001; Hartmann, Wiesner, & Wiesner-Steiner, 2007; Stepulevage, 2001). The first effort, to keep males and females separated, is exemplified in "girls only day" at a local computer club or same-sex math and science classes in some schools. The assumption is that creating a bounded and protected space for female youth will ensure that females are not intimidated by males who may appear to be more confident and competent. The intention is to provide equitable access to tools and materials in mixed-gender settings. The second effort is based on children's gendered toy preferences from a very young age. The assumption is that if only girls would take up LEGOs and science kits instead of Barbie dolls and crafting kits, we would not see the stark gender disparities in STEM pathways later; in other words, if girls just played more with boys' toys, gender scripts would change.

Both of these efforts are problematic, positioning girls within a cultural deficit model that either presupposes that girls need to be protected because they are weak and/or that girls need to change to become more like their male counterparts. Current research suggests a new path forward, one that takes a strength orientation to girls and the tools, materials, and practices that have historically been valued in feminine communities of practice. Across the dyads studied, we found that that gender scripts within electronics and computing were not absolutely fixed, as is assumed in much of the research, but rather that gender scripts are socially situated within tools, materials, and practices.

CONCLUSION

This work offers a glimpse of the transformative power of considering how tools—bearing traces of their histories of use and access—mediate youth's interactions and participation in classroom spaces. In this case, e-textile toolkits successfully flip the gendered scripts about who had hands-on access to electronics materials and tools by honoring girls' historic practices and, in doing so, expanded the ways into complex electronics and computing content. This seemingly small change in the materials and tools produces a rippling effect on the youth's classroom practices. Moreover, classrooms, clubs, and after-school settings should consider how altering materials and tools may situate STEM practices in cultural contexts that broaden participation patterns and offer youth multiple entry points and opportunities to perform identities that are socially valued across communities of practice and their gendered histories.

REFERENCES

Anderson, C. (2012). *Makers: The new industrial revolution*. New York, NY: Random House.

Andersson, B., & Karrqvist, C. (1979). *Elektriska Kretsar* (Electric Circuits). EKNA Report No 2, University of Gothenburg, Mölndal, Sweden.

Asoko, H. (1996). Developing scientific concepts in the primary classroom: Teaching about electric circuits. In G. Welford, J. Osborne, & P. Scott (Eds.), *Research in science education in Europe* (pp. 36–49). London: Falmer Press.

Baafi, E., & Millner, A. (2011). Modkit: A toolkit for tinkering with tangibles & connecting communities. In *Proc. 5th Int'l Conf. Tangible, Embedded, and Embodied Interaction* (TEI 11) (349-352). ACM.

Banzi, M. (2008). *Getting Started with Arduino* (1st ed.). Text Only.

Bardzell, S. (2010). Feminist HCI: Taking Stock and Outlining an Agenda for Design. In *Proceedings of the 28th International Conference on Human Factors in Computing Systems* (pp. 1301–1310). Atlanta, GA: ACM. doi:10.1145/1753326.1753521

Bardzell, S. (2013). E-Textiles and the body: Feminist technologies in design research. In L. Buechley, K. Peppler, M. Eisenberg, & Y. Kafai (Eds.), Textile Messages: Dispatches from the World of E-Textiles and Education. Academic Press.

Beaudry, M. C. (2006). *Findings: The material culture of needlework and sewing*. Princeton, NJ: Yale University Press.

Buccholz, B., Shively, K., Peppler, K., & Wohlwend, K. (2014). Hands on, hands off: Gendered access in sewing and electronics practices. *Mind, Culture, and Activity*, *21*(4), 278–297. doi:10.1080/10749039.2014.939762

Buechley, L. (2006). A construction kit for electronic textiles. In *Proceedings of IEEE International Symposium on Wearable Computers* (ISWC). Montreux, Switzerland: IEEE.

Buechley, L. (2010). Questioning invisibility. *Computer*, *43*(4), 84–86. doi:10.1109/MC.2010.114

Buechley, L. (2013). Lilypad arduino: E-textiles for everyone. In L. Buechley, K. Peppler, M. Eisenberg, & Y. Kafai (Eds.), Textile Messages: Dispatches from the World of E-Textiles and Education. Academic Press.

Buechley, L., & Eisenberg, M. (2009). Fabric PCBs, electronic sequins, and socket buttons: Techniques for e-textile craft. *Personal and Ubiquitous Computing*, *13*(2), 133–150. doi:10.1007/s00779-007-0181-0

Buechley, L., Elumeze, N., & Eisenberg, M. (2006). Electronic/computational textiles and children's crafts. In *Proceedings of the 2006 Conference on Interaction Design and Children* (pp. 49-56). Tampere, Finland: ACM. doi:10.1145/1139073.1139091

Buechley, L., Jacobs, J., & Mako Hill, B. (2013). Lilypad in the wild: Technology DIY, e-textiles, and gender. In L. Buechley, K. Peppler, M. Eisenberg, & Y. Kafai (Eds.), Textile Messages: Dispatches from the World of E-Textiles and Education. Academic Press.

Buechley, L., & Mako Hill, B. (2010). LilyPad in the wild: How hardware's long tail is supporting new engineering and design communities. In *Proceedings of the Conference on Designing Interactive Systems* (pp. 199-207). ACM Press. doi:10.1145/1858171.1858206

Buechley, L., Peppler, K. A., Eisenberg, M., & Kafai, Y. B. (Eds.). (2013). *Textile Messages: Dispatches from the World of E-Textiles and Education*. New York: Peter Lang.

Buechley, L., & Qiu, J. (2013). *Sew Electric*. Cambridge, MA: HLT Press.

Chalayan, H. (2011). *From Fashion and Back*. Bss Bijutsu.

Chung, Y. (2005). *Silken Threads: A History of Embroidery in China, Korea, Japan, and Vietnam*. New York: Harry N. Abrams.

Clegg, S. (2001). Theorising the machine: Gender, education and computing. *Gender and Education*, *13*(3), 307–324. doi:10.1080/09540250120063580

Connell, R. W., & Messerschmidt, J. W. (2005). Hegemonic masculinity: Rethinking the concept. *Gender & Society*, *19*(6), 829–859. doi:10.1177/0891243205278639

Craig, K. (2013). *Know It All Bag*. Retrieved from http://www.knitty.com/ISSUEss10/PATT-knowitall.php

Design, D. (2013). *When technology meets sensuality*. Paper presented at the Smart Fabrics Conference, Barcelona, Spain.

Digby, G. (1964). *Elizabethan Embroidery*. New York: Yoseloff.

Dougherty, D. (2013). The maker mindset. In M. Honey & D. E. Kanter (Eds.), *Design, make, play: Growing the next generation of STEM innovators* (pp. 7–11). New York, NY: Routledge.

Eisenberg, M., Eisenberg, A., & Huang, Y. (2013). Bringing e-textiles into engineering education. In L. Buechley, K. Peppler, M. Eisenberg, & Y. Kafai (Eds.), *Textile Messages: Dispatches from the World of E-Textiles and Education*.

Elumeze, N. (2013). Traveling light: Making textiles programmable "through the air.". In L. Buechley, K. Peppler, M. Eisenberg, & Y. Kafai (Eds.), *Textile Messages: Dispatches from the World of E-Textiles and Education*.

Eng, D. (2009). *Fashion Geek: Clothes Accessories Tech*. Cincinnati, OH: North Lights Books.

Eng, D. (2013). *Fairytale Fashion*. Retrieved from www.FairytaleFashion.org

Essinger, J. (2007). *Jacquard's Web: How a Hand-Loom Led to the Birth of the Information Age*. New York: Oxford University Press.

Evans, J. (1978). Teaching electricity with batteries and bulbs. *The Physics Teacher*, *16*(1), 15–22. doi:10.1119/1.2339794

Fisch, A. (1996). *Textile Techniques in Metal.* Asheville, NC: Lark Books.

Fisher, A., & Margolis, J. (2002). Unlocking the clubhouse: The Carnegie Mellon experience. ACM SIGCSE Bulletin Women and Computing, 34(2), 79-83.

Foster, P. N. (1995a). Industrial arts/technology education as a social study: The original intent? *Journal of Technology Education, 6*(2), 4–18.

Foster, P. N. (1995b). The founders of industrial arts in the US. *Journal of Technology Education, 7*(1), 6–21.

Frauenfelder, M. (2010). *Made by Hand: Searching for Meaning in a Throwaway World.* Portfolio Hardcover.

Fredette, N., & Lochhead, J. (1980). Students' conceptions of simple circuits. *The Physics Teacher, 18*(3), 194–198. doi:10.1119/1.2340470

Gere, C., & Rudoe, J. (2010). *Jewelry in the Age of Queen Victoria: A Mirror to the World.* London: British Museum Press.

Harris, J. (Ed.). (1993). *Textiles, 5,000 Years: An International History and Illustrated Survey.* New York: H.N. Abrams.

Hartmann, S., Wiesner, H., & Wiesner-Steiner, A. (2007). Robotics and gender: The use of robotics for the advancement of equal opportunities in the classroom. In Gender Designs IT Construction and Deconstruction of Information Society (pp. 175-188). Academic Press.

Instructables.com & the Editors at MAKE Magazine. (2008). The Best of Instructables Volume I: Do-It-Yourself Projects from the World's Biggest Show & Tell. Authors.

Kafai, Y., Fields, D., & Searle, K. (2012). Making technology visible: Connecting the learning of crafts, circuitry, and coding in youth e-textile designs. In *Proceedings of the International Conference of the Learning Sciences (ICLS).* Sydney, Australia: Academic Press.

Kafai, Y., Fields, D., & Searle, K. (2014). Electronic textiles as disruptive designs: Supporting and challenging maker activities in schools. *Harvard Educational Review, 84*(4), 532–556. doi:10.17763/haer.84.4.46m7372370214783

Kafai, Y., Lee, E., Searle, K., Fields, D., Kaplan, E., and Lui, D. (2014). A crafts-oriented approach to computing in high school: Introducing computational concepts, practices, and perspectives with electronic textiles. *ACM Transactions on Computing Education, 14*(1). DOI: 10.1145/2576874

Kafai, Y., & Peppler, K. (2014). Transparency reconsidered: Creative, critical, and connected making with e-textiles. In M. Boler & M. Ratto (Eds.), *DIY Citizenship* (pp. 179–188). Cambridge, MA: MIT Press.

Kafai, Y., Searle, K., Kaplan, E., Fields, D., Lee, E., & Lui, D. (2013). Cupcake cushions, Scooby Doo shirts, and soft boomboxes: E-textiles in high school to promote computational concepts, practices, and perceptions. In *Proceeding of the 44th ACM Technical Symposium on Computer Science Education.* ACM. Doi:10.1145/2445196.2445291

Kaufmann, B., & Buechley, L. 2010. Amarino: A toolkit for the rapid prototyping of mobile ubiquitous computing. In Proceedings of Mobile HCI. Lisbon, Portugal: Academic Press. doi:10.1145/1851600.1851652

Khoja, S., Wainwright, C., Brosing, J., & Barlow, J. (2012). Changing girls' attitudes towards computer science. *Journal of Computing Sciences in Colleges, 28*(1), 210–216.

Kuznetsov, S., and Paulos, E. (2010). *Rise of the Expert Amateur: DIY Projects, Communities, and Cultures.* Paper presented at ACM NordiCHI, Reykjavík, Iceland.

Layne, L., Vostral, S., & Boyer, K. (Eds.). (2010). *Feminist Technology.* University of Ilinois Press.

Levine, F., & Heimerl, C. (2008). *Handmade Nation: The Rise of DIY, Art, Craft, and Design.* New York: Princeton Architectural Press.

Lewis, A., & Lin, F. (2008). *SwitchCraft: Battery-Powered Crafts to make and Sew.* New York: Crown Publishing Group.

Lindsay, E. (2013). The space between us: Electronic music + modern dance + e-textiles. In L. Buechley, K. Peppler, M. Eisenberg, & Y. Kafai (Eds.), *Textile Messages: Dispatches from the World of E-Textiles and Education.*

Maloney, J., Peppler, K., Kafai, Y. B., Resnick, M., & Rusk, N. (2008). *Programming by choice: Urban youth learning programming with scratch. Published in the.* Portland, OR: Proceedings by the ACM Special Interest Group on Computer Science Education. doi:10.1145/1352135.1352260

Marcu, G., Kaufman, S. J., Lee, J. K., Black, R. W., Dourish, P., Hayes, G. R., & Richardson, D. J. (2010, March). Design and evaluation of a computer science and engineering course for middle school girls. In *Proceedings of the 41st ACM technical symposium on computer science education* (pp. 234–238). New York, NY: ACM. doi:10.1145/1734263.1734344

Marculescu, D., Marculescu, R., Zamora, N., Stanley-Marbell, P., Kholsa, P., Park, S., ... (2003). Electronic textiles: A platform for pervasive computing. *Proceedings of the IEEE.* citeseer. ist.psu.edu/marculescu03electronic.html

Margolis, J., & Fisher, A. (2001). *Unlocking the Clubhouse: Women in Computing.* Boston, MA: MIT press.

Marvin, C. (1990). *When Old Technologies Were New: Thinking About Electric Communication in the Late Nineteenth Century.* New York: Oxford University Press.

McGaw, J. (2003/1996). Reconceiving technology: Why feminine technologies matter. *Gender and Archaeology,* 52–75.

National Research Council of the National Academies. (2011). *A Framework for K-12 science education: Practices, crosscutting concepts, and core ideas.* Washington, DC: National Academies Press.

Ngai, G., Chan, S., & Ng, V. (2013). Designing i*CATch: A multipurpose, education-friendly construction kit for physical and wearable computing. AC Trans. *Computers & Education, 13*(2). doi:10.1145/2483710.2483712

Ngai, G., Chan, S., Ng, V., Cheung, J., Choy, S., Lau, W., & Tse, J. (2010) I*CATch: A scalable plug-n-play wearable computing framework for novices and children. In *Proceedings of the 28th International Conference on Human Factors in Computing Systems* (pp. 443-452). Atlanta, GA: ACM.

Orth, M. (2013). Adventures in electronic textiles. In L. Buechley, K. Peppler, M. Eisenberg, & Y. Kafai (Eds.), Textile Messages: Dispatches from the World of E-Textiles and Education. Academic Press.

Orth, M., Post, R., & Cooper, E. (1998). Fabric computing interfaces. In Proceedings of CHI 98 Conference Summary on Human Factors in Computing Systems (pp. 331-332). New York: ACM. doi:10.1145/286498.286800

Osborne, R. (1981). Children's ideas about electric current. *New Zealand Science Teacher, 29*, 12–19.

Osborne, R. (1983). Towards modifying children's ideas about electric current. *Research in Science & Technological Education, 1*(1), 73–82. doi:10.1080/0263514830010108

Osborne, R., Tasker, R., & Schollum, B. (1981). *Video: Electric current*, working paper no. 51, *Learning in Science Projects*. Hamilton, New Zealand: SERA, University of Waikato.

Pacelli, M., Loriga, G., Taccini, N., & Paradiso, R. (2006). Sensing fabrics for monitoring physiological and biomechanical variables: E-textile solutions. In *Proceedings of the 3rd IEEE EMBS Intl Summer School and Symposium on Medical Devices and Biosensors*. Boston, MA: ACM. doi:10.1109/ISSMDBS.2006.360082

Paechter, C. (2003). Masculinities and femininities as communities of practice. *Women's Studies International Forum, 26*(1), 69–77. doi:10.1016/S0277-5395(02)00356-4

Pakhchyan, S. (2008). *Fashioning Technology: A DIY Intro to Smart Crafting*. Cambridge, MA: O'Reilly Media.

Papadopoulos, D. (2007). Wearable technologies, portable architectures and the vicissitudes of the space between. *Architectural Design, 77*(4), 62–67. doi:10.1002/ad.488

Papert, S. (1980). *Mindstorms: Children, computers, and powerful ideas*. New York: Basic Books.

Peppler, K. (2010). The new fundamentals: Introducing computation into arts education. In E. Clapp & M. J. Bellino (Eds.), 20Under40: Reinventing the Arts and Arts Education for the 21st Century. Bloomington, IN: AuthorHouse.

Peppler, K. (2013). STEAM-powered computing education: Using e-textiles to integrate the arts and STEM. *IEEE Computer, 46*(9), 38–43. doi:10.1109/MC.2013.257

Peppler, K. (2014). *New Creativity Paradigms: Arts Learning in the Digital Age*. New York, NY: Peter Lang Publishing.

Peppler, K., & Bender, S. (2013). Maker movement spreads innovation one project at a time. *Phi Delta Kappan, 95*(3), 22–27. doi:10.1177/003172171309500306

Peppler, K., & Danish, J. (2013). E-textiles for educators: Participatory simulations with e-puppetry. In L. Buechley, K. Peppler, M. Eisenberg, & Y. Kafai (Eds.), *Textile Messages: Dispatches from the World of E-Textiles and Education* (pp. 133–141). New York, NY: Peter Lang Publishing.

Peppler, K., & Glosson, D. (2013a). Stitching circuits: Learning about circuitry through e-textile materials. *Journal of Science Education and Technology, 22*(5), 751–763. doi:10.1007/s10956-012-9428-2

Peppler, K., & Glosson, D. (2013b). Learning about circuitry with e-textiles. In M. Knobel & C. Lankshear (Eds.), *The New Literacies Reader*. New York, NY: Peter Lang Publishing.

Peppler, K., Gresalfi, M., Salen Tekinbaş, K., & Santo, R. (2014). *Soft Circuits: Crafting E-Fashion with DIY Electronics*. Cambridge, MA: MIT Press.

Peppler, K., Sharpe, L., & Glosson, D. (2013). E-textiles and the new fundamentals of fine arts. In L. Buechley, K. Peppler, M. Eisenberg, & Y. Kafai (Eds.), *Textile Messages: Dispatches from the World of E-Textiles and Education* (pp. 107–117). New York, NY: Peter Lang Publishing.

Peppler, K., Tan, V., Thompson, N., & Bender, S. (2015). *New tools for circuitry learning: evaluating the efficacy of circuitry construction kits.* Paper Presentation at the 2015 American Educational Research Association Conference.

Perner-Wilson, H., & Buechley, L. (2013). Handcrafting textile sensors. In L. Buechley, K. Peppler, M. Eisenberg, & Y. Kafai (Eds.), *Textile Messages: Dispatches from the World of E-Textiles and Education.*

Post, R., & Orth, M. (1997). Smart fabric, or "wearable clothing." In *Proceedings of the IEEE International Symposium on Wearable Computers (ISWC)* (pp. 167-168). IEEE.

Post, R., Orth, M., Russo, P., & Gershenfeld, N. (2000). E-broidery: Design and fabrication of textile-based computing. *IBM Systems Journal, 39*(3-4), 840–860. doi:10.1147/sj.393.0840

Reichel, M., Schel, H., and Gruter, T. (2006). Smart fashion and learning about digital culture. *Current Developments in Technology-Assisted Education,* 1-5.

Schelhowe, H., Katterfeldt, E. S., Dittert, N., & Reichel, M. (2013). EduWear: E-textiles in youth sports and theater. In L. Buechley, K. Peppler, M. Eisenberg, & Y. Kafai (Eds.), Textile Messages: Dispatches from the World of E-Textiles and Education. Academic Press.

Scollon, R. (2001). *Mediated Discourse: The Nexus of Practice.* London: Routledge. doi:10.4324/9780203420065

Shepardson, D. P., & Moje, E. B. (1994). The nature of fourth graders' understandings of electric circuits. *Science Education, 78*(5), 489–514. doi:10.1002/sce.3730780505

Shipstone, D. (1984). A study of children's understanding of electricity in simple DC circuits. *European Journal of Science Education, 6*(2), 185–198. doi:10.1080/0140528840060208

Smith, P. (1968). *Body Covering. Museum of Contemporary Crafts.* New York: The American Craft Council.

Starner, T. (2002). Wearable computers: No longer science fiction. *IEEE Pervasive Computing / IEEE Computer Society [and] IEEE Communications Society, 1*(1), 86–88. doi:10.1109/MPRV.2002.993148

Stepulevage, L. (2001). Gender/technology relations: Complicating the gender binary. *Gender and Education, 13*(3), 325–338. doi:10.1080/09540250120082525

Thiberghien, A., & Delacote, G. (1976). Manipulations et representations de circuits electriques simples chez des enfants de 7 a 12 ans. *Revue Française de Pédagogie, 34*(1), 32–44. doi:10.3406/rfp.1976.1613

Turkle, S., & Papert, S. (1992). Epistemological pluralism and the revaluation of the concrete. *The Journal of Mathematical Behavior, 11*(1), 3–33.

Weaver, A. C. A., & Prey, J. C. (2013). Fostering gender diversity in computing. *Computer, 46*(3), 22–23.

Weinberger, C. J. (2004). Just ask! Why surveyed women did not pursue IT courses or careers. *Technology and Society Magazine, IEEE, 23*(2), 28–35. doi:10.1109/MTAS.2004.1304399

ADDITIONAL READING

Buechley, L., Peppler, K., Eisenberg, M., & Kafai, Y. (Eds.), *Textile Messages: Dispatches from the World of E-Textiles and Education*. New York, NY: Peter Lang Publishing.

Peppler, K. (2014). *New Creativity Paradigms: Arts Learning in the Digital Age*. New York, NY: Peter Lang Publishing.

Peppler, K., Gresalfi, M., Salen Tekinbaş, K., & Santo, R. (2014). *Soft Circuits: Crafting E-Fashion with DIY Electronics*. Cambridge, MA: MIT Press.

Peppler, K., Salen Tekinbaş, K., Gresalfi, M., & Santo, R. (2014). *Short Circuits: Crafting E-Puppets with DIY Electronics*. Cambridge, MA: MIT Press.

KEY TERMS AND DEFINITIONS

Arduino: A microcontroller board with pins that connect to electronics or computers, using text-based coding environments to sense and control something in the physical world. In the chapter we discuss LilyPad Arduinos, simple boards that can be sewn into fabric and control lights, sounds, and movements of the textiles.

Coding: Also known as *computer programming*. Creating a language that describes the instructions or program used in software; in this chapter, coding ranges from complex codes performed by technicians to the e-textiles codes related to Modkit or LilyPad Arduinos.

DIY: Also known as do-it-yourself. The method of building, modifying, or repairing something without the aid of experts or professionals. DIY has been closely aligned with the Maker Movement.

E-Textiles: Also known as *electric textiles* or *smart textiles*. Everyday textiles and clothes that have electric components embedded in them;

Maker Movement: The name given to the increasing number of people employing DIY techniques and processes to develop unique technology products. Educators use this to engage the natural inclinations of children and the power of learning by doing. *See also DIY.*

STEM: The curricular disciplines of science, technology, engineering, and math, fields where women and minorities are often underrepresented.

Chapter 12
Virtual Worlds and Online Videogames for Children and Young People:
Promises and Challenges

Guy Merchant
Sheffield Hallam University, UK

ABSTRACT

Online virtual worlds and games provide opportunities for new kinds of interaction, and new forms of play and learning, and they are becoming a common feature in the lives of many children and young people. This chapter explores the issues that this sort of virtual play raises for researchers and educators, and the main themes that have emerged through empirical investigation. I focus on children and young people within the age range covered by compulsory schooling, providing illustrative examples of virtual environments that promote play and learning as a way of underlining some key areas of interest. Drawing on work from a range of theoretical and disciplinary perspectives the chapter emphasises how these environments have much in common with other imagined worlds and suggests that looking at the ways in which the virtual is embedded in everyday contexts for meaning making provides an important direction for future research.

1. WHAT IS A SUCCINCT OVERVIEW OF THE RESEARCH?

Virtual worlds and video games are high profile and popular forms of entertainment in the new global mediascape. They attract large numbers of children and young people, and this has led to interest in some quarters and concern in others as we grapple with the promises and challenges of new kinds of virtual play. Developers and entrepreneurs are designing increasingly sophisticated virtual environments, and so it seems timely to review the key findings that emerge from empirical and theoretical work, and to address those issues in meaning making and learning that are of interest to parents and educators. In what follows I contribute to this endeavour by looking critically at the specific promises and challenges of using

DOI: 10.4018/978-1-4666-8310-5.ch012

computer-generated virtual worlds and online videogames with children and young people for educational purposes. The research base in this area is still in its infancy, but we can now draw on studies of children in the early years, of teenagers and adults – studies located in a range of different settings and jurisdictions. This body of work outlines the kinds of understandings that virtual play can foster, and points to how it is integrated into everyday lives, as well as how it might be absorbed into more formal educational practice. However, first hand experience of virtual worlds and videogames is alien to many parents and educators and the media reaction to immersive online play is often one of moral panic (Gillen & Merchant, 2013). As a result it is necessary to be clear about what constitutes or defines these environments, and to explore some of the popular myths and misconceptions that have attached to these new forms of play. I begin with a focus on these issues.

'This Insubstantial Pageant': Understanding Virtual Worlds

In Shakespeare's *Tempest*, the magician Prospero refers to the play itself as an 'insubstantial pageant' and in a much-quoted speech draws out parallels between theatre and life itself. The dramatic performance, and the imaginary world that is conjured up by it, is seen as an insubstantial pageant, a cast of characters involved in a sequence of events that we temporarily believe in. A play could be seen as a prototypical virtual world. As an event it is real enough, it takes place in space and time with all the material supports of a theatre or similar venue; members of the audience are embodied and present, but yet the world they are transported into is constructed in their individual imaginations, and filtered through their own particular lived experiences.

Drama, in common with other art forms, has the potential to entertain and enrich our lives as well as to educate and enlighten us, even to the extent of challenging or changing our world view.

Of course it may not always do this - it may not touch everyone equally, and there is evidently enough 'good' and 'bad' drama performance to create lucrative livelihoods for critics! Nonetheless the enduring popularity of drama and other narrative media such as books, films and videogames reminds us of the significance of imagined worlds in our lives. I want to argue that virtual worlds and video games, rather than being radically new and hard to comprehend, are simply a recent manifestation of this same phenomenon. Although their realisation *is* new – in the sense that virtual worlds are created from pixels and mediated through screens - the desire to engage in world building, and the cognitive processes involved in meaning making are inherently similar to those at work in constructing other imagined worlds (Gillen & Merchant, 2013).

But for all this similarity, virtual worlds and videogames have introduced a new dimension. We now no longer simply consume the text, we 'play' or create it as we go along (Mackey, 2002). It is as if we had taken on a role in the drama and can then dictate the course of events, seeing things from our character's point of view, or indeed from multiple points of view. In short our actions can influence what we see on the screen. In this way virtual worlds and videogames have many similarities to each other, both being computer-mediated environments in which players have at least some degree of agency. This agency, dictated of course by opportunities and constraints imposed by the game design, is often achieved by adopting a character, or avatar, that can be moved around the screen and can interact with other characters or objects. Although it is possible to engage with virtual worlds and videogames offline, their current popularity can be largely attributed to the fact that online connectivity provides opportunities for play and interaction with others who are not in the same location, as well as those who are.

The technical literature on virtual play draws a distinction between Massively Multiplayer Online Games (MMOGs) and Multi-User Virtual Environments (MUVEs). MMOGs include the hugely popular *World of Warcraft* with its 7 million active accounts (Satista, 2014) as well as newcomers like *Clash of the Clans,* currently strong in the rapidly expanding mobile games market. The most popular MUVEs are usually referred to as virtual worlds (*Second Life* and *Active Worlds* are popular examples), and they are distinguished from videogames by the simple fact that they "have no prescribed structuring of activity and allow varying degrees of creative freedom" (White & Le Cornu, 2010, p. 184). So, although games may develop in virtual world environments, they are not part of the basic architecture. In this way, virtual worlds place a greater overt emphasis on sociality, the building of community, and the co-construction of the environment itself (as in *Minecraft*).

Morningstar and Farmer who designed one of the first virtual worlds, Lucasfilm's *Habitat,* imagined the growth of a virtual world community in which:

... users can communicate, play games, go on adventures, fall in love, get married, get divorced, start businesses, found religions, wage wars, protest against them, and experiment with self-government. (Morningstar & Farmer, [1991] 2008, p.1.)

In *Habitat,* users were shown on-screen as a simple figure or avatar. This idea of an avatar that represents or in some accounts 'is' the user, strongly associates with both MUVEs and MMOGs. With technological development both avatar design and on-screen movement have become ever more sophisticated, enabling players to develop both life-like and fantastic representations (see Figure 1) and movement.

In *Second Life,* for example, it is possible to create a wide range of avatars using human and animal forms (see Boellstorff, 2008). Body shapes, skin tones and attire can be exchanged or bought at any time. Some 'residents' spend a lot of time developing and modifying their avatar's appearance, although this isn't exactly a pre-requisite for participation. By way of contrast, another popular virtual world, *Club Penguin,* focuses on different features, and all users are represented in the same way, by the same basic avatar – a penguin - although as we shall see later, this can be 'personalised'

Figure 1. A meeting in Second Life showing a range of avatars

too. In MMOGs avatar representation is usually linked to the game genre. So, in *World of Warcraft* dwarves, elves and orcs tie in with the fantasy-adventure theme, whereas the videogame family *Grand Theft Auto* uses a contemporary American look for its playable characters' escapades in Liberty City (Merchant, 2014).

In a similar way, the screen environment of virtual worlds varies considerably from the flat cartoon-like scenes in *Club Penguin* to the elaborate three-dimensional universe of *Second Life*. In *Second Life* residents have constructed complex environments that replicate houses, huts, public buildings and shopping malls as well as more fanciful settings. As the technology has developed, so the possibilities have increased, and these various virtual environments have created their own niche audiences, often on a global scale, spawning a significant fan-base usually connected in both on- and off-line communities (Steinkuehler, 2007). It is not untypical, then, for virtual world and gaming activity to involve side-by-side collaboration with friends, either informally or in after-school clubs, as well as online (see Burnett & Bailey, 2014).

Despite their obvious popularity and attraction, both virtual worlds and online video games have provoked negative reactions from mainstream media (Gillen & Merchant, 2013). On the one hand their immersive quality has generated the fear that large numbers of children and young people are spending endless hours online, squandering money on upgrades and accessories, and on the other that they are becoming morally degenerate through over-exposure to sex and violence. There is little evidence to support any of these claims, but they do build on isolated cases, and play into a more generalised moral panic in which narratives about the Internet and new technology as a 'corrosive' force in society predominate (see Palmer, 2006 for example). Although there are clear safety and security issues associated with any online activity (Livingstone, 2009), there is little to indicate that the virtual environments

under consideration are any more risky than other sites. Internet addiction, just like TV addiction before it, seems to be more of a reaction to new media than an actual condition. Furthermore, video gaming and virtual world play, once seen as solitary, anti-social and isolated pursuits, turn out to be highly social, collaborative activities (Schott & Kambouri, 2006).

The idea that virtual environments are simply about banal and passive entertainment has been challenged by a number of academic researchers. The work of Gee (2003) has been particularly influential in arguing that popular videogames are often built on sound learning principles and promote sophisticated reasoning and problem solving. This has undoubtedly contributed to the growth in educational research on virtual play, as well as the rising popularity of 'gamification', in which game principles are applied to drive formal or informal learning (Abrams & Walsh, 2014). As video gaming comes of age, there is a growing impulse to recognise their textual possibilities, sometimes as a way of supporting more familiar curricular goals such as those associated with the English curriculum (Beavis, 2014) and at others as a new art form requiring new methods of analysis. In the latter case the emergence of literary videogames, which use game mechanics and digital media to drive the narrative are a striking example of a new hybrid textual form (Enslinn, 2014).

To summarise then, I have argued that videogames and virtual worlds, rather than being radically new, are best seen as the most recent technologies for creating imagined worlds. Their distinctiveness lies in their dependence on the screen and in their potential for engaging participants in shaping the text, by modifying the environment, interacting with others and dictating the course of events. In this respect, the centrality of avatars in virtual play is worthy of note, and further exploration. Although videogames and virtual worlds have much in common, the emphasis on an underlying game narrative and a set of objectives or challenges is what distinguishes the former from the latter. However, it remains the case that players often use game environments simply to 'hang out'; and conversely virtual world residents may introduce game elements into their environments. The boundary between MUVEs and MMOGs is then fuzzy, to say the least. Finally, I have suggested that concerns about addiction, over-exposure to sex and violence, and social isolation are rooted in moral panics – reactions to what appear to be new and unfamiliar practices.

Empirical research on these online environments crosses disciplinary boundaries and yet there is no comprehensive and systematic literature review currently available. Despite this researchers have looked at specific themes such as the literature on the use of video games for learning (e.g.: Mitchell & Savill-Smith, 2004), that on possible links between aggression and video games (e.g.: Bensley & Van Eenwyk, 2001), and the use of virtual worlds in education (e.g.: Kim, Lee & Thomas, 2012). Arguably the current state of research is one of diversity rather than depth. But yet there are a number of emerging themes in virtual world and video game research that relate to the focus of this chapter. These concern the social dimensions of virtual play – who is playing and who they are playing with; what they are playing and learning and how their learning might be related to other areas of activity; and how we might better understand the nature of virtual play itself.

The Social Dimensions of Virtual Play

Popular perceptions of gaming and virtual world play as a solitary activity have been largely discredited through empirical research. For example, Tu-ukkanen et al. (2010) observed how young people are socially active in virtual worlds, and Schott & Kambouri (2003) in their ethnography of gamers argue for a focus on the 'social envelope' of gam-

ing, showing how even player-to-game interactions often take place in front of a real-time audience of peers. Furthermore, the increasing popularity of virtual worlds and games has led some to think of them as 'new play spaces' (Kafai, 2010, p.4) and given the global spread of virtual play (Apperley, 2014) it is easy to imagine that their appeal is a universal phenomenon. Surprisingly though, there is a shortage of detailed demographic evidence for this, although there are plenty of headline-grabbing statistics. Organisations like the US-based Pew Internet Project provide regular, impressionistic updates on a whole range of related issues. For instance, in an influential report on video games, Pew's researchers claimed that:

Video gaming is pervasive in the lives of American teens—young teens and older teens, girls and boys, and teens from across the socioeconomic spectrum. Opportunities for gaming are everywhere, and teens are playing video games frequently. When asked, half of all teens reported playing a video game "yesterday." Those who play daily typically play for an hour or more. (Lenhart, et. al., 2008, p.1.)

Whilst this undoubtedly helps us to think about the growing significance of video gaming, it also restricts our view to a particular time and place. Given the rapid changes that sweep through popular digital culture, it is difficult to know if this is still the case, or whether and how factors such as the rise of social networking and the take up of mobile technology have impacted on this. In their critical review of this and similar work, Warschauer & Matuchniak (2010) encourage us to take a closer look at how race, gender, and socio-economic status pattern access and use of technology. The implication being that we would be well advised to be somewhat cautious in relation to claims about the widespread popularity of virtual play - it is significant in different ways to different segments of the population.

One pressing area of concern is the apparent gendered nature of virtual play, although there is some evidence to suggest that this is changing. For instance, video game players are no longer predominantly male teenagers (Casell & Jenkins, 1998) – in a recent report the average age of an American video game player was estimated as 31, with nearly half of the gamers being female (Entertainment Software Association, 2014). However, it is still generally accepted that girls gaming habits and practices are different to boys, they prefer different kinds of games and that boys play more frequently and for longer periods of time (Hayes, 2013). Given that some sources suggest that 75% of game developers are male this is perhaps not surprising. There is some resistance to this, particularly with the growing interest in text-based games using software like *Twine* which has provided an important space for women designers.

Research on specific genres and populations highlights key variations in virtual play. For example, Stein et al. (2012) in a survey of over a thousand sports gamers between the ages of 18 and 31 found that they were predominantly white and male; Bertozzi (2012; 2014) has carefully charted the significance of first person shooter and other predation games in the lives of young women, noting their increased popularity and their potential for empowerment; whereas Marsh's (2013) study of young children's play in a virtual world which is discussed in the next section adds to this complex and diverse picture. These sorts of studies point to the patterning of interest and activity and contribute to a nuanced understanding of an increasingly popular pursuit.

The rise of virtual play is consistently reported in larger studies. A recent survey of children and young people between the ages of 5 and 15 in the UK shows the growing popularity of online games (OfCom, 20013) whilst the Interactive Games and Entertainment Association in Australia claims that 93% of homes in their study have a device for playing computer games, and

that 73% of parents talk about games with their children (IGEA 2014). Yet, in another initiative, Livingstone et al. (2011), who surveyed children and their parents in 25 countries in Europe, point to a less-dramatic take up. Admittedly their work is broader in focus – but they do profile children's engagement in virtual play and note that this was represented in only 23% of their sample.

Making international comparisons is, of course, fraught with difficulty and perhaps quibbling over percentages is not particularly helpful in this instance. However, what does seem clear is that online gaming is *increasing* in popularity, although perhaps *unevenly* across different populations. Put together with industry figures for the number of subscriptions for MUVEs, virtual play seems to be part of the everyday life of many children and young people. Having said this we cannot assume that this is the case for *all* children or even that it is experienced in the same way and to the same frequency by those who do engage. For this reason, the accounts, that follow are predominantly qualitative, and focus on the situated practices associated with video games and virtual worlds.

What Are They Playing and What Are They Learning?

As scholars begin to acknowledge the heterogeneous nature of virtual play, researchers are illuminating the range of learning that takes place in and around these environments. Whilst early work followed Gee's (2003) ideas about the learning principles enshrined in 'good' games, more recent studies highlight specific kinds of learning that emerge from game play. Following Carpenter (2009), who identified the parallels between social networks and social learning environments, researchers have focused on such diverse topics as civic participation and learning about citizenship (Tuukkanen et al., 2010), the development of epistemic games (Boots & Strobel, 2014), the use of virtual worlds in higher education (Beck

& Perkins, 2014; Kirriemuir, 2010), and virtual play in the development of elementary school literacy (Merchant, 2009). In short, attention has shifted from an interest in what is learnt in and about games to describing the kinds of learning that might be achieved through playing them. As a result it is not uncommon to find discussions of the role of game play in promoting anything from health awareness to legal studies, from sports science to STEM subjects.

Although the notion of learning transfer has exercised the best minds in psychology and education, the relationship between what we might call virtual learning and everyday life has, as a result, become a key area of interest. Whilst research on sports gaming may not address formal learning, it serves to highlight how such activity is interwoven with on-going interest, other forms of play and fandom (Stein et al. 2012). So whilst there is no single template to describe how virtual play relates to other aspects of gamers' lives (see Lange, 2011), current thinking has begun to problematise the virtual/real binary (Merchant et al., 2014). As Lemke observes in his commentary on research on *Whyville*:

Too often we hear it argued that what players learn in virtual spaces is worthless because it has no application in the "real' world – a world, these critics seem to assume, where what is real to us excludes our experience of the virtual. (Lemke, 2010, p. 151)

Perspectives of this sort are encouraging researchers to think about how virtual spaces are embedded in people's lives and how we can develop more sophisticated understandings of virtual play and, in turn, the sorts of research methods that are going to most productive in this endeavour.

How Might We Better Understand Virtual Play?

As we have seen, a number of influential studies have focused on the detailed description of specific, situated practices. Schott & Kambouri's (2003) emphasis on the 'social envelope' of gaming is one such approach, whereas the micro-ethnographic focus on events, human and non-human actors offered by Giddings (2009) is an alternative. Leander & McKim (2003) grapple with the central issue of how learners move between and across online and offline contexts, and their 'connective ethnography' offers some important ways of conceptualising this movement.

Elsewhere it has been suggested that researchers ignore game design at their peril (Sheridan & Rowsell, 2010), and that our understanding of virtual worlds and online games must take account of what sorts of play, agency and identity performance is prompted, possible, or proscribed by their design. This has led to research on game design (e.g.: Thorhague, 2013), on game-related practices such as modding (Gee & Hayes, 2011) and the use of cheats. Further work has followed the idea of design principles for serious games and this is reflected in the work of Annetta (2010) and Boots & Strobel (2014).

2. WHAT ARE THE CURRENT ISSUES IN THE FIELD RAISED BY THESE STUDIES?

Most of the research referred to here is influenced either directly or indirectly by ideas about 'new literacies' (Lankshear & Knobel, 2006) and 'media literacies' (Buckingham, 2003). Together they represent a perspective on the meaning making practices involved in the consumption, production and distribution of new media and the habits of mind that have grown up around them. Given the multimodal nature of new media (Kress, 2003) there has been plenty of debate about how this re-defines the term literacy, the implications for education, and even conjecture about the future of alphabetic print literacy (Merchant, 2007). These issues are not of immediate concern, but yet they do serve as background to what follows.

New literacy practices have certainly diversified over the last ten years and often academic research has struggled to keep pace. Despite this, virtual play *has* attracted considerable attention, partly because of its apparent 'newness', but also because the environments in which it takes place seem to capture the attention and imagination of large numbers of children and young people. As indicated above, Gee's (2003) work has been a major influence, and although this focuses on the world of video gaming, much of it is equally applicable to virtual worlds. The sophistication of his body of work is such that it speaks to other new literacy practices, too, if not to education as a whole. The fact that not all children and young people are avid gamers does not disturb Gee's basic argument, although the suggestion that gaming can be more rewarding than school is provocative to say the least.

I do not attempt a detailed summary of Gee's ideas here, but focus instead on two central claims that are made in his work. They are most clearly articulated in the book *What Video Games Have to Teach us about Learning and Literacy* (2003), and are as follows: 1) video games can be powerful learning environments because they are based on a sophisticated understanding of how we learn; and 2) the learning principles involved in video game design can be applied to other environments such as schools. Of these two claims, it is probably the first that has attracted the most attention, if only because it is a very positive statement about a popular practice that is often, as we have seen, demonized in public debate. My concern here with exploring the use of online videogames and virtual worlds resonates with this first claim – that is, that they can both be powerful learning environments (see Dede et al., 2006), although I do consider the second claim later on.

In the discipline of education, the notion that new technologies require new literacies is widely debated (eg: Lankshear & Knobel, 2006; Merchant, 2007) and often draws on observations and studies

of situated insider practices in everyday contexts. There is less work that traces these practices as they cross into the official domains of education, or explores how they might be translated or adapted to address specifically educational purposes. The ambitions of texts like Carr et al.'s (2006) work on computer games and my own on virtual worlds (Merchant, 2009; 2010) move in this direction, and invite further sustained empirical investigation. More detailed accounts, however, remain the province of insider researchers, such as Boellstorff (2008), Pearce & Artemesia (2010) and Nardi (2010), who have become participants in the virtual environments they study.

The meaning making practices associated with computer gameplay and virtual worlds constitute a distinct subset of the research on new literacies. Steinkuehler (2006; 2007) makes a contribution to our understanding of this with her exploration of the 'constellation of literacy practices' that are involved in and associated with gaming, whereas Marsh's (2008) work on *Club Penguin*, Gillen's (2009) study of *Teen Second Life*, and my own explorations of *Active Worlds* (Merchant, 2009) investigate the diverse literacy practices that constitute and accompany virtual play. These, and other similar studies, show that young people find these virtual environments compelling, and that they engage in sophisticated multimedia practices that often spill out into different aspects of their life including real world play, traditional forms of writing and other online activity (Burnett & Merchant, 2014). The implications of this work for formal education are considerable, particularly if the growth trends of the 'metaverse' continue (see fig. 2). Educators may need to take these new experiences of literacy into account if only to acknowledge their role in learners' lives. But they may also want to incorporate some gaming and some virtual world play into school life, and in this respect the claims made by Gee (2003) about the learning that takes place in gaming are important.

Figure 2. A screenshot from Club Penguin showing the arctic environment and penguin avatars

In another strand of research and scholarship, the media theorist Henry Jenkins has developed the idea that technological innovation, coupled with wider societal trends, has led to the emergence of what he calls 'participatory culture'. An influential publication, often referred to as The White Paper, offers the following definition: a participatory culture is "one in which members believe their contributions matter, and feel some degree of social connection with one another." (Jenkins et al., 2006, p.3). The argument made is that the shift from individual expression to collaborative community involvement characterises both youth engagement with new media and the skills that will be necessary for future economic success and civic engagement. Virtual world and video game research, such as that undertaken by Black, 2010; Marsh, 2010; Steinkuehler, 2011; and Ochsner & Martin, 2013, has described and illustrated the mechanics of this participation and how it works in establishing communities:

1. With relatively low barriers to artistic and civic engagement
2. With strong support for creating and sharing one's creations with others
3. With some type of informal mentorship whereby what is known by the most experienced is passed along to novices
4. Where members believe their contribution matters
5. Where members feel some degree of social connection with one another (at least they care what other people think about what they have created). (Jenkins, et al., 2006, p.7)

If Jenkins' thesis about participatory culture is right then developing such practices and the habits of mind, skills and competences that are involved become an essential part of what have been described as C21st literacies (Burnett et al., 2014). Gameplay in virtual environments and the constellation of literacy practices involved are an arena for the development of this kind of participation. The importance of making pedagogical connections with virtual play then becomes significant. The burning questions for educators will be about *what* kinds of digital work to develop and *how* to go about it. Squire identifies this in his study of video games in the classroom when he outlines the challenge for educators in terms of "how we can use games more effectively as educational tools" (Squire, 2005, n.p).

In my own work I have drawn attention to some of the obstacles to embedding virtual world gameplay in the classroom (Merchant, 2009, 2010) making similar points to those advanced by O'Brien & Scharber, who argue that:

A major pothole in digital literacies is that the institutionalized structures of schools are often incompatible with the purposes and enactments of digital literacies. Many digital literacies practices defy the traditional scheduling or organizational routines of schools. (O'Brien & Scharber, 2008, p.67)

In some respects the same argument surfaces again in Squire's collection of case studies of educational games (Squire, 2012). He seems to suggest that despite all their benefits for learning, their most natural home is in after-school clubs and other non-formal settings. However, Squire does offer the sort of detail that has, to date, been missing from the field. For instance, he is clear that there *are* specific features and properties that can be used to describe and define 'educational games', he provides a useful model to account for game-based learning, and outlines a learning trajectory.

In what follows I consider three rather different virtual environments that demonstrate some of the key characteristics of virtual world and video game play. They are chosen in order to illustrate what has gone before and to highlight specific issues – but not because they are in any sense representative. What is sometimes referred to as the 'metaverse', the totality of virtual environments, is both sizeable

and varied, and shows an increased tendency to reach out into niche markets (KZero, 2013). The three environments I explore highlight facets of this expanding metaverse. I begin by looking at a virtual world that is specifically aimed at young children. *Club Penguin,* which is owned by the Disney Corporation, is widely considered to be the most popular virtual world in the under-10 age range. This is followed by an exploration of *Skillville*, a rather different type of virtual environment - one that employs the principles of gamification to develop economic awareness in teenagers. I conclude by reflecting on the virtual world *Barnsborough*, created locally, in the UK, with colleagues using the *Active Worlds* platform. This virtual world was designed for classrooms, and specifically aimed to develop literacy with elementary school students.

The work of Pearce and Artemisia (2010) provides a useful lens to look at these examples through. Pearce argues that we should pay attention to the ways in which virtual environments are designed - the implication being that design both enables and constrains what is possible. Of course, in some environments users *become* designers as they build, modify and variously contribute to that environment as well as how it is used and described – but this could simply be seen as an extension of the design principle, since even in environments like *Second Life* and *Minecraft,* in which building is highly prized, players are limited to the in-world tools that are available. Pearce suggests that virtual environments are emergent in nature, in that the cultures that grow up in and around them are continuously forming and re-forming, often on a global or transnational scale. Finally, Pearce develops the idea of 'communities of play'. She argues that such communities have a long and important history, but that they have adapted and in some senses been transformed through online interaction. Whilst acknowledging that these communities arise in a variety of contexts, for the purpose of this chapter, I follow Pearce in using the term to describe groups in which digital and networked media such as MUVEs and MMOGs support play and play-related activities and interactions.

Penguin Adventures: Young Children in Virtual Worlds

The virtual world, *Club Penguin,* is aimed at 6-14 year olds and provides a safe, ad-free environment in which children can "play games, have fun and interact" (Club Penguin, n.d.). Joining the world involves adopting and naming a penguin, inhabiting an igloo, and exploring the arctic environment. With something in the region of 170 million registered accounts, *Club Penguin* has members spread across 190 countries (KZero, 2013). The majority of these accounts are free, although paid membership gives access to additional features allowing members to purchase virtual clothing, furniture, and pets called "puffles" using an in-game currency. Unlike *Second Life, Club Penguin* does not simulate a three dimensional world (as Figure 2 shows), but yet it is designed to represent movement, and uses different screens to create a varied environment for penguin-avatars.

As Marsh observes, the fact that the design uses icons and symbols, rather than written text makes it easy for very young children to navigate:

Symbols, such as arrows, are used throughout the world to guide penguins and every page contains icons that link to a map of the world, the newspaper Club Penguin Times and a 'Moderator,' who can be contacted if penguins wish to complain about the behaviour of others in the world. The navigation bar at the bottom of the screen contains icons that enable children to chat with other penguins, to use emoticons, to throw snowballs, to contact other penguins in order to request that they become friends, and to navigate to their avatar's home, their igloo. (Marsh, 2013, p.79.)

Because of *Club Penguin*'s focus on young children it prides itself on its safety procedures – and these are wide-ranging, including the above-mentioned moderator contact, chat vocabulary restrictions, and identity protection protocols. Moderators are active and online all the time (although not necessarily visible) and have the power to ban, mute or expel users from *Club Penguin*. So although it is possible to join *Club Penguin* as an adult, all activity is carefully monitored. Inappropriate behaviour is not tolerated - the environment is designed with the principles of online safety in mind.

Up to this point I have referred to *Club Penguin* as a virtual world, but in-world games and activities are released at regular intervals, and by virtue of this, the world is sometimes described as a MMOG. Clearly it boasts a large play community and incorporates gaming elements, and certainly the way in which games are refreshed, and news updates appear in *Club Penguin Times*, work together to convey the sense of emergence. Although its basic design lacks a game structure – there is no over-arching purpose or trajectory, it could well be that the events that are staged support its emergent nature and may have contributed to its popularity. Marsh's (2013) study of 5-11 year old members of *Club Penguin* outlines key features of the learning that occurs in the world. Through games and interaction she suggests that children develop the new literacies associated with participatory culture and that these enable children to productively engage with the online environment, 'to make friends, to express themselves and to engage in pleasurable interactions with a variety of multimodal texts on a regular basis.' (Marsh, 2013, p.84).

Despite all this, *Club Penguin* is not without its critics. Some have argued that, as another arm of the Disney empire, it is further evidence of the disneyfication of childhood (see Giroux, 2001), in which a consumerist ideology is promulgated and continually recycled. For instance, as in *Second Life*, the use of an in-world currency implicitly values the accumulation of wealth, which enables members to buy clothing and enhance their avatar's home. Another related, but more subtle critique of *Club Penguin* centres on the use of the so-called 'freemium' model, in which the service is initially made free of charge, but requires a subscription for additional functionality and virtual goods. Because *Club Penguin* is aimed at children it has been suggested that this revenue is dependent on pester power – once 'hooked', children will put pressure on adults to buy them a subscription. Nonetheless, these criticisms aside, *Club Penguin* still enjoys huge popularity and clearly provides a focus for a new form of digital play which appears to have a range of benefits (Marsh, 2010; 2013).

Pedagogic Innovation: Gamification and Economic Awareness

Earlier in this chapter, we saw how Gee claims that the learning principles embedded in video game design could be applied in or transferred to other contexts (Gee, 2003). This idea has been taken up by the 'gamification' movement which argues that applying 'game mechanics' to a range of different contexts improves user-engagement and can stimulate behaviour change and conceptual learning (Hamari, et al., 2014). In the following example, gamification is used to solve a specific educational problem - the teaching of economic awareness in schools in Belgium. Economic awareness, and specifically financial literacy, is a required part of cross-curricular study in this context (Flemish Ministry of Education and Training, 2010). However, schools find it almost impossible to meet these expectations for two reasons. Firstly, because the curriculum is already overcrowded there is little time to include another dimension, and secondly, because most teachers feel that they are not properly qualified to teach financial literacy (Palmaers, 2014).

Skillville was developed by the EdICT group at Limburg Catholic University and provides a virtual environment for Belgian schools and their students, to address this particular challenge. The EdICT group, with support from KBC, one of Belgium's largest banks, designed *Skillville* using the principles of game mechanics. *Skillville* demands little from teachers and is predicated on the idea that students will learn from online engagement, peer interaction and reflection on their real world experience. The design team drew on current literature on game mechanics (see Table 1, below) in building *Skillville*.

Aimed at students between the ages of 12 and 18, *Skillville* is based on activities and events related to the players' ages. For example, they receive weekly 'pocket money', apply for a student job when they are 16 - or a real job, with taxable pay, when they are 18. Although everyday financial management is important in *Skillville*, other factors come into play, too. For example, players might lose their wallet, or crash their scooter, thus incurring unexpected costs. They also have to manage their health, and make 'sensible' choices when shopping for food. In this way real-life elements are integrated into the game. Score bars, leader boards and challenges are also built in to the game design in order to motivate the students.

Figure 3 shows the *Skillville* home screen. On the bottom left is the player's avatar and clickable icons for various functions. Rotating clockwise from the left of the screen there is:

- An exit button: to leave *Skillville*.
- The budget controller: to register incoming and outgoing transactions.
- *Skillville* Bank: to transfer money between bank accounts and the wallet.
- *Skillville* Shop: to buy foods, electronics, and other virtual goods.
- My purchases: to provide an overview of all items purchased.

Table 1. Example of game mechanics

Fast Feedback	• Encourage users to continue or adjust their activities • Congratulate users for reaching goals • Encourage the next step to a milestone
Transparency	• Show users exactly where they stand in relation to others • Use individual and team profiles to show progress in real-time and historically • Use leader boards to show ranking and other metrics
Goals	• Have clear short and long term goals • Use challenges to give users a purpose for interaction • Underline what is possible and what is valued
Badges	Use badges as an indicator of accomplishment of a skill
Levelling	• Provide levels to indicate achievements and progression • Use levels to identify status within a community • Use levels to introduce new missions and challenges
On-Boarding	• Provide easy entry-level play • Encourage users to learn by playing
Competition	• Raise the stakes for accomplishing a goal by showing users how they compare to others, as individuals or in teams. • Encourage competition with time-based, team and individualized leader boards. (Where do I rank? How can I overtake my closest competitor?)
Collaboration	• Connect users as a team to accomplish larger tasks • Encourage knowledge-sharing
Community	Build community in such as way that it gives meaning to other game mechanics (badges, leader board etc.)
Points	• Save scores to recognise status and accumulate to purchase real or virtual goods • Earn points through activities, sharing, contributing

(Adapted from Bunchball, 2014)

Figure 3. Screenshot of Skillville showing, financial management data and avatar functions

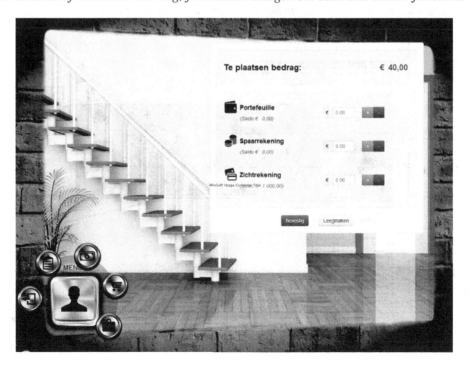

In addition to this, players can access the *Skillville* Library which contains web resources, and reference documents as well as *Skillville* Training for resources for assessing and developing life-skills.

Central to *Skillville* is the way in which it has been designed to develop age-appropriate financial literacy, and we have seen how it uses game mechanics to achieve this. But developing a community of play remains in the hands of the school students who are using it. In common with many other educational resources, creating a context that supports the game's underpinning values and a community that gives meaning to the game mechanics is a considerable challenge. This contrasts with successful commercial games that already have an established play community that newcomers are apprenticed to, and which is supported by a network of communication systems both in the virtual world itself, and in the constellation of literacy practices that surround it (Steinkuehler, 2007).

Crossing Boundaries: Virtual Worlds in the Classroom

The final example is based on my own work on the use of the three dimensional virtual world *Barnsborough* with elementary school children. Like *Skillville*, *Barnsborough* was designed by a group of educators working in collaboration with private sector developers. It was built with *Active Worlds* software, and can be navigated from a standard keyboard by directing the movement of onscreen avatars. As Figure 4 shows, this virtual world simulates a contemporary urban environment. A number of literacies are designed into the environment including: tool tips, available by mousing-over objects, environmental texts, such as shop signs, graffiti, logos, posters, and advertisements, and hyperlinks, such as webpages, phone messages, and music clips. Off the shelf avatars, each with a unique point of view in the world, can be used by children to communicate with each other through a 'chat' function, which is displayed in instant-message format beneath the main display, with recent utterances also appearing in speech balloons above their heads.

Figure 4. An annotated screenshot of Barnsborough showing some of its features.

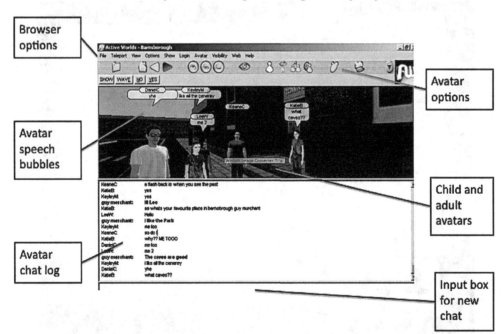

In a succession of classroom-based projects (Merchant, 2009, Merchant, 2010 & Burnett & Merchant, 2014) teachers introduced *Barnsborough* by suggesting that it had been hurriedly and mysteriously abandoned by its previous inhabitants. The broad objective for children was to solve this mystery by collecting evidence available in the world in a number of media and textual forms. The texts located in the virtual world provided child-avatars with a number of possible accounts and solutions to the problem of why *Barnsborough* had been abandoned, which included a major biohazard, an alien abduction, and a political or big business disaster.

In some ways our work in *Barnsborough* succeeded in demonstrating how new literacies could be embedded in the classroom – children were engaged in problem-solving in a virtual environment, meeting and communicating with onscreen avatars, and interacting through synchronous small-group chat. It also provided good illustrations of the collaborative potential of virtual play with children often working in teams or temporary groupings to explore the environment. It was noted that they became immersed in the world in ways that are sometimes observed in drama activities and gaming (Carroll, 2002; Merchant, 2009). Not only did children find *Barnsborough* enjoyable, teachers were enthusiastic, too. Yet it was also clear that the teachers' enthusiasm for *Barnsborough* was tempered by other factors – factors that were not directly concerned with the concept of new literacies or the use of a virtual world per se. The first of these was to do with the fall-out from curriculum reform, and the associated innovation fatigue; the second was about curriculum 'fit'; and the third about access to hardware. These are explored below.

Successive waves of reforms have buffeted the English school system in recent years, and teachers have borne the brunt of this, writing schemes of work to comply with new curriculum requirements, adapting to new modes and criteria for assessment, and being subject to ever more exacting systems of accountability. The climate has not been particularly favourable for other innovations, and clearly something as different as virtual world gameplay raises all sorts of challenges. Despite this, creative teachers are hard to discourage, and in successive *Barnsborough* projects there have been no shortage of volunteers. But immersive gameplay takes time, its benefits are hard to measure, and teachers are often left with the question of how to justify the time spent in virtual play in what has become a highly structured curriculum. Finally, even though there has been considerable investment in school computing in England and Wales, virtual world work was often beset by intermittent hardware problems. Keeping class sets of desktop or laptop computers serviceable poses a considerable institutional challenge, particularly in times of economic uncertainty.

As with *Skillville* it was difficult to establish a strong community of play in *Barnsborough*. Where this did occur it was often manufactured by the teacher - through class discussion and related writing projects, but often because of the constraints of the school timetable this was time-limited. It seems then that Pearce's notion of the emergent quality of a virtual play culture is particularly difficult to replicate in the school environment. Current organisational structures and institutional practices in schools do seem incompatible with the rhythms and characteristics of virtual play, and this is probably why some of the more productive educational research now takes place in after-school clubs and other settings (see, for example Hollett & Ehret, 2014; Wohlwend, 2013)

3. WHAT ARE THE GAPS IN THE EXTANT RESEARCH AND DIRECTIONS FOR FUTURE RESEARCH?

As we have seen, video games and virtual worlds occupy an important place in the lives of many children and young people. Imaginary realms are culturally significant in that they educate and entertain us, and have the capacity to enrich our lives. In this sense these virtual environments provide a context for the development of new communities of play (Pearce & Artemisia, 2010) – communities that may be co-present, dispersed or a hybrid of both. The alleged dangers of virtual play are predominantly based on moral panics that have little empirical validity. Throughout this chapter it has been argued that these virtual spaces provide opportunities for the sorts of active engagement, production and interaction that are hallmarks of an emerging participatory culture (Jenkins et al., 2006). At their best they nurture communicative experiences that are important in contemporary life, and provide an arena for problem-solving and higher order thinking skills (Squire, 2012). However, not all videogames do this, and like some virtual worlds, they *may* simply entertain their players. At their worst they provide unhelpful models of consumerism or gender (Carrington & Hodgetts, 2010). As a result both parents and educators will want to know the conditions and characteristics that can make engagement in virtual environments productive for those in their care. Unfortunately, there is little overall evidence to go on here, and certainly insufficient to make judgements about specific games or worlds.

In the previous section I looked at three examples of virtual environments to highlight some of the pressing issues in this field. Based on this it might be concluded that popular, commercial games and virtual worlds have more potential than their educational equivalents. In the world of media entertainment the level of investment allows for a degree of design sophistication, product development and customer care that are beyond the reach of most educational environments. However, they are forced to compete in the open market and because of this their aims and values may not necessarily be primarily educational. In contrast, online environments that promote virtual play with a specific educational purpose, particularly when they are targeted at

schools, have the potential to engage the young in powerful learning, but they often find it difficult to grow authentic communities of play and struggle to find a place in standard educational routines. Identifying what is educational in virtual play remains a priority, and models for how such play can cross the boundaries between formal and non-formal, on- and off-line contexts is needed if our understanding is to develop further.

Researchers need to generate more in-depth studies of virtual play, and particularly those that focus on how this is situated in the day to day lives of children and young people. A particular gap concerns young children. As we have seen, the work of Marsh (2002; 2010) on *Club Penguin* begins to chart the territory, but this is a rapidly expanding market and there is certainly more scope for the rich description of young children's virtual play. Children of all ages can now access virtual worlds, and their activity is far from passive. As Burnett & Bailey's (2014) work on *Minecraft* shows, making in-world content involves a complex of technical skill and creativity that connects screen-based activity with real world interaction. Understanding more about how design and content creation skills develop is another important area. In the world of gaming, Burn (2009) makes an important contribution, and studies of game making, such as that produced by Buckingham, Burn & Pelletier (2011) need to be built upon so that we can identify possible learning trajectories.

If virtual play is to be seen as a new kind of digital capital (Merchant, 2007) – as a way of developing foundational literacies for social and cultural participation, then it is important to know how this capital is currently distributed. Following from the work of Warschauer & Matuchniak (2010), careful analysis of how access and use is patterned can complement more situated studies of communities of play to build up a picture of how practices vary in and between social groups. It may then be necessary to take steps to ensure that digital technology does not perpetuate or magnify existing social inequities.

4. WHAT ARE THE RECOMMENDATIONS/ IMPLICATIONS FOR EDUCATION, CIVIC ENGAGEMENT (GLOBAL AND LOCAL), SOCIAL PRACTICE, AND POLICY?

In this chapter I have tried to illustrate the diversity of virtual environments, focusing on those that fall into the rather loose categories of MUVEs and MMOGs. This diversity is, of course, strongly determined by the design affordances of different worlds, and these affordances construct and constrain the ways in which meanings are made, as well as the parameters for action and interaction. For example, the interactive dimension of virtual worlds, such as *Barnsborough,* contrasts with the highly individualised avatar work of *Skillville*. But even though *Barnsborough* allows for plenty of user interaction, opportunities for modifying the world, uploading content, or building (as in *Minecraft*) are not available. There are also contrasting aesthetics across these virtual spaces. The cartoon-like designs of *Club Penguin* differ sharply from the representational qualities of *Second Life*. Such diversity confounds attempts to see virtual worlds or video games as a singular phenomenon. This all goes to illustrate some of the difficulties that attach to the work of building robust categories in an area that is developing so rapidly and unpredictably. It also supports the view that life online is as diverse as life offline, if indeed the two can be held separate in the first place. Perhaps it could be argued that the essence of meaning making remains relatively stable - at least from a cognitive perspective - but the rapid multiplication and diversification of textual spaces produces new forms and these certainly warrant more sophisticated description.

Virtual worlds and video games are part of a digital culture that is in a constant state of flux. *BarbieGirls* and *Teen Second Life* no longer exist, *World of Warcraft* membership is in decline, while more successful games, like *Grand Theft Auto,* continue to thrive. Acknowledging the ephemeral nature of these virtual environments seems to be a necessary condition for researching this field. Part of this can be attributed to rapid changes in technology, but part, I suspect, is due to the restless nature of popular taste in a fluid cultural climate. Shifts in the political economy are influential too, since they determine developers' appetite to invest in innovation. In the entertainment industry a new product must sell, and in the increasingly marketised world of education a new product must be shown to 'make a difference' – more often than not in the narrowly defined measures of high stakes testing. But despite all this, when we consider the skills that will be important for education and civic engagement in the future, there is little doubt that they will involve the sorts of literacies that are developed in and through virtual play.

In their landmark text, Lankshear & Knobel (2006) describe these literacies as new communicative practices and new mindsets, and show how they underpin a wide range of activity that crosses the boundaries of formal/informal learning, of work/play and of on/offline. Characterised by fluid movement across different spaces, new literacies involve actions and interactions that interweave with activity in the physical environment, creating a rich tapestry of meanings (see Martin et al., 2013). So although the boundary between online and offline activity has been described as a porous membrane (Castronova, 2005), I suggest that there is even more fluidity than the membrane metaphor implies – perhaps a state of affairs that is, in essence, little different from the way in which we navigate our way through the rich textual spaces of the contemporary urban environment, as a largely continuous experience. All this suggests a kind of educational experience which is far removed from that currently provided by the Anglophone school systems of North America, the UK and Australasia, in which literacy is predominantly conceived of in terms of the logic of alphabetic print.

In the opening section of this chapter I reflected on the cultural significance of imagined worlds, and the ways in which they entertain, enrich and educate us. The role of the imagination, and the capacity for creative engagement offered by new media, has been described in detail by Willett, Robinson, & Marsh (2008). By looking more specifically at virtual interactions we can see how imagination, learning and learner identities can be shaped through playful, and often self-motivated, activity. This is perhaps best illustrated through the descriptions of informal and less-bounded practices, such as those that constellate around virtual worlds and gaming 'in the wild' (Beavis, 2013). But it does seem that innovative educators are able to draw on these practices in classrooms, although they may experience some conflict with entrenched routines and structures (Merchant, 2010; Beavis, 2013). The extent to which new habits of mind imply new school pedagogies certainly warrants further investigation (see Squire, 2005). In general, though, it seems to be the case that more tightly defined conceptions of learning, coupled with more extensive controls – often as a response to discourses of risk – continue to characterize educational initiatives that incorporate virtual play. To counter this, I suggest that we need to re-state the value of play in learning, and to acknowledge its inherently social nature. But of course, education also has a role in developing learners' critical faculties and this requires careful consideration, too. I explore these three themes below, before looking in more depth at what schools systems might address.

Recognising the Importance of Play

I have argued that on- and off-line play is important in developing the sorts of understandings of multimodal texts that are central to participatory culture (Jenkins et al., 2006). Whether virtual play involves an element of production, such as planning and design, or whether it is simply undertaken as a participant, the game-like quality remains an important feature. Underscoring this is a restatement of the relationship between play and learning. As Vygotsky (1987) suggested, opportunities for creative and imaginative exploration are important, not only for our psychological wellbeing, but also in providing opportunities to reflect upon or critique other aspects of our lives; these opportunities are an important and often undervalued part of learning.

Identity play such as that involved in developing the appearance and activity of one's avatar, or building and furnishing a virtual home are significant aspects of the imaginative act of world making. In some environments, such as *Club Penguin*, dressing a character and acquiring possessions or attributes can become part of developing a sort of narrative history. The avatars that stand for us, but are not us, are representations that may not quite have a life of their own, or exist independently, but yet they quickly develop characteristics and recognizable routines and collect around them a history of use that patterns interactions with others.

Often, virtual play has an immersive quality in which players are drawn into their imaginary worlds in what Coleridge once described as the 'willing suspension of disbelief', and this has many similarities to the traditional forms of play observed in young children. But at the same time we have seen how this virtual play spills out into, and enriches more familiar kinds of play (see Willet et al., 2013). But it is not simply the case of considering young children's play since, as Pearce & Artemesia (2009) point out, play is not just the province of childhood. Adolescents and adults are deeply involved in communities of play, too. In fact it could be argued that some of our most powerful learning experiences grow out of these social affiliations.

The Social Nature of Virtual Play

It has long been thought that social interaction and learning are inextricably linked. The social dimension of virtual play could well increase learning opportunities, and in some cases it clearly enables collaborative problem solving and strategizing. Challenges such as those set up in *Barnsborough*, or the invitation to organize a raid in *World of Warcraft* (see Martin, et al. 2013), or simply the need to collect or trade objects invariably depends upon collaboration and interaction. Such challenges can be complex and demanding. In fact, the level of challenge may be something akin to what Gee describes as being pleasantly frustrating.

Learning works best when new challenges are pleasantly frustrating in the sense of being felt by learners to be at the outer edge of, but within, their 'regime of competence'. That is, these challenges feel hard, but 'doable'. (Gee, 2005, p. 10)

In many of the studies described in this chapter, challenges become 'doable' only through the collective action of networked individuals. In short, the virtual spaces I have described work to mediate social interaction, and to extend real-world connections and they are united by the ways in which new literacies are being used to create, develop and populate virtual spaces. I suggest then, that sophisticated uses of video games and virtual worlds are by nature social as individuals become embedded in communities of play.

Developing a Critical Perspective

For all the possibilities and learning benefits they may offer, virtual environments are not, however, value-free. As with any designed space they are informed by a worldview in which particular identity positions are favoured (and others not), and particular representations are made available (Holland, Lachicotte, Skinner, & Cain, 2001). This is not to say that individuals, such as the children and young people in the studies reported here, do not have agency – in fact I argue strongly that they do – but we must recognize that this agency is acted out along or against, the grain of a set of

norms and values. When considering commercial or institutional environments, it is important, then, to acknowledge the pedagogical dimension, whether that is explicit or hidden. In this sense I follow Giroux and Pollock in suggesting that it is crucially important not lose sight of

... how learning occurs by providing the ideas and narratives that shape how people see the world and themselves... (Giroux & Pollock, 2010, p.5)

This is certainly true for video games and virtual worlds in which these ideas and narratives are often foregrounded, providing significant and powerful opportunities for critique. Although such work may seem pressing when we look at gendered consumerism in *Barbie Girls*, (Carrington & Hodgetts, 2010), or more straightforward when we consider educational projects such as *Barnsborough* or *Skillville*, the underlying concern is the same. Individuals enact their identities in and through their interactions with each other; but these identity performances are strongly shaped by the contexts that they operate within.

This raises the question of whether there is space for critical practice in virtual play and other social media. It may be the case that the sort of approach described by Burnett & Merchant (2011) constitutes a way forward. Here we argued that existing paradigms of critical literacy and critical media literacy are restricted in their ability to engage with the fluid and densely interwoven spaces of social media. In its place we proposed a practice-based model that focuses on the interplay between purposes, contexts, and resources. This conception of social media practice is based on a view of how identities are formed and performed, and how these are in turn embedded in social networks and has important implications for both parents and educators. Whether this model offers a way forward is as yet untested, but the centrality of encouraging a critical perspective remains. Parents and educators have a moral duty to encourage safe, ethical and advantageous practice, and children and young people have a right to expect their guidance.

Table 2. A Charter for Literacy Education

Dimensions of Literacy in Experience and Action	Qualities of Empowering Literacy Education
Literacies as multiple	Empowering literacy education involves recognition of the *linguistic, social and cultural resources* learners bring to the classroom, whilst encouraging them to diversify the range of communicative practices in which they participate.
Multiple modes and media	Empowering literacy education involves understanding how socially recognisable meanings are produced through the orchestration of semiotic resources.
Provisionality	Empowering literacy education involves a range of activity that includes improvisation and experimentation as well as the production of polished texts.
Multiple authorship	Empowering literacy education values collaboration in text making and is emancipatory in the way is facilitates access to others' texts and ideas.
Objects, bodies and affect	Empowering literacy education involves recognition of the *affective, embodied* and *material* dimensions of meaning making.
Social	Empowering literacy education involves engaging with others in a variety of different ways.
Socially-situated	Empowering literacy education involves exploring how you position yourself and how you are positioned by others through texts.
Unruly	Empowering literacy education occurs within *safe, supportive spaces* that promote experimentation.
Changing	Empowering literacy education involves developing an understanding of the changing nature of meaning making.

(From Burnett et al., 2014)

Back to School: Policy Development

In recent years, there have been a number of influential proposals from educators and researchers working in the field of new literacies aimed at generating curricular and pedagogical designs that incorporate new communicative practices (e.g. Cope & Kalantzis, 1999; Jenkins et al, 2006; Lankshear & Knobel, 2010). Burnett et al. (2014) add to this work by using research-based notions of literacy to inform ongoing national and transnational debates about 21st Century skills. They have generated a set of foundational principles – described as a charter - that sit well with the sorts of understandings developed through video games and virtual worlds (see Table 2).

When we look at the dimensions and qualities listed in the charter in the light of what this chapter has to say about video game and virtual world research there is a clear overlap. A pedagogy and school curriculum that is built on the qualities identified here as 'empowering' could well embrace virtual play, as well as other social media, addressing some of the promises and challenges that have been explored. In the meantime, we are dependent on the hard work and enthusiasm of lone innovators within the education system, as well as the creative work done outside of formal schooling. It is, of course, vitally important that we continue to document and celebrate this, because it helps to build a body of evidence that demonstrates how we can build on the positive features of these virtual environments to create meaningful and motivating educational experiences for all children and young people.

REFERENCES

Abrams, S., & Walsh, S. (2014). Gamified vocabulary: Online resources and enriched language learning. *Journal of Adolescent & Adult Literacy*, *58*(1), 49–58. doi:10.1002/jaal.315

Annetta, L. (2010). The I's have it: A framework for serious educational game design. *Review of General Psychology*, *14*(2), 105–112. doi:10.1037/a0018985

Apperley, T. (2014). Understanding digital games as education technologies: capitalizing on popular culture. In P. Benson & A. Chik (Eds.), *Popular Culture, Pedagogy and Teacher Education: International perspectives* (pp. 66–82). Abingdon: Routledge.

Beavis, C. (2013). Multiliteracies in the wild: learning from computer games. In G. Merchant, J. Gillen, J. Marsh, & J. Davies (Eds.), *Virtual Literacies: interactive spaces for children and young people* (pp. 57–74). Abingdon: Routledge.

Beavis, C. (2014). Literature, imagination and computer Games: video games and the English/Literature curriculum. In C. Burnett, J. Davies, G. Merchant, & J. Rowsell, J. (Eds.), New literacies across the globe (pp.88-102). Abingdon: Routledge.

Beck, D., & Perkins, R. (2014). Review of educational research methods in desktop virtual world environments; framing the past to provide future direction. *Journal of Virtual Worlds Research*, *7*(1), 1–9.

Bensley, L., & Van Eenwyk, J. (2001). Video games and real-life aggression: Review of the literature. *The Journal of Adolescent Health*, *29*(4), 244–257. doi:10.1016/S1054-139X(01)00239-7 PMID:11587908

Bertozzi, E. (2012). Killing for girls: Predation play and female empowerment. *Bulletin of Science and Technology*, *32*(6), 447–454. doi:10.1177/0270467612469072

Bertozzi, E. (2014). The feeling of being hunted: Pleasures and potentialities of predation play. *Games and Culture*, *9*(6), 429–441. doi:10.1177/1555412014549578

Black, R. (2010). The language of Webkinz: Early childhood literacy in an online virtual world. *Digital Culture & Education*, *2*(1), 7–24.

Boellstorff, T. (2008). *Coming of Age in Second Life: An Anthropologist Explores the Virtually Human*. Princeton: Princeton University Press.

Boots, N., & Strobel, J. (2014). Equipping the designers of the future: Best practices of epistemic video game design. *Games and Culture*, *9*(3), 167–181.

Buckingham, D. (2003). *Media Education: literacy, learning and contemporary culture*. Cambridge: Polity Press.

Buckingham, D., Burn, A., & Pelletier, C. (2011). Case Study on the Impact of the Making Games Project. London: Institute of Education. Retrieved from http://www.ioe.ac.uk/research_expertise/ioe_rd_a4_mgames_0511.pdf

Bunchball. (2014). *What is gamification?* Retrieved from http://www.bunchball.com/gamification

Burn, A. (2009). *Making New Media: Creative Production and Digital Literacies*. New York: Peter Lang.

Burnett, C. (2009). Research into literacy and technology in primary classrooms: An exploration of understandings generated by recent studies. *Journal of Research in Reading*, *32*(1), 22–37. doi:10.1111/j.1467-9817.2008.01379.x

Burnett, C., & Bailey, C. (2014). Conceptualising collaboration in hybrid sites: playing *Minecraft* together and apart in a primary classroom. In C. Burnett, J. Davies, G. Merchant, & J. Rowsell (Eds.), *New Literacies across the Globe* (pp. 50–71). Abingdon: Routledge.

Burnett, C., Davies, J., Merchant, G., & Rowsell, J. (Eds.). (2014). *New Literacies across the Globe*. Abingdon: Routledge.

Burnett, C., & Merchant, G. (2011). Is there a space for critical literacy in the context of new media? *English. Practice and Critique, 10*(1), 41–57.

Burnett, C., & Merchant, G. (2014). Points of view: Reconceptualising literacies through an exploration of adult and child interactions in a virtual world. *Journal of Research in Reading, 37*(1), 36–50. doi:10.1111/jrir.12006

Carpenter, B. (2009). Living and learning in interesting times. *Journal of Virtual Worlds Research, 2*(1), 4–5.

Carr, D., Buckingham, D., Burn, A., & Schott, G. (Eds.). (2006). Computer Games: text, narrative and play. Cambridge, MA: Polity Press.

Carrington, V., & Hodgetts, K. (2010). Literacy-lite in BarbieGirls™. *British Journal of Sociology of Education, 31*(6), 671–682. doi:10.1080/0142 5692.2010.515109

Cassell, J., & Jenkins, H. (Eds.). (1998). *From Barbie to Mortal Kombat: Gender and computer games*. Cambridge, MA: MIT.

Castronova, E. (2005). *Synthetic Worlds: the Business and Culture of Online Games*. London: University of Chicago Press.

Club Penguin. (n.d.). *About Club Penguin*. Retrieved from http://www.clubpenguin.com/company/about

Cope, B., & Kalantzis, M. (Eds.). (1999). *Multiliteracies: Literacy Learning and the Design of Social Futures*. London: Macmillan.

Dede, C., Clarke, J., Ketelhut, D., Nelson, B., & Bowman, C. (2006). *Fostering Motivation, Learning and Transfer in Multi-User Virtual Environments*. Paper given at the 2006 AERA Conference, San Francisco, CA.

Ensslin, A. (2014). *Literary Gaming*. London: MIT Press.

Entertainment Software Association. (2014). *2014 essential facts about the computer and video game industry*. Retrieved from http://www.theesa.com/category/research/

Flemish Ministry of Education and Training. (2010). *Aims of the cross-curricular subjects*. Retrieved from http://www.ond.vlaanderen.be/curriculum/publicaties/voet/voet2010.pdf

Gee, J. (2003). *What videogames have to teach us about learning and literacy*. New York: Palgrave Macmillan.

Gee, J. (2005). Learning by Design: Good videogames as learning machines. *E-learning, 2*(1), 5–16. doi:10.2304/elea.2005.2.1.5

Gee, J., & Hayes, E. (2011). *Language and learning in the digital age*. Abingdon: Routledge.

Giddings, S. (2009). Events and collusions: A glossary for the microethnography of video game play. *Games and Culture, 4*(2), 144–157. doi:10.1177/1555412008325485

Gillen, J. (2009). Literacy practices in Schome Park: A virtual literacy ethnography. *Journal of Research in Reading, 32*(1), 57–74. doi:10.1111/j.1467-9817.2008.01381.x

Gillen, J., & Merchant, G. (2013). From virtual histories to virtual literacies. In G. Merchant, J. Gillen, J. Marsh, & J. Davies (Eds.), *Virtual Literacies: interactive spaces for children and young people* (pp. 9–27). Abingdon: Routledge.

Giroux, H. (2001). *The Mouse That Roared: Disney and the End of Innocence.* New York: Rowman & Littlefield.

Giroux, H. A., & Pollock, G. (2010). *The mouse that roared: Disney and the End of Innocence* (2nd ed.). New York: Rowman & Littlefield.

Hamari, J., Koivisto, J., & Sarsa, H. (2014). Does Gamification Work? – A Literature Review of Empirical Studies on Gamification. *Proceedings of the 47th Hawaii International Conference on System Sciences.* doi:10.1109/HICSS.2014.377

Hayes, E. (2013). A new look at girls, gaming, and literacies. In B. Guzzetti & T. Bean (Eds.), *Adolescent Literacies and the Gendered Self: (re)constructing identities through multimodal literacy practices* (pp. 101–108). Abingdon: Routledge.

Holland, D., Lachicotte, W., Skinner, D., & Cain, C. (2001). *Identity and Agency in Cultural Worlds.* Cambridge, MA: Harvard University Press.

Hollett, T. & Ehret, C (2014). Bean's World: (Mine)crafting affective atmospheres for gameplay, learning, and care in a children's hospital. *New Media and Society.* Doi 1461444814535192

IGEA. (2014). *Digital Australia.* Retrieved from http://www.igea.net/wp-content/uploads/2013/11/Digital-Australia-2014-DA14.pdf

Jenkins, H. (2006b). *Confronting the challenges of participatory culture: media education for the 21ˢᵗ century.* Chicago: MacArthur Foundation. Available at: http://www.pewinternet.org/files/old-media//Files/Reports/2008/PIP_Teens_Games_and_Civics_Report_FINAL.pdf.pdf

Kafai, Y. (2010). World of Whyville: An introduction to tween virtual life. *Games and Culture, 5*(1), 3–22. doi:10.1177/1555412009351264

Kim, S., Lee, J., & Thomas, M. (2012). Between purpose and method: A review of educational research. *Journal of Virtual Worlds Research, 5*(1), 1–8.

Kirriemuir, J. (2010). UK university and college technical support for *Second Life* developers and users. *Educational Research, 52*(2), 215–227. doi:10.1080/00131881.2010.482756

Kress, G. (2003). *Literacy in the New Media Age.* Abingdon: Routledge. doi:10.4324/9780203164754

KZero. (2013). *Universe Chart.* Retrieved from http://www.kzero.co.uk/blog/universe-chart-q4-2011-avg-user-age-10-15/

Lange, P. (2011). Learning real life lessons from online games. *Games and Culture, 6*(1), 17–37. doi:10.1177/1555412010377320

Lankshear, C., & Knobel, M. (2006). *New Literacies: Everyday Practices and Classroom Learning* (2nd ed.). Maidenhead: Open University Press.

Lankshear, C., & Knobel, M. (2010). *New Literacies: Everyday Practices and Social Learning* (3rd ed.). Maidenhead: Open University Press.

Leander, K., & McKim, K. (2003). Tracing the everyday 'sitings' of adolescents on the Internet: A strategic adaptation of ethnography across online and offline spaces. *Education Communication and Information, 3*(2), 211–240. doi:10.1080/14636310303140

Lemke, J. (2010). Lessons from *Whyville*: A hermeneutics of our mixed reality. *Games and Culture, 6*(1), 149–157. doi:10.1177/1555412010361944

Lenhart, A., Kahne, J., Middaugh, E., Macgill, A., Evans, C., & Vitak, J. (2008). *Teens, Video Games, and Civics*. Washington, DC: Pew Internet & American Life Project. Retrieved from http://www.pewinternet.org/files/old-media/Files/Reports/2008/PIP_Teens_Games_and_Civics_Report_FINAL.pdf.pdf

Livingstone, S. (2009). *Children and the Internet: Great expectations, challenging realities*. Cambridge: Polity Press.

Livingstone, S., Haddon, L., Gorzig, A., & Olafsson, K. (2011). *EU Kids Online*. Retrieved from http://www.lse.ac.uk/media%40lse/research/EUKidsOnline/EU%20Kids%20II%20(2009-11)/EUKidsOnlineIIReports/Final%20report.pdf

Mackey, M. (2002). *Literacies Across Media: Playing the text*. Abingdon: Routledge. doi:10.4324/9780203218976

Marsh, J. (2010). Young children's play in online virtual worlds. *Journal of Early Childhood Research*, *8*(1), 23–39. doi:10.1177/1476718X09345406

Marsh, J. (2013). Countering Chaos in *Club Penguin*. In G. Merchant, J. Gillen, J. Marsh, & J. Davies (Eds.), *Virtual Literacies: interactive spaces for children and young people* (pp. 73–88). Abingdon: Routledge.

Merchant, G. (2007). Writing the Future in the Digital Age. *Literacy*, *41*(3), 118–128. doi:10.1111/j.1467-9345.2007.00469.x

Merchant, G. (2009). Literacy in Virtual Worlds. *Journal of Research in Reading*, *32*(1), 38–56. doi:10.1111/j.1467-9817.2008.01380.x

Merchant, G. (2010). 3D Virtual worlds as environments for literacy teaching. *Education Research*, *52*(2), 135–150. doi:10.1080/00131881.2010.482739

Merchant, G. (2014). The Trashmaster: Literacy and new media. *Language and Education*, *27*(2), 144–160. doi:10.1080/09500782.2012.760586

Merchant, G., Gillen, J., Marsh, J., & Davies, J. (Eds.). (2014). *Virtual Literacies: interactive spaces for children and young people*. Abingdon: Routledge.

Mitchell, A., & Savill-Smith, C. (2004). *The use of computer and video games for learning: a review of the literature*. London: Learning and Skills Development Agency.

Morningstar, C., & Farmer, F. R. (2008). The lessons of Lucasfilm's *Habitat*. *Journal of Virtual Worlds Research*, *1*(1), 1–20.

Nardi, B. (2010). *My Life as a Night Elf Priest: An Anthropological Account of World of Warcraft*. Michigan: University of Michigan Press.

O'Brien, D., & Scharber, C. (2008). Digital literacies go to school: Potholes and possibilities. *Journal of Adolescent & Adult Literacy*, *52*(1), 66–68. doi:10.1598/JAAL.52.1.7

Ochsner, A., & Martin, C. (2013). Learning and cultural participation in *Mass Effect* and *Elder Scrolls* affinity spaces. In W. Kaminski & M. Lorber (Eds.), *Gamebased Learning: Clash of Realities 2012* (pp. 97–106). Munich: Kopäd Verlag.

Ofcom. (2013). *Children and Parents: Media Use and Attitudes Report*. Retrieved from http://stakeholders.ofcom.org.uk/binaries/research/media-literacy/october-2013/research07Oct2013.pdf

Palmaers, D. (2014). *Playing a Serious Game to Enhance Financial Literacy: a case study of Skillville*. (Unpublished dissertation). Sheffield Hallam University, Sheffield, UK.

Palmer, S. (2006). *Toxic Childhood: how modern life is damaging our children and what we can do about it*. London: Orion.

Pearce, C. & Artemesia. (2010). *Communities of Play: Emergent Cultures in Multiplayer Games and Virtual Worlds*. Cambridge, MA: MIT Press.

Schott, G., & Kambouri, M. (2003). Moving between the spectral and the material plane. *Convergence*, *9*(3), 41–55.

Schott, G., & Kambouri, M. (2006). Social play and learning. In D. Carr, D. Buckingham, A. Burn, & G. Schott (Eds.), *Computer Games: text, narrative and play* (pp. 119–132). Cambridge, MA: Polity Press.

Sheridan, M., & Rowsell, J. (2010). *Design Literacies: Learning and Innovation in the Digital Age. Abungdon*. Routledge.

Squire, K. (2005). Changing the Game: What Happens When Video Games Enter the Classroom? *Innovate: Journal of Online Education*, *1*(6). Retrieved from http://www.editlib.org/j/ISSN-1552-3233/v/1/n/6/

Squire, K. (2012). *Video games and learning: Teaching and participatory culture in the digital age*. New York: Teachers College Press.

Statista. (2014). *Number of World of Warcarft subscribers from 1st quarter of 2005 to 2nd quarter of 2014*. Retrieved from http://www.statista.com/statistics/276601/number-of-world-of-warcraft-subscribers-by-quarter/

Stein, A., Mitgutsch, K., & Consalvo, M. (2012). Who are sports gamers? A large scale study of sports videogame players. *Convergence*, *19*(3), 345–353.

Steinkuehler, C. (2006). Massively multiplayer online gaming as participation in a discourse. *Mind, Culture, and Activity*, *13*(1), 38–52. doi:10.1207/s15327884mca1301_4

Steinkuehler, C. (2007). Massively multiplayer online games as a constellation of literacy practices. *E-Learning and Digital Media*, *4*(3), 297–318.

Steinkuehler, C. A. (2011). Video games and digital literacies. *Journal of Adolescent & Adult Literacy*, *54*(1), 61–63. doi:10.1598/JAAL.54.1.7

Thorhague, A. (2013). The rules of the game – the rules of the player. *Games and Culture*, *8*(6), 371–391. doi:10.1177/1555412013493497

Tuukkanen, T., Iqbal, A., & Kankaanranta, M. (2010). A framework for children's participation in virtual worlds. *Journal of Virtual Worlds Research*, *3*(2), 4–26.

Vygotsky, L. S. (1987). The collected works of L. S. Vygotsky: Problems of general psychology (vol. 1; R. W. Rieber & A. S. Carton Eds., N. Minick, Trans.). New York: Plenum Press.

Warschauer, M., & Matuchniak, T. (2010). New technology and digital worlds: Analyzing evidence of equity in access, use, and outcomes. *Review of Research in Education*, *34*(1), 179–225. doi:10.3102/0091732X09349791

White, D., & Le Cornu, A. (2010). Eventedness and disjuncture in virtual worlds. *Educational Research*, *52*(2), 183–196. doi:10.1080/00131881.2010.482755

Willett, R., Richards, C., Marsh, J., Burn, A., & Bishop, J. (2013). *Children, media and playground cultures: Ethnographic studies of school playtimes*. Basingstoke: Palgrave. doi:10.1057/9781137318077

Willett, R., Robinson, M., & Marsh, J. (Eds.). (2008). *Play, Creativity and Digital Cultures*. London: Routledge.

KEY TERMS AND DEFINITIONS

Avatar: The on screen image or character used to represent an individual player in a virtual world or online game.

Gamification: The use of video game principles or designs in the structuring of a learning experience (see Abrams & Walsh, 2014).

MMOG: Abbreviation of 'massively multiplayer online game' referring to a persistent Internet-based game played by large numbers.

MUVE: Abbreviation of 'multi-user virtual virtual environment' referring to a persistent internet-based virtual world characterised by community and world-building activity (see virtual world).

New Literacies: Communicative practices associated with new digital media, often described as new mindsets (see Lankshear & Knobel, 2006; 2010).

Online Video Game: A digitally-mediated game that depends on its players being online.

Predation Game: A video game that involves activity related to chasing, capturing other players or game-based characters.

Social Envelope: A term used by Schott & Kambouri (2003) to describe the social activity that takes place in and around a video game.

Sports Game: A video game based on actions and activities associated with the world of sport.

Virtual Play: Onscreen activity that takes place in a videogame or virtual world (see Pearce & Artemesia, 2010).

Virtual World: An internet based MUVE that has no prescribed structuring of activity (see White & LeCornu, 2010).

Chapter 13
Digital Storytelling

Alan Davis
University of Colorado – Denver, USA

Leslie Foley
Grand Canyon University, USA

ABSTRACT

Digital storytelling, especially in the form of short personally-narrated stories first pioneered by the Center for Digital Storytelling in Berkeley in 1993, is a practice that has now expanded throughout English speaking countries and Western Europe, and has a smaller but growing presence in the developing world. This review examines the origins of the practice and early dissemination, and its current uses in community-based storytelling, education, and by cultural institutions. Research regarding the impacts and benefits of digital storytelling and relationships between storytelling, cognition and identity, and mediating technologies are examined. Current issues in the field, including issues of voice, ownership, power relationships, and dissemination are considered, along with possible future directions for research and implications for social practice and policy.

INTRODUCTION

In the broadest sense, digital storytelling refers to the use of digital media to produce and disseminate stories. That general definition encompasses a wide spectrum of uses of digital media: uses by corporations to control their public image and promote products, by politicians and interest groups to persuade, by artists as a creative medium, by non-profit groups to promote community development, by educators as an instructional tool and learning activity, and by academic researchers to speak to non-academic audiences. Digital stories are prominent in the entertainment industry, from computer games and motion pictures to animated cartoon shows. Smartphones and dissemination platforms like YouTube have given rise to an unprecedented explosion in participatory digital storytelling by non-professionals. The Pew Research Internet Project (2013) reported that 18% of adults in the United States have created videos and posted them online, and of these, 23% were scripted. A previous survey by the same organization reported that one in four teens that use the Internet records and uploads video to the Web (Lenhardt, 2012). The ways that such products are produced, disseminated, and viewed continue to change at a rapid pace, driven by reciprocal changes in technologies and the activities they mediate (Wertsch, 1998).

DOI: 10.4018/978-1-4666-8310-5.ch013

A more focused historical meaning of the term *digital storytelling* refers to a grassroots movement that used multi-media digital tools to help ordinary people tell their own "true stories," especially people who lacked access to the equipment and technical expertise required to produce and disseminate such stories in the not distant past. Digital storytelling as a phrase denoting an organized practice arose from the collaboration of Dana Atchley and Joe Lambert in California in the 1990s (Lambert, 2006), culminating in the founding of the Center for Digital Storytelling (CDS) in Berkeley in 1998. The influence of CDS has been acknowledged by most people writing about digital storytelling today, including most of the authors of the works included in this review. The origin story of CDS, paraphrased from Lambert's (2006) account, provides insights into elements of motivation and purpose, format, and processes that continue to influence digital storytelling today.

Lambert (2006, p. 2) described his childhood home as "an oasis of liberal friendliness in the desert of 1950s Texas conservatism." He immersed himself in folk music, especially songs that told stories of working people, headed to San Francisco in 1976, and became involved in the People's Theater Coalition. In 1986, he and three friends started Life on the Water, a theater company experimenting with solo performance, and it was there that he encountered Dana Atchley. Atchley had been traveling around the US collecting stories of offbeat Americans and presenting them on college campuses and community centers in multi-media shows. In 1990, he had an idea for a multi-media show about his own life, to be called *Next Exit*, and he brought it to Lambert at Life on the Water. Lambert could not obtain funding to produce it, but the two began to share ideas as Atchley produced the show himself and Lambert included it in a solo performance festival. By 1992, the San Francisco Bay area was experiencing the "digital tsunami" of Silicon Valley, and Atchley was refining the multi-media aspects of his show. He attended meetings of the newly

formed International Interactive Communications Society, and exchanged ideas with people bringing digital technology to performance arts.

In 1993, Atchley was invited to perform in a National Video Festival in Los Angeles, and to lead a three-day workshop there in the new Digital Media lab of the American Film Institute, helping people make short personal video stories, inspired by the example of his own "digital story". Lambert and two associates skilled in digital technology helped him prepare for the workshop and facilitate it. Ten people participated, and each produced a digital story. Lambert found the experience to be unlike anything he had previously experienced:

The sense of transformation of the material, and of accomplishment, went well beyond the familiar forms of creative activity I could reference. And even as the tools themselves frustrated me, I knew that this activity had a special power that could be shaped into a formal creative practice. (Lambert, 2006, p. 10)

Monte Fay Hallis produced a three-minute digital story at that first workshop about her friend Tanya Shaw, a woman struggling with AIDS, who died shortly before the story's screening. The story was personal, with emotional importance to the teller, and it and made an emotional connection with the viewer. It was simple and spare in a way that was aesthetically pleasing. It also personalized a larger issue of social justice.

From this beginning, Lambert left theater work to devote himself to continue the work of helping ordinary people to create their own digital stories. He and Atchley co-founded the Center for Digital Storytelling (CDS) as a formal organization in Berkeley in 1998, making use of intensive workshops to enable people who normally lacked technical expertise and access to digital video editing software to make digital stories. They typically screened the story of Tanya and other selected stories from early workshops (Lambert, 2006), to model elements of narrative content (personal, focused, emotionally significant) and digital elements (voiced narration, still images, two to three minutes in length). The CDS estimated that by 2014 some 25,000 digital stories had been produced in association with the Center for Digital Storytelling alone (D. Weinshenker, Personal Communication, November 24, 2014).

Digital storytelling loosely inspired by the model of the Center for Digital Storytelling (CDS) has expanded worldwide, and most of the published literature using the phrase *digital storytelling* refers to a short multi-media product of the type pioneered by CDS: a voiced narration telling a story accompanied by visual images viewed on a screen and lasting about three minutes. Production of digital stories has been described in schools, universities, community centers, museums, libraries, health organizations, non-profit organizations and non-governmental development and relief organizations (NGOs), churches, and multi-media centers such as CDS. The practice was introduced into the United Kingdom by Daniel Meadows of the Cardiff University School of Journalism after visiting the Center for Digital Storytelling in Berkeley. Beginning in 2001, Cardiff University and the BBC sponsored *Capture Wales* (Meadows & Kidd, 2009), which made hundreds of personal digital stories about life in Wales available online. A subsequent BBC project throughout the UK, *Telling Lives*, created a large collection of digital stories by UK residents available through the Internet (Thumin, 2008). Similar projects were undertaken in Scandinavia in the early 2000s including faith-based stories in Norway (Kaare & Lundby, 2008). Since then, digital storytelling has been facilitated by hundreds of organizations throughout the world, including several large grants from the Ford Foundation in 2013. McWilliam (2009) recently surveyed 300 different programs worldwide facilitating digital storytelling and maintaining an active online presence.

Much of the research and scholarship regarding digital storytelling can be characterized as addressing aspects of a small number of broad questions:

- What explicit and implicit purposes does digital storytelling serve?
- How does collective digital storytelling serve marginalized and disempowered groups?
- What issues of privacy, authorship, control, and risk arise in the facilitation of digital storytelling, especially with members of disempowered groups?
- How is digital storytelling used in educational settings, and with what effects?
- How does digital storytelling serve as a potentially transformative developmental resource for the storyteller?
- How can digital storytelling serve as a research approach for scholars to promote new knowledge and influence policy making?
- What is the relationship between the activities in which storytelling is embedded, the nature of the stories themselves and the technology available to produce and disseminate them?

These questions loosely correspond to disciplinary and institutional domains, and are reflected in the major sections that organize this chapter. The relationships between medium, message, and activity are largely discussed within the disciplinary domains of communication theory and sociological media studies. The instrumental purposes of digital storytelling are most prominently considered within educational research. Digital storytelling is now becoming commonplace in both K-12 and higher education settings, especially in the context of language arts and social studies activities in elementary schools, after school clubs and youth organizations with teens, and in a wide and expanding number of contexts in institutions of higher education. The transformative potential of digital storytelling may be understood as an inquiry within the broader body of personal narrative theory and self-reflection within psychology, with implications for both educators and therapists. Finally, collective digital storytelling frequently draws on critical theory and purposes of social justice, with an emphasis on group empowerment and community support. Questions of ethics, protection of participants, and tensions between the purposes of participants, facilitators, and funders apply across several categories, but recently have been discussed most prominently by those employing digital storytelling in the service of disempowered groups.

BACKGROUND

Digital Storytelling and Community-Based Narratives

The use of digital storytelling by different cultural and social communities to "capture their own stories, using approaches and methods that reflect both historical cultural practices and contemporary expressions and ideas in these communities" has been advocated by the Center for Digital Storytelling since its inception (Lambert, 2009, p. 96). Purposes may include creating a collection of individual accounts of life within a shared community (Meadows & Kidd, 2009), promotion of mental and physical well-being (Gubrium, 2009; Hardy & Sumner, 2014), promotion of human rights and breaking down prejudices (American Friends Service Committee, 2014), empowering disempowered groups to define and disseminate their own collective and individual stories to counter stories and impressions of them created by others (American Friends Service Committee, 2014), to convey perceptions of a community to funders, program managers, or scholars as part

of an evaluation or participatory action research effort (Dibley, 2011; Gubrium & Otañez, 2013; T. Lewin, 2011), to promote democracy and participatory government (M. A. Clarke, 2009) and to promote reflective practice and foster cohesion and collaboration within a community of practice (Freidus & Hlubinka, 2002).

Similar purposes underlie the practice of *photovoice*, a multi-media approach first developed in 1992 by Caroline Wang and Mary Ann Burris to empower rural women in China to influence policies (Wang & Burris, 1992). Photovoice has been employed widely as a methodology in which marginalized or disempowered participants use photography in a joint project to portray their experiences and concerns (Mitchell, 2008), and there is apparently a more extensive scholarly literature about its use in participatory action research and community development than there is for digital storytelling (Wilcox, 2009). A primary distinction is that digital storytelling results in a narrated video presentation in story form, whereas photovoice results in a collection of photographs with captions that may be presented in exhibitions, online, or in print (Rudkin & Davis, 2007).

Community-based stories generally involve bringing together participants who share an important element of shared experience (e.g., refugees from Somalia, women who have experienced sexual assault, transgendered persons) into a workshop setting. A central element of the process is participation in a *story circle* (Lambert, 2013), in which participants share personal experiences as potential ideas for digital stories in an atmosphere of confidentiality and trust. The interactive process of the story circle has been interpreted as revealing and enacting social co-construction of identity, as participants make choices about what is significant about their individual stories, what elements are shared across their individual stories, and how experiences can be shaped and framed for sharing with an audience (Freidus & Hlubinka, 2002; Gubrium, 2009). Freidus and Hlubinka (2002) described a *meta-narrative* that may emerge from the group's recognition of common experiences as individual experiences are shared. For example, a collection of digital stories by Somali Bantu refugees in Baltimore, Maryland (American Friends Service Committee, 2008) portrayed a collective story of oppression and exodus from Somalia and life in a refugee camp before coming to the United States, along with individual variations of how life was after arriving in the United States.

Facilitators of community-based digital storytelling have documented benefits for participants. Freidus and Hlubinka (2002) described how joint participation in digital storytelling enable participants to come into a stronger collaborative relationship with one another, suggesting that the practice can strengthen communities of learners within organizational contexts. Participants in story circles experience emotional support and solidarity through the sharing of experience that can be part of a healing process (Gubrium, 2009) and can co-construct positive assertions of identity that counter positioning by dominant groups (T. Lewin, 2011). Wilcox (2009) conducted a systematic evaluation of three community development projects in which youth made digital stories about issues in their communities in California. In all three, she found a new degree of understanding about community-based issues, access to resources and technology that allowed community members to expand skill-sets. Through sharing their story in small group settings, participants gained a greater sense of ownership of their experiences and increased participation in future decisions about their communities.

Several writers have considered the potential value of digital storytelling to inform a broader community, particularly potential allies, professional care givers, and policy makers, about the perspectives of members of a less empowered community in order to further understanding, often with the aim of improving treatment, policies and programs. When employed for this purpose, digital storytelling becomes a technique for *participatory*

action research, with historical roots in the work of Kurt Lewin (1946). *Participatory* action research is distinguished from other forms of action research by an emphasis on enlisting those most directly affected by a problem in describing and analyzing the problem and bringing about change (Reason & Bradbury, 2008). Examples of the use of digital storytelling in this tradition include disseminating stories of immigrants and refugees publicly via the Internet (American Friends Service Committee, 2008; 2014), sharing patients' digital stories with healthcare providers (Hardy & Sumner, 2014), facilitating digital stories by youth in California to develop community pride and awareness of community development efforts (Wilcox, 2009); and using digital stories by Maori community members as feedback to policy makers in New Zealand regarding changes within Maori social networks and to NGO program personnel and government officials in Bangladesh and South Africa (Lewin, 2011). In these contexts, especially when policy makers or service providers are intended audiences, digital storytelling can be a technique for participatory action research by bringing the voices and viewpoints of participants into decision making processes.

Digital Storytelling in Educational Settings

Screen media such as smartphones and computer games have become commonplace in the figured worlds of youth throughout the developed world. Fashions, popular culture heroes such as athletes, musicians and actors, and narratives that figure large in popular culture are known to youth today primarily through screen media, and the importance of these media as new literacies are increasingly recognized by educators (Hull & Schultz, 2002; Jenkins, Puroshotma, Weigel, Clinton, & Robison, 2009). Messages communicated through screen media have a strong impact in shaping youths' opinions about fashion, sexuality, and status, and provide a rich source of narrative motifs which young people take up in their own storytelling to address issues in their own lives (Diamondstone, 2004; Dyson, 1997). For these reasons, there is evidence that youth associate screen media with high interest and high status. Digital storytelling taps into youths' associations with screen media as preferred means of communication.

There is growing use of digital storytelling as an educational activity in youth centers and after-school programs (Davis & Weinshenker, 2012; Hull & Katz, 2006) and within educational institutions, both in K-12 schools and in universities. In a recent survey of institutions offering digital storytelling programs and maintaining an active online presence, 55 programs were in K-12 schools (McWilliam, 2009). As a practice that developed first outside of institutional learning and has been brought into the classroom with the associated constraints of formal learning objectives, grading, teacher control, and accountability concerns, different purposes and questions arise (Erstad & Selseth, 2008). In this section, we address digital storytelling in K-12 schooling in relationship to new understandings of literacy and 21st century skills, and student agency, voice, and engagement. Finally, we consider digital storytelling in higher education.

New Literacies and Multiliteracies

The development of portable computers and digital communications in the last decades of the 20th century led to calls for the integration of technology into schooling and descriptions of generally inconsistent but promising uses (Leu Jr., 2000, 2002; Schachter & Kasper, 2014; Valmont & Wepner, 2000). The Common Core State Standards (2014) now include the use of new technologies and new literate practices. New literacies include the use of technical tools and a new mindset that focuses on cultural and social relations that stem from valuing participation, collaboration, dispersion, and distributed expertise of literacy practices (Lankshear & Knobel, 2006).

A call to re-think the meaning of literacy and its relationship to schooling that has proven highly influential was formulated by a group of ten educators meeting for a week in New London, New Hampshire in 1994 who became known as the New London Group. They published their position paper in *Harvard Education Review* (New London Group, 1996), and subsequently as a book (New London Group, 2000). Arguing that the mission of education is to prepare all students to participate fully in public, community, and economic life, the New London Group identified ways in which technology and globalization were fundamentally changing the sorts of literacies needed to support full participation in those three domains. In a world characterized by both local diversity and global connectedness, people are more likely to communicate across languages and cultures and need to operate flexibly across speech registers and social contexts. Modern communication regularly includes images, text, and sound, and full participation entails being able to employ these modalities in communication as well as to interpret and critique them. Work environments increasingly emphasize flexibility, continuous learning, teamwork, and the adoption of new technologies. Boundaries between public and private blur. People's identities are multi-layered as they participate in multiple and overlapping communities, calling for facility with multiple discourses (New London Group, 2000).

The New London Group proposed *design* as the basic metaphor for developing a pedagogy of multiliteracies. Design refers both to the form of products and to the processes for arriving at them. Design changes over time, and responds to particular problems and needs, but draws on principles of both science and art to arrive at products that work and are pleasing. Teachers need to see themselves as designers of learning activities and learning environments, and students need to be designers within those learning environments, intentionally drawing on available technologies, modalities, and discourses for different purposes and audiences (New London Group, 2000).

Digital storytelling fits well with the vision of multiliteracies expressed by the New London Group in several respects. It employs screen technologies attractive to youth and allows them to author within those technologies in ways not possible by simply texting, or exchanging pictures or videos (Hagood, 2009; Nucera & Lee, 2014; Thoman & Jolls, 2004). As a personal expression directed at a real audience and employing the author's own voice, digital storytelling develops personal agency, encourages reflection on identity, and choices regarding voice and register. As a process of planning and assembling elements of text, images, transitions, and soundtrack, it is an experience in design.

Defining agency as the capacity to make a difference in respect to cultural practices, Erstad and Silseth (2008) focused on the stand students take when expressing themselves through digital storytelling. They argued that digital storytelling provides opportunities for greater agency in comparison with most classroom activities because it privileges the student's interpretation before an audience, highlights the student's personal voice, and raises the student's voice to an authoritative plane within the classroom context, supported by multiple modalities. Others have noted the importance of student agency and voice (Banaszweski, 2002) particularly in respect to students who had greater facility with visual and oral expression than with the written word (Banaszweski, 2002; Erstad & Silseth, 2008; Sylvester & Greenidge, 2009). Researchers have also observed that students who created digital stories in the classroom demonstrated increased engagement and confidence (Foley, 2013; Frazel, 2010; Sylvester & Greenidge, 2009; Vasudevan, Schultz, & Bateman, 2010). Foley (2013) studied the use of digital storytelling to develop multimodal literacies of first and second-grade students. The students developed confidence in their traditional literacy skills, as well as multimodal literacies, including selecting among fonts, images, and transitions. Students began to see themselves as writers with important information to share.

The development of a digital story engages the student in potentially complex processes of design. The student needs to plan the structure of the story, integrate visual and narrative elements, anticipate audience, develop a point of view, and write a script, a task posing cognitive demands associated with significant benefits for students (Jonassen, Howland, Marra, & Crismond, 2008). Mayer (2014) argued that the use of multiple sensory modalities, drawing on different parts of the brain, further enhances the learning experience.

Digital storytelling has become one of many uses of new technologies in classrooms. Students make use of the form to tell autobiographical stories (Kajder, 2004), but also to invent myths (Kulla-Abbott & Polman, 2008) to explain mathematical concepts (Dreon, Kerper & Landis, 2011), describe and connect personal meanings to historical events such as the Holocaust (Levin, 2003), to investigate environmental issues (Kulla-Abbott & Polman, 2008) and to describe and respond to art (Chung, 2007).

One well-designed comparison study (Ballast, Stephens, & Radcliffe, 2008) found that participation in digital storytelling improved students' writing, apparently through the time and attention given to developing and revising the script in anticipation of screening the finished product before an audience. The researchers found that the writing of sixth grade students as measured by a scored writing sample improved relative to a control group following participation in a six-week writing unit that culminated in a digital story.

Pahl and Rowsell (2010) emphasized the potential of digital storytelling to enable students to make emotional and conceptual connections between the classroom and their lives outside of school. Drawing on the construct of *artifact* as an object with special meaning associated with time and place, they analyzed examples from New Jersey and United Kingdom of students using digital stories to make visible and explicit connections between parts of their lives that had seemed unconnected. In one, a Latino high school student studying *The Odyssey* likened Ulysses's quest to his own struggles to succeed at football, and Athena's protection of Ulysses to his older brother's support of him. In another, parents and children together made digital stories about artifacts in their homes and screened the stories at the primary school. Drawing on Bourdieu's (1990) construct of *habitus*, Pahl and Rowsell (2010) argued that the processes of reflecting on elements of their out-of-school lives and presenting them to audiences within the school context supported shifts in dispositions associated with each context.

Darvin and Norton (2014) propose that the elevation of students' lived experience and cultural perspectives through digital storytelling can create a *third space* for immigrant students in the classroom. Third space (Bhabha, 1994; Gutierrez, 2008) is a discourse space that draws on both dominant cultural resources and dominant language and patterns of discourse, and the cultural resources and discourse of the family and community of origin of the student. Darvin and Norton (2014) described a three-month *Literacy through Digital Storytelling* program in a Vancouver, Canada secondary school with a predominantly immigrant student population, in which youth first read stories of migrant experience, and then created and screened digital stories of their own experience, narrated in the language of their choice, with English subtitles. The activity enacted a third space in which the experiences, identities, and language of the students were salient at the same time students developed multimodal literacies valued by the school.

Educators in several continents are using digital stories as an instructional resource to develop students' receptive and expressive language in both first and second languages. Resources available on the Internet allow teachers to make use of stories developed by others, and often to develop and contribute stories by their own students. For example, *Scribjab.com* is a website and iPad ap-plication developed by Canadian scholars Toohey and Dagenais at Simon Fraser University, allowing young students to read and create subtitled digital stories using multiple languages. The African Storybook Project (http://www.saide.org.za/african-storybook-project), established by the South African Institute for Disease Education, provides young learners in sub-Saharan Africa open-access digital stories in both African languages and English. Kindersite.org, developed by Ziv Avidor, provides digital stories and other resources for teaching English to young children.

An emerging body of comparative studies have examined the effects of digital stories on second language acquisition. Yang and Wu (2012) studied the effects of digital storytelling as a means of teaching English to students in Taiwan employing an experimental design, and found significant effects on English achievement, critical thinking, and learning motivation in comparison to a lecture-based approach. Verdugo and Belmonte (2007), studying the use of digital stories from the Internet (Kindersite.org) in teaching English to six-year-old students in Spain (n = 220), found moderate to high effect sizes in comparison with students with teacher-led instruction. Similar results have been reported with elementary students studying English in Taiwan (Tsou & Tzeng, 2006). These results from international studies raise possibility that similar effects might be obtained in the United States and other English-dominant countries for the use of digital storytelling in teaching English to speakers of other languages.

Digital Storytelling in Higher Education

Increasing use of digital storytelling is reported in higher education. McWilliam's (2009) survey identified 68 colleges, professional training schools, and universities with digital storytelling programs with active online presences. Within universities, the majority of programs were associated with teacher preparation programs, especially in North America. The second largest group of programs were in media production departments (McWilliam, 2009). Many universities also employ digital storytelling as a learning activity within courses. A short list of examples includes film study at Hamilton College (Matthews-DeNatale, 2008), teacher education in Japan (Susono, Ikawa, & Kagami, 2011), humanities courses in Australia (R. G. Clarke & Thomas, 2012), and applied anthropology courses in Colorado (Otañez, 2011). Robin (2008) and Rudnicki et al. (2006) have provided descriptions of a wide range of uses of digital storytelling in higher education.

Rina Benmayor (2008) has proposed that digital storytelling become a signature pedagogy for the humanities, arguing that it represents an assets-based social pedagogy with the potential to empower and transform students intellectually, creatively, and culturally. Clarke and Thomas (2012), drawing on Benmayor, evaluated the use of digital storytelling with undergraduates in humanities courses in Australia, and found that the anticipated benefits were realized and confirmed by the participating students. Students commented that the digital narrative allowed them to bring a more personal perspective to the critique of literature and that the activity caused them to reflect on their own identity.

Benmayor (2012) has written extensively about the use of personal digital storytelling with Latino students in higher education, using the Spanish word *testimonio* in place of *storytelling* to convey the meaning of a significant personal account. The activity leads students to examine their personal experience and sense of identity in an atmosphere of mutual trust that is confirming and empowering. The use of visual and oral modalities in addition to written text also draws on students' strengths, and the activity can lead students to make strong personal connections to content in Latino literature or ethnic studies courses. Describing her Latina Life Stories course, Benmayor writes:

Teaching testimonio to the YouTube generations is a happy endeavor. The marriage of multimedia and testimonio has turned the Latina Life Stories into a space of active learning and creativity, giving voice—figuratively and literally—to young Latin@ and other students of color who rarely encounter a space in the academy to tell their truths and be heard. The digital world offers a democratizing opportunity for young Latin@s to tell their stories in their preferred "language" of multimedia. Moreover, the digital medium offers many more possibilities for authorship than the traditional publication format that Latin@s found, and still do find, so hard to break into (Benmayor, 2012, p. 521).

This example could potentially be extended to the use of digital storytelling with other groups of students who may be wrestling with establishing an identity within higher education such as first year students, first generation students, and women majoring in male-dominated fields.

Digital Storytelling in Cultural Institutions

McWilliam (2009) identified 51 digital storytelling programs hosted by cultural institutions including libraries (40), media centers or film boards (6) and museums (5). Most of these described themselves has *historical* digital storytelling programs, collecting digital stories to document life in the community at a point in time. For example, six California libraries participated in the *California of the Past* project, running workshops for community members to tell personal stories in order to form a historical collection. Similarly, a program in Malmo, Norway ran workshops to create a collection of stories of the history of the city. *Capture Wales* (Meadows & Kidd, 2009), perhaps the first large-scale effort of this type, collected 404 personal stories in 2001, all still available online at the time of this writing. A survey of participants indicated that 79% thought the experience would have "a lasting impact" on them (Meadows & Kidd, 2009, p. 111). A similar program, the Australian Centre for the Moving Image, collects and exhibits personal digital stories of Australians (Simondson, 2009), and another operates through Museu da Pessoa (Museum of the Person) in São Paulo, Brazil (Clarke, 2009).

There are a number of resources online that discuss elements of digital storytelling and its learning applications. *Educational Uses of Digital Storytelling* at the University of Houston (http://digitalstorytelling.coe.uh.edu) is a comprehensive website including a summary of digital examples, software, elements, lesson plans and tips. The Center for Digital Storytelling (httl://storycenter.org) provides examples of stories and features the Digital Storytelling Cookbook, discussing story elements and approaches to scripting and digitizing story elements.

The Center for Digital Storytelling (Storycenter.org) offers various public workshops in an effort to engage more participants in digital storytelling. The value of the human voice is vital in all workshops ranging from education to public health. For example, public health participants learn the value of first-person multimedia narratives in public health education and policy advocacy in a workshop model. Researchers and community practitioners explore how digital storytelling can enhance public health promotion by first creating digital stories and turning them into videos to give insight into complex health issues in an attempt to drive changes in behavior, social norms, and policy. The Embodied Story Workshop focuses on awareness of body, spirit, and life experience including a combination of yoga, energy work, movement, story sharing, writing, photography, audio recording, and performance. The one-day Snapshot Story Workshop challenges participants to create a digital story based on a single photograph.

Digital Storytelling as a Transformative Developmental Resource

Several researchers have suggested that digital storytelling has the potential to serve as a significant resource in the process of identity change and identity development (Davis, 2004; Davis & Weinshenker, 2012; DeGennaro, 2008; Hull & Katz, 2006). The term *transformative learning* has been used by adult learning theorists (Illeris, 2014; Mezirow, 2000) to denote positive change that involves a shift in identity, and in this sense digital storytelling is claimed to serve as a transformative resource for the participant, contributing to lasting change in the sense of self.

Theoretical support for the relationship of digital storytelling to transformative learning can be drawn from Bruner's (1990) narrative theory and from Bakhtin's dialogic theory of identity construction (Holquist, 1990). According to Bruner (1990), human beings conceptualize experiences as narratives, and the narrative form is fundamental to making sense of experiences and retrieving them in memories. Bartlett's (1932) classic studies of memory demonstrated that our framing of memory in narratives serves not only to retrieve memories, but also shapes memory by altering our recollections into canonical representations of the social world. Shotter (1990) argued that this framing served a social function, so that memories can be more readily shared with others. The process of recall and sharing involves both literal memory and interpretation (Bruner, 1990). As we narrate, we interpret what things mean, evaluate their significance, and infer why they happened. The process of authoring a digital story involves a more intense, focused, and prolonged experience of personal narration than one ordinarily engages in, strengthening its potential for self-reflection and interpretation.

Personal narrative is at once born out of experience and gives shape to experience (Davis & Weinshenker, 2012). Ochs and Capps (1996), in their analysis of the relationship between narrative and identity, argued that reflective awareness of one's past and future is shaped by one's narrative framing of experience:

Spinning out their tellings through choice of words, degree of elaboration, attribution of causality and sequentiality, and the foregrounding and backgrounding of emotions, circumstances and behavior, narrators build novel understandings of themselves-in-the-world. In this manner, selves evolve in the time frame of a single telling as well as in the course of the many tellings that eventually compose a life (Ochs & Capps, 1996, p. 22).

In short, we are the actor in our own stories, and it is the stories as well as the objective actions that constitute a life and an identity.

Recent empirical research has provided a more detailed account of how stories shape identity. Daily diary studies and repeated recordings of conversations of married couples indicate that nearly all life events experienced as significant are shared with someone in the form of a personal story within 24 hours (McLean, Pasupathi, & Pals, 2007). Listener behavior (attentive or non-attentive) affects how much tellers elaborate their stories, impacting subsequent memories (Pasupathi & Hoyt, 2009). Negative stories are more readily remembered than positive stories, are told more often, and have more impact than positive stories on the sense of self (Fivush, 2004). McLean, Pasupathi, and Pals (2007) hypothesized that telling stories that arrive at positive resolutions of negative themes in the presence of attentive, supportive audiences have the greatest potential for positive transformations of self-concept.

An emerging body of qualitative research on the impacts of digital storytelling on identity support these findings from psychologists. Davis and Weinshenker (Davis, 2004; Davis & Weinshenker, 2012) described through detailed case studies how the day-by-day processes of script development, revision, and eventual showing of digital stories

before a supportive audience of peers were associated with positive re-constructions of self with long term effects. Hull and Katz (2006) used case study methodology to document similarly transformative effects. Davis and Weinshenker (2012) argued that the time, concentration, and technical decisions required to produce personal digital stories contribute to their transformative potential for the storyteller in comparison to other types of narratives. A digital story becomes "fixed" in a way that is not true of oral stories or written text. The oral story can vary each time it is told, and allows the author the opportunity to re-construe with each telling. The digital story, in contrast, involves a complex linking of narrative and imagery, and is difficult to change. Once it is complete, its "telling" does not require the participation of the storyteller: it stands as a work of art, a representation apart from the teller, an "object" for reflection and critique. The fact that it can require significant planning and several days to complete can add to its significance to the teller.

Sociological Media Studies

Inquiry into digital storytelling from the perspective of sociological media studies is well represented in an anthology edited by Knut Lundby (2008), *Digital Storytelling, Mediatized Stories*. The line of inquiry builds upon Vygotsky's (1934/1978) observation that human activity is mediated by physical and conceptual tools, including language and other symbols, and by Wertch's (1998) observation that activity and tools develop in a reciprocal relationship over time. Given these understandings, it is not surprising that the ancient practice of storytelling, at once activity and tool, leads to the invention of new ways of mediating stories, and that our notions of storytelling are in turn shaped by the new mediational tools that become available (Erstad & Wertsch, 2008). Several questions arise: How does the use of digital technologies affect the content and interpretation of personal storytelling? As digital storytelling becomes more familiar and widespread, how do emerging themes and genres come to shape our interpretations of *personal* stories told by *ordinary* people in *community*? How do broader familiar contexts of commercial storytelling in television, movies, and computer games, combined with greater access to digital photography, recording and editing impact our tacit notions of *quality* and originality in digital storytelling?

Multimodality and Cultural Tools

At the heart of a story is a sequence of events. Yet the same sequence of events, expressed as a written text, an oral telling, or a digital story combining voice narrative, visual images, and perhaps music and sound effects, can convey different messages to an audience. Each of the modal elements – voice, image, sound track – draws on its own implicit semiotic "grammar" (Kress, 2003; Kress & van Leeuwen, 2001). The same sentence spoken in rap cadence to a hip-hop rhythm track conveys something different about both speaker and message than the same words spoken slowly and quietly. The phrase, "She headed off alone" illustrated by an image of a woman leaving a bar at night conveys a different feeling than the same phrase illustrated by a hot air balloon rising in a misty morning. Multi-modal communication provides a much richer symbolic palette than written or spoken text alone, but requires additional aesthetic choices. Hull and Nelson (2005) analyzed how a multimodal text can create a different system of signification, one that transcends the collective contribution of its constituent parts. The meaning that a viewer or listener experiences transcends what is possible via each mode separately.

Digital storytelling by individuals occurs within cultural contexts, *performance spaces* (Erstad & Wertsch, 2008; Goffman, 1959) or *MediaSpaces* (Couldry & McCarthy, 2004; Lundby, 2009) that include individuals' familiarity with commercial media, multimedia tools, and digital stories made by others available at particular times and places. These *affordances* (Gibson, 1979/1986) are cultural tools that shape the individual storyteller's thinking about potential stories implicitly or explicitly, as the storyteller selects from available *schematic narrative templates* (Erstad & Wertsch, 2008). The personal story emerges as an individual variation within a social genre.

Most digital storytelling by individuals takes place in digitally-rich societies such as the United States, Northern Europe, and Australia, places where people are familiar with genres of film and television and have a growing proficiency in the language of media (Lundby, 2009). But this cultural context also is reflected in internalized standards for what constitutes interesting or worthwhile digital story when, for example, a sponsoring organization is selecting digital stories by *ordinary people* for dissemination or display. Nancy Thumin (2009) pointed out the paradox of institutions seeking stories by ordinary people, when the implicit standards for interesting stories include a tension or contradiction beyond ordinary life and some level of technical artistry relative to the commercial digital productions that we encounter daily. The result is to showcase stories that are out of the ordinary while celebrating them as portrayals of ordinary experience.

Stig Hjarvard (2004) has used *mediatization* to focus attention on how communications media come to impact (*mediatize*) the social practices that they play a part in representing. Political campaigns are shaped by the constraints and affordances of television coverage. Weddings take on features that make them ready for re-mediation, or imitate television versions of such events (Couldry, 2008). Similarly, limitations of the workshop format, Internet bandwidth and storage, impose pressures to limit the length of digital stories, and awareness of the possibility of unintended and undesired audiences, both present and future, may lead storytellers to hold back personal material (Couldry, 2008).

Researchers in the tradition of sociological media studies are interested in how digital storytelling's contexts and processes of production become associated with styles of interpretation and meaning, associated social linkages, and implications for power and legitimation (Couldry, 2008; Drotner, 2008).

Digital storytelling has been used as a means for engaging in critical reflection among various social groups including social workers (La Rose, 2013), community activists (Sawchuk, 2013), and filmmakers (Washington & Keon, 2014). Their stories serve as examples of the mediation and mediatization of social practice. Digital stories allow authors to mediatize their writing, to use technology to perform traditional literacy practices. In doing so, these practices were also mediated, changed, and adjusted by the technology, and by digital media culture (Baym, 2010; Lundby, 2008; Markham & Baym, 2009). The politics of the storymakers were revealed in the stories, as well. As accounts were co-constructed and shared with others, the digital stories mediated and mediatized reflective, empowerment, and advocacy practices illustrating the significance of political orientation in shaping perspectives in the text. The stories were also mediated by the digital culture that became a part of the individuals' perceptions through their involvement in digital media.

CURRENT ISSUES IN THE FIELD

The salient issues arising in scholarship on digital storytelling vary substantially by disciplinary orientation. The use of digital storytelling for community development and group empowerment has raised important issues around (a) confidentiality and ethnical ownership of stories, (b) the influence of funders and sponsoring agencies on the content of stories and the processes through which they are produced, and (c) dissemination of stories and their impacts on decision makers and other audiences. In education, digital storytelling

remains one of many potential ways in which digital technologies may be employed in classrooms to develop students' facility with new tools of communication and presenting knowledge, in addition to promoting self-reflection. Many voices have called for explicit attention to developing students' new literacies, and established lists of 21st Century Skills include use of technology by students to develop and communicate knowledge. At the same time, there appears to be little effort to assess students' abilities in these areas.

Issues in Community-Based Digital Storytelling

The Issue of Voice

A commonly expressed goal for digital storytelling is to elevate the *authentic voice* of people whose voices have been silenced or minimized by dominant social structures. In a micro-analysis of the processes of script development in digital storytelling in an after-school program for middle school urban youth, Davis (2004) showed how story scripts emerged over extended periods of conversation and revision involving suggestions from adult facilitators. Adult influence was aimed at leading youth to reflect on their experiences and decide why they were meaningful, and at helping youth to weave images and ideas identified by the youth into a narrative form, all with realization that the stories would not be significant to the youth unless they owned them and believed them. Does this collaboration undermine the story as representing the *authentic voice* of the youth? Gubrium, Krause, and Jernigan (2014) have described conflicting understandings of *voice* between those who believe that each person has an authentic voice reflecting the true self, and those who view identity as socially constructed and shifting. Gubrium et al. (2014) argued for helping participants to strive for a *strategically* authentic voice in their stories, one not based on the assumption of an essential self apart from the influence of others, but a voice the teller believes in and also one that speaks strategically so that her message will be clear and persuasive. A role of the facilitator is to help the teller find a voice that is both authentic and strategic. The discussion is illustrative of the choices facing facilitators of digital storytelling.

Issues of Ethics and Risk

The process of creating and sharing stories within disempowered groups raises complex ethical questions of risk, confidentiality, trust, and ownership, which are explored in depth in *Community-Based Multiliteracies and Digital Media Projects* (Pleasants & Salter, 2014). Renuka Bery (Bery, 1995), writing before the advent of YouTube, identified a set of ethical questions to be considered by facilitators of participatory media. Fifteen years later, Sam Gregory (2010) raised ethical concerns about the proliferation of video on the Internet and drew attention to the need to balance freedom of expression with rights of privacy and inherent dangers in disseminating images of individuals engaged in activities and causes that could expose them to danger. Amy Hill (2014) used case studies of community-based digital storytelling to describe her shift from a position of wanting to "surface rarely heard stories in the service of justice", a stance she came to describe as naïve, to a much more cautionary stance governed by clearly articulated principles. In her examples, a teenager from California creates a digital story about his former life as a gang member and wants to include photos of his friends. Women in Nepal, a country with a very high incidence of violence against women and a stigma against women who have suffered sexual abuse, create digital stories about experiences of sexual violence that could have severely negative consequences for them if viewed by outsiders. At a digital storytelling workshop in South Africa for women with HIV/AIDS, one woman felt betrayed when her digital story was shared with members of the organization's staff who had not been present when she first created it. The examples highlight the complexity of safeguarding storytellers from their own desire to reveal information that can put them or others at risk, the difficulty in communicating information in advance about who might view a story, the impossibility of knowing in advance how some people will respond to one's story, and matters of ownership when a participant agrees to share her story and later changes her mind.

Funders' Goals, Participants' Goals

A related issue involves funding, and tensions between funders' goals and participants' goals. Community based digital storytelling often involves collaboration among community members, a non-profit organization that initiates and facilitates the process, and funders (typically foundations or government agencies). More than 52 foundations are now members of Grantmakers in Film and Electronic Media (GREM), foundations that fund media projects, including digital storytelling. Funders may impose goals and priorities for projects. Facilitating organizations, seeking funding, set forth goals and describe products and processes of dissemination in proposals in order to please funders, often without input from potential participants. Wilcox (2009) has raised the following questions: What kind of influence should foundations have over the focus of community based digital storytelling? How do foundation criteria affect the stories that are being told? How does the relationship between the grantee and the funder affect the extent to which the stories are distributed?

Once funding is obtained and participants come together with the facilitation of an organization, the goals of funders and facilitators, and perceptions of status and expertise become part of the context of the *politics of collaboration* as participants discuss themes, story lines, and potential audiences in the process of making community-based digital stories (Miller, Luchs, & Jalea, 2012). The *social location* of each participant, reflecting group affiliations and associated status, (Lee & Miller, 2014) is reflected in what decisions are made and how they come about.

Influencing Action

A final issue regards the dissemination of community-based digital stories and their role in shaping public opinion and influencing social action. Participants and funders often support community-based storytelling as a means of raising awareness and creating a community of support among participants and also changing perceptions and policies in broader social spheres. As we have pointed out, differences among participants may qualify this latter goal. Yet even when participants agree to the dissemination of their stories, active efforts to bring the stories to a wider audience through publicity, Internet positioning, and strategic use of social media may fall short (Wilcox, 2009) and no follow-up is done to gauge impact.

Issues in Education

In contrast to community-based digital storytelling, the practice of digital storytelling in schools and universities has become quite varied in implementation and has moved away from the workshop model pioneered by the Center for Digital Storytelling and the use of *story circle* as a means of shaping personal stories within a community of trust and safety. This brings into question how digital storytelling in schools is different from other forms of multimedia production by students, and whether digital storytelling is best thought of mainly as an issue of integrating technology into instruction. In that context, it shares important concerns with all other technological innovations in schooling, including issues of cost and teacher preparation. Whereas pens and paper have remained inexpensive and essentially the same for the past 50 years, the software for recording and compiling digital stories and the

platforms on which they are produced and viewed develop from year to year. These changes represent investment costs to schools, and challenges for preparing teachers to facilitate their use smoothly and inefficiently with large groups of students without the assistance of special grants to bring in outside assistance.

With the adoption of the Common Core State Standards in many states across the nation, emphasis has been placed on students' use of information and communication technologies, or ICTs (Leu, Kinzer, Coiro, & Cammack, 2004). ICTs are gaining momentum as an integral element to teaching and learning along with the notions that being literate now encompasses technological skills (Dalton, 2012). In addition, the Common Core State Standards highlight students' abilities to create both print and non-print texts through the integration of traditional and new literacies practices (Dalton, 2012). If digital storytelling is to take its place as a regular part of the repertoire of new literacy and student expression, technological support and procedural knowledge must become more widely available, and more attention paid to evaluating the proficiencies of students in digital production. At present, it is difficult to conduct research on the technological proficiencies acquired by students through digital storytelling, due to a lack of institutionalized measures.

FUTURE RESEARCH DIRECTIONS

Because the *digital storytelling* process is historically associated with the workshop model pioneered by the Center for Digital Storytelling, most of the research reviewed above treats digital storytelling as a planned endeavor rather than a societal phenomenon, undertaken intentionally for instrumental purposes. Over the past 15 years a rapidly expanding literature has treated digital storytelling as a novel technique, describing new uses with different groups for different purposes. Nearly all such studies have claimed benefits for participants and for audiences, and most have emphasized the processes through which those benefits may be realized. Very few have provided a carefully considered theoretical framework drawing the connections between processes and outcomes, and very few have brought disciplined attention to documenting or measuring outcomes in ways that would allow an examination of causal inferences. It seems to us that the expansion of descriptive studies may be approaching its peak potential, and that the field will benefit from studies linking theory, practice, and results employing disciplined research designs. Within each of the domains of practice for digital storytelling described above, the claimed benefits of the practice can be examined in order to clarify the relationship of theory to practice, and to test how widely the benefits actually are realized, under what circumstances, and at what cost.

K-12 Education

The studies and reports of the use of digital storytelling in schools, detailed above, report six main types of benefits: (a) student authoring in respect to new literacies, with students developing skills in using multiple modalities and technologies to produce and share their own expressive work in a variety of subject areas; (b) increased proficiency in writing; (c) improved content knowledge in respect to topics conveyed through digital stories, such as history; (d) improved learning of second languages; (e) improved student engagement, and (f) personal self-reflection. We discuss potential directions for research in each of these areas.

Student Authoring within New Literacies

Digital storytelling employs written text, oral production, and visual images, modalities that draw upon different parts of the brain (Williams, 2010) and may contribute to more efficient learning when used in combination (Mayer, 2014). In our review, few authors drew explicitly upon cognitive theory

supporting multi-media learning, theory reviewed in several chapters of the *Cambridge Handbook of Multimedia Learning* (Mayer, 2014). Research is needed that compares digital storytelling to other types of multimedia authoring available for use in classrooms. Does the use of visual *images* (as opposed to visual *text*, as in traditional Power Point presentations) along with spoken words lead to different and more efficient learning for both the author and the audience? If multimedia authoring (including digital storytelling) requires more time and expense than more conventional report writing and oral presentations by students, is this time and expense justified by evidence of learning outcomes beyond the importance of developing competence with the technology? Can we document with careful research that students with learning challenges related to reading and writing express (a) their personal stories and (b) their knowledge in content areas more competently through digital storytelling than through writing alone? Research addressing these questions could both guide practice and, depending on the findings, encourage greater financial support.

Writing

Although digital stories are not primarily written products, writing is usually involved in their production. Scripts are typically drafted and revised several times before they are recorded as voice tracks. Ballast et al. (2008), in a well-designed study discussed above, found that sixth-grade students engaged in a digital story unit performed higher on scored writing samples than a control group. Research to replicate these results with different grade levels, writing topics, and types of students would be valuable, because a concern with digital storytelling and with multimedia production in general is that it takes instructional time from traditional literacy learning, especially writing. It is reasonable that the use of the technology and the goal of screening a finished production before peers could lead students take more attention and care with the steps of drafting and revision than for a written story or report, resulting in improvements in writing.

Improved Content Knowledge

As described earlier in this chapter, digital storytelling has been used by students to communicate their understandings regarding history, mythology, science, and other academic subjects, but we are not aware of research studies that systematically studied the trade-offs between digital storytelling and other ways of developing and communicating subject knowledge. Comparisons would also be valuable between first-person digital narratives (including ones in which students assumed the identity of someone else, such as a person living at the time of the Civil War), and third-person narratives.

Second Language Learning

A small but well-designed body of studies, described previously in this review, suggests strong potential for the use of digital storytelling in the teaching of second languages, both as expressive tools as students develop and share their own stories, and as receptive tools, as students watch stories developed by others. The studies we reviewed involved students in non-English speaking countries learning English. Research on the use of digital storytelling with speakers of other languages living in English speaking countries as means of developing language skills is needed. The use of a single set of images with double soundtracks, one in the student's home language and another in the target language, has the advantage of elevating both languages, and has implications for developing biliteracy in immigrant students and speakers of tribal languages with declining populations of speakers or few written resources.

Student Engagement, Self-Reflection, and Agency

Digital storytelling has been described as empowering to students (Ballast et al., 2008; Nucera & Lee, 2014). As discussed above, digital storytelling enables students to author their own stories employing digital media and present them to audiences – acts of agency that encourage the author to draw on her own cultural perspectives and resources, including images and language. This suggests significant potential for improving academic performance of students from marginalized groups. This potential could easily be undermined by practices that are overly prescriptive and evaluative, and research on the potential of digital storytelling for marginalized youth has mainly taken place in out-of-school settings, however. Under what conditions do youth from marginalized groups display agency and engagement with digital storytelling within classroom settings? How can trust and safety be established in classroom settings to encourage self-reflection in digital storytelling without incurring risks? What evidence is there that the use of digital storytelling is particularly advantageous to children from marginalized groups in furthering academic learning?

Finally, little is known about how schools organize to implement digital storytelling. As the use of digital storytelling grows, it shifts from being an innovative practice piloted by a single teacher, to an organized effort involving several facilitators. Collaborations among library media specialists, computer teachers, and classroom teachers in regards to digital storytelling could be explored and described (Bromley, Faughnan, Ham, Miller, Armstrong, Crandall, Garrison, & Marrone, 2014).

Transformative Impacts on Identity

Following efforts by Jerome Bruner (1990) to formalize and consolidate work on the role of narrative in respect to memory, experience and identity within psychology (described above in this chapter), a lively field of narrative psychology has emerged with defined constructs and a growing body of empirical research on relationships among those constructs (Hevern, Josselson, & McAdams, 2013; McLean et al., 2007). Studies in the field have begun to address questions such as: Do stories about negative experiences have more transformative potential than positive stories? How does awareness of audience shape stories and impact their significance to the teller? How can digital storytelling be incorporated into transformative practices such as Alcoholics Anonymous and other approaches involving recurring testimonials before peers? Does storytelling bring experiences into long-term memory more effectively than other approaches to learning? Do men process personal stories differently than women? How do answers to each of these questions vary within cultural contexts? Narrative psychologists are addressing these questions, but not with specific attention to digital storytelling. How does digital storytelling compare to other forms of personal narrative (chatting with friends, keeping a diary, testifying at an altar call in a Baptist church, blogging, posting Facebook status updates) in respect to evoking reflection and shaping identity? How and in what ways does the social context of digital storytelling (e.g., story circle in a voluntary setting as opposed to a project in a class) shape the personal impact of the experience?

Further Research on Community-Based Digital Storytelling

The themes of individual and community empowerment and community change run through much of the writing about community-based digital storytelling, as reviewed above. Research

that described in detail what forms empowerment takes, both phenomenologically as experienced by the participants, and externally as observed by researchers, would be an important contribution. Recognizing that current evidence of impacts on participants is stronger than evidence of impacts on policy makers and broader audiences, Wilcox (2009) has called for more research on how digital storytelling increases knowledge about issues impacting underrepresented communities and how digital stories creating spaces for public discussion and action. How and to what extent are digital stories amplifying underserved voices? Heather Pleasants (Personal Communication, November 24, 2014) has hypothesized a three-stage trajectory of empowerment, through which participants first develop self-awareness through objectifying and sharing personal experience through digital story production, then come to see themselves as participating in a community of shared experience and drawing strength and confidence from that sense of group solidarity. Finally, participants may to take action individually or collectively such as advocating, reaching out to influence others, or participating in community organizing. Research on what roles digital storytelling might play in that trajectory of empowerment would be useful to the field.

CONCLUSION

Taken as a whole, descriptions of digital storytelling as a guided practice, and research on that practice in its varied forms and contexts, suggests a vital and growing activity that has moved from origins in the United States to other English speaking countries, and now to a growing list of countries worldwide. Nonetheless, apart from isolated examples, there is little evidence that the practice has had widespread impacts on education, civic engagement, or public policy, all areas that digital storytelling practitioners have set out to influence. There is evidence of significant potential, still in early stages of realization.

Perhaps the arena in which the implications of digital storytelling may be most auspicious is its use in higher education. McWilliam's (2009) survey identified 68 colleges, professional training schools, and universities with digital storytelling programs with active online presences, and there are many additional examples of universities in which digital storytelling is being taught as a course in itself, used as a research tool, or employed as a significant activity within a course. Such activities are actively promoted by catalyst institutions such as the University of Houston (digitalstorytelling.coe.uh.edu). Several factors favor the expansion of digital storytelling in higher education beyond multi-media programs. Faculty can integrate digital storytelling into their classes without institutional impediments, adult students can give consent to share personal stories and bring their own digital devices, technical assistance is readily available, and uses internal to the institution can be done without incurring costs. At the same time, university faculty are in ideal positions to make use of digital storytelling in participatory research, work for which some external funding is available. To the extent university schools of education begin to incorporate digital storytelling into teacher preparation programs (along with other pedagogical uses of multimedia technology) and other areas of professional preparation such as public health, universities may serve as the sort of catalyst for extending the practice in the way the Center for Digital Storytelling has done historically.

Within K-12 education, digital storytelling has largely untapped potential for all students within the expansion of students' digital literacy. But we believe it has particular promise students from marginalized groups, especially for students learning English as a second language. In the early stages of language learning, digital storytelling can serve as a highly engaging tool for creating and sharing stories, both personal and fictitious. In higher grades, when students are dealing with questions of identity, overcoming obstacles,

clarifying goals, and making choices about their futures, the combination of student authorship and agency, writing and revising a script, employing multiple modalities, and having an authentic audience for one's expressive productions can be a powerful combination. Perhaps the greatest obstacle to carrying out this potential is not the lack of access of low income students to digital devices with which to capture images and edit video, but rather the incessant accountability pressures that can discourage allocation of time to expressive production and create formal, evaluative environments that interfere with trust and authentic personal expression.

Civic engagement has been inherent in the practice of digital storytelling since its onset. Capture Wales (Meadows & Kidd, 2009), for example, involved hundreds of Welsh citizens recording personal stories about their lives and communities. Such large-scale projects have generally come and gone with little notice of their passing, because they are dependent on external funding that is not sustained, however. Non-profit organizations sponsor digital storytelling projects with civic engagement and individual and group empowerment as goals, but as discussed previously, the dissemination of stories to broad or influential audiences is a challenge for such projects, as is sustained funding. They are likely to persevere, but on a small scale and with limited impact, not because they do not have important potential, but because to grow in sustainable ways they must either serve the needs of participants in such clear ways that participants will seek them out and help pay for them, or they must find continuing funding sources.

At its core, it may be the transformative potential of digital storytelling for individuals and groups who participate in it seeking to understand themselves and to make sense of their experiences, especially experiences of dealing with hardships and obstacles, that will persevere and remain at the heart of the practice. Although we have not found articles about its specific use in narrative therapy, its therapeutic potential has been attested to by many (Davis & Weinshenker, 2012; Lambert, 2013). This potential has brought paying middle class customers to CDS workshops for more than 20 years, and is a reminder that there is something very satisfying about making a short movie about an important event in your own life.

REFERENCES

American Friends Service Committee. (2008). *Somali Bantu refugees speak*. Retrieved from http://www.umbc.edu/blogs/digitalstories/2008/12/somali_bantu_refugees_speak_th.html

American Friends Service Committee. (2014). *Storyology: Digital storytelling by immigrants and refugees*. Retrieved from http://www.afsc.org/story/storyology-digital-storytelling-immigrants-and-refugees

Ballast, K., Stephens, L., & Radcliffe, R. (2008). *The effects of digital storytelling on sixth grade students' writing and their attitudes about writing*. Paper presented at the Society for Information Technology & Teacher Education International Conference, Las Vegas, NV.

Banaszweski, T. (2002). *Digital storytelling finds its place in the classroom*. MultiMedia Schools.

Bartlett, F. (1932). *Remembering: A study in social and experimental psychology*. Cambridge, UK: Cambridge University Press.

Benmayor, R. (2008). Digital storytelling as a signature pedagogy for the new humanities. *Arts and Humanities in Higher Education*, 7(2), 188–204. doi:10.1177/1474022208088648

Benmayor, R. (2012). Digital testimonio as a signature pedagogy for Latin@ studies. *Equity & Excellence in Education*, 45(3), 507–524. doi:10.1080/10665684.2012.698180

Bery, R. (1995). Chapter. In L. W. R. Slocum & D. Rocheleau (Eds.), Power, process and participation: Tools for change (pp. 64–80). London: Intermediate Technology Publications.

Bhabha, H. (1994). *The location of culture*. London: Routledge.

Bourdieu, P. (1990). *The logic of practice*. Palo Alto, CA: Stanford University Press.

Bromley, K., Faughnan, M., Ham, S., Miller, M., Armstrong, T., Crandall, C., & Marrone, N. et al. (2014). Literature circles go digital. *The Reading Teacher*, 68(3), 229–236. doi:10.1002/trtr.1312

Bruner, J. (1990). *Acts of meaning*. Cambridge, MA: Harvard University Press.

Chung, S. K. (2007). Art education technology: Digital storytelling. *Art Education*, 60(2), 17–22.

Clarke, M. A. (2009). Developing digital storytelling in Brazil. In J. Hartley & K. McWilliam (Eds.), *Digital storytelling around the world* (pp. 91–117). Malden, MA: Wiley-Blackwell.

Clarke, R. G., & Thomas, S. (2012). Digital narrative and the humanities: An evaluation of the use of digital storytelling in an Australian undergraduate literacy studies program. *Higher Education Studies*, 2(3), 30–43. doi:10.5539/hes.v2n3p30

Common Core State Standards Initiative. (2014). *Preparing America's students for success*. Retrieved November, 2014, from http://www.corestandards.org/

Couldry, N., & McCarthy, A. (2004). Introduction: Orientations: Mapping MediaSpace. In N. Couldry & A. McCarthy (Eds.), *MediaSpace, place, scale and culture in a media age* (pp. 1–18). London: Routledge.

Darvin, R., & Norton, B. (2014). Transnational identity and migrant learners: The promise of digital storytelling. *Education Matters*, 2, 55–66.

Davis, A. (2004). Co-authoring identity: Digital storytelling in an urban middle school *Technology. Humanities, Education, and Narrative, 1*(1), 1–21.

Davis, A., & Weinshenker, D. (2012). Digital storytelling and authoring identity. In C. Ching & Foley (Eds.), Technology and identity: Research on the development and exploration of selves in a digital world (pp. 47-64). Cambridge, UK: Cambridge University Press. doi:10.1017/CBO9781139027656.005

DeGennaro, D. (2008). The dialectics of informing identity in an urban youth digital storytelling workshop. *E-learning, 5*(4), 429–444. doi:10.2304/elea.2008.5.4.429

Diamondstone, J. (2004). *Jasmine makes a scary movie: A multi-modal analysis of an adolescent's popular culture literacy.* Paper presented at the National Council of Teachers of English Assembly for Research (NCTEAR), Berkeley, CA.

Dibley, R. (2011). *Using digital media to report back information-rich research and evaluation results.* Paper presented at the Australasian Evaluation Society Conference, Sydney, Australia. Retrieved from http://www.communityresearch.org.nz/research/using-digital-media-to-report-back-information-rich-research-and-evaluation-results/

Dyson, A. (1997). *Writing superheroes: Contemporary childhood, popular culture, and classroom literacy.* New York: Teachers College Press.

Erstad, O., & Silseth, K. (2008). Agency in digital storytelling: Challenging the educational context. In K. Lundby (Ed.), *Digital storytelling, mediatized stories* (pp. 213–232). New York: Peter Lang.

Erstad, O., & Wertsch, J. V. (2008). Tales of mediation: Narrative and digital media as cultural tools. In K. Lundby (Ed.), *Digital storytellin, mediatized stories* (pp. 21–40). New York: Peter Lang.

Fivush, R. (2004). The silenced self: Constructing self from memories spoken and unspoken. In D. R. Beike, J. M. Lampinen, & D. A. Behrend (Eds.), *The self and memory: Studies in self and identity* (pp. 75–93). New York: Psychology.

Foley, L. M. (2013). Digital storytelling in primary-grade classrooms (Ph.D. Dissertation). Phoenix, AZ: Arizona State University. Retrieved from http://gradworks.umi.com/35/60/3560250.html

Frazel, M. (2010). *Digital storytelling guide for educators.* Washington, DC: International Society for Technology in Education.

Freidus, N., & Hlubinka, M. (2002). Digital storytelling for reflective practice in communities of learners. *Association for Computing Machinery SIGGROUP Bulletin, 23*(2), 24–26. doi:10.1145/962185.962195

Gibson, J. (1979/1986). *The ecological approach to visual perception.* Hillsdale, NJ: Lawrence Erlbaum Associates.

Goffman, E. (1959). *The presentation of self in everyday life.* New York: Doubleday.

Gregory, S. (2010). Cameras everywhere: Ubiquitous video documentation of human rights, new forms of video advocacy, and considerations of safety, security, dignity and consent. *Journal of Human Rights Practice, 2*(2), 191–207. doi:10.1093/jhuman/huq002

Gubrium, A. (2009). Digital storytelling: An emergent method for health promotion research and practice. *Health Promotion Practice, 10*(2), 186–191. doi:10.1177/1524839909332600 PMID:19372280

Gubrium, A., Krause, E., & Jernigan, K. (2014). Strategic authenticity and voice: New ways of seeing and being seen as young mothers through digital storytelling. *Sexuality Research & Social Policy*, *11*(4), 337–347. doi:10.1007/s13178-014-0161-x PMID:25506294

Gubrium, A., & Otañez, M. (2013). Digital storytelling. In A. Gubrium & K. Harper (Eds.), *Participatory visual and digital methods* (pp. 125–150). Walnut Creek, CA: Left Coast Press.

Gutierrez, K. (2008). Developing a sociocritical literacy in the Third Space. *Reading Research Quarterly*, *43*(2), 148–164. doi:10.1598/RRQ.43.2.3

Hagood, M. C. (2009). *New literacies practices: Designing literacy learning*. New York: Peter Lang.

Hardy, P., & Sumner, T. (2014). Our stories, ourselves: Exploring identities, sharing experiences and building relationships through patient voices. In H. M. Pleasants & D. E. Salter (Eds.), *Community-based multiliteracies and digital media probjects: Questioning assumptions and exploring realities* (pp. 65–86). New York: Peter Lang.

Hevern, V., Josselson, R., & McAdams, D. (2013). Narrative. In D. Dunn (Ed.), *Oxford bibliographies in psychology*. New York: Oxford University Press.

Holquist, M. (1990). *Dialogism: Bakhtin and his world* (2nd ed.). New York: Routledge. doi:10.4324/9780203330340

Hull, G., & Katz, M.-L. (2006). Crafting and agentive self: Case studies of digital storytelling. *Research in the Teaching of English*, *41*, 43–81.

Hull, G., & Nelson, M. (2005). Locating the semiotic power of multimodality. *Written Communication*, *22*(2), 224–261. doi:10.1177/0741088304274170

Hull, G., & Schultz, K. (2002). Connecting school with out-of-school worlds. In G. Hull & K. Schultz (Eds.), *School's out! Bridging out of school literacies with classroom practice* (pp. 32–60). New York: Teachers Coillege Press.

Illeris, K. (2014). *Transformative learning and identity*. New York: Routledge.

Jenkins, H., Puroshotma, R., Weigel, M., Clinton, K., & Robison, A. (2009). *Confronting the challenges of participatory culture: Media education for the 21st century*. Cambridge: MIT Press.

Jonassen, D., Howland, J., Marra, R., & Crismond, D. (2008). *Meaningful learning with technology*. Columbus, OH: Pearson.

Kaare, B. H., & Lundby, K. (2008). Mediatized lives: Autobiography and assumed authenticity in digital storytelling. In K. Lundby (Ed.), *Digital storytelling, mediatized lives* (Vol. 52, pp. 105–122). New York: Peter Lang.

Kajder, S. B. (2004). Enter here: Personal narrative and digital storytelling. *English Journal*, *93*(3), 64–68. doi:10.2307/4128811

Kress, G. (2003). *Literacy in the new media age*. London: Routledge. doi:10.4324/9780203164754

Kress, G., & van Leeuwen, T. (2001). *Multimodal discourse: The modes and media of contemporary communication*. Oxford University Press.

Kulla-Abbott, T., & Polman, J. (2008). Engaging student voice and fulfilling curriculum goals with digital stories. *Technology, Humanities, Education, and Narrative*. Retrieved from http://thenjournal.org/feature/160/

Lambert, J. (2006). *Digital storytelling: Capturing lives, creating community*. New York: Routledge.

Lambert, J. (2013). *Digital storytelling: Capturing lives, creating community* (4th ed.). New York: Routledge.

Lankshear, C., & Knobel, M. (2006). *New Literacies: Everyday practices and classroom learning* (2nd ed.). Maidenhead, UK: Open University Press.

Lee, E., & Miller, L. (2014). Entry point: Parfticipatory media-making with queer and trans refugees: Social locations, agendas, and thinking structurally. In H. M. Pleasants & D. E. Salter (Eds.), *Community-based multiliteracies and digital edia projects: Questioning assumptions and exploring realities* (Vol. 63, pp. 45–64). New York: Peter Lang.

Lenhardt, A. (2012). Teens and online video. *Pew Internet and American Life Project*. Retrieved from http://www.pewinternet.org/Reports/2012/Teens-and-online-video.aspx

Leu, D. J. Jr. (2000). Literacy and technology: Deictic consequences for literacy education in an information age. In M. L. Kamil, P. B. Mosenthal, P. D. Pearson, & R. Barr (Eds.), *Handbook of reading research* (Vol. 3, pp. 310–336). Newark, DE: International Reading Association.

Leu, D. J., Jr. (2002). The new literacies: Research on reading instruction with the Internet. In A. E. AFarnstrup & S. J. Samules (Eds.), Handbook of reading research (Vol. 3, pp. 743-770). Mahwah, NJ: Erlbaum.

Levin, H. (2003). Making history come alive. *Learning and Leading with Technology*, *5*, 175–185.

Lewin, K. (1946). Action research and minority problems. *The Journal of Social Issues*, *2*(4), 34–46. doi:10.1111/j.1540-4560.1946.tb02295.x

Lewin, T. (2011). Digital storytelling. *Participatory Learning and Action, 63*, 54-62.

Lundby, K. (2009). The matrices of digital storytelling: Examples from Scandinavia. In J. Harley & K. McWilliam (Eds.), *Story circle: Digital storytelling around the world* (pp. 176–187). Chichester, UK: Wiley-Blackwell. doi:10.1002/9781444310580.ch12

Matthews-DeNatale, G. (2008). *Digital storytelling: Tips and resources* Retrieved from https://net.educause.edu/ir/library/pdf/ELI08167B.pdf

Mayer, R. (2014). Cognitive theory of multimedia learning. In R. Meyer (Ed.), *The Cambridge handbook of multimedia learning* (pp. 43–71). Cambridge, UK: Cambridge University Press.

McLean, K., Pasupathi, M., & Pals, J. (2007). Selves creating stories creating selves: A process model of self development. *Personality and Social Psychology Review*, *11*(3), 262–278. doi:10.1177/1088868307301034 PMID:18453464

McWilliam, K. (2009). The global diffusion of a community media practice: Digital storytelling online. In J. Harley & K. McWilliam (Eds.), *Story circle* (pp. 37–76). Chichester, UK: Wiley-Blackwell. doi:10.1002/9781444310580.ch3

Meadows, D., & Kidd, J. (2009). "Capture Wales": The BBC digital storytelling project. In J. Hartley & K. McWilliam (Eds.), *Story circle: Digital storytelling around the world* (pp. 91–117). Malden, MA: Wiley & Sons. doi:10.1002/9781444310580.ch5

Mezirow, J. (2000). *Learning as transformation*. New York: Jossey Bass.

Miller, L., Luchs, M., & Jalea, G. D. (2012). *Mapping memories: Participatory media, place-based stories, and refugee youth*. Montreal: Concordia University Press.

Mitchell, C. (2008). Getting the picture and changing the picture: Visual methodologies and educational research in South Africa. *South African Journal of Education, 28*, 365–383.

New London Group. (1996). A pedagogy of multiliteracies: Designing social futures. *Harvard Educational Review, 66*(1), 60–92. doi:10.17763/haer.66.1.17370n67v22j160u

New London Group. (2000). A pedagogy of multiliteracies: Designing social futures. In B. Cope & M. Kalantzis (Eds.), *Multiliteracies: Literacy learning and the design of social futures* (pp. 9–37). New York: Routledge.

Nucera, D. J., & Lee, J. (2014). I transform myself, I transform the world around me. In H. M. Pleasants & D. E. Salter (Eds.), *Community-based multiliteracies and digital media projects* (pp. 181–202). New York: Peter Lang.

Ochs, E., & Capps, L. (1996). Narrating the self. *Annual Review of Anthropology, 29*(1), 19–43. doi:10.1146/annurev.anthro.25.1.19

Otañez, M. (2011). Ethical consumption and academic production. *Anthropology News, 56*, 26–42. doi:10.1111/j.1556-3502.2011.52426.x

Pahl, K., & Rowsell, J. (2010). *Artifactual literacies.* New York: Teachers College Press.

Pasupathi, M., & Hoyt, T. (2009). The development of narrative identity in late adolescence and emergent adulthood: The continued importance of listeners. *Developmental Psychology, 45*(2), 558–574. doi:10.1037/a0014431 PMID:19271839

Reason, P., & Bradbury, H. (2008). Introduction. In P. Reason & H. Bradbury (Eds.), *The SAGE handbook of action research: Participant inquiry and practice* (pp. 5–10). Los Angeles, CA: SAGE. doi:10.4135/9781848607934

Robin, B. (2008). The effective uses of digital storytelling as a teaching and learning tool. In J. Flood, S. B. Heath, & D. Lapp (Eds.), *Handbook of research on teaching literacy through the communicative and visual arts* (Vol. 2, pp. 429–440). New York: Lawrence Erlbaum Associates.

Rudkin, J., & Davis, A. (2007). Photography as a tool for understanding youth connections to their neighborhoods. *Community, Youth, and Environments, 17*, 107–123.

Rudnicki, A., Cozart, A., Ganesh, A., Markello, C., Marsh, S., McNeil, S., . . . Robin, B. (2006). *The buzz continues: The diffusion of digital storytelling across disciplines and colleges at the University of Houston.* Paper presented at the International Conference of the Society for Information Technology and Teacher Education.

Schachter, J., & Kasper, J. (2014). Finding voice: Building literacies and communities inside and outside the classroom. In H. M. Pleasants & D. E. Salter (Eds.), *Community-based multiliteracies and digital media projects* (Vol. 63, pp. 181–202). New York: Peter Lang.

Shotter, J. (1990). The social construction of forgetting and remembering. In D. Middleton & D. Edwards (Eds.), *Collective memory* (pp. 120–138). London: SAGE.

Simondson, H. (2009). Digital storytelling at the Australian Centre for the Moving Image. In J. Hartley & K. McWilliam (Eds.), *Story circle: Digital storytelling around the world* (pp. 118–123). Chichester, UK: Wiley-Blackwell. doi:10.1002/9781444310580.ch6

Susono, H., Ikawa, T., & Kagami, A. (2011). *Digital storytelling workshop for Japanese inservice teachers.* Paper presented at the Global Learn Asia Pacific.

Sylvester, R., & Greenidge, W. (2009). Digital storytelling: Extending the potential for struggling writers. *The Reading Teacher*, *4*(4), 284–295. doi:10.1598/RT.63.4.3

Thoman, E., & Jolls, T. (2004). Media literacy: A national priority for a changing world. *The American Behavioral Scientist*, *48*(1), 18–29. doi:10.1177/0002764204267246

Thumin, N. (2008). It's good for them to know my story: Cultural mediation as tension. In K. Lundby (Ed.), *Digital storytelling, mediatized stories* (pp. 85–104). New York: Peter Lange.

Thumin, N. (2009). Exploring self-representations in Wales and London: Tension in the text. In J. Hartley & K. McWilliam (Eds.), *Story circle: Digital storytelling around the world* (pp. 205–218). Chichester, UK: Wiley-Blackwell. doi:10.1002/9781444310580.ch14

Tsou, W., & Tzeng, Y. (2006). Applying a multimedia storytelling website in foreign language learning. *Computers & Education*, *47*(1), 17–28. doi:10.1016/j.compedu.2004.08.013

Valmont, W. J., & Wepner, S. B. (2000). Using technology to support literacy learning. In S. B. Wepner, W. J. Valmont, & R. Thurlwo (Eds.), *Linking literacy and technology: A guide for K-8 classrooms* (pp. 2–18). Newark, DE: International Reading Association.

Vasudevan, L., Schultz, K., & Bateman, J. (2010). Through multimodal storytelling rethinking composing in a digital age: Athoring literate identities. *Written Communication*, *27*, 442–465. doi:10.1177/0741088310378217

Verdugo, D. R., & Belmonte, I. (2007). Using digital stories to improve listening comprehension with Spanish young learners of English. *Language Learning & Technology*, *11*, 87–101.

Vygotsky, L. S. (1934/1978). *Mind in society*. Cambridge, MA: Harvard University Press.

Wang, C., & Burris, M. A. (1992). Empowerment through photo novella: Portraits of participation. *Health Education & Behavior*, *21*(2), 171–186. doi:10.1177/109019819402100204 PMID:8021146

Wertsch, J. V. (1998). *Mind as action*. Oxford, UK: Oxford University Press.

Wilcox, W. (2009). Digital storytelling: A comparative case study in three nothern California communities (MA Thesis). Davis, CA: University of California Davis. Retrieved from http://www.escholarship.org/uc/item/71w6n7qd

Williams, D. (2010). The speaking brain. In D. A. Sousa (Ed.), *Mind,brain, and education* (pp. 85–112). Bloomington, IN: Solution Tree Press.

Yang, Y.-T., & Wu, W.-C. (2012). Digital storytelling for enhancing student academic achievement, critical thinking, and learning motivation: A year-long experimental study. *Computers & Education*, *59*(2), 339–352. doi:10.1016/j.compedu.2011.12.012

ADDITIONAL READING

Ching, C., & Foley, B. (2012). *Constructing the self in a digital world*. Cambridge: Cambridge University Press. doi:10.1017/CBO9781139027656

Hartley, J., & McWilliam, K. (2009). *Story circle: Digital storytelling around the world*. Chichester, England: Wiley-Blackwell. doi:10.1002/9781444310580

Lambert, J. (2013). *Digital storytelling: Capturing lives, creating community*. Berkeley, CA: Digital Diner Press.

Lundby, K. (2008). *Digital storytelling, mediatized stories*. New York: Peter Lang.

Pleasants, H., & Salter, D. (2014). *Community-based multiliteracies and digital media projects*. New York: Peter Lang.

Testimonio (Spanish) *In Latin America, a personal narrative from the heart, a significant autobiographical story.*

KEY TERMS AND DEFINITIONS

Community of Practice: A phrase introduced by Jean Lave and Etienne Wenger in 1991 to refer to a sense of shared identity through participation in a domain of social production, such as an occupation, in which craft knowledge was developed and promulgated within the group.

Community-Based Narratives: Stories authored within distinctive cultural and social communities, often shaped within a social process of storytelling, and reflecting historical cultural practices or important shared aspects of experience.

Digital Storytelling: The practice of creating and disseminating short multimodal digital narratives (usually first person narratives) with voice narration and visual images.

Meta-Narrative: A story consisting of the defining common experiences shared by a group of persons.

Multiliteracies: A term introduced by the New London Group of educators in 1996 to emphasize that full participation in a global world connected through new technologies required a broad and flexible notion of "literacy": proficiency in communicating within and across multiple cultural and social contexts and making use of a variety of mediating technologies and modalities.

Narrative Psychology: A branch of psychology concerned with how persons make use of stories in interpreting, remembering, sharing, and coping with experience.

Participatory Action Research: A type of action research in which those most directly affected by a problem are actively involved in describing and analyzing the problem and bringing about change.

Transformative Learning: Learning characterized by a shift in the identity or self-concept of the learner, in contrast to processes in which the learner becomes more proficient or knowledgeable but does not undergo a shift in identity.

Chapter 14

Use of Apps and Devices for Fostering Mobile Learning of Literacy Practices

Richard Beach
University of Minnesota, USA

Jill Castek
Portland State University, USA

ABSTRACT

Given the increased use of apps and mobile devices in the classroom, this chapter reviews research on secondary and college students' uses of educational apps employed with mobile devices in the classroom supporting mobile learning (m-learning). It focuses on research analyses of m-learning activities fostered through ubiquity/authenticity, portability, and personalization/adaptivity of apps and mobile devices fostering collaboration/interactivity, multimodality, and shared productivity. These practices serve to enhance information search and acquisition, reading digital texts, formulating and sharing responses to texts, shared productivity, and language learning. While there is some research documenting how m-learning serves to foster these literacy practices, there remains a need for further research on how effective design of m-learning activities supports literacy learning, as well as how larger economic and policy issues shape or impede effective m-learning.

SUCCINCT OVERVIEW OF THE RESEARCH

Use of apps on mobile devices employed in educational spaces abound, making mobile learning a rich area for exploration, for example, how digital video apps serve to create videos or curation apps support acquisition of information. However demonstrating the ways that these apps can support learning is complex. To examine the

connections between use of apps on mobile devices and learning, we have drawn across existing areas of research we have created a map to organize the complex terrain of mobile learning (m-learning) and its associated considerations (see Figure 1). In creating this map, we thought carefully about how researchers and educators might go about analyzing apps in terms their learning potential and also about ways of learning that are uniquely fostered by the use of apps.

DOI: 10.4018/978-1-4666-8310-5.ch014

Figure 1.

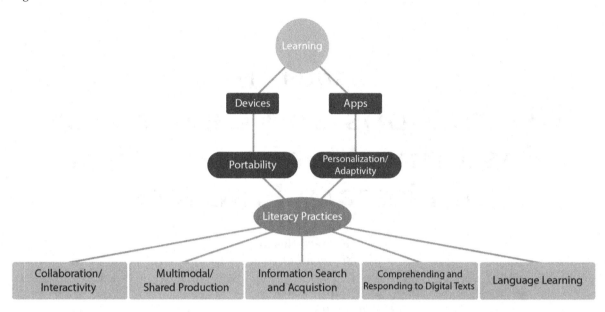

We recognize there are a variety of ways to examine mobile learning (m-learning). In this chapter, we focus on how m-learning is mediated through activities involving the use of apps and mobile devices to foster certain literacy practices. For the purpose of this chapter, we define m-learning as learning that can occur across different physical or geographical spaces so that students are not limited to learning simply within the classroom (Miller & Doering, 2014). Decoupling the learner from learning primarily in the classroom fosters a shift in focus to learning in a range of different contexts. There is therefore a need for research on how to design activities that serve to mediate and exploit the ubiquitous use of mobile devices to foster literacy practices.

For this chapter, we have limited our review of research on uses of devices and apps to secondary and college students, including middle-schoolers, recognizing that there is considerable attention on use of devices and apps for children (see Ly & Vaala, 2014, as an example of an analysis of use of apps for literacy and language learning by young children and emergent readers through age eight).

THE INCREASED FOCUS ON MOBILE LEARNING

One of the major shifts in the use of technology in the past three years has been the increased use of apps as well as tablet and smartphone devices. Mobile devices have certain features--portability, cameras, touch screens, GPS, and other applications that teachers can employ to foster constructivist and connectivist learning (Ito et al., 2013). Eighty percent of U.S. students in grades 9-12 and 65% of U.S. students grades 6-8 have access to a smartphone, while 45% of U.S. students grades 9-12 and 52% of grades 6-8 have access to a tablet (Devaney, 2014). Seventy seven percent of teachers indicate that use of these mobile devices enhances motivation for learning and 76% find that they help to address diverse learning styles (EdTech, 2013). Fifty eight percent of middle school students and 42% of high school students report using tablets regularly in their classrooms while 58% of middle school students and 75% of high school students report using smartphones regularly in the classroom (Pearson, 2014). Ninety percent of students perceive use of tablets as changing how they will learn in the future and 89% agree that the use of tablets enhances their engagement with learning (Pearson, 2014).

Eighty nine percent of high schools students have personal access to Internet-connected smart phones; 60% have access to laptops; and 50% have access to tablets (Riedel, 2014). Sixty percent of students use mobile devices for research; 43%, for educational games; and 40%for collaboration with their peers. Given many school's BYOD (bring your own device) policies, students are using devices both outside and inside of schools as members of a "participatory culture" (Jenkins, 2006). Kalantzis and Cope (2012) describe these students as members of a "Generation P" (Nielsen & Webb, 2011) who "do as much writing as reading in their spare time—and reading and writing are fused as integrated practices in social networking sites, blogs, and text messages (pp. 9 -10). Rather than perceiving practices such as texting as having a negative impact on school writing quality, research indicates that texting can contribute to school writing, particularly when students are aware of the need to engage in code-switching from formal to informal language usage across contexts (Wood, Kemp, & Plester, 2013).

Much of this increase in use of apps and mobile devices in schools derives from the use of apps and mobile devices within the larger population. An analysis of results from a Pew survey found that people regularly employ apps and devices to check news, weather, sports, or stock updates (73.9%), communicate with social contacts (65%), learn something related to their interests (63.3%), or acquire information about a destination--museums, festivals, historical sites, parks, etc. (52.9%), with the latter related to their actual visits to these sites (Lai, 2014).

There has also been a marked increase in the uses of mobile devices in schools, particularly with the adoption of bring-your-own-device school (BYOD) policies identified to be a significant trend for 2014-2015 by the Horizon Report survey

analysis (Johnson et al., 2014). A survey of K-12 teachers found that 70.5% supported use of cell phone in their classrooms, a shift from previous perceptions of cell phones as a disruption, although only a small percentage of teachers actually use cell phones to support their instruction (Thomas, et al., 2013).

Schools are also investing in m-learning; South Korea provides extensive teacher training in digital learning and will be phasing out print textbooks by 2016; Turkey plans to distribute ten million tablets to students by 2015, while Thailand will distribute 13 million mobile devices to students by 2015 (Devaney, 2014).

In schools in developing countries that may not have computer hardware, the use of cellphones or smartphone devices is having a particularly significant effect on learning (West & Chew, 2014). An analysis of the use of mobile phones in seven developing countries (Ethiopia, Ghana, India, Kenya, Nigeria, Pakistan, Zimbabwe) found that most people employ their phones to engage in reading because they do not have access to print texts, even though most of these texts are in English (West & Chew, 2014). In South Africa, as part of the m4Lit (mobile phones for literacy) project, students used their phones to respond to 21 chapters of a mobile novel by discussing the unfolding plot, leaving comments, and voting in polls, as well as submitting their own writing to complete sequel story ideas (Walton, 2010). Through their interactions, adolescent participants learned to engage in new forms of linguistic inter-actions associated with romantic talk as well as sharing photos. Another study of South African women's use of phones found that the women perceived their use of their phones for texting as a primary literacy practice that supported their work and family lives (Velghe, 2014).

However, in countries such as South Africa, there continue to be class disparities related to access to and use of digital devices. A comparison study of children of an upper-middle-class family with a low-income family in South Africa identified a wide gap in terms of not only access to digital devices but also the use of certain literacy practices with the upper-middle-class family. The upper-middle-class children were able to engage in both extensive communication and production practices while their low-income counterparts, with only limited access to cell phones, had access to minimum amounts of information (Lemphane & Prinsloo, 2013).

How Use of Apps and Mobile Devices Fosters M-Learning

There is certainly a synergetic relationship between iOS, Android OS, or Chrome OS apps that requires some understanding of the use of mobile devices—smartphones, tablets, or iPod Touches (Beach & O'Brien, 2014). Additionally, devices' mobility/portability, and the intuitive design for use were found to be beneficial (Hutchison & Beschorner, 2014).

There remains a need to identify how features of apps and devices actually serve to enhance m-learning activities as distinct from status-quo learning activities. Doing so involves going beyond simply the use of apps and devices to consider how m-learning mediates learning across different contexts in space and time (Yu, Lee, & Ewing, 2015). As recommended by the Aspen Institute Task Force on Learning and the Internet (2014), rather than placing technology at the center of learning, it is important to place the student at the center of learning. That task force also recommended that students should have access to learning networks and that these networks need to provide students with the relevant resources for their learning. Similarly the *Connected Learning: An Agenda for Research and Design* report (Ito et al., 2013) posited the need to focus on "connected learning" as driven by students' interests, passions, the building of social relationships, civic engagement, and academic achievement.

Use of mobile devices also shapes teachers adopting alternative instructional methods in terms of how they integrate use of devices to support instruction. An analysis of students' use of iPads in British schools identified significant gains in students' work and engagement in learning and collaboration (Clarke et al., 2013; Webb, 2012). This occurred through use of multimodal production as well as through the purposeful, focused nature of app design that supported the teacher's planning. Students reported using iPads most frequently for writing notes/essays, making presentations, and using the calculator and dictionary; they were more likely to report tasks using the iPad than did instructors (Clarke et al., 2013). Another study examining classroom uses of iPads in twelve learning projects found that iPads supported media creation and editing through geo-tagging and sharing photos, video editing and sharing, video calls, music creation and performance; augmented reality using GPS and compass to add points of interest to a digital map; and productivity and collaboration curation, presentations, and publications (Cochrane, Narayan, & Oldfield, 2013).

Use of mobile devices can also provide low-income students with access to relevant information if they do not have wi-fi access in their homes (Barseghian, 2013). However, a survey of 2,400 middle and high school students by the Pew Research Center found that while 52% of teachers in higher income schools report students using phones to access information, only 35% of teachers in lower-income schools report students using their phones to access information (Purcell et al., 2013). Forty nine percent of teachers in lower-income schools report that their schools employ filters blocking access to certain sites; 33% report that their schools have rules limiting use of phones, use of filters and rules that are less likely to be in use in higher-income schools; and 39% report that their schools are "behind the curve" in implementing use of digital tools for instruction, compared to only 15% of teachers in higher income schools.

Given these class-based disparities in uses of devices, 84% of all teachers in the survey perceived a widening gap through unequal access and use of technology between lower and upper income schools. These results suggests that online access and related use of mobile devices varies according to school districts' socio-economic status related to districts' technology support, creating a digital divide that serves to perpetuate the income gap between upper-income families versus middle-income families (Merchant, 2012; Purcell et al., 2013).

FEATURES OF MOBILE DEVICES ENHANCING M-LEARNING

There are a number of features of mobile devices that enhance m-learning.

Ubiquity

The fact that devices are ubiquitous means that students can transport them and use them to support learning across different contexts, for example, taking photos or video clips on a field trip. However, while college students in one study found that use of mobile devices broadened their way of communicating and learning beyond the classroom, they also expressed their frustration with faculty who were not open to employing mobile learning in their classrooms (Gikas & Grant, 2013). In another study, while high school students expressed positive perceptions in one study of the use of social media apps in their classes for interactive, collaborative learning, only 42.2% expressed positive attitudes about how these apps were actually used in their classrooms (Mao, 2014).

This suggests the need for enhanced understanding and use of instructional methods on how to exploit use of the ubiquity of devices in

different contexts (Kearney, Schuck, Burden, & Aubusson, 2012; McLain, 2014). This includes methods on how students can participate across different virtual worlds that mimic lived-world contexts as evident in the popularity of game-like m-learning apps (Pachler, Bachmair, & Cook, 2010). Students in Jackson Hole, Wyoming, who were studying the topic of "dark matter" engaged in a virtual field trip using Google+ Hangouts and the Google Education Connected Classrooms program to interact with physicists at the SLAC National Accelerator Laboratory to experience demonstrations of the use of the lab's 2-mile-long linear accelerator as well as a space telescope to study "dark matter" (Freeberg, 2014).

Portability

Because mobile devices are highly portable, students can employ these devices in a range of different spaces beyond the classroom, so that, for example, they can listen to recordings while engaged in other activities, record data or images on field trips, or interact with others at any time (Nielsen & Webb, 2011). College students noted that use of texts on their iPads afforded them with more access to information and interaction with peers than when they were using traditional textbooks (Angst & Malinowski, 2010). High school students using smartphones studied 40 minutes more per week than did students without access to smartphones (StudyBlue, 2011). An analysis of the use of mobile devices by 500 students, ages 12-16, engaged in informal, personalized learning in a geography project studying neighborhoods and communities using mobile devices for geocaching noted the benefits of devices' portability (Jones et al., 2013). The use of GPS science apps for collecting data in natural habitats, for example, and pollution levels in the water or air, allows students to engage in scientific study in these habitats (McLain, 2014).

Personalization/Adaptivity

Personalization refers to the degree to which students can customize their learning according to their own level of control, choice, self-regulation, and sense of agency (Kearney et al., 2012). For example, students participating in the iChoose (http://iChooseTech.Weebly.com) project select their own learning objectives and apps designed to achieve those objectives, providing them with a sense of autonomy and control over their learning (Bisson & Vazquez, 2013).

An emerging set of apps and devices have built-in algorithms that adjust and accommodate to individual differences in learners' abilities or knowledge as a student employs an app or device in a manner similar to adaptive technology assessments where the assessment itself adjusts according to the students performance. One example involves the use of adaptive textbooks developed by the OpenStax project (http://cnx.org) at Rice University (Rutlin, 2014). When students do not do well on their understanding of certain topics, they are provided with additional explanations and practice, as well as the use of quizzes based on previously acquired knowledge. Use of apps and devices with built-in algorithms can also benefit students with advanced abilities or knowledge so that they can move over or advance ahead of certain familiar material.

These three features of apps and mobile devices—their ubiquity, portability, and personalization/adaptivity for fostering learning literary learning leads to the question whether use of apps and devices transfer from their uses in everyday, largely social contexts to uses in school contexts (Merchant, 2012). The degree to which such transfer will occur depends on the degree to which schools are open to experiential, hands-on learning activities that exploit use of apps and devices for "locating information 'in the field,' in so-called augmented reality applications and using audio-visual capture as an alternative mode of recording" (Merchant, 2012, p. 777).

Conceptualizing M-learning as Creating Alternative Learning Spaces

Whether such transfer occurs entails rethinking the limitations of traditional classroom spaces to provide students with opportunities for m-leaning across a range of different lived-world and virtual contexts. This suggests that m-learning needs to go beyond just uses of mobile apps or devices to provide instruction to a focus on creating alternative learning spaces exploiting the affordances of apps and devices.

As suggested in the Framework for the Rational Analysis of Mobile Education (FRAME) model, m-learning serves to support constructivist, contextualized learning through interactivity and collaboration across all contexts (Koole, 2009). Such learning requires creating learning spaces based on three components

- The user's or learner's sense of agency to make changes based on how they appropriate uses of m-learning.
- The everyday social and cultural practices users employ in their lived-world experiences as shaped by m-learning in learning spaces.
- The social-cultural and technological structures of institutions mediating their experiences in these spaces. (London Mobile Learning Group, 2014).

USE OF APPS AND DEVICES TO SUPPORT LITERACY PRACTICES

Given the need to articulate instructional methods and ways to support use of apps and mobile devices for m-learning in these alternative learning spaces, in this chapter, we focus on how use of apps and devices serve to support learning the literacy practices of collaboration/interactivity; multimodal, shared production; information search and acquisition, comprehending and responding to digital texts, and language learning.

Collaboration/Interactivity

Use of apps and mobile devices foster the literacy practices of collaboration and interactivity through shared, collaborative response to texts and experiences as well construction of texts (Lai et al., 2013). For example, students can employ annotation apps to encourage collaborative responses to the same text so that students are sharing and modeling different ways of interpreting that text (Beach & O'Brien, 2014; Castek & Beach, 2013), benefitting from interactions with peers with certain practices they may lack (Castek, Coiro, Guzniczak, & Bradshaw, 2012) as well as engaging in collaborative construction of texts.

Students also employ mobile devices in collaborative, multiplayer digital games to each contribute to solving problems in ways that enhance their collaborative learning abilities (Hsu & Shih, 2013). Students can play games such as the Up River game created on the ARIS mobile game platform (http://arisgames.org) (Wagler & Mathews, 2011); one of four UbiqGames biology games (http://education.mit.edu/projects/ubiquitous-games) (Rosenheck, 2011); and Mentira (http://mentira.org), a murder mystery game set in New Mexico involving learning Spanish.

Students can also employ apps and devices to engage in collaborative responses through the use of virtual simulations of natural or physical realities, for example virtual representations of the solar system as well as biological, chemistry, or physics experiments. In using these apps, students are not limited to when, where, and how they experience certain phenomena. A study of 152 high school students who used the SolarWalk 3D app on iPads to study simulated aspects of scale in space compared to 1,184 students who used more traditional instruction found significant differences in students' understanding of scale in space using the iPads (Schneps, et al., 2014).

Use of apps and mobile devices also enhances interactivity between students, teachers, and parents for sharing information (Gikas & Grant, 2013). 74% of university students in five countries indicated that reachability was what they "like most" about their smartphones (Baron, 2011). For example, students can use the Google Classroom (http://tinyurl.com/nswmg7q) app to submit their assignments using their mobile devices to teachers using the Google Apps for Education. Use of Twitter for sending reminders and extending class discussions in college classes resulted in higher levels of engagement and class grades than in classes without Twitter (Junco, Heibergert, & Loken, 2011). Use of school texting apps such as those employed in the OneVille Project in Somerville, Massachusetts was perceived positively by students as a reflection that their school and teachers desire to support their success in school through reminders about completing assignments (Pollack, 2011). Students in a history class used social and mobile technologies for productive interactions associated with museum visiting (Charitonos, Blake, Scanlon, & Jones, 2012). Interactivity also occurs through curation of content or artifacts to create what Pachler et al., (2012) define as "mobile portfolios" of learning used within and outside of the classroom to foster further reflections.

Multimodal Shared Production

Students also employ apps and devices for multimodal productions (Kress, 2003) to take and view photos or video, record and listen to audio, and access and create multimodal e-books (Simpson et al., 2013). For example, teachers can create "learning trails" for virtual field trips based on the use of photos tied to GPS locations (Li et al., 2013).

The portability of apps and mobile devices allow students to capture or create images, video, or audio in natural/outdoors contexts. A comparison of learning about solar cells using a desktop computer in a lab, versus use of an iPad in a courtyard, found that students had a higher willingness to continue learning using the iPad as opposed to use of a desktop computer given the iPad's portability for use in a courtyard (Sung & Mayer, 2013).

Use of multimodal features is particularly supportive of science instruction (Johnson, et al., 2013). Students employed iPads in a biology course to create stop-motion videos about cell processes in ways that enhanced their understanding of the mitosis and meiosis processes (Deaton et al., 2013). Students studying human and animal anatomy can employ apps for analyzing and manipulating 3D visual representations of the body as well as instructional videos providing information about specific aspects of the body (Lewis et al., 2014). 6th graders' use of Edmodo, Evernote, and Skitch apps, and taking notes/photos and sharing observations in studying fish anatomy as part of a BYOD model, supported productive, inquiry based learning (Song, 2014). Or, for studying astronomy, students employing pinch-and-zoom manipulation of Solar Walk virtual 3D simulations of the solar system on tablets found that students' understanding of astronomy concepts was significantly higher than results from students engaged in traditional instruction (Schneps et al., 2014). Comparison of college students' perceptions of conducting motion experiments using iPads and the Vernier Video Physics app in a Physics college versus conducting the same experiments using traditional physical methods using ticker tapes found that students much preferred using the video analysis, particularly in terms of efficiency in creating the videos. Creating the videos gave them more time to discuss the results than when they had to complete the more time-consuming traditional methods of creating and annotating videos (Ramos & Devers, 2014).

Apps and devices can also be used to record or capture body movements. One example is the unofficially-named SciPlay app for use in physics instruction, which is being developed for launch in 2015 by the design firm Local Projects and the SciPlay research center (Cairney, 2014). In using this app, students record themselves engaged in physical activities such as jumping or throwing a ball to then use data analysis tools provided by the app to measure and analyze different aspects of their motions. This app reflects the future development of apps identified by the 2014 Horizon Report (Johnson et al., 2014) involving use of "quantified self" or "wearable" technologies (p. 44) that record individuals' activities, for example, their sleep, movement, dietary, heart rate, and step count, that could be used in conjunction with health, fitness, or medical education programs.

Students also use apps and devices to create digital texts--images, literary texts, slideshows, videos, podcasts, and other forms of production to engage in critique or parody. In producing digital texts, students aim to achieve positive audience response, and in the process are displaying competence to peers, teachers, and other adults in ways that enhance their sense of agency. An analysis of the use of iPads at the college level over a two-year period by twenty-seven instructors identified the benefits of cameras and microphones to produce digital stories, documentary videos, photo essays, and multimedia presentations (Wagoner et al., 2012).

This sort of sharing produces positive audience uptake associated with fostering civic engagement. For example, students in the Mobile Action Lab at Youth Radio in Oakland, California, devised the iOS Forage City (http://www.foragecity.com) app designed to acquire and share information about gathering excess food grown in trees in Oakland for redistributing to people through food banks or homeless shelters (Soep, 2014). Using the App Inventor app, Youth Radio participants also designed the Android All Day Play (http://tinyurl.com/lz82nrp) app for streaming hip-hop/eclectic music to publicize the work of certain young musicians in Oakland. And, students in the Youth Speaks spoken word organization created the Android VoxPop (http://tinyurl.com/msjy4yh) app for use in sharing new stories for certain areas of the world where such stories may not receive impartial coverage.

Information Search and Acquisition

Another primary literacy practice involves searching for and acquiring information. Given the ubiquity and portability of devices, students can readily access information "on the fly" (Geurtz & Foote, 2014) using database, news/magazine curation, and Wikipedia apps to acquire relevant information (Bomhold, 2013). Or, they can employ "citizen apps" designed to collect data related to understanding transportation, weather events, water/electricity consumption, or use of government services that can be used to identify and address the nature and quality of local services for studying community issues (Desouz & Bhagwatwar, 2012).

Ease of use in accessing information enhances students' attitudes towards learning. A comparison of the effects of use of iPads/iPods supporting "here and now" mobile learning versus computer-based instruction on undergraduates' achievement in art (based on acquiring information about different paintings) indicated that while conducting searches using a computer generated higher positive achievement outcomes, use of the iPad/iPod generated higher positive attitude outcomes, suggesting the importance of considering students' attitudes related to the benefits of m-learning (Martin & Ertzberger, 2013). A key factor supporting effective searches has to do with an app's interface simplicity related to usability. Use of the Boopsie app for library searches found that students considered its portability and simplicity to be preferable to their library's conventional search sites (Miller, Vogh, & Jennings, 2013).

Related to the importance of creating alternative learning spaces mediated by uses of apps and devices, schools and museums are increasingly focused on creating "information spaces" enhanced "through storage capacity, through networking capabilities, and through sensors built into the device that capture and process data in ways that humans cannot" (Mundie & Hooper, 2014, p. 14). For example, visitors in museum exhibits can employ apps and mobile devices to acquire and experience extensive additional information/videos about an exhibit through uses of apps and mobile devices (Mundie & Hooper, 2014, p. 14).

Students also employ virtual/augmented (AR) apps with devices to experience virtual places or sites to acquire information or collect data related to science inquiry. In an "ecomobile" project, students collected data from a local pond and used mobile devices with an augmented reality application to observe virtual information and media associated with environmental analysis of the pond's water quality, an experience that resulted in superior understanding of water quality analysis and more positive attitudes compared to previous analyses without the m-learning experiences (Kamarainen, et al., 2013).

Comprehending and Responding to Digital Texts

A number of studies have examined the use of digital reading devices--iPads, Kindle eBook Reader, etc., on students' reading processes and comprehension. This research indicates that reading digital texts through mobile apps and devices involves more interactive, collaborative, and multimodal literacy practices than reading print texts (Rowsell, 2014), while other research points to some of the limitations of digital reading (Mangen, et al., 2014).

One study comparing college students' reading on an iPad and Kindle versus print texts found that while reading times were faster with print texts, they perceived the iPad as the most usable, with the Kindle and print texts perceived as next most usable. Differences in text formatting had no effect on comprehension (Connell, Bayliss, & Farmer, 2012). A comparison of ELF adolescents' use of reading in an Extensive Reading Program (ERP) on a mobile tablet versus a desktop found that students using the tablet achieved higher reading achievement, as well as more productive use of online activities and more positive attitudes towards reading (Lin, 2014). The results favored the mobile group who not only outperformed the desktop group in online activities and reading achievement but also showed greater appreciation of participation in the online ERP than students using desktops (Lin, 2014).

A qualitative analysis of the reading experience itself indicates that when reading texts on an e-reader device, there needs to be a synergy between the device and the e-book text formatting to provide readers with positive reading engagement (MacWilliam, 2013). This suggests the importance of the design of instructional materials and texts for use on e-reader devices. Based on their experiences using mobile e-books, college students expressed positive experiences particularly in terms of a sense of self-efficacy. They reported that that reading e-books, involved reading texts in non-linear ways, and making social, collaborative connections with peers about their learning through note-sharing, comments, and IMing (Kissinger, 2013). It is also the case that for some students with dyslexia with visual attention deficits, reading on a device that allow the reader to make adjustments so that only several words are displayed on a line served to focus their attention in ways that enhanced their reading speed and comprehension (Schneps at al., 2013).

Students also employ apps or device features for formulating and sharing their responses to texts (Chen & Chen, 2014; Korkey, 2014; Konnikova, 2014). For example, annotation apps such as Annotate PDF, GoodReader, Readdle, or Notetaker HD as well as annotation tools associated with Diigo, DocAS, or VoiceThread can be used to add annotations to highlighted sections of a text for sharing with others. In a study of 6th grade students' use of annotations (Castek, Beach, Cotanch, & Scott, 2014), students used the Diigo app to highlight and add sticky-note questions and connections to texts in conjunction with other aspects of science learning. Findings showed that students used the annotation app to pose questions, formulate claims, and request evidence from peers

to answer questions or support claims. These results suggest that the process of collaborative annotation encourages students' documentation, critique, and refinement of ideas, which can aid learners in close reading of science texts. An analysis of Diigo annotations types showed that students used annotations in a variety of ways: 34% questioning, 22% integrating/connecting, 13% evaluating, 10% determining important ideas, 9% inferring, 8% reacting to others' comments, and 4% monitoring.

The fact that students' sticky-note annotations were targeted to specific sentences in the text indicates that these apps helped students identify specific language, allowing them to "determine important ideas," as well as "infer," "integrate," or "evaluate" specific information in the text. Use of the annotation apps served as a more efficient approach to annotating texts than use of handwritten annotations and produced a trail of thinking that students could readily share with others, enhancing productivity. These and other collaboratively used apps can help students build conceptual understanding and communicate ideas through the use of concept-mapping, note-taking/annotation, and screen-casting activities that allowed students to access information and create their own digital products that included rich visual representations (Castek & Beach, 2013).

Use of apps and devices also allows for virtual simulation of lived-world problems, for example, simulation of science experiments associated with experiential learning (McLain, 2014; Srisawasdi & Sornkatha, 2014). For example, the ThinknLearn app was designed to help students generate hypotheses as they participate in abductive science inquiry investigations requiring them to continually formulate alternative hypotheses while acquiring new data from their experiments. Students employing this app demonstrated superior use of abductive thinking processes when compared to a control group (Ahmed & Parsons, 2013). In a related study, use of an annotation and interactive discussion scaffolding tool (CRAS-RAIDS) for collaboratively formulating and sharing annotations resulted in significantly higher comprehension and engagement by fifth graders (Chen & Chen, 2014).

Mobile Augmented Reality (AR) apps such as Layar, Wikitude.me, or Junaio that can superimpose or overlay certain information or "pins" onto real world representations or texts (Chinthammit & Thomas, 2014) are also being used to mesh virtual with lived-world experiences and texts. For example, the MagicBook literary texts include tagged content that, when viewed through a camera, provide additional visual representations or animations elaborating on or extending the story content.

Use of AR enhances the reading experience in tangible ways. When reading a text about an audience viewing a movie in a theater, a reader could view a clip of that movie (Chinthammit & Thomas, 2014). Students can also engage in responding to AR tours or narratives such as Google Lit Trips, Literary London, *The 21 Steps* (Cummings, 2008), or *The Westwood Experience* (Allen, Tsai, Hinman, & Azuma, 2010). In the latter, locations within Westwood, California are superimposed with images of previous historical images that also include narratives by the current mayor of Westwood (http://tinyurl.com/myub6em).

Language Learning

M-learning also assists language learning for English language learner (ELL) students by providing them with information and rules related to use of English instantly on their mobile devices given that the portability of devices can enhance frequent, regular use of relatively casual language practice. Use of the Grammar Clinic app provided college ELL students in a writing class with grammar rules, resulting in positive gains in their self-editing and error reductions (Li & Hegelheimer, 2013). University students in Saudi Arabia employing the TalkEnglish app demonstrated higher English proficiency through uses of the app than control group students no using the app (Al-Jarf, 2012).

A comparison of high school students in Taiwan learning English in an extensive reading program either reading on an iPad or a desktop found that students using the iPads were more engaged and improved their reading to a greater degree than students using a desktop (Lin, 2014). Key factors influencing these differences were the higher level of collaborative post-reading discussions, the value of portability where students could read in different settings, and the multimodal features of texts on the iPad that helped them comprehend unfamiliar vocabulary.

At the same time, a review of studies on uses of m-learning for language learning points to the challenge of students not being motivated to employ devices typically employed for personal, private, or social reasons as opposed to use to complete academic tasks (Ushioda, 2013). It is also the case that the research reviewed indicated superficial engagement given how the content is broken into small chunks or tasks and the limitations of a small screen and keyboard.

WHAT ARE THE CURRENT ISSUES IN THE FIELD RAISED BY THESE STUDIES?

There are a number of issues raised by this research regarding the effectiveness of the use of apps and devices in fostering learning. The Mobile Learning Group (Pachler, Bachmair, and Cook, 2010) posits that use of mobile apps and devices in school contexts does not necessarily result in innovative learning when the traditional design of schooling and instruction limits potential uses of m-learning. They perceive a major tension occurring between the formal, status-quo school curriculum and institutional practices, and the informal learning practices occurring through m-learning in everyday life. However, they equate schoolwork with formal learning versus non-school work with informal learning, a false binary in that non-school work can replicate formal learning processes occurring in school.

A related issue has to do with how researchers are framing what constitutes the pedagogical or learning purposes for employing apps or devices for academic purposes, as opposed to students' own social communication/networking purposes. While it is certainly the case that students use apps and mobile devices primarily for their own social communication/networking purposes rather than for educational purposes (Bicen & Kocakoyun, 2013), it has become increasingly difficult to clearly distinguish between pedagogical and social uses of apps and devices when social uses can also support pedagogical goals.

It may also be the case that use of m-learning practices may vary in terms of supporting personalization and authenticity. One survey of teachers found that that they perceive authenticity as highly supported by m-learning with collaboration, networking, and student agency less so (Kearney, Burden, Rai, 2015). One reason for these perceptions of support for personalization and authenticity relates to students' ownership of their own devices for storage of their work and use for individual learning at their own pace and ability level (Kearney, Burden, Rai, 2015).

Classifying Use of Apps for Learning

Given the many thousands of iOS and Android apps available on the Apple Apps Store or Android Play Store, another issue has to do with knowing how to identify and classify apps in ways the provide valid and reliable information for researchers and educators. While commercial classification systems typically focus on subject matter and/or grade level, more useful systems for teachers would identify potential purposes associated with using apps related to pedagogical goals or the TPACK framework related to the integration of Content Knowledge (CK), Pedagogical Knowledge (PK), and Technology Knowledge (TK) (Cherner, Dix, & Lee, 2014).

Given the need for an alternative classification system that would be useful for teachers based on an analysis of the purpose and worth of apps,

Cherner, Dix, & Lee (2014) developed and validated a system based on three categories according to Bloome's learning taxonomy—"skill-based" that foster memorization, recall, test-preparation, and skill-drill activities associated with Remembering and Understanding; "content-based" that foster providing access to data, information, or knowledge associated with Applying and Analyzing; and "function-based" that foster constructivist or experiential learning.

The challenge in creating these classification systems has to do with whether they capture how uses of apps and devices represent a collective, collaborative activity as opposed to focusing only on individual students' uses of apps or devices (Warner, 2014). Case-study analyses of three adolescents use of iPhones based on how they support portability, social interactivity, context sensitivity (acquiring data unique to certain contexts, connectivity, and individuality, and customized scaffolding for inquiry), found that use of the iPhones support learning by helping with access to information, social networking, and participating as contributors of knowledge for others (Squire & Dikkers, 2012).

Classification systems also need to identify the degree to which the use of apps serve to support certain ways of learning only made possible through use of those apps. As Brad McLain (2014) posits,

The power of mobile apps for education is not to be found in viewing them as tools for the delivery of more of the same educational pedagogies we currently use, but rather as vehicles for new kinds of learning experiences (p. 196).

McLain distinguishes between what he describes as "replicant" versus "extender" apps (p. 196). "Replicant" apps are those that simply replicate or reify ways of learning made possible by other tools such as flash-cards or calculators. These apps reify traditional instructional methods and criteria for learning, for example, the degree to which students acquire certain content or skills using flash-card apps. "Extender" apps "extend the learning experience in ways not otherwise possible except through app technology (p. 196); they require a focus on new, alternative learning experiences made possible through the use of apps. McLain cites the example of an astronomy app such as StarWalk that allows students unique experiences with observing the night sky through providing different kinds of data about planets and stars.

These distinctions reflect the contrast between the use of technology tools as a *substitution* or *augmentation* of another existing tool for certain activities—for example, a flash card or calculator, versus *modification* or *redefinition* of learning activities mediated by uses of a digital tool (Puentedura, 2011).

Classification systems also need to examine the degree to which apps enhance student engagement with learning (Pegrum et al., 2013). This entails use of qualitative research methods to capture students' particular experiences in employing apps. Screencasting apps such as ShowMe or Explain Everything for creating think-aloud recordings of students' thinking about learning tasks have been found to enhance student engagement (Abrams, 2014). Observational and interview techniques could be employed to determine students' specific uses of apps and devices for learning in different lived-world contexts. For example, screen capture programs that run in the background of students' devices could collect data about use of their devices. These micro-analyses could then be supplemented with retrospective think-alouds, narrative interviews, and in the moment observations.

An analysis of preservice science teachers' experiences in using ten different science apps—four chemistry, four physics, and two biology apps, focused on their level of engagement in science activities fostered through these apps (Baran & Khan, 2014). Preservice teachers were observed using these apps in outdoor and classroom contexts; their levels of engagement were coded by observers. Specifically, teachers employed the Project Noah app to locate and identify local flora and fauna; they then took digital photos of certain flora and fauna to add to the Project Noah database for their region. Teachers also employed the AcceleroGauge app designed to determine 3D acceleration and gravity values by comparing their own movement going down a set of stairs to movement in an elevator. In addition, they used the Distant Suns app that projected the night sky within their classroom so that they could use the app to identify certain stars/sans, constellations, planets, and moons.

Based on their experience with the ten apps, the teachers formulated their own criteria for evaluating their experience with these apps, generating the criteria of usability, integration/relevance to the curriculum, entertainment value, ability to engage users, usefulness for outdoors, clarity/ease of use, relevance to real world, compatibility, content/repertoire, and extras (p. 271). In applying these criteria, they rated those apps such as the Project Noah, AcceleroGauge, and Distant Suns more highly than other apps as supporting hands-on, interactive activity, as well as experiential learning outside the classroom.

In a similar study, twelve science teachers evaluated students' use of apps, using the Mobile App Selection for Science (MASS) framework that focuses on social-cultural aspects of learning related to the use of situated, authentic, personalized science learning activities (Kearney, Schuck, Burden, & Aubusson, 2012). The evaluation was made using the application of six criteria related to app use: 1) accuracy, 2) relevance of content, 3) sharing findings, 4) feedback, 5) scientific inquiry and practices and 6) usability (Green, et al., 2014). A comparison with the Evaluation Rubric for Mobile Applications rubric (Walker, 2011) found that similar assessments served to validate use of the MASS framework.

This qualitative assessment of apps based on teachers' uses of apps represents needed future research on specific practices associated with use of apps for particular purposes. When applied to students' use of apps, this research could generate insights into the kinds of learning fostered through uses of apps as well as development of classification systems for educators related to the kinds of learning fostered by uses of apps.

HOW DESIGN OF CLASSROOM SPACES INFLUENCES DESIGN OF CLASSROOM ACTIVITIES

Another issue important to m-learning has to do with how the pedagogical and physical design of the classroom space influences the design of activities in ways that exploit uses of apps or devices (Leander & Hollett, 2013). If either the activity and/or the classroom spaces are not designed to support effective use of apps or devices, learning potential may not be fully realized. An analysis of use of apps for augmented reality participation in a traditional museum space indicated that use of lecture podcasts supported relatively solitary activities while the use of Twitter interactions and multi-player games involved more collaboration (Kearney et al., 2012).

This issue has led to the recognition of the limitations of traditional classroom, museum, library, or school spaces for students accessing, creating, and sharing information and texts across different spaces using apps and devices, requiring physical redesign of traditional spaces to accommodate the use of apps and devices (Leander & Hollett, 2013). For example, a classroom at Case Western University was transformed to create an "active collaboration room" with an interactive whiteboard, projection screens, tables for three to six students, and video cameras that automatically pan to project persons who are speaking (Nastu, 2012). However, analysis of teachers and student interaction in a redesigned classroom found that teachers still employed the same familiar lessons and interaction patterns as in traditional classrooms (Julian, 2013), suggesting the importance of teacher attitudes towards use of redesigned learning spaces.

Use of E-Book Readers

Another important m-learning issue has to do with the effective use of e-book reader apps in fostering reading comprehension (Schugar & Schugar, 2014). As previously noted, comparisons of reading of a mystery short story on a Kindle versus a print text version finds that adult readers demonstrated significantly lower recall using the Kindle than for print texts (Mangen, et al., 2014), suggesting the need for more research on how use of devices influence reading comprehension.

The Evolution of Reading in the Age of Digitisation (E-READ) research project focuses European researchers attention on this issue. Because some students still prefer print texts, embedding 2D barcodes into texts that are then scanned using mobile devices, can encourage readers to acquire additional information or access animations thus enhancing responses to those texts (Uluyol & Agca, 2012). One question in this research is the degree to which automatic text summarization to condense the length and quantity of text (to highlight key ideas for reading on mobile devices) enhances reading comprehension (Yang et al., 2013). An analysis of one approach for analyzing use of text summarization indicated that users perceived the text summaries as supporting mobile learning (Yang et al., 2013). Given the ways in which texts are condensed or reduced for use on mobile devices, there is a need for more research on this topic.

Support for Special Needs Learners

Similar issues occur in the analysis of use of apps and devices to understand uses of m-learning by students with special learning needs. Mobile devices themselves have certain accessibility features for students with visual, hearing, or physical impairments, for example, on iOS or Android devices, there are various features for reading aloud texts (Beach & O'Brien, 2014).

These features can be accessed through bar codes and can increase sound, enlarge texts, alter touch commands, or change colors. These accessibility features are also found on certain apps (Kumar & Owston, 2014), particularly apps that can be customized to adapt to individual students particular learning needs (Fernandez-Lopez et al., 2013). Use of iOS apps tailored to meet the needs of LD struggling readers employing the remedial reading program Second Chance Reading resulted in significant gains in their reading ability (Retter et al., 2013).

Text-to-speech, speech-to-text, and video/audio apps that exploit multimodality are particularly useful for students with visual or hearing issues (Abrams, 2014; Hecker & Engstrom, 2011). For example, the BrainPop app illustrative videos included use of captions and the Toontastic app for creating animations included specific step-by-step instructions (Kumar & Owston, 2014). The MyVoice app that involved students inputting certain words that were then linked with pictures and audio of these words enhanced motivation of 7th -12th grade students in special education classes (Campigotto, et al., 2013). Students with disabilities and autism benefited from using an iPad to create and view videos of themselves solving math problems (Burton et al., 2013). A comparison of students with emotional disturbances using worksheets versus iPads for solving math problems found higher levels of achievement and motivation in using the iPads (Haydon, et al., 2012).

While these accessibility audio, speech, visual, and touch features of apps and devices provide supportive accommodations for special needs students, the remaining challenge relates to how busy teachers can create alternative instructional activities exploiting the use of these apps and devices and make use of these accommodations based on determining unique learning challenges for particular students.

WHAT ARE THE GAPS IN THE EXTANT RESEARCH AND DIRECTIONS FOR FUTURE RESEARCH?

Given the relative newness of m-learning and research on m-learning, there remains a number of gaps associated with conducting research on m-learning. A major gap in the research has to do with the lack of understanding of the specific learning processes involved in the use of apps (Green et al., 2014) given both positive (Huang, Lin, & Cheng, 2010; Hwang & Chang, 2011) and less positive effects (Park, Parsons, & Ryu, 2010) of apps on learning outcomes. Such research needs to go beyond a focus on the technology features "in" the apps to analysis of the instructional activities mediated "by" uses of the apps (Green, et al., 2014; Sung & Mayer, 2013).

In conducting this research, researchers could document how particular aspects of an activity mediated through use of an app and/or device are best scaffolded and how students' ability to use an app or device evolves over a period of time. In our own research on students' uses of Diigo digital sticky-note annotations while reading science texts (Castek & Beach, 2013; Castek et al., 2014), the practices of collaboration and multimodality were associated with sharing/responding to each other's questions and comments. Collaboration was achieved through the teacher's scaffolding of the activity, the fact that students could view the yellow sticky-note icons on the text, and open up the digital to and respond to others' annotations. Also important was the students' familiarity with how to employ the Diigo sticky-notes for sharing responses and how to use the digital space to foster dialogue and collaboration.

Another gap in the research has to do with the use of short-term research studies that may not capture students' long-term ability to learn to effectively employ an app or device. An analysis of 35 adolescents' uses of a mobile tablet device over the period of year found a steady increase in their digital media literacy levels, but acquiring effective use of accessing information and interacting productively required on-going, persistent instruction over time (Park & Burford, 2013). This suggests the need for research focusing on how students' gain familiarity with apps and devices over time so as to make this process more efficient and effective, an aspect that is often overlooked in short-term studies. Students need multiple experiences with apps and devices to learn their features and use them optimally in the service of deep learning (Cochrane et al., 2015).

There is also only limited research on how engaging in these text or apps creation projects enhances students' engagement. Drawing on qualitative analysis of students' engagement in app development, Vakil (2014) examined how creation of apps within Google's App Inventor for Android (AIA) in an after-school program served to foster critical inquiry. For example, one student employed the Google Maps creation apps to create a Google Map, something that resulted in positive uptake in ways that enhanced his sense of agency. Students in another study used the GameSalad tool during a semester course to create game apps, resulting in significant increases in their engagement, interest, understanding, and ability to design games (Dekhan, Xu, & Yin, 2013).

This research indicates that students are most likely to be engaged in creating texts when they draw on and transfer their prior experiences with genre features of familiar texts or apps they believe will results in positive audience response. Israel, et al. (2013) demonstrated that 5th graders who were asked to generate ideas for creating apps to support STEM instruction, were most likely to propose game-like apps involving use of leveled play; use of videos, pop-up images for word definitions; and use of multiplayer, collaborative platforms, features that reflected students' awareness of the need to embed assistive features to engage players in playing games (Israel, et al., 2013).

There is also a need for research on individual differences in how teachers and/or students employ use of apps or devices. Individual teachers may employ the same apps or devices in quite different ways based on their instructional methods, teaching philosophy, or expertise in technology integration. An ethnographic analysis of two high school English teachers uses of iPad and iOS apps during the first year of use of iPads in their school found that they varied their uses of iPads and apps in significant ways (Russell & Hughes, 2014). In one teacher's class, students most frequently employed browser (Safari), annotation (NeuAnnotate), word-processing (Pages, Notes), and English-subject-related apps (Celtx, Aesop's Fables) (p. 297), using these apps for acquiring information about, sharing annotations, and generating essays, with the teacher's students engaged in multimodal production in creating a video in response to reading *Beowulf*. In another teacher's class, students employed their iPads as e-readers as well as using annotation apps to add annotations to texts, and email to share responses to texts. The researchers noted that a key factor shaping differences in the teachers' and students' uses of iPads and apps was the lack of restrictions on how and which apps students could employ, infusing a sense of choice in learning, despite the occasional off-task use of the iPads.

WHAT ARE THE RECOMMENDATIONS/IMPLICATIONS FOR EDUCATION, CIVIC ENGAGEMENT (GLOBAL AND LOCAL), SOCIAL PRACTICE, AND POLICY?

The increased use of m-learning has major sociological and economic implications for the future of schooling and society. One of the major implications of m-learning is that it can transform classroom learning in terms of space and time by drawing on students' own uses of apps and devices outside of the classroom for their own social purposes. An examination of 620 Korean and American students' use of m-learning practices outside their classes found that learners sought more uses of m-learning within their classes—what the researchers referred to as a "hybrid shift" towards classroom instruction associated with more informal, personalized, situated, and collaborative learning in the classroom (Biddix, Chung, & Park, 2015). Students wanted more uses of interactivity with instructors and peers through social networking sites or apps; easy, rapid access to course materials using their mobile devices; and the ability to submit their work using their devices, recommendations that entail the need for increased use of hybrid instruction that meshes students uses of apps and devices outside the classroom with their uses within the classroom.

Use of m-learning also serves to personalize instruction by fostering students' formulation of their own goals for learning. Analysis of adult learners engaged in geocaching using their mobile devices for learning about aspects of natural landscapes defined their own learning goals and uses of their devices for geocaching to achieve those goals, serving to transform these natural setting into contexts for learning (Jones, Scanlon, & Clough, 2013).

The degree to which use of m-learning can serve to transform classroom learning may depend on the degree to which schools adopt top-down versus bottom-up implementation strategies (Pachler et al., 2012). One advantage of top-down, large-scale, district-wide purchases of apps and devices for all students is that in low-income districts, students may then benefit from having access to apps and devices. On the other hand, top-down implementation can be problematic, as evident in difficulties encountered in the large-scale rollout of iPads for students in the Los Angeles school district, resulting in teacher skepticism about use of iPads (Blume, 2013).

District policies towards the use of apps and devices are often driven by a hyperbolic "boosterism" discourse (Wright & Parchoma, 2011) constituting ways in which technology itself will serve to enhance learning that focuses on use of an app or device isolated from activities in which they are employed. Some of this discourse derives from a consumerism promoted by technology companies based on creating needs for technology use that is assumed will address disparities in the quality of instruction within schools. However, as previously noted, the disparities in access and use of app and devices between higher versus lower-income schools (Merchant, 2012; Purcell et al., 2013) evident in the finding that only 17% of students attend schools that provide students with their own device (Pearson, 2014) may override any attempt to address these disparities.

District-wide policies can also limit students' uses of their own devices ("BYOD" policies), resulting in students perceiving school as distinct from their informal learning outside of school (Pachler et al, 2012). Use of more bottom-up strategies that draw on students' use of their own use of apps and devices for use in school can result in transfer of self-directed, informal learning into school contexts, but may privilege students who can afford to own their own apps and devices (Pachler et al, 2012).

Addressing these local disparities across school districts suggests the need for statewide or national policies designed in insure equity in students' access to and use of apps and devices. This includes governments and school district formulating effective policies regarding bring-your-own-devices (BYOD) (Ismail, 2013). As of March, 2014, there was a 30% increase in BYOD use in American schools over the previous year, with 56% of districts adopting BYOD policies (Center for Digital Education, 2014). A review of research on uses of mobile learning afforded by uses of these devices found that students' use of their own devices can foster personalized learning, enabling transfer of work between home and school, reducing school's technology costs, and enhancing student motivation and engagement (Hwang & Wu, 2014).

It is also important that schools and governments recognize the challenge of the "digital divide" related to limited access to and use of apps and devices based on socio-economic factors, resulting in differences in social capital defined as people having access to interpersonal or community resources that provide certain benefits or support for achieving their goals (Putnam & Feldstein, 2004). These inequities can also occur within and across developing countries. Lack of access to print texts, computers, or broadband access in these countries has led to the relatively high use of mobile devices for learning in these countries (Velghe, 2014; Walton, 2010), but there remains a need to understand how m-learning benefits students in these countries and whether curriculum can be developed that exploits m-learning in ways that will engage students to acquire certain literacy practices.

People can use m-learning to acquire social capital through online communication and social networking with others (Jung, Chan-Olmsted, & Kim, 2013). Survey research of smartphone users in South Korea found that users who were younger, employed more innovative strategies, and had higher consumption skills were more likely to download and use more apps; income and education level had no effects on downloading apps. At the same time, while the number of apps downloaded did not contribute to enhanced social capital, how certain apps were employed and the use of communication and new/information apps did contribute to enhanced social capital (Jung et al, 2013).

Given an expanded definition of social capital as the ability to employ resources to effectively communicate and interact with others (Lee, 2014), all of this suggests the need to go beyond simply framing the "digital divide" only in terms of access

or ownership of apps or devices to also focus on people's learning to employ apps and devices for communication with others and information access enhancing their social capital. This requires an increased focus on professional development for teachers on effective m-learning practices, as well as providing adults in libraries and adult learning centers with instruction on ways to employ apps and devices to interact with others and acquire relevant information consistent with one's goals.

This professional development could focus on helping teachers plan instructional activities in terms of selecting and using devices are consistent with their particular goals as well as being able to identify and predict constraints involving use of devices (Hutchison & Woodward, 2013). Such training may result in teachers not only employing m-learning more effectively but also adopting more student-centered instruction. Based on training of science teachers over a two year period compared with teachers who did not receive training found while 57% of teachers and 48% of students of teachers who did not receive the training were employing technology when observed by researchers, for teachers who were trained, 73% of students and 48% of teachers were using technology during observation periods (Meyer, 2013). One reason that students in the latter group were using technology more on their own was that 59% of the teachers who were trained increased the amount of individualized instruction they offered and 43% were using fewer lectures. It was also the case that 52% of their students increased in their proficiency with m-learning resulting in being more likely to using m-learning for working on their projects during their free time, resulting in students having more positive views of the value of m-learning than students of non-trained teachers who did not implement m-learning.

An analysis of the planning processes involving use of mobile devices employed by science teachers in a professional development workshop and as they implemented these plans in their teaching indicated that use of the devices enhanced accessibility to current information for devising science lessons (Ekanayake & Wishart, 2014). Teachers also expanded alternative ways to represent science subject matter to their students by employing more activities involving students providing their own data. For example, students used their devices to collect images of household chemicals for use in a chemistry lesson; teachers checked with colleagues on whether certain teaching aids actually worked on each other's devices. The teachers also recognized the variation in students' technology skills, resulting in their providing students additional time to practice uses of their devices.

An examination of their students' participation indicated enhanced student engagement associated with their bringing in images of household chemicals, using teacher-developed instructions and videos to support individualized learning, providing their teachers with images and videos using Bluetooth to demonstrate learning, and answering assessment questions on their devices for instant feedback and correction of misconceptions.

CONCLUSION

Throughout this review, we have placed learning mediated by app at the center of the discussion of apps, devices, and m-learning more generally. The research reviewed suggests there is potential for the use of these technologies to not only enhance but also transform learning (Puentedura, 2011). However, this transformative power lies not in the apps or devices themselves but in the design of the activities that govern their use and the literacy practices they foster. When it comes to the use of apps and devices, activity design must consider how mobile devices employed with use of apps such as portability, touch, image/video production capabilities, and ease of use, among others as well as consideration of individual differences in students' ability to employ certain apps. We offer this review to help the field better understand the landscape of m-learning and to inspire additional research in this emerging area.

REFERENCES

Abrams, S. S. (2014). Integrating virtual and traditional learning in 6-12 classrooms: A layered literacies approach to multimodal meaning making. New York: Routledge.

Ahmed, S., & Parsons, D. (2013). Abductive science inquiry using mobile devices in the classroom. *Computers & Education*, *63*, 62–72. doi:10.1016/j. compedu.2012.11.017

Al-Jarf, R. (2012). Mobile technology and student autonomy in oral skill acquisition. In J. Díaz-Vera (Ed.), *Left to my own devices: Learner autonomy and mobile-assisted language learning innovation and leadership in English language teaching* (pp. 105–130). Bingley, UK: Emerald Group.

Allen, R., Tsai, Y.-T., Hinman, R., & Azuma, R. (2010). The Westwood experience: Connecting story to locations via mixed reality. In *Proceedings of the International Symposium on Mixed and Augmented Reality* (pp. 39-46). Seoul, Korea: Institute of Electrical and Electronics Engineers.

Angst, C., & Malinowski, E. (2010). *Findings from eReader Project, Phase 1: Use of iPads in MGT40700, Project Management," University of Notre Dame Working Paper Series*. South Bend, IN: University of Notre Dame. Retrieved from http://www.nd.edu/~cangst/NotreDame_iPad_ Report_01-06-11.pdf

Aspen Institute Task Force on Learning and the Internet. (2014). *Learner at the center of a networked world*. Washington, DC: The Aspen Institute.

Baran, E., & Khan, S. (2014). Going mobile in science teacher education. In C. Miller & A. Doering (Eds.), *The new landscape of mobile learning* (pp. 258–275). New York: Routledge.

Baron, N. S. (2011). Concerns about mobile phones: A cross–national study. *First Monday*, *16*(8). doi:10.5210/fm.v16i8.3335

Barseghian, T. (2013, March 13). *For low-income kids, access to devices could be the equalizer* [web log comment]. Retrieved from http://tinyurl.com/cosebth

Beach, R., & O'Brien, D. (2014). *Using apps for learning across the curriculum: A literacy-based framework and guide.* New York: Routledge.

Beach, R., & O'Brien, D. (2015b). Enhancing struggling students' engagement through the affordances of interactivity, connectivity, and collaboration. *Reading & Writing Quarterly, 31*(2), 119–134. doi:10.1080/10573569.2014.962200

Bicen, H., & Kocakoyun, S. (2013). The evaluation of the most used mobile devices applications by students. *Procedia: Social and Behavioral Sciences, 89,* 756–760. doi:10.1016/j.sbspro.2013.08.928

Biddix, J. P., Chung, C. J., & Park, H. W. (2015). The hybrid shift: Evidencing a student-driven restructuring of the college classroom. *Computers & Education, 80,* 162–175. doi:10.1016/j.compedu.2014.08.016

Bisson, R., & Vazquez, A. W. (2013, December 10). iChoose: Academic choice and iPads. Paper presented at the TIES Conference, Minneapolis, MN.

Blume, H. (2013, December 1). *Mixed reaction to iPad rollout from L.A. teachers and administrators* [web log comment]. Retrieved from http://tinyurl.com/k6xlcrg

Bomhold, C. R. (2013). Educational use of smartphone technology: A survey of mobile phone application use by undergraduate university students. *Program: Electronic Library & Information Systems, 47*(4), 424–436. doi:10.1108/PROG-01-2013-0003

Burton, C. E., Anderson, D. H., Prater, M. A., & Dyches, T. T. (2013). Video self-modeling on an iPad to teach functional math skills to adolescents with autism and intellectual disability. *Focus on Autism and Other Developmental Disabilities, 28*(2), 67–77. doi:10.1177/1088357613478829

Cairney, G. (2014, August 12). *App seeks to take complexity out of teaching physics* [web log comment]. Retrieved from http://tinyurl.com/mxzvs52

Campigotto, R., McEwenb, R., & Demmans Eppa, C. (2013). Especially social: Exploring the use of an iOS application in special needs classrooms. *Computers & Education, 60*(1), 74–86. doi:10.1016/j.compedu.2012.08.002

Castek, J., & Beach, R. (2013). Using apps to support disciplinary learning and science learning. *Journal of Adolescent & Adult Literacy, 56*(7), 544–554. doi:10.1002/JAAL.180

Castek, J., Beach, R., Cotanch, H., & Scott, J. (2014). Exploiting the affordances of multimodal tools for writing in the science classroom. In R. S. Anderson & C. Mims (Eds.), *Handbook of research on digital tools for writing instruction in K-12 settings* (pp. 80–101). Hershey, PA: IGI Global.

Castek, J., Coiro, J., Guzniczak, L., & Bradshaw, C. (2012). Examining peer collaboration in online inquiry. *The Educational Forum, 76*(4), 479–496. doi:10.1080/00131725.2012.707756

Center for Digital Education. (2014). *Digital school districts survey identifies innovative uses of technology.* Author. Retrieved from http://tinyurl.com/k8a37by

Charitonos, K., Blake, C., Scanlon, E., & Jones, A. (2012). Museum learning via social and mobile technologies: (How) can online interactions enhance the visitor experience? *British Journal of Educational Technology, 43*(5), 802–819. doi:10.1111/j.1467-8535.2012.01360.x

Chen, C.-M., & Chen, F.-Y. (2014). Enhancing digital reading performance with a collaborative reading annotation system. *Computers & Education*, *77*, 67–81. doi:10.1016/j.compedu.2014.04.010

Cherner, T., Dix, J., & Lee, C. (2014). Cleaning up that mess: A framework for classifying educational apps. *Contemporary Issues in Technology & Teacher Education*, *14*(2). Retrieved from http://www.citejournal.org/vol14/iss2/general/article1.cfm

Chinthammit, W., & Thomas, A. (2014). Augmented reality in the English classroom. In L. Unsworth & A. Thomas (Eds.), *English teaching & new literacies pedagogies: Interpreting and authoring digital multimedia narratives* (pp. 213–231). New York: Peter Lang.

Clarke, B., Svanaes, S., Zimmermann, S., & Crowther, K. (2013). *One-to-one tablets in secondary schools: An evaluation study, Stage 3: April-September 2013. Family Kids and Youth, UK*. Sussex: UK: Tablets for Schools. Retrieved from http://www.tabletsforschools.org.uk

Cochrane, T., Guinibert, M., Simeti, C., Brannigan, R., & Kala, A. (2015). Mobile Social Media as a Catalyst for Collaborative Curriculum Redesign. In J. Keengwe & M. Maxfield (Eds.), *Advancing higher education with mobile learning technologies: Cases, trends, and inquiry-based methods* (pp. 1–21). Hershey, PA: Information Science Reference; doi:10.4018/978-1-4666-6284-1.ch001

Cochrane, T., Narayan, V., & Oldfield, J. (2013). iPadagogy: Appropriating the iPad within pedagogical contexts. *International Journal of Mobile Learning and Organisation*, *7*(1), 48–65. doi:10.1504/IJMLO.2013.051573

Connell, C., Bayliss, L., & Farmer, W. (2012). Effects of ebook readers and tablet computers on reading comprehension. *International Journal of Instructional Media*, *39*(2), 131–140.

Deaton, C. C. M., Deaton, B. E., Ivankovic, D., & Norris, F. A. (2013). Creating stop-motion videos with iPads to support students' understanding of cell processes: "Because you have to know what you're talking about to be able to do it. *Journal of Digital Learning in Teacher Education*, *30*(2), 67–73. doi:10.1080/21532974.2013.10784729

Dekhan, S., Xu, X., & Yin, M. (2013). Mobile app development to increase student engagement and problem solving skills. *Journal of Information Systems Education*, *24*(4), 299.

Desouz, K. C., & Bhagwatwar, A. (2012). Citizen apps to solve complex urban problems. *Journal of Urban Technology*, *19*(3), 107–136. doi:10.1080/10630732.2012.673056

Devaney, L. (2014, September 3). *Mobile learning's major impact* [web log comment]. Retrieved from http://tinyurl.com/mshraao

EdTech. (2013, December 24). *Mobile and education development infographic* [web log comment]. Retrieved from http://tinyw.in/obaO

Ekanayake, T. M. S. S. K. Y., & Wishart, J. M. (2014). Developing teachers' pedagogical practice in teaching science lessons with mobile phones. *Technology, Pedagogy and Education*, *23*(2), 131–150. doi:10.1080/1475939X.2013.810366

Fernandez-Lopez, A., Rodriguez-Fortiz, M. J., Rodriguez-Almendros, M. L., & Martinez-Segura, M. J. (2013). Mobile learning technology based on iOS devices to support students with special education. *Computers & Education*, *67*, 77–90. doi:10.1016/j.compedu.2012.09.014

Freeberg, A. (2014, February 6). *Virtual field trips take students into the labs* [web log comment]. Retrieved from http://tinyurl.com/mbya9vo

Geurtz, R., & Foote, C. (2014). Librarian technology leadership in the adoption of iPads in a high school. In C. Miller & A. Doering (Eds.), *The new landscape of mobile learning* (pp. 276–291). New York: Routledge.

Gikas, J., & Grant, M. M. (2013). Mobile computing devices in higher education: Student perspectives on learning with cellphones, smartphones & social media. *The Internet and Higher Education*, *19*, 18–26. doi:10.1016/j.iheduc.2013.06.002

Green, L. S., Hechter, R. P., Tysinger, P. D., & Chassereau, K. D. (2014). Mobile app selection for 5th through 12th grade science: The development of the MASS rubric. *Computers & Education*, *75*, 65–71. doi:10.1016/j.compedu.2014.02.007

Hahn, J. (2010). Information seeking with Wikipedia on the iPod Touch. *RSR. Reference Services Review*, *38*(2), 284–298. doi:10.1108/00907321011045043

Haydon, T., Hawkins, R., Denune, H., Kimener, L., McCoy, D., & Basham, J. (2012). A comparison of iPads and worksheets on math skills of high school students with emotional disturbance. *Behavioral Disorders*, *37*(4), 232–243.

Hecker, L., & Engstrom, E. U. (2011). Technology that supports literacy instruction and learning. In J. R. Birsh (Ed.), *Multisensory teaching of basic language skills* (3rd ed., pp. 657–683). Baltimore: Brookes Publishing Company.

Holden, C., & Sykes, J. (2011). Mentira: Prototyping language–based locative gameplay. In S. Dikkers, J. Martin, & B. Coutler (Eds.), *Mobile media learning: Amazing uses of mobile devices for learning* (pp. 111–130). Pittsburgh, PA: ETC Press.

Hsu, J.-L., & Shih, Y.-J. (2013). Developing computer adventure education games on mobile devices for conducting cooperative problem-solving activities. *International Journal of Mobile Learning Organisation*, *7*(2), 81–98. doi:10.1504/IJMLO.2013.055616

Huang, Y.-M., Lin, Y.-T., & Cheng, S.-C. (2010). Effectiveness of a mobile plant learning system in a science curriculum in Taiwanese elementary education. *Computers & Education*, *54*(1), 47–58. doi:10.1016/j.compedu.2009.07.006

Hutchison, A., & Beschorner, B. (2014). Using the iPad as a tool to support literacy instruction. *Technology, Pedagogy and Education*. doi:10.1080/1475939X.2014.918561

Hutchison, A., & Woodward, L. (2013). A planning cycle for integrating digital technology into literacy instruction. *The Reading Teacher*, *67*(6), 455–464. doi:10.1002/trtr.1225

Hwang, G. J., & Chang, H. F. (2011). A formative assessment-based mobile learning approach to improving the learning attitudes and achievements of students. *Computers & Education*, *56*(4), 1023–1031. doi:10.1016/j.compedu.2010.12.002

Hwang, G.-J., & Chang, H.-F. (2011). A formative assessment-based mobile learning approach to improving the learning attitudes and achievements of students. *Computers & Education*, *56*(4), 1023–1031. doi:10.1016/j.compedu.2010.12.002

Hwang, G.-J., & Wu, P.-H. (2014). Applications, impacts and trends of mobile technology-enhanced learning: A review of 2008-2012 publications in selected SSCI journals. *International Journal of Mobile Learning Organisation*, *8*(2), 83–95. doi:10.1504/IJMLO.2014.062346

Ismail, I., Azizan, S. N., & Azman, N. (2013). Mobile phone as pedagogical tools: Are teachers ready? *International Education Studies*, *6*(3), 36–47. doi:10.5539/ies.v6n3p36

Israel, M., Marino, M. T., Basham, J. D., & Spivak, W. (2013). Fifth graders as app designers: How diverse learners conceptualize educational apps. *Journal of Research on Technology in Education, 46*(1), 53–80. doi:10.1080/15391523.2013.10782613

Ito, M., Gutierrez, K., Livingstone, S., Punel, B., Rhodes, J., & Salen, K. … Watkins, S. C. (2013). Connected learning: An agenda for research and design. Irvine, CA: The Digital Media and Learning HUB Reports on Connected Learning.

Johnson, L., Adams Becker, S., Cummins, M., Estrada, V., Freeman, A., & Ludgate, H. (2013). *NMC Horizon Report: 2013 K-12 Edition*. Austin, TX: The New Media Consortium.

Johnson, L., Adams Becker, S., Estrada, V., & Freeman, A. (2014). NMC Horizon Report: 2014 K-12 Edition. Austin, TX: The New Media Consortium. Retrieved from http://tinyurl.com/k4lp6fn

Johnson, L., Adams Becker, S., Estrada, V., & Martín, S. (2013). Technology outlook for STEM+Education 2013-2018: An NMC Horizon Project Sector Analysis. Austin, TX: The New Media Consortium. Retrieved from http://tinyw.in/ByT0

Johnston, N., & Marsh, S. (2014). Using iBooks and iPad apps to embed information literacy into an EFL foundations course. *New Library World, 115*(1), 51–60. doi:10.1108/NLW-09-2013-0071

Jones, A. C., Scanlon, E., & Clough, G. (2013). Mobile learning: Two case studies of supporting inquiry learning in informal and semiformal settings. *Computers & Education, 61,* 21–32. doi:10.1016/j.compedu.2012.08.008

Julian, S. (2013). Reinventing classroom space to re-energise information literacy instruction. *Journal of Information Literacy, 7*(1), 69–82. doi:10.11645/7.1.1720

Junco, R., Heiberger, G., & Koken, E. (2011). The effect of Twitter on college student engagement and grades. *Journal of Computer Assisted Learning, 27*(2), 119–132. doi:10.1111/j.1365-2729.2010.00387.x

Jung, J., Chan-Olmsted, S., & Kim, Y. (2013). From access to utilization: Factors affecting smartphone application use and its impacts on social and human capital acquisition in South Korea. *Journalism & Mass Communication Quarterly, 90*(4), 715–735. doi:10.1177/1077699013503163

Kalantzis, M., & Cope, B. (2012). *Literacies.* New York: Cambridge University Press. doi:10.1017/CBO9781139196581

Kamarainen, A. M., Metcalf, S., Grotzer, T., Browne, A., Mazzuca, D., Tutwiler, M. S., & Dede, C. (2013). EcoMOBILE: Integrating augmented reality and probeware with environmental education field trips. *Computers & Education, 68,* 545–556. doi:10.1016/j.compedu.2013.02.018

Kearney, M., Burden, K., & Rai, T. (2015). Investigating teachers' adoption of signature mobile pedagogies. *Computers & Education, 80,* 48–57. doi:10.1016/j.compedu.2014.08.009

Kearney, M., Schuck, S., Burden, K., & Aubusson, P. (2012). Viewing mobile learning from a pedagogical perspective. *Research in Learning Technology, 20,* 1–17.

Kim, D., Rueckert, D., Kim, D.-J., & Seo, D. (2013). Students' perceptions and experiences of mobile learning. *Language Learning & Technology, 17*(3), 52–73.

Kissinger, J. S. (2013). The social & mobile learning experiences of students using mobile e-books. *Journal of Asynchronous Learning Networks, 17*(1), 155–170.

Konnikova, M. (2014, July 16). Being a better online reader. *The New Yorker.* Retrieved from http://tinyurl.com/mm26ahr

Koole, M. (2009). A model for framing mobile learning. In M. Ally (Ed.), *Mobile learning: Transforming the delivery of education and training* (Vol. 1, pp. 25–47). Edmonton, Alberta: Alberta University Press.

Korkey, H. (2014, September 9). *Can students "go deep" with digital reading?* [web log comment]. Retrieved from http://tinyurl.com/m35qkff

Kress, G. (2003). *Literacy in the New Media Age*. New York: Routledge. doi:10.4324/9780203164754

Kumar, K., & Owston, R. (2014). Accessibility evaluation of iOS apps for education. In C. Miller & A. Doering (Eds.), *The new landscape of mobile learning* (pp. 208–224). New York: Routledge.

Lai, C.-H. (2014). An integrated approach to untangling mediated connectedness with online and mobile media. *Computers in Human Behavior, 31*, 20–26. doi:10.1016/j.chb.2013.10.023

Lai, C.-H., Chu, C.-M., Luo, P.-P., & Chen, W.-H. (2013). Learners' acceptance of mobile technology supported collaborative learning. *International Journal of Mobile Learning Organisation, 7*(3/4), 277–291. doi:10.1504/IJMLO.2013.057166

Leander, K., & Hollett, T. (2013). Designing new spaces for literacy learning. In P. Dunston, S. K. Fullerton, C. C. Bates, P. M. Stecker, M. W. Cole, A. H. Hall, et al. (Eds.), 62nd yearbook of the Literacy Research Association (pp. 29-42). Altamonte Springs, FL: Literacy Research Association.

Lee, M. (2014). Bringing the best of two worlds together for social capital research in education Social network analysis and symbolic interactionism. *Educational Researcher, 43*(9), 454–464. doi:10.3102/0013189X14557889

Lemphane, P., & Prinsloo, M. (2013). *Children's digital literacy practices in unequal South African settings*. Tilburg, Netherlands: University of Tilburg, Tilburg Papers in Cultural Studies #60. Retrieved from http://tinyurl.com/q5uxzov

Lewis, T. L., Burnett, B., Tunstall, R. G., & Abrahams, P. H. (2014). Complementing anatomy education using three-dimensional. *Clinical Anatomy (New York, N.Y.), 27*(3), 313–320. doi:10.1002/ca.22256 PMID:23661327

Li, Y., Guo, A., Lee, J. A., & Negara, G. P. K. (2013). A platform on the cloud for self-creation of mobile interactive learning trails. *International Journal of Mobile Learning Organisation, 7*(1), 66–80. doi:10.1504/IJMLO.2013.051574

Li, Z., & Hegelheimer, V. (2013). Mobile-assisted grammar exercises: Effects on self-editing in L2 writing. *Language Learning & Technology, 17*(3), 135–156.

Lin, C.-C. (2014). Learning English reading in a mobile-assisted extensive reading program. *Computers & Education, 78*, 48–59. doi:10.1016/j.compedu.2014.05.004

London Mobile Learning Group. (2014). *Theory: Mobile learning* [web log comment]. Retrieved from http://www.londonmobilelearning.net/#theory.php

Ly, A., & Vaala, A. (2014, August 15). *What's in store today: A snapshot of kids' language & literacy apps, Part 1*. Washington, DC: New America's Ed Policy Program and the Joan Ganz Cooney Center at Sesame Workshop. Retrieved from http://tinyurl.com/nlxs4wu

MacWilliam, A. (2013). The engaged reader. *Publishing Research Quarterly, 29*(1), 1–11. doi:10.1007/s12109-013-9305-8

Magley, G. (2011, October 3). *Grade 8 mobile one-to-one with iPads: Component of the Millis schools personalized learning initiative.* Millisp, MA: Millisp Public Schools. Retrieved from http://tinyurl.com/k7jfato

Mangen, A., Robinet, P., Olivier, G., & Velay, J.-L. (2014, July 21-25). *Mystery story reading in pocket print book and on Kindle: Possible impact on chronological events memory.* Paper presented at The International Society for the Empirical Study of Literature and Media, Turin, Italy. Retrieved from http://tinyurl.com/llvaeav

Mao, J. (2014). Social media for learning: A mixed methods study on high school students' technology affordances and perspectives. *Computers in Human Behavior, 33,* 213–223. doi:10.1016/j.chb.2014.01.002

Martin, F., & Ertzberger, J. (2013). Here and now mobile learning: An experimental study on the use of mobile technology. *Computers & Education, 68,* 76–85. doi:10.1016/j.compedu.2013.04.021

McLain, B. (2014). Delineation of evaluation criteria for educational apps in STEM education. In C. Miller & A. Doering (Eds.), *The new landscape of mobile learning* (pp. 192–207). New York: Routledge.

Merchant, G. (2012). Mobile practices in everyday life: Popular digital technologies and schooling revisited. *British Journal of Educational Technology, 43*(5), 770–782. doi:10.1111/j.1467-8535.2012.01352.x

Meyer, L. (2013, June 27). Report: Professional development for mobile learning improves student engagement and interest in STEM subjects. *THE Journal.* Retrieved from http://tinyurl.com/jwg27vv

Miller, C., & Doering, A. (Eds.), *The new landscape of mobile learning.* New York: Routledge.

Miller, R. E., Vogh, B. S., & Jennings, E. J. (2013). Library in an app: Testing the usability of Boopsie as a mobile library application. *Journal of Web Librarianship, 7*(2), 142–153. doi:10.1080/19322909.2013.779526

Mundie, J., & Hooper, S. (2014). The potential of connected mobile learning. In C. Miller & A. Doering (Eds.), *The new landscape of mobile learning* (pp. 8–18). New York: Routledge.

Nastu, J. (2012, October 29). *How "collaborative learning" is transforming higher education* [web log comment]. Retrieved from http://tinyurl.com/owyg9ao

Nielsen, L., & Webb, W. (2011). *Teaching generation text: Using cell phones to enhance learning.* New York: John Wiley.

Pachler, N., Bachmair, B., & Cook, J. (2010). *Mobile learning: Structures, agency, practices.* New York: Springer. doi:10.1007/978-1-4419-0585-7

Pachler, N., Seipold, J., & Bachmair, B. (2012). Mobile Learning. Some theoretical and practical considerations. In K. Friedrich, M. Ranieri, N., Pachler, N., & P. de Theux (Eds.), *The "my mobile" handbook: Guidelines and scenarios for mobile learning in adult education* (pp. 11-16). Retrieved from http://www.mymobile-project.eu/IMG/pdf/Handbook_print.pdf

Park, S., & Burford, S. (2013). A longitudinal study on the uses of mobile tablet devices and changes in digital media literacy of young adults. *Educational Media International, 50*(4), 266–280. doi:10.1080/09523987.2013.862365

Pearson. (2014, May 9). *Pearson student mobile device survey: National report: Students in grades 4-12*. Author. Retrieved from http://tinyw.in/GJul

Pegrum, M., Oakley, G., & Faulkner, R. (2013). Schools going mobile: A study of the adoption of mobile handheld technologies in Western Australian independent schools. *Australasian Journal of Educational Technology*, 29(1), 66–81.

Pollock, M. (2011). Research day: Exploring the potential of texting for student-teacher communication. Somerville, MA: The OneVille Project. Retrieved from http://wiki.oneville.org/main/The_OneVille_Project

Puentedura, R. R. (2011). *A matrix model for designing and assessing network-enhanced courses*. Retrieved from http://www.hippasus.com

Purcell, K., Heaps, A., Buchanan, J., & Friedrich, L. (2013). How teachers are using technology at home and in their classrooms. Washington, DC: Pew Research Center Internet Project. Retrieved from http://tinyurl.com/laqo2kb

Putnam, R. D., & Feldstein, L. (2004). *Better together: Restoring the American community*. New York: Simon & Schuster.

Ramos, R., & Devers, D. (2014). iPad-enabled experiments in an undergraduate physics laboratory. In C. Miller & A. Doering (Eds.), The new landscape of mobile learning (pp. 334-352). New York: Routledge.

Retter, S., Anderson, C., & Kieran, L. (2013). IPad use for accelerating gains in reading skills of secondary students with learning disabilities. *Journal of Educational Multimedia and Hypermedia*, 22(4), 443–463.

Rosenheck, L. (2011). Beetles, beasties and bunnies: Ubiquitous games for biology prototyping language-based locative gameplay. In S. Dikkers, J. Martin, & B. Coutler (Eds.), *Mobile media learning: Amazing uses of mobile devices for learning* (pp. 77–96). Pittsburgh, PA: ETC Press.

Rowsell, J. (2014). Toward a phenomenology of contemporary reading. *Australian Journal of Language & Literacy*, 37(2), 117–127.

Russell, G., & Hughes, J. (2014). iTeach and iLearn with iPads in secondary English language arts. In C. Miller & A. Doering (Eds.), The new landscape of mobile learning (pp. 292-307). New York: Routledge.

Rutkin, A. (2014, August 14). *Digital textbooks adapt to your level as you learn* [web log comment]. Retrieved from http://tinyurl.com/pl225a9

Schneps, M. H., Ruel, J., Sonnert, G., Dussault, M., Griffin, M., & Sadler, P. M. (2014). Conceptualizing astronomical scale: Virtual simulations on handheld tablet computers reverse misconceptions. *Computers & Education*, 70, 269–280. doi:10.1016/j.compedu.2013.09.001

Schneps, M. H., Thomson, J. M., Chen, C., Sonnert, G., & Pomplun, M. (2013). E-Readers are more effective than paper for some with dyslexia. *PLoS ONE*, 8(9), e75634. doi:10.1371/journal.pone.0075634 PMID:24058697

Schugar, H. R., & Schugar, J. T. (2014). Reading in the post-PC era: Students' comprehension of interactive e-books. Paper presented as the American Educational Research Association, Philadelphia, PA.

Simpson, A., Walsh, M., & Rowsell, J. (2013). The digital reading path: Researching modes and multidirectionality with iPads. *Literacy*, *47*(3), 123–130. doi:10.1111/lit.12009

Soep, L. (2014, February 21). *Youth productions in digital-age civics*. Paper presented at the University of Minnesota Learning Technologies Media Lab. Retrieved from http://tinyurl.com/oys39ar

Song, Y. (2014). "Bring Your Own Device (BYOD)" for seamless science inquiry in a primary school. *Computers & Education*, *74*, 50–60. doi:10.1016/j.compedu.2014.01.005

Squire, K., & Dikkers, S. (2012). Amplifications of learning: Use of mobile media devices among youth. *Convergence (London)*, *18*(4), 445–464. doi:10.1177/1354856511429646

Srisawasdi, N., & Sornkhatha, P. (2014). The effect of simulation-based inquiry on students' conceptual learning and its potential applications in mobile learning. *International Journal of Mobile Learning Organisation*, *8*(1), 28–49. doi:10.1504/IJMLO.2014.059996

StudyBlue. (2011). *StudyBlue study report* [web log comment]. Retrieved from http://tinyurl.com/7l9vp8b

Sung, E., & Mayer, R. E. (2013). Online multimedia learning with mobile devices and desktop computers: An experimental test of Clark's methods-not-media hypothesis. *Computers in Human Behavior*, *29*(3), 639–647. doi:10.1016/j.chb.2012.10.022

Thomas, K. M., O'Bannon, B. W., & Bolton, N. (2013). Cell phones in the classroom: Teachers' perspectives of inclusion, benefits, and barriers. *Computers in the Schools: Interdisciplinary Journal of Practice, Theory, and Applied Research*, *30*(4), 295–308. doi:10.1080/07380569.2013.844637

Uluyol, C., & Agca, R. K. (2012). Integrating mobile multimedia into textbooks: 2D barcodes. *Computers & Education*, *59*(4), 1192–1198. doi:10.1016/j.compedu.2012.05.018

Ushioda, E. (2013). Motivation matters in mobile language learning: A brief commentary. *Language Learning & Technology*, *17*(3), 1–5. Retrieved from http://llt.msu.edu/issues/october2013/commentary.pdf

Vakil, S. (2014). A critical pedagogy approach for engaging urban youth in mobile app development in an after-school program. *Equity & Excellence in Education*, *47*(1), 31–45. doi:10.1080/10665684.2014.866869

Velghe, R. (2014). "I wanna go in the phone": Literacy acquisition, informal learning processes, "voice" and mobile phone appropriation in a South African. *Ethnography and Education*, *9*(1), 111–126. doi:10.1080/17457823.2013.836456

Wagler, M., & Mathews, J. (2011). Up river: Place, ethnography, and design in the St. Louis River estuary. In S. Dikkers, J. Martin, & B. Coutler (Eds.), *Mobile media learning: Amazing uses of mobile devices for learning* (pp. 39–60). Pittsburgh, PA: ETC Press.

Wagoner, T., Schwalbe, A., Hoover, S., & Ernst, D. (2012). CEHD iPad Initiative: Year two report. Minneapolis, MN: College of Education and Human Development, University of Minnesota. Retrieved from http://www.cehd.umn.edu/Mobile/About.html

Walker, H. (2011). Evaluating the effectiveness of apps for mobile devices. *Journal of Special Education Technology*, *26*(4), 59–63.

Walton, M. (2010). *Mobile literacies & South African teens: Leisure reading, writing, and MXit chatting for teens in Langa and Gugulethu*. Durbanville, South Africa: Shuttleworth Foundation m4Lit Project. Retrieved from http://tinyw.in/lJmr

Warner, J. (2014). *Networked, social, and multimodal: Adolescents composing across spaces.* (Unpublished doctoral dissertation), Teachers College, Columbia University, New York.

Webb, J. (2012). The iPad as a tool for education: a case study. Nottingham, UK: Naace. Retrieved from http://www.naace.co.uk/publications/long-fieldipadresearch

West, M., & Chew, H. E. (2014). Reading in the Mobile Era: A study of mobile reading in developing countries. Paris: United Nations Educational, Scientific, and Cultural Organization; Retrieved from http://tinyw.in/qdSw

Wood, C., Kemp, N., & Plester, B. (2013). *Text messaging and literacy: The evidence.* New York: Routledge.

Wright, S., & Parchoma, G. (2011). Technologies for learning? An actor-network theory critique of "affordances" in research on mobile learning. *Research in Learning Technology*, *19*(3), 247–258. doi:10.1080/21567069.2011.624168

Yang, G., Chen, N.-S., Erkki Sutinen, K., Anderson, T., & Wen, D. (2013). The effectiveness of automatic text summarization in mobile learning contexts. *Computers & Education*, *68*, 233–243. doi:10.1016/j.compedu.2013.05.012

Yu, C., Lee, S. J., & Ewing, C. (2015). Mobile learning: Trends, issues, and challenges in teaching and learning. In J. Keengwe & M. Maxfield (Eds.), *Advancing higher education with mobile learning technologies: Cases, trends, and inquiry-based methods* (pp. 60–87). Hershey, PA: Information Science Reference; doi:10.4018/978-1-4666-6284-1.ch004

KEY TERMS AND DEFINITIONS

Annotation: Marking up text to add highlights and individual comments, connections, and questions.

Apps: Specialized programs employed on iOS, Android, Chrome OS, or Windows platforms for use on mobile devices.

Connected Learning: Learning through transfer of experiences, knowledge, and literacy practices across school, home, community, and peer-group worlds.

Digital Text: Text (including images, sound, video, and other multimodal features) read on a screen, can be on website or text read on a downloadable PDF document.

Literacy Practices: Practices involving literacy learning associated with understanding and creating texts in social events involving prior knowledge, beliefs, attitudes, and social relationships.

M-Learning: Mobile learning that takes place when using apps or a mobile device.

Mobile Devices: Small portable digital mechanisms such as phones or tablets that provide access to the web, apps, and other software.

Multimodality: Using visual, auditory, textual, and image-based ways of representation for the purposes of communicating with and engaging audiences.

Personalization/Adaptivity: Opportunities to customize ways of using apps to meet individual preferences.

Portability: The ability to use a digital device flexibly in different locations.

Ubiquity/Authenticity: An everyday practice that involves real and meaningful use of an app (not simply for an assignment).

Chapter 15

Deviously Deviant:
The Strange Tapestry that is deviantART.com

Brian Lee Jones
Marana Unified School District, USA

ABSTRACT

This chapter presents the unique case of deviantART.com – a popular social networking and image-sharing platform for artists. The chapter introduces and describes the platform, its history, and some of the features the platform offers. It forwards a brief summation of current research, outlines issues emerging from that research, explores the strength and weaknesses of that research, and discusses some of the many difficulties related to researching the platform and its members. The chapter includes a discussion of "creativity" and the economically centric rhetoric and misconceptions latent in hyped popular discourse surrounding the rise of a "creative economy." A discussion of educational issues from an art education perspective is also included in the chapter, which concludes with a presentation of larger social and policy issues related to deviantART.com.

INTRODUCTION

DeviantART(dA) is a global social networking collective of more than 32 million members, known as *deviants*, and 291 million user-produced artifacts, known as *deviations,* uploaded by dA members (dA, 2014). Deviations include digital and non-digital art, such as drawings, paintings, photographs, sculptures, photo-manipulations, fan art and video game designs. The current dA database includes 2,400 descriptive categories to classify and index deviations. (Additional forms of cultural production uploaded to dA include a seemingly innumerable and evolving list of media, genres, and styles including role-playing activities, poetry, fiction, animation, comics, skins, tattoos, graffiti, original characters, wallpaper, stock images, artisan crafts, member resources, tutorials, commentary, posters, graphic design, illustration, industrial design, theater design, web interfaces, architectural designs, and ceramics.) When deviants create and envision deviations that require new descriptors, dA staff add new categories Bazargan, 2011). When deviants upload new deviations, the site obliges them to tag the work with descriptive and searchable categories, some

DOI: 10.4018/978-1-4666-8310-5.ch015

of which are listed above. Tags build an indexed hierarchy which aides semantic search paths within the site for deviants and visitors.

Scholars seeking to build a picture of dA for dA outsiders have likened the platform to a kind of artist's alley (Perkel, 2011), or an exhibition hall at an art or comic convention; a global exhibition space where anyone over 13-years of age can set up a *digital booth* and display work for free (Jones, 2012). Artists establish online digital homepages – similar to booths at a craft or art fair - where they display their work and provide opportunity for personal interaction. As with booths at an artist conventions, online visitors many pass on by (click on to another artist's home page), stop and look at the artist's work (clicking through the artist's work and reading the artist's commentary with each image), or collect the artist's work for their own collection. Visitors may also engage the artist in an online conversation in an asynchronous version of starting a discussion at an artist's booth. Key informants interviewed by Jones found the art convention analogy an accurate and insightful description of the dA site.

Outsiders to dA often misunderstand the platform's name as descriptive of the content posted on the site. For dA CEO and co-founder Angelo Sotira, known as *spyed* (dA) in dA, deviants indicated not aberrant works of art, but a welcoming online collective for cultural producers whose work and identity remained outside the purview and concern of more culturally enfranchised art markets, institutions and practitioners. The merging of "deviant" and "art" in the platform's name lead to confusion among outsiders who have misunderstood the name *deviantART* as descriptive of the kinds of the content posted on dA (Bazargan, 2011). Instead, the title intended a welcoming space for self-identified outsiders - disenfranchised artists and creative producers. Free membership invited artists into a welcoming art world (Becker, 1984; Danto, 1964) where deviating from the norm tapped a communitarian internet culture (Castells, 2001) of artists and creative individuals. Originally envisioned as a music-sharing site in 2000, dA founders drew inspiration from rock iconoclast Frank Zappa's statement: "Without deviation from the norm, progress is not possible" (Bazargan, 2011; Wang, 2011; yokom, 2005). Rather than aberrant content and perverse membership, visitors to dA encounter a lavish display of aesthetic production, art, and visual culture. Visitors encounter deviants representing various levels of achievement and development from 13-year-olds drawing with crayons to professional designers and artists and everything in between.

"Deviating from the norm" culture remains a centerpiece of dA's identity. On site's 14th birthday in August of 2014 *spyed* wrote:

We [dA] are the movement for the liberation of creative expression.

We believe that art is for everyone, and we're creating the cultural context for how it is created, discovered and shared.

Artists love us because we are an inclusive and supportive community. We help them find their identity through self-expression. We provide the tools, resources and exposure to enable them to become better, more successful artists. We inspire people to create art by feeding their creativity. (Sotira, 2014, para 4)

"DeviantART" signals *deviating* - a charge against the social mechanisms that establish (presumably) a belief in a monolithic institutional art world; a world that enfranchise some cultural practices while dismissing others (Wang, 2011). That deviation ethos is coded into the platform's insider diction and jargon. Members are identified as *deviants* (italics for emphasis). Deviants' uploaded cultural products identified as *deviations*. The dA front page recognizes individual deviants for *deviousness, e.g.,* outstanding commitment and service to the dA collective. Staff and volunteers identify Daily *Deviations* to showcase 25 works they deem worthy of daily recognition. Deviant's mailboxes fill with *deviation* stacks - graphically represented as a stack of cards filled with new deviations from the deviant's *deviant* WATCH (dA) list. Each stack prioritized by the latest uploaded deviation from watched deviants. Since it first went live, dA has boasted its *devious* service to the art and skin community on the dA front page.

Devious jargon is not without criticism. Some outsider and deviant artists bemoan the site's name and devotion to deviant diction as a liability. Some complain that "deviant" might evoke misconceptions among potential clients and employers viewing an artist's dA portfolio (Bazargan, 2011). For founder *spyed*, the name remains central to the site's guiding ethos (yokom, 2005). Rather than change the name, *spyed* and dA staff favor promoting public awareness of the site, setting a positive connotation for the term "deviant," and maintaining the communal and alternative art world ethos (Bazargan, 2011; yokom, 2005).

Non-deviants' preconceptions have persisted to pester dA for years. The platform has struggled with representing the differing needs and conflicts between amateur, young teen and professional artists. Its popularity with youth amateur artists established grounds for public critics that negatively influenced outsiders' perception of the site as favoring anime, manga, and child art over professional artists, designers, and other (supposedly) more sophisticated producers of visual culture. Furthermore, a common misperception of dA as a site that permits and, in some cases, promotes "art theft," also negatively impacted outsider perceptions of the site (Jones, 2012; Owens, 2012; Perkel, 2011).

Art theft remains a common criticism of dA and a reason to avoid the site. Deviants have long argued that site administration has not adequately responded to reported forms of art theft. While there is official policy on copyright available, the issue of art theft seems far more nuanced. The dA copyright policy (http://about.deviantart.com/

policy/copyright/) outlines the site's legal responsibilities when the owner of the copyrighted source challenges the display or use of their work. Per the policy, the dA site administrators do not arbitrate or take a position on legal infringement accusations. Rather, they clarify existing copyright law as part of dA policy ("Etiquette Policy," n.d.). The denial of art theft is striking when contrasted to other policies involving speech acts. For example, dA policy prohibits commentary considered to be *inherently disrespectful, aggressive, or otherwise abusive.* Also prohibited is commentary that *potentially* could escalate into an *aggressive or abusive situation.* While policy states artwork must be original it refers to legal and legitimate claims of ownership as requirements for identifying violations. Among deviant's, however, the issue of theft is pressing and the community continues to develop norms and rules. The topic of the nuanced nature of art theft on dA and its implications for new social technologies is presented in the final section of this chapter.

Statistics on dA membership and member engagement are impressive. As of August 7, 2014, dA boasted 291-million deviations uploaded by 32-million registered members (deviantArt.com). According to Internet analytics by Alexa.com, as of August 10, 2014, dA ranked 153rd in web traffic (The next most globally popular site - artmajeur. com - ranked 722 globally). The dA site had a bounce rate (percentage of visitors that enter and leave the site without visiting other pages) of 38%. The dA site averaged 10 page-views per visitor and visitors remained on the site for an average of 5:54 minutes. When compared to the Internet average, both males and females were similarly represented on dA. Visitors with some or no college were over-represented, and visitors with graduate education were under-represented. Eighteen to twenty-four-year-olds are over represented on dA when compared to the overall Internet population. The majority of dA users reside in the United States (28%); followed by India (8.3%), France (3.6%), Germany (3.5%), and the United

Kingdom (3.4%). According to Alexa.com whites are overrepresented and Hispanics are slightly overrepresented.

In contrast to dA and "deviating from the norm," Artmajeur.com, the second most popular site for visual art according to Alexa.com, is a global gallery for artists to market, sell, and promote their artwork and reputation. In contrast to the large amount of digital art on dA, the majority of the work on Artmajeur represents traditional media – paintings and sculptures. Unlike dA where gender representation is roughly equal to the overall Internet population, women are highly overrepresented on Artmajeur. Furthermore, most users access the site from school locations and users with graduate degrees are highly overrepresented. Artmajeur launched the same year as dA, late 2000, and survived the entrepreneurial and investment insecurity of the dot-com bubble of 2001. Artmajeur transitioned from French language to English in 2001 on the front page. However, the site offered users five languages to select from in their individual galleries. The early site resembled the frames and blog roll of images and categories used by dA at the time. The most striking difference between Artmajeur and dA is the ideological orientation of both sites. The dA site favors a "hacker culture" (Castells, 2001) and Artmajeur is oriented to an "entrepreneurial culture." While dA clearly favored the counter cultural force of free music sharing online, Artmajeur sought out artists seeking recognition, promotion, and sales.

Both researchers and entrepreneurs will find dA's historical development also telling. Early manifestations of social media in the form recognizable today included Netscape and AOL in the mid 1990s. At its founding, dA provided:

- Personalized web pages for members – concurrently with Artmajeur.com, one year before Friendster, three years before MySpace, and four years before Facebook.

- Galleries for user submitted photos and artwork – concurrently with Artmajeur.com, four years before Flickr, and five years before YouTube.
- Individual subdomain names for members - seven years before Tumblr.
- Small personal ID icons - six years before Twitter. ("The brief history of social media," n.d.; Wang, 2011).

That is not to suggest that dA's early features were visionary. Many remediated features found on other sites at the time. Two years prior to dA's launch, sixdegrees.com offered a social networking website and AOL was founded in 1985. While AOL offered a closed platform forum for community membership online, Netscape offered a personal start page. By 2000, dA's rows and columns resembled Sixdegrees' and Netscape's. By 2000, Netscape offered chat and web-mail, features that also appeared on dA. Sixdegrees applied the social theory of contact and influence, including appropriating the theory's popular name e.g. *Six Degrees of Separation*, to the development of social media platforms. This allowed users to create a "personal on-line community where you have the ability to interact, communicate and share information and experiences with millions of other members from around the world" ("Internet Archive," n.d.). Strikingly, concurrent with the launch of dA, Artmajeur.com offered a site for professional artists oriented to promotion, marketing, and the sale of artwork. During the 2001 bust of the dot-com bubble, dA and Artmajeur while sixdegrees faltered irrecoverably. Both sites' popularity swelled in 2005. In 2014, Artmajer's popularity decreased while dA's continued to swell. Other differences include Artmajeur's membership that resided primarily in France (59%) followed by Russia (8%) while dA membership resided primarily in the U.S. (40%) followed by India (8%).

The dA platform outfits deviants with an array of features; too many to fully outline here. Many dA features are implicitly social in that the collective behavior of deviants influences visitor interactions and experiences because deviations become visible as they are most often filtered by popularity. As popularity impacts the images displayed on the dA front page, selection of deviations presented on the front page is based on the social behavior of visitors and deviant's search paths. Visitors and deviants can alter the front-page selections using site filters for popularity in weeks, months, or all time. Visitors and deviants may also observe real-time uploads by refreshing the front page after setting the filter to do so. As new images arrive faster than most browsers can refresh, it is possible to watch new images arrive in a matter of seconds. The dA site provides various search tools that can be used in a variety of combinations including click-through on image thumbnails, semantic searches, and spontaneous paths to images from the front page or other deviant's home pages. Semantic searchers depend on the tags supplied by the poster deviant and the titles of the works. On dA, tags build a hierarchical index based on site provided vocabulary, a narrow set of tags, and deviant provided vocabulary, a broad user vocabulary in titles, to build a folksonomy (a collaborative system for annotating content). A closed set of site provided tags can be criticized as creating an unbending and awkward indexing system that limits and perhaps misdirects both the artist and the visitor. The dA administrators counter this concern in at least two ways. First by nesting tags based on media, content, and artist intention and, secondly, by assisting searchers' strategy for finding content by offering filters and searcher provided terms. Nonetheless, finding content depends on the visitor's application of search strategies, the site's provisions for searching and tagging, and the deviant's selection of tags and titling of deviations. Deviants other paths to content involve deviant uses of the site.

Every deviation carries artist-provided tags from 20 categories (Digital Art, Traditional Art, Photography, Artisan Craft, Literature, Film & Animation, Motion Books, Flash, Designs & Interfaces, customization, Cartoons, & Comics, Manga & Anime, Anthro, Fan Art, Resources & Stock Images, Community Projects, Contests, Journals, DeviantART Related, and Scraps) and more than 2,000 sub-categories nested within the 20 main categories. For example, the category of digital art contains 11 sub-categories, each with its own additional sub-categories. Tags equip visitors and deviants with search paths to content following category links provided on the front page. Tags appear listed below each deviation and provide users links to similar images. Thus, users can follow intuitive and seemingly spontaneous search paths following click-troughs by tags and images. It is likely that some deviants misdirect searchers with non-sequitur tags intended to hide their deviations from searches (Lange, 2007). More overtly social features include tools for drawing and painting with peers in real-time, chat rooms, user established groups, threaded comments on home pages, individual deviations, galleries, journal space, a gallery of favourites (dA), visual inbox with daily uploads from watched deviants, and dA Notes, a message systems for deviant-to-deviant private communication. On average, dA users visit ten pages on the site (Alexa.com).

Deviants combine various surprisingly complex strategies for searching that exploit site provisions in untraditional hierarchical categories and provide access to content semantic search tools bypass. To do so, deviants join interests groups established by other deviants, build collections of favored artwork, and watch other deviants of shared affinities or interests. As members of user-created dA groups, deviants receive daily notifications of new posts to that group. Deviants also receive daily notifications of new posts from other deviants they watch. Deviants search and click-through other deviants fav (dA) galleries, which are visible on each deviant's home page (Jones, 2012). Many use the front page as a starting point for serendipitous and intuitive click-through behaviors. All of these behaviors reveal ways that deviants strategize to collaboratively develop alternative uses of the site's features and maximize opportunities to encounter content and deviants they find compelling. These complex and collaborative paths to new content transcend conventional understandings of folksonomy based on tagging and retrieval algorithms. They indicate the evolution of complex user-co-constructed strategies that align with Perkel's identification of a tension between deviants and dA administration. They also indicate social behavior, and the need for sites to design social behavior, that transcend semantic conceptualizing of large databases of user annotated images. Furthermore, it demonstrates that sites like dA, as well as other sites, suffer messy and awkward searches based on user provided sematic tags.

Another limitation of dA search features that inadvertently stimulates alternatives to semantic paths is the site's use of popularity to rank search responses. Nearly all-semantic search paths on dA rank responses by popularity. Popularity restricts searches to an infinitesimal representation of the sites millions of deviations. The development of user behaviors to locate content using alternative strategies suggests deviants finding ways around the limitations of ranking by popularity and that deviants want access to work passed by dA search algorithms. Given that search features privilege an infinitesimal representation of the thousands of daily uploads on dA, users locating alternative approaches to content seem a natural development. It also suggests the sophisticated awareness of both the site's provisions and methods for combining those provisions to access a broader range of responses than traditional algorithm-designed searches provides.

Search reciprocity exists on dA. Deviants desire more than to locate content; they often want their work to be found by others. By joining groups,

faving, and watching, deviants not only subvert semantic search limitations, but also provide a deviant a greater chance of being discovered by others. In such ways, social behavior on platforms of user created content challenge the little fish in a big pound phenomenon.

Unlike social bookmarking sites such as delicious, locating content serendipitously, the deviant's group affiliations selection of watchers and faved work gallery are deeply embedded in the deviants' home page identity. Locating content by click-through impulses often involves visiting the other deviant's home page which provides not only access to their favs, but the visited artists own work, her or his identity markers, country, gender, sometimes age, journal entries, and sometimes their personal likes for music, operating systems, software and hardware, favorite movies and music and so on. In this way serendipitous search behavior is highly social and unpredictable. The dA site also provides additional features that depend on being discovered by others.

Some site features promote commercial opportunities for deviants. The dA site provides members the opportunity to purchase digital reproductions, cards, mugs, t-shirts, and the like, from other deviants. The platform also provides sharing tools that enable users to link deviations to other social media sites. The practice of using sharing tools was highly irksome for some deviants (Perkel, 2011). (Contesting infrastructural changes is a perennial practice among self-appointed deviant-guardians and protectors of the dA ideology and is evident in numerous deviant rants in journals, threaded comments, and cartoons.) Deviants create other commercial opportunities the site did not intend. For example, commissioning other deviants to produce a work of art is a popular practice among deviants.

Self-reported demographics by deviants are often publically available on deviant's home pages. Additional quantitative information gathered by dA are often available from a deviant's personal page, e.g., the number of deviations uploaded, comments, page views, scraps, watchers, forum posts, critiques, and faves. Paying deviants can select to hide some of the more detailed statistics from public view. Nonetheless, the array of potentially public quantitative-data is extensive and included the deviation that was most often viewed and how often it was viewed, which deviation is most faved, how often the deviant uploads, what day the deviant is most likely to upload deviations, and the month a deviant is most active as well as numerous other statistics. Statistics also include the behavior of site visitors including how many faves and comments are received per deviation, how many comments, favourites, deviation views, and page views the deviant has received.

OVERVIEW OF THE RESEARCH

While much research exists on social media and an emerging body of work on image-sharing platforms specifically, there exists a dearth of research specific to dA. With a handful of exceptions, most of the published research comes from an emerging *internet generation of scholars* (Castells, 2001), many of who are or were graduate students at the time of publishing. Studies include, evaluating and designing technologies to "visualize scientifically" (Manovich, n.d.), evaluating dA as a site for college distance learning (Mavrommati & Fotaris, 2012), studies of dA as a casual and unofficial learning environment (Jones, 2012, in press; Herr-Stephenson & Perkel, 2008), and the co-construction of site infrastructure by members (Perkel, 2011). Such sparse and widely dispersed research provides an outline of early research that is presented in the following paragraphs as well as some analogous research that provides insights that both clarify dA and provoke additional questions toward dA.

An obvious entry point here is research on image-sharing sites, those that emphasize photo sharing over social interaction. Related research on social technologies and image-sharing sites such as Flickr do exist. Exploring Flickr, Davies (2007) argued photo-sharing sites reveal the boundaries of public and private. Van House and Davis (2005) analyzed the social life of 60 users of camera phones over a 10-month period. Their study identified the users behavior revealed that participants used phones to capture memories, communicate with others, and for personal self-expression. Most deviations on dA are far more labor-intensive cultural products than the simple click, post, and chat social-image sharing on platforms such as Facebook and Instagram. Comparing dA to such sites is complicated as dA is, by a matter of degrees, not a platform oriented primarily toward social interaction. While fine art photographers populate dA (Leadbeater and Miller identified photography as one of the fastest growing pro-am communities, especially among retirees), it is the centering of youth art on dA that is minimally represented on other image-sharing platforms. Researchers have noted the unique case of dA and oriented research tools to working with meta-data of images.

A team of researchers combined Cultural Analytics and Social Network Theory with the intention of providing technological tools for extracting visual features and information from deviations using computer vision and machine learning. The methods and open-source *toolkit* assembled by the research team are highly technical and designed by computer engineers. Researchers designed or adopted a technological toolkit to analyze and visually represent large samples of images, often batches in the millions.

The toolkit extracted visual features of images such as brightness and contrast, image edges, and hue intensity. Narrowing the large amount of digital information and file size of digital images to discrete and selective image properties enabled analysis of large sets of images. Early difficulties required methods to narrow the sampling to limited groupings. The Salah team[1] reduced the pool of deviant to core deviants, those active and highly socially integrated within the collective and groups within the collective. To manage the unwieldy data, the team identified and eliminated abandoned dA accounts and non-paying members on the pretense that the latter represented less committed deviants. Social network analysis provided further grouping of samples by identifying the most integrated groups of deviants and the most integrated deviants within those groups. The research team also used deviation tags for selecting image samples. Comparative analysis provided opportunity to identify possible contradictions between the tags and the social network groups' in which deviants tagged those images.

Salah's team openly admits that looking for similarities between samples of images may result in inconsistent comparisons dependent on the groups and types of images. For example, comparison between traditional artists and digital artists provided evidence of differences in the use of value (digital artists represented darker use of values than traditional artists). Comparing artist's use of value between digital artists as a group might not provide the similar discrepancies. As deviations include the date of the upload, the research team believes temporal changes in an artist's work are also analyzable using the toolkit. This is an important statement as Almila Salah and Albert Salah (2013) also claim the combination of visual analysis software and other social network theories may provide insights into how innovation propagates in the dA collective and between highly integrated deviants and what makes particular artistic innovations successfully disseminated.

Dan Perkel's 2011 dissertation titled *Making art, creating infrastructure: DeviantART and the production of the web* focused on two broad and interrelated questions; how dA shaped the social identities of deviants as creative practitioners and how deviants who strove to establish recognition as creative practitioners on the site shaped the platform's infrastructure. Drawing on a rich breadth of social theorists, Perkel conceptualizes infrastructure as both the technological features

and social practices by which things become infrastructure. He sought to move beyond conceptions of dA as one of stable technological features toward the less-stable, and more nuanced, world of deviant's practices that highlight ambiguities and tensions related to the platforms mutually constructed infrastructure. He identifies *tensions* in these instabilities, a recurring theme in his dissertation.

To frame the world of creative practitioners, Perkel draws on Becker's (1984) description of art worlds. Becker's art world concept forwards an institutional aesthetic theory. Though he does not fully identify it as such, the institutional theory of art argues enfranchised organizations and institutions establish the conditions by which art is produced, distributed, defined, and received. Art critics, curators, museums, galleries, conservators, and artists are all members in a larger social network that makes art a viable cultural product.

Similar to Becker, Perkel argues that in order to be recognized as an artist and creative practitioner in an art community, the artist must cultivate what the community recognizes as artistic practices. On dA, Perkel argues, becoming an artist requires attracting recognition and popularity in order to profit symbolically and, in some cases, financially. Perkel identifies a paradox as differing and similar art worlds sometimes clash and sometimes coalesce on the platform and artists struggle with maintaining identity and respect as autonomous artists, a conceptual hold over from Romanticism, and the platform's affordances that hinder democratic and participator culture for many deviants.

Perkel follows Becker's conception of two differing kinds of production, craft artisans and Artists with a capital "A." While the high art world highly values artist originality, uniqueness, individual genius, and personal expression, craft artisans value technical virtuosity and technical skill. Perkel located similar tension among deviants regarding learning. This tension was evident in differing deviant's perspective on deviant-produced tutorials. Perkel found a conflict between deviants regarding tutorials and how deviants ontologically oriented themselves to learning from tutorials and critiques. The conflict was evident in deviant's perspectives on learning by critiques (social resources) or by tutorials (material resources). Attitudes toward tutorials evidenced an ambiguity with some deviants perceiving tutorials as part of learning by self-direction and others equating use of any tutorials to constricting the opportunity to discover unique solutions to visual problems by working it out on ones' own.

Perkel's findings "illustrate flaws in conventional accounts of creativity in a world with the web—accounts that fail to recognize the active, contested, and ongoing work underlying the mutual production of creative practice and the web" (p. 1). Perkel also levels soft criticism toward social media and cultural studies theorists such as Jenkins (1992, 2009) for oversimplifying terms including community and participatory culture, and forwarding overly romantic and revolutionary conceptions of social media regarding user empowerment. *spyed* forwarded a similar vision of empowerment and dA.

Jones' (2012) case study of 12 deviants from seven countries is a short interdisciplinary dissertation focused on emerging 21st century literacies among art learners. Jones writes from an art education perspective and sought to identify deviant behaviors related to many deviants' claims that dA offered a unique space to improve as an artist. Jones forwarded to two broad research questions: "(a) What art-related skills, concepts, and dispositions do members acquire on dA? and (b) Which new literacy practices do members use in the acquisition of art-related skills, concepts, knowledge, and dispositions?" (abstract). Jones' findings aligned with many of Perkel's findings relating to art theft, the propagation of user-produced learning resources intended explicitly for the educational benefits of other users, and deviants' self-identified value for self-autonomy over personal improvement and learning.

Jones identified deviants' *practicing* at professional behaviors that are common to freelance artists among youth deviants - taking commissions, setting up complex pricing structures, branding, building an audience, and so on. Participants identified these behaviors as practicing for the real world. Many participants describe the great care taken to present work of the highest quality on dA, and great care in keeping galleries up-to-date. This keeps in mind many deviant's ultimate goal of attracting attention as professional opportunities might depend on the quality of presentation on dA. A seeming conflict between deviant's argument that dA is a place to improve and a platform to attract potentially professional attention suggested professional behavior was also part of learning on dA for some deviants. Jones identified Knobel and Lankshears' (2003) argument that new social media practices reflect an epistemological shift among youth from propositional knowledge - knowing what, to performance knowledge - knowing how to get things done. Jones also identified some deviants that resisted professional aims and insisted they used the site to improve without professional ambitions. Some of the professional practice behaviors embodied Castell's conception of an Internet entrepreneurial culture. Overall, a conflict existed between professional aspirations and the desire to produce art of professional quality exclusively for personal pleasure among the interviewed members. Yet, even among the latter group, professional standards for production and final products was a goal.

Jones examined how deviants search for inspirational and motivational content on dA. This behavior followed a *spontaneous wandering* of using various search features to seemingly randomly search the site for serendipitous discoveries. This wandering fit with the analogy of an exhibition hall at an art convention. Perkel also argued for a similar analogy of dA as an Artist Alley.

Jones identified learning practices used by deviants including learning by observation. This included both learning simply by exposure to different kinds and styles of deviations. Observational strategies included dissecting and emulating other deviants' deviations. Some learned using feedback and critiques, though the latter required some effort to cultivate. Deviants in Jones' study understood feedback as dA provided statistics that indicated the interest of other deviants while critiques indicated specific criticism of individual artwork (see Perkel on feedback and critiques.) Lastly, deviants learned by making what Jones labeled durable learning resources. In a later article, Jones (in press) titles the same as Collective Learning Resources.

Jones' analysis of learning resources compliments Perkel (2011) and Herr-Stephensons and Perkels' (2008) analysis of tutorials and walk-throughs by identifying the learning that producers of these resources acquire in the course of *making* the resources. He identified works in progress, tutorials, and improvement memes as forms of deviant-produced learning resources. Drawing on Becker (1984), he identified learning experiences that producers, not the end user, of collective learning resources experience. Through making learning resources for other deviants, producers learned to externalize an internal dialogue that artist's usually give little attention (Becker, 1984). Learning resource producers become attentive to personal metacognitive thinking regarding the making process. In later work (Jones, 2015), he uses multimodal analysis (Jewitt, 2009) to identify the formal qualities of deviant-produced learning resources and the visual strategies for reflection that are structurally established by the improvement meme template's graphic-structure of rows and columns of empty frames into which users place her or his artwork. Improvement memes demand equalization of images for comparison, which in turn affect how a deviant user of the template self-reflects on her or his art-making process over the years. In addition to improvement memes, Jones also recognizes one deviant's use of video screen capture, and live-stream demonstrations for her audience of interested fans; particularly the

re-presentation of that demonstration through the addition of music, increased frame-rate, and the added compliment of the song lyrics that expand the work's possible meanings. The overall affect shares little similarity with commercially produced artist demonstration videos, but does celebrate the artist's skill and abilities.

In his dissertation, Jones includes a brief section on feminist concepts of *grrrl* power ("grrl" being a replacement for the popularization of the pejorative "girl power" in popular broadcast media) in the work of three deviant artists. Of particular interest is one interviewee's fan art and representation of a homosexual and cross-dressing character from an obscure Japanese video game. Jones argues that rather than exploiting stereotypes, the artist's refashioning of the character transforms the character into a tragic fool, a masquerade of overworked stereotypes of homosexuality and femininity.

Mavrommati and Fotaris (2012) evaluated dA as a distance education platform for teaching a graphic design class at the university level. Assignments were posted, turned in, and peer-to-peer critiqued on dA. Overall, the research indicated the advantage of using dA as a distance platform including access to an overview of the work by peers and peer-to-peer communication. While some students indicated discouragement at a lack of comments, most reported classmate comments as a positive feature, especially in building a sense of peer community. Students did indicate a negative aspect of using dA as a learning platform that related to the lack of attention from the larger dA collective. Overall, Mavrommati and Fotaris concluded that dA offered a positive environment for distance learning.

CURRENT ISSUES IN THE FIELD

Three broad fields of interest emerge in the research; education, web infrastructure, and meta-data analysis of image databases. Both quantitative and qualitative approaches are published in peer-reviewed journals. Overall, the studies portray dA as a complex platform that blends cultural production, creative practitioners, and online social technologies centered on sharing images. Together, these studies present strikingly different theoretical, methodological, and research interests. The dA site appears to be a vastly complex unit of investigation which suggests dA resists generalization both internally (for example photographers and youth fan artists both have some points of contact, photographing fan cosplay or fan artist accessing stock photography for anatomical references, and divergent groups with little overtly social interaction) and externally. The dA bears strong differences to other image-sharing sites and popular social media platforms where individuals favor posting pictures from everyday life.

First, an emerging topic of interest in research on the dA site is education as schools, rather than home or work, as the most likely physical access locations for dA users ("Alexa.com"). Such statistics may not be as counter to popular conceptions of the site as a platform of leisure learning for children as we might think. As 18 to 24-year-olds are overrepresented among dA users, it is possible that dA serves as an image-sharing site for design ideas and inspiration among college art students. The dA site's resources include abundant deviant produced tutorials and other educational resources that provide guidance in the production of images and that deviants exploit the site's database for inspiration (Jones, in press; Perkel, 2011). The dA site's tutorials and educational recourses seem more abundant than on other image-sharing sites. The dA administrators have argued that dA contains more online Adobe tutorials for users than Adobe (the manufacturer of Photoshop, InDesign, and Illustrator) provides (Bazargan, 2011). Deviants have claimed the platform is used to locate inspiration and that deviants insist the dA site is a virtual space where novice artists join to improve in their art production. Taken together, the possibility that dA is merging into

institutional (so-called formal) school settings as a site of educational importance for students into the college classroom seems likely. It is striking that this is one more example of the quickly changing social life of technology forcing education back on its heels. Of course, the possibility that junior faculty with prior experience with dA from its outset may be exploiting the site for images.

Given that increasing inclusion in college classrooms of multimodal forms of communication and presentation, dA may provide a resource for quickly acquiring digital imagery in disciplines not traditionally associated with visual art or communication. If the hypothesis is forwarded here, for college students, dA is a visual culture form of a Wiki. Furthermore, *spyed* (Sotira, 2014), and dA staff (Bazargan, 2011) identify dA as a site for education and deviants identified personal artistic improvement as one of the central benefits of membership. Deviants are producing sophisticated learning resources (Jones, 2015; Perkel, 2011; Perkel & Herr-Stephenson, 2008) as a form of everyday online learning toward personal learning interests. DeviantART staff and management indicate intentions to cultivate and empower dA as an educational site (Bazargan, 2011; Wang, 2011). Perkel and Jones' work suggest user's production of increasingly sophisticated learning resources is an area of burgeoning interest. Jones' work identifies the rise of emergent *new literacies* and *multimodal literacies* among dA users that will likely impact institutional forms of art education.

Furthermore, staff encourages deviants to produce and promote tutorials. Formal, institutional, educational practitioners have sought to co-opt dA as a learning platform (Mavrommati & Fotaris, 2012) and may find user-produced learning resources as an area of interest as instructional tasks for students. Certainly, exploring the use of social media platforms for the creation of educational resources is relevant to teacher preparation.

Second, Perkel's work argues that users shape the infrastructure of dA in both contentious and co-operative behaviors. Jones identified search paths for images as an area of possible interest. Internet users increasingly search for visual as well as semantic content through major search engines. Image search behavior in large databases of images will likely interest web designers and researchers in library science. As many deviants search based on serendipitous explorations of the site for surprise discoveries, research on how users search image databases will likely provide insights into the differences between how individuals search images verses text sources of information. How, for example, do users search for specific image-based information? How do they search through images serendipitously for personal pleasure? What features, and how do deviants use them, to locate image content? How do users manipulate text and image filters to locate desired images? How much tolerance for non-equatorial search results will users endure? How do deviants rely on social features such as other deviant's favorites or threaded links to locate similar content?

Third, the interest lies in social network theory and visual image analysis software (Salah et al., 2012). Salah's search for tools and the application of those tools for researching how image-based content coalesces into patterns out of metadata sets of images suggests images contain evidence of social behavior. Salah's work raises both issues and promise for researching metadata of large and divergent image databases, image metadata. The dA site offers a unique location for explorative, quantitative uses of software analysis. As Salah's work advances, the use of social networking theory to identify surprising insights into how deviants group, who the dA power users are, and what arcs between power might users indicate. How do power users communicate using social features, which social features do they exploit, and how does this influence manifest in user-produced cultural-products? Such work may complement Perkel's identification of user's co-production of the site's infrastructure and what learners actually gain from tutorials and participation in groups. Does, for example, fan artist's work conform in terms of composition, color schemes, light to dark ranges, and so on? Aligning social influence with evidence of image influence would offer an interdisciplinary and mixed-method approach and greatly strengthen claims of influence of power users on the cultural products produced along various arcs. Locating additional ways to further this research seems both promising and daunting. A need for interdisciplinary research that uses such tools to assist in answering authentic research questions seems a pressing need. Solid interdisciplinary research in this direction would greatly assist claims of research value that the toolkit might offer.

GAPS IN EXTANT RESEARCH AND POSSIBLE DIRECTIONS FOR FUTURE RESEARCH

The most obvious deficiency in current dA research is the lack of seasoned researchers. Potentially, the board lack of attention as a research field will change as a growing Internet generation of scholars (Castells, 2001) develops professional trajectories and academic careers. Nonetheless, other social platform sites like Facebook and social image-sharing sites like Flickr and YouTube garnish increasing research attention and an expanding body of published studies. It is also likely that lack of attention from popular media and news organizations sustains dA's underground position in scholarship. The diversity of populations, groupings, media, and forms of interaction on dA frustrate any effort to build a comprehensive research image of the site and its users. Certainly, a researcher's orientation to the site greatly influences how such matters are worked out.

Some research discussed below reveals weaknesses in interdisciplinary approaches due to lack of a depth of knowledge in a given discipline. Some of the research discussed below follows orientations to the site that carry sometimes latent and sometimes-overt economic ideologies. Here are some of these weaknesses in current research.

Much of the work wanders into the disciplines of aesthetics and art theory – both of which are unstable grounds with steep learning curves for any scholar outside these disciplines. The toolkit Salah brings forward bares an aesthetic ideology similar to *Formalism*. Formalism in visual aesthetics holds that formal qualities – visual and sensorial experiences of color scheme, line, composition, value, balance, and so on constitute the most salient qualities of aesthetic objects. Most current scholars and theorist in visual art find formalism profoundly limiting and biased toward the rise of Abstract Expressionism. The visualization toolkit described by Salah removes the bulk of available image properties through converting the image into a single property, e.g., light to dark values, shape edges, areas of contrast, hues, and the like. Salah's claim that emotional qualities can be identified using the toolkit is also formalistic, e.g., emotional reactions to images are fundamentally based on an image's visual properties and that these qualities can be isolated from gestalt experience. While the Salah team's initial trials intended applying the toolkit to dA as a case study test of the toolkit's potential, later articles make stronger and over reaching claims as to the toolkit's potential. While not entirely an unworthy approach for explorative methods, lack of compelling examples and currently relevant research questions from scholars in non-computer engineering fields remains pressing to validating the toolkits potential as an interdisciplinary research instrument. How data mining software fits with research in the humanities, art history, art criticism, and visual culture is unclear. Its value to Internet industries, e.g., fingerprinting copyright infringement, aiding search technologies, and Internet marketing seems most promising to stakeholders interested in such issues.

Becker's art world presents its own difficulties for Perkel and Jones. The difficulty in applying Becker's Institutional Theory of aesthetics is Becker's perception of a singular *Art World*. A perception that did not foresee the disruption the Internet would foist on the enfranchised art world of museums, galleries, art history, and so on. Nor could it foresee the rise of the Internet and the global awareness and participation in everyday cultural-production and dispersal of the same. There exist seemingly innumerable art worlds today and many are not enfranchised by elite art experts. Many art worlds are active, overlap, and conflict on dA and most develop unique peculiarities. Salah too, draws on the myth of a singular art world system and goes so far as to comparing dA to the 19th century Paris Salon des Refuses that exhibited artworks rejected from the highly influential – and politically sanctioned – 1863 Paris Salon (Almilia A. Salah, 2010). While limited parallel between dA and the Salon des Refuses might be conceivable to some scholars, rejected salon artists desired recognition from the politically sanctioned show and to display officially rejected works. The Refuses is far from *spyed's* vision of dA as a "global undercurrent of creativity" that intends to structure a "movement for liberation of creative expression" and "where art starts" (Sotira, 2014). The diversity of art worlds on dA and the mix of everyday cultural-production demands theoretical and research orientations that avoid defaulting to aesthetic theories centered around elitist art enfranchisement that will distort a good research image of dA.

Noting such weaknesses, ways forward are possible. As discussed earlier in this paper, tagging and social search behavior are of interest on dA as deviants seem to exploit alternative paths to content that go beyond site provided semantic search algorithms. These alternatives paths to content seem deeply rooted in deviants' personal identity as presented on home pages and artworks. Such highly collaborative and deeply personal depictions of crowd sourcing and collective and collaborative intelligence are of interest. Such issues beg for attention to the mundane and everyday uses of dA by visitors and deviants alike – the everyday "vernacular" of users (Bugress, 2006). One possible research direction might use Mayfield's (Flew, 2005, p. 32) law of participation to measure levels of social engagement and influence. Exploring the trajectory of deviants from collective intelligence to collaborative intelligence using Mayfield's law of participation - from readers to leaders - on the site seems possible using network theory and software to gather and analyze metadata longitudinally. Another approach might explore flows of information using dA memes. A meme is "an idea, behavior, style, or usage that spreads from person to person within a culture" (meme, 2012). Unlike memes on the Internet, memes on dA are titled "meme" by the deviant author (Jones, in press). On dA memes are pervasive and range from humorous to educational. The role of humor in child art as social acts is also of interest.

Henry Jenkin's (1992, 2009) identification of *participatory culture* has gained widespread attention and aligns with behavior found on dA. Jenkins claimed producers and consumers build new relationships that empower consumers who often produce personal cultural products that extend narratives found in commercially produced and popular narratives (popular culture). Jenkins described characteristics of participatory culture including; low barriers to community engagement, strong systems of support for creating and sharing, some form of informal mentorship for sharing expertise from experts to novices, valuing the contribution of all members, and a strong sense of social connection between members. Furthermore, that such communities fostered the development of new skills such as distributed cognition, collective intelligence, playful problem solving, networking, negotiating, using trans media platforms and others. Jenkin's outline resonates strongly with dA behaviors. Perkel, however, while not rejecting Jenkin's model identified some contradictions and limitations of a participatory culture approach to dA. Gee and Hayes (2011) framed a similar model to Jenkins participatory culture. Gee and Hayes reframed such participatory groups as passionate affinity *spaces*. Identifying "spaces" of interaction rather than as cultural groups seems prom-

ising. On dA some affinity spaces orient around specific popular images and narratives while others center on media, genre, style, techniques, or subjects matter. Leadbeater and Miller (2004) identified pro-amateurs communities in Britain – not specifically associated with Internet or social technologies per se – from astronomers to crafters within which individuals seek personal knowledge and seriousness alongside enfranchised professionals. Leadbeater and Miller identified levels of engagement and seriousness from amateur to pro-amateur; the latter adopting professional practices. Jones identified professional practices among deviants that remediate professional roles between deviants. The development of professional seriousness and ways youth transition from posting child artwork to professional behaviors offers potential for studies of dA.

As noted above and discussed in the next section, copyright and art theft are of interest on dA. Lawrence Lessig (2004, 2008) argued that the free access to code and the physical layers of the Internet promoted conditions for innovative production as individuals and groups built on the ideas of others in an open-source ethos. End to end development established a decentralized network that challenged corporate control – especially large media conglomerates like Disney and Sony. Lessig argued that favoring those that disrupted the power structures would lead to positive economic outcomes – a hybrid economy – and the benefits of *fee culture*. Such disrupters and their innovative instincts are best empowered by freeing culture from past systems of control. Lessig was a central force behind Creative Commons (CC) licensing which empowered the everyday producer of content to proactively provide legal permission for work to be reused, remixed, and reworked without the need to secure permission from the author. dA adopted CC licensing by making it an option for deviants when uploading a new deviation. The need in dA was pressing as some deviants produced stock photos or other content that were specifically produced and posted for re-use by other artists. A less tidy, and perhaps more pessimistic perspective, than Lessig's optimistic free culture is Tiziana Terranova' (2000) critical theory approach and her identification of *free labor* – a complex emergence of voluntary and unwaged labor that is both an "enjoyed and exploited" (p. 33) in late capitalist economies. How these concepts operate – if at all - on dA is not clear and as deviants adopt practices such as marketing, cultivating an audience of watchers, taking commissions and so forth shape dA as a worthy site to explore such concerns and how individuals perceive and seek to leverage naive economic opportunities for personal rewards. Are deviants being exploited and how? The increasing number of deviants linking to personal Etsy sites oriented to selling personal products and crafts beg for further research as well. Furthermore, dA offers a unique microcosm of the disruption of copyright by members and the ways member's police and establishes community norms regarding copyright and art theft.

Studies of dA visitors - non-members - are missing. Numerous individuals visit dA during any day. Nothing is published about visitors as they leave only a gestural footprint of their activities – gestures evident in pageviews and popularity evidenced in search paths. Analytics from Alexa suggest that the majority of visitors to dA visit the site from the physical location of schools rather than home or work. What such activities involves, who is doing it, and what they use dA for are topics of potential interest.

As a site of learning, dA is of interest to education. Deviants identify improvement as a central benefit of dA membership. New Literacy Scholars envision the technology and behavior of users as new literacies. Jones (in press) is one example New Literacy Studies applied to dA. Along these lines, dA is a site of highly informal *not school* learning (Sefton-Green, 2013). Sefton-Green argued that research on learning not occurring in schools, so called informal learning, suffers as little of that research uses established theories of learning relevant to the context. Formal institutionalized learning in schools favor narrow theoretical conceptions of learning. Sefton-Green argued that perspective must broaden if schools are to value the forms of learning occurring out of school on sites like dA and locate *points of correspondence.* Furthermore, that learning in not-school settings like dA is far less influenced by formal organization than inside institutional school settings. Especially on dA, that unlike after school or community arts programs, imposes minimal learning structure beyond the infrastructure of the site. How these differing settings, and all the variations between them, interact in youths' everyday lives – between school and not school, remains unclear and needs research. Much of the work on New Litercies Studies follows along similar interests (Cazden et al., 1996; Coiro, Knobel, Lankshear, & Leu, 2009; Knobel & Lankshear, 2003, 2007; Leu, Kinzer, Coiro, & Cammack, 2004; Leu, O'Bryne, Zawlinski, McVerry, & Everett-Cacopardo, 2009)

One possible interest for researcher is the role of not-school learning and formal learning as youth transition to adulthood (Stefton-Green, 2013). Deviants begin to import practices that natively mimic professional market driven practices in the form of commissions and cultivating an audience as they mature and gain importance in the dA community. The rise of such practices speaks to the developing of identity and autonomy as deviants seek to convert their cultural products and knowledge into capital. So too, as deviants begin to police and protect those productions from the exploitation individual or corporate art theft.

Deviant's insistence on autonomy as learners – a do-it-yourself (diy) dA ethos (see Perkel and Jones) – suggests conflicts with formal art instructions. They suggest that deviant's expect differing outcomes from dA membership than from their art teachers. Jones (in press) argues this difference may lead to deviants to seek art teachers as resources of information related to the deviant's personal learning trajectory and desires rather than as teachers of mandated curriculum that deviants may negotiate as they make sense of school learning in the context of their personal learning desires. How students negotiate such differences begs for future research. While tech savvy educators may leverage differences between not school and school learning as an argument for needed reform or a force of conflict with school learning, students likely negotiate the difference in nuanced ways teachers do not currently understand. Youth may also simply compartmentalize the two worlds. They current attention to 'lifelong learning' and 21st-century 'skills' brings to bare strong questions of the learner identity and power in traditional institutionalized education settings against not school learning contexts.

As a site where deviants remix and disrupt popular narratives through humor and parody dA offers potential for production, dialogue, and critique of visual culture images and narratives. Progressive educators seeking to democratize education and tap the disruptive potential of new technologies regarding class, gender, sexual orientation, and racial inequalities may find sites like dA of interests. So too, cultural theorists looking to identify such issues as represented in youth's own cultural products.

Interested researchers may find two approaches to dA phenomenon useful. Slater and Miller (2000) conducted a landmark study of Internet use in Trinidad. Their work points to the potential and importance of recognizing that the Internet is not a single cyberspace but one of many real-world technologies used by a diverse population of individuals that are immersed in the routines of daily life. As Miller and Slater state of the Internet, it is being used *somewhere* and *someplace*. Perkel's work leans in this direction as he visited deviants in various physical locations. An ethnography immersed in the lives of deviants in the context of their daily life remains a potential research approach. Boellsorff's (2008) landmark ethnography of Second Life contrasts with Miller and Slater. Boellsorff develops a traditional ethnography of the Second Life as a closed site – which he justi-

fies based on his research intentions. Though not an ethnography, Jones' case study approach addressed dA as a self-contained site. His focus was on what deviants *do* on dA. The point made here is that research related to dA, especially from the Miller and Slater orientation is needed.

RECOMMENDATIONS/IMPLICATIONS FOR EDUCATION, CIVIC ENGAGEMENT, SOCIAL PRACTICE ECONOMICS, AND POLICY

This section focuses on two components of discourses that potentially mislead conceptualizing the future and significance of dA: (a) Popular conceptions of creativity and the potential of creative production on the Internet - misconceptions that are historically based in notions of what artists do, who artists are and are largely framed in a discourse that is oriented toward economic competitiveness; and (b) The emphasis dA Inc. places on education and the burgeoning interest in 21st century "skills," "workplace readiness," or "competencies" - especially with an interest in exploiting the power of social media for institutional purposes. Yet, epistemological and ontological conflicts of ideologies and practices between schooling and social technologies exist. Taken together, the two misperceptions from both business and education identify two massively powerful institutional interests and frame how popular discourse may conceptualize dA and deviants. Even critiques of new economic relationships of every-day cultural production such as Leadbeater and Miller argue that garnishing social capital by individuals through their participation in pro-am interest groups is ultimately economically advantageous as individuals convert social capital into financial capital and are better positioned and networked to recover from unemployment and transition to second careers. Flew (2008), drawing on the work of Miller and Slater, has pointed out the focus on western conceptions of the social and online technologies that favor a neo-liberal interest to the exclusion of global uses of social media in the daily lives of individuals world wide. The point made here is that such ideas and research agendas that import economic interests are likely missing what youth do and are doing on dA as well as how these young artists consider the financial potential of their work. At what ages do deviant youth begin to use commercial diction - terms such as "commissions" – and when do they begin to convert social capital gained by recognition from peers to conceptualizing the possible financial returns from cultural productions? Which deviants resist, how, and why? In what ways do the dA's administration and volunteers facilitate the transition from making and posting work for personal pleasure as child expression to building recognition and symbolic forms of actual capital?

Populist discourse in business often conceptualizes artists as the *exemplum virtitus* of creativity practices. Much of the popular discourse surrounding creative practices turns on arguments grounded in economic discourse. This conception of artists betrays an implicit discourse oriented toward the appropriation of *creativity* for business interests. It also provides a caution to researchers in oversimplifying conceptions of creative cultural production. The economic appropriation of creativity in popular discourse is especially evident among business consultants, inspirational speakers, and gurus promising that creativity leads to economic competitiveness during an era witnessing the rise of a "creative class" (Florida, 2002). Florida's conception of a creative class disposes the majority of the world's population to the non-creative classes and creativity as under the ownership of an elite class.)

Other likeminded business leaders include Daniel Pink. Pink (2004) argued that the MFA was the new MBA and that artists were, or should be, the executives that corporations and businesses need to employ to thrive. Pink, following hemispherical or lateralization of the brain (right hemisphere is creative while the left is logical), argued for the economic value of creativity. Furthermore, those right-brained individuals will *rule the world*. Scholars in psychology have dismissed this notion of lateralization of the brain. Furthermore, Pink's conception pulled from larger myths associating artists and mental illness. Such myths date back to the rise of Romanticism when artists were held as a counter-balance to the industrial revolution and industrialization's genesis in the scientific enlightenment (Efland, 1990). Such conceptions are evidenced in the title of Goya's iconic 1799 etching *The Sleep of Reason Produces Monsters*. Kantian romanticism argued that artists carry the gift of being irrational and must be free to defy the rules of scientific thinking –the artist attends to the sublime in nature and her or his emotional experience and dreams. As such artists produced work as if they were a protected class of unique individuals with unique capacities – divine like abilities - to create as if by fiat (out of nothing). The era granted artists permission to live outside societal expectations and norms - especially claiming autonomy over their lives, work, and ideas. This is largely the idea Pink builds on. Another thinker of a similar mindset is Ken Robinson.

Robinson, author of the popular *The Element* (2009) and popular TED talks, betrays the business world's interest in creativity and, more importantly, business' interest in following artists as models of creative producers. Humanities, art history, criticism and philosophy have abandoned notions of artists as the embodiment of creativity, an argument central to both Pink and Robinson. In scholarship in humanities and art education "creativity" has become dated and a pejorative term. Robinson points to the loss of interest in drawing among adolescents as evidence that schools kill creativity. The argument reveals inattention to developmental psychology that identified developmental and social changes among adolescents that explain why many youth stop drawing around the age of 11 (Lowenfeld & Brittain, 1964). Youth abandon drawing at the age when they identify the ability to draw realistically as the ability that distinguishes artists from non-artists. Part of the developmental argument contains a sociocultural component in that most adolescents arrive at the conclusion that they are not artistic and thus abandon drawing at the same ages. Adolescent abandonment of drawing is largely a global and cross-cultural phenomenon. Toku (2001) suggests that in Japan - where more youth continue drawing into adolescence and drawings reveal more complex strategies for representing 3D space on a 2D surface - this tendency is abating to some degree as more and more adolescents continue to draw into their later teen years. Various explanations include the visual nature of Japanese written language based on *kanji,* visual characters, and traditional Japanese strategies for representing space visually as evident in *Ukioye* (floating world) prints. It is possible that engagement with popular culture, rather than schooling, influences youths' every-day drawing behaviors is also at play. Much of teen drawing in Japan is from slavish copying of manga and anime – neither free-expression nor the popular conception of art production as the mark of creativity and creative thinking. Nonetheless, Robinson's insistence that stopping drawing is the evidence of schools killing creativity hinges on the fallacy that drawing *is* creativity. Robinson's populist argument that schools kill creativity is largely a rhetorical vice that some in the business community and politics rally around.

The point stressed here is not a critique of 21st century business practices per se, but that such perceptions is founded on misconceptions of what artists do, how they envision their work, and conventional bracketing of what qualifies as creativity for youth. These notions are easily imported into dA and held by many deviants as well. The point emphasized here is that discourse surrounding creativity and cultural production on the Internet is often framed in neo-liberal and western entrepreneurial perceptions of creativity.

It is possible to nudge the conceptions of dA outside an economic framework. Burgess (2006) identified a *vernacular of creativity* - creativity found in an individual's application of media tools and equipment to everyday ends. For Burgess, everyday creativity serves as a way for an individual to announce their social existence through sharing in a cultural context. In effect, digitally touching is a way for individuals to *becoming real* to others socially through the application of natively acquired understandings of story telling. Individual acquire the skills to use these technologies from consuming media, e.g., video, music and cinema. Burgess is particularly focused on Digital Storytelling. In a similar spirit, Erstad, Gillje, Sefton-Green and Vasbø (2009) argued for the idea of *learning lives* – a narrative basis for learning, identity, and agency grounded in an individual's lifelong learning trajectory. Burgess argues that attending to the *mundane* rather than exemplar is the more useful approach. Rather than attending to the high profile exemplars of deviant success stories – like popular power user deviants or those securing financial success – researching the everyday deviant, the near anonymous deviant, is where democratic empowerment resides (vernacular rather than creative class). Such scholarship would look to dignifying the work of the anonymous deviant – the seemingly mundane user where rich, life biographies reside, should the lens be moved from economic frameworks of highbrow creativity, neo-liberal, and elitist constructs.

Bugress' work also suggests that groups and individuals less self-regulated by adulthood, education, and professional experiences and expectations, offer metaphorically rich content and textual productions for examination. For example, the storytelling of older adults reveals more self-regulatory and measured digital storytelling, selection of images, and presentation than that of younger storytellers. As dA is populated by youth as young as 13 and often prior to consistent formal art education, exploring the intersection between popular and everyday experience offers a site of rich potential. At the intersection slippages between consumption and production, between pro and amateur, and between traditional conceptions of an audience as a destination of media and exist today. Burgess argued conceptions of media based on economic models are insufficient when analyzing the everyday uses of media today. Rather than distribution from source to audience models, a participatory circulation model is required. Hartley (2008) identified shifts in historical ideologies from modern to global versions of the economic "value chain" model (production, distribution and consumer). He points out a shift in meaning from the original definition of producers and consumers to one where there is a creative contribution by the consumer themselves making them a pro-sumer. Interestingly, Harley's value chain model argues that the seeming power of a pro-sumer is an illusion. On dA, what has shifted in contemporary times is not the production to consumption arrangement, but the source of sense making – engagement with popular imagery transfers the responsibility of defining meaning from the producer to the consumer – so much that deviants do not question the right to recreate, remix, redact, and repurpose published sources for their own ends and purposes.

As presented in the beginning of this chapter, art theft and copyright issues on dA present a struggle between the grassroots of members and dA administration. The nuanced conflict carries implications for emerging social technologies that post and distribute user generated cultural productions. According to dA beta-tester and ten-year dA member *lauraneato* (2010), theft varies from malicious dA identity thieves claiming to be another deviant to inexperienced members who simply do not know the rules of the site or the appropriate uses of site features – for example, using ones gallery as a depository for copyrighted or other deviant's activity. Members on other platforms like Flickr, Tumblr, or Photobucket commonly accept such behavior. Between these extremes exists a range of behavior and ambiguities that involve both the accused thief's intentions (naive or malicious) and the way the work is represented on a deviant's page.

Deviant *lauranteto* (2010) identified four general levels of theft. She identifies "Type A" as the Photobucket thief that either did not know how to use the site appropriately or defiantly argue they can use their dA home page as they wish. "Type B" is the "I altered yours so it is now mine" thief. Type B thieves range from those that altered the image in a minimal way such as changing a color to those "bashing" on other's work as a form of trolling (offending others to provoke the community into a dramatically heated often emotionally charged arguments). Luaranteto identifies "Type C" thieves as those who trace, copy, or color the source and claim the altering makes it theirs. These types of thieves range from coloring published and copyrighted manga, copying others work as a form of learning from the original artists, justifying copying by linking and recognizing the source work, claiming they simply forgot to reference the source, or deliberately misrepresenting the altered work as their own inspiration and talent. "Type D" are the "I am the real artist" types that range from claiming the similarity to the source is coincidental, invoking a victim status claiming that the source was actually derivative of the copied work, claiming they are the actual source artists and simply moved to a new id and home page. *Lauraneato's* categories reveal both the characteristics of infringement and the moral and ethical issues latent in the accused thieves' intentions. Individual deviants differ on where to draw the line regarding what qualifies as art theft and many would not classify Type A as acts of theft. Perkel (2011) argued difficulties in identifying art theft among deviants centered on a moral framework for identifying theft held by deviants. The moral framework contrasts strongly with legal frameworks centered on issues of copyright and intellectual property infringement – which protects business rather than individual interests. The contrast is evident in the extent to which deviants guard against theft by posting warnings, setting and posting personal policies, and raising awareness of art theft within the dA collective. In kind, dA administration provided some options for creative commons licensing and watermarking deviations. Such provisions contrast with other platform provisions that seem to enable art thievery. Sharing features allowed users to easily link to others' work to Facebook, Tumblr, Twitter, Pinterest, reddit, Google+, StumbleUpon, and LiveJournal accounts. Many deviants strongly criticized the sharing features as facilitating art theft (Herr- Stephenson & Perkel, 2008; Perkel, 2011). Perkel found some deviants welcomed and benefitted financially from the having their work shared by others across platforms while others disliked the loss of control over images. It seems possible that disquieted deviants viewed the dA as a closed social collective that protected deviations from outside attention and possible misuse. Many of the safeguards established by deviants and the site administration – warnings, clearly marked as Creative Commons icons, and raising the collective's awareness of shared norms and values – are removed when visitors and other deviants reposted deviations on outside media platforms. The conflict between deviants also suggests that some deviants may extend a fragile trust between artists that they do not extend to the larger social media universe of non-artists.

One clear example of the conflict between the site and the users was *Spyed's* (Sotira, 2009) response to criticisms that the site facilitated art theft - he denied that it even existed as a valid concept. *Spyed* insisted art theft "is not a term" and redirected deviants to the legal descriptions of intellectual infringement. Using infringement as the standard, *Spyed* attempted to redefine – and effectively deny – an issue the collective found as highly problematic. *Spyed* dismissed the legitimacy of the criticisms against the site's share features as simple "dArama." He also admitted his denial of art theft and firm position on legal guidelines. Five years later, the site's reputation as a platform for thievery remains a popular criticism of dA despite dA provisions for reporting deviations for bing a "misplaced deviation," "permission issues," or "my work used" (Stock-By-Crystal, 2011) and many non-dA artists state this reason not to join the site or the reason they closed their dA accounts (Bazargan, 2011).

The divide between CEO and deviants is complex. Much of the larger discourse surrounding the ease of copying, reusing, repurposing, and remixing copyrighted content often pitted large media corporations against individuals. Media corporations, not the individual artists, held the copyrights in these cases and media corporations had the legal heft, financial reserve, and risks to profit to litigate against individual's reuse of media – big business versus individual's freedoms and participatory forms of media consumption. In contrast, art theft on dA is clearly different as it pits individuals against individuals and resides in a struggle among deviants to police the norms and values deviants constructed socially amidst rising concerns within the collective. It also stands as a critique of *Spyed's* denial of art theft. The criticism *Spyed* attempt to divert reveals a misunderstanding of what deviants want – help from dA administration in policing and protecting against theft by punishing accused thieves. However, dA administration's refusals to punish or remove deviants until legal courts confirm infringement to protect deviants against spurious accusations of thievery. A generous interpretation of *Spyed's* response would note that protecting freedom of use aligned with the site's original ethos of deviating from the norm and the site's original conception as music-sharing site. A less generous interpretation would note the emphasis on legal argument as a direct denial of member's concerns. The second seems more likely as theft occurs between members and by non-deviant visitors to the site. Many deviants – most with only partial or no college education – likely have little access or finances for legal cases. Some deviants have strongly criticized dA's evolution as increasingly taking on features and aesthetics common to mainstream social media platforms such as Facebook. These conflicts seem to reveal that some deviants view the site as a protected online habitat for artists. It also outlines a possible divide between amateurs and professionals on the site. Deviant amateurs seek a protected space to grow as artists in the safety of an *espre de corpes* of peers while more accomplished deviants seek recognition with a cross platform and global reach.

As dA is a platform for peer-to-peer sharing and distribution it is positioned in a global debate regarding intellectual property in an era of easy reuse, repurposing, and redistribution of content (arguably central to dA as a site of cultural production by individuals). Flew (2008) and Lessig (2004) point to the economic consequences of conservative legislation regarding copyright including what Lessig mocked as the *Mickey Mouse Protection Act* (*Sonny Bono Law* of 1998) which extended Disney's financial monopoly of Mickey's copyright 50 years from the date of the artist's death. Disney's history, according to Lessig, of extending copyright at the historical threshold of Mickey Mouse's impending entry into public domain resulted in 11 legal extensions of copyright since 1928. For Lessig, a free culture established a protected public domain in which creativity thrived as individuals had open opportunity to build on prior innovations and the work of (Flew, 2006; Lessig 2004). The *"Mickey Protection Act"* passed despite protest from economists who argued the law would restrict innovation and, thus, economic prosperity. In essence, the legal protection of public domain dating back to the 18th century was turned on its head and now protected corporate control over individual artist's ownership. As deviants such as *Lauraneto* develop sophisticated structures to classify art theft, a curious set of deviant values emerges that speak to larger issues of what infringement means in the 21st century as well as the need for collaboration to establish rules for conscientious cultural producers that the complexities of legal infringement cannot provide. Deviants are defining the roles not just to identify and punish infringers, but also to provide guidance for new members seeking acceptance within

the dA community and desiring to avoid the art theft label. The point here is that deviants built structures and definitions to protect ownership of cultural products as a response to the limitations of copyright law in the 21st century.

Rather than favoring innovative formal artistic progress or serving a gift economy that benefits exploitation by corporate interest, how the every-day-youth becomes real to other youths through sharing cultural productions online seems a far more promising research orientation. Rather than focusing on power users and influence, innovation may reside at the intersection of remediating the everyday. Some youth may not be interested in enfranchisement or recognition as much as being identified as being real in a digital world. dA might serve as a digital playground where such becoming real to others take place. In this way, dA is a site more broadly important than just to art and design. While business interests exist in the infrastructure of the Internet and social technologies, exploiting free labor for the everyday user remains more nuanced, broadly social, and contains a vast array of products not directly exploitable or directly influencing power users.

Such economic arguments and initiatives have a history in art education. Based on cultural insecurities in the U.S. and Britain at the outset of the Industrial Revolution in the late 1800s to early 1900s, interest in the establishment of schools that focused on design and architecture arose (Efland, 1990). Cultural insecurities were an acute concern in the "new world" which desired to demonstrate cultural legitimacy and address cultural insecurities rising in contrast to the "old world's" rich history of European art and architecture. The sensed cultural insecurity empowered an establishment of "art and design" schools in both the United Kingdom – where fears that France had advanced artisans and designers - and United States. The United Kingdom developed a two-tiered system dividing decorative arts from fine arts. The United States merged decorative and artisan arts with fine arts under a single roof. Some of these schools remain today and are highly respected - among them Pratt Institute and the Rhode Island School of Design.

In 1875, a group of unsatisfied students in the United States broke from the National Academy of Design and established the Art Students League. Students criticized the schools removal of life drawing from curriculum and, interestingly, restricted access to the collection of artworks and books. The league quickly established a policy of *unselfish sharing* of student knowledge between peers (Efland, 1990). Presumably, the communal spirit may have been an indicator of budding artists' resistance to an emphasis on methods oriented to artisan – rather than traditional fine art - training. It also suggests a top-down organization at the National Academy. While conditions are decidedly different with dA, the communal spirit on dA shares sympathy with the Art Student League's policy of unselfish sharing among peers. It also reveals artists' demand for blending autonomy and community in ways that align with some deviants understanding of the site.

The exodus to the Art Students League may indicate artists' struggling to define artistic identity situated against industrialization. It situates amidst contested ideas of what artists do at a very practical level – pedagogy. Entwined in these events is the apparent struggle for fine vs. industrial arts. However, these tremors of discontent may have more to do with autonomy rather than debates of the fine art high road against the industrial low road. Such debates are likely irrelevant to deviants who engage with popular culture and new technologies easily.

The point made here is that potential conflicts of interest exist in and about dA and these conflicts reflect multiple possible ideologies and agendas. Like most things deviant, such agendas are complex and are difficult to classify easily. Economic views of digital technologies may further muddy the waters, but cannot be ignored, when examining dA as an intersection of multiple cultural identities. Some deviants do exhibit professional behaviors.

Others resist them. Most seem caught in between. The dA site is minimally researched that offers multiple opportunities. How what is "professional" and what is "amateur" (see Leadbeater & Miller, 2004) interacts is a pressing curiosity. The dA remains clouded in questions. It does not easily fit other models - historical, technical, or theoretical - without quickly presenting conflicting populations and evidence. It is unique among popular social media sites as it favors – at least in appearance and publically stated visions – communal more than capitalistic ideology that, ironically, remains an entrepreneurial success story. It contains both communitarian independence and social integration. Deviants claim a high value for autonomy over learning, but appear to welcome strong restrictions on the way and kinds of cultural products they produce. As a pedagogical site, dA remains open to deeper inquiry and its impact on how individuals gain knowledge and skills outside formal settings is under early conceptions that ought to forge more nuanced analysis. The dA site cautions against business ideology in discourse when framing the site while still presenting remediation of professional practice and language. Researchers will likely encounter dA as a quantum site of hide and seek, this population, but not that population, this medium, but not that medium.

So too, conceptualizing dA from an educational perspective offers other difficulties and contradictions. Framing deviants as collaborative learners and peer-to-peer learners without careful and critical examination of the ontological and epistemological differences between formal schooling and the everyday learning outside of schools is suspect. When researching learning in *not-in-school* settings researchers risk defaulting to models of learning biased toward the kinds of learning occurring in school settings (Sefton-Green, 2013). The same may be true of professional and amateur practices on dA. Leadbeater & Miller's (2004) description of the complex relationship and sometimes partnership between amateur and professional astronomers serves as one example. Photography might offer another, more specific example. So too the presence of professional marketing and business practices among many deviants – taking commissions, nurturing a fan base, cultivating and attracting new watchers- is another. Relationships mediated between professional artists – freelance or employed – working in gaming, graphic novels, and design occurring on dA seem a worthy unit of exploration. Conceptualizing dA as an exploitable educational space and resource seem valuable topics of inquiry given schools are the most likely access point. Despite this, many dA pages established for and by students from educational institutions such as the Rhode Island School of Design and the School of the Art Institute of Chicago lack watchers, members, and are largely abandoned spaces and groups. The educational issues related to dA also bring the pro-am lifestyle, e.g., leisure learning, second careers, and exploring possible careers to the forefront of policy questions for education (Leadbeater & Miller, 2004).

It is also valuable to consider the disturbances that new technologies place on "not school" (Stefon-Green, 2013) learning settings such as afterschool or community organized learning. These too are organized learning settings that enjoy some measure of freedom that formalized curriculum from government (public) schools are mandated by law to provide. "Not school"-learning in organized settings also carries its own ideologies and can suffer the same blindness to the social aspects of the everyday learning of youth. Some youth have more home and peer access to the social technologies and the literacies that accompany learning outside schools while others in economically disenfranchised settings do not. Those with home experiences, access to technologies such as digital scanners, digital drawing tables, quality digital cameras, and the software and apps to fully utilize the potential of these technologies – all of which are required for participation on dA – clearly have profound advantages in the era of social media. So too, the

skills required of such technologies to connect, participate, influence, share, co-labor, and discuss personal cultural productions in ways that expand social capital advantage youth engaged with passionate affinity spaces (Gee & Hayes, 2011) and participatory culture (Jenkins, 2009). Such constitute new literacies (Knobel & Lankshear, 2003) that require instruction. "Not school"-settings for organized learning also face questions of how to proceed in this new era. Perhaps more so than formal curriculum and instruction in government schools, not school settings, might face more need to integrate new literacies – especially access to technologies, collective spaces, and expertise to guide youth in entering participatory environments such as dA. Furthermore, alternative private and charter schools may develop a greater interest in social technologies and participatory culture online than government schools. Alternative schools may have more quick-footed responses and novel teaching ideologies that more easily fit new social technologies than government-regulated schools under conservative and modernist models of instruction.

Scholars on dA face a pressing need to explicate how youth at all levels of education from K to graduate and diverse settings from government, alternative charter, private, home and the unschooling movement and dA seems an interesting case. The dA in particular, with deviant's insistence that the site is a place to improve, get inspired, honor and police learning autonomy, and deviant-made learning resources seems a site of interest. Such interest can extend beyond learning in the visual arts. This includes college and university uses of dA. Research on faculty uses of social technologies by Moran, Seaman, and Tinti-Kane (2011) are a starting point. There is a need for research on how dA fits into students' larger social media practices in both academic and personal uses. To what extent are students posting products assigned in class? To what extent are they exploiting content to meet assignment requirements? To what extent are professors including or exploiting dA or other social media platforms for classroom use? To what extent might faculty be using dA as a resource behind the purview of students and vice versa – how are students using dA for classwork outside the purview of their instructors? How are students crowd sourcing to solve visual problems related to classwork? In school, such situations provide institutional conflicts for teachers, administrators and policy.

The paths forward for education and social technologies are of interest. Notions of "not school" and formal education are in conflict – will schools retreat to traditional test, teach, reteach, and factory notions of "standardized" products (students) or move to more progressive and truly child-centered education? How will information flows related to knowledge and skill development outside traditional institutional publishers deal with the vast array of interest-driven learning – the learning lives and digital-learning biographies of youth today. Such concerns reside in the larger reality that sites like dA illuminate.

Arguably, dA permits only a tapestry of empirical, qualitative, interpretive, and theoretical conceptualizations that must be viewed together. Hopefully, this chapter serves as a call to add threads to that tapestry of research in the spirit of deviousness and the strange phenomenon that is deviantART.com. In addition, hopefully it forwards some context for policy changes in education and understanding of what learning lives and lifelong learning look like today. Perhaps dA challenges artist Dubuffet's criticism of a narrow conception of art. Dubufett wrote, "What culture lacks is a taste for the anonymous, innumerable germinations" that lie just outside the light of what officially passes for enfranchised "art." The dA seems to welcome the innumerable and practically anonymous. At risk of too heavily revealing the author's views, dA offers a site where cultural production celebrates the everyday individual as they make life meaningful for themselves. It also contains contradictions in the light of capitalistic

takeovers of sites such as dA – YouTube is a solid example of what might be ahead for dA. dA - its history among other sites, its image sharing infrastructure, educational desires of deviants, its flow of knowledge within the community, its co-constructed infrastructure, complex relationship to art theft and copyright over cultural production in a free-labor economy, its diverse generational divide between young teens and young adults, its array of users from pros to amateurs, its self-policing of collective norms that build a sense of community, and the interest divides from building financial to social capital among its members – provides a unique site of everyday cultural production.

REFERENCES

Bazargan, K. (2011, June 13). *DeviantArt: Creating community around creativity* [Audio podcast]. Retrieved from https://itunes.apple.com/us/podcast/lgm-2011-audio/id450991073?mt=2

Becker, H. S. (1984). *Art worlds*. Oakland, CA: University of California Press.

Boellstorff, T. (2008). *Coming of age in Second Life: An anthropologist explores the virtually human*. Woodstock, NJ: Princeton University Press.

Burgess, J. (2006). Hearing ordinary voices: Cultural studies, vernacular creativity and digital storytelling. *Continuum (Perth)*, *20*(2), 201–214. doi:10.1080/10304310600641737

Castells, M. (2001). *The Internet galaxy: Reflections on the Internet, business, and society*. New York, NY: Oxford University Press, Inc. doi:10.1007/978-3-322-89613-1

Coiro, J., Knobel, M., Lankshear, C., & Leu, D. (2009). *Handbook of research on new literacies*. New York, NY: Routledge.

Danto, A. (1964). The artworld. *The Journal of Philosophy*, *61*(19), 571–584. doi:10.2307/2022937

Davies, J. (2007). Display, identity and the everyday: Self-presentation through online image sharing. *Studies in the Cultural Politics of Education, 28*(4), 549–564. doi:10.1080/01596300701625305

Efland, A. (1990). *A history of art education: Intellectual and social currents in teaching the visual arts.* New York, NY: Teachers College Press.

Erstad, O., Gilje, Ø., Sefton-Green, J., & Vasbø, K. (2009). Exploring 'learning lives': Community, identity, literacy and meaning. *Literacy, 43*(2), 100–106. doi:10.1111/j.1741-4369.2009.00518.x

Etiquette Policy. (n.d.). Retrieved from http://about.deviantart.com/policy/etiquette/

Flew, T. (2005). *New media: An introduction.* Oxford University Press.

Florida, R. L. (2002). *The rise of the creative class and how it's transforming work, leisure, community and everyday life.* New York, NY: Basic books.

Gee, J. P., & Hayes, E. R. (2011). *Language and learning in the digital age.* New York, NY: Routledge.

Hartley, J. (2008). *Television truths: Forms of knowledge in popular culture.* Middlesex, MA: Blackwell Publishing. doi:10.1002/9780470694183

Herr-Stephenson, B., & Perkel, D. (2008). *Peer pedagogy in an interest-driven community: The practices and problems of online tutorials.* Paper presented at the Medai@Ise Fifth Anniversary Conference. Retrieved from http://eprints.lse.ac.uk/21576/1/perkel-herrstephenson-peerpedagogy%28LSEROversion%29.pdf

Internet Archive. (n.d.). Retrieved from http://archive.org

Jenkins, H. (1992). *Textual poachers: Television fans & participatory culture.* New York, NY: Routledge.

Jenkins, H. (2009). *Confronting the challenges of participatory culture: Media education for the 21st century.* Cambridge, MA: The MIT Press.

Jewitt, C. (Ed.). (2009). *The Routledge handbook of multimodal analysis.* New York, NY: Routledge.

Jones, B. (2012). *Spontaneous wanderers in the digital metropolis: A case study of the new literacy practices of youth artists learning on a social media platform* (Dissertation). Arizona State University, Tempe, AZ. Retrieved from ASU Digital Repository.

Jones, B. (in press). Collective learning resources: Connecting social-learning practices in deviantART to art education. *Studies in Art Education.*

Knobel, M., & Lankshear, C. (2003). *New literacies: Changing knowledge and classroom learning.* Philadelphia, PA: Open University Press.

Knobel, M., & Lankshear, C. (2007). Online memes, affinities and culture production. In M. Knobel & C. Lankshear (Eds.), *A New Literacies Sampler* (Vol. 29, pp. 199–227). New York, NY: Peter Lang.

Lauraneato. (2010, December 16). *The different categories of art theft* [deviantART journal]. Retrieved from http://www.deviantart.com/browse/all/#/journal/The-Different-Categories-of-Art-Theft-214241001?hf=1

Leadbeater, C., & Miller, P. (2004). *The pro-am revolution: How enthusiasts are changing our economy and society.* London, UK: Demos.

Lessig, L. (2004). *Free culture: How big media uses technology and the law to lock down culture and control creativity.* New York, NY: Penguin.

Lessig, L. (2008). *Remix: Making art and commerce thrive in the hybrid economy.* New York, NY: Penguin. doi:10.5040/9781849662505

Leu, D., Kinzer, C., Coiro, J., & Cammack, D. (2004). Toward a theory of new literacies emerging from the Internet and other information and communication technologies. *Theoretical Models and Processes of Reading, 5*(1), 1570–1613.

Leu, D., J., O'Bryne, I., Zawilinski, L., McVerry, G., & Everett-Cacopardo, H. (2009). Expanding the new literacies conversation. *Educational Researcher, 38*(4), .264-269.

Lowenfeld, V., & Brittain, W. (1964). *Creative and Mental Growth*. New York, NY: Macmillan.

Manovich, L. (n.d.). *Visualization methods for media studies*. Retrieved July 22, 2014, from https://www.academia.edu/2800483/Visualization_Methods_for_Media_Studies

Mavrommati, I., & Fotaris, P. (2012). Teaching design from a distance: The deviantArt case of Virtual Design Studio. *IEEE Learning Technology Newsletter, 14*(2), 24–25.

meme. (2012). In *Merriam-Webster.com*. Retrieved from http://www.merriam-webster.com/dictionary/meme

Moran, M., Seaman, J., & Tinti-Kane, H. (2011). *Teaching, learning, and sharing: How today's higher education faculty use social media*. Boston, MA: Pearson Learning Solutions.

Owens, T. (2012, September 17). *Sharing, theft, and creativity: deviantART's share wars and how an online arts community thinks about their work*. Retrieved from http://blogs.loc.gov/digitalpreservation/2012/09/sharing-theft-and-creativity-deviantarts-share-wars-and-how-an-online-arts-community-thinks-about-their-work/

Perkel, D. (2011). *Making art, creating infrastructure: deviantART and the production of the Web* (Dissertation). University of California, Berkeley. Retrieved from eScholarship UC. (6fg9f99202)

Pink, D. (2004). The MFA is the new MBA. *Harvard Business Review, 82*(2), 21–22.

Robinson, K. (2009). *The element: How finding your passion changes everything*. New York, NY: Penguin.

Salah, A. (2010, July 5). *The online potential of art creation and dissemination: deviantART as the next art venue*. Presented at the Electronic Visualization and the arts. Retrieved from http://www.bcs.org/upload/pdf/ewic_ev10_s1paper3.pdf

Salah, A. (2013). Flow of innovation in deviantArt: Following artists on an online social network site. *Mind & Society, 12*(1), 137–149. doi:10.1007/s11299-013-0113-9

Salah, A., Salah, A. A., Buter, B., Dijkshoorn, N., Modolo, D., Nguyen, Q., & van de Poel, B. et al. (2012). DeviantArt in spotlight: A network of artists. *Leonardo, 45*(5), 486–487. doi:10.1162/LEON_a_00454

Slater, D., & Miller, D. (2000). *The Internet: An ethnographic approach*. Oxford, NY: Berg.

Sotira, A. (2009, August 11). *Update: Quick post on art theft and share tools* [deviantART journal]. Retrieved from http://hq.deviantart.com/journal/Update-Quick-Post-on-Art-Theft-and-Share-Tools-230838615

Sotira, A. (2014, August 8). *The deviantART community turns 14* [deviantART journal]. Retrieved from http://spyed.deviantart.com/journal/The-DeviantArt-Community-Turns-14-473124195

Stock-By-Crystal. (2011, March 12). *How to report art theft on dA* [deviantART post]. Retrieved from http://stock-by-crystal.deviantart.com/art/How-to-report-art-theft-on-dA-200713154

Terranova, T. (2000). Free labor: Producing culture for the digital economy. *Social Text, 18*(2), 33–58. doi:10.1215/01642472-18-2_63-33

Van House, N. A., & Davis, M. (2005). The social life of cameraphone images. In *Proceedings of the Pervasive Image Capture and Sharing: New Social Practices and Implications for Technology Workshop (PICS 2005) at the Seventh International Conference on Ubiquitous Computing (UbiComp 2005)*. Retrieved from http://web.mit.edu

Wang, J. (2011). *Innovator: DeviantART's Angelo Sotira* [Electronic magazine]. Retrieved June 26, 2014, from http://www.entrepreneur.com/article/217859

yokom. (2005, January 16). *Angelo Sotira, interviewed* [deviantART blog post]. Retrieved from http://yokom.deviantart.com/art/Angelo-Sotira-Interviewed-14204533

KEY TERMS AND DEFINITIONS

Deviant: deviantART member (paying or free).

deviantART: Image sharing and social networking platform for artists.

Deviation: Uploaded artwork or artifact produced and posted by a deviantART member.

Exemplum Virtitus: A moral or virtuous exemplar to be emulated.

Learning Lives: Identified by Erstad, Gillje, Sefton-Green and Vasbø (2009) as the narrative basis for learning, identity, and agency in the context of a learner's personal life narrative.

Online Collectives: An online grouping centered on common goals. Used here as an alternative to what is often referred to as online *communities*. Communities indicate social qualities and individual sense of community that may or may not be present in larger collectives.

Vernacular Creativity: Identified by Burgess (2006) as the everyday (mundane) creativity of individuals as use social technologies.

ENDNOTE

[1] I use "Salah team" to represent the various scholars associated with this work. Different articles from the "team" attribute authorship to various researchers. I use "Salah team" as shorthand as the published articles appear to reference the same work though different scholars are associated with different articles. The most recent articles are by Salah and Salah.

Chapter 16
Children and Youth Making Digital Media for the Social Good

Jill Denner
Education, Training, Research, USA

Jacob Martinez
Digital NEST, USA

ABSTRACT

This chapter describes how children and youth are using digital media to address inequity in their schools, communities, and in society. The chapter begins with a review of the historical and cultural roots of children making digital media for the social good, and situates the approach in the context of other civic and community-based movements. The next section focuses on the range of ways that children and youth are making digital media, including who is participating, and the social and institutional factors involved. The next sections describe the benefits for the participants and for society, as well as the barriers to broader participation. Two case studies highlight key strategies for engaging marginalized youth in making digital media for the social good, and ways to expand the popularity of this approach. The chapter concludes with suggestions for future research, and the broader implications for education, civic engagement, social practice and policy.

INTRODUCTION

This chapter builds on a long history of youth-led movements to address issues of social justice in their schools, communities, and beyond. Efforts to reframe youth in terms of their agency and impact have had a profound effect on how they are viewed and on what researchers study (Ginwright, Noguera, & Cammarota, 2006; Giroux,

2003; Tuck & Wang, 2013). This view of youth has become increasingly relevant as we witness a growing access to opportunities to create content with and for large and diverse audiences, which has exploded with the digital media outlets now available through mobile devices. Although these two movements--social justice and digital media--have some obvious points of intersection, they are rarely talked about together.

DOI: 10.4018/978-1-4666-8310-5.ch016

In this chapter, we focus on the implications of children and youth making, not just using digital media. Our approach extends a long history of media studies that shows the way that media production is not neutral. For example, Morrell (2002) describes how the critical teaching of popular culture makes it a site for resisting injustice, an approach that is now captured in the DIY (do-it-yourself) movement in digital media and technology. Lankshear and Knobel (2008) describe DIY as a movement where novices reclaim the authority previously held by trained experts, as they express themselves through mechanisms that include podcasting, photography, music videos, and animation. In school settings the DIY movement has explored ways to use activities that include blogs, videos, and game making to engage youth and promote new literacies (Guzzetti, Elliott, & Welsch, 2010). Outside of school, DIY media creation often provides an outlet for creativity and self-expression through animated stories and e-textiles (Kafai & Peppler, 2011; Kafai & Peppler, 2014). To a great extent, the DIY movement has focused on artifacts produced by "everyday people to meet their own goals and personal satisfaction" (Lankshear & Knobel, 2008, p. 10). However, the excitement about DIY digital media is also about its potentially transformative role.

When youth create, not just use digital media, they are engaging in what others have called authentic learning experiences, which can have a transformative role for both the learner and the society that they aim to impact. Creating new media can take the form of questioning mainstream media using animated storytelling (Kafai, Fields, & Burke, 2010) and creating disruptive technologies such as encryption software for text messages (Milberry, 2014). For some, DIY digital media involves taking action without the gaze of those in power (Ratto & Boler, 2014), while others rely on adult guidance and access to resources. In a seminal article, Blikstein (2008) built on the work of Paulo Freire and Seymour Papert to explore the ways that digital media can be used for emancipation, particularly among youth from less privileged communities. He describes how social transformation happens when youth go beyond using technologies to designing personally meaningful devices, using the example of youth in Brazil who created a newspaper and a video documentary to raise awareness about issues of social justice in their community that they believed were important to address.

In this chapter, we shine the spotlight on the transformative power of digital media for addressing issues of social inequity, particularly when put in the hands of young people. While the use of digital media for the social good is thriving in adult populations, the review that follows shows that it is also growing among children and youth, who have increasing access to mobile and child-friendly technologies. In particular, there is a growing interest in the ways in which youth are making digital media for the social good. For the purpose of this chapter, *making* includes youth using digital tools for a range of activities, such as to write stories, make games, create online communities, build apps, create blogs, contribute to crowdsourcing sites, and produce images. Our focus is on pre-college students, so in most cases, the young people are not doing these activities themselves—they are working with peers, teachers, and adults. Thus, we include within the DIY acronym activities that involve making digital media in collaboration with other people. This chapter will both summarize research and provide general and specific examples of how children and youth are working together to make digital media for the social good, how this connects to and departs from a history of social justice movements, and the social conditions that foster engagement.

The following questions will be addressed:

- What are the historical and cultural roots of children and youth making digital media for the social good?

- How are children and youth making digital media and how is it connected to the social good?
- What are the benefits and barriers to digital media production by children and youth?

The chapter includes a definition of what we mean by the "social good." Research on children and youth using digital media for social good is fairly new, and mostly descriptive. Where possible, we highlight variation in age, gender, culture, and socioeconomic status. In addition, we will discuss how to expand the popularity of making digital media in ways that benefit society, and include two case studies that describe efforts to increase access for marginalized youth to create transformative media. The next section describes the additional research that is needed to advance this field. The chapter concludes with recommendations for educators, researchers, and policy makers on how to increase the frequency and diversity of young people making digital media for the social good.

OVERVIEW OF THE RESEARCH

Historical and Cultural Roots

The material presented in this chapter builds on a long history that includes both academic theories and community-driven efforts to create social change. Academic researchers have developed and elaborated on resistance theory as a way to describe how young peoples' actions are often a logical reaction to oppression and inequity. This view, which was given wide attention after the publication of key articles by Willis (1977) and Fine (1991), focuses on youth agency in response to structural inequalities. The significance of this work is that it raised the possibility that youth actions, such as dropping out of school, getting pregnant, or taking low-paying jobs, should not be interpreted simply as an act of self-destruction or a sign of limited cognitive development. An

alternative view is that youth were often carefully analyzing their situations and choosing to forge an educational or career path that was based on their values, or their sense of self. In other words, many of these youth were taking action in an effort to reclaim a sense of power and identity, however, given their limited tools, the result often had negative consequences for themselves or those around them.

Fine (2014) has written extensively about the contradictions inherent in resistance, which can result simultaneously in disrupting and becoming part of cycles of inequity. To increase the likelihood that resistance can have positive, transformational results, many have argued for the use of a critical pedagogy, which starts from the lived experiences of marginalized youth and engages them in a critical dialogue (Freire, 1970). The emphasis is on voices that are usually not heard, such as poor and urban youth, and on helping them take action using a medium that is familiar to them (e.g., music or film), in order to resist injustice (Morrell, 2002). Much of this work builds on the writings of Giroux (2003), who long ago argued for the need to engage youth in a dialogue to inform social change and help them recognize what he called the oppression of the mainstream media on today's youth. He argued that youth resistance can be harnessed to address the abuses of power to transform society for all, rather than result in greater marginalization. These works emphasize that by raising critical consciousness and creating spaces of opportunity, youth will be motivated and empowered to play an important role in community action for social change.

Community is at the heart of many social justice movements that look to address issues of inequality or injustice. Successful social change efforts are driven by a collective that is fueled by each individual's awareness of the historical and cultural roots of inequities (Mercado & Reyes, 2010). In contrast to popular descriptions of the individual hero or heroine that makes social change, most efforts take place within a broader social network or context. For example, activism, particularly by youth in poor and urban communities with economic and systematic disparities, comes from collective reflection, action, and healing that takes place when individuals come together to discuss inequalities or violations of social justice (Ginwright, 2010). This coming together shows individuals that they are not alone, and promotes critical reflection about a current situation, and often reveals the roots of social inequality (Ginwight & Cammarota, 2002). It also results in a centralization of skills and knowledge to collectively impact the inequality. These views of youth agency, resistance, and community provide an important context for interpreting more recent examples of youth-driven activities, which are increasingly more likely to incorporate technology. As we show in the rest of this chapter, digital media has not replaced social movements; in many cases it is being used to strengthen these movements.

What Is the "Social Good?"

The focus in this chapter on the social good is part of a growing recognition of the ways in which youth are leading social change, as well as a renewed call for more youth to participate in civic affairs and the political process. It goes beyond examples of youth participation to explore how youth are taking action to address inequity. In an earlier article, we identified a continuum of involvement by youth in social change efforts (Denner & Bean, 2010). On one end of the continuum is *community service*, where youth help others in their community but there is no explicit connection to political systems or social change. A little further along the continuum is *service learning*, where involvement in the community has clearly identified learning objectives and opportunities for reflection that could include political analysis, but the goal is not to promote critical thinking about the roots of social inequality. What these approaches have in common is that they both focus on changing

the youth and meeting immediate service needs, rather than on making lasting change in systems or structures. On the other hand, *civic engagement* involves the active participation of youth with others to improve their schools and communities. And *civic activism* typically involves building a critical consciousness, and focuses on social change efforts that are a direct response to an inequity at the local, regional, or global level. Civic activism is also sometimes an effort to address an immediate social injustice or problem and may or may not involve a long-term engagement or critical evaluation of the roots of the injustice (Wheeler, 2003).

In this chapter, we focus on actions that address broader issues, whether they are political, structural, or social. Following the continuum described above, we will include examples of youth involvement that range from civic engagement to civic activism. Although recent research has found that few are civically engaged (Livingstone, 2010; Malin et al., 2014), a wide range of youth-led efforts to make social change have been documented (Cammarota & Fine, 2008; Denner & Bean, 2010; Ginwright & Cammarota, 2007; Sherrod, Torney-Purta, & Flanagan, 2010). Building on this work, Ginwright and Cammarota (2002) created a model that can be used to describe three different stages of action. In their youth development social justice model, youth move from self-awareness to social awareness, and finally global awareness as they develop agency and the skills to negotiate, protest, and challenge institutionalized forms of social inequity. Thus, social change typically begins with awareness, identity exploration, and a critique of existing structures, before it moves to action.

The availability of new media has led to new forms of civic engagement that manifest in online communities and networks (Papaioannou, 2013). Because self-awareness is a critical part of the social change process, this chapter will include examples of digital media creation that may not directly change systems of power and privilege, but are a first step in that process. Weis and Fine (1993) have clearly shown how self expression, particularly by people whose voices are typically silent, is one strategy for initiating both individual and social change. Thus, our definition of the "social good" includes efforts that have the potential to disrupt structural forces of oppression ranging from the local to the global, regardless of whether there is research that shows their impact on society. In addition, building on Fine (2014), we consider an action to be connected to the social good, even if it is not clear that it is driven by the intention to make social change.

What Does DIY Digital Media Look Like for Children and Youth?

Digital media has given youth a global platform to reveal and take action in response to injustice, and this is particularly important for youth with no other political outlet, and those who feel excluded from politics (Buckingham, 2000). One of the most exciting parts of increased accessibility to digital media is that children and youth are using technology in new and unexpected ways, including as a way to make content or products that disrupt or challenge the adult-driven world of digital media, as well as products that help address injustice and a lack of resources or opportunities in their communities.

In this section, we describe how children and youth are making digital media, in ways that range from self-expression to activism. Despite the growth in content creation, it is still being done by a relatively small subset of children and youth. A recent survey of youth in the US found that 1 in 6 are involved in "active expression, such as organizing an online group or discussion, starting a website, or creating original media to share online" (Cohen & Kahne, 2012). That study found that 11% had started a political group in a social media site, 6% wrote an article or sent a video about a political topic to an online news site, 7% wrote an email or blog about a political

issue, and 7% expressed their political views in an event like a poetry slam or music event (Cohen & Kahne, 2012). A study in the UK had similar findings. Livingstone (2010) did focus groups and surveyed a large number of 9-19 year olds in the UK and found that very few are interested in civic or political issues. Among those that go online at least once a week, half have visited a website about something like a charity, human rights issue, or the environment, but the outcome was usually just to get information. Only 35% did something as a result of visiting the site, and only 23% created content (sent an email or joined a chat discussion). There is limited data on who are producing media content, but a recent study of Canadian youth showed that although almost all the participants could access the internet outside of school, their activities varied, it was the older and more affluent youth who were more likely to be creating content (Steeves, 2012).

There are a variety of ways in which children and youth are making digital media that have implications for the social good. One popular approach is for youth to engage in participatory action research to collect information that they then use to create change (Whyte, 1991). In one example, young women worked as a collective to do research about gentrification in their neighborhood, and used that data to create websites that "speak back" to different audiences that play a role in these developments (Cahill, Rios-Moore, & Threatts, 2008). Another example is of high school students who conducted research on the inequities at their school that limit access and opportunity, and then created digital media projects (e.g., a documentary) to share the results of their research (Romero et al., 2008). When the students presented their projects to key decision makers, it led to structural changes that improved the safety of their school, as well as the learning environment (Romero et al., 2008). And in a third example, middle school students used surveys and interviews to collect information that informed the creation of news media broadcasts that were designed to challenge unfair decisions at their school (e.g., school dress code, recess time) (Jenson, Dayha, & Fisher, 2014a). These examples show how participatory action research can fuel youth-driven digital media production, but the activities are typically initiated by and carefully monitored by adults.

Activities that involve making zines, videos, or blog posts are more likely to be initiated by young people, with less oversight or control by persons in power. Thus, these forms of digital media are often used by youth who want to interrogate dominant discourses that are perceived to limit their access or opportunity. For example, Guzzetti and Gamboa (2004) describe how girls create and distribute zines on the internet (and on paper) to raise awareness and incite others to act on issues that are important to them, but are typically ignored by the mainstream media. Similarly, Edell, Brown, & Tolman (2013) describe how teens and young women challenge media representations of girls' bodies by creating blog posts, online petitions, and presentations that are distributed online. And Banet-Weiser (2011) describes how girls create and post videos online and claims this is a way of "mocking celebrity as well as beauty culture" and "allows girls to both perform gendered identity and to point out its contradictions" (p. 8). Because the videos are not polished by adults, they capture the complexity of the expectations that girls perceive as they simultaneously embrace and challenge societal ideals about beauty.

More readily accessible technologies have been used, particularly by poor and marginalized youth. Mitchell et al. (2010) describe a group of rural girls in South Africa who worked to impact the HIV/AIDS epidemic by writing blog posts that included challenges to media stereotypes about who gets AIDS. Others have described how youth use mobile devices to create visual images and micro-blogging (e.g., Twitter) to capture and share incidents of injustice, in an effort to mobilize millions of voices for social change (Diaz-Ortiz & Stone, 2011; Salazar, 2010). Youth Radio is

another example of how young people are creating media that adds to and critiques mainstream news coverage. For example, Youth Radio's Emails from Kosovo series, which told the story of war in Serbia through the eyes of young people, was broadcast on NPR and influenced international politics (Soep & Chávez, 2010). These are all examples of how youth are engaging in disruptive and potentially transformative acts by circumventing the dominant media and producing and distributing their own stories.

Other ways that youth create digital media for social change is in the production of interactive products that others can use, like games and apps. In 1995, a foundational book on computer game programming called Minds in Play (Kafai, 1995) described how children can create games to teach younger children about math or science. Since then, a growing number of freely available, and novice-friendly game authoring tools such as Scratch, GameMaker, and Alice, has led to an increasing number of computer game programming classes, both in and after school; some of the games address social justice issues. For example, a program for First Nations high school students in the US provided the resources for them to create digital games that tell and rework traditional stories from their culture (Lameman, Lewis & Fragnito, 2010). In another US high school class, students created mobile games to advocate for an environmental issue in their community. Mathews (2010) found that when they made a game "…about an issue that was important to them and included their voices, the students felt like they were able to 'push back' against the city" (p. 99). Similarly, girls in an afterschool class were motivated to create games that could be used teach younger students how to navigate the challenges of middle school, including unequal treatment by teachers and administrators (Denner et al., 2005). And in more recent programs, youth are creating apps that address structural inequities, such as limited opportunities and access to after school activities (Van Wart, Vakil, & Parikh, 2014).

Like prior social justice movements, a key aspect of youth making digital media is the role of social context, and the ways that it enables and constrains the nature of what is made and the impact it has. Jenkins et al. (2009) have described how children and youth contribute to and shape the content of online digital media as part of a participatory culture. He described participatory cultures as having "relatively low barriers to artistic expression and civic engagement, strong support for creating and sharing one's creations, and some type of informal mentorship whereby what is known by the most experienced is passed along to novices." For example, participatory politics are described as "interactive, peer-based acts through which individuals and groups seek to exert both voice and influence on issues of public concern. Importantly, these acts are not guided by deference to elites or formal institutions" (Cohen & Kahne, 2012). Websites like www.change.org provide a space for youth to rally support for causes that demand a response from or change by corporations, educational institutions, and political groups. Participation in these groups has led youth to create online petitions that directly challenge or protest giant media corporations (Earl & Schussman, 2008).

These movements are taking place primarily online, through actions like blog posts, creating videos, or starting a new political group. For example, Jenkins (2014) describes what he calls "fan activism," and provides an example of a global community of youth who use metaphors from the Harry Potter books to mobilize and raise funds, often rewriting parts of the narrative. And Kafai & Burke (2013) describe the ScratchEd online community as a form of "computational participation," where youth design, create, and remix digital media products in collaboration with others.

As these studies have shown, digital media can provide a tool for self expression, civic engagement, and activism. The examples described here show only some of the many possible ways that children and youth can use digital media to make a difference in the social, cultural, economic, and political issues that affect their daily lives. In the next section, we review some key issues raised by these studies, including the benefits and barriers, and use two case studies to highlight some promising strategies for engaging more children and youth in the production of digital media that can lead to positive societal change.

CURRENT ISSUES RAISED BY THESE STUDIES

What Are the Benefits of Making Digital Media for the Social Good?

The majority of existing research focuses on the benefits of engagement in different kinds of digital media production for the children and youth that are involved. Kafai and Peppler (2011) identified four categories of participatory competencies that are necessary for full participation in DIY media production: technical, critical, creative, and ethical practices. Technical competencies include coding, debugging, and repurposing; critical competencies include reworking and remixing media; creative competencies include applying artistic principles and connecting multimodal sign systems; and ethical practices include crediting ownership and providing inside information. A small body of research shows the range of ways that making digital media, particularly for the social good, can build these competencies. We briefly summarize the results of these studies below.

The different competencies can be found in a range of digital media production activities. For example, studies have shown that when children program games they engage with computer science concepts and develop skills such as programming and debugging (Denner, Werner, & Ortiz, 2012; Feng & Chen, 2013). Similarly, writing blogs can increase young peoples' knowledge about how to identify things that they can do in their own communities, and a sense of empowerment that they can make a difference (Mitchell et al., 2010). And making an environmental mobile game (Mathews, 2010) or building an app (Van Wart et al., 2014) can increase students' awareness about and ability to analyze social issues, as well as build their technical understanding. Similarly, creative competencies that include self expression and making artistic choices are fostered through activities like making e-textiles. For example, Kafai and Peppler (2014) describe how youth "redefine their position within established power structures" while creating products that involve sewing, fabric, circuits and codes (p. 180).

Critical practices that directly challenge organizational or political structures involve remixing and deconstructing, and are found in activities such as making Zines (Chidgey, 2014) or do-it-yourself news (Annany, 2014). Although no known formal research has examined the benefits of these activities for the development of critical competencies, records of online viewing suggest they have wide impact. For example, the most popular video by 9-year-old Kid President on Youtube has been viewed over 34,000,000 times and has likely mobilized a generation of young children from racial/ethnic minority groups to become critical and active citizens. These competencies prepare youth, particularly those from poor and underserved communities, with workforce competencies that can have great implications for the economic prosperity of their communities. Other potential benefits of the development of these competencies include increased knowledge and confidence, a more critical or analytic perspective on social justice, and changes in attitudes.

The benefits of youth-led digital media production for the social good are harder to gauge. There are many case studies of how youth are changing conversations and mobilizing adult action (Ginwright et al., 2006; Romero et al., 2008; Soep & Chávez, 2010). However, it is not possible to confirm causation, or whether an external factor caused both of these actions, or whether the result is generalizable beyond that particular situation. While there are several anecdotal examples of how digital media projects have had an impact on social issues, there is not enough research to describe the actual benefits to society.

What Are the Barriers to Making Digital Media for the Social Good?

Research also highlights some of the challenges to productive engagement, which include structural and relational factors that limit access and support. In an analysis of youth activism, Gordon (2008) concludes that mobility plays a major role in who participates. For example, girls and younger students tend to have greater restrictions on where they go (both online and physically) and who they interact with. Thus, in an era of fear about cyberbullying, accessing inappropriate material and sexual predators, efforts to protect children can have the unintended consequence of also limiting their opportunity to engage with transformative social and digital media. Others have also described the ways that adults control youth's access to DIY media production, and the importance of understanding how they both support and constrain opportunity and action (Jenson et al., 2014a; Livingstone & Helsper, 2008). In particular, challenges include school-based power relations that silence youth voices, as well as limited access to technology or adults with expertise in digital media (Jenson, Dayha, & Fisher, 2014b).

Economic factors also determine who has access to computers and unrestricted wifi. Hispanic youth and those with household incomes less than $30,000 a year are the least likely to have internet access, and African American youth are most likely to access the internet on a cell phone (Madden et al., 2013). Not surprisingly, studies show that youth are more likely to be creating digital content when they are older and come from more affluent families (Steeves, 2012). Transparency about the barriers to the productive use of digital media for the social good is rare;

probably because the adults writing about these activities are part of the barriers. Building on a legacy of youth-led social justice efforts, adults must maintain a critical perspective on their own role, and the ways that they both constrain and create possibilities for authentic spaces in which children and youth, particularly those from groups whose voices are underrepresented, can create and distribute digital media.

CASE STUDIES

In this section, we highlight two examples of how to meaningfully involve youth in the creation of digital media for the social good. These examples are intended to illustrate contemporary approaches to using a critical pedagogy that motivates marginalized youth to build the skills and become creators of digital products that will benefit their communities and society as a whole. These cases were selected for several reasons. One is that they are designed to overcome many of the barriers to making digital media for the social good described earlier. Second, in contrast to most writings on critical pedagogy that focus primarily on teenagers or young adults, the examples include youth from elementary through high school. Finally, the programs focus on digital media production by Hispanic/Latino youth, whose experiences have been surprisingly absent from critical media studies.

Case #1: CSteach – Computer Science for the Social Good

CSteach is an afterschool class where elementary students from underrepresented groups learn to create digital media to address issues of social justice. It uses a near peer teaching model that includes high school students who are from the community and often know the younger children in the program, either through their extended family or neighborhood. The goal is to foster

capacities, identities, and relationships to use the tools of computer science for positive social change, among both the 5th grade and high school students. The class has been implemented 10 times so far in a school district that serves mostly Latino, low income students. To date, participants have included approximately 300 elementary school students (ages 9-11 years), and 30 high school students between the ages 15-17.

The program uses critical pedagogy to help students identify areas of injustice and opportunity in their community, and to create a message using digital media. CSteach draws on research in mathematics that shows how creating learning experiences that are culturally relevant and connect with social justice issues can engage students in learning in a way that is deep, meaningful, and that contributes to the development of a positive identity (Leonard et al., 2010). It also builds on examples of "computing for the social good" in college (Goldweber et al., 2011), and is the first known effort to integrate computer science and social justice in elementary schools. Thus, one of the goals is to help students recognize how computer programming (coding) can be relevant to their lives and that it can be used to make changes or create things that will help their family and community. Specific goals are that students will: a) learn to identify and understand advocacy needs and opportunities in their schools and/or community, b) understand some of the ways that computer science can help address these needs, and c) develop a sense of responsibility and motivation to use the tools of computer science for the social good.

Social justice concepts are introduced in age-appropriate ways to help students understand and generate ideas about how technology can be used for the social good of their school. Because the program targets 10-11 year old children, it uses terms that are recognizable to the students. For example, the "definition" of social justice in CSteach is that it is something that a student believes is unfair in their community and needs to be changed or improved. It should be relevant, and ideally personally meaningful to them. To this end, the program teaches four "big ideas" about social justice that are developmentally appropriate for young children:

- **Fairness:** Students learn the difference between having a complaint or a dislike, and situations that are a result of inequality in people's opportunities, due to bias, unequal distribution of power, or other privileges.
- **Community:** Students focus on an issue that is personally meaningful and impacts themselves or people they are connected to. Given their limited mobility outside the school, the 5th grade students are encouraged to think about fairness at their school.
- **Empowerment:** Students learn about other young people who believe that they can make (and are making) real change, which builds their own motivation, including the development of an identity as a leader or change agent.
- **Action:** Students learn that collective action is the most effective way to make social change, and that change can happen by working with others and leveraging both social and computer networks.

The 13-week curriculum guides students through the exploration of social justice both from a local and a global perspective. They are introduced to the topics by watching short videos with examples of how technology is being used by young people to solve problems around the world, as well as children and youth engaged in efforts to improve their community. These short videos highlight the ways in which the power of technology can be leveraged to build community support for a local issue, and how technology can be the vehicle to disseminate information to a community. The activities are framed within a context that the students understand and can relate to--they identify circumstances that they or others consider to be unfair at their school.

A series of activities were designed to scaffold students' developing understanding of social justice, and how they can be involved in social change. The students move from self awareness to social awareness--the first two stages of action in Ginwright and Cammarota's (2002) model of youth development social justice. The activities are delivered by high school students, and are at an appropriate developmental level to help students think about their school as a space where everyone has an equal right to learn and participate. The high school students draw on their own experiences to help the younger students reflect on what is important to them, and then guide them through activities to explore what makes them feel good and helps them learn at school. Then students reflect on things that are unfair, and what prevents them and others from feeling good and having equal opportunities to learn at school. They identify the factors that get in the way of having a safe and fair learning and social environment. Finally, the students work together to identify solutions to those barriers in order to make their school more "awesome."

It is these "awesome" ideas that are incorporated into a digital multimedia project--an animation that students design and then code using the Scratch programming tool. The projects are designed to send a message about something they see as unfair at their school, why, and how it should be changed. The final digital media projects are shared with their peers, teachers, and administrators at school, as well as with their families. The program creates a space for children to contextualize and localize social justice issues in their own language, with support from older students in their community, and gives them the tools and resources to write a message using digital media that can be used as a first step toward social change.

Case #2: The Digital NEST

Digital NEST (Nurturing Entrepreneurial Skills with Technology) creates sustainable and scalable technology centers in low income communities in California, with the goal of engaging, empowering, and preparing youth to create digital media that will fuel local economic development. It is a community-based hub that provides a safe and collaborative learning environment and opportunities for people between the ages of 12-24 to enter a common space where they can work together to build digital media products for the benefit of themselves and their community. The long-term goal is to bring prosperity to underserved communities by teaching technological and entrepreneurial skills to youth and young adults.

The Digital NEST started in an agricultural community where few families can afford to buy their children a computer or get reliable internet, and even fewer can provide expensive software that requires regular updates and maintenance. The community lacks the infrastructure to provide the public with high speed internet, so many motivated high school and college students sit outside businesses or on weekends on the closed campus of the local community college in order to find a connection that will allow them to do their homework. Due to these limitations, the community has few high tech professionals; those who left the community to get an education or pursue work experience have few incentives or opportunities to return to work in their home town.

The Digital NEST is modeled after successful technology companies that inspire creativity and innovation, and provides its members with state-of-the-art technology in a safe space that gets them off the streets. There are four major components. The NEST provides access to: 1) *Technology.* Youth use laptops to access professional, multimedia software, take online computing and digital media courses, visit social networking sites, create original digital media projects, and connect with peers and professionals with similar interests.

2) *Technology education.* Youth meet and take classes from mentors who represent leading digital media and technology companies, such as Google, Netflix, and Smith Micro Software, and they have access to thousands of online courses. The youth can choose among classes on digital film making, digital game design, networking, mobile application development, web site design, and graphic design. 3) *Leadership opportunities.* Youth take on leadership roles both within and outside the NEST. For example, local and regional companies hire youth to work as consultants and gain real-world experience by building digital media products and providing technology support services, which infuse youth voice into local business and fuel community economic development. Youth also learn leadership skills that they apply by directing the activities at the NEST and mentoring younger students. 4) *A safe and creative space outside of school.* The center is centrally located, and run primarily by young adults, providing a safe and productive place where youth can create digital media and reinvent their futures.

As an example of youth leadership, members developed an ideology to guide how the space would be used. Together they wrote the following statement: "As Members of the Digital NEST, we commit to bettering our community by becoming innovators and utilizing technology for the benefit of ourselves and others, providing a safe and collaborative learning environment, maintaining a positive perception about our community, and providing service to our local and global community." While adult participation is a critical part of the Digital NEST, particularly for connecting youth with resources and helping them to establish a process, youth leadership has been essential for creating a place that does not reproduce the structural inequalities that many of these youth experience in formal institutions, like school.

There are some commonalities that run across these two case studies. First, both use an intergenerational model that builds on cultural strengths. This model is based on the work of Bourdieu (1986) that shows there are resources and social capital in poor and marginalized communities, even if they are not valued by the dominant culture. The use of near peers from the local community not only helps to deliver the digital media skills in a language that is familiar to them, it provides youth with more experienced (but still young) people from whom they learn how to navigate challenges and create opportunities that allow them to pursue their goals and still maintain ties to their family and culture (Cooper, 2011). A second commonality across these case studies is that they aim to foster empowerment with digital media among individuals by creating access, building their technical skills, and then scaffolding opportunities for them to use those tools to participate as active citizens in their community. A third similarity is that both CSteach and the Digital NEST recognize the importance of creating a safe space where different kinds of skills and interests are valued. This means that there are opportunities and mentors, regardless of whether a person is interested in the more technical aspects of digital media that involve programming, the more artistic aspects that involve images and music, or the more social aspects that involve leading groups and building networks.

How Can the Popularity of Making Digital Media in Ways that Benefit Society Be Expanded?

Although much of the digital media created for the social good is youth-driven, adults play a crucial role in creating equitable opportunities. Youth with limited access to digital media need adults to set up opportunities and structures that they can realistically use. Although most schools in the US have computers and internet access, firewalls block access to websites that promote social networking and social change. Libraries are another access point, but many have limited hours, or cannot be safely reached by youth from different neighborhoods, and few are accessible

to children or youth without parental supervision. As shown in the case studies, effective strategies include providing opportunities to take some introductory courses or workshops, to work with more experienced youth, and to create project-based digital media content that can easily be accomplished even with little technology knowledge. Other organizations like Global Minimum (www. gmin.org) are dedicated to building the capacity of young people to solve problems affecting their communities using innovative methods that often include digital media and technology. In Africa, they foster intergenerational teams that have built a range of solutions including a communication platform through social networks and apps to connect poor high school students with university students, and luminescent boards to create light for emergency service providers to safely navigate through informal settlements. And the TakingITGlobal program combines digital youth engagement with global education and social innovation; a study found that participation led to the creation of digital media online, and the use of the tools to make change in their communities (Raynes-Goldie & Walker, 2008). To increase the number of youth that are making digital media for the social good, we need organizations like these, that leverage the desire of many youth to take action to improve conditions for themselves and their families.

However, not all efforts to engage children and youth in digital media production create the space or the guidance to connect these activities to social change; the results depend in part on the motivation of the adults involved. For example, Fisherkeller (2013) identified multiple reasons that adults have created opportunities for youth to produce their own media. These include: to increase children's civic engagement or political participation, to create opportunities for self-expression and creativity, and to motivate children to engage in and persist in complex digital environments for some other outcomes, such as to learn about computation, to build confidence with computing, or to increase media literacy. Clearly, it is not necessary for every digital media class to focus on how it can be used to address social injustice. However, when adults set up the opportunity and structure for youth to create digital media, they have to be conscious about the ways in which they are controlling it, so that youth can drive the content that is created.

GAPS IN THE RESEARCH AND DIRECTIONS FOR FUTURE RESEARCH

There are several limitations of existing research that prevent us from guiding efforts to effectively engage children and youth in digital media production for the social good. In particular, we know little about why youth participate, what they learn, or the benefits to society. We also have limited knowledge of how the answers to these questions will vary, depending on the kinds of media that youth produce.

Some of the limitations are methodological. For example, most existing studies are small, in-depth descriptions of a group or program, and it is not possible to generalize the findings from most studies due to a lack of diversity in the participants, self-selection of children and youth into the activities, and small sample sizes, which often rely on case studies of one or two children. A range of methodological approaches are needed to provide both in-depth and generalizable findings. We need both large studies to understand who is making digital media for the social good and how, as well as in-depth studies to understand the benefits to both the youth and society as a whole.

In addition, we need more studies of youth designing and developing new technologies for the social good. Soep (2015) makes the important point that "…it's important to disaggregate what we mean by media, that we include technology creation as a kind of media production, and that we pinpoint specific considerations related to telling digital stories versus creating digital tools

and platforms" (p. 30). Indeed, creating products like digital games and apps has been linked to various kinds of computational learning and thinking (Grover & Pea, 2013; Werner, Denner, & Campe, 2014). However, the focus of most of these efforts has been on building the capacities of individuals, rather than on the implications of their products for social change—who uses them, how, and what are the resulting changes in people, institutions, or systems?

There are several additional directions for future research. For example, we know little about how and why youth create digital media for the social good—the factors that lead or enable them to design and develop products. We also know little about the kinds of programs, curriculum, or institutional structures that increase the likelihood that youth will create digital media that aims to address injustice or improve lives. Research is also needed on the potential risks or backlash in response to efforts by youth to use digital media for the social good. Few have described who responds to their creations and how the nature of this response varies across communities and power structures. This information is important to understand if we are to increase the number and diversity of youth who engage in these practices.

Despite the emphasis in the research on the importance of social factors, there is very little information about how the family and the school foster the creation of digital media. This is particularly important because Livingstone (2010) found that it was schools and parents that were the greatest influencers on youth's interest in and participation in politics. Thus, we need research on the role that parents, siblings, and other family members play in where, when, and how youth create digital media for the social good. While studies have shown that parents can create barriers, little is known about how they (or other family member) create opportunities, either by being role models through their own digital media creation, or by sending their children to classes where they can get the skills and support. In addition, there is a need for research on whether participation looks different if it is youth-generated compared to when it is happening in an adult-led class or program. Part of this research should be an investigation into the role of privilege and adult control in creating digital media for the social good.

Although most of this research has focused on the transformative power of digital media production, there is rarely discussion about the institutional resources or level of adult support that are necessary for young people to successfully complete and share a project. A few have called for more dialogue about this, and have highlighted the ways that institutional structures can limit this work (Jenson et al., 2014a). But additional transparency and documentation of these factors will go a long way toward creating learning environments where young people can create digital media that has a positive influence on themselves and the things they care about.

Similarly, research is needed on effective educational practices and pedagogies. While some teachers are integrating DIY media into their classroom (Guzzetti et al., 2010) little is known about how to support these efforts to be effective for different kinds of students. We also need research on whether students take these experiences outside the school, or the extent to which they involve creating media for the social good. The existing research is also missing a developmental perspective on the most appropriate strategies for introducing concepts of social justice and civic engagement to children at different ages. Additional dialogue with children of all ages is needed to incorporate terminology that is familiar to them.

Fine (2014) recommends taking a long-term view to understand the factors leading up to youth resistance, as well as the consequences of those actions. Thus, the next stage of research should not only analyze the digital media content or products created by youth, but also understand the circumstances (both supports and challenges) that led to the creation of the product, as well as what happened, both to the individual and to society,

as a result of those creations. Drawing on these limitations, we will make recommendations for next steps to fill these research gaps.

IMPLICATIONS AND RECOMMENDATIONS FOR EDUCATION, CIVIC ENGAGEMENT, SOCIAL PRACTICE, AND POLICY

There are several implications for educators, parents, policymakers, and companies that make digital media tools. Youth, particularly those from poor communities, need both the support and the resources to use digital media for the social good. Educators and parents can increase the likelihood that their children's digital media use will have a social justice component if they engage youth as leaders in the decision-making about the content and use of their digital media. The best way to promote the use of digital media for the social good involves striking a balance between trying to guide and direct their activities to increase their impact, and supporting youth's critical consciousness, creativity, and self expression. We have described some of those physical and online spaces in this chapter. For policymakers to create and sustain efforts that connect digital media use with the social good, they should break down institutional barriers (e.g., lack of computer centers in underserved communities, high cost of internet) of accessing technology and create financial support for efforts that tie digital media and social justice. And companies can increase the ease with which their tools can be used for the social good by offering free or drastically reducing the cost of software for youth, and providing training and examples of how the software can be used to address social justice issues.

Creating opportunities for the meaningful engagement of youth that are underrepresented in the careers that shape the digital future is an act of social justice itself. Members of underserved communities do not have equal access to the high paying and growing number of technology-related careers. The act of engaging youth from these communities is one way to address the social justice issue but it needs to be done meaningfully and deeply. It must build on existing cultural and social capital, which means having local leaders involved at every stage, and putting youth in authentic decision making roles.

ACKNOWLEDGMENT

This material is based upon work supported by the National Science Foundation under Grant No. CNS-1240756.

REFERENCES

Annany, M. (2014). Critical news making and the paradox of "do-it-yourself-news". In M. Ratto & M. Boler (Eds.), *DIY Citizenship: Critical making and social media* (pp. 359–372). Cambridge, MA: MIT Press.

Banet-Weiser, S. (2011). Branding the post-feminist self: girls' video production and YouTube. In *Mediated girlhoods: New explorations of girls' media culture* (pp. 277-294). Academic Press.

Blikstein, P. (2008). Travels in Troy with Freire: Technology as an agent of emancipation. In P. Noguera & C. A. Torres (Eds.), *Social justice education for teachers: Paulo Freire and the possible dream*. Rotterdam, Netherlands: Sense.

Bourdieu, P. (1986). The forms of capital. In J. G. Richardson (Ed.), *Handbook of theory and research for the sociology of education* (pp. 241–258). New York, NY: Greenwood Press.

Buckingham, D. (2000). *The making of citizens: Young people, news and politics*. London: Routledge.

Cahill, C., Rios-Moore, I., & Threatts, T. (2008). Different eyes/open eyes: Community-based participatory action research. In J. Cammarota & M. Fine (Eds.), *Revolutionizing Education: Youth participatory action research in motion* (pp. 89–124). New York, NY: Routledge.

Cammarota, J., & Fine, M. (2008). *Revolutionizing education: Youth participatory action research in motion*. New York, NY: Routledge.

Chidgey, R. (2014). Developing communities of resistance? Maker pedagogies, do-it-yourself feminism, and DIY citizenship. In M. Ratto & M. Boler (Eds.), *DIY Citizenship: Critical making and social media* (pp. 101–114). Cambridge, MA: MIT Press.

Cohen, C. J., & Kahne, J. (2012). *Participatory politics: New media and youth political action*. Retrieved on September 15, 2014 from http://ypp.dmlcentral.net/sites/default/files/publications/Participatory_Politics_Report.pdf

Cooper, C. R. (2011). *Bridging multiple worlds: Cultures, identities, and pathways to college*. Oxford University Press. doi:10.1093/acprof:oso/9780195080209.001.0001

Denner, J., & Bean, S. (2010). The young women's leadership alliance: Political socialization in three U.S. high schools. In A. Ittell, H. Merkens, L. Stecher, & J. Zinnecker (Eds.), *Jahrbuch Jugendforschung* (pp. 85–103). Germany: VS Verlag. doi:10.1007/978-3-531-92320-8_4

Denner, J., Werner, L., Bean, S., & Campe, S. (2005). The Girls Creating Games Program: Strategies for engaging middle school girls in information technology. *Frontiers: A Journal of Women's Studies*, 26(1), 90–98.

Denner, J., Werner, L., & Ortiz, E. (2012). Computer games created by middle school girls: Can they be used to measure understanding of computer science concepts? *Computers & Education*, 58(1), 240–249. doi:10.1016/j.compedu.2011.08.006

Diaz-Ortiz, C., & Stone, B. (2011). *Twitter for good: Change the world one tweet at a time*. San Francisco, CA: Jossey-Bass.

Earl, J., & Schussman, A. (2008). Contesting cultural control: Youth culture and online petitioning. In W. L. Bennett (Ed.), *Civic life online: Learning how digital media can engage youth* (pp. 71–96). Cambridge, MA: MIT Press.

Edell, D., Brown, L. M., & Tolman, D. (2013). Embodying sexualisation: When theory meets practice in intergenerational feminist activism. *Feminist Theory*, *14*(3), 275–284. doi:10.1177/1464700113499844

Feng, C., & Chen, M. (2013). The effects of goal specificity and scaffolding on programming performance and self regulation in game design. *British Journal of Educational Technology*, *45*(2), 285–302. doi:10.1111/bjet.12022

Fine, M. (1991). *Framing dropouts: Notes on the politics of an urban high school*. SUNY Press.

Fine, M. (2014). An intimate memoir of resistance theory. In E. Tuck & K. W. Yang (Eds.), *Youth resistance research and theories of change* (pp. 46–58). New York, NY: Routledge.

Fisherkeller, J. (2013). Young people producing media: Spontaneous and project-sponsored media creation around the world. In D. Lemish (Ed.), *The Routledge International Handbook of Children, Adolescents, and Media* (pp. 344–350). London: Routledge.

Freire, P. (1970). *Pedagogy of the oppressed*. New York: Continuum.

Ginwright, S. (2010). Peace out to revolution! Activism among African American youth: An argument for radical healing. *Young*, *18*(1), 77–96. doi:10.1177/110330880901800106

Ginwright, S., & Cammarota, J. (2002). New terrain in youth development: The promise of a social justice approach. *Social Justice Journal*, *29*(4), 82–95.

Ginwright, S., & Cammarota, J. (2007). Youth activism in the urban community: Learning critical civic praxis within community organizations. *International Journal of Qualitative Studies in Education*, *20*(6), 693–710. doi:10.1080/09518390701630833

Ginwright, S., Noguera, P., & Cammarota, J. (2006). *Beyond resistance! Youth activism and community change*. New York, NY: Routledge.

Giroux, H. (2003). *The abandoned generation: Democracy beyond the culture of fear*. Palgrave Macmillan.

Goldweber, M., Davoli, R., Little, J. C., Riedesel, C., Walker, H., Cross, G., & Von Konsky, B. R. (2011). Enhancing the social issues components in our computing curriculum: Computing for the social good. *ACM Inroads*, *2*(1), 64–82. doi:10.1145/1929887.1929907

Gordon, H. R. (2008). Gendered paths to teenage political participation: Parental power, civic mobility, and youth activism. *Gender & Society*, *22*(1), 31–55. doi:10.1177/0891243207311046

Grover, S., & Pea, R. (2013). Computational Thinking in K–12 A Review of the State of the Field. *Educational Researcher*, *42*(1), 38–43. doi:10.3102/0013189X12463051

Guzzetti, B. E., & Welsch. (2010). DIY media in the classroom: New literacies across content areas. New York, NY: Teachers College Press.

Guzzetti, B. J., & Gamboa, M. (2004). Zines for social justice: Adolescent girls writing on their own. *Reading Research Quarterly*, *39*(4), 408–435. doi:10.1598/RRQ.39.4.4

Jenkins, H. (2014). Fan activism as participatory politics: The case of the Harry Potter Alliance. In M. Ratto & M. Boler (Eds.), *DIY Citizenship: Critical making and social media* (pp. 65–74). Cambridge, MA: MIT Press.

Jenkins, H., Purushotma, R., Weigel, M., Clinton, K., & Robison, A. J. (2009). *Confronting the challenges of participatory culture: Media education for the 21ˢᵗ century.* The John D. and Catherine T. MacArthur Foundation Reports on Digital Media and Learning.

Jenson, J., Dahya, N., & Fisher, S. (2014a). Power struggles: Knowledge production in a DIY news club. In M. Ratto & M. Boler (Eds.), *DIY citizenship: Critical making and social media* (pp. 169–178). Cambridge, MA: The MIT Press.

Jenson, J., Dahya, N., & Fisher, S. (2014b). Valuing production values: A 'do it yourself' media production club. *Learning, Media and Technology*, *39*(2), 215–228. doi:10.1080/17439884.2013.799486

Kafai, Y. B. (1995). *Minds in Play: Computer game design as a context for children's learning.* New Jersey: Erlbaum.

Kafai, Y. B., & Burke, Q. (2013). The social turn in K-12 programming: Moving from computational thinking to computational participation. *SIGCSE*, *2013*, 603–608.

Kafai, Y. B., Fields, D. A., & Burke, W. Q. (2010). Entering the clubhouse: Case studies of young programmers joining the online Scratch communities. *Journal of Organizational and End User Computing*, *22*(2), 21–35. doi:10.4018/joeuc.2010101906

Kafai, Y. B., & Peppler, K. (2011). Youth, technology, and DIY: Developing participatory competencies in creative media production. *Review of Research in Education*, *35*(1), 89–119. doi:10.3102/0091732X10383211

Kafai, Y. B., & Peppler, K. (2014). Transparency reconsidered: Creative, critical, and connecting making with e-textiles. In M. Ratto. & M. Boler (Eds.), DIY Citizenship: Critical making and social media (pp. 179-188). Cambridge, MA: MIT Press.

Lameman, B. A., Lewis, J. E., & Fragnito, S. (2010). Skins 1.0: A curriculum for designing games with First Nations Youth. Paper presented at FuturePlay 2010, Vancouver, Canada.

Lankshear, C., & Knobel, M. (2008). *Digital literacies: Concepts, practices, and policies* (Vol. 30). Peter Lang.

Leonard, J., Brooks, W., Barnes-Johnson, J., & Berry, R. Q. (2010). The nuances and complexities of teaching mathematics for cultural relevance and social justice. *Journal of Teacher Education*, *61*(3), 261–270. doi:10.1177/0022487109359927

Livingstone, S. (2010). Interactivity and participation on the Internet: young people's response to the civic sphere. In P. Dahlgren (Ed.), *Young citizens and new media: Learning for democratic participation* (pp. 103–124). London, UK: Routledge.

Livingstone, S., & Helsper, E. J. (2008). Parental mediation of children's internet use. *Journal of Broadcasting & Electronic Media*, *52*(4), 581–599. doi:10.1080/08838150802437396

Madden, M., Lenhart, A., Duggan, M., Cortesi, S., & Gasser, U. (2013). *Teens and technology 2013.* Retrieved on January 2, 2015 from http://www.pewinternet.org/2013/03/13/teens-and-technology-2013/

Malin. (2014). *Youth civic development and education.* Retrieved on July 26, 2014 from https://coa.stanford.edu/sites/default/files/Civic%20Education%20report.pdf

Mathews, J. M. (2010). Using a studio-based pedagogy to engage students in the design of mobile-based media. *English Teaching*, *9*(1), 87–102.

Mercado, C. I., & Reyes, L. O. (2010). Latino community activism in the twenty-first century. In E. Murillo Jr et al. (Eds.), *Handbook of Latinos and Education: Theory, research, and practice* (pp. 250–261). New York, NY: Routledge.

Milberry, K. (2014). (Re)making the Internet: Free software and the social factory hack. In M. Ratto & M. Boler (Eds.), *DIY Citizenship: Critical making and social media* (pp. 53–63). Cambridge, MA: MIT Press.

Mitchell, C., Pascarella, De Lange, N., & Stuart, J. (2010). We wanted other people to learn from us: Girls blogging in rural South Africa in the age of AIDS. In S. Mazzarella (Ed.), Girl Wide Web 2.0: Revisiting girls, the internet, and the negotiation of identity (pp. 161-182). New York, NY: Peter Lang.

Morrell, E. (2002). Toward a critical pedagogy of popular culture: Literacy development among urban youth. *Journal of Adolescent & Adult Literacy*, 72–77.

Papaioannou, T. (2013). Media and civic engagement: The role of Web 2.0 technologies in fostering youth participation. In D. Lemish (Ed.), *The Routledge International Handbook of Children, Adolescents, and Media* (pp. 351–358). London: Routledge.

Ratto, M., & Boler, M. (Eds.). (2014). *DIY Citizenship: Critical making and social media.* Cambridge, MA: MIT Press.

Raynes-Goldie, K., & Walker, L. (2008). Our space: Online civic engagement tools for youth. In W. L. Bennett (Ed.), *Civic life online: Learning how digital media can engage youth* (pp. 161–188). Cambridge, MA: MIT Press.

Romero, A., Cammarota, J., Dominguez, K., Valdez, J., Ramirez, G., & Hernandez, L. (2008). "The opportunity if not the right to see" The Social Justice Education Project. In J. Cammarota & M. Fine (Eds.), *Revolutionizing Education: Youth participatory action research in motion* (pp. 131–151). New York, NY: Routledge.

Salazar, L. (2010). *Taking IT mobile: Youth, mobile phones, and social change.* Retrieved on September 26, 2014 from http://www.tigweb.org/resources/toolkits/view.html?ToolkitID=2937

Sherrod, L., Torney-Purta, J., & Flanagan, C. (2010). *Handbook of research on civic engagement in youth.* Hoboken, NJ: Wiley. doi:10.1002/9780470767603

Soep, E. (2015). Phones aren't smart until you tell them what to do. In E. Middaugh & B. Kirshner (Eds.), *youthaction: Becoming political in the digital age* (pp. 25–41). Charlotte, NC: Information Age Publishing.

Soep, E., & Chávez, V. (2010). *Drop that knowledge: Youth Radio stories.* Berkeley, CA: University of California Press.

Steeves, V. (2012). *Young Canadians in a wired world.* Retrieved on August 28, 2014 from http://mediasmarts.ca/sites/default/files/pdfs/publication-report/full/YCWWIII-youth-parents.pdf

Tuck, E., & Wang, K. W. (2013). *Youth resistance research and theories of change.* New York, NY: Routledge.

Van Wart, S., Vakil, S., & Parikh, T. S. (2014). Apps for social justice: Motivating computer science learning with design and real-world problem solving. Paper presented at ITiCSE '14, Uppsala, Sweden.

Weis, L., & Fine, M. (Eds.). (1993). *Beyond silenced voices: Class, race, and gender in United States schools*. SUNY Press.

Werner, L., Denner, J., & Campe, S. (2014). Children programming games: A strategy for measuring computational learning. *ACM Transactions on Computing Education*, *14*(4), 24. doi:10.1145/2677091

Wheeler, W. (2003). Youth leadership for development: Civic activism as a component of youth development programming and a strategy for strengthening civil society. In F. Jacobs, D. Werlieb, & R. M. Lerner (Eds.), Handbook of Applied Developmental Science (2nd ed.; pp. 491–505). Academic Press.

Whyte, W. F. E. (1991). *Participatory action research*. Sage Publications, Inc.

Willis, P. E. (1977). *Learning to labor: How working class kids get working class jobs*. New York: Columbia University Press.

KEY TERMS AND DEFINITIONS

Digital Media: Newscasts, games, blogs, music, films, images, animated stories.

DIY: Do-it-yourself digital media.

Marginalized: A person or group of people whose perspectives are outside the mainstream.

Participatory Culture: A community characterized by creative expression and civic engagement.

Social Justice: Equality in terms of wealth, opportunities and privileges.

Social Media: Internet and mobile-based tools for sharing and discussing ideas.

Youth Agency: Active participation of young people in overcoming injustice.

Chapter 17
The Appification of Literacy

David Gerard O'Brien
University of Minnesota, USA

Megan McDonald Van Deventer
University of Minnesota, USA

ABSTRACT

Appification represents the rapid movement of digital tools and media from a Web-based platform to mobile apps. While appification makes the former Web-based tools and apps more accessible, and improves users' quality of life, it also undermines traditional literacy skills and practices associated with print literacies. After defining appification and presenting examples, the chapter explores how appification impacts literacy in the broader society and critiques how schools, via standards, are adapting to the broader appification. Apps and appification play a significant role in changing globally what is meant by literacy. Yet, in the US, schools and educational policy are not keeping up with the rapid transition. Although schools are increasingly embracing the idea of apps and portable devices like tablets, there is little systematic connection between using the new technologies in schools and improving literacy required to be proficient in the app-o-verse.

There are currently about 1.2 million apps in Apple's App Store with a total of 75 billion downloads to date, putting it neck and neck with Google Play (Perez, 2014). By the year 2016, it is estimated that over 196 million smart phones will be in use in the US, and this number should rise to 220 million by 2018 (Statista, 2014). Worldwide, there are 1.75 billion smartphone users (eMarketer, 2014). App use and downloads of apps are dramatically increasing. It is projected that app downloads by 2017 will hit between 200-270 billion—up from about 200 billion in 2013 (Salz, 2014).

App does not seem significant enough to be a word because it is only part of the word *application*—yet it is now such an important word that it vied for the recognition of word of the year and won that honor in the 2010 competition by the American Dialect society (2011). *Appification* does not refer merely to the proliferation of apps or putting more app icons on your smartphone. Rather, it refers to a fundamental shift in how we access and use information and media, specifically how we are moving from using the Web as a vast information server by the internet as a "flow

DOI: 10.4018/978-1-4666-8310-5.ch017

medium" (Kosner, 2012). The Web, rather than being the primary access interface, is increasingly becoming the back-end service for apps. Technicians and programmers have made the distinction between native apps and web apps. Native apps are programs that run on a mobile device's operating system; they are written specifically for a device and reside on the device. All of those apps that need space in the mobile device memory and run locally on the device are native apps. Web apps, as the name states, are apps that are internet-enabled and dependent and can be accessed via a device browser. Web apps automate web sites functions. A well-known example one of these is the app for Google Maps. To users, whether appification relies on the Internet or on local programming, is not so noticeable in terms of the app interface; but the functions of some apps are entirely dependent on a Internet. A web app like *Hootsuite*, which manages ones social media, is clearly a web app because it is totally dependent on the Internet-based social networks. But the mobile app further automates the process.

When average users acquire apps through an app store, they do not connect the term back to applications or the more anachronistic notion of apps as little *programs*. People still ask, "What exactly are apps?" and are told that they are like programs, like tools; they are ways of automating practical approaches to meet a particular need or interest or just to facilitate fun. These users are not necessarily aware that some app programs are ways of consolidating existing web apps, unless they use both the web app in the browser and in a mobile app. Google maps is an example. Each app affords both positive and negative affordances in terms of traditional literacy practices.

In this chapter we examine the impact of digital media, in the form of apps, on literacy by looking applications in general, then how it is related to schooled literacy; and, finally, by bridging it with how appification is impacting literacy in the broader society. Apps, like other digital tools, are cast mostly in a positive light. But for every positive

affordance, there is an equal, and usually necessary, negative affordance—what James Gibson (1986), who coined the term "affordance," calls the "good or ill" aspect of affordances.

At the time of this writing, Apple Watch was the newest app device. The Apple Watch affords extreme portability; it also affords such a small display that it cannot communicate as much print-based information per screen as an iPhone or iPod Touch. Apple Watch is the most publicized entry in the expanding classes of wearable devices. As such, it promises to afford a unique synergy that goes with being part of one's person; it could redefine our habitus. With it, we are not inconvenienced by actually having to reach into a pocket to pull out such a large and inconvenient device as a smartphone. A short while ago, smartphones were viewed as svelte, sleek, and shiny. With the arrival of Apple Watch smartphones may eventually become positioned as sometimes necessary but somewhat unwieldy, as large, and not so accessible compared to the Watch. Last week a smartphone was viewed as much more portable; now, with Apple Watch, an iPad mini might seem a gargantuan digital dinosaur. And so it goes with applications and their relation to mobility.

Apple Watch will introduce novel literate practices not directly linked to the traditional practices like reading words embedded in syntactic structures. Apple Watch will afford direct contact and synchronicity with everything through very small texts and pictures; Watch users will be able to send new kinds of semiotic messages. With the Watch, the reason reading texts will be downplayed in relation to other visuals, and sensors and haptic feedback, is that the Watch's screen is--well, the size of a watch screen--because that is what we expect a watch screen to be. If Apple Watch just displayed chronometrical information with hands or digital time, it would fail to meet the life-changing expectation of previous Apple devices. But Apple Watch is much more; it is a key exemplar of appification and what to expect as the process of appification continues. Below we will discuss other apps, most of them not as intimately integrated into ones habitus as Watch but, nevertheless, examples of the affordance of portability of Watch, and devices that promise a profound impact on literacy engagement and practices.

SUCCINCT REVIEW OF RESEARCH: THE FUTURE OF LITERACY IN AN APP-CENTERED WORLD

Because of apps and the way they package and define digital media and literacy, new literacy practices are emerging that engender new kinds of literate engagement and new competencies (Leu, Kinzer, Coiro, Castek, & Henry, 2013). Children, youth, and adults all benefit from these new media via apps, but usually to the detriment of some time-honored print-centric practices at the heart of our learning and a significant part of the essence human culture. We continue to explore these positive and negative affordances below, by first framing the discussion with cybernetics and the networking of humans.

Peter F. Hamilton (2012) in the book *Great North Road* constructs a future world that many critics say is a believable view of our possible future relationship to digital technologies and apps in about 130 years. In that future world, the emerging *Internet of things* has morphed into a world in which we *are* the things—we all have nodes, or IP address-like connections. These private Electronic Identities (EIs) link us to the net and our body meshes, retinal sensors, and processors are all part of the network. We can share our perceptual data to communicate with others instantaneously. Although we still have identities outside of the net and make the usual sentient decisions to use various technologies, the ecosystem is a collective of experiences and digital data streams that connect everyone.

In *Great North Road*, the EI is the central app that controls and monitors other apps, but apps are part of our identities, a bioelectronics connection to the world. Granted, any view of life in the future is limited by the restriction of how we envision possibilities grounded in both our current experiences and where we have been in our relationship to technologies. But Hamilton's world is a viable outcome of the current trajectory of apps and connectivity. We explore this further with a focus on the present.

Aside from the role of apps in organizing and proliferating media consumption overall, apps have replaced or automated countless tasks ranging from reading a children's book to organizing a grocery list, to controlling and monitoring home security systems and appliances, to checking one's biometrics related to life style. As apps have automated tasks and afforded more "efficiency" in our daily lives they have also replaced many other digital spaces—mostly Web sites where we used to go to read to get static content. Apps are replacing larger pieces of digital real estate that included lots of print on relatively large screens, to less print on small screens and replacing the functionality of those web pages with other modalities more suited to small screens—or, they are replacing linguistic information with icons.

Apple Watch, mentioned previously, is the most extreme example of shrinking digital viewing space. The Internet of things, and, most recently what Elgan (2015) calls the Internet of Self, specifically the Quantified Self, fully eliminate linguistic modes and language in communication. For example, Elgan notes that each day we render lots of biometric data, and apps use biometric sensors to compile data like blood pressure, heart rate, skin surface temperature, respiratory patterns and even sleep patterns. The analyses of these Quantified Self data by software within apps provides information about health and life styles But the compelling point Elgan makes, an assertion that is the remarkably similar to the EI in *Great North Road*, is that Quantified Self data can be used to command the objects in the Internet of Things *directly*. In short, apps provide an interface for people to communicate directly with things based on our biometrically indicated states and needs. An app that works with a biometric monitor knows when you are waking and turns on the light next to your bedside. The next step in the Internet of things, with us as things, is networked bio-electronic communication among humans that bypasses traditional written and oral language.

The appification of everything is leading to the transformation of the Web into an "App-o-verse." The App-o-verse is a term that Kosner (2012) uses to name the new digital space we live in where apps increasingly replace Websites. Instead of the Web being our primary user interface, it becomes an underlying service layer for apps, which become the new user interfaces; and in the app-o-verse, more and more Websites, places and spaces that are essentially linked pages, will be replaced by apps. Ironically, just as researchers are starting to examine the challenges of reading "online," (Leu et al., 2013) a lot of what is online is being absorbed by apps—some of our reasons for going online are being eroded. Certainly this plays into Leu's notion of deixis (Leu, 2000) which points to the challenge and even impracticality of studying something like literacy in the age of rapid digital transformations when it is such a moving target.

Once we figure out the challenges of reading web pages, navigating multimodal information, and synthesizing across online intertexts to do research on a topic, apps will eliminate that digital space and replace the computer screen real estate with smaller spaces requiring more efficient forms of communication using less traditional semiotic resources—e.g., touch informational or emotive icons. The once-clear distinction between so-called native apps and Web apps is increasingly blurred as the power and versatility of apps is tied to web server back-ends. In general, appification is lauded as a way to make our lives more efficient.

But appification both simplifies and complicates our lives. One of the authors, David, has an smartphone app that monitors the temperature of grilled foods out on his patio via a Bluetooth connection that complicates the previously easy task of just periodically walking out to his deck to eyeball burgers and flipping them. We typically believe that digitization simplifies our lives, or makes our lives easier, but most of the apps we select and download are forgotten or discarded. New apps that duplicate the functions of previously acquired apps are purchased that app consumers do not remember purchasing.

Information sharing, or sharing what has traditionally been called knowledge, has traditionally relied considerably on literacy processes tied to print and cognitive, linguistic, and psycholinguistic skills employed with connected written discourse. Print texts, through their history, have gone from being very hard to acquire to being so portable that most of them, including classic texts or even rare texts, are available digitally. The increasing connectivity (Anderson and Rainie, 2014) means that we can access more information, more immediately, and with bandwidth that supports visual modalities. But the most daunting negative affordance is that we have an increasing amount of information and a decreasing amount of *knowledge* (Mitra, 2013). To give just a small sampling of what has happened in appification, we discuss some app categories

SOME BROAD CATEGORIES OF APPS

Books

Includes e-books, graphic novels, comics, "Bedtime Stories." These apps range from digital spaces that seem like traditional books to highly interactive spaces in which readers "step inside" the story and become part of the action. Many of them explore multimodality via animations of scenes and characters, music, and include "kara-oke" mode in which words light up as narrators read them. All of the tablet versions allow readers to interact via screen touch gestures. Many of the children's book apps have "Read to Me" or "Read it Myself" modes with narrators that boldly step into the app to replace parent readers--a literacy practice that is antithetical to early literacy experiences and supporting young readers (Israelson, 2014). The karaoke feature, which is sometimes erroneously designed to keep a reader on task and at the right point on the page, actually disrupts fluency; and replacing parents weakens the early bond and positive feeling around socialization and reading. The power of the visual media, including animations, replaces visualization and mental imagery, which has been shown to be powerful in comprehension (Sadoski & Pavio, 2001). One book titled *The Fantastic Flying Books of Mr. Morris Lessmore* (Joyce, 2012) is a traditional text that is extended to video and movie-like visuals when viewed through an iPad app associated with the book; this integration of traditional texts with technology invites children to read simultaneously with viewing the media but also distracts from the book. What is cast as interactive and engaging, also supplants some basic processes proven in comprehension research. Therefore, the negative affordance is that replacing linguistic communication with visual representations promises to negatively impact our time-tested abilities to read longer connected discourse. At the same time, mobile reading of print text is on the increase with 32% of cell phone users 18 years or older reporting that they read books on phones (Zickuhr & Rainie, 2014)

Entertainment

In this large category, a lot of media network "channels" or other streaming media sources have been appified. These provide organized access to information about a show on that network, video clips, video of entire episodes, written synopses,

and extras in which cast members of programs provide background information on episodes. Some provide access to databases of information about the media, including synopses of plots and information about cast members. In the category of entertainment are games or other sorts of "trivialities" (Kosner, 2012). However, as app design, just like web design in its earliest days, becomes less the domain of tech enthusiasts and more in line with knowledge workers designing what they need, more of the app volume will shift to categories that we might now label as productivity and business.

Many apps in this category are solely for pleasure and often include classic video game offerings such as Angry Birds. These games that can be played on devices are not as complex as computer or console-based video games. Video games that have a positive impact on literacy have this effect because of their designers' rigorous involvement in understanding how to motivate and engage users, to immerse them in narratives of virtual worlds, to energize them to use resources and strategies to advance to the next level, and to provide membership with others who share interests and goals in affinity spaces (Gee, 2007; Squire, 2011). Even though most game apps on mobile devices are designed to entertain and pass the time and are not designed to be as sophisticated as games on game consoles, as mobile device processors become more powerful and smart phones more affordable, the gaming industry is moving more and more to mobile devices.

Some apps, like Instagram, Pinterest, or You-Tube produce visuals, such as pictures or videos, as publishable content. Previously, when a person wanted to learn how to install a new product, such as a garbage disposal, or try a new recipe, they would have to read a manual to research how to perform the task. This technical reading would elicit detailed, focused reading that promoted close reading to follow the explanatory steps. These apps now employ pictorials; diagrams and videos that replace the literacy skills previously required to access and understand information.

Popular apps like Twitter serve the main purpose of replacing longer coherent discourse with *textoids* in social media platforms. Historically, a textoid was a short, contrived text overloaded with information and constructed specifically for assessments of comprehension. It was considered a poor representation of reading and writing in the real world of texts. Textoids were not actually found in day-to-day reading. At present, textoids are crucial communications. All of the little digital texts created while texting, tweeting, or writing posts on social networking sites are textoids. Whereas text messages are print-based textoids, SMS are multimodal textoids. Facebook is largely based on publishing textoids. Reading and writing textoids, like the art of texting in general, fragments information from the traditional literacy style of complete sentences, paragraphs, and punctuation while affording instant communication to millions of people.

Lifestyle

Here one finds apps that automate refilling prescriptions, automate shopping at favorite stores while highlighting special discounts and deals, and lead potential real estate buyers to a particular neighborhood by presenting listings on homes before they actually appear in the market—all based on multiple desirability variables that narrow the search. This category includes apps that automate how you select makeup by turning your smartphone into a makeup mirror in which you see what applications of makeup look like. Lifestyle apps facilitate decisions by condensing and providing information before consumers commit to purchases, personal goals, or pursue new interests.

This huge category has subcategories like *Happiness and Well Being* with apps that produce inspirational quotations for each day, access subliminal recordings that enhance learning or improve relaxation. It also includes apps pertaining to things like *Religion and Spirituality*, and *Holidays*, *Weddings* and other Special Occasions.

There are also dating apps integrated with existing social media. Many of these apps encourage more intertextual reading across similar apps when, for instance, shoppers look for deals across various store apps—the power of the app to synthesize this information to avoid the real world practicality of going to one store and reading product information before buying something. To be even more convincing, some of these apps link to important texts on topics written by various experts to lend the app more credibility.

Google Maps and other atlas or mapping apps now have the power to replace navigation guides in cars for free. With voice-guidance and visuals, drivers are liberated from reading Road Atlas maps or written directions to successfully arrive at a destination. Before, the literacy practice of interpreting maps and pinpointing locations required some memorization, step-by-step processes, and the ability to interpret geographical maps through translating verbal and visual directions. This preservation of literacy afforded through maps and directions has been lost due to app technologies that use global positioning systems (GPS) satellites to pinpoint navigation, requiring little engagement from the app user.

Apps that report the weather are growing in popularity as they are updated in real-time. In the past, readers would have to examine the forecast and read a short description in the newspaper that spans the entire day. But now apps provide images that represent the weather and everything is communicated through images and textoids. The predictive nature of traditional printed forecasts, written in a way that would explain weather moments and expectations, is digitally replaced with something like a smiling sun to represent warm temperatures.

Even such an intimate experience as purchasing a house can now be accomplished through apps. Previously homebuyers would develop a relationship with their realtor and digest handouts and packets about houses, neighborhoods, and school districts. Purchasing a house required mentors in the field to guide homebuyers through the challenge of interpreting this vast material. Then, this information would be synthesized to secure the perfect house for a particular buyer. Apps like Zillow now replace the hard work of engaging with literacy practices involved in purchasing a first home with graphs, visuals, and colorful demographics that summarize all of this research on homeownership, houses, and location into fragmented pieces of information. A Zillow app user can scroll through listings of houses and receive these pieces of information that have been stripped of context and pertinent details passively, allowing the app to identify ideal houses.

Apps respond to the trends and needs of consumers. For example, when sports are in season, apps are developed to track the playoffs. Such apps exist for the NFL, World Series, and March Madness. Previously, when teams were playing in a final series, a fan would spend time comparing scores across teams and matching up players with potential points earned to calculate the winner. Groups of sports fans would rally around score sheets performing complex literacy tasks to predict and evaluate which teams were in the lead, or how the fan could stay competitive once their favorite team was eliminated. Social interactions were based on understanding complex sources of information. Now, apps automatically update and refresh themselves, with built in "what-if" scenarios where all users input minimal data to receive the detailed information described above.

Education

What appears under this tag to represent the broad field in which we work? This category includes everything from a listing of iTunes U courses on Apple iOS apps to Apps for Teachers, offering tools from basic work apps like word processing apps, note taking tools, to coursework and student assignment and assessment management tools. Under the subcategory of Preschool and Kindergarten, one can find an amazing menagerie of

apps that attempt to hook parents. For example, one finds apps on everything from helping pre-toddlers learn sounds of animals via kinesthetic and tactile (touching animal images on screen) interactions, building sight vocabulary, apps that present sometimes strange multimodal versions of classic children's books, and approaches to early reading through phonemic awareness and phonics, often applied in ways that defy existing educational practices and research but sell millions of copies of apps to parents. Many of these apps have the potential to undermine literacy instruction and practices used by teachers, or in the case of apps targeting preschoolers, negatively affect their perceptual processing, language development, and engagement before they get to school.

As of yet, it is unclear what sorts of literacy skills and practices are promoted by apps while some traditional reading and writing practices are undermined. Print texts within apps is are often textoids rather than extended discourse. It is clearer, based on work by fellow educators, that app design for education by non-educators can produce some strange approaches to teaching and learning literacy without the benefit of research or knowledge of "best practices." It is also clear that teachers who know best practices submit to the appification and the glitzy multimodal affordances sometimes based on the recommendations from peers, in spite of the questionable approaches apps take (Israelson, 2014). Below, we discuss broadly some of the negative and positive affordances associated with appification of literacy.

CURRENT ISSUES RAISED BY STUDIES: A CLOSER LOOK AT THE AFFORDANCES OF THE APPIFICATION OF LITERACY

As noted, although apps might get us to read *something*, more often, it is unlikely that the something is extended, printed discourse. It is increasingly likely to be an abbreviated versions of traditional print—textoids like text messages and Tweets. Apple Watch Glances and Quick Replies fit into the category, along with a range of slightly more extended texts. With apps, it also more likely that the reading is multimodal rather than purely linguistic. The same is true of writing. The apps for the Apple Watch have features that will replace text and typical written language with haptics and *emoji videos*: Apple brags, "You won't just see and respond to messages, calls, and notification, easily and intuitively. You will actually feel them. With Apple Watch, every exchange is less about reading words on a screen and more about making a genuine connection." (Apple, Inc., 2014). Against the backdrop of a relatively large body of research that clearly defines the challenges of skilled reading of print, literacy is now at turning point where much, and soon most, of students' reading of both informational and narrative texts will occur in digital environments either in apps, e-books, or online.

Although literacy researchers know a lot about reading print, the field is just embarking on research programs involving digital reading that will allow them to complement or supplant what is already known about reading print in general and reading-to-learn in particular (O'Brien, Ortmann, & Rummel, 2014). As just noted, Leu and his colleagues (Leu, 2000; Leu & Kinzer, Leu et al., 2011) have aptly termed this relatively new phase of research *deictic* to acknowledge that these new digital literacies are elusive because they are so rapidly unfolding and evolving. Just when researchers start to figure out a particular digital context and tools that make it possible, and study them, the whole milieu changes. And even if researchers did start to make progress on the optimal skills and strategies needed to read multimodally in what we now call "online" spaces, the shift to apps will present whole new set of challenges.

But what are the features of digital texts with multimodal affordances that distinguish them from print texts? Or, in the case of apps, how do multimodal texts relying more on visual symbols other than alphabetic writing change what is meant by literacy and literacy practices? The chapter now moves to examining these differences to describe the literacy practices needed to read these texts.

1. *Digital texts are increasingly multimodal.* Print occurs with other media in creative juxtapositions, with accompanying links or navigation tools allowing readers to rapidly traverse modalities by linking to pictures, other graphics, and video. As noted, these multimodal texts still include print and require the skills necessary in reading print, but it is likely that the proportion of print text to other media texts will decrease significantly in the immediate future, especially in light of appification. To give an example from the field of education, the key design decisions in creating educational apps will be selecting the balance of modalities to best represent information, position ideas within a conceptual domain, and incorporate ways of engaging learners to maximize their comprehension. It is, currently, unclear even what research agendas can best investigate how appification's multimodal affordances, with portable devices and small viewing areas, will replace or modify our existing theoretical frameworks and notions about how children and youth learn to read and write digitally.

2. *Textoids are replacing longer printed discourse.* We discussed textoids earlier. In online textbooks or course systems, as well as in more recent standalone e-textbooks or e-course apps, the amount of longer print discourse is decreasing as pieces of text are written more concisely or condensed into segments. As noted already, the term *textoid*, which had a negative connotation, is now integral to literacy with apps. Now textoids are taking on a whole new life as integral reading bits presented to more

flexibly introduce print with other media. Textoids extensively abbreviate longer discourse, afford portablilty allowing them to be recursively reconstructed and shared immediately with thousands or even millions of readers.

3. *Portable texts on portable devices are replacing static, standalone texts.* Until relatively recently students bought or rented textbooks and carried them back and forth to school. Even the typical online versions of these books have been merely electronic duplications of the pages using, for example, the .pdf format. But with the more interactive digital reading and writing environments it is increasing likely that readers will assume writers' stances, write responses to existing texts, or write texts in response to things they read, including peer texts and share their texts online (Beach & O'Brien, 2015). Many apps afford this reader-as-writer/writer-as-reader interactivity.

The term portable text eludes a standard definition. Adobe's Portable Document Format (pdf), embodies the original affordance. A document that previously took the form of a printed stack of pages could be turned into an electronic document, an image of the print document that could be easily transported to other formats and across digital space. But the complementary and more compelling affordance is that you can continue to change the document, edit it, embellish it, insert queries into it, annotate it and then send it on. The portable text is evolving as it "travels." It is media that is more spreadable (Jenkins, Ford, & Green, 2013). That is, the digital format and the Internet are technical aspects that enable sharing of ones portable content, but also the cultural shift about the accessibility, ownership, and participatory nature of media mean that a portable texts is more likely be taken up, changed, and redistributed.

These portable texts are already everywhere; look no further than texting and Tweets. And look at how these portable texts appear and are elaborated upon and reconstructed in social networking. Portable texts, like the more commercially written counterparts, are usually textoids rather than longer discourse. But the fact that they are communally constructed, reconstructed, and shared is a huge contrast to static standalone texts that have prevailed for centuries. The other positive affordance is that portable texts can be accessed and changed via portable devices.

4. *Intertexts are becoming the nexus of meaning.* With the increase in appification and textoids and the portability of these texts, for example, short news summaries on an iPad or iPhone, previous theories and frameworks for how readers comprehend what they read will be turned upside down since those theories relate to reading extended print organized in print-centric artifacts like chapters and textbooks (O'Brien, et al. 2014). In traditional notions of reading, emphasis is placed on both the content and authority in single texts. An framework by Beach and O'Brien (2015) discuss the relations among digital reading, reading e-textbooks and texts in apps, as intertextuality and intermediality. Historically, intertextuality considers any print text as part of the larger sociocultural context--the social textuality, from which is was created. Each text is both the absorption of and the transformation of another (Kristeva, 1980). No reader interprets a single text without this broader social textuality and, increasingly, readers are likely to change texts they encounter due to the affordances of new technologies. In the case of reading digital textoids in apps or online, or hyperlinking to texts, linking from print texts to media, and using as-you-go note taking and annotation tools in apps, the notion of intermediality--intertextuality with print and other media, applies.

Understanding and learning are not simply the result of interacting with a single text, or even considering the text within the world of all texts that could have influenced it; rather, the construction of meaning happens from two sources, what Still & Worton (1990) called the double axis of intertexts: new texts enter the intertextual field via authors or via readers. With portable texts in apps, the number of authors and readers could increase almost exponentially. So what a reader learns and understands is more and more likely to be an intertextual composite rather than as something represented in a single text. Put more technically, an individual app user's understanding in this multimodal space, is the integrative, and transformative construction she or he makes from all of the multimodal texts, print, visual, video--read in the learning space (an e-book, an online site, an experience across sites) and interjects into the textual field based on her or his total textual experience. The learning ramifications of this intermedial transformation are huge.

The days of delving into a single, linear text are not gone, but may be on the wane. The key to reading proficiently henceforth is more likely to be the ability to read intertextually via textoids, to integrate understanding, across apps, web pages or sites, across e-textbook pages and media spaces, and to construct a new permanent representation via multimodal intertexts (van Meter & Firetto, 2008). Put another way, reading proficiently, during the actual intermedial reading is the ability to maintain a coherent multimodal intertextual loop (Hayes-Roth & Thorndyke, 1979; van Meter & Firetto, 2008) building on one's knowledge and understanding, and organizing that knowledge, as one reads from text to text across modalities. The literacy proficiency needed to do this kind of reading is so new, and readers have so little practice at it, that it unfolding as the appification of literacy develops.

5. *Digital texts are situated and participatory.* An important aspect of so-called new literacy studies (NLS) (Gee, 1990) is that reading, as

well as writing and any other literate enactment, is a socially situated practice (Barton, 1994; Barton, Hamilton, & Ivanic, 2000; Gee, 1996) and is automatically linked to the social institutions and power relations that sustain it. A text, then, is both an artifact of a practice that created it and a dynamic component of a situated practice in which it is read. A chapter in a biology book represents officially approved, "scientifically based" research and accumulated knowledge synthesized and reported, in an officially approved and adopted textbook that is aligned to a school district's standards.

These "official knowledge" texts (Apple, 1993) used in school comprise the bulk of what has been the key artifact of school curricula--textbooks. In reading traditional textbooks, both teachers and students have implicitly agreed to one take on an immense, complex knowledge domain through one textual lens. Against the backdrop of this institutionalized notion of reading, depending on the teacher, the lesson structure, the social dynamics of collaborative groups and the purposes and activities aligned with the reading, the practice of reading a text can be a very rich experience that varies across settings. Appified, digital reading, portable texts, and intermediality all question and critique the idea that officially represented knowledge is enough or even possible when readers and writers-as-participants constantly construct new texts and modify existing texts, transforming printed renditions into multimodal forms.

6. *E-book affordances enhance learning.* There are positive digital affordances of e-books not available with print texts that can serve to enhance learning (Gleeson, 2012). Readers can bookmark and highlight sections of a book for later reference and sharing with others. They can then annotate highlighted sections to create a repository of these annotations as well as share these annotations

with others. They can search a text for certain words or topics linked to outside reference texts such as Wikipedia, as well as look up word definitions. And, in using PDF files, they can share and store files using a range of cloud services as well as employ different annotation tools.

Within five years, the features of digital texts and digital reading will be at the forefront of curriculum planning in school districts and, hopefully, factor strongly into how educators assess students' proficiencies in school. These features and the processes they engender will also be the topic of a lot of exciting research. Research on the use of app-based media in broader society, and how these practices impact children, youth, and adults, and youth, as well as adults, are already underway in projects such as the *Pew Internet and American Life Project*.

GAPS IN THE EXTANT RESEARCH: THE APPS GENERATION IN THE INSTITUTION OF THE SCHOOL

Prior to the integration of apps into our daily lives, in the conduct of daily tasks, we often engaged in challenging literacy tasks to learn information needed to do jobs, to shop, to learn how to use things. As noted, apps have increasingly streamlined and simplified many tasks that required more involved literacy practices by supplanting the traditional practices involved in things like doing research, technical reading, and engaging in formal communication. Depending on both your progression into the landscape of apps and the degree of recent nostalgia you have for traditional artifacts of literacy like magazines and books, this appification of literacy no longer affords the types of engagement and immersion in daily literacy practices that we once had. But to what extent do educational goals and school policies reflect or work against the appification in the broader world?

Currently, 43 states have adopted the Common Core State Standards (CCSS) for English Language Arts which aim to prepare students for the literacy skills required in the 21st century (National Governors Association Center [NGA Center] for Best Practices & Council of Chief State School Officers [CCSSO], 2010). Simultaneously, many schools are adopting technology tools and policies intended to enhance literacy engagement in the intersection of literacy technologies and the CCSS. With so many processes automated or bypassed by apps in the broader culture, as a global society, we will question the importance of schooled knowledge as it has been traditionally defined in school curricula--most of it print-based and organized in textbooks. Is it more important to construct deep understanding by reading, writing, and discussing within and around textbooks? Or is it simply more efficient to access app-abbreviated information as needed?

Following is a question recently posed by Williamson (2013): What is the future of the curriculum in the digital age? He notes that one view of curriculum sees the school curriculum as a microcosm of what is important in wider society-- "what it elects to remember about its past, what it believes about its present, what it hopes and desires for its future" (p. 2-3). Consider the popularized terms like *touch-of-a-finger, global information access, learning in the mediashpere,* or *multimodality*; then consider that large transnational tech companies (e.g., Google, Apple, Microsoft) with large amounts of capital, provide access to information *and* define the forms that it will take. Also consider that these companies have education programs, designed to define school curricula that they believe will keep up with rapidly changing educational innovations. Apps and portable devices will encompass and embody that goal. And literacy practices defined by or supportive of these apps will eventually predominate in what will become the educational curriculum.

In contrast to the apps that smartphone users have downloaded most often, are apps that are explicitly employed for the purpose of learning in educational settings. Many schools are adopting technology tools and policies intended to enhance literacy engagement in the classroom. Adopting technology leads to apps often being used in classrooms for individual and collaborative learning opportunities. With the purpose of supporting learning, these apps can diverge from the purposes and platforms of the socially popular apps listed above.

In conjunction with the Common Core State Standards (CCSS) being adopted by forty-three states, there is concern for the technology to align with the standards' goals. The English Language Arts standards aim to prepare students for the literacy skills required in the 21st century (National Governors Association Center [NGA Center] for Best Practices & Council of Chief State School Officers [CCSSO], 2010). As discussed at length above, the literacy skills of the 21st century are currently being redefined based on persons' interactions with the multimodal platforms.

The current issues in the field are that schools are adopting both CCSS and technology practices and policies with the goal of enhancing literacy—or using literacy to support learning. A key unaddressed question is whether these practices and their supporting policies enhance educational literacy practices, and whether these two adjacent sets of policies can be simultaneously implemented. Educators must navigate a balance of implementing the Common Core literacy standards and technology, which can lead to new classroom learning dynamics.

There is not a Common Core Literacy Standard that directly promotes or encourages the use of technology or media (Dalton, 2012). However, implicit in the CCSS goal "to prepare all students for success in college, career, and life" (CCSS, 2010, www.corestandards.org) is to ensure students are knowledgeable and comfortable operating technology and media to successfully navigate their future endeavors. Therefore, the standards can complement both technological and print literacy practices depending on the school's technology policy, the teacher's self-efficacy in teaching through both print and multimodal resources, and how accessible technology is for the particular school population.

Because the CCSS can be implemented in both print-based and media-based classrooms, defining acceptable literacy practices is left to the discretion of educational stakeholders. Standards and assessments do not necessarily provide guidance to help educators prepare kids for the multimodal world of apps outside of school and reading visual media. What the CCSS do call for, though, is preserving traditional notions of text and literacy practices. Unlike the appification of our social literacy practices, the CCSS attempt to maintain traditional literacy practices. If students are prepared to navigate more challenging text and literacy interactions, then these skills should translate to multimodal platforms and apps.

The CCSS Literacy Standards underscore the importance of close reading, promoting and reading nonfiction texts, and synthesizing information across multiple texts. These literacy skills and strategies represent the type of automatized process that apps are now preforming for readers. The CCSS supports these three literacy practices as representations of the types of skills and strategies citizens supposedly need to be successful today and in the future. Each literacy skill and strategy will be briefly examined, and then an educational app that supports this type of literacy will be discussed to estimate whether traditional literacy practices can in fact support the social literacy practices that are currently so prevalent in society. Do students benefit from the aims of the CCSS in promoting and teaching traditional literacy practices?

Close reading has been one of the most discussed topics since the publication and adoptions of the CCSS. For example, under the subheading "Key Ideas and Details" the CCSS documents states that students are expected to "read closely to determine what the text says explicitly and to make logical inferences from it; and cite specific textual evidence when writing or speaking to support conclusion drawn from the text" (CCSS, 2010, www.corestandards.org, p. 35). The importance of being able to refer directly to the text to find answers, or information, is a critical skill according to the CCSS. As previously mentioned, prior to the appification of literacy, reading closely for details was a valuable skill in ensuring correct directions or understanding technical manuals. The CCSS still uphold the traditional literacy practice of close reading.

There are several educational apps that support the traditional notion of close reading and help students meet the aims of the CCSS. For example, the iPad app Subtext allows a teacher to enhance an e-text with their own commentary, which can include questions regarding the text, vocabulary assistance, or a link to YouTube video. By utilizing Subtext's interactive reading experience, teachers can model how close reading should be accomplished during the reading task. This way, readers are supported as they begin to define close reading for themselves with an expert reader guiding their initial attempts at navigate challenging texts. Being able to support literacy at the exact moment a reader experiences crisis is a positive affordance of education applications such as Subtext. Another Web 2.0 site that is similar is activelylearn.com, the name of which implies the interactive process that helps build and maintain close reading skills.

The CCSS emphasize reading informational texts (Gewertz, 2012) more than educational policy in the past. Due to relatively recent educational research that has demonstrated the lack of exposure to nonfiction texts in school (Duke, 2004), informational texts have been predominant in the K-12 curriculum. Therefore, the CCSS promotes more exposure to nonfiction texts in hopes that this will prepare students for the literacy demands of college and the workplace. Accessing timely and specific nonfiction texts is easier through digital devices, especially when context should be provided to enhance the nonfiction text.

Apps such as Pocket or Flipboard allow students to save material on the web to access later offline. Apps that allow students to access material offline may help equalize who has access to nonfiction texts outside of the classroom. Also, providing an offline option allows students longer amounts of time to digest and navigate complex informational texts. Educational apps can help teachers collect a wide variety of nonfictional sources, organize them in the most effective way for the content to be delivered, and help students navigate multiple sources. The app Learnist allows teachers to create file folders of interactive information such as TedTalks, instructional videos, historic speeches, website excerpts, and multimodal presentations to assist students in exploring nonfictional texts in a structured way. Navigating nonfiction texts, whether historic or contemporary, can feel intimidating as source documents are often challenging texts. Through apps such as Learnist, teachers can support students in their initial investigations of nonfictional texts that will allow students to gain confidence as they explore knowledge across texts, modes, and sources to compare and contrast information.

The complex skill of synthesizing information has become automated by apps. No longer does an individual have to personally examine all characteristics of a home for purchase, as apps and Web 2.0 tools already complete comparisons and data collection for the consumer. As apps afford less personalized investment in synthesizing material, readers loose the ability to read and compile knowledge across multiple sources. The CCSS aim to strengthen the skill of synthesizing material across multiple texts to encourage students to identify key concepts and critique multiple perspectives.

Apps and Internet tools such as Evernote and Notability help with the written aspect of synthesizing material. Evernote and Notability are accessible online and through devices, which allow for students to access their notes through multiple platforms. Evernote communicates across devices, so notes from your phone and computer are synced automatically, while Notability syncs with Gmail or Dropbox easily. Allowing students to keep track of their written notes, thoughts, and connections as they read texts supports the skill of synthesizing information in a multimodal, technological world.

Gaps and Directions for Future Research

As noted, schools are increasingly embracing the idea of apps and tablet devices, but there is little systematic connection between using the new technologies and improving literacy or learning in general (Murphy, 2014). Standardized assessments that are used, and will continue to be used, do not tap the new literacies that students are learning via apps and working in digital spaces; and we still lack adequate assessments of competency with digital new literacies (Leu, Kinzer, Coiro, Castek, & Henry, 2013). Hence, there will continue to be a disconnect between the situated literacy practices supported by apps generally and literacy skills taught in school.

And even the progress Leu and colleagues (2013) have made on defining online reading processes and assessing online reading and other new literacies cannot keep up with the rapidly morphing genres of apps which, as we have noted, are replacing web pages. And with the proliferation of apps, it is hard to predict what kinds of literacy to study. Leu and his colleagues note that new literacies rarely find their way into the standard language arts curriculum because we have yet to keep up with the dynamic way they are changing literacy and unable to match assessments geared toward them with proficiency in practices like reading and writing. So new literacies, via apps and tablet devices, Chromebooks, or similar devices are add-ons, rather than an integral part

of the school curriculum. What is more, many of the commercial apps are neither designed by educators nor based on "best practices" supported by research. There are few guaranteed approaches to selecting quality apps that promote literacy in school (Israelson, 2014).

In spite of the rapid appification of the broader culture, school curricula are still largely based on single textbooks and standardized, high-stakes assessments tap skills mapped onto standards that position literacy as more of an autonomous set of skills (Street, 1984) than as socially and culturally-situated practices. Apps for everyday use are exemplars of new literacies; hence they are fit more to what Street (1984) defines as ideological literacies, drawing on and helping to construct situated literacies practices fit to specific daily tasks, work, and entertainment choices in the broader culture.

A recent study found that digital content represents about 42 percent of the non-hardware ed-tech market, up from 36 percent in 2010-11 (Herold, 2014). But with the Common Core Standards tied to assessments, just like they have done with commercial print curricula, digital curricula for schools are mapped onto the standards and publishers produce what the education market demands. The trend, as predicted, is that digital media and apps in school produced by commercial publishers will be fit more to the status quo of standards and assessments than to the kinds of situated literacy practices evolving in the world of apps outside of education that take advantage of the unique affordances of digital media and digital spaces. That said, there are both education-specific and more general apps that can and are being used in education and these have transformative potential (Beach & O'Brien, 2015)

Apple's promotional video for iBooks textbooks released in 2012, inspired teachers to talk about what engages them with teaching and learning and, most importantly, what engages students. The teachers doing testimonials in the promotional video quickly segue to the downside of traditional textbooks: Textbooks are outdated, static, expensive, and subject to adoption cycles that restrict the currency of students' knowledge and teachers' creativity. And, also, the books are heavy. They weigh down students' backpacks and most parents have read or heard reports about how these backpacks will cause orthopedic problems that start with first graders carrying backpacks almost bigger than them. The Apple video teachers go one step further and note that because of the weight of the backpack, students might just stop using the books because of their disdain for carrying them around.

But where are we with the appification of school textbooks? In tapping the huge textbook market, Apple has done what all critics of traditional textbooks have done, long before the availability of e-textbook authoring tools like iBooks Author. Since the existence of textbooks specifically tailored to instruction, educators have commented on how disengaging they are and how teachers use them selectively and often bypass them with lecture, recitations, and similar discourse (Alvermann & Moore, 1991; Wade & Moje, 2000; Moje, Stockdill, Kim, & Kim, 2011). Ever since computer labs appeared in schools in the 1980s educators have had a vision of replacing print with other media, or at least using variations of print juxtaposed with other "richer" media. Textbooks have persisted, and will persist for some time, surely longer than they should, because the books are the very core of the institutionalized notion of what a curriculum is, how it is organized, and how teachers should think about the topical domains they teach. Most of the blogs and podcasts that have focused on both commercial education publishers' and tech companies' forays into education have noted that textbook publishers are also a huge industry controlled by relatively few larger companies, most of which apparently have already negotiated some agreements with Apple.

Ultimately, and likely sooner than later because of iPads and other tablet devices, or the large array of "ultrabook" notebook computers, traditional print textbooks, the centuries old artifacts of teaching and learning, will fade away. They will be replaced by multimodal platforms in the form of apps. But right now those apps share some of the disengaging features of textbooks, introduce some new features that have negative affordances related to learning, and struggle to organize complex school curricula (Beach & O'Brien, 2015).

But the question that we must address globally is not so much the political or economic implications of the disappearance of the traditional textbook industry, but the implications its replacement has for student engagement and learning. Almost everything we think of when we envision *textbooks* will be transformed into something else. Among many affordances promised by multimodal texts in apps are these: (a) fast fluid navigation; (b) beautiful graphics; and (c) a better and easier way to take notes and use those notes. These are the most currently publicized set of affordances designed into e-textbooks because the designers could design with the features given the technology available. But do these features, in and of themselves, make the multimodal texts more educationally sound or more engaging?

On the surface, it seems like a no-brainer that "fast fluid" navigation is a huge advantage. But to what extent does the ability to rapidly navigate out of where you are currently studying something in print, or focused deeply on slowly reading a piece of complex print text, also afford some negatives like taking your perceptual span and your brain away from what you were engaging with? We have to keep in mind that print texts, as linear presentations of content, also used built-in features to engage students with difficult concepts (e.g., topic signaling, vocabulary support, marginal glossing) and controlling navigation to the next page.

We can all agree that beautiful graphics are important and something that traditional print texts do not support as well as e-Books. But there is research about the positive and negative app affordance with regard to the types and placement of graphics or other visual elements in relation to print (Beach & O'Brien, 2015). Again, if a reader is concentrating on an important or difficult piece of text, to what degree can the attention and engagement needed to deeply comprehend it be jeopardized by an engaging graphic or other visual element like a video?

Finally, availability and highlighting and note taking/annotation tools in a range of apps in both iOS and android operating systems is particularly important. Since highlighting and note taking are taken as time-tested studying techniques, most people assume that if tools are available that make them more accessible, that students will learn more with them. But research indicates clearly that the use of study approaches like highlighting and note taking with traditional texts, require instruction about the texts, instruction in procedures based on texts and learners' goals, guided practice at processing text with the study tools, and individual practice for students to use the tools more effectively independently (Anderson & Armbruster, 1984; Bohay, Blakely, Tamplin, & Radvansky, 2011). If they are so easy and available, could it be that students will halt the fluency of their reading by stopping to highlight or write notes? Or that they will rely more on a possible overabundance of highlights ineffectively executed or copious notes that do not reflect the importance levels of topics in a text?

RECOMMENDATIONS/ IMPLICATIONS FOR EDUCATION AND CIVIC ENGAGEMENT

There is an increased tendency that application interfaces, either standalone applications or those connected to web page back ends, are referred to as apps. A primary focus of marketing cell phones and data plans is the apps, and apps epitomize progress in our mobile, digital, multimodal world. However, it is apparent that as we make progress, we also take steps backward in terms of how literacy is used to support communication and learning. It seems that for every positive affordance of the appification of society, there is an equally important negative affordance that reminds us that progress in appification takes something away from what we traditionally and almost romantically define as literate engagement as it is historically situated in print and the life of the book.

Scholars in education and related fields have negatively critiqued the way schools have adopted autonomous models of literacy in the traditional curriculum. The hope, among educationists in general, is that schools, as they increasingly use apps, will realize more synchronicity with the broader digital, multimodal society and teach students to proficiently use the technologies that are now part of day-to-day life in technically developed societies. Instead, schools have either resisted the appification, sticking with traditional print-centric curricula, or have leaned toward commercially designed apps that actually reinforce autonomous literacy skills and standards that originate within the print-centric status quo.

The appification of the broader societies of technologically advanced parts of the globe, have moved more toward an ideological position with hundreds of thousands of apps used to meet specific socially situated needs and to support literacy practices needed to live from day-to-day and engage in work and related tasks and support certain lifestyles. However, the institution of the school and formal education has used appification to mostly support the status quo by automating the acquisition of skills and mapping instruction on standards.

REFERENCES

Alvermann, D. E., & Moore, D. W. (1991). Secondary school reading. In R. Barr, M. L. Kamil, P. Mosenthal, & P. D. Pearson (Eds.), *Handbook of reading research* (Vol. 2, pp. 951–983). New York: Longman.

American Dialect Society. (2011). *"App" 2010 Word of the Year, as voted by the American Dialect Society*. Retrieved December 8, 2014, from http://www.americandialect.org/American-Dialect-Society-2010-Word-of-the-Year-PRESS-RELEASE

Anderson, J., & Rainie, L. (2014). *The Internet of things will thrive by 2025*. Washington, DC: Pew Research Center's Internet and American Life Project.

Anderson, T. H., & Armbruster, B. B. (1984). Studying. In P. D. Pearson, R. Barr, M. L. Kamil, & P. Mosenthal (Eds.), *Handbook of Reading Research* (pp. 657–679). New York: Longman.

Apple, M. W. (1993). *Official knowledge: Democratic education in a conservative age*. New York: Routledge.

Apple, Inc. (2015). *Ad: Apple Watch Features*. Retrieved January 15, 2015 from https://www.apple.com/in/watch/features/

Barton, D. (1994). *Literacy: An introduction to the ecology of written language*. Cambridge, MA: Blackwell.

Barton, D., & Hamilton, M. (2000). Literacy practices. In D. Barton, M. Hamilton, & R. Ivanic (Eds.), *Situated Literacies: Reading and writing in context* (pp. 7–15). London: Routledge.

Beach, R., & O'Brien, D. (2015). *Using apps for learning across the curriculum: A literacy-based framework and guide*. New York: Routledge.

Bohay, M., Blakely, D. P., Tamplin, A. K., & Radvansky, G. A. (2011). Note taking, review, memory, and comprehension. *The American Journal of Psychology*, *124*(1), 63–73. doi:10.5406/amerjpsyc.124.1.0063 PMID:21506451

Common Core State Standards Initiative. (2010). Common core standards for English language arts & literacy in history/social studies, science, and technical subjects. Washington, DC: Council of Chief State School Officers (CCSSO).

Dalton, B. (2012). Multimodal composition and the common core state standards. *The Reading Teacher*, *66*(4), 333–339. doi:10.1002/TRTR.01129

Duke, N. K. (2004). The case for informational text. *Educational Leadership*, *61*(6), 40–45.

Elgan, M. (2015). Here comes the Internet of self. *Computerworld*. Retrieved January 14, 2015 from http://www.computerworld.com/article/2867234/here-comes-the-internet-of-self.html

eMarketer. (2014). *Smartphone Users Worldwide will Total 1.73 Billon*. Retrieved November 10, 2014 from http://www.emarketer.com/Article/Smartphone-Users-Worldwide-Will-Total-175-Billion-2014/1010536

Gee, J. P. (1990). *Social linguistics and literacies: Ideology in discourses*. Bristol, PA: Falmer.

Gee, J. P. (1996). *Social linguistic and literacies: Ideology in discourses* (2nd ed.). Bristol, PA: Taylor & Francis.

Gee, J. P. (2007). *What video games have to teach us about literacy and learning* (2nd ed.). New York: Palgrave Macmillan.

Gewertz, C. (2012). Districts Gear up for Shift to Informational Texts. *Education Digest: Essential Readings Condensed for Quick Review*, *78*(1), 10–14.

Gibson, J. J. (1986). *The ecological approach to visual perception*. New York: Taylor & Francis Group.

Gleeson, M. (2012). *iPads (or other devices) and literature circles – co-starring Edmodo*. Mr. G Online. Retrieved April 7, 2012 from http://mgleeson.edublogs.org/2012/04/03/ipads-and-literature-circles

Hamilton, P. F. (2012). *Great north road*. New York: Del Rey.

Hayes-Roth, B., & Thorndyke, P. H. (1979). Integration of knowledge from text. *Journal of Verbal Learning and Verbal Behavior*, *18*(1), 91–108. doi:10.1016/S0022-5371(79)90594-2

Herold, B. (2014, June 9). 2014). Digital content providers ride the wave of rising revenues. *Education Week*, 14–15.

Israelson, M. (2014). *A Study of Teachers' Integration of App Affordances and Early Literacy Best Practices*. (Unpublished doctoral dissertation). University of Minnesota, Minneapolis, MN.

Jenkins, H., Ford, S., & Green, J. (2013). *Spreadable media: Creating value and meaning in a networked culture*. New York: New York University Press.

Kosner, A. W. (2012). *The Appification of everything will transform the world's 360 million web sites*. Retrieved August 22, 2014 from http://www.forbes.com/sites/anthonykosner/2012/12/16/forecast-2013-the-appification-of-everything-will-turn-the-web-into-an-app-o-verse/

Kristeva, J. (1980). *Desire in language: A semiotic approach to literature and art*. New York: Columbia University Press.

Leu, D. J. (2000). Literacy and technology: Deictic consequences for literacy education in an information age. In M. L. Kamil, P. Mosenthal, & R. Barr (Eds.), Handbook of Reading Research (vol. 3). Mahwah, NJ: Lawrence Erlbaum.

Leu, D. J. Jr, & Kinzer, C. K. (2000). The convergence of literacy instruction with networked technologies for information and communication. *Reading Research Quarterly*, *35*(1), 108–127. doi:10.1598/RRQ.35.1.8

Leu, D. J., Kinzer, C. K., Coiro, J., Castek, J., & Henry, L. A. (2013). New literacies: A dual-level theory of the changing nature of literacy instruction, and assessment. In D. E. Alvermann, N. J. Unrau, & R. Ruddell (Eds.), *Theoretical Models and Processes of Reading* (pp. 1150–1181). Newark, DE: International Reading Association. doi:10.1598/0710.42

Leu, D. J., McVerry, G. W., O'Byrne, I., Kiili, C., & Zawilinski, L., Everett-Cacopardo, Kennedy, C., & Forzani, E. (2011). The new literacies of online reading comprehension: Expanding the literacy and learning curriculum. *Journal of Adolescent & Adult Literacy*, *55*(1), 5–14.

Mitra, S. (2013). Beyond the hole in the wall: A Q&A with 2013 TED Prize Winner. *TED Blog*. Retrieved January 15, 2015 from http://blog.ted.com/2013/03/04/before-the-hole-in-the-wall-a-qa-with-2013-ted-prize-winner-sugata-mitra/

Moje, E. B., Stockdill, D., Kim, K., & Kim, H.-j. (2011). *The role of text in disciplinary learning The Handbook of Reading Research* (Vol. 4, pp. 453–486). New York: Routledge.

Murphy, M. E. (2014, August). Why some schools are selling their iPads. *The Atlantic*. Accessed Oct 15, 2014 from http://www.theatlantic.com/education/archive/2014/08/whats-the-best-device-for-interactive-learning/375567/

O'Brien, D., Ortmann, L., & Rummel, A. (2014). *Disciplinary Literacies: Beyond the Print-Centric Era*. Paper presented at the Annual Meeting, Literacy Research Association, Marco Island, FL.

Perez, S. (2014). *iTunes App Store now has 1.2 Million apps, has 75 billion downloads to date*. Retrieved on October 10, 2014 from http://techcrunch.com/2014/06/02/itunes-app-store-now-has-1-2-million-apps-has-seen-75-billion-downloads-to-date/

Sadoski, M., & Paivio, A. (2001). *Imagery and text: A dual coding theory of reading and writing*. Mahwah, NJ: Lawrence Erlbaum Associates.

Salz. (2014). The Importance of "Push" in the App Age. *eContent Magazine*. Accessed Jan 25, 2015 at http://www.econtentmag.com/Articles/Column/Agile-Minds/The-Importance-of-Push-in-the-App-Age-99018.htm

Squire, K. (2011). Designed cultures. In C. SteinKuehler, K. Squire & S. Barab (Eds.), Games, learning, and society learning and meaning in the digital age (pp. 10-31). New York: Cambridge University Press.

Statista. (2014). *Number of smartphone users in the US from 2010 to 2018*. Retrieved October 22, 2014 from http://www.statista.com/statistics/201182/forecast-of-smartphone-users-in-the-us/

Still, J., & Worton, M. (1990). Introduction. In M. Worton & J. Still (Eds.), *Intertextuality: Theories and Practice* (pp. 1–44). Manchester, UK: Manchester University Press.

Street, B. V. (1984). *Literacy in theory and practice*. Cambridge, UK: Cambridge University Press.

van Meter, P. N., & Firetto, C. (2008). Intertextuality and the study of new literacies. In J. Coiro, M. Knobel, C. Lankshear, & D. J. Leu (Eds.), *Handbook of Research on New Literacies* (pp. 1079–1092). New York: Lawrence Erlbaum.

Wade, S. E., & Moje, E. B. (2000). The role of text in classroom learning. In M. L. Kamil, P. B. Mosenthal, P. D. Pearson, & R. Barr (Eds.), *Handbook of reading research* (Vol. 3, pp. 609–627). Mahwah, NJ: Lawrence Erlbaum.

Williamson, B. (2013). *The future of the curriculum: School knowledge in the digital age* (M. Press, Ed.). Cambridge, MA: John D. and Catherine T. MacArthur Foundation.

KEY TERMS AND DEFINITIONS

App: A program that runs on a mobile device or interfaces a Web site to a mobile device. Native apps are programs that run on a mobile device's operating system and reside there. Web apps are Internet-enabled apps that are on mobile devices but can also be accessed via a mobile device or computer browser.

Appification: The replacement of Websites and Web pages with programs that run on mobile operating systems and mobile devises. With appification instead of the Web being a user's primary user interface, it becomes an underlying service layer for apps, which become the new user interface.

App-o-Verse: A reference to the digital world in which an increasing use of apps will replace Websites.

Common Core State Standards: A set of standard constructed by representatives of states, via the National Governors Association (NGA) Center for Best Practices and the Council of Chief State School Officers (CCSSO) including governors and state commissioners of education. The standards are intended to provide more consistency across the US states in education standards.

Digital Literacies: The literacy practices needed to be successful in working with digital tools and in digital spaces, including reading and writing digital texts, understanding how to understand and use online information, and use apps.

Multimodality: A reference to the use of various ways to construct and communicate using print, visual, auditory, or even performance modes in combinations. Although the term if often associated with digital modes, it has also been used to distinguish between print and other visual modes that appear in genres like graphic novels.

Portable Texts: A document that previously took the form of a printed stack of pages that is now in a digital format an digitally transportable. For example a portable document file (pdf) is an image of a print document that could be easily transported to other formats and across digital space. An equally important affordance of these documents is that you can continue to change the document, edit it, embellish it, insert queries into it, annotate it and then send it on. The portable text is evolving as it "travels."

Chapter 18

New and Strange Sorts of Texts:
The Shaping and Reshaping of Digital and Multimodal Books and Young Adult Novels

Melanie Kittrell Hundley
Vanderbilt University, USA

Teri Holbrook
Georgia State University, USA

ABSTRACT

Dennis Baron (1999) writes about the impact of digital technology on literacy practices and thus is a good exemplar for considering how communication technologies are changing the ways in which stories are told. In this chapter, we argue that young adult literature authors and readers are currently in what Baron terms an inventive stage as they devise new ways of producing storied texts. Young adult authors, aware of their readers as avid, exploring, and savvy tech users, experiment with text formats to appeal to readers growing up in a digital "participatory culture" (Jenkins, Purushotma, Weigel, Clinton & Robins, 2009). In a cultural climate where the very notion of what constitutes a book is changing, our chapter responds to Baron's (2009) claim that readers and writers are in the process of "[learning] to trust a new technology and the new and strange sorts of texts that it produces" (p. x).

For many of us, the computer revolution came long ago, and it has left its mark on the way we do things with words.

(Baron, 2009, p. 15)

Books as cultural tools are part of the shaping and reshaping of cultures and the stories those cultures tell. Recent changes in communication technologies have raised the alarm that *the book* as a format is in danger. Readers accustomed to the terse prose of Tweets and the speedy delivery of ebooks to their tablets, the worry goes, may

DOI: 10.4018/978-1-4666-8310-5.ch018

lose interest in the long form of literary prose. However, the book per se is not as fragile and unchangeable as many fear; books have already proven that they can both cause and survive cultural shifts. In observing the power and resilience of the book, Richard Nash (2014) pointed out

Books withstood the disruption of new modes of storytelling—the cinema, the TV set. And books have been the disruptor themselves many times, disrupting the Roman Church and upending the French aristocracy, the medieval medical establishment, then the nineteenth-century medical establishment. (para. 35)

Thus, as Nash asserted, the tensions surrounding contemporary developing communication technologies and their ongoing influence on the shape and form of the book echo the tensions expressed in previous moments of cultural change.

Two videos, both available on YouTube at the time of this chapter's writing, demonstrate this current moment of cultural tension surrounding the book. The first video, a piece of Norwegian sketch comedy originally broadcast in 2001 called "The Medieval Helpdesk" (NRK, 2007), shows a befuddled monk seeking expert advice on how to use the new technology of the codex. He expresses delight and frustration as he labors to understand the page-turning functions of the unfamiliar format. The second video, a more recent ad by Ikea (Ikea Singapore, 2014), features a serene speaker explaining the ease of use of the company's paper-and-ink catalog, referred to as not an iBook or an ebook but as a "bookbook."

The popularity of both videos (YouTube views combined are in excess of 20 million) points to the contested present in which practitioners of the book form--both readers and makers--find themselves. The videos' humor hinges on the ongoing anxious relationship between the book community and the technolog(ies) at its creative disposal. In the 2001 "Medieval Helpdesk" video, social satirists reflected the helplessness readers

felt towards perplexing new digital formats and related practices (D'Arcens, 2014); in the 2014 Ikea work, marketers tapped into a perceived consumer nostalgia for the out-of-fashion process of turning a page. In less than 15 years, readers went from bewildered babes in the woods to wistful old hands.

But while readers and writers today are increasingly turning to portable technology for the consumption and distribution of texts, discussions within book communities over the nature and role of the book in the digital era are by no means settled. Instead, they continue to intensify. At the heart of the discussion is the very structure of texts and modes of content in the digital age and, as a result, the qualities and types of experiences available to readers and writers. Print-based books, by the nature of their physical make-up, are predominantly linear, ordered, and bounded while digital and electronic texts--which feature multimodal communication and linking capabilities--can be multi-sensory, changeable, impermanent, flexible, and unbounded. Creators, academics, publishers, and users wrestle with this overarching problem: Given that the book form is a technology that directs extensive aspects of human experience, what are the effects when that technology is radically altered, when the components of "bookness" are profoundly disrupted? Said differently, what happens when the structure of the book, which Marshall McLuhan (1960) argued was responsible for human constructs ranging from the assembly line to romantic love, is displaced by newer technologies of knowledge? Underlying these concerns is an even more daunting inquiry: If, since its inception, the technology of the book has guided how humans make knowledge, then how can the features of digital communication technology support humans "to begin to think differently" (McLuhan, 1960) and what repercussions might that thinking differently bring?

The scope of these questions is vast, which perhaps adds to the current jitteriness of the discussion. Dennis Baron (2009) comfortingly reminds us that we are in the process of learning to "trust" these emerging communication technologies and the "new and strange sorts of texts" (p. x) made possible by them. In this chapter, we start by looking at some of the tensions surrounding the impact of digital technologies on the book format and how those tensions might be framed within stages of technological development. We give an overview of early electronic literature as a response on the part of authors wanting to experiment with what new literacy technologies make possible. Recognizing the impact of Internet and computer use on young people, we position readers of young adult (YA) literature as integral to literary experimentation taken up by creators of YA novels seeking to engage and respond to their Internet-fluent audience. We will look at how such text-related trends as transmedia and user-developed content point to the need for research, particularly educational research, to inform practices around the cultivation of students as text participants (Jenkins, Purushotma, Weigel, Clinton, & Robison, 2009). Finally, we will examine conversations around standards and policy that suggest educators can create generous spaces of learning that include young adult literature and digital media so that students can participate in and eventually lead this present technological moment.

WHAT IS A SUCCINCT OVERVIEW OF THE RESEARCH?

Stages of Communication Technologies

We find it useful to view the changes impacting notions of the book and other textual formats through Baron's (1999) stages of literacy and communication technologies. Baron argued that with new technology, "we are thrown into excitement and confusion as we try it on, try it out, reject it, and then adapt it to our lives—and, of course, adapt our lives to it" (p. 16). He posited that literacy technologies go through similar stages of development, whether they involve making marks in clay or displaying pixels on a screen: the stages of invention, accessibility, function, and authentication.

High costs and small numbers of early adopters usually mark the beginning invention stage of new communication technologies, when "practitioners keep [the technology] to themselves...either on purpose or because nobody else has any use for it" (Baron, 1999, p. 16). After periods of relatively exclusive use, this "priestly" class adapts and mediates the technology so that it becomes more generally functional, primarily by presenting the technology as similar to existing communication practices. Costs drop, and as the public recognizes the usefulness of the technology, they respond by developing new literacy practices. "Only then does the technology come into its own, no longer imitating the previous forms given us by the earlier communication technology, but creating new forms and new possibilities for communication" (p. 16). As the practices associated with the new forms become prevalent, the technology undergoes an authentication stage, where segments within a given society negotiate appropriate use and work to establish trustworthiness of the technology by combatting fraud and other illegal operations.

As an example, Baron (1999) used the pencil. Early pencil production involved "proprietary secrets as closely guarded as any Macintosh code" (p. 18) and required increasingly fine-tuned experimentation in lead mixtures, wood selections, production equipment, extrusion processes, and finishing elements, such as built-in erasers and painted exteriors. Over the 250-year course of its development, "the humble wood pencil...developed from a curiosity of use to cabinet-makers, artists and note-takers into a tool so universally employed for writing that we seldom give it any thought" (p. 18). As part of the pencil's incorporation into social use, users experimented with it, making decisions about where it was useful and trustworthy (e.g., in schools) and where it was not (e.g., in legal documents).

Like pencils, Baron (1999) argued, computers went through their invention and "priestly" stages when only a few used them, but their access and functionality expanded as users acquired the emerging technologies, experimented with them, and expanded their function. Currently, computer-based technologies are in the midst of an intense authentication stage as users—including institutions such as governments, educational bodies, corporations, and religious entities—engage in negotiations around possible and acceptable practices. Trustworthiness is an ongoing development; the International Society for Technology in Education (ISTE) sets standards for technology use in schools that include "safe, legal, and responsible use of information and technology" (ISTE, 2007) and cyber crime is listed by the U.S. Department of Justice as a top priority (United States Department of Justice, n.d.).

Viewed Through Stages: Early Hypertext Fiction as Invention

Baron's stages are recurrent, concurrent, and inexact, as can be seen in the varied cycles between contemporary technological innovations and the users who adopt, adapt, and distribute them. With this entanglement noted, the stages nonetheless provide a useful lens for considering the impact of digital and electronic technologies on the form of the book. In moving from printed page to pixeled screen, authors in the last quarter of the 20th century entered a "curiosity of use" stage (Baron, 1999, p. 18), akin to the experimentation Baron attributed to 16th century cabinet-makers exploring the affordances of the newly invented pencil.

In 1987, author Michael Joyce plunged into the inventive stage of digital book forms when he wrote what is generally considered the first hypertext fiction, *afternoon, a story*. Hypertext fiction takes advantage of the linking functions available via computer codes and software to create an interactive text. Instead of the assumption made by print authors that readers will follow a word-by-word, sentence-by-sentence path through a piece of writing, hypertext fiction authors programmed hyperlinks into their writing that allowed readers to move from site to site (or node to node) within a text. In *afternoon*, Joyce used a nodal textual architecture (via the early hypertext software Storyspace) to construct a network of multiple pathways through the story. Depending on the links readers chose, the narrative--and the experience of the story--changed.

Joyce (1991) envisioned a flowering of hypertext fiction where the reader-as-writer would "[give] birth to the true electronic text" (para. 25). This reader was better termed, Joyce said, as an interlocutor who would have a "reciprocal relationship" (para. 32) with the author and co-construct the text as she read. In this way, hypertext fiction put the author's authority under pressure. The architecture of hypertext fiction, which relied on the reader to make choices and to retrace pathways for different effects, encouraged a deliberately different alliance between author and reader than the one engendered by fixed and linear print texts. Writing about the impact of hypertext on fiction, Joyce said, "The book is dead, long live the book" (para. 9). In this statement was the recognition of transformational writing technology, the prediction that while *the book* might be disappearing, it would be remade based on the interactive possibilities afforded by electronic and digital technology.

Around the same time, new media theorist Jay David Bolter (1991a) also saw the impact emerging electronic technologies would have on traditional print books, placing the development of electronic literature within a historical context:

Electronic technology remakes the book in two senses. It gives us a new kind of book by changing the surface on which we write and the rhythms with which we read. It also adds to our historical understanding of the book by providing us with a new form that we can compare to printed books, manuscripts, and earlier forms of writing. (p. 3-4)

As an example of such comparisons, Bolter cited the period following the invention of the printing press, during which printers continued to produce texts bearing the same characteristics as handwritten manuscripts. "It took a few generations," Bolter noted, "for printers to realize that their new technology made possible a different writing space" (p. 3), one that allowed them to present written words in ways that were markedly different from earlier manually scribed texts.

Hypertext as Laboratory

Bolter and Joyce were both writing during what author Robert Coover (1999) described as the golden age of literary hypertext, the decade before the development of commercially available browsers that made the Internet--and its increasingly multimodal, user-produced content--widely accessible. In the 1980s and 1990s, hypertext was taken up by several authors as a new technology of reading and writing that could change the textual landscape. Hyperfiction writers such as Stuart Moulthrop (*Victory Garden*), Judy Malloy (*Uncle Roger* and *its name was Penelope*), and Shelley Jackson (*Patchwork Girl*) created hypertexts that were nodal and linked, but primarily print-based, a hallmark of early writers experimenting with the new electronic technologies. George Landow (1992/2006) and other early hypertext theorists (e.g. Bolter, 1991a, 1991b; Joyce, 1995; Moulthrop, 1994) saw hypertext as a "laboratory in which to test…ideas" regarding "textuality, narrative, and the roles or functions of reader and writer" (p. 2). This laboratory produced a variety of metaphors to describe hypertext: non-linear text (Nelson, 1981), a structure of structures (Bolter, 1991a), an event (Morgan, 2000), and a network of possibilities (Hayles, 2002), among others.

The energy behind the early days of hypertext fiction pointed to the profundity with which emerging technologies were impacting notions of the book and, along with it, literacy. James

Gee (2003) maintained that "we never just read or write…we always read or write *something in some way*" (p. 14). Hypertext, with its focus on text architecture, interactivity, indeterminancy, and reader-as-writer authorship, changed both the *something* (product) that was written or read and the *some way* (process) in which that product was created and consumed.

Hypertext as Transformational Technology

The enthusiasm with which early hypertext authors and theorists engaged in their inquiries point to the transformational nature of the electronic technologies they were employing. Landow (1997) argued that hypertext "calls into question ideas of plot and story current since Aristotle" (p. 181). Instead of the traditional novel's fixed page and predictable order of printed words, hypertext resisted closure by offering readers a "field of linkage and associational play whose meaning depends upon permutations" (Moulthrop, 1991, p. 260). Instead of the traditional book's claim of a clear differentiation between author and reader, hypertext intentionally fused the two, requiring the reader to make overt decisions to navigate the text. Instead of the absolute authority of the lone author, hypertext exploded the boundaries of text by not allowing a single point of view. Hypertext permitted authors to demonstrate that the notions of plot and story in Western culture, made so commonplace as to be considered common sense, were the function of print technology, and therefore open to transformation by new technological developments.

"Print fiction," wrote Bolter and Joyce (1987), "is proud of its rigidity," and since hypertext could not depend on fixity as a core attribute, it "must therefore draw its aesthetic strength from its capacity for change" (p. 49). Communication researcher Johndan Johnson Eilola (1994) saw the impact of hypertext thusly:

[Hypertext provided the] opportunity to remap [our] conceptions of literacy, to reconsider the complex, interdependent nature of the ties between technology, society, and the individual in the acts of writing, reading and thinking. Adding the concept of hypertext to theory does not replace other definitions or conceptions of writing and reading; it opens those definitions up to debate and change." (p. 204)

During the golden age of hypertext, the debate was enjoined. The traditional book was to be disrupted as authors took into their artistry the affordances and constraints of emerging electronic communication technologies.

Tensions in the Accessibility Stage

Using Baron's (1999) stages of literacy technology, the experimentation that is fertile during the invention stage undergoes pressure as a technology becomes more widely accessible and adopted. As more people take up a technology, it spreads into general use, but some of the earlier innovations may be dampened as adopters map it onto familiar, existing practices. With digital literacy technology, this movement can be seen in Coover's (1999) description of hypertext fiction's transition into what he called the silver age:

Silver ages are said to follow upon golden ages as marriage and family follow upon romance, and last longer but not forever. They are characterized by a retreat from radical visions and a return to major elements of the preceding tradition — while retaining a fascination with surface elements of the golden age innovations, by a great diffusion and popularization of its diluted principles and their embodiment in institutions, and by a prolific widespread output in the name of what went before, though no longer that thing exactly. (para. 4)

In Coover's view, the silver age of hyperfiction was ushered in "almost overnight" (para. 14) by the emergence of Internet accessibility, along with browsers, html code, laptops with large memory

banks, and other technological developments that made hypermedia--with its multimodal, massively linked social networks--a practicable avenue for human expression.

Influence of the Internet

Whereas the 1980s had seen hypertext fiction develop from a "daring" and "frivolous" form to one that was "a serious and sensible" use of computer technology (Bolter & Joyce, 1987, p. 41), by the dawn of the 20th century, hypertext was "used more to access hypermedia as enhancements for more or less linear narratives, when it's not launching the reader out into the mazy outer space of the World Wide Web, never to be seen again" (Coover, 1999, para. 15). Coover argued that such an environment, where hyperlinks were synonymous with surfing the Web, was not conducive to the kinds of literary thinking taken up by early hypertext authors.

[The Web] tends to be a noisy, restless, opportunistic, superficial, e-commerce-driven, chaotic realm, dominated by hacks, pitchmen and pretenders, in which the quiet voice of literature cannot easily be heard or, if heard by chance, attended to for more than a moment or two. Literature is meditative and the Net is riven by ceaseless hype and chatter. Literature has a shape, and the Net is shapeless. The discrete object is gone, there's only this vast disorderly sprawl, about as appealing as a scatter of old magazines on a table in the dentist's lounge. (para. 15)

As the multimodal, hypermedia features of the Web became more usable, Coover claimed, writers (and readers) would generate texts that did not privilege the word but were constructed to share space with images and sound. While these "wondrous and provocative invasions of text by sound and image" (para. 22) were not wholly welcomed by Coover, he nonetheless saw them as opportunities for authors to experiment and develop the technological tools at their disposal.

Response to Born-Digital Literature

The stage seemed set, as it were, for a maturing of electronic literature into more general use as authors and readers accepted digital and multimodal texts as commonplace literary forms. However, that maturing did not necessarily take the form or occur with the speed that the early hypertext community predicted. One expectation was for a robust industry of born-digital literature, defined by Katherine Hayles (2008) as a "first generation digital object created on a computer and (usually) meant to be read on a computer" (p. 3). In the first 15 years of the 21st century, the development of the field of born-digital literature has been uneven. YouTube (n.d.) reports that 100 hours of video are uploaded daily to viewers who watch 6 billion hours a month, but the growth of born-digital literature has been less secure. In the emerging field of transmedia, for example, technological barriers and wary publishers are among the challenges transmedia creators navigate as the form strives to take hold (Piesing, 2012). Numbers of readers who purchase e-books may be growing, but it is harder to get a handle on numbers of readers of born-digital literature (Bell, 2014). In a reflection on the field of electronic literature, Scott Rettberg (2009) wrote, "Electronic literature has not found a large popular audience, and it is entirely possible that it never will" (para. 6).

Referencing the popularity of the e-book platform, where many books are electronic versions of print texts, Bolter (2010) noted that the introduction of new technology does not necessarily mean that new forms will be taken up.

You could say that e-books change everything. You could say that they are magical and revolutionary. You could also say that they change nothing. In much the same way the digital cinema could be said to be simply the perfectly projected digital version of traditional Hollywood film, the e-book could be said to be .... the digital remediation of the printed book. (Bolter, 2010)

Through remediation rather than transformation, Bolter posited, "the community may accept this change of technology without rethinking the form or cultural position of the book at all." This resistance to rethinking the book, he argued, can be seen by the muted response to born-digital literature by the traditional academic and literary establishment, which has remained committed to print forms. In this light, Joyce's earlier ironic statement becomes commutative: the book is dead = long live the book.

ONGOING STAGES OF INVENTION AND AUTHENTICATION

Despite an expressed disappointment by early adopters of hypertext literary forms, contemporary users continue to take up new communication technologies and manipulate them for their own purposes. Indeed, in terms of novels and other storytelling media, computer-based technologies are arguably still in an ongoing "curiosity of use" stage, in which authors, illustrators and creative teams are experimenting to see just what is possible. As Rettberg (2009) observed,

Electronic literature has forked down a multitude of paths, so many in fact that it has become difficult to describe the field in terms of distinct genres. In comparison to other literary cultures, e-lit culture is still marginal, produced by a comparatively small group of writers dispersed around the globe, often working in isolation. (para. 4)

And yet, Rettberg continued, the field is growing as indicated by the increasing number of dissertations, festivals, and examples of work being produced. Whereas early hypertext blended new capabilities (branching and linking) with more familiar forms (established patterns of print texts with few images and sounds), born-digital literature now encompasses a full range of multimodal features and exists in multiple formats and platforms as creators continue to challenge the form and structure of the print novel.

In the midst of this literary experimentation, issues of trustworthiness and authentication are also in play. A National Endowment for the Arts report (2007) queried the role of technology in American reading trends within the context of those trends' "considerable consequences" (p. 5). Educators are examining the role communication and literacy technologies play in reading practices through the affordances of multimodal digital texts (e.g., O'Brien & Voss, 2011), in relation to students with disabilities (e.g., Schneps, Thomson, Chen, Sonnert, & Pomplun, 2013), and in regards to national literacy standards (e.g., Dalton, 2012/2013, 2013). Awards and recognitions tackle questions of literary quality and merit (e.g., Electronic Literature Organization, 2014). In this way, participants in the field of digital texts find themselves navigating through recursive--if messy--stages of development to gain permanence.

WHAT ARE THE CURRENT ISSUES IN THE FIELD RAISED BY THESE STUDIES?

To discuss the current issues involving the impact of digital technology on the book, we focus on one literary field--the young adult novel. Writing in the 1960s, McLuhan (1960, 1964/1994) argued that electronic media had transformational effects on its users, and because young people of his era grew up as television viewers, they engaged with the world differently than previous generations whose experiences were molded by print technology. We take up McLuhan's construct of youth in the electronic age to suggest that audiences for young adult novels, having grown up as computer users, have different expectations of and experiences with texts than readers from previous generations. As a result, young adult literature has

become a site for a rich curiosity of use stage as authors experiment with text forms and practices aimed at these readers.

In this section, we look to young adult literature--in its curiosity of use period--to consider how technology is impacting the form and function of contemporary narrative. We give an overview of data as evidence of adolescents as avid users of digital technology. We examine specific examples of young adult literature to consider how technology-derived subgenres are incorporated within print-based narratives, how technology is used to disrupt and replace narrative structures, and how technology allows new ways to read and participate in narrative formats within storyworld and across platforms.

Adolescent Readers as Technology Users

Considerable data indicates the prevalence of online participation by teens and young adults. Recent Pew reports shed light on the amount of time young people spend on the Internet and the types of activities in which they engage while online. Ninety-five percent of American teens ages 12-17 use the Internet, while 76% of respondents in that age group report using social networking sites and 77% report having cell phones. In the 18-29 age group, 96% report being Internet users, while 84% use social networking sites, and 97% report having cell phones (Anderson & Rainie, 2012). In addition, 57% of teens are "content creators" who employ the Internet to make blogs and web pages; distribute personal artwork, narratives, and videos; and craft mash-ups (Lenhart & Madden, 2005).

With their audience so connected to digital technology, it is not surprising to see YA authors experimenting with digital-related features in their texts, effectively engaging in an invention stage. In a recent newspaper article, publishing experts laid out two trends in the production of digital texts that, if taken together, can point to how digitally-derived young adult literature is in a generative curiosity of use period. The first is the emergence of Tumblr as a venue for creative work, particularly for fanfiction. Tumblr has developed into "a co-creation, self-publishing platform" (Rafferty, qtd. in Flood, 2014, para. 2). Oftentimes working collaboratively, "thousands of people are...producing a lot of short-form, episodic fiction and hundreds of thousands more are reading it.... Tumblr allows this creativity to explode, making it very easy for readers and publishers to discover real talent and energy there" (para. 2). Industry observers note that the site's image-based orientation makes it "increasingly important" for people in creative fields (Bercovici, 2013). Industry data indicates that Tumblr users skew toward a younger demographic, with 46% of the 34 million contributors/users worldwide between the ages of 16 and 24 (Smith, 2013). Whether these young adult users are posting individually created content, working collaboratively to generate content, or engaging with and reposting other users' content, they are involved in a complex fertile sphere of content creation.

A second trend identified by digital publishing experts is the continued struggle of "anything involving location-based storytelling, intrinsic and overt gamelike interactivity, augmented reality, and 'born digital' fiction" (Franklin, qtd. in Flood, 2014, para. 4). However, experts noted, "these experiments" can be commercially viable if done well (para. 4).

We see in these two trends an incentive and logic for young adult literature authors to be experimenting with digitally-related and born-digital texts. An audience that is actively engaged online and who makes up approaching 50% of the users of a noted creative site are more than readers. Many of them are part of what Henry Jenkins et al. (2009) termed a "participatory culture:"

A participatory culture is a culture with relatively low barriers to artistic expression and civic engagement, strong support for creating and shar-

ing one's creations, and some type of informal mentorship whereby what is known by the most experienced is passed along to novices. A participatory culture is also one in which members believe their contributions matter, and feel some degree of social connection with one another (at the least they care what other people think about what they have created). (p. xi)

These participatory teens are not only reading online, they are reposting and linking. They aren't only consuming, they are taking the tools of production into their own hands, sometimes in commentary, sometimes in collaboration, sometimes in individually created works in which they seek out and reciprocate with feedback. This atmosphere is fast-paced, public, and messy--and it is into this oxygen that young adult literature authors enter, curious and motivated, trying to find formats, textual elements, and narratives that will reach their readers.

Echoing McLuhan, Ong (1982) contended that "[t]echnologies are not mere exterior aids, but also interior transformations of consciousness, and never more than when they affect the word" (p. 315). Miskec (2007) argued that today's adolescents "have lived a distinct way of knowing the world because of their connection to technology--a very different experience than those in the generations that preceded them" (p. 7). The digital connection that shapes adolescents' way of seeing the world also shapes how they see books and stories told across multiple media. Texts no longer are defined as words on paper, presumably (and falsely) created by a lone author. For adolescent readers, texts can be multimodal, interactive, hyperlinked, dispersed, revisable, rhizomatic, and nodal, which renders insufficient the concepts of print-only modes of text production and bounded, fixed texts.

But, as Jenkins et al. argued (2009), "the computer does not operate in a vacuum" (p. 7). Incorporating digital technologies into text creation "necessarily affects our relationship with every other communications technology, changing how we feel about what can or should be done with pencils and paper, chalk and blackboard, books, films, recordings" (p. 7). Changing familiar formats and creating new possibilities for stories by shifting from words on paper to more multimodal and digital formats changes the tools people use to structure consciousness. YA authors are involved in this consciousness restructuring as they use media that transforms text into new shapes and forms, thus building on the ways their readers--media-savvy teens--engage with and make sense of the world.

New and Strange Books and Young Adult Novels

The affordances of digital media—linking, interactivity, connectivity, sound, animation, and immediacy of information—provide opportunities for readers to explore and engage with texts in an expanded textual landscape. The pervasiveness of digital media and the ease with which readers can navigate digital texts allows for different kinds of movements through texts. The linear movement through a text, facilitated by the familiar structure of a book, is shifted when the text is moved to a digital format; modes can be combined within the same framework; navigation among and out of screens can be as easy as following a link. This redefines the structures of the story and challenges the expectations for what readers do as they read. This remaking of a path through a book challenges the linear structure of the book as well as the long-established traditions associated with linearity—tension, transitions, etc. Glazier (2002) noted that what "writing *is* becomes altered by how it is physically written through its production technology" (p. 4). What is necessary in one format becomes obsolete in another as the way in which text is created alters and shapes what stories can be told.

The use of digital technology in and for books and YA novels is increasingly complex as authors explore the composing possibilities of digital technologies. "Many young adult authors utilize the affordances of digital media—non-linearity, lack of closure, narrative dispersed across multiple genres, disrupted narrative flow, and images that carry narrative weight—to situate their texts in larger digital contexts" (Parsons and Hundley, 2012, p. 242). These affordances provide young adult authors with other tools, not bounded by the shape and form of the book, to tell their stories. Changing the tools of storytelling illustrates Bolter's (1991a) argument that technology allows for a "new kind of book by changing the surface on which we write" (p. 3-4). Thus, what stories can be told and what tools can be used to tell them reconstructs expectations of the book. As readers become more and more fluent in social media such as texting, Facebook, blogging, etc., authors are beginning to incorporate those reading experiences into the texts they create. Authors are also considering the ways in which multiple media formats can be combined to tell stories; for example, authors may use print and video side-by-side to tell a particular story. Additionally, some authors are experimenting with digital only text structures and exploring what stories can be told using web-based storytelling. In this section, we will examine ways in which technology is currently shaping and reshaping the narrative structures authors are using to construct the novels.

Technology Subgenres within Print-Based Narrative

The description of today's teenager often discusses the ways in which that teenager engages with the digital world, focusing, in particular, on teen participation in social media. Sweeney (2010) argued,

The students that we teach today are products of a very different environment, one in which the ability to stay connected with others is constant and communication takes many forms. Writing, for adolescents who live in an age of digital communication, has taken on new importance and plays a prominent role in the way they socialize, share information, and structure their communication. (p. 121)

The texts these adolescents create and the narratives they construct across media provide an alternative paradigm for the structure of the book. This way of knowing the world, connected, interactive, and immediate, shapes their expectations of text and media. The influence of social media—Twitter, instant messaging, texting, Facebook, Instagram, etc.—shape the teen as both reader of multiple media texts and also as creator of those texts. The tropes and protocols of social media become a part of their expectations of composing for that media.

Social Media Tropes Used in Narrative

Authors such as Todd Strasser, Alex Bradley, Adele Griffin, Ken Baker, and Mari Mancusi incorporate the tropes of social media into the structure of their narrative. These authors use email, blogs, Twitter, and instant messaging (IM) within what are essentially traditional print texts to explain events, provide conflict, and push their characters to action. The role and use of social media in the context of the story relies on a reader who is familiar with the protocols of that media. Incorporating social media as a component of the text adds to the complexity in two ways; it disrupts the narrative flow and it challenges the reader to construct the story across multiple genres. Understanding social media as different genres of communication requires a reader who is relatively fluent in how those media are used in daily interactions. While many students "do not recognize this type of communication as writing"

(Sweeney, 2010, p. 124), they are familiar with the expectations of a Facebook status update, an instant message, a Tweet, etc. "Writing," Sweeney (2010) acknowledged, "is an integral part of students' lives today due to their use of texting and social networking sites" (p. 124). YA authors recognize their readers' engagement with these forms of social media and make the choice to include these formats. This increases the authenticity of the adolescent characters' experiences in the text while also providing composing tools for the author.

Strasser's (2011) murder mystery *Kill You Last* uses texting and email in the narrative structure to provide both clues to the mystery and to create suspense for the reader. The novel opens with a prologue that provides an example of each. Shelby, the main character, receives a text from a boy she is interested in dating and a short email from someone who tells her, "I like you, Shelby Sloan. If I have to kill you, I'll kill you last" (prologue). The tone of the text and the email provide immediate contrasts; the text is friendly and uses text speak while the email is threatening and uses complete sentences. When Shelby receives the second threatening email, she shows both to her friend who asks, "Who sends e-mails?" (p. 2). This question establishes the expectation that texting is new and current while email technology is older, providing a clue to the identity of the person making the threats. Later, some emails from that character feature text speak but others do not. Shelby confronts Ashley, a classmate who has admitted to sending her threatening emails, and learns that there are two people sending threats using similar screen names. Shelby and Ashley compare the patterns for texting and the use of sentences. The emails that use text speak are clearly from a teenager. The emails that actually threaten Shelby are written in more formal speech. This important clue is hidden in the text expectations; Ashley treats the short emails as though they are text messages and uses the accepted protocols for texts; the killer treats emails as short letters and uses the accepted format for letters. Recognizing the protocols and expectations of different subgenres as both a tool for storytelling and as a clue within the narrative requires a writer who is familiar with textual expectations and knows how to manipulate social media features. It also calls upon readers to know and recognize those protocols and expectations in order to engage with the story.

Wish You Were Dead (Strasser, 2009) builds on the expectations of social media and the ease with which online participants can hide their identities. The novel, another murder mystery, uses layers of social media to create the story. Blogs, blog comments, screen names, text messages, and Facebook are embedded in the narrative. An anonymous blogger posts how much she hates a popular girl, and the popular girl disappears. Characters text each other, post comments to the blog, and refer to Facebook. The juxtaposition of the social media tools that are used by the characters or referred to by the characters establish authenticity. Social media is employed in multiple ways and in multiple contexts by teens so the layered use of social media in this novel contributes to an interactive feel as well as a sense of reality. The readers see the blog posts that detail a very stressed teen girl's struggles at fitting in; the accompanying comments mirror the kinds of typical blog responses seen in online spaces. The blog comments range from caring to hostile. The ability to hide or create different identities is an intrinsic aspect of social media, and authors use this ability to create/recreate their characters.

24 Girls in 7 Days (Bradley, 2006) uses the anonymity of social media to explore how protagonist Jack can connect with multiple girls in a short period of time. Jack openly acknowledges that his love life is awful; his friends decide to help him find a date to the prom. While he is talking to, emailing, and meeting the girls on his friends' lists, he receives emails and instant messages from Fancypants. Over the course of the seven days, he falls in love with Fancypants without knowing who she actually is IRL (in real life). When her identity is revealed, it challenges his established relationship with her because he has to re-examine it with the lens of what he knows about Fancypants. This ability to hide one's identity behind a screen name in order to develop a relationship challenges the expected social mores.

The destructive power of social media is highlighted in Cann's (2004) *Text Game*; in this novel, a devious fellow student uses insidious text messages to break up Melissa and Ben just as they start their relationship. The texts interrupt Melissa's day, and this highlights both the anonymity of texting and the immediacy of the messages. The texts continue over several weeks; Melissa doesn't know who is sending them or if she can trust Ben. The constant comments about how Ben is going to break up with her, how ugly she is, and how she can't trust him disrupt Melissa's life as well as the narrative flow of the story. Visually, the texts are in bold and inset from the other paragraphs. Each text is preceded by a symbol for a text message. The visual style signals the use of social media and the interruption of the narrative flow.

Facebook and texting take center stage in Griffin's (2010) *The Julian Game*. Raye is a new student at an elite private school. On a whim, she creates a Facebook profile for the imaginary Elizabeth, describing her as an exchange student from Poland. Raye creates such a believable profile that Elizabeth is suddenly "friended" by most of the popular people at her new school. This set up, which eventually leads to Raye's duplicity being discovered, allows the author to depict the ease with which social media can be used in cyber-bullying. When presented with the opportunity to "destroy" another character, Raye muses that she is "[p]rotected and anonymous, a ghostwriter without fingerprints" (p. 191). The author relies on the reader to bring certain knowledge and experiences to the text: an understanding of the protocols of social media such as posting, following, commenting, friending; familiarity with cyber-bullying through news stories or personal experiences; and awareness of the ubiquity and inescapability of social media.

Mancusi's (2008) *Gamer Girl* incorporates the instant messaging components of a gaming environment. The author weaves a traditional narrative, game play--including the instant messaging between players--and manga to create a story about identity and relationships online. This story relies on the reader's understanding of the role of instant messaging in game play and recognition of how closely players identify with their characters. The main character Maddy moves in and out of identities and uses gaming plots to create a fanfiction manga, reflecting similar practices by adolescent readers. Without an understanding of these digital literacy practices, the reader would not be able to weave the storylines together to see how integral the gamer identity is to those who participate. The adolescent reader, as a participant in these forms of digital practices, is able to construct meaning across the texts.

Incorporating social media into more familiar narrative structures allows authors to bring to bear multiple levels of engagement and understanding to the narrative; this level of experimentation with the tools requires not just author exploration but also reader fluency.

Blogs and Blogging as Tropes Used in Narrative

Like other social media tools, blogs provide an opportunity for a character to express his or her opinion or to comment on what someone else has posted. The characteristics of blogs provide an opportunity for authors to explore the private/public nature of social media, the longer structure of blog posts as opposed to Twitter or Facebook, or insight into a character's secret thoughts. Shana Norris, Cathleen Davitt Bell, and Robynn Clairday are authors who use blogs to reveal secrets and explore character motivation.

In Norris's (2008) *Something to Blog About*, main character Libby has had a pretty rough few weeks. She's set her hair on fire in a horrible chemistry lab accident. Not only that, she did it in front of the boy she really likes. Her mother is dating her arch-enemy's father. Libby does what many teens do when they feel overwhelmed by their lives--she writes about it in a blog. Norris incorporates Libby's blog into the narrative, building on the expectations that blogs are places for characters to explore the way they are feeling about events; in this particular text, the author equates blogs with diaries. Just as a teen expects her diary to be secret, so too does Libby expect her blog to be secret. When this expectation is violated and the blog becomes public, Libby recognizes a key aspect of online posting; nothing is ever really private. In this way, the author engages with the public/private nature of writing.

The speed in which the divide between public/private writing can be dismantled is illustrated in Bell's (2011) *Little Blog on the Prairie*. Main character Gen begins blogging as a way to vent her feelings about being forced to participate in a pioneer summer camp. Her blog gradually increases in popularity until she has over 500,000 followers. The author uses the rapid rise in popularity of Gen's blog to show how social media interactions can become news stories themselves. For example, the author picks up on how blogs can lead to social activism when Gen writes about the possibility of having to kill Pumpkin, a chicken that lives on the farm, and almost immediately someone a creates a "Save Pumpkin" Facebook page with almost 20,000 followers. Gen's blog takes on a life of its own, spawning Facebook pages, news stories, and a reality television show. In this way, the story explodes the public/private nature of blogging and demonstrates how online texts can become memes or other social markers.

Genesis Bell, the main character in Clairday's (2005) *Confessions of a Boyfriend Stealer*, knows exactly how public blogs can be and uses that to her advantage. She writes her blog posts, not to deal with her emotional issues with her family, but rather to tell her side of an ongoing battle with her ex-best friends. Genesis uses the public nature of the blog to control the public story of how she "stole" her two best-friends' boyfriends. She also uses the blog to explore her thinking behind the movies and documentaries that she makes as class projects. She talks explicitly to the reader of her blog, and, while there are comments on her blog, she does not have a dramatic moment where her blog is shared with the other characters. Clairday's Genesis differs from Norris's Libby and Bell's Gen because she understands how blogs can be used. She tells the reader in the first post that she is there to tell her side of the story. In this instance, the author uses the reader's understanding that blogs and social media are ways to talk directly to the public in order propel the story.

In these examples, we can see how readers must be familiar with the tropes of social media in order to figure out how to situate the media within the context of the story. Young adult authors play with the reader's understanding of the media to provide authenticity to their teen characters but also to challenge traditional narrative formats.

Technology to Replace the Narrative

Just as some print authors eschew paragraphs and chapter structures and choose to write novels in verse or in diary or letter formats, some young adult authors choose to use the formats of social media as the tool to tell their story. Authors such as Lauren Myracle and Elizabeth Rudnick do more than incorporate social media into the narrative structure of their novels; they use social media to replace the traditional narrative format. For readers who are not active users of social media, this can be disorienting. The visual layout of the pages of these novels resembles the on-screen look of instant messenger, Twitter, emails, and blogs. For the reader, this establishes how the novel should be read and seamed together. The visual cues are necessary to provide the roadmap for the novel.

Myracle's (2005) *ttyl* is the first in a four-book series about Maddie, Angela, and Zoe; what is unique about this series is that each book is told entirely in IM format. There are no paragraphs or chapter breaks. The conversations are divided by dates rather than chapter headings. Tools such as narration, description, and transition are replaced by IMs. The use of IMs as the way in which the story is told alters how the reader learns about characters and how tension is developed. Choosing a different platform for constructing the story both limits and expands what the author can do in the telling of the story. Relying entirely on what Maddie, Angela, and Zoe say in their IMs means that everything that happens in the story is reported action occurring off-screen. If the characters attend a party, the reader does not see them at the party, rather the reader sees what the characters say about the party. The characters have screen names, use emoticons, and visually represent their actions with short phrases framed by asterisks. This method of storytelling relies on a reader who is a fluent user of instant messaging and understands not only how to read IMs but also how to combine multiple people's IMs into a coherent story.

Rudnick's (2010) *Tweet Heart*, like *ttyl*, requires readers to seam parts of the narrative together. However, *Tweet Heart* does not rely on a single format of social media to construct the text. Rather, it combines IM, Twitter, emails, and blogs. *Tweet Heart* is a multi-genre, multimodal text constructed entirely of multiple forms of social media. The story is built across several platforms of social media, and when "media platforms converge, the varying platforms provide opportunities to tell different parts of a story in different ways" (Groenke and Maples, 2010, p. 40). *Tweet Heart* relies on readers who are as familiar with social media as the characters are.

Technology to Reshape the Narrative

The incorporation of video and animation in a more traditional print text allows for the technology to reshape the story that is being told. Multi-platform novels are texts in which more than one platform are used to tell the story; the platforms work together to create the story but components of the text exist only in a single platform. For example, *Skeleton Creek*, Carman's (2009) multi-platform novel, follows Ryan and Sarah as they try to solve a mystery in their small town. The story, told in both print and video, requires the reader to seam those two platforms together to create the single story. The readers get part of the story from Ryan's journal and part of the story from Sarah's videos. Neither is complete without the other. The print component of the novel is designed to look like a journal; the cover is marbled to resemble a composition book and the font looks like handwriting. The pages are lined. Images and typed notes look as though they are pasted or taped in. At certain points in the novel, readers are directed to an online site where they type in a specific password to gain access to Sarah's videos. The videos exist only online; however, there are references to them in the print text, and all of the passwords that a reader needs in order to access the videos are in the print text. The interaction between print and video and the juxtaposition of the two platforms create a story that exists in the intersections of each platform. The two platforms do not retell what happened in the other; rather they build on or contradict the other. The reader constructs the story from the two platforms. The narrative in this novel is dispersed across the two media formats, raising questions about how the media work together, how the author constructs the text, and how the reader reads across media. Additionally, the text challenges the physical idea of a book as it exists in both print and digital formats.

While the *Skeleton Creek* series uses print and video to create the story, *BZRK* (Grant, 2013) and *Virus on Orbis* (Haarsma, 2008) use digital media to build and supplement the world of the novel. *BZRK,* the story of a group of rebellious teens who are fighting for their right to be human in a world in which biotechnology and nanotechnology control people, is accompanied by an app that allows the reader to play in the world created by the book. *Virus on Orbis,* the adventures of

Johnny Turnbull as he negotiates an alien world, has a companion video game that lets the readers play in the world of the novel but requires them to bring information from the novel to the video game. With both *BZRK* and *Virus on Orbis*, the novel can exist without the app or game, but the game does not work without the text. The world of the book gives shape and form to the games and, in order to play the games, the reader must have read the book.

Like *BZRK* and *Virus on Orbis, The Survivors* (Havard, 2011) uses technology to supplement the world of the print novel; however, this novel has both a print and app version of the text. The actual text of the novel and the text of the app are the same; however, the app layers on additional information, extending the text. A reader can click on watermark symbols embedded in the text to see a Google map of the setting, hear referenced songs, see a character's Facebook page, or follow a character on Twitter. Additionally, the reader can see the author's notes, supplemental information on a historical event, and reference materials the author used to research and develop the story. The considerations of authorship and the boundaries of a text are challenged by the ways in traditional narrative formats are reshaped by the inclusion of technology as components of the narrative structure.

Ruby Skye, P.I. (http://rubyskyepi.com/) produced by Karen Walton, Jill Golick, and Steven Golick (2010-2012) is a series designed to be an online, video version of familiar girl detective stories. Ruby, a modern-day Nancy Drew or Trixie Belden, solves mysteries in her local neighborhood and school. The video series takes on the tropes of both print detective series and television detective series. Each season is divided into short episodes that serve as a video-chapter that readers can access on the teen detective's home page. The video-chapters follow the kinds of chapter patterns that teen detective novels follow; each one ends with a question, cliffhanger, or clue that may or may not turn out to be significant. The main character talks both to the other characters and to the viewer. While the story itself exists in video format only, the web site and accompanying media provide transmedia extensions of the story. The reader can follow particular characters, learn about other girl detectives, read blog posts about female activists, and participate in social media interactions with other viewers. The structure of this text challenges the expectations of traditional print narratives.

Technology to Read, Co-Construct, and Explore the Narrative

Authors, particularly young adult authors, have embraced the communicative aspects of digital media to create stories that exist across multiple platforms, to connect with their readers, and to allow for reader participation. Many authors have extensive web sites designed to support the storyworlds created in their novels. Authors such as Laurie Halse Anderson, Rick Riordin, John Green, and J.K. Rowling take advantage of the affordances of digital media to engage with their readers; they provide additional information about their stories and their characters as well as interactive sites for the readers to engage in the texts. Readers expect authors to give them more—more story, more access, more connections. The expectation is that the book is one format of the story situated in a larger digital world. Readers follow authors and characters on Twitter and Facebook and respond to author blogs; they play games and interact with other fans of novels on online sites. Adolescent readers expect more than a book.

Participating in Storyworlds

Texts such as *The Collider Comics* (Garley, Stewart, Gowran, Tempest, Pickering, and Simmonds, 2012), and *The Collider Quest* (Bernardo, Scott, Neves, Gomes, Azevedo, and Cantwell, 2012) exist as a constellation of online graphic novels, apps, games, and web sites. Each individual media format contains a rich and complete story; however, these stories interact to create a larger, interconnected storyworld. Experiences with the graphic novel give the players information to guide gameplay and interactions on the web sites. The narrative is not a singular story extended across multiple media formats as in *Skeleton Creek*; the juxtaposition of text and video game play does not extend the narrative as it does in *Virus on Orbis*. Instead, each media format in The Collider world stands alone. The formats, however, are stronger when read together.

As more authors, artists, and game designers come together to create storyworlds, this kind of multi-platform storytelling and world creation will become more common. The kinds of reader participation in the storyworld of the text opens up new composing opportunities as well as for reader creation and connection. Because the storyworld of a novel extends beyond the text, it creates a larger participation space for the reader. The reader may read the text, play a game, read the graphic novels, or write fanfiction. Because the world exists in multiple formats and platforms, the reader has greater opportunity for choice. The question for the reader to consider is not how to read the multiple formats to create stories but rather how to consider multiple storylines within a storyworld.

The multiple sites that support storyworlds designed to extend reader experiences with an author or authors' work allow spaces for readers to create fanfiction. Fanfiction, as a component of these large storyworlds, extends the worlds of the novel and allows for the participatory creation of story. In digital environments, the lines between author/reader/composer are blurred and fluid, illustrating Jenkins' (2006) argument that we can't "talk about media producers and consumers as occupying separate roles" (p. 3). Jenkins explained that we should "see [producers and consumers] as participants who interact with each other according to a new set of rules that none of us fully understands" (p. 3). Jodi Lynn Anderson (2010) allowed readers of her online novel *Loser/Queen* to vote on particular plot elements and included their responses in subsequent installments. This invitation to participate in the creation of the novel "pushes the boundaries of reader co-construction to a new level" and builds on some of the key features of social media—interactivity, connectivity, and participation (Parsons and Hundley, 2012, p. 243). The final print version of the novel incorporated the readers' collaborative choices into the text. While Anderson's choice to allow her readers to co-construct the text does not explicitly connect to the readers' creation of fanfiction, it blurs the lines between author and reader by opening up the participatory possibilities. Fanfiction extends this participation and further blurs the lines, although the author's invitation to create is not necessarily a part of that format. Readers can develop stories based on characters and worlds created by authors without the author's explicit invitation to do so.

Transmedia

Jenkins (2007) explained that

> ... [t]ransmedia storytelling represents a process where integral elements of a fiction get dispersed systematically across multiple delivery channels for the purpose of creating a unified and coordinated entertainment experience. Ideally, each medium makes it own unique contribution to the unfolding of the story. (para. 3)

This definition focuses on the ways in which the familiar components of fiction get taken up and used in stories spread out across several media—video, web sites, games, text, image, etc. What is particularly interesting about the definition is the emphasis on how each medium is expected to carry narrative weight in the ways in which the story develops. Each medium provides a way of looking at the story through a new lens and level of participation, bringing with it the genre-like

expectations about what this medium can do for the story. What does a video make possible in the narrative that a single image does not? This expands the composing options for the writer while also expanding the participation options for the reader. *Collapsus, Inanimate Alice, The Cainsville Files, The Julian Year,* and *The Memory Machine* are narratives that push at structural boundaries; they exist in electronic format as apps, e-books, and online stories. These stories exist across multiple platforms, genres, and modes and require reader participation to construct the narrative.

As writers, artists, and composers experiment and play with the composing possibilities for storytelling, readers are provided with a dizzying array of "texts" with which to play and participate, raising questions such as, Is this a story or a game? Is this a movie or a game or a story? The either/or binary are subsumed in transmedia storytelling into an and/and/and construction.

For example, *Collapsus* (www.collapsus.com), directed by Tommy Pallotta, is an online multimedia text; the director of the text describes *Collapsus* as "transmedia story" and as an "annotated film" (Pallotta, 2011, np). The story is told through a mix of character videos, graphic-novel style animations, documentary clips, blogs, articles, and text. There is also an interactive component that forces readers to make choices on the issues surrounding energy usage. The screen is divided into three panels with the central panel providing the fiction component of the story. The reader is introduced to characters through a mix of video, text, and animations. The panels to the left and right of the central screen contain additional components of the story—an interactive panel that pushes readers to make choices and a panel that contains blogs, articles, documentaries, and other texts that provide character development, additional data about the issues, and plot components that ratchet up the reader's stress level. The multiple media formats in this story work together to create the story.

Kate Pullinger and Chris Joseph's (2011) *Inanimate Alice* (http://www.inanimatealice.com/), an online serial story about young Alice and her growing up in various countries, uses words, images, sounds, movement, games, and animation to create a story that exists across the modes. This story, read on screen, is structured in episodes that provide glimpses into Alice's family life, her friendships, and, among other events, her father's disappearance. The complexity of the story depends on the interactions of the modes. For example, the episodes' strategic use of sound both foregrounds tension and supports the other events happening in the story. The use of whispering, knocking, and wind are subtle and powerful. As a reader, the sounds often blend into the background and at strategic moments increase in volume or completely disappear. In either case, the sound becomes an integral part of the narrative structure.

In *The Cainsville Files* (2014), Kelley Armstrong, author of adult and young adult fantasy novels, explores the storytelling possibilities of graphic novels, animations, sound, and explicit game-like reader choice. Just as early hypertext incorporated linking and allowed readers and writers to "reconsider the writer's use of sequence in order to control the passage of readers through the text" (Snyder, 1996, p. 66) so, too, does the use of explicit reader choice in sections of this story guide the reader's navigation. The app opens with a scene of protagonist Jenn's new office; we learn that she is a former police office now turned private investigator. At several points in each section, the reader is given the option to choose how Jenn will respond to another character's actions or whether or not she will explore particular locations for clues. This use of choice, often a component of video games, allows the reader to co-create the narrative; some choices will end the story within just a few screens while others will take the reader deeper into the mystery. The table of contents for this story is a series of visual images of locations in which some action in the story occurs. The story can be read and reread and the story itself will change as the reader chooses a different path through the mystery.

Like *The Cainsville Files*, Gregory Lamberson's *The Julian Year* (2014) relies on explicit reader choice to construct the narrative. The use of the visual table of contents for *The Cainsville Files* provides a way for the reader to orient herself in the text; *The Julian Year* uses a technology called Tree Branching technology to provide the reader a visual map of where she has been in the text. Tree-branching, like hypertext linking, is based on nodes and branching pathways. *The Julian Year* must be read using MMG Sidekick, an app that allows the reader to read and participate in the text. While the choices in *The Julian Year* are not as extensive as *Collapsus* or *The Cainsville Files*, the use of the tree branching technology provides a way for authors to reconceptualize narrative as fluid, branching, and not fixed.

Denise Chapman Weston's (2014) *The Memory Machine*, a multigenre, multimodal ibook, tells the story of Anna, her autistic brother, and her grandfather. The text uses journal entries, sound, images, and video to construct a story about memory, memory loss, and family. The reader of this story does not choose to construct the story path, rather, she chooses to explore small tangents and moments that bring richness and depth to the idea of memory and the small details that create a life. The narrative spine of *The Memory Machine* is a journal format, but the entries incorporate more than text. The reader must figure out the arch of the story via the intersections of modes and genres created by the author. The author provides navigational directions for the reader as well as color coded text markers to indicate additional information.

WHAT ARE THE GAPS IN THE EXTANT RESEARCH AND DIRECTIONS FOR FUTURE RESEARCH?

The participatory and transmedia texts described here are textually subversive because they form and "[re-form] with successive readings, no two readings are alike" (Snyder, 1996, p. 93). Readers may or may not start and end at the same point in the text in successive readings. Because the texts shift based on reader choice, they are not fixed; they are performative. Each iterative reading is a new performance, an event in the making. Morgan (2000) contended that "hypertext is always an event—a text just in the process of becoming as we read and ceasing to exist in that sequence when we quit the program" (p. 133). The idea of text as an event contrasts with the seeming fixedness of traditional print texts.

As the digital tools used to create these kinds of texts become more ubiquitous, more writers will work to create texts that exist across platforms and incorporate multiple paths, genres, and modes. The contrast between the apparent fixedness of traditional print formats and the text-as-event formats of these kinds of digital texts provide both a current issue for authors and readers as well as areas of future research. Learning to construct a text that is performative is challenging for the author; applying the reading and participation strategies that are part of the participatory culture in which they are engaging is challenging for readers; redefining what authorship, reader, and text means in this environment provides a challenge for researchers as well. Just as the use of the codex reshaped the work that authors and scholars could do and provided opportunities for new text forms such as the novel, so, too, will these participatory and transmedia texts provide

new ways of composing for authors and readers, and raise new questions about form and authorship for researchers.

Gee (2003) made the case that video games are "a new form of art. They will not replace books; they will sit beside them, interact with, and change them and their role in society" (p. 204). Similarly, the authors described above are exploring digital media tools to develop "a new form of art" and storytelling, one that sits beside and interacts with the more familiar forms of text. They are situating multiple platforms beside and within texts to explore narrative possibilities. As Jenkins (2006) argued, "Old media are not being displaced. Rather, their functions and status are shifted by the introduction of new technologies" (p. 14). Due to the current exploration of what is possible, new digital technologies have become part of the author's and reader's toolkit.

What this means for researchers is multifaceted. Drawing from McLuhan's (1960) assertion that communication technologies are implicated in a wide-range of human constructs, what relational practices and structures will digital text formats generate? Do communication technologies, as McLuhan posited, propel people to think differently, and if so, how might that difference be conceptualized? What discourses and organizing structures might develop around the changing notions of the book? How might the ways in which people create and use emerging text formats impact such institutions as media, government, and education—and vice versa? In a partial consideration of that last question, we give a brief overview of how educational discourses are being impacted by the social practices arising around text forms made possible by communication technologies.

WHAT ARE THE RECOMMENDATIONS/ IMPLICATIONS FOR EDUCATION, CIVIC ENGAGEMENT (GLOBAL AND LOCAL), SOCIAL PRACTICE, AND POLICY?

In the current intense curiosity of use stage, YA authors are experimenting with form and participation, responding to the perceived media literacy practices of their readers. They draw from established technology tropes, remixing them with print conventions and within print formats. They explore and try out the affordances of computer-based technologies, including the Internet, to test the elasticity of narrative. As literacy educators, we posit this question: If authors and creative teams are engaged in a curiosity of use stage as they make moves within their art form to reach their young adult audience, what are the implications for educators concerned with the cultivation of students' literacy practices in the digital age?

We respond to this question by taking up Jenkins' et al. (2009) work on participatory culture to suggest that engagement with these "new and strange sorts of texts" (Baron, 2009, p. x) could be a critical component of students' in-school and out-of-school education. We will explore the ideas of participatory culture as it relates to adolescents who are reading, writing, communicating, and composing within a participatory culture. We will suggest that notions of a parallel pedagogy (Leander, 2009) can be used to productively consider the tensions emerging between "old" and "new" literacy practices in K-12 instruction and the role digital-related literature can play. Finally, we will look briefly at current structures operating within U.S. education--explicitly the Common Core State Standards--and how digital young adult literature can be harnessed to aid in the development of students' digital literacy practices.

Learning in a Participatory Culture

In their influential MacArthur Foundation report entitled "Confronting the Challenges of Participatory Culture," Jenkins et al. (2009) offered a general overview of youth digital practices for educators concerned with new media literacies. They suggested a definition of 21st century literacy that built on earlier constructs:

A definition of twenty-first century literacy offered by the New Media Consortium (2005) is "the set of abilities and skills where aural, visual, and digital literacy overlap. These include the ability to understand the power of images and sounds, to recognize and use that power, to manipulate and transform digital media, to distribute them pervasively, and to easily adapt them to new forms" (p. 8). We would modify this definition in two ways. First, textual literacy remains a central skill in the twenty-first century. Before students can engage with the new participatory culture, they must be able to read and write. Youth must expand their required competencies, not push aside old skills to make room for the new. Second, new media literacies should be considered a social skill. (p. 19)

Noting that educators frequently focus on the digital divide--that is, students' equitable access to digital technology--as a dominant topic, Jenkins's team argued that more crucial was the question of participation. "A focus on expanding access to new technologies carries us only so far if we do not also foster the skills and cultural knowledge necessary to deploy those tools toward our own ends" (p. 8). Instead of the digital haves and have-nots that were the concern of digital divide conversations, students are more likely to be divided into groups "for whom the Internet is an increasingly rich, diverse, engaging and stimulating resource... and those for whom it remains a narrow, unengaging, if occasionally useful, resource of rather less significance" (Livingstone & Bober, qtd. in Jenkins et al., p. 17).

Engaging in the participatory culture of the Internet allows students to develop "cultural competencies and social skills needed for full involvement" (Jenkins et al., 2009, p. xiii) in their own era. This engagement may include participating in online communities, creating and posting individually- or collaboratively-created digital works, developing new knowledge in formal or informal teams, and contributing to the circulation and form of media through blogging and other venues. The effects of the participatory culture creates "a new form of the hidden curriculum" (p. xii), whereby some students are prepared with the skills needed to be active and effective members of their societies and others are not. While traditional curriculum has frequently focused on individual achievement and work, a participatory culture perspective privileges community involvement and social skills over individual expression. This shift creates different types of skills that students should cultivate. Among these, according to the authors, are play (experimenting to solve problems), appropriation (sampling and remixing content), multitasking (scanning to identify details), distributed cognition (interacting with tools to expand cognition), transmedia navigation (following information and narratives across modalities), and networking (searching, synthesizing, and disseminating information).

Jenkins et al. further noted that some educators argue students will learn digital media practices outside of school and on their own. The authors countered, however, with three issues that they claimed make concerted pedagogical attention necessary:

1. **The Participation Gap:** The unequal access to "opportunities, experiences, skills, and knowledge" needed for societal participation (p. xii)
2. **The Transparency Problem:** A need to focus on students' awareness of how "media shape perceptions of the world" (p. xii)

3. **The Ethics Challenge:** The need for socialization and professionalization processes to support students as they develop ethical norms as "media makers and community participants" (p. xiii)

To respond to these issues and to support students as they cultivate new cultural competencies requires a systemic and creative approach on the part of schools, policy makers, community organizations, and families.

Working and Expanding School Learning Structures

Literacy education in schools has long addressed the three concerns identified by Jenkins's team, albeit primarily in the context of print literacy. Literacies are conventionally understood as social practices and engagements, media (texts) as motivated shapers of perception and knowledge is the backbone of critical literacy, and the ethical norms of reading and writing are part of standard language arts curricula. Now, however, schools are tasked with considering those concepts anew within the digital environment.

Kevin Leander (2009) posed a question no doubt opined by many educators:

[How] can we possibly fit more into an already overcrowded curriculum, even if we do decide to buy into an expanded definition of what it means to be literate (Kinzer and Leander, 2003)? Behind such [a question] is a key issue with important consequences: how do we imagine the relationship of so-called 'new literacies' (Lankshear and Knobel, 2003) to more conventional print-based literacies? (p. 147)

Leander noted four "stances" toward the incorporation of new literacies into language arts classes: resistance, replacement, return, and remediation. The resistance stance privileges the reading and writing of print-based texts. The replacement stance takes the position that print-based texts are essentially antiquated and should be replaced with the kinds of texts that are among the "native, everyday practices of youth" (p. 148), such as blogs and multimedia genres. The return stance has a print-centric focus that understands new literacy practices as means to develop print-based literacies; in other words, print genres are valued as the ultimate guide to knowledge production. The remediation stance reflects an understanding that elements of conventional media are "communicated, or mediated once again" through newer forms. In other words, "the new is never entirely apart from the old" (p. 148).

Remediation also entails recognizing that we are currently in need of understanding the modes of thinking and learning that we want our students to engage in, and consider which media, including print, still and moving images, music, voice, embodied performance, or other that might best 'mediate' such modes of thinking and learning. (p. 148)

Educators taking a remediation stance are "agnostic" (p. 148) in the face of multiple media, more interested in the processes, meanings, and effects of media than a favoring of a single form.

Adopting a remediation stance, Leander went on to describe the concept of a parallel pedagogy, in which "old and new literacy practices, including print texts and visual texts, may be fruitfully taught side by side, rather than the 'old' being a precursor to the new or being replaced by it" (p. 149). This move to a parallel pedagogy works at a meta level. Rather than focusing on the specific products of specific media, Leander's notion of parallel pedagogy asks students to explore how certain aspects of texts have "powerful purchase across media" (p. 160). How, for example, might argument be conveyed through image without a reliance on words (Hundley & Holbrook, 2013)? How is time conveyed differently through visuals, transitions, or print? By taking up a parallel pedagogy, Leander suggested, teachers might be able to address the scheduling issue that makes adding digital literacy instruction so daunting.

Other educators have also argued for the importance of making instructional space for new literacies (e.g., Hicks, 2013; Hundley, Smith, & Holbrook, 2013; Selfe, 2007; Wysocki & Lynch, 2012). As one example, Troy Hicks and Franki Sibberson use the conventional reading/writing workshop model to create time and structure for digital composition in their classrooms (Hicks & Sibberson, 2015).

The question of the place of digital-related literature in language arts classrooms can be found in the arguments presented above. If students need to develop the competencies and social skills to navigate and affect the cultural currents of their time, then should literature generated in response to technological affordances be part of that work? If online communities have developed around the stories told in transmedic young adult literature, should the social practices that govern those communities be seen as both in-school and out-of-school learning? If it is important for students to engage in critical literacy, understanding that no text is neutral and that texts shape cultural perceptions, should the hypermedia/multimodal texts in which they engage be open to their informed scrutiny? And finally, if students are already participating in a curiosity of use stage as they craft and distribute their own works, should these practices be brought under the auspices of their classroom curriculum? Undergirding these questions is the belief that schools have a responsibility to support students' cultural competencies around technology as they explore literature as a means of constructing themselves and the societies in which they live.

Digital Literacies and the Common Core

Considering those questions cannot be done outside the structures of assessment and standards, including the Common Core State Standards (CCSS). While the CCSS standards are used in the United States, they were developed within a global context and raise issues relevant in international educational settings. Educators and educational researchers have examined how the CCSS seemingly position digital literacy and technology, noting that the standards in these areas are vague and broad, which can be both a bonus and a problem (Avila & Moore, 2012; Dalton, 2012/2013; Pandya & Auckerman, 2014). In addition, some see tensions in language arts instruction that stem from the kinds of assessments mandated by educational stakeholders and policymakers, nationally as well as internationally. For example, Leander (2009) surmised that the resistance stance toward new literacies curricula may be less a fear of technology than a pragmatic response to standardized assessments that favor conventional print literacy practices.

In the face of what could be seen as moves to restrict and deprofessionalize teachers, educators are advocating ways of reading the emerging standards for flexibility and space. Jessica Van Cleave and Sarah Bridges-Rhoads (in press) encouraged teachers to ask "different questions of the CCSS" by positioning it

... as a living document that can be read again and again with an eye toward all sorts of literacy teaching and learning in classrooms....[We], as teachers, can begin to think and speak ourselves as authors of the CCSS and thus become participants in writing its history. (p. 42)

By engaging in conversations about what the CCSS can be, teachers can actively make the standards in the talking and teaching of them.

In this vein, educators are finding ways of navigating these institutionalized structures to bring digital and new literacies into the classrooms. Expressing an emerging view, Dalton (2012/2013) wrote that while the CCSS does not include an explicit standard addressing technology, "the standards assume that being literate means being digitally literate." The standards can be read, she maintained, to understand technology as not supplemental to literacy development, "but rather...deeply infused throughout teaching, curriculum, and learning" (p. 333). Working with the notion that digital literacy is an assumed aspect of curriculum, Dalton operated within the "open-endedness" (p. 333) of the standards to design projects that permitted students to develop as digital composers.

JuliAnna Avila and Michael Moore (2012) argued that looking at the CCSS with critical and digital literacies in mind could "offset some of the stifling aspects of standardization" (p. 28). Noting that digital literacy held a "relatively low profile" in the standards, they maintained educators nonetheless had the power to "shape the standards toward a stronger inclusion of both digital and critical literacies" (p. 29), thereby helping students prepare to be active agents in civic life. Similar to Dalton, Avila and Moore enacted the stance that the Common Core's language arts standards can be read to include--even assume--digital and new literacies, a position which then opens opportunities for teachers to create classrooms in which students explore and craft digital multimodal texts.

Drawing from Luke and Freebody's work on the four resource model, Jessica Zacher Pandya and Maren Aukerman (2014) argued that the CCSS were written to promote some aspects of technology use but not others. Luke and Freebody (1999) posited that readers and writers rely on four types of competencies or families of practices as they engage and produce texts: coding, pragmatic, semantic, and critical. Each of these families of practices are necessary but not sufficient in and of themselves, Luke and Freebody argued, for the development of literate citizens. The practices also change depending on prevailing notions of literacy, impacted by the communication tools adopted by societies.

In their examination of the CCSS, Pandya and Aukerman (2014) maintained that the standards promote technological use in the development of pragmatic ("the ability to use texts to get things done" [p. 429]) and semantic ("the ability to make meaning from and with texts" [p. 429]) competencies. However, the standards provide less focus on coding ("the ability to decode words, including knowledge of...keyboard layout and keyboarding" [p. 429]) and critical ("the ability to critique and analyze texts...[and] the knowledge that texts are never neutral" [p. 429]) competencies. While they acknowleged that "optimistic" (p. 431) educators see room in the CCSS for critical literacy around technology use, Pandya and Aukerman are less encouraged, concerned that teachers may not be able to find space if such foci are not required.

If, as many researchers argue, digital and new literacies are assumed in the CCSS, then how can educators find that space in their day-to-day teaching so students can develop as active, involved, responsible participants in the digital age? Like Pandya and Aukerman, we find reason to be skeptical as we watch schools enact mandated instruction and narrow interpretations of the CCSS. However, we also believe that teachers can work against constricted understandings of the standards in their selection of texts and related practices. We suggest that bringing digitally-derived and born-digital literature into English Language Arts classes can involve students in complex and productive literacy practices. Referring to Jenkins et al.'s (2009) list of key technology-related skills, we see that by engaging students in the types of experimental texts created by young adult literature authors, teachers can support students as they cultivate such skills as play, appropriation, multitasking, distributed cognition, transmedia navigation, and networking.

Furthermore, reading/writing workshops that immerse students in not only the reading of such texts but the creation of them as well can go far to address Jenkins et al.'s gaps in participation, transparency, and ethics. Instead of relying on out-of-school and home-based spaces to provide students access to online participation, schools can engage student participation through the affinity groups that develop around young adult literature, immersing them in online communities that critique and expand the narratives, positioning students as active co-creators of texts and the shapers of discourse. By engaging students in critical conversations around young adult literature, including experimental texts, they can explore the systems of power and normativity that make no text neutral. And by incorporating these texts--and the online communities and practices they include--into classrooms, teachers can support students as they explore the ethics of being content producers and responsible participants in digital environments.

In this chapter we have posited that YA authors are engaged in a curiosity of use process in response to their tech-savvy adolescent readers. But it's interesting to note that as they experiment and invent, their work may, in time, reach other audiences. A recent study discussed in *Publisher's Weekly* (2012) explained that

... fully 55% of buyers of works that publishers designate for kids aged 12 to 17 -- known as YA books -- are 18 or older, with the largest segment aged 30 to 44, a group that alone accounted for 28% of YA sales. And adults aren't just purchasing for others -- when asked about the intended recipient, they report that 78% of the time they are purchasing books for their own reading. (para. 1)

While young adult authors are exploring the options for digital media in storytelling and using tools that their intended audience are employing in their daily lives, their audience extends beyond just adolescents. Over half of the books identified as books for young adults are bought by adults, purchased for themselves. As authors experiment with digital media in storytelling, they are reshaping reader expectations and helping determine which storytelling tools will become more than a curiosity of use, not just for a segment of readers but for larger audiences. Similarly, Jenkins and other scholars working in the intersections of digital technology and the literacy practices of adolescents and young adults point to inquiries that can be taken up by researchers looking at the larger question of the changing nature of the book. For example, more research is needed on the shifting relationship between author and reader in the digital age: *In participatory cultures, what counts as authorship? When books are reconceptualized within notions of transmedia, how is the author function taken up and performed? How do reading practices--and the construct of reader itself--change in the context of transmedia and/ or dispersed texts?*

As Nash (2014) noted, books have been a part of culture and a disruption of culture. The jitteriness of the current era, therefore, is nothing new; extending back to the Greeks, observers have fretted over the effects of new communication technologies, including the at-one-time new technology of the book. While, as Coover (1992) worried, contemporary digital technologies seem fragile in their short life cycle, the book is not fragile. Books are extraordinarily resilient. Put to use by motivated humans, books do change the world.

That said, some of the forms and features of texts do change, and in those changes are new possibilities for human agency. One of the exciting aspects of living in a time of curiosity and inventiveness is seeing those possibilities erupt. It could be said that readers and composers of young adult literature are in the business of eruptions. In critiquing the publishing business, Nash (2014) reminded,

A business born out of the invention of mechanical reproduction transforms and transcends the very circumstances of its inception, and again has the potential to continue to transform and transcend itself--to disrupt industries like education.... By defining books as against technology, we deny our true selves, We deny the power of the book. Let's restore to publishing its true reputation--not as a hedge against the future, not as a bulwark against radical change, not as a citadel amidst the barbarians, but rather as the future at hand, as the radical agent of change....(para. 52)

What we see in the work (and play) of adolescent readers and young adult authors as they actively explore and authenticate digital media tools is the remaking and remixing of what a book can be. The book is dead; long live the book.

REFERENCES

Anderson, J., & Rainie, L. (2012, Feb. 29). *Main findings: Teens, technology, and human potential in 2020*. Pew Research Internet Project. Retrieved from http://www.pewinternet.org/2012/02/29/main-findings-teens-technology-and-human-potential-in-2020/

Anderson, J. L., & Lee, B. (Illus.) (2010). Loser/Queen. New York: Simon & Schuster, 2010.

Anderson, L. H. (1999). *Speak*. New York: Farrar, Straus & Giroux.

Armstrong, K. (2014). *The Cainsville files* [ibook]. Retrieved from itunes.apple.com

Avila, J., & Moore, M. (2012). Critical literacy, digital literacies, and Common Core State Standards: A workable union? *Theory into Practice*, *51*(1), 27–33. doi:10.1080/00405841.2012.636332

Baron, D. (1999). From pencils to pixels: The stages of literacy technologies. In G. Hawisher & C. Selfe (Eds.), *Passions, pedagogies, and 21st century technologies* (pp. 15–33). Logan, UT: Utah State University Press.

Baron, D. (2009). *A better pencil: Readers, writers, and the digital revolution*. Oxford, UK: Oxford University Press.

Bell, A. (2014, August 8). *Reading digital fiction*. Retrieved from http://www.digitalreadingnetwork. com/reading-digital-fiction/

Bell, C. D. (2010). *Little blog on the prairie*. New York: Bloomsbury.

Bercovici, J. (2013, Jan. 3). Do you need a Tumblr? *Forbes*. Retrieved from http://www.forbes.com/ sites/jeffbercovici/2013/01/02/do-you-need-a-tumblr/

Bernardo, N., Scott, C., Neves, F., Gomes, P., Azevedo, S., & Cantwell, D. (2012). *Collider quest* [mobile application software]. Retrieved from itunes.apple.com

Bolter, J. D. (1991a). *Writing space: The computer, hypertext, and the history of writing*. Hillsdale, NJ: L. Erlbaum Associates.

Bolter, J. D. (1991b). Topographic writing: Hypertext and the electronic writing space. In G. Landow & P. Delaney (Eds.), *Hypermedia and literary studies*. Cambridge, MA: The MIT Press.

Bolter, J. D. (2010). *Elite and popular: Digital art and literature in the era of social and locative media*. Keynote speech at Kingston University, London, UK. [video] Retrieved from http://vimeo. com/22554435

Bolter, J. D., & Joyce, M. (1987). Hypertext and creative writing. In *Proceedings of the ACM Conference on Hypertext* (pp. 41-50). doi doi:10.1145/317426.317431

Bradley, A. (2006). *24 girls in 7 days*. New York: Speak.

Buckingham, D. (2011). Foreword. In M. Thomas (Ed.), *Deconstructing digital natives* (pp. ix–xi). New York: Routledge.

Cann, K. (2004). *Text game*. Minneapolis, MN: Stoke Books.

Carman, P. (2009). *Skeleton Creek*. New York: Scholastic.

Clairday, R. (2005). *Confessions of a boyfriend stealer*. New York: Delacorte.

Coover, R. (1999). *Literary hypertext: The passing of the golden age*. Keynote Address, Digital Arts and Culture, Atlanta, GA. Retrieved from http:// www.nickm.com/vox/golden_age.html

D'Arcens, L. (2014). *Comic medievalism: Laughing at the Middle Ages*. Woodbridge, UK: Boydell & Brewer, Ltd.

Dalton, B. (2012/2013). Multimodal composition and the Common Core State Standards. *The Reading Teacher*, *66*(4), 333–339. doi:10.1002/ TRTR.01129

Dalton, B. (2013). Engaging children in close reading: Multimodal commentaries and illustration remix. *The Reading Teacher*, *66*(8), 642–649. doi:10.1002/trtr.1172

Electronic Literature Organization. (2014, June 21). *Announcing winners of 1st Coover & Hayles awards!* Retrieved from http://eliterature. org/2014/06/announcing-winners-of-1st-coover-hayles-awards/

Flood, A. (2013, Jan. 10). Digital publishing: The experts' view of what's next. *The Guardian*. Retrieved from http://www.theguardian. com/books/2014/jan/10/digital-publishing-next-industry-revolution

Garley, M., Stewart, R. H., Gowran, G., Tempest, J., Pickering, W., & Simmonds, M. (2012). *Collider Comics* [Mobile application software]. Retrieved from itunes.apple.com

Gee, J. P. (2003). *What video games have to teach us about learning and literacy* (1st ed.). New York: Palgrave Macmillan.

Glazier, L. P. (2002). *Digital poetics: the making of e-poetries.* Tuscaloosa, AL: University of Alabama Press.

Grant, M. (2013). *BZRK.* New York: Egmont.

Green, J., & Levithan, D. (2010). *Will Grayson, Will Grayson.* New York: Dutton.

Griffin, A. (2010). *The Julian game.* New York: Putnam.

Groenke, S. L., & Maples, J. (2010). Young adult literature goes digital: Will teen reading ever be the same? *ALAN Review, 37*(3), 38–44.

Haarsma, P. J. (2008). *The softwire: Virus on Orbis.* Somerville, MA: Candlewick Press.

Havard, A. (2011). *The survivors.* Nashville, TN: Chafie Press.

Hayles, N. K. (2002). *Writing machines.* Cambridge, MA: The MIT Press.

Hayles, N. K. (2008). *Electronic literature: New horizons for the literary.* Notre Dame, Indiana: University of Notre Dame.

Hicks, T. (2013). *Crafting digital writing.* Portsmouth, NH: Heinemann.

Hicks, T., & Sibberson, F. (2015). Students as writers and composers: Workshopping in the digital age. *Language Arts, 92*(3), 221–228.

Hundley, M., & Holbrook, T. (2013). Set in stone or set in motion? Multimodal and digital writing with pre-service English teachers. *Journal of Adolescent & Adult Literacy, 56*(6), 492–501. doi:10.1002/JAAL.171

Hundley, M., & Parsons, L. (in press). Reading with blurred boundaries: Digital & visual culture influence on young adult literature. In J. Hayn & J. Kaplan (Eds.), *Adolescent Literature Today.* New York: Rowman & Littlefield.

Hundley, M., Smith, B., & Holbrook, T. (2013). Re-Imagine Writing: Multimodal Literary Analysis in English Education. In K. Pytash & R. Ferdig (Eds.), *Exploring technology for writing and writing instruction.* Hershey, PA: IGI Global.

ISTE. (2007). *ISTE standards-students.* Retrieved from http://www.iste.org/standards/standards-for-students

Jackson, S. (1996). *Patchwork Girl: by Mary/Shelley/and Herself.* [CD-ROM]. Watertown, MA: Eastgate Systems, Inc.

Jenkins, H. (2006). *Convergence culture: Where old and new media collide.* New York: New York University Press.

Jenkins, H. (2007, March 22). *Transmedia storytelling* [blog post]. Retrieved from http://henryjenkins.org/2007/03/transmedia_storytelling_101.html

Jenkins, H., Purushotma, R., Weigel, M., Clinton, K., & Robison, A. J. (2009). Confronting the challenges of participatory culture: Media education for the 21st century. Cambridge, MA: The MIT Press. Retrieved from https://mitpress.mit.edu/sites/default/files/titles/free_download/9780262513623_Confronting_the_Challenges.pdf

Johnson-Eilola, J. (1994). Reading and writing in hypertext: Vertigo and euphoria. In C. Selfe & S. Hilligloss (Eds.), *Literacy and computers* (pp. 195–219). New York: Modern Language Association of America.

Joyce, M. (1991). Notes toward an unwritten nonlinear electronic text, "The Ends of Print Culture" (a work in progress). *Postmodern Culture, 2*(1).

Joyce, M. (1995). *Of two minds: Hypertext pedagogy and poetics*. Ann Arbor, MI: University of Michigan Press.

Joyce, M. (1996/1987). *Afternoon, a story*. [CD-ROM]. Watertown, MA: Eastgate Systems. (Originally published 1987)

Kist, W. (2013). New literacies and the Common Core. *Educational Leadership*, *70*(6), 38–43.

Lamberson, G. (2014). *The Julian year* [MMG Sidekick version]. Retrieved from itunes.apple.com

Landow, G. P. (1997). Hypertext 2.0 (Rev., amplified ed.). Baltimore, MD: The Johns Hopkins University Press.

Landow, G. P. (2006). *Hypertext 3.0: Critical and new media in an era of globalization*. Baltimore, MD: The Johns Hopkins University Press. (Original work published 1992)

Leander, K. (2009). Composing with old and new media: toward a parallel pedagogy. In V. Carrington & M. Robinson (Eds.), Digital literacies: Social learning and classroom practices (pp. 147-162). Los Angeles, CA: Sage. doi:10.4135/9781446288238.n10

Lenhart, A., & Madden, M. (2005). Teen content creators and consumers. *Pew Internet & American Life Project*. Retrieved from http://www.pewinternet.org/~/media//Files/Reports/2005/PIP_Teens_Content_Cr eation.pdf.pdf

Lenhart, A., Purcell, K., Smith, A., & Zickuhr, K. (2010). Social media and young adults. *Pew Internet & American Life Project*. Retrieved from http://www.pewinternet.org/Reports/2010/Social-Media-and-Young-Adults.aspx

Luke, A., & Freebody, P. (1999). *Further notes on the four resources model*. Retrieved from http://www.readingonline.org/research/lukefreebody.html

Malloy, J. (1986). *Uncle Roger*. Retrieved from http://www.well.com/user/jmalloy/uncleroger/partytop.html

Malloy, J. (1993). Its name was Penelope. Watertown, MA: Eastgate Systems, Inc. (Original exhibition version 1989)

Mancusi, M. (2010). *Gamer girl*. New York.

McLuhan, M. (1960, May 18). *The global village* [Video file]. Retrieved from http://www.cbc.ca/archives/categories/arts-entertainment/media/marshall-mcluhan-the- man-and-his-message/world-is-a-global-village.html

McLuhan, M. (1994). *Understanding media: The extensions of man* (T. Gordon, Ed.). Berkeley, CA: Gingko Press. (Original work published 1964)

Miskec, J. (2007). YA by Generation Y: New writers for new readers. *ALAN Review*, *35*(3), 7–14.

Morgan, Wendy. (2000). Electronic tools for dismantling the Master's House: Poststructuralist Feminist Research and Hypertext Poetics. In E. A. St.Pierre & W. S. Pillow (Eds.), Working the ruins: Feminist poststructural theory and methods in education (pp. 130-149). New York: Routledge.

Moulthrop, S. (1991). The politics of hypertext. In G. Hawisher & C. Selfe (Eds.), *Evolving perspectives on computers and composition studies* (pp. 253–271). Urbana, IL: NCTE.

Moulthrop, S. (1991). *Victory garden*. Watertown, MA: Eastgate Systems, Inc.

Moulthrop, S. (1994). Rhizome and resistance: Hypertext and the dreams of a new culture. In G. P. Landow (Ed.), *Hyper/text/theory* (pp. 299–319). Baltimore, MD: The John Hopkins University Press.

Myracle, L. (2004). ttyl. New York: Amulet.

Nash, R. (2014). What is the business of literature? *The Virginia Quarterly Review, 90*(4). Retrieved from http://www.vqronline.org/articles/what-business-literature

National Endowment for the Arts. (2007). *To read or not to read: A question of national consequence.* Retrieved from http://arts.gov/sites/default/files/ToRead.pdf

Nelson, T. H. (1981). *Literary machines.* Swatchmore, PA: Theodor H. Nelson.

New Study: 55% of YA Books Bought by Adults. (2012, September 13). Retrieved from http://www.publishersweekly.com/pw/by-topic/childrens/childrens-industry- news/article/53937-new-study-55-of-ya-books-bought-by-adults.html

Norris, S. (2008). *Something to blog about.* New York: Amulet.

NRK. (2007, February 26). *Medieval helpdesk with English subtitles* [Video file]. Retrieved from http://www.youtube.com/watch?v=pQHXSjbQvQ. (Originally broadcast in 2001.)

O'Brien, D., & Voss, S. (2011). Reading multimodally: What is afforded? *Journal of Adolescent & Adult Literacy, 55*(1), 75–78. doi:10.1598/JAAL.55.1.9

Ong, W. J. (1982). *Orality and literacy: The technologizing of the word.* New York: Routledge. doi:10.4324/9780203328064

Pallotta, T. (2011, June 6). *Walkthrough.* Retrieved from http://www.submarinechannel.com/transmedia/collapsus-walkthrough-with-tommy-pallotta/

Pandya, J. Z., & Auckerman, M. (2014). A four resources analysis of technology in the CCSS. *Language Arts, 91*(6), 429–435.

Piesing, M. (2012). Despite promise, transmedia publishing still mostly a mess. *Publishing Perspectives.* Retrieved from http://publishingperspectives.com/2012/12/despite-promise-transmedia-publishing-still-mostly-a-mess/

Prensky, M. (2011). Digital wisdom and homo sapiens digital. In M. Thomas (Ed.), *Deconstructing digital natives* (pp. 15–29). New York: Routledge.

Pullinger, K., & Joseph, C. (2011). *Inanimate Alice.* Retrieved from http://www.inanimatealice.com/

Rettberg, S. (2009). Communitizing electronic literature. *Digital Humanities Quarterly, 3*(2). Retrieved from http://www.digitalhumanities.org/dhq/vol/3/2/000046/000046.html

Riordan, R. (2005). *The lightning thief.* New York: Scholastic.

Rowling, J. K. (1999). *Harry Potter and the sorcerer's stone.* New York: Scholastic, Inc.

Rudnick, E. (2010). *Tweet Heart.* New York: Disney/Hyperion.

Schneps, M. H., Thomson, J. M., Chen, C., Sonnert, G., & Pomplun, M. (2013). E-Readers are more effective than paper for some with dyslexia. *PLoS ONE, 8*(9), e75634. doi:10.1371/journal.pone.0075634 PMID:24058697

Selfe, C. (2007). *Multimodal composition: Resources for teachers.* Cresskill, NJ: Hampton Press.

Singapore, I. (2014, September 3). *Experience the power of a bookbook* [Video file]. Retrieved from https://www.youtube.com/watch?v=MOXQo7nURs0

Smith, C. (2013, Dec. 13). Tumblr Offers Advertisers A Major Advantage: Young Users, Who Spend Tons Of Time On The Site. *Business Insider.* Retrieved from http://www.businessinsider.com/tumblr-and-social-media-demographics-2013-12#ixzz3I8FQlCOH

Snyder, I. (1996). *Hypertext: the electronic labyrinth*. Carlton South, Australia: Melbourne University Press.

Strasser, T. (2009). *Wish you were dead*. New York: Egmont.

Strasser, T. (2011). *Kill you last*. New York: Egmont.

Sweeney, S. M. (2010). Writing for the instant messaging and text messaging generation: Using new literacies to support writing instruction. *Journal of Adolescent & Adult Literacy, 54*(2), 121–130. doi:10.1598/JAAL.54.2.4

United States Department of Justice. (n.d.). *Cyber crime*. Retrieved http://www.justice.gov/usao/briefing_room/cc/

Van Cleave, J. & Bridges-Rhoads, S. (in press). Rewriting the Common Core State Standards for Tomorrow's Literacies. *English Journal, 104*(2), 41-47.

Walton, K., Golick, J., & Golick, S. (Producers). (2010-2012). *Ruby Skye, P.I.* [Webisode series]. Retrieved from http://rubyskyepi.com

Weston, D. C. (2014). *The memory machine* [ibook]. Retrieved from itunes.apple.com

Wysocki, A. & Lynch. (2012). *Design, compose, advocate*. New York: Longman.

YouTube. (n.d.). *Statistics*. Retrieved https://www.youtube.com/yt/press/statistics.html

KEY TERMS AND DEFINITIONS

Codex: Early text form comprised of stitched sheets or pages.

E-Book: Short for "electronic book"; e-books are accessible on digital devices such as computers, tablets, and smart phones and may either be electronic versions of print texts or texts designed to be published in an electronic format.

Hypermedia: An interactive digital or electronic text that includes hyperlinks to other digital or electronic media such as print, videos, image files, and sound files.

Hypertext: An interactive digital or electronic text that includes hyperlinks to other digital or electronic texts; sometimes used synonymously with hypermedia.

Interactive Book: An electronic or digital book designed to include active reader participation via links or embedded reader-enacted functions.

Non-Linear Text: A text designed to disrupt chronological flow or conventional textual sequencing.

Participatory Culture: Term developed by Henry Jenkins to describe contemporary cultures where members of a society do not only consume media content but also create and distribute it.

Story App: Digital application designed to tell a narrative or story, usually employing print, images and sound. Frequently, story apps are also interactive and non-linear.

Transmedia Storytelling: A form of narrative in which the story is told across multiple media platforms (e.g., books, films, websites, story apps) and usually across multiple media forms (e.g., video, audio, print).

Chapter 19
Collaborative Writing:
Wikis and the Co-Construction of Meaning

Katina Zammit
Western Sydney University, Australia

ABSTRACT

As people, of all ages, take advantage of the opportunities offered by Web 2.0 to be active participants in the process of knowledge building, they become publishers and producers of knowledge not simply consumers of information. In this chapter I will draw upon Bruns and Humphrey's (2007) concept of produsage and the four capacities of produsers as a frame through which to consider the use of wikis for collaborative writing and the social construction of meaning in an online environment. In presenting an overview of the literature on wikis in educational, work and interest-group (affinity spaces) contexts, the issues and gaps, connections will be made between these two concepts and other complementary ideas. While the chapter focuses, primarily, on wiki usage in educational contexts commentary is also included on wikis in workplace environments and for interest-groups (affinity spaces).

INTRODUCTION

In the information age of the 21st century, knowledge is a powerful tool that is ever changing. We can no longer know everything or even hope to be able to achieve an outcome without the support of others: their intellectual input, their critique of our ideas, their suggested directions, and their contribution to an end product. We are no longer silos of knowledge transmitting this knowledge to others but are part of knowledge building communities, contributing together for the advancement of society. As such the skills and capacities to work in a knowledge building community are

essential for students to learn throughout their education, from the early years of school through to university.

The online environments that offer opportunities for people to connect with each other and create spaces for the exchange and development of knowledge are part of what is collectively known as Web 2.0. Examples of Web 2.0 platforms are blogs, forums, Google docs and wikis. Web 2.0 encourages individual users to coordinate with others by creating spaces for user collaboration and the means for them to explore, combine, annotate, edit, splice and mix a range of communication modes, such as images, sound, video

DOI: 10.4018/978-1-4666-8310-5.ch019

and writing re-expressing ideas and creating new content (Cole, 2009; Crook et al., 2008; Greenhow, Robelia, & Hughes, 2009; Tay & Allen, 2011). It is the active participation in communities of practice (Crook et al., 2008; Wenger, 1999) that affords the potential for greater conceptual understanding because what is created collaboratively is greater than what could be produced independently (Kalanztis & Cope, 2012; Thornton, 2013). Involvement in these communities, builds an individual's repertoire of practices.

As people, of all ages, take advantage of the opportunities offered by Web 2.0 to be active participants in the process of knowledge building, they become publishers and producers of knowledge not simply consumers of information (Cole, 2009; Forte & Bruckman, 2007; Greenhow et al., 2009), blurring the boundaries between the two, and becoming "produsers"(users/producers) (Bruns & Humphrey, 2007). Produsage, as Bruns and Humphrey (2007) point out, involves the "collaborative and continuous building and extending of existing content in pursuit of further improvement" (p. 2). It has four fundamental characteristics that are not characteristic of traditional linear modes of production and work where individual ownership of knowledge is valued. The four characteristics of produsage are:

1. *It is community based.*
2. *Participants occupy fluid roles participating as is appropriate to their personal skills, interests, and knowledges.*
3. *The "artifacts" are unfinished.*
4. *What is produced is common property. (Bruns & Humphreys, 2007, p. 2)*

Produsage occurs within a 'participatory culture' (Jenkins, Clinton, Purushotma, Robison, & Weigel, 2006) enabled by Web 2.0 technology. Involvement in a participatory culture occurs when people have a social connection with others, share ideas and believe their contributions matter. Within their varied communities, people

contribute to knowledge building and knowledge sharing through participatory, collaborative, and distributed practices (Greenhow et al., 2009; Jenkins et al., 2006; Thornton, 2013). Participatory cultures can be identified as:

- *Affiliations* — memberships, formal and informal, in online communities centered around various forms of media, (such as Facebook, message boards, metagaming, game clans).
- *Expressions* — producing new creative forms, (such as digital sampling, skinning and modding, fan videomaking, fan fiction writing, zines, mash-ups).
- *Collaborative Problem-solving* — working together in teams, formal and informal, to complete tasks and develop new knowledge (such as through Wikipedia, alternative reality gaming, spoiling).
- *Circulations* — Shaping the flow of media (such as podcasting, blogging). (Jenkins et al., 2006, p. 3)

Whether in an educational environment, a social environment, an organizational or workplace environment, members involved in knowledge building through the deployment of Web 2.0 technology need to learn the skills and capacities to negotiate these spaces. They also need to consider these spaces an advantage to them and the learning or work practices (Stocker, Richter, Hoefler, & Tochtermann, 2012). Educational environments are more able to provide support and opportunities for produsage than corporate environments, as they are more flexible and dynamic and hence better placed to develop participatory cultures and form communities of practices.

Bruns and Humphrey (2007) suggest four capacities that students require in order to be produsers in collaborative environments, which promote learning in the information age. They are the capacities to be:

1. **Creative:** Content (artistic, information, knowledge) creation and the development of creative capacities.
2. **Collaborative:** Developing the capacity to know when, where and with whom to collaborate, and under what circumstances not to do so.
3. **Critical:** Developing sufficient critical capacities to establish the appropriate context for their engagement in produsage processes. This requires a critical stance both towards potential collaborators and their work… and towards their own creative and collaborative abilities and existing work portfolio.
4. **Communicative:** An explicit focus on effective and successful communication between participants… to be both constructively critical, and able to communicate about the collaborative and creative processes (a meta-level skill) (p. 3).

In this chapter I will draw upon Bruns and Humphrey's (2007) concept of produsage and the four capacities of produsers as a frame through which I consider the use of wikis for collaborative writing and the social construction of meaning in an online environment. In presenting an overview of the literature on wikis in educational, work and interest-group (affinity spaces) contexts, the issues and gaps, I will attempt to make connections with these two concepts and other complementary ideas. While I focus the chapter, primarily, on wiki usage in educational contexts I also include commentary on wikis in workplace environments and affinity spaces.

BACKGROUND

Wikis are a Web 2.0 technology that can facilitate collaborative construction of meaning, foster produsers that use and create content, and enable a participatory culture to be promoted in a classroom or organization. The word "wiki" comes from the Hawaiian word *wiki wiki* meaning "to hurry," and wikis certainly enable rapid and easy authoring direct to the Web (Parker & Chao, 2007; Wheeler, Yeomans, & Wheeler, 2008). They are a cost-effective and easy means of enabling co-construction of a text that uses a WYSWYG (what you see is what you get) interface (Malaga, 2010), depending on the choice of wiki platform (see Figure 1 & 2). Most wiki programs use similar affordances to word processing programs making them easy to use and requiring only a limited amount of workplace training (Lundin, 2008; Morgan & Smith, 2008; Standing & Kiniti, 2011; Thornton, 2013). Additional affordances are included that assist tracking of text changes (History section) and enable communication across time and place (Discussion or Comments section) between student-creators of a wiki page,

Figure 1. Example of a Wikispace page

Figure 2. Example of a Twiki page

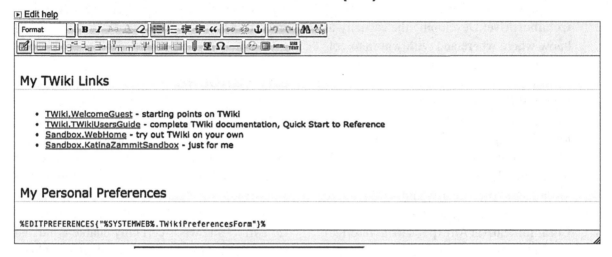

between educator and student-creators, between members of an organizational team or an affinity (interest-based) group. Further extensions can be added to a wiki to customize it to meet an organization or enterprise's purpose, for example links to internal document repositories; computing capabilities, such as algorithms, web services support; special pages such as a sand box for users to practice wiki editing; and other affordances such as a RSS feed, multi-page handling and content rating (Lykourentzou, Dagka, Papadaki, Lepouras, & Vassilakis, 2012).

Wikis in education are created as teacher resource sites, teacher centered content delivery devices, sites for individual student presentations and portfolios with limited collaboration and sites for groups that are truly collaborative in the co-construction of a text (Reich, Murnane, & Willett, 2012). For workplaces and affinity spaces, wikis tend to be resource sites, spaces for organizational knowledge building and knowledge sharing that capture tacit and previously undocumented knowledge of workers as well as explicit knowledge (Grudin & Poole, 2010) and for working on a solution, an issue or shared passion (Oschner & Martin, 2013). Affinity wikis can also be researched-based, drawing on the knowledge of experts to solve a solution or share results, for example Wang's gene-function wiki to pool resources (2006, cited inBoulos, Maramba, & Wheeler, 2006) and formal mathematical wiki (Alama, Brink, Mamane, & Urban, 2011).

Wikis shift students in educational contexts from being *consumers* of the Internet to *creators* (Lamb & Johnson, 2009;Pifarre & Fisher, 2011) or *produsers* (Bruns & Humphreys, 2007). Students work together in a technologically mediated social space (Wheeler et al, 2008) either synchronously or asynchronously, in geographically close or distanced locations, to construct their knowledge base, clarify ideas and provide feedback to each other using the affordances of the wiki (Engstrom & Jewett, 2005; Huang & Nakazawa, 2010; Lucey & Shifflet, 2013; McPherson, 2012; Thomas, 2013). Students publish content direct to the Web, including text, images and hyperlinks; to edit existing content; expand content; create pages; post links to a new page or outside web sites; track changes; and to return to previous versions; suggest changes, post responses and discuss options; and co-construct knowledge as students build and edit their collective work in a single environment

(Arnold, Ducate, & Kost, 2012; Hazari, North, & Moreland, 2009; Lundin, 2008; Mak & Coniam, 2008; Morgan & Smith, 2008; Pifarre & Fisher, 2011; Wheeler et al., 2008).

Google docs could also be used as an online platform for students to use in the co-construction of knowledge but the affordances are more limited than those of a wiki. Limitations of Google docs relate to the design of the final product, management of multiple documents or pages within the one site for knowledge management, the choice of media that can be included, and users can't return to previous versions or view/review the decision making strategies employed during the creation of a document. While users of Google docs are co-creators of a text, usually a written text, they are not limited in their produsage, as they do not develop a knowledge base using a range of modes and affordances, make changes to that knowledge base over time and share that knowledge more widely.

The affordances of wikis can assist collaborative writing, providing opportunities for groups of students to "continuously reflect, review, publish and observe cumulative written results as they unfold in the production process" (Thomas, 2013, p. 21). Their use can challenge the traditional interaction both in and out of the classroom (Lundin, 2008; Mak & Coniam 2008) because they encourage a teaching paradigm shift from traditional didactic teaching and learning to more transformative, active and collaborative learning (Jung & Suzuki, 2014; Lundin, 2008).

The educator's role is thus changing when wikis are used as a learning environment, as with other Web 2.0 platforms, from one of instructor, to one of facilitator, moderator or even partner (Bruns & Humphrey, 2007; Hadjerrouit, 2013; Huang & Nakazawa, 2010; Wheeler Et al., 2008).

Wikis provide opportunities for teachers to become more active during the process of creating a text, providing continuous feedback, and not just focused on the assessment of a final product created by an individual (Zammit, 2010b). Teachers become equal participants with students, sharing power and control over content, and contribute to the development of a community of practice where students are part of a knowledge building discourse (Forte & Bruckman, 2007; Scardamalia & Bereiter, 1994). Such communities of practices, that involve students in co-construction of knowledge, acknowledge students can be knowledge-creators and that information can flow between them as participants not just through a 'central authority'. As Bruns and Humphrey (2007) point out "traditional and rigid teacher/learner, staff/student, university/client dichotomies are counter-productive in the co-creative, collaborative process of produsage" (p. 3).

Workplaces that utilize wikis as part of an organization's knowledge management strategy or for coordination and completion of projects also shift the management style hierarchical to more transformative and distributive leadership. They build a trusting culture where employees have a voice in the organization (Grace, 2009; Lykourentzou et al., 2012) and the knowledge of employees is seen as a valuable strategic resource (Stocker et al., 2012; Yates, Wagner, & Majchrzak, 2010). Innovation can be encouraged and supported through the use of wikis in an organization (Standing & Kiniti, 2011). Wikis enable employees and teams to work in a similar way to students, developing and working within communities of practice that facilitate knowledge-building discourse.

While used for different purposes than educational contexts, wikis in workplaces also shift employees from consumers of information to produsers. The same shift can be identified in wiki-based affinity spaces, such as the Marvel wiki (http://marvel.wikia.com), ChemWiki (http://chemwiki.ucdavis.edu/) and Elder Scrolls wiki (http://elderscrolls.wikia.com), for the people who use these spaces and build upon the knowledge of the community, co-constructing the information as they collaborate.

Wikis and Collaborative Learning

Members of a collaborative group share a common goal, pool their knowledge, share participation, accountability and resources (McPherson, 2012; Arnold et al, 2012). As McPherson (2012) points out "collaboration enables insights and solutions that only teamwork can produce" (p. 3). Collaborative learning offers numerous benefits for students, which equally apply to employees in organizations. These include:

1. *Increased involvement and motivation*
2. *Enhanced critical thinking skills,*
3. *Promotion of problem-solving skills*
4. *Encouraging student learning and achievement (Cole, 2009; De Witt et al, 2014; Hadjerrouit, 2013)*

Drawing on socio-cultural approaches to learning, researchers have demonstrated that wikis in education can promote collaborative learning and provide students with opportunities to learn as a result of social interaction and the support of others (Hadjerrouit, 2013; Thomas, 2013). Lund (2008) comments, "a wiki has the potential to advance and realize a collective ZPD [Zone of Proximal Development] but its features and affordances must be socially enacted" (p. 40). Social-based learning requires students to work together, with others, and can't be enacted by a single student creating a wiki page. It requires "learning dialogues" (Crook Et al., 2008, p. 31). A wiki can be the platform to develop these learning dialogues assisting student groups to communicate and develop their "paper" more effectively (Malaga, 2010), as they participate in collaboratively building resources (Parker & Chao, 2007).

What constitutes collaboration in a wiki depends upon the purpose of the wiki in an organization or education context and the learning design outcomes, and time frame for achieving the goal. Working truly collaboratively is a complex task. It is challenging and time-consuming but has the potential for students to achieve a better quality end product (Arnold Et al., 2012; Hadjerrouit, 2013). If a group chooses to divide a task up into sections and allocate each section to a group member, who in turn focuses on revising their own contributions to the text, then the group is working cooperatively (Arnold Et al., 2012). Tay and Allen (2011) call this "collective individualism" (p. 160). Parks, Hamers, and Huot-Lemonnier (2003, cited in McPherson 2012, p. 5) classify collaboration into the four types of:

- **Joint Collaboration:** Writers work together on a text and are equally responsible for its construction;
- **Parallel Collaboration:** Writers do not have equal responsibility while working on the same project;
- **Incidental Collaboration:** Usually results from spontaneous requests for momentary assistance; and,
- **Covert Collaboration:** Involves the acquisition of information from documents while creating text.

Joint and covert collaboration builds "collective intelligence" (Jenkins et al., 2006) and can be compared to students and others developing creative and critical capacities (Bruns & Humphreys, 2007). In general, studies in educational contexts consider genuine collaboration to be 'better' than cooperation. But in practice, it is more complex than this and it may be more beneficial to consider them as complementary depending on the phase in the learning sequence.

Studies investigating collaboration during wiki construction in education contexts frequently use taxonomies to analyze the collaborative and revision process using the audit trails in the history, comment and/or discussion sections of a wiki as a record of the collaboration. These affordances are also used to ascertain the form of collaboration: whether it is cooperation (individuals work on separate aspects to complete the task) or 'true

Table 1. Taxonomies of collaboration or cooperation

Mak and Coniam (2008) ESL High School Learners in Hong Kong	Pifarre and Fisher (2011) Spanish Primary-Aged Students (9-10 Years Old)	Arnold et al (2012) University Students Studying Intermediate German	Woo et al (2013) Chinese Primary-Aged Students' in Hong Kong Studying English
1) **Adding ideas** –new content is contributed. (2) **Expanding ideas** –existing ideas are built on or reworked in some way (3) **Reorganizing ideas** – editing and organizing takes place such as text being moved around, a topic sentence added etc (4) **Correcting errors** –amendments are made to grammar, spelling and punctuation, but no new content is contributed (p. 451)	**Surface changes** (i) Formal (spelling, punctuation) (ii) Meaning-preserving (addition, deletion, substitution, restructuring, reversion) **Text-based changes** (i) Micro-structure (addition, deletion, substitution, restructuring, reversion) (ii) Macro-structure (addition, deletion, substitution, restructuring, reversion).	**Formal or surface changes**: format, spelling, punctuation, revisions to grammar, such as verbs, nominal/ adjectival endings, word order, lexical revision, spelling, and, translation, **Meaning or stylistic changes**: additions, reordering, meaning-developing changes, significant content additions, content deletions, factual correction	(1) **Content meaning or global**, feedback related to idea development, audience, purpose, and organization of writing (2) **Surface or local**, comments related to copy-editing (e.g. wording, grammar, and punctuation). *e. Evaluations*, commented on features of writing; *f. Clarifications*, probed for explanations and justifications; *g. Suggestions*, pointed out the direction for changes; *h. Alterations*, provided specific changes (p. 284-285) + revision-oriented comments, that were likely to lead to revision; and non-revision-oriented

collaboration' (each member of the group or team work on all aspects of the wiki) or a combination of the two, during co-construction of meaning. In a workplace, this will depend on whether it is knowledge management or project-based use of a wiki and whether it is a well-established organization or start-up company. Most research classify changes based on the categories of meaning and surface changes (see Table 1).

Mak and Coniam (2008) found that most contributions involved students adding new ideas (meaning change) and least contributions involved correcting others' errors (surface change). These findings imply that students were working cooperatively rather than truly collaboratively.

In contrast, Woo et al (2013) found that, similar to other studies (Arnold et al., 2012), the most common revisions were surface level changes including spelling, punctuation and grammar. In addition, their findings revealed "a complex collaborative process during the actual composition of writing and not just during the reviewing process of an already completed text" (p. 303).

From their analysis, Arnold et al (2012) found that the wiki composition process demonstrated a more complex picture of collaboration, with a combination of collaborative and cooperative writing. A large majority of the students (75%) made revisions to their own as well as to other writers' text, which indicated that the majority of students took a collaborative approach to group work. However, they noted that almost two thirds of all revisions were made to the students' own writing, meaning that the majority of revisions were based in cooperation rather than collaboration. Similar to Woo et al (2013), there were more formal or surface revisions than meaning or stylistic revisions made to others' writing. In relation to meaning revisions, students used a more cooperative approach when making changes to content. Students felt less inhibited to correct the formal mistakes of their group mates while they considered meaning-based revisions more problematic, maybe even off limits. This could also be associated with students' lack of knowledge of the topic which constrains their ability to make constructive meaning changes because they may not feel confident about the field to contribute or change another's writing (Zammit, 2010b).

Affordances that Facilitate Collaboration

Studies of electronic learning environments and their designs, such as wikis, have identified affordances that facilitate collaboration and task success (Table 2). Kirschner, Strijbos, Krejins, and Beers' (2004) classification of affordances associated with the design of electronic collaborative learning environments, categorize them into technological, educational and social affordances. Technological affordances relate to the usability of the electronic collaborative learning environment, such as the tools incorporated into a wiki. They are the affordances of the system that allows tasks to be accomplished in an efficient and effective way, and make it easy for a user to learn and control (p. 50). Educational affordances are instrumental in determining if and how individual and team learning (e.g., collaborative learning) can take place (p. 51). Social affordances are the properties of electronic collaborative learning environments that act as social-contextual facilitators relevant for the learner's social interaction (p. 51). Understandings of all three affordances, not just the technological, are necessary to facilitate collaboration and co-construction of knowledge.

Building on the work of Kirshner et al (2004), Bower (2008) further identified a set of sub-categories for technological affordances. He categorised technological affordances into media, spatial, temporal, navigational, emphasis, synthesis, and access-control affordances, calling them e-learning technology affordances. Bower (2008) then classified each technological affordance according to the degree of interaction they enabled (Table 2) referring to them as either static/instructive ('affordances that allow fixed representations and one way transmission of information') or collaborative/productive ("affordances that allow flexible representations that can be adjusted and shared") (p. 7) but acknowledging visually that some of the affordances are in between. Bower noted that the list was not exhaustive nor were the categories absolute. These e-learning technological affordances contribute to students' and others ability to collaboratively write or create a multimodal text in an online environment, and each of the collaborative/ productive affordances and 'abilities' are tools available in a wiki, and not found in Google docs.

Fu et al (2013), adding to the work of Bower (2008), found in their study, five categories of educational affordances, and two for social affordances associated with wikis that supported collaboration. The educational affordances were:

1. Group project management: Students are able to designate and schedule the assignment.
2. Group report co-construction: Students are able to participate in the document revision at will.
3. Information sharing: Students are able to publish links to sources
4. Knowledge sharing: Students are able to post their insights and interpretations on a concept or topic
5. Feedback sharing: Students are able to request and provide feedback between each other.

The social affordances were:

1. Communication: Students can communicate online within a platform.
2. Motivation: Students can enhance motivation among group members (p. 89).

The expanded list of technology, educational and social affordances provide additional understanding of the skills required by students to enhance their ability to co-construct meaning collaboratively using a wiki. Being able to utilize all these affordances assist students to develop

Table 2. Affordances that support collaboration

Kirschner, Strijbos, Krejins, and Beers' (2004) p 50-51			
Technological affordances: relate to the usability of the electronic collaborative learning environment, such as the tools incorporated into a wiki. **Educational affordances:** instrumental in determining if and how individual and team learning (e.g., collaborative learning) can take place. **Social affordances:** the properties of electronic collaborative learning environments that act as social-contextual facilitators relevant for the learner's social interaction.			
Bower (2008, p. 6-7) **[building on Kirschner et al, 2004]**			
Technological Affordances: Static/Instructive			**Collaborative/ Productive**
Media affordances	read-ability view-ability listen-ability watch-ability		write-ability draw-ability speak-ability video-produce-ability
Spatial affordances		resize-ability move-ability	
Temporal affordances	playback-ability	accessibility	record-ability synchronous-ability
Navigational affordances	browse-ability search-ability	data-manipulation-ability	link-ability
Emphasis affordances	highlight-ability		
Synthesis affordances		combine-ability integrate-ability	
Access-control affordances			permission-ability share-ability
Fu et al (2013, p. 89) **[building on Kirschner et al, 2004; adding to Bower, 2008]**			
Educational affordances: 1. Group project management: Students are able to designate and schedule the assignment. 2. Group report co-construction: Students are able to participate in the document revision at will. 3. Information sharing: Students are able to publish links to sources 4. Knowledge sharing: Students are able to post their insights and interpretations on a concept or topic 5. Feedback sharing: Students are able to request and provide feedback between each other. **Social affordances:** 1. Communication: Students can communicate online within a platform. 2. Motivation: Students can enhance motivation among group members			

the four capacities of a produser: creative, collaborative, critical and communicative (Bruns & Humphreys, 2007).

Advantages of Wikis

For students' to contribute to the 'collective wisdom' (Dede, 2009), they require skills to generate and share knowledge, for communal reflection and social dialogue. They require 21st century skills and new literacies that are 'multiple, dynamic, and malleable' (National Council for the Teaching of English [NCTE], 2008; Partnership for 21st Century Skills, 2011). Wikis can support students' development of new literacies as well as facilitate collaborative learning. Being literate today requires students to have more than just print literacy (Lankshear & Knobel, 2006; Zammit, 2010a). Students need to acquire digital literacy, media literacy, information literacy, and critical literacy skills (Lankshear & Knobel, 2006; Zammit, 2008) that can be deployed as needed in education or workplace context or affinity spaces. These new literacies build on traditional print and paper-based literacy (Castek, 2006; Coiro, 2003; Jenkins et al., 2006).

Jenkins Et al. (2006) identified 11 core skills associated with a participatory culture and 21st century learning. They view these core skills as "shift(ing) the focus of literacy from one of individual expression to community involvement" (p. 4). These core skills can be very effectively supported through the technological, educational and social affordances of wikis and complement Bruns and Humphrey's (2006) capacities of a produser. They are:

- *Play: The capacity to experiment with one's surroundings as a form of problem solving*
- *Performance: The ability to adopt alternative identities for the purpose of improvisation and discovery*
- *Simulation: The ability to interpret and construct dynamic models of real-world processes*
- *Appropriation: The ability to meaningfully sample and remix media content*
- *Multitasking: The ability to scan one's environment and shift focus as needed to salient details.*
- *Distributed Cognition: The ability to interact meaningfully with tools that expand mental capacities*
- *Collective Intelligence: The ability to pool knowledge and compare notes with others toward a common goal*
- *Judgment: The ability to evaluate the reliability and credibility of different information sources*
- *Transmedia Navigation: The ability to follow the flow of stories and information across multiple modalities*
- *Networking: The ability to search for, synthesize, and disseminate information*

- *Negotiation: The ability to travel across diverse communities, discerning and respecting multiple perspectives, and grasping and following alternative norms. (p. 4)*

In addition, studies in education have found that through the use of wikis students are more engaged with the writing process (Morgan & Smith, 2008), whether it is in English, or another language, such as German (Kessler, 2009), Japanese (Jung & Suzuki, 2014) or Chinese (Fu, Chu, & Kang, 2013). Wikis in education have been shown to:

- Energize reluctant learners (Lamb & Johnson, 2009; Zammit, 2010b)
- Promote group synergy (Lamb & Johnson, 2009; Mak & Coniam, 2008)
- Allow for differentiation of learning (McPherson, 2012; Thornton, 2013)
- Encourage authentic and inquiry-based learning (Cress & Kimmerle, 2008; Lamb & Johnson, 2009; Thomas, 2013)
- Help students with reading and writing, including evaluation and revision skills (Hazari et al., 2009; Lamb & Johnson, 2009; Manion & Selfe, 2012; Pifarre & Fisher, 2011; Thomas, 2013; Woo, Chu, & Li, 2013)
- Develop students' skills of reflection (Hazari et al., 2009; Lamb & Johnson, 2009; Pifarre & Fisher, 2011; Thomas, 2013)

Wikis in workplaces also provide benefits to large organizations and small to medium enterprises (SMEs), from well-established corporations such as IBM, Pfizer, Cisco Systems (Standing & Kiniti, 2011) as well as start-up companies. When wikis have been chosen as a solution by an organization the pays off can be measurable, such as financial and customer-related, as well as "immeasurable" or "value-added", such as reputation (Grace, 2009). Studies have found benefits for organizational processes as well as other benefits that come from a participatory culture and one that supports corporate produsers. These include:

- Knowledge codification and knowledge management, which involves building and organizing explicit and tacit knowledge that exists in various parts of a corporation (Grudin & Poole, 2010; Lykourentzou et al., 2012);
- Facilitation of collaboration among units or groups within and between organizations, across time and locations (Grace, 2009; Grudin & Poole, 2010), including the creation of large complex or technical documents, policies and procedures (Grace, 2009), and development of communities of practice (Lykourentzou et al., 2012);
- Development and maintenance of dynamic information systems and processes that change over time (Grace, 2009; Lykourentzou et al., 2012; Standing & Kiniti, 2011);
- Management activities, such as decision making and team or project-based planning (Boulos et al., 2006; Grudin & Poole, 2010; Stocker et al., 2012), which enables a common record of a project and an audit trail of decisions (Grace, 2009; Lykourentzou et al., 2012) that can then be used for training purposes (Lykourentzou et al., 2012), as well as overcoming version confusion often associated with email attachments (Grace, 2009; Lykourentzou et al., 2012)
- Solution of novel and non-routine problems and crisis management (Grace, 2009; Lykourentzou et al., 2012; Standing & Kiniti, 2011);
- Interaction with third parties that enhance communication with customers and vendors, such a help desk, facilitation of advertising, participatory publications (Grudin & Poole, 2010; Lykourentzou et al., 2012);

- Increased two way communication between management and other staff (Grace, 2009), with greater transparency of knowledge and knowledge holders (Stocker et al., 2012);
- Increased employee satisfaction, recognition, and enhanced reputation, and team spirit (Lykourentzou et al., 2012; Standing & Kiniti, 2011).

Wikis can facilitate collaborative or cooperative writing, with both resulting in the creation of a text that involves co-construction of meaning, but each enhances different skills and capacities. The choice of which form of collaboration is promoted relates strongly to the design of learning (pedagogy) and task design (curriculum), which encourages students to approach a task and make decisions about how to work together as a group. In fact the pedagogy, curriculum and assessment practices employed within studies also varied considerably. From open-ended design that left decisions about topic and process up to students to more specific guidelines and details for students to follow as part of the process and completion of a task. Selection of type of collaboration in a workplace is guided by the purpose of the wiki and the roles people take in order to achieve the organizational or business goal.

CURRENT ISSUES RAISED IN THE FIELD

Simply using a wiki in a classroom does not necessarily promote collaboration and co-construction of knowledge by students and teacher or support students as produsers. Issues within the field of collaborative writing and co-constructing meaning using a wiki environment are associated with how to develop a knowledge building community and community of practice. These include issues around what is the 'best' form of collaboration, development of students' skills and capacities that enhance learning, content creation and collaboration in a wiki environment, learning design (pedagogy, curriculum and assessment) to support a shift in educational discourse from individual competitiveness to group collaboration.

While studies acknowledge that using wikis in education promotes collaborative learning and facilitates collaborative writing, the nature of the collaboration was problematized. Collaborative learning may be considered an ill-defined concept (Witney & Smallbone, 2011), but it is generally accepted that genuine collaboration involves students working as a team to complete a task collectively, with mutual engagement and responsibility (Hadjerrouit, 2013; Fu Et al., 2013; McPherson, 2012; Lund, 2008; Cole, 2009). Crook Et al. (2008) note private learning versus collaborative learning as one of the tensions associated with using Web 2.0 in education. If a group divides a task up into sections and allocates each section to a group member, who in turn focuses on revising their own contributions to the text, is this collaboration? Is this form of collaboration, also known as working cooperatively or as coordination (Crook Et al., 2008), a means to develop "collective intelligence" (Jenkins et al., 2006) better than genuine collaboration? When is cooperation more useful than genuine collaboration and in which contexts do you choose one over the other or use both?

As Reich, Murnane & Willett (2012, p.11) found, many educational wikis are resource sites and not truly collaborative spaces. In their study they investigated 255 wikis used in primary and secondary schools and found only a very small percentage (1%) represented a truly collaborative space. The other types were: (a) failed wikis, trial wikis, and teacher resource sites (40%); (b) teacher centered content delivery devices (34%); (c) individual student presentations and portfolios with limited collaboration (25%).

While wikis support different types of collaborative practices, there are issues to be dealt with associated with students' learning to work in a wiki environment. Some of the issues identified are:

- Students' resistance to having their contributions altered or deleted by other group members (Grant, 2009; Lucey & Shifflet, 2013; Mak & Coniam, 2008; Parker & Chao, 2007; Wheeler et al., 2008)
- Students' reluctance to edit other's work for fear of being wrong, thought of as cheating or shaming other students (Bruns & Humphreys, 2007; DeWitt, Siraj, & Alias, 2014; Grant, 2009; Jung & Suzuki, 2014; Lund, 2008; McPherson, 2012; Witney & Smallbone, 2011)
- Students' frustration due to technical difficulties, such as
  ◦ The limited capacity of the free wiki software to support multiple users editing simultaneously (McPherson, 2012; Wheeler et al., 2008; Zammit, 2010b)
  ◦ The difficulty of designing a page, in particular the organization and use of multimodal components (Austin, Smyth, Rickard, Quirk-Bolt, & Metcalfe, 2010; Bruns & Humphreys, 2007; Fu et al., 2013)
  ◦ Network problems (Fu et al., 2013; Li, Chu, & Ki, 2014)
- Students contributing only when in class and access issues at home (Wheeler Et al., 2008; Austin, Et al. 2010)
- Students' tendency to read only those pages to which they have contributed (Wheeler Et al., 2008)
- Students' lack of knowledge of the technological affordances and the time to learn how the wiki works (Cole, 2009; Forte & Bruckman, 2007; Fu et al., 2013; Lucey & Shifflet, 2013; Ruth & Houghton, 2009)
- Students' expectations of transmission pedagogy, curriculum and assessment based in traditional print-based models (Arnold et al., 2012; Forte & Bruckman, 2007; Grant, 2009; Jenkins et al., 2006; Jung & Suzuki, 2014; Lund, 2008; Manion & Selfe, 2012; McPherson, 2012; Tay & Allen, 2011)

As Manion & Selfe (2012, p. 32) noted these difficulties with the human (social) and technological affordances can also became productive moments of discussion. While the technological affordance of usability is a necessary factor when designing learning environments it is not sufficient to facilitate collaboration and collaborative learning (Kirshner Et al., 2004). The technology affords learning and education when it mediates social and educational contexts. As such, the educational and social affordances are as important or if not more important in supporting students collaboratively creating a text using a wiki. All three affordances (technological, social and educational) need to be considered by educators in the design of learning. Issues associated with the social as well as the technological affordances are also relevant for organizations and SMEs in relation to knowledge sharing (Stocker et al., 2012).

Providing enabling opportunities for students to be active constructors of knowledge, that is to be produsers, does not mean relinquishing the responsibility of teachers for learning and teaching (Manion & Selfe, 2012). In fact designing learning to support collaboration and co-construction of knowledge becomes more essential, in order for students to develop the skills required to work and sustain their activity, to use wiki affordances effectively and to improve the outcomes for students (Cole, 2009; Grant 2009; Hadjerrouit, 2013; Huang & Nakazawa 2010; Witney & Smallbone, 2011; Woo Et al., 2013). It can also encompass opportunities for discussion of the issues mentioned above as well as others as they arise.

Messages about the form of collaboration are embedded within the learning design and the activities. In contexts where teachers always make the decisions, students may find it difficult to adjust to a collaborative learning approach. Teachers may also find it difficult to adjust so that they "do not stand outside the learning process (as teachers often do), but rather participate actively" (Scardamalia & Bereiter, 1994, p. 274). Opportunities for students to explicitly learn the

new skills associated with Web 2.0 in context are also required because learning to interpret information as well as becoming skilled at collaboratively producing knowledge and being active constructors of multimodal texts is probably beyond students' educational experience (Forte & Bruckman, 2007). In addition, students need skills to know "when and how to use which technologies and knowing which forms and functions are most appropriate for one's purposes" (Greenhow et al., 2009, p. 248).

As teachers plan for learning, they make decisions about the content, its organization, pacing and how to learn, choosing between teacher-led control over these decisions (strong framing) to student-led (weaker framing) with greater options for students to take control of the learning (Bernstein, 1990). Teachers most often choose the content and almost always choose the assessments. When using wikis in an education context, decisions about pacing, content, and task completion provide opportunities for movement to occur between strong and weak framing, like waves. Wikis may be able to promote significant shifts in teaching practices: from a traditional transmissive pedagogy to a transformational one; from teacher-based control or management of educational experience to shared or learner control (Crook et al., 2008); from assessment focused on individualized written texts to group-based multimodal creations. But the current educational discourse does not promote socially-supported learning and assessment as legitimate. As Crook et al. (2008) comment there is a tension here in relation to *Private learning versus collaborative learning,* noting that "while teachers are expected to reproduce conditions of collaborative thinking similar to work... they are also expected to assess the achievement and potential of individual learners" (p. 37).

Issues raised by the literature in relation to wikis in workplaces are not the same as those for the use of wikis in educational contexts or affinity spaces. While there are a few in common, such as employees being uncertain about the editing of others' contributions (Grudin & Poole, 2010), training on the affordances and the types of collaboration to be deployed, most are different. When an organization selects a wiki it is not to develop 21st century skills of their employees but as a solution to an organizational issue associated with knowledge management, project management or other organizational reason as mentioned in the previous section. A main issue for organizations is the necessity for a clear business goal to be articulated for the use of a wiki, which needs to be well communicated throughout the organization (Standing & Kiniti, 2011; Stocker et al., 2012).

While the organizational benefit may be communicated, employees need to see (and believe) that the choice of a wiki is justified and will meet the intended purpose (Grace, 2009; Grudin & Poole, 2010; Stocker et al., 2012). Employees need to know how the wiki will help them with their work, how it will be incorporated into their daily work pattern or if it is an extra not just how it will benefit the organization (Standing & Kiniti, 2011) whether management has made the decision or it is a fellow employee. Issues specifically related to organizations and SMEs include:

- Developing a culture of collaboration (Standing & Kiniti, 2011) and drawing on the repertoire of practices in organizations which vary according to the industry (Stocker et al., 2012);
- Security and legal issues, including legislative requirements and privacy of clients (Boulos et al., 2006; Lykourentzou et al., 2012) and of user activities and project processes (Lykourentzou et al., 2012);
- Alignment of expectations of managers and individual contributors (Grudin & Poole, 2010), such as
  - Who pays for the time to learn and contribute (Standing & Kiniti, 2011)
  - Communication strategies and incentives employed (Lykourentzou et al., 2012)

  - Lack of clear guidelines and policies on wiki use (Lykourentzou et al., 2012; Standing & Kiniti, 2011)
- Content organization and its flexibility over time as content structure may need to change as wiki grows, the company develops and/ or when different team members have different views about its organization (Grudin & Poole, 2010);
- Position of wiki in existing information ecology, in relation to email, document repositories, intranet site, hallway conversations (Grudin & Poole, 2010) and within the corporate culture (Lykourentzou et al., 2012);
- Currency of information provided which impacts on reputation if there is old content or it is not updated (Grudin & Poole, 2010);
- Wikis ill-suited for some tasks, such as complex formatting, professional polish (Grudin & Poole, 2010) and deciding when to use a wiki and not and/ or which wiki platform to use;
- How to start or work in with other technology currently in use and how to migrate material and how much material should be populated before others begin to use the wiki (Stocker et al., 2012);
- Wiki usability and accessibility that impacts on employee familiarization and participation (Lykourentzou et al., 2012; Standing & Kiniti, 2011);
- Quality control of the information (Lykourentzou et al., 2012; Standing & Kiniti, 2011).

These are often glossed over by referring to the need for policies around procedures and workflow to be developed as part of the implementation process, but little work has been conducted on the effectiveness of such policies. Policies around contributing to affinity space wikis, such as the Marvel wiki (http://marvel.wikia.com/ Category:Policies) and the Elder Scrolls wiki (http://elderscrolls.wikia.com/wiki/The_Elder_Scrolls_Wiki:Policies_and_guidelines), are already in place that provide guidelines to assist the communal co-construction of knowledge, the terminology to use, as well as story-lines. Interest-based affinity space membership and contributions are also member-checked which may limit a new produser's creativity, critique and communication. Research into how new members develop their 'voice' and begin their produsage in an affinity space wiki is an area for investigation, as well as how to gain credence to become an expert within an 'elitist' view of the wiki users (Pellicone & Ahn, 2010). The controls placed on affinity space contributors does also limit vandalism, or the posting of fraudulent and incorrect information, which can be an issue for Wikipedia, but is not seen as a major issue for corporations or education contexts as users are known via their logon and their contributions can be tracked.

IMPLICATIONS AND RECOMMENDATIONS FOR EDUCATION, CIVIC ENGAGEMENT, SOCIAL PRACTICE AND POLICY

Recommendations and implications within educational and workplace contexts will be considered in this section. Well-used affinity spaces appear to have policies in place around co-construction and the scope of members' use of creativity, critique and communicative capacities in an attempt to educate their new members.

In large organizations and SME contexts, it is suggested that policies are needed to assist managers and workers actively support the effective usage of a wiki for either knowledge management or/and project management. Policies and procedures will need to be developed to address the issues identified earlier in this chapter, especially in relation to the incentives and integration into the work environment and work tasks for individuals or teams. Apart from policies, established organizations may need to look at how the wiki fits into their overall information structure, critically analyzing their current information architecture. As part of the interrogation, managers and users need to consider how and for what purposes wikis can provide a solution; how to ensure migration to the wiki is achieved, promoted and supported, for example how much information needs to be pre-populated, how to get people to participate; and what content organizational structure will support both flexibility over time and assist to maintain currency of the information. While most wikis use a familiar interface of a word document, organizations will need to consider how to provide training to new and current employees at all levels, and possibly in different locations, in time and space.

For educational contexts, the recommendations and implications can be viewed as supporting educators to use wikis as part of the learning space for students that promote the learning and development of the four capacities of produsers (creativity, collaborative, critical and communicative) (Bruns & Humphreys, 2007) and the core skills of a 21st century learner (Jenkins et al., 2006). The support and policy development in education revolves around professional learning of teachers already in the system and the role of teacher educators in providing learning opportunities for preservice teachers to take into the classroom, from both the theoretical and practical perspective.

Planning for change to classroom practices is essential in order to ensure that pedagogy, curriculum and assessment contribute to a transformative, 21st century pedagogy. Educators will need to closely consider both their designs for learning (pedagogy) and task design (curriculum) in order to include explicit teaching and learning of skills associated with knowledge building and sharing using wikis, including the technological, educational and social affordances (Fu et al., 2013; Kirschner, Strijbos, Krejins, & Beers, 2004). Wikis themselves can't force students to collaborate even if the learning environment encourages collaboration. A pedagogical approach, that includes attention to the task design, is important to lead students to collaboration (Grant, 2009; Hadjer-rouit, 2013; Judd, Kennedy, & Cropper, 2010).

Teachers' learning design that support students as produsers and to practice core skills, such as distributed cognition, collective intelligence and negotiation are critical as is the teaching of learning design. In addition, the learning design needs to take into account activities that scaffold students' understandings of how to construct the target text within the content area, and their understandings of the affordances of the different semiotic modes.

The changes that can occur as a result of the careful planning of learning and task design that incorporates the use of wikis to collaboratively co-construct meaning influence the (hidden) messages that students receive about their ability, who controls the curriculum and the pace of learning, who has the knowledge, and who has a voice in what is learnt and how (Zammit, 2011). The structuring of the pedagogic discourse, the framing and classification of knowledge (Bernstein, 1975, 1990) are also keys to making significant change to classroom practices and student outcomes, at all levels of education, not just in primary or secondary schools. The provision and withdrawal of scaffolding as part of the learning design supports a flexible, cyclical model of scaffolding.

Throughout the implementation of a curriculum where students and teacher work towards co-construction of knowledge and collaborative writing of a text, there are times when students need explicit instruction and scaffolding, where strong framing is required, and times when this support can be withdrawn and weaker framing is enacted. When planning a learning design teachers and preservice teachers as part of their education course need to consider: When will strong framing be used to scaffold students' learning and when will weaker framing be employed, thus providing engaging messages (The Fair Go Project, 2006) to students about their ability, control over learning and a voice in what they study and when? Will

there be a phase where the teacher and students work together to jointly construct a wiki before students in pairs or small groups collaboratively create a wiki? How will students be supported to learn about the topic, the text, to develop core skills and capacities? How will students be assessed? What outcomes related to both process and product (target text) will the learning design sequence explicitly teach students in order for them to demonstrate achievement? What education discourses will need to be taken into consideration in order to actively work against them?

These shifts in learning design around pedagogy, curriculum and assessment can be challenging if skills are not in students' repertoire of shared practices (Grant, 2009) or funds of knowledge (Moll, Amanti, Neff, & Gonzalez, 1992) and teachers have to work against the institutionalized discourse of competition (Arnold Et al., 2012; Grant, 2009). One suggestion is for teachers to explicitly scaffold students' collaborative processes through discussions about "how they can contribute to the group and establish a set of expectations for the project"(Wheeler Et al, 2008, p. 444) or include in the leaning design a "thinking together" approach (Pifarre and Fisher, 2011, 464) at the beginning of the intervention, which scaffolds students' ability to learn how to collaborate. Discussions can prepare students so they make an effort to "share, discuss, take each other's opinion and revise each others' writing" (Pifarre and Fisher, 2011, p. 464) when using a wiki. Austin Et al. (2010) also found that when teachers planned 'regular high-quality social discourse' activities they developed trust building which enabled students to provide constructive feedback and develop as a community of learners.

While there is no one perfect learning design, examples can be useful for educators and preservice teachers to reflect upon and adapt. Wiki pedagogical models can demonstrate how to provide support across different phases of the learning design. Sharing of 'successful' models and frameworks as well as publications of problems that arise and possible solutions, through wiki or publication or professional organizations websites, conferences or publications, could provide educators with a basis upon which to plan, trial and evaluate their learning designs and associated activities. These will probably need support from educational systems, especially in provision of time to plan learning designs within teaching hours.

For example, Hadjerrouit (2013, pp. 45-46) suggests a pedagogical process to support planning and implementation of wikis. While this model provides a step-by-step process, adjustments need to be incorporated especially in relation to the provision of scaffolding about how the text (written or multimodal) is constructed; supporting students to contribute when they do not know much about the topic or support topic selection (step 3); and the support for learning how to develop the topic, especially around development of new literacies, such as information literacy, reading on-line, and critical literacy (step 8). Thornton (2013, pp. 55-56) suggests a more global pedagogical model, called the 4E Wiki Writing Model for undergraduate students, to support a class's collaborative writing of a text. Similar to Hadjerrouit's model, students may require scaffolding about how the text (written or multimodal) is constructed and the affordances of different communication modes, in order to better meet the assessment outcome. Meanings are orchestrated through the selection and configuration of modes, choosing one semiotic mode over another because "there is a good reason to use *this* form for *that* meaning" (Kress, 2010, p. 5). Students may also need information literacy, critical literacy skills and visual literacy, especially relating to design of the wiki page. The inclusion of discussion about types of collaboration may also be beneficial. Different models or frameworks may also be more relevant to different levels of schooling.

Alternative pedagogies also have potential to support collaborative writing and creation of a multimodal text using a wiki environment, such as Zammit's (2010a) *New Learning Environ-ments Curriculum and Pedagogical Framework* and Kalanztis and Cope's (2005) *Learning by Design* approach. Both these frameworks are based on explicit teaching of the organization and features of different communication modes and multimodality with an emphasis on scaffolding students' creation of a text in any medium. These multiliteracies pedagogical models can provide support for teachers to plan and select their pedagogy, curriculum and scaffolding for assessment, with assessment for learning and assessment as learning. Both provide guidance about how to move teachers and students from the known to the unknown. Their guidelines are not as specific as those suggested by Hadjerrouit (2013) and Thornton (2013), but the exemplars they include can be adapted for different educational contexts. They are also not designed with wikis in mind nor the collaboration skills but could be adapted to specifically address co-construction of meaning and creation of a text using a wiki. The phases of learning they suggest can guide teachers to reflect and consider inclusion of different modes, processes and mediums as part of the learning design, what skills need to be explicitly taught or learnt by students and how to scaffold this learning within a specific time frame.

In addition, educators can't assume that students will appreciate learning how to work differently, to be produsers. Success in a traditional approach may deter students from taking up a more socially oriented learning approach as they see the possibility of "not" succeeding (Halse, Denson, Howard, & Zammit, 2010; Herrington, Oliver, & Reeves, 2003). Students may actively challenge or passively work against changes to assessment because of their previous educational experiences (see for example, Mak & Coniam, 2008). These views need to be considered in the planning of the learning and task design and the delivery of the curriculum.

For example, Manion and Selfe (2012) suggest assessment approaches should help teachers to think "differently about how we teach and how we engage our students as they learn" (p. 26). Working with three academics teaching different courses at university, they co-designed the workflow of the courses to develop the habits and values they wanted students to take up in relation to knowledge building within the classroom and in the field. They "used regular, diverse and distributed methods of assessment to gauge student learning and carefully guide the students' project along the way" (p. 33). They "provided guidance to students in the assessment process, preparing students to both practice the inquiry of the discipline and discern the criteria by which practitioners within the field evaluate each other's work." Selfe's students, however, began with a very traditional view of assessment and they had to be convinced about this new way of learning and being assessed. Similary, Tay and Allen (2011) also noted that if university teaching was to change the mindset of students in relation to what was valued, such as working together, then assessment needed to reflect that view.

FUTURE RESEARCH DIRECTIONS

Most studies on the use of wikis in education, for collaborative writing and co-construction of knowledge have been conducted in higher education contexts, with an increasing but limited amount of research being conducted in secondary schools and less in the primary years (elementary/lower middle schools). Research in the early years, that is, in grades 1-3 is even scarcer. More recent research involving students in the secondary, primary and early years is needed. The studies referred to in this chapter are also implemented over a range of times: from 8 hours to 3 weeks to 3 terms making the results difficult to compare.

A more limited number of studies have been conducted on the use of wikis in workplaces from large organizations to small and medium enterprises (SMEs) and for continued professional learning (see for example, Boulos et al., 2006). Research on the use of wikis in participatory cultures (Jenkins et al., 2006) around affiliations and expressions based on interest areas (affinity spaces) and collaborative problem-solving communities (such as Wang's gene wiki cited in Boulos et al., 2006) is also very limited. Affinity- based wikis could be considered excellent examples of produsage in practice where people both use the knowledge and produce or rework the content. They also have strict guidelines on what to include and how to write, as well as encourage active reporting of vandalism but they are not sites where research is conducted or as a basis for research.

Lykourentzou et al. (2012) have identified gaps in the use of wikis by large organizations and SMEs that could inform future research. They note that there is a need to:

- Measure the return on investment produced through the use of a corporate wiki, as well as the added value that a wiki can gain an enterprise;
- The identification of the base factors affecting a wiki's success, from all levels of the organization from top management to wiki users;
- The development of a detailed framework for the selection of the most appropriate corporate wiki platform;
- How wikis merge with social networks, as well as other technology such as handheld devices;
- What features and the number of features corporate wikis need in order to enhance them and their use. (p.45 – 47)

In educational contexts, there are gaps relating to the design of learning that develops students' core skills (Jenkins et al., 2006) and their creative, collaborative, critical and communicative capacities (Bruns & Humphrey, 2007). Studies need to undertake the next step and provide ideas for implementation of learning designs, such as:

- How to develop students' capacities to collaborate, especially if geographically distant;
- How to enable students to make choices with whom they work;
- How to choose which mode/s to use, and/ or how to support students to choose;
- How to support or build students' confidence in an education context to provide contributions or meaning changes to others' wikis or wikipages;
- Strategies that enable students to delve into and across a topic or field that encourages and demonstrates how to share information found when not on their own topic of investigation or even if it is on the same topic, especially for assessment purposes.
- How to work against educational discourse of an institution and students' beliefs about learning and assessment

To support students' creative capacities educators need to ensure students are explicitly taught the skills to create texts, whether in writing or deploying multiple modes, using the affordances of a wiki so they can use this knowledge to critique their own and others' contributions and assist them to communicate their views on the text being co-constructed. It can't be assumed that students know how to use technology to create texts for education purposes just because they use it for social reasons. Crooke et al. (2008) have two tensions relating to these gaps, which they termed "Digital native versus digital immigrant" noting that *"Pupils are caricatured as self-assured natives while teachers are portrayed as less confident immigrants"* (p. 39) and "Rip-mix-burn versus cut-tweak-paste" which focuses on "How the learner's own perspective or voice can be cultivated in a digital realm that allows such easy integration of pre-formed material" (p. 42).

Learning designs that incorporate the scaffolding of students' understandings of how texts are constructed, including deconstruction of the text

teachers want students to produce, need designing, trialing and evaluation, especially in the early years and primary school years. These studies would be relevant for teachers implementing curricula that include multimodal text creation (see for example, Australian Curriculum Assessment and Reporting Authority (ACARA), 2012). In those studies that focus on co-creation of knowledge through collaboratively producing a written text using a wiki, students were rarely provided with explicit instruction on how to create a successful example of the text that was to be assessed.

If the complex nature of collaboration is also considered then it appears that 'successful' learning designs of teachers using wikis for collaborative writing have initially provided strong framing with the explicit teaching of certain core skills and capacities, which also allow students to take up opportunities to control their own learning (weaker framing) (see as an example, Pifarre & Fisher, 2011). However this is an implied reading of those studies that acknowledge the complex nature of collaboration when students use wikis to co-construct meaning. While wikis can facilitate moving from teacher-led instruction to weaker framing where students have greater control over their own learning or share control with the teacher in a collaborative manner to create a text, many studies do not acknowledge the complex nature of collaboration focusing on one type of collaboration and analyzing wiki data only to demonstrate if students are using true collaboration or cooperation and judging the nature of the revisions.

Achievement of successful outcomes in writing or creating a text for a specific purpose are the result of explicit scaffolding of how the text is organized and the key language features, in addition to the wiki's technological affordances. If the aim is for students to create a multimodal text, then students require an understanding of the affordances of multiple modes of representation, and scaffolding of their understandings of the 'grammars' of the different modes and how to work with the wiki affordances to communicate, critique and create the text. Teachers need to develop students' understandings of the affordances of the different semiotic modes, the language to describe them and the technology (Zammit, 2015).

With an understanding of how the written, spoken, visual, and audio modes represent separately and in combination convey powerful meanings, students may be more successful with creating, critiquing, communicating and selecting the most appropriate design using the most apt modes to convey their meaning (Kress, 2010). These understandings may also provide students with the skills to be able to make more meaningful revisions beyond surface level changes of spelling and grammar But research needs to be conducted to further affirm this position and consider how educators can plan for such learning? And what experiences work in which contexts and in which content areas? How can learners be scaffolded across time and space for teachers working with students geographically distanced, not in the same class?. One possibility would be to consider connecting research on new literacies, and multiliteracies (New London Group, 2000; Zammit, 2010a), with a wiki environment.

In considering the intersection between students' critical and communicative capacities with their creative, it would also be useful to investigate the decision-making processes of students using a wiki around selection of modes to create the meaning they wanted to convey and to demonstrate their knowledge. This direction could also provide useful for research of organizational and affinity space wikis. Students, and employees, can communicate through other means to negotiate their roles, and discuss the co-construction of a wiki or wiki page, whether they are in close proximity or geographically distant, such as face-to-face, mobiles, SMS, Skype (Hadjerrouit 2013; Huang & Nakazawa 2010). Larusson and Alterman (2009) found students' online interactions were interspersed with many offline activities, which supported their collaboration online by building and maintaining a common view, but this was not

a focus of their study. If students are working in close proximity to each other, such as in the same classroom or computer laboratory, students can talk to each other as part of the decision-making and collaborative process. Why would students type a question or suggestion, or go to another computer to revise the text if they can just ask their partner or group member face-to-face? Students may also work together on the same computer searching for information, discussing the construction of the text, deciding on changes, and making revisions to their co-constructed text and / or take turns to use the computer. The reasons for using these other modes should be part of investigations to develop a more robust wiki pedagogy. The findings may in turn assist with further development of wiki platforms that include these other modes, such as face-to-face communication, moving beyond written communication for geographically distanced members of a group.

Current research is also limited due to its use of data from audit trails in the history, comment and discussion pages. This data provides only a limited view of the actual collaboration and communicative strategies students employ, as noted in the previous paragraph. Other methods of gathering data need to be conducted in addition to analyses of audit trails, such as interviews with students and teachers or journals kept that record processes that include all communicative strategies employed during collaboration. Many of the other communicative strategies may be observable in class, but most will not be, especially if out of school contexts are also to taken into consideration. Studies on the interplay and mediation of meanings across modes of communication, including the wiki, would be a valuable contribution to the field extending it beyond the technological.

As noted earlier, boundaries between school and out of school can be blurred when students use wikis to construct knowledge and build a knowledge community, with the concomitant weakening in framing of knowledge as strictly school-related. Collaboratively constructing texts at any place and at any time and how this contributes to students' engagement in learning and learning outcomes could provide rich ground for investigation. Those studies that analyze collaborative practices of students using a wiki tend to report on the school-based collaboration analyzing the contributions of students during school with little investigation of the out-of-school planning, contributions and revisions that take place in concert with in class work. In fact students may prefer to work in an out of school context, such as home, because they can work on the wiki with less chance of losing their work. Students may also prefer to work at home for other reasons not yet known.

Research also emphasizes the importance of teaching students, at any age, how to collaborate. However, there is less information reported that documents a range of examples of how students have successfully learned to collaborate or be communicative, or document the strategies across educational contexts. In fact the older the student, the more emphasis there may need to be on developing their ability for 'genuine' collaboration in comparison to co-operation. Secondary students and university students have spent many years of their education in a traditional, competitive, individualized assessment educational environment. Working against the prevailing educational discourse is challenging and examples of how wikis and learning designs can support change to the traditional practices and views could provide support for teachers wanting to make a change to socially constructed learning.

CONCLUSION

Wikis can promote collaborative writing practices and the co-construction of knowledge but simply providing students with a wiki to create a text does not in itself ensure effective collaborative writing, or creation of a successful written or multimodal text or pages. Wikis can facilitate produsage, sup-

port the learning of the capacities of being creative, critical, collaborative and communicative, and core skills of 21st century literacy necessary for work and active participation in our networked global society. They can prepare students to become knowledge workers that possess the ability to be flexible and think differently. Teachers hold the key to improving students' capabilities to work in a socially-supported learning environment that promotes collective cognition and a community of practice, that is promoted in organizational and affinity space wikis. Knowledge building communities in the classroom require teachers to explicitly plan to scaffold students' understandings of the technological, educational and social affordances of wikis as well as the affordances of a range of communication modes for learning. There are still tensions that need to be considered during planning of learning design. There is still the educational policy and system requirements that promote a different educational discourse to that promoted through a co-construction of knowledge approach. Technology of itself does not solve these issues. Knowledge building and knowledge sharing communities in the workplace also need to consider the prevailing discourses if organizations and SMEs are to build a culture of trust and to incorporate knowledge management into the daily work practices of employees.

REFERENCES

Alama, J., Brink, K., Mamane, L., & Urban, J. (2011). *Large formal wikis: Issues and solutions*. Paper presented at the Intelligent Computer Mathematics, Bertinoro, Italy. doi:10.1007/978-3-642-22673-1_10

Arnold, N., Ducate, L., & Kost, C. (2012). Collaboration or cooperation? Analzing group dynamics and revision processes in wikis. *CALICO Journal*, *29*(3), 431–448. doi:10.11139/cj.29.3.431-448

Austin, R., Smyth, J., Rickard, A., Quirk-Bolt, N., & Metcalfe, N. (2010). Collaborative digital learning in schools: Teacher perceptions of purpose and effectiveness. *Technology, Pedagogy and Education, 19*(3), 327–343. doi:10.1080/1475939X.2010.513765

Australian Curriculum Assessment and Reporting Authority (ACARA). (2012). *The Australian Curriculum: English* Retrieved from http://www.australiancurriculum.edu.au/English/Rationale

Bernstein, B. (1975). Class, Codes and Control: Vol. 3. *Towards a Theory of Educational Transmissions*. London: Routledge & Kegan Paul.

Bernstein, B. (1990). *The Structuring of Pedagogic Discourse: Class, Codes and Control* (Vol. 4). London: Routledge. doi:10.4324/9780203011263

Boulos, M., Maramba, I., & Wheeler, S. (2006). Wikis, blogs and podcasts: A new generation of web-based toosl for virtual collaborative clinical practice and education. *BMC Medical Education, 6*(41). Retrieved from http://www.biomedical-central.com/1472-6920/6/41 doi:10.1186/1472-6920-6-41 PMID:16911779

Bower, M. (2008). Affordance analysis – matching learning tasks with learning technologies. *Educational Media International, 45*(1), 3–15. doi:10.1080/09523980701847115

Bruns, A., & Humphreys, S. (2007). *Building collaborative capacities in learners: The M/cyclopedia Project revisited*. Paper presented at the WikiSym '07, Montréal, Canada.

Castek, J. (2006). *The changing nature of reading comprehension: Examining the acquisition of new literacies in a 7th grade science classroom*. Paper presented at the National Reading Conference Los Angeles 2006, Los Angeles, CA.

Coiro, J. (2003). Reading comprehension on the Internet: Expanding our understanding of reading comprehension to encompass new literacies. *The Reading Teacher, 56*(5), 458–464.

Cole, M. (2009). Using Wiki technology to support student engagement: Lessons from the trenches. *Computers & Education, 52*(1), 141–146. doi:10.1016/j.compedu.2008.07.003

Cress, U., & Kimmerle, J. (2008). A systemic and cognitive view on collaborative knowledge building with wikis. *Computer-Supported Learning, 3*, 105-122. doi: I 0.1 007/s11412-007-9035-z

Crook, C., Cummings, J., Fisher, T., Graber, R., Harrison, C., Lewin, C., & Sharples, M. (2008). *Web 2.0 technologies for learning: The current landscape – opportunities, challenges and tensions WEb 2.0 technologies for learning at Key Stages 3 and 4* (p. 72). BECTA.

Dede, C. (2009). Comments on Greenhow, Robelia, and Hughes: Technologies That Facilitate Generating Knowledge and Possibly Wisdom. *Educational Researcher, 38*(4), 260–263. doi:10.3102/0013189X09336672

DeWitt, D., Siraj, S., & Alias, N. (2014). Collaborative mLearning: A Module for Learning Secondary School Science. *Journal of Educational Technology & Society, 17*(1), 89–101.

Engstrom, M. E., & Jewett, D. (2005). Collaborative learning the wiki way. *TechTrends, 49*(6), 12–15.

Forte, A., & Bruckman, A. (2007). *Constructing Text: Wiki as a toolkit for (collaborative?) learning*. Paper presented at the WikiSym '07 - Wikis at Work in the World: Open, Organic, Participatory Media for the 21st Century, Montreal, Canada. Retrieved from http://www.wikisym.org/ws2007/proceedings.html

Fu, H., Chu, S., & Kang, W. (2013). Affordances and Constraints of a Wiki for Primary-school Students' Group Projects. *Journal of Educational Technology & Society*, *16*(4), 85–96.

Grace, T. P. L. (2009). Wikis as a knowledge management tool. *Journal of Knowledge Management*, *13*(4), 64–74. doi:10.1108/13673270910971833

Grant, L. (2009). 'I dont care do ur own page!' A case study of using wikis for collaborative work in a UK secondary school. *Learning, Media and Technology*, *34*(2), 105–117. doi:10.1080/17439880902923564

Greenhow, C., Robelia, B., & Hughes, J. E. (2009). Learning, Teaching, and Scholarship in a Digital Age: Web 2.0 and Classroom Research: What Path Should We Take Now? *Educational Researcher*, *38*(4), 246–259. doi:10.3102/0013189X09336671

Grudin, J., & Poole, E. (2010). Wikis at work: Success factors and challenges of enterprise wikis. In ACM (Ed.), *WikiSym '10: Proceedings of the 6th international symposium on Wikis and open collaboration* (pp. Article 5). Gdansk, Poland: ACM. Retrieved from http://dl.acm.org/citation.cfm?id=1832780

Hadjerrouit, S. (2013). A framework for assessing the pedagogical effectiveness of wiki-based collaborative writing: Results and implications. *Interdisciplinary Journal of E-Learning and Learning Objects*, *9*, 29–49.

Halse, C., Denson, N., Howard, S., & Zammit, K. (2010). *Evaluation of The Centre for Learning and Innovation Avaya immersive environment project*. Sydney: University of Western Sydney.

Hazari, S., North, A., & Moreland, D. (2009). Investigating Pedagogical Value of Wiki Technology. *Journal of Information Systems Education*, *20*(2), 187–198.

Herrington, J., Oliver, R., & Reeves, T. (2003). Patterns of engagement in authentic online learning communities. *Australasian Journal of Educational Technology*, *19*(1), 59–71.

Huang, W-H., & Nakazawa, K. (2010). An empirical analysis on how learners interact in wiki in a graduate level online course. *Interactive Learning Environments*, *18*(3), 233-244. doi:10.1080/10494820.2010.500520

Jenkins, H., Clinton, K., Purushotma, R., Robison, A., & Weigel, M. (2006). *Confronting the Challenges of Participatory Culture: Media Education for the 21st Century Building the Field of Digital Media and Learning* (p. 68). Chicago, IL: The John D. and Catherine T. Macarthur Foundation.

Judd, T., Kennedy, G., & Cropper, S. (2010). Using wikis for collaborative learning: Assessing collaboration through contribution. *Australasian Journal of Educational Technology*, *26*(3), 341–354.

Jung, I., & Suzuki, Y. (2014). Scaffolding strategies for wiki-based collaboration: Action research in a multicultural Japanese language program. *British Journal of Educational Technology*, 1–10. doi:10.1111/bjet.12175

Kalantzis, M., & Cope, B. (2005). *Learning by design*. Melbourne: Victorian Schools Innovation Commission and Common Ground Publishing.

Kalanztis, M., & Cope, B. (2012). *New learning: Elements of a science of education* (2nd ed.). Melbourne: Cambridge Univesity Press.

Kessler, G. (2009). Student-initiated attention to form in wiki-based collaborative writing. *Language Learning & Technology*, *13*(1), 79–95.

Kirschner, P., Strijbos, J.-W., Krejins, K., & Beers, P. (2004). Designing Electronic Collaborative Learning Environments. *Educational Technology Research and Development*, *52*(3), 47–66. doi:10.1007/BF02504675

Kress, G. (2010). *Multimodality: A social semiotic approach to contemporary communication.* Abingdon, UK: Routledge.

Lamb, A., & Johnson, L. (2009). Wikis and collaborative inquiry. *School Library Media Activities Monthly, 8*(April), 48–51.

Lankshear, C., & Knobel, M. (2006). *New literacies: Everyday practices and classroom learning* (2nd ed.). Maidenhead, UK: Open University Press.

Larusson, J., & Alterman, R. (2009). Wikis to support the "collaborative' part of collaborative learning. *Computer-Supported Collaborative Learning, 4,* 371-402. doi: 10.1 007/s11412-009-9076-6

Li, X., Chu, S., & Ki, W. W. (2014). The effects of a wiki-based collaborative process writing pedagogy on writing ability and attitudes among upper primary school students in Mainland China. *Computers & Education, 77,* 151–169. doi:10.1016/j.compedu.2014.04.019

Lucey, T., & Shifflet, R. (2013). Wiki resources: Using the Internet as a tool for educational collaboration and professional development. In L. Ngo, S. Goldstein & L. Portugal (Eds.), *E-collaboration in Teaching and Learning* (pp. 56-74): Edulogue. Retrieved from http://www.Edulogue.com

Lund, A. (2008). Wikis: A collective approach to language production. *ReCALL, 20*(1), 35–54. doi:10.1017/S0958344008000414

Lundin, R. (2008). Teaching with Wikis: Toward a Networked Pedagogy. *Computers and Composition, 25*(4), 432–448. doi:10.1016/j.compcom.2008.06.001

Lykourentzou, I., Dagka, F., Papadaki, K., Lepouras, G., & Vassilakis, C. (2012). Wikis in enterprise settings: A survey. *Enterprise Information Systems, 6*(1), 1–53. doi:10.1080/17517575 .2011.580008

Mak, B., & Coniam, D. (2008). Using wikis to enhance and develop writing skills among secondary school students in Hong Kong. *System, 36*(3), 437–455. doi:10.1016/j.system.2008.02.004

Malaga, R. (2010). Choosing a wiki platform for student projects - Lessons learned. *Contemporary Issues In Education Research, 3*(2), 49–54.

Manion, C., & Selfe, R. (2012). Sharing an Assessment Ecology: Digital Media, Wikis, and the Social Work of Knowledge. *Technical Communication Quarterly, 21*(1), 25–45. doi:10.108 0/10572252.2012.626756

McPherson, C. (2012). *Using a wiki to facilitate student collaboration in an upper elementary art project: A case study.* Academic Press.

Moll, L., Amanti, C., Neff, D., & Gonzalez, N. (1992). Funds of knowledge for teaching: Using a qualitative approach to connect homes and classrooms. *Theory into Practice, 31*(2), 132–141. doi:10.1080/00405849209543534

Morgan, B., & Smith, R. (2008). A wiki for classroom writing. *The Reading Teacher, 62*(1), 80–82. doi:10.1598/RT.62.1.10

National Council for the Teaching of English (NCTE). (2008). *The NCTE definition of 21st century literacies.* Retrieved from http://www. ncte.org/positions/statements/21stcentdefinition

New London Group. (2000). A Pedagogy of Multiliteracies: Designing Social Futures. In B. Cope & M. Kalantzis (Eds.), *Multiliteracies: LIteracy Learning and Design Social Futures* (pp. 9–37). Melbourne: Macmillan.

Oschner, A., & Martin, C. (2013, 23 - 25 May 2012). *Learning and cultural participation in Mass Effect and Elder Scrolls affinity spaces.* Paper presented at the Clash of Realities 4th International Computer Game Conference, Cologne, Germany.

Parker, K. R., & Chao, J. T. (2007). Wiki as a teaching tool. *Interdisciplinary Journal of Knowledge and Learning Objects, 3*, 57–72.

Partnership for 21st Century Skills. (2011). *Framework for 21st century learning.* Retrieved 24.09.2014, 2014, from http://www.p21.org/our-work/p21-framework

Pellicone, A., & Ahn, J. (2010). *Construction and community: Investigating interaction in a Minecraft affinity space.* Retrieved from http://ahnjune.com/wp-content/uploads/2014/05/Pellicone-Ahn-GLS-Final.pdf

Pifarre, M., & Fisher, R. (2011). Breaking up the writing process: How wikis can support understanding the composition and revision strategies of young writers. *Language and Education, 25*(5), 451–466. doi:10.1080/09500782.2011.585240

Reich, J., Murnane, R., & Willett, J. (2012). The state of wiki usage in U.S. K-12 schools: Leveraging Web 2.0 data warehouses to assess quality and equity in online learning environments. *Educational Researcher, 41*(7), 7–15. doi:10.3102/0013189X11427083

Ruth, A., & Houghton, L. (2009). The wiki way of learning. *Australasian Journal of Educational Technology, 25*(2), 135–152.

Scardamalia, M., & Bereiter, C. (1994). Computer support for knowledge-building communities. *Journal of the Learning Sciences, 3*(3), 265–283. doi:10.1207/s15327809jls0303_3

Standing, C., & Kiniti, S. (2011). How can organizations use wikis for innovation? *Technovation, 31*(7), 287–295. doi:10.1016/j.technovation.2011.02.005

Stocker, A., Richter, A., Hoefler, P., & Tochtermann, K. (2012). Exploring appropriation of enterprise wikis: A multiple case study. *Computer Supported Cooperative Work, 21*(2-3), 317–356. doi:10.1007/s10606-012-9159-1

Tay, E., & Allen, M. (2011). Designing social media into university learning: Technology of collaboration or collaboration for technology. *Educational Media International, 48*(3), 151–163. doi:10.1080/09523987.2011.607319

The Fair Go Project (Ed.). (2006). *School is for me:Pathways to student engagement.* Sydney: NSW Department of Education and Training.

Thomas, S. (2013). What's in a Wiki for me? How a Wiki can be used to enhance a language learning classroom and student collaboration. *The Journal of Teachers Helping Teachers, 1*(1), 11–32.

Thornton, J. (2013). The 4E wiki writing model. *Curriculum and Teaching Dialogue, 15*(1 & 2), 49–62.

Wenger, E. (1999). *Communities of practice: Learning, meaning and identity.* Cambridge, UK: Cambridge University Press.

Wheeler, S., Yeomans, P., & Wheeler, D. (2008). The good, the bad and the wiki: Evaluating student generated content for collaborative learning. *British Journal of Educational Technology, 39*(6), 987–995. doi:10.1111/j.1467-8535.2007.00799.x

Witney, D., & Smallbone, T. (2011). Wiki work: Can using wikis enhance student collaboration for group assignment tasks? *Innovations in Education and Teaching International, 48*(1), 101–110. doi:10.1080/14703297.2010.543765

Woo, M. M., Chu, S., & Li, X. (2013). Peer-feedback and revision process in a wiki mediated collaborative writing. *Educational Technology Research and Development, 61*(2), 279–309. doi:10.1007/s11423-012-9285-y

Yates, D., Wagner, C., & Majchrzak, A. (2010). Factors affecting shapers of organizationsl wikis. *Journal of the American Society for Information Science and Technology, 61*(3), 543–554. doi:10.1002/asi.21266

Zammit, K. (2008). *Under construction: A world without walls*. Paper presented at the ASLA Online III Virtual Conference - Digital literacy strand – Keynote paper. Retrieved from http://www.asla.org.au/pd/online2008/program.htm

Zammit, K. (2010a). New Learning Environments Framework: Integrating multiliteracies into the curriculum. *Pedagogies*, *5*(4), 325–337. doi:10.1080/1554480X.2010.509479

Zammit, K. (2010b). *Working with wikis: Collaborative writing in the 21st Century*. Paper presented at the Key Competencies in the Knowledge Society: IFIP Advances in Information and Communication Technology, Brisbane, Australia.

Zammit, K. (2011). Connecting multiliteracies and engagement of students from low socio-economic backgrounds: Using Bernstein's pedagogic discourse as a bridge. *Language and Education*, *25*(3), 203–220. doi:10.1080/09500782.2011.560945

Zammit, K. (2015). Extending students' semiotic understandings: Learning about and creating multimodal texts. In P. Trifonas (Ed.), *International Handbook of Semiotics*. London: Springer. doi:10.1007/978-94-017-9404-6_62

KEY TERMS AND DEFINITIONS

21st Century Literacies: The skills and understandings required for an individual to effectively participate and work in the 21st century, including information literacy, digital literacy, critical literacy, the ability to collaborate and solve problems.

Affordances: The resources specific to a mode or form of technology that are used in the creation of a text and for meaning making.

Capacities: The ability to undertake an action, complete an activity or understand something.

Collaboration: The practice of individuals working together on a task, problem or project working towards the completion of the desired outcomes, solution or goals.

Communities of Practice: A group of people interested in the same field, interest or process who learn from each other, supporting each other's learning and together develop knowledge, understandings and skills.

Knowledge Building: The practice of building the knowledge base of a person, institution or organization in order to support the core work of the individual, institution or organization.

Knowledge Management: The practice of managing the information developed by employees in a workforce so that it can be easily stored, retrieved and archived for others within the company to use.

Multiliteracies: The literacies and pedagogies associated with the understanding and use of a range of semiotic modes, including the written, spoken, audio, visual, gestural and combinations of these modes.

Produsage: The practice of being both a user and producer of online (Internet) content.

Produsers: People who both use or consume information from an online environment (the Internet) and also produce or create information for others to use.

Chapter 20
Instant Messaging and Texting

Gloria E. Jacobs
Portland State University, USA

ABSTRACT

This chapter contains an examination of the research into texting and instant messaging. Instant messaging and texting are shown to be powerful technologies for maintaining relationships, building identities, and functioning within an information based society. The author raises questions about the implications of these social practices for those individuals who remain on the digital margins. The chapter provides an overview of the research, including a brief history of the technology and a theoretical framing of the terms used to discuss the phenomenon. A discussion of who uses instant messaging and why, and what the research has found regarding the conventions of use associated with instant messaging and texting follows. The chapter ends with a discussion of the current issues in the field, locates gaps in the research, and identifies implications and recommendations for education, civic engagement, social practice, and policy.

INSTANT MESSAGING AND TEXTING

A close friend lives on the opposite coast of the United States from me. We used to call each other infrequently, but now we converse several times a week. The reason for this shift is that our conversations take place via a combination of Facebook Messenger and text messaging rather than by voice. We no longer have to coordinate across time zones or personal schedules. If one of us thinks of something to say, we can send a message. Sometimes our messages are quick check-ins, but there are other times when we will have extended conversations that take place over the course of days. Sometimes our conversations happen in real-time and other times there are long gaps of time between messages. She uses her mobile telephone for all her online communication, and I switch between my smartphone, personal laptop, and office computer depending on where I am and what my schedule demands. My friend and I have become part of the "always on" (Baron, 2008) community made possible by the advent of the Internet, mobile telephony, and media convergence as exemplified by smartphones and a growing number of mobile applications (apps).

DOI: 10.4018/978-1-4666-8310-5.ch020

Our exchanges also exemplify the changing social practices that are emerging out of a constantly connected world.

According to the Pew Internet and American Life Project (Fox & Rainie, 2014), 87% of Americans use the Internet, and of those, 67% say online communication has strengthened relationships with friends and family. Along with the penetration of the Internet into daily life, mobile telephones have become a ubiquitous aspect of 21st century living within both developed and developing countries (Ling & Baron, 2013). Mobile telephones are owned by 90% of American adults, 58% of adults own smartphones (Pew Internet Research Project, 2014a), and 23% of American youth own smartphones (Lenhart, 2012b). These technological shifts are important when considering the nature of online communication practices such as instant messaging and text messaging.

In this chapter, I focus on instant messaging and text messaging as forms of one-to-one communication that are afforded by easy access to Internet connected computers and mobile telephones. I consider the implications of these technologies especially for those who continue to be disengaged from digital technology. Specifically, I strive to understand what the implications are for *not* using these technologies.

The chapter begins with an overview of the research. This overview includes a brief history of the technologies followed by a theoretical framing of the terms associated with instant messaging and texting. I then explore the question of whether it matters that people do or do not use instant messaging and texting. The second section of this chapter explores the literature into the nature of people's engagement in instant messaging and texting. The review of the literature is followed by a discussion of the current issues in the field raised by the research, and directions for future research are identified. The chapter ends with recommendations and implications for education, social practice, civic engagement, and policy.

OVERVIEW OF THE RESEARCH

In the late 1990s, when I first became interested in instant messaging practices among youth and what it means for literacy development, there were few studies on the phenomena. Most of the computer mediated communication (CMC) research was into chat (originally Internet Relay Chat or IRC), which became popular in the early 1990s when America Online was launched. Chat involved a group of individuals communicating simultaneously (synchronously) within "rooms" based around a specific topic. It was within the chat environment that many of the conventions now associated with instant messaging and texting were developed: abbreviations (cuz for because), initialisms (LOL), and short, rapid exchanges. Instant messaging and text messaging users adopted these conventions even though the functionalities and purposes differ. For example, instant messaging and texting were designed for one-to-one communication; however, multiple instant messaging and texting conversations can occur simultaneously and texts can be sent to groups of individuals. As such, social practices unique to each mode of communication also developed.

A BRIEF HISTORY

According to Baron (2013), instant messaging began in the 1980s with the ability to message one another through mainframe computers. Instant messaging, as we know it today, became a social phenomenon with the introduction of ICQ in 1996 and AIM (America Online Instant Messenger). A number of similar services were available during the heyday of instant messaging, but AIM was the primary platform for most users in the United States. In 2004, the Pew Internet and American Life Project (Shui & Lenhart, 2004) reported that instant messaging was replacing email as the dominant form of online communication; however, less than 10 years later, Lenhart (2012a) reported that texting was the preferred communication tool for teens and that instant messaging was becoming less popular.

This drop in interest in instant messaging co-occurred with the development of instant messaging functionality being integrated into a number of broader platforms such as Facebook and multiplayer online games (Petronzio, 2012). For example, Facebook has a message function built into the computer-based system that is connected to the Messenger application for smartphones. Online games also have a messenger function built into the interface that allows players to communicate outside the action being performed within the game. By 2012, AIM was all but extinct and no longer supported by America Online (Abbruzzese, 2014), and in 2013, MSN Messenger, another popular instant messaging platform was shutdown for most users and was completely ended in 2014 when the last of the Chinese users were transferred to Skype (Chowdhry, 2014).

It is possible that texting will follow a pattern similar to that of instant messaging. Nonetheless, the popularity grew in tandem with significant changes in the technology that supports the practice. In 1993, Nokia debuted the first mobile telephone with texting capabilities. Predictive texting was introduced in 1995, and telephones with a QWERTY keyboard became available in 1997. With predictive texting, the telephone suggests a word based on the first letters entered by the user; more recent versions also suggest words based on the context of the sentence. QWERTY keyboards are the standard keyboard layout for typewriters and computers in countries that use the Latin alphabet. QWERTY refers to the first six letters on the top left row of alphabetic keys. The turning point in texting use, however, was in 1999 when it became possible for text messages to cross networks. Prior to 1999, mobile users only could send messages to those within their mobile provider's network, thus limiting the number of people with whom they could text. However, in

1999 it became possible for text messages to cross networks or be sent to anyone, regardless of cell phone provider. When this technological barrier was removed, texting used increased dramatically.

Texting soon surpassed instant messaging as the most popular mode of communication, and a 2008 Nielsen report (In U.S. SMS Texting Tops) indicated that Americans increased texting use by 450% over two years. According to the Pew Internet and American Life Project (Lenhart, 2012b), texting has become the dominant form of communication among teens. However, by 2012, there was evidence of a decline of short message service (SMS), the technical name for texting, as its functionality was subsumed by other services (such as iMessage on iPhones and Facebook Messenger) (Luckerson, 2012). Now, it appears that instant messaging may be on the rise again but in a different form through mobile messaging services such as "Whatsapp."

Whatsapp, Messenger (associated with Facebook), and similar smartphone applications allow users to send messages, images, video, and audio to other individuals who have the application downloaded on their smartphone or other mobile device. Information about the geographical location of the users can also be shared. Both sender and recipient must have the same messaging application in order to communicate, thus limiting who messages can be sent to. Despite that limitation, the messaging applications are growing in popularity because traditional texting may incur fees. Messaging applications allow the users to send messages for free.

Thus, the use of particular technologies appear to shift depending on how easy it is to use the technology to maintain contact with key individuals, cost, and how integrated it is with other activities such as social media and gaming. As Herring (2013) argued, "CMC [computer mediated communication] itself has been undergoing a shift, from occurrence in stand-alone clients such as emailers and instant messaging programs to juxtaposition with other content, often of an information or entertainment nature, in converged media platforms, where it is typically secondary, by design, to other information or entertainment-related activities" (p. 4). Herring calls this convergent media computer-mediated communication (CMCMC).

A THEORETICAL FRAMING OF TERMS

Although Herring's (2013) use of CMCMC is descriptive and accurate, the set of initials feels as if it is a bit of an alphabet soup. Thus, I continue to use the term computer mediated communication (CMC) when discussing instant messaging and texting with the recognition that these tools can be used on a variety of platforms and across a range of hardware such as desktops, laptops, tablets, mobile (cell) phones, and smartphones.

Herring (2013) also used the term "Discourse 2.0" (p. 4) to capture how the Web 2.0, or interactive Internet, in which individuals are content producers as well as consumers, affects how people use language and text. Investigation into Discourse 2.0 may provide insights into disruptive technologies or innovations (Christensen, 1997) that may be contributing to the development of new social norms and practices as well as challenges to existing power structures. The concept of disruptive technologies comes out of the business field, but is now being applied to education and health care. Disruptive technologies are innovations that challenge the status quo by introducing simpler, more convenient, more accessible, and more affordable ways of accomplishing goals (Christensen, 1997).

In this case, power is understood through a Foucaldian lens where power is a fluid set of relationships rather than a case of one group or person having power and another being without (Foucault, 1980). Castells (2000) argued that flexibility can be both liberating or repressive if "the rewriters of the rules are always the powers that

be" (p. 71). If rules are being rewritten, those who are observers can never figure out what the rules are, thus putting them at a disadvantage. However, if the users rewrite the rules, then power shifts. Therefore, instant messaging and texting may be disruptive, and the social practices associated with those tools may be ways of changing social and political relationships. More specifically, the ability to share information in ways that circumvent official channels may provide a means for challenging the status quo. I return to this proposition in the issues and implications sections of this chapter.

Additionally, the term Discourse 2.0 evokes Gee's (1999) stance that Discourse includes ways of "behaving, interacting, valuing, thinking, believing, speaking, and often reading and writing that are accepted as instantiations of particular roles.... Discourses are ways of being 'people like us.'... Discourses operate to integrate and sort persons, groups, and society" (p. viii - ix). Thus, Discourse 2.0 describes a way of using language within the world of Web 2.0 that marks them as members of the Web 2.0 community. People's engagement or lack of engagement with a particular technology is seen as integral to the membership within a particular Discourse community. To take up a particular practice, such as texting, means shifting community membership and identity. Furthermore, the way language is used as one engages in a technological practice also marks identity and community membership. For example, youth using acronyms (pos for parents over shoulder) identifies them as a member of a group who knows the terms and are facile in using those terms. It also marks those who are unfamiliar with the terms as outsiders.

Although the theoretical stance through which I view instant messaging and texting is consistent with that captured within the Discourse 2.0 terminology, I find the term to be too broad for discussing the specific practices of instant messaging and texting. The difficulty in finding a descriptive term for the phenomena of online discourse is evident in the variety of terms applied to the language of CMC: textspeak or netspeak (Crystal, 2004), textese (Drouin, 2011), textisms (Wood, Kemp, & Plester, 2013). For the sake of consistency, I use the term textisms when discussing the specific language practices of instant messaging and texting. When discussing the broader aspects of language and technology, I use Discourse 2.0. Moving between these two terms, I argue, allows me to address the micro and macro level concerns of research into people's engagement with the technologies.

I further suggest that using the word Discourse captures the sociocultural nature of the language and literacy practices associated with instant messaging and texting rather than being narrowly focused on the technological affordances of the phenomenon. The term textisms allows for a close examination of the specific language and literacy choices of individuals within the larger sociocultural context.

This theoretical stance is grounded in the new literacies perspective (Leu, Kinzer, Coiro, & Cammack, 2004) of technology and the new literacies. Leu et al. defined the new literacies as follows:

The new literacies of the Internet and other ICTs include the skills, strategies, and dispositions necessary to successfully use and adapt to the rapidly changing information and communication technologies and contexts that continuously emerge in our world and influence all areas of our personal and professional lives. These new literacies allow us to use the Internet and other ICTs to identify important questions, locate information, critically evaluate the usefulness of that information, synthesize information to answer those questions, and then communicate the answers to others. (p. 1572)

The new literacies, of which instant messaging and texting are a part, thus describe the broader literacy practices in which Discourse 2.0 and textisms exist.

A final and less theoretical point about terminology involves the dichotomous terms of synchronous and asynchronous. Originally, synchronous and asynchronous were used to identify the way data is transmitted. However, the terms have come to be associated with how people send and receive messages. Email is typically considered asynchronous in that the message is sent and exists in the receiver's inbox until it is retrieved and read. Texting has also been considered to be asynchronous because the text is sent and resides in the receiver's phone until it is read. The receiver can respond to the email or text at any time. Conversely, synchronous communication occurs when sender and receiver are online at the same time and send and receive messages in real time, such as in a chat room. However, I argue these terms are no longer useful because, within the state of being constantly connected, individuals often exchange emails in real-time, and those emails can resemble conversations. Texts, which were originally considered asynchronous, now often are exchanged in real time. Similarly, messages sent over instant messaging programs stay in a person's in-box until they are read, thus those conversations can be asynchronous. Thus, I do not use these terms in this chapter.

DOES IT MATTER WHETHER PEOPLE USE INSTANT MESSAGING AND TEXTING?

What is apparent from the history of instant messaging and texting is that technological platforms may change, but the social function of maintaining contact across time and space remains important. The past 14 years of technology development and scholarly research has also demonstrated that Discourse 2.0 is persistent even if the specifics of what constitutes textisms change. What I wish to do with this chapter is turn attention to the implications of these technologies and the accompanying discourse for those individuals who continue to be disengaged from digital technology. Ling (2008) asked, "Should we be concerned that the elderly don't text?" Similarly, in this chapter I ask, should we be concerned about *anyone* who does not text or otherwise use digital technology? What are the implications of instant messaging and texting for the individuals and for society at large, and conversely, what are the implications for *not* using these technologies?

The remainder of this chapter explores the literature into the nature of people's engagement in instant messaging and texting. The review of the literature is followed by a discussion of the current issues in the field raised by the research, and directions for future research are identified. The chapter ends with recommendations and implications for education, social practice, civic engagement, and policy.

This literature review is not intended to be a comprehensive investigation into the research conducted into instant messaging and texting since the inception of the technologies. Instead, I focus on the research that is particularly salient for understanding the role of instant messaging and texting within emerging social practices and questions of engagement and power. I include older studies to establish the historical trajectory of the research, but focus primarily on the most recent work to identify questions and implications for future consideration. For those interested in a more comprehensive exploration of the literature, Porath's (2011) review of texting research provides a solid overview, especially as related to the world of educational technology, and Wood et al. (2013) have provided deep background and insights into the relationship between text messaging and literacy. Baron (2013) has similarly provided a thorough examination of instant messaging through the lens of pragmatics. Although there has been a significant increase in the number of photos and videos sent through applications such as Instagram and Snapchat since the integration of cameras into mobile phones, I exclude the research into those practices primarily because the

phenomenon appears to be inherently different from traditional texting and instant messaging.

I begin the literature review with a discussion of who uses instant messaging and texting followed by an examination of why people use those communications technologies. The third section reviews the literature on the conventions of use associated with instant messaging and texting, and the final section of the literature review considers research that directly applies instant messaging and texting to educational settings.

WHO USES INSTANT MESSAGING AND TEXTING

Ling (2010) and Ling, Bertel, and Sundsoy (2012) called texting a life phase medium with a "standing wave" of teens representing the heaviest users; use becomes more moderate as people age. In the United States, the use of texting has been increasing among boys and older teens. Additionally, Blacks followed by Hispanics are leading the increase in texting within the United States (Lenhart, 2012b). This shift in demographics raises the issue of shifting power relations. As more members of minority populations are able to participate in information sharing activities, questions arise as to what this might mean for engagement in United States society at large. This is an area that has been under researched and under theorized.

According to Lenhart (2012b), 63% of U.S. teens say they exchange texts daily. Additionally, Lenhart reported that only 22% of teens use instant messaging, and approximately 40% (2 out of 5 respondents) reported that they never use instant messaging. Ling et al. (2012), who used metered data to discover text usage patterns in Norway, found that teens also have the most text partners and text across genders more than any other group (Ling et al., 2012).

Analysis of Norwegian metered data showed a drop in texting use when individuals moved into young adulthood, even if they were heavy users of text when they were younger (Ling, 2010; Ling et al., 2012). Ling proposed that this drop in use might be related to the life phase wherein young adults experience greater demands on their time due to parenthood and professional obligations. Contrary to expected patterns, however, Ling identified an increase in texting among middle-aged adults. Because Ling was analyzing metered data, he was not able to see the content of the messages, but he proposed that the increase was due to preteen children using their parents' phones for texting.

Although Ling et al. (2012) cautioned that the findings are limited in generalizability because they were gathered from Norway, a small and homogenous country, the findings raise additional questions about how "the mobile phone is an instrument of the intimate sphere" (p. 295). As is discussed in more detail in the section about why people use instant messaging and texting, Ling argued that texting supports the development of close ties at the expense of interaction with weaker connections. Whether this is the case, however, should be further explored, especially in light of Ling's (2008) argument that older adults are being systematically left out of the intimate sphere because of design, through a series of assumptions, and because of technological affordances and constraints.

Findings from Norway and the United States were similar. Ling's (2008) and Ling et al.'s (2012) data showed that older adults (65+) do not text at all, and Smith (2014) found that only 11% of older adults own smartphones. For adults older than 65, landline telephones remain the preferred method of communication. Ling proposed that there may several reasons why older adults eschew texting: there may not be others within their age cohort with whom to text, or the technological affordances of landlines may be more attractive than texting. However, the data from Smith's study indicated that younger, more highly educated, and affluent seniors have substantial technology assets and had a positive view of technology. Conversely, those who are older, less affluent, and who have

significant health and disability challenges are largely disconnected from technology physically and psychologically (Smith, 2014).

Smith's (2014) report showed that challenges for seniors include the physical, skepticism, and difficulties learning new technologies, but once seniors get online, technology becomes an integral part of their lives. The Pew Internet and American Life study did show that even though smartphones are not popular among older adults, tablets and ebook readers are. To date, no research has been conducted into the reasons for this, but the work of the Literacy, Language, and Technology Research Group (Castek, Withers, Pendell, Pizzolato, Jacobs & Reder, 2013) indicated that vision limitations are a challenge for older adults acquiring digital literacy. Therefore, the ability to enlarge text on tablets and ereaders may increase the functionality of these devices for older adults. Thus, if older adults are to be brought into the intimate sphere of texting, such affordances should be made clear to users.

Whereas Ling's (2008) concern was that older adults are being left out of the intimate sphere, Smith (2014) suggested the issue is much larger:

As the internet plays an increasingly central role in connecting Americans of all ages to news and information, government services, health resources, and opportunities for social support, these divisions are noteworthy—particularly for the many organizations and individual caregivers who serve the older adult population. (para. 3)

Contributing factors to the exclusion of older adults may be assumptions that social networks wind down as a person ages and that older adults may be reluctant to use seemingly complex devices, a situation compounded by older adults' tendency to own older mobile phone models not conducive to texting (Ling, 2008). Furthermore, Ling noted that when older adults do own mobile telephones, they see those phones as a safety device rather than a communication tool; as such, mobile telephones are seen as an unwelcome addition that does not fit easily into well established life patterns. This reluctance to engage with mobile technology and CMC practices such as texting or instant messaging may limit older adults ability to access different resources.

The apparent systematic exclusion of segments of the population was also reflected in the work of Durkin, Conti-Ramsden, and Walker (2011). Durkin et al. raised issues similar to Ling's (2008) in their investigation of how adolescents with and without specific language impairment (SLI) use texting. Durken et al. found that adolescents with SLI were less likely to respond to a text than their typically developing peers, composed shorter texts, and used less text language than typically developing youth. Similar to Ling's (2010) concern about older adults being systematically left out of the intimate sphere, Durkin et al. expressed concern that youth with SLI are at greater risk of social marginalization and thus may need support if they are to adopt new communication technologies. The authors suggested that although significant hurdles to participation in texting practices exist for youth with SLI, once those youth experience the interpersonal benefits that texting can afford, their engagement increases. Smith (2014) likewise found that once senior adults experienced the benefits of online engagement, they regularly used the technology.

Overall, texting and instant messaging are practices closely aligned with youth, although young adults and middle-aged adults do use the technologies to some extent. Although Ling (2010) and Ling et al. (2012) claimed use people texted less as they moved into adulthood, it remains to be seen whether the population who grew up with CMC as an everyday practice will follow that same pattern. Regardless of the numbers of people who do use text and messaging, within the United States there are segments of the population who remain outsiders.

WHY PEOPLE USE INSTANT MESSAGING AND TEXTING

Tannen (2013), Turner, Abrams, Katic, and Donovan (2014), and Voida, Newstetter, and Mynatt (2002) among others have noted that digital writing is a combination of written and conversational languages that "epitomizes small talk" (Turner et al., p. 174). The research has indicated that like small talk there are social roles that instant messaging and texting play. These roles include building and maintaining relationships, and constructing identity. Although the term small talk implies triviality, as the research indicates, the implications of engagement with CMCs can be significant.

- **Building and Maintaining Relationships:** Ling (2010) indicated that the heaviest users of texting are youth and that use drops as individuals become older. An explanation for this phenomenon is that relationship building is an important aspect of adolescence as individuals begin to separate from their immediate family. As such, any tool that supports relationship building may be attractive to youth. Ito and Okabe (2010) argued that mobile messaging or texting allows youth to overcome or resist some of the adult imposed regulations that govern their everyday lives.

Ito and colleagues conducted decade long ethnographic research into the mobile practices of Japanese youth. This work provides insight into the meaning of mobile messaging, whether through texting or instant messaging, within the lives of those who use it (Ito & Daiskue, 2003, 2005; Ito & Okabe, 2010). According to Ito and colleagues, mobile technology extends existing social patterns and is driven by historical, social, and cultural factors rather than anything inherent within the technology. More specifically, Ito theorized how the "power geometries of existing places of home, school, and public places" (p. 2) contribute to the ways mobile technology is used and the meanings users impart to the technology. The research of Ito and Daiskue (2003, 2005) and Ito and Okabe (2010) indicated that the Japanese youth use texting as a way to resist the control of parents and society. Mobile messaging allows the youth to stay in constant contact with one another while functioning within a highly regulated home and society.

An example of this type of behavior is when youth exchange messages while in the presence of family. These messages may say little more than "What's up," contain complaints about family members, or an exchange of jokes or updates about current activities. No instrumental information is exchanged, but the continual contact allows the youth to establish and maintain a connection with peers while being co-present with family.

Although Sacco and Ismail (2014) found that face-to-face interactions provide more basic needs satisfaction when compared to instant messaging, they also found that instant messaging met more social needs than no interaction at all. However, individuals do not use instant messaging and texting to build relationships where none exist; in fact, most texts are sent to a small group of friends (Grinter & Eldridge, 2003; Ling et al., 2012) and teens who used either instant messaging or texting also tended to be heavy users of voice calls (Lenhart, 2012b). Furthermore, instant messaging and texting do not appear to be substitutes for social interaction; socially isolated adolescents who had few offline connections tended not to use instant messaging or texting (Bryant, Sanders-Jackson, & Smallwood, 2006; Sacco & Ismail, 2014).

Instant messaging and texting have become tools for those individuals who are already connected. Ling et al. (2012) argued that texting is used among youth for a variety of situations that require simple and "under the radar" communication (p. 282). Generally, texting is used to coordinate interaction, send and receive reminders, and maintain social contact (Licoppe, 2004). In general, youth find texting useful as a way to maintain social relationships and manage everyday life (Ling et al. 2012). However, the number of social relationships maintained through texting appears to be small. Ling et al. found that about 50% of texts go to only five people; thus youth may be sending a high number of texts, but they are not reaching out to a wide range of people. Moreover, most people text others who are the same gender as they and tend to only text people who are within their age cohort (Ling et al., 2012). Thus, texting and instant messaging appear to support existing social networks and may even contribute to the narrowing of an individual's world by limiting opportunities to engage with people outside the intimate sphere.

These findings led Ling et al. (2012) to argue that texting has become central to teen culture because it provides them with a constant link to their peers while allowing them to operate outside of the surveillance of adults, acts consistent with the developmental need of youth in western cultures to separate from families and align with peers. This finding is consistent with research into instant messaging. Dolev-Cohen and Barak (2013) found, "IMing, whether through designated programs or through social network chat procedures, form an inseparable part of the contemporary adolescent's world and youngsters use it to fulfill their need to share, include, receive information, and experience belonging" (p. 62). Similarly, Quan-Haase and Young (2010) and Mesch, Talmud, and Quan-Haase (2012) recognized instant messaging being a tool for social gratification. Thus, instant messaging and texting appear to serve similar purposes.

However, Brito (2012) found that youth see a difference between the two modes of communication. In general, like the adults in Ling et al.'s (2012) study, the young adolescents in Brito's study saw texting as being utilitarian whereas instant messaging was portrayed as having more social consequences. These differences are apparent in Turner et al.'s (2014) findings that texting has features that are distinct from instant messaging or text: texting is comparatively short, has a relative concentration of nonstandard typographic markers, and is predominantly oriented toward small-talk and the building of solidarity. Whether these differences hold as mobile instant messaging, which closely resembles texting, takes hold remains to be seen. It may be that instant messaging conducted through a computer was seen as having more social consequences because the act of sitting at a computer and intentionally engaging in the act of instant messaging may support exchanges that are more socially oriented. The mobile nature of texting may be a contributing factor to the patterns identified by Brito.

Social context is also a contributing factor to how instant messaging and texting is used. Lauricella and Kay (2013) examined how university students used texting and instant messaging for academic purposes with peers and faculty and found students preferred texting to instant messaging, and they tended to text weekly with instructors and daily with peers. Furthermore, although the students said they found both instant messaging and texting to be useful, the students rarely used instant messaging with instructors, and only used it weekly with peers. Their overall usage patterns may be reflective of the decline of instant messaging as a whole, but of more interest is that Lauricella and Kay's finding suggests that the university students may be in a transitional stage where they used instant messaging and texting for social purposes among peers but take on the more adult-like attitude of using the tools for instrumental purposes when interacting with faculty. As Quan-Haase and Young (2010) argued, users adopt multiple forms of communication depending on how each tool meets specific social and emotional needs.

For example, Pettigrew (2014) found that text messaging was a way to maintain connectedness within close interpersonal relationships. Contrary to other studies that suggested texting was for instrumental purposes among adults, Pettigrew found that texting is less about transactional purposes and more about relationship maintenance. Pettigrew's research suggested that texting is conducive to relationship building because it allows for perpetual contact and is direct, discreet, and private. Additionally, Pettigrew (2014) found that texting was useful because it was only a temporary distraction from the in-place experience and afforded users the opportunity to evaluate a text before responding. In comparison, a voice call is a significant interruption that requires an immediate response by the receiver. As Pettigrew (2014) argued, "an [text] alert does not necessitate a response. It merely creates the potential for a response" (p. 707), and that "response should not be automatic or necessarily immediate but should be informed, intentional, and thoughtful (p. 711). Thus, communicating through text messages allows interlocutors to formulate a response that will be supportive of their goals for the relationship.

Pettigrew's findings are consistent with that of Didomenico and Boase (2013) who examined how the asynchronous nature of mobile texting allowed study participants to manage social space. Specifically, they found that response to a text was strategically determined within the turn-taking process of a physical gathering of friends. As DiDomenico and Boase noted, telephone calls are intrusive in that the receiver must choose between answering the summons and suspending engagement with the co-present individuals or ignoring the call. However, with texting, a receiver can remain engaged in the co-present conversation and respond to the text at a time when full attention is not needed. DiDomenico and Boase referred to this as a "dynamic switching and blurring" (p. 129) that may point to emerging social norms. Thus, it appears that the social act of texting is strategically determined based on a variety of factors. As Turner et al. (2014) argued, research should go beyond the superficial fascination with the technology and look for a deeper engagement with the cultural contexts and communicative practices in which people engage.

In that shared language use is a marker of identity and community membership (Gee, 1996), another way to gain insights into how texting and instant messaging serve to build relationships is through a consideration of language convergence. Riordan, Markman, and Stewart (2012) investigated how the language of interlocutors converged over time during instant messaging conversation and found that interlocutors tended to converge structurally as well as lexically. They argued that convergence influences the perception of rapport that exists between interlocutors. This finding is consistent with Lewis and Fabos's (2000, 2005) discussion of how Sam, their study participant, consciously changed her language during instant messaging to match that of her conversational partner in order to achieve acceptance or build social status. Like Lewis and Fabos, Riordan et al. found that pace or speed of response was also an important area of convergence. Moreover, Riordan et al. found that convergence decreased over the course of a conversation when the interlocutors disagreed and that convergence was also lower with individuals who did not know one another personally. Using convergence as a tool for analyzing CMC conversations provides insights into how individuals make meaning within a seemingly lean medium. By matching language, structure, and pace, individuals engaged in CMC are able to build perceptions and create solidarity.

Finally, studies have investigated the types of relationships supported by the use of instant messaging and texting. Mesch et al. (2012) argued that online communication modes such as instant messaging are used primarily to maintain existing ties with individuals who are already known and with whom close ties have been established. Social ties, which social network theory (Haythornthwaite, 2005) describes as being weak, strong, or latent, are built through repeated interaction. Bryant et

al. (2006) found that both instant messaging and texting youth did not create more ties; instead, instant messaging and texting appeared to support existing ties only, a finding consistent with Grinter and Eldridge (2003) and Ling et al. (2012). The reasons for this may be situated within the way information communication technology (ICT) use reflects socio-structural elements such as the norms of social engagement (Mesch et al., 2012). For instance, Mesch et al. found that in Canada, the majority of instant messaging was conducted with close ties, a finding consistent with that of Ling et al.'s (2012) work in Norway. However, in Israel, instant messaging consisted of a mix of close and distant ties. In both cases, however, face-to-face meetings preceded contact via instant messaging, thus indicating that individuals tend not to exchange messages with people they do not know.

- **Managing Emotions:** That people text or instant message only those people who are known may be related to the finding that instant messaging has been shown to be an effective emotional outlet (Dolev-Cohen & Barak, 2013), something unlikely to occur between people with weak ties. Although Bryant et al. (2006) and Sacco and Ismail found that socially isolated youth tended not to use CMC, Dolev-Cohen and Barak (2013) found that introverted participants in particular profited from using instant messaging as a way to attain emotional relief. They argued that using the Internet to expose "the real me" (p. 59) is psychologically important because it can lead to self-acceptance, a feeling of belonging, and a sense of self-determination. Furthermore, Dolev-Cohen and Barak suggested that instant messaging, as a form of writing, has value because writing itself has therapeutic value. Thus, it appears that using instant messaging or texting may be beneficial to the group of individuals who most are apt not to use it. If instant messaging or texting are to be useful for supporting the emotional needs of individuals, those individuals must be part of a community for whom CMC is a viable form of communication.

- **Sexting:** Although not an area of focus in this chapter, the practice of sexting deserves mention in that it is an area of increasing interest among those who work with youth. Sexting is the use of texts to send sexually explicit messages. A Pew Internet and American Life report (2014b) indicated that sexting behavior is most common among 18 to 25-year-olds and drops steadily across age cohorts. Additionally, Lenhart (2009) found that among teens, aged 12-17, 4% have sent sexually suggestive messages and 15% have received such messages; the percentage of those sending and receiving texts increases as the teens age. Given these statistics, it is clear that sexting, while not widely practiced, is not uncommon. The meanings and implications of sexting appear to be embedded within the context of the senders and recipients and thus should be considered accordingly. For instance, among college students, sexting correlates with insecure romantic relationships (Drouin & Landgraff, 2012) and is predictive of sexual behaviors among teens (Temple, 2012; Temple & Choi, 2014). According to Temple and Choi (2014) sexting may be emerging as a "new normal part of adolescent sexual development and not strictly limited to at-risk adolescents" (p. 5) as well as being predictive of sexual activity. If this proposition holds, sexting too should be considered a discursive marker.
- **Cyberbullying:** The research into bullying through the use of texting and instant messaging generally falls within the broader category of cyberbullying. Cyberbullying is highly visible and emotionally charged and texting has been shown to be a tool of choice for cyberbullies (Whittaker & Kowalski, 2015). Whereas the research discussed thus far in this section has focused on the use of instant messaging and texting as a way to build relationships, cyberbullying, like bullying in general serves to position targeted individuals as an outsider or other. According to Slonje, Smith, & Frisen, (2013), bullying is intentional and is based on an imbalance of power wherein the victim is unable to act defensively. Pyzalski (2012) defined cyberbullying as repeated acts of online aggression, conducted over a longer period of time, have negative intentions, and represent an imbalance of power. Cyberbullying is particularly harmful because it can occur anonymously and can be spread more readily by bystanders who exacerbate the bullying by passing along the damaging digital information (Slonje et al., 2013). This results in a larger audience for the spurious information, which can result in high levels of anxiety within the victim. Additionally, Slonje et al. pointed out that once a spurious comment has been sent into cyberspace, it remains there, thus contributing to feelings of powerless.

A number of studies have placed the percentage of youth who have experienced cyberbullying at 19% to 25% with the majority of cyberbullying being experienced during the early teens and by girls (Rivers & Noret, 2010). Cyberbullying peaks during adolescence (Slonje et al, 2012), thus most research on cyberbullying has been conducted among middle school and high school students. However, many students reported experiencing cyberbullying for the first time during college (Kowalski, Giumetti, Schroeder, & Reese, 2013).

Victims of cyberbullying typically are known to the perpetrators. Pyzalski (2012), who studied Polish 15-year-olds, and Whittaker and Kowalski

(2015), who studied U.S. college students, both found that most cyberbullying predominantly occurred between friends. Strangers or random individuals also were the targets, but less so than known individuals. Slonje et al. (2013) found that in most cases cyberbullying started with face-to-face conflicts, which then expanded to tools such as texting.

Instant messaging had been the most frequently used venue for cyberbullying (Kowalski & Limber, 2007), but by 2015 cyberbullying had shifted to texting and social media such as Twitter (Whittaker & Kowalski, 2015). Specifically, Whittaker and Kowalski (2015) found that among college students, texting (56.8%) was the most commonly used platform for cyberbullying, and instant messaging (2.3%) was seldom mentioned. This finding reflects the falling popularity of instant messaging as a tool for peer-to-peer communication. Given the shifting technology of choice for cyberbullying, Whittaker and Kowalski (2015) argued

As new modes of technology emerge, new means of cyberbullying appear. Additionally, the modes likely reflect age-related trends. The most often used technological tools among ninth graders may differ from seniors in college. (p. 16).

Whittaker and Kowalski argued that the venue for cyberbullying is tied closely to the popularity of a particular a given technology. As such, Pyzalski's argument for a reformulation of the "prevalent paradigm that restricts electronic aggression to cyberbullying and understands it as peer aggression" (p. 313) should be seriously considered by researchers, educators, and mental health professionals.

Similarly, Kowalski, Giumetti, Schroeder, and Lattanner (2014) argued that research into cyberbullying is fragmented and under-theorized. They suggested that there is a need for understanding the incremental impact of cyberbullying on key behavioral and psychological outcomes. In light of these arguments, understanding people's use of technologies such as texting to target others may be symptomatic of larger issues within the context of the perpetrator's and recipient's lives.

Additionally, the research has indicated that age affects how individuals respond to cyberbullying. Kowaski and Limber (2007) found that most middle school students responded to cyberbullying by doing nothing, but Whittaker and Kowalski's (2015) work with college students showed the most common response was to block the individual followed by reporting the perpetrator. Younger adolescents reported were unlikely to report cyberbullying because they believed adults would not do anything. These differences could be accounted for by the developmental differences between young adolescents and college students.

Although cyberbullying is a significant problem, the research indicates that it should not be regarded as a single type of behavior but instead should be understood as occurring differently in different contexts (Whittaker & Kowalski, 2015). For instance, schools have struggled with taking action against cyberbullying because such behaviors ostensibly occur off the school grounds. However, recent court cases have cleared the way for schools to respond to cyberbullying that impacts the school environment (Hinduja & Patchin, 2015). Moreover, schools and other institutions are beginning to understand that cyberbullying behaviors are part of the larger social and cultural system rather than being an outgrowth of technology.

- **Constructing Identity:** Identity construction has been theorized through a variety of psychological and social lenses. Work in identity construction and literacy practices, and instant messaging and texting use in particular, often is grounded in the sociocultural perspectives wherein identity is constructed through Discourse (Gee, 2000-2001). Within this perspective language is used to identify oneself or someone else as a way of being or belonging to a particular group (Alvermann, Marshall, McLean, Huddleston, Joaquin, & Bishop, 2012). For example, an immigrant youth might use instant messaging or texting to experiment with American idioms thus demonstrating a growing identification with U. S. popular culture.

Work into identity construction and CMC using the concept of Discourse identity (Alvermann et al. 2012; Gee, 2000-2001) has been key to providing significant insights into the nature of language that occurs outside formal instructional settings. Lam's (2009) examination of the CMC practices of transnational youth has shown that digital literacy practices are part of youth's larger communicative repertoire used to "position themselves and navigate an interconnected and changing world" (p. 823). Lewis and Fabos (2000, 2005), who worked with youth in the Midwestern United States, also showed that instant messaging serves to position youth within a social network and to build a desired identity. Similarly, Jacobs (2004, 2006) found that engagement in instant messaging contributed to the development of what Gee (2000) called portfolio people who have a set of skills and dispositions necessary for success in an information based society.

These three sets of studies were concerned with what instant messaging practices mean in the every day life of users and the role instant messaging use plays in identity development (Jacobs, 2004, 2006; Lam, 2000, 2009; Lewis & Fabos, 2000, 2005). Specifically, Lam's study focused on the implications of instant messaging for an adolescent immigrant living in the United States and learning English. Lam argued that through engagement with instant messaging, the study participant was able to construct an identity as a competent English speaker, an identity denied him as an English language learner within the school system. Lewis and Fabos's study analyzed the experiences of an adolescent girl who used instant messaging to sustain her social network

and to build social status. They found that the study participant shifted her use of language and the conventions of writing depending with whom she was exchanging messaging. Jacobs (2006, 2008) found that instant messaging was part of a repertoire of practices that the study participant used as she positioned herself for the future. In all three studies, the authors argued that the specifics of instant messaging conventions were less important than how the literacy and language practices were used to support the development of the individual as a literate subject within the world of new literacies. As such, using a CMC such as instant messaging and texting is not just about staying in touch with a group of friends; it becomes an integral part of demonstrating that the user is part of a particular group that uses language and technology in certain ways. When considered through the lens of identity construction, it may be that older adults' resistance to the use of texting and instant messaging is less about the barriers of the technology and more that technology use is inconsistent with their constructed identities and discourse communities.

The research into why people use instant messaging and texting has indicated that these CMC modes are used to build and maintain relationships within communities for whom instant messaging and texting are accepted and even preferred ways to communicate. By participating in these communities and following the discursive norms of the community, individuals are able to build Discourse identities that identify them as being a member of a particular community.

CONVENTIONS OF USE

One of the most persistent and prolific areas of research into instant messaging and texting has been around the conventions of use and what those conventions mean for language and literacy development. These discursive norms have become identified as markers of membership within communities of CMC users. This area of research began when Baron (1984) identified CMC as a possible source of language change. Voida et al. (2002) were among the first to argue that instant messaging represents the collision of verbal and written communication, and Tagliamonte & Denis (2008) called texting a hybrid register that includes formal and informal language. Tannen (2013) claimed that the "the discourse of digital media interaction is characterized by written linguistic phenomena analogous to those I have identified as constituting conversational style in spoken interaction" (p. 100). Given the hybrid nature of instant messaging and texting, researchers into the language conventions of those forms have often considered the relationship between the spoken and the written. However, few have considered how those language conventions are markers of identity or markers of membership within a Discourse community.

The early research focused on the language used within chat rooms and how people negotiated turn-taking (Herring, 1999) within environments in which prosodic and paralinguistic cues (facial expressions, gestures, vocal tone, etc.) were absent. Early research also delved into how individuals and were able to make sense of the emotional content of a message despite the lean nature of the medium (Walther, 1996). Later, when instant messaging became popular among youth in the late 1990s and early 2000s, a "moral panic" (Thurlow, 2006) arose in the popular press concerning the infiltration of CMC language into academic writing.

Thurlow and Poff (2011) framed the popular discourse around CMC language within the larger issue of people's belief systems.

... both media discourse and other popular commentary prioritize and exaggerate the look of text messaging language – its supposedly distinctive lexical and typographic style. Notwithstanding this, everyday talk about texting does offer important insights into people's beliefs (and concerns)

about language (and technology) which, as Pennycook (2004) notes, performativity establishes the meanings of language itself. It is for this reason that the study of texting warrants continued research interest, especially from discourse analysts and other language and communication scholars. (p. 180)

The concerns voiced in the media discourse are somewhat justified based on the fact that 85% of all 12 to 17-year-olds use some form of textisms when sending messages (Lenhart, Arafeh, Smith, & McGill, 2008). However, what is missed by those voicing those concerns is the reality that many youth do not consider instant messaging or texting to be a form of writing (Lenhart et al. 2008). This finding is significant given the research of Savas (2011), who considered how contextual and individual factors shape linguistic variation with CMC. Savas found that those individuals who viewed CMC as a type of written language tended to write in ways consistent with standard written English, and those who viewed CMC as a form of spoken language applied the norms of spoken language to their CMC messages. Thus, the concerns voiced by educators and the popular press may be related to the differences between how adults and youth view the practices of instant messaging and texting. Furthermore, the views one holds about the relationship of CMC to writing may be indicative of one's Discourse community.

Nonetheless, concerns about the relationship between CMC, language, and literacy are worth considering given Herring's (2013) argument that most of what is online is actually familiar, including discourse patterns such as spelling variations or interactional differences between genders. Discourse 2.0, it seems, is not necessarily new; instead, it may reflect language and literacy practices already in place among different groups or be an extension of pragmatic needs of different groups. For example, Turner et al. (2014) argued that texting language use has been conventionalized among adolescent users and is driven by three pragmatic maxims: (a) brevity and speed, (b) a playful informal register, and (c) phonological approximation. Specifically, Turner et al. argued that users engage in purposeful writing that shows an awareness of audience, efficiency in communication, expression of personal voice, and inclusion within a community of practice. Texting, therefore, is used strategically within a specific context.

An example of the conventionalization of textisms can be found in the work of Haas, Takayoshi, Carr, Hudson, and Pollock (2011) who conducted a rich study of the language of instant messaging. Haas et al. analyzed a 32,000-word corpus of university students' instant messages. They identified a 15-item taxonomy of language features and frequency patterns and argued that these features provide cues for the interpretation of how the message is to be interpreted. In the article, Haas et al. focused on the features of eye dialect, slang, emoticons and meta-markings as paralinguistic cues.

Haas et al. (2011) defined eye dialect as "deliberate, non-standard spelling used to suggest pronunciation or, more precisely, to draw attention to associations between a character's ways of pronouncing words and certain regional and cultural dialect" (p. 386). In eye dialect, letters can be added or subtracted from words to indicate sounds (such as partay for party). Meta-markings, Haas et al. explained are those parts of the message where the interlocutor steps outside of the message to comment on the message. These include elements such as an asterisk (*) to indicate a spelling correction. Emoticons, which will be discussed later in this chapter, also were considered meta-markers in that they serve to comment on the message. According to Haas et al.

... the language features of IM most often serve to establish the tone of the exchange as a whole, to attach emotional meaning to utterances, and to smooth the communication. By writing into the language (in often innovative and creative ways) paralinguistic cues, the participants in our study work to clarify, or more precisely disambiguate, meaning. (p. 393)

It must be remembered, however, that to make sense of these cues the interlocutors must be inculcated into the practices of the community. Without such understanding, the paralinguistic cues may be seen as being meaningless or nonsensical.

Making sense of these cues is paramount when engaged in instant messaging and texting. The role of cue interpretation is apparent in the instant messaging research of Nguyen and Fussell (2014) who found there are a number of lexical and structural cues that indicate high or low involvement in a conversation. Specifically, they found that high involvement conversations resulted in higher word use, a finding consistent with Jacobs (2004). Jacobs found that those messages with high emotional content tended to be longer and have more complex grammatical structures. Nguyen and Fussell also found high involvement messages included fewer personal pronouns, more definite articles, more assent words, and more cognitive mechanism words. They suggested that these cues provide interlocutors with a sense of how involved the conversational partner was in a messaging exchange. Thus, interlocutors not only learn how to interpret a message, but also learn to judge the affective stance of their conversational partner. As such, Nguyen and Fussell's work demonstrated that the conventions of use within CMC exchanges are not arbitrary but instead serve important functions within the social context of use.

The conventions of use serve the multiple purposes of identifying community membership as well as serving to facilitate meaning making. Cues are embedded within the lexical and structural choices made by interlocutors, and these cues are learned through engagement in CMC language and literacy practices (Jacobs, 2004, 2006). However, engagement in these practices has lead to questions as to the impact on language and literacy development.

- **Textisms and Literacy Development:** A major concern with youth's use of textisms is whether it negatively affects literacy development. Drouin (2011) defined textese (textisms) as an abbreviated vocabulary that includes initialisms (lol), homophones (gr8 for great), contractions (cuz for because), and the deletion of unnecessary words, vowels, punctuation, and capitalization. She argued that many of the spelling conventions resemble children's inventive spelling, thus revealing the literacy skills that support the use of these forms (Crystal, 2008). This section reviews research into aspects of the relationship between textisms and literacy development including reading ability, spelling ability, grammatical knowledge, and awareness of how language works. I propose that a larger consideration of the research literature indicates that rather than impacting literacy development either positively or negatively as some have argued, texting and instant messaging become part of the repertoire of literacy practices that youth engage in that marks them as members of an information based society (Jacobs, 2008).

- **Reading Ability:** In light of the federal mandates to increase the literacy levels of children, as measured by a narrow set of quantified measures, it is not unsurprising that researchers have been interested in the relationship between reading ability and texting or instant messaging. Two studies into texting and reading ability revealed interesting correlations between children's ability to decode and encode texts and their ability to read traditional texts. These findings indicate that the desire to use textisms

may supersede ease of use, thus indicating that use of textisms may be more closely related to Discourse identity (Gee, 2000-2001) than the supposed functionalities of texting.

For example, although the rise of textisms is often associated with the need for speed in producing texts, Kemp and Bushnell (2011) found that children took longer and made more errors when reading messages written using textisms than in conventional English. Also, contrary to popular perception, the children were no faster at writing textisms than when writing conventional English. Kemp and Bushnell also found that individuals' texting experience did increase writing speed, but did not increase reading speed. Finally, Kemp and Bushnell found that better literacy skills overall were associated with greater reading speed and accuracy when reading textisms. This finding was corroborated by Coe and Oakhill's (2011) comparative study of the texting habits of 10 and 11-year-olds in England.

Coe and Oakhill (2011) compared the texting habits of students identified as proficient readers were to those identified as struggling readers. They examined the frequency and type of text devised and the speed at which the students could read messages in comparison to their ability to read formal English. They found that the less skilled readers spent more minutes a day using cell phones but were less competent at producing and understanding textisms. Conversely, the proficient readers used more textisms and were faster at both reading texts and formal English. It is important to remember that the research of Kemp and Bushnell (2011) and Coe and Oakhill (2011) do not demonstrate causality; texting was not shown to have either a negative or positive impact on reading ability. Instead, this research implies that strong readers are able to make use and make sense of text across contexts and struggling readers struggle within both contexts. Furthermore, the fact that struggling readers spent more time using the cell phones (Coe & Oakhill, 2011) indicated that the struggling readers were motivated to engage in the practice even though it was more challenging.

- **Language Awareness:** The evidence has indicated that one reason for the positive relationship between textisms and literacy is that in order to use texting conventions such as homophones (gr8 for great), individuals need to have a phonemic awareness. Plester, Lerkkanen, Linjama, Rasku-Puttonen, and Littleton (2011) provided unique insights into the relationship between language and texting with their study of Finnish and English preteens. They found that the Finnish participants appeared to use the same proportion of textisms as their UK English speaking peers, but the Finnish text register closely resembled spoken Finnish, which is substantially different from written Finnish. The text patterns of the UK English speaking participants did not apply spoken English language variations in their texting and instead included more phonological play with homophones (U for you), which Finnish does not afford. Despite these differences between language users, the authors found that the data showed a positive relation between the textism ratio and literacy measures.

Further insight into the relationship between language and textisms is provided in the work of Okuyama (2013). Okuyama noted that the nonverbal features of texting tend to be based on the texting of hearing adolescents. Earlier research, as Okuyama noted, had found that a higher percentage of deaf university students used texting for relaxation, relief from boredom, or for the security of being able to reach someone in case of emergency, and hearing students, in comparison, used texting more for social contact. Furthermore,

Okuyama noted that deaf high school students had reported that texting supported an increased level of independence and improved English literacy skills. Additionally, as Quan-Haas and Young (2010) found, texting provided a level of social gratification for both hearing and deaf students.

Despite the seeming utility of texting, some deaf teens noted a lack of knowledge about the exact meanings of certain acronyms and abbreviations used in texting (Henderson-Summet et al., 2007). In Okuyama's (2013) study, the study participants indicated that they did not use textisms or emoticons because they are not integrated into the hearing world that uses textisms. However, Okuyama found that the text messages of the participants contained nonconventional grammar that echoed that of sign language. Okuyama argued that the study demonstrated that deaf students did adopt texting as a form of communication and were not discouraged by having to write in a second language and, in fact, created texts that reflected their first language. Okuyama argued,

... rather than dismissing these features simply as "errors" in English, we should keep in mind that deaf texters who proficiently sign on a daily basis do indeed engage in linguistic creativity in texting, but in a slightly different way from their non-signing counterparts. Moreover, considering the unconventional nature of texting and its flexibility to allow for the vernacular style of language, we need to avoid focusing on the low English literacy levels of this adolescent population. Instead, we need to look for the distinct textisms commonly used among signing deaf teens and investigate how and when such constructs occur. (p. 1236)

These findings are consistent with the concept of Discourse identities. How language is used within texting and instant messaging appears to be closely related to community membership.

- **Spelling Ability:** The unconventional use of language within texting and instant messaging has contributed to the moral panic identified by Thurlow (2006). Spelling, in particular, is an area the popular press has focused on (Jacobs, 2004). Wood, Jackson, Hart, Plester, and Wilde (2011) investigated the effect of texting on 9 and 10-year-olds' reading, spelling and phonological processing skills. This short-term project, in which the children were provided with cell phones for texting, showed that engaging in texting did not significantly advantage or disadvantage literacy development. However, they did find that textism use was positively linked to spelling development, and the number of messages sent and received was linked to lexical retrieval skills. The authors suggested this relationship might exist because texting supports increased engagement with written language and phonemic knowledge. Specifically, to use a nonconventional spelling such as "gr8" for great requires phonemic awareness. Furthermore, engaging in texting allows children and youth to play with language thus building sensitivity to and knowledge of how language works. Varnhagen, McFall, Pugh, Routledge, Sumida-MacDonald, and Kwong (2010) also investigated the relationship between texting and spelling and found that typographic and spelling errors were uncommon and that spelling ability was not related to language used within instant messaging. Thus, they too argued that the use of textisms does not have a harmful effect on conventional written language.

- **Grammar Knowledge:** Instant messaging and texting also are associated with nonconventional grammar use. These include aspects such as nonstandard use of punctuation or lack of punctuation, lack of capitalization, ungrammatical word forms (I going now), and word reduction (gonna) (Kemp, Wood, Waldron, 2014). There have

been conflicting results from several studies, but on the whole, the evidence has been tending to show there is either no relationship between texting and grammatical knowledge or a positive relationship.

For example, Cingel and Sundar (2012) found that 11 and 12-year-olds who were heavy users of textisms had a negative relationship between the use of textisms and scores on a grammar assessment (Cingel & Sundar, 2012). However, Cingel and Sundar acknowledged that it might be that youth who are weaker in grammar use more textisms than those youth who have strong grammar skills. A more comprehensive study into the relationship between texting and grammar was conducted by Kemp et al. (2014). Kemp et al. (2014) collected data from 244 British children, adolescents, and young adults in order to ascertain whether grammatical errors in texting was related to their performance on tasks of grammatical knowledge. They found that the variance of grammatical violations in texts was inconsistently predicted by the results of the grammatical tasks. Specifically, they found that children who made poor grammar choices on the task also tended to make more errors in their texting. No relationship was found between the results of the task and the texting of secondary students, and the results of the university students followed that of the younger children. As such, the authors were unable to conclude whether the use of unconventional grammar during texting is a predictor of poor grammatical abilities.

Kemp et al.'s findings are intriguing given Ling's (2010) suggestion that texting is associated with life phase. Further research is needed to understand the impact of life phase on formal grammar knowledge and the use of texting. For example, textisms appear to have an impact on children who are at a formative stage of literacy development, but have less impact on older adolescents and then more impact on university students. Additionally, there is evidence that texting has a positive relationship with the literacy skills of adults (Powell and Dixon, 2011). Because the extant studies tend to be short-term, longitudinal studies of texting practices and grammar development may provide additional insights. Additionally, ethnographic studies of texting and instant messaging use across life phases may provide more insights into the development of grammatical knowledge in relation to everyday literacy practices.

- **Pragmatic Knowledge:** Part of the problem facing researchers into instant messaging, texting, and textisms is the conflation between the larger practice of communicating using ICTs and the actual language used. Drouin (2011) sought to "disentangle text messaging from textese and examine the relations between these variables and literacy" (p. 72). Like Lewis and Fabos (2000, 2005) and Grace, Kemp, Martin, and Parrila (2013), Drouin found that college undergraduates were able to recognize when to use textisms and when not to. More specifically, Drouin found that the study participants were sensitive in their use of language and changed their language depending on their intended recipient. The students tended to use textisms more in messages to friends and rarely when communicating with professors. Drouin argued, "it does not appear that textese just seeps out into writing everywhere and in equal amounts; instead, the average person uses textese thoughtfully, and more often within the contexts deemed appropriate" (p. 72). She suggested that those individuals who use textisms in inappropriate contexts may not view those contexts as inappropriate, thus revealing a limited pragmatic knowledge.
- **Emoticons and Other Paralinguistic Cues:** Another aspect of CMC conventions that are prevalent in instant messaging and texting is the use of paralinguistic

cues. These include the use of emoticons and other cues that provide information concerning the intended tone of a message.

Emoticons are graphic representations of facial expressions (Walther & D'Addario, 2001). Originally, users add emoticons to messages as a way to substitute for the nonverbal cues missing from CMC. For example, a smiley face) would be added to indicate the interlocutor was smiling when the message was sent and that the message should be interpreted accordingly. However, Walther and D'Addario, (2001) found that emoticons had little impact on message interpretation, especially when the verbal content is negative. Walther and D'Addorio's findings were refuted by a later study by Derks, Bos, and von Grumbkow (2008), who found that emoticons do serve as proxies for nonverbal behavior by strengthening the intensity of a message. Derks et al. also found that interlocutors can create ambiguity and express sarcasm by juxtaposing a verbal message that carries one connotation with an emoticon that carries another. The shifts in findings remain unexplained, however, one explanation may be that in the years between Walther and D'Addario's research and Derks et al.'s, users became savvier in their use and interpretation of emoticons.

- **Why Conventions of Use Are Important:** The ongoing conversation about the conventions of use within communication modes such as instant messaging and texting has suggested that these conventions have meaning beyond the concerns about whether they impact literacy development. As Lewis and Fabos (2005) suggested, the "young people we studied used language in complex ways in order to negotiate multiple messages and interweave these conversations into larger, overarching story lines" (p. 482). Thus, the use of the conventions unique to instant messaging and texting not only mark an individual as a member of a particular discourse community, but it also contributes to their social identity and their place in a larger connected society. And if being a member of a connected society is necessary for engagement in the world, it then becomes important to consider what happens to those who are not connected.

INSTANT MESSAGING, TEXTING, AND THE TENDENCY TO MULTITASK

The always on nature of texting or instant messaging contributes significantly to the tendency to multitask, an issue long been an area of interest among researchers and a concern among educators and parents. Of particular interest for educators is the impact of multitasking on learning.

Junco and Cotten (2012) researched the relationship between multitasking and academic performance among college students and found that students who reported spending a large among of time using Facebook or texting while studying had lower GPAs than those who limited their time online. Junco and Cotten indicated that the assumption is that engaging in texting or Facebook while studying may tax cognitive processing and preclude deeper learning. However, rather than condemning the act of multitasking, the authors suggested that the type and purpose of ICT use matters in terms of educational impacts. That is, using an ICT to support learning differs from using an ICT to procrastinate. As with other research discussed in this chapter, Junco and Cotten did not establish a causal relationship between the use of texting and poor GPAs. It may be that students who are weaker learners or who have less effective study skills may turn to texting or Facebook to procrastinate or to alleviate the stress of studying.

To provide clearer insights into multitasking behaviors, Rosen, Carrier, and Cheever (2013) conducted a minute-by-minute assessment of on-task behavior, off-task technology use, and open computer windows as university students were studying. They found that participants averaged less than six minutes on task prior to switching. Most of the switching, according to Rosen et al. was due to distractions including social media, texting, and preference for task-switching. Furthermore, student dispositions appeared to be a significant factor in the amount of task-switching. Those individuals who preferred to task-switch had more distracting technologies available and those students with relatively high use of study strategies were more likely to stay on-task. Thus, the evidence does not support the supposition that texting or instant messaging causes poor study skills or lower grades; it is not unlikely that weaker students are more apt to multitask.

Additionally, it is unclear how the cultural contexts of an educational setting impacts students' use of ICTs. In cultural contexts where individuals are expected to be in constant contact, to cut oneself off from communication may have social consequences. As such, to better understand the nature of multitasking, it is important to ask what the larger implications of the practice are.

EDUCATIONAL APPLICATIONS OF INSTANT MESSAGING AND TEXTING

Using ICTs and CMC for direct educational applications has been a significant interest of researchers and practitioners. Much of the research discussed in the previous sections have implications for education even though the studies may not have been explicitly about using instant messaging and texting in educational settings for educational purposes. Those implications are discussed in the second section of this chapter. In this section, I focus on a few studies that examined how instant messaging or texting can be used to support educational goals within educational settings.

The research generally has indicated that direct application of texting or instant messaging for teaching and learning activities is not successful;

however one area of education that shows promise for the use of CMCs such as instant messaging and texting is that of second language acquisition. As Lam's (2007, 2009) work shows, engaging with language online allows individuals to construct an identity as a proficient language user. However, I do not include research that directly interrogates the application of CMCs for second language acquisition because the body of research is significant and beyond the scope of this chapter. The areas I focus on are tutoring, collaborative learning, and engagement.

- **Supporting Online Tutoring:** Hrastinski and Stembom (2013) considered how instant messaging could be used to support a low-cost one-to-one tutoring model. The research drew on a Vygotskian model of working within the zone of proximal development to support the math learning among older students. Coaching or tutoring was supplied by preservice teachers at a university. The study indicated that instant messaging was a less than satisfactory way to support the students' learning because the coaches found it difficult to identify the appropriate learning level of the student. This especially was true if they were simultaneously coaching more than one student. As such, the ability to hold multiple conversations and multitask while instant messaging was found to be a constraint for the more intensive interaction required for effective tutoring or coaching.

- **Collaborative Learning:** Kim, Lee, and Kim (2014) compared student interactions across an electronic bulletin board system, computer based instant messaging, and mobile instant messaging to determine the effects of the technology on collaborative learning processes. They found that those participants who participated on a bulletin board system enacted more cognitive and metacognitive interactions than those us-

ing computer-based or mobile instant messaging; however, those using instant messaging enacted more social and affective interactions. This finding is consistent with the research discussed earlier that indicates instant messaging and texting are used generally for affective purposes. As such, it may be that attempting to use an affective tool such as instant messaging and texting for academic purposes may not be an efficacious use of technology.

- **Promoting Engagement:** Rambe and Bere (2013) looked to using mobile technology and mobile instant messaging to broaden academic participation. Students in an information technology class at a South African university used a mobile instant messaging application to increase lecturer-student and student-to-student participation in formal and informal spaces. The intent was to create learning communities for knowledge creation and to shift the instructor's pedagogical approach. However, they found that the instructors expressed resentment because the technology broke the boundaries between personal life and academic life when students used the application to contact them after hours. The students were also ambivalent about using the application on a wider scale.

WHAT ARE THE CURRENT ISSUES IN THE FIELD RAISED BY THESE STUDIES?

Despite large number of studies into instant messaging and texting, there are a number of issues that remain relevant for researchers. One that should always be considered is, where are these practices heading? As the historical progression of both modes of communication has shown, Discourse 2.0 is constantly shifting due to technological developments and social change. Scholars who limit their research to the superficial aspects of the technology will soon find their work to be irrelevant. Thus, it is important to continually consider how these practices fit within the larger communications ecology. Furthermore, it is not enough to know what people are doing or even why they are doing it. Research must continue to push forward in developing understandings of what these practices mean to individuals and how those practices fit within sociocultural contexts.

- **Engagement:** A second issue that must be considered by the field is what these practices mean for individuals who are not engaged. To co-opt Ling's (2008) question, does it matter whether vulnerable populations text? If texting and instant messaging are tools of the intimate sphere, if they are used for identity construction and relationship building, where do people who do not use ICTs fall within society? Zickuhr (2013) reported that 15% of the population in the United States do not use the Internet or email; are these individuals also disconnected from others because they do not text or use instant messaging? This question is even more salient for older individuals, especially as the American population ages.

- **Convergence:** Another issue to be considered by the field is the growing convergence as identified by Herring (2013). If technologies such as instant messaging and texting are being subsumed by other platforms, what does it mean for the development of research questions and methodologies? Is it worthwhile to continue separating out questions concerning conventions of use or the role of a particular technology without considering how it is embedded within other platforms? For instance, do players of massive multiplayer online games use the messaging function differently than people who use stand-alone messaging systems? And if so, what does it mean?

WHAT ARE THE GAPS IN THE EXTANT RESEARCH AND DIRECTIONS FOR FUTURE RESEARCH?

Much of the research into instant messaging and texting is based on self-reported data, metered data, corpus analysis, or experimental designs. Only a few studies drew on ethnographic methods that provide deeper insights into the cultural nature of instant messaging and texting use. However, conducting ethnographic studies would be difficult given the intimate nature of texting and instant messaging. Thus, the findings of all studies should be viewed with some measure of skepticism and be accompanied with a resistance to generalization.

The research into instant messaging and texting have indicated that there is a set of language practices associated with the communication modes. The question that arises is how these language practices fit within the larger context of Discourse 2.0. The language of blogging differs from the language of texting because the intended audiences differ. If this is the case, what does this mean as we try to make sense of the 2.0 world? Is it sufficient to leave learning the various online discourses to chance or is there a need to teach the nuances of Discourse 2.0, particularly to those who come from marginalized populations and have less access to online practices.

Yet another area of research that should be considered is the shifting demographic of texting use. Lenhart (2012b) reported that the increase in texting is being led by Blacks followed by Hispanics. This shift in the demographics of texting may be due, in part, to the penetration of mobile phones into all strata of society. If this is the case, how should the field respond to these shifts? The literature clearly shows that the majority of research into instant messaging has been conducted among adolescents and university students. However, if the demographics of use are shifting, the research focus should also shift, especially in light of the sociocultural nature of language use. For example, some studies showed gender effects (Kimbrough et al. 2013) and other studies (Mesch et al., 2012) showed no gender effects. Why should we continue considering gender effects in texting? How might these differences provide insights into the nature of gender construction and identity?

Furthermore, as the demographics of texting shift, questions arise as to how different groups will affect Discourse 2.0. As Durkin et al. (2011), Plester et al. (2011), and Okuyama (2013) noted, an individual's language has a direct relation to the way they construct instant messages and texts. Thus, will the bilingualism of Hispanics or the patterns of African American English affect the conventions and structures of the language used in texting and instant messaging? And if it does, why does it matter? Will texting, as a tool of the intimate sphere, contribute to further divisions between groups, or will a new more inclusive language of the Internet emerge?

Finally, consideration should be given to the emerging social norms (DiDomenico & Boase, 2013) that are accompanying the use of instant messaging and texting. The moral panic identified by Thurlow (2006) may be an artifact of a generation that does not understand the new social norms and is applying an outdated set of assumptions to modes of communication that they don't yet understand.

WHAT ARE THE RECOMMENDATIONS/ IMPLICATIONS FOR EDUCATION, CIVIC ENGAGEMENT (GLOBAL AND LOCAL), SOCIAL PRACTICE, AND POLICY?

There are a number of recommendations and implications for social practice, education, civic engagement, and policy that should be considered in light of the extant research on instant messaging and texting. I examine these four areas through the lens of the question of what engagement and lack of engagement means for individuals, communities, and society as a whole.

- **Social Practice:** Implications and recommendations for social practice have been interwoven into the literature review presented in this chapter. In this section, I compile those implications and recommendations in order to provide a cohesive summary.

Instant messaging and texting may exemplify the changing social norms exchanges of the always on world. As the research of DiDomenico and Boase (2013) indicated, the ways individuals integrate texting or instant messaging into their every day lives reflect new ways of interacting that may not be understandable to those who do not use those tools. Furthermore, the increasing importance of the internet in American society suggests that those who are not connected will be unable to access resources that are increasingly accessible only online. Thus, instant messaging and texting, as tools of the intimate sphere, may serve as an easy and attractive entry into the world of online communication.

Additionally, the research has indicated that instant messaging and texting serve many of the same purposes as small talk. These seemingly trivial exchanges are the mortar that holds people together. Instant messaging and texting have been shown to assist in building and maintaining relationships and constructing identity. Thus engaging in these CMC practices allows individuals to identify as members of a technological society. This is not to say that people cannot build relationships or construct identity without using CMCs. What the research has shown is that using CMCs builds a particular type of relationship and particular types of identities that may serve to position individuals for success in today's information society; those who do not engage in these practices are positioned as outsiders. Although some individuals may choose not to engage in CMC practices for any number of reasons, it should be a conscious and autonomous decision driven by personal preference rather than a position forced by economic or social circumstances.

The decision not to be in constant contact should be made as carefully as the decision to be always on. As Turner et al. (2014) suggested, researchers should investigate the cultural contexts and communicative practices in which people engage. Specifically, the research has not yet identified how the cultural contexts of a setting impacts use of ICTs. For example, in contexts where individuals are expected to be in constant contact, to cut oneself off from communication may have social consequences. However, being in constant contact also has implications for involvement in face-to-face activities and circumstances that require uninterrupted attention. Thus, youth and adults should give deep consideration to when to be connected, when to disconnect, and when and how to multitask effectively.

- **Education:** Although there is a growing body of research into the use of social media for second language learning, investigations into the use of tools such as instant messaging and texting for other pedagogical purposes have not yet yielded evidence of promising practices. As the research has demonstrated, users of text and instant messaging are at best ambivalent about using a social tool for educational purposes. As Knobel and Lankshear (2006) noted in their discussion of blogging as a tool for teaching, care should be taken by educators when appropriating Web 2.0 practices. Knobel and Lankshear argued that pedagogizing a practice originally done for pleasure removes the social context associated with the practice. In that instant messaging and texting, as the research has demonstrated, are used for social gratification, taking these practices and using them in

teaching situations risks removing the social meaning associated with the practice.

Rather than attempting to use instant messaging or texting in educational settings, it may be wiser to use what student know about language and literacy, as demonstrated in their ability to text, to foster engagement with learning. The research has shown that instant messaging and texting have a ludic quality wherein users develop playful approaches to language use in order to express ideas and emotions. Bringing this sense of play into educational settings may be more fruitful than using the actual technologies. For example, activities such as having students turn a scene from a play, novel, or nonfiction article into a series of text messages allow for youth to play with language and demonstrate their facility with the language. However, such activities should be approached with care because those activities might marginalize the youth who do not have access to the technology or who have not engaged with the practices in a sustained way.

Additionally, consideration should be given to the less visible and understood ways that individuals may be engaging in with texting or instant messaging. As Lam (2009) argued, "An expanded view of the linguistic resources of youth of migrant backgrounds would lead us to reconsider how our educational practices may leverage these young people's communicative repertoires as resources for elarning instead of keeping them invisible or marginalized in the classroom. (p. 823). Such expanded views hold promise for a range of individuals and a range of ways of thinking and communicating that can position people for success in a world not yet envisioned.

- **Civic Engagement:** Understanding the role of texting and instant messaging as a tool for civic engagement is in its infancy and perhaps represents one of the most promising areas of research. This is especially salient given the ubiquity of the mobile phone, which takes on a significant role in street protests (Neumayer & Stald, 2014). Furthermore, given the research that instant messaging and texting are tools for relationship building and are part of the everyday practices of a significant number of people, there is immense potential for using these tools for mobilizing groups to take social action. A few studies have examined the role of texting within events such as the Egyptian revolution (Khamis & Vaughn, 2011) and the 2012 United States presidential election (Cogburn & Espinoza-Vasquez, 2011). The Khamis and Vaughn (2011) study indicated that texting is part of the emergence of the citizen journalist and that users invent measures to overcome barriers put in place by governmental agencies. Cogburn and Espinoza-Vasquez (2011), however, demonstrated how a savvy media team was able to mobilize a grass-roots movement using texting as well as other CMC tools to serve mainstream political ends.

In light of these early studies of an emerging but important phenomenon, researchers should consider conducting naturalistic research into how people use mobile instant messaging and texting in situations that may be chaotic. A question to be explored could include investigating whether the purpose shifts in these situations. Specifically, if texting is a tool of the intimate sphere, how are texts used to mobilize large groups of people? Thus, the development of research into civic engagement and mobile communication tools may also lead to the development of new approaches and reasons for research. Furthermore, consideration of texting and instant messaging as tools for civic engagement should also take into account those individuals who do not engage in either of those practices. Organizations or movements dependent on digital technology and social media may fail to reach key individuals in

the community. As such, instant messaging and texting need to be understood as part of a larger ecology of communication forms used to support civic engagement.

- **Policy:** Texting and instant messaging are tools that support the intimate sphere but have implications for social practice, education, and civic engagement; therefore, it is clear that policies should be put in place to support those populations who continue to be excluded from engagement in the digital world. Some policies have already been put in place, but limited time frames and funding reduces long-term impact. One of these was the 2010 Broadband Opportunities Program (BTOP) (National Telecommunications and Information Administration, n.d.). BTOP was developed to expand access to broadband services in the United States. The BTOP program included the enhancement and expansion of public computer centers and the support of training programs designed to introduce vulnerable populations to the digital world. While such programs are a move in the right direction, that funding stream has ended and programs have had to find other sources of revenue. Even if this funding stream was still in place, it is unclear whether practices such as texting and instant messaging would be supported by the program in that those ICTs do not have a clear connection to job preparation.

The tendency among policy makers, researchers, and educators is to focus on youth when considering digital technologies. However, the research indicates that those who are in the margins of digital technology use are adults. Thus policymakers within the realm of adult education should turn some attention to bringing adults into the digital realm. The BTOP program did this to some extent, but addition policy support is needed.

Adult job readiness is administered by the Office of Career, Technical, and Adult Education (OCTAE), which provides support for adults who need additional education in order to become better prepared for the workforce (Office of Career, Technical, and Adult Education, 2014). Additionally, the Workforce Innovation and Opportunities Act (U.S. Department of Labor Employment and Training Administration, 2014) and the *Ready to Work: Job-Driven Training and American Opportunity* reform (2014) call for "creating onramps to fill America's highest demand jobs" (p. 21). This upskilling is intended to offer opportunities for all U.S. citizens, regardless of age, to learn the skills to become employed within the information technology sector. However, learning skills such as texting are typically seen as being outside the purview of such programs. This way of thinking, unfortunately, may be shortsighted in that simple practices such as texting and instant messaging may be gateway practices that introduce individuals to the world of computers and the Internet. Thus, policies that support programs broader than workforce readiness may be appropriate.

Finally, policies should be put into place to support building connections with older adults. As the population ages, health issues become more salient and the risk of isolation increases. Although texting and instant messaging may not be the most appropriate tools for all older adults, those tools should not be ignored based on assumptions about the interest or abilities of older individuals. As the research has shown, once older adults become convinced of the usefulness and relevance of a technology, they are apt to take it up.

Although I have focused on policies for adults and older adults, policies should also be put into place that support the appropriate use of texting and instant messaging among youth. These include policy considerations for areas such as sexting, cyberbullying, and texting while driving. Cyberbullying has been recognized as being part of a larger problem of bullying with the added complication that it happens in a virtual space that is minimally regulated by schools or parents. As such, action has already been taken to allow schools to address cyberbullying that impacts the learning environment. Similar policies are being considered and put into place for sexting. Laws have also been enacted against texting and driving and have been accompanied by public awareness campaigns to stop the behaviors.

Often the use of ICTs among youth is seen as a distraction; however, as the research has shown, instant messaging and texting are part of a repertoire of practices that tend to support the development of language and literacy. However, these ICTs do appear to be distracting when individuals do not have skills in place that support learning; in these cases the use of instant messaging and texting may in fact be symptomatic of larger learning issues rather than being causative. Thus policies should support the continued development of strong language and literacy skills within the context of youths' educational lives with a recognition that the use of ICTs supports their social, emotional, and academic growth.

CONCLUSION

I began this chapter with a brief description of the way my friend and I use texting to transcend the limitations of time and geographic distance. Because of texting, our relationship has continued to build and our emotional tie is stronger than it was before we were able to text on a regular basis. Although she and I are both middle-aged White women, the details of our lives are significantly different in terms of health, education, and socioeconomic status. Yet, we both use mobile technology to text one another, and it is that practice that provides opportunities for growth for both of us. Our use of texting is deeply embedded within the contexts of our lives and our relationship with one another.

I end this chapter by returning to the beginning because this literature review has led me to see that it is time to push forward toward deeper understandings of the nature of Discourse 2.0 as used within the intimate sphere and its implications for society at large. It is unclear where the practices of instant messaging and texting will go. Instant messaging has morphed into mobile instant messaging, and new applications are apt to replace whatever is popular at the time of this writing. Texting, as originally conceived, also is becoming subsumed by other technologies. Both forms of CMC have become integrated into a wide range of applications and platforms that allow people to stay in contact in whatever ways fits best within their lives. However, despite the growing number of people who use texting or some form of instant messaging, there remain groups who have been systematically excluded from engagement or even deciding whether to engage or not. Whether it matters if someone texts or sends instant messaging should be determined by individuals and the community in which they belong. What is most important is that people can be connected in ways that are personally meaningful and allow them to have a positive impact on their lives and within society.

REFERENCES

Abbruzzese, J. (2014). *The rise and fall of AIM: The breakthrough AOL never wanted.* Retrieved from http://mashable.com/2014/04/15/aim-history/

Alvermann, D. E., Marshall, J. D., McLean, C., Huddleston, A. P., Joaquin, J., & Bishop, J. (2012). Adolescents' web-based literacies, identity construction, and skill development. *Literacy Research and Instruction*, *51*(3), 179–195. doi:1 0.1080/19388071.2010.523135

Baron, N. (1984). Computer-mediated communication as a force in language change. *Visible Language*, *XVIII*(2), 118–141.

Baron, N. (2008). *Always on: Language in an online and mobile world.* New York: Oxford University Press. doi:10.1093/acprof:o so/9780195313055.001.0001

Baron, N. S. (2013). Instant messaging. In S. Herring, D. Stein, & T. Virtanen (Eds.), *Pragmatics of Computer Mediated Communication* (pp. 136–161). Berlin, Germany: De Gruyter. doi:10.1515/9783110214468.135

Brito, P. Q. (2012). Tweens' characterization of digital technologies. *Computers & Education*, *59*(2), 580–593. doi:10.1016/j.compedu.2012.03.005

Bryant, J. A., Sanders Jackson, A., & Smallwood, A. M. K. (2006). IMing, Text Messaging, and Adolescent Social Networks. *Journal of Computer-Mediated Communication*, *11*(2), 577–592. doi:10.1111/j.1083-6101.2006.00028.x

Castek, J., Withers, E., Pendell, K., Pizzolato, D., Jacobs, G., & Reder, S. (2014, March). *Conquering the computer: Digital literacy acquisition among vulnerable adult learners.* Paper presented at the annual meeting of the American Association of Applied Linguistics, Portland, OR.

Castells, M. (2000). The rise of the network society (2nd ed.; Vol. 1). Oxford, UK: Blackwell.

Chowdhry, A. (2014). *MSN Messenger is completely shutting down on October 31st.* Retrieved from http://www.forbes.com/sites/amitchowdhry/2014/08/31/msn-messenger-is-completely-shutting-down-on-october-31st/

Christensen, C. M. (1997). *The innovator's dilemma: When new technologies cause firms to fail.* Boston, MA: Harvard Business School Press.

Cingel, D. P., & Sundar, S. S. (2012). Texting, techspeak, and tweens: The relationship between text messaging and English grammar skills. *New Media & Society*, *14*(8), 1304–1320. doi:10.1177/1461444812442927

Coe, J. E. L., & Oakhill, J. V. (2011). "txtN is ez f u no h2 rd": The relation between reading ability and text-messaging behaviour. *Journal of Computer Assisted Learning*, 27(1), 4–17. doi:10.1111/j.1365-2729.2010.00404.x

Cogburn, D. L., & Espinoza-Vasquez, F. K. (2011). From Networked Nominee to Networked Nation: Examining the Impact of Web 2.0 and Social Media on Political Participation and Civic Engagement in the 2008 Obama Campaign. *Journal of Political Marketing*, 10(1-2), 189–213. doi:10.1080/1537 7857.2011.540224

Crystal, D. (2004). *A glossary of netspeak and textspeak*. Edinburgh, UK: Edinburgh University Press.

Crystal, D. (2008). Texting. *ELT Journal*, 62(1), 77–83. doi:10.1093/elt/ccm080

Derks, D., Bos, A. E. R., & von Grumbkow, J. (2007). Emoticons and Online Message Interpretation. *Social Science Computer Review*, 26(3), 379–388. doi:10.1177/0894439307311611

DiDomenico, S., & Boase, J. (2013). Bringing mobiles into the conversation. In D. Tannen & A. M. Trester (Eds.), *Discourse 2.0: Language and New Media* (pp. 119–132). Washington, DC: Georgetown University Press.

Dolev-Cohen, M., & Barak, A. (2013). Adolescents' use of Instant Messaging as a means of emotional relief. *Computers in Human Behavior*, 29(1), 58–63. doi:10.1016/j.chb.2012.07.016

Drouin, M., & Landgraff, C. (2012). Texting, sexting, and attachment in college students' romantic relationships. *Computers in Human Behavior*, 28(2), 444–449. doi:10.1016/j.chb.2011.10.015

Drouin, M. A. (2011). College students' text messaging, use of textese and literacy skills. *Journal of Computer Assisted Learning*, 27(1), 67–75. doi:10.1111/j.1365-2729.2010.00399.x

Durkin, K., Conti-Ramsden, G., & Walker, J. (2011). Txt lang: Texting, textism use and literacy abilities in adolescents with and without specific language impairment. *Journal of Computer Assisted Learning*, 27(1), 49–57. doi:10.1111/j.1365-2729.2010.00397.x

Foucault, M. (1980). *Power/Knowledge* (C. Gordon, Trans.). New York, NY: The Harvester Press.

Fox, S., & Rainie, L. (2014). The web at 25 in the U.S. Washington, DC: Pew Internet and American Life Project. Retrieved from http://www.pewinternet.org/2014/02/27/the-web-at-25-in-the-u-s/

Gee, J. P. (1999). Discourses and social languages. In *An introduction to discourse analysis: Theory and method* (pp. 11–39). New York: Routledge.

Gee, J. P. (2000). Teenagers in new times: A new literacy studies perspective. *Journal of Adolescent & Adult Literacy*, 43(5), 412–420.

Gee, J. P. (2000–2001). Identity as an analytic lens for research in education. *Review of Research in Education*, 25, 99–125.

Grace, A., Kemp, N., Martin, F. H., & Parrila, R. (2013). Undergraduate's attitudes to text messaging language use and intrusions of textisms into formal writing. *New Media & Society*. doi:10.1177/1461444813516832

Grinter, R., & Eldridge, M. (2003). Wan2tlk?: everyday text messaging. In *Proceedings of the Conference on Human Factors in Computing Systems CHI 03* (pp. 441–448). ACM. doi:10.1145/642611.642688

Haas, C., Takayoshi, P., Carr, B., Hudson, K., & Pollock, R. (2011). Young People's Everyday Literacies: The Language Features of Instant Messaging. Research In The Teaching Of English. *Research in the Teaching of English*, 45(4), 378–404.

Haythornthwaite, C. (2005). Social networks and internet connectivity effects. *Information, Communication & Society, 8*(2), 125-147. doi:10.1080/13691180500146185

Henderson-Summet, V., Grinter, R. E., Carroll, J., & Starner, T. (2007). Electronic communication: Themes from a case study of the deaf community. *Lecture Notes in Computer Science, 4662*(Part I), 347–360. doi:10.1007/978-3-540-74796-3_33

Herring, S. (1999). Interactional coherence in CMC. *Journal of Computer-Mediated Communication, 4*.

Herring, S. (2013). Discourse in Web 2.0: Familiar, reconfigured, and emergent. In D. Tannen & A. M. Trester (Eds.), *Discourse 2.0: Language and New Media* (pp. 1–15). Washington, DC: Georgetown University Press.

Hinduja, S., & Patchin, J. W. (2015). *Cyberbullying legislation and case law: Implications for school policy and practice*. Retrieved from http://www.cyberbullying.us/cyberbullying-legal-issues.pdf

Hrastinski, S., & Stenbom, S. (2013). Student–student online coaching: Conceptualizing an emerging learning activity. *The Internet and Higher Education, 16*, 66–69. doi:10.1016/j.iheduc.2012.02.003

In U. S. SMS texting tops mobile phone calling. (2008). Retrieved from http://www.nielsen.com/us/en/insights/news/2008/in-us-text-messaging-tops-mobile-phone-calling.html

Ito, M., & Daisuke, O. (2003). Mobile phones, Japanese Youth, and the replacement of social contact. In R. Ling (Ed.), *Front Stage - Back Stage: Mobile Communication and the Renegotiation of the Public Sphere*. Grimstad, Norway. Retrieved from http://www.itofisher.com/mito/

Ito, M., & Daisuke, O. (2005). *Personal, portable, pedestrian: Mobile phones in Japanese life*. Cambridge, MA: MIT Press.

Ito, M., & Okabe, D. (2010). Intimate connections: Contextualizing Japanese youth and mobile messaging. In R. Harper, L. Palen, & A. Taylor (Eds.), *Inside the text: Social perspectives on SMS in the mobile age* (pp. 127–145). Dordrecht, The Netherlands: Springer.

Jacobs, G. (2008). We Learn What We Do: Developing a Repertoire of Writing Practices in an Instant Messaging World. *Journal of Adolescent & Adult Literacy, 52*(3), 203–211. Retrieved from papers://8823b2b3-0f26-4eac-b58e-76a95997f0e0/Paper/p1570

Jacobs, G. E. (2004). Complicating contexts: Issues of methodology in researching the language and literacies of instant messaging. *Reading Research Quarterly, 39*(4), 394–406. doi:10.1598/RRQ.39.4.3

Jacobs, G. E. (2006). Fast Times and Digital Literacy : Construction Within Instant Messaging. *Journal of Literacy Research, 38*(2), 171–196. doi:10.1207/s15548430jlr3802_3

Junco, R., & Cotten, S. R. (2012). No A 4 U: The relationship between multitasking and academic performance. *Computers & Education, 59*(2), 505–514. doi:10.1016/j.compedu.2011.12.023

Kemp, N., & Bushnell, C. (2011). Children's text messaging: Abbreviations, input methods and links with literacy. *Journal of Computer Assisted Learning, 27*(1), 18–27. doi:10.1111/j.1365-2729.2010.00400.x

Kemp, N., Wood, C., & Waldron, S. (2014). Do I Know Its Wrong: Children'S and Adults' Use of Unconventional Grammar in Text Messaging. *Reading and Writing, 27*(9), 1585–1602. doi:10.1007/s11145-014-9508-1

Khamis, S., & Vaughn, K. (2011). Cyberactivism in the Egyptian Revolution: How Civic Engagement and Citizen Journalism Tilted the Balance. *Arab Media & Society, 14*. Retrieved from http://www.arabmediasociety.com/index.php?article=769&p=0

Kim, H., Lee, M., & Kim, M. (2014). Effects of Mobile Instant Messaging on Collaborative Learning Processes and Outcomes : The Case of South Korea. *Education Technology & Society*, *17*(2), 31–42.

Kimbrough, A. M., Guadagno, R. E., Muscanell, N. L., & Dill, J. (2013). Gender differences in mediated communication: Women connect more than do men. *Computers in Human Behavior*, *29*(3), 896–900. doi:10.1016/j.chb.2012.12.005

Knobel, M., & Lankshear, C. (2006). Weblog worlds and constructions of effective and powerful writing: Cross with care, and only where signs permit. In K. Pahl & J. Rowsell (Eds.), *Travel Notes from the New Literacy Studies: Instances of Practice* (pp. 72–92). Clevedon, UK: Multilingual Matters.

Kowalski, R. M., Giumetti, G. W., Schroeder, A. N., & Lattanner, M. R. (2014). Bullying in the digital age: A critical review and meta-analysis of cyberbullying research among youth. *Psychological Bulletin*, *140*(4), 1073–1137. doi:10.1037/a0035618 PMID:24512111

Kowalski, R. M., Giumetti, G. W., Schroeder, A. W., & Reese, H. H. (2012). Cyber bullying among college students: Evidence domains of college life. In C. Wankel & L. Wankel (Eds.), *Misbehavior online in higher education* (pp. 293–321). Bingley, UK: Emerald. doi:10.1108/S2044-9968(2012)0000005016

Kowalski, R. M., & Limber, S. P. (2007). Electronic bullying among middle school students. *The Journal of Adolescent Health*, *41*(6), 22–30. doi:10.1016/j.jadohealth.2007.08.017 PMID:18047942

Lam, W. S. E. (2000). L2 literacy and the design of the self: A case study of a teenage writing on the Internet. *Teachers of English to Speakers of Other Languages*, *34*(3), 457–482. Retrieved from papers://8823b2b3-0f26-4eac-b58e-76a95997f0e0/Paper/p2147

Lam, W. S. E. (2009). Multiliteracies on instant messaging in negotiating local, translocal, and transnational affiliations: A case of an adolescent immigrant. *Reading Research Quarterly*, *44*(4), 377–397. doi:10.1598/RRQ.44.4.5

Lauricella, S., & Kay, R. (2013). Exploring the use of text and instant messaging in higher education classrooms. *Research in Learning Technology*, *21*(0), 1–18. doi:10.3402/rlt.v21i0.19061

Lenhart, A. (2012a). *Communication Choices*. Retrieved from http://www.pewinternet.org/2012/03/19/communication-choices/

Lenhart, A. (2012b). Teens, Smartphones & Texting. Washington, DC: Pew Internet and American Life Project. Retrieved from http://pewinternet.org/Reports/2012/Teens-and-smartphones.aspx

Lenhart, A., Arafeh, S., Smith, A., & Macgill, A. R. (2008). *Writing, technology and teens, 83*. Retrieved from papers://8823b2b3-0f26-4eac-b58e-76a95997f0e0/Paper/p59

Leu, D., Kinzer, C. K., Coiro, J., & Cammack, D. (2009). Reading Online - New Literacies_ Toward a Theory of New Literacies. *Theoretical Models and Processes of Reading*, 41. Retrieved from papers://8823b2b3-0f26-4eac-b58e-76a95997f0e0/Paper/p761

Lewis, C., & Fabos, B. (2000). But will it work in the heartland? A response and illustration. *Journal of Adolescent & Adult Literacy*, *43*, 462–469.

Lewis, C., & Fabos, B. (2005). Instant messaging, literacies, and social identities. *Reading Research Quarterly*, *40*(4), 470–501. doi:10.1598/RRQ.40.4.5

Licoppe, C. (2004). 'Connected' presence. The emergence of a new repertoire for managing social relationships in a changing communication technoscape. *Environment and Planning. D, Society & Space*, *22*(1), 135–156. doi:10.1068/d323t

Ling, R. (2008). Should we be concerned that the elderly don't text? *The Information Society, 24*(5), 334–341. doi:10.1080/01972240802356125

Ling, R. (2010). Texting as a life phase medium. *Journal of Computer-Mediated Communication, 15*(2), 277–292. doi:10.1111/j.1083-6101.2010.01520.x

Ling, R., & Baron, N. S. (2013). Mobile phone communication. In S. Herring, D. Stein, & T. Virtanen (Eds.), *Pragmatics of Computer Mediated Communication* (pp. 192–215). Berlin, Germany: De Gruyter. doi:10.1515/9783110214468.191

Ling, R., Bertel, T. F., & Sundsoy, P. R. (2012). The socio-demographics of texting: An analysis of traffic data. *New Media & Society, 14*(2), 281–298. doi:10.1177/1461444811412711

Luckerson, V. (2012). *OMG: Traditional text messaging is on the decline*. Retrieved from http://business.time.com/2012/11/15/omg-traditional-text-messaging-is-on-the-decline/

Mesch, G. S., Talmud, I., & Quan-Haase, A. (2012). Instant messaging social networks: Individual, relational, and cultural characteristics. *Journal of Social and Personal Relationships, 29*(6), 736–759. doi:10.1177/0265407512448263

National Telecommunications and Information Administration. (n.d.). *Broadband USA: Connecting America's Communities*. Retrieved from http://www2.ntia.doc.gov/

Neumayer, C., & Stald, G. (2014). The mobile phone in street protest: Texting, tweeting, tracking, and tracing. *Mobile Media & Communication, 2*(2), 117–133. doi:10.1177/2050157913513255

Nguyen, D. T., & Fussell, S. R. (2014). Lexical Cues of Interaction Involvement in Dyadic Instant Messaging Conversations. *Discourse Processes, 51*(5-6), 468–493. doi:10.1080/0163853X.2014.912544

Office of Career, Technical, and Adult Education: Workforce Innovation and Opportunities Act. (2014). Retrieved from http://www2.ed.gov/about/offices/list/ovae/pi/AdultEd/wioa-reauthorization.html

Okuyama, Y. (2013). A case study of US deaf teens' text messaging: Their innovations and adoption of texisms. *New Media & Society, 15*(8), 1224–1240. doi:10.1177/1461444813480014

Petronzio, M. (2012). *A brief history of instant messaging*. Retrieved from http://mashable.com/2012/10/25/instant-messaging-history/

Pettigrew, J. (2014). Text messaging and connectedness within close interpersonal relationships. *Marriage & Family Review, 45*(6-8), 697–716. doi:10.1080/01494920903224269

Pew Internet Research Project. (2014a). *Mobile technology fact sheet*. Washington, DC: Author. Retrieved from http://www.pewinternet.org/fact-sheets/mobile-technology-fact-sheet/

Pew Internet Research Project. (2014b). *Couples and texting*. Washington, DC: Author. Retrieved from http://www.pewinternet.org/2014/02/11/couples-the-internet-and-social-media/pi_14-02-11_techrelationships_435/

Plester, B., Lerkkanen, M.-K., Linjama, L. J., Rasku-Puttonen, H., & Littleton, K. (2011). Finnish and UK English pre-teen children's text message language and its relationship with their literacy skills. *Journal of Computer Assisted Learning, 27*(1), 37–48. doi:10.1111/j.1365-2729.2010.00402.x

Porath, S. (2011). Text Messaging and Teenagers: A Review of the Literature. *Journal of the Research Center for Educational Technology, 7*, 86–99.

Powell, D., & Dixon, M. (2011). Does SMS text messaging help or harm adults' knowledge of standard spelling? *Journal of Computer Assisted Learning, 27*(1), 58–66. doi:10.1111/j.1365-2729.2010.00403.x

Pyzalski, J. (2012). From cyberbullying to electronic aggression: Typology of the phenomenon. *Emotional & Behavioural Difficulties*, *17*(3-4), 305–317. doi:10.1080/13632752.2012.704319

Quan-Haase, A., & Young, A. L. (2010). Uses and Gratifications of Social Media: A Comparison of Facebook and Instant Messaging. *Bulletin of Science, Technology & Society*, *30*(5), 350–361. doi:10.1177/0270467610380009

Rambe, P., & Bere, A. (2013). Using mobile instant messaging to leverage learner participation and transform pedagogy at a South African University of Technology. *British Journal of Educational Technology*, *44*(4), 544–561. doi:10.1111/bjet.12057

Riordan, M. A., Markman, K. M., & Stewart, C. O. (2012). Communication Accommodation in Instant Messaging: An Examination of Temporal Convergence. *Journal of Language and Social Psychology*, *32*(1), 84–95. doi:10.1177/0261927X12462695

Rivers, I., & Noret, N. (2010). "I h8 u": findings from a five-year study of text and email bullying. *British Educational Research Journal*, *36*(4), 643–671. doi:10.1080/01411920903071918

Rosen, L. D., Mark Carrier, L., & Cheever, N. A. (2013). Facebook and texting made me do it: Media-induced task-switching while studying. *Computers in Human Behavior*, *29*(3), 948–958. doi:10.1016/j.chb.2012.12.001

Sacco, D. F., & Ismail, M. M. (2014). Social belongingness satisfaction as a function of interaction medium: Face-to-face interactions facilitate greater social belonging and interaction enjoyment compared to instant messaging. *Computers in Human Behavior*, *36*, 359–364. doi:10.1016/j.chb.2014.04.004

Savas, P. (2011). A case study of contextual and individual factors that shape linguistic variation in synchronous text-based computer-mediated communication. *Journal of Pragmatics*, *43*(1), 298–313. doi:10.1016/j.pragma.2010.07.018

Shui, E., & Lenhart, A. (2004). How Americans use instant messaging. Washington, DC: Pew Internet & American Life Project. Retrieved from http://www.pewinternet.org/Reports/2004/How-Americans-Use-Instant-Messaging.aspx

Slonje, R., Smith, P. K., & Frisen, A. (2013). The nature of cyberbullying, and strategies for prevention. *Computers in Human Behavior*, *29*(1), 26–32. doi:10.1016/j.chb.2012.05.024

Smith, A. (2014). Older adults and technology. Washington, DC: Pew Internet and American Life Project. Retrieved from http://www.pewinternet.org/2014/04/03/older-adults-and-technology-use/

Tagliamonte, S. A., & Denis, D. (2008). Linguistic ruin? LOL! Instant messaging and teen language. *American Speech*, *83*(1), 3–34. doi:10.1215/00031283-2008-001

Tannen, D. (2013). The medium is the metamessage: Conversational style in new media interaction. In D. Tannen & A. M. Trester (Eds.), *Discourse 2.0: Language and New Media* (pp. 99–117). Washington, DC: Georgetown University Press.

Temple, J. R., & Choi, H. (2014). Longitudinal association between teen sexting and sexual behavior. *Pediatrics*, *134*(5), e1287–e1292. doi:10.1542/peds.2014-1974 PMID:25287459

Temple, J. R., Paul, J. A., van den Berg, P., Le, V. D., McElhany, A., & Temple, B. W. (2012). Teen sexting and its association with sexual behaviors. *Archives of Pediatrics & Adolescent Medicine*, *166*(9). doi:10.1001/archpediatrics.2012.835 PMID:22751805

Thurlow, C. (2006). From statistical panic to moral panic: The metadiscursive construction and popular exaggeration of new media language in the print media. *Journal of Computer-Mediated Communication*, *11*(3), 1–39. doi:10.1111/j.1083-6101.2006.00031.x

Thurlow, C., & Poff, M. (2011). Text messaging. In S. C. Herring, D. Stein, & T. Virtanen (Eds.), *Handbook of the pragmatics of CMC* (pp. 163–189). Berlin, Germany: Mouton de Gruyter.

Turner, K. H., Abrams, S. S., Katic, E., & Donovan, M. J. (2014). Demystifying digitalk: The what and why of the language teens use in digital writing. *Journal of Literacy Research*, *46*(2), 157–193. doi:10.1177/1086296X14534061

U.S. Department of Labor Employment and Training Administration. (2014) *Workforce Innovation and Opportunity Act*. Washington, DC: Author. Retrieved from http://www.doleta.gov/wioa/pdf/WIOA-Overview.pdf

Varnhagen, C. K., McFall, P. P., Pugh, N., Routledge, L., Sumida-MacDonald, H., & Kwong, T. E. (2010). Lol: New language and spelling in instant messaging. *Reading and Writing*, *23*(6), 719–733. doi:10.1007/s11145-009-9181-y

Voida, A., Newstetter, W. C., & Mynatt, E. D. (2002). *When conventions collide: The tensions of instant messaging attributed*. Paper presented at the CHI Conference, Minneapolis, MN.

Vygotsky, Walther, J. D. (1996). Computer-mediated communication: Impersonal, interpersonal, and hyperpersonal interaction. *Communication Research*, *25*(1), 3–43.

Walther, J. B., & D'Addario, K. P. (2001). The Impacts of Emoticons on Message Interpretation in Computer-Mediated Communication. *Social Science Computer Review*, *19*(3), 324–347. doi:10.1177/089443930101900307

Whittaker, E., & Kowalski, R. M. (2014). Cyberbullying Via Social Media. *Journal of School Violence*, *14*(1), 11–29. doi:10.1080/15388220.2014.949377

Wood, C., Jackson, E., Hart, L., Plester, B., & Wilde, L. (2011). The effect of text messaging on 9- and 10-year-old children's reading, spelling and phonological processing skills. *Journal of Computer Assisted Learning*, *27*(1), 28–36. doi:10.1111/j.1365-2729.2010.00398.x

Wood, C., Kemp, N., & Plester, B. (2013). *Text messaging and literacy: The evidence*. New York, NY: Routledge.

Zickuhr, K. (2013). Who's not online and why. Washington, DC: Pew Internet and American Life Project. Retrieved from http://www.pewinternet.org/2013/09/25/whos-not-online-and-why/

KEY TERMS AND DEFINITIONS

Computer Mediated Communication (CMC): Human communication that occurs through the use of two or more electronic devices (Walther, 1996).

Discourse 2.0: How the interactive Internet, in which individuals are content producers as well as consumers, affects how people use language and text (Herring, 2013).

Disruptive Technologies: Innovations that challenge the status quo by introducing simpler, more convenient, more accessible, and more affordable ways of accomplishing goals (Christensen, 1997).

Instant Messaging: A form of CMC that uses a mobile application or computer program to send messages between one or more individuals. All conversational partners must be logged in to the same application or program.

Media Convergence: The development of computer programs, mobile applications, and electronic devices that brings multiple functionalities into one device, program, or application. Smartphones exemplify media convergence in that within one device, an individual is able to communicate by voice, text, image, access the Internet, download and listen to music or podcasts, play games, read books, etc.

Predictive Typing/Texting: A functionality within mobile devices that provides the typist with a word based on the first letters entered by the user or words based on the context of the sentence.

Texting: Sending short messages between mobile devices using short messaging service (SMS). Unlike instant messaging, which requires users to be signed-in on the same application, any mobile device enabled with SMS can receive a text from any with a similarly enabled mobile device.

Section 3
Issues Associated with Digital Media

Chapter 21
Cyberbullying and Internet Safety

Deirdre M. Kelly
University of British Columbia, Canada

Chrissie Arnold
University of British Columbia, Canada

ABSTRACT

The chapter considers cyberbullying in relation to Internet safety, concentrating on recent, high quality empirical studies. The review discusses conventional debates over how to define cyberbullying, arguing to limit the term to repeated, electronically-mediated incidents involving intention to harm and a power imbalance between bully and victim. It also takes note of the critical perspective that cyberbullying— through its generic and individualistic framing—deflects attention from the racism, sexism, ableism, and heterosexism that can motivate or exacerbate the problem of such bullying. The review concludes that: (a) cyberbullying, rigorously defined, is a phenomenon that is less pervasive and dire than widely believed; and (b) cyber-aggression and online harassment are more prevalent, yet understudied. Fueled by various societal inequalities, these latter forms of online abuse require urgent public attention. The chapter's recommendations are informed by a view of young people as apprentice citizens, who learn democratic participation by practicing it.

INTRODUCTION

What is cyberbullying? We thought to begin this chapter with a compelling vignette that we could refer back to, as we discussed the research. But we were stymied trying to draw from an actual case discussed in the media or legal briefs, or to select a fictional story, a hypothetical incident used in survey research, or a rich description from a qualitative study.

All the high-profile media cases linked to cyberbullying told stories of misogyny, racism, and homophobia so severe as to constitute serious criminal acts better dealt with by the justice system, rather than the relatively less serious incidents more amenable to an educational approach that the term *cyberbullying* conjured. Complicating matters still further, the real-life cases that received media attention usually ended in suicide by the victim—misleadingly implying that cyberbullying

DOI: 10.4018/978-1-4666-8310-5.ch021

causes suicide. We initially thought of selecting one of these stories, because they had actually happened, would be widely known, and would highlight the gravity of the underlying issues. We began to realize that this strategy is common in the research literature. Wingate, Minney, and Guadagno (2013), for example, begin their review article by recounting the story of Jamey Rodemeyer, a 14-year-old who had come out as gay and been subject to homophobic bullying by peers at school and online—later, after Jamey's suicide, the bullying was investigated as criminal harassment. Wong-Lo and Bullock (2014) introduce their topic of bystander culture in cyberbullying by referencing Amanda Todd, the 15-year-old whose video, titled *My Story: Struggling, Bullying, Suicide, and Self Harm*, garnered over a million viewers after Amanda committed suicide. Other researchers mention cases like these that end in suicide in their conclusion; for example, Wright and Burnham (2012) do this to underscore for *The Professional Counselor* audience the importance of earliest possible "cyberbullying interventions" (p. 175).

We also turned to fiction as a possible source. J. K. Rowling's (2012) novel *The Casual Vacancy,* in various reviews, has been said to contain a subplot about cyberbullying. One of the teenage characters, Sukhvinder Jawanda, is subjected to bullying at school and tormented daily with anonymous, hateful postings to her Facebook wall. Over the course of the book, Sukhvinder is subjected to racist, sexist, and homophobic epithets, insults to her family's Sikh religion and national origin, and demeaning comments about her body (hairy, fat) and dyslexia. While Rowling makes clear that Sukhvinder has other reasons besides the acts of her "anonymous cyber-torturer" (p. 132) to be depressed, the cyberbullying does contribute significantly to her self-loathing, slicing her arms with a razor blade, and suicidal thoughts.

If fiction and high-profile media cases tend to the extreme yet also, in their detail, hint at patterns of online harassment and abuse that

amount to hate crimes and institutional forms of oppression, then hypothetical vignettes developed for research purposes achieve nearly the opposite effects. In trying to devise a scenario with broad resonance, researchers, often by design, strip the cyberbullying incident of context. For example, Price and colleagues (2014) used the animation *Broken Friendship*, wherein Katie passes along her best friend's password to "the beautiful people," who then use it to create humiliating images and emails of Katie's friend, and these are then spread among teens at the school. The authors explain that the figures in the animation were "deliberately shown in silhouette to ensure the removal of any identifying cultural context, allowing for personal identification and interpretation of the scenario from any situation" (p. 5). Unfortunately, as we will discuss in more detail in a later section, this may have the effect of obscuring the complex workings of power, including who gets to belong to the "beautiful people" and by what means. From this more critical sociocultural perspective, the term *cyberbullying* serves as a euphemism for phenomena better described as, for example, *online sexual harassment*, where "harassment is based on unequal, gendered power relations within and between the sexes" (Kelly, Pomerantz, & Currie, 2006, p. 21).

Does this mean we abandon the term *cyberbullying* altogether? In what follows, we will argue for provisionally retaining the term, particularly if tightly defined, for reasons related to maturity, whether defined by age, life experiences, or both. First, the term *bullying* conjures images of the schoolyard bully stealing a weaker child's lunch money; it thus associates the activities covered by the term with young people, giving it an advantage over more legalistic terms like *harassment* by reminding adults that proposed remedies should be seen within a developmentally appropriate frame. Imagine a young person reading through the comments section of various online news sites, which are rife with incivility; afterwards, he makes obnoxious comments about his fellow players in an online multiplayer game like *Grand Theft Auto* (itself full of violence and sexist and racist stereotypes). It is conceivable that he might repeatedly "trash talk" a peer online without fully realizing the distress he may be inflicting (Runions, 2013). Indeed, without knowing more details, this "common, albeit immature, give-and-take among adolescents" (Waldman, 2012, p. 709) may not, as we will discuss later, constitute cyberbullying.

Second, young people, as they build their identities, draw from their perceptions of difference as they interact with parents, teachers, and peers and interpret messages from educational, religious, justice, and other key social institutions. While not their only resource, they do use everyday forms of discrimination as a means of gaining status. "Connolly (2006) has shown, for example, how boys aged five and six appropriated discursive resources (including improvising upon racist ideas and practices) to construct their gender identities and regulate the behavior of their peers" (Kelly & Brooks, 2009, p. 204). In this, they are drawing from the wider social context, where adults and adult-run institutions are heavily implicated. Thus, while everyday forms of discrimination should neither be ignored nor trivialized, we argue for not leaping ahead and labeling these acts in ways that put the blame too quickly on the individuals involved by categorizing them as simply "perpetrators" or "victims"—a path that leads too easily to draconian measures and criminalization of young people.

In what follows, we will navigate between these two broad ideas of, on the one hand, cyberbullying, rigorously defined, as a phenomenon that is less pervasive and dire than widely believed (Sabella, Patchin, & Hinduja, 2013), and, on the other hand, online incivility and harassment that is, sadly, more common and underpinned by various societal inequalities that require public attention. Our discussion will be informed by a view of young people as apprentice and, at times, de facto citizens (Kelly, 2014) whose agency needs to borne in mind as we consider the research on

cyberbullying and Internet safety and our recommendations for education, civic engagement, social practice, and policy in light of this review.

OVERVIEW OF THE RESEARCH

The two concepts that are the focus of this chapter—*cyberbullying* and *Internet safety*—each might be thought of as shifting goalposts, where the indicated terrain is fought over, claimed and reclaimed, expanding and contracting accordingly. For example, online predators were more the concern in the mid-1990s, whereas cyberbullying in recent years has become the more prominent issue seen to be compromising the safety of young people online (Facer, 2012; Livingstone, Kirwil, Ponte, & Staksrud, 2014). In the US, 35 states enacted legislation that addressed cyberbullying in the period 2006-2010 (National Conference of State Legislatures, 2014; cf. Hinduja & Patchin, 2014).

Life Online: Putting Internet Safety and Cyberbullying in Context

Internet usage is now nearly universal among young people in North America. In the United States, 95% of those aged 12 to 17 are online, increasingly via portable devices (Madden, Lenhart, Duggan, Cortesi, & Gasser, 2013). In Canada, 99% of students in grades 4-11 are able to access the Internet outside of school (Steeves, 2014b). When researchers inquire more generally into what life online is like for children and young people, the overall picture is surprisingly positive, given the prominence given to dangers in the mainstream media and on the public policy agenda. Almeida and colleagues, for example, conducted 158 interviews with children and youth (aged 8 to 17) in Portugal about their various Internet activities at home and in school. A key finding was the intertwining of children's online and offline activities: for instance, their "virtual" social networking experiences enhanced and multiplied their peer relations in the "real" world, and those interviewed did not mention cyberbullying at all (Almeida, Delicado, de Almeida Alves, & Carvalo, 2014, pp. 14-15; see also the summary of research in Festl & Quandt, 2013, p. 103; Keipi & Oksanen, 2014).

In nationally representative surveys that aim for broad measures of online experience, teens are noticeably more likely to report positive experiences than negative ones. In the US, 57% of teen social media users said they have had an experience online that made them feel good about themselves, and 37% reported having had an online experience that made them feel closer to another person (Madden, Lenhart, Cortesi, et al., 2013, p. 73). In Canada, very high percentages of both boys (90%) and girls (89%) in grades 4-11 agreed that they "knew how to protect [themselves] online" (Steeves, 2014b, p. 5).

When asked about the types of risks that concern them on the Internet, young people's list overlaps with, but adds to and sometimes reorders, the list that adults might provide on their behalf, helping to create a more complete and nuanced picture of the issues that constitute Internet safety. The EU Kids Online survey, for example, has explored the changing mix of opportunities and risks that young people encounter via the Internet, providing a helpful classification of risks according to content, contact, and conduct (Livingstone, Haddon, & Görzig, 2012). *Content risks* include encountering pornography, violent or gory imagery, hateful messages (including racist and misogynist content), websites that induce worries over body image, unwanted popup ads and commercials, and so on. *Contact risks* include strangers, usually adults, attempting to engage with youth online, which might include pretending to be someone younger for nefarious reasons (e.g., sexual harassment, coercion, pedophilia). *Conduct risks* occur more in the context of young people's daily encounters with each other online (i.e., peer to peer) and include incivility, name-calling, threats or other nasty behavior, having one's account

hacked or privacy violated, and cyberbullying. In the EU Kids Online survey, respondents aged 9 to 16 were asked about what bothered people their age online, and over half (55%) of the risks they mentioned were related to content (especially violence and pornography), 19% to conduct, and 14% to contact; the concerns shifted significantly by age, with older children more likely to report being bothered by inter-personal risks as compared with content-related ones (Livingstone et al., 2014, pp. 277-278).

The mix of risks varies by the type of Internet platform or activity; the *affordances* (or opportunities to perform particular actions in particular environments) of social networking sites, for example, are comparatively likely to be linked with conduct risks such as cyberbullying (Livingstone et al., 2014, p. 283). In the US, 80% of online teens (aged 12-18) are users of social media sites (Lenhart et al., 2011). In Canada, of students in grades 4-11 the proportion with their own Facebook account rises steadily with age, from 67% in grade 7 to 95% in grade 11 (Steeves, 2014c). As already mentioned, young people report positive experiences using social media. But in Canada, 23% of grade 4-11 students also reported that they had said or done "something mean or cruel to someone online," while 37% reported that someone had said or done "something mean or cruel to them online that made them feel" bad about themselves (Steeves, 2014a, p. 2). And in the US, while 69% of teens who use social media think that peers are "mostly kind to each other" on social network sites, 15% report having been the target of "online meanness" over the last year (Lenhart et al., 2011, p. 3).

Of course, researchers might dispute whether these survey items necessarily measure cyberbullying as such. Some feminist scholars have suggested that the problem of pervasive online vitriol or "e-bile" is not adequately captured by the term *cyberbullying* and is threatening the public presence of women and other marginalized groups in society (Jane, 2014). Other scholars have raised concerns of "alarmism" and whether "the problems should be defined as being unique to technology" (Finkelhor, 2014, p. 655).

The varied conceptualizations are not surprising because, in reality, a continuum of behaviors exists, ranging from annoying or disappointing to severe, persistent, and pervasive attacks on others. At what point on the continuum does an incident make the leap from being one of poor judgment to one that we would call cyberbullying – or even one that may be criminal? (Sabella et al., 2013, p. 2704)

As will be discussed in the next sections, rates of cyberbullying vary widely based on differences in how researchers conceive of and define the phenomenon, how they measure it, and how they go about deciding who to ask as well as characteristics of who is asked (issues of sampling).

Prevalence Rates and Change over Time

The field of cyberbullying is still comparatively new, and researchers have not come to consensus on what constitutes cyberbullying (or even that it should be called that). Before turning to the specifics of this debate, we provide a sense of prevalence rates and their variance, drawing from recent reviews of the scholarly literature done by leading experts. Kowalski and colleagues (2014) did a comprehensive and systematic review and provide a table summarizing cyberbullying prevalence estimates and characteristics of 166 existing studies done in countries throughout the world, published through 2012. They document the "highly variable" prevalence rates, both of engaging in cyberbullying behavior and being victimized by it, and while they did not venture a general estimate for perpetration in this review article, they cited a range of 10% to 40% for cyberbullying victimization (Kowalski, Schroeder, Giumetti, & Lattanner, 2014, p. 1108). Patchin and

Hinduja (2014), in a review of prevalence rates, found that cyberbullying rates ranged from 1.2% to 44.1%, with an average rate of 15.2% (median of 13.7%) across 42 peer-reviewed journal articles; victimization rates ranged from 2.3% to 72%, with an average rate of 21.3% (median of 15.8%) across 51 peer-reviewed journal articles. In an earlier review of peer-reviewed research reports focused only on victimization, Tokunaga (2010) estimated that 20 to 40% of all youths have experienced cyberbullying at least once in their lives. Livingstone and Smith, scholars based in the UK, focused their review on research published since 2008; they concluded "that occasional or one-off occurrences [of victimization] may be reported by over 20% of young people but serious or recent or repeated incidents are reported by only around 5%, less than for traditional bullying" (2014, p. 639).

What about prevalence rates over time? There is some data to suggest that rates increased during the period 2000-2005 (Smith, 2012). During this period, the issue of cyberbullying came onto the radar of researchers, the term itself having been coined by Bill Belsey, the founder of bullying. org, circa 2000 (www.cyberbullying.ca). In more recent years, however, experts agree that there has not been a clear increase (or decrease) in the prevalence rates of cyberbullying—a fact all the more striking in that this same time period has seen the introduction and rapid uptake of portable technologies (Hinduja & Patchin, 2012; Livingstone & Smith, 2014, p. 642; Olweus, 2012a, b; Smith, 2012).

What Is Cyberbullying?

The field has been dominated to date by psychologists influenced by the work done on what has come to be called "traditional" (offline, face-to-face) bullying, influenced by the work of Dan Olweus (e.g., 1993) in Norway. The definition of traditional bullying usually highlights it as aggressive behavior that (1) is *repeated*, (2) is *intended* to cause harm or to dominate, and (3) involves a *power imbalance* between bully and victim. *Cyberbullying*, then, shares these elements but is carried out using electronic communication technologies to threaten, humiliate, or harass others who "cannot easily defend" themselves (Smith et al., 2008, p. 376). Given the nature of online communication, however, the three elements of repetition, intention, and power imbalance have had to be elaborated in ways that make sense in this comparatively new and still evolving context.

Repetition

If someone posts an embarrassing photo or a mean comment about another person on one occasion, this would not be seen as bullying, because the action was not repeated. Some researchers have pointed out, however, that in an online environment, the photo or comment could be forwarded to others and, if not removed from a public forum, the victim might be faced with it over and over again. So, what counts as repetition might differ from a repeated attack by one perpetrator (Dredge, Gleeson, & de la Piedad Garcia, 2014; Langos, 2012; Wingate et al., 2013, p. 90, citing Menesini & Spiel, 2012).

Intention to Harm

Repetition links to intention to cause harm. A one-time insult can sometimes be explained as a joke-gone-wrong, but if the behavior is repeated, it indicates a pattern of directed aggression. Complicating matters, social cues are not as visible online; offline, potential aggressors might realize they have hurt another's feelings if they look sad, while potential victims can hear a tone that helps them interpret whether a comment was meant as something other than playful teasing.

Power Imbalance

Traditional bullying assumes that the bully has superior power based on physical strength, num-

bers, age or grade, popularity at school, or other markers of social status (as we discuss in later sections, critical scholars have raised concerns that the bullying construct should focus on *institutional* power as well as these *relational* power inequities). Determining power imbalance online is complicated by the degree of anonymity that is possible in that environment, and some researchers have argued that the criterion can be dispensed with (Wingate et al., 2013). Yet, many other researchers have demonstrated the salience of power differentials as a defining criterion (e.g., Menesini et al., 2012; Pieschl, Porsch, Kahl, & Klockenbusch, 2013; Ybarra, Espelage, & Mitchell, 2014), seeing anonymity as a contributor to power imbalance (Slonje, Smith, & Frisén, 2013, p. 27).

While Olweus's construct of traditional bullying has been highly influential in the effort to define cyberbullying, Menesini has raised the issue of whether building mainly from this construct has introduced a bias. The Italy-based researcher pointedly asked, "How and to what extent might cyberbullying be underestimated if we neglect its specificity? How and to what extent can the studies on cyberbullying help us deepen the knowledge of bullying as a whole problem?" (2012, p. 544). From this perspective, Menesini and other researchers in Europe and around the world have explored how electronically-mediated communication differs from in-person communication, inquiring into the implications for how to define cyberbullying. In particular, they have highlighted as potentially meaningful to the perceptions of those involved in cyberbullying: (a) greater anonymity of the bully and witnesses, (b) potential intensity (no safe time or place), (c) scale of publicity (larger audience), and (d) missing social cues (less direct feedback from victims and witnesses) (Kowalski et al., 2014; Mehari, Farrell, & Le, 2014; Menesini, 2012; Nocentini et al., 2010; Schultze-Krumbholz, Hoher, Fiebig, & Scheithauer, 2014; Slonje et al., 2013; Sticca & Perren, 2013; Thomas, Connor, & Scott, 2014). While to date these have not been shown to be essential definitional criteria, they have been seen as potential factors that might deepen understanding of the nature and severity of the aggression as well as the motivations for, and consequences of, cyberbullying.

Greater Anonymity

Anonymity online varies by degree, from *full anonymity*, to *pseudonymity* (where one uses a fictional username, avatar, or both), to *visual anonymity* (where physical characteristics are hidden or unavailable) (Keipi & Oksanen, 2014, p. 1099). This feature of online communication affords users the opportunity to engage in cyberbullying with less accountability and fewer repercussions (Runions, 2013), because users are less likely to fear punishment by authority figures or retaliation by their targets (Wright, 2013), and even witnesses do not necessarily know who they are (Mehari et al., 2014, p. 403). Studies done with young adults have provided some evidence that believing one's actions to be truly anonymous does predict cyber-aggressive behavior over time (Barlett, Gentile, & Chew, 2014; Wright, 2013). Further, some researchers have suggested that a repeated threat from an anonymous person can induce more fear and feelings of helplessness in the victim, possibly due to their perceiving less control over the situation (Sticca & Perren, 2013). At the same time, however, studies have shown that most school-age victims of cyberbullying know their bullies (for a recap, see Cassidy, Faucher, & Jackson, 2013, p. 579), and that some people who engage in *offline* bullying (e.g., spreading hurtful rumors around school) successfully hide their identities from their victims (Ybarra, Mitchell, & Espelage, 2012). Further, recent studies have found that young people do not perceive anonymity to be very important "in determining victim-perpetrator relationships and the seriousness of the behavior" (Bryce & Fraser, 2013, p. 783; see also Compton, Campbell, & Mergler, 2014).

No Time or Space Limitations

Researchers have theorized that the 24/7 feature of the Internet might mean that those being cyberbullied feel no relief, that there is no safe space or time. In a US national survey that measured relative rates of online and offline bullying, Ybarra and colleagues found, however, that only a small (but, nevertheless, concerning) 5% of young people reported being bullied in multiple environments (Ybarra et al., 2012, p. 211).

Greater Publicity

Researchers have posited that the potentially wider audience for cruel or embarrassing incidents might make cyberbullying worse for its victims. The evidence for this, so far, is mixed. In the national study just mentioned, over twice as many youth who reported having been bullied *at school* said they felt "extremely upset" by the most serious incident as compared to youth bullied online (Ybarra et al., 2012, p. 210). In an experimental study based on hypothetical scenarios, Sticca and Perren (2013) found that youth in grades 7-8 ranked as worse (more distressing) public bullying scenarios, whether online or offline. The publicity, rather than the medium of communication, was their main concern. In addition, although the incident that goes viral on the Internet might be "potentially the most harmful," the literature suggests that "Most cyberbullying attacks still happen in a localized online context" (Festl & Quandt, 2013, p. 123 n. 3; see also Slonje et al., 2013, p. 27).

Missing or Ambiguous Social Cues

Citing the theoretical work of Suler on the "online disinhibition effect," many researchers have discussed the way that visible witnesses and the nearby presence of authority figures can serve as barriers to aggression offline, but online where these are often absent, people may feel more free to cyberbully (e.g., Barlett et al., 2014; Mehari et al., 2014, p. 402). Tone of voice and facial expressions, including eye contact, gestures, and body language influence face-to-face communication, but these social cues are missing from much electronically-mediated communication. As discussed earlier, this can lead to miscommunication or lack of understanding of intentions. Potential bullies may not get direct feedback that their behavior is being read as hurtful; in many online situations, they will not see emotional reactions that might prompt an empathic response (Mehari et al., 2014; Runions, 2013). At the same time, to the extent that some potential bullies online do not have unmediated social reinforcement from bystanders, they may be more motivated to act in offline situations.

How Is Cyberbullying Measured?

The lack of consensus among bullying researchers of cyberbullying's defining characteristics and relevant dimensions is reflected in the wide-ranging and inconsistent ways it has been measured (for reviews, see Kowalski et al., 2014; Mehari et al., 2014; Thomas et al., 2014). In a systematic review of studies (published before late 2010) with instruments that assessed cyberbullying, Berne and colleagues (2013, p. 329) located 44 definitions with the following criteria:

- Occurs via electronic media: 42
- Intention to harm: 40
- Repeated behavior: 25
- Power imbalance: 13
- 24/7 nature: 0
- Anonymity: 0
- Wider audience: 0

With so many measurement tools failing to include the key definitional criteria, researchers have sometimes conflated cyberbullying with peer conflict (Sabella et al., 2013) or more general peer "cyber-aggression" (Runions, 2013; Thomas et al., 2014; Ybarra et al., 2014). Ybarra and colleagues have conducted a series of studies aimed to sort through the confusion. They found, importantly, that including a list of cyberbullying behaviors *without* using the word *bully* or a definition of bullying leads to inflated prevalence rates. They recommend using the word *bully* (with or without a definition) and then directly measuring such criteria as power imbalance and repetition to reduce misclassification (Ybarra, boyd, Korchmaros, & Oppenheim, 2012; see also Kowalski et al., 2014). In a later study, Ybarra and colleagues found that generalized peer aggression (Internet harassment) and cyberbullying overlapped, with the latter the more specific and consequential form. This study provided particularly convincing evidence for why prevalence rates vary so widely, because it assessed both concepts (generalized peer aggression and cyberbullying) "separately within the same study using the same sampling and data collection methodology; and measure time frame" (Ybarra et al., 2014, p. 294).

These findings are in line with the idea that cyberbullying is not itself a distinct *type* (or new form) of bullying but should be considered under the more general definition of bullying (Kowalski et al., 2014; Thomas et al., 2014, p. 10). Rather, the *medium of communication* is an additional dimension of bullying (elements of which might be measured), where three well-documented forms of bullying can be expressed in-person or electronically: (a) *physical*, (b) *relational*, and (c) *verbal* (Mehari et al., 2014). While some researchers argue that cyberbullying consists mainly of relational bullying (social exclusion, rumor spreading) (e.g., Talwar, Gomez-Garibello, &

Shariff, 2014), Mehari and colleagues argue that even physical bullying can occur electronically. They give as examples sending violent pictures or issuing threats of physical violence (2014, pp. 404, 406).

When cyberbullying is defined and measured in a way that takes into account intention, repetition, and power imbalance, prevalence rates are much lower. For example, Olweus found that only 4.1–5.0% of youth experienced victimization, while 2.5–3.2% of youth could be classified as bullies (2012a), with a very high proportion of those involved in cyberbullying also involved in traditional bullying (Olweus, 2012a, b; see also Hinduja & Patchin, 2012; Kowalski et al., 2014, p. 1107).

This is not to say that citizens should not be concerned about the more general phenomenon of peer cyber-aggression, particularly if it is directed against people on the grounds of race, gender, real or perceived sexuality, national origin, religion, physical or mental disability, and other grounds where discrimination is prohibited by law (for further discussion, see the Issues section below). Indeed, group-interview studies have found that young people labeled as *cyberbullying* a one-time incident, if severe or highly publicized (Dredge et al., 2014; Nocentini et al., 2010; Menesini et al., 2012; but see Olweus, 2012a, pp. 531-532). Rather than confuse the issue, however, we suggest (following Waldman, 2012) labeling a one-time serious incident a *cyberattack*, reserving the term *cyberbullying* only for repeated cyberattacks. See Figure 1 for a conceptual map of how these various ideas relate to one another.

To recap, there has been a lack of consensus regarding the concept of cyberbullying and its definition and therefore how to measure it. To date, these differences have made it difficult to make meaningful comparisons of findings across studies and therefore to draw firm conclusions, but we do want to comment on a few trends, because we think the available evidence can quell certain anxieties and provisionally inform efforts at prevention and intervention.

Figure 1. Conceptual map of terms and ideas related to cyberbullying

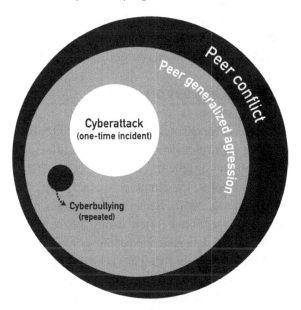

Age Differences and School Transitions

The available research suggests that cyberbullying is at its worst in grades 7 through 10, late middle school and early high school (Kowalski et al., 2014, p. 1125; see also Cassidy, Jackson, & Brown, 2009; Steeves, 2014a). This is an age when traditional bullying is also peaking, and Juvonen and Graham (2014), in a comprehensive review of school bullying, note that middle school or the transition from elementary to secondary school are times when young people are preoccupied with establishing their place in the social hierarchy. This is in line with social dominance theory, wherein "bullying perpetration can be considered a strategic behavior that enables youths to gain and maintain a dominant position within their group" (p. 164). This suggests that during periods of "social reorganization and uncertainty," such as the transition from elementary to middle school or to high school, bullying behaviors aimed at enhancing one's status would be most prevalent (p. 164). "On the basis of the current evidence," as Juvonen and Graham note, "it is difficult to determine whether these transitions involve mainly environmental changes (e.g., larger schools, increased anonymity) or whether the combination of environmental and developmental (e.g., pubertal) changes is involved in the creation of social hierarchies based on aggression" (p. 165).

Potential Impact on Victims

A number of recent reviews have correlated cyberbullying with a plethora of psychosocial, affective, and academic problems (Kowalski et al., 2014, esp. pp. 1114-1115; Slonje et al., 2013, pp. 29-30; Tokunaga, 2010). Because most studies have been cross-sectional (often using self-reported questionnaire data generated at one point in time) and because cyberbullying has been defined in so many ways, the research on cyberbullying victimization has been "replete with mixed findings" (Tokunaga, 2010, p. 282). For these reasons, we must be cautious at this stage about the negative impacts attributed to cyberbullying victimization.

That said, and to focus here only on mental health, there are a number of cross-sectional studies showing significant associations between involvement in cyberbullying, as either a victim or bully, and symptoms of depression and suicidal ideation, independent of involvement in traditional bullying (Bonanno & Hymel, 2013; Bauman, Toomey, & Walker, 2013). In a 2-year longitudinal study of both traditional and cyberbullying victimization in the Netherlands, researchers (Bannink, Broeren, van de Looij-Jansen, de Waart, & Raat, 2014) found that among girls—but not boys—both traditional bullying and cyberbullying victimization were associated with mental health problems, after controlling for baseline mental health. The study demonstrated that, for both boys and girls, traditional bullying victimization--but not cyberbullying victimization--was associated with suicidal ideation, after controlling for baseline suicidal ideation. In an observational study, Sinyor, Schaffer, and Cheung (2014) reviewed coroner records for all suicide deaths in youth aged between 10 and 19 in the city of Toronto

from 1998 to 2011. They identified bullying as a contributing factor in fewer than 5 deaths (5.3%) and detected no deaths where cyberbullying was involved. Depression, however, was detected in two out of every five cases. The authors highlight "the need to view suicide in youth as arising from a complex interplay of various biological, psychological, and social factors of which bullying is only one" (p. 632). While cyberbullying does not cause suicide, it may "exacerbate instability and hopelessness in the minds of adolescents already struggling with stressful life circumstances" (Hinduja & Patchin, 2010, as cited in Sabella et al., 2013, pp. 2705-2706).

Critical Sociocultural Perspectives

As seen so far, much of the research in the field of cyberbullying has been done by psychologists, building on traditional bullying research and focusing mainly on personality variables and other individual characteristics. While this body of literature explores important dimensions of the phenomenon, it is crucial to recognize that cyberbullying is not just an individual-based problem, but also needs to be understood in a wider social context, drawing on research from such disciplines as media and cultural studies and sociology. An important part of this work, to date, has been raising questions about: (a) how the problem has been discussed and named; (b) who benefits and who loses from this framing; and (c) what solutions follow logically and which ones are less widely imaginable. When the problem is named as *cyberbullying* and children's safety is said to be at risk, families' emotions are roused, and "both liberals and conservatives can be rallied to the cause — conservatives to restore discipline, liberals to protect the weak" (McCaskell, 2012, p. 61).

From a critical sociocultural perspective, while cyberbullying discourse addresses issues of violence, it can—through its generic framing—occlude attention to the racism, sexism, ableism (discrimination against people with disabilities), and heterosexism that can motivate or exacerbate the problem of such bullying (see, e.g., Moy, 2008; Bickmore, 2011). If people treat cyberbullying as mainly about personality traits and mental or behavioral disorders, and sharply divide "perpetrators" from "victims," critical scholars worry that this contributes to "a general trend to label children, particularly in a culture that tends to psycho-pathologize behaviors" (Brown, Chesney-Lind, & Stein, 2007, p. 1260). In this way, too, naming cyberbullying as the problem negates other problems, such as "pathological social conditions" (Edelman, 1988, p. 27). For example, Stack (2012) does not diminish bullying as an issue, but she details a number of policy issues (such as child poverty, inequitable service provision to Aboriginal children) and names the more pressing concern to be "how adults continue to support policies that adversely impact their kids" (para. 1).

A number of scholars have suggested that we are currently in the midst of a "moral panic" (Cohen, 2002/1972) about cyberbullying. Phases in this *moral panic* process include: (a) mainstream media sensationalizing youth violence, which (b) fuels concerns among the general public, (c) anxieties run high across the ideological spectrum, and (d) public support builds for authorities, including politicians, to take action and restore a sense of social order. These critical scholars have proposed to reframe the public discussion to emphasize instead "children's rights and capacities to engage in democratic debates about the nature of an online public space in which they are already participating" (Facer, 2012, p. 397; see also Kelly, 2010; McCaskell, 2012; Stack, in press). What is meant by democracy—and by extension, the relation of children and youth to democracy, as well as the nature of democratic education—however, is often unspecified (Kelly, 2014).

CURRENT ISSUES IN THE FIELD

The question of how to address the issue of cyberbullying is a contentious one, with several facets to consider. Our goal in this section is neither to offer the reader the "right" answer nor to put the debates to rest. Rather, we hope to outline some of the tensions that arise when trying to address cyberbullying and to illustrate them with grounded examples of what different policymakers, educators, and corporations are doing in response. We aim to call into question some of the decisions and responses that have arisen due to the moral panic that surrounds cyberbullying, calling for a more even-handed approach to the issue.

Balancing Freedom of Expression with the Safety of Persons

One of the primary considerations when considering how to address cyberbullying and, in turn, potentially regulating people's online activities, is the question of whether it is constitutionally valid to do so. In Canada, the right to freely express one's opinion is a fundamental freedom protected under section 2 of the *Canadian Charter of Rights and Freedoms*. In the United States, it is protected under the First Amendment to the US Constitution. These protections are in place to ensure the ability of people to participate in what has been called the "marketplace of ideas" in a liberal and democratic society, built on the belief that forms of political expression contribute to democracy by encouraging opposing views. The "marketplace of ideas" theory holds that "the best test of truth is the power of the thought to get itself accepted in the competition of the market" (Oliver Wendell Holmes, dissenting in *Abrams v. United States*, 1919, quoted in Jaffe, 2013, p. 281). According to this logic, ideas, interactions, and assertions on the Internet should not be regulated, nor do they need to be attached to their authors, because their legitimacy should only be determined by their marketability. Jaffe (2013) questions this position, asking if the marketplace should be the arbiter of the truth—and, ultimately, the safety of young people—in the context of cyberbullying.

The arguments above are based on a conceptualization of the marketplace as a neutral space, one in which all points of view have equal opportunity to be taken as truth; further, the marketplace of ideas theory assumes no responsibility for the fact that the exchange of ideas can lead to harm. Particularly, it does not account for the insidious ways that relations of power are embedded in online exchanges, nor for the reality that threats to one's safety are not experienced equally by all groups. To address this, some regulations do currently exist to regulate discourse on the Internet. In the Canadian context, for example, freedom of expression is limited in cases of hate speech, which is public communication that vilifies individuals based on their membership in a social group. The courts in Canada have acknowledged that hate speech stifles discourse and curtails the ability of the affected group to participate in the "marketplace of ideas" by shutting down dialogue and making it difficult or impossible for members of the vulnerable group to respond. While this protection does exist, a great deal of the behavior labeled *cyberbullying* would not be considered extreme nor targeted enough to qualify as hate speech. As such, an important topic of debate is whether further regulations are needed to govern online spaces to prevent cyberbullying. In framing this debate, it is important to remember that in order for such regulations to be deemed constitutionally valid, they would have to reasonably justify their limit to free speech. Legal scholars have noted that defamation, intentional affliction of distress, and threats are not protected under the First Amendment as valuable speech (Citron, 2009; Waldman, 2012).

Intertwined with the debate on freedom of expression is whether one should have the right to remain anonymous online. It has been argued that the ability to be anonymous is a key motivator to engage in online vitriol and cyberbullying (Barlett et al., 2014; Wright, 2013), in turn prompting calls for intermediaries (e.g., website hosts) to curtail anonymity in order to increase safety for users. There are, however, several arguments in favor of maintaining anonymity online. For example, Kates (2013) argues that anonymity is crucial insofar as it facilitates a more honest public debate. She calls into question the *Huffington Post's* recent decision to remove the ability to comment anonymously on its site, where three-quarters of comments contributed, according to a former managing editor, "contained unpublishable levels of vitriol" sent by "trolls" (Soni, 2013). Reflecting on her own experience, Kates asserts, "When I leave quotations on the Internet that are traceable to me, I tend to leave too many positives…If I had to identify myself every time I went online and left a comment my behaviour would change and I'd leave a trail of false positives" (p. 32). It is primarily her concern for truth that drives her defense of anonymity: "If anonymity provides a vehicle for truth, it should be respected" (p. 32).

While Kates' argument is perhaps less directly connected to the experiences of youth online and the cyberbullying debate, there is also a strong case to be made that anonymity can serve to protect particularly vulnerable youth, allowing them to use the Internet to explore their identities in ways that they would otherwise be unable to do. Imagine, for example, the situation of a young person who is questioning their sexuality or gender identity, living in a small rural community where they do not know of anyone who has experienced what they are going through. Online anonymity allows for the potential to connect with communities of people who can ultimately become a support or lifeline for young people when they are going through particularly tumultuous periods in their lives. It is often being anonymous that makes participation in these communities safe, allowing young people to connect with others in similar circumstances without risking their participation becoming public within their own personal spheres (e.g., Driver, 2007).

Creating Effective Legal Remedies without Infringing on Privacy Rights

Over the past several years, cyberbullying has been thrust onto the public agenda through several horrific, high-profile cases of online abuse involving teens. Many of the stories that have captured the national imagination in both Canada (for example, Amanda Todd and Rehtaeh Parsons) and the USA (for example, Tyler Clementi) have been those in which teens have died by suicide. These cases have spurred a moral panic, resulting in sometimes hasty responses from government officials and policymakers (Facer, 2012; Mc-Caskell, 2012; and see example below). Under the banner of fighting cyberbullying and keeping our children safe, these responses often include problematic provisions that heavily infringe on privacy rights. While the cases referred to above certainly deserve redress, we question whether they are necessarily cases of cyberbullying, or whether they are in fact more aptly categorized as serious crimes; Amanda Todd, for example, was subjected to sexual extortion and blackmail by an adult Internet predator (Surbramaniam & Whalen, 2014). The conflation of such incidents with more common, everyday acts of peer-to-peer aggression contributes to a moral panic that, in some cases, triggers extreme responses with unintended consequences.

In the Canadian context, for example, the response at the federal level has been the recent enactment into law of Bill C-13, the *Protecting Canadians from Online Crime Act*. The Conservative government has repeatedly touted this legislation as needed to protect, as one federal minister put it, "our most vulnerable citizens—our children and grandchildren—from acts of cyberbullying and other forms of online exploitation" (Department of Justice Canada, 2014). Politicians repeatedly

elicited support for the bill by invoking the names of Amanda Todd and Rehtaeh Parsons. The Act creates a new criminal offence of "knowingly" distributing an "intimate image" (nude, sexually explicit) of a person without the depicted person's consent and where they have "a reasonable expectation of privacy." This was meant to combat cases of "revenge porn." The Act also extends the criminalization of hate speech, which had been based on color, race, religion, ethnic origin, or sexual orientation but now also includes national origin, age, sex, and mental or physical disability (Nicol & Valiquet, 2014, sec. 2.1.7).

At the same time, the Act provides various investigative tools that enhance police powers, including a provision that broadens "the scope of warrantless, voluntary disclosure of personal information by ISPs [Internet Service Providers] to law enforcement" (West Coast LEAF, 2014, p. 13). While the cyberbullying safeguards have received broad support, the "lawful access" provisions have been criticized by Canada's Privacy Commissioner (Payton, 2014), civil liberties groups, equality rights organizations, Internet law experts (Geist, 2014), and even Amanda Todd's mother (now a victims' rights advocate) on the grounds that privacy rights are jeopardized. As Patriquin (2014) comments, "the government shoehorned increased Internet surveillance powers into an anti-bullying bill, which would grant legal immunity to telecommunications companies that voluntarily hand over customer data. The bill would also further lower the standards of evidence for police officers seeking to monitor Internet activities" (para. 5).

Not only did the government leverage public concern over cyberbullying to push through controversial legislation increasing its surveillance powers, the degree to which this Act actually addresses *youth* cyberbullying is also questionable. Indeed, it is primarily concerned with *adults* sharing intimate images non-consensually and with privacy rights. It would not change the current child pornography laws in Canada that make it illegal for people under 18 to share, for example, a nude photo of themselves with another person under 18, even if they wish to (e.g., "sexting" a sexually intimate partner), because youth under 18 are deemed by law to be unable to consent to participation in pornography (West Coast LEAF, 2014, p. 39). While authorities in Canada have not so far been using criminal law to prosecute consensual sharing of intimate images of teens by other teens, this has not been the case in the United States (Bailey & Hanna, 2011, p. 408). Slane (2013) analyzes the conceptual challenges raised by legal responses to malicious (as opposed to consensual) sexting, arguing that "we all have a right to both protection from sexual victimization and from undue interference with sexual expression" (p. 117).

Finding the Appropriate Role of the School in Addressing Cyberbullying

The responsibility of schools to address incidents of cyberbullying is a contentious issue. On one side is the argument that cyberbullying often happens outside of the school, both beyond the limits of school property and outside of school hours. Willard (2012) notes this can sometimes result in school administrators' dismissing the problem, based on the assumption that it is "off-campus, not my job" (p. 46). Yet Willard insists that this attitude stems from a lack of understanding of the legal standards, which require the school to get involved if "the off-campus speech is clearly preventing" a "child from feeling safe at school" (p. 45). A further argument is that incidents at school appear to trigger cyberbullying, which is then carried over into online exchanges (Cassidy et al., 2009). In the Canadian context, the "courts have long recognized that schools owe a duty of care to their students, and have held that the standard of care owed by a school to a student is that of a 'reasonably prudent or careful parent'" (West Coast LEAF, 2014, p. 46). This holds school boards and provincial ministries of education accountable

under the law of negligence, wherein they must take "reasonable steps to counter foreseeable risks of injury to those to whom a duty of care is owed" (West Coast LEAF, 2014, p. 46). As such, schools are required to have comprehensive policies in place to deal with discrimination, harassment, and abusive behavior; if a student can show that the school has breached this standard of care, s/he could conceivably make a claim against the school for negligence.

The role of the school in addressing cyberbullying can take many forms and ultimately needs to be multi-faceted in nature, engaging multiple stakeholders, including parents, police, Internet service providers, "e-safety" organizations, policymakers, news media, and researchers (Vandebosch, 2014; see also Moreno, Egan, Bare, Young, & Cox, 2013). The response taken by a school will necessarily vary, depending on whether the action is preventative or reactive in nature. Willard (2012) advocates for a restorative justice approach to responding to individual instances of cyberbullying, arguing that the primary objective for schools to consider when addressing cyberbullying should be to have the harm stopped. She maintains that it is important not to get too focused on merely disciplining the student who is cyberbullying, as this can have unintended consequences. She notes, for example, that sometimes the move to suspend a student for cyberbullying can simply lead to more vengeful forms of online retaliation (p. 46).

Exploring the Responsibility of ICT Corporations to Combat Cyberbullying

While a great deal of attention in combating cyberbullying has been directed toward schools and individual actors, an actor that is often minimized in the debate on how to address the issue of cyberbullying is the corporation. Whether it is an Internet Service Provider (ISP) or a specific Social Networking Site (SNS), such as Facebook or Twitter, a great deal of cyberbullying takes place under the purview of major corporations with significant resources at their disposal. This section explores the existing legal responsibilities of corporations in combating cyberbullying and online harassment, and asks what role they could and should play in addressing this issue.

At present, corporations that operate in the online space (for example, social networking sites or web-hosting services), are not completely free from regulation or responsibility; however, it is quite difficult to hold them legally accountable for content hosted on their sites. In the US, corporations are protected by section 230 of the *Communications Decency Act*, which "exempts ISPs from liability for user-generated content" (West Coast LEAF, 2014, p. 77; see also Jaffe, 2013). This means that as long as the content on a website is authored by a third party, the blogging platforms, forums, and ISPs cannot be held legally responsible for that content. There are some exceptions to this immunity from responsibility; it does not apply to "violations of child pornography, obscenity, criminal or intellectual property laws" (West Coast LEAF, 2014, p. 77). There have been calls to get rid of this section and thus for victims of severe cyberbullying (e.g., revenge porn or hate speech) to be able to hold websites responsible for the content they host. Those opposed to changing this law argue that it would "allow public figures to sue Wikipedia over misleading content or businesses to sue Yelp, in addition to individual reviewers, for libel based on negative reviews" (ibid.).

An extended example here will provide more detail and context to explore the possible role corporations might play in addressing the issue of cyberbullying. In an article in *The Atlantic* about the hunt for solutions to cyberbullying, Emily Bazelon (2013) tells the story of a worker from the Youth Services Bureau in Middletown, Connecticut, who was trying to deal with a gossip Facebook page created at a local high school. The worker determined that the content of the page was breaking Facebook's policy against bullying and

harassment and thus appealed to the corporation on two separate occasions to have it taken down, to no avail. Bazelon uses this story to explore the question of whether massive social networking sites such as Facebook might develop a more systematic approach to addressing cyberbullying online, rather than simply dealing with and responding to posts one by one. On her visit to the department that deals with Hate and Harassment at Facebook, she is assured that "Facebook does not style itself as the public square, where people can say anything they want, short of libel or slander. It's much more like a mall, where private security guards can throw you out" (p. 84). The head of the department also speaks to the challenge of regulating online behavior in a context as massive as Facebook. He notes that it is difficult to discern what kinds of behavior constitute worrisome forms of bullying, due to everything being so contextual, tone of voice being lost in online interactions, and Facebook's reluctance to infringe on people's freedom of speech.

While these are certainly challenges that corporations like Facebook face, equality rights groups, among others, argue that they are not insurmountable, provided that financial incentives and political pressures are brought to bear. "These are some of the most lucrative companies in the world," West Coast LEAF (Women's Legal Education and Action Fund) asserts. "They . . . attract some of the brightest and most creative minds to come and work with them. As the EU 'right to forget' [or 'right to be forgotten'] case shows, they can respond to orders to change their practices. The capacity is there; what's missing is the incentive or requirement to make change" (2014, p. 79).

How Best to Educate Young People about Cyberbullying

Perhaps the most pressing issue in the field right now in terms of addressing cyberbullying is how best to educate young people about it. Educators and parents are faced with the dilemma of needing young people to know that there are indeed dangers involved with using the Internet and participating in online communities, while also recognizing that online participation is an important aspect of young people's lives that is not about to go away. Further, they must recognize that cyberbullying is an issue that can affect youths' lives, while refraining from feeding into the moral panic that surrounds it. In a discussion about the use of bullying discourse, Moy (2008) raises the concern that it is most often dealt with in the realm of the private, failing to attend to structural inequalities at the source of much violence and oppression. Moy recognizes, however, that talk about bullying provides a place to begin conversations in schools and other educational settings with young people, teachers, administrators, and parents about underlying issues of discrimination. Moy's argument can be extended to the cyberbullying discourse. Jane (2014), for example, recognizes the power of the term *cyberbullying*, noting that alternative phrases like *online vitriol* or *misogyny* are rarely taken seriously in wider public discussion. While there is certainly a risk of feeding a moral panic about digital technology and obscuring the structural underpinnings of the violence by employing the term *cyberbullying,* it can also be used to mobilize people to have productive conversations about making the Internet a safer space for all people.

In discussing potential methods for addressing cyberbullying, Facer (2012) argues, "We need to recognise that any debate in this area will be inadequate if it is framed around an idea of the child only as innocent, vulnerable and biddable" (p. 410). Further, she asserts, "we need to begin to have richer conversations with young people themselves about what it means to participate in public space and the risks, the powers and consequences of such participation" (p. 410). Doing this requires adults to recognize young people as the experts of their own experience as well as to show a genuine interest in the way they perceive

and interpret their experiences online (for further discussion, see the Recommendations section).

GAPS IN THE EXTANT RESEARCH AND DIRECTIONS FOR FUTURE RESEARCH

A number of recent literature reviews on cyberbullying have called for more involvement of children and youth in research. For example, Slonje et al. (2013) conclude: "There is the potential to make more use of young people themselves, not only as participants in focus groups, but also by involving them as researchers themselves, in the design of the study, and gathering data" (p. 31). We agree with this recommendation but call specifically for more ethnographic research with young people about their life online, building on the work of sociologists like danah boyd (2008). What are the realities of life online for young people today? From their perspectives, what dilemmas do they face in participating in online spaces? What opportunities does their participation afford them (e.g., a means for self-expression, creativity, and connecting to other people)? What dangers, if any, do they perceive? What might be the gaps in their knowledge about how their participation could influence their lives in the future? How might they participate in nuanced discussion about how they can foster safer spaces online, while also recognizing pressures that their social circles place on them? Rather than assume that cyberbullying is a concern, this more open-ended, in-depth approach allows the concerns of young people to drive the conversation that might ensue from this research agenda.

As already noted, the preponderance of the research in this area has been done by educational psychologists doing quantitative work. Several recent literature reviews by leaders in the field have noted its under-theorization. Kowalski and colleagues (2014) concluded the literature "lacks theoretical focus" (p. 1073); Mehari et al. (2014)

found "no unified theoretical framework to move the field of cyberbullying forward" (p. 1), and Slonje et al. (2013) noted that the field "lacks an overall theoretical approach" (p. 31). A few studies have begun to emerge from the disciplines of law (e.g., Jaffe, 2013), cultural and media studies (e.g., Stack, in press), public health (e.g., Moreno et al., 2013), criminology (e.g., Navarro & Jasinski, 2013), and sociology (e.g., Facer, 2012)—a welcome addition, in that these studies have often been qualitative or conceptual and have pointed to structural factors and explanations, thus complementing the individual focus emphasized in the psychological research. We need more such studies, with an aim of theorizing a continuum of cyber violence. Feminist researchers have made a start on this, based on empirical studies of gendered violence in offline settings. They have noted what constitutes sexual harassment and argued that groping, unwanted sexualized comments, and epithets create a hostile climate, with sexual assault and rape further along the continuum of gender-based violence in terms of severity (Gådin, 2011, p. 58; Brown et al., 20007).

The feminist work theorizing gendered violence in offline settings needs to be brought into conversation with work being done on electronically-mediated violence. Examples of the latter include research on e-bile (Jane, 2014), cyber misogyny (West Coast LEAF, 2014), cyber gender harassment (Citron, 2009), cyberbullying between intimate partners in teen dating relationships (Alvarez, 2012) or cyber dating abuse (Zweig, Lachman, Yahner, & Dank, 2013). How do these proliferating constructs relate to each other, and with what implications for how we think about violence?

A related research direction is to bring together the mounting evidence of the hostile climate for women and other marginalized groups on the Internet, with those who dare to name their experiences as racism, sexism, and homophobia being singled out for relentless cyber attacks (e.g., Blackhorse, 2014; Citron, 2009, p. 380). The Pew Internet and American Life Project has documented a digital gender safety gap, where young women (aged 18-24), especially those belonging to racialized minority groups, "experience particularly severe forms of online harassment," such as stalking (Duggan et al., 2014, p. 15). In addition, "women were more likely than men to find their most recent experience with online harassment extremely or very upsetting—38% of harassed women said so of their most recent experience, compared with 17% of harassed men" (p. 7; see also Steeves, 2014a). This finding dovetails with survey and experimental studies showing that girls and young women are significantly more negatively affected and distressed by cyberbullying incidents, with bullying involving images the most emotionally distressing (Bauman & Newman, 2013; Pieschl et al., 2013).

We recommend longitudinal research to investigate the long-term effects on children of growing up at a time when online incivility and hostility are pervasive in contemporary culture. Indeed, there is evidence that young people see online harassment as a "relatively routine" part of their "online relationships and experiences" (Bryce & Fraser, 2013, p. 785). Almost half (46%) of students in one study agreed or strongly agreed that "Cyber-bullying is a normal part of the online world. There is nothing anyone can do to stop it" (Cassidy et al., 2009, p. 397). Are children becoming quickly inured to online harassment, and are certain groups more at risk due to this possible desensitization, because they learn over time to treat as normal attacks on their core identities?

Indeed, it is not uncommon for adults as well as peers to advise those experiencing online harassment to toughen up or to see incidents as harmless name-calling, teasing, or joking. This can add insult to injury, "because it delegitimizes the suffering experienced by the target in the first instance, while providing an additional insult in the accusation that the complainant lacks a sense of humour and/or is hypersensitive" (Jane, 2014, p. 539). A high proportion of online vitriol amounts to racism and misogyny (Citron, 2009; Jane, 2014; West Coast LEAF, 2014). For example, when feminists critique sexism in videogames, they endure serious and sustained online threats such as we saw in the GamerGate campaign. Indeed, experimental studies have shown that young men are more likely to sexually harass women online if their female chat partner is a feminist and their privileged status as male has been threatened (Siebler, Sabelus, & Bohner, 2008). All this raises long-term concerns about the silencing of women and minority groups in public discourse. At a time when public life is so highly mediated, does cyberbullying systematically discourage the full presence of certain people in online environments, and with what implications for participatory democracy?

We also recommend legal analysis and conceptual and evaluation studies of the proliferating anti-cyberbullying legislation and school- and district-based policies and responses. Shariff (2013) has raised questions about the necessity, value, and impact of emerging laws and notes, in the Canadian context, that financial or educational resources rarely seem to accompany requirements to develop safety plans. Perren et al. (2012) found, in their literature review, a relative paucity of "empirical evidence concerning the success of [anti-cyberbullying] responses" (p. 290).

Do these new laws and policies "allocate more resources to surveillance and control than to facilitation of healthy relationships or conflict/peace learning" (Bickmore, 2011, p. 648)? Are structures of support, such as mental health care, provided (Stack, in press)? Are the policies put into place to combat cyberbullying being enforced unevenly, having a disproportionate impact on racialized minority and low-income students? Are mandated guidelines necessarily being put into practice, or strategically ignored, and if so, with what effects? For example, Smith et al. (2012) did a content analysis of school anti-bullying policies in England and followed up. Even when schools were required by national law to specify certain kinds of bullying (e.g., homophobic, racist, sexist, based on disability or faith) so that they would be more likely to be addressed, many school policies did not cover cyberbullying or "prejudice or identity-based bullying," although mention of these had increased over time (p. 67).

RECOMMENDATIONS AND IMPLICATIONS

The issues encompassed by Internet safety are complicated, all the more so because, as we have argued, cyberbullying and related forms of interpersonal violence need, ultimately, to be understood in relation to unjust social structures and institutional contexts as roots of bullying. As a way of focusing, in what follows we will explore what digital citizenship might mean, drawing from a critical media education approach that distinguishes between *protectionism* (youth as future citizen) and *preparation* (youth as apprentice or de facto citizen) (Kelly, 2014). The protectionist perspective on social networking, for example, emphasizes risks and the role of adults in helping youth to manage those risks. Understandably, parents and teachers want to protect children and youth from potentially harmful representations and cyberbullying, to shield them from being asked to think in narrow, consumerist ways that make them feel bad about themselves, because they do not measure up to some impossible ideal. Neglected in this protectionist approach, however, is a concern to prepare young people for understanding and engaging in the media culture, which offers increasing opportunities for creativity and participation as media producers, not just as consumers. Here, we argue "that we can pursue the aims of both protection (understood as achieved through critical dialogues with youth about their positive and negative experiences . . .) and preparation, simultaneously" (Kelly, 2010, p. 278). We emphasize the importance of listening to young people and encouraging their participation in society, as we outline some recommendations in the interconnected domains of education, social practice and policy, and civic engagement.

Education

Although, as discussed above, more research is needed on what prevention and intervention responses are most effective, we want to suggest some important guidelines. While the language of *cyberbullying* might draw a broader audience initially, it is less likely to focus on systemic inequities or call to mind existing legal remedies (McCaskell, 2012). It is important educationally, therefore, to link an anti-bullying curriculum to existing human rights codes and what Citron (2009) calls "a cyber civil rights agenda." Focusing on anti-discrimination and strengthening equity initiatives provides the bridge between various types of cyberbullying and forms of oppression, a bridge currently lacking in many jurisdictions.

Take the case of "cyber misogyny" and on-line sexual harassment that is directed primarily, but not exclusively, at girls and women (Citron, 2009; Duggan et al., 2014; Jane, 2014; Kelly et al., 2006; Mantilla, 2013; Stack, in press; West Coast LEAF, 2014). Compared to bullying, sexual harassment is rarely discussed as happening among youth (Brown et al., 2007; Gådin, 2011). Surveys done with young people on traditional bullying and cyberbullying rarely include items that measure the three main forms that comprise sexual harassment (gender harassment, sexual coercion, and unwanted sexual attention), which are comparatively well researched among adult populations offline (Barak, 2005). An exception is the study by Ybarra and colleagues (2012) that allowed for comparisons of bullying and unwanted sexual experiences online and offline among a US national sample of youth. They concluded that sexual harassment was a concern online and offline: rates of "unwanted sexual experiences in the past year" were the same at school as on-line, both 18% (p. 211). Feminist scholars have

argued that naming such specific harms—rather than assuming they are covered under the term *bullying*—lends legitimacy to the experiences of those who are targeted, "validating their suffering by acknowledging the damage to their autonomy, livelihood, identity, dignity, and well-being" (Citron, 2009, p. 411).

Schools might communicate this in a variety of ways. In Vancouver, BC, for example, public schools have students and their parents or guardians sign an *Internet Safety Agreement*, outlining responsibilities and privileges, including that "Student users have the right to access information that is free from hate propaganda, sexist, homophobic, racist, pornographic or obscene content" (unpublished, 2014). Schools will need to take gender, age, and cultural differences into account when planning interventions against sexist bullying (which often operates alongside racist and homophobic bullying) as well as prevention programs (Gådin, 2011; Steeves, 2014b, pp. 5-6; cf. Shapka & Law, 2013, p. 735). For this, teachers would need resources and professional development to understand and educate about how bullying often draws from, and operates in tandem with, institutionalized forms of discrimination based on gender, race, sexuality, and disability, and how these markers of power and status, in turn, are embedded in the social relations of school and schooling.

Given, for example, that older teens are more likely to agree that while sexist and racist content online is "wrong," it is "not their place to say anything" (Steeves, 2014b, p. 8), educators need to approach interventions creatively, using participatory methods. Play-building, ethno-drama, and other theatre strategies have been used successfully to prompt various audiences of high school students and educators to engage with anti-discrimination education (Gallagher, 2004; Goldstein, 2010; Perkins, 2012). Gallagher explains that drama allows participants to explore conflict in messy, unpredictable, but, ultimately, productive ways. "Rather than repressing or pathologizing one's often-healthy desire to differentiate oneself from others, drama can work towards exploration of the diverse positions and investments in the room, the conflicts between the frames of reference students bring to their work and their relationship to larger systems of oppression and social exclusion" (2004, p. 28).

Another creative, participatory educational strategy is peer involvement. Peer-led approaches, particularly those implemented in collaboration with supportive teachers, have shown promise in reducing cyberbullying (Menesini, Nocentini, & Palladino, 2012; Slonje et al., 2013, p. 31). In one study, trained peer educators in high school (average age 16) took initiative to involve whole classes, working to produce, for example, an online forum, a peer-to-peer counseling space, "a short movie on cyberbullying, a guide for safer use of e-mail and social networks, and a poster against cyberbullying" (Menesini et al., 2012, p. 317). Such media production projects can promote a sense of agency and citizenship in youth (Kelly, 2010, p. 296). In addition, this type of peer involvement can counter feelings of student powerlessness, because it de-centers the teacher as sole authority as well as generates "newfound respect for their peers as co-teachers (people with knowledge) as well as co-learners (people willing to listen to their ideas)" (Kelly, 2012, pp. 148-149).

A related, peer-facilitation approach is taken in the TrendShift workshop, developed by West Coast LEAF based on focus group interviews with youth conducted at local schools and with youth-serving organizations (http://www.westcoastleaf.org/our-workshop/trendshift/). Intended for high school students, TrendShift aims to foster dialogue about what it means to be a young person online today, to unpack the term *cyberbullying* by discussing the structural conditions that promote such forms of interpersonal aggression, and to inform young people of their legal rights and responsibilities online. The workshop uses a peer-facilitation model, delivered by trained facilitators aged 18 to 24. It

seeks to create a safe space where young people can relate to the facilitators and expect to discuss issues in a realistic way, without having their concerns dismissed as juvenile or feeling that they are being overly protected by adults. TrendShift thus responds to young people's feeling that they are told at every turn not to "cyberbully" without adults grasping or respecting the way they make use of online social networks (see boyd, 2008; boyd & Marwick, 2011). Indeed, ethnographers have found that high school students associate the term *bullying* with middle school and immaturity and feel diminished and stigmatized by being defined as a bully or victim (Marwick & boyd, 2011).

Social Practice and Policy

Alongside the curricular opportunities to recognize children and youth as potential change agents within, across, and beyond classrooms, we recommend a youth-as-apprentice citizenship approach to creating and implementing Internet safety policies. This means creating opportunities for children and youth to do democracy within and beyond the school, recognizing them as, in the here and now, knowing subjects and political actors. Here, we take some inspiration from John Oliver Secondary School in Vancouver, BC, where public inner-city high school students co-created with teachers, over the course of a school year, their own Digital Code of Conduct, after disturbing racial remarks were posted on Twitter (Rossi, 2013, 2014). John Oliver hosted school-wide assemblies and smaller student discussion groups to discuss the problem of online incivility and what kindness online might look like. "All 1,100 students at the school wrote 10 statements about how they would act online. Each classroom submitted its top 10 statements, and student leaders and teachers synthesized the final statements for the code" (Rossi, 2014, para. 9). When students are involved in the creation of school-wide policy, they are more likely to support it (Kelly, 2014). As a student leader at John Oliver told a reporter,

"When the students created the code of conduct, the students said 'I choose to be a better citizen online,' 'I choose to not bully people online' and I think it's much more powerful when students choose to do it because it's a voluntary thing, and they're not being forced to participate in this" (Singh-Joseph, 2014, para. 11).

Of course, letting students take the lead on setting community standards needs to be done in collaboration with school adults. For example, at John Oliver administrators will decide, on a case-by-case basis, on the consequences for inappropriate use of social media (Rossi, 2013). Ideally, administrators will use disciplinary measures in line with the positive school culture, such that they are widely considered fair and in proportion to any harm done (Citron, 2009, p. 414). School, district, and state and provincial administrators also need to take the lead in rethinking organizational arrangements that might, however unintentionally, contribute to cyberbullying based on invidious distinctions based on gender, race, sexuality, and ability (e.g., cruel statements about those placed in special education). For example, sexual harassment is exacerbated by structural problems and institutional practices, but these are not within the control of young people to change (Gådin, 2011, p. 65).

Another policy area is the regulation of online safety through technology. Again, our recommendations are informed by thinking through the implications for digital citizenship and how various proposals embed particular views about young people and their ability to navigate and participate in online spaces. We draw on van den Berg's (2014) discussion of the range of technical tools proposed to increase children's Internet safety. She makes a useful distinction between "technological influencing" (p. 68) that relies on techno-regulation (more stringent) from that which aims to persuade (less stringent).

By *techno-regulation* van den Berg means "the process of hard-coding normative or legal codes into technologies to make certain behav-

iours impossible and prompt others," leaving no room for users to maneuver (p. 72). The unstated assumption in this approach is that children and youth need protection, because they are incapable of navigating the tortuous world of the Internet on their own and thus need to be sheltered from its content or stopped altogether from participating in it in harmful ways. Examples of techno-regulation include: (a) the development of Internet browsers, computers, and tablets designed specifically for young people that operate in a separate online world without the capability to interact with the wider web (e.g., KidZui, p. 77); (b) the use of parental monitoring controls (p. 75); and (c) the use of programming to disallow young people from posting content identified as cyberbullying. In the latter case, a company like Facebook could conceivably use automated monitoring techniques to remove or block postings deemed to be cyberbullying or online harassment (Van Royen, Poels, Daelemans, & Vandebosch, 2015).

Conceiving youth as apprentice citizens, who learn democratic participation by practicing it, would necessitate a different form of online regulation, an approach van den Berg (2014) calls *persuading* and *nudging*. Technical means might prompt young people to pause to consider certain choices and courses of action flagged as risky when they "color outside the lines," to use van den Berg's metaphor. A social networking site might remind "users of the size and makeup of the audience that will view a message once it is posted"; this "gently nudges these users in the direction of greater safety, of improved privacy protection and more privacy awareness" (van den Berg, 2014, p. 71).

Another example, discussed in Bazelon (2013), is the use of algorithms to lightly guide users toward actions online deemed to enhance their safety and wellbeing; Henry Lieberman, a computer scientist at MIT, is exploring the possibility of providing users with prompts when they are about to post something that an interface identifies as cyberbullying or abuse. Rather than simply blocking the activity, the technology would flag to the user that it thinks the behavior may be a form of cyberbullying and delay the posting for a minute or two. In this time, the user could decide whether or not to continue with the post or to revoke it. Lieberman calls this "ladders of reflection," borrowing the term from philosopher Donald Schön (Bazelon, 2013, p. 87).

These persuasive technologies allow social media users to remain the decision maker, while helping them learn to manage statements that are made on a whim yet may result in more harm than intended. Forms of regulation that allow users to remain in control of their experience respect the ability of young people to make their own decisions. Social network users are more likely to see persuasive tools as fairer than techno-regulation, because network providers have given adequate explanations for decisions or procedures; van Laer (2013) calls this "informational justice." That is, forms of intervention that ask the social media user (regardless of age) to reflect on what they are doing, but still allow them to make their own decisions about how to proceed, are generally met with less resistance than interventions that leave the user with no alternatives. We agree with van den Berg (2014) that persuasive technical tools are preferable to techno-regulation—in tandem with inter-generational conversations—because they enhance young people's reflective capacities so necessary to democratic citizenship. In her words, "(older) children and teenagers would have more freedom to experiment and discover and in the process to become more competent, risk-aware and resilient while protective measures for their security would still be in place" (p. 83).

Civic Engagement

The recommendations we have made so far are in line with encouraging youth civic engagement, whether in local or global arenas. They involve treating children and youth as collaborators and knowers in classrooms, schools, and in online spaces, enabling them to apprentice as democratic citizens. If adults are to lay the proper groundwork for youth civic engagement, we need to ensure that the conversations and debates that unfold are not contrived or limited only to those students who already have high status within the school, such as athletes or members of the honor society (Kelly, 2014). We know, for example that the increased use of zero-tolerance discipline policies has led to a disproportionate number of racialized-minority, low-income youth being pushed out of school, often due to minor infractions (Casella, 2003; Cassidy & Jackson, 2005; Losen, 2011; Templeton & Dohrn, 2010). All young people deserve to be able to contribute to, question, and challenge the fairness of such policies.

To sum up, public concern continues to mount about cyberbullying, as evidenced by news stories and public policy responses at the local, state/provincial, and national levels. This underscores the importance of wider dissemination of carefully done research, because this might promote the need for, and inform, a wider continuum of more nuanced policy responses. We need good professional judgment to be exercised in defining and dealing with cyberbullying, rather than sweeping zero-tolerance policies that have been shown to be applied in disproportionately harsh ways towards marginalized children and youth.

REFERENCES

Almeida, A. N. d., Delicado, A., de Almeida Alves, N., & Carvalo, T. (2014). Internet, children and space: Revisiting generational attributes and boundaries. *New Media & Society*, 1–18. doi:10.1177/1461444814528293

Alvarez, A. R. G. (2012). "IH8U": Confronting cyberbullying and exploring the use of cybertools in teen dating relationships. *Journal of Clinical Psychology*, *68*(11), 1205–1215. doi:10.1002/jclp.21920 PMID:22961672

Bailey, J., & Hanna, M. (2011). The gendered dimensions of sexting: Assessing the applicability of Canada's child pornography provisions. *Canadian Journal of Women and the Law*, *23*(2), 405–441. doi:10.3138/cjwl.23.2.405

Bannink, R., Broeren, S., van de Looij-Jansen, P. M., de Waart, F. G., & Raat, H. (2014). Cyber and traditional bullying victimization as a risk factor for mental health problems and suicidal ideation in adolescents. *PLoS ONE*, *9*(4), e94026. doi:10.1371/journal.pone.0094026 PMID:24718563

Barak, A. (2005). Sexual harassment on the internet. *Social Science Computer Review*, *23*(1), 77–92. doi:10.1177/0894439304271540

Barlett, C. P., Gentile, D. A., & Chew, C. (2014). Predicting cyberbullying from anonymity. *Psychology of Popular Media Culture*. doi:10.1037/ppm0000055

Bauman, S., & Newman, M. L. (2013). Testing assumptions about cyberbullying: Perceived distress associated with acts of conventional and cyber bullying. *Psychology of Violence*, *3*(1), 27–38. doi:10.1037/a0029867

Bauman, S., Toomey, R. B., & Walker, J. L. (2013). Associations among bullying, cyberbullying, and suicide in high school students. *Journal of Adolescence*, *36*(2), 341–350. doi:10.1016/j.adolescence.2012.12.001 PMID:23332116

Bazelon, E. (2013, March). How to stop the bullies. *Atlantic (Boston, Mass.)*, 82–90.

Berne, S., Frisén, A., Schultze-Krumbholz, A., Scheithauer, H., Naruskov, K., Luik, P., & Zukauskiene, R. et al. (2013). Cyberbullying assessment instruments: A systematic review. *Aggression and Violent Behavior*, *18*(2), 320–334. doi:10.1016/j.avb.2012.11.022

Bickmore, K. (2011). Policies and programming for safer schools: Are "antibullying" approaches impeding education for peacebuilding? *Educational Policy*, *25*(4), 648–687. doi:10.1177/0895904810374849

Blackhorse, A. (2014, December 22). My hostile, aggressive, racist, sexist hate mail. *The Tyee*. Retrieved from http://thetyee.ca/Opinion/2014/12/22/Native-American-Sports-Mascots/?utm_source=daily&utm_medium=email&utm_campaign=221214

Bonanno, R. A., & Hymel, S. (2013). Cyber bullying and internalizing difficulties: Above and beyond the impact of traditional forms of bullying. *Journal of Youth and Adolescence*, *42*(5), 685–697. doi:10.1007/s10964-013-9937-1 PMID:23512485

boyd, d., & Marwick, A. E. (2011). *Social privacy in networked publics: Teens' attitudes, practices, and strategies*. Paper presented at the A decade in internet time: Symposium on the dynamics of the internet and society, Oxford, UK. http://papers.ssrn.com/sol3/papers.cfm?abstract_id=1925128

boyd, d. (2008). Why youth ♥ social network sites: The role of networked publics in teenage social life. In D. Buckingham (Ed.), *Youth, identity, and digital media* (pp. 119-142). Cambridge, MA: MIT Press.

Brown, L. M., Chesney-Lind, M., & Stein, N. (2007). Patriarchy matters: Toward a gendered theory of teen violence and victimization. *Violence Against Women*, *13*(12), 1249–1273. doi:10.1177/1077801207310430 PMID:18046042

Bryce, J., & Fraser, J. (2013). "It's common sense that it's wrong": Young people's perceptions and experiences of cyberbullying. *Cyberpsychology, Behavior, and Social Networking, 16*(11), 783–787. doi:10.1089/cyber.2012.0275 PMID:23745618

Casella, R. (2003). Zero tolerance policy in schools: Rationale, consequences, and alternatives. *Teachers College Record, 105*(5), 872–892. doi:10.1111/1467-9620.00271

Cassidy, W., Faucher, C., & Jackson, M. (2013). Cyberbullying among youth: A comprehensive review of current international research and its implications and application to policy and practice. *School Psychology International, 34*(6), 575–612. doi:10.1177/0143034313479697

Cassidy, W., & Jackson, M. (2005). The need for equality in education: An intersectionality examination of labeling and zero tolerance practices. *McGill Journal of Education, 40*(3), 445–466.

Cassidy, W., Jackson, M., & Brown, K. N. (2009). Sticks and stones can break my bones, but how can pixels hurt me?: Students' experiences with cyber-bullying. *School Psychology International, 30*(4), 383–402. doi:10.1177/0143034309106948

Citron, D. K. (2009). Law's expressive value in combating cyber gender harassment. *Michigan Law Review, 108*(3), 373–415.

Cohen, S. (2002). *Folk devils and moral panics: The creation of the mods and rockers* (3rd ed.). London: Routledge. (Original work published 1972)

Compton, L., Campbell, M., & Mergler, A. (2014). Teacher, parent and student perceptions of the motives of cyberbullies. *Social Psychology of Education, 17*(3), 383–400. doi:10.1007/s11218-014-9254-x

Department of Justice Canada. (2014). *Government of Canada highlights royal assent of bill to help law enforcement protect victims of online crime.* Retrieved from Government of Canada website: http://news.gc.ca/web/article-en.do?nid=913359&_ga=1.66908974.1410492497.1419632791

Dredge, R., Gleeson, J., & de la Piedad Garcia, X. (2014). Cyberbullying in social networking sites: An adolescent victim's perspective. *Computers in Human Behavior, 36*, 13–20. doi:10.1016/j.chb.2014.03.026

Driver, S. (2007). *Queer girls and popular culture: Reading, resisting, and creating media.* New York: Peter Lang.

Duggan, M., Rainie, L., Smith, A., Funk, C., Lenhart, A., & Madden, M. (2014). *Online harassment* (p. 63). Pew Research Center.

Edelman, M. (1988). *Constructing the political spectacle.* Chicago: University of Chicago Press.

Facer, K. (2012). After the moral panic? Reframing the debate about child safety online. *Discourse (Berkeley, Calif.), 33*(3), 397–413. doi:10.1080/01596306.2012.681899

Festl, R., & Quandt, T. (2013). Social relations and cyberbullying: The influence of individual and structural attributes on victimization and perpetration via the Internet. *Human Communication Research, 39*(1), 101–126. doi:10.1111/j.1468-2958.2012.01442.x

Finkelhor, D. (2014). Commentary: Cause for alarm? Youth and internet risk research—A commentary on Livingstone and Smith (2014). *Journal of Child Psychology and Psychiatry, and Allied Disciplines, 55*(6), 655–658. doi:10.1111/jcpp.12260 PMID:24840173

Gådin, K. G. (2011). Peer sexual harassment in schools: Normalization of gender practices in a neoliberal time. In S. Fahlgren, A. Johansson, & D. Mulinari (Eds.), *Normalization and "outsider-hood": Feminist readings of a neoliberal welfare state* (pp. 58–67). Bentham Science Publishers. doi:10.2174/97816080527901110101010058

Gallagher, K. (2004). Bullying and its compatriots: Racism, sexism, and homophobia. *Orbit (Amsterdam, Netherlands)*, *34*, 28–31.

Geist, M. (2014). Telecoms offer to build surveillance tools into networks. *The Tyee*. Retrieved from http://thetyee.ca/Mediacheck/2014/12/17/Surveillance-Tools-in-Networks/

Goldstein, T. (2010). Snakes and ladders: A performed ethnography. *International Journal of Critical Pedagogy*, *3*(1), 68–113.

Hinduja, S., & Patchin, J. (2014). State cyberbullying laws: A brief review of state cyberbullying laws and policies (pp. 1–19)., Retrieved from http://cyberbullying.us/Bullying_and_Cyberbullying_Laws.pdf

Hinduja, S., & Patchin, J. W. (2012). Cyberbullying: Neither an epidemic nor a rarity. *European Journal of Developmental Psychology*, *9*(5), 539–543. doi:10.1080/17405629.2012.706448

Jaffe, E. M. (2013). Imposing a duty in an online world: Holding the web host liable for cyberbullying. *Hastings Communications & Entertainment Law Journal*, *35*(2), 277–302.

Jane, E. A. (2014). "Your a ugly, whorish, slut": Understanding e-bile. *Feminist Media Studies*, *14*(4), 531–546. doi:10.1080/14680777.2012.741073

Juvonen, J., & Graham, S. (2014). Bullying in schools: The power of bullies and the plight of victims. *Annual Review of Psychology*, *65*(1), 159–185. doi:10.1146/annurev-psych-010213-115030 PMID:23937767

Kates, A. (2013). Web users should have the right to remain anonymous in cyberspace. *Engineering & Technology*, *8*(9), 32–32. doi:10.1049/et.2013.0927

Keipi, T., & Oksanen, A. (2014). Self-exploration, anonymity and risks in the online setting: Analysis of narratives by 14–18-year olds. *Journal of Youth Studies*, *17*(8), 1097–1113. doi:10.1080/13676261.2014.881988

Kelly, D. M. (2010). Media representation and the case for critical media education. In M. C. Courtland & T. Gambell (Eds.), *Literature, media, and multiliteracies in adolescent language arts* (pp. 277–303). Vancouver: Pacific Education Press.

Kelly, D. M. (2012). Teaching for social justice: Translating an anti-oppression approach into practice. *Our Schools/Our Selves, 21*(2), 135-154.

Kelly, D. M. (2014). Alternative learning contexts and the goals of democracy in education. In J. A. Vadeboncoeur (Ed.), Learning in and across contexts: Reimagining education. New York: Teachers College Press.

Kelly, D. M., & Brooks, M. (2009). How young is too young? Exploring beginning teachers' assumptions about young children and teaching for social justice. *Equity & Excellence in Education*, *42*(2), 202–216. doi:10.1080/10665680902739683

Kelly, D. M., Pomerantz, S., & Currie, D. H. (2006). "No boundaries"? Girls' interactive, online learning about femininities. *Youth & Society*, *38*(1), 3–28. doi:10.1177/0044118X05283482

Kowalski, R. M., Schroeder, A. N., Giumetti, G. W., & Lattanner, M. R. (2014). Bullying in the digital age: A critical review and meta-analysis of cyberbullying research among youth. *Psychological Bulletin*, *140*(4), 1073–1137. doi:10.1037/a0035618 PMID:24512111

Langos, C. (2012). Cyberbullying: The challenge to define. *Cyberpsychology, Behavior, and Social Networking, 15*(6), 285–289. doi:10.1089/cyber.2011.0588 PMID:22703033

Lenhart, A., Madden, M., Smith, A., Purcell, K., Zickuhr, K., & Rainie, L. (2011). *Teens, kindness and cruelty on social network sites: How American teens navigate the new world of "digital citizenship"*. Washington, DC: Pew Research Center.

Livingstone, S., Kirwil, L., Ponte, C., & Staksrud, E. (2014). In their own words: What bothers children online? *European Journal of Communication, 29*(3), 271–288. doi:10.1177/0267323114521045

Livingstone, S., & Smith, P. K. (2014). Annual research review: Harms experienced by child users of online and mobile technologies: The nature, prevalence and management of sexual and aggressive risks in the digital age. *Journal of Child Psychology and Psychiatry, and Allied Disciplines, 55*(6), 635–654. doi:10.1111/jcpp.12197 PMID:24438579

Livingstone, S. M., Haddon, L., & Görzig, A. (Eds.). (2012). *Children, risk and safety on the internet: Research and policy challenges in comparative perspective*. Chicago, IL: Policy Press. doi:10.1332/policypress/9781847428837.001.0001

Losen, D. J. (2011). *Discipline policies, successful schools, and racial justice*. Boulder, CO: National Education Policy Center.

Madden, M., Lenhart, A., Cortesi, S., Gasser, U., Duggan, M., Smith, A., & Beaton, M. (2013). *Teens, social media, and privacy*. Washington, DC: Pew Research Center.

Madden, M., Lenhart, A., Duggan, M., Cortesi, S., & Gasser, U. (2013). *Teens and technology 2013*. Washington, DC: Pew Research Center.

Mantilla, K. (2013). Gendertrolling: Misogyny adapts to new media. *Feminist Studies, 39*(2), 563–570.

McCaskell, T. (2012). The politics of *common cause*: Using "values framing" to understand the battle over bullying in our schools. *Our Schools/Our Selves, 21*(4), 45-78.

Mehari, K. R., Farrell, A. D., & Le, A.-T. H. (2014). Cyberbullying among adolescents: Measures in search of a construct. *Psychology of Violence*. doi: 10.1037/a0037521.supp

Menesini, E. (2012). Cyberbullying: The right value of the phenomenon. Comments on the paper "Cyberbullying: An overrated phenomenon?". *European Journal of Developmental Psychology, 9*(5), 544–552. doi:10.1080/17405629.2012.706449

Menesini, E., Nocentini, A., & Palladino, B. E. (2012). Empowering students against bullying and cyberbullying: Evaluation of an Italian peer-led model. *International Journal of Conflict and Violence, 6*(2), 314–320.

Menesini, E., Nocentini, A., Palladino, B. E., Frisén, A., Berne, S., Ortega-Ruiz, R., & Smith, P. K. et al. (2012). Cyberbullying definition among adolescents: A comparison across six European countries. *Cyberpsychology, Behavior, and Social Networking, 15*(9), 455–462. doi:10.1089/cyber.2012.0040 PMID:22817693

Moreno, M. A., Egan, K. G., Bare, K., Young, H. N., & Cox, E. D. (2013). Internet safety education for youth: Stakeholder perspectives. *BMC Public Health, 13*(1), 1–6. doi:10.1186/1471-2458-13-543 PMID:23738647

Moy, L. C. (2008). Disrupting "bully" talk: Progressive practices and transformative spaces for anti-violence work in schools (doctoral dissertation). Vancouver: University of British Columbia; Retrieved from http://hdl.handle.net/2429/5739

National Conference of State Legislatures. (2014). *Cyberbullying enacted legislation: 2006-2010*. Washington, DC: Retrieved from http://www.ncsl.org/research/education/cyberbullying.aspx

Navarro, J. N., & Jasinski, J. L. (2013). Why girls? Using routine activities theory to predict cyberbullying experiences between girls and boys. *Women & Criminal Justice, 23*(4), 286–303. doi:10.1080/08974454.2013.784225

Nicol, J., & Valiquet, D. (2013). *Legislative summary of Bill C-13: An Act to amend the Criminal Code, the Canada Evidence Act, the Competition Act and the Mutual Legal Assistance in Criminal Matters Act.* Retrieved from Library of Parliament website: http://www.parl.gc.ca/Content/LOP/LegislativeSummaries/41/2/c13-e.pdf

Nocentini, A., Calmaestra, J., Schultze-Krumbholz, A., Scheithauer, H., Ortega, R., & Menesini, E. (2010). Cyberbullying: Labels, behaviours and definition in three European countries. *Australian Journal of Guidance & Counselling, 20*(2), 129–142. doi:10.1375/ajgc.20.2.129

Olweus, D. (1993). *Bullying at school: What we know and what we can do.* Oxford: Blackwell Publishers.

Olweus, D. (2012a). Cyberbullying: An overrated phenomenon? *European Journal of Developmental Psychology, 9*(5), 520–538. doi:10.1080/17405629.2012.682358

Olweus, D. (2012b). Comments on cyberbullying article: A rejoinder. *European Journal of Developmental Psychology, 9*(5), 559–568. doi:10.1080/17405629.2012.705086

Patchin, J., & Hinduja, S. (2014). *Cyberbullying facts.* Retrieved from http://cyberbullying.us/facts/

Patriquin, M. (2014, November 7). Don't overreact, Canada. *New York Times.* Retrieved from http://www.nytimes.com/2014/11/08/opinion/dont-overreact-canada.html?emc=eta1&_r=0

Payton, L. (2014, November 20). Cyberbullying bill raises alarm for privacy commissioner. *CBC News.* Retrieved from http://www.cbc.ca/news/politics/cyberbullying-bill-raises-alarm-for-privacy-commissioner-1.2842034

Perkins, C. (2013). How school principals understand and respond to homophobia: A study of one B.C. public school district using ethnodrama (doctoral dissertation). Vancouver, Canada: University of British Columbia; Retrieved from http://hdl.handle.net/2429/43383

Perren, S., Corcoran, L., Cowie, H., Dehue, F., Garcia, D. J., McGuckin, C., & Völlink, T. et al. (2012). Tackling cyberbullying: Review of empirical evidence regarding successful responses by students, parents, and schools. *International Journal of Conflict and Violence, 6*(2), 283–292.

Pieschl, S., Porsch, T., Kahl, T., & Klockenbusch, R. (2013). Relevant dimensions of cyberbullying—Results from two experimental studies. *Journal of Applied Developmental Psychology, 34*(5), 241–252. doi:10.1016/j.appdev.2013.04.002

Price, D., Green, D., Spears, B., Scrimgeour, M., Barnes, A., Geer, R., & Johnson, B. (2014). A qualitative exploration of cyber-bystanders and moral engagement. *Australian Journal of Guidance & Counselling, 24*(1), 1–17. doi:10.1017/jgc.2013.18

Rossi, C. (2013, September 18). High school gets social media 101 course: Disturbing Twitter trend prompted lesson. *Vancouver Sun.* Retrieved from http://www.vancouversun.com/technology/High+school+gets+social+media+course/8925397/story.html

Rossi, C. (2014, February 27). School creates digital code. *Vancouver Courier.* Retrieved from http://www.vancourier.com/news/school-creates-digital-code-1.869932

Rowling, J. K. (2012). *The casual vacancy*. New York: Little, Brown and Company.

Runions, K. C. (2013). Toward a conceptual model of motive and self-control in cyber-aggression: Rage, revenge, reward, and recreation. *Journal of Youth and Adolescence, 42*(5), 751–771. doi:10.1007/s10964-013-9936-2 PMID:23526207

Sabella, R. A., Patchin, J. W., & Hinduja, S. (2013). Cyberbullying myths and realities. *Computers in Human Behavior, 29*(6), 2703–2711. doi:10.1016/j.chb.2013.06.040

Schultze-Krumbholz, A., Hoher, J., Fiebig, J., & Scheithauer, H. (2014). How do adolescents in Germany define cyberbullying? A focus-group study of adolescents from a German major city. *Praxis der Kinderpsychologie und Kinderpsychiatrie, 63*(5), 361–378. PMID:24877777

Shapka, J. D., & Law, D. M. (2013). Does one size fit all? Ethnic differences in parenting behaviors and motivations for adolescent engagement in cyberbullying. *Journal of Youth and Adolescence, 42*(5), 723–738. doi:10.1007/s10964-013-9928-2 PMID:23479327

Shariff, S. (2013). Review of *Cyberbullying prevention and response: Expert perspectives. New Media & Society, 15*(1), 154–156. doi:10.1177/1461444812459453c

Siebler, F., Sabelus, S., & Bohner, G. (2008). A refined computer harassment paradigm: Validation, and test of hypotheses about target characteristics. *Psychology of Women Quarterly, 32*(1), 22–35. doi:10.1111/j.1471-6402.2007.00404.x

Singh-Joseph, R. (2014). Technology: The good, the bad & the ugly. *Darpan: Reflecting South Asian Lifestyle*. Retrieved from http://www.darpanmagazine.com/lifestyle/tech/technology-the-good-the-bad-the-ugly/

Sinyor, M., Schaffer, A., & Cheung, A. H. (2014). An observational study of bullying as a contributing factor in youth suicide in Toronto. *Canadian Journal of Psychiatry, 59*(12), 632–638. PMID:25702362

Slane, A. (2013). Sexting and the law in Canada. *The Canadian Journal of Human Sexuality, 22*(3), 117–122. doi:10.3138/cjhs.22.3.C01

Slonje, R., Smith, P. K., & Frisén, A. (2013). The nature of cyberbullying, and strategies for prevention. *Computers in Human Behavior, 29*(1), 26–32. doi:10.1016/j.chb.2012.05.024

Smith, P. K. (2012). Cyberbullying: Challenges and opportunities for a research program—A response to Olweus (2012). *European Journal of Developmental Psychology, 9*(5), 553–558. doi:10.1080/17405629.2012.689821

Smith, P. K., Mahdavi, J., Carvalho, M., Fisher, S., Russell, S., & Tippett, N. (2008). Cyberbullying: Its nature and impact in secondary school pupils. *Journal of Child Psychology and Psychiatry, and Allied Disciplines, 49*(4), 376–385. doi:10.1111/j.1469-7610.2007.01846.x PMID:18363945

Soni, J. (2013). The reason HuffPost is ending anonymous accounts. *The Huffington Post*. Retrieved from http://www.huffingtonpost.com/jimmy-soni/why-is-huffpost-ending-an_b_3817979.html

Stack, M. (2012, February 26). Who are the real bullies? *The Mark*. http://pioneers.themarknews.com/articles/8209-who-are-the-real-bullies/#.VF0IxPnF98E

Stack, M. (2015 in press). "Vomitorium of venom": Framing culpable youth, bewildered adults and the death of Amanda Todd. In D. S. Coombs & S. Collister (Eds.), *Debates for the digital age: The good, the bad, and the ugly of our online world* (Vol. 2). Santa Barbara, CA: Praeger.

Steeves, V. (2014a). *Young Canadians in a wired world, phase III: Cyberbullying: Dealing with online meanness, cruelty and threats.* Ottawa, Canada: MediaSmarts.

Steeves, V. (2014b). *Young Canadians in a wired world, phase III: Encountering racist and sexist content online.* Ottawa, Canada: MediaSmarts.

Steeves, V. (2014c). *Young Canadians in a wired world, phase III: Life online.* Ottawa, Canada: MediaSmarts.

Sticca, F., & Perren, S. (2013). Is cyberbullying worse than traditional bullying? Examining the differential roles of medium, publicity, and anonymity for the perceived severity of bullying. *Journal of Youth and Adolescence, 42*(5), 739–750. doi:10.1007/s10964-012-9867-3 PMID:23184483

Surbramaniam, V., & Whalen, J. (2014, December 4). Dutch man suspected of tormenting Amanda Todd had 75 other victims, Facebook report says. *CBC.* Retrieved from http://www.cbc.ca/news/canada/dutch-man-suspected-of-tormenting-amanda-todd-had-75-other-victims-facebook-report-says-1.2857281

Talwar, V., Gomez-Garibello, C., & Shariff, S. (2014). Adolescents' moral evaluations and ratings of cyberbullying: The effect of veracity and intentionality behind the event. *Computers in Human Behavior, 36,* 122–128. doi:10.1016/j.chb.2014.03.046

Templeton, R., & Dohrn, B. (2010). Activist interventions: Community organizing against "zero tolerance" policies. In J. A. Sandlin, B. D. Schultz, & J. Burdick (Eds.), *Handbook of public pedagogy: Education and learning beyond schooling* (pp. 420–433). New York: Routledge.

Thomas, H. J., Connor, J. P., & Scott, J. G. (2014). Integrating traditional bullying and cyberbullying: Challenges of definition and measurement in adolescents – A review. *Educational Psychology Review,* 1–18.

Tokunaga, R. S. (2010). Following you home from school: A critical review and synthesis of research on cyberbullying victimization. *Computers in Human Behavior, 26*(3), 277–287. doi:10.1016/j.chb.2009.11.014

van den Berg, B. (2014). Colouring inside the lines: Using technology to regulate children's behaviour online. In S. van der Hof, B. van den Berg, & B. Schermer (Eds.), *Minding minors wandering the web: Regulating online child safety* (pp. 67–87). The Hague: Springer. doi:10.1007/978-94-6265-005-3_4

van Laer, T. (2014). The means to justify the end: Combating cyber harassment in social media. *Journal of Business Ethics, 3123*(1), 85–98. doi:10.1007/s10551-013-1806-z

Van Royen, K., Poels, K., Daelemans, W., & Vandebosch, H. (2015). Automatic monitoring of cyberbullying on social networking sites: From technological feasibility to desirability. *Telematics and Informatics, 32*(1), 89–97. doi:10.1016/j.tele.2014.04.002

Vandebosch, H. (2014). Addressing cyberbullying using a multi-stakeholder approach: The Flemish case. In S. van der Hof, B. van den Berg, & B. Schermer (Eds.), *Minding minors wandering the web: Regulating online child safety* (pp. 245–262). The Hague: Springer. doi:10.1007/978-94-6265-005-3_14

Waldman, A. E. (2012). Hostile educational environments. *Maryland Law Review (Baltimore, Md.), 71*(3), 705–771.

West Coast, L. E. A. F. (2014). *Cybermisogyny: Using and strengthening Canadian legal responses to gendered hate and harassment online.* Vancouver, BC: West Coast LEAF.

Willard, N. (2012). Cyberbullying and the law. In J. Patchin & S. Hinduja (Eds.), *Cyberbullying prevention and response: Expert perspectives* (pp. 36–56). New York: Routledge.

Wingate, V. S., Minney, J. A., & Guadagno, R. E. (2013). Sticks and stones may break your bones, but words will always hurt you: A review of cyberbullying. *Social Influence*, 8(2-3), 87–106. doi:10.1080/15534510.2012.730491

Wong-Lo, M., & Bullock, L. M. (2014). Digital metamorphosis: Examination of the bystander culture in cyberbullying. *Aggression and Violent Behavior*, *19*(4), 418–422. doi:10.1016/j.avb.2014.06.007

Wright, M. F. (2013). The relationship between young adults' beliefs about anonymity and subsequent cyber aggression. *Cyberpsychology, Behavior, and Social Networking*, *16*(12), 858–862. doi:10.1089/cyber.2013.0009 PMID:23849002

Wright, V. H., & Burnham, J. J. (2012). Cyberbullying prevention: The development of virtual scenarios for counselors in middle schools. *Professional Counselor: Research & Practice*, *2*(2), 169–177. doi:10.15241/vhw.2.2.169

Ybarra, M. L., Boyd, D., Korchmaros, J. D., & Oppenheim, J. K. (2012). Defining and measuring cyberbullying within the larger context of bullying victimization. *The Journal of Adolescent Health*, *51*(1), 53–58. doi:10.1016/j.jadohealth.2011.12.031 PMID:22727077

Ybarra, M. L., Espelage, D. L., & Mitchell, K. J. (2014). Differentiating youth who are bullied from other victims of peer-aggression: The importance of differential power and repetition. *The Journal of Adolescent Health*, *55*(2), 293–300. doi:10.1016/j.jadohealth.2014.02.009 PMID:24726463

Ybarra, M. L., Mitchell, K. J., & Espelage, D. (2012). Comparisons of bully and unwanted sexual experiences online and offline among a national sample of youth. In Ö. Özdemir (Ed.), *Complementary pediatrics* (pp. 203–216). Rijeka, Croatia: InTech.

Zweig, J. M., Lachman, P., Yahner, J., & Dank, M. (2013). Correlates of cyber dating abuse among teens. *Journal of Youth and Adolescence*, *43*(8), 1306–1321. doi:10.1007/s10964-013-0047-x PMID:24198083

KEY TERMS AND DEFINITIONS

Citizenship, Children and Youth: Civic identity in relation to democracy, which varies by how democracy is envisioned. When young people are seen as *future citizen-consumers*, adults act to protect and prepare children by teaching them how to manage risks and about democratic virtues such as respect and tolerance. When young people are seen as *apprentice citizens*, adults encourage them to learn democracy by practicing it. Positioning young people as *de facto citizens* means recognizing contexts where they are already full-fledged political actors and knowing subjects.

Cyber-Aggression: General peer-to-peer aggression that occurs online and consists in one-off occurrences or happens occasionally but where there is not a power imbalance between the aggressor and the target of aggression or where there is no intention to inflict harm or distress.

Cyberattack: A one-time yet serious incident of aggression where the aggressor intended harm and a power imbalance is present. It does not constitute cyberbullying due to its one-off occurrence.

Cyberbullying: Like traditional (offline) bullying, it is aggressive behavior that is repeated, intended to cause harm, and involves a power imbalance between bully and victim. It is distinguished by its occurrence through online contact. The electronic means of communication spotlights additional elements of potential relevance (i.e., greater anonymity, scale of publicity, missing or ambiguous social cues, 24/7 feature of the Internet) for understanding the nature, severity, and impact of the online name-calling, threats, and acts meant to embarrass, harass, or humiliate.

Harassment, Identity-Based: Repeated acts (such as contacting, tracking, or threatening someone) that annoy and distress the recipient and that are based on the victim's membership in a social group. Harassment becomes criminal when the behavior causes the person targeted to become reasonably fearful for her or his safety. See also, *sexual harassment, online.*

Hate Speech: Public communication that vilifies individuals based on their membership in a social group. In Canada, the federal Criminal Code prohibits hate speech against "identifiable groups" based on color, race, religion, ethnic origin, sexual orientation, national origin, age, sex, and mental or physical disability (but not gender identity). See also *harassment, identity-based.*

Moral Panic: Stanley Cohen's concept of a process whereby mainstream media sensationalize a putative social crisis (e.g., youth violence), fueling concerns among the public across an ideological spectrum, and building support for authorities, including politicians, to take action and restore a sense of social order. Examples include cyberbullying or digital technologies as highly risky in the hands of children and youth.

Online Safety Risks: These have been classified according to content, contact, and conduct.

Conduct risks occur in daily encounters among peers, with cyberbullying being the prime example. *Content risks* include encountering pornography, unwanted commercials, violent or gory images, hate-mongering websites, and so on. *Contact risks* include strangers attempting to engage with young people online for nefarious reasons, including grooming for pedophilia and sexual harassment and coercion.

Sexting: Sending sexually explicit text messages or intimate images of oneself—full or partial nude shots or sexy poses—to another person via cell phone, usually consensually. When a former intimate partner shares these sexually explicit messages or images non-consensually with other people intending to humiliate the subject depicted, this has been labeled *revenge porn.*

Sexual Harassment, Online: Consists in unwanted sexualized comments, threats of sexual violence (e.g., rape), misogynist epithets, and sexist insults that create a hostile climate or digital gender safety gap. Aimed at enforcing gender boundaries in cyberspace, it is based on unequal, gendered power relations within and between the sexes and takes three main forms: unwanted sexual attention, sexual coercion, and gender harassment. See also *harassment, identity-based.*

Chapter 22
Diversification and Nuanced Inequities in Digital Media Use in the United States

Eliane Rubinstein-Avila
University of Arizona, USA

Aurora Sartori
University of Arizona, USA

ABSTRACT

This chapter explores access to, and engagement with, digital media by United States' (U.S.) by non-mainstream populations. Framing the issue from a sociotechnical standpoint, the authors explore how engagement with digital media is shaped by socioeconomic status (taking into account confounding factors, such as race and ethnicity, and social and geographical ecologies). The authors highlight studies that focus on the robust digital practices with which nonmainstream populations already engage, and to which they contribute. One example is how some black Twitter users engage in signifyin'–a culturally specific linguistic practice—as a means of performing racial identity online. The authors also problematize concepts such as the new digital divide and digital exclusion, and finally, reiterate that a universal roll-out of high speed broadband alone will not necessarily lead to further engagement with digital media for ALL populations. In fact, the authors claim that providing more or faster access is likely not enough to prevent the entrenchment of a global digital underclass.

This chapter explores the ways in which non-mainstream populations in the United States (U.S.) access and engage with ICT and digital media. For the purpose of this chapter, the term nonmainstream population refers to racial/ethnic and linguistic minority groups, who are also low-income or poor (i.e., hovering on or below the poverty line), and/or infrequent Internet users. The authors also problematize two related concepts of *digital divide* and *digital exclusion*.

Although the term digital media has been used and described across the literature for over a decade, its definition remains nebulous. Digital media cannot be defined solely as digitized content, but rather must include a discussion its salient features—namely its interactivity and abil-

DOI: 10.4018/978-1-4666-8310-5.ch022

ity to foster collaboration and "group forming" networks (Smith, 2013). Rather than explicitly defining digital media, scholars often refer to it by providing a parenthetical lists of examples, such as "blogging, digital comics, digital photography, digital videos, video game design, information visualization, etc." (Sims, 2014, p. 673). Such lists, however, are ever-changing, as new types of digital media are constantly appearing on the scene. *The John Hopkins Guide to Digital Media* (Ryan et. al, 2014) for example, has over 150 entries, which range from the familiar (social networking sites, wikis) to the more obscure (e.g., digital installation art and machinima). Due to the dynamic nature of digital media, therefore, our definition remains broad and inclusive, encompassing most media that require a broadband connection and, at least for now, hardware such as desktops or laptops, smartphones or tablets to access it.

Currently, the most salient features of digital media include its affordance to access a global audience, providing individuals or groups the opportunity to: (1) create/produce, (2) congregate and share interests and ideas, (3) swap and sell information and goods, and (4) express one's individual/community voice through a social platform. An important and exciting aspect of digital media (viewed as dangerous by some) is that it allows anyone with a fast broadband connection to engage actively in, and even help shape, current political, cultural, social, and economic scenes. Thus, as digital media becomes increasingly influential for all aspects of public life, its equitable access becomes ever more vital. To put it succinctly, our chapter focuses on the intersection between race/ethnicity and social economic status (SES) and with access to and engagement with ICT (Information and Communication Technology) and digital media.

Since the international exploration of this topic is beyond the scope of our chapter, we therefore restricted our search to scholarship conducted in U.S. contexts. To retrieve relevant sources across several growing bodies of literature, we searched various academic databases using keywords such as: *digital media, information and computer technology (ICT), digital divide,* combined with terms such as *access, use,* and *engagement.* We then cross-referenced the sources we retrieved with keywords that relate to nonmainstream populations (i.e., *Hispanics, Latinas/Latinos, Blacks, African Americans, Native Americans, American Indians, Indigenous,* and *poor/ low-income* (including whites). This process yielded a range of sources that included academic journal articles, research reports and chapters in academic books.

WHAT IS THE SUCCINCT OVERVIEW OF THE RESEARCH?

Nonmainstream Populations Access to (ICT): An Incidental Predecessor to Digital Media

In the early 2000s the phrase 'digital divide' referred to a binary notion of access, or lack of access, that various demographic groups had to the Internet (Rubinstein-Avila, 2011). However, as access, per se, has become less of an issue, especially compared to the issue of speed, software, and advanced multiliteracies, the term 'digital divide' has become more nuanced. Although scholars from different disciplines have contributed to our understanding of the ways in which digital media is used across race/ethnic groups, and especially socioeconomic lines, ICT access and engagement among the most vulnerable groups (e.g., the poor, elderly, and disabled) have by no means been resolved.

Because the use of digital media is reliant upon ICT, and because such a large portion of the extant research focuses on the digital divide, we find it is essential to explore ICT use among nonmainstream populations as a foreground into a more detailed discussion about the ways in which nonmainstream populations are using digital media. Therefore, in this section, we explore the digital divide as it is conceptualized both in terms of access to the Internet in general, and to broadband and mobile technology specifically. After presenting the demographic trends, we reflect on the limitations of quantitative results that are not contextualized in social theory, and attempt to frame the issue from a sociotechnical standpoint, exploring how engagement with ICT and digital media is shaped by socioeconomic status in the U.S. (with obvious confounding factors, such as race and ethnicity).

Factors Affecting Access

Predictably, overall ICT use by adults in every racial group and income bracket has increased astronomically since the 1990's. Based on the telephone survey by the Pew Internet & American Life Project conducted by Princeton Survey Research Associates International (PSRAI) of a representative sample of 1,006 adults, a full 87% of adults were online in 2014, versus just 14% in 1995 (Fox & Rainie, 2014). Gaps in access continue to persist, however, given multiple demographic factors (Zickhur & Smith 2012). According to the U.S. Census Bureau (2012), Internet use varies dramatically by race, 82.9% for Asians (25 and older), 80.3% for whites, 68.2% for blacks, 64% for Latinos/as. Native Americans currently have the lowest rate of Internet use, with 49.36% of all households having home access, and 59.69% accessing the Internet at all (NTIA 2013).

Some scholars have found that amongst the Latino/a population, language barriers may impact online rate and use (Livingston, Parker, & Fox 2009; Warschauer & Matuchniak 2010). A report issued by the Pew Internet and American Life Project describes the extent to which English literacy correlates to higher levels of Internet use for Latino/a adults in the U.S. The research for the report relied on three datasets derived from landline surveys conducted by International Communications Research: (1) 2006 National Survey of Latinas/os – 2,000, (2) 2006 Hispanic Religion Survey – 4,016, and (3) 2008 Post-Election Survey

– 1,540. According to the report, all three surveys used similar methodologies, targeting Latinas/os ages 18 and older who were given the option of responding in English, Spanish or a combination of the two languages. The report's findings showed that the majority (81%) of adult Latinos/as who could read English very well used the Internet in 2008. Approximately half of those (52%) who reported not being able to read English well went online, compared to 24% of those who reported being unable to read English at all (Livingston et al., 2009). Spanish reading proficiency, however, does not seem to play as important of a role to Internet access; 62% of those who reported being able to read in Spanish very well reported going online, compared to 67% who read it pretty well, 62% who claimed not to read it well, and 66% who claimed did not read Spanish at all. Based on this data, the report noted that literacy levels per se did not appear to impact Internet use for Latinas; however, low English literacy seemed to be a hindrance (Livingston et al., 2009, figure 5, section 2).

Overall, gaps in access seem to be narrowing but still exist (Livingston et al. 2009; Lopez et al. 2013; Zickuhr & Smith 2012). The use of ICT seems to fluctuate depending on variables such as race (Smith 2014), age (Zickhur & Smith 2012), level of educational attainment (Livingston, Parker, & Fox 2009), English language fluency (Fairlie et al., 2006), and income (Warschauer & Matuchniak 2010). Social economic status (SES) seems to be a major factor. When variables such as income and educational levels are controlled for, differences in Internet use between racial groups all but disappear (NTIA 2013). Rates of internet usage amongst Latinas/os, African Americans, and whites with similar income and education levels are virtually the same (Livingston 2010; Smith 2014). The strongest negative predictors for internet use are not being a member of a certain racial or ethnic group, but rather having a low household income (under $20,000 per year), being over 65 years old, and not having completed high school

(Zickhur & Smith 2012). There is little doubt that Internet use is most positively correlated with income: 97% of those earning $75,000 or more use the internet, while only 60% of those living in household earning less than $30,000 annually are internet users (Zickhur & Smith 2012). At the higher income levels, regular Internet access and usage becomes the norm (Livingston, Parker, and Fox 2009).

Types of Access and Connections

Internet access, however, occurs across a broad spectrum, and under widely varying technological and social conditions. Substantial differences exist between connecting through dial-up, high and higher-speed broadband, and using public computers at a library or community centers. As Warschauer and Matuchniak (2010) suggest, the types of connections to which people have access shape their engagement. As an example, the authors cite research reporting that while 62% of adults with broadband went online to look up information about the 2008 election, only 37% of those with a dial-up connection did so (Warschauer & Matuchniak, 2010). Not surprisingly, access to high-speed (broadband) varies considerably along the lines of race/ethnicity, income, location, and level of education (NTIA 2013). Whites generally have higher rates of access (65%), followed by blacks (52%), and Latinas/os (45%) (Livingston, 2010). Since race/ethnicity and SES are highly confounded among households earning less than $25,000 annually, 45% had a broadband connection, compared to 94% of those making $100,000 or more (NTIA 2013). Rural households also have lower rates of broadband access (58%) compared to their urban counterparts (72%). Not surprisingly, research highlighting educational attainment follows a similar pattern (NTIA 2013).

The rise of mobile technology, however, has provided yet another route to connect to and partake in digital media. In fact, the use of cell phones has reached near-parity across all racial groups. As of 2010, 85% of whites owned a cell phone while 79% of blacks and 76% of Latinas/os reported owning a cell phone (Livingston 2010). Basing its findings on a telephone survey of 2,252 adults in 2013, PSRAI found that 91% of all Americans now own a cell phone; in fact, they found that the percentage of cell phone owners that use their phones to access the Internet is around 63%--doubled since 2009 (Duggan & Smith, 2013). With the advent of smartphones and the capacity to connect from almost anywhere, primarily reliance on less expensive phones, rather than computers, to access the Internet has become a noticeable phenomenon—not only in the U.S., but also world-wide. This group of "cell-mostly" Internet users is comprised primarily of younger individuals who are under 30, non-whites, and those with relatively low incomes and lower education levels (Duggan & Smith, 2013). The researchers found that among this group, 60% of respondents were Hispanics, 43% were African Americans, compared with 27% of whites. Level of education seems to be negatively correlated to "cell-mostly" users. In other words, those with higher educational attainments are less likely to connect primarily via their phones; 45% of cell-mostly users had earned a high school diploma or less, and only 21% were college graduates (Duggan & Smith, 2013). On the other hand, the trend in computer ownership provides almost the opposite scenario. According to the 2011 U.S. Census, 76% of all households had a computer; African American and Latino/a households, however, were less likely to have computers (62% and 63%, respectively), as were households with incomes lower than $25,000 (52%) (NTIA 2013).

A Matter of Social Justice

Why is Internet access a matter of social justice? It has been widely acknowledged that access to the Internet is a useful tool in people's lives (Fox & Rainie 2014), but why, *exactly*, is the issue of the digital divide so important? Beyond the fact that so many functions are constantly relocating to the digital realm (e.g., healthcare, taxes, education), we are also in the process of shifting from an industrial to an informational economy, making digital literacy an increasingly invaluable set of skills for employment (Warschauer & Matuchniak 2010, citing Castells, 1996). According to the U.S. Bureau of Labor Statistics, the demand for manual labor is steadily decreasing, as industries such as manufacturing and construction are two of the most rapidly shrinking businesses in terms of net employment (Watson, 2012). Occupations that require the use of information technology, on the other hand, continue to grow; this increase seems impervious even to widespread economic recessions (Csorny, 2013).

In a study conducted as part of the Children and Technology Project, in which ICT use was defined as "computer and internet use, video-game playing, and cell-phone use" (Jackson et al. 2008, p. 438), the authors examined race and gender differences across the nature of use. The authors also explored the extent to which the intensity of engagement in particular activities could predict academic performance. For example, levels of ICT use were found to be significantly lower in general among African American male youth than among other groups. The study was based on a survey of 515 children (172 African Americans and 343 whites) with an average age of 12. The authors found ICT use, in general, to be positively correlated to academic performance (Jackson et al. 2008). With regards to intensity of use, survey results revealed that white students had been engaging with ICT for a longer period of time compared to African American students. Overall, the authors found that males had been using computers longer than females. A race by gender interaction revealed that African American males engaged in fewer activities, with one exception—playing videogames, the only activity that was the linked to lower academic performance in their study (Jackson et al. 2008).

Thus, the new, more nuanced digital divide can be seen as a major obstacle to equal opportunity in future employment. The full benefits afforded by ICT are constantly changing and widespread, and beyond the scope of our chapter. Scholarship on this topic ranges from how engagement with digital media is imperative for social and economic participation in a networked public culture (Ito et al., 2009) to the role of online social media in the cultivation of pro-democratic behaviors (Monforti & Marichal 2014). Based on a cursory glance of occupational patterns and current educational trends, it seems safe to assert that equitable access to ICT is indeed a matter of social justice. Analyzing how such nuanced factors shape the digital divide on a larger scale, however, requires sizable resources. The Digital Youth Project (DYP) is one notable example of such a project. A seminal three-year ethnographic study, the DYP investigated how youth participate in the "new media ecology," a term used to highlight the extent to which digital media is embedded in the lives of youth in a world where technologies, infrastructure, and everyday practices of young people are interrelated (Ito et al, 2009). The project, part of a $50 million initiative funded by the MacArthur Foundation to study learning and digital media, was unique both in terms of its large scale and in terms of its adherence to qualitative methodologies. Drawing upon extensive data collected in 23 different case studies completed by 28 researchers/collaborators, the DYP describes the new media practices of a wide range of diverse populations of youth, spanning from middle-class families in suburban Silicon Valley, to poor teens living in urban LA. The focus of the project, however, was to document practices that were observed broadly, across multiple case studies. The specificities of each research site were largely glazed over in the attempt to provide a more generalizable portrait of youth engagement with digital media. For this reason, while some of the individual case studies that comprise the Digital Youth Project are highly relevant to the focus of this chapter, the conclusions as a whole are too general to really depict any specific trends regarding how low-income and minority populations interact with digital media.

That being said, there are some underlying points made about the importance of certain *types* of access to digital media that have far-reaching implications when considering how socioeconomic status may shape one's use of technology. Having consistent "lightweight" access to digital tools, for example, was determined by the researchers to be a necessary precondition for participating in networked public spaces (Ito et al. 2009). The researchers concluded that "[w]hen kids lack access to the Internet at home, and public libraries and schools block sites that are central to their social communication, they are doubly handicapped in their efforts to participate in common culture and sociability" (2009, p. 74). The authors assert that engaging in social and recreational activities online, not just accessing "serious" (p. 75) information, is an important aspect of participating in public life in the digital age, in addition to being a crucial starting point for self-expression and digital media creation (Ito et al., 2009).

CURRENT ISSUES IN THE FIELD RAISED BY THESE STUDIES

U.S. Nonmainstream Populations' Engagement with Digital Media

One of the many issues this contemporary scholarship raises is our lack of understanding of the ways in which vulnerable groups *are* accessing ICT and digital media (and for what purposes). While there is quite a substantial body of scholarship about how nonmainstream populations are *not* using digital media (see above discussion on the digital divide), there is a notable dearth of research regarding the many ways in which ethnic/racial minorities and low-income individuals are taking up digital tools actively. For example,

there are relatively few studies focusing on how nonmainstream populations in the U.S. use mobile technology. One of the few is a study of Latina immigrant farmworkers by Garcia (2011). Based on the analysis of in-depth interviews with six women in southeastern Ohio, Garcia sought to document how immigrant women use ICT and digital media through their mobile phones. Text messaging was a common form of communication amongst these research participants, specifically for those who were living in the U.S. while attempting to maintain contact with family members in the home country (Garcia, 2011). Additionally, this research revealed that mobile phones connected these farmworkers to information and news relating to their current status as immigrants. Mobile phones also provided the participants a means to locate transportation, which is essential for immigrants who are unable to obtain drivers licenses. Garcia (2011) also found that in many instances, however, the men (husbands, etc.) maintained ownership of the phones and controlled access to the phones—especially when there was only one mobile phone per household. Access to mobile phones, therefore, only appeared to strengthen the hierarchical relations between men and women.

Small scale, qualitative studies such as this one provide an essential dimension to a comprehensive understanding of the state of digital media in the U.S. Rather than simply underscoring the lack of engagement with digital media, studies such as this are needed to illuminate the nuances of *how* vulnerable populations use the technology to which they have access. Information about adult populations is especially scarce, as research on this topic focuses almost entirely on youth.

Social Media: Diversification or Segmentation?

Another issue that contemporary studies have brought to a head is the idealized myth that the incorporeal nature of the web would function as the ultimate democratizing arena, making invisible most, if not all, forms of social differences. However, recent studies illustrate that this is not the case. Social networking sites (SNSs), which have virtually exploded in popularity over the past several years—a phenomenon that was aided in part by the simultaneous proliferation of mobile technology – have been a fertile arena for scholarship on social relations. According to the Pew Research Internet Project, 73% of adults who are online use some kind of social networking site (Duggan & Smith 2013b). Though Facebook remains the favorite overall, marked diversification has taken place. As of recent findings, 42% of online adult users engage in multiple social networking sites such as LinkedIn, Twitter, Pinterest, and Instagram. Which platform people choose, and why, yields surprisingly complex and layered social findings. In fact, an emerging body of scholarship is exploring the ways in which offline social divisions are being reproduced in the digital realm (Duggan & Smith 2013b).

As it stands, it turns out that the SNS people choose are not a matter of random chance, but rather a confluence of multiple demographic and social factors such as race, class, gender, and age (boyd, 2012). Drawing upon four years of ethnographic data collected in diverse communities across the country, boyd (2012) focused on the role of social media in the lives of American teens. Based on her extensive data, which included 2,000 hours of observation of online practices, 103 formal semi-structured interviews, and analyses of 10,000 randomly selected MySpace profiles, boyd offers a qualitative illustration of how the social network site adoption by teens reflects a broader discourse of race and class in the U.S. In fact, boyd's (2012) analysis of teens' perceptions of different SNSs - specifically MySpace and Facebook – focuses specifically on the classed and racialized terminology teens used to describe the sites. For example, boyd (2012) documents that white teens tended to describe MySpace in overtly classed and racialized terms, as being "for the riffraff," folks from "the other side of the

tracks," and "ghetto" (boyd, 2012, p. 204 – 220). According to boyd (2012), MySpace, which preceded Facebook by several years, had evolved to embody an "urban late-night culture." Its cachet among teens was mostly derived from the site's association with the freedom and maturity of the 20- to 30-something crowd, its first adopters (p. 206). The origins of Facebook, on the other hand, created in the hallowed halls of an Ivy League college and initially restricted to use by Harvard students, imbued the network with a safer, more elite and exclusive image (boyd, 2012).

By 2006-2007, once Facebook was opened to all users, there was a definitive trend among generally white and more affluent teens to choose Facebook over MySpace. Users from less privileged backgrounds, who identified themselves as belonging to a subculture, preferred MySpace overall (boyd 2012). boyd frames this trend by drawing an intentionally provocative analogy between the movement of mainstream teens from MySpace to Facebook as "white flight," a term that refers to the historical exodus of white city dwellers to the suburbs in the 1960's. boyd (2012) asserts that teens who fled MySpace to join Facebook, were often motivated by many of the same fundamental issues (as the white suburban families fleeing the urban centers)—fear and anxiety, social networks, institutional incentives, and racism (boyd, 2012). Though boyd admits to the limitations of the metaphor, she illuminates several interesting parallels: equating the "American Dream" of the suburbs with the "teen Dream" of collegiate maturity, represented by Facebook. The urban "decay" of cities is likened to the influx of spam into MySpace ("digital graffiti"), in both cases serving as signs of disrepair or feeling unsafe (boyd 2012, p. 219).

Related to the issue of social segmentation raised by contemporary studies is the sociological concept of "homophily," referring to the tendency of individuals to befriend those who are most like themselves. boyd (2012) points out that socializing in the U.S., for both youth and adults, is organized along lines of race and ethnicity (boyd 2012). Thus, the self-segregation of youth into homophilic social groups within school spaces is replicated online, as teens connect virtually with pre-existing networks of friends, following established race and class-based social boundaries (boyd 2012). Using extensive statistical analyses, Hargittai's (2012) work also illuminates the systematic segmentation of youth into distinct social networking sites among first year college students. Harigittai (2012) administered a paper survey to two diverse cohorts of college students, reaching 1,060 students in 2007 and 1,115 in 2009. The data was collected from students at the University of Illinois in Chicago, which she cites as being one of the most ethnically diverse universities in the U.S. (according to U.S. News and World Report 2009). In fact, less than half of each cohort sampled was white, with levels of parental education varying substantially (Hargittai 2012). In addition to obtaining students' demographic information, the survey included questions about the social context of Internet use (e.g. home access, time students spent online, and their knowledge and use of social networking sites). Echoing boyd's (2012) work, Hargittai (2012) found that SNS use varied strikingly along racial and ethnic lines: Latino/a students were significantly more likely to use MySpace and less likely to use Facebook than their white counterparts. However, the opposite was true for Asian and Asian American students. African American students were also much more likely than white students to use MySpace, though most (91% in 2009) also reported having Facebook accounts (Hargittai 2012). MySpace was also significantly more popular among those students whose parents had less than a high school education (56% in 2009, compared to 26% of students whose parents held graduate degrees), a factor used as a proxy for SES (socioeconomic status) or class (Hargittai 2012). Once again, the study shows that offline social divisions are reproduced in the digital realm, the implications of which Hargittai (2012) describes in pragmatic terms: if college

professors, employers, or government agencies assume that information is transmitted most effectively by using specific SNS, populations who utilize alternate sites are likely to be systematically excluded from receiving the message.

Assuming Racialized Identities

With 271 million active users, Twitter is widely considered the most popular of the microblogging sites. This genre of digital media is defined by enforcing users to conform their posts to limits of extreme brevity: 140 characters (Twitter.com; Croxall 2014). By electing to follow a given user, that individual's short posts (or "tweets") thereby appear on a continuously updated feed on one's homepage, known as a timeline. Interaction between users consists of "retweeting," (i.e., publicly copying someone's tweets or by replying to another user's tweets by using the @reply feature). The hashtag, created by using the symbol "#," marks phrases and indicates the topic of a tweet, thus allowing users to search for specific topics and follow them.

Given the severe limitations the platform places on the length of the message, one may question whether anything of importance can be communicated. However, Croxall (2014) claims that the medium lends itself to a sharing of day-to-day life that allow users to deepen relationships with each other over time—developing a sense of "ambient intimacy." In fact, Twitter has in large part transcended any indictments of triviality by its role in organizing, disseminating, and publicizing a number of well-known large-scale social acts with very real-world impact (e.g., the revolution in Egypt). The real-time updates of Twitter can function to enable "*social* proprioception" (Croxall, 2014, italics in the original). Literally, proprioception is a term used to describe an individual's sense of the relative location of her/his body. In this sense, Twitter enables proprioception of a group of people. The platform's real-time, continuously updated feeds enable a collective awareness of a networked public. This renders the coordination of large-scale public actions possible by providing groups of people a sense of self (Croxall, 2014). This specific affordance by Twitter is especially interesting for the purposes of this chapter. It begs us to question *how* a live, continuously updated, and widely used social media platform can function to both reflect, as well as actively shape, cultural identities across an increasingly multicultural, multiracial, and multilingual world.

Of all the social media sites, Twitter has experienced a marked rise in popularity across the U.S., especially amongst African Americans; 34% of black American Internet users report having Twitter accounts, compared to only 18% of the overall population of adult Internet users (Duggan & Smith 2013b). Racialized hashtags are frequently featured in Twitter's list of "trending topics," often showcasing black American culture (Florini 2014; Sharma, 2013). The "Black Twitter" phenomenon has emerged as a much-discussed topic amongst journalists and bloggers (Florini 2014). In her study of "Black Twitter" timelines, Florini (2014) archived and analyzed the timelines of black Twitter users, examining how participants engaged in a specific Black American cultural practice – *signifyin'* – as a means of performing racial identity online. Florini defines *signifyin'* as a "genre of linguistic performance that allows for the communication of multiple levels of meaning simultaneously, most frequently involving word-play and misdirection" (2014, p. 224). A playful and witty genre, with deep roots in Black American cultural traditions, Florini (2014) underscores signifyin' as a mode of interaction that enables Black Twitter users to "align themselves with Black oral traditions, to index Black cultural practices, to enact Black subjectivities, and to communicate shared knowledge and experiences" (p. 224). Signifyin' often incorporates Black popular culture references, requiring background knowledge and cultural competencies from those engaging in the practice to render the multiple levels of meaning comprehensible. However, Florini (2014) avoids

contributing to the idea that "Black Twitter" is homogenous and monolithic, claiming that the use of signifyin' is a choice on the part of many individual users of color to perform a racial identity in a context that does not require the user to disclose race membership explicitly. The choice to invoke Black cultural traditions, therefore, can be interpreted as a means of resisting marginalization and invisibility (Florini 2014).

Florini's (2014) study reveals the ways in which engagement with social media can be used to perform a racial identity, ensuring that race remains visible online. In fact, Florini (2014) interprets the performance of a collective Black identity online as an active rejection of the prevalent "colorblindness" that is so entrenched in contemporary U.S. racial discourses. Employing modes of communication like signifyin', writing tweets in Black Vernacular English (BVE), and indexing Black cultural knowledge are all ways of asserting a racialized identity, and thereby communicating that race, as well as racial inequality, continue to shape Black people's experiences (Florini 2014).

Florini's (2014) study is not only innovative and insightful, but it also approaches research on digital media from a perspective of resource, not deficit. As the author points out, most studies about minorities and digital media tend to portray "people of color as technological outsiders" and to "obscure the many people of color who are online" (Florini, 2014, p. 224). In fact, even a brief foray into recent scholarship certainly conveys this clearly—a trend that is especially apparent in research regarding African American males (Patton, Eschmann & Butler 2013; Smith 2014; Jackson et al. 2008).

An example of academic research that frames African American males' engagement with digital media negatively is Patton, Eschmann, and Butler's study (2013). Patton et al. (2013) explored how social media (primarily Facebook, MySpace, Twitter, and YouTube), has been repurposed by urban men—mostly African American—to function as a stage for what they call "Internet banging," defined as gang-affiliated communication. The authors claim that the intent of such posts are to promote gang affiliation, boast about or threaten violent acts, or network with other gang members (Patton et al. 2013). The authors also draw parallels between Internet banging and "hip hop identity," which the authors define as a collective urban masculine identity that is "rebellious," "assertive," and "antagonistic toward many other aspects of American culture" (p. A57). In addition, the authors claimed that hip-hop identity, "along with unemployment and poor educational opportunities ... fuels the behavior we currently see among African American men on the Internet" (p. A57). The problem with such research is that it fails to contextualize the "Internet banging" phenomenon as only one (uncommon) use out of the *many* ways in which African American men engage with digital media. Because research that focuses on African Americans' digital media use is so scant, it seems particularly troubling that the few extant studies seem to focus on topics already sensationalized in popular media.

GAPS IN THE EXTANT RESEARCH AND DIRECTIONS FOR FUTURE RESEARCH

Engagement of Low-Income Youth with Digital Media (in Classrooms and After-School Contexts)

Much of the research on nonmainstream populations and digital media focuses on youth within educational settings. It is important, however, that such research not be conducted using deficit models, but instead, from a lens that takes into account the robust digital practices with which youth already engage and to which they contribute. For example, descriptive studies (e.g., Tripp & Herr-Stephenson, 2009) seek to document how low-income and minority youth are currently using digital media both in school and out of school,

highlighting the unexpected obstacles youth often face at home and at school, as well as the youths' own resourcefulness. Another area of scholarly focus that would add to the gaps in our knowledge are data-driven classroom-based studies, analyzing how instructors of under-funded, urban schools are using digital media production projects to make schooling more relevant for marginalized populations and as a way to engage students as critical, socially aware citizens (e.g., Turner, 2012; and Schmier, 2014). In addition to classroom-based approaches, we need more studies that analyze how extracurricular programs have attempted to cultivate digital literacy skills in low-income and minority populations by supplementing instruction in formal educational settings with academic summer camps (Baker, Staiano, & Calvert, 2011), after-school clubs (Vickery, 2014), and youth development agencies (Soep, 2011).

Despite widely varying degrees of access, many youth seem to be finding ways to interact with digital media in diverse and interesting ways. In their case studies of two low-income Latino middle school students, Tripp and Herr-Stephenson (2009) illustrate the participants' nuanced engagement with digital media (in and out of school) despite economic barriers. The case studies sought to examine how youth who do not have easy access to computers, Internet, and media production software, still manage to interact with digital media in ways that are both creative and personally meaningful. Drawing from ethnographic research from the 2005-2006 academic school year, and informed by *genres of participation* - defined as modes of engagement that shape how technology is framed, understood, and operated within mediated spaces (Tripp & Herr-Stephenson, 2009, citing Ito et al., forthcoming) - the study highlighted how youth approached technology differently within and across diverse settings. A great distinction lay between youth-driven genres of participation, which were voluntary, self-directed, and motivated by youths' interests, and adult-driven genres of participation, which were organized around adults' goals for young people (e.g., academic educational software) (Tripp & Herr-Stephenson, 2009). How this 'second digital divide' (Tripp & Herr-Stephenson, 2009, citing Buckingham, 2007) is navigated by both young people and parents, teachers, and other figures of authority is an increasingly salient issue and frames much of the research on youth and digital media (e.g., Ito et al, 2009).

Though they would be lumped together demographically, the two participants studied by Tripp and Herr-Stephenson (2009) illustrate the extent to which youths' personal use of digital media is unique, driven by highly individualized interests, experiences, and skills. The subject of the first case study, James, displayed a tendency of disengagement with the adult-driven new media-related school assignments. James utilized his limited access to digital media at school to listen to music, find information on bands, and also maintain a social networking page. While James' home was not equipped with Internet access (his parents citing both economic obstacles and a desire to keep their son out of trouble), he was able to gain access at friends' homes to support his music interests and engage in social networking. The second research participant, Michelle, had a computer and Internet access at home. Unlike James, her time at home—and especially her whereabouts online—were rigorously regulated and monitored by her mother. Also unlike James, Michelle was more engaged with school assignments that utilized new media. Michelle was able to maintain a social networking page to communicate with her friends, despite her mother's concerns.

Interestingly, significant barriers to access experienced by both James and Michelle were sociocultural, rather than physical or economic obstacles. As documented in similar studies of technology and family dynamics (see Tripp, 2011), the parents of both participants attempted to firmly regulate their children's internet use, maintaining that it be restricted to mostly academic pursuits and limiting online activities that were perceived

as somehow "risky," such as exploring social media sites (Tripp & Herr-Stephenson, 2009). The school's approach to engagement with digital media also provided limited opportunities for students to connect in-school assignments with out-of-school interests, and primarily involved students in adult-driven genres of participation. The researchers thus conclude that the incorporation digital media into academic settings does not alone make schooling more relevant or interesting to students (Tripp & Herr-Stephenson, 2009). Young peoples' existing knowledge and interests need to be taken into account, as do sociocultural and institutional constraints (Tripp & Herr-Stephenson, 2009).

How student interests and out-of-school literacy practices can be incorporated into classroom pursuits is precisely the focus of Turner's (2012) year-long ethnographic study of an urban middle school's multimodal media production (MMP) class. Focusing on the experiences of 'Gina,' a female African-American student in the MMP class, Turner analyzed the how the class structure encouraged students to reframe their out of school literacy practices as tools for knowledge production and learning in an academic setting. The school that was the site of the MMP class was attended primarily by students whose families lived below the poverty line and had highly variable access to technology at home. Most students were African American and Latino (Turner 2012).

Significantly, Turner notes that the class instructor's ultimate objective was to foster critical thinking – specifically a critical perspective on popular media - through the use of new technologies. The class's principal assignment involved students working together to conduct community research projects. These projects incited students to investigate important issues in their community and then use MMPs – which included "documentaries, digital stories, Hip Hop music, digital video poetry, music videos, multi-user digital environments (MUVEs), public service announcements, youth radio, Web sites, blogs, wikis, and other emergent technologies used in multimodal designs" – to express and analyze their findings (Turner, 2012, p. 498). Grounded in a theoretical framework that included critical media literacies, Turner's (2012) study draws connections between multimodal literacy learning and issues of social justice, thus directly impacting the lives of youth. As a pedagogical approach framing the MMP class, critical media literacies entailed enabling students to critique media as text, becoming increasingly aware of their own patterns of media consumption, and ultimately having students create their own narratives (Goodman, 2003; Turner, 2012). Turner (2012) identified students' engagement with social justice issues (such as inequality in urban education and racial justice) through the production of their MMPs, which served to indicate the burgeoning critical literacies that the students developed while researching, analyzing, and documenting community issues. This progression is clearly illustrated in the media produced by Gina (the focal participant), whose early work largely consisted of love songs and music videos heavily influenced by commercial Hip Hop and only moderately critical of how the genre portrayed females (Turner 2012). By the semester's end, however, after completing a community research project on homeless youth, Turner (2012) describes Gina's songs "We Strugglin'" and "My Community" as critically addressing heavy issues such as inequality in urban education, racial justice, traumatic life experiences, and popular culture as resistance.

By analyzing the students' MMPs created over the course of a year, Turner was able to track how students engaged with texts differently over time, and observe how the course fostered the development of social consciousness. MMPs allowed students to use the "stylistics of modern youth culture" to cultivate new and traditional literacy skills, providing the students with an avenue for participating in their own "socially, culturally, historically, and politically situated practices that may have been unavailable in previous curricular

frameworks" (Turner, 2012, p. 504). As in Tripp and Herr-Stephenson's (2009) study, Turner similarly illustrated that merely incorporating technology and media production into a course does not alone translate to increased student interest and course relevance. In this case, the instructor's own pedagogical stance and incorporation of critical social justice issues were essential factors shaping student experiences in the media production class.

In other words, the research literature would benefit from more studies that value nonmainstream students' media practices outside of school settings. Formal school settings too often marginalize students' interests in favor of focusing on adult-driven genres of participation. This limited focus and enactment of restrictive policies regarding technology use and digital media in school disproportionately impacts low-income students, who may not have consistent, superfast, and autonomous use of high-speed Internet outside of school.

For example, Schmier's (2014) 18-month ethnography of a single classroom documented how the instructor of a digital media studies class in an urban public middle school incorporated student interests - namely, popular culture - into the curriculum. Building upon studies by Morrell and Duncan-Andrade (2006) and Marsh (2005), Schmier's work contributes to the body of evidence that supports bringing popular culture into the classroom as an effective means of empowering youth as critical media consumers and strengthening students' academic literacy skills (Schmier, 2014). Schmier (2014) also incorporated the concept of "connected learning" (Ito et al., 2013), which proposes fusing student interests and passions with the curriculum as a way to create new educational, economic, and political opportunities for traditionally marginalized populations of learners. Collaboration and networking also play an important role in the connected learning framework as skills necessary to be literate in the 21st century (Schmier, 2104;

citing the New London Group, 1996), and making supportive learning communities a central aspect of Schmier's (2014) study.

The class studied by Schmier (2014) was principally engaged in exploring both traditional and new media journalistic practices, such as podcasting. The researcher focused on three students who were immigrants or children of immigrants, with origins in Nigeria, El Salvador, and Honduras. Schmier observed these students' literacy practices in various contexts - online, in the classroom, and in spaces outside of school. Other data collection included focus group discussions, interviews, and the collection of texts produced by the students. Significantly, each of the three focal students maintained highly active online presences outside of school, consistently updating their personal blogs and participating in social media as forms of recreation.

As in Turner's (2012) study, the transformational affordances of digital media emerged when students were permitted to draw upon their interests, skills, and personal experiences in the classroom. Encouraged by their instructor to report on topics that were personally meaningful to them, Schmier describes how the students were able to leverage their out-of-school literacy practices to reposition themselves as "successful author[s], designer[s], and leader[s] in the classroom," and as experts within specific online communities (Schmier, 2014, p. 43). For those youth who were failing their core classes and generally regarded as struggling students, this repositioning as competent and insightful authors and activists was especially significant (Schmier, 2014). Two of the female students in particular became deeply engaged in documenting instances of inequity in their community, and were inspired to produce texts such as an anti-drug public service announcement, a podcast regarding the school's understaffing, and a documentary about a community mural project orchestrated to cover graffiti (Schmier, 2014).

When digital media studies incorporate student interests they serve as an important bridge for students to leverage their community cultural knowledge and out-of-school literacy practices within an academic setting. Digital media production in schools can also function as a creative outlet for expression and a platform for the cultivation of critical social awareness. Through the digital media studies class, the students "honed their ability to publish for multiple audiences," (Schmier, 2014, p. 45), bringing in popular culture artifacts and practices to design multimodal texts that persuasively addressed a wide range of locally relevant topics and positioned the students as community activists. The researcher's concluding suggestions for teachers include allowing for student choice in writing topics and modes of presentation, making peer feedback more rewarding (as in online forums) rather than an "artificial step in linear writing process," and having students work together to create texts that reflect the needs of their communities (Schmier, 2014, p. 46).

Extracurricular Digital Media Programs

There is little doubt that mobile devices, high-speed internet, and personal computers all transform how, why, when, and what students learn, but to what degree schools should support (or restrict) media practices and engagement remains a contentious issue (Vickery 2014). Because of the often limited and heavily monitored nature of technology access in schools, programs offered during the summer, after school, and by youth development agencies play an especially important role in providing marginalized youth with the resources and support necessary to develop digital literacy skills. The academic summer program studied by Baker, Staiano, and Calvert (2011) is one example of how a supplementary program can successfully combine digital media production skills with an environment that reaffirms youths' commitment to and positive perceptions of school.

The study followed 24 low-income, urban African American adolescents who attended the summer program, focusing on how the adolescents expressed themselves through digital media, and analyzing both the form and content of their digital productions (Baker, Staiano, & Calvert 2011). The researchers preface their study with a description of the various challenges confronted by low-income urban African American students, such as high drop-out rates (citing Chapman, Laird, & Kewal Ramani 2010), under-resourced schools that fostered negative academic self-concepts (citing Baker 1998), inadequate programs for high-achieving academic students (citing Ford & Webb, 1994), and exposure to deviant peers due to a lack of supervised settings for peer interaction (citing Brody et al., 2001).

The 24 students, all between the ages of 12 and 18, were randomly selected from a summer camp college-preparatory program that recruited students from a low-income neighborhood in a large metropolitan city. Held at a local university, the summer program provided academic and family mentoring support with the goal of fostering the skills and motivation necessary to graduate high school and pursue further education (Baker, Staiano, & Calvert 2011). The 24 youth who participated in the study were assigned to a digital production course as part of their daily summer camp schedule. The course was led by a professional filmmaker and editor who instructed students to create digital films about their summer experience, encouraging the participants to include whatever content they liked, though filming was restricted to the campus area. The students used digital cameras, mini digital video cameras, and iMovie editing software to create their digital productions (Baker et al., 2011).

The researchers found that the students' digital productions expressed overwhelmingly positive academic views, which was attributed to the sup-portive academic environment and positive peer relationships fostered by the program (Baker, et al., 2011). The productions also featured montage styles, foregrounded music, and other design features that mimicked much of the media consumed by the students (Baker, et al., 2011). In this sense, the use of digital media here is fundamentally distinct from its position studied by Turner (2012) and Schmier (2014). Without the emphasis on *critical* media literacy described by Turner (2012), the digital media productions of the summer academic program served more as a direct reflection of the media consumed by the youth, as well as an expression of how peer relationships and perceptions of school were correlated in the lives of the participants. While research like Turner's (2012) and Schmier's (2014) demonstrate how digital media production can function as a platform for consideration of social justice issues and inciting students to become more critically aware, the digital productions created in the summer program studied by Baker et al. (2011) functioned more as unmediated modes of communication and expression, surely made more interesting because of their association with forms of popular media consumed by youth recreationally.

The context in which learning takes place has an obvious impact on the modes of participation taken up by students as they interact with digital media. Informal learning environments like after-school clubs, precisely because of their less regulated structure, can serve as vital resources to support students as they develop new digital skills and learn to navigate social networks online and offline (Vickery 2014). Significantly, these affordances can also lead to the expansion of youth's social capital, which plays a vital role in enabling economic upward mobility, particularly for minority youth (Vickery, 2014, citing Hargittai, 2011; Laureau, 2003). In addition to the accumulation of social capital, digital literacies are also cited as enhancing political participation, and in general encompassing a set of skills and ways of interacting with technology that create more equitable futures for young people (Vickery, 2014, citing DiMaggio, Hargittai, Celeste, & Shafer, 2004).

As part of the Digital Edge Project—a large-scale research project designed to analyze teens' media ecologies in both formal and informal learning environments –Vickery (2014) studied Texas City High School's (TCHS) after-school digital media club for eight months. The researcher observed and interviewed participants from three formal technology courses and two informal after-school clubs at TCHS, which was described as "a large, low-performing, economically challenged, and ethnically diverse, Hispanic-majority, public high school" (Vickery, 2014, p. 82). Vickery's focal participants were a multiracial group of 9 female and 9 male participants, all of whom had unreliable access to computers and the internet in their homes. The after-school digital media club (DMC), therefore, was a particularly vital resource for these students, who otherwise would not have had sufficient access to technology in order to develop digital literacy skills beyond what was available to them in school.

Within the DMC, students were free to engage in low-stakes, interest-driven participation in an environment that facilitated experimentation and a trial-and-error approach to learning (Vickery, 2014). The learning environment of the DMC was distinct from the formal technology classes not only in that the work was ungraded, but also in that it encouraged students to work more collaboratively, teaching each other and cooperatively organizing large-scale projects like scripting, shooting, and editing short films (Vickery, 2014). The club's adult mentor also reached out to nonprofit and community organizations, creating opportunities for youth to work on projects like PSAs for local organizations and thereby expanding students' offline social networks to include professionals in the local community (Vickery, 2014). This networking feature of the club's activities additionally led the adult mentor

to provide the students with instruction on how to communicate professionally with the press and potential donors (Vickery, 2014).

RECOMMENDATIONS/ IMPLICATIONS FOR EDUCATION, CIVIC ENGAGEMENT (GLOBAL AND LOCAL), SOCIAL PRACTICE, AND POLICY

Overall, the informal learning environment provided by the digital studies club was crucial to the development of students' digital literacies because it allowed for the freedom to collaborate, explore, and creatively experiment with digital media in a way that formal, curriculum-based, teacher-as-expert technology courses did not (Vickery, 2014). The researcher writes that spaces like the DMC "help bridge students' out-of-school and in-school learning by providing a space that students can explore, look up online tutorials, and help each other, but in a space that also offers adult guidance and support." (Vickery, 2014, p. 91).

Beyond underscoring the importance of after-school technology clubs, Vickery's (2014) study touches on the more fundamental issue of how digital media and networked technology are regarded by educational institutions at large, and how to support students' digital skills whilst retaining some control over how those skills are used and to what end. Throughout the study, a noticeable gap became increasingly apparent between how technology was regarded in the informal DMC and the school's official policies, which mandated that social media sites and video sharing sites remained blocked on all school computers (Vickery, 2014). The school's restrictive policies primarily affected those students with no or precarious home Internet access, the consequence of which was that these students were unable to distribute their work online, thereby preventing them from obtaining valuable feedback from the online community. The blocking of social media also inhibited the development of students' network literacies and stymied their opportunities to fully understand how intellectual property functions in the digital realm (Vickery 2014).

Vickery's study demonstrates how the participation gap is constantly evolving as online networks become more complex and new skills are increasingly necessary. After-school clubs can function to help minimize these gaps by providing the kind of access necessary to cultivate digital literacies. However, students who do not have the time to participate in extracurricular programs, because of financial constraints, jobs, and familial obligations, are still excluded (Rubinstein-Avila, 2006). For this reason, Vickery (2014) asserts that formal education environments need to provide opportunities for youth to engage with digital media in meaningful ways.

Programs that partner with schools and incorporate services for out-of-school youth and recent high school graduates are therefore an important piece of the puzzle. One such program that provides minority and low-income youth with opportunities to study, explore, and create digital media is Youth Radio, a transmedia production company and youth development agency with headquarters in Oakland, California (Soep, 2011). Youth Radio, which has bureaus in L.A., Washington D.C., and Atlanta, involves young people all over the country in producing a weekly live radio show entitled *Youth in Control*. The show features stories written by youth, who also create associated playlists, videos, photos, and online posts on a weekly basis (Soep, 2011). The organization primarily recruits low-income youth and young people of color to participate in the program, seeking to provide a viable and empowering educational alternative to students who attend "economically abandoned schools" in urban areas (Soep, 2011, p. 9). Youth Radio participants progress through specialized courses in digital media and production, taking

part in workshops, presentations, and professional development opportunities and eventually becoming eligible for paid positions as peer educators, media makers, and engineers (Soep 2011). As program participants, youth receive individualized education and career counseling, as well as community college credit for some courses. With 1,200 participants and over 30 million weekly listeners, Youth Radio has expanded extensively since its inception in 1992; *Youth in Control* is broadcast via commercial, public, and community-supported radio stations, and is also available on various social media sites, blogs, and iTunes (Soep 2011).

In addition to the radio show and associated media, Youth Radio has several side projects that involve youth in more advanced collaborative technological projects. Perhaps the most impressive of these is the Mobile Action Lab, which pairs students with experts to create locally-relevant apps for mobile devices (Soep, 2011). One app that is currently being created by the Lab, for example, addresses issues of food justice, using crowdsourcing to harvest excess, unused fruit from neighborhood yards and then redistribute the produce to local community members in need (Soep, 2011).

Soep, who is the senior producer and research director at Youth Radio writes that "with the right mix of supportive peers, professional colleagues, and nimble institutions, [young people] can, and do, translate their digital media activities into acts of citizenship and collective work toward public good" (Soep, 2011, p. 11). She argues that digital and mobile tools are increasingly vital for directing the flow of resources and enacting social change. Engaging young people—especially those who would otherwise lack access to digital networked technology—in such types of projects, provides crucial opportunities to take an active part in "democratic life" (Soep, 2011, p. 8). Supportive educational environments that incorporate crucial twenty-first century literacies relevant to youth, and encourage them to engage critically into their lived realities, not only result in relevant learning experiences, but are also likely to render education more equitable for nonmainstream youth.

Beyond Access: Social, Political, Economic, and Cultural Issues

It is clear that as we near the middle of the second decade of the 21ˢᵗ century, the digital divide is more than a simplistic binary issue of access. Providing public infrastructure to improve rates of broadband adoption is an important measure, but only scratches the surface. The issue of digital disparity is more complex and must consider how technology is taken up and used by individuals and communities, and how different forms of inequity intersect. In an article focusing on digital inequality, Halford and Savage (2010) articulate that: "… the transformational potential of ICT requires capacity building to overcome the effects of other, independent, structural sources of disadvantage" (p. 940). The writers point out that recent research underscores the notion that mere access does not afford the same advantages to all users (Halford & Savage, 2010, citing DiMaggio & Hargittai, 2001; Hargittai, 2008). Thus, the digital divide implies not only differential access to digital technology, but also differential use, affordances, advantages, and outcomes. The authors' recommendations for further research involve deconstructing predetermined ideas of social categories and moving toward a more nuanced understanding of how lines of knowledge/power interact with technology within specific contexts (Halford & Savage, 2010).

Similarly, Gilbert (2010) argued that digital and urban inequalities are mutually constituted, and that research into the "digital divide" needs to take into account social complexities, which include relations of power, scale, and an analysis of place (Gilbert, 2010). Focusing on the daily lives of individuals, Gilbert (2010) proposed that future research ought to examine how social networks and digital capacities do or do not develop, and how the developments of those capacities are either

helped or hindered by community resources on a local, regional, national, and global scale (Gilbert, 2010). Recommending that the digital divide needs to be situated within a broader theory of inequality, she is critical of the fact that most research on the digital divide remains merely descriptive, and relies on static notions of racialized/gendered social categories. Gilbert demonstrates that many (quantitative) studies lack the analytic depiction of "the have-nots" as differentiated individuals that possess agency (Gilbert, 2010).

Discerning how to investigate the sociocultural nature of technology, however, is a somewhat ambiguous task. One possible framework for such a task is to use the concept of a *technology identity*, a term proposed by Goode (2010) and defined as a blend of belief systems including (1) beliefs about one's technology skills, (2) beliefs about opportunities and constraints to using technology, (3) beliefs about the importance of technology, and (4) beliefs about one's own motivation to learn more about technology. Using qualitative data from a mixed-methods study conducted at an urban West Coast research university that had a high rate of enrollment of low-income students, Goode (2010) collected data on three students from diverse backgrounds and with varying relationships with technology. Goode (2010) focused specifically on each participants' family practices and experiences, tracing how these impacted the students' technology identities. The findings illustrated that students with positive technology identities tended to thrive, while those with negative technology identities struggled, an imbalance that may impact students' future opportunities (Goode, 2010). Goode also underscored the perpetuation of the digital divide, and the role of universities in reproducing digital inequalities.

Policies to Minimize the Digital Divide and Encourage Digital (Media) Inclusion

The federal government has also acknowledged the digital divide as a troubling issue, and has responded with several large-scale policies intended to counteract disparities in access to broadband internet connections. Around 2008 – 2009, the US government officially recognized that its market-driven approach to broadband service provision, a deregulatory strategy used since 1996, had led to robust investment in the industry, but highly uneven provision of services across the country. To ameliorate this glaring disparity in broadband access nationwide, the American Recovery and Reinvestment Act (ARRA) of 2009 allotted $7.2 billion of stimulus funding to extend broadband Internet access and for broadband projects. These funds were funneled into two programs, the Broadband Technology Opportunities Program (BTOP), to be administered by NTIA, and the Broadband Initiative Program (BIP), to be administered by the Rural Utilities Service (RUS) of the Department of Agriculture (LaRose et al., 2014). BTOP was to target groups that been empirically shown to disproportionately lack access to broadband connections, such as low-income communities and minorities, as well as those who had gotten less attention in discussions of the digital divide, such as senior citizens, children, and the differentially abled (LaRose et al., 2014). In a federal report published in 2014 analyzing the effectiveness of the programs five years after the BTOP and BIP were initiated, researchers concluded that while the BTOP was successful in expanding access to broadband overall, it did *not* succeed in increasing access to for minority groups. Moreover, the report determined that such programs did not effectively increase broadband adoption in rural areas unless public education efforts about its benefits were simultaneously undertaken (LaRose et al. 2014).

The BTOP-funded programs that were most successful, therefore, not only provided the physical infrastructure and economic subsidies for broadband, but also included initiatives to develop the technological skills of participants. San Francisco's Community Living Campaign (CLC), for example, used a grant from BTOP to provide computers with Internet access at senior and community center and housing sites across the city (Jobling 2014). The CLC found that holding intimate, focused, and nonthreatening trainings in multiple languages (English, Spanish, and Cantonese) and exposing participants to online resources that were relevant to their lives were all important aspects of facilitating digital literacy among the seniors. The three most significant features of the CLC's approach seem to be that (1) the center developed their classes based on the needs and desires of that specific community, building sessions around student goals like learning how to video conference with relatives in another county, or how to see photos of grandchildren on Facebook; (2) the trainings were limited in scope, often focusing on a single skill, and allowing for extensive time to practice that skill; and (3) the CLC integrated technology into other activities, such as healthy aging workshops (Jobling, 2014). Clearly, simply providing the technology would not have been enough to induce seniors to become tech-savvy. Instead, the endeavor required a comprehensive approach, one that was contextually specific, accessible, and tailored to the needs of the target community.

Is a Global Digital Underclass Emerging?

Although our discussion about nonmainstream populations' access to, and engagement with, ICT and digital media was focused on the U.S., we found a U.K.-based site, the LSE Media Policy Project: http://www.lse.ac.uk/media%40lse/documents/MPP/LSEMPPBrief3.pdf that focuses on similar issues to the ones we raise throughout this chapter. For example, a media policy brief, titled "The Emergence of a Digital Underclass" by Ellen Helsper underscored important global issues, not only relevant to the U.K. or the E.U., but also to the U.S., and the rest of the global community. While Helsper and other scholars and researchers point out that infrastructure policies and improved access are necessary, they also raise essential questions, such as: Are these policies sufficient to achieve digital inclusion? Are there particular groups of individuals who are likely to be left behind in this race for ever-increasing broadband speeds?

Currently the healthy, young, well-educated professionals with higher incomes are the ones who are more likely to engage with, and contribute to digital media, through high-speed broadband. Those with health problems, the elderly, low income ethnic/racial minority groups, in manual labor occupations or those with few educational qualifications tend to incorporate the Internet into fewer aspects of their everyday lives (even if their use and engagement has increased). They are becoming relatively more disadvantaged compared to mainstream Internet users. In other words, the information rich are made richer while the digital poor become, comparatively, poorer. This group's message is extremely relevant to our chapter; they claim that universal roll-out of high speed broadband will not automatically lead to increased Internet use nor encourage digital critical skills or deeper engagement with ICTs and digital media for all. To conclude our discussion and pose a direction for future work, we end with the question: what can, or should, be done to avoid the entrenchment of a global digital underclass?

REFERENCES

Baker, C. M., Staiano, A. E., & Calvert, S. L. (2011). Digital expression among urban, low-income African American adolescents. *Journal of Black Studies*, *42*(4), 530–547. doi:10.1177/0021934710384994 PMID:21910270

boyd, d. (2012). White flight in networked publics: How race and class shaped American teenage engagement with MySpace and Facebook. In L. Nakamura & P. Chow-White (Eds.), *Race After the Internet*. New York: Routledge,

Croxall, B. (2014). Twitter, Tumblr, and microblogging. In M. Ryan, L. Emerson, B. J. Robertson, & I. Ebrary (Eds.), *The Johns Hopkins Guide to Digital Media*. Baltimore, MD: The John Hopkins University Press.

Duggan, M., & Smith, A. (2013a). *Cell internet use 2013*. Washington, DC: Pew Research Internet Project. Retrieved July 15, 2014 from http://www.pewinternet.org/2013/09/16/cell-internet-use-2013/

Duggan, M., & Smith, A. (2013b). *Social media update 2013*. Washington, DC: Pew Research Internet Project. Retrieved July 10, 2014 from http://www.pewinternet.org/2013/12/30/social-media-update-2013/

Fairlie, R. W., London, R., Rosner, R., Pastor, M., & University of California Santa Cruz. (2006). *Crossing the divide: Immigrant youth and digital disparity in California*. Santa Cruz, CA: Center for Justice, Tolerance, and Community, University of California, Santa Cruz.

Florini, S. (2014). Tweets, tweeps, and signifyin': Communication and cultural performance on "Black twitter". *Television & New Media*, *15*(3), 223–237. doi:10.1177/1527476413480247

Fox, S., & Rainie, L. (2014). *The web at 25 in the U.S.* Washington, DC: Pew Research Internet Project. Retrieved July 20, 2014 from http://www.pewinternet.org/2014/02/27/the-web-at-25-in-the-u-s/

Garcia, O. P. (2011). Gender digital divide: The role of mobile phones among Latina farm workers in southeast Ohio. *Gender, Technology and Development*, *15*(1), 53–74. doi:10.1177/097185241101500103

Goode, J. (2010). The digital identity divide: How technology knowledge impacts college students. *New Media & Society*, *12*(3), 497–513. doi:10.1177/1461444809343560

Hargittai, E. (2012). Open doors, closed spaces? Differentiated adoption of social network sites by user background. In L. Nakamura & P. Chow-White (Eds.), *Race After the Internet* (pp. 223–245). New York: Routledge.

Itō, M. (2009). *Living and Learning with New Media: Summary of Findings from the Digital Youth Project.* Cambridge, MA: MIT Press.

Jackson, L. A., Zhao, Y., Kolenic, A., Fitzgerald, H. E., Harold, R., & Von, E. A. (2008). Race, gender, and information technology use: the new digital divide. *Cyberpsychology & Behavior: The Impact of the Internet, Multimedia, and Virtual Reality on Behavior and Society, 11*(4), 437–442.

Livingston, G. (2010). *Latinos and digital technology, 2010.* Washington, DC: Pew Research Hispanic Trends Project. Retrieved May 31, 2014 from http://www.pewhispanic.org/2011/02/09/latinos-and-digital-technology-2010/

Livingston, G., Parker, K., & Fox, S. (2009). *Latinos online, 2006-2008: Narrowing the gap.* Washington, DC: Pew Research Hispanic Trends Project. Retrieved May 31, 2014 from http://www.pewhispanic.org/2009/12/22/latinos-online-2006-2008- narrowing-the-gap/

Lopez, M. H., Gonzalez-Barrera, A., & Patten, E. (2013). *Closing the digital divide: Latinos and technology adoption.* Washington, DC: Pew Research Hispanic Trends Project. Retrieved May 31, 2014 from http://www.pewhispanic.org/2013/03/07/closing-the-digital-divide-latinos-and-technology-adoption/

Patton, D., Eschmann, R., & Butler, D. (2013). Internet banging: New trends in social media, gang violence, masculinity and hip hop. *Computers in Human Behavior, 29*(5), A54–A59. doi:10.1016/j.chb.2012.12.035

Rubinstein- Ávila, E. (2007). In their words, sounds and images: After-school literacy programs for urban youth. In B. Guzzetti (Ed.), Literacy for a new millennium: Adolescent literacy. Greenwood Publishers.

Rubinstein- Ávila, E. (2011). Exploring (public) Internet use among low-income youth in Brazil, Argentina, and Chile. In D. Alvermann & K. Hinchman (Eds.), Reconceptualizing the literacies in adolescents' lives: Bridging the everyday/academic divide (3rd ed.; pp. 49 -63). Routledge.

Ryan, M., Emerson, L., Robertson, B. J., & Ebrary, I. (2014). *The Johns Hopkins Guide to Digital Media.* Baltimore, MD: The John Hopkins University Press.

Schmier, S. (2014). Popular culture in a digital media studies classroom. *Literacy, 48*(1), 4–39. doi:10.1111/lit.12025

Sims, C. (2014). From differentiated use to differentiating practices: Negotiating legitimate participation and the production of privileged identities. *Information Communication and Society, 17*(6), 670–682. doi:10.1080/1369118X.2013.808363

Smith, A. (2013). *Smartphone Ownership 2013.* Washington, DC: Pew Research Internet Project. Retrieved June 24, 2014 from http://www.pewinternet.org/2013/06/05/smartphone-ownership-2013/

Smith, A. (2014). *African Americans and technology use.* Washington, DC: Pew Research Internet Project. Retrieved May 31, 2014 from http://www.pewinternet.org/2014/01/06/african-americans-and-technology-use/

Smith, R. (2013). *What is Digital Media?* Retrieved December 13, 2014 from http://thecdm.ca/news/faculty-news/2013/10/15/what-is-digital-media

Soep, E. (2011). Youth media goes mobile. *National Civic Review*, *100*(3), 8–11. doi:10.1002/ncr.20073

Tripp, L. M. (2011). "The computer is not for you to be looking around, it is for Schoolwork": Challenges for digital inclusion as Latino immigrant families negotiate children's access to the internet. *New Media & Society*, *13*(4), 552–567. doi:10.1177/1461444810375293

Tripp, L. M., & Herr-Stephenson, R. (2009). Making access meaningful: Latino young people using digital media at home and at school. *Journal of Computer-Mediated Communication*, *14*(4), 1190–1207. doi:10.1111/j.1083-6101.2009.01486.x

Turner, K. C. N. (2012). Multimodal Hip Hop Productions as Media Literacies. *The Educational Forum*, *76*(4), 497–509. doi:10.1080/00131725.2012.708617

U.S. Census Bureau. (2012). *Computer and internet access in the United States*. Retrieved from https://www.census.gov/hhes/computer/publications/2012.html

Vickery, J. R. (2014). The role of after-school digital media clubs in closing participation gaps and expanding social networks. *Equity & Excellence in Education*, *47*(1), 78–95. doi:10.1080/10665684.2013.866870

Warschauer, M., & Matuchniak, T. (2010). New technology and digital worlds: Analyzing evidence of equity in access, use, and outcomes. *Review of Research in Education*, *34*(1), 179–225. doi:10.3102/0091732X09349791

Zickuhr, K., & Smith, A. (2012). *Digital differences*. Washington, DC: Pew Research Internet Project. Retrieved May 31, 2014 from http://www.pewinternet.org/2012/04/13/digital-differences/

Zickuhr, Z. (2013). *Who's not online and why*. Washington, DC: Pew Research Internet Project. Retrieved July 6, 2014 from http://www.pewinternet.org/2013/09/25/whos-not-online-and-why/

KEY TERMS AND DEFINITIONS

Cell-Mostly Users: Internet users who connect primarily or only through their cellphones. Cell-mostly users tend to be younger and low-income.

Digital Underclass: Vulnerable populations who are infrequent (or non) Internet users. Despite improvement in infrastructure policy and greater access, digital inclusion is not likely to include all groups, and even create an additional barrier to social mobility.

Homophily: The idea that similarity leads to connectivity. In other words, the tendency of individuals to bond with each other who are similar in regards to social factors such as: age, class, ethnicity, gender, and/or organizational roles.

New Media Ecology: The study of complex communication technologies and systems as cultural environments.

Nonmainstream Populations: Language or ethnic groups that are not a part of the white, abled, middle class population in power.

Racialized (Online) Identities: Are often conveyed actively by members of minoritized groups, from a position of social and political resistance to their marginalization by mainstream society.

'Second' Digital Divide: White the initial (first) digital divide revealed a gap between the "haves and the have nots" (those who had access to Internet connectivity and those who did not, the 'second' reveals a gap between those with more or less ICT skills.

Social Proprioception: Awareness of the spatial positioning of a group in order to organize/coordinate themselves.

Chapter 23
The Role of Mobile Learning in Promoting Literacy and Human Rights for Women and Girls

Judith M. Dunkerly-Bean
Old Dominion University, USA

Helen Crompton
Old Dominion University, USA

ABSTRACT

In this chapter the authors review the fairly recent advances in combating illiteracy around the globe through the use of e-readers and mobile phones most recently in the Worldreader program and the United Nations Educational Scientific and Cultural Organization (UNESCO) mobile phone reading initiatives. Situated in human rights and utilizing the lens of transnational feminist discourse which addresses globalization and the hegemonic, monolithic portrayals of "third world" women as passive and in need of the global North's intervention, the authors explore the ways in which the use of digital media provides increased access to books, and other texts and applications in both English and native languages for people in developing countries. However, while advances in combating illiteracy through the use of e-readers, mobile phones and other mobile learning initiatives are promising, the tensions and power imbalances of digital literacies, which resources are available by whom, for whom and why, must also be examined.

INTRODUCTION

Literacy is a human right, a tool of personal empowerment through expression as well as a means to social, cultural and human development. Yet the nature and use of literacy, for whom, under which circumstances and for what purposes is a contentious question that depends greatly on the social views, cultural capital, politics, and temporality of both its teachers, students and the communities of discourse in which they participate (Foucault, 1972;Gee, 1996)). In short, who is considered literate and what literac(ies) are considered to be worth knowing are dependent

DOI: 10.4018/978-1-4666-8310-5.ch023

on dominant societal, and in an age of globalization, transnational constructs.. Carl Kaestle (1991) points to the inherently social and political aspects of literacy in stating,

Literacy is discriminatory with regard to both access and content. Problems of discrimination are not resolved just because access is achieved; there is a cultural price tag to literacy. Thus, whether literacy is liberating or constraining depends in part whether it is used as an instrument of conformity or creativity. (p. 30)

That is to say that the mere access to literacy does not guarantee that access to the liberatory potential of literacy is achieved as well. Rather, access is a necessary but not sufficient condition for liberation.

In discussing the plurality of literacy and the nature of being literate, the United Nations Educational, Scientific and Cultural Organization (UNESCO) posits, "the way literacy is defined influences the goals and strategies adopted and the programs designed by policy makers as well as the teaching and learning methodologies curricula, and materials employed by practitioners. Its definition also determines how progress or achievements in overcoming illiteracy will be monitored or assessed" (UNESCO, 2004, p. 12). According to recent international data compiled by UNESCO, there are currently 773.5 million adults globally who are functionally illiterate. Of that number, 63.8% are women. 123.2 million children are illiterate, 61/3% of them are girls. The lowest literacy rates worldwide are found in Sub-Saharan Africa and in South and West Asia (United Nations Educational, Scientific and Cultural Organization [UNESCO], 2013). The significance of these numbers to the struggle for the recognition of human rights for women cannot be ignored (Kelleher, 2014). Addressing global illiteracy, especially for women and girls

is a necessary, but not sufficient component in recognizing the human rights, especially in regard to the education of all.

In this chapter we review the advances in combating illiteracy around the globe through the use of mobile learning initiatives such as e-readers and mobile phones, most recently in the *Worldreader* program as well as in UNESCO's mobile reading initiatives (West & Chew, 2014). We utilize the lens of transnational feminist discourse (Hesford & Kozol, 2005; Swarr & Nagar, 2010) that addresses the effects of globalization and the hegemonic and monolithic portrayals of "third world" women as passive and in need of the global North's intervention. Additionally, while advances in combating illiteracy through the use of e-readers and other mobile devices are promising, the tensions and power imbalances of digital literacies, especially in developing countries must also be examined. Intrinsic to this examination is the recognition of the multifaceted interconnections between global flows, particularly of information and ideas, when digital media "travel" from one locale to another, far removed not only in place but in resources and power as well.

BACKGROUND

Thus, to begin, we situate this review in the affordances and limitations of human rights discourse, especially as it relates to women and girls. Building upon the themes and tensions particular to the human rights discourse, we discuss the ways in which transnational feminisms speak to the effect of globalization and the contexts of both the local and the global, as well as the public and private sphere. Having established the lens in which we situate digital media in this review of the literature, we explore mobile learning initiatives as sites where the promise of digital media may have to attend to concerns around the "reproduction of gender, class and racial inequality" (Blackmore, 2005; p. 244) even as they strive for global literacy.

Human Rights

The notion of human rights recognized today was established with the United Nation's *Universal Declaration of Human Rights* (UDHR) in 1948 written in the aftermath of the Second World War. Although the primary intent of the document was to prevent a recurrence of the human rights travesties that occurred during WWII, the UDHR also provided for education as a human right stating in Article 26:

(1) Everyone has the right to education. Education shall be free, at least in the elementary and fundamental stages. Elementary education shall be compulsory. Technical and professional education shall be made generally available and higher education shall be equally accessible to all on the basis of merit.

(2) Education shall be directed to the full development of the human personality and to the strengthening of respect for human rights and fundamental freedoms. It shall promote understanding, tolerance and friendship among all nations, racial or religious groups, and shall further the activities of the United Nations for the maintenance of peace.

(3) Parents have a prior right to choose the kind of education that shall be given to their children. (United Nations, resolution 217A [III], 1948)

As Fionnuala Waldron (2010) elaborates, these documents provide a global framework for providing education for all, and just as importantly, education for the purpose of creating and protecting a more just global citizenry.

In this age of globalization, where identities are both global, local and contested spaces within each, (Beck, 2010, 2002, p. 36; see also Apple, Kenway, Singh, 2005), the ways in which

literacies are constructed, created and by whom, become increasingly crucial. Yet, to be literate and have access to literacy is a necessary, but not a sufficient condition for individual, societal, and indeed, global betterment and advancement. For literacy to fulfill its promise also requires change in political and social structures that underlie and perpetuate inequality; it must be constructed as a right (Bhola, 2008). As Katerina Tomasveski, the late Special Rapporteur to the United Nation argued:

The right to an education is a bridge to all human rights: education is indispensible for effective political participation and for enabling individuals to sustain themselves; it is the key to preserving languages and religions; it is the foundation for eliminating discrimination. It is the key to unlocking all other human rights (Tomaseveski, 2003, p. 172).

In contextualizing literacy instruction, especially in the global context, we place a human rights-based approach to literacy education if not on a continuum with critical pedagogy and social justice, then certainly from a similar lineage of ideals. However, there is a distinct difference between the auspices of critical pedagogy and a human rights based approach: while critical pedagogy espouses similar ideals and resulting practices (i.e. praxis, social justice, etc,) they remain contextualized to a particular nation-state. A human rights based approach situates education in a geo-political framework that claims literacy as indivisible from other *universal* human rights including the social, cultural, civil & political (UNESCO/UNICEF, 2007).

However, despite the laudable goals espoused within the human rights education discourse, it is not without critique especially around issues of access, inclusion and equality for both men and women, boys and girls. We turn now to the ways in which transnational feminism speaks to the effects of globalization and to some scholar's critiques of the public/private, political/cultural aspects of human rights-based discourse in education, in general and literacy in particular.

Globalization and Transnational Feminism

Globalization may be characterized by the extensive movement or flow of information, ideas, images, capital, and people across increasingly permeable political borders due to economic and technological change (Castells, 1996; Luke, 2002). The speed, durability, flexibility and mutability of these transnational flows and networks affect almost every aspect of local and global life, *albeit*, unevenly to the effect that the global and the local are not experienced as polarities, but rather as mutually influencing spaces (Beck, 2002; Harper & Dunkerly, 2010).

Transnational feminism has emerged largely as a response to international and global feminism that has been critiqued as "rigidly adhering to nation-state borders and ignoring and paying inadequate attention to the effects of globalization" in the former, and for "prioritizing northern feminist agendas…and for homogenizing women's struggles for sociopolitical justice, especially in colonial and neocolonial contexts" (Nagar & Swarr, 2010, p. 4). In other words, transnational feminism speaks to the hegemonic and monolithic portrayal of "Third World women" as passive victims and instead seeks to recast and highlight their activism and agency in such a way that transnational solidarity and collaborations can be reached. As Nayereh Tohidi (2005) explains," the concept of transnational feminism offers the desirability and possibility of a political solidarity of feminists across the globe that transcends class, race, sexuality and national boundaries" (Tohidi, 2005, p. 5)

Thus, transnational feminism is concerned with "the interdependence of the global and the local – how each is implicated in the other – and how the "local, private and domestic are constituted

in relation to global systems and conversely, how such systems must be read for their particular locational inflection" (Hesford & Kozol, 2005, p. 15). However, it is in the realm of particular locational inflection as well as in the interplay of local/global and the public/private sphere in human rights discourse, especially around education, that transnational feminists critiques systems that may perpetuate inequality and continue to portray women in a monolithic manner. We turn now to those critiques surrounding human rights discourse as well as to the corporatization of non-governmental agencies (NGO's) and the "NGOization" of development in the Third World.

Transnational Feminist Critique of Human Rights Discourse

Despite the overarching goals of human rights that would appear on the surface to be without reproof, Blackmore (2005) argues that the human rights movement has all too often focused on political and civic rights that largely impact men in the public sphere and less on rights that most impact women in the economic, social and cultural spheres such as those that relate to education, childcare and domestic violence. As she contends:

Education policy discourses, for example, distinguish the human *right* to a basic education, but rarely calls upon the right to an "inclusive" education, one that is about empowerment, that recognizes girls' and women's needs as well as interests. The latter would have as a fundamental proposition of a more inclusive human rights discourse the development of individual agency that would be about participation, inclusive curriculums, as well as just outcomes, essential tenets of education for democratic citizenship. But there is little challenge within current human rights discourses to change the dispositions of education away from social selection and the reproduction of gender, class and racial inequality. The dominant view is that access to education means equality (p. 244).

In recognizing the importance of literacy acquisition in recognizing both private/public sphere human rights, the development of a literate female global population is imperative in creating a space for women and girls to move limited definitions of citizenship and rights into the discourse of a global society (Dunkerly & Harper, 2013). Yet, paradoxically, it is in that space of reform and development that women become a "project" and their literacy an "objective" that negates their agency and instead positions them as in need of the Global North's salvation.

Transnational Feminist Critique of Non-Governmental Organizations (NGOs)

Since the 1980's, non-governmental agencies have become one of the primary vehicles though which funding for development, including mobile learning initiatives are delivered (Peake & De Souza, 2010). Indeed, organizations such as the *United Nations Foundation*, a public charity that supports United Nation's efforts has invested and or raised over 1.5 billion dollars over the past decade, delivered to the UN and UN partners including NGO affiliates (The United Nations Foundation website, n.d.). Although there is considerable diversity among NGOs, their developers and funding sources, the extent to which they have also become corporatized and act as extensions of the state in regard to labor and resources is well documented (Farrington, Bebbington, Wellard, & Lewis, 1993). Additionally, the role of donors in influencing the direction, meaning and legitimacy of the organization without being "on the ground" is also of concern, especially in regard to local agency vs. NGO objectives (Hilhorst, 2003). As the *Sangtin Writers* (a collective of women researchers and activists in India) ask: "What does it mean when NGOs or movements begin to determine for a village which issues it should mobilize around and which people should it work with? Whose village?

Whose issues? Whose empowerment? And who is authorized to claim credit for that empowerment? (Reena, Nagar, Singh, & Surbala, 2010, p. 134).

Another issue is raised by Linda Peake and Karen de Souza, who voice concerns about the corporatization of NGOs and the attendant practices of establishing benchmarks, outcomes and plans for sustainable development. While these and other aspects are certainly a necessary component of organizational structure, they "at the same time, neatly package it up into projects that deal, for example with "women" or other apparently discrete aspects of development for disconnected periods of time (Peake & De Souza, 2010, p. 110).

Ultimately, however, the most essential concern of transnational feminism in regard to the work of some NGOs comes down to the collapsing of women's issues into singular, simplistic and monolithic categories. The *Sangtin Writers* offer a succinct and passionate argument against this:

When women's issues are collapsed into a pre-designated gender and a pre-marked body, and "feminist activism" is gathered and piled into a predetermined list of issues and when a complex political and cultural economy at local and global scales becomes associated with such a classification, feminism becomes an institutionalized structure, a bureaucracy, and a commerce that feeds the status quo. A compartmentalization of poverty and violence along the lines of gender helps sustain the existing caste-and class- based structures of privilege and deprivation (Reena et al., 2010, p. 140).

As we turn now to a review of the extant literature, we do so through the lens of transnational feminisms and against the backdrop of historical human rights efforts. Throughout this review, we will utilize that lens to interrogate local v. global voice, the construction of womanhood and girlhood, the proliferation of the Global North's perspective at the possible expense of local knowledge; and the ways in which technology, while indeed liberating in some regards, may hold the potential for inadvertent hegemony as well.

OVERVIEW OF CURRENT RESEARCH

In reviewing the uses of digital media in promoting the human rights of women and girls through increased literacy, we begin with an overview of the research conducted around the utilization of mobile phones both in formal education and in personal use as a promising conduit for recognizing international literacy goals, most notable those of UNESCO's *Education for All* initiative that relate to mobile learning, namely:

- Improving levels of adult and youth literacy: how mobile technologies can support literacy development and increase reading opportunities.
- Improving the quality of education: How mobile technologies can support teachers and their professional development.
- Achieving gender parity and equality in education: how mobile technologies can support equal access to and achievement in basic education of good quality for all, in particular for women and girls.

While the use of either personally owned, or organization distributed, mobile phones to provide access to books of all varieties has been in existence for a few years, the utilization of electronic readers (e-readers) is a bit more recent. *WorldReader* is one such program, and is the largest in global reach and influence to date. Given that the impetus for e-reader initiative build from research around utilizing mobile phones for literacy access and learning, we begin by offering an overview of mobile learning in general and then discussing

the advances in mobile reading globally in particular. We then turn to developments in utilizing e-readers in formal school settings in developing countries. While there is not a substantial body of research on the use of digital media and the use of personal electronic devices such as mobile phones and e-readers in promoting literacy and human rights for women and girls, what exists offers a hint both tantalizing and cautionary of what may be possible in the near future.

Mobile Learning

Mobile devices can now be used to provide learning to those who have been previously unable to access traditional learning opportunities for reasons of location, finance, disability, or infrastructure. In 1972, Kay created a concept model of the Dynabook, the first handheld multimedia computer intended for learning that could be used outside the typical constraints of the classroom. Kay described some of the functions of this portable computer:

Imagine having your own self-contained knowledge manipulator in a portable package the size and shape of an ordinary notebook. Suppose it had enough power to outrace your senses of sight and hearing, enough capacity to store for later retrieval thousands of page-equivalents of reference materials, poems, letters, recipes, records, drawings, animations, musical scores, waveforms, dynamic simulations, and anything else you would like to remember and change. (Kay & Goldberg, 1977/2001, p. 167)

From the initial conception of the Dynabook, mobile devices were soon developed that have extended the capabilities described by Kay & Goldberg. Over a relatively short period of time, mobile learning has changed the learning landscape. In this section, a brief overview of recent history presents the achievements of the research community and global agencies, such as UNESCO, USAID, and the World Bank, in reviewing, articulating, and promoting mobile learning across the globe.

Mobile Learning Initiatives: From 2003

In 2003, there were a number of mobile learning initiatives taking place in countries across the globe. These research initiatives typically used a basic mobile phone that had phone and SMS capabilities. Many of these researchers were responding to the call to provide an education to children in developing nations. At the United Nations Millennium Summit in 2000, development goals were written and signed by 189 heads of state from across the world. From those eight goals, one was to provide primary schooling for all children by 2015. In 2000, this was a difficult target, as there was typically very little to no access to basic schooling for many children in places. For example, four out of every ten primary-aged children in the Sub-Sahara do not attend school (UNESCO, 2011). Information Communication Technology (ICT) resources have not always been available to support training and encourage schooling despite the advocacy efforts from the Department for International Development UK, UNESCO and the World Bank.

There is a paucity of trained teachers and resources in many rural locations to provide education to the students. In 2003, a *Text 2 Teaching* program was funded by Nokia. This program was intended to bring teaching resources to provide education to poor families in rural locations with a low population density. These areas lack even the basic Internet access to have access to educational resources. The main component of the program is to provide the teachers with access to videos that can be downloaded at high speeds using the cellular network. From the basic mobile phones provided to the teachers, these videos, of expert teachers explaining mathematics, science, and

English concepts, could be broadcast on large screens for the students to watch. The initiative started in the Philippines but since has expanded to India, Chile, Nigeria, and Columbia.

To better understand how technology can provide better access and quality to teacher education in sub-Saharan Africa, *Deep Impact: An investigation of the use of information and communication technologies* (Leach, 2005) was conducted in Bangladesh. Similar to the *Text 2 Teaching* program, teachers were provided with basic mobile phones. The teachers used these to connect with a tutor and peers to share photos and short videos of teaching practice. The researchers reported that the use of mobile phones provided benefit to the teachers through the facilitation of contextualized, constructive, situated, and collaborative learning enabled by the use of the mobile devices.

Mobile Learning Initiatives: 2011-2014

The mobile learning work of global agencies has increased greatly since 2011 and those efforts include: a) drawing together mobile learning researchers and scholars to better understand what we know about mobile learning and how it can be used to extend and enhance learning and providing opportunities to access appropriate learning around the globe, and b) produce publications to share what is known about mobile learning with policy makers, educational leaders, and other stakeholders. The following table provides some examples of the work of global agencies since January 2011 (see Table 1).

Since 2000, there has been a rise in the number of mobile learning implementations connected with the concomitant emergence of new devices. This is not to say that cutting edge technologies are ubiquitous in these developing countries; but that the speed of new technological devices has driven down the cost of the past generation technologies making devices such as the basic mobile phone

Table 1. Global mobile learning initiatives

Year	Agency	Action
Feb. 2011		World Mobile Congress (held annually)
Aug. 2011	USAID	The first m4Ed4Dev symposium in Washington DC
Nov. 2011	World Innovation Summit for Education	Debate focused on mobiles, education and the hard-to-reach
Dec. 2011	UNESCO	The First Mobile Learning Week
2011	World Bank	eTransform Africa
2012	World Economic Forum	Accelerating the Adoption of Mobile learning: A call for collective and collaborative Action
2012	GSMA	Report on Transforming learning through mEducation
Mar. 2012	UNESCO hosted by CoSN	International Symposium
Early 2012	UNESCO	Funded by Nokia commissioned regional reviews to capture the global state of mobile learning.
Sept. 2012	USAID	mEducation Alliance Symposium
Feb. 2013	UNESCO & USAID	Symposium focused on Education for All goals related to mobile learning- mobiles for literacy
2013	UNESCO	UNESCO Policy Guidelines
2013	UNESCO	Publication on literacy for women and girls
2013	UNESCO	Publication on youth workforce development
2013	UNESCO	Publication on literacy

Table adapted from Crompton, H. (in press). The global mobile story so far. *In Mobiles for lifelong learning & skills development*. United Nations International Telecommunications Union (ITU). Geneva, Switzerland.

affordable and accessible in many developing countries. In addition, mobile network operators have been competing to provide connectivity to the global south, resulting in reduced prices. These changes have seen a rise of a new technological infrastructure in many developing countries.

Mobile Learning Initiatives to Support Women and Girls

In the past decade, a number of researchers have responded to calls for gender equilibrium, to design mobile learning initiatives to support women and girls. From a review of published information and data, it appears that these initiatives have focused on empowering women and girls by providing information about health, finance, and general education. This section provides the reader with examples of efforts in these areas.

Health

In many developing countries, crucial healthcare issues are often addressed by family members and the local community who do not have the training or knowledge to ensure the well-being of the individuals. In Timor-Leste, pregnancy is a life or death reality with many women and babies dying in the first few hours or days after the birth. In an effort to support the women in this region, Health Alliance International (HAI), a US based NGO, won a USAID grant to connect women with midwives. The team created an internet-based program to send out bi- weekly SMS messages to the pregnant women with information and advice on postpartum and newborn care. The messages were sent in Tetun; the widely spoken language in that area. *Liga Inan* (connecting mothers in Tetun) or *Mobile Moms*, is a four year initiative from 2011 (see http://www.healthallianceinter-national.org/blog/post/mobile-moms-liga-inan/ for more information)

MomConnect is a similar mobile learning initiative in South Africa. Supported by UNICEF Kwazulu-Natal Department of Health connect pregnant women and healthcare workers via SMS. However, unlike the women in Timor-Leste, these women can get access to healthcare. The messages help the women keep track of appointments and reminders to visit the clinics for regular check-ups (see http://www.unicef.org/southafrica/media_14102.html)

Sexual and reproductive health is essential to the wellbeing of a person and especially for young people. However, gaining access to accurate information can be difficult with many relying on peer information, due to cultural/social stigma or taboos. *Learning about Living* (LaL) is a OneWorld initiative that provides information about sexual and reproductive health and rights (www.oneworld.org) Young people may access information and a question and answer service via SMS and social media platforms (e.g. Facebook). LaL was launched in 2007 in Nigeria and is now implemented in Senegal, Morocco, Mali, Egypt, and Cambodia

Financial

New media is providing an opportunity for women and girls to compete with their male counterparts. By providing information to young girls they can make informed choices about their futures and pursue aspirations beyond a final goal of marriage. Launched in 2009, *Nokia Life* offers information and educational opportunities to people in China, India, Indonesia, and Nigeria. This initiative gives guidance to women who are interested in starting a small business and become economically active. The information is provided in 18 languages and bespoke to the culture and needs of women living in particular communities.

In Kenya, the *Open Kenya Initiative* offers open educational resources to enable girls to solve issues in their communities. These girls are also provided with a peer mentor to help guide them in achieving these goals. In South Africa, *ShetheGeek* is an initiative funded by ITU that is a blog-based community of women who seek to empower women through technology. Girls are also being encouraged to gain financially from exploiting new media. In Uganda, *GirlGeek-Kampala* was founded in 2012 by a small group of technology leaders. Women in Uganda feel that they are discouraged from entering into computer science with the lack of scholarship and female mentors contributing to a gender gap (Ochwa-Echel, 2011). *GirlGeekKampala* encourage the culture of programming and coding among female university students.

General Education

Mobile learning initiatives have been introduced around the globe to support women and girls in learning general educational concepts, such as literacy and mathematics.

Aligned to Education for All goals, UNESCO started a project to answer pertinent questions on how mobile learning can be used to appropriately and effectively support women and girls in education. This initiative was designed to answer three questions: 1) How should effective mobile learning initiatives for women and girls be designed? 2) How can they be created in gender-sensitive and sustainable ways? and 3) What barriers need to be addressed and what pre-conditions need to be in place for successful implementation?

The *Mobile Literacy Program* was a one-year program specifically targeted at improving the literacy skills of women living in villages in rural Afghanistan. Afghanistan has the lowest literacy rates in the world with an estimated 43.1% of men and just 12.6% of women being considered literate. After mobile phone use rose from 1% to over 18 million active mobile phone users in 2012, this telecommunications infrastructure was used to provide access to the under-served population in Afghanistan. This initiative used a combination of classes and literacy tasks using mobile phones. The participants received assignments texted to their phones that involved topics relevant to the daily lives of the women in the group. This helped the learners understand that literacy was a practical skill for everyday life.

UNESCO also implemented a *Mobile-Based Post Literacy Program* in Pakistan in 2009. Gender disparity in literacy is high in Pakistan with 69% of males and 45% of females over 15 years of age literate (see http://www.pbs.gov.pk/content/pakistan-social-and-living-standards-measurement (Pakistan Bureau of Statistics, 2012-2013). The disparity was high in urban populations but the greatest difference was in the rural population.

The literacy program has two stages. In the first stage, women attend a basic literacy course with face-to-face training on how to write the alphabet and to read with emphasis on phonics. In the second stage, the women are given a mobile phone to begin a two-month mobile-based literacy program. The women receive SMS messages six to eight times per day on topics including Islamic teaching, numeracy, health, general knowledge, local government, beauty tips, food recipes, and jokes. As the messages are received, the women read the messages, practice writing the messages, and respond to questions.

Lower income, rural children were targeted in a literacy initiative in North India. In this program, children who attended an after school program were each given a cellphone with English Language Learning games pre-loaded. The mobile devices were loaned to the children for five months to support language learning with games (Kam, Kumar, et al, 2009). Gaming was also the focus of *M4Girls*, a project to bridge the gap between boys and girls mathematical competencies in underserved communities in South Africa

(Zelezny-Green, 2013). Girls were given mobile phones with curriculum aligned mathematical content in games and videos to boost achievement.

Developing a sense of community when learning is important for women as they have a space to network, talk and be heard, and listen to others (Fletcher, 1999). However, developing learning communities can be difficult due to cultural and location restraints. Mobile devices can provide opportunities to overcome these barriers and empower women and girls. The *Pink Phone Project* in Cambodia is an initiative to train women leaders to use mobile devices to share ideas, resources, and information. Since 2010, *Oxfam Cambodia and Women for Prosperity*, a local NGO, have taken the Pink Phone Project to women in three provinces-Kratie, Kampong Thom, and Stung Treng. In these locations, men are more likely to have mobile phones than women and domestic violence is common. This initiative provides mobile phones to women and these phones are painted bright pink to discourage men from using them (see http://policy-practice.oxfam.org.uk/blog/2012/03/pink-telephones-in-cambodia).

Mobile Reading

Although the Internet and other mobile learning advances have provided a greater number of people with access to more information in recent times, than in all of the physical libraries ever in existence there still remain vast populations that lack connectivity and access to the internet and to the necessary technology and computers need to access it. Despite the seemingly ubiquitous presence of the Internet, only 40 percent of the world's population is online and in developing countries 16 percent fewer women than men use the Internet (ITU, 2013). Moreover, the discrepancy and inequality in access is as disturbing as it is predictable. Currently in Africa only 7 per cent of households are connected to the Internet, compared with 77 per cent in Europe (West &

Chew, 2014). Thus, millions remain functionally isolated from textual resources that are foundational to education, employment and engagement in the globalized world.

Given the unequal and indeed, in some locales, impractical access to computers and the Internet, mobile phones have become one of the primary means of accessing text when books and libraries are either non-existent or too expensive to stock and maintain. The difference in access to traditional libraries globally depicts the rather dismal nature of equality in access: In the United Kingdom for example, the ratio of libraries to population is 1:15,000 citizens. In Nigeria, that ratio is 1: 1, 350,000 (UNESCO, 2013). However, recent data from the United Nations indicate that of the an estimated global population of 7 billion, over 6 billion people now have access to a working mobile phone. For the sake of comparison, 4.5 billion people have access to a toilet (UNESCO, 2013). In order to capitalize on the existence of even basic mobile phone ownership and usage, corporations such as Nokia have partnered with UNESCO and the non-profit organization World Reader to utilize a mobile reading app to provide access to text for whom print based books are inaccessible. *Worldreader Mobile* (WRM) is an application that allows people to access books and stories from a wide variety of mobile phones, including inexpensive feature phones. In order to determine the effectiveness of mobile reading in developing areas, UNESCO conducted a large survey of mobile reader users to determine who was reading, what they were reading and how the users of mobile reading felt about the experience of reading on mobile device. On average, WRM had 334,000 active users per month. In order to utilize WRM, users download the free application, which is stored in the memory of the phone. It is important to note, that while *Worldreader* Mobile (WRM) provides *access* to over 6,000 digital titles, mobile data connection and the resulting expense

is required of the user. Although the majority of the titles available through the app are free, most of the books are not downloadable, nor can they be read offline.

The study conducted by UNESCO in partnership with *Worldreader* and Nokia was designed as an "in-app" survey with the following criteria: low literacy rates for adults and youth, and a minimum of 6,000 established *Worldreader* users per month. Seven countries were selected for participation based on those criteria: Ethiopia, Ghana, India, Kenya, Nigeria, Pakistan and Zimbabwe. Although Kenya and Zimbabwe have distinctly lower adult illiteracy rates (13% and 8% respectively, other countries fare much worse. In Ethiopia, for example, the adult illiteracy rate is over 60 percent for the total population and over 70 percent for women; in Pakistan the illiteracy rate is 45 percent for all adults and 60 percent for women. (UNESCO, 2013). Overall, the average illiteracy rates for adults in the countries included in this study are 34 percent or approximately one third of the total population (see Figure 1).

Perhaps not surprisingly, the illiteracy rates for youth in the countries surveyed are similar to those of the adults. Again, Kenya and Zimbabwe have youth illiteracy rates far below the averages found in the other nations surveyed, while Ethiopia has the greatest percentage of illiterate youth at approximately 45%. Overall, the average youth illiteracy rate for all seven countries included in the study is 20 percent, or one-fifth of the population. The rates for each country included are summarized in Figure 2.

In order to conduct the survey, users were issued an invitation that appeared on their mobile device and their reading frequency was tracked by monitoring usage. 4,333 readers in the seven countries completed the survey and were monitored. Of those, 3,332 were men and 1,001 were women. Readers of both genders were categorized in the following way:

Figure 1. Adult illiteracy rates in developing countries

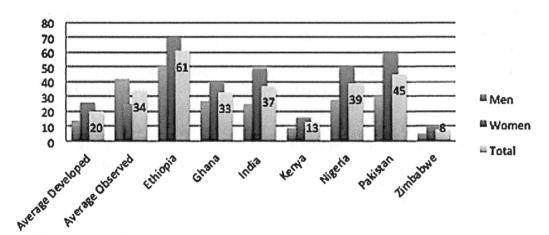

Figure 2. Youth illiteracy rates in developing countries

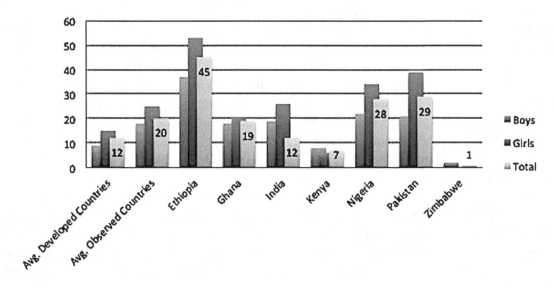

- Occasional Readers – read 2–4 times per month
- Frequent Readers – read 5–20 times per month
- Habitual Readers – read 21–40 times per month
- Power Readers – read more than 40 times per month

The researchers tracked usage in order to compare actual time spent reading with self-reported attitudes and perceptions towards mobile reading. Following the survey, researchers attempted to conduct qualitative follow-up phone interviews with those designated as frequent readers, however, the response rate was poor and resulted in only a total of seventeen interviews. A small incentive in the form of mobile credit equal to US $0.50 was offered to those completing the survey, which could be used to purchase books. Despite the limitations of only including readers using the *Worldreader* mobile app, the results of the study present credible data in assessing the demographics of users, the frequency with which they engage in mobile reading and their attitudes towards reading on mobile devices.

Mobile Reader Demographics

In general, mobile reading demographics closely mirrored mobile phone ownership in the countries represented in the study. On average, there are approximately three male mobile readers for every female. This gender difference is narrowest in Nigeria and Zimbabwe with the ratio of two male readers for every female, while in Ethiopia and India the gap is the widest at nine males for every female. However, women used mobile phones for reading more frequently and for more diverse reasons than did men. This is encouraging, as it highlights the potential of mobile reading to provide women and girls with greater opportunities for literacy and for civic participation. Indeed, the gender balance shifts to a female majority across countries when viewing reading activity. Among the top 2,000 active readers, over 59 percent are female; among the top 1,000 active readers, 72 percent are female; and among the top 100 active readers, 80 percent are female. As West and Chew (2014) explain:

On average, women spent 207 minutes per month reading on their mobile phones during the three-month period of the study. Men, by contrast, read about 33 minutes per month. Women also tended to read more frequently and for longer periods at a time. During the study period, men read 3 to 4 times a month for around 10 minutes each time, while women read around 11 times per month for about 19 minutes each time. In terms of hours read per month, women performed 66 per cent of the total reading completed during the study period, despite the fact that they only constitute 23 percent of the total readers (p.30).

In addition to gender differences, this study also captured difference in age and educational attain-

ment. Perhaps not surprisingly, the participants in this study tended to have achieved a higher level of education than the respective national average – 24% of respondents reported having a bachelor's degree of higher. In comparison, the average for higher education degrees across nations involved was 8.7%. Surprisingly though, reading time diminished for those who had obtained a bachelor's degree in comparison to those still in secondary (high) school. The researchers posit that this may be due to young people studying for entrance exams for bachelor education programs therefore accessing greater amounts of text for longer periods of time). A similar pattern was observed in those readers who were in or preparing for master's or doctoral programs. An interesting theory posed by the researchers is that as higher education is obtained, printed books and other texts are more accessible and digital reading is used less.

These finding also align with findings related to the age of the readers in question. Across and within countries, users of digital reading were typically young. The average age of participants in this study was 24. Over 90 percent of the survey respondents were under the age of 35, and two-thirds of respondents were under 24 years old. Across all countries, fewer than 1 in 10 mobile respondents were over the age of 35 (West & Chew, 2014). These findings align with the illiteracy rates for adults and youth discussed earlier. It would stand to reason that with lower illiteracy rates, and a higher likelihood of having and using a mobile phone for a variety of reasons, younger people would be more likely to utilize their phones for the purpose of reading.

Attitudes Towards and Purposes for Mobile Reading

Generally speaking, the results from this study indicated that people enjoyed reading on their mobile phones, with those that reported a greater affinity for reading in general, having the value of reading reinforced. For those who reported not caring for reading traditional text, the results indicated a better attitude towards reading on a mobile phone. This is another encouraging finding from this study in regard to greater self-efficacy in reading, especially in terms of promoting literacy for women and girls. Although fewer women owned mobile phones, a greater percentage of women (65%) than men (45%) reported that they enjoyed reading in general and 69% of women reported enjoying reading more on a mobile device than in traditional print-based books. While not within the scope of the study, the authors do posit that the significant difference in reading on mobile devices between men and women may be cultural and stem from issues regarding the education and literacy of women and girls:

It is possible that these gender differences can be attributed, at least in part, to specific cultural factors that make mobile reading particularly appealing to women. In countries and communities where female education is still a contentious subject, reading on mobile phones may be more socially acceptable than reading physical books, since it appears no different from reading text messages, and other people cannot see the titles of the books (West & Chew, 2013, p. 46).

In addition to the guise of other activities that may be more socially acceptable than reading, mobile phones as conduits of information may also provide women and girls with access to texts that may not be deemed appropriate by family and community members, such as those addressing sexuality, reproductive issues, or other health related concerns.

In examining respondents' purposes for reading as found in the study, some surprising trends emerge. The most notable is the use of mobile phones to access books to read to children. Over 33% of those surveyed said that they used their mobile phones to read to their children, and 34% said that they would if more children's books were available. The surprise here is that the majority of these respondents were men. While that figure

may be linked to the overall ownership of mobile phones, it is distinct contrast to perceived gender roles and responsibilities towards child rearing. In any case, the use of mobile phones as a means of promoting early literacy in developing countries cannot be overlooked and is one area for further research.

While individuals of both genders utilized their mobile readers for a variety of purposes across many genres, trends in search terms and usage indicate that readers are most frequently searching for and reading romance novels, textbooks, short stories, global bestsellers, health information, career advice, religious materials most predominantly. Of those, romance, religion and educational materials are the most frequently accessed. While these finding may mirror perceived differences or stereotypes in reading preferences and topics between genders, it is also the case that the *Worldreader* app has a greater number of titles in these topic areas available and less in non-fiction or current affairs. This again, may be a topic for further research as more topics and genres become available across mobile reading applications.

Barriers to Mobile Reading

Despite the benefits associated with mobile reading and learning, there are barriers as well. Perhaps not unsurprisingly, the greatest perceived barriers to utilizing mobile phone for reading relate to connectivity, choice and cost of use. For younger readers (under the age of 19) and men, lack of desirable content was reported as the most frequent barrier to reading via mobile phone. 60 percent of men and 64 percent of young people found that the reading material available was not of primary interest, compared to 45 percent of women. These findings may not be surprising given the relatively small amount of non-fiction and even less material specifically targeted to a young adult (YA literature) audience. Additionally, most readers reported that they would like to see more content written by local authors in local languages available. This is an important finding and speaks to one of the critiques around mobile reading – who determines the content, the purposes and the availability of texts in the mobile applications? As we will discuss later in this chapter, technology cannot be simply imported from one locale to another without consideration of local knowledge.

Second to limited content, mobile readers found that connectivity issues impacted their ability to read on their phones. 53 percent of all users cited frequent connectivity issues as an impediment to reading. While this is not surprising given the "cloud" based nature of the application, it does have implications for the impact of digital reading to extend the access and availability of text. Related to connectivity are issues of airtime costs incurred by mobile phone reading apps. Although determining an exact price for reading a book on a mobile phone is difficult due to variance in plans, locale, etc., it is estimated that the cost of reading a book through the *Worldreader* or similar programs is approximately two to three cents in US currency. While certainly a concern especially in countries with high poverty rates, the cost of reading a book on a mobile phone is much lower than the cost of an average print book. This is reflected in the 18 to 34 percent of respondents who reported worrying about airtime costs 'frequently' or 'sometimes' in the study.

While the findings of this robust study illuminate the ways in which mobile phones may be utilized to secure greater access for a greater number of people to a variety of books, it does not address mobile reading in libraries and formal education (school) settings. We turn now to the use of e-reader initiatives in developing countries. Similar to the research on mobile reading, the largest studies have been undertaken by NGO's and non-profit organizations. While this does not diminish the findings, their significance or the benefits achieved, it does present some particular issues related to power, access and the "top-down"

nature of these projects, especially in regard to local knowledge and culture. This is especially salient given the almost monopolizing influence of non-profit agencies such as *Worldreader*, especially when in partnership with global organizations such as UNESCO and USAID.

E-Reader Initiatives

Project LEAP

Project LEAP, which stands for "Libraries, e-Reading, Activities and Partnership," was a pilot program implemented by *Worldreader* in partnership with eight public and community libraries in Western Kenya, and funded by the Bill and Melinda Gates Foundation. LEAP tested the use, function and adoption of e- readers in the participating libraries in an effort to understand and investigate the potential and feasibility of library e-reader programs across Kenya and sub-Saharan Africa. One of the stated goals of this initiative was to increase reading through libraries, and therefore improve literacy skills and ameliorate the effects of illiteracy on poverty, health, gender equality and social and economic stability (Jaffe, Lowe, and Tam, 2014)

Early in 2014 *Worldreader* contributed 200 e-readers (each preloaded with 200 digital book titles) to the selected pilot libraries, for a total of 40,000 books. In this study the following key findings were reported:

- Diversity and size of library collections and the need for more technology programs as priority concerns prior to the e-reader program initiative.
- Young people (determined in the study to be under the age of 25) were the primary users of the e-readers, and points to an important need to engage young people.
- Of almost equal importance to issues of access and availability, both library patrons and staff stressed the importance and value

of social interactions and the ability to discuss what was being read, and to obtain technical assistance when required.

Despite the numerous positive findings associated with LEAP, concerns and challenges also arose. One of the most prevalent concerns centered on access issues in rural areas. While it may be expected that larger urban centers would have greater numbers of patrons, and thus require a greater number of e-readers, rural areas tended to attract more people coming greater distances to read, only to find limited availability and access. Another challenge was to provide readers with texts written by African authors. While *Worldreader* has partnered with over one hundred African authors to digitize their work, the demand is still outpacing the supply and speaks to concerns around who has the power to determine what is available to readers in the developing world. Lastly, there was somewhat of a cultural "disconnect" between views on the value and place for printed text in societies where social interaction and oral storytelling are highly valued. This is in keeping with Totemeyer's (1994) observation:

Books and libraries are often seen as redundant in societies that are mainly based on oral traditions and practices. In such societies, people stop reading once formal education is completed as they derive more pleasure from the oral and performing arts – talking, singing, dancing, socializing – than from the rather private and individual reading of a book (p. 54).

What is interesting to note, then, is that even given the attractive (from a Global North perception) addition of technology in the form of e-readers, the mismatch between what is valued remains. We will discuss this at greater length later in this chapter, however, it is important to bear in mind the incongruity of practice and beliefs when technology becomes a placed resource that may or may not take into consideration the hegemony involved in imposing practice not inherently a part of local practice.

iRead Ghana

Project LEAP examined the distribution of pre-loaded e-readers to both rural and urban libraries in locales through areas of Kenya. *iRead Ghana* represented the introduction of e-readers into the classes and curriculum of elementary schools in Ghana. The iREAD (Impact on Reading of E-Readers And Digital content) Ghana Study was a pilot study conducted from October 2010 to July 2011. It was categorized as a Global Development Alliance (GDA) program between the United States Agency for International Development (USAID) and *Worldreader,* as a non-profit organization. This study gave purposively sampled (n=481) Ghana public school students access to books through e-readers. While USAID and *Worldreader* conducted this study; ILC Africa, a private company, was responsible for monitoring and evaluation of the study as it progressed. The report is available at: http://www.worldreader.org/uploads/WorldreaderILCUSAIDiREADFinalReportJan-2012.pdf.

Generally speaking, the majority of students and teachers from the *iREAD Ghana* had positive experiences with the e-reader and expressed the belief that there is a place for digital media and e-reader technology in the Ghanaian school system. However, some negative effects were also reported, mainly from the teachers involved in the study. Figure 3 summarizes both positive and negative findings in this study.

The report concluded that there were positive effects from the short term to the long term in promoting both reading and literacy skills. Namely, the study concluded that:

In the short-term, students have immediate and reliable access to books for academic and personal

Figure 3. Successes and challenges of the iREAD Ghana project

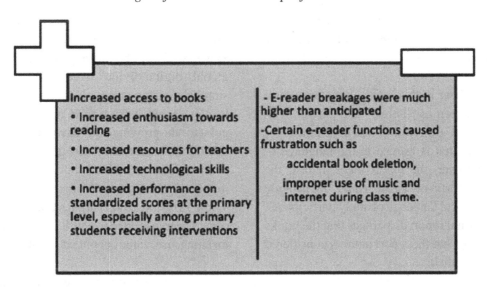

Increased access to books

• Increased enthusiasm towards reading

• Increased resources for teachers

• Increased technological skills

• Increased performance on standardized scores at the primary level, especially among primary students receiving interventions

- E-reader breakages were much higher than anticipated

-Certain e-reader functions caused frustration such as

accidental book deletion,

improper use of music and internet during class time.

---

use, without having to depend on the traditional paper book system that is currently practiced. In the medium-term, student and teachers have access to reading materials and teaching resources that facilitate and significantly accelerate the learning process, since students are able to have direct access to information in a home setting. In the long-term, final evaluation data strongly suggest that when the device is introduced and managed properly among primary level students, it has the potential to improve reading performance, and more importantly increase enthusiasm for reading as a lifetime habit (p. 7).

While these are certainly laudable goals in promoting literacy, they do not take into account local knowledge or value the literacies that students bring to school. Thus, while benefits are apparent and measurable, the conclusions may once more raise the spectre of a monolithic portrayal of those in developing countries as being in need of the Global North's intervention. This stance becomes more apparent later in the study's report on socio-cultural limitations regarding language and what they term as "unsupportive home environments".

Note that the report negatively frames both the uses of other languages as well as home practices in agricultural communities that may place more importance on activities other than reading (emphasis added):

Socio-Cultural Limitations

- *English language limitations: While English is the official language of Ghana, it is the second language for most if not all project-affected students and teachers. English language limitations were especially significant for primary students who use English for the first time in primary class 4.*
- *Potentially unsupportive home environments: As many project-affected students are from agricultural families, **their home environments may not appreciate reading as an activity**. For example, students may spend more time at home performing family chores and agricultural tasks rather than engaging with their e-readers.*

*Additionally, students whose parents have limited English and literacy skills may be **unable to actively incorporate the device into home life**. (p. 22).*

Thus, we hear in this report that agricultural tasks are not seen as "literate" and parents with limited English are creating an environment for their children that is framed in the language of deficit. Moreover, the report takes to task the admirable efforts of *Worldreader* to provide books in the local language of study participants. Indeed, the final report disparages that the books may not be in what the report authors considered "standard" English:

Findings within this report demonstrate that many students had an affinity towards African reading material because it was representative of their culture. A concern, however, is that many of the locally authored texts had grammatical, syntactical, and typographical errors that do not present a positive model for young readers (p. 24).

Again, while initiatives such as *iRead Ghana* do provide greater access to literacy, we must ask whose literacies are being privileged? Earlier in this chapter we made the argument that literacy is tantamount to the realization of human rights especially for women and girls. However, it would also seem necessary to ensure that in attempting to secure those rights, we do not inadvertently engage in practices that subvert the values of societies that may not view literacy in the same way. We turn now to a discussion of the issues, such as this one, that arise when technology is transported as value-laden to various locales.

SOLUTIONS AND RECOMMENDATIONS

One of the issues raised by examining the role of digital media in contributing to the increased literacy, and thus greater civic engagement of women and girls globally lies in the notion of digital technologies as placed resources (Prinsloo & Rowsell, 2012); as well as in the concept of a global "digital divide" which cannot be bridged simply by making technology available in distant locales. Bonny Norton and Carrie-Jane Williams point to "the growing body of work which suggests that digital resources are not directly transferable from well resourced to poorly resourced communities" (Norton & Williams, 2012, p. 315). While Prinsloo (2005) argues that new literacies cannot be transported to new locales and have their meaning, use, value or context simply reproduced:

At the level of practice, the new literacies are never reproduced in their entirety across different contexts. They function as artifacts and as signs that are embedded in local relations that are themselves shaped by larger social dynamics of power, status, access to resources and social mobility. They are placed resources. (Prinsloo 2005, p.96)

In making this argument, Prinsloo refutes the attractive generality and seamless transferability of skill-based new literacies such as the ability to "use the Internet and other ICT's to identify important questions, locate information, critically evaluate the usefulness of that information, synthesize information to answer questions, and then communicate the answers to others (Leu *et al*, 2004; p.1570). While these skills and may seem like a *panacea* for global illiteracy issues, they do not necessarily take in to account the situated and enculturated nature of of digital practice, especially as it pertains to literacy. Thus, Prinsloo's distinction is crucial to this review, as the majority of the extant literature are reports and other various publications by international NGOs and other organizations who may be more inclined to discuss the affordances for users of digital literacies in developing nations, but reluctant to discuss the "constraints that mark their status as persons located on the globalised periphery (Prinsloo & Rowsell, 2012; p. 271). However, it is imperative not to view the notion of placed resources or the global digital divide as coming from a discourse of deficit or disadvantage. Rather, the research around new literacies and digital literacies/ technologies as placed resources allows for the exploration of possibilities when the settings of use are recognized rather than homogenized in function and affordance. Snyder and Prinsloo (2007) speak to this and encourage researchers and practitioners alike to attend to the variety and nuanced contexts in which people engage in digital media practices and resist the notion that availability of technology equates with access and equality:

When computers or other media are inserted in a particular setting, to bring about certain results, they encounter situated social practices that do not necessarily result in these resources being used in a way that promotes social development and participation, as might be conceived by the implementers. Digital divide logic overemphasizes the importance of the physical presence of computers and connectivity to the exclusion of other factors that allow people to use electronic media for meaningful ends. (Snyder & Prinsloo, 2007, p. 174).

In tandem to notion of digital media and literacies as placed resources, we must also consider the role of culture and what "counts" as knowledge and literacy to people in developing parts of the world. Mobile learning has been demonstrated to enhance and extend learning and related activities in various settings in many ways. Yet as Traxler (2013) posits, mobile learning may transmit certain cultural and pedagogical assumptions and values related to education inherent in Western models, that may not reflect the culture of the locales in which mobile reading has been placed. Questions such as, "What is worth learning?" "How is it to be learnt?" "Who can teach it?" "How can competence be expressed?" implicitly define that culture's conception of learning, and thus of knowing" (Traxler, 2013, p. 49).

Additionally, given that language and literacy are primary markers of a particular culture, there is often an uneasy tension between globally predominant languages such as English, and a local language and/or dialect. Indeed, education and enculturation are often synonymous with each other. Thus, there is a fine line between offering new technologies to be incorporated into existing cultures and social systems and imposing them in a manner which may subvert or replace them. As Traxler succinctly argues:

These technologies project the pedagogies, strictly speaking perhaps the epistemologies, of outsiders into communities that of course already have their own learning. There is a risk that mobile technologies delivering learning in this way represent either a Trojan horse or a cargo cult that threatens or undermines a fragile educational ecosystem. The issue is not one of emerging markets or developing regions per se but of fragile cultures (or sub-cultures or even counter cultures) and their capacity to negotiate an optimal balance between the preservation of language, heritage and culture on the one hand and engagement with the wider world and the global knowledge economy, on the other. (Traxler, 2013; p. 49)

It is in that delicate balance of local preservation and global engagement that may present the biggest challenge for mobile reading and e-reader initiatives as we move forward into new research. In doing so it is valuable to remain cognizant of their situated and contextualized use in ways that may further illuminate the affordance and challenges of digital media and literacies as placed resources.

FUTURE RESEARCH DIRECTIONS

At myworld.org, the United Nations is asking the public what priorities should be the future priorities for international development. In 2013, the top two choices were education at 27% and then ICT 22%. Education and technology are tools for personal empowerment and holistic development that should be available to females as well as males. In the past decade, there has been a rise in the number of mobile learning initiatives taking place around the world. Researchers have accepted the call to empower women and girls with the use of mobile devices. Projects have become more culturally appropriate than their predecessors, with attention to language and social norms of those communities and societies. However, this research is still relatively new with many areas remaining unexplored. Researchers need to draw from what knowledge we have gathered to offer communities and cultures richer learning opportunities. Researchers need to also learn from implementations that have not worked to support gender equality as well as the challenges and hurdles to working with individuals and communities in developing countries. This information will help to provide a depth to the collective understanding and toward the design of future successful mobile learning initiatives.

At UNESCO's Mobile Learning Week 2014, Traxler and Crompton (in press) conducted research to pull together the expert opinions of those attending the policy forum. One of the discussion topics focused on the ethics of research and Traxler and Crompton pointed out the Golden Rule vs. the Platinum Rule. The Golden Rule reminds us to treat others how we would wish to be treated, however, the Platinum Rule reminds us that how a person may wish to be treated may not be the same as what they would actually want due to cultural differences. As one participant stated:

Ethics are rules set out by a population. Most of the time those rules are coming from powerful societies pushing forward those rules as be-

ing 'good practice' or 'philosophically sound'. However, what works for some populations, might not work for others, and each context can have unexpected negative effects of well-meant ethical guidelines that are provided in a research project. As such ethical guidelines should have some freedom in their conceptualization, allowing the target population to provide their insights and their ethical views

As researchers travel to foreign countries, they need to remember the Platinum Rule and find out more about that country and what is and is not appropriate when conducting research.

To support researchers in conducting future research that is culturally respectful Traxler and Crompton (in press) posit that local researcher capacity is built. Furthermore, they point out that local researcher capacity will not only be culturally respectful but provide a more accurate understanding of local socio-cultural contexts in data collection and the final analysis. With this in mind, future research will benefit from local women and girls being involved in conducting the research in addition to the local women and girls who are the study participants. This will contribute to the transnational feminist discourse (Hesford & Kozol, 2005; Swarr & Nagar, 2010) that the women and girls are taking lead role in the research. This can be difficult in countries where research is not highly valued or a well-paid occupation, but this can be supported in the future as local women and girls can join outside research teams and be well compensated for their time.

A dominant concern for future research lies in the relative lack of scholarship investigating digital media as a vehicle for the literacy and rights of women and girls. Currently, the majority of the extant research is conducted by NGO's and/or non-profits, aligned with corporate interests (ie; *Nokia, Amazon*, etc.) Without negating the contributions made by these reports, it is difficult to ignore the inherent biases and interest served by them. While all research reflects the subjectivity of the author or entity conducting the research, there is a noticeable gap in a critical or socio-cultural perspective reflected in the existing literature cited here. Indeed, very little attention is given to the particularities of context or participants. Likewise, it is difficult to determine what, if any local voice, experience and input may have been contributed or even solicited. Thus, there is a profound need for more independent research especially that which is context –based around access and equality to digital media and the variety of literacies afforded by it. Indeed, as Traxler (2013) argues, the pervasiveness and ubiquitous nature of mobile devices and the learning made possible through them, also potentially devalues the pedagogical when "there is an app for that." Where then, is the place for expert, long-term professional development and mentoring. Traxler posits that when content alone is privileged:

There is a risk that the role and impact of the research community becomes marginal. This is important because as we use mobiles for international development (italics in the original) we will encounter and probably ignore local theories of learning, theories embedded in their traditions and culture and expressing their ideas about what to learn, where, when and why, and how to learn, and who from (p.58).

Traxler sees this as a risk because it denies the opportunity to learn from and with other cultures and traditions while assuming that pedagogy will keep track with technology. This notion of pedagogy and "who decides" how and what to learn, who from and what is worth knowing brings us to our next issue for further study.

Another key issues related to mobile learning and digital media is the notion of who decides content to be shared, how to share it and to what extent (if any) is local knowledge and context solicited and represented in the content. In the case of BYOT or individuals selecting which apps to use, how and why, the question may not be as important. However, in the case of initiatives where the content of mobile readers is predetermined and or can be user selected albeit from a predetermined "library", there does seem to be a pronounced risk of imposing a Global North perspective, rather than a local one. Similarly, questions of perception regarding the "developer" and the "developing" may inadvertently re-ascribe age-old power relationships between North and South.

As Prinsloo and Rowsell (2012) state, "it is only through a situated and local account of digital praxis can we begin to see tensions, power imbalances and, at the same time, idiosyncratic use and understanding of the digital" (p.274). Those power imbalances become more complex and problematic when gender is also considered, especially in regard to who is heard and who is not. Judith Butler (1990) reminds us, "what qualifies as 'gender' …attests to a pervasively normative operation of power" (p. xxi). This operation of power is still very much evident in digital context, perhaps in some ways, even exacerbated due to issues of access. Additional research is needed then in regard to how gender is enacted across individual and group contexts in digital spaces (Krasny, 2013). Moreover, Krasny states there is a need for research "investigating the extent to which electronic texts fulfills its promise of providing for gender-free communication and whether virtual learning environments allow for more equitable gender participation" (p. 65). In exploring these issues among others raised in this volume, the potential for digital media and mobile learning to address the human rights and literacy for women and girls globally may begin to be realized.

CONCLUSION

In this chapter we reviewed the relatively recent advances in combating illiteracy and lack of access to a variety of resources through mobile learning and e-reading initiatives. In doing so, we utilized the lens of transnational feminism and human rights discourse to both illuminate and problematize those advances, especially as they relate to women and girls globally. The role of transnational feminisms in critiquing human rights discourse as well as the methods and objectives of NGOs is invaluable in examining what role digital media, mobile reading, and the use of e-readers may have in promoting literacy and human rights for women and girls. Most salient to these critiques, especially as they relate to corporate and NGO involvement and influence is the risk of privileging the Global North's perspectives and interests over local cultures, customs and values. Additionally, it must be remembered and bears reiteration that access is not synonymous with equity, especially for women and girls in the so-termed "developing world".

Thus in considering the potential for digital media and the variety of mobile learning initiatives now in practice, we offer the following as recommendations, realizing that the implications of widely used mobile reading and learning are continuing to grow exponentially:

- Consider the power dynamics in providing supportive interventions. Researchers from developed countries need to be cognizant of perceptions of power especially when working with people in developing countries.
- Consider the role of women and girls in mobile learning initiatives to play the part of the provider (the interventionist) as well as the participants in these studies. This will avoid the perceptions of men having the power in conducting the research.
- Empathize with women and girls respecting local cultures and practices. This will ensure that they are treated in a way they would like to be treated and not how the researchers, who are probably from a different culture, would like to be treated.

- Identify ways to normalize technology use with women and girls. Create a culture of technology ownership and use. This may seem contradictory to earlier points about respecting the local culture, however, there are times when local cultures may be exacerbating oppressive ideas that women and girls are less important to their male counterparts. For example, the Pink Phone Project in Cambodia was used to show the local people that phones were not just a device for the male population.
- Develop strategies of technology use to promote literacy in women and girls. Connect these strategies with positive culturally relevant practices. In this chapter, there are many examples of literacy initiatives connecting to cultural norms. A good example was the Mobile Literacy program in Afghanistan. In this study women were learning basic literacy skills by receiving SMS messages that contained topics such as Islamic teaching, food recipes, beauty tips, and health facts that would be interesting and relevant to the women in the study.
- Learn from failed projects and why they failed. It is important to share details of studies that have not worked and why they did not work as this will avoid researchers wasting time on projects that have failed in the past. Instead, the researchers can learn from past research failures to instead direct their efforts to initiatives that may be successful.
- Remember that projects that worked in one community will not necessarily work in other communities that appear similar. One of the main themes from this work is that what will work for women and girls in one community may not necessarily work for women and girls in another community. Even as researchers work with a population in the same country, each city, town, and village may be different.

In conclusion, we look to the promise of mobile learning, digital media and initiatives to promote equitable access to literacy and other human rights, but we do so with a sense of caution and remain cognizant that the potential for hegemony often walks beside even the noblest of intentions. However, as girls and women continue to exercise agency to alter the status quo, we are reminded of a poem written by a 15 year-old girl called "Luckline", who sued her government for failing to protect her from her rapist (Armstrong, 2014, p. 34-35):

Here I Come

Walking down through history to eternity

From paradise to the city of goods

Victorious, glorious, serious and pious

Elegant, full of grace and truth

The centerpiece and masterpiece of literature

Glowing, growing and flowing

Here, there, everywhere

Cheering millions everyday

The book of books that I am

For all women and girls, victorious, glorious, serious and pious, we dedicate this review in the hope for the full and ultimate realization of their rights as humans and global citizens.

REFERENCES

Apple, M., Kenway, J., & Singh, M. (2005). *Globalizing Education: Policies, pedagogies, & politics*. New York: Peter Lang.

Armstrong, S. (2014). *Uprising: A new age is dawning fro every mother's daughter*. New York, NY: St. Thomas Press.

Beck, U. (2002). The cosmopolitan society and its enemies. *Theory, Culture & Society*, *19*(1-2), 25–44. doi:10.1177/026327640201900101

Bhola, H. S. (2008). Adult literacy for sustainable development: Creating a knowledgebased discourse for action. In Signposts to literacy for sustainable development. UNESCO Institute for Lifelong Earning.

Blackmore, J. (2005). Feminist strategic rethinking of human rights discourses in education. In W. Hesford & W. Kozol (Eds.), *Just Advocacy: Women's human rights, transnational feminisms and the politics of representation* (pp. 243–265). New Brunswick, NJ: Rutgers Univesity Press.

Blackmore, J. (2005). Feminist strategic rethinking of human rights discourses in education. In W. Hesford & W. Kozol (Eds.), *Just Advocacy: Women's human rights, transnational feminisms and the politics of representation* (pp. 243–265). New Brunswick, NJ: Rutgers Univesity Press.

Butler, J. (1990). *Gender trouble: Feminism and the subversion of identity*. London: Routledge.

Castells, M. (1996). *Rise of the network society*. Cambridge, UK: Blackwell.

Dunkerly, J., & Harper, H. (2013). The girl citizen-reader: Gender and literacy education for 21st century citizenship. In B. Guzzetti & T. W. Bean (Eds.), *Adolescent Literacies and the Gendered self: (Re)constructing identities through multimodal literacy practices*. New York: Routledge.

Farrington, J. W., Bebbington, A., Wellard, K., & Lewis, D. L. (1993). *Reluctant partners?:Non governmental organizations: The state and sustatinable agriculture*. London: Routledge.

Fletcher, J. K. (1999). *Disappearing acts: Gender, power and relational power at work*. Cambridge, MA: MIT Press.

Foucault, M. (1972). *The Archeology of knowledge and the discourse on language*. New York, NY: Pantheon.

Gee, J. (1996). *Social linguistics and literacies*. London: Falmer Press.

Grewal, I., & Kaplan, C. (2001). Global identities: Theorizing transnational studies of sexuality. *GLQ Archive*, *4*(4), 663–679. doi:10.1215/10642684-7-4-663

Harper, H., & Dunkerly, J. (2010). Educating the world: Teachers and their work as defined by the United Nations Educational, Scientific and Cultural Organization (UNESCO). *Current Issues in Comparative Education*, *4*, 56–65.

Health Alliance International. (2012). *Mobile moms*. Retrieved from http://www.healthallianceinternational.org/blog/post/mobile-moms-liga-inan/

Hesford, W. S., & Kozol, W. (Eds.). (2005). *Introduction. In Just advocacy: Women's human rights, transnational feminism and the politics of representation* (pp. 1–29). New Brunswick, NJ: Rutgers University Press.

Hilhorst, D. (2003). *The real world of NGOs: Discourses, diversity and development*. London: Zed Books.

Jaffe, S., Lowe, Z., & Tam, T. (2014). *Project LEAP: Libraries, e-reading, activities, partnership baseline report*. Retrieved August 18, 2014 from http://cdn.worldreader.org/wp-content/uploads/2014/08/Project-LEAP-Baseline-Report_2.pdf

Kaestle, C. (1991). *Literacy in the United States: Readers and reading since 1880*. New Haven, CT: Yale University Press.

Kam, M., Kumar, A., Jain, S., Mathur, A., & Canny, J. (2009). Improving literacy in rural India: Cellphone games in an afterschool program. In *Proceedings of IEEE/ACM Conference on Information and Communication Technology and Development* (ICTD 09). Doha, Qatar: IEEE.

Kay, A. & Goldberg, A. (1977/2001). Personal dynamic media. *IEEE Computer – COMPUTER*, *10*(3), 31-41. DOI: 10.1109/C-M.1977.217672

Kelleher, F. (2014, June 17). The literacy injustice: 493 million women still can't read [magazine]. *The Guardian*. Retrieved from http://www.theguardian.com/global-development-professionals-network/2014/jun/17/literacy-women-illiteracy-development

Krasny, K. (2013). *Gender and literacy: A handbook fro educators and parents*. Santa Barbara, CA: Praeger.

Leach, J. (2005). *Deep impact: An investigation of the use of information and communication technologies* [Report]. London: The Department for International Development.

Leu, D. J., Kinzer, C. K., Coiro, J., & Cammack, D. A. (2004). Toward a theory of new literacies emerging from the Internet and other information and communication technologies. In R. B. Ruddell & N. Unrau (Eds.), *Theoretical Models and Processes of Reading* (5th ed.; pp. 1568–1611). Newark, DE: International Reading Association.

Luke, A. (2002). Curriculum, Ethics, Metanarrative: Teaching and Learning Beyond the Nation. *Curriculum Perspectives*, *22*(1), 49–55.

Nokia. (n.d.). *Text 2 Teach*. Retrieved from http/:www.text2teach.org.ph:%3Fpage_id=2

Norton, B., & Williams, C. (2012). Digital identities, student investments and eGranary as placed resources. *Language and Education*, *26*(4), 315–329. doi:10.1080/09500782.2012.691514

Ochwa-Echel, J. (2011). Exploring the Gender Gap in Computer Science Education in Uganda. *International Journal Of Gender, Science, Technology (Elmsford, N.Y.), 3*(2). Retrieved from http://genderandset.open.ac.uk/index.php/genderandset/article/view/119

OXFAM. (2012, March 7). *Using pink phones to empower women and girls in Cambodia.* Retrieved from http://policy-practice.oxfam.org.uk/blog/2012/03/pink-telephones-in-cambodia

Pakistan Bureau of Statistics. (2013). *2012-2013 Literacy rates.* Retrieved from http://www.pbs.gov.pk/sites/default/files/pslm/publications/pslm_prov_dist_2012-13/education/2.14b.pdf

Peake, L., & De Souza, K. (2010). Feminist academic and activist praxis in service of the transnational. In A. Swarr & R. Nagar (Eds.), *Critical transnational feminist praxis* (pp. 105–123). Albany, NY: State University of New York Press.

Prinsloo, M. (2005). The new literacies as placed resources. *Perspectives in Education, 23*(4), 87–98.

Prinsloo, M., & Rowsell, J. (2012). Digital literacies and placed resources in the globalised periphery. *Language and Education, 26*(4), 271-277.

Reena, N. R., Singh, R., & Surbala. (2010). Still playing with fire: Intersectionality, activism and NGOized feminisim. In A. Swarr & R. Nagar (Eds.), Critical transnational feminist praxis (pp. 124-143). Albany, NY: State University of New York Press.

Snyder, I., & Prinsloo, M. (2007). Young peoples engagement with digital literacies in marginal contexts in a globalised world. *Language and Education, 21*(3), 171–179. doi:10.2167/le745.0

UNICEF South Africa. (2013). *Supporting pregnant women's journey to motherhood.* Retrieved from http://www.unicef.org/southafrica/media_14102.html

Swarr, A. L., & Nagar, R. (Eds.). (2010). *Introduction: Theorizing treansnational feminist praxis. In Critical transnational feminist praxis* (pp. 1–20). Albany, NY: State University of New York Press.

The United Nations Foundation website. (n.d.). Retrieved from www.unfoundation.org/faq.html

Tohidi, N. (2005, May). *Transnational feminism: A range of disciplinary perspectives.* Paper presented at Symposium conducted at the University of California, Los Angeles, Los Angeles, CA. Retrieved from http://www.humnet.ucla.edu/humnet/cmcs/#index.html

Tomasevski, K. (2003). *Education denied.* London: Zed Books.

Totemyer, G. (1994). Challenges for democracy: Decentralization and empowerment in Africa. *Regional Development Dialogue, 15,* 49–61.

Traxler, J. (2013). mLearning: Solutions for international development - rethinking the thinking. *Digital Culture & Education, 5*(2), 74–85.

Traxler, J. (2014). Mobile learning in international development. In A. Tsinakos & M. Ally (Eds.) *Global Mobile Learning Issues and Trends.* Retrieved from http://www.meducationalliance.org/content/global-mobile-learning-implementations-and-trends

Traxler, J., & Crompton, H., (in press). *Research in Mobile Learning.* United Nations Educational, Scientific, and Cultural Organization (UNESCO).

UNESCO. (2013). *Adult and Youth Literacy* [Fact sheet]. UNESCO Institute for Statistics.

UNESCO/UNICEF. (2007). *A human rights-based approach to education: A framework for the realization of children's right to education and rights in education. United Nations Educational, Scientific and Cultural Organization. United Nations Children's Fund.* London: United Nation's Children's Fund.

UNICEF. (2012). *Moms Connect.* Retrieved from: http://www.unicef.org/southafrica/media_14102.html)

USAID. (2012). *iREAD Ghana study: final evaluation report* [Report]. Retrieved from http://www.worldreader.org/uploads/Worldreader%20ILC%20USAID%20iREAD%20Final%20Report%20Jan-2012.pdf

Waldron, F. (2010). Introduction. In F. Waldron & B. Ruane (Eds.), *Human rights education: Reflections on theory and practice* (pp. 1–14). Dublin, Ireland: The Liffey Press.

West, M., & Chew, H. E. (2014). *Reading in the mobile era: A study of mobile reading in developing countries* [Report]. Retrieved from http://www.unesco.org/new/en/unesco/themes/icts/m4ed/mobile-reading/reading-in-the-mobile-era/

Zelezny-Green. (2013, February13). Boosting mobile learning potential for women and girls: Lingering considerations. *E-learning Africa.* Retrieved from http://www.elearning-africa.com/eLA_Newsportal/boosting-mobile-learning-potential-for-women-and-girls-in-africa-lingering-considerations/

ADDITIONAL READING

Ally, M., & Tsinakos, A. (2013) *Global Mobile Learning Implementations and Trends*, China Central Radio & TV University Press, Beijing China 10 2013, ISBN 978-7-304-06343-6 available online: http://en.crtvu.edu.cn/images/stories/globalmobilelearning.pdf

Ally, M., & Tsinakos, A. (Eds.). (2014) *Increasing Access through Mobile Learning.* Commonwealth of Learning http://www.col.org/PublicationDocuments/pub_Mobile%20Learning_web.pdf

Bean, T. W., Dunkerly-Bean, J., & Harper, H. J. (2014). Teaching young adult literature: Developing students as world citizens. Thousand Oaks, CA: SAGE.

Bennett, J., & Hart, S. N. (2001). Respectful learning communities: Laying the foundations of human rights, democracy and peace in the new millennium. In S. Hart, C. P. Cohen, M. F. Erickson, & M. Flekkoy (Eds.), *Children's Rights in Education.* London: Kingsley Publishers.

Berge, Z., & Muilenburg, L. Y. (Eds.). (2013). *Handbook of Mobile Learning.* New York: Routledge.

Black, S. E., & Brainerd, E. (2002). *Importing Equality?: The impact globalization on gender discrimination.* Cambridge: National Bureau of Economic Research Blackmore, J. (1999). Localization/globalization and the midwife state: strategic dilemmas for state feminism in education? *Journal of Education Policy, 14*(1), 33–54.

Cherland, M. R., & Harper, H. J. (2007). *Advocacy research in literacy education: Seeking higher ground.* Mahwah, New Jersey: Lawrence Erlbaum Associates.

Dallas, Texas Gibson, M.A. & Rojas, A.R. (2006). Globalization, immigration and the education of "new" immigrants in the 21st century. *Current Issues in Comparative Education, 9*(1), 69–76.

Dua, E. & Trotz, D.A. (2002). Transnational pedagogy: doing political work in women's studies: an interview with Chandra Talpade Mohanty." *Atlantis.* Spring/Summer (2), 66 – 77.

Feree, M., & Tripp, A. M. (2006). Global feminism: transnational women's activism, organizing, and human rights. New York: New York University Press.

Fernandes, E. (2013). *Transnational feminism in the United States: Knowledge, ethics and power.* New York: New York University Press.

Freeman, C. (2000). *High Tech and High Heels in the Global Economy: Women, Work, and Pink-Collar Identities in the Caribbean.* Durham: Duke. doi:10.1215/9780822380290

Grewal, I. (2005). *Transnational America: Feminisms, Diasporas, Neoliberalisms.* Durham: Duke. doi:10.1215/9780822386544

Hart, R. (1992). Children's participation: from tokenism to citizenship. Innocenti Paper, No. 4 UNICEF International Child Development Centre: Italy

Hicks, D. (2002). *Reading lives: Working class children and literacy learning.* New York: Teachers College Press.

Hicks, D. (2003). Thirty years of global education: A reminder of key principles and precedents. *Educational Review, 55*(3), 265–275. doi:10.1080/0013191032000118929

Hicks, D., & Holden, C. (2006). *The challenge of global education: Issues, principles and practice.* New York: Routledge.

Hull, G. A., & Stornaiuolo, A. (2010). Literate arts in a global world. *Journal of Adolescent & Adult Literacy, 54*(2), 85–97. doi:10.1598/JAAL.54.2.1

Jimenez, R., Smith, P., & Teague, B. (2009). Transnational and community literacies for teachers. *Journal of Adolescent & Adult Literacy, 53*(1), 16–28. doi:10.1598/JAAL.53.1.2

Kinshuk, R. Huang & M. Spector (eds) (2013). Reshaping Learning - The Frontiers of Learning Technologies in a Global Context, Springer

Mackenzie, A. (2004). *Citizens All? Children's rights and citizenship education An endline survey of curriculum and practice in a sample of UK schools.* London: UNICEF.

Marshall, S., & Kinuthia, W. (Eds.). (2013). *On the Move: Mobile Learning for Development.* Hershey, PA: IGI Global.

Moghadam, V. M. (2005). *Globalizing women: Transnational feminist networks: themes in global social change.* Baltimore, Md.: Johns Hopkins University Press.

Mohanty, C. T. (2003). *Feminism without Borders: Decolonizing Theory, Practicing Solidarity.* Durham: Duke University Press. doi:10.1215/9780822384649

Mundy, K., Manion, C., Masemann, V., & Haggerty, M. (2007). *Charting global education in Canada's elementary schools: Provincial, district and school level perspectives.* UNICEF OISE/UT.

Pachler, N., Cook, J., & Traxler, J. (2015). Key Issues. In *Mobile Learning: Research And Practice.* London: Continuum.

Parrenas, R. S. (2005). *Children of global migration: Transnational families and gendered woes.* Stanford: Stanford University Press.

Parsons, D. (Ed.). (2013). *Innovations in Mobile Educational Technologies and Applications.* IGI Global. doi:10.4018/978-1-4666-2139-8

Quinn, C. (2012). *The mobile academy: mLearning for higher education.* San Francisco, CA, USA: Jossey-Bass.

Tierney, R. (2006). Global/Cultural teachers creating possibilities: Reading worlds, reading selves, and learning to teach. *Pedagogies, 1*(1), 77–87. doi:10.1207/s15544818ped0101_11

Traxler, J., & Kukulska-Hulme, A. (Eds.). (2015). *Mobile Learning: The Next Generation.* New York: Routledge. doi:10.4018/978-1-4666-8239-9.ch042

Traxler, J. & Wishart, J. (2011) *Making Mobile Learning Work: Case Studies of Practice,* Bristol: ESCAlate (HEA Education Subject Centre).

Waldron, F., & Ruane, B. (Eds.). (2010). *Human Rights education: Reflections on theory and practice. Dublin: Liffey.* Mobile: Learning.

KEY TERMS AND DEFINITIONS

Education for All (EFA): A UNESCO initiative and global commitment to provide quality basic education for all children, youth and adults. At the World Education Forum (Dakar, 2000), 164 governments pledged to achieve EFA and identified six goals to be met by 2015.

Globalization: A condition of the permeability of social, economic and political borders. It is characterized by the extensive movement or flow of information, ideas, images, capital, and people across increasingly permeable political borders due to economic and technological change.

Human Rights: The idea of human rights recognized today was established with the United Nation's *Universal Declaration of Human Rights* (UDHR) in 1948 written after the Second World War. The primary intent of the document was to prevent a recurrence of the human rights travesties that occurred during WWII. However, the UDHR also provides for the recognition of 30 human rights, including the right to education.

Literacy: Literacy is a human right, a tool of personal empowerment through expression as well as a means to social, cultural and human development. Broadly defined, it is the ability to read, comprehend and act upon a variety of texts and contexts.

Mobile Learning: The utilization of mobile devices to provide learning to those who have been previously unable to access traditional learning opportunities for reasons of location, finance, disability, or infrastructure.

Non-Government Organization (NGO): A citizen-based association that operates independent of governments, typically to deliver resources or serve a social or political purpose. NGOs may be classified as either operational NGOs, which usually address development projects, or advocacy NGOs, which are concerned with promoting a cause.

Transnational Feminisms: This wave of feminism has emerged largely as a response to international and global feminism. It speaks to the hegemonic and monolithic portrayal of "Third World women" as passive victims. Instead, it aims to recast and highlight activism and agency in such a way that transnational solidarity and collaborations can be reached.

Chapter 24
Social Media for Promoting Grassroots Political Movements and Social Change

Amir Manzoor
Bahria University, Pakistan

ABSTRACT

In light of many recent Internet-led revolutions, the Internet and its tools of social media have been heralded as instrumental in facilitating the uprisings. This chapter provides a close examination of the social media role in grass roots political and social change movements. The chapter discusses the ways activists have used social media tools for organizing and generating awareness of political mobilization and the characteristics of social networking that can be harnessed in a particular cultural and historical context to achieve collective political actions. The chapter also discusses long-established theories of communication to explain how social networking tools became appealing to the activists in these Internet-led movements. The chapter will look at various Internet-led political movements around the globe to demonstrate the enormous potential of social networking tools to facilitate and expedite political mobilization.

INTRODUCTION

Social media is defined as a group of Internet-based applications that build on the ideological and technological foundations of Web 2.0 and that allow the creation and exchange of user-generated content (Kaplan & Haenlein, 2010, p. 61). Social media tools include social networking sites such as Facebook, micro blogging sites like Twitter and Instagram, video sharing sites like YouTube, and image sharing sites such as Flickr and Tumblr. Social media studies are a relatively young but growing field (Kaplan & Haenlein, 2010). In June 2010, 22% of time spent online was spent using social media and blog sites worldwide (Neilson, 2010). Grove (2010) estimated the global average time spent per person on social media sites in 2010 was nearly five and a half hours per month.

DOI: 10.4018/978-1-4666-8310-5.ch024

However, by early 2014 the average time spent on social media sites dropped to 3.6 hours per day (Brendan Butler, 2014).

The recent Internet-led uprisings have fostered an ongoing dialogue about the role of social networking tools for promoting grassroots political movements and social change (Conover, 2013). Social media is now being considered an undeniable force for good. According to (MacKinnon, 2011), Wael Ghonim, Google executive in Egypt, famously declared right after Egyptian President Hosni Mubarak stepped down in February,, "If you want to liberate a society just give them the Internet" (p.1). The Internet proved to be an effective weapon of the masses against their authoritarian leaders. According to the New York Times, such use of Internet was the 21st-century way to resolve conflict. As (Kristof, 2009) put it, "On one side are government thugs firing bullets and on the other side are young protesters firing tweets" (p. 1). We have also witnessed Twitter revolutions (i.e. different revolutions and protests, all of which were coordinated using Twitter) in which the young tech-savvy generations monopolized the digital gap to challenge their archaic authoritarian governments. Some examples of such revolutions include 2009 Moldova civil unrest,2009 Iranian election protests (also known as Green Revolution),2010 Tunisian revolution (also known as Jasmine Revolution), Egyptian Revolution of 2011, and Euromaidan Revolution of Ukraine in 2013. The initial success of such Internet-led revolutions has brought a great deal of attention to the role of social media and the Internet in fostering grass root political change. Nevertheless, such potential of change is dependent on the extent to which social media and the Internet is (Gibson, 2013).

The Internet-led uprisings in the Middle East (e.g., Egypt) and North Africa (e.g., Libya and Tunisia) brought significant developments in all these countries. Scholars in the academy continue to debate the role of social media in these upris-

ings. Because these events are recent, available data and analysis about the role of social media and the Internet in grass root political and social change is limited. Prior to such events, research concerned with social media as a vehicle for social change was largely speculative in nature. One key issue is the manner in which social media became the source of information. Meaning, the source of information was ordinary citizens who for the very first time in their history used social media more than mainstream media to react to and even cover the events of political revolutions (Hassan, 2013).

This phenomenon of social networking as a political and social change agent is very significant. We see after centuries a technological innovation used as a tool for change. The social networking tools such as Twitter, Facebook, YouTube, and personal blogs have been used as an insider perspective to the ongoing revolutions. Revolutions can occur without Internet or technology. Revolutions have been taking place before the advent of social media. The advent of social media provided a crucial facilitator role by bringing together distant people and providing gathering real time information. The data about the use of these tools as source of information, a part from their established use for socializing, provides significant evidence of their relevance in mobilizing political movements and bringing change. However, the social media tools can not only be repressed by the governments but also used in their favor. Therefore, a logical analysis of this phenomenon is needed to establish a critical perspective about the history and novelty of this phenomenon of social networking for political and social change.

This chapter aims to understand the connection between technology, society, and political movements through the creation of a network society and analyze the extent to which social media can play a positive role in grassroots political change by analyzing various case studies from different countries. The chapter also discusses the characteristics of social media that can be harnessed in a particular cultural and historical context to achieve collective political actions.

BACKGROUND

Social Media Tools

Facebook

Facebook, a social network, emerged in 2004 as a way to connect with fellow students. Initially adopted by high school and college students, the social network now has 1.35 billion monthly active users., making it the premiere social media service in the world. If Facebook were a country, it would be the third largest behind China and India. Facebook users interact with other users, or "Facebook friends" by updating their "status", writing on other members "walls" or sending direct personal messages. Users are able to create and join interest groups, 'like' pages, import and search for contacts, and upload photos and videos. The average user is connected to 80 community pages, groups and events. Despite being a US-based product, Facebook users are mostly located outside USA. A crucial aspect of the social media role in various Internet-led uprisings was the use of mobile phones. In this regard it is important to note that in 2011 more than 350 million users of Facebook used their mobile phones to access their accounts (Storck, 2011; Finau, Prasad, Logan, & Cox, 2014).

Twitter

Launched in July 2006, Twitter is a real-time online social networking and microblogging service that has grown to 284 million monthly active users and 500 million Tweets sent per day as of 2014. Users can exchange photos, videos, and communicate via "Tweets" which are short posts limited to 140 characters. Uses can also embed media links in their tweets. Twitter users can "follow" or essentially subscribe to the updates of other users. These other users may include conventional media sources, such as Newsweek, celebrities, and friends. Additionally, tweets can be categorized using "hashtags" (e.g. #egypt) which group posts together by topic or type (Chebib & Sohail, 2011) or user-identified key words that clue readers in to what others think is important. Twitter provides very personal communication where uses choose whom they want to follow. This selection creates a unique experience specific to each user. This unique experience is dependent on various factors related to use of Twitter such as time of Twitter user, frequency to cheek Twitter feeds, the Twitter followers, and the user interface used to access Twitter. Due to this flexibility, norms among Twitter users quickly emerge and fade away (Jenkins, 2010). Since Twitter can be accessed using both computer and mobile phones, it is a lightweight communication tool especially helpful in crisis situation.

YouTube

YouTube was founded in 2005 and provides a forum for the distribution of video content of various types. YouTube was the first website dedicated solely to uploading and sharing personal video. Over 3 billion videos were viewed each day on YouTube, reaching 700 billion playbacks in 2010 and 100 hours of video were uploaded to YouTube every minute in 2014 (YouTube Statistics, 2014). As well as uploading and viewing media, users can also leave comments on videos. In 2014, YouTube was the third most frequented website online (Alexa, 2014).

Weblogs

Blogs are short form of weblogs. Belong are an easy-to-use content management tools that provides instant addition of content to a website via a web interface. Blogs do not require any programming or technical skills (Wyld, 2007). All you need is Internet access and typing skills. Such easiness of creating blogs has resulted in proliferation of personal blogs globally. In Arab region alone, there were 35,000 active blogs in 2009, growing to 40,000 by 2010 (OpenArab.Net, n.d.).

An average person, with little or no advanced computer skills, can have good success using social media services and independent blogging. This is one reason why these social media services and independent blogging have become attractive for common people. Using social media services and independent blogging, content can be created and accessed with as little as a smartphone; and it can be easily intertwined. Links to videos posted on YouTube can be embedded in blogs, Facebook, and Twitter. A Twitter post can appear on a Facebook page. In other words, large numbers of people can be contacted easily and inexpensively via a variety of services.

Social Media and Communication

International media and academic circles acknowledge the role of social media tools in various political movements. However, there are different opinions regarding effectiveness of these tools in aiding political mobilization and social change. Social media communication has brought politicians and political parties closer to their voters. Politicians can communicate fast and reach citizens in a targeted manner without an intermediate role of mass media. Citizens are using social media to post reactions, feedback, and participate in conversations and debates. Despite increased presence of social media, online political engagement is largely restricted to people who are already political activists online. For example, in most European states, television and newspapers (both offline and online) are still the most important source of political information for citizens. While social media use in some cases has resulted in toppling of authoritative regimes (such as the case of revolution in Egypt and Tunisia) in some

cases the similar success was not achieved (such as in case of political uprising in Bahrain and Saudi Arabia) (Reuter & Szakonyi, 2013).

Nature and Benefits of Social Media Communication

Communication using social media tools is different from communication using traditional ways of communication such as TV, newspapers, and radio. First, communication using social media tools is two way communication where use can also respond to messages in real time. Second, receivers of information obtained from social media are not necessarily prone for action. This is even true for people who virtually join group. These uncommitted users of social media can join a Facebook group or follow a twitter feed. Doing so can provide them some anonymity without physically participating in a resolution (Papic & Noonan, 2011).

Communication using social media provides some important benefits for political and social change. Online groups can be trained, recruited, and organized at much less costs (Papic & Noonan, 2011). A large number of users of social media tools makes it easy to convince recruits to find or join another social media site (Greeley, 2011). Findings recruits online is also easy because groups are normally formed around shared causes or interests (Mainwaring, 2011).

People active online are also likely active group participants. In a study, Pew research center found that 80% of Internet users participated in groups. Participation from social media users was even more active, with 82% of social network sites and 85% users of Twitter participated in group activities (Rainie, Purcell, & Smith, 2011). Uses were more likely to engage in group activities if they fell that their participation can make meaningful difference (Rainie et al., 2011).

In many crisis situation, such as Haiti earthquake or Mumbai attacks, users broadcasted information to a large number of people. This information was not pushed to a specific group of people (Hughes & Palen, 2009). This communication was different from the traditional way of communication using social media. In the context of disaster, such type of communication cane be every important for tactical, emotional, and community building purposes (Palen & Liu, 2007).

Activists who use social media for social change can use them to plan in-real-life and in-virtual-life meetings, keep followers informed about events and news, and gain followers. Social media use can increase users' self-efficacy to join a cause because, in part, their peers' involvement and actions are transparent. It can also be useful by giving an on-the-ground view to people not culturally or physically close to the users.

Social media also lowers traditional socio-economic barriers to commanding the spotlight. You do not have to "be somebody" to "be somebody" on social media. Politicians, governments, and activists all look to tap into the potential of social media. The Internet and social media has re-constituted the construction of social relationships especially among young people. Social media is also producing radical changes in how communication is produced, mediated, and received. Under such circumstances, state power becomes more porous and there is less control. Internet and social media provide a source of political energy that posits a new relationship between the new media technologies, politics, and public life (Giroux, 2009). These digital technologies influence the formation and activities of civil society groups: mobs, movements, and civil society organizations. While mass popular protests are by no means a new phenomenon, digital tools are facilitating their formation (Etling, Faris, & Palfrey, 2010).

Theories of Communication

There exists many established theories of communication, such as Lasswell's functionalist theory of media and Granovetter's theory of weak ties that can be used to explain the use of social media

as a vehicle for organization and mobilization of people. Both of these theories are based on sociology and were developed before the advent of social media. Still these theories are adequate to explain why social media was chose as a tool of communication by activists during various Internet led political movements.

Laswell's theory provides an analytical framework for communication that is based on the multi-faceted question "who says what in which channel to whom with what effect?" (Mattelart & Mattelart 1998, p.5). Laswell's framework involves content analysis to provide on objective systematic and quantitative description of the manifest content of communication (Mattelart & Mattelart, 1998). According to Lasswell there are three functions of communication in society; (1) Surveillance of the environment, (2) Correlation of components of society, and (3) Cultural transmission from one generation to the next. Social media has a profound influence on youth outlook, behavior, education, practices etc. as the social media keep on changing and innovating, the youth are influenced and the flow is also the reverse. every time youth acquire new style etc., the media watchdogs would know and update / upload their images, stories etc. they go on looking for new trends so as to keep youth captivated. And, this is rather successful. Although, Lasswell's model is simple and easy, the disadvantage of his model is the lack of feedback.

Manual Castell's network theory (Castells, 1996) can also be used to explain the important characteristics of social media that are useful for political activism. Social network can help create weak ties, support anonymity provided by the Internet, and provide online communication that is egalitarian in nature. According to Castells (1996), weak ties are useful in providing information and opening up opportunities at a low cost. The advantage of the Internet is that it allows the forging of weak ties with strangers, in an egalitarian pattern of interaction where social characteristics are less influential in framing, or even blocking communication. The strength of a tie is based on a combination of the amount of time, the emotional intensity, the intimacy (mutual confiding), and the reciprocal services which characterize the tie (Granovetter, 1973). Social media networks are based on these weak ties- acquaintances with other people whom one might share common interests or goals with, or may have mutual friends. The strength in weak ties lies in their ability to introduce us to new ideas and new information, and the Internet allows these ties to be forged with incredible speed over vast geographical barriers (Gladwell, 2010).

Granovetter (1973) analyzed the link between micro-level interactions and macro- level patterns in social networks, concluding with the strength of weak ties lies in their potential for diffusion, social mobility, political organization, and social cohesion in general, across different networks. People can have two types of ties with the people around them (such as friends and family). Weak ties are loose acquaintances that one can use e.g. to provide creative ideas or transfer knowledge. Strong ties exist with trusted friends and family. Strong ties can be used by a person for emotional health and join hand for a common cause such as relief efforts in a crisis. Applying Granovetter's theory to political mobilization, gathering of thousands of protesters would not have been possible if activists would have spoken only to their close friends and family. By capitalizing on the weak ties forged online through social networks, such as Facebook and Twitter, the activists were able not only to circulate their calls for political mobilization, but also began a dialogue that fostered the attitude for political activism in communities. A conclusion of Granovetter's study that is germane to the Internet-led movements is that weak ties are more likely to link members of different small groups than are strong ones, which tend to be concentrated within particular groups. Weak ties established online allowed different oppositional

factions to connect over a common goal of ousting repressive regimes, and to translate this into political mobilization.

According to Gladwell (2010), weak ties do not help people create social change. What matters most is the extent to which someone is personally connected with the movement to create social change. However, if strong ties are essential for social change and social media does not create those required strong ties, perhaps people have fewer strong ties now than they did previously. McPherson, Smith-Lovin, & Brashears (2004) found three times increase in the number of people who believed there was no one with whom they could discuss important matters. According to findings of McPherson et al. (2004), one important factor affecting people relationships and ties could be the modern technology (e.g. computer and mobile phone). While technology has provided opportunities to network with people across geographical boundaries it has lowered the possibility of face to face communication with people around us such as family, friends, neighbors etc. Usage of internet has even interfered with communication in home. We can see a post familial family where family members spend time interacting with electronic gadgets of communication rather than communicating with each other. This suggests that ubiquity of technology may foster wider, less localized weak ties and not the strong, tightly interconnected confidant ties.

Still we may have use of weak ties generated due to ubiquity of technology. One example is the crisis situations such as Haiti earthquake. Many people who donated money had little or no strong ties with the country. Communication using social media, such as blog post, status updates, and tweets from peers, motivated them to do good deeds. Clearly a network of weak ties generated this awareness and motivation to do good deeds. Individuals can have strong positions within a network despite their less strong commitment to a cause. There individual can fill certain rules defined as a result of spread of awareness due to the network of weak ties. A small donation may not make a signification impact on relief efforts but sharing of such donation on social media may attract many to follow the same path and donate (Srinivansan, 2010).

Social Media and Media Culture in the World

In order to understand the significance of social media tools, we must understand the use of social media in the context of media culture in different parts of the world.

According to Lewis (2005), the single most important development is the adoption of modern communications. Though, the world Internet penetration has increased dramatically over the last several years, the technological capabilities of modern life that are taken for granted in highly developed societies, have progressed in a relatively short span of time and have not been embraced by the authoritarian governments that dominate many significant regions of the world (such as Middle East). The rapid development of print and visual media in these regions has made the ruling elite fear the Internet as a conduit for political and moral subversion.

As Internet access has proliferated across these regions, a highly ambivalent and complex relationship between media and governments has developed, in which autocracies have encouraged Internet penetration in the name of economic development, while simultaneously attempting to maintain control over the spread of information and media sources (Khamis & Vaughn, 2011). This complex relationship between increasing Internet accessibility and a complementary increase in suppression of online freedom has led to a culture of subversion, an emerging cyberworld that knows no physical boundaries (Salmon, Fernandez, & Post, 2010) based on online social networking. With a lack of truly independent and representa-

tive media, disenfranchised youths have searched for an alternative method of participation in the public and political spheres (Storck, 2011).

CURRENT ISSUES OF SOCIAL MEDIA USE FOR SOCIAL AND POLITICAL CHANGE

Social Media for Political Change

Social media such as Facebook, Twitter and Wikis have become important political tools for citizens in countries with limitations and restrictions on media and freedom of speech (Khondker 2011; Strandberg, 2013; Stromback & Aelst, 2013). Citizens in many countries employ social media sites to voice their opinions, criticize policies, engage with their governments and even expose corrupt practices (Cave 2012; Logan 2012; Swegger, 2013; Thompson, 2013). Social media while primarily used as a social networking platform has become a popular means for citizens to discuss political issues, air dissent against politicians and government policies and even expose government corruption. Social media is thus increasingly playing an important role in how citizens become aware of information, how citizens engage in the political process and even to some extent how governments feel accountable to the public. This is especially so as various regions of the world are undergoing an ICT (Information, Communications and Technology) revolution with a number of major ICT developments. The increased availability of internet and mobile access is spurring the use of social media. Cave (2012) finds that ICT, specifically social media, is being used to enhance accountability and transparency by exposing negligence, poor service delivery, and corruption. The Arab spring in the Middle East is an example of the impact of social media in politics (Maghrabi and Salam 2011; Bruns, Highfield & Burgess, 2013; Wolfsfeld, Segev & Sheafer, 2013). Social media played an important role in the Arab Spring by enabling political activists in these countries to air their grievances, organize, and coordinate protests and also to share their plight with the world (Khondker, 2011; Wolfsfeld, 2014). Thus, social media is playing an important role in the facilitation of political change.

Studies that have examined the potential for social media to facilitate political change have largely been conducted in developed countries (Kushin & Yamamoto, 2010), and have produced mixed findings. These studies have examined issues such as social media as a campaign tool by political candidates (Stieglitz et al. 2012) and the offline political effect of online political discussions (Bimber & Copeland, 2013). Some authors argue that social media has significantly changed how democracy is achieved (Shirky 2011). A few studies have cited the example of how social media was able to implement democratic change in the Middle East (Maghrabi and Salam 2011; Howard et al. 2011). Social media has provided a mechanism for public dissent to be communicated. This is especially the case in countries absent of free media, civil society actors, and formal mechanisms for citizens to engage in the political process (Kaplan & Haenlein, 2010; Vaccari et al., 2013). In these countries, information that is published by the media is usually censored and comprises of government propaganda. Social media allows citizens to discuss, share, and communicate issues that are censored from traditional media. Social media also allows citizens to criticize government policies and hold government officials to account. Social media has also been used to expose corruption and engender greater transparency (Cave 2012; Logan 2012).

Issues of Social Media in Grassroots Political Movements

In order to fully evaluate the role of social media tools in the grassroots political movements, four visible issues can be identified: social media as an organizational tool, as an alternative press and

outlet for citizen journalism, a tool for generating awareness both regionally and internationally, and social media as a democratic medium.

Social Media as an Organizational Tool

The relative speed at which many Internet-led political uprisings occurred is one of the defining characteristics of these uprisings. In Tunisia, the uprising took 28 days. In Libya, the uprising took roughly 9 months. While in Egypt it took mere 18 days. Effective use of social media networks was central to the acceleration of these uprisings. Social networks provided a form of organizational infrastructure that initially started as virtual networks and finally transposed to the offline networks. Activists of these uprisings successfully capitalized the strengths of social network sites notably "many-to-many" communication capabilities and the speed with which information can be transferred and spread.

In Egypt, Wael Ghonim's Facebook group "We Are All Khaled Said" was created in memory of Khaled Said, a 28-year-old Egyptian from the coastal city of Alexandria, Egypt, who was tortured to death at the hands of two police officers during Egypt uprising. This group served as an organizational platform that attracted like-minded individuals to connect over a common interest to commemorate Khaled Said. This evolved into a common interest in forming an opposition to the Egyptian police force, which evolved into a movement to force Mubarak to step down. Activists in Lebanon began to unite with the goal of ousting the sectarian system. These activists managed to reach around 15,000 people through a Facebook group entitled "In favor of ousting the Lebanese sectarian system–towards a secular system." The group was comprised of youth from different sects, regions, and cultural backgrounds (Naim, 2011). However, the sectarian and divided nature of Lebanese youth partisanship rendered it difficult to use social media to mobilize young people through a common goal (Galey, 2011; Srinavasan,

2014). Social media played a different role in Tunisia and Egypt's anti-government protests than in Libya and Yemen. There was not the kind of strong tradition of online activism in Libya and Yemen as there is in other Arab countries (Riley, 2011). In Libya, there was a lack of Internet infrastructure, online access was difficult, and the Gadhafi regime had limited social media. In Yemen, government controls and extreme poverty limited Internet use (Riley, 2011). Unfortunately, in these countries, technological barriers to social media coupled with severe totalitarian regimes stymied reform efforts.

Sandwiched between Romania and Ukraine, Moldova emerged as an independent republic following the collapse of the USSR in 1991. The first widely recognized use of social media as a tool of political revolution occurred in Moldova in 2009. Activists used Facebook, LiveJournal (an electronic diary service/social network), and Twitter to organize protests and bring attention to the political unrest in the former Soviet republic. Interestingly enough, during the protests, Russian-language Tweeters debated the role of social networking tools in organizing the demonstration (Hodge, 2009).

On January 17, 2001, during the impeachment trial of Philippine President Joseph Estrada, loyalists in the Philippine Congress voted to set aside key evidence against him. Less than two hours after the decision, activists, with the help of forwarded text messages, were able to organize a protest at a major crossroads in Manila. Over the next few days, over a million people arrived. The public's ability to coordinate such a massive and rapid response, in which close to seven million text messages were sent that week, so alarmed the country's legislators that they reversed course and allowed the evidence to be presented. The event marked the first time that social media had helped force out a national leader (Shirky, 2011). On January 20, 2011, Estrada resigned.

Not only did social media provided the organizational infrastructure, but also it provided a crucial platform for potential protesters to network with one another and share their common grievances. Once individuals found out that other people would be protesting, they were more likely to join themselves. Eventually, a tipping point occurred, when the protest or activity became self-reinforcing, and increased without further direct organization or action by the leadership (Duncombe, 2011). The spread of communication using social media to offline communities was essential to reach the majority of population that, in many cases, remains offline. Very traditional forms of spreading information such as distributing flyers to citizen on the streets were also used by the activists. Every user was a potential re-broadcaster that broadcasted information to his own real world social network. The conclusion to be drawn here is that successful socio-political movements must be based on grassroots organizational structures. These structures starts offline and use both offline and online organizational tactics. On the must part, social media was a tool for acceleration and facilitation of socio political movement.

Social Media as an Alternative Press

With its low entry barriers, social media tools provide an accessible platform for citizen journalism, defined as the use of digital media tools to report on events on the ground, uploading text and videos directly to the Internet or feeding the information and videos to media outlets (Khamis & Vaughn, 2011). The dialogue taking place via Facebook, Twitter and other social media networks was used by the mainstream media as a source during the height of the protests in various Internet-led political movements. During Egypt uprising, Al-Jazeera relied on reputed bloggers and Twitter users for real-time coverage of events, by using Sharek, a citizen's media platform that received and filtered through submissions by citizen journalists. Though there were obvious accuracy issues related to citizen journalism, the implication for the role of social media within the uprising is that it allowed for those directly involved to shape their own narrative and expose themselves to an international audience. Social media place the tools of documentation and truth-telling into the hands of ordinary citizens, social media networks create linked activists who can contest the narrative- crafting and information-controlling capabilities of authoritarian regimes (Duncombe, 2011)·

In the political uprising of Egypt, Twitter was used by activists as a platform of discussions about events happening on the ground. Activists capitalized on Twitter's mobile-phone enabled social media to not only send regular tweet updates but also share other forms of medial such as photographs and videos. These examples aptly demonstrate the role of alternate press played by Twitter users. There user self published their own accounts of the uprising. This self published information served as their own narratives of events exposed to audience at both local and global level. This way social media allowed literally real time following of events by the user across geographical boundaries (Storck, 2011).

Although Tunisia's government practiced some of the most repressive Internet censorship, the country had one of the most connected populations in the region outside the Gulf; 33% of the population was online, 16% on Facebook and 18% using Twitter. Although the Tunisian regime blocked YouTube during the month of unrest, it did not entirely block Internet access, and seasoned cyber activists played bridging roles, re-posting videos and Facebook content about protests from closed loops of private networks to twitter and online news portals with greater reach (Oxford Analytica, 2011). Also, Tunisia witnessed a sudden eight percent surge in the number of Facebook users during the first two weeks of unrest, coupled with a shift in the usage turned from merely social in nature into primarily political (Khaleej Times, 2011).

During uprising in Egypt, the government shut down the Internet. At that time, individuals outside the country came forward and use technology to provide continuous coverage of the events. That helped continue the momentum of the political movement. According to Time Magazine (2011), social media plays a significant role for people outside the borders. These people can use social medial to bring context, understanding, and analysis of the situation. However, this new sphere of citizen journalism have also brought the issues of accuracy and anonymity. Previously unheard individuals have used anonymity provided by Internet to express their dissent without any fear of any backlash from the government. At the same time, there is a possibility that this anonymity can be abused. Take one example of Tom MacMaster, 40, a married U.S. student at the University of Edinburg. He created in February 2011 Amina Abdallah Arraf al Omari, a fictional character or hoax persona. MacMaster presented himself as a Syrian-American blogger, identifying herself as a lesbian on her weblog "A Gay Girl In Damascus" and blogging in support of increased civil and political freedom for Syrians. During the 2011 Syrian uprising, a posting on the blog purportedly by "Amina's" cousin claimed that Amina was abducted on 6 June 2011. The online response in the community, mainstream media, and social networking websites was rapid and extensive. His posts caught the attention of the world amassing thousands of followers and news organizations. On June 12, The Electronic Intifada published evidence for its claims that "Amina" was the product of one or both of husband-wife team Tom MacMaster and Britta Froelicher. McMaster initially denied this, but later that day the blog was updated with MacMaster's admission that he was the sole author of the blog.

Social media proponents promoted the technology's role in the Iranian unrest, but a closer look reveals a more complicated picture. Although there was a great deal of excitement about the role of Twitter in Iran after the presidential election evidence indicated that twitter conversation about the Iranian protest occurred mostly among those in the West, and most likely was not used by Iranians to organize. Instead, Twitter and other social media were used to report protest events as they unfolded, replacing the foreign press and also creating international support for the movement (Etling et al., 2010). Research into the Iranian blogosphere showed that political and religious conservatives were no less prominent than regime critics (Etling, Palfrey & Faris, 2009). While the movement was unsuccessful in forcing change, it continued to exist, still using social media as a way to communicate within Iran and with others around the world who are sympathetic to their cause.

In Moldova, word had been spreading rapidly via Twitter and other online networking services. The official media carried no coverage, but accounts, pictures, and video of the rally were appearing in real time on Twitter and YouTube (Mungiu-Pippidi & Munteanu, 2009). Although the protestors failed to prompt a change of leadership or a new election, they got the world to focus on a small, remote country, and digital activism became recognized as a source of political power.

Social Media as a Tool to Generate Awareness

Much attention has been paid to the role that the Internet has played in generating awareness of various Internet-led uprisings. Movements started online were transposed to offline movements where they gained momentum and attention. In Egypt, the majority of Facebook users agreed that Facebook was used most effectively to raise awareness of the causes of the movements within the country (Mourtada & Salem, 2011). Take example of Facebook group "We Are All Khaled Said Khaled". Khaled became the symbol for many Egyptians who dreamed to see their country free of brutality, torture, and ill treatment. This Facebook group quickly attracted more then 500, 000 members. The group spread photos of

Khaled's disfigured corpse on the Internet. This Facebook group exploited Facebook to engage users in a powerful cyber activism campaign against an authoritarian government of Egypt. Howard (2010) defines cyberactivism as "the act of using the internet to advance a political cause that is difficult to advance offline," adding that "the goal of such activism is often to create intellectually and emotionally compelling digital artifacts that tell stories of injustice, interpret history, and advocate for particular political outcomes." (p.145). The important difference between cyber activism and mobilization is that mobilization is focused on planning, execution, and facilitation of actions. Cyber activism helps in fostering and promoting civic engagement that in turn results in various forms of civic mobilization. Therefore both concepts are closely interrelated. The use of Facebook group "We are All Khaled Said Khaled" for political motives sparked a new consciousness that provided serious consequences for polities in Egypt and networking capabilities of Facebook.

It was found that those Egyptians who admit to not using social media still vouched for social media as a platform where they could enjoy free expression of political will. This shows a wider change in social consciousness of people who took part in that uprising in Egypt. Egyptian public used online tools to challenge the repressive and corrupt monopolies of power in Egypt (Chebib & Sohail, 2011). A clear and definite shift in attitude towards authorities was observed. It has been argued that this shift in attitude was collective and driven by use of social media. Social media played an important role in formulating this collective shift in social consciousness. Thus, cyberactivists were able to capitalize on the accelerating effect of social networking online to formulate a social movement that could be transferred to the offline community and then manifested in political action. Many ordinary people not particularly politically active and kept their dissent limited to discussions with friends about their dissatisfaction with the government. However, an important shift took place once they realized via Facebook that this dissatisfaction was manifest in the nation.

A final element to address is the ways in which social media, whether intentionally or unintentionally raised awareness of the ongoing political uprisings in the international community. The need for social networking tools to continue political mobilization was made evident when Western corporations Google and Twitter teamed together to offer "Speak2Tweet" services after President Mubarak shut down Internet access across the nation. The involvement of powerful non-state, transnational actors in the domestic politics was very significant for activists who were able to continue their plight against the state.

US government recognized the role of new media as a source of information in authoritative states when US Secretory of State Hillary Clinton issued a request to twitter and asked to delay a planned site maintenance. This request came in the wake of protests in Iran against controversial presidential elections of 2009. The delay in twitter's site maintenance was meant to provide Iranian protestors an opportunity to communicate via social network. It also allowed US government to access information from Iran, where US had no official diplomatic presence for last three decades (McElroy, 2009). Thus. Social media acted as a significant source of information for both civilians and governments.

Social Media as Democratic Medium

Globalization affects different stakeholders in different ways. In a similar fashion, Internet stimulates different users in different ways. The two states may react in entirely different ways to the use of Internet as a pro-democracy-tool (Morozov, 2011). Activists in Tunisia and Egypt were apparently able to exploit the benefits of social media. However activists in Bahrain and

Saudi Arabia, in an attempt to replicate the same strategies, were not able to reap the same benefits of social media.

Egypt is one example of social media use to voice political dissent. In 2009, Iranian protestors initiated the green movement in which Twitter was used as a forum to register their protest against the controversial presidential elections. The use of social media by green movement to spread democratic sentiment was lauded by US and other western governments. This was because it fit nicely with motives and policies of western governments. However, in the after math of Iranian presidential elections, green movements lost its momentum and quickly faded into the background. Barack Obama made history in 2008 presidential elections of USA. He was the first presidential candidate to effectively use social media as a major campaign strategy. Given how ubiquitous social media is today, interacting with people on social media (such as sending voting reminders on Twitter) was a big deal in 2008. On the announcement of Obama's candidacy in 2007, Twitter had only just started and there wasn't even an iPhone yet. Four years later in 2012, the number of American adults who used social media increased from 37% to 69%. In 2012, 66% of American social media users were actively engaged in political activism online. This population was estimated to be the equivalent of 39% of all American adults. In 2008, McCain's campaign was as social-media-deaf as Obama's was social-media-savvy. While the Republican candidate Romney's campaign tried to replicate the 2008 success story of Obama, they did not achieve the traction that the Democrats did (Mejova, Srinivasan, & Boynton, 2013). Obama dominated the social media space because his team got how networks work. The real power of social media is not in the number of posts or Tweets but in user engagement measured by content spreadability. For example, Obama logged twice as many Facebook "Likes" and nearly 20 times as many re-tweets as Romney. With his existing social media base and spreadable content, Obama had far superior reach (Pamela Rutledge, 2013; Graber & Dunaway, 2014, Gulati & Williams, 2013).

In 2014, more than 200 Nigerian schoolgirls were kidnapped from their boarding school by armed Islamist militants. The event became an issue of international importance, with a $300,000 (£177,000) cash reward offered to anyone who could help locate and rescue the girls. Social media played a pivotal role in forcing the issue onto the agenda of world leaders. Hundreds of thousands of people (including the first lady Michelle Obama) posted images of themselves holding pieces of paper with the #BringBackOurGirls hashtag written on it on Facebook, Instagram and Twitter (Collins, 2014). But the attention of the world outside Nigeria soon faded. Journalists moved on to other stories; the hashtag stopped trending, a reflection that social media is failing. As the New Yorker's Naunihal Singh put it, "a viral hashtag, it seems, is a fever that breaks quickly." (Gary Nauer, 2014, p.1).

Trayvon Martin, a 17-year-old kid from Miami, was shot and killed by a neighborhood watch volunteer in Sanford, Florida on February 26, 2012. A massive social media campaign started against the killing of Martin. On Twitter, there had been more than 600,000 mentions of the case. A single "Justice for Trayvon Martin" Facebook page was created and brought in more than 82,000 "likes" alone (Gray, 2012). On August 14, Obama spoke to the nation, urging both law enforcement officers and protesters to take a step back and think. On August 9, 2014, Brown, 18 and unarmed, was shot to death by a Ferguson police officer. By the next day, it was national news, reported by every major news outlet across the United States. The story skipped over classic media filters and, in some ways, the public was driving the story through social media, and the media was following public cues. It took less than a week for Brown's death to go from the streets of suburban Missouri to the White House. That speaks volumes about the

shifting dynamics in how these stories are told. In big part, this was due to a group of media-savvy, grassroots organizers that arose after the failures of the media response in 2012 and the shooting of Oscar Grant in Oakland, California, in 2009. The Million Hoodies Movement for Justice was established in March 2012, immediately after Martin's death became national news (Elijah Wolfson, 2014). These examples are a clear proof of the fact that to sustain online activism and to transform it into an offline reality is a difficult proposition (Afouxenidis, 2014; Anduiza, Cristancho, & Sabucedo, 2013; Ceron, Curini, Iacus, & Porro, 2014; Enjolras, Steen-Johnsen, & Wollebæk, 2013; Lim, 2013).

In another case, we witnessed the use of networking capabilities of social media in 2011 London roots where police officers used social media extensively to communicate with each other and to get information from public about the riots. In fact, we also see similarities between London riots and Egyptian uprising. Besides the use of social media both were triggered by the unjustified death of a young man. In addition, in both scenarios the governments made efforts to shut down access to social media tools. The Egyptian government implemented a full nationwide Internet blackout. In UK, the government vowed to do whatever it takes to end the unrest, including blocking access to social media sites (Halliday, 2011). This comparison shows that context is very important when it comes to judge the potential of social media and Internet as force for good. In the case of Egypt the use of social media and Internet by activists was landed by western governments as a force to promote and entrench democracy. However in the case of London, the same tools were treated by western governments as foes when used to fuel civil unrest in London.

It is also important to note that the Internet cannot be considered as a universal remedy for all political ills, especially regarding authoritarian regimes. Internet is a tool without a handle (Morozov, 2012). While Internet possess enormous liberating potential, harnessing this potential and translating it into political reality is a much harder task to accomplish. Different contexts give rise to different problems and thus need custom-made solutions and strategies. In Egypt, social media did play a role in organizing the protests and bringing to the attention of the international community, voices that had previously not been given a platform for dissent.

However, many years after revolution, chaos and protest continued in Egypt. The young Egyptian activists were upset by the results of the poll. Their political imagination and demands were not reflected in the polls. This situation echoed concerns of people that many deep rooted political and economic issues were behind the civic unrest in Egypt. Internet and social media played an important role in strengthening pro-democracy movement. However, it would be a mistake to think that Internet and social media alone can solve these issues.

Social Media and Social Change

Social media has significantly altered communication. This change has brought significant media attention in the recent past. Notably the Mumbai attacks, the Iranian presidential election protects in 2009, and the Haiti earthquake were situations where communication was significantly facilitated by social media. Using social media tools, people can connect and unite in a crisis situation, raise global awareness of an issue, and usurp authoritarian governments. Social media tools can provide can be provide night information at the right time e.g. location of a hospital for people injured in an accident. The awareness of a cause generated by social media can be used to raise funds for the cause. Using social media everyone can be a journalist (Finau, Prasad, Logan, & Cox, 2014).

However, transparent nature of communication using social media can also be dangerous as rumors can quickly spread on social media. For example, criminals can use social media to observe police activity by spreading false rumors. Additionally, though social media can increase awareness of an issue we cannot say for sure whether social media actually puts people in action.

There are other issues involved in the use of social media for social change. One such issue is the ability of social media companies to handle crisis situations. Twitter was praised after they delayed a schedule site maintenance activity on the request of US Department of State. The purpose of this delay was to avoid interruption of communication in Iran during protests on presidential election. However, Facebook faced severe criticism on their real name policy. This real name policy forced activists to use their real name on their Facebook accounts. Violations could result in account deletion even if non-use of real name was for safety propose.

Many believe that social change can be facilitated through new ways of communication provided by social media. Twitter co-founder Biz Stone thought that social media lowers the barriers for activism. Still many believe that social media has little role in creating social changes and real social change come from people on the ground. According to Gladwell (2010) online social networks creates only weak ties that are not sufficient for actual action. Gladwell argued that online social media communication tools have been given unnecessary importance for their role in creating social change and the role of communication itself to create social change has been under emphasized. According to Gladwell (2010), "Where activists were once defined by their causes, they are now defined by their tools" (p. 2). Shirky (2009) argues that the way social media changed the communication significantly impacted the way people create change: "Group action gives human society its particular character, and anything that changes the way groups get things done will affect society as a whole" (Shirky, 2009, p. 23). So, while there is no doubt that people are using social media for communication, has it produced significant changes in the way social changes is created by activists?

Studies suggest that social media usage is context dependent (Kaplan & Haenlein, 2010; Shirky 2011). Furthermore, rapid ICT developments in many regions of the world suggest that the use of social media in these regions will increase. Social media could thus play a significant role in the political, social, and economic development of countries.

Issues of Social Media Use for Social Change

In order fully evaluate the role of social media tools for bringing social change; following visible issues can be identified.

Motivating Action for Social Change

Social change requires a lot of work. To be effective, revolutions requires organization, funding, and support from masses (Papic & Noonan, 2011). Even a well organization revaluation need to go through an activist process of social transformation. This process includes information acquisition, knowledge development, transfer and sharing; ideation and thought leadership; empathy and emotional connection; and the spread of credible ideas that inspire cognitive dissonance (Leggio, 2008).

To motivate social change, a mass appeal is needed. People need to be convinced that their participation will make a difference. This convincing is especially important if people participation involves experience of personal discomfort. This task is not small and becomes very complicated in case of large groups (such as the ones involved in a political protest). In case of large groups, contribution made to the action of each individual member of group has no discernable impact on the overall success of the group. A rational person will not bear the cost of participation in the group

(such as individual's time) knowing that he/she will enjoy the public good even if he/she do not make a meaningful participation in the group (Finkel & Muller, 1989).

Gladwell (2010) argues that communication tools, used by people, are often overemphasized for their role in bringing social change. The people behind social change are often underemphasized. Regardless of the tools used for planning and organizing social change, same basic principles of motivation must be applied to bring change. Social media tools can make the task of communication easier but the same tools cannot help much in convincing the people to participate especially when participation involves personal risks.

The Influence of the Media

Social media tools have been praised for the ability to reach many people, but the transition from reach to action is debated. The argument over whether or not the media influences social change is not new. Lazarsfeld & Merton (2000) argued that the mass media could cause audiences to become knowledgeable about a subject, but take no action. They argued that media create no social change, but instead works to enforce existing social values. To understand this argument one need to analyze the overabundance of information streaming on social media. For example, a Twitter feed can possibly provide an individual a false sense of understating rather than bring this individual towards action. For example, people might learn on Twitter about the killing of a protestor in Iran but not be compelled to join the protest because of the feeling that they are already involved.

Today people see abundant information on many things happening around them. In this case, prioritization of attention becomes a difficult task. According to (ReadWrite, 2009), the question arises "How does an Internet junkie, news organization, or political operative monitor rapidly evolving real-time events, from the crucial details to the bigger picture? More importantly, how can a data stream be turned into real-time action, reaching the people who need it, when they need it, and in a form they can easily digest?" (p.1). In this regard, social media is different from traditional channels of communication (such as TV and newspapers) because there is no editor on social media. This is good because social media can give voice to those who many not otherwise have one. However, those voice many be combined unreliable.

Cultural Differences in Social Media Use

Cultural difference exists, across countries, in the use of social media tools. These cultural differences profoundly impact the way people use social media. According to Sheedy (2011), cultural differences can affect communication from five aspects. These aspects include design language, language subtitles, Internet performance, and face and avatars. Due to their cultural differences, people use social media differently. While Facebook may consider all Facebook friends equal, many cultures have different expectation for different relationship. Such different anticipations can cause different perceptions of strength of social media and change the way different cultures may use social media for social change.

Legitimacy of Social Media

The wide reaching broadcast provided by social media is one strong factor why social media is preferred to disseminate information in a crisis. For example, Al Jazeera English, which offers coverage of the Middle East, often when no other media will or can, is not carried by any major American cable or satellite companies (Rich, 2011). In this case, the social media presence of Al Jazeera becomes indispensable to get real-time information about a crisis in the Middle East. Transparent form of communication, provided by

social media, is changing the way people receive and interact with news and information, but one that is only now being seen as legitimate.

The Digital Divide

The digital divide refers to the potential for a divide between those connected to the Internet and those not connected, sometimes worded as the divide between the information have's and have's not (Steyaert, 2002). Digital divide is one significant challenge in using social media for social change. A large digital divide severely limits the social media use for social change.

Policy Implications

Today social media sites, such as Facebook, Twitter and YouTube provide vast amount of shared information. Much of this information is provided by citizens acting as journalist. The content provided by these citizen journalist cannot be hold to ethical standard of traditional journalists. For years, privacy concerns have been on the center stage of the debate concerning social media use. As social media has become more integrated into people communication, more complex issue have arisen (Madrigal, 2011).

US Secretary of State Hillary Clinton's historic speech in January 2010 on internet freedom was celebrated as an unequivocal policy statement on global free speech and expression. Hillary Clinton said, "New technologies do not take sides in the struggle for freedom and progress but the United States does (Yee, 2011, p.1). This statement reiterates the point made by Gladwell that we tend to personify social media tools instead of actions (Gladwell, 2010). It also raises important questions about the regulation of social media. Social media platforms do offer constitutional protections such as freedom of expression (Greeley, 2011). These platforms are also used worldwide. The questions arises as to which country's rule should be followed when the social media platform developed in Country A is used a user in Country B?

Another question that concerns use of social media for social change is that who has a right to have a social media presence. Obviously, any use of social media for threatening or abusive purposes cannot be allowed. However, who is going to decide the rules to determine what constitutes an unacceptable behavior on social media platforms? Some social media platforms follow non-transparent policies on the issue of deleting accounts. That makes the issue complicated. For example, Facebook removes a user's account if another user "report" an abuse. In case a user account is removed, Facebook makes no contact with the removed user. The only option available to the removed user is to send an email to disabled@facebook.com with a reinstatement request (York, 2010).

Such policies of social media sites can have serious consequences for activists using social media for social change. The opposition can easily have an activist's Facebook account removed if they don't approve the activist organizing event and relaying messages. This way, the source of information could be cut off and group would be forced to find another way of communication. Facebook's real name policy also caused a stir when Facebook disabled the account of popular Chinese blogger and activist Michael Anti because he was not using his legal name, Zhao Jing (Tran, 2011). For activists, this real name policy brings serious threats to their secrecy, privacy, and the revolutions that organize. This is because the transparent nature of social media communication allows governments to see what activists are doing and take action against them if they deem necessary. Even social media platforms providers can turn against individuals if they feel that the content posted is inappropriate. As an example, Twitter suspended the account of Guy Adams, a British journalist, who criticized NBC's Olympics coverage. Adams encouraged his followers to email an NBC executive and express their disappoint-

ment. Adams also took a step further: He included the email of Gary Zenkel, the president of NBC Olympics. Twitter suspended Guy's account by saying "Your Twitter account has been suspended for posting an individual's private information such as private email address." After getting his account suspended, Guy responded by saying that he found Zenkel's email address on Google where it was publicly available. Later on, Twitter reinstated Guy's account. Twitter acknowledged it had flunked the situation by actively reporting the offending tweet to NBC, with which it had been working in partnership for the Olympics (Mott, 2012).

Other social media platforms, such as Twitter, YouTube, and LinkedIn do not offer account verification and do not follow strict real name policies. LinkedIn policy says "Create a user profile for anyone other than a natural person" (LinkedIn, n.d.). This creates different problems for activists— one cannot be sure that people are who they say they are. The similar confusion was caused during Green Movement in Iran when rumors of government impersonating activists were spread on social media.

In some cases, social media platforms may be asked by governments or law enforcement to turn over some user information or to help identify criminals. Facebook hasn't implemented special tools or processes for activists. According to Facebook's Chief Security Officer Joe Sullivan "We get requests all the time in a few different contexts where people would like to impersonate someone else. Police wanting to go undercover or human rights activists, say. And we, just based on our core mission and core product, don't want to allow that. That's just not what Facebook is. Facebook is a place where people connect with real people in their lives using their real identities (Madrigal, 2011, p.3). Twitter attempts to notify users if they have to release any records or information about them. As Biz Stone, co-founder of Twitter, stated "Our goal is to instantly connect people everywhere to what is most meaningful to them. For this to happen, freedom of expression is essential."…"Our position on freedom of expression carries with it a mandate to protect our users' right to speak freely and preserve their ability to contest having their private information revealed.". "While we may need to release information as required by law, we try to notify Twitter users before handing over their information whenever we can so they have a fair chance to fight the request if they so choose" (Stone, 2011, p.1).

RECOMMENDATIONS/ IMPLICATIONS FOR EDUCATION, CIVIC ENGAGEMENT, SOCIAL PRACTICE, AND POLICY

As civil unrest continues, Twitter remains an outlet for citizen journalism, while protesters continue their struggle for political legitimacy. Change in political culture undergoes a lengthy and challenging process and history suggests that f change cannot be expected with one year of the start of the political movement for change. Undoubtedly, the use of social media and Internet have accelerated aspects of social change and revolution. However, the capabilities of social media and Internet for a long term change are yet to be demonstrated. Perhaps the most important and successful contribution of social media is that it has allowed a more independent press to flourish. One of the essential corollaries of a democratic society is an independent and transparent media. Social media has played a key role of a watch dug on repressive governments (Iskander, 2011). Therefore, social media can be regarded as important tools for political protest. However, social media cannot be treated as a form of social activism that is not dependent on the individuals who use social media. The use of social media is an example of how speeches, articles, images, and documents are constantly being recorded and placed online to create an accessible archive of information. This

has a cathartic effect for a society that has operated under oppression and censorship (Iskander, 2011).

Following are some of the recommendations for using social media as a political and social change agent.

First, we should remember that there were people behind the social media tools used for social change. However, credit is generally given to the tools used for political and social change and not the people behind them. Social media tools can be used to raise awareness, appeal masses, rise funding, and bring people together. However, to personify these tool mean that we underestimate the participation costs and risks that activists bear.

Second, the best social media tools can do is to raise world awareness of an issue and we witnessed that in the case of uprisings in Egypt, Tunisia, Iran, Ukraine etc. Perhaps the most significant impact of online protests was that rest of the world got to know a view from the ground. This impact was evident in case of fund raising for Haiti earthquake victims and raising world awareness of the protests on Iranian presidential election.

Third, social media tools allow users to help each other, regardless of location and this potential of social media tools should be leveraged to its maximum possible extent. During Mumbai attacks of 2008, people used social media to get help to needy people and provide information to each other. In Egypt, social media helped protesters exchange information about possible dangers and to get medical help to people in need. Nevertheless people's ability to help each other using social media was not limited by geographical boundaries. People in many countries actively observed the revolution in Egypt and helped activists in different ways. People set up proxies, hacked government website, and raised awareness about the cause of Egyptian activists. Additionally, this increased awareness can work to incite politicians. Politicians can become more vocal and open with their reaction to revolution and situation they witness on social media.

Fourth, social media use for political and social change can be dangerous and therefore activists must consider this when planning to use social media tools in their movements. It is clear that many policies of social media sites, such as real name policy, are in direct conflict with the interests of activists. These policies pose great dangers to activists as governments can use social media to spy on, misinform, or incriminate activists. Social media use in Egypt helped bring massive organizing and action. It may appear that use of online tools, such as social media, to bring social change is not dangerous However, that doesn't seem to be true. In Egypt, post-Mubarak era was even more dangerous for activists using social media. New York Times on April 11, 2011 reported that a young Egyptian blogger Maikel Nabi was sentenced to there years in jail. The reason behind the sentence was a blog written by Nabi, describing Egyptian army's abuse of female detainees. The evidence presented in the court against Nabi included screen shots of his personal Facebook page and blog (Robert Mackey, 2011). The situation may be even worse in other countries. According to Facebook's Chief of Security Joe Sullivan, "When you step back and think about how Internet traffic is routed around the world, an astonishing amount is susceptible to government access" (Madrigal, 2011, p.3). Therefore, social media must not be mistaken as either a perfect method for social change communication or a trend that will quickly pass.

GAPS IN EXISTING RESEARCH

One important aspect of Internet-led revolutions is that the costs of organizing are lowering and allowing decentralized forces of ordinary people actually push revolution. However, such organizations have slim chances of becoming long lasting structures, which, for example, can become political parties after the revolution.

Visionaries such as Manuel Castells (Castells, 2009) and Marshall McLuhan (McLuhan, 2001) predicted the transformative convergence of media and technology on society. However, at least taking the Egyptian Revolution as example, the factors of organizational presence, boots on the ground, community outreach and face to face interactions are crucial factors in creating and sustaining social change-- still more important than the magic of networking and social media, or leaderless protest movements spurred by technology. The Muslim Brotherhood came late to the revolution, was relatively unskilled at the use of social media in comparison to the young protestors of the Arab street, but nevertheless has been able to grasp the reins of government in Egypt.

According to Manuel Castells conceptualization of network configurations, new political movements allow previously disconnected, undeveloped political identities to take shape and rise to a prominent position. This is particularly applicable to those countries where religions and ethnic divides previously prevented networking. For example, many Arab regimes banned the creation of political parties and limited the right to associate or create civil rights groups. Social media helped such groups discover one another and break the psychological barrier of fear between them. In Tunisia, conversations about liberty, democracy and revolution on blogs and on twitter often immediately preceded mass protests. According to Rosenberg (2011) social media has three uses: It is an efficient and cheap way to give members information. It also conveys to members the highly motivating realization that they have big numbers so that they feel more excited and less fearful than people unaware they are part of a very big group. And it is an efficient way to transfer skills and information.

According to Shirky (2011) "The more promising way to think about social media is as long-term tools that can strengthen civil society and the public sphere" and "social media can compensate for the disadvantages of undisciplined groups by reducing the costs of coordination" (, p.2). The anti-Estrada movement in the Philippines used the ease of sending and forwarding text messages to organize a massive group with no need (and no time) for standard managerial control. As a result, larger, looser groups can now take on some kinds of coordinated action, such as protest movements and public media campaigns that were previously reserved for formal organizations. For political movements, one of the main forms of coordination is what the military calls "shared awareness," the ability of each member of a group to not only understand the situation at hand but also understand that everyone else does, too. Social media increase shared awareness by propagating messages through social networks. The anti-Aznar protests in Spain gained momentum so quickly precisely because the millions of people spreading the message were not part of a hierarchical organization (Shirky, 2011). While the state can shut down easily the unorthodox tools, shutting down tools in broad use involve risk of politicizing a large number of people who were not active politically before. Another impact of shutting down such tools is that it draws external attention from citizens and governments outside the country or the region to that country or region to the place that is experiencing protest or conflict. The real threat of this attention is the external reaction that authoritarian governments will have to face.

The rise of social media in this latest wave of political mayhem has brought considerable criticism from political theorists and social scientists. The critics argue that techno utopians overstate what the technology can do and understand the conditions for use of technology. There are, broadly speaking, two arguments against the idea that social media will make a difference in national politics and social fabric of the society. The first is that the tools are themselves ineffective, and the second is that they produce as much harm to democratization as good, because repressive governments are becoming better at using these tools

to suppress dissent. The critique of ineffectiveness, most recently offered by Malcolm Gladwell in The New Yorker, concentrates on examples of what has been termed "slacktivism," whereby casual participants seek social change through low-cost activities, such as joining Facebook's "Save Darfur" group, that are long on bumper-sticker sentiment and short on any useful action. According to Gladwell (2010), "platforms of social media are built around weak ties. Social networks are effective at increasing participation—by lessening the level of motivation that participation requires." (p. 3). In his point of view, the type of relationships created by use of social media were not conducive to the sustained, hierarchical, and high-risk behavior needed to make real social change. The second critique of social media as tools for political improvement points to the fact that the state is gaining increasingly sophisticated means of monitoring, interdicting, or co-opting these tools. The use of social media is just as likely to strengthen authoritarian regimes as it is to weaken them. For example, the Chinese government has spent considerable effort perfecting several systems for controlling political threats from social media (Shirky, 2011).

Social media tools suffer from one significant weakness. Using these tools to bring political change require people to have close personal connection to bring an action. This is especially true if the action is risky and difficult. We see many successful examples of the use of social media tools for political change. However, we also see many examples where activists failed to achieve the desired political results e.g. the political movement of Belarus in March 2006. The movement was against the allegedly rigged election of President Aleksandr Lukashenko. The movement first swelled, then faltered, leaving Lukashenko more determined than ever to control social media. During the June 2009 uprising of the Green Movement in Iran, activists used every possible technological coordinating tool to protest the controversial presidential election.

The movement ultimately brought to heel by a violent crackdown. In the Red Shirt movement of Thailand in 2010, the social media savvy activists occupied the downtown Bangkok. Again, the movement ultimately brought to heel by a violent crackdown, killing dozens. The structure of social media tools also puts limits on political activism. Take example of Twitter. "There are so many messages streaming through at any moment that any single entry is unlikely to break through the din, and the limit of 140 characters -- part of the service's charm and the secret of its success -- militates against sustained argument and nuance." (Etling et al., 2009, p.2)

FUTURE RESEARCH AREAS

The Internet-led revolutions raise questions about whether citizen journalism is activism and whether participants can be journalists. The fact that social media users do not have to be vetted or held to ethical standards is both a problem and a blessing. An area that needs further research is how the rules of social media will be established and how they will be embraced by the next generation of social media users, both in crises and times that are more peaceful.

A further study of the use of social media in politics post-uprising could investigate the role of social networking in establishing new political parties or civil society groups, a process that has proven itself the main obstacle to protesters gaining political legitimacy.

While it is established that the social media strengthen a political movement and bring social change it is still unclear whether social media is more empowering to leadership or the supporters of a movement. This is a research area that needs further investigation.

While the number of social media users is increasing still, there is a large number of people who don't use social media. If social media be-comes the only successful mechanism to cause social change, what happens to those who do not have access to social media? This question is very important for future uses of social media in politics and needs further investigation.

Another area that needs to be researched is the relative preference of cyber activism and conventional political activism in bringing the social and political change. Should we consider cyber-activism a lesser/inferior form of activism, compared to physical on-the-street type of political activism? The answer to this question is crucial for the future role of social media as a political and social change agent.

CONCLUSION

The advent of technology and the rise of social media are changing the political landscape around the world. Social media is empowering citizens to voice their opinions, participate in the political process, and allowing some governments to engage with citizens in a more responsive and interactive manner. The role and power of social media in political and social change is just beginning. Social media has the potential to transform national political processes, to foster greater engagement with Governments, to develop new forms of enhanced transparency, democracy and accountability and usher in an era of political change.

The debate over whether or not the emergence of social media has changed the way people communicate for political and social change has received heightened attention.

This chapter examined use of social media in several recent cases that received worldwide attention. By analyzing the way the activists utilized the tools of social media through established theories of communication, one can see how the inherent characteristics of social media and the Internet were able to foster the necessary requirements for collective action. However, despite its success in organizing the uprisings, it would seem from the current situation in various cases that social media has been less useful in translating the needs and demands of protesters into political reality.

Several key issues related to the use and role of social media for political and social change were discussed. Though there is a range of opinion as to how influential social media was in generating political mobilization in various Internet-led political movements, it is argued that its main roles were in providing an organizational infrastructure, as a form of alternative press, and as generating awareness both domestically and internationally of the ongoing revolution. Social media tools are often personified, but for political and social change to occur there must be people behind the tools.

Social media can increase world awareness of an issue and allows people to help each other regardless of location. Social media can help start the change process but to make change happen is a task much harder than imagined. When analyzing the role of Internet in political activism it is important to know what the history tells us. A review of history tells us that behind any political activism there have always been people willing to decide that its time to stand up to the powers and publicly voice the dissent despite risk of imprisonment, death or torture. Protests, when effective, are the end of a process, rather than a replacement for it. Political freedom has to be accompanied by a society literate enough and densely connected enough to discuss the issues presented to the public. The cyber-verse gives no side a decisive, unassailable advantage. For groups that have felt powerless against repressive regimes, social media's technological leveling of the political playing field provides one of the most important components of any successful revolution – hope.

The founders of Facebook, Twitter, and YouTube did not create their products with the intent of starting revolutions and ousting repressive regimes. They probably never thought of playing a role in the revolution by providing their products as vehicles for change. The people behind the revolution were the ones that initiated the idea of revolution and chose their tools / medium of communication for the revolution. Irrespective of the choice of tools/medium of communication, the ultimate strength of a movement is determined by the will for activism.

For all that it does, social media is no "silver bullet" when it comes to political and social change. The use of social media tools does not have a single predetermined outcome. Therefore, attempts to outline their effects on political and social action are too often reduced to conflicting anecdotes. Social media has limited impact at best on an important factor affecting nascent revolutions – a regime's willingness to use force to squelch protests.

A way forward for the Internet-led movements for political and social change in repressive regimes is to gain influence to the extent that they are able to avoid the scrutiny and controls of the state. A challenge for improving their prospects in closed societies that must rely on decentralized networks is to adapt, emulate, and transfer the benefits of highly organized civil society groups. It is important because in repressive regimes bottom-up decentralized organizing is more likely to survive.

REFERENCES

Afouxenidis, A. (2014). Social Media and Political Participation: An Investigation of Small Scale Activism in Greece. *Advances in Applied Sociology, 04*(01), 1–4. doi:10.4236/aasoci.2014.41001

Alexa. (2014, September 27). *Alexa Top 500 Global Sites*. Retrieved September 27, 2014, from http://www.alexa.com/topsites

Anduiza, E., Cristancho, C., & Sabucedo, J. M. (2013). Mobilization through online social networks: The political protest of the indignados in Spain. *Information Communication and Society*, *17*(6), 750–764. doi:10.1080/136911 8X.2013.808360

Bimber, B., & Copeland, L. (2013). Digital media and traditional political participation over time in the US. *Journal of Information Technology & Politics*, *10*(2), 125–137. doi:10.1080/19331681 .2013.769925

Bruns, A., Highfield, T., & Burgess, J. (2013). The Arab Spring and Social Media Audiences English and Arabic Twitter Users and Their Networks. *The American Behavioral Scientist*, *57*(7), 871–898. doi:10.1177/0002764213479374

Castells, M. (1996). *Rise of The Network Society*. Malden, MA: Wiley-Blackwell.

Castells. (2009). *The Power of Identity* (2nd ed.). Wiley-Blackwell.

Cave, D. (2012). *Digital islands: how the Pacific's ICT revolution is transforming the region*. Retrieved September 27, 2014, from http://www.lowyinstitute.org/publications/digital-islands-how-pacifics-ict-revolution-transforming-region

Ceron, A., Curini, L., Iacus, S. M., & Porro, G. (2014). Every tweet counts? How sentiment analysis of social media can improve our knowledge of citizens' political preferences with an application to Italy and France. *New Media & Society*, *16*(2), 340–358. doi:10.1177/1461444813480466

Chebib, N. K., & Sohail, R. M. (2011). The reasons social media contributed to the 2011 Egyptian revolution. *International Journal of Business Research and Management*, *2*, 139–162.

Collins, M. (2014, May 9). *#BringBackOurGirls: the power of a social media campaign*. Retrieved January 24, 2015, from http://www.theguardian.com/voluntary-sector-network/2014/may/09/bringbackourgirls-power-of-social-media

Conover, M. D. (2013). *Digital democracy: The structure and dynamics of political communication in a large scale social media stream*. Indiana University. Retrieved from http://gradworks.umi.com/35/68/3568779.html

Duncombe, C. (2011). The Twitter revolution? Social media, representation and crisis in Iran and Libya. In *Australian Political Science Association Conference (APSA) 2011* (pp. 1–12). Australian National University, School of Politics and International Relations.

Enjolras, B., Steen-Johnsen, K., & Wollebæk, D. (2013). Social media and mobilization to offline demonstrations: Transcending participatory divides? *New Media & Society*, *15*(6), 890–908. doi:10.1177/1461444812462844

Etling, B., Faris, R. M., & Palfrey, J. G. (2010). *Political Change in the Digital Age: The Fragility and Promise of Online Organizing*. Retrieved from http://dash.harvard.edu/handle/1/4609956

Etling, J. P. B., & Faris, R. (2009, June 21). Why Twitter Won't Bring Revolution to Iran. *The Washington Post*. Retrieved from http://www.washingtonpost.com/wp-dyn/content/article/2009/06/19/AR2009061901598.html

Finau, G., Prasad, A., Logan, S., & Cox, J. (2014). Social Media and e-Democracy in Fiji, Solomon Islands and Vanuatu. *AMCIS 2014 Proceedings*. Retrieved from http://aisel.aisnet.org/amcis2014/SocioTechnicalIssues/GeneralPresentations/6

Finkel, S. E., & Muller, E. N. (1998). Rational choice and the dynamics of collective political action: Evaluating alternative models with panel data. *The American Political Science Review*, *92*(1), 37–49. doi:10.2307/2585927

Galey, P. (2011, March 16). Grasp of social media not enough to instigate change in Lebanon. *The Daily Star, Lebanon News*. Retrieved from http://www.dailystar.com.lb/News/Lebanon-News/2011/Mar-16/134603-grasp-of-social-media-not-enough-to-instigate-change-in-lebanon.ashx#axzz3EVTBDyid

Gary Nauer. (2014, August 7). *Hashtag campaign didn't "bring back our girls"*. Retrieved January 24, 2015, from http://www.indystar.com/story/opinion/2014/08/07/hashtag-campaign-bring-back-girls/13717045/

Gibson, R. K. (2013). Party Change, Social Media and the Rise of "Citizen-initiated" Campaigning. *Party Politics*. doi:10.1177/1354068812472575

Giroux, H. A. (2009). The Iranian uprisings and the challenge of the new media: Rethinking the politics of representation. *Fast Capitalism, 5*(2).

Gladwell, M. (2010, September 27). *Small Change*. Retrieved September 26, 2014, from http://www.newyorker.com/magazine/2010/10/04/small-change-3

Graber, D. A., & Dunaway, J. L. (2014). *Mass Media and American Politics*. Los Angeles : Washington, DC: CQ Press.

Granovetter, M. S. (1973). The strength of weak ties. *American Journal of Sociology*, *78*(6), 1360–1380. doi:10.1086/225469

Gray, M. (2012, March 26). Social Media: The Muscle Behind the Trayvon Martin Movement. *Time*. Retrieved from http://newsfeed.time.com/2012/03/26/social-media-the-muscle-behind-the-trayvon-martin-movement/

Greeley, B. (2011, February 2). The Fallacy of Facebook Diplomacy. *BusinessWeek: Magazine*. Retrieved from http://www.businessweek.com/magazine/content/11_07/b4215008414536.htm

Grove, J. V. (2010, March 19). *Social Networking Usage Surges Globally [STATS]*. Retrieved September 27, 2014, from http://mashable.com/2010/03/19/global-social-media-usage/

Gulati, G. J., & Williams, C. B. (2013). Social Media and Campaign 2012 Developments and Trends for Facebook Adoption. *Social Science Computer Review*, *31*(5), 577–588. doi:10.1177/0894439313489258

Halliday, J. (2011, August 11). David Cameron considers banning suspected rioters from social media. *The Guardian*. Retrieved from http://www.theguardian.com/media/2011/aug/11/david-cameron-rioters-social-media

Hassan, R. (2013). New Media and Political Revival: The Middle East Story. *Journal of Mass Communication & Journalism*, *03*(03). doi:10.4172/2165-7912.1000e135

Hodge, N. (2009, April 8). *Inside Moldova's Twitter Revolution*. Retrieved September 27, 2014, from http://www.wired.com/2009/04/inside-moldovas/

Howard, P. N. (2010). *The Digital Origins of Dictatorship and Democracy: Information Technology and Political Islam*. Oxford, UK: Oxford University Press.

Howard, P. N., Duffy, A., Freelon, D., Hussain, M., Mari, W., & Mazaid, M. (2011). *Opening closed regimes: What was the role of social media during the Arab Spring?* Academic Press.

Hughes, A. L., & Palen, L. (2009). Twitter adoption and use in mass convergence and emergency events. *International Journal of Emergency Management*, *6*(3), 248–260. doi:10.1504/IJEM.2009.031564

Iskander, E. (2011). Connecting the national and the virtual: Can Facebook activism remain relevant after Egypt's January 25 uprising? *International Journal of Communication, 5*, 13–15.

Jenkins, H. (2010, October 6). *Perhaps a revolution is not what we need | MIT Center for Civic Media.* Retrieved from https://civic.mit.edu/blog/henry/perhaps-a-revolution-is-not-what-we-need

Kaplan, A. M., & Haenlein, M. (2010). Users of the world, unite! The challenges and opportunities of Social Media. *Business Horizons, 53*(1), 59–68. doi:10.1016/j.bushor.2009.09.003

Khaleej Times. (2011, March 2). *Social media a catalyst for political reforms.* Retrieved from http://www.khaleejtimes.com/DisplayArticle09.asp?xfile=data/theuae/2011/March/theuae_March27.xml&section=theuae

Khamis, S., & Vaughn, K. (2011). Cyberactivism in the Egyptian revolution: How civic engagement and citizen journalism tilted the balance. *Arab Media and Society, 13*(3).

Khondker, H. H. (2011). Role of the new media in the Arab Spring. *Globalizations, 8*(5), 675–679. doi:10.1080/14747731.2011.621287

Kristof, N. D. (2009, June 18). Tear Down This Cyberwall! *The New York Times.* Retrieved from http://www.nytimes.com/2009/06/18/opinion/18kristof.html

Kushin, M. J., & Yamamoto, M. (2010). Did social media really matter? College students' use of online media and political decision making in the 2008 election. *Mass Communication & Society, 13*(5), 608–630. doi:10.1080/1520543 6.2010.516863

Lazarsfeld, P. F., & Merton, R. K. (2000). Mass communication, popular taste and organized social action. *Media Studies Reading (Sunderland),* 22–23.

Leggio, J. (2008, November 28). *Mumbai attack coverage demonstrates (good and bad) maturation point of social media.* Retrieved January 25, 2015, from http://www.zdnet.com/article/mumbai-attack-coverage-demonstrates-good-and-bad-maturation-point-of-social-media/

Lewis, B. (2005, June). Freedom and Justice in the Modern Middle East. *Foreign Affairs.* Retrieved from http://www.foreignaffairs.com/articles/60796/bernard-lewis/freedom-and-justice-in-the-modern-middle-east

Lim, M. (2013). Many Clicks but Little Sticks: Social Media Activism in Indonesia. *Journal of Contemporary Asia, 43*(4), 636–657. doi:10.108 0/00472336.2013.769386

LinkedIn. (n.d.). *Has anyone been Linked to a fake profile?* Retrieved September 26, 2014, from http://www.linkedin.com/groups/Has-anyone-been-Linked-fake-4812009.S.211395951

Logan, S. (2012). *Rausim! Digital politics in Papua New Guinea.* Academic Press.

MacKinnon, R. (2011, July 31). *Our Web freedom at the mercy of tech giants.* Retrieved from http://www.cnn.com/2011/OPINION/07/31/mackinnon.tech.freedom/index.html

Madrigal, A. C. (2011, January 24). *The Inside Story of How Facebook Responded to Tunisian Hacks.* Retrieved September 26, 2014, from http://www.theatlantic.com/technology/archive/2011/01/the-inside-story-of-how-facebook-responded-to-tunisian-hacks/70044/2/

Maghrabi, R., & Salam, A. F. (2011). *Social Media, Social Movement and Political Change: The Case of 2011 Cairo Revolt.* Academic Press.

Mainwaring, S. (2011). *Egypt: Social Media as a Life or Death Proposition.* Retrieved September 27, 2014, from http://www.fastcompany.com/1724837/egypt-social-media-life-or-death-proposition

Mattelart, A., & Mattelart, M. (1998). *Theories of Communication: A Short Introduction*. London: SAGE Publications Ltd.

McElroy, B. D. (2009, June 16). *Twitter maintained service during Iranian elections after US State Dept request*. Retrieved from http://www.telegraph.co.uk/technology/twitter/5552733/Twitter-maintained-service-during-Iranian-elections-after-US-State-Dept-request.html

McLuhan, M. (2001). *The Medium is the Massage* (9th ed.). Corte Madera, CA: Gingko Press.

McPherson, M., Smith-Lovin, L., & Brashears, M. E. (2006). Social isolation in America: Changes in core discussion networks over two decades. *American Sociological Review*, *71*(3), 353–375. doi:10.1177/000312240607100301

Mejova, Y., Srinivasan, P., & Boynton, B. (2013). GOP Primary Season on Twitter: "Popular" Political Sentiment in Social Media. In *Proceedings of the Sixth ACM International Conference on Web Search and Data Mining* (pp. 517–526). New York, NY: ACM. doi:10.1145/2433396.2433463

Morozov, E. (2012). *The Net Delusion: The Dark Side of Internet Freedom (Reprint edition.)*. New York: Public Affairs.

Mott, P. (2012, August 6). *Freedom of Speech Doesn't Mean a Thing to Twitter -- Or Does It?* Retrieved September 26, 2014, from http://www.huffingtonpost.com/patrick-mott/freedom-of-speech-doesnt-_b_1739207.html

Mourtada, R., & Salem, F. (2011). Civil movements: The impact of Facebook and Twitter. *Arab Social Media Report*, *1*(2), 1–30.

Mungiu-Pippidi, A., & Munteanu, I. (2009). Moldova's "Twitter Revolution". *Journal of Democracy*, *20*(3), 136–142. doi:10.1353/jod.0.0102

Naim, H. (2011, May 17). *Social media creating social awareness in the Arab world by Hani Naim - Common Ground News Service*. Retrieved September 27, 2014, from http://www.commongroundnews.org/article.php?id=29759&lan=en&sp=0

Neilson. (2010, June 15). *Social NetworksBlogs Now Account for One in Every Four and a Half Minutes Online*. Retrieved September 27, 2014, from http://www.nielsen.com/us/en/insights/news/2010/social-media-accounts-for-22-percent-of-time-online.html

OpenArab.Net. (n.d.). *Arabic Blogs: An Embodiment of Freedom of Expression*. Retrieved September 27, 2014, from http://old.openarab.net/en/node/366

Oxford Analytica. (2011, February 9). *Middle East: Social media outwit authoritarianism* [Text]. Retrieved September 27, 2014, from https://www.oxan.com/display.aspx?ItemID=DB166066

Palen, L., & Liu, S. B. (2007). Citizen communications in crisis: anticipating a future of ICT-supported public participation. In *Proceedings of the SIGCHI conference on Human factors in computing systems* (pp. 727–736). ACM. doi:10.1145/1240624.1240736

Palfrey, J., Etling, B., & Faris, R. (2009, June 21). Reading Twitter in Tehran? Why the Real Revolution is on the Streets – and Offline. *Washington Post*.

Pamela Rutledge. (2013, January 25). *How Obama Won the Social Media Battle in the 2012 Presidential Campaign*. Retrieved from http://mprcenter.org/blog/2013/01/how-obama-won-the-social-media-battle-in-the-2012-presidential-campaign/

Papic, M., & Noonan, S. (2011, February 3). *Social Media as a Tool for Protest*. Retrieved September 27, 2014, from http://www.stratfor.com/weekly/20110202-social-media-tool-protest

Rainie, L., Purcell, K., & Smith, A. (2011). *The Social Side of the Internet*. Retrieved from http://www.pewinternet.org/2011/01/18/the-social-side-of-the-internet/

ReadWrite. (2009, July 25). *Evolution of a Revolution: Visualizing Millions of Iran Tweets*. Retrieved September 26, 2014, from http://readwrite.com/2009/07/25/evolution_revolution_visualizing_millions_iran_tweets

Reuter, O. J., & Szakonyi, D. (2013). Online Social Media and Political Awareness in Authoritarian Regimes. *British Journal of Political Science, FirstView*, 1–23. doi:10.1017/S0007123413000203

Rich, F. (2011, February 5). Wallflowers at the Revolution. *The New York Times*. Retrieved from http://www.nytimes.com/2011/02/06/opinion/06rich.html

Riley, S. (2011, Oct 31). Social media one key to the arab spring IT-savvy population it played bigger role in Tunisia, Egypt than in Libya, Yemen, some say. *Investor's Business Daily*, p. A06. Retrieved from http://proxy.consortiumlibrary.org/docview/915383384?accountid=14473

Robert Mackey. (2011, April 11). *Blogger Jailed for Insulting Egypt's Military*. Retrieved from http://thelede.blogs.nytimes.com/2011/04/11/blogger-jailed-for-insulting-egypts-military-is-pro-israel/

Rosenberg, T. (2011, July 12). *Friends in Revolution*. Retrieved September 26, 2014, from http://opinionator.blogs.nytimes.com/2011/07/12/friends-in-revolution/

Salmon, C. T., Fernandez, L., & Post, L. A. (2010). Mobilizing public will across borders: Roles and functions of communication processes and technologies. *Journal of Borderland Studies*, *25*(3-4), 159–170. doi:10.1080/08865655.2010.9695778

Sheedy, C. S. (2011). *Social media for social change: A case study of social media use in the 2011 Egyptian revolution*. A Capstone Project Presented to the Faculty of the School of Communication, American University.

Shirky, C. (2009). *Here comes everybody: The power of organizing without organizations*. Penguin.

Shirky, C. (2011, February). The Political Power of Social Media. *Foreign Affairs*. Retrieved from http://www.foreignaffairs.com/articles/67038/clay-shirky/the-political-power-of-social-media

Srinivasan, R. (2010, September 28). *Say You Want To Tweet a Revolution?* Retrieved from http://rameshsrinivasan.org/say-you-want-to-tweet-a-revolution/

Srinivasan, R. (2014). What Tahrir Square Has Done for Social Media: A 2012 Snapshot in the Struggle for Political Power in Egypt. *The Information Society*, *30*(1), 71–80. doi:10.1080/01972243.2013.856363

Steyaert, J. (2002). Inequality and the digital divide: myths and realities. *Advocacy, Activism and the Internet*, 199–211.

Stieglitz, S., & Dang-Xuan, L. (2013). Social media and political communication: A social media analytics framework. *Social Network Analysis and Mining*, *3*(4), 1277–1291. doi:10.1007/s13278-012-0079-3

Stone, B. (2011, January 28). *The Tweets Must Flow*. Retrieved September 26, 2014, from https://blog.twitter.com/2011/tweets-must-flow

Storck, M. (2011). *The role of social media in political mobilisation: a case study of the January 2011 Egyptian uprising*. University of St Andrews.

Strandberg, K. (2013). A social media revolution or just a case of history repeating itself? The use of social media in the 2011 Finnish parliamentary elections. *New Media & Society, 15*(8), 1329–1347. doi:10.1177/1461444812470612

Strömbäck, J., & Aelst, P. V. (2013). Why political parties adapt to the media Exploring the fourth dimension of mediatization. *International Communication Gazette, 75*(4), 341–358. doi:10.1177/1748048513482266

Swigger, N. (2013). The Online Citizen: Is Social Media Changing Citizens' Beliefs About Democratic Values? *Political Behavior, 35*(3), 589–603. doi:10.1007/s11109-012-9208-y

Thompson, J. B. (2013). *Media and Modernity: A Social Theory of the Media.* John Wiley & Sons.

Time Magazine. (2011, February 22). Meet the Man Tweeting Egypt's Voices to the World. *Time.* Retrieved from http://content.time.com/time/specials/packages/article/0,28804,2045328_2045333_2045489,00.html

Tran, T. (2011, March 8). *China blogger angered over losing Facebook account.* Retrieved January 25, 2015, from http://www.washingtontimes.com/news/2011/mar/8/china-blogger-angered-over-losing-facebook-account/

Vaccari, C., Valeriani, A., Barberá, P., Bonneau, R., Jost, J. T., Nagler, J., & Tucker, J. (2013). Social media and political communication: A survey of Twitter users during the 2013 Italian general election. *Rivista Italiana Di Scienza Politica*, (3). doi:10.1426/75245

Wolfsfeld, G. (2014). *Making Sense of Media and Politics: Five Principles in Political Communication.* Taylor & Francis.

Wolfsfeld, G., Segev, E., & Sheafer, T. (2013). Social Media and the Arab Spring Politics Comes First. *The International Journal of Press/Politics, 18*(2), 115–137. doi:10.1177/1940161212471716

Wolfson, E. (2014, August 15). *How Lessons From Trayvon Helped Make Ferguson News.* Retrieved January 24, 2015, from http://www.newsweek.com/how-lessons-trayvon-helped-make-ferguson-news-264942

Wyld, D. C. (2007). *The blogging revolution: Government in the age of Web 2.0.* IBM Center for the Business of Government.

Yee, A. (2011, March 14). *Where does the west stand on global freedom of expression?* Retrieved September 26, 2014, from https://www.opendemocracy.net/andy-yee/where-does-west-stand-on-global-freedom-of-expression

York, J. (2010, April 8). *On Facebook Deactivations.* Retrieved from http://jilliancyork.com/2010/04/08/on-facebook-deactivations/

YouTube Statistics. (n.d.). Retrieved from http://www.youtube.com/t/press_statistics

KEY TERMS AND DEFINITIONS

Citizen Journalism: It refers to the gathering, writing, editing, production and distribution of news and information by people not trained as professional journalists. Source:http://www2.uncp.edu/home/acurtis/Courses/ResourcesForCourses/Journalism/CitizenJournalism.html.

Civic Engagement: Civic engagement refers to promoting quality of community life through both political and non-political processes. Sources: http://www.nytimes.com/ref/college/collegespecial2/coll_aascu_defi.html.

Cyberactivism: It refers to the use of e-mail, blogs and social networking sites to publicize a cause by disseminating information quickly that is unavailable through traditional news sources. Sources: http://www.pcmag.com/encyclopedia/term/63075/cyberactivism.

Social Change: It refers to the transformation of culture and social institutions over time. Source: http://education-portal.com/academy/lesson/what-is-social-change-forms-definition-quiz.html.

Social Media: Social media refers to the collection of online communication channels dedicated to community-based input, interaction, content-sharing and collaboration. Source: http://whatis.techtarget.com/definition/social-media.

Social Policy: It refers to an interdisciplinary and applied subject concerned with the analysis of societies' responses to social need. Source: http://www.lse.ac.uk/socialPolicy/aboutUs/introduction.aspx.

Social Practice: Social practice is a theory within psychology that seeks to determine the link between practice and context within social situations. Source: http://en.wikipedia.org/wiki/Social_Practice.

Chapter 25
Social Media and Gender Issues

Lynne M. Webb
Florida International University, USA

Nicholas Temple
Central Washington University, USA

ABSTRACT

Using Performance Theory as an explanatory basis, this essay explicates the performance of gender in social media beginning with the gendered history of digital technologies and an articulation of the social media venues' unique affordances for gender performance. Then, the chapter reviews the scientific research examining gendered online behavior in social media noting opportunities for enacting traditional sex role stereotypes and thus socializing others to do so as well as opportunities to enact equality and thus disseminating calls for liberation and increased equality between the sexes in all aspects of social life. Facebook, blogs, and online games are examined in detail as exemplars of specific social media cites of gender performance.

INTRODUCTION

Equity between the sexes has dramatically increased across the last 150 years. From the suffragist movement in the United States in the late 1800s to the United Nations' on-going human rights campaign for women (http://www.un.org/womenwatch/directory/human_rights_of_women_3009.htm), legal and social changes have led to increased professional and social opportunities for both men and women. Now that logging on to social media has become a daily activity for so many global citizens; researchers are examining how men and women engage in these online activities as well as how such engagement impacts

equality between the sexes. This chapter reviews the social scientific examinations of gender issues in social media and thus discusses research related to biological sex, gender, sexuality, sexual preferences, and sexual identification. Such a review allows the reader to access the extent to which social media serve as sites of socialization into traditional gender roles as well as sites to enact equality and to disseminate liberation rhetoric.

One theory that allows understanding of how online venues provide opportunities for individual users to enact gender is Performance Theory. If users perform gender online, they have opportunities to engage in a wide variety of performances from traditional sex role behaviors to widely divergent,

DOI: 10.4018/978-1-4666-8310-5.ch025

gendered behaviors such as gender-bending, and performances between these extremes. Below we offer a more in depth explanation of Performance Theory and its application to gendered behavior as a prelude to examining gendered behavior on social media.

Performance theory (Bell, 2008; Schechner, 2003) guides and informs our interpretation of the research reviewed in this chapter. Butler's theory of gender performativity (1990) argues that humans enact gender identities through expression and performance (Wood, 2009). Butler makes a clear distinction between biological sex and gender: whereas biological sex (male, female) is a mere accident of birth, gender is produced and maintained through cultural discourses of masculinity, femininity, and androgyny. Humans enact gender via multiple forms of expression within societal inscriptions of gender (Menard-Warwick, 2007). Performative theory posits that gender is not specifically something humans *have,* but rather, something they *do* (Menard-Warwick). Gender is an active expression of identity and an outward performance (Bell, 2006); the central claim of the theory states that without the performance of gender, there is no gender (Wood, 2009). Through performance, individuals may enact traditional sex roles and thus maintain the status quo. Conversely, innovators can perform gendered identities that represent increased equality between the sexes, such as stay-at-home Dad and female software designer.

We are not the first scholars to rely on Performance Theory as a viable explanation for social life. Drawing on the many traditions of performance theory (Bell, 2008), previous scholars examined performances across a variety of social concerns including gender (Hans et al., 2011; Morris, 1995) and identity (Litt, 2012) as well as across a wide range of settings including traditional mass media (Aleman, 2010) and social media (Hans et al., 2011; Litt, 2012).

Individuals perform various aspects of social identity simultaneously. For example, the first author of this essay performs as a married female professor on her BlackBoard account. Multiple aspects of identity *frequently* interact with and co-occur with gender, including biological sex, sexual orientation, sexuality, and sexual identity. These performances are so frequently associated, one with the other, that researchers often focus their investigation specifically on one of these *associated* aspects of gender identity in an attempt to gain insight into gender. Furthermore, researchers sometimes treat these associated aspects of gender identity (biological sex, sexual orientation, sexuality, and sexual identity) as if they are the same thing as gender. Unfortunately, much of the research examining gender issues in social media suffers from these limitations; many researchers report differences by biological sex or differences by marital status rather than examining issues of gender directly.

Additionally, it is important to note that additional aspects of social identity can shape gender performance. For example, race and class often limit and shape how individuals enact their feminine and/or masculine identities. Issues of race and class are important in and of themselves as potential influences on users' online behavior as well as influences on gendered behaviors. Unfortunately, race and class as aspects of identity performance, while very important and worthy of examination in and of themselves, are beyond the scope of this essay. Furthermore, it is important to note that much of the research on gender issues in social media examines the online behavior of white middle-class users.

The ever-changing nature of the Internet and the ability to freely navigate among online cultures permits the fluidness of gender to be realized and experienced (Bailey & Telford, 2007). The Internet can be viewed as a space with liberating potential, where gender can be performed in new ways (Hans et al., 2011); innovative identities can be imagined by online representation (White, 2003) and gendered scripts can be re-conceptualized (Bruckman, 1993; Kelly, Pomerantz, & Currie, 2006; Loureiro

& Ribeiro, 2014). Such experimentation typically challenges mainstream conceptions of gender. Indeed, many scholars have argued that both male and female users communicate online in ways that "replicate and disrupt" established gender practices (Anderson & Buzzanell, 2007, p. 32).

The pervasive nature of the Internet in the Western world, with ubiquitous free wifi and the wide-spread use of social media, creates opportunities for a wide variety of gender enactments beyond work and family contexts and issues. Users' sexual orientation, sexuality, and sexual identity can be displayed in numerous ways across multiple websites where users can gain audience for their performances and can find social support for both traditional (e.g., mommy blogs) and nontraditional performances (e.g., transgendered identities).

Additionally, the Internet, as mass medium, provides a space for gendered social issues to receive widespread attention. Social media sites allow information-provision, engagement, and discussion of ideas outside the status-quo gendered discourse. Thus, social media can provide forums for voices that are often overlooked or silenced in society (i.e., lesbian teens). Additionally, the Internet allows for networking and establishing a sense of connection necessary for movements enacting social change. For example, the materialization of modern feminism is "marked by the emergence of networks and contacts which need no centralized organizations and evade its structures of command control" (Bailey & Telford, 2007, p. 259). From this viewpoint, the Internet is a space of gender liberation where gender can be performed, conceptualized, and theorized in innovative ways.

The purpose of this chapter is to review the scholarly reports relevant to gender and social media, noting evidence of online gender performances, pointing out to the reader which social media venues offer unique affordances for gender performance as well as extent to which the performances represent enactment of existing gender norms and/or increased equality between the sexes. Immediately below, a brief history of gendered online behavior is presented as preface to the review.

BACKGROUND

When the 21st century began, technology was predominantly male-dominated; primarily male engineers developed both the hardware and software of social media. Additionally, as early as 2000, in a sample of 185 users from 84 U.S. families, men reported spending almost twice as many hours per week online at home as women (Kayany & Yelsma, 2000). Because of these inequities, technological advancements can be viewed as masculine tools of power (Bailey & Telford, 2007). Despite steps to increase equity, men continue to dominate in specialized fields of technology such as software design (Anderson & Buzzanell, 2007) and many online venues are viewed as masculine (Taylor, 2004)—making the Internet appear to be a male-occupied space. Some feminists have argued that because of female exclusion, technology reflects a patriarchal hierarchy that produces tools of oppression detrimental to women (i.e., pornography; Podlas, 2000).

However, in the more recent era of technological growth, women comprise an increasing percentage of the Internet population. Since 2001, male versus female access to the Internet has reached parity (U. S. Department of Commerce, 2004). The data regarding relational use of online technologies is especially interesting. The 2000 Pew Internet and American Life project reported that women use the Internet to maintain relationships more than men. Among 713 college students, women were four to five times more likely than men to use social networking websites (Tufekci, 2008b). Women report more Facebook "friends" than men and report spending more time on Facebook than men, regardless of the size of their networks (Acar, 2008). Another recent survey of college students documented no differences between male versus female reports of the amount of time spent online communicating with romantic partners (Sidelinger, Ayash, & Tibbles, 2008). Furthermore, women and men spend equal time playing online games (Williams, Consalvo, Caplan, & Yee, 2009). Contemporary feminists view these multiple measures of online equity as indicating that the Internet can provide a space for women's empowerment and agency (Hans et al., 2011), given that it provides "unparalleled mechanisms for widespread dissemination and communication" (Bailey & Telford, 2007, p. 244). With the advent of Internet 2.0 and its emphasis on user-produced content, social media that facilitate online interaction among users have flourished (Lind, 2012); these venues offer users of both sexes a multiplicity of opportunities to interact and spread their ideas far and wide. Below the affordances of social media as venues for gender performance are reviewed. Then appears a review of the research on gender issues and social media with blogs, Facebook, and online games serving as exemplars.

SOCIAL MEDIA AND GENDER

Some feminist commentators praise the rise of social media, including websites such as Facebook, because they privilege expressiveness and social skills, traits often considered feminine (Zacharias & Arthurs, 2008). Indeed, women outnumber men in social media. One global study reported that 76% of online women use social media, as compared to 70% of online men (Vollman, Abraham, & Mörn 2010). Similarly, Junco, Merson, & Salter (2010) found that women spend more time on social networking sites than men. Feminists hoped that social media (websites that facilitate user interaction) would serve as spaces to empower young women to carve out their own identities that might counter mainstream media stereotypes; indeed, some hoped that women could construct new or altered definitions of what

it ultimately means to be a "girl" (Scott-Dixon, 2002; Koskela, 2004). They could do this by exchanging comments, building relationships, and exchanging social capital (Bailey et al., 2013; Senft, 2008) via social media. As a result of the potential offered by this relatively new media technology, Senft (2008) posited that diverse narratives written by girls themselves could begin to upset the dominant, stereotypical definitions of "girl" and perhaps even challenge gender-based constraints that hinder social equality.

Women are clearly enthusiastic in their use of social media technology, and have utilized it in meaningful ways to enhance their social lives (Bailey et al., 2013). There is a wide plethora of social media platforms to choose from, including (but certainly not limited to) Facebook, Tumblr, Google Plus, Twitter, Vine, and the wide array of online dating sites such as eHarmony. However, one key point to note about many of these sites is that they are both mainstream and corporate.

Corporate, mainstream websites tend to contain large amounts of advertising, and that advertising often portrays pre-existing stereotypes of what it is to be a "man" or a "woman". Given that women use social media in greater numbers and at a higher intensity than men, it seems likely that they bear more of the brunt of exposure to repeated messages reinforcing these gender norms. Evidence suggests that young women internalize the commercial images that they see in advertisements here and incorporate the stereotypes into their online social presentation to varying degrees (Ringrose, 2010). Ringrose concluded that "positioning the self as always 'up for it' and the 'performance of confident sexual agency' has shifted to become a *key regulative*" (2010, p. 176). Thus, women may experience a visual imperative to present the self as sexy on social networking sites. Girls in online spaces also reproduce other common stereotypes of femininity (Bailey et al., 2013). Often, they place emphasis on being attractive and having attractive friends (Manago, Graham, Greenfield, & Salimkhan, 2008), present themselves as eager to please males (Kapidizic & Herring, 2011), and generally work to look like a happy, carefree, and sexy but not sexual.

Thus, social media has proved to be a "mixed bag" offering and at times encouraging the enactment of traditional gender roles as well as, at other times, providing opportunities to "give voice" to users' unique ideas, including both men and women who may be uncomfortable communicating in face-to-face public venues. Despite its mixed reviews, social media in general offer multiple unique affordances that allow liberating gendered behaviors that are rarely readily available offline. Such affordances include as the following:

- Many venues offer *unfettered access to a mass audience* for the promotion of individual voices that might otherwise be silenced (such as gay teens) as well as public spaces for the organization of gendered social movements (e.g., the Arab Spring that advocated for increased women's rights).

- *Gender-bending* occurs when biological males pose as female, biological female pose as males, or either sex poses nongendered. Offline gender-bending occurs (e.g., cross-dressing), but gender-bending is more common online where fewer nonverbal cues are available to unmask the behavior. Samp, Wittenberg, and Gillett (2003) reported that feminine, masculine, and androgynous individuals were equally likely to engage in gender-bending. Online gender-bending allows for the critical examination of social constructions of gender and potentially contributes to the long-term destabilization of the way society currently constructs gender (Danet, 1998). The act of gender-bending allows individuals to gather skills, tools, and data to challenge rigid notions of gender and sexuality. The performance of an alternative gender

identity through online interactions can "defamiliarize" individuals with their real life gender role (Bruckman, 1993), allowing users to address their sexuality and to interact in ways that he/she would not be comfortable doing in offline, as well as to understand the way sexual politics work in society (Danet, 1998).

- Young, Griffin-Shelley, Cooper, O'Mara, and Buchanan (2000) defined *cybersex* as "two online users engaging in private discourse about sexual fantasies. The dialogue is usually accompanied by self-stimulation" (p. 60). Cybersex requires the articulation of sexual desire to the extent that would be most unusual in face-to-face encounter. Both married and unmarried men and women participate in cybersex (Millner, 2008), resulting in a wide variety of sexual encounters online. Multiple websites match partners who desire single-single dating, affairs between partners married to others, online sexual encounters, and so on. Cybersex covers a wide range of relationships including but not limited to cyber romances (Gibbs, Ellison, & Heino, 2006) and cyber affairs (Young et al., 2000), yet many cybersex partners never meet offline. When and if they meet, the relationships are often of very short duration. In contrast, cyber partners who establish emotionally connected relationships often interact online for a very long time (Barta & Kiene, 2005). Thus, many social media sites offers opportunities to develop relationships with others who enjoy uncommon relational and sexual practices that users might be hesitant to explore in offline venues, including various polyamory practices (multiple loving partners) (Ritchie & Baker, 2006), homosexuality (Ashford, 2006; Walker, 2009), and exploitative relationships (Brookey & Cannon, 2009), as well as sexual practices beyond the status quo.

- Social media provides important information *tools for managing complex multifaced lives* with both family and work responsibilities (Edley & Houston, 2011). Using online coordination, both men and women maintain demanding professional positions while they become increasingly engaged with their children's lives and care of older or disabled relatives.

- Because access to social media is free and relatively easy, many non-profit organizations maintain a social media presence. To facilitate working parents' success in enacting increased engagement in family life, educational, recreational, and healthcare *organizations engage social media* as a means of information distribution and co-ordination (Atkinson et al., 2009; Palmen & Kouri, 2012). Additionally, nonprofit agencies that advocate for equality between the sexes (includegender.org), greater opportunities for women (now.org), and/or the rights of individuals engaged in nontraditional gender enactments (http://transequality.org) also maintain an online presence via social media.

The same affordances that facilitate liberation also present some noteworthy challenges to users. A partial listing of such challenges that relate closely to gender are noted below:

- *Hiring decisions based in part on users' online profiles* have become increasingly common. Given that online information exists almost indefinitely and given that any information posted online can be retrieved by an experienced corporate hacker, any hint of unconventionality in sexual or gendered behavior may have financial consequences for users.

- *Deception* is common in social media, as users can enact inaccurately positive self-presentations that are accepted more easily online than they would be offline (Gibbs et al., 2006). Women typically lie for safety concerns and men lie to boost their socioeconomic status, but both sexes believe that lying about such factors allows for openness and honesty regarding the more important matters of their emotional experiences and sexual desires (Ben-Ze'ev, 2004). Gibbs et al. (2006) concluded that "the Internet is the medium for identity manipulation" (p. 169), including gender-bending.

- *Online dating* sites bring gender directly to the fore as the convention of dating is heavily tied to gender roles (Fullick, 2013). Whitty (2007) argued that users on these sites are quite strategic in the ways in which they present themselves as they seek to attract the ideal romantic partner. Hancock and Toma (2009) report that both men and women exert a high level of control over their profiles in an effort to present their best possible or ideal selves (Toma & Hancock, 2011). However, Fullick (2013) points out online daters are well aware that they are putting themselves out there for consumption in a consumption based culture, and as such must sell themselves. Part of:selling" involves mimicking how other media sell gender.

- *Internet infidelity* takes many forms—cyber affairs among them. According to Limacher and Wright (2006), "infidelity can be understood as a breach of trust between a couple, in which the secrecy and lies become the culprit in destroying the relationship, not necessarily the sex" (p. 314). Although the Internet can be used for factual sexual education, it also can be used for emotional and sexual maladaptive behaviors associated with cybersex (Millner, 2008). Some internet users spend up to 10 hours per week engaged in cybersexual relationships (Cooper, Boies, Maheu, & Greenfield, 2000). Biological sex "is a good predictor of motivation for infidelity" (Barta & Kiene, 2005, p. 341); women are more likely to engage in infidelity when they experience emotional dissatisfaction in their primary relationship; men are more likely to be sexually motivated.

- *Online pornography* is widely available on the Internet and the pornography websites are often formatted as social media to facilitate interaction. Multiple researchers have documented that adolescent and young adult males are more likely than females to view sexually explicit online content (e.g., Boies, 2002; Peter & Valkenburg, 2006). Men are more likely than women to seek visual sexual depictions as a means to experience sexual arousal for masturbation; women are more likely to seek out erotic narratives and chat rooms than men; women are less likely than men to self-stimulate when using online materials (Barta & Kiene, 2005). Men often think of pornography on the Internet as mere visual stimulation for masturbation with no emotional attachment (Limacher & Wright, 2006); however, female offline romantic partners often hold an alternative viewpoint. "Getting caught" using pornography can transform a safe and loving relationship into one of mistrust and distance. Wives who catch their husbands using Internet pornography typically perceive themselves as unpleasing to their husbands and experience emotional pain by the husband's "involvement" with another woman.

In sum, social media offer multiple unique affordances that allow liberating gendered behaviors that are rarely readily available offline. However, such affordances come with some noteworthy challenges. To explain how gendered perfor-

mances occur in such environments the following sections of the chapter discuss in detail research findings relevant to three widely popular and well-researched social media: blogs, Facebook, and online games.

EXEMPLARS: FACEBOOK, BLOGS, GAMING

This section of the chapter discusses in detail how gender is performed in three prominent and well researched social media venues: blogs, Facebook, and online games. Each venue is discussed in some detail to reveal its unique affordances that offer both opportunities and challenges to increased equality between the sexes.

Gender and Blogs

Because identity arises from "publicly validated performances," users can enact gender identity through blogging (García-Gómez, 2009, p. 613). Bloggers present their performative gendered identities through both visual and discursive means (van Doorn, van Zoonen, & Wyatt, 2007) as they create and write their blogs. Via such performances, bloggers can enact a wide range of gendered performances from traditional sex-roles, such as expected behaviors in the "cult of femininity" on teen-agers' blogs (Gomez, 2010, p. 135) or push the boundaries of permitted gendered behavior in repressive regimes (Riegert & Ramsey, 2013). From 2000 to 2005, the number of blogs grew from 100,000 to more than 4 million (Woods, 2005). Riley (2005) reported about half a million blogs in Australia and 2.5 million blogs in the U. K. In 2009, more than 12 million adults in the U. S. maintained a blog (Schechter, 2009).

From the beginning, scholars have characterized blogs as a powerful medium of communication (Kline & Burstein, 2005; Rodzvilla, 2002; Rosenberg, 2009; Woods, 2005), as blogs provide an individual mass media outlet for every blogger. Because blog participants directly engage in knowledge production, and because blogs typically limit content to specific and narrow foci, blogs lend themselves to community formation. Blogs form online communities around a specific theme, idea, or industry activity (Droge et al., 2010; Vickery, 2010), where a "sense of community is developed through interactions with like-minded people" (Kaye, 2005, p. 76), such as bloggers writing on feminist business practices. Bloggers perform gender for their audience of readers via their writing; readers can become familiar and friendly with bloggers after reading their posts regularly and respond with their own performances of gender. Through blogging, authors invite audience members (typically fellow bloggers who write on the same or similar subject matter) to discuss, share, and support one another (Lopez, 2009). Thus, blogs have the potential to become sites of enlightenment and liberation.

- **Gendered Use of Blogs:** Twelve million Americans report blogging (Lehhart & Fox, 2006); men and women blog approximately equally (Haferkamp & Krämer, 2008). In displaying online identities, almost all bloggers reveal their gender on their blogs (Kleeman, 2007). In addition to explicitly stating gender, blog creators employ various forms of nonverbal behaviors (e.g., colors, backgrounds, fonts, and pictures) that perform gendered identity. For example, a self-proclaimed "girly girl" could select a pink background for her blog.

Gender is performed quite distinctively in the context of blogs. Males are more likely to write filter blogs (Karlsson, 2007; Wei, 2009), containing primarily information external to the author such as news and political events; the blog content is "filtered in that certain items are discussed and others are excluded. Political blogs, for example, often link to the websites of traditional media sources, such as newspapers. Filter blogs typically are written by men (Herring, Kouper, Scheidt, & Wright, 2004). Therefore, when traditional media outlets quote political filter blogs, as they often do (Tucker, 2009), the media outlets are usually repeating male voices (Herring et al., 2004). Similarly, more published academic research examines male blogs than female blogs (Lopez, 2009).

Gender can be performed via linguistic practices (Motschenbacher, 2009) and multiple studies document such practices by males:

- Herring and Paolillo (2006) found that filter blogs favored by men had more "male" stylistic features, such as statements and restatements of facts.
- Van Doorn et al. (2007) found that male authors carefully avoided being too "emotional," focusing their blogs on information and ideas.
- In a study of British bloggers, Pedersen and Macafee (2007) report that men's blog content focuses on sharing information, providing opinions, and highlighting links. This finding paints a gendered picture for how males share information through blogging—a picture consistent with typical ways males communicate in offline interactions. Tannen (1990) argues men engage in report talk, giving information and opinions as a means of gaining or sustaining status.
- Men evoke gender identities using facts and emotionless language versus women who employ expressive and inclusive language. Amir, Abidin, Darus, and Ismail (2012) reported finding such "differences in language use among teenage bloggers" (p. 105).

Medical blogs serve as a prime example of how men perform masculinity on blogs. Kovic, Lulic, and Brumini surveyed medical blogs, defined as "a blog whose main topic was related to health or medicine" (2008, p. 2), and discovered that 59% of medical bloggers were male; 74% of the bloggers reported being motivated to post on medical blogs to share knowledge and skills, and 56% by the desire of gaining insights from others. (Respondents could choose more than one motivation; therefore the percent total exceeds 100%). Two-thirds of medical bloggers received attention from the news media about their blogs.

It could be argued that males were more likely to participate in these medical blogs because the nature of these blogs aligns with a masculine communication style, allowing the authors to perform their gender through their blogs. Because men are more likely to write filter blogs (Pedersen & Macafee, 2007; van Doorn et al., 2007), they also are more likely to be seen as credible bloggers (Armstrong & McAdams, 2009). In short, male bloggers are seen as information transmitters and form blogging relationships based on sharing of information and the credibility of that information.

Women, on the other hand, are more likely to write journal blogs, or diary blogs (Attwood, 2009; Karlsson, 2007; Wei, 2009). Such blogs describe personal life; their content primarily originates with the blogger rather than external sources. However, unlike traditional diaries, journal blogs do not have the connotation of privacy and instead seek an online, mass audience. Women are more likely to blog to document their lives, for self-expression, and to pass time (Li, 2007) than to provide information. For example, female bloggers write about their experiences with infertility (e.g., Turner Channel, 2010) and empty-nest syndrome (e.g., The Pioneer Woman, 2010).

Diary blogs are personal and emotion-laden, creating "readerly attachment" (Karlsson, 2007, p. 139). Journal bloggers invite their readers to identify with and relate to the author through comments (Webb & Lee, 2011). Readers who habitually read these blogs are more likely to be female (Karlsson, 2007), and the creation of support networks on such blogs is consistent with the communal, relational communication characteristic of women.

Female communication style allows women to share, create, and maintain relationships, bring others into the conversation, and respond to ideas (Wood, 2009). Through journal blogging, reading blogs regularly, and leaving feedback, women engage in rapport-talk, described by Tannen as "negotiations for closeness in which people try to seek and give confirmation and support, and to reach consensus" (1990, p. 25). Blogs can provide a shared emotional connection (Stavrositu & Sundar, 2008), where members of the blog community share life experiences and events. One blog feature that aids relationship building (van Doorn et al., 2007) is the 'blogroll' (a list of links that allows the user to add others' blogs to their blogroll, creating a network of blogs sometimes called the "blogosphere"). The use of blogrolls "fosters a reciprocal relationship" where people add each other's blogs to their blogrolls (p. 146).

The language of women's blogs plays a central role in the performance of their gendered identities as the "features of 'women's language' are powerful resources to linguistically index female identities" (Motschenbacher, 2009, p. 19). Teen girls' diary blogs provide an obvious example of feminine gender performance via statements such as "I am a woman, not a girl!" and "Since I was a little girl" (García-Gómez, 2009, p. 615). Also, women's language is more inclusive and expressive, passive, cooperative, and accommodating (Herring & Paolillo, 2006) than the language used by male bloggers. Women bloggers construct their gendered identities using sexualized imagery and words, often while talking about domesticity and taking care of the home (van Doorn et al., 2007). This juxtaposed mix creates a unique female gender identity combining traditional views of women such as the mother and sex object (Wood, 2009).

- **Female Empowerment via Blogging:** Women can experience liberation and validation through blogging (Hans, Lee, Tinker, & Webb, 2011), as "blogging's ultimate product is empowerment" (Kline & Burstein, 2005, p. 248). Walters (2011) described blogs as "a site for everyday activism" (p. 363). Although women may feel marginalized and underrepresented in the offline public sphere, blogs can empower women by emphasizing knowledge important to women and organizing groups of like-minded women in the cyber public-sphere (Stavrositu & Sundar, 2008). For example mommy blogs (i.e., blogs predominantly about family life written by women) serve as one venue for such organizing. Thousands of mothers embrace blogging as a form of communication, documentation, and socialization as well as a means of producing income (Neff, 2008); they blog to communicate about their families, to document their rites of passage as mothers, and to provide and receive advise on difficult challenges in private life. Thus, mothers are experiencing empowerment in the blogosphere and their efforts are enjoying increased scholarly attention (Camahort, 2006; Friedman & Calixte, 2009; Hammond, 2010; Kline & Burstein, 2005; Lee & Webb, 2012, 2014; Lopez, 2009; Moravec, 2011; Thompson, 2007; Webb & Lee, 2011).

Lee and Webb (2014) argue that mommy bloggers are redefining motherhood in the 21st century. In mainstream U. S. culture, motherhood is typically viewed as a private and domestic matter (Lopez, 2009). However, by chronicling maternal events in the public realm via blogs, bloggers redefine the meaning of motherhood. As mommy bloggers display their own online maternal identity, they typically present a very different picture from motherhood as presented in mainstream media. "Instead of the loving mother, we see women who are frazzled by the demands of their newborn baby, who have no clue what to do when their child gets sick, who suffer from postpartum depression and whose hormones rage uncontrollably" (Lopez, p. 732). Readers see blog-

gers' "work in progress" identities as the authentic voices of maternity in the 21st century (Moravec, 2011)—voices that paint realistic pictures of child-rearing while "having a life" (Lopez, 2009).

- **Women's Movements on Blogs:** Given that the traditional media misrepresented and underrepresented women, blogs provide a meaningful, alternative public platform for women's voices (Stavrositu & Sundar, 2008). Indeed, female sexual liberation can be enacted via blogging. Attwood (2009) studied women's sex blogs, and sex "blooks" (blogs turned into books). Attwood describes "blooks" as "the world's fastest growing new kind of book" (p. 5). Through these blogs and blooks, female authors emphasize sexual openness, empowerment, and pleasure. In these venues, women authors redefine their sexuality and femininity by writing publically about what many people would consider the most intimate and personal form of social life.

Blogs provide a vital venue for gendered self-expression, especially in countries that limit freedom of expression (Monteiro, 2008). Some women in Egypt, Saudi Arabia, and Jordan blog to enact their liberated identities and to publically critique repressive gender roles (Riegert & Ramsey, 2013). Some of these blogs provide forums for political activism, while others are centers of expression, featuring short stories and prose. One female blogger describes blogging as a haven:

Blogs don't only give you the chance to hide, they give you another valuable thing: a space without a title. But what happens after a while of creating the blog you find yourself in the midst of what you once escaped. The pseudo name is no longer a curtain that hides you, but it becomes the name of the being exposed by the posts, one after the other. You gain an identity among your neighbors in blogging—an identity made more defined and clear by every new post. I want to blog for ten years and remain, to the tenth year, thinking about this place as my own place where my rules apply, and that I could, if I desired, post blank posts. (p. 50)

These female bloggers find refuge, identity, and comfort in their blogs. When the blog quoted above was blocked by the Saudi Arabian government, its author began emailing new posts from her cell phone. Readers wanted to stay connected to the author, so they desired to read her posts however posted. Thus, blogging can give repressed women power and voice.

- **Video Blogs or Vlogs:** Vlogs, or video logs, allow users to post in video form (Molyneaux, O'Donnell, & Gibson, 2009) accompanied by text-based comments (Kendall, 2008). Most vlogs focus on personal content. In a study on Youtube vlogs, men posted vlogs more than women (Molyneaux et al., 2009). However, female vloggers were more likely to interact with other vloggers by asking questions and re-sponding. The quality of vlogs also differs along sex lines. Vlogs created by men had better sound quality; women created more interactive vlogs with better image quality. Men vlog about public and technology-related topics; women vlog about personal matters. Despite gender differences in the content and creation of vlogs, both men and women reported feeling a part of the Youtube community.

Blogs and vlogs offer a gender performance platform that is open to the public, whereas other social media, such as Facebook allows users to carefully select the "friends" who will witness their gendered identity performances. With thousands of blogs competing for readership, users may prefer posting on Facebook, a social utility with wider reach than any individual blog, and a documented faithful following.

Gender and Facebook

One of the most important social media trends of the past decade was the rise of the social media website, Facebook. Facebook, one of the fastest growing and most ubiquitous websites in the world, provides a variety of ways for users to display identity (e.g., Boupha, Grisso, Morris, Webb, & Zakeri, 2013), network (e.g., Webb, Wilson, Hodges, Smith, & Zakeri, 2012), and maintain relationships (e.g., Ledbetter & Mazer, 2014). A pure social media outlet, the site provides multiple ways to discover and locate known individuals, groups, and organizations; after finding these entities, users can interact or maintain privacy and simply follow their updates.

"Checking Facebook" can become "deeply integrated in users' daily lives through specific routines and rituals" (Debatin, Lovejoy, Horn, & Hughes, 2009, p. 83). According to one survey of college students, 81% of Facebook users log on to the site on any given day (Sheldon, 2009) and they spend an average of 49 minutes per day on the website. Additionally, the site is synced with other social networking sites such as Twitter and Instagram so that users can post content simultaneously to multiple sites.

Unlike many social networking sites, Facebook provides a template to assist new users in the creation of their personal homepages, or their "profile pages," as they are called in Facebook's vernacular. Users are prompted to answer questions about demographic information (name, birth date, sex, job, where they went to school), popular culture interests (favorite TV shows, movies, quotes) and social information (relational status). However, the new user is never asked information about nationality, ethnicity, or race. Users can elect to provide as much or as little of this information as they prefer, and can select privacy settings that determine who sees what information within and outside of their created Facebook network. However, the site prompts users for information that they did not provide initially, implying that a complete profile is ideal to the Facebook organization. Personalizing profile pages allows users to display identity and users can modify the content of their homepages at any time. Men and women also may differ in how they design and interpret profiles. In an analysis of profiles of 13 to 30 years old users, males and females were equally likely to provide basic profile information such as name, e-mail address, hometown and a profile picture (Taraszow, Aristodemou, Shitta, Laouris, & Arsoy, 2010). Perhaps for safety reasons, women were less likely to reveal locator information such as a home address and mobile telephone number (Taraszow et al., 2010).

- **Building Facebook Networks:** Users can send a "friend request" to any other Facebook user, and if accepted, the two users are listed as friends on Facebook. Female users are less likely than male users to accept friendship requests from strangers (Ongun & Demirag, 2014). Currently, Facebook reports that the average user has 130 friends (Facebook, 2011), but networks can vary greatly from one to five thousand friends. Kee et al.'s research (2013) documents the most users' "networks" are actually comprised of tightly bound groups (e.g., immediate family or a close circle of friends) within large, diverse social aggregations (e.g., extended family or everyone-you-know-at-work).

While Facebook friendships can form entirely online, it is more often the case that a Facebook relationship supports a pre-existing offline relationship (Ellison, Steinfield, & Lampe, 2007; Haythornthwaite, 2005; Lampe, Ellison, & Steinfield, 2006). Facebook friends range from established

intimate relationships to acquaintances. Users perceive that when they are Facebook friends with offline friends and family members, the relationships improve with Facebook use (Waters & Ackerman, 2011).

- **Identity Presentation:** Users broadcast their gendered identities on Facebook via connectivity and narrative (van Dijck, 2013). The unique affordances of Facebook software facilitates connection and narrative, in part, by encouraging photo uploads, status updates, and check-ins. College students who engage in one of these activities such as posting pictures tend to do many more activities (Webb, et al., 2012); in short, users often go "all in" employing multiple connectivity devises. Users control the exact type and amount of information they display (Zhao, Grasmmucks, & Martina, 2008), thus allowing them to craft positive presentations of identity to display to other users (Jones, Remland, & Sanford, 2007).

Gender identity is displayed, in part, via pictures. Rose et al. (2012) found that the pictures uploaded to Facebook as profile pictures contain previously identified gendered traits. Specifically, males often upload pictures that make them seem active, dominant, and independent; females focus more on pictures that make them look attractive and dependent (Rose et al., 2012). Bailey et al. (2013) claim that the, "traditional 'girl' is well established in online spaces" (2013, p. 95), and other research points to the traditional "male" being present as well. However, Strano (2008) found that women often engage in impression management via their profile pictures more than men. Given the harsh judgment women receive for deviating from pre-existing gender expectations, this finding seems to make sense. While both men and women perform gender in social network spaces, women are under more pressure to do so and to conform to what is shown to them through the advertising and other media.

As Garcia-Gomez (2011) noted, sexuality is one aspect of identity; she reported that female teenagers discursively construct sexuality on Facebook primarily via language used when relating to other girls. Observing the identity disclosure of other users can reduce uncertainty by allowing insight into potential responses, attitudes, and behaviors in future interactions (Sheldon, 2009). Researchers describe the users' payoff for self-disclosure in identity presentations as potential gain in "social capital" or the making of connections with potential "pay off" (Aubrey & Rill, 2013; Ellison et al., 2007; Jiang & de Bruijn, 2014). By self-disclosing, users gain social capital but potentially reduce online privacy (Ellison, Steinfeld, & Lampe, 2007; Steinfield, Ellison, & Lampe, 2008).

- **Privacy:** Because Facebook gathers data on its users from profiles and posting activities, the site has come under intense media scrutiny for its privacy policies and changes to those policies. An increased number of users modified their Facebook privacy settings following that media scrutiny (boyd & Hargittai, 2010). O'Brian and Torres (2012) report that over half of Facebook users they surveyed reported a high level of privacy awareness. Mohamed and Ahmad (2012) reported than female users were more likely than male users to increase privacy settings rather than rely on Facebook's default settings that allow for maximum information sharing.

Limiting visibility may allow users to feel more comfortable self-disclosing (Stritzke, Nguyen, & Durkin, 2004). Indeed, Debatin, Lovejoy, Horn, & Hughes (2009) reported that Facebook users "claimed to understand privacy issues, yet reported uploading large amounts of personal information" (p. 83). Tufekci's (2008a) survey results revealed

that users may employ a wide variety of methods to ensure privacy including the use of coded language, nick names, and adjusting post visibility via official privacy settings *rather than* limit the amount of information they disclosure. Indeed, users employ a wide variety of methods for managing privacy such as excluding contact information in profiles and untagging themselves in pictures (Young & Quan-Hasse, 2013). In sum, multiple studies document that Facebook users perceive themselves as knowledgeable about privacy issues and as savoy users who effectively maintain their desired level of privacy though both conventional and unconventional methods.

- **Gendered Usage and Performances:** Young adult men and women appear to use Facebook in equal numbers (Hargittai, 2008), but they may differ in how they use it. Women versus men spend more online time engaged in social networking (Acar, 2008). Female college students spend more time communicating with others on social networking sites than male college students (Acar, 2008). College women express affection on Facebook more than their male counterparts; additionally, they perceive Facebook affection as more appropriate than college men (Mansson & Myers, 2011).

College women received and accepted more friendship requests than men (Acar, 2008). College men reported using Facebook to locate and initiate relationships with potential dating partners, whereas college women reported using Facebook to maintain existing relationships (Sheldon, 2009). Among college students, both men and women were more likely to initiate Facebook friendships with opposite-sex users with attractive versus unattractive profile pictures (Wang, Moon, Kwon, Evans, & Stefanone, 2010).

How do strangers interpret the comments that friends write on users' profiles? Both male and female college students viewed negative comments by friends on a user's profile about the users' moral behavior as influencing the profile owners' attractiveness (Walther, vander Heide, Kim, Westerman, & Tong, 2008). Specifically, the negative comments decreased the attractive of female profile owners and increased the attractiveness of male profile owners.

Any user can elect to create a sex-free or gender-neutral Facebook profile. In such situations, users must choose their language carefully because their talk style could reveal their gender (Thomson, 2006; Loureiro & Ribeiro, 2014). Furthermore, stereotypical content of messages also leads to deconstructions and assignments of online gender. For example, a user discussing cooking is likely to be decoded as female, whereas a user discussing sports is likely to be decoded as male. Once manifest, gender can play a role in user relationships on Facebook.

Facebook enjoys widespread acceptance among users world-wide; in contrast, a smaller number of users play online games. Nonetheless, interactive online games offer a commercial social media based on competition with a strong appeal and unique affordances for gendered performance such the necessarily to create an avatar to represent the self. In the next section we discuss these affordances and the resultant gender performances as we review the social scientific research about online gaming.

Gender and Gaming

In 2012, feminist activist Anita Sarkeesian began a project, "Tropes Versus Women In Video Games," to explore sexism in video games via multiple in depth videos. She launched a Kickstarter with the goal of raising $6000 for her work, and instead raised 25 times that amount (Liss-Schultz, 2014). Because of her critique of the portrayal of women in online games, Sarkeesain received death threats and rape threats; she experienced attempts to collect and publically distribute her home address and phone number. In 2014, she went into hiding in response to the sheer amount of misogynist hate she received (Campbell, 2014). Sarkeesian's experience exemplifies the popular attention that the topic of gender and gaming is currently receiving. While Sarkeesian's work focuses on the sexism in games in the popular sphere, academic research focuses on how the gaming experience itself is highly gendered in three ways: (1) who is allowed to enjoy video games, (2) how players may behave within the game, and (3) how those who play video games enact gender within the more "anonymous" digital environment.

Online gaming began as mechanized one-person card games such as solitaire, evolved into one-person video games such as early Mario, jumped to player-versus-machine game such as online chess in the 1990s, and then took the social-media leap to player-versus-player games with interaction between players, allowing users to select their opponents, discuss rules and potential rule violations, congratulate winners, and across-games, develop on-going relationships. With the advent of massive multi-player online role-playing games (MMORPG), the conversion from online games as diversion to online gaming as a social media was complete. Today, with real-time voice communication between players, users form teams, go on quests together, develop antagonist relationships with serial opponents and collegial relationships with fellow players from around the world. Given that many MMORPG are commercial and proprietary, other social media, such as Facebook, do not offer them as part of the possible ways for users to interact. Instead Facebook purchased and offers versions of simpler games that are far less expensive to own and operate.

As the technology and the culture of gaming progresses, it becomes more and more social; for example, games often have entire communities of message boards, Facebook pages, and other arenas of online communication devoted to them. Additionally, gaming is increasingly social itself. For example, Playstation Network and Xbox Live both allow users to post images, videos, and commentary on their experiences playing the games. Other users respond to these postings, and people can develop friend lists. In this way, gaming has becomes a social medium.

Below, the chapter discusses how, in a very real way, gender is policed within the gaming subculture, both in terms of how the genders are represented in the games as Sarkeesian noted, and how men and women play the games. However, it is important to note that the literature reviewed below carries with it the implicit assumption that MMORPG is a more masculine space in which women are making inroads. While this be true of MMORPG, casual gaming such as Facebook games and games for smart phones have seen a very large influx of female gamers. These spaces do not see some of the misogyny directed at female gamers that is represented in many of the studies below. As such, additional research is needed to further clarify the increasing complex social media phenomenon of online gaming.

- **Portrayals of Gaming Characters:** As Olgetree and Drake (2007) argue, "gender differences in participation and character portrayals potentially impact the lives of youth in a variety of ways" (p.537). Unfortunately, such representations of gender can often be stereotyped and can lead to misleading expectations of gender identity, beauty standards, sex appeal, and even gender-related violence (Beasley & Standley, 2002; Dietz, 1998). Such stereotypes extend to the websites designed to promote the commercial MMORPG. Robinson, Callister, Clark, and Phillips (2008) reported that these websites portray female characters in highly sexualized ways and male characters far outnumber female characters. Perhaps gaming companies are simply identifying their base, as more men identify as gamers than women (Shaw, 2011). From promotion to execu-

tion, games identify males as the primary audience and imply a woman's place within the gaming world. To participate, women must fill the position outlined for them or potentially face the kind of backlash Sarkeesian faced when she spoke out against these articulated gender roles.

- **Activities in Gaming Per Se:** The experience of playing the games is as gendered as the games themselves. Although women and men spend equal time playing online games (Williams et al., 2009), women largely perceive video games as gendered male (Thornham, 2008; Royse, Lee, Undrahbuyan, Hopson, & Consalvo, 2007). In an ethnographic study, Thornham (2008) found that both men and women play video games quite competently, but women ask for help and instruction as a means of eliciting social interaction from male gamers. Such requests offer male gamers the opportunity to demonstrate expertise. Both males and females in Thornham's study played out specific gender roles when gaming. However, as more women have entered the realm of video gaming, they have adopted a multiplicity of roles. Yates and Littleton (2001) call upon researchers to examine how players construct the very act of gaming and how such constructions may impact and challenge their sense of self, including their own gendered identities. To answer this call, Royce et al. (2007) conducted a study about the levels of play in video games and how women approach this phenomenon in a medium that is clearly skewed towards male gamers. Their findings identified distinct attitudes towards gaming that corresponded with three different levels of play:
  - Female gamers who identified as power gamers due to their heavy amounts of play had no problems integrating video games and gender identity be-

cause they took far more control over the experience in the characters they created. These gamers valued choice and control, and seemed to choose characters that were feminine and sexy as well as strong. For these female gamers, digital games were not a problematic technology because they were able to embody femininity in their lives as they performed masculinity in their gaming behavior. The performance of gender was a choice for these women—a preferred negotiation with the technology. They felt empowered, rather than at the mercy of a gendered gaming experience.

○ By contrast, the second category of moderate gamers identified by Royce et al. (2007) exercised control as well. However, instead of control over characters within the game, these gamers controlled the types of games they played. They enacted control at the environmental level. These gamers tended to reinscribe traditional gender divisions by assigning certain genres of games like fantasy and violent games to men, while they claimed ownership over what they perceive as more feminine games such as puzzle and problem-solving games.

○ Finally, those women who identified as non-gamers perceived the entire gaming experience as a male one, and thus displayed no interest in it.

Nonetheless, it is "impossible for researchers to make ready conclusions about how digital games may operate as 'technologies of gender,' for they seem to operate in different ways for different women" (Royce et al., 2007, p. 560). Kerr (2003) concurs; she reported that women tend to contest and appropriate gaming technology for their own means.

• **Gendered Interactions between Gamers:** The technology of gaming is always improving, however, and with improvements come new ways in which gender must be negotiated. Until this point, the discussion has for the most part focused on the relationship between the player and the game. Online gaming has become more and more of a reality, from MMORPG to console services that allow for many games to have a multiplayer element that can involve playing with anyone from within the nation and sometimes around the world. For example, Xbox Live, the service that allows Xbox players to connect and game with other Xbox players, recently reached 46 million subscriptions (Agnello, 2013); more than half of all Xbox owners have an Xbox Live subscription. With this service, and others like it, comes the ability to communicate orally via a headset (as opposed to textually, as has been more common with MMORPGs). Due to the general lack of a keyboard with consoles, oral communication is the preferred method of communication among users while playing. Such online gaming experiences have arguably moved gaming into the social media sphere.

With the rise of *interactive* online gaming comes the question of how players will perform beyond the games themselves and how they will interact with a vast community of people playing the same game. This is a far different, more dynamic performance than the living room gamers Thornham (2008) studied. At the same time, however, voices are easily identified as male or female, and thus a level of anonymity disappears. Williams et al. (2007) reports that in real-time voice chat, other gamers respond to voice as a gendered identity cue. Kuznekoff and Rose (2012) played neutral audio responses of a man speaking and a woman speaking while playing games on the Xbox Live network; the female voice received three times more negative comments than the male voice or no voice at all. Many comments about the female voice contained specific gendered insults, such as "whore" or "slut".

Williams, Caplan, and Xiong (2009) reported that male players were more verbally aggressive in general in some online multiplayer games than female players. Perhaps voice communication technology allows male gamers to be even more active participants in gendering the gaming experience. Furthermore, Gray (2012) noted that in promotional materials for the games, female characters are sexualized; now the anonymous male voice can and does hurl negative sexualized insults at female voices. Such behavior stands in contrast to Thornham (2008)'s living room gamers, where gender was enacted as a form of expertise within gaming. The verbal insults directed at women in an environment that allows for relatively anonymous voice communication may mark MMORPG as a contested gender space; here we have male voices attempting to bully and police gender roles for female voices.

Given that heavy female gamers seek to define their own gaming experience, conflict over the nature of the gendered gaming experience seems inevitable. As Kuznekoff and Rose (2012) point out, more research is needed in this area. They claim that, "past research has not fully examined the content generated by gamers and instead has focused on that content created by game developers" (p. 553). With online gaming, gamers communally create a large portion of their own experience, and as such the virtual gaming environment becomes a socially constructed space. Based on the research cited above, gender is an important part of that social construction.

- **Gender-Bending:** While voice chat has made it more difficult for gamers to mask their offline gender identity in online gaming spaces, it has not prevented gender-bending entirely. Given that MMORPGs

often rely primarily on text-based chat only, gender-bending while gaming has become quite common. Yee (2004) reported that, in massive online games, one out of every two female characters is played by a man. One reason male players cite for gender-bending is that female characters receive more assistance and free gifts while playing. Gender-bending requires a conscious, careful performance to avoid being outed, however (Motschenbacher, 2009; Remington, 2009).

Researchers have offered numerous rationales for gender-bending in cyberspace. Motivations themselves can be gendered, as they can reflect deferential treatment of men and women in contemporary American society. Men might gender-bend because they desire the attention garnered by a female identity (Danet, 1998) or because they desire the power achieved in misrepresentation or intentionally deceiving others. Women might gender-bend to be more comfortable enacting aggression or or enjoy the power typically accorded males. Additionally, adopting a masculine identity allows women to avoid online sexual harassment (Danet, 1998). Furthermore, gender-bending allows individuals to experiment with gendered social norms such as differing levels of self-disclosure. Because it is considered more socially acceptable for a woman to self-disclose at a high level than for a man, a man wishing to self-disclose extensively can assume the identity of a woman to avoid questioning. Users can gender-bend to "try on" new ways of communicating in their offline as well as online, personal relationships (Hans et al., 2011). Thus, gender-bending allows users to enact relationships in ways perceived as desirable online but undesirable in offline venues.

For those who adhere to traditional gender roles (i.e., biological males enact masculine behaviors, biological females enact feminine behaviors), gender-bending is unfathomable and confusing because gender-benders fail to fit easily or readily into existing cognitive categories. "I log in and now I'm a woman. And I'd log off and I'm a man again" (Bruckman, 1993). Gender-benders display "improper" gender identity in a society that considers gender an important part of human interaction (Bruckman, 1993); thus, gender-bending can be viewed as a form of resistance (Rothman, 1993) that poses a threat to the social structure. Gender-benders can develop identity based on performance of unconventionally gendered representations and accordingly can be socially reprimanded and pathologized by evaluators (Plante, 2006).

Ibanez (2012) suggests that when users perform online gender and race different from their offline self, such performances can provide new knowledge of other people's gendered identities. As mentioned above, however, more research is needed in the content gamers create for themselves within the gaming environment, and this includes the performance of gender. Much of the current research centers on the female experience in the masculine environment, and perhaps with good reason. The female experience offers an insight into how gender functions within gaming.

- **Performing Gender While Gaming:** Questions arise as to what it means to perform gender in an environment that is in every aspect gendered as masculine. Given that female gamers often perceive that they must conform to masculine expectations, even when controlling their own gaming experience. When masquerading as a woman, however, male players must conform to male expectations regarding women. This kind of performance would necessarily involve some tensions and heavy reliance on stereotypes – the very stereotypes perpetuated by the gaming medium. It is possible to resist sexual and gender norms in cyberspace, but unfortunately those very norms also can be and often are reproduced instead of challenged (Brookey & Cannon, 2009; Martey & Consalvo, 2011; Martey,

Stromer-Galley, Banks, Wu, & Consalvo, 2014; Stabile, 2014). In addition, created characters tend to be disproportionately male and white, meaning that females and minorities are underrepresented (Waddell, Ivory, Conde, Long, & McDonnell, 2014). This kind of lopsided representation can lead to skewed perceptions of offline social reality (Waddell et al., 2014).

There is no doubt that both men and women are playing video games. Some, such as Norris (2004), suggest that the hostile environment toward women within online video games might be a reason why more women are not playing them, but that environment does not preclude female participation entirely, or even mostly. Evidence of this diversity can be found in the recent debate over changes to the popular MMORPG *World of Warcraft* (WoW) that sought to eliminate sexist and gendered dialogue. Some gamers lauded the changes as a step forward, while others opposed the changes as the result of feminist killjoys (Braithwaite, 2014). Braithwaite concluded that those opposed to the changes sought to reinforce gender power dynamics. Similarly, Eklund (2011) noted that the study of gender within spaces such as WoW must involve an examination of sexuality; although heterosexual norms and rules typically apply within that online gaming space, there are opportunities for queer performance.

In other parts of the world, separate genres of MMORPGs are marketed to cater to different genders. For example, in Taiwan there are "Kawaii Online Role Playing Games" that target females and "Simulated Online Role Playing Games" that target males (Hou, 2012). While availability of targeted games demonstrates interest on the part of females, it also exemplifies gender roles being reinforced through specific targeting. How gender is performed in increasingly multiplayer gaming environments should be of great interest to scholars concerned with this continually evolving performance context.

Gaming, Facebook, and blogs each offer unique affordances for the performance of gender and each witnesses distinct types of performance. The three exemplars offer diverse models of how affordances impact performances as well as the diversity of gendered performances. The existing findings are interesting but more research is needed.

GAPS IN THE EXTANT RESEARCH AND DIRECTIONS FOR FUTURE RESEARCH

The detailed review of the relevant social scientific research offers evidence that users perform gender in multiple social media venues and that some of those performances reinforce existing sex role stereotypes (such as the sexualized female avatars in WoW) while others promote increased equality (such as the liberation blogs). Additionally, the detailed descriptions of three specific social media clarified the notion of specific affordances; examples linked those affordances to specific kinds of gendered performances (e.g., women not listing cell phone numbers on Facebook). However, the exact links between affordances of specific social media and the types of performances they promote remains largely undocumented. Future research to address this knowledge gap would assist innovators in knowing where to invest their online efforts.

- **Gaps in Gender and Blogs Research:** Much has been written about what kinds of blogs male and female writers tend to create. As mentioned above, statistical evidence tells us who is writing what kinds of blogs. However, further research that examines blogs beyond the simplistic demarcation of filter versus diary blogs could prove helpful in understanding online gendered performances. As ideas of gender become more and more nuanced, so too must blogs as gendered spaces. Older bi-naries may cease to apply or may apply in new and different ways. More nuanced research might include the following ideas:

o Miller (1984) first articulated the notion that topical genre itself is used rhetorically as a form of social action. Miller's work offers one approach for investigating how blog genres themselves may be gendered and to address the question of how a much wider variety of blog types that are being used generically also can be employed to rhetorically construct and articulate gender. At the moment, filter blogs and diary blogs seem to reinforce existing gender norms and stereotypes, but are there genres of blogs that challenge such stereotypes?

- If researchers examined blog genres that are not typically defined by gender, such as environmental blogs, they might (or might not) find evidence of gender performance. If such performances occur, how do they differ from those in clearly gendered spaces?

- Does labeling a blog influence how potential readers see the blog *in terms of potential gendered performances* that are permitted there? For example, does labeling blogs "sexist" versus "liberation" versus "traditionally gendered" prompt readers to perceive an implied rhetorical invitation to engage in certain types of gendered behaviors?

- Another area for possible research, stemming from the research into women's movements via blogs, is looking at blogs as digital but rhetorical spaces. Such research could examine questions such as how is this space conceptualized and how it becomes gendered (or not) within such conceptualizations of the space.

- **Gaps in Gender and Facebook Research:** Rarely has gender been the focal point of research on Facebook. Instead, issues of gender tended to surface in studies about usage. Thus, we know that women use Facebook more than men but there are many other avenues of potential research. Below are a few suggestions for further exploration.

  ◦ Do expectations of privacy vary among the genders? The concept of privacy and perceptions of it on Facebook has been studied in some depth, but not with an eye towards gender. The few differences by biological sex that have emerged were incidental findings.

  ◦ Given that privacy, relationship building, and gender issues intersect on Facebook, more in depth examination of existing findings are in order. For example, females accept more friend requests; does this mean that privacy is of less concern? Or is "networking" of greater concern? Is there some other motivation?

  ◦ Many studies examine how users display identity on Facebook but rarely is gender the focus of such studies. Studies of ethnicity displays (Boupha et al., 2013) could be nuanced to include differential performances of gender.

  ◦ Facebook itself has recently included an increased array of sexuality options to choose from as users craft their profiles. Sexuality affords the opportunity to practice gender performance. Will users change their options, and thus their gender per-

formances, with the advent of these increased options? Will new users employ them or continue to favor traditional options?

  ◦ Users middle-age and older comprise the fastest growing age segment on Facebook. Thus, examining Facebook behavior affords researchers to opportunity to study gendered performances among an unstudied online population.

- **Gaps in Gender and Gaming Research:** As mentioned at the start of the gaming section, there seem to be implicit assumptions in the literature of gaming as a masculine space. Much like the more traditional forms of social media (if any form of social media can be labeled "traditional"), gaming is a quickly evolving social platform. Females may dominate certain parts of the space, such as casual games, but research is needed to verify or disprove this idea, and to examine the performance of gender in new gaming spaces not automatically assumed "masculine". Perhaps the assumption of gaming as a masculine space no longer holds true in light of newer gaming experiences. What are the experiences of the feminine gender in these frontiers? What is the masculine reaction to the new gaming spaces? How will gender factor into the social construction of these new spaces? How do race and gender intersect in social gaming spaces? These questions and more are the issues that should drive future research into the social medium of gaming.

- **General Directions for Future Research:** In addition to the specific suggestions above, there are some obvious gaps in the research across multiple social media venues. Below three are highlighted:

  ◦ The increased linkages between social media, such as a Facebook status update containing a link to a blog post, may further reinforce gender beliefs and behaviors; conversely, delivering the same message on multiple venues may prompt users to rejection of messages. The potential impact of social media linkages and their relationship to gender preferences is unknown and awaits exploration.

  ◦ The vast majority of research examining gender issues in social media focuses on women and women's experiences. There are reasonable and laudable reasons for this focus; nonetheless, with males comprising approximately 49% of the human specie, attention to their gendered performances will provide additional insights.

  ◦ Furthermore, research could track how gender performances evolve over time.

  ◦ Finally, the vast amount of research on gender and social media published thus far reports differences between the biological sexes rather than engaging more nuanced assessments of gender or concerns of sexual identification. Moving to more sophisticated conceptualizations and measurement will rapidly increase scholars understanding of online gendered performances.

SOLUTIONS AND RECOMMENDATIONS

Given the tremendous popularity of social media, especially among impressionable adolescents and young adults, it seems reasonable to continue researching these so called new media and to play close attention to performances of gender, race, and class in these online spaces. Conversely,

the same social media that elicit powerful, liberating gender performances also present many challenges, such as online deception. Therefore, social media engagement should be thoughtful but not avoidant.

Social media provide venues for interaction and performance. They are neutral. Users can employ social media to benefit and to harm themselves and others. Collectively, users, groups, and organizations can employ social media as instruments to maintain the status quo or to move in directions of positive change. Regardless of the users' goals, the following specific recommendations apply:

- Change agents who desire to promote increased gender equality should develop an online presence that spans multiple media. Employing multiple media simultaneously allows for the reinforcement of promoted ideas as well as the potential to reach multiple audiences. On these websites, they might offer models of preferred gendered performances as well as provide positive feedback to the positive performances they see.

- Similarly, agencies that assist men and women in their efforts to achieve equity might "advertise" their services on social media, especially on websites where equality is sorely lacking such as dating websites and online gaming websites. Providing information about their services in a place where those services are needed may lead to a significant increase in clientele.

- Finally, socializing agents such as educators, parents, coaches, and religious leaders might reasonably participate in social media as users so that they can appreciate their mentees' online experiences, especially as they pertain to societal and peer pressure to conform to gender and sexual expectations. When the time comes to educate young adults about the role of social media in sexualization and gender exploitation, socializing agents can build their credibility by speaking from first-hand knowledge of social media venues.

CONCLUSION

The performance of gender is endemic to social media of all kinds, including blogs, Facebook, and online games. Some users employ social media venues to challenge existing gender stereotypes and to defy prevailing social norms; other users reproduce existing sex role stereotypes on social media—sometimes because gender performances are policed either by the software itself or by fellow users. Instead of challenging gender roles, many social media, such as online games, reconstruct them along familiar lines through corporate advertising and social pressure. In those cases, most of the pressure to conform is directed to women; at this point in time, the scholarly focus also lies with female users. However, more research on the phenomenon would establish the effect of the performance of gender in these spaces on both users and programmer.

REFERENCES

Acar, A. (2008). Antecedents and consequences of online social networking behavior: The case of Facebook. *Journal of Website Promotion, 3*(1-2), 62–83. doi:10.1080/15533610802052654

Agnello, A. J. (2014). *Recent results give Microsoft a compelling defense for the always-online next Xbox*. Digital Trends 2013. Available from http://www.digitaltrends.com/gaming/xbox-360-sales-and-xbox-live-membership-numbers-give-microsoft-a-compelling-defense-for-the-always-online-next-xbox/

Aleman, S. M. (2010). Americans in brown bodies: An analysis of journalistic performances of whiteness. *Southwestern Mass Communication Journal, 26*(1), 1–18.

Amir, Z., Abidin, H., Darus, S., & Ismail, K. (2012). Gender differences in the language use of Malaysian teen bloggers. *GEMA Online Journal of Language Studies, 12*, 105–124.

Anderson, W. K. Z., & Buzzanell, P. M. (2007). "Outcast among outcasts": Identity, gender, and leadership in a mac users group. *Women & Language, 30*, 32–45.

Armstrong, C. L., & McAdams, M. J. (2009). Blogs of information: How gender cues and individual motivations influence perceptions of credibility. *Journal of Computer-Mediated Communication, 14*(3), 435–456. doi:10.1111/j.1083-6101.2009.01448.x

Ashford, C. (2006). The only gay in the village: Sexuality and the net. *Information & Communications Technology Law, 15*(3), 275–289. doi:10.1080/13600830600961202

Atkinson, N. L., Saperstein, S. L., Desmond, S. M., Gold, R. S., Billing, A. S., & Tian, J. (2009). Rural ehealth nutrition education for limited-income families: An iterative and user-centered design approach. *Journal of Medical Internet Research, 11*(2), 5. doi:10.2196/jmir.1148 PMID:19632974

Attwood, F. (2009). Intimate adventures: Sex blogs, sex "blooks" and women's sexual narration. *European Journal of Cultural Studies, 12*(1), 5–20. doi:10.1177/1367549408098702

Aubrey, J. S., & Rill, L. (2013). Investigating relations between Facebook use and social capital among college undergraduates. *Communication Quarterly, 61*(4), 479–496. doi:10.1080/014633 73.2013.801869

Bailey, J., Steeves, V., Burkell, J., & Regan, P. (2013). Negotiating with gender stereotypes on social networking sites: From "bicycle face" to Facebook. *The Journal of Communication Inquiry, 37*(2), 91–112. doi:10.1177/0196859912473777

Bailey, J., & Telford, A. (2007). What's so cyber about it: Reflections on cyberfeminism contribution to legal studies. *Canadian Journal of Women and the Law, 19*, 243–272.

Barta, W., & Kiene, S. (2005). Motivations for infidelity in heterosexual dating couples: The roles of gender, personality differences, and sociosexual orientation. *Journal of Social and Personal Relationships, 22*(3), 339–360. doi:10.1177/0265407505052440

Beasley, B., & Standley, T. C. (2002). Shirts vs. skins: Clothing as an indicator of gender role stereotyping in video games. *Mass Communication & Society, 5*(3), 279–293. doi:10.1207/S15327825MCS0503_3

Ben-Ze'ev, A. (2004). *Love online: Emotions on the Internet.* Cambridge, UK: Cambridge University Press. doi:10.1017/CBO9780511489785

Boies, S. C. (2002). University students' uses of and reactions to online sexual information and entertainment: Links to online and offline sexual behavior. *The Canadian Journal of Human Sexuality, 11*, 77–89.

Boupha, S., Grisso, A. D., Morris, J., Webb, L. M., & Zakeri, M. (2013). How college students display ethnic identity on Facebook. In R. A. Lind (Ed.), *Race/Gender/Media: Considering diversity across audiences, content, and producers* (3rd ed., pp. 107–112). Boston, MA: Pearson.

boyd, d., & Hargittai, E. (2010). Facebook privacy settings: Who cares? *First Monday, 15*(8), 1.

Braithwaite, A. (2014). "Seriously, get out": Feminists on the forums and the War(craft) on women. *New Media & Society, 16*(5), 703–718. doi:10.1177/1461444813489503

Brookey, R. A., & Cannon, K. L. (2009). Sex lives in Second Life. *Critical Studies in Mass Communication, 26*(2), 145–164. doi:10.1080/15295030902860260

Bruckman, A. S. (1993), *Gender-swapping on the Internet.* Retrieved from www.inform.umd.edu/EdRes/Topic/WomensStudies/Computing/Articl/gender-swapping

Butler, J. (1990). Subversive bodily acts. In J. Butler (Ed.), *Gender trouble: Feminism and the subversion of identity* (pp. 163–180). New York: Routledge.

Camahort, E. (2006). *BlogHer '06 session discussion Mommyblogging is a radical act! On day two.* Retrieved from http://blogher.org/node/5563

Campbell, C. (2014). *Sarkeesian driven out of home by online abuse and death threats.* Polygon 2014. Available from http://www.polygon.com/2014/8/27/6075679/sarkeesian-driven-out-of-home-by-online-abuse-and-death-threats

Cooper, A., Boies, S., Maheu, M., & Greenfield, D. (2000). Sexuality and the Internet: The next sexual revolution. In F. Muscarella & L. Szuchman (Eds.), *Psychological perspectives on human sexuality* (pp. 519–545). New York: Wiley.

Danet, B. (1998). Text as mask: Gender, play, and performance on the Internet. In S. G. Jones (Ed.), *CyberSociety 2.0: Revising computer-mediated communication and community* (pp. 129–158). Thousand Oaks, CA: Sage. doi:10.4135/9781452243689.n5

Debatin, B., Lovejoy, J. P., Horn, A. K., & Hughes, B. N. (2009). Facebook and online privacy: Attitudes, behaviors, and unintended consequences. *Journal of Computer-Mediated Communication*, *15*(1), 83–108. doi:10.1111/j.1083-6101.2009.01494.x

Dietz, T. L. (1998). An examination of violence and gender role portrayals in video games: Implications for gender socialization and aggressive behavior. *Sex Roles*, *38*(5/6), 425–442. doi:10.1023/A:1018709905920

Droge, C., Stanko, M. A., & Pollitte, W. A. (2010). Lead users and early adopters on the web: The role of new technology product blogs. *Journal of Product Innovation Management*, *27*(1), 66–82. doi:10.1111/j.1540-5885.2009.00700.x

Edley, P. P., & Houston, R. (2011). The more things change, the more they stay the same: The role of ICTs in work and family connections. In K. B. Wright & L. M. Webb (Eds.), *Computer-mediated communication in personal relationships* (pp. 194–221). New York: Peter Lang.

Eklund, L. (2011). Doing gender in cyberspace: The performance of gender by female *World of Warcraft* players. *Convergence (London)*, *17*(3), 323–342. doi:10.1177/1354856511406472

Ellison, N. B., Steinfield, C., & Lampe, C. (2007). The benefits of Facebook "friends:" Social capital and college students' use of online social network sites. *Journal of Computer-Mediated Communication*, *12*(4), 1143–1168. doi:10.1111/j.1083-6101.2007.00367.x

Facebook, Inc. From http://www.facebook.com/press/info.php?statistics

Friedman, M., & Calixte, S. (Eds.). (2009). *Mothering and blogging: The radical act of the mommyblog*. Toronto, Canada: Demeter Press.

Fullick, M. (2013). "Gendering" the self in online dating discourse. *Canadian Journal of Communication*, *38*, 545–562.

García-Gómez, A. (2009). Teenage girls' personal weblog writing: Truly a new gender discourse? *Information Communication and Society*, *12*(5), 611–638. doi:10.1080/13691180802266657

García-Gómez, A. (2011). Regulating girlhood: Evaluative language, discourses of gender socialization and relational aggression. *European Journal of Women's Studies*, *18*(3), 243–264. doi:10.1177/1350506811405817

Gibbs, J., Ellison, N., & Heino, R. (2006). Self-presentation in online personals: The role of anticipated future interaction, self-disclosure, and perceived success in Internet dating. *Communication Research*, *33*(2), 152–177. doi:10.1177/0093650205285368

Gomez, A. G. (2010). Disembodiment and cyberspace: Gendered discourses in female teenagers' personal information disclosure. *Discourse & Society*, *21*(2), 135–160. doi:10.1177/0957926509353844

Gray, K. L. (2012). Intersecting oppressions and online communities. *Information. Technology & Society*, *15*, 411–428.

Haferkamp, N., & Krämer, N. (2008, May). *Entering the blogosphere: Motives for reading, writing, and commenting.* Paper presented at the Meeting of the International Communication Association, Montreal, Canada.

Hammond, L. (2010). Mommyblogging is a radical act. In J. F. Stitt & P. R. Powell (Eds.), *Mothers who deliver: Feminist interventions in public and interpersonal discourse* (pp. 77–98). Albany, NY: State University of New York Press.

Hancock, J. T., & Toma, C. L. (2009). Putting your best face forward: The accuracy of online dating photographs. *Journal of Communication*, *59*(2), 367–386. doi:10.1111/j.1460-2466.2009.01420.x

Hans, M. L., Lee, B. D., Tinker, K. A., & Webb, L. M. (2011). Online performances of gender: Blogs, gender-bending, and cybersex as relational exemplars. In K. B. Wright & L. M. Webb (Eds.), *Computer mediated communication in personal relationships* (pp. 302–323). New York: Peter Lang Publishers.

Hargittai, E. (2008). Whose space? Differences among users and non-users of social network sites. *Journal of Computer-Mediated Communication*, *13*(1), 276–297. doi:10.1111/j.1083-6101.2007.00396.x

Haythornthwaite, C. (2005). Social networks and internet connectivity effects. *Information Communication and Society*, *8*(2), 125–147. doi:10.1080/13691180500146185

Herring, S. C., Kouper, I., Scheidt, L. A., & Wright, E. L. (2004) Women and children last: The discursive construction of weblogs. *Into the blogosphere: Rhetoric, community and culture of weblogs.* Retrieved from http://blog.lib.umn.edu/blogosphere/women_and_children.html

Herring, S. C., & Paolillo, J. C. (2006). Gender and genre variation in weblogs. *Journal of Sociolinguistics*, *10*(4), 439–459. doi:10.1111/j.1467-9841.2006.00287.x

Hookway, N. (2008). "Entering the blogosphere": Some strategies for using blogs in social research. *Qualitative Research*, *8*(1), 91–113. doi:10.1177/1468794107085298

Hou, C. I. (2012). Gendered avatars: Representation of gender differences between cartoons and simulated online role playing games in Taiwan. *China Media Research*, *8*(3), 81–91.

Jiang, J., & de Bruijn, O. (2014). Facebook helps: A case study of cross-cultural social networking and social capital. *Information Communication and Society*, *17*(6), 732–749. doi:10.1080/1369118X.2013.830636

Jones, T. S., Remland, M. S., & Sanford, R. (2007). *Interpersonal communication through the life span.* Boston: Houghton Mifflin.

Junco, R., Merson, D., & Salter, D. (2010). The effect of gender, ethnicity, and income on college students' use of communication technologies. *Cyberpsychology, Behavior, and Social Networking*, *13*(6), 619–627. doi:10.1089/cyber.2009.0357 PMID:21142986

Kapidzic, S., & Herring, S. C. (2011). Gender, communication, and self-presentation in teen chatrooms revisited: Have patterns changed? *Journal of Computer-Mediated Communication*, *17*(1), 39–59. doi:10.1111/j.1083-6101.2011.01561.x

Karlsson, L. (2007). Desperately seeking sameness: The processes and pleasures of identification in women's diary blog reading. *Feminist Media Studies*, *7*(2), 137–153. doi:10.1080/14680770701287019

Kayany, J. M., & Yelsma, P. (2000). Displacement effects of online media in the socio-technical contexts of households. *Journal of Broadcasting & Electronic Media*, *44*(2), 215–229. doi:10.1207/s15506878jobem4402_4

Kaye, B. (2005). It's a blog, blog, blog, blog world. *Atlantic Journal of Communication*, *13*, 73–95. doi:10.1207/s15456889ajc1302_2

Kee, K. F., Sparks, L., Struppa, D. C., & Mannucci, M. (2013). Social groups, social media, and higher dimensional social structures: A simplicial model of social aggregation for computational communication research. *Communication Quarterly*, *61*(1), 35–58. doi:10.1080/01463373.2012.719566

Kelly, D. M., Pomerantz, S., & Currie, D. H. (2006). "No boundaries"? Girls' interactive, online learning about femininities. *Youth & Society*, *38*(1), 3–28. doi:10.1177/0044118X05283482

Kendall, L. (2008). Beyond media producers and consumers: Online multimedia productions as interpersonal communication. *Information Communication and Society*, *11*(2), 207–220. doi:10.1080/13691180801937084

Kerr, A. (2003). Women just want to have fun: A study of adult female players of digital games. In M. Copier & J. Raessens (Eds.), Level Up: Digital Games Research Conference (p. 270-285). Utrecht: University of Utrecht.

Kleman, E. (2007). *Journaling for the world (wide web) to see: A proposed model of self-disclosure intimacy in blogs*. Paper presented at the 93rd National Communication Association Conference, Chicago, IL.

Kline, D., & Burstein, D. (2005). *Blog! How the newest media revolution is changing politics, business and culture*. New York: CDS Books.

Koskela, H. (2004). Webcams, TV shows, and mobile phones. Empowering exhibitionism. *Surveillance & Society*, *2*, 199–215.

Kovic, I., Lulic, I., & Brumini, G. (2008). Examining the medical blogosphere: An online survey of medical bloggers. *Journal of Medical Internet Research*, *10*(3), e28. doi:10.2196/jmir.1118 PMID:18812312

Kuznekoff, J. H., & Rose, L. M. (2012). Communication in multiplayer gaming: Examining Player responses to gender cues. *New Media & Society*, *15*(4), 541–556. doi:10.1177/1461444812458271

Lampe, C., Ellison, N., & Steinfield, C. (2006, November). A Face (book) in the crowd: Social searching vs. social browsing. In *Proceedings of the 2006 20th anniversary conference on Computer supported cooperative work* (pp. 167-170). doi:10.1145/1180875.1180901

Ledbetter, A. M., & Mazer, J. P. (2014). Do online communication attitudes mitigate the association between Facebook use and relational interdependence? An extension of media multiplexity theory. *New Media & Society*, *16*(5), 806–822. doi:10.1177/1461444813495159

Lee, B. D., & Webb, L. M. (2012). The ICC (identity, content, community) theory of blog participation. In R. A. Lind (Ed.), *Producing theory: The intersection of audiences and production in a digital world* (pp. 177–193). New York: Peter Lang Publishers.

Lee, B. S., & Webb, L. M. (2014). Mommy bloggers: Who they are, what they write about, and how they are shaping motherhood in the 21st century. In A. R. Martinez & L. J. Miller (Eds.), Gender in a transitional era: Changes and challenges (pp. 41-57). Lanham, MD: Lexington.

Li, D. (2007). *Why do you blog: A uses-and-gratifications inquiry into bloggers' motivations*. Paper presented at the International Communication Association Convention, San Francisco, CA.

Limacher, L., & Wright, L. (2006). Exploring the therapeutic family intervention of commendations. *Journal of Family Nursing*, *12*(3), 307–331. doi:10.1177/1074840706291696 PMID:16837697

Lind, R. A. (2012). Produsing theory in a digital world: Illustrating *homo irretitus*. In R. A. Lind (Ed.), *Produsing theory: The intersection of audiences and production in a digital world* (pp. 1–14). New York: Peter Lang Publishers.

Liss-Schultz, N. (2014). This woman was threatened with rape after calling out sexist video games - and then something inspiring happened. *Mother Jones*. Available from http://www.motherjones.com/media/2014/05/pop-culture-anita-sarkeesian-video-games-sexism-tropes-online-harassement-feminist

Litt, E. (2012). *Knock, knock*. Who's there? The imagined audience. *Journal of Broadcasting & Electronic Media, 56*(3), 330–345. doi:10.1080/08838151.2012.705195

Livingstone, S. (2008). Taking risky opportunities in youthful content creation: Teenagers' use of social networking sites for intimacy, privacy, and self-expression. *New Media & Society, 10*(3), 393–411. doi:10.1177/1461444808089415

Lopez, L. K. (2009). The radical act of "mommy blogging": Redefining motherhood through the blogosphere. *New Media & Society, 11*(5), 729–747. doi:10.1177/1461444809105349

Loureiro, S. M. C., & Ribeiro, L. (2014). Virtual atmosphere: The effect of pleasure, arousal, and delight on word-of-mouth. *Journal of Promotion Management, 20*(4), 452–469. doi:10.1080/10496491.2014.930283

Manago, A. M., Graham, M., Greenfield, P. M., & Salimkhan, G. (2008). Self-presentation and gender on MySpace. *Journal of Applied Developmental Psychology, 29*(6), 446–458. doi:10.1016/j.appdev.2008.07.001

Mansson, D. H., & Myers, S. A. (2011). An initial examination of college students' expressions of affection through Facebook. *The Southern Communication Journal, 76*(2), 155–168. doi:10.1080/10417940903317710

Martey, R. M., & Consalvo, M. (2011). Performing the looking-glass self: Avatar appearance and group identity in *Second Life. Popular Communication, 9*(3), 165–180. doi:10.1080/15405702.2011.583830

Martey, R. M., Stromer-Galley, J., Banks, J., Wu, J., & Consalvo, M. (2014). The strategic female: Gender-switching and player behavior in online games. *Information. Technology & Society, 17*, 286–300.

Menard-Warwick, J. (2007). "My little sister had a disaster, she had a baby": Gendered performance, relational identities, and dialogic voicing. *Narrative Inquiry, 17*(2), 279–297. doi:10.1075/ni.17.2.07men

Miller, C. R. (1984). Genre as social action. *The Quarterly Journal of Speech, 70*(2), 151–176. doi:10.1080/00335638409383686

Millner, V. (2008). Internet infidelity: A case of intimacy with detachment. *The Family Journal (Alexandria, Va.), 16*(1), 78–82. doi:10.1177/1066480707308918

Mohamed, N., & Ahmad, I. H. (2012). Information privacy concerns, antecedents and privacy measure use in social networking sites: Evidence from Malaysia. *Computers in Human Behavior, 28*(6), 2366–2375. doi:10.1016/j.chb.2012.07.008

Molyneaux, H., O'Donnell, S., & Gibson, K. (2009). YouTube vlogs: An analysis of the gender divide. *Media Report to Women, 37*, 6–11.

Monteiro, B. (2008). Blogs and female expression in the Middle East. *Media Development, 55*, 47–53.

Moravec, M. (Ed.). (2011). *Motherhood online: How online communities shape modern motherhood*. Newcastle upon Tyne, UK: Cambridge Scholars Publishing.

Morris, R. C. (1995). All made up: Performance theory and the new anthropology of sex and gender. *Annual Review of Anthropology, 24*(1), 567–592. doi:10.1146/annurev.an.24.100195.003031

Motschenbacher, H. (2009). Speaking of the gendered body: The performative construction of commercial femininities and masculinities via body-part vocabulary. *Language in Society, 38*(01), 1–22. doi:10.1017/S0047404508090015

Neff, J. (2008). P&G relies on power of mommy bloggers. *Advertising Age, 79*, 4–24.

Norris, K. O. (2004). Gender stereotypes, aggression, and computer games: An online survey of women. *Cyberpsychology & Behavior*, *7*(6), 714–727. doi:10.1089/cpb.2004.7.714 PMID:15687807

O'Brien, D., & Torres, A. M. (2012). Social networking and online privacy: Facebook users' perceptions. *Irish Journal of Management*, *31*(2), 63–97.

Ogletree, S. M., & Drake, R. (2007). College students video game participation and perceptions: Gender differences and implications. *Sex Roles*, *56*(7-8), 537–542. doi:10.1007/s11199-007-9193-5

Ongun, E., & Demirag, A. (2014). An evaluation of Facebook users' blocking tendencies regarding their privacy and security settings. *Global Media Journal*, *5*, 263–280.

Palmen, M., & Kouri, P. (2012). Maternity clinic going online: Mothers' experiences of social media and online health information for parental support in Finland. *Journal of Communication in Health Care*, *5*(3), 190–198. doi:10.1179/1753807612Y.0000000013

Pedersen, S., & Macafee, C. (2007). Gender differences in British blogging. *Journal of Computer-Mediated Communication*, *12*(4), 1472–1492. doi:10.1111/j.1083-6101.2007.00382.x

Peter, J., & Valkenburg, P. M. (2006). Adolescents' exposure to sexually explicit online material and recreational attitudes toward sex. *Journal of Communication*, *56*(4), 639–660. doi:10.1111/j.1460-2466.2006.00313.x

Pew Internet and American Life Project. (2000, May). *Tracking online life: How women use the Internet to cultivate relationships with family and friends*. Retrieved from Pew Internet and American Life website: http://www.pewinternet.org

Plante, R. F. (2006). Sexual spanking, the self, and the construction of deviance. *Journal of Homosexuality*, *50*(2/3), 59–79. doi:10.1300/J082v50n02_04 PMID:16803759

Podlas, K. (2000). Mistresses of their domain: How female entrepreneurs in cyberporn are initiating a gender power shift. *Cyberpsychology & Behavior*, *3*(5), 847–854. doi:10.1089/10949310050191827

Remington, A. (2009). Gender-bending gamers dress for success. In *The book of odds: The odds of everyday life*. Retrieved from http://www.bookofodds.com/Daily-Life-Activities/Entertainment-Media/Articles/A0008-Gender-Bending-Gamers-Dress-for-Success

Riegert, K., & Ramsey, G. (2013). Activists, individualists, and comics: The counter-publicness of Lebanese blogs. *Television & New Media*, *14*(4), 286–303. doi:10.1177/1527476412463447

Riley, D. (2005). The Blog Herald blog count October 2005: Over 100 million blogs created. *Blog Herald*. Retrieved from http://www.blogherald.com/2005/10/10/the-blog-herald-blog-count-october-2005/

Ringrose, J. (2010). Sluts, whores, fat slags, and Playboy bunnies: Teen girls' negotiation of "sexy" on social networking sites and at school. In C. Jackson, C. Paechter, & E. Renold (Eds.), Girls and education 3-16: Continuing concerns, new agendas (pp. 170-182). New York, NY: McGraw Hill Open University Press.

Ritchie, A., & Barker, M. (2006). "There aren't words for what we do or how we feel so we have to make them up": Constructing polyamorous languages in a culture of compulsory monogamy. *Sexualities*, *9*(5), 584–601. doi:10.1177/1363460706069987

Robinson, T., Callister, M., Clark, B., & Phillips, J. (2008). Violence, sexuality, and gender stereotyping: A content analysis of official video game web sites. *Web Journal of Mass Communication Research, 13*, 1–17.

Rodzvilla, J. (Ed.). (2002). *We've got blog: How weblogs are changing our culture.* Cambridge, MA: Perseus Books Group.

Rose, J., Mackey-Kallis, S., Shyles, L., Barry, K., Biagini, D., Hart, C., & Jack, L. (2012). Face it: The impact of gender on social media images. *Communication Quarterly, 60*(5), 588–607. doi:10.1080/01463373.2012.725005

Rosenberg, S. (2009). *Say everything: How blogging began, what it's becoming, and why it matters.* New York: Crown Publishers.

Rothman, R. A. (1993). *Inequity and stratification: Class, color, and gender.* Englewood Cliffs, NJ: Prentice Hall.

Royal, C. (2005). A meta-analysis of journal articles intersecting issues of Internet and gender. *Journal of Technical Writing and Communication, 35*(4), 403–429. doi:10.2190/3RBM-XKEQ-TRAF-E8GN

Royse, P., Lee, J., Undrahbuyan, B., Hopson, M., & Consalvo, M. (2007). Women and games: Technologies of the gendered self. *New Media & Society, 9*(4), 555–576. doi:10.1177/1461444807080322

Samp, J. A., Wittenberg, E. M., & Gillett, D. L. (2003). Presenting and monitoring a gender-defined self on the Internet. *Communication Research Reports, 20*(1), 1–12. doi:10.1080/08824090309388794

Schecter, D. (2009). They blog, I blog, we all blog. *Nieman Reports, 63*, 93–95.

Scott-Dixon, K. (2002). Turbo chicks: Talkin' 'bout my generation. *Herizons*, 16-19.

Senft, T. M. (2008). *Camgirls: Celebrity and community in the age of social networks.* New York, NY: Peter Lang.

Sheldon, P. (2009). Maintain or develop new relationships? *Rocky Mountain Communication Review, 6*, 51–56.

Sidelinger, R. J., Ayash, G., & Tibbles, D. (2008). Couples go online: Relational maintenance behaviors and relational characteristics use in dating relationships. *Human Communication, 11*, 341–356.

Stabile, C. (2014). "I will own you": Accountability in massively multiplayer online games. *Television & New Media, 15*(1), 43–57. doi:10.1177/1527476413488457

Stavrositu, C., & Sundar, S. S. (2008). Can blogs empower women? Designing agency-enhancing and community-building interfaces. In *CHI 2008 Proceedings of the Conference on Human Factors in Computing Systems: Works in progress* (pp. 2781–2786). Retrieved from http://delivery.acm.org/10.1145/1360000/1358761/p2781-stavrositu.pdf?key1=1358761&key2=5505519621&coll=GUIDE&dl=GUIDE&CFID=80978056&CFTOKEN=37792974

Strano, M. (2008). User descriptions and interpretations of self-presentation through Facebook profile images. *Cyberpsychology: Journal of Psychological Research in Cyberspace, 2*(2).

Stritzke, W. G. K., Nguyen, A., & Durkin, K. (2004). Shyness and computer-mediated communication: A self-presentational theory perspective. *Media Psychology, 6*(1), 1–22. doi:10.1207/s1532785xmep0601_1

Tannen, D. (1990). *You just don't understand: Women and men in conversation.* New York: William Morrow.

Taraszow, T., Aristodemou, E., Shitta, G., Laouris, Y., & Arsoy, A. (2010). Disclosure of personal and contact information by young people in social networking sites: An analysis using Facebook profiles as an example. *International Journal of Media and Cultural Politics*, 6(1), 81–102. doi:10.1386/macp.6.1.81/1

Taylor, R. (2004, May 11). Is blog a masculine noun? *The Guardian*. Retrieved from http://politics.guardian.co.uk/comment/story/0,9115,1214393,00.html

The Pioneer Woman. (2010, September 15). *Crying my eyes out* [Web log post]. Retrieved from http://thepioneerwoman.com/blog/2010/09/crying-my-eyes-out/

The Turner Channel. (2010, February 9). *Infertility...* [Web log post]. Retrieved from http://mattandjuleeturner.blogspot.com/2010/02/infertility.html

Thompson, S. (2007). Mommy blogs: A marketer's dream. *Advertising Age*, 78, 6–11.

Thomson, R. (2006). The effect of topic of discussion on gendered language in computer-mediated communication discussion. *Journal of Language and Social Psychology*, 25(2), 167–178. doi:10.1177/0261927X06286452

Thornham, H. (2008). Gaming, gender, and geeks. *Feminist Media Studies*, 8(2), 127–142. doi:10.1080/14680770801980505

Toma, C. L., & Hancock, J. T. (2011). A new twist on love's labor: Self-presentation in online dating profiles. In K. B. Wright & L. M. Webb (Eds.), *Computer mediated communication in personal relationships* (pp. 41–55). New York: Peter Lang Publishers.

Tucker, J. S. (2009). Foreward. In M. Friedman & S. Calixte (Eds.), *Mothering and blogging: The radical act of the mommyblog* (pp. 1–20). Toronto, Canada: Demeter Press.

Tufekci, Z. (2008a). Can you see me now? Audience and disclosure regulation in online social network sites. *Bulletin of Science, Technology & Society*, 28(1), 20–36. doi:10.1177/0270467607311484

Tufekci, Z. (2008b). Grooming, gossip, Facebook and Myspace: What can we learn about these sites from those who won't assimilate? *Information Communication and Society*, 11(4), 544–564. doi:10.1080/13691180801999050

U.S. Department of Commerce. (2004). *A nation online: Entering the broadband age*. Retrieved from http://www.ntia.doc.gov/reports/anol/NationOnlineBroadband04.htm

van Dijck, J. (2013). 'You have one identity': Performing the self on Facebook and LinkedIn. *Media Culture & Society*, 35(2), 199–215. doi:10.1177/0163443712468605

van Doorn, N., van Zoonen, L., & Wyatt, S. (2007). Writing from experience: Presentations of gender identity on weblogs. *European Journal of Women's Studies*, 14(2), 143–159. doi:10.1177/1350506807075819

Vickery, J. R. (2010). Blogrings as virtual communities for adolescent girls. In S. R. Mazzarella (Ed.), *Girl wide Web 2.0: Revisiting girls, the Internet, and the negotiation of identity* (pp. 183–200). New York, NY: Peter Lang.

Vollman, A., Abraham, L., & Mörn, M. P. (2014). *Women on the web: How women are shaping the internet*. Available from http://www.comscore.com/Press_Events/Presentations_Whitepapers/2010/Women_on_the_Web_How_Women_are_Shaping_the_Internet

Waddell, T. F., Ivory, J. D., Conde, R., Long, C., & McDonnell, R. (2014). White man's virtual world: A systemic content analysis of gender and race in massively multiplayer online games. *Journal of Virtual Worlds Research*, 7(2), 1–14.

Walters, S. (2011). Everyday life, Everyday death. *Feminist Media Studies, 11*(3), 363–378. doi:10.1080/14680777.2010.542341

Walther, J. B., van der Heide, B., Kim, S., Westerman, D., & Tong, S. (2008). The role of friends' appearance and behavior on evaluations of individuals on Facebook: Are we known by the company we keep? *Human Communication Research, 34*(1), 28–49. doi:10.1111/j.1468-2958.2007.00312.x

Wang, S. S., Moon, S. I., Kwon, K. H., Evans, C. A., & Stefanone, M. A. (2010). Face off: Implications of visual cues on initiating friendship on Facebook. *Computers in Human Behavior, 26*(2), 226–234. doi:10.1016/j.chb.2009.10.001

Waters, S., & Ackerman, J. (2011). Exploring privacy management on Facebook: Motivations and perceived consequences of voluntary disclosure. *Journal of Computer-Mediated Communication, 17*(1), 101–115. doi:10.1111/j.1083-6101.2011.01559.x

Webb, L. M., & Lee, B. S. (2011). Mommy blogs: The centrality of community in the performance of online maternity. In M. Moravec (Ed.), *Motherhood online: How online communities shape modern motherhood* (pp. 244–257). Newcastle upon Tyne, UK: Cambridge Scholars.

Webb, L. M., Wilson, M. L., Hodges, M., Smith, P. A., & Zakeri, M. (2012). Facebook: How college students work it. In H. S. Noor Al-Deen & J. A. Hendricks (Eds.), Social media: Usage and impact (p. 3-22). Lanham: MD: Lexington.

Wei, L. (2009). Filter blogs vs. personal journals: Understanding the knowledge production gap on the Internet. *Journal of Computer-Mediated Communication, 14*(3), 532–558. doi:10.1111/j.1083-6101.2009.01452.x

White, M. (2003). Too close to see: Men, women and webcams. *New Media & Society, 5*(1), 105–121. doi:10.1177/1461444803005001901

Whitty, M. (2007). Introduction. In M. T. Whitty, A. J. Baker, & J. A. Inman (Eds.), *Online Matchmaking* (pp. 1–14). New York, NY: Palgrave Macmillan. doi:10.1057/9780230206182

Williams, D., Caplan, S., & Xiong, L. (2007). Can you hear me now? The impact of voice in an online gaming community. *Human Communication Research, 33*(4), 427–449. doi:10.1111/j.1468-2958.2007.00306.x

Williams, D., Consalvo, M., Caplan, S., & Yee, N. (2009). Looking for gender: Gender roles and behaviors among online gamers. *Journal of Communication, 59*(4), 700–725. doi:10.1111/j.1460-2466.2009.01453.x

Wood, J. (2009). *Gendered lives: Communication, gender, and culture.* Boston: Wadsworth.

Woods, J. (2005). Digital influencers: Business communicators dare overlook the power of blogs? *Communication World, 22*, 26-30. Retrieved from http://www.iabc.com/cw/

Yates, S., & Littleton, K. (2001). Understanding computer game cultures: A situated approach. In E. Green & A. Adam (Eds.), *Virtual gender: Technology, consumption, and identity* (pp. 103–123). London: Routledge.

Yee, N. (2004). *Daedalus Gateway: The Psychology of MMORPGs.* Retrieved October, 27, 2009 from http://www.nickyee.com/daedalus/gateway_genderbend.html

Young, A. L., & Quan-Haase, A. (2009). *Information revelation and internet privacy concerns on social network sites: A case study of Facebook.* Retrieved March 5, 2011, from http://www.iisi.de/fileadmin/IISI/upload/2009/p265.pdf

Young, K. (2008). Internet sex addiction: Risk factors, stages of development, and treatment. *The American Behavioral Scientist, 52*(1), 21–37. doi:10.1177/0002764208321339

Young, K., Griffin-Shelley, E., Cooper, A., O'Mara, J., & Buchanan, J. (2000). Online infidelity: A new dimension in couple relationships with implications for evaluation and treatment. *Sexual Addiction & Compulsivity*, 7(1-2), 59–74. doi:10.1080/10720160008400207

Zacharias, U., & Arthurs, J. (2008). The new architectures of intimacy? Social networking sites and genders. *Feminist Media Studies*, 8, 197–202. doi:10.1080/14680770801980612

Zhao, S. Y., Grasmucks, S., & Martina, J. (2008). Identity construction of Facebook: Digital empowerment in anchored relationships. *Computers in Human Behavior*, 24(5), 1816–1836. doi:10.1016/j.chb.2008.02.012

KEY TERMS AND DEFINITIONS

Blog: Website where the owner (i.e., the blogger) posts content (text, pictures, links) related to a specific topic on a frequent and regular basis; posts are displayed in reverse chronological order and readers' comments are encouraged.

Gender (vs. Biological Sex): Whereas biological sex (male or female) is a mere accident of birth, humans enact gender via multiple modes of expression within societal inscriptions of gender as performed through words and actions.

Gender-Bending: Biological males pose as female, biological female pose as males, or individuals pose as nongendered.

Multi-Player Online Gaming: An online game in which the number of simultaneous players is unlimited.

Online Gaming: Games played exclusively on the Internet, such as World of Warcraft, and typically involve fiction, role playing and unusual skills.

Performance Theory: Butler's theory of gender performativity (1990) argues that humans create gender identities through expression and performance, typically within the confines of cultural expectations and limitations.

Relationship Maintenance: "Keep up with" and "stay in touch with" relational partners.

Social Capital: The making of connections with potential "pay off."

Social Media: Websites that facilitate user interaction.

Compilation of References

21. *st Century Skills Map*. (2011, March). Retrieved from https://www.actfl.org/sites/default/files/pdfs/21stCenturySkillsMap/p21_worldlanguagesmap.pdf

Abbruzzese, J. (2014). *The rise and fall of AIM: The breakthrough AOL never wanted.* Retrieved from http://mashable.com/2014/04/15/aim-history/

Abrams, A. (2009). *The portfolio builder 2 for PowerPoint:Templates for creating digital portfolios with PowerPoint.* Retrieved from http://www.arnieabrams.net/portfolio/Chapter1-%20PB_overview.pdf

Abrams, S. S. (2014). Integrating virtual and traditional learning in 6-12 classrooms: A layered literacies approach to multimodal meaning making. New York: Routledge.

Abrams, S., & Walsh, S. (2014). Gamified vocabulary: Online resources and enriched language learning. *Journal of Adolescent & Adult Literacy*, *58*(1), 49–58. doi:10.1002/jaal.315

Acar, A. (2008). Antecedents and consequences of online social networking behavior: The case of Facebook. *Journal of Website Promotion*, *3*(1-2), 62–83. doi:10.1080/15533610802052654

Acquisti, A., & Gross, R. (2005, November). *Information revelation and privacy in online social networks.* Paper presented in the ACM Workshop on Privacy in the Electronic Society, Alexandria, VA.

Adams, C. (2010). Cyberbullying: How to make it stop. *Instructor*, *120*(2), 44–49.

Adams, J. C., & Webster, A. R. (2012). What do students learn about programming from game, music video, and storytelling projects? In *Proceedings of the 43rd ACM Technical Symposium on Computer Science Education* (pp. 643–648). New York, NY: ACM. doi:10.1145/2157136.2157319

Afouxenidis, A. (2014). Social Media and Political Participation: An Investigation of Small Scale Activism in Greece. *Advances in Applied Sociology*, *04*(01), 1–4. doi:10.4236/aasoci.2014.41001

Aghaei, S., Nematbakhsh, M. A., & Farsani, H. K. (2012). Evolution of the world wide web: From Web 1.0 to Web 4.0. *International Journal of Web & Semantic Technology*, *3*(1), 1–10. doi:10.5121/ijwest.2012.3101

Agnello, A. J. (2014). *Recent results give Microsoft a compelling defense for the always-online next Xbox.* Digital Trends 2013. Available from http://www.digitaltrends.com/gaming/xbox-360-sales-and-xbox-live-membership-numbers-give-microsoft-a-compelling-defense-for-the-always-online-next-xbox/

Ahmed, S., & Parsons, D. (2013). Abductive science inquiry using mobile devices in the classroom. *Computers & Education*, *63*, 62–72. doi:10.1016/j.compedu.2012.11.017

Alama, J., Brink, K., Mamane, L., & Urban, J. (2011). *Large formal wikis: Issues and solutions.* Paper presented at the Intelligent Computer Mathematics, Bertinoro, Italy. doi:10.1007/978-3-642-22673-1_10

Alam, I. (2011). Higher education and digital divide in India. *Journal of Library and Information Science, 1*(2), 133–139.

Alam, M., & Prasad, N. R. (2007). Convergence transforms digital home: Techno-economic impact. *Wireless Personal Communications, 44*(1), 75–93. doi:10.1007/s11277-007-9380-2

Alasraj, A., Freeman, M., & Chandler, P. (2013). Optimising layered integrated instructional design through the application of cognitive load theory. *Toulouse:Proceedings from the 6th International Cognitive Load Theory Conference.*

Aleman, S. M. (2010). Americans in brown bodies: An analysis of journalistic performances of whiteness. *Southwestern Mass Communication Journal, 26*(1), 1–18.

Alessi, S. M., & Trollip, S. R. (2001). *Multimedia for learning: Methods and development.* Needham Heights, MA: Pearson.

Alexa. (2014, September 27). *Alexa Top 500 Global Sites.* Retrieved September 27, 2014, from http://www.alexa.com/topsites

Alexander, J., & Parsehian, S. (2014). Content-driven commerce: Differentiating and driving sales with content in commerce. *FitForCommerce.* Retrieved from http://www.fitforcommerce.com/whitepaper-signup-weblinc-content-driven-commerce.html

Alexander, C. (2014). Student-created digital media and engagement in middle school history. *Computers in the Schools, 31*(3), 154–172. doi:10.1080/07380569.2014.932652

Al-Jarf, R. (2012). Mobile technology and student autonomy in oral skill acquisition. In J. Díaz-Vera (Ed.), *Left to my own devices: Learner autonomy and mobile-assisted language learning innovation and leadership in English language teaching* (pp. 105–130). Bingley, UK: Emerald Group.

Alkire, S., & Foster, J. (2009). Counting and multidimensional poverty measurement. *Oxford Poverty & Human Development Initiative (OPHI).* Retrieved from http://www.ophi.org.uk/wp-content/uploads/OPHI-wp32.pdf

Allen, R., Tsai, Y.-T., Hinman, R., & Azuma, R. (2010). The Westwood experience: Connecting story to locations via mixed reality. In *Proceedings of the International Symposium on Mixed and Augmented Reality* (pp. 39-46). Seoul, Korea: Institute of Electrical and Electronics Engineers.

Almeida, A. N. d., Delicado, A., de Almeida Alves, N., & Carvalo, T. (2014). Internet, children and space: Revisiting generational attributes and boundaries. *New Media & Society*, 1–18. doi:10.1177/1461444814528293

Alvarez, A. R. G. (2012). "IH8U": Confronting cyberbullying and exploring the use of cybertools in teen dating relationships. *Journal of Clinical Psychology, 68*(11), 1205–1215. doi:10.1002/jclp.21920 PMID:22961672

Alvermann, D. E., Beach, C. L., & Johnson, J. (2014). *Becoming 3lectric.* Retrieved from www.becoming3lectric.com

Alvermann, D. E. (2008). Why bother theorizing about adolescents' online literacies for classroom practice and research? *Journal of Adolescent & Adult Literacy, 52*(1), 8–19. doi:10.1598/JAAL.52.1.2

Alvermann, D. E. (2011). Moving on, keeping pace: Youth's literate identities and multimodal digital texts. In S. Abrams & J. Rowsell (Eds.), *Rethinking identity and literacy education in the 21st century. National Society for the Study of Education Yearbook* (Vol. 110, part I (pp. 109–128). New York, NY: Columbia University, Teachers College.

Alvermann, D. E. (Ed.). (2010). *Adolescents' online literacies: Connecting classrooms, digital media, & popular culture.* New York, NY: Peter Lang.

Alvermann, D. E., & Hagood, M. C. (2000). Critical media literacy: Research, theory, and practice in 'new times'. *The Journal of Educational Research, 93*(3), 193–205. doi:10.1080/00220670009598707

Alvermann, D. E., Marshall, J. D., McLean, C., Huddleston, A. P., Joaquin, J., & Bishop, J. (2012). Adolescents' web-based literacies, identity construction, and skill development. *Literacy Research and Instruction, 51*(3), 179–195. doi:10.1080/19388071.2010.523135

Alvermann, D. E., & Moore, D. W. (1991). Secondary school reading. In R. Barr, M. L. Kamil, P. Mosenthal, & P. D. Pearson (Eds.), *Handbook of reading research* (Vol. 2, pp. 951–983). New York: Longman.

Alvermann, D., Hutchins, R. J., & DeBlasio, R. (2012). Adolescents' engagement with Web 2.0 and social media: Research, theory, and practice. *Research in the Schools*, *19*(1), 33–44.

Alzouma, G. (2005). Myths of digital technologies in Africa: Leapfrogging development? *Global Media and Communication*, *1*(3), 339–356. doi:10.1177/1742766505058128

American Dialect Society. (2011). *"App" 2010 Word of the Year, as voted by the American Dialect Society*. Retrieved December 8, 2014, from http://www.americandialect.org/American-Dialect-Society-2010-Word-of-the-Year-PRESS-RELEASE

American Friends Service Committee. (2008). *Somali Bantu refugees speak*. Retrieved from http://www.umbc.edu/blogs/digitalstories/2008/12/somali_bantu_refugees_speak_th.html

American Friends Service Committee. (2014). *Storyology: Digital storytelling by immigrants and refugees*. Retrieved from http://www.afsc.org/story/storyology-digital-storytelling-immigrants-and-refugees

Amiel, T. (2006). Mistaking computers for technology: Technology literacy and the digital divide. *Association for the Advancement of Computing in Education*, *14*(3), 235-256. Retrieved from http://www.editlib.org/p/6155/

Amir, Z., Abidin, H., Darus, S., & Ismail, K. (2012). Gender differences in the language use of Malaysian teen bloggers. *GEMA Online Journal of Language Studies*, *12*, 105–124.

Ananiadou, K., & Claro, M. (2009). 21st century skills and competences for new millennium learners in OECD countries. *OECD Education Working Papers*, *41*, 1-34. Retrieved from http://www.oecd.org/officialdocuments/publicdisplaydocumentpdf/?cote=EDU/WKP(2009)20&doclanguage=en

Anderson, J. L., & Lee, B. (Illus.) (2010). Loser/Queen. New York: Simon & Schuster, 2010.

Anderson, J. Q., Boyles, J. L., & Rainie, L. (2012, July 27). *The future impact of the Internet on higher education: Experts expect more-efficient collaborative environments and new grading schemes; they worry about massive online courses, the shift away from on-campus life*. Retrieved from http://pewinternet.org/~/media//Files/Reports/2012/PIP_Future_of_Higher_Ed.pdf

Anderson, J., & Rainie, L. (2012, Feb. 29). *Main findings: Teens, technology, and human potential in 2020*. Pew Research Internet Project. Retrieved from http://www.pewinternet.org/2012/02/29/main-findings-teens-technology-and-human- potential-in-2020/

Anderson, C. (2012). *Makers: The new industrial revolution*. New York, NY: Random House.

Anderson, E. (2011). *The cosmopolitan canopy: Race and identity in everyday life*. New York: W. W. Norton & Company.

Anderson, J., & Rainie, L. (2014). *The Internet of things will thrive by 2025*. Washington, DC: Pew Research Center's Internet and American Life Project.

Anderson, L. H. (1999). *Speak*. New York: Farrar, Straus & Giroux.

Anderson, T. H., & Armbruster, B. B. (1984). Studying. In P. D. Pearson, R. Barr, M. L. Kamil, & P. Mosenthal (Eds.), *Handbook of Reading Research* (pp. 657–679). New York: Longman.

Anderson, W. K. Z., & Buzzanell, P. M. (2007). "Outcast among outcasts": Identity, gender, and leadership in a mac users group. *Women & Language*, *30*, 32–45.

Andersson, B., & Karrqvist, C. (1979). *Elektriska Kretsar (Electric Circuits)*. EKNA Report No 2, University of Gothenburg, Mölndal, Sweden.

Anduiza, E., Cristancho, C., & Sabucedo, J. M. (2013). Mobilization through online social networks: The political protest of the indignados in Spain. *Information Communication and Society*, *17*(6), 750–764. doi:10.1080/1369118X.2013.808360

Angst, C., & Malinowski, E. (2010). *Findings from eReader Project, Phase 1: Use of iPads in MGT40700, Project Management," University of Notre Dame Working Paper Series.* South Bend, IN: University of Notre Dame. Retrieved from http://www.nd.edu/~cangst/Notre-Dame_iPad_Report_01-06-11.pdf

Annany, M. (2014). Critical news making and the paradox of "do-it-yourself-news". In M. Ratto & M. Boler (Eds.), *DIY Citizenship: Critical making and social media* (pp. 359–372). Cambridge, MA: MIT Press.

Annetta, L. (2010). The I's have it: A framework for serious educational game design. *Review of General Psychology, 14*(2), 105–112. doi:10.1037/a0018985

Antin, J., & Churchill, E. F. (2011). Badges in social media: A psychological perspective. *Gamification Research Network.* Retrieved from http://gamification-research. org/wp-content/uploads/2011/04/03-Antin-Churchill.pdf

Apperley, T. (2014). Understanding digital games as education technologies: capitalizing on popular culture. In P. Benson & A. Chik (Eds.), *Popular Culture, Pedagogy and Teacher Education: International perspectives* (pp. 66–82). Abingdon: Routledge.

Appiah, K. A. (2006). *Cosmopolitanism: Ethics in a world of strangers.* New York: W. W. Norton.

Apple, Inc. (2015). *Ad: Apple Watch Features.* Retrieved January 15, 2015 from https://www.apple.com/in/watch/features/

Apple. (2015). *Get your game face on.* Retrieved from http://www.apple.com/ipod-touch/from-the-app-store/

Apple, M. W. (1993). *Official knowledge: Democratic education in a conservative age.* New York: Routledge.

Apple, M., Kenway, J., & Singh, M. (2005). *Globalizing Education: Policies, pedagogies, & politics.* New York: Peter Lang.

Armstrong, K. (2014). *The Cainsville files* [ibook]. Retrieved from itunes.apple.com

Armstrong, S. (2014). *Uprising: A new age is dawning fro every mother's daughter.* New York, NY: St. Thomas Press.

Armstrong, C. L., & McAdams, M. J. (2009). Blogs of information: How gender cues and individual motivations influence perceptions of credibility. *Journal of Computer-Mediated Communication, 14*(3), 435–456. doi:10.1111/j.1083-6101.2009.01448.x

Arnold, N., Ducate, L., & Kost, C. (2012). Collaboration or cooperation? Analzing group dynamics and revision processes in wikis. *CALICO Journal, 29*(3), 431–448. doi:10.11139/cj.29.3.431-448

Arthur, C. (2014). UK launches largest study of mobile phone effects on children's brains. *The Guardian.* Retrieved from http://www.theguardian.com/technology/2014/may/20/uk-launches-largest-study-of-mobile-phone-effects-on-childrens-brains

Asghari, R., & Gedeon, S. (2010). Significance and impact of Internet on the entrepreneurial process: E-entrepreneurship and completely digital entrepreneurship. In A. Kakouris (Ed.), Proceedings of the 5th European Conference on Innovation and Entrepreneurship (pp. 70–76). Reading, UK: Academic Publishing Limited. Retrieved from http://academic-conferences.org/pdfs/ECIE10-abstract%20booklet.pdf

Ashford, C. (2006). The only gay in the village: Sexuality and the net. *Information & Communications Technology Law, 15*(3), 275–289. doi:10.1080/13600830600961202

Asia-Pacific Economic Cooperation. (2014). *Human resources working group: 21st century competencies.* Retrieved from http://hrd.apec.org/index.php/21st_Century_Competencies

Asoko, H. (1996). Developing scientific concepts in the primary classroom: Teaching about electric circuits. In G. Welford, J. Osborne, & P. Scott (Eds.), *Research in science education in Europe* (pp. 36–49). London: Falmer Press.

Aspen Institute Task Force on Learning and the Internet. (2014). *Learner at the center of a networked world.* Washington, DC: The Aspen Institute.

Association of American Colleges and Universities (AACU). (2013). *It takes more than a major: Employer priorities for college learning and student success: Overview and key findings.* Retrieved from http://www.aacu.org/leap/presidentstrust/compact/2013SurveySummary

Association of College and Research Libraries. (2011). *ACRL visual literacy competency standards for higher education.* Retrieved from http://www.ala.org/acrl/standards/visualliteracy

Atkinson, R. D., & McKay, A. S. (2007, March). *Digital prosperity: Understanding the economic benefits of the information technology revolution.* Retrieved from http://www.itif.org/files/digital_prosperity.pdf

Atkinson, N. L., Saperstein, S. L., Desmond, S. M., Gold, R. S., Billing, A. S., & Tian, J. (2009). Rural ehealth nutrition education for limited-income families: An iterative and user-centered design approach. *Journal of Medical Internet Research, 11*(2), 5. doi:10.2196/jmir.1148 PMID:19632974

Attwood, F. (2009). Intimate adventures: Sex blogs, sex "blooks" and women's sexual narration. *European Journal of Cultural Studies, 12*(1), 5–20. doi:10.1177/1367549408098702

Aubrey, J. S., & Rill, L. (2013). Investigating relations between Facebook use and social capital among college undergraduates. *Communication Quarterly, 61*(4), 479–496. doi:10.1080/01463373.2013.801869

Audsley, S., Fernando, K., Maxson, B., Robinson, B., & Varney, K. (2013). An examination of Coursera as an information environment: Does Coursera fulfill its mission to provide open education to all? *The Serials Librarian: From the Printed Page to the Digital Age, 65*(2), 136–166. doi:10.1080/0361526X.2013.781979

Aufderheide, P., & Jaszi, P. (2008). *Recut, reframe, recycle: Quoting copyrighted material in user-generated video.* Washington, DC: American University, Center for Social Media, School of Communication.

Aurasma. (2013a). *About Us.* Retrieved from http://www.aurasma.com/about-us/

Ausburn, L. J., & Ausburn, F. B. (2014). Technical perspectives on theory in screen-based virtual reality environments: Leading from the future in VHRD. *Advances in Developing Human Resources, 16*(3), 371–390. doi:10.1177/1523422314532125

Austin, R., Smyth, J., Rickard, A., Quirk-Bolt, N., & Metcalfe, N. (2010). Collaborative digital learning in schools: Teacher perceptions of purpose and effectiveness. *Technology, Pedagogy and Education, 19*(3), 327–343. doi:10.1080/1475939X.2010.513765

Australian Curriculum Assessment and Reporting Authority (ACARA). (2012). *The Australian Curriculum: English* Retrieved from http://www.australiancurriculum.edu.au/English/Rationale

Au, W. (2011). Teaching under the new Taylorism: High-stakes testing and the standardization of the 21st century curriculum. *Journal of Curriculum Studies, 43*(1), 25–45. doi:10.1080/00220272.2010.521261

Avila, J., & Moore, M. (2012). Critical literacy, digital literacies, and Common Core State Standards: A workable union? *Theory into Practice, 51*(1), 27–33. doi:10.1080/00405841.2012.636332

Azevedo, R., Moos, D., Greene, J., Winters, F., & Cromley, J. (2008). Why is externally-facilitated regulated learning more effective than self-regulated learning with hypermedia? *Educational Technology Research and Development, 56*(1), 45–72. doi:10.1007/s11423-007-9067-0

Baafi, E., & Millner, A. (2011). Modkit: A toolkit for tinkering with tangibles & connecting communities. In *Proc. 5th Int'l Conf. Tangible, Embedded, and Embodied Interaction* (TEI 11) (349-352). ACM.

Baildon, M., & Damico, J. S. (2011). *Social studies as new literacies in a global society: Relational cosmopolitanism in the classroom.* New York: Routledge.

Bailey, J., & Hanna, M. (2011). The gendered dimensions of sexting: Assessing the applicability of Canada's child pornography provisions. *Canadian Journal of Women and the Law, 23*(2), 405–441. doi:10.3138/cjwl.23.2.405

Bailey, J., Steeves, V., Burkell, J., & Regan, P. (2013). Negotiating with gender stereotypes on social networking sites: From "bicycle face" to Facebook. *The Journal of Communication Inquiry, 37*(2), 91–112. doi:10.1177/0196859912473777

Bailey, J., & Telford, A. (2007). What's so cyber about it: Reflections on cyberfeminism contribution to legal studies. *Canadian Journal of Women and the Law, 19*, 243–272.

Baker, E. A. (2012, November). *Dragons, iPads, and literacy, O-My: Examining the feasibility of voice recognition apps in a first-grade classroom.* Paper presented at the meeting of the Literacy Research Association, San Diego, CA.

Baker, E. A. (2013a, October). *That was then: Definitions, explorations, and prognostications of literacies.* Paper presented at the meeting of the Kentucky Reading Association, Lexington, KY.

Baker, E. A. (2013b, April). *Traversing time and space: An ontological analysis of traditional and new literacies.* Paper presented at the meeting of Digital Classics Association, Buffalo, NY.

Baker, E. A. (2013c, December). *Voice recognition apps: A systems theory exploration of grapho-semantic awareness.* Paper presented at the meeting of the Literacy Research Association, Dallas, TX.

Baker, E. A. (2014, December). *Siri got it wrong!: Dialogic negotiations among first-grade authors using voice recognition to compose.* Paper presented at the meeting of the Literacy Research Association, Marco Island, FL.

Baker, E. A., & Dooley, C. (2010, March 1). Teaching language arts in a high stakes era. *Voice of Literacy* [Podcast]. Retrieved from http://voiceofliteracy.org

Baker, E. A., & Monte-Sano, C. (2012, October 1). Writing prompts that help adolescents think as historians. *Voice of Literacy* [Podcast]. Retrieved from http://voiceofliteracy.org

Baker, E. A., & Pacheco, M. (2011, January 3). How elementary bilingual literacy teachers negotiate policy with students' needs. *Voice of Literacy* [Podcast]. Retrieved from http://voiceofliteracy.org

Baker, E. A., & Shanahan, C. (2012, January 16). Gleaning insights from historians, mathematicians, and chemists about how they read within their disciplines. *Voice of Literacy* [Podcast]. Retrieved from http://voiceofliteracy.org

Baker, E. A., Schmidt, R., & Whitmore, K. (2011, January 17). The language of struggle in search of hope for teachers. *Voice of Literacy* [Podcast]. Retrieved from http://voiceofliteracy.org

Baker, E. A., Vogler, J., & Schallert, D. (2014, January 20). The democratization of classrooms: Examining online discussions. *Voice of Literacy* [Podcast]. Retrieved from http://voiceofliteracy.org

Baker, C. M., Staiano, A. E., & Calvert, S. L. (2011). Digital expression among urban, low-income African American adolescents. *Journal of Black Studies, 42*(4), 530–547. doi:10.1177/0021934710384994 PMID:21910270

Baker, E. A. (2001). The nature of literacy in a technology rich classroom. *Reading Research and Instruction, 40*(3), 153–179.

Baker, E. A. (2003). Integrating literacy and technology: Making a match between software and classroom. *Reading & Writing Quarterly, 19*(2), 193–197. doi:10.1080/10573560308221

Baker, E. A. (2007a). Elementary classroom web sites: Support for literacy within and beyond the classroom. *Journal of Literacy Research, 39*(1), 1–38.

Baker, E. A. (2007b). Support for new literacies, cultural expectations, and pedagogy: Potential and features for classroom web sites. *New England Reading Association Journal, 43*(2), 56–62.

Baker, E. A. (2010a). New literacies, new insights: An exploration of traditional and new perspectives. In E. A. Baker (Ed.), *The new literacies: Multiple perspectives on research and practice* (pp. 285–311). New York: Guilford Press.

Baker, E. A. (Ed.). (2010b). *The new literacies: Multiple perspectives on research and practice.* New York: Guilford Press.

Baker, E. A., Pearson, P. D., & Rozendal, M. S. (2010). Theoretical perspectives and literacy studies: An exploration of roles and insights. In E. A. Baker (Ed.), *The new literacies: Multiple perspectives on research and practice* (pp. 1–22). New York: Guilford Press.

Baker, E. A., Rozendal, M., & Whitenack, J. (2000). Audience awareness in a technology rich elementary classroom. *Journal of Literacy Research, 32*(3), 395–419. doi:10.1080/10862960009548086

Bakhtin, M. M. (1981). *The dialogic imagination* (M. Holquist, Ed., M. Holquist & C. Emerson, Trans.). Austin, TX: University of Texas Press.

Ballast, K., Stephens, L., & Radcliffe, R. (2008). *The effects of digital storytelling on sixth grade students' writing and their attitudes about writing.* Paper presented at the Society for Information Technology & Teacher Education International Conference, Las Vegas, NV.

Banaji, S., Burn, A., & Buckingham, D. (2010). *The rhetorics of creativity: A literature review* (2nd ed.). London: Creativity, Culture and Education.

Banaszweski, T. (2002). *Digital storytelling finds its place in the classroom.* MultiMedia Schools.

Banet-Weiser, S. (2011). Branding the post-feminist self: girls' video production and YouTube. In *Mediated girlhoods: New explorations of girls' media culture* (pp. 277-294). Academic Press.

Banks, J. (2003, May). *Negotiating participatory culture in the new media environment: Auran and the Trainz online community an (im)possible relation.* Paper presented in *Digital Arts Conference*, Melbourne.

Bannink, R., Broeren, S., van de Looij-Jansen, P. M., de Waart, F. G., & Raat, H. (2014). Cyber and traditional bullying victimization as a risk factor for mental health problems and suicidal ideation in adolescents. *PLoS ONE, 9*(4), e94026. doi:10.1371/journal.pone.0094026 PMID:24718563

Banzi, M. (2008). *Getting Started with Arduino* (1st ed.). Text Only.

Barak, A. (2005). Sexual harassment on the internet. *Social Science Computer Review, 23*(1), 77–92. doi:10.1177/0894439304271540

Baran, E., & Khan, S. (2014). Going mobile in science teacher education. In C. Miller & A. Doering (Eds.), *The new landscape of mobile learning* (pp. 258–275). New York: Routledge.

Bardzell, S. (2010). Feminist HCI: Taking Stock and Outlining an Agenda for Design. In *Proceedings of the 28th International Conference on Human Factors in Computing Systems* (pp. 1301–1310). Atlanta, GA: ACM. doi:10.1145/1753326.1753521

Bardzell, S. (2013). E-Textiles and the body: Feminist technologies in design research. In L. Buechley, K. Peppler, M. Eisenberg, & Y. Kafai (Eds.), Textile Messages: Dispatches from the World of E-Textiles and Education. Academic Press.

Barlett, C. P., Gentile, D. A., & Chew, C. (2014). Predicting cyberbullying from anonymity. *Psychology of Popular Media Culture.* doi:10.1037/ppm0000055

Barlett, R. M., & Strough, J. (2003). Multimedia versus traditional course instruction in introductory Social Psychology. *Teaching of Psychology, 30*(4), 335–338. doi:10.1207/S15328023TOP3004_07

Baron, D. (1999). From pencils to pixels: The stages of literacy technologies. In G. Hawisher & C. Selfe (Eds.), *Passions, pedagogies, and 21st century technologies* (pp. 15–33). Logan, UT: Utah State University Press.

Baron, D. (2009). *A better pencil: Readers, writers, and the digital revolution.* Oxford, UK: Oxford University Press.

Baron, N. (1984). Computer-mediated communication as a force in language change. *Visible Language, XVIII*(2), 118–141.

Baron, N. (2008). *Always on: Language in an online and mobile world.* New York: Oxford University Press. doi:10.1093/acprof:oso/9780195313055.001.0001

Baron, N. S. (2011). Concerns about mobile phones: A cross–national study. *First Monday, 16*(8). doi:10.5210/fm.v16i8.3335

Baron, N. S. (2013). Instant messaging. In S. Herring, D. Stein, & T. Virtanen (Eds.), *Pragmatics of Computer Mediated Communication* (pp. 136–161). Berlin, Germany: De Gruyter. doi:10.1515/9783110214468.135

Barrett, H. (2011). *Balancing the two faces of ePortfolios.* Retrieved from http://electronicportfolios.org/balance/balancingarticle2.pdf

Barseghian, T. (2013, March 13). *For low-income kids, access to devices could be the equalizer* [web log comment]. Retrieved from http://tinyurl.com/cosebth

Barta, W., & Kiene, S. (2005). Motivations for infidelity in heterosexual dating couples: The roles of gender, personality differences, and sociosexual orientation. *Journal of Social and Personal Relationships, 22*(3), 339–360. doi:10.1177/0265407505052440

Bartlett, F. (1932). *Remembering: A study in social and experimental psychology.* Cambridge, UK: Cambridge University Press.

Barton, D. (1994). *Literacy: An introduction to the ecology of written language.* Cambridge, MA: Blackwell.

Barton, D., & Hamilton, M. (2000). Literacy practices. In D. Barton, M. Hamilton, & R. Ivanic (Eds.), *Situated Literacies: Reading and writing in context* (pp. 7–15). London: Routledge.

Barton, D., Hamilton, M., & Ivanic, R. (Eds.). (2000). *Situated literacies: Reading and writing in context.* London: Routledge.

Basawapatna, A. R., Koh, K. H., & Repenning, A. (2010). Using scalable game design to teach computer science from middle school to graduate school. In *Proceedings from The Fifteenth Annual Conference on Innovation and Technology in Computer Science Education* (pp. 224-228). New York, NY: ACM. doi:10.1145/1822090.1822154

Basno. (2014). *Create digital badges that recognize employee milestones.* Retrieved from http://basno.com/employers

Bauman, S., & Newman, M. L. (2013). Testing assumptions about cyberbullying: Perceived distress associated with acts of conventional and cyber bullying. *Psychology of Violence, 3*(1), 27–38. doi:10.1037/a0029867

Bauman, S., Toomey, R. B., & Walker, J. L. (2013). Associations among bullying, cyberbullying, and suicide in high school students. *Journal of Adolescence, 36*(2), 341–350. doi:10.1016/j.adolescence.2012.12.001 PMID:23332116

Baverstock, A., & Steinitz, J. (2013). Who are the self-publishers? *Learned Publishing, 26*(3), 211–223. doi:10.1087/20130310

Bazargan, K. (2011, June 13). *DeviantArt: Creating community around creativity* [Audio podcast]. Retrieved from https://itunes.apple.com/us/podcast/lgm-2011-audio/id450991073?mt=2

Bazelon, E. (2013, March). How to stop the bullies. *Atlantic (Boston, Mass.),* 82–90.

Beach, R., & O'Brien, D. (2014). *Using apps for learning across the curriculum: A literacy-based framework and guide.* New York: Routledge.

Beach, R., & O'Brien, D. (2015b). Enhancing struggling students' engagement through the affordances of interactivity, connectivity, and collaboration. *Reading & Writing Quarterly, 31*(2), 119–134. doi:10.1080/10573569.2014.962200

Beale, A. V., & Hall, K. R. (2007). Cyberbullying: What school administrators (and parents) can do. *The Clearing House: A Journal of Educational Strategies, Issues and Ideas, 81*(1), 8–1. doi:10.3200/TCHS.81.1.8-12

Bean, T. W., & Dunkerly-Bean, J. (in press). Expanding conceptions of adolescent literacy research and practice: Cosmopolitan theory in educational contexts. *Australian Journal of Language and Literacy.*

Bean, T. W., Dunkerly-Bean, J., & Harper, H. J. (2014). *Teaching young adult literature.* Thousand Oaks, CA: SAGE.

Beasley, B., & Standley, T. C. (2002). Shirts vs. skins: Clothing as an indicator of gender role stereotyping in video games. *Mass Communication & Society, 5*(3), 279–293. doi:10.1207/S15327825MCS0503_3

Beaudry, M. C. (2006). *Findings: The material culture of needlework and sewing.* Princeton, NJ: Yale University Press.

Beavis, C. (2014). Literature, imagination and computer Games: video games and the English/Literature curriculum. In C. Burnett, J. Davies, G. Merchant, & J. Rowsell, J. (Eds.), New literacies across the globe (pp.88-102). Abingdon: Routledge.

Beavis, C. (2013). Multiliteracies in the wild: learning from computer games. In G. Merchant, J. Gillen, J. Marsh, & J. Davies (Eds.), *Virtual Literacies: interactive spaces for children and young people* (pp. 57–74). Abingdon: Routledge.

Beck, D., & Perkins, R. (2014). Review of educational research methods in desktop virtual world environments; framing the past to provide future direction. *Journal of Virtual Worlds Research, 7*(1), 1–9.

Becker, H. S. (1984). *Art worlds*. Oakland, CA: University of California Press.

Beck, U. (2002). The cosmopolitan society and its enemies. *Theory, Culture & Society, 19*(1-2), 25–44. doi:10.1177/026327640201900101

Beck, U. (2012). *World at risk*. Cambridge, UK: Polity Press.

Beck, U., & Sznaider, N. (2010). Unpacking cosmopolitanism and the social sciences: A research agenda. *The British Journal of Sociology, 61*(1), 381–403. doi:10.1111/j.1468-4446.2009.01250.x PMID:20092506

Beegel, J. (2014). *Infographics for Dummies*. Hoboken, NJ: John Wiley & Sons, Inc.

Bell, A. (2014, August 8). *Reading digital fiction*. Retrieved from http://www.digitalreadingnetwork.com/reading-digital-fiction/

Bell, M. A. (2013). Picture this! Using Instagram with students. *Internet@Schools, 20*(4), 23–25.

Bell, C. D. (2010). *Little blog on the prairie*. New York: Bloomsbury.

Benkler, Y. (2006). The wealth of networks: How social production transforms markets and freedom. New Haven, CT: Yale University Press. Retrieved from http://www.benkler.org/Benkler_Wealth_Of_Networks.pdf

Benmayor, R. (2008). Digital storytelling as a signature pedagogy for the new humanities. *Arts and Humanities in Higher Education, 7*(2), 188–204. doi:10.1177/1474022208088648

Benmayor, R. (2012). Digital testimonio as a signature pedagogy for Latin@ studies. *Equity & Excellence in Education, 45*(3), 507–524. doi:10.1080/10665684.2012.698180

Bennet, S., Maton, K., & Kervin, L. (2008). The 'digital natives': A critical review of the evidence. *British Journal of Educational Technology, 39*(5), 775–786. doi:10.1111/j.1467-8535.2007.00793.x

Bennett, S. (2014, August, 4). North Korea, Iran, China, Pakistan, Turkey - countries who block social media. *Mediabistro*. Retrieved from http://www.mediabistro.com/alltwitter/countries-social-media-banned_b59035

Bennett, J. (2010). *Vibrant matter*. Durham, NC: Duke University Press.

Bennett, S., Bishop, A., Dalgarno, B., Waycott, J., & Kennedy, G. (2012). Implementing Web 2.0 technologies in higher education: A collective case study. *Computers & Education, 59*(2), 524–534. doi:10.1016/j.compedu.2011.12.022

Bennett, V. E., Koh, K., & Repenning, A. (2013). Computing creativity: Divergence in computational thinking. In *Proceedings from The 44th ACM Technical Symposium on Computer Science Education* (pp. 359–364). New York, NY: ACM. doi:10.1145/2445196.2445302

Bennett, W. L., Freelon, D., & Wells, C. (2010). Changing citizen identity and the rise of a participatory media culture. In L. R. Sherrod, J. Torney-Purta, & C. A. Flanagan (Eds.), *Handbook of research on civic engagement in youth* (pp. 393–423). Hoboken, JH: John Wiley & Sons. doi:10.1002/9780470767603.ch15

Bennett, W. L., & Segerberg, A. (2011). Digital media and the personalization of collective action: Social technology and the organization of protests against the global economic crisis. *Information Communication and Society, 14*(6), 770–799. doi:10.1080/1369118X.2011.579141

Bensley, L., & Van Eenwyk, J. (2001). Video games and real-life aggression: Review of the literature. *The Journal of Adolescent Health, 29*(4), 244–257. doi:10.1016/S1054-139X(01)00239-7 PMID:11587908

Ben-Ze'ev, A. (2004). *Love online: Emotions on the Internet*. Cambridge, UK: Cambridge University Press. doi:10.1017/CBO9780511489785

Bercovici, J. (2013, Jan. 3). Do you need a Tumblr? *Forbes*. Retrieved from http://www.forbes.com/sites/jeffbercovici/2013/01/02/do-you-need-a-tumblr/

Bercovici, J. (2014). Inside Pinterest: The coming ad colossus that could dwarf Twitter and Facebook. *Forbes, 194*(6), 70–82. Retrieved from http://www.forbes.com/sites/jeffbercovici/2014/10/15/inside-pinterest-the-coming-ad-colossus-that-could-dwarf-twitter-and-facebook/

Berland, J. (2000). Cultural technologies and the "evolution" of technological cultures. In A. Herman & T. Swiss (Eds.), *The world wide web and contemporary cultural theory* (pp. 235–258). New York, NY: Routledge.

Bernardo, N., Scott, C., Neves, F., Gomes, P., Azevedo, S., & Cantwell, D. (2012). *Collider quest* [mobile application software]. Retrieved from itunes.apple.com

Berners-Lee, T., & Fischetti, M. (1999). *Weaving the Web: The original design and ultimate destiny of the World Wide Web by its inventor*. San Francisco: Harper San Francisco.

Berne, S., Frisén, A., Schultze-Krumbholz, A., Scheithauer, H., Naruskov, K., Luik, P., & Zukauskiene, R. et al. (2013). Cyberbullying assessment instruments: A systematic review. *Aggression and Violent Behavior*, *18*(2), 320–334. doi:10.1016/j.avb.2012.11.022

Bernstein, B. (1975). Class, Codes and Control: Vol. 3. *Towards a Theory of Educational Transmissions*. London: Routledge & Kegan Paul.

Bernstein, B. (1990). *The Structuring of Pedagogic Discourse: Class, Codes and Control* (Vol. 4). London: Routledge. doi:10.4324/9780203011263

Berry, D. M. (2011). The computational turn: Thinking about the digital humanities. *Culture Machine*, *12*, 1–22.

Berson, M. (2006). Enhancing democracy with technology in the social studies. *The International Journal of Social Education*, *21*(1), vii–viii.

Bertot, J. C., Jaeger, P. T., Munson, S., & Glaisyer, T. (2010). Engaging the public in open government: The policy and government application of social media technology for government transparency. *IEEE Computer*, *43*(11), 53–59. doi:10.1109/MC.2010.325

Bertozzi, E. (2012). Killing for girls: Predation play and female empowerment. *Bulletin of Science and Technology*, *32*(6), 447–454. doi:10.1177/0270467612469072

Bertozzi, E. (2014). The feeling of being hunted: Pleasures and potentialities of predation play. *Games and Culture*, *9*(6), 429–441. doi:10.1177/1555412014549578

Bery, R. (1995). Chapter. In L. W. R. Slocum & D. Rocheleau (Eds.), Power, process and participation: Tools for change (pp. 64–80). London: Intermediate Technology Publications.

Bhabha, H. (1994). *The location of culture*. London: Routledge.

Bhola, H. S. (2008). Adult literacy for sustainable development: Creating a knowledgebased discourse for action. In Signposts to literacy for sustainable development. UNESCO Institute for Lifelong Earning.

Bicen, H., & Kocakoyun, S. (2013). The evaluation of the most used mobile devices applications by students. *Procedia: Social and Behavioral Sciences*, *89*, 756–760. doi:10.1016/j.sbspro.2013.08.928

Bickmore, K. (2011). Policies and programming for safer schools: Are "antibullying" approaches impeding education for peacebuilding? *Educational Policy*, *25*(4), 648–687. doi:10.1177/0895904810374849

Biddix, J. P., Chung, C. J., & Park, H. W. (2015). The hybrid shift: Evidencing a student-driven restructuring of the college classroom. *Computers & Education*, *80*, 162–175. doi:10.1016/j.compedu.2014.08.016

Biesdorf, S., & Niedermann, F. (2014, July). *Healthcare's digital future*. McKinsey & Company. Retrieved from http://www.mckinsey.com/insights/health_systems_and_services/healthcares_digital_future

Bigum, C., Knobel, M., Lankshear, C., & Rowan, L. (2003). Literacy, technology and the economics of attention. *L1-Educational Studies in Language and Literature*, *3*(1/2), 95–122. doi:10.1023/A:1024588324175

Biller, G., Gorlenko, L., & McColgin, D. (2014, Nov.). *Data visualization: The new literacy*. The Artefact Group. Retrieved from http://www.artefactgroup.com/content/data-visualization-the-new-literacy/

Bimber, B., & Copeland, L. (2013). Digital media and traditional political participation over time in the US. *Journal of Information Technology & Politics*, *10*(2), 125–137. doi:10.1080/19331681.2013.769925

Bisson, R., & Vazquez, A. W. (2013, December 10). iChoose: Academic choice and iPads. Paper presented at the TIES Conference, Minneapolis, MN.

Bjerede, M., & Bondi, T. (2012). Learning is personal: Stories of android tablet use in the 5th grade. *Learning Untethered*. Retrieved from http://www.learninguntethered.com/?p=24

Björk, B., Welling, P., Laakso, M., Majlender, P., Hedlund, T., & Guðnason, G. (2010). Open access to the scientific journal literature: Situation 2009. *PLoS ONE, 5*(6), e11273. doi:10.1371/journal.pone.0011273 PMID:20585653

Blackhorse, A. (2014, December 22). My hostile, aggressive, racist, sexist hate mail. *The Tyee*. Retrieved from http://thetyee.ca/Opinion/2014/12/22/Native-American-Sports-Mascots/?utm_source=daily&utm_medium=email&utm_campaign=221214

Blackmore, J. (2005). Feminist strategic rethinking of human rights discourses in education. In W. Hesford & W. Kozol (Eds.), *Just Advocacy: Women's human rights, transnational feminisms and the politics of representation* (pp. 243–265). New Brunswick, NJ: Rutgers Univesity Press.

Black, R. W. (2008). *Adolescents and online fan fiction.* New York: Peter Lang.

Black, R. W. (2010). The language of Webkinz: Early childhood literacy in an online virtual world.[DCE]. *Digital Culture & Education, 2*(1), 7–24.

Black, S. R., & Yasukawa, K. (2011). A tale of two councils: Alternative discourses on the 'literacy crisis' in Australian workplaces. *International Journal of Training Research, 9*(3), 218–233. doi:10.5172/ijtr.9.3.218

Blake, A., & Quiros, M. (2012). Boundary objects to guide sustainable technology-supported participatory development for poverty alleviation in the context of digital divides. *Electronic Journal of Information Systems in Developing Countries, 51*(1), 1-25. Retrieved from http://www.academia.edu/5632559/Boundary_Objects_to_Guide_Sustainable_Technology-Supported_Participatory_Development_for_Poverty_Alleviation_in_the_Context_of_Digital_Divides

Bleed, R. (2005). Visual literacy in higher education. *ELI Explorations*, 1-11. Retrieved from http://net.educause.edu/ir/library/pdf/ELI4001.pdf

Blikstein, P. (2013). *Seymour Papert's legacy: Thinking about learning, and learning about thinking*. Retrieved from https://tltl.stanford.edu/content/seymour-papert-s-legacy-thinking-about-learning-and-learning-about-thinking

Blikstein, P. (2008). Travels in Troy with Freire: Technology as an agent of emancipation. In P. Noguera & C. A. Torres (Eds.), *Social justice education for teachers: Paulo Freire and the possible dream*. Rotterdam, Netherlands: Sense.

Block, B. (2014). *The visual story: creating the visual structure of film, TV and digital media*. CRC Press.

Bloomberg, T. V. (2014). *Wearable technology seen as biggest trend in 2014*. [video]. Retrieved from http://www.bloomberg.com/video/wearable-technology-seen-as-biggest-trend-in-2014-xsbl35YaToS8p2PQZ2551Q.htmlhttp://www.bloomberg.com/video/wearable-technology-seen-as-biggest-trend-in-2014-xsbl35YaToS8p-2PQZ2551Q.html

Blume, H. (2013, December 1*). Mixed reaction to iPad rollout from L.A. teachers and administrators* [web log comment]. Retrieved from http://tinyurl.com/k6xlcrg

Bodnar, J., & Doshi, A. (2011). Asking the right questions: A critique of Facebook, social media, and libraries. *Public Services Quarterly, 7*(3-4), 37-41. doi:101.1080/15228959.2011.623594

Boellstorff, T. (2008). *Coming of Age in Second Life: An Anthropologist Explores the Virtually Human*. Princeton: Princeton University Press.

Bohay, M., Blakely, D. P., Tamplin, A. K., & Radvansky, G. A. (2011). Note taking, review, memory, and comprehension. *The American Journal of Psychology, 124*(1), 63–73. doi:10.5406/amerjpsyc.124.1.0063 PMID:21506451

Boies, S. C. (2002). University students' uses of and reactions to online sexual information and entertainment: Links to online and offline sexual behavior. *The Canadian Journal of Human Sexuality, 11*, 77–89.

Boler, M. (Ed.). (2010). *Digital media and democracy*. Cambridge, MA: MIT Press.

Bolt, D., & Crawford, R. (2000). *Digital divide: Computers and our children's future*. York: TV Books.

Bolter, J. D. (2010). *Elite and popular: Digital art and literature in the era of social and locative media*. Keynote speech at Kingston University, London, UK. [video] Retrieved from http://vimeo.com/22554435

Bolter, J. D. (1991a). *Writing space: The computer, hypertext, and the history of writing.* Hillsdale, NJ: L. Erlbaum Associates.

Bolter, J. D. (1991b). Topographic writing: Hypertext and the electronic writing space. In G. Landow & P. Delaney (Eds.), *Hypermedia and literary studies.* Cambridge, MA: The MIT Press.

Bolter, J. D., & Joyce, M. (1987). Hypertext and creative writing. In *Proceedings of the ACM Conference on Hypertext* (pp. 41-50). doi doi:10.1145/317426.317431

Bomhold, C. R. (2013). Educational use of smartphone technology: A survey of mobile phone application use by undergraduate university students. *Program: Electronic Library & Information Systems, 47*(4), 424–436. doi:10.1108/PROG-01-2013-0003

Bonanno, R. A., & Hymel, S. (2013). Cyber bullying and internalizing difficulties: Above and beyond the impact of traditional forms of bullying. *Journal of Youth and Adolescence, 42*(5), 685–697. doi:10.1007/s10964-013-9937-1 PMID:23512485

BooksARalive. (2013). *Posts: Augmented reality books.* Retrieved from http://www.booksaralive.com/

Boots, N., & Strobel, J. (2014). Equipping the designers of the future: Best practices of epistemic video game design. *Games and Culture, 9*(3), 167–181.

Borovoy, A. (2013). *Five-Minute film festival: Vine and Instagram video in the classroom.* Edutopia. Retrieved from http://www.edutopia.org/blog/film-festival-vine-instagram-video-education

Borovoy, A. E., & Cronin, A. (2011, November). *Resources for understanding the common core state standards | Edutopia.* Retrieved October 2014, from http://www.edutopia.org/common-core-state-standards-resources

Borsheim-Black, C., Macaluso, M., & Petrone, R. (2014). Critical literature pedagogy: Teaching canonical literature for critical literacy. *Journal of Adolescent & Adult Literacy, 58*(2), 123–133. doi:10.1002/jaal.323

Borup, J., West, R. E., & Graham, C. R. (2012). Improving online social presence through asynchronous video. *The Internet and Higher Education, 15*(3), 195–203. doi:10.1016/j.iheduc.2011.11.001

Boulos, M., Maramba, I., & Wheeler, S. (2006). Wikis, blogs and podcasts: A new generation of web-based toosl for virtual collaborative clinical practice and education. *BMC Medical Education, 6*(41). Retrieved from http://www.biomedicalcentral.com/1472-6920/6/41 doi:10.1186/1472-6920-6-41 PMID:16911779

Boupha, S., Grisso, A. D., Morris, J., Webb, L. M., & Zakeri, M. (2013). How college students display ethnic identity on Facebook. In R. A. Lind (Ed.), *Race/Gender/Media: Considering diversity across audiences, content, and producers* (3rd ed., pp. 107–112). Boston, MA: Pearson.

Bourdieu, P. (1986). The forms of capital. In J. G. Richardson (Ed.), *Handbook of theory and research for the sociology of education* (pp. 241–258). New York, NY: Greenwood Press.

Bourdieu, P. (1990). *The logic of practice.* Palo Alto, CA: Stanford University Press.

Bourdieu, P., & Johnson, R. (1993). *The field of cultural production: Essays on art and literature.* New York: Columbia University Press.

Bower, M. (2008). Affordance analysis – matching learning tasks with learning technologies. *Educational Media International, 45*(1), 3–15. doi:10.1080/09523980701847115

boyd, d. (2008). Why youth ♥ social network sites: The role of networked publics in teenage social life. In D. Buckingham (Ed.), *Youth, identity, and digital media* (pp. 119-142). Cambridge, MA: MIT Press.

boyd, d. (2012). White flight in networked publics: How race and class shaped American teenage engagement with MySpace and Facebook. In L. Nakamura & P. Chow-White (Eds.), *Race After the Internet.* New York: Routledge,

boyd, d., & Hargittai, E. (2010). Facebook privacy settings: Who cares? *First Monday, 15*(8), 1.

boyd, d., & Marwick, A. E. (2011). *Social privacy in networked publics: Teens' attitudes, practices, and strategies.* Paper presented at the A decade in internet time: Symposium on the dynamics of the internet and society, Oxford, UK. http://papers.ssrn.com/sol3/papers.cfm?abstract_id=1925128

Bradley, A. (2006). *24 girls in 7 days.* New York: Speak.

Bradsher, K., & Mozur, P. (2014, September 21). China clamps down on web, pinching companies like Google. *New York Times*. Retrieved from http://www.nytimes.com/2014/09/22/business/international/china-clamps-down-on-web-pinching-companies-like-google.html?_r=0

Braidotti, R. (2013). *The posthuman*. Cambridge, UK: Polity.

Braithwaite, A. (2014). "Seriously, get out": Feminists on the forums and the War(craft) on women. *New Media & Society*, *16*(5), 703–718. doi:10.1177/1461444813489503

Brandt, D., & Clinton, K. (2002). Limits of the local: Expanding perspectives on literacy as a social practice. *Journal of Literacy Research*, *34*(3), 337–356. doi:10.1207/s15548430jlr3403_4

Breznitz, S. M., & Noonan, D. S. (2013, June). *Arts districts, universities, and the rise of digital media*. Retrieved from http://scholarworks.iupui.edu/bitstream/handle/1805/3567/breznitz-2013-arts.pdf?sequence=1

Brito, P. Q. (2012). Tweens' characterization of digital technologies. *Computers & Education*, *59*(2), 580–593. doi:10.1016/j.compedu.2012.03.005

Bromley, K., Faughnan, M., Ham, S., Miller, M., Armstrong, T., Crandall, C., & Marrone, N. et al. (2014). Literature circles go digital. *The Reading Teacher*, *68*(3), 229–236. doi:10.1002/trtr.1312

Brookey, R. A., & Cannon, K. L. (2009). Sex lives in Second Life. *Critical Studies in Mass Communication*, *26*(2), 145–164. doi:10.1080/15295030902860260

Broussard, M. (2014). *Why e-books are banned in my digital journalism class*. Retrieved from http://www.newrepublic.com/article/116309/data-journalim-professor-wont-assign-e-books-heres-why

Brown, A. E., & Grant, G. (2010). Highlighting the duality of the ICT and development research Agenda. *Information Technology for Development*, *16*(2), 96–111. doi:10.1080/02681101003687793

Brown, J., & Duguid, P. (2002). *The social life of information*. New York: Harvard Business School Press.

Brown, K., Jackson, M., & Cassidy, W. (2006). Cyberbullying: Developing policy to direct responses that are equitable and effective in addressing this special form of bullying. *Canadian Journal of Educational Administration and Policy*, *57*, 1–36.

Brown, L. M., Chesney-Lind, M., & Stein, N. (2007). Patriarchy matters: Toward a gendered theory of teen violence and victimization. *Violence Against Women*, *13*(12), 1249–1273. doi:10.1177/1077801207310430 PMID:18046042

Bruckman, A. S. (1993), *Gender-swapping on the Internet*. Retrieved from www.inform.umd.edu/EdRes/Topic/WomensStudies/Computing/Articl/gender-swapping

Brumberger, E. (2011). Visual Literacy and the digital native: An examination of the millennial learner. *Journal of Visual Literacy*, *30*(1), 19–46.

Bruner, J. (1986). *Actual minds, possible worlds*. MA: The President and Fellows of Harvard College.

Bruner, J. (1990). *Acts of meaning*. Cambridge, MA: Harvard University Press.

Bruns, A., & Humphreys, S. (2007). *Building collaborative capacities in learners: The M/cyclopedia Project revisited*. Paper presented at the WikiSym '07, Montréal, Canada.

Bruns, A., Highfield, T., & Burgess, J. (2013). The Arab Spring and Social Media Audiences English and Arabic Twitter Users and Their Networks. *The American Behavioral Scientist*, *57*(7), 871–898. doi:10.1177/0002764213479374

Bryant, S. L., Forte, A., & Bruckman, A. (2005). Becoming Wikipedian: Transformation of participation in a collaborative online encyclopedia. In *Proceedings of the 2005 International ACM/SIGGROUP Conference on Supporting Group Work* (pp. 1-10). ACM. Retrieved from http://dl.acm.org/citation.cfm?id=1099205

Bryant, J. A., Sanders Jackson, A., & Smallwood, A. M. K. (2006). IMing, Text Messaging, and Adolescent Social Networks. *Journal of Computer-Mediated Communication*, *11*(2), 577–592. doi:10.1111/j.1083-6101.2006.00028.x

Bryce, J., & Fraser, J. (2013). "It's common sense that it's wrong": Young people's perceptions and experiences of cyberbullying. *Cyberpsychology, Behavior, and Social Networking, 16*(11), 783–787. doi:10.1089/cyber.2012.0275 PMID:23745618

Brynjolfsson, E., & McAfee, A. (2012). Big data's management revolution. *Harvard Business Review*. Retrieved from https://hbr.org/2012/09/big-datas-management-revolutio

Brynjolfsson, E., Hu, Y. J., & Smith, M. D. (2003). Consumer surplus in the digital economy: Estimating the value of increased product variety at online booksellers. *Management Science*. Retrieved from http://papers.ssrn.com/sol3/papers.cfm?abstract_id=400940

Brynjolfsson, E., & McAfee, A. (2012). *Race against the machine: How the digital revolution is accelerating innovation, driving productivity, and irreversibly transforming employment and the economy*. Lexington, MA: Digital Frontier Press.

Bryson, M., Petrina, S., Braundy, M., & de Castell, S. (2003). Conditions for Success?: Gender in technology-intensive courses in British Columbia secondary schools. *Canadian Journal of Science, Mathematics, and Technology Education, 3*(2), 185–193. doi:10.1080/14926150309556559

Buccholz, B., Shively, K., Peppler, K., & Wohlwend, K. (2014). Hands on, hands off: Gendered access in sewing and electronics practices. *Mind, Culture, and Activity, 21*(4), 278–297. doi:10.1080/10749039.2014.939762

Buckhingham, J. (2014). Open digital badges for the uninitiated. *Teaching English as a Second Language, 18*(1). Retrieved from http://tesl-ej.org/pdf/ej69/int.pdf

Buckingham, D., Burn, A., & Pelletier, C. (2011). Case Study on the Impact of the Making Games Project. London: Institute of Education. Retrieved from http://www.ioe.ac.uk/research_expertise/ioe_rd_a4_mgames_0511.pdf

Buckingham, D. (2000). *The making of citizens: Young people, news and politics*. London: Routledge.

Buckingham, D. (2003). *Media Education: literacy, learning and contemporary culture*. Cambridge: Polity Press.

Buckingham, D. (2007). Media education goes digital: An introduction. *Learning, Media and Technology, 32*(2), 111–119. doi:10.1080/17439880701343006

Buckingham, D. (2011). Foreword. In M. Thomas (Ed.), *Deconstructing digital natives* (pp. ix–xi). New York: Routledge.

Buckingham, D., & Burn, A. (2007). Game-literacy in theory and practice. *Journal of Educational Multimedia and Hypermedia, 16*, 323–349.

Buckingham, D., & Willett, R. (2006). *Digital generations: Children, young people, and the new media*. Mahwah, NJ: Lawrence Erlbaum Associates.

Buechley, L. (2006). A construction kit for electronic textiles. In *Proceedings of IEEE International Symposium on Wearable Computers* (ISWC). Montreux, Switzerland: IEEE.

Buechley, L. (2013). Lilypad arduino: E-textiles for everyone. In L. Buechley, K. Peppler, M. Eisenberg, & Y. Kafai (Eds.), Textile Messages: Dispatches from the World of E-Textiles and Education. Academic Press.

Buechley, L., Jacobs, J., & Mako Hill, B. (2013). Lilypad in the wild: Technology DIY, e-textiles, and gender. In L. Buechley, K. Peppler, M. Eisenberg, & Y. Kafai (Eds.), Textile Messages: Dispatches from the World of E-Textiles and Education. Academic Press.

Buechley, L. (2010). Questioning invisibility. *Computer, 43*(4), 84–86. doi:10.1109/MC.2010.114

Buechley, L., & Eisenberg, M. (2009). Fabric PCBs, electronic sequins, and socket buttons: Techniques for e-textile craft. *Personal and Ubiquitous Computing, 13*(2), 133–150. doi:10.1007/s00779-007-0181-0

Buechley, L., Elumeze, N., & Eisenberg, M. (2006). Electronic/computational textiles and children's crafts. In *Proceedings of the 2006 Conference on Interaction Design and Children* (pp. 49-56). Tampere, Finland: ACM. doi:10.1145/1139073.1139091

Buechley, L., Peppler, K. A., Eisenberg, M., & Kafai, Y. B. (Eds.). (2013). *Textile Messages: Dispatches from the World of E-Textiles and Education*. New York: Peter Lang.

Buechley, L., & Qiu, J. (2013). *Sew Electric*. Cambridge, MA: HLT Press.

Bull, J. G., & Kozak, R. A. (2014). Comparative life cycle assessments: The case of paper and digital media. *Environmental Impact Assessment Review*, *45*, 10–18. doi:10.1016/j.eiar.2013.10.001

Bunchball. (2014). *What is gamification?* Retrieved from http://www.bunchball.com/gamification

Burden, T. (2013). K-12 Teachers Uncertain about how to connect with student and parents via social media. *Business Wire*. Retrieved from http://www.businesswire.com/news/home/20140114005604/en/K-12-Teachers-Uncertain-Connect-Students-Parents-Social#.VB-tqC5dVUO

Burgess, J. (2006). Hearing ordinary voices: Cultural studies, vernacular creativity and digital storytelling. *Continuum (Perth)*, *20*(2), 201–214. doi:10.1080/10304310600641737

Burke, A. (2010). Children's construction of identity in virtual play worlds–a classroom perspective. *Language and Literature*, *15*(1), 58–73.

Burke, Q., & Kafai, Y. B. (2014). Decade of game making for learning: From tools to communities. In M. C. Angelides & H. Aguis (Eds.), *Handbook of digital games* (pp. 689–709). New York: Wiley-IEEE Press. doi:10.1002/9781118796443.ch26

Burmark, L. (2002). *Visual literacy. Learn to see, see to learn*. Alexandria, VA: ASCD.

Burn, A., & Pelletier, C. (2011). Case study on the impact of the Making Games Project. London: Institute of Education, University of London. Retrieved from http://www.ioe.ac.uk/research_expertise/ioe_rd_a4_mgames_0511.pdf

Burn, A. (2008). The case of Rebellion: Researching multimodal texts. In J. Coiro, M. Knobel, C. Lankshear, & D. J. Leu (Eds.), *Handbook of research on new literacies* (pp. 149–177). London: Taylor & Francis.

Burn, A. (2009). *Making New Media: Creative Production and Digital Literacies*. New York: Peter Lang.

Burn, A., & Buckingham, D. (2007). Towards game-literacy: Creative game authoring in English and Media classrooms. *English Drama Media*, *7*, 40–46.

Burnett, C. (2009). Research into literacy and technology in primary classrooms: An exploration of understandings generated by recent studies. *Journal of Research in Reading*, *32*(1), 22–37. doi:10.1111/j.1467-9817.2008.01379.x

Burnett, C. (2010). Technology and literacy in early childhood educational settings: A review of research. *Journal of Early Childhood Literacy*, *10*(3), 247–270. doi:10.1177/1468798410372154

Burnett, C. (2011). Pre-service teachers' digital literacy practices: Exploring contingency in identity and digital literacy in and out of educational contexts. *Language and Education*, *25*(5), 433–449. doi:10.1080/09500078 2.2011.584347

Burnett, C. (2014). Investigating pupils' interactions around digital texts: A spatial perspective on the "classroom-ness" of digital literacy practices in schools. *Educational Review*, *66*(2), 192–209. doi:10.1080/0013 1911.2013.768959

Burnett, C. (in press). (Im)materializing literacies. In J. Rowsell & K. Pahl (Eds.), *The Routledge Handbook of Literacy Studies*. London, UK: Routledge.

Burnett, C., & Bailey, C. (2014). Conceptualising collaboration in hybrid sites: playing *Minecraft* together and apart in a primary classroom. In C. Burnett, J. Davies, G. Merchant, & J. Rowsell (Eds.), *New Literacies across the Globe* (pp. 50–71). Abingdon: Routledge.

Burnett, C., Davies, J., Merchant, G., & Rowsell, J. (Eds.). (2014). *New Literacies across the Globe*. Abingdon: Routledge.

Burnett, C., Dickinson, P., Myers, J., & Merchant, G. (2006). Digital connections: Transforming literacy in the primary school. *Cambridge Journal of Education*, *36*(1), 11–29. doi:10.1080/03057640500491120

Burnett, C., & Merchant, G. (2011). Is there a space for critical literacy in the context of new media? *English. Practice and Critique*, *10*(1), 41–57.

Burnett, C., & Merchant, G. (2014). Points of view: Reconceptualising literacies through an exploration of adult and child interactions in a virtual world. *Journal of Research in Reading*, *37*(1), 36–50. doi:10.1111/jrir.12006

Burton, C. E., Anderson, D. H., Prater, M. A., & Dyches, T. T. (2013). Video self-modeling on an iPad to teach functional math skills to adolescents with autism and intellectual disability. *Focus on Autism and Other Developmental Disabilities, 28*(2), 67–77. doi:10.1177/1088357613478829

Butler, C. (2004). *Henri Lefebvre: Spatial politics, everyday life, and the right to the city.* New York, NY: Routledge.

Butler, J. (1990). *Gender trouble: Feminism and the subversion of identity.* London: Routledge.

Butler, J. (1990). Subversive bodily acts. In J. Butler (Ed.), *Gender trouble: Feminism and the subversion of identity* (pp. 163–180). New York: Routledge.

Cabral, J. (2008). Is generation Y addicted to social media? *The Future of Children, 18*, 125.

Cahill, C., Rios-Moore, I., & Threatts, T. (2008). Different eyes/open eyes: Community-based participatory action research. In J. Cammarota & M. Fine (Eds.), *Revolutionizing Education: Youth participatory action research in motion* (pp. 89–124). New York, NY: Routledge.

Cairney, G. (2014, August 12). *App seeks to take complexity out of teaching physics* [web log comment]. Retrieved from http://tinyurl.com/mxzvs52

Cake, M. (n.d.). *Web 1.0, Web 2.0, Web 3.0 and Web 4.0 explained.* Retrieved from http://www.wisdomnetworks.im/economic-development/internet-evolution

Camahort, E. (2006). *BlogHer '06 session discussion Mommyblogging is a radical act! On day two.* Retrieved from http://blogher.org/node/5563

Cammarota, J., & Fine, M. (2008). *Revolutionizing education: Youth participatory action research in motion.* New York, NY: Routledge.

Campbell, C. (2014). *Sarkeesian driven out of home by online abuse and death threats.* Polygon 2014. Available from http://www.polygon.com/2014/8/27/6075679/sarkeesian-driven-out-of-home-by-online-abuse-and-death-threats

Campigotto, R., McEwenb, R., & Demmans Eppa, C. (2013). Especially social: Exploring the use of an iOS application in special needs classrooms. *Computers & Education, 60*(1), 74–86. doi:10.1016/j.compedu.2012.08.002

Cann, K. (2004). *Text game.* Minneapolis, MN: Stoke Books.

Caperton, I. H. (2012). Toward a theory of game-media literacy: Playing and building as reading and writing. *The Journal of Media Literacy, 59*, 18–27.

Carey, K. (2012). Show me your badge. *The New York Times.* Retrieved from http://www.nytimes.com/2012/11/04/education/edlife/show-me-your-badge.html?_r=0

Carlsson, B. (2004). The digital economy: What is new and what is not? *Structural Change and Economic Dynamics, 15*(3), 245–264. doi:10.1016/j.strueco.2004.02.001

Carman, P. (2009). *Skeleton Creek.* New York: Scholastic.

Carolan, S., & Evain, C. (2013). Self-publishing: Opportunities and threats in a new age of mass culture. *Publishing Research Quarterly, 29*(4), 285–300. doi:10.1007/s12109-013-9326-3

Carpenter, B. E. (1996). *Architectural principles of the Internet.* Retrieved from http://www.rfc-editor.org/rfc/rfc1958.txt

Carpenter, B. (2009). Living and learning in interesting times. *Journal of Virtual Worlds Research, 2*(1), 4–5.

Carpentier, N. (2009). Participation is not enough: The conditions of possibility of mediated participatory practices. *European Journal of Communication, 24*(4), 407–420. doi:10.1177/0267323109345682

Carpentier, N. (Ed.). (2011). *Media and participation: A site of ideological-democratic struggle.* Intellect Books.

Carr, D., Buckingham, D., Burn, A., & Schott, G. (Eds.). (2006). Computer Games: text, narrative and play. Cambridge, MA: Polity Press.

Carrington, V., & Hodgetts, K. (2010). Literacy-lite in BarbieGirls™. *British Journal of Sociology of Education, 31*(6), 671–682. doi:10.1080/01425692.2010.515109

Carrington, V., & Luke, A. (1997). Literacy and Bourdieu's sociological theory: A reframing. *Language and Education, 11*(2), 96–112. doi:10.1080/09500789708666721

Carrington, V., & Robinson, M. (2009). *Digital literacies: Social learning and classroom practices.* Los Angeles: SAGE Publications. doi:10.4135/9781446288238

Carter, P.L., & Reardon, S.F. (2014, September). *Inequality matters*. Palo Alto, CA: Stanford University.

Casella, R. (2003). Zero tolerance policy in schools: Rationale, consequences, and alternatives. *Teachers College Record*, *105*(5), 872–892. doi:10.1111/1467-9620.00271

Cassell, J., & Jenkins, H. (Eds.). (1998). *From Barbie to Mortal Kombat: Gender and computer games*. Cambridge, MA: MIT.

Cassidy, W., Faucher, C., & Jackson, M. (2013). Cyberbullying among youth: A comprehensive review of current international research and its implications and application to policy and practice. *School Psychology International*, *34*(6), 575–612. doi:10.1177/0143034313479697

Cassidy, W., & Jackson, M. (2005). The need for equality in education: An intersectionality examination of labeling and zero tolerance practices. *McGill Journal of Education*, *40*(3), 445–466.

Cassidy, W., Jackson, M., & Brown, K. N. (2009). Sticks and stones can break my bones, but how can pixels hurt me?: Students' experiences with cyber-bullying. *School Psychology International*, *30*(4), 383–402. doi:10.1177/0143034309106948

Cassoni, A. & Ramada, C. (2012). *Digital money and its impact on local economic variables: The case of Uruguay*. Academic Press.

Castek, J. (2006). *The changing nature of reading comprehension: Examining the acquisition of new literacies in a 7th grade science classroom*. Paper presented at the National Reading Conference Los Angeles 2006, Los Angeles, CA.

Castek, J., Withers, E., Pendell, K., Pizzolato, D., Jacobs, G., & Reder, S. (2014, March). *Conquering the computer: Digital literacy acquisition among vulnerable adult learners*. Paper presented at the annual meeting of the American Association of Applied Linguistics, Portland, OR.

Castek, J., & Beach, R. (2013). Using apps to support disciplinary learning and science learning. *Journal of Adolescent & Adult Literacy*, *56*(7), 544–554. doi:10.1002/JAAL.180

Castek, J., Beach, R., Cotanch, H., & Scott, J. (2014). Exploiting the affordances of multimodal tools for writing in the science classroom. In R. S. Anderson & C. Mims (Eds.), *Handbook of research on digital tools for writing instruction in K-12 settings* (pp. 80–101). Hershey, PA: IGI Global.

Castek, J., Coiro, J., Guzniczak, L., & Bradshaw, C. (2012). Examining peer collaboration in online inquiry. *The Educational Forum*, *76*(4), 479–496. doi:10.1080/00131725.2012.707756

Castells, M. (2000). The rise of the network society (2nd ed.; Vol. 1). Oxford, UK: Blackwell.

Castells. (2009). *The Power of Identity* (2nd ed.). Wiley-Blackwell.

Castells, M. (1996). *Rise of The Network Society*. Malden, MA: Wiley-Blackwell.

Castells, M. (2001). *The Internet galaxy: Reflections on the Internet, business, and society*. New York, NY: Oxford University Press, Inc. doi:10.1007/978-3-322-89613-1

Castells, M. (2010). The rise of the Fourth World: Informational capitalism, poverty, and social exclusion. In *End of millennium* (2nd ed.; Vol. 3, pp. 3–49). Oxford, UK: Wiley-Blackwell; doi:10.1002/9781444323436.ch2

Castronova, E. (2005). *Synthetic Worlds: the Business and Culture of Online Games*. London: University of Chicago Press.

Cavalier, R., & Weber, K. (2002). Learning, media, and the case of Dax Cowart: A comparison of text, film, and interactive multimedia. *Interactive Learning Environments*, *10*(3), 243–262. doi:10.1076/ilee.10.3.243.8763

Cave, D. (2012). *Digital islands: how the Pacific's ICT revolution is transforming the region*. Retrieved September 27, 2014, from http://www.lowyinstitute.org/publications/digital-islands-how-pacifics-ict-revolution-transforming-region

Center for Collective Intelligence. (2014). MIT. Retrieved October 20, 2014 from http://cci.mit.edu/

Center for Digital Education. (2014). *Digital school districts survey identifies innovative uses of technology*. Author. Retrieved from http://tinyurl.com/k8a37by

Central Intelligence Agency (CIA). (2012). *CIA—The world fact book: United States.* Retrieved from https://www.cia.gov/library/publications/the-world-factbook/geos/us.html

Ceron, A., Curini, L., Iacus, S. M., & Porro, G. (2014). Every tweet counts? How sentiment analysis of social media can improve our knowledge of citizens' political preferences with an application to Italy and France. *New Media & Society, 16*(2), 340–358. doi:10.1177/1461444813480466

Cervetti, G., Pardales, M. J., & Damico, J. (2001, April). A tale of differences: Comparing the traditions, perspectives, and educational goals of critical reading and critical literacy. *Reading Online, 4*(9). Retrieved from http://www.reading.org/articles/art_index.asp?HREF=/articles/cervetti/ index.html

Chalayan, H. (2011). *From Fashion and Back.* Bss Bijutsu.

Chambers, J. (2013). Foreword. In B. Bilbao-Osorio, S. Dutta, & B. lanvin (Eds.), The global information technology report, 2013 (pp. ix-x). Academic Press.

Chandler-Olcott, K., & Mahar, D. (2003). Adolescents' *anime*-inspired "fanfictions": An exploration of multiliteracies. *Journal of Adolescent & Adult Literacy, 46,* 556–566.

Chapman, R. B., Slaymaker, T., & Overseas Development Institute. (2002). *ICTs and rural development: Review of the literature, current interventions and opportunities for action.* London: ODI. Retrieved from http://www.odi.org/sites/odi.org.uk/files/odi-assets/publications-opinion-files/2670.pdf

Charitonos, K., Blake, C., Scanlon, E., & Jones, A. (2012). Museum learning via social and mobile technologies: (How) can online interactions enhance the visitor experience? *British Journal of Educational Technology, 43*(5), 802–819. doi:10.1111/j.1467-8535.2012.01360.x

Chebib, N. K., & Sohail, R. M. (2011). The reasons social media contributed to the 2011 Egyptian revolution. *International Journal of Business Research and Management, 2,* 139–162.

Chen, C.-M., & Chen, F.-Y. (2014). Enhancing digital reading performance with a collaborative reading annotation system. *Computers & Education, 77,* 67–81. doi:10.1016/j.compedu.2014.04.010

Chen, G. M., & Zhang, K. (2010). New media and cultural identity in the global society. In R. Taiwo (Ed.), *Handbook of Research on Discourse Behavior and Digital Communication: Language Structures and Social Interaction* (pp. 801–815). Hershey, PA: Idea Group Inc. doi:10.4018/978-1-61520-773-2.ch051

Chen, H., Chiang, R., & Storey, V. C. (2012). Business intelligence and analytics: From big data to big impact. *Management Information Systems Quarterly, 4*(36), 1165–1188.

Cherner, T., Dix, J., & Lee, C. (2014). Cleaning up that mess: A framework for classifying educational apps. *Contemporary Issues in Technology & Teacher Education, 14*(2). Retrieved from http://www.citejournal.org/vol14/iss2/general/article1.cfm

Chesney, K. (2010). *Boys of Fall-CMA Awards 2010-HD Quality.* Available from YouTube.

Chicago Art Department. (2013). *What is a badge?* Retrieved from https://www.youtube.com/watch?v=HgLLq7ybDtc#t=125

Chidgey, R. (2014). Developing communities of resistance? Maker pedagogies, do-it-yourself feminism, and DIY citizenship. In M. Ratto & M. Boler (Eds.), *DIY Citizenship: Critical making and social media* (pp. 101–114). Cambridge, MA: MIT Press.

Chie, D. (2014). The perils and pitfalls of BYOD in your workplace. Retrieved from Christensen, C. (2008). Disruptive innovation and catalytic change in higher education. *Forum for the Future of Higher Education,* 43-46. Retrieved from http://www.paloaltostaffingtech.com/news-insights/thought-leadership/the-perils-and-pitfalls-of-byod-in-your-workplace/http://net.educause.edu/ir/library/pdf/ff0810s.pdf

Chinthammit, W., & Thomas, A. (2014). Augmented reality in the English classroom. In L. Unsworth & A. Thomas (Eds.), *English teaching & new literacies pedagogies: Interpreting and authoring digital multimedia narratives* (pp. 213–231). New York: Peter Lang.

Chowdhry, A. (2014). *MSN Messenger is completely shutting down on October 31st.* Retrieved from http://www.forbes.com/sites/amitchowdhry/2014/08/31/msn-messenger-is-completely-shutting-down-on-october-31st/

Christensen, C. M. (1997). *The innovator's dilemma: When new technologies cause firms to fail.* Boston, MA: Harvard Business School Press.

Christensen, C. M. (2008). *Disruptive diplomas: The future of education.* New York: McGraw Hill.

Chuang, H., & Ku, H. (2011). The effect of computer-based multimedia instruction with Chinese character recognition. *Educational Media International*, *48*(1), 27–41. doi:10.1080/09523987.2011.549676

Chung, S. K. (2007). Art education technology: Digital storytelling. *Art Education*, *60*(2), 17–22.

Chung, Y. (2005). *Silken Threads: A History of Embroidery in China, Korea, Japan, and Vietnam.* New York: Harry N. Abrams.

Cingel, D. P., & Sundar, S. S. (2012). Texting, techspeak, and tweens: The relationship between text messaging and English grammar skills. *New Media & Society*, *14*(8), 1304–1320. doi:10.1177/1461444812442927

Cisco. (2014). *Cisco visual networking index: Global mobile data traffic forecast update, 2013-2018.* Retrieved from http://www.cisco.com/c/en/us/solutions/collateral/service-provider/visual-networking-index-vni/white_paper_c11-520862.html

Cities of Learning. (2014). *One summer, more than 100,000 badges and a movement is born.* Retrieved from http://citiesoflearning.org/learn/

Citron, D. K. (2009). Law's expressive value in combating cyber gender harassment. *Michigan Law Review*, *108*(3), 373–415.

Clairday, R. (2005). *Confessions of a boyfriend stealer.* New York: Delacorte.

Clarke, B., Svanaes, S., Zimmermann, S., & Crowther, K. (2013). *One-to-one tablets in secondary schools: An evaluation study, Stage 3: April-September 2013. Family Kids and Youth, UK.* Sussex: UK: Tablets for Schools. Retrieved from http://www.tabletsforschools.org.uk

Clarke, M. A. (2009). Developing digital storytelling in Brazil. In J. Hartley & K. McWilliam (Eds.), *Digital storytelling around the world* (pp. 91–117). Malden, MA: Wiley-Blackwell.

Clarke, R. G., & Thomas, S. (2012). Digital narrative and the humanities: An evaluation of the use of digital storytelling in an Australian undergraduate literacy studies program. *Higher Education Studies*, *2*(3), 30–43. doi:10.5539/hes.v2n3p30

Clark, R. E. (1994). Media will never influence learning. *Educational Technology Research and Development*, *42*(2), 21–29. doi:10.1007/BF02299088

Clark, R. E., & Feldon, D. F. (2005). Five common but questionable principles of multimedia learning. In R. E. Mayer (Ed.), *The Cambridge handbook of multimedia learning* (pp. 97–116). New York, NY: Cambridge University Press. doi:10.1017/CBO9780511816819.007

Clegg, S. (2001). Theorising the machine: Gender, education and computing. *Gender and Education*, *13*(3), 307–324. doi:10.1080/09540250120063580

Clemons, E., Reddi, S., & Row, M. (1993). The impact of information technology on the organization of economic activity: The move to the middle hypothesis. *Journal of Management Information Systems*, (10): 9–35.

Club Penguin. (n.d.). *About Club Penguin.* Retrieved from http://www.clubpenguin.com/company/about

CNET.com. (2014). *Wearable tech.* CNET. Retrieved from http://www.cnet.com/topics/wearable-tech/

Cochrane, T., Guinibert, M., Simeti, C., Brannigan, R., & Kala, A. (2015). Mobile Social Media as a Catalyst for Collaborative Curriculum Redesign. In J. Keengwe & M. Maxfield (Eds.), *Advancing higher education with mobile learning technologies: Cases, trends, and inquiry-based methods* (pp. 1–21). Hershey, PA: Information Science Reference; doi:10.4018/978-1-4666-6284-1.ch001

Cochrane, T., Narayan, V., & Oldfield, J. (2013). iPadagogy: Appropriating the iPad within pedagogical contexts. *International Journal of Mobile Learning and Organisation*, *7*(1), 48–65. doi:10.1504/IJMLO.2013.051573

Coe, J. E. L., & Oakhill, J. V. (2011). "txtN is ez f u no h2 rd": The relation between reading ability and text-messaging behaviour. *Journal of Computer Assisted Learning*, *27*(1), 4–17. doi:10.1111/j.1365-2729.2010.00404.x

Cogburn, D. L., & Espinoza-Vasquez, F. K. (2011). From Networked Nominee to Networked Nation: Examining the Impact of Web 2.0 and Social Media on Political Participation and Civic Engagement in the 2008 Obama Campaign. *Journal of Political Marketing*, *10*(1-2), 189–213. doi:10.1080/15377857.2011.540224

Cohen, C. J., & Kahne, J. (2012). *Participatory politics: New media and youth political action*. Retrieved on September 15, 2014 from http://ypp.dmlcentral.net/sites/default/files/publications/Participatory_Politics_Report.pdf

Cohen, S. (2002). *Folk devils and moral panics: The creation of the mods and rockers* (3rd ed.). London: Routledge. (Original work published 1972)

Cohn, E. R., & Hibbits, B. (2004). Beyond the electronic portfolio: A lifetime personal web space. *Educause Review Online*. Retrieved from http://www.educause.edu/ero/article/beyond-electronic-portfolio-lifetime-personal-web-space

Coiro, J., Karchmer, R. A., & Walpole, S. (2009). *Critically evaluating educational technologies for literacy learning*. Retrieved from newliteracies.uconn.edu/coiro/handbookeval.pdf

Coiro, J. (2003). Reading comprehension on the Internet: Expanding our understanding of reading comprehension to encompass new literacies. *The Reading Teacher*, *56*(5), 458–464.

Coiro, J., Knobel, M., Lankshear, C., & Leu, D. J. (Eds.). (2008). *Handbook of research on new literacies*. New York: Taylor and Francis Group.

Cole, M. (2009). Using Wiki technology to support student engagement: Lessons from the trenches. *Computers & Education*, *52*(1), 141–146. doi:10.1016/j.compedu.2008.07.003

Coleman, E. G. (2010). Ethnographic approaches to digital media. *Annual Review of Anthropology*, *39*(1), 487–505. doi:10.1146/annurev.anthro.012809.104945

Collins, G, & Quan-Haase. (2014). Are social media ubiquitous in academic libraries? A longitudinal study of adoption and usage patterns. *Journal of Web Librarianship*, *8*(1), 48-68. doi: 10.1.1080/19322909.2014.873663

Collins, G. (2012). *Social media use by Ontario university libraries: Challenges and ethical considerations*. Paper presented at the Annual Conference of CAIS. Retrieved from http://www.cais-acsi.ca/proceedings/2012/caisacsi2012_submission_117.pdf

Collins, M. (2014, May 9). *#BringBackOurGirls: the power of a social media campaign*. Retrieved January 24, 2015, from http://www.theguardian.com/voluntary-sector-network/2014/may/09/bringbackourgirls-power-of-social-media

Collins, S. A., Yoon, S., Rockoff, M. L., Nocenti, D., & Bakken, S. (2014). Digital divide and information needs for improving family support among the poor and underserved. *Health Informatics Journal*, 1–11. PMID:24935213

Common Core State Standards Initiative. (2010). Common core standards for English language arts & literacy in history/social studies, science, and technical subjects. Washington, DC: Council of Chief State School Officers (CCSSO).

Common Core State Standards Initiative. (2012). *Common Core State Standards Initiative: Preparing America's students for college and career*. Retrieved from http://www.corestandards.org

Common Core State Standards Initiative. (2014). *Myths vs facts*. Retrieved from http://www.corestandards.org/about-the-standards/myths-vs-facts/

Common Core State Standards Initiative. (2014). *Preparing America's students for success*. Retrieved November, 2014, from http://www.corestandards.org/

Common Sense Media. (2012). *Children, teens, and entertainment media: The view from the classroom*. Retrieved from https://www.commonsensemedia.org/research/children-teens-and-entertainment-media-the-view-from-the-classroom

Common Sense Media. (2014). *Trillion dollar footprint*. Retrieved from https://www.commonsensemedia.org/educators/lesson/trillion-dollar-footprint-6-8

Compaine, B. M. (2001). *Re-examining the digital divide* (130). Retrieved from Research Affiliate, Internet and Telecoms Convergence Consortium, MIT. Retrieved from http://digital.mit.edu/research/papers/130%20Compaine,%20Digital%20Divide.pdf

Compton, L., Campbell, M., & Mergler, A. (2014). Teacher, parent and student perceptions of the motives of cyberbullies. *Social Psychology of Education, 17*(3), 383–400. doi:10.1007/s11218-014-9254-x

Connell, C., Bayliss, L., & Farmer, W. (2012). Effects of ebook readers and tablet computers on reading comprehension. *International Journal of Instructional Media, 39*(2), 131–140.

Connell, R. W., & Messerschmidt, J. W. (2005). Hegemonic masculinity: Rethinking the concept. *Gender & Society, 19*(6), 829–859. doi:10.1177/0891243205278639

Conover, M. D. (2013). *Digital democracy: The structure and dynamics of political communication in a large scale social media stream.* Indiana University. Retrieved from http://gradworks.umi.com/35/68/3568779.html

Considine, D., Horton, J., & Moorman, G. (2009). Teaching and reaching the millennial generation through media literacy. *Journal of Adolescent & Adult Literacy, 52*(6), 471–472. doi:10.1598/JAAL.52.6.2

Cook, G. (2013). *The best American infographics.* New York: Houghton Mifflin Harcourt.

Cooper, A., Boies, S., Maheu, M., & Greenfield, D. (2000). Sexuality and the Internet: The next sexual revolution. In F. Muscarella & L. Szuchman (Eds.), *Psychological perspectives on human sexuality* (pp. 519–545). New York: Wiley.

Cooper, C. R. (2011). *Bridging multiple worlds: Cultures, identities, and pathways to college.* Oxford University Press. doi:10.1093/acprof:oso/9780195080209.001.0001

Coover, R. (1999). *Literary hypertext: The passing of the golden age.* Keynote Address, Digital Arts and Culture, Atlanta, GA. Retrieved from http://www.nickm.com/vox/golden_age.html

Cope, B., & Kalantzis, M. (Eds.). (1999). *Multiliteracies: Literacy Learning and the Design of Social Futures.* London: Macmillan.

Copeland, M. (2014). *New Under Armour ad featuring Misty Copeland promotes female empowerment.* Available from YouTube: www.youtube.com/watch?v=52tc3STY3fc

Corbett, D., & Higgins, R. (2006). *Portfolio life: The new path to work, purpose, and passion after 50.* Jossey-Bass.

Cordes, C., & Miller, E. (2000). *Fool's Gold: A critical look at computers in childhood (Report).* College Park, MD: Alliance for Childhood.

Cormode, G., & Krishnamurthy, B. (2008). Key differences between Web 1.0 and Web 2.0. *First Monday, 13*(6). doi:10.5210/fm.v13i6.2125

Cottrell, T. (2014). *An assessment of the effect of multimedia on critical thinking outcomes. (Doctoral dissertation).* Retrieved from Dissertations & Theses: A&I. (AAT 3624781).

Couldry, N. (2012). *Media, society, world: Social theory and digital media practice.* Cambridge, UK: Polity Press.

Couldry, N., & McCarthy, A. (2004). Introduction: Orientations: Mapping MediaSpace. In N. Couldry & A. McCarthy (Eds.), *MediaSpace, place, scale and culture in a media age* (pp. 1–18). London: Routledge.

Coursera. (2014). *About Us.* Retrieved September 2 from https://www.coursera.org/about/partners

Cox, V. K., May, R. C., Kroder, S. L., & Franklin, G. M. (2010). Following the paper trail: Measuring the economic and environmental impact of digital content delivery. *Technological Developments in Networking. Education and Automation, 37-41.* doi:10.1007/978-90-481-9151-2_7

Craig, K. (2013). *Know It All Bag.* Retrieved from http://www.knitty.com/ISSUEss10/PATTknowitall.php

Creative Commons. (n.d.). *Creative commons.* Retrieved from https://creativecommons.org

Cress, U., & Kimmerle, J. (2008). A systemic and cognitive view on collaborative knowledge building with wikis. *Computer-Supported Learning, 3,* 105-122. doi:10.1007/s11412-007-9035-z

Cronbach, L. J. (1951). Coefficient alpha and the internal structure of tests. *Psychometrika, 16*(3), 297–334. doi:10.1007/BF02310555

Crook, J. (2014). Vine finally lets you import video from your camera roll. *TechCrunch*. Retrieved from http://techcrunch.com/2014/08/20/with-a-billion-loops-every-day-vine-finally-lets-users-import-video-from-their-camera/

Crook, C., Cummings, J., Fisher, T., Graber, R., Harrison, C., Lewin, C., & Sharples, M. (2008). *Web 2.0 technologies for learning: The current landscape – opportunities, challenges and tensions WEb 2.0 technologies for learning at Key Stages 3 and 4* (p. 72). BECTA.

Croxall, B. (2014). Twitter, Tumblr, and microblogging. In M. Ryan, L. Emerson, B. J. Robertson, & I. Ebrary (Eds.), *The Johns Hopkins Guide to Digital Media*. Baltimore, MD: The John Hopkins University Press.

Crystal, D. (2004). *A glossary of netspeak and textspeak*. Edinburgh, UK: Edinburgh University Press.

Crystal, D. (2008). Texting. *ELT Journal*, *62*(1), 77–83. doi:10.1093/elt/ccm080

Cukier, K., & Mayer-Schonberger, V. (2013). *Big data: a revolution that will transform how we live, work, and think*. Houghton Mifflin Harcourt.

Cumps, B., Vanden Eynde, O., & Viaene, S. (2013). Impact of e-waste on the operating model of a "close the digital divide" organisation. *ECIS 2013 Completed Research, 71*. Retrieved from http://aisel.aisnet.org/cgi/viewcontent.cgi?article=1294&context=ecis2013_cr

Czernich, N., Falck, O., Kretschmer, T., & Woessmann, L. (2011). Broadband Infrastructure and Economic Growth. *The Economic Journal*, *121*(552), 505–532. doi:10.1111/j.1468-0297.2011.02420.x

D'Arcens, L. (2014). *Comic medievalism: Laughing at the Middle Ages*. Woodbridge, UK: Boydell & Brewer, Ltd.

Dabbagh, N., & Kitsantas, A. (2012). Personal learning environments, social media, and self-regulated learning: A natural formula for connecting formal and informal learning. *The Internet and Higher Education*, *15*(1), 3–8. doi:10.1016/j.iheduc.2011.06.002

Daher, W. (2014). Students' adoption of social networks as environments for learning and teaching: The case of the Facebook. *International Journal of Emerging Technologies in Learning*, *9*(4), 16–24. doi:10.3991/ijet.v9i8.3722

Dahlstrom, E., Walker, J. D., & Dziuban, C. (2013). ECAR study of undergraduate students and information technology, 2013. Louisville, CO: Educause Center for Analysis and Research. Retrieved from https://net.educause.edu/ir/library/pdf/ERS1302/ERS1302.pdf

Dallas Museum of Art. (2014). *Dallas Museum of Art partners with Grace Museum in Abilene, TX to expand friends membership program*. Retrieved from http://www.dm-art.org/press-release/dallas-museum-art-partners-grace-museum-abilene-tx-expand-friends-membership-program

Dalton, B. (2012). Multimodal composition and the common core state standards. *The Reading Teacher*, *66*(4), 333–339. doi:10.1002/TRTR.01129

Dalton, B. (2013). Engaging children in close reading: Multimodal commentaries and illustration remix. *The Reading Teacher*, *66*(8), 642–649. doi:10.1002/trtr.1172

Damico, J. S., & Baldwin, M. (2013). Content literacy for the 21st Century: Evacuation, elevation, and relational cosmopolitan in the classroom. *Journal of Adolescent & Adult Literacy*, *55*(3), 232–243. doi:10.1002/JAAL.00028

Danaher, B., Dhanasobhon, S., Smith, M. D., & Telang, R. (2010). Converting pirates without cannibalizing purchasers: The impact of digital distribution on physical sales and internet piracy. *Marketing Science*. Retrieved from http://www.heinz.cmu.edu/~rtelang/ms_nbc.pdf

Danby, S., Davidson, C., Theobald, M., Scriven, B., Cobb-Moore, C., & Houen, S. … Thorpe, K. (2013). Talk in activity during young children's use of digital technologies at home. *Australian Journal of Communication, 40*(2). Retrieved from http://www.austjourcomm.org/index.php/ajc/article/view/4

Danet, B. (1998). Text as mask: Gender, play, and performance on the Internet. In S. G. Jones (Ed.), *CyberSociety 2.0: Revising computer-mediated communication and community* (pp. 129–158). Thousand Oaks, CA: Sage. doi:10.4135/9781452243689.n5

Danto, A. (1964). The artworld. *The Journal of Philosophy*, *61*(19), 571–584. doi:10.2307/2022937

Darvin, R., & Norton, B. (2014). Transnational identity and migrant learners: The promise of digital storytelling. *Education Matters*, *2*, 55–66.

Dasgupta, S., Lall, S., & Wheeler, D. (2001). Policy reform, economic growth, and the digital divide: An econometric analysis. *The World Bank Development Research Group Infrastructure and Environment, 2567,* 1-18. Retrieved from http://books.google.com/books?id=4v-04WJ4U BEC&pg=PP2&dq=Dasgupta,+Lall,+%26+Wheele r,+2001&hl=en&sa=X&ei=etBSVOrON8ergwTqiY OIBQ&ved=0CB0Q6AEwAA#v=onepage&q=Dasg upta%2C%20Lall%2C%20%26%20Wheeler%2C%20 2001&f=false

Davenport, T. (2013). *Data is worthless if you don't communicate it.* Harvard Business Review. Retrieved from http://blogs.hbr.org/2013/06/data-is-worthless-if-you-dont/

Davidson, R. (2014). Using infographics in the science classroom. *Science Teacher (Normal, Ill.), 81*(3), 34–39. doi:10.2505/4/tst14_081_03_34

Davies, A., Fidler, D., & Gorbis, M. (2011). *Future work skills 2020. Institute for the Future for University of Phoenix Research Institute.* Retrieved from http://www. iftf.org/uploads/media/SR-1382A_UPRI_future_work_ skills_sm.pdf

Davies, J. (2007). Display, identity and the everyday: Self-presentation through online image sharing. *Studies in the Cultural Politics of Education, 28*(4), 549–564. doi:10.1080/01596300701625305

Davis, A., & Weinshenker, D. (2012). Digital storytelling and authoring identity. In C. Ching & Foley (Eds.), Technology and identity: Research on the development and exploration of selves in a digital world (pp. 47-64). Cambridge, UK: Cambridge University Press. doi:10.1017/ CBO9781139027656.005

Davis, A. (2004). Co-authoring identity: Digital storytelling in an urban middle school *Technology. Humanities, Education, and Narrative, 1*(1), 1–21.

Dawkins, R. (1976). *The selfish gene.* New York, NY: Oxford University Press.

de Castell, S., & Jenson, J. (2004). Paying attention to attention: New economies for learning. *Educational Theory, 54*(4), 381–397. doi:10.1111/j.0013-2004.2004.00026.x

De Vinck, S., & Lindmark, S. (2014). *Innovation in the film sector: What lessons from the past tell us about Hollywood's digital future–and what that means for Europe.* Cheltenham, UK: Edward Elgar Publishing.

Deaton, C. C. M., Deaton, B. E., Ivankovic, D., & Norris, F. A. (2013). Creating stop-motion videos with iPads to support students' understanding of cell processes: "Because you have to know what you're talking about to be able to do it. *Journal of Digital Learning in Teacher Education, 30*(2), 67–73. doi:10.1080/21532974.2013.10784729

Debatin, B., Lovejoy, J. P., Horn, A. K., & Hughes, B. N. (2009). Facebook and online privacy: Attitudes, behaviors, and unintended consequences. *Journal of Computer-Mediated Communication, 15*(1), 83–108. doi:10.1111/j.1083-6101.2009.01494.x

Dede, C., Clarke, J., Ketelhut, D., Nelson, B., & Bowman, C. (2006). *Fostering Motivation, Learning and Transfer in Multi-User Virtual Environments.* Paper given at the 2006 AERA Conference, San Francisco, CA.

Dede, C. (2009). Comments on Greenhow, Robelia, and Hughes: Technologies That Facilitate Generating Knowledge and Possibly Wisdom. *Educational Researcher, 38*(4), 260–263. doi:10.3102/0013189X09336672

DeFranco, M. (2014). Don't be rude, adopt wearables at your workplace. *Forbes.* Retrieved from http://www. forbes.com/sites/michaeldefranco/2014/08/05/dont-be-rude-adopt-wearables-at-your-workplace/

DeGennaro, D. (2008). Learning designs: An analysis of youth-initiated technology use. *Journal of Research on Technology in Education, 41*(1), 1–20. doi:10.1080/153 91523.2008.10782520

DeGennaro, D. (2008). The dialectics of informing identity in an urban youth digital storytelling workship. *E-learning, 5*(4), 429–444. doi:10.2304/elea.2008.5.4.429

Dekhane, S., & Xu, X. (2012). Engaging students in computing using Gamesalad: A pilot study. *Journal of Computing Sciences in Colleges, 28,* 117–123.

Dekhan, S., Xu, X., & Yin, M. (2013). Mobile app development to increase student engagement and problem solving skills. *Journal of Information Systems Education, 24*(4), 299.

Delaney, D., & Leitner, H. (1997). The political construction of scale. *Political Geography*, *16*(2), 93–97. doi:10.1016/S0962-6298(96)00045-5

Delanty, G. (2006). The cosmopolitan imagination: Critical cosmopolitanism and social theory. *The British Journal of Sociology*, *5*(1), 25–47. doi:10.1111/j.1468-4446.2006.00092.x PMID:16506995

Delello, J. A. (2013, May). *Case study: Students digitally archive newly minted classroom management skills*. Pathbrite Inc. Retrieved from http://partner.pearson.com/sites/default/files/UTT%20Case%20Study%20EDU_v2.pdf

Delello, J. A. (2014). Insights from pre-service teachers using science-based augmented reality. *Journal of Computers in Education*, *1*(4), 295–311. doi:10.1007/s40692-014-0021-y

Delello, J. A., & McWhorter, R. R. (2013). New visual social media for the higher education classroom. In G. Mallia (Ed.), *The Social Classroom: Integrating Social Network Use in Education*. Hershey, PA: IGI Global.

Delello, J. A., & McWhorter, R. R. (2014, August). Creating virtual communities of practice with the visual social media platform Pinterest. *International Journal of Social Media and Interactive Learning Environments*, *2*(3), 216. doi:10.1504/IJSMILE.2014.064205

Delello, J. A., McWhorter, R. R., & Camp, K. (2014). Social media as a classroom learning tool. *International Journal on E-Learning*.

Deleuze, G., & Guattari, F. (1987). *A thousand plateaus: Capitalism and schizophrenia*. Minneapolis, MN: University of Minneapolis Press.

Dembo, S., & Bellow, A. (2013). *Untangling the web*. Thousand Oaks, CA: Corwin Press.

Denner, J., & Bean, S. (2010). The young women's leadership alliance: Political socialization in three U.S. high schools. In A. Ittell, H. Merkens, L. Stecher, & J. Zinnecker (Eds.), *Jahrbuch Jugend-forschung* (pp. 85–103). Germany: VS Verlag. doi:10.1007/978-3-531-92320-8_4

Denner, J., Werner, L., Bean, S., & Campe, S. (2005). The Girls Creating Games Program: Strategies for engaging middle school girls in information technology. *Frontiers: A Journal of Women's Studies*, *26*(1), 90–98.

Denner, J., Werner, L., & Ortiz, E. (2012). Computer games created by middle school girls: Can they be used to measure understanding of computer science concepts? *Computers & Education*, *58*(1), 240–249. doi:10.1016/j.compedu.2011.08.006

Dennett, D. (2002). Dangerous memes. *TED*. Retrieved from http://www.ted.com/talks/dan_dennett_on_dangerous_memes?language=en

Department of Justice Canada. (2014). *Government of Canada highlights royal assent of bill to help law enforcement protect victims of online crime*. Retrieved from Government of Canada website: http://news.gc.ca/web/article-en.do?nid=913359&_ga=1.66908974.1410492497.1419632791

Derks, D., Bos, A. E. R., & von Grumbkow, J. (2007). Emoticons and Online Message Interpretation. *Social Science Computer Review*, *26*(3), 379–388. doi:10.1177/0894439307311611

Design, D. (2013). *When technology meets sensuality*. Paper presented at the Smart Fabrics Conference, Barcelona, Spain.

Desouz, K. C., & Bhagwatwar, A. (2012). Citizen apps to solve complex urban problems. *Journal of Urban Technology*, *19*(3), 107–136. doi:10.1080/10630732.2012.673056

Devaney, L. (2014, September 3). *Mobile learning's major impact* [web log comment]. Retrieved from http://tinyurl.com/mshraao

Dewey, J. (1897). My pedagogic creed. *The School Journal*, *54*(3), 7780.

Dewey, J. (1909). *How we think*. Boston, MA: D.C. Heath.

Dewey, J. (1916). *Democracy and education: An introduction to the philosophy of education*. New York, NY: MacMillan.

Dewey, J. (1938). *Experience and education*. New York: Simon & Schuster.

DeWitt, D., Siraj, S., & Alias, N. (2014). Collaborative mLearning: A Module for Learning Secondary School Science. *Journal of Educational Technology & Society*, *17*(1), 89–101.

Dezuanni, M. (2014). The building blocks of digital media literacy: Socio-material participation and the production of media knowledge. *Journal of Curriculum Studies*. doi:10.1080/00220272.2014.966152

Dezuanni, M., Kapitzke, C., & Iyer, R. (2010). Copyright, digital media literacies and preservice teacher education. *Digital Culture & Education*, 2(2), 230–245.

Diamondstone, J. (2004). *Jasmine makes a scary movie: A multi-modal analysis of an adolescent's popular culture literacy*. Paper presented at the National Council of Teachers of English Assembly for Research (NCTEAR), Berkeley, CA.

Diaz-Ortiz, C., & Stone, B. (2011). *Twitter for good: Change the world one tweet at a time*. San Francisco, CA: Jossey-Bass.

Dibley, R. (2011). *Using digital media to report back information-rich research and evaluation results*. Paper presented at the Australasian Evaluation Society Conference, Sydney, Australia. Retrieved from http://www.communityresearch.org.nz/research/using-digital-media-to-report-back-information-rich-research-and-evaluation-results/

DiDomenico, S., & Boase, J. (2013). Bringing mobiles into the conversation. In D. Tannen & A. M. Trester (Eds.), *Discourse 2.0: Language and New Media* (pp. 119–132). Washington, DC: Georgetown University Press.

Dietz, T. L. (1998). An examination of violence and gender role portrayals in video games: Implications for gender socialization and aggressive behavior. *Sex Roles*, 38(5/6), 425–442. doi:10.1023/A:1018709905920

Digby, G. (1964). *Elizabethan Embroidery*. New York: Yoseloff.

Digital Marketing Ramblings. (2014). *DMR directory of social network, app and digital stats: WordPress stats and facts*. Retrieved from http://expandedramblings.com/index.php/business-directory/?listing=wordpress&wpbdp_sort=field-10

DiNucci, D. (1999). Fragmented Future. *Print*, 53(4), 32.

DiSalvo, B. J., Crowley, K., & Norwood, R. (2008). Learning in context: Digital games and young black men. *Games and Culture*, 3(2), 131–141. doi:10.1177/1555412008314130

DiSalvo, B., & Bruckman, A. (2010). Race and gender in play practices: Young African American males. In *Proceedings of the Fifth International Conference on the Foundations of Digital Games* (pp. 56–63). New York, NY: ACM. doi:10.1145/1822348.1822356

Dixon, J., & Keyes, D. (2013). The permanent disruption of social media. *Stanford Social Innovation Review*. Retrieved from http://www.ssireview.org/articles/entry/the_permanent_disruption_of_social_media

Dixon, , Correa, T., Straubhaar, J., Covarrubias, L., Graber, D., Spence, J., & Rojas, V. (2014). Gendered space: The digital divide between male and female users in internet public access sites. *Journal of Computer-Mediated Communication*, 19(4), 991–1009. doi:10.1111/jcc4.12088

Dobson, T., & Willinsky, J. (2009). Digital literacy. In D. Olson & N. Torrance (Eds.), *Cambridge Handbook on Literacy*. Cambridge, UK: Cambridge University Press. doi:10.1017/CBO9780511609664.017

Dogoriti, E., & Pange, J. (2014). Considerations for online English language learning: the use of Facebook in formal and informal settings in higher education. In G. Mallia (Ed.), *The Social Classroom: Integrating Social Network Use in Education*. Hershey, PA: IGI Global. doi:10.4018/978-1-4666-4904-0.ch008

Dolev-Cohen, M., & Barak, A. (2013). Adolescents' use of Instant Messaging as a means of emotional relief. *Computers in Human Behavior*, 29(1), 58–63. doi:10.1016/j.chb.2012.07.016

Donaldson, M. C. (1978). *Children's minds*. New York, NY: Norton.

Donston-Miller, D. (2014). Workplace wearables: The pros and cons for businesses. *Techpage One*. Retrieved from http://techpageone.dell.com/technology/workplace-wearables-the-pros-and-cons-for-businesses/#.VDUkHvldW1g

Dougherty, D. (2013). The maker mindset. In M. Honey & D. E. Kanter (Eds.), *Design, make, play: Growing the next generation of STEM innovators* (pp. 7–11). New York, NY: Routledge.

Dowd, N. (2013). Social media: Libraries are posting, but Is anyone listening? *Library Journal*. Retrieved from http://lj.libraryjournal.com/2013/05/marketing/social-media-libraries-are-posting-but-is-anyone-listening/#_

Dredge, R., Gleeson, J., & de la Piedad Garcia, X. (2014). Cyberbullying in social networking sites: An adolescent victim's perspective. *Computers in Human Behavior*, *36*, 13–20. doi:10.1016/j.chb.2014.03.026

Drew, S. (2013). Open up the ceiling on the common core state standards: Preparing students for 21st-century literacy-now. *Journal of Adolescent & Adult Literacy*, *56*(4), 321–330. doi:10.1002/JAAL.00145

Driscoll, M. (2005). *Psychology of learning for instruction* (3rd ed.). Boston: Pearson Education.

Driver, S. (2007). *Queer girls and popular culture: Reading, resisting, and creating media*. New York: Peter Lang.

Droge, C., Stanko, M. A., & Pollitte, W. A. (2010). Lead users and early adopters on the web: The role of new technology product blogs. *Journal of Product Innovation Management*, *27*(1), 66–82. doi:10.1111/j.1540-5885.2009.00700.x

Drouin, M. A. (2011). College students' text messaging, use of textese and literacy skills. *Journal of Computer Assisted Learning*, *27*(1), 67–75. doi:10.1111/j.1365-2729.2010.00399.x

Drouin, M., & Landgraff, C. (2012). Texting, sexting, and attachment in college students' romantic relationships. *Computers in Human Behavior*, *28*(2), 444–449. doi:10.1016/j.chb.2011.10.015

Duff, P. A. (2003). Intertextuality and hybrid discourses: The infusion of pop culture in educational discourse. *Linguistics and Education*, *14*(3-4), 231–276. doi:10.1016/j.linged.2004.02.005

Duggan, M. (2013, October 28). Photos and video sharing grow online. *Pew Internet Research Project*. Retrieved from http://www.pewinternet.org/fact-sheets/social-networking-fact-sheet/

Duggan, M., & Brenner, J. (2013, February 14). The demographics of social media users - 2012. *Pew Research Center*. Retrieved from www.pewinternet.org/2013/02/14/the-demographics-of-social-media-users-2012

Duggan, M., & Smith, A. (2013a). *Cell internet use 2013*. Washington, DC: Pew Research Internet Project. Retrieved July 15, 2014 from http://www.pewinternet.org/2013/09/16/cell-internet-use-2013/

Duggan, M., & Smith, A. (2013b). *Social media update 2013*. Washington, DC: Pew Research Internet Project. Retrieved July 10, 2014 from http://www.pewinternet.org/2013/12/30/social-media-update-2013/

Duggan, M., Rainie, L., Smith, A., Funk, C., Lenhart, A., & Madden, M. (2014). *Online harassment* (p. 63). Pew Research Center.

Duke, N. K. (2004). The case for informational text. *Educational Leadership*, *61*(6), 40–45.

Duncombe, C. (2011). The Twitter revolution? Social media, representation and crisis in Iran and Libya. In *Australian Political Science Association Conference (APSA) 2011* (pp. 1–12). Australian National University, School of Politics and International Relations.

Dunkerly-Bean, J. M., Bean, T., & Alnajjar, K. (2014). Seeking asylum: Adolescents explore the crossroads of human rights education and cosmopolitan critical literacy. *Journal of Adolescent & Adult Literacy*, *58*(3), 230–241. doi:10.1002/jaal.349

Dunkerly, J., & Harper, H. (2013). The girl citizen-reader: Gender and literacy education for 21st century citizenship. In B. Guzzetti & T. W. Bean (Eds.), *Adolescent Literacies and the Gendered self: (Re)constructing identities through multimodal literacy practices*. New York: Routledge.

Dunleavy, M., & Dede, C. (2014). Augmented reality teaching and learning. In *Handbook of research on educational communications and technology* (pp. 735–745). NY: Springer. doi:10.1007/978-1-4614-3185-5_59

Dunn, H. S. (2010). Information literacy and the digital divide: Challenging e-exclusion in the Global South. In E. Ferro, Y. Dwivedi, J. Gil-Garcia, & M. Williams (Eds.), *Handbook of Research on Overcoming Digital Divides: Constructing an Equitable and Competitive Information Society* (pp. 326–344). Hershey, PA: Information Science Reference; doi:10.4018/978-1-60566-699-0.ch018

Durkin, K., Conti-Ramsden, G., & Walker, J. (2011). Txt lang: Texting, textism use and literacy abilities in adolescents with and without specific language impairment. *Journal of Computer Assisted Learning*, 27(1), 49–57. doi:10.1111/j.1365-2729.2010.00397.x

Dyson, A. (1997). *Writing superheroes: Contemporary childhood, popular culture, and classroom literacy*. New York: Teachers College Press.

Earl, J., & Schussman, A. (2008). Contesting cultural control: Youth culture and online petitioning. In W. L. Bennett (Ed.), *Civic life online: Learning how digital media can engage youth* (pp. 71–96). Cambridge, MA: MIT Press.

Edell, D., Brown, L. M., & Tolman, D. (2013). Embodying sexualisation: When theory meets practice in intergenerational feminist activism. *Feminist Theory*, 14(3), 275–284. doi:10.1177/1464700113499844

Edelman, M. (1988). *Constructing the political spectacle*. Chicago: University of Chicago Press.

Edley, P. P., & Houston, R. (2011). The more things change, the more they stay the same: The role of ICTs in work and family connections. In K. B. Wright & L. M. Webb (Eds.), *Computer-mediated communication in personal relationships* (pp. 194–221). New York: Peter Lang.

EdTech. (2013, December 24). *Mobile and education development infographic* [web log comment]. Retrieved from http://tinyw.in/obaO

EducatorsTechnology.com. (2014). *Facebook has just released a new iPad app called Paper*. Retrieved from http://www.educatorstechnology.com/2014/02/facebook-has-just-released-new-ipad-app.html

Edwards, S. (2010). "Numberjacks are on their way": A cultural historical reflection on contemporary society and the early childhood curriculum. *Pedagogy, Culture & Society*, 18(3), 261–272. doi:10.1080/14681366.2010.504649

Edwards, S. (2013). Post-industrial play: Understanding the relationship between traditional and converged forms of play in the early years. In *Children's virtual worlds: Culture, learning and participation* (pp. 10–25). New York, NY: Peter Lang Publishing.

EdX. (2014). *Schools and Partners*. Retrieved from https://www.edx.org/schools-partners

EEOC. (2014). Social media is part of today's workplace but its use may raise employment discrimination concerns. *U.S. Equal Employment Opportunity Commission*. Retrieved from http://www.eeoc.gov/eeoc/newsroom/release/3-12-14.cfm

Efland, A. (1990). *A history of art education: Intellectual and social currents in teaching the visual arts*. New York, NY: Teachers College Press.

Eisenberg, M., Eisenberg, A., & Huang, Y. (2013). Bringing e-textiles into engineering education. In L. Buechley, K. Peppler, M. Eisenberg, & Y. Kafai (Eds.), *Textile Messages: Dispatches from the World of E-Textiles and Education*.

Ekanayake, T. M. S. S. K. Y., & Wishart, J. M. (2014). Developing teachers' pedagogical practice in teaching science lessons with mobile phones. *Technology, Pedagogy and Education*, 23(2), 131–150. doi:10.1080/1475939X.2013.810366

Eklund, L. (2011). Doing gender in cyberspace: The performance of gender by female *World of Warcraft* players. *Convergence (London)*, 17(3), 323–342. doi:10.1177/1354856511406472

Ekström, A., Jülich, S., Lundgren, F., & Wisselgren, P. (Eds.). (2012). *History of participatory media: Politics and publics, 1750–2000*. Routledge.

Elden, S. (2004). *Understanding Henri Lefebvre: Theory and the possible*. London: Continuum.

Electronic Literature Organization. (2014, June 21). *Announcing winners of 1st Coover & Hayles awards!* Retrieved from http://eliterature.org/2014/06/announcing-winners-of-1st-coover-hayles-awards/

Elgan, M. (2015). Here comes the Internet of self. *Computerworld*. Retrieved January 14, 2015 from http://www.computerworld.com/article/2867234/here-comes-the-internet-of-self.html

Eliasson, G., Johansson, D., & Taymaz, E. (2004, September). Simulating the new economy. *Structural Change and Economic Dynamics*, 15(3), 289–314. doi:10.1016/j.strueco.2004.01.002

Ellison, N. B., Steinfield, C., & Lampe, C. (2007). The benefits of Facebook "friends:" Social capital and college students' use of online social network sites. *Journal of Computer-Mediated Communication*, *12*(4), 1143–1168. doi:10.1111/j.1083-6101.2007.00367.x

Elumeze, N. (2013). Traveling light: Making textiles programmable "through the air.". In L. Buechley, K. Peppler, M. Eisenberg, & Y. Kafai (Eds.), *Textile Messages: Dispatches from the World of E-Textiles and Education*.

eMarketer. (2014). *Smartphone Users Worldwide will Total 1.73 Billon*. Retrieved November 10, 2014 from http://www.emarketer.com/Article/Smartphone-Users-Worldwide-Will-Total-175-Billion-2014/1010536

Encyclopædia Britannica, Inc. (EBI). (2006). *Fatally flawed: Refuting the recent study on encyclopedic accuracy by the journal Nature*. Retrieved from http://corporate.britannica.com/britannica_nature_response.pdf

Eng, D. (2013). *Fairytale Fashion*. Retrieved from www.FairytaleFashion.org

Eng, D. (2009). *Fashion Geek: Clothes Accessories Tech*. Cincinnati, OH: North Lights Books.

Engstrom, M. E., & Jewett, D. (2005). Collaborative learning the wiki way. *TechTrends*, *49*(6), 12–15.

Enjolras, B., Steen-Johnsen, K., & Wollebæk, D. (2013). Social media and mobilization to offline demonstrations: Transcending participatory divides? *New Media & Society*, *15*(6), 890–908. doi:10.1177/1461444812462844

Ensslin, A. (2014). *Literary Gaming*. London: MIT Press.

Entertainment Software Association. (2014). *2013 Industry facts*. Retrieved from http://www.theesa.com/facts/

Entertainment Software Association. (2014). *2014 essential facts about the computer and video game industry*. Retrieved from http://www.theesa.com/category/research/

Epstein, D., Nisbet, E. C., & Gillespie, T. (2011). Who's responsible for the digital divide? Public perceptions and policy implications. *The Information Society*, *27*(2), 92–194. doi:10.1080/01972243.2011.548695

Erstad, O., Gilje, Ø., Sefton-Green, J., & Vasbø, K. (2009). Exploring 'learning lives': Community, identity, literacy and meaning. *Literacy*, *43*(2), 100–106. doi:10.1111/j.1741-4369.2009.00518.x

Erstad, O., & Silseth, K. (2008). Agency in digital storytelling: Challenging the educational context. In K. Lundby (Ed.), *Digital storytelling, mediatized stories* (pp. 213–232). New York: Peter Lang.

Erstad, O., & Wertsch, J. V. (2008). Tales of mediation: Narrative and digital media as cultural tools. In K. Lundby (Ed.), *Digital storytellin, mediatized stories* (pp. 21–40). New York: Peter Lang.

Esenlauer, V. J. (2011). Multimodality and social actions in 'personal publishing' text: From the German 'Poetry Album' to Web 2.0 'Social Network Sites. In K. L. O' Halloran & B. A. Smith (Eds.), *Multimodal studies: Exploring issues and domains* (pp. 131–152). New York: Routledge.

Essinger, J. (2007). *Jacquard's Web: How a Hand-Loom Led to the Birth of the Information Age*. New York: Oxford University Press.

Esteves, J. (2014). *Did You Know? 2014*. Retrieved from http://www.youtube.com/watch?v=XrJjfDUzD7M

Ethereal. (n.d.). In *Merriam-Webster.com*. Retrieved from http://www.merriam-webster.com/dictionary/ethereal

Etiquette Policy. (n.d.). Retrieved from http://about.deviantart.com/policy/etiquette/

Etling, B., Faris, R. M., & Palfrey, J. G. (2010). *Political Change in the Digital Age: The Fragility and Promise of Online Organizing*. Retrieved from http://dash.harvard.edu/handle/1/4609956

Etling, J. P. B., & Faris, R. (2009, June 21). Why Twitter Won't Bring Revolution to Iran. *The Washington Post*. Retrieved from http://www.washingtonpost.com/wp-dyn/content/article/2009/06/19/AR2009061901598.html

Ettlinger, N. (2008). The predicament of firms in the new and old economies: A critical inquiry into traditional binaries in the study of the space-economy. *Progress in Human Geography*, *32*(1), 45–69. doi:10.1177/0309132507083506

European Commission. (2014). *Economic stability and growth*. Retrieved from http://ec.europa.eu/economy_finance/euro/why/stability_growth/index_en.htm

Evans, J. (1978). Teaching electricity with batteries and bulbs. *The Physics Teacher, 16*(1), 15–22. doi:10.1119/1.2339794

Everhart, D. (2014). *Badges: Bridging the gap between higher ed and the workforce*. Retrieved from http://blog.blackboard.com/badges-bridging-gap-higher-ed-workforce

Facebook Statistics. (2014). *KISSmetrics*. Retrieved from blog.kissmetrics.com/facebook-statistics

Facebook, Inc. From http://www.facebook.com/press/info.php?statistics

Facebook. (2014). *Introducing paper*. Retrieved from https://www.facebook.com/paper

Facer, K. (2012). After the moral panic? Reframing the debate about child safety online. *Discourse (Berkeley, Calif.), 33*(3), 397–413. doi:10.1080/01596306.2012.681899

Fain, P. (2012). Big data's arrival. *Inside higher ed.* Retrieved from https://www.insidehighered.com/news/2012/02/01/using-big-data-predict-online-student-success

Fairlie, R. W., London, R., Rosner, R., Pastor, M., & University of California Santa Cruz. (2006). *Crossing the divide: Immigrant youth and digital disparity in California*. Santa Cruz, CA: Center for Justice, Tolerance, and Community, University of California, Santa Cruz.

Fang, I. (1997). *A history of mass communication: Six information revolutions*. Boston: Focal Press.

Farrell, D., & Barton, D. (2012). *Education to employment: Designing a system that works*. Retrieved from http://mckinseyonsociety.com/downloads/reports/Education/Education-to-Employment_FINAL.pdf

Farrington, J. W., Bebbington, A., Wellard, K., & Lewis, D. L. (1993). *Reluctant partners?:Non governmental organizations: The state and sustainable agriculture*. London: Routledge.

Fattal, L. F. (2012). What does amazing look like? Illustrator studies in pre-service teacher education. *Journal of Visual Literacy, 31*(2), 17–22.

Faye, M. (2000). *Developing national information and communication infrastructure: Policies and plans in Africa*. Paper presented at the Nigeria NICI Workshop.

Felt, L. J., Vartabedian, V., Literat, I., & Mehta, R. (2012). Explore locally, excel digitally: A participatory learning after school program for engaging citizenship on and offline. *Journal of Media Literacy Education, 4*(3), 213–228.

Feng, C., & Chen, M. (2014). The effects of goal specificity and scaffolding on programming performance and self-regulation in game design. *British Journal of Educational Technology, 45*(2), 285–302. doi:10.1111/bjet.12022

Fernandez, J. (2009). A SWOT analysis for social media in libraries. *Online, 33*(5), 35-37. Retrieved from http://search.proquest.com/docview/199913917?accountid=45950

Fernandez-Lopez, A., Rodriguez-Fortiz, M. J., Rodriguez-Almendros, M. L., & Martinez-Segura, M. J. (2013). Mobile learning technology based on iOS devices to support students with special education. *Computers & Education, 67*, 77–90. doi:10.1016/j.compedu.2012.09.014

Festl, R., & Quandt, T. (2013). Social relations and cyberbullying: The influence of individual and structural attributes on victimization and perpetration via the Internet. *Human Communication Research, 39*(1), 101–126. doi:10.1111/j.1468-2958.2012.01442.x

Fewkes, A. M., & McCabe, M. (2012). Facebook: Learning tool or distraction? *Journal of Digital Learning in Teacher Education, 28*(3), 92–98.

Fiegerman, S. (2013, August 20). Vine tops 40 million users. *Mashable*. Retrieved from http://mashable.com/2013/08/20/vine-40-million-registered-users/

Finau, G., Prasad, A., Logan, S., & Cox, J. (2014). Social Media and e-Democracy in Fiji, Solomon Islands and Vanuatu. *AMCIS 2014 Proceedings*. Retrieved from http://aisel.aisnet.org/amcis2014/SocioTechnicalIssues/GeneralPresentations/6

Fine, M. (1991). *Framing dropouts: Notes on the politics of an urban high school*. SUNY Press.

Fine, M. (2014). An intimate memoir of resistance theory. In E. Tuck & K. W. Yang (Eds.), *Youth resistance research and theories of change* (pp. 46–58). New York, NY: Routledge.

Finkelhor, D. (2014). Commentary: Cause for alarm? Youth and internet risk research—A commentary on Livingstone and Smith (2014). *Journal of Child Psychology and Psychiatry, and Allied Disciplines, 55*(6), 655–658. doi:10.1111/jcpp.12260 PMID:24840173

Finkel, S. E., & Muller, E. N. (1998). Rational choice and the dynamics of collective political action: Evaluating alternative models with panel data. *The American Political Science Review, 92*(1), 37–49. doi:10.2307/2585927

Fisch, A. (1996). *Textile Techniques in Metal.* Asheville, NC: Lark Books.

Fisher, A., & Margolis, J. (2002). Unlocking the clubhouse: The Carnegie Mellon experience. ACM SIGCSE Bulletin Women and Computing, 34(2), 79-83.

Fisherkeller, J. (2013). Young people producing media: Spontaneous and project-sponsored media creation around the world. In D. Lemish (Ed.), *The Routledge International Handbook of Children, Adolescents, and Media* (pp. 344–350). London: Routledge.

Fivush, R. (2004). The silenced self: Constructing self from memories spoken and unspoken. In D. R. Beike, J. M. Lampinen, & D. A. Behrend (Eds.), *The self and memory: Studies in self and identity* (pp. 75–93). New York: Psychology.

Flanagan, B., & Calandra, B. (2005). Podcasting in the classroom. *Learning and Leading with Technology, 20–25.*

Flatow, I. (2008, March 21). *Web privacy concerns prompt Facebook changes* [Talk show]. Retrieved from http://www.highbeam.com/doc/1P1-150730298.html

Fleckenstein, K. S. (2003). *Embodied literacies: Image-word and a poetics of teaching.* Carbondale: Southern Illinois University Press.

Flemish Ministry of Education and Training. (2010). *Aims of the cross-curricular subjects.* Retrieved from http://www.ond.vlaanderen.be/curriculum/publicaties/voet/voet2010.pdf

Fletcher, J. K. (1999). *Disappearing acts: Gender, power and relational power at work.* Cambridge, MA: MIT Press.

Flew, T. (2014). *Fast Times at Virtual U: Digital Media, Markets and the Future of Higher Education in the West Report.* Retrieved from http://184.168.109.199:8080/xmlui/bitstream/handle/123456789/2244/EJ577677.pdf?sequence=1

Flew, T. (2005). *New media: An introduction.* Oxford University Press.

Flew, T., & Humphreys, S. (2005). Games: Technology, industry, culture. In *New media: An introduction* (pp. 101–114). South Melbourne: Oxford University Press.

Flood, A. (2012). *Enhanced ebooks are bad for children finds American study.* Retrieved from http://www.theguardian.com/books/2012/jun/07/enhanced-ebooks-bad-for-children

Flood, A. (2013, Jan. 10). Digital publishing: The experts' view of what's next. *The Guardian.* Retrieved from http://www.theguardian.com/books/2014/jan/10/digital-publishing-next- industry-revolution

Florida Senate, President Office. (2013). *Senators and business leaders discuss expanding career and professional education initiatives* [press release]. Retrieved from http://www.flsenate.gov/Media/PressReleases/Show/1392

Florida, R. L. (2002). *The rise of the creative class and how it's transforming work, leisure, community and everyday life.* New York, NY: Basic books.

Florini, S. (2014). Tweets, tweeps, and signifyin': Communication and cultural performance on "Black twitter". *Television & New Media, 15*(3), 223–237. doi:10.1177/1527476413480247

Foley, L. M. (2013). Digital storytelling in primary-grade classrooms (Ph.D. Dissertation). Phoenix, AZ: Arizona State University. Retrieved from http://gradworks.umi.com/35/60/3560250.html

Foray, D., & Lundvall, B.-A. (1996). The knowledge-based economy: From the economics of knowledge to the learning economy. In Organization for Economic Co-operation and Development (Ed.), Employment and growth in the knowledge-based economy (pp. 11-32). Paris: OECD.

Forte, A., & Bruckman, A. (2007). *Constructing Text: Wiki as a toolkit for (collaborative?) learning.* Paper presented at the WikiSym'07 - Wikis at Work in the World: Open, Organic, Participatory Media for the 21st Century, Montreal, Canada. Retrieved from http://www.wikisym.org/ws2007/proceedings.html

Forzani, E., & Burlingame, C. (2012, December). *Evaluating representative state samples of seventh-grade students' ability to critically evaluate online information.* Paper presented at the annual meeting of the Literacy Research Association, San Diego, CA.

Foster, J. C. (2013). The promise of digital badges. *Techniques: Connecting Education & Careers, 88*(8), 30.

Foster, N. F., & Gibbons, S. (2005). Understanding faculty to improve content recruitment for institutional repositories. *D-Lib Magazine, 11*(1). doi:10.1045/january2005-foster

Foster, P. N. (1995a). Industrial arts/technology education as a social study: The original intent? *Journal of Technology Education, 6*(2), 4–18.

Foster, P. N. (1995b). The founders of industrial arts in the US. *Journal of Technology Education, 7*(1), 6–21.

Foucault, M. (1972). *The Archeology of knowledge and the discourse on language.* New York, NY: Pantheon.

Foucault, M. (1980). *Power/Knowledge* (C. Gordon, Trans.). New York, NY: The Harvester Press.

Fowler, A., & Cusack, B. (2011). Kodu game lab: improving the motivation for learning programming concepts. In *Proceedings of the 6th International Conference on Foundations of Digital Games* (pp. 238–240). New York: ACM. doi:10.1145/2159365.2159398

Fox, S., & Rainie, L. (2014). The web at 25 in the U.S. Washington, DC: Pew Internet and American Life Project. Retrieved from http://www.pewinternet.org/2014/02/27/the-web-at-25-in-the-u-s/

Fox, S., & Rainie, L. (2014). *The web at 25 in the U.S.* Washington, DC: Pew Research Internet Project. Retrieved July 20, 2014 from http://www.pewinternet.org/2014/02/27/the-web-at-25-in-the-u-s/

Frauenfelder, M. (2010). *Made by Hand: Searching for Meaning in a Throwaway World.* Portfolio Hardcover.

Frazel, M. (2010). *Digital storytelling guide for educators.* Washington, DC: International Society for Technology in Education.

Fredette, N., & Lochhead, J. (1980). Students' conceptions of simple circuits. *The Physics Teacher, 18*(3), 194–198. doi:10.1119/1.2340470

Freeberg, A. (2014, February 6). *Virtual field trips take students into the labs* [web log comment]. Retrieved from http://tinyurl.com/mbya9vo

Freidus, N., & Hlubinka, M. (2002). Digital storytelling for reflective practice in communities of learners. *Association for Computing Machinery SIGGROUP Bulletin, 23*(2), 24–26. doi:10.1145/962185.962195

Freire, P. (1970). *Pedagogy of the oppressed.* New York: Continuum.

Frey, C. B., & Osborne, M. A. (2013). *The future of employment: How susceptible are jobs to computerization?* Retrieved from http://www.futuretech.ox.ac.uk/sites/futuretech.ox.ac.uk/files/The_Future_of_Employment_OMS_Working_Paper_1.pdf

Friedman, M., & Calixte, S. (Eds.). (2009). *Mothering and blogging: The radical act of the mommyblog.* Toronto, Canada: Demeter Press.

Fristoe, T., Denner, J., MacLaurin, M., Mateas, M., & Wardrip-Fruin, N. (2011). Say it with systems: Expanding Kodu's expressive power through gender-inclusive mechanics. In *Proceedings from The 6th International Conference on Foundations of Digital Games* (pp. 227–234). New York, NY: ACM. doi:10.1145/2159365.2159396

Fuchs, C., & Horak, E. (2006). Informational capitalism and the digital divide in Africa. *Masaryk University Journal of Law and Technology,* 11-32. Retrieved from https://mujlt.law.muni.cz/storage/1205244869_sb_s02-fuchs.pdf

Fuchs, C., Hofkirchner, W., Schafranek, M., Raffl, C., Sandoval, M., & Bichler, R. (2010). Theoretical foundations of the web: Cognition, communication, and co-operation. Towards an understanding of Web 1.0, 2.0, 3.0. *Future Internet, 2*(1), 1–59. doi:10.3390/fi2010041

Fu, H., Chu, S., & Kang, W. (2013). Affordances and Constraints of a Wiki for Primary-school Students' Group Projects. *Journal of Educational Technology & Society, 16*(4), 85–96.

Fukuda-Parr, S. (2003). The Human development paradigm: Operationalizing Sen's ideas on capabilities. *Feminist Economics*, *9*(2), 301–317. doi:10.1080/1354570022000077980

Fullick, M. (2013). "Gendering" the self in online dating discourse. *Canadian Journal of Communication*, *38*, 545–562.

Gabriel, M. A., Campbell, B., Wiebe, S., MacDonald, R., & McAuley, A. (2012). The role of digital technologies in learning: Expectations of first year university students. *Canadian Journal of Learning & Technology, 38*(1), 1–18.

Gådin, K. G. (2011). Peer sexual harassment in schools: Normalization of gender practices in a neoliberal time. In S. Fahlgren, A. Johansson, & D. Mulinari (Eds.), *Normalization and "outsiderhood": Feminist readings of a neoliberal welfare state* (pp. 58–67). Bentham Science Publishers. doi:10.2174/978160805279011101010058

Gadrey, J. (2003). *New economy, new myth*. London: Routledge.

Galey, P. (2011, March 16). Grasp of social media not enough to instigate change in Lebanon. *The Daily Star, Lebanon News*. Retrieved from http://www.dailystar.com.lb/News/Lebanon-News/2011/Mar-16/134603-grasp-of-social-media-not-enough-to-instigate-change-in-lebanon.ashx#axzz3EVTBDyid

Gallagher, B. (2014). 10 sexist memes we should probably stop using. *Complex*. Retrieved from http://www.complex.com/pop-culture/2014/02/sexist-memes-we-should-probably-stop-using/

Gallagher, K. (2004). Bullying and its compatriots: Racism, sexism, and homophobia. *Orbit (Amsterdam, Netherlands), 34*, 28–31.

Galperin, H., & Rojas, F. (2011). Broadband policies in Latin America and the Caribbean. In V. Jordán, H. Galperin, & W. Peres (Eds.), Fast-tracking the digital revolution: Broadband for Latin America and the Caribbean. Santiago, Chile: United Nations. Retrieved from http://repositorio.cepal.org/bitstream/handle/11362/35351/S2011329_en.pdf?sequence=1

Games, A. (2013, March). *Understanding the evolution of adolescents' computational thinking skills within the Globaloria educational game design environment*. Retrieved from Globaloria_ComputationalThinkingSkills_Games_Mar2013.pdf

Games, I. A. (2009). *21st century language and literacy in Gamestar Mechanic: Middle school students' appropriation through play of the discourse of computer game designers* (Doctoral dissertation). Retrieved from ProQuest Dissertations and Theses. (3384100)

Games, A. (2010). Bug or feature: The role of Gamestar Mechanic's material dialog on the metacognitive game design strategies of players. *E-Learning and Digital Media*, *7*(1), 49–66. doi:10.2304/elea.2010.7.1.49

Games, I. A. (2010). Gamestar mechanic: Learning a designer mindset through communicational competence with the language of games. *Learning, Media and Technology, 35*(1), 31–52. doi:10.1080/17439880903567774

Gannes, L. (2006, October 26). Jawed Karim: How YouTube took off. *Gigaom*. Retrieved from https://gigaom.com/2006/10/26/jawed-karim-how-youtube-took-off/

Gao, F., Luo, T., & Zhang, K. (2012). Tweeting for learning: A critical analysis of research on microblogging in education published in 2008 –2011. *British Journal of Educational Technology, 43*(5), 783–801. doi:10.1111/j.1467-8535.2012.01357.x

García-Gómez, A. (2009). Teenage girls' personal weblog writing: Truly a new gender discourse? *Information Communication and Society*, *12*(5), 611–638. doi:10.1080/13691180802266657

García-Gómez, A. (2011). Regulating girlhood: Evaluative language, discourses of gender socialization and relational aggression. *European Journal of Women's Studies, 18*(3), 243–264. doi:10.1177/1350506811405817

Garcia, O. P. (2011). Gender digital divide: The role of mobile phones among Latina farm workers in southeast Ohio. *Gender, Technology and Development, 15*(1), 53–74. doi:10.1177/097185241101500103

Gardner, H. (n.d.). *Changing minds: The art and science of changing our own and other people's minds*. Boston: Harvard Business School Press.

Gardner, H. (1985). *Frames of mind: The theory of multiple intelligences*. New York, NY: Basic Books.

Gargiulo, R., & Metcalf, D. (2012). *Teaching in today's inclusive classrooms: A universal design for learning approach*. Cengage Learning.

Garley, M., Stewart, R. H., Gowran, G., Tempest, J., Pickering, W., & Simmonds, M. (2012). *Collider Comics* [Mobile application software]. Retrieved from itunes.apple.com

Gartner. (2012). *Gartner says big data creates big jobs: 4.4 million IT jobs globally to support big data by 2015*. Retrieved from http://www.gartner.com/newsroom/id/2207915

Gary Nauer. (2014, August 7). *Hashtag campaign didn't "bring back our girls"*. Retrieved January 24, 2015, from http://www.indystar.com/story/opinion/2014/08/07/hashtag-campaign-bring-back-girls/13717045/

Gee, J. (2005). Learning by Design: Good videogames as learning machines. *E-learning*, *2*(1), 5–16. doi:10.2304/elea.2005.2.1.5

Gee, J. P. (1990). *Social linguistics and and literacies: Ideology in discourses*. London: Falmer.

Gee, J. P. (1999). Discourses and social languages. In *An introduction to discourse analysis: Theory and method* (pp. 11–39). New York: Routledge.

Gee, J. P. (2000). Teenagers in new times: A new literacy studies perspective. *Journal of Adolescent & Adult Literacy*, *43*(5), 412–420.

Gee, J. P. (2000–2001). Identity as an analytic lens for research in education. *Review of Research in Education*, *25*, 99–125.

Gee, J. P. (2007). *What video games have to teach us about literacy and learning* (2nd ed.). New York: Palgrave Macmillan.

Gee, J. P. (2010). A situated sociocultural approach to literacy and technology. In E. A. Baker (Ed.), *The new literacies: Multiple perspectives on research and practice* (pp. 165–193). New York: Guilford Press.

Gee, J. P., & Hayes, E. (2012). Passionate affinity groups. In C. Steinkuehler, K. Squire, & S. Barab (Eds.), *Games, learning, and society: Learning and meaning in the digital age* (pp. 129–153). London: Cambridge University Press. doi:10.1017/CBO9781139031127.015

Gee, J. P., & Hayes, E. R. (2009). "No quitting without saving after bad events": Gaming paradigms and learning in *The Sims*. *International Journal of Learning and Media*, *1*(3), 1–17. doi:10.1162/ijlm_a_00024

Gee, J. P., Hull, G., & Lankshear, C. (1996). *The new work order: Behind the language of the new capitalism*. Boulder, CO: Westview.

Gee, J., & Hayes, E. (2010). *Women as gamers: The Sims and 21st century learning*. New York: Palgrave Macmillan.

Gee, J., & Hayes, E. (2011). *Language and learning in the digital age*. Abingdon: Routledge.

Geist, M. (2014). Telecoms offer to build surveillance tools into networks. *The Tyee*. Retrieved from http://thetyee.ca/Mediacheck/2014/12/17/Surveillance-Tools-in-Networks/

Gere, C., & Rudoe, J. (2010). *Jewelry in the Age of Queen Victoria: A Mirror to the World*. London: British Museum Press.

Gerjets, P., Scheiter, K., & Schuh, J. (2008). Information comparisons in example-based hypermedia environments: Supporting learners with processing prompts and an interactive comparison tool. *Educational Technology Research and Development*, *56*(1), 73–92. doi:10.1007/s11423-007-9068-z

Geurtz, R., & Foote, C. (2014). Librarian technology leadership in the adoption of iPads in a high school. In C. Miller & A. Doering (Eds.), *The new landscape of mobile learning* (pp. 276–291). New York: Routledge.

Gewertz, C. (2012). Districts Gear up for Shift to Informational Texts. *Education Digest: Essential Readings Condensed for Quick Review*, *78*(1), 10–14.

Geyer-Schulz, A., Neumann, A., Heitmann, A., & Stroborn, K. (2004). *Strategic positioning options for scientific libraries in markets of scientific and technical information: The economic impact of digitization*. Retrieved from https://journals.tdl.org/jodi/index.php/jodi/article/view/101/100

Ghonim, W. (2012). *Revolution 2.0: The power of the people is greater than the people in power: A memoir.* New York: Houghton Mifflin Harcourt.

Gibbs, J., Ellison, N., & Heino, R. (2006). Self-presentation in online personals: The role of anticipated future interaction, self-disclosure, and perceived success in Internet dating. *Communication Research, 33*(2), 152–177. doi:10.1177/0093650205285368

Gibson, M., & Owens, K. (2009). The importance of critically examining what it now means to be visually literate. In *Conference Proceedings from Power 2 Empowerment: Critical Literacy in Visual Culture.* Dallas, TX: Academic Press.

Gibson, J. (1979/1986). *The ecological approach to visual perception.* Hillsdale, NJ: Lawrence Erlbaum Associates.

Gibson, R. K. (2013). Party Change, Social Media and the Rise of "Citizen-initiated" Campaigning. *Party Politics.* doi:10.1177/1354068812472575

Giddings, S. (2009). Events and collusions: A glossary for the microethnography of video game play. *Games and Culture, 4*(2), 144–157. doi:10.1177/1555412008325485

Gikas, J., & Grant, M. M. (2013). Mobile computing devices in higher education: Student perspectives on learning with cellphones, smartphones & social media. *The Internet and Higher Education, 19*, 18–26. doi:10.1016/j.iheduc.2013.06.002

Giles, J. (2005). *Special report: Internet encyclopaedias go head to head.* Retrieved from http://www.nature.com/nature/journal/v438/n7070/full/438900a.html

Gillen, J. (2009). Literacy practices in Schome Park: A virtual literacy ethnography. *Journal of Research in Reading, 32*(1), 57–74. doi:10.1111/j.1467-9817.2008.01381.x

Gillen, J., & Merchant, G. (2013). From virtual histories to virtual literacies. In G. Merchant, J. Gillen, J. Marsh, & J. Davies (Eds.), *Virtual Literacies: interactive spaces for children and young people* (pp. 9–27). Abingdon: Routledge.

Gillmor, D. (2006). *We the media: Grassroots journalism by the people, for the people.* O'Reilly Media, Inc.

Ginwright, S. (2010). Peace out to revolution! Activism among African American youth: An argument for radical healing. *Young, 18*(1), 77–96. doi:10.1177/110330880901800106

Ginwright, S., & Cammarota, J. (2002). New terrain in youth development: The promise of a social justice approach. *Social Justice Journal, 29*(4), 82–95.

Ginwright, S., & Cammarota, J. (2007). Youth activism in the urban community: Learning critical civic praxis within community organizations. *International Journal of Qualitative Studies in Education, 20*(6), 693–710. doi:10.1080/09518390701630833

Ginwright, S., Noguera, P., & Cammarota, J. (2006). *Beyond resistance! Youth activism and community change.* New York, NY: Routledge.

Giroux, H. A. (2009). The Iranian uprisings and the challenge of the new media: Rethinking the politics of representation. *Fast Capitalism, 5*(2).

Giroux, H. (2001). *The Mouse That Roared: Disney and the End of Innocence.* New York: Rowman & Littlefield.

Giroux, H. (2003). *The abandoned generation: Democracy beyond the culture of fear.* Palgrave Macmillan.

Gladwell, M. (2010, September 27). *Small Change.* Retrieved September 26, 2014, from http://www.newyorker.com/magazine/2010/10/04/small-change-3

Glaser, M. (2006, September 27). Your guide to citizen journalism. *Mediashift.* Retrieved from http://www.pbs.org/mediashift/2006/09/your-guide-to-citizen-journalism270/

Glaser, R. (1976). Components of a psychology of instruction: Toward a science of design. *Review of Educational Research, 46*(1), 29–39. doi:10.3102/00346543046001001

Glazier, L. P. (2002). *Digital poetics: the making of e-poetries.* Tuscaloosa, AL: University of Alabama Press.

Gleeson, M. (2012). *iPads (or other devices) and literature circles – co-starring Edmodo.* Mr. G Online. Retrieved April 7, 2012 from http://mgleeson.edublogs.org/2012/04/03/ipads-and-literature-circles

Goffman, E. (1959). *The presentation of self in everyday life.* New York: Doubleday.

Goldhaber, M. H. (1997). The attention economy and the net. *First Monday*, 2(4). doi:10.5210/fm.v2i4.519

Gold, M. K. (Ed.). (2012). *Debates in the digital humanities*. Minneapolis: U of Minnesota Press.

Goldman, R., Pea, R., Barron, B., & Derry, S. J. (Eds.). (2014). *Video research in the learning sciences*. NY: Routledge.

Goldstein, T. (2010). Snakes and ladders: A performed ethnography. *International Journal of Critical Pedagogy*, 3(1), 68–113.

Goldweber, M., Davoli, R., Little, J. C., Riedesel, C., Walker, H., Cross, G., & Von Konsky, B. R. (2011). Enhancing the social issues components in our computing curriculum: Computing for the social good. *ACM Inroads*, 2(1), 64–82. doi:10.1145/1929887.1929907

Golumbia, D. (2014). Characteristics of digital media. In M. L. Ryan, L. Emerson, & B. J. Robertson (Eds.), *The John Hopkins guide to digital media*. Baltimore, MD: John Hopkins University Press.

Gomes, L. F. (2011). Digital literacy and sustainability: The *vozes que ecoam* project. In M. L. Soares & L. Petarnella (Eds.), *Schooling for sustainable development in South America: Policies, actions and educational experiences* (pp. 205–217). Dordrecht, Netherlands: Springer. doi:10.1007/978-94-007-1754-1_13

Gomez, A. G. (2010). Disembodiment and cyberspace: Gendered discourses in female teenagers' personal information disclosure. *Discourse & Society*, 21(2), 135–160. doi:10.1177/0957926509353844

Gonzalez-Mena, J. (2005). *Foundations of early childhood education: Teaching children in a diverse society*. Boston, MA: McGraw-Hill.

González, N., Moll, L. C., & Amanti, C. (2005). *Funds of knowledge: Theorizing practice in households, communities, and classrooms*. Mahwah, NJ: L. Erlbaum Associates.

Goode, J. (2010). The digital identity divide: How technology knowledge impacts college students. *New Media & Society*, 12(3), 497–513. doi:10.1177/1461444809343560

Google. (2013). *Celebrating Google Play's first birthday*. Retrieved from http://googleblog.blogspot.com/2013/03/celebrating-google-plays-first-birthday.html

Gordon, R. J. (2000, August). *NBER Working Paper Series: Does the "New Economy" measure up to the great inventions of the past?* Retrieved from http://www.nber.org/papers/w7833.pdf

Gordon, H. R. (2008). Gendered paths to teenage political participation: Parental power, civic mobility, and youth activism. *Gender & Society*, 22(1), 31–55. doi:10.1177/0891243207311046

Gosney, J. W. (2005). *Beyond reality: A guide to alternate reality gaming*. Boston, MA: Course Technology Press.

Gould, J. E. (2012, September 13). *Actor Tim Dax on Sam Bacile and "Innocence of Muslims"*. Retrieved from http://nation.time.com/2012/09/13/the-making-of-innocence-of-muslims-one-actors-story/

Graber, D. A., & Dunaway, J. L. (2014). *Mass Media and American Politics*. Los Angeles : Washington, DC: CQ Press.

Grace, A., Kemp, N., Martin, F. H., & Parrila, R. (2013). Undergraduate's attitudes to text messaging language use and intrusions of textisms into formal writing. *New Media & Society*. doi:10.1177/1461444813516832

Grace, T. P. L. (2009). Wikis as a knowledge management tool. *Journal of Knowledge Management*, 13(4), 64–74. doi:10.1108/13673270910971833

Graff, H. J. (1979). *The literacy myth: Literacy and social structure in the nineteenth century city*. New York, NY: Academic Press.

Graff, H. J. (2011). *Literacy myths, legacies, & lessons: New studies on literacy*. New Brunswick, NJ: Transaction Publishers.

Graham, L., & Metaxas, P. T. (2003). Of course it's true: I saw it on the Internet! *Communications of the ACM*, 46(5), 71–75. doi:10.1145/769800.769804

Granovetter, M. S. (1973). The strength of weak ties. *American Journal of Sociology*, 78(6), 1360–1380. doi:10.1086/225469

Grant, L. (2009). 'I dont care do ur own page!' A case study of using wikis for collaborative work in a UK secondary school. *Learning, Media and Technology*, 34(2), 105–117. doi:10.1080/17439880902923564

Grant, M. (2013). *BZRK*. New York: Egmont.

Gray, M. (2012, March 26). Social Media: The Muscle Behind the Trayvon Martin Movement. *Time*. Retrieved from http://newsfeed.time.com/2012/03/26/social-media-the-muscle-behind-the-trayvon-martin-movement/

Gray, P. (1999). *Johann Gutenberg (c. 1395-1468)*. Retrieved August 16 from http://content.time.com/time/magazine/article/0,9171,36527,00.html

Gray, K. L. (2012). Intersecting oppressions and online communities. *Information. Technology & Society, 15*, 411–428.

Greeley, B. (2011, February 2). The Fallacy of Facebook Diplomacy. *BusinessWeek: Magazine*. Retrieved from http://www.businessweek.com/magazine/content/11_07/b4215008414536.htm

Greenhow, C. (2008). Commentary: Connecting formal and informal learning in the age of participatory media: A response to Bull et al. *Contemporary Issues in Technology & Teacher Education, 8*(3). Retrieved from http://www.citejournal.org/vol8/iss3/editorial/article1.cfm

Greenhow, C., Robelia, B., & Hughes, J. E. (2009). Learning, Teaching, and Scholarship in a Digital Age: Web 2.0 and Classroom Research: What Path Should We Take Now? *Educational Researcher, 38*(4), 246–259. doi:10.3102/0013189X09336671

Green, J., & Levithan, D. (2010). *Will Grayson, Will Grayson*. New York: Dutton.

Green, L. S., Hechter, R. P., Tysinger, P. D., & Chassereau, K. D. (2014). Mobile app selection for 5th through 12th grade science: The development of the MASS rubric. *Computers & Education, 75*, 65–71. doi:10.1016/j.compedu.2014.02.007

Greenwald, G. (2014). Should Twitter, Facebook, and Google executives be the arbiters of what we see and read? *The Intercept*. Retrieved from https://firstlook.org/theintercept/2014/08/21/twitter-facebook-executives-arbiters-see-read/

Gregory, S. (2010). Cameras everywhere: Ubiquitous video documentation of human rights, new forms of video advocacy, and considerations of safety, security, dignity and consent. *Journal of Human Rights Practice, 2*(2), 191–207. doi:10.1093/jhuman/huq002

Grewal, I., & Kaplan, C. (2001). Global identities: Theorizing transnational studies of sexuality. *GLQ Archive, 4*(4), 663–679. doi:10.1215/10642684-7-4-663

Griffin, A. (2010). *The Julian game*. New York: Putnam.

Griffiths, M., Davies, M., & Chappell, D. (2003). Breaking the stereotype: The case of online gaming. *Cyberpsychology & Behavior, 6*(1), 81–91. doi:10.1089/109493103321167992 PMID:12650566

Grimes, S. M., & Shade, L. R. (2005). Neopian economics of play: Children's cyberpets and online communities as immersive advertising in NeoPets.com. *International Journal of Media & Cultural Politics, 1*(2), 181–198. doi:10.1386/macp.1.2.181/1

Grimshaw, D. J., & Gudza, L. D. (2010). Local voices enhance knowledge uptake: Sharing local content in local voices. *Electronic Journal of Information Systems in Developing Countries, 40*, 1–12.

Grinter, R., & Eldridge, M. (2003). Wan2tlk?: everyday text messaging. In *Proceedings of the Conference on Human Factors in Computing Systems CHI 03* (pp. 441–448). ACM. doi:10.1145/642611.642688

Groenke, S. L., & Maples, J. (2010). Young adult literature goes digital: Will teen reading ever be the same? *ALAN Review, 37*(3), 38–44.

Grove, J. V. (2010, March 19). *Social Networking Usage Surges Globally [STATS]*. Retrieved September 27, 2014, from http://mashable.com/2010/03/19/global-social-media-usage/

Grover, S., & Pea, R. (2013). Computational Thinking in K–12 A Review of the State of the Field. *Educational Researcher, 42*(1), 38–43. doi:10.3102/0013189X12463051

Gruber, H., & Koutroumpis, P. (2011). Mobile telecommunications and the impact on economic development. *Economic Policy, 26*(67), 387–426. http://onlinelibrary.wiley.com/doi/10.1111/j.1468-0327.2011.00266.x/abstract doi:10.1111/j.1468-0327.2011.00266.x

Grudin, J., & Poole, E. (2010). Wikis at work: Success factors and challenges of enterprise wikis. In ACM (Ed.), *WikiSym '10: Proceedings of the 6th international symposium on Wikis and open collaboration* (pp. Article 5). Gdansk, Poland: ACM. Retrieved from http://dl.acm.org/citation.cfm?id=1832780

Grunfeld, H. (2011). *The contribution of information and communication technologies for development (ICT4D) projects to capabilities, empowerment and sustainability: a case study of iREACH in Cambodia* (Doctoral dissertation, Victoria University, Melbourne, Australia). Retrieved from http://vuir.vu.edu.au/19359/

Gubrium, A. (2009). Digital storytelling: An emergent method for health promotion research and practice. *Health Promotion Practice*, *10*(2), 186–191. doi:10.1177/1524839909332600 PMID:19372280

Gubrium, A., Krause, E., & Jernigan, K. (2014). Strategic authenticity and voice: New ways of seeing and being seen as young mothers through digital storytelling. *Sexuality Research & Social Policy*, *11*(4), 337–347. doi:10.1007/s13178-014-0161-x PMID:25506294

Gubrium, A., & Otañez, M. (2013). Digital storytelling. In A. Gubrium & K. Harper (Eds.), *Participatory visual and digital methods* (pp. 125–150). Walnut Creek, CA: Left Coast Press.

Guerrieri, P., & Bentivegna, S. (2011). *The economic impact of digital technologies: Measuring inclusion and diffusion in Europe* (E. Elgar, Ed.). Cheltenham, UK: Edward Elgar Publishing. doi:10.4337/9780857935236

Guillen, M. F., & Suarez, S. L. (2005). Explaining the global digital divide: Economic, political and sociological drivers of cross-national Internet use. *Social Forces*, *84*(2), 681–708. doi:10.1353/sof.2006.0015

Gulati, G. J., & Williams, C. B. (2013). Social Media and Campaign 2012 Developments and Trends for Facebook Adoption. *Social Science Computer Review*, *31*(5), 577–588. doi:10.1177/0894439313489258

Gutierrez, K. (2008). Developing a sociocritical literacy in the Third Space. *Reading Research Quarterly*, *43*(2), 148–164. doi:10.1598/RRQ.43.2.3

Gu, X., Zhu, Y., & Guo, X. (2013). Meeting the "digital natives": Understanding the acceptance of technology in classrooms. *Journal of Educational Technology & Society*, *16*(1), 392–402.

Guzzetti, B. E., & Welsch. (2010). DIY media in the classroom: New literacies across content areas. New York, NY: Teachers College Press.

Guzzetti, B. J. (2010). Feminist perspectives on the new literacies. In E. A. Baker (Ed.), *The new literacies: Multiple perspectives on research and practice* (pp. 242–264). New York: Guilford Press.

Guzzetti, B. J., & Gamboa, M. (2004). Zines for social justice: Adolescent girls writing on their own. *Reading Research Quarterly*, *39*(4), 408–435. doi:10.1598/RRQ.39.4.4

Haarsma, P. J. (2008). *The softwire: Virus on Orbis*. Somerville, MA: Candlewick Press.

Haas, C., Takayoshi, P., Carr, B., Hudson, K., & Pollock, R. (2011). Young People's Everyday Literacies: The Language Features of Instant Messaging. Research In The Teaching Of English. *Research in the Teaching of English*, *45*(4), 378–404.

Habermas, J. (1975). *Legitimation crisis*. London, England: Beacon Press.

Hackett, R. (2014). Showdown at the B.Y.O.D. corral. *Fortune*. Retrieved from http://fortune.com/2014/07/24/bring-your-own-device-byod-enterprise-showdown/

Hadjerrouit, S. (2013). A framework for assessing the pedagogical effectiveness of wiki-based collaborative writing: Results and implications. *Interdisciplinary Journal of E-Learning and Learning Objects*, *9*, 29–49.

Haferkamp, N., & Krämer, N. (2008, May). *Entering the blogosphere: Motives for reading, writing, and commenting*. Paper presented at the Meeting of the International Communication Association, Montreal, Canada.

Hagood, M. C. (2009). *New literacies practices: Designing literacy learning*. New York: Peter Lang.

Hahn, J. (2010). Information seeking with Wikipedia on the iPod Touch. *RSR. Reference Services Review*, *38*(2), 284–298. doi:10.1108/00907321011045043

Halliday, J. (2011, August 11). David Cameron considers banning suspected rioters from social media. *The Guardian*. Retrieved from http://www.theguardian.com/media/2011/aug/11/david-cameron-rioters-social-media

Halliday, M. A. K. (1977). *Learning how to mean: Explorations in the development of language*. New York: Elsevier.

Hall, R. (2013). Educational technology and the enclosure of academic labour inside public higher education. *Journal for Critical Education Policy Studies*, *11*(3), 52–82. Retrieved from http://www.jceps.com/wp-content/uploads/PDFs/11-3-03.pdf

Hall, R., Atkins, L., & Fraser, J. (2014). Defining a self-evaluation digital literacy framework for secondary educators: The DigiLit Leicester project. *The Journal of the Association for Learning Technology*, *22*(21440). Retrieved from https://www.dora.dmu.ac.uk/handle/2086/9892

Hall, S. (1973). *Encoding and decoding in the television discourse*. Birmingham, UK: Centre for Contemporary Cultural Studies.

Halse, C., Denson, N., Howard, S., & Zammit, K. (2010). *Evaluation of The Centre for Learning and Innovation Avaya immersive environment project*. Sydney: University of Western Sydney.

Hamari, J., Koivisto, J., & Sarsa, H. (2014). Does Gamification Work? – A Literature Review of Empirical Studies on Gamification. *Proceedings of the 47th Hawaii International Conference on System Sciences*. doi:10.1109/HICSS.2014.377

Hamdoun, A., Mangeni, S., & Dwivedi, Y. K. (2013). Insights into sustainable energy-capacity trends towards bridging the digital divide a perspective of the need for green broadband communications in Sub Saharan Africa. In *Proceedings of International Conference on Computing, Electrical and Electronics Engineering (ICCEEE)* (pp. 459-463). ICCEEE. doi:10.1109/ICCEEE.2013.6633982

Hamel, J. Y. (2010). *ICT4D and the human development and capabilities approach: The potentials of information and communication technology*. Human development research paper 2010/37, UNDP. Retrieved from http://hdr.undp.org/sites/default/files/hdrp_2010_37.pdf

Hamilton, P. F. (2012). *Great north road*. New York: Del Rey.

Hammond, L. (2010). Mommyblogging is a radical act. In J. F. Stitt & P. R. Powell (Eds.), *Mothers who deliver: Feminist interventions in public and interpersonal discourse* (pp. 77–98). Albany, NY: State University of New York Press.

Hampton, K., Rainie, L., Lu, W., Dwyer, M., Shin, I., & Purcell, K. (2014). Social Media and the 'Spiral of Silence'. *Pew Internet Research Project*. Retrieved from http://www.pewinternet.org/files/2014/08/PI_Social-networks-and-debate_082614.pdf

Hancock, J. T., & Toma, C. L. (2009). Putting your best face forward: The accuracy of online dating photographs. *Journal of Communication*, *59*(2), 367–386. doi:10.1111/j.1460-2466.2009.01420.x

Han, J., Choi, D., Chun, B., Kwon, T., Kim, H., & Choi, Y. (2014). Collecting, organizing, and sharing pins in Pinterest: Interest-driven or social-driven? *Performance Evaluation Review*, *42*(1), 15–27. doi:10.1145/2637364.2591996

Hansen, D. T. (2008). Curriculum and the idea of cosmopolitan inheritance. *Journal of Curriculum Studies*, *40*(3), 289–312. doi:10.1080/00220270802036643

Hansen, D. T. (2014). Theme issue: Cosmopolitanism as cultural creativity: New modes of educational practice in globalizing times. *Curriculum Inquiry*, *44*(1), 1–14. doi:10.1111/curi.12039

Hansen, M. B. (2012). *Bodies in code: Interfaces with digital media*. NY: Routledge.

Hans, M. L., Lee, B. D., Tinker, K. A., & Webb, L. M. (2011). Online performances of gender: Blogs, gender-bending, and cybersex as relational exemplars. In K. B. Wright & L. M. Webb (Eds.), *Computer mediated communication in personal relationships* (pp. 302–323). New York: Peter Lang Publishers.

Hardy, P., & Sumner, T. (2014). Our stories, ourselves: Exploring identities, sharing experiences and building relationships through patient voices. In H. M. Pleasants & D. E. Salter (Eds.), *Community-based multiliteracies and digital media probjects: Questioning assumptions and exploring realities* (pp. 65–86). New York: Peter Lang.

Harel, I., & Papert, S. (Eds.). (1991). *Constructionism*. New York, NY: Ablex Publishing.

Hargittai, E. (2008). Whose space? Differences among users and non-users of social network sites. *Journal of Computer-Mediated Communication*, *13*(1), 276–297. doi:10.1111/j.1083-6101.2007.00396.x

Hargittai, E. (2012). Open doors, closed spaces? Differentiated adoption of social network sites by user background. In L. Nakamura & P. Chow-White (Eds.), *Race After the Internet* (pp. 223–245). New York: Routledge.

Harlan, M. A. (2014). Standing on a corner. *Teacher Librarian, 42*(1), 38–42. Retrieved from http://search.proquest.com/docview/1610735348?accountid=45950

Harper, H., Bean, T. W., & Dunkerly, J. (2010). Cosmopolitanism, globalization, and the field of adolescent literacy. *Canadian and International Education. Education Canadienne et Internationale, 39*(3), 1–13.

Harper, H., & Dunkerly, J. (2010). Educating the world: Teachers and their work as defined by the United Nations Educational, Scientific and Cultural Organization (UNESCO). *Current Issues in Comparative Education, 4*, 56–65.

Harris, R. W., & United Nations Development Programme. (2004). *Information and communication technologies for poverty alleviation*. Kuala Lumpur: United Nations Development Programme's Asia-Pacific Development Information Programme. Retrieved from http://en.wikibooks.org/wiki/Information_and_Communication_Technologies_for_Poverty_Alleviation

Harris, J. (Ed.). (1993). *Textiles, 5,000 Years: An International History and Illustrated Survey*. New York: H.N. Abrams.

Harris, K. (2008). Using social networking sites as student engagement tools. *Diverse Issues in Higher Education, 25*(18), 4.

Harrison, K. (2014). Online negotiations of infertility: Knowledge production in (in) fertility[Blog post]. *Convergence (London), 20*(3), 337–351. doi:10.1177/1354856514531400

Hart Research Associates. (2013). *It takes more than a major: Employer priorities for college learning and student success*. Retrieved from http://www.aacu.org/leap/documents/2013_EmployerSurvey.pdf

Hartley, J. (2008). *Television truths: Forms of knowledge in popular culture*. Middlesex, MA: Blackwell Publishing. doi:10.1002/9780470694183

Hartman, D. K., Morsink, P. M., & Zheng, J. (2010). From print to pixels: The evolution of cognitive conceptions of reading comprehension. In E. A. Baker (Ed.), *The new literacies: Multiple perspectives on research and practice* (pp. 131–164). New York: Guilford Press.

Hartmann, S., Wiesner, H., & Wiesner-Steiner, A. (2007). Robotics and gender: The use of robotics for the advancement of equal opportunities in the classroom. In Gender Designs IT Construction and Deconstruction of Information Society (pp. 175-188). Academic Press.

Hartnell-Young, E., & Vetere, F. (2008). A means of personalizing learning: Incorporating old and new literacies in the curriculum with mobile phones. *Curriculum Journal, 19*(4), 283–292. doi:10.1080/09585170802509872

Harven, M. (2014). Digital badges gain traction in higher education. *EdTech Times*. Retrieved from http://edtechtimes.com/2014/03/28/digital-badges-gain-traction-higher-education/

Harwood, D. (2015). Crayons & iPads: Children's meaning making in the digital world. *An Leanbh Óg (The Young Child) Journal, 9*(1), 107-120.

Hassan, R. (2013). New Media and Political Revival: The Middle East Story. *Journal of Mass Communication & Journalism, 03*(03). doi:10.4172/2165-7912.1000e135

Hatch, J. A. (2002). *Doing qualitative research in education settings*. Albany, NY: State University of New York Press.

Hattwig, D., Burgess, J., Bussert, K., & Medaille, A. (2011). *ACRL Visual Literacy Competency Standards for Higher Education*. Retrieved from http://www.ala.org/acrl/standards/visualliteracy

Havard, A. (2011). *The survivors*. Nashville, TN: Chafie Press.

Haydon, T., Hawkins, R., Denune, H., Kimener, L., McCoy, D., & Basham, J. (2012). A comparison of iPads and worksheets on math skills of high school students with emotional disturbance. *Behavioral Disorders, 37*(4), 232–243.

Hayes, E. (2013). A new look at girls, gaming, and literacies. In B. Guzzetti & T. Bean (Eds.), *Adolescent Literacies and the Gendered Self: (re)constructing identities through multimodal literacy practices* (pp. 101–108). Abingdon: Routledge.

Hayes, E. R. (2008). Game content creation and IT proficiency: An exploratory study. *Computers & Education*, *5*(1), 97–108. doi:10.1016/j.compedu.2007.04.002

Hayes, E. R., & Games, I. A. (2008). Making computer games and design thinking: A review of current software and strategies. *Games and Culture*, *3*(3-4), 309–332. doi:10.1177/1555412008317312

Hayes, E., & Lee, Y. (2012). Specialist language acquisition and trajectories of IT learning in a Sims fan site. In E. Hayes & S. Duncan (Eds.), *Learning in video game affinity spaces* (pp. 186–211). New York: Peter Lang.

Hayes-Roth, B., & Thorndyke, P. H. (1979). Integration of knowledge from text. *Journal of Verbal Learning and Verbal Behavior*, *18*(1), 91–108. doi:10.1016/S0022-5371(79)90594-2

Hayles, N. K. (2002). *Writing machines*. Cambridge, MA: The MIT Press.

Hayles, N. K. (2008). *Electronic literature: New horizons for the literary*. Notre Dame, Indiana: University of Notre Dame.

Hayles, N. K. (2012). *How we think: Digital media and contemporary technogenesis*. Chicago: University of Chicago Press. doi:10.7208/chicago/9780226321370.001.0001

Haythornthwaite, C. (2005). Social networks and internet connectivity effects. *Information, Communication & Society*, *8*(2), 125-147. doi:10.1080/13691180500146185

Hazari, S., North, A., & Moreland, D. (2009). Investigating Pedagogical Value of Wiki Technology. *Journal of Information Systems Education*, *20*(2), 187–198.

Health Alliance International. (2012). *Mobile moms*. Retrieved from http://www.healthallianceinternational.org/blog/post/mobile-moms-liga-inan/

Hebberd, L. (2013). *How to recruit using Instagram [5 simple steps]*. Retrieved from http://theundercoverrecruiter.com/how-to-recruit-using-instagram-in-5-simple-steps/

Hecker, L., & Engstrom, E. U. (2011). Technology that supports literacy instruction and learning. In J. R. Birsh (Ed.), *Multisensory teaching of basic language skills* (3rd ed., pp. 657–683). Baltimore: Brookes Publishing Company.

Heeks, R. (2010). Do information and communication technologies (ICTs) contribute to development? *Journal of International Development*, *22*(5), 625–640. doi:10.1002/jid.1716

Heer, J., Bostock, M., & Ogievetsky, V. (2010). A tour through the visualization zoo. *Communications of the ACM*, *53*(6), 59–67. doi:10.1145/1743546.1743567

Hegarty, M., & Just, M. A. (1993). Constructing mental models from text and diagrams. *Journal of Memory and Language*, *32*(6), 717–742. doi:10.1006/jmla.1993.1036

Henderson-Summet, V., Grinter, R. E., Carroll, J., & Starner, T. (2007). Electronic communication: Themes from a case study of the deaf community. *Lecture Notes in Computer Science*, *4662*(Part I), 347–360. doi:10.1007/978-3-540-74796-3_33

Henn, S. (2012, April 18). From Silicon Valley, a new approach to education. *National Public Radio*. Retrieved from http://www.npr.org/blogs/alltechconsidered/2012/04/18/150846845/from-silicon-valley-a-new-approach-to-education

Herman, A. (1999). So much for the magic of technology and the free market: The world wide web and the corporate media system. In A. Herman (Ed.), *The World Wide Web and contemporary cultural theory: Magic, metaphor, power*. New York, NY: Routledge.

Herold, B. (2014). Student mobile device usage outpacing school tech programs, survey finds. *Education Week*. Retrieved from http://blogs.edweek.org/edweek/DigitalEducation/2014/09/student_mobile_device_usage_survey_pearson.html

Herold, B. (2014, June9). 2014). Digital content providers ride the wave of rising revenues. *Education Week*, 14–15.

Herring, S. C., Kouper, I., Scheidt, L. A., & Wright, E. L. (2004) Women and children last: The discursive construction of weblogs. *Into the blogosphere: Rhetoric, community and culture of weblogs*. Retrieved from http://blog.lib.umn.edu/blogosphere/women_and_children.html

Herring, S. (1999). Interactional coherence in CMC. *Journal of Computer-Mediated Communication, 4*.

Herring, S. (2013). Discourse in Web 2.0: Familiar, reconfigured, and emergent. In D. Tannen & A. M. Trester (Eds.), *Discourse 2.0: Language and New Media* (pp. 1–15). Washington, DC: Georgetown University Press.

Herring, S. C., & Paolillo, J. C. (2006). Gender and genre variation in weblogs. *Journal of Sociolinguistics, 10*(4), 439–459. doi:10.1111/j.1467-9841.2006.00287.x

Herrington, J., Oliver, R., & Reeves, T. (2003). Patterns of engagement in authentic online learning communities. *Australasian Journal of Educational Technology, 19*(1), 59–71.

Herr-Stephenson, B., & Perkel, D. (2008). *Peer pedagogy in an interest-driven community: The practices and problems of online tutorials.* Paper presented at the Medai@Ise Fifth Anniversary Conference. Retrieved from http://eprints.lse.ac.uk/21576/1/perkel-herrstephenson-peerpedagogy%28LSEROversion%29.pdf

Hesford, W. S., & Kozol, W. (Eds.). (2005). *Introduction. In Just advocacy: Women's human rights, transnational feminism and the politics of representation* (pp. 1–29). New Brunswick, NJ: Rutgers University Press.

Hestres, L. (2008, March). *The blogs of war: Online activism, agenda setting and the Iraq war.* Paper presented at the meeting of the International Studies Association, San Francisco, CA.

Hevern, V., Josselson, R., & McAdams, D. (2013). Narrative. In D. Dunn (Ed.), *Oxford bibliographies in psychology.* New York: Oxford University Press.

Hewlett-Packard Development Company. (2004). *The power of visual communication.* Retrieved from http://www.hp.com/large/ipg/assets/bus-solutions/power-of-visual-communication.pdf

Hicks, T. (2013). *Crafting digital writing.* Portsmouth, NH: Heinemann.

Hicks, T., & Sibberson, F. (2015). Students as writers and composers: Workshopping in the digital age. *Language Arts, 92*(3), 221–228.

Hilhorst, D. (2003). *The real world of NGOs: Discourses, diversity and development.* London: Zed Books.

Hinduja, S., & Patchin, J. (2014). State cyberbullying laws: A brief review of state cyberbullying laws and policies (pp. 1–19)., Retrieved from http://cyberbullying.us/Bullying_and_Cyberbullying_Laws.pdf

Hinduja, S., & Patchin, J. W. (2015). *Cyberbullying legislation and case law: Implications for school policy and practice.* Retrieved from http://www.cyberbullying.us/cyberbullying-legal-issues.pdf

Hinduja, S., & Patchin, J. W. (2012). Cyberbullying: Neither an epidemic nor a rarity. *European Journal of Developmental Psychology, 9*(5), 539–543. doi:10.1080/17405629.2012.706448

Hine, C. (2000). *Virtual ethnography.* London, UK: Sage.

HITLabNZ. (2013). *colAR.* Retrieved from http://www.hitlabnz.org/index.php/products/colar

Hobbs, R. (2010). *Digital and media literacy: A plan of action. A white paper on the digital and media literacy recommendations of the Knight Commission on the information needs of communities in a democracy.* Washington, DC: The Aspen Institute, Communications and Society Program.

Hobbs, R. (2007). *Reading the media: Media literacy in high school English.* New York: Teachers College Press.

Hobbs, R. (2010). *Copyright clarity: How fair use supports digital learning.* Thousand Oaks, CA: Corwin.

Hodge, N. (2009, April 8). *Inside Moldova's Twitter Revolution.* Retrieved September 27, 2014, from http://www.wired.com/2009/04/inside-moldovas/

Holden, C., & Sykes, J. (2011). Mentira: Prototyping language–based locative gameplay. In S. Dikkers, J. Martin, & B. Coutler (Eds.), *Mobile media learning: Amazing uses of mobile devices for learning* (pp. 111–130). Pittsburgh, PA: ETC Press.

Holdings, N. (2012). *State of social media: The social media report.* The Nielsen Company. Retrieved from http://www.nielsen.com/content/dam/corporate/us/en/reports- downloads/20 1 2-Reports/The-Social-Media-Report-2012.pdf

Holland, D., Lachicotte, W., Skinner, D., & Cain, C. (2001). *Identity and Agency in Cultural Worlds.* Cambridge, MA: Harvard University Press.

Hollett, T. & Ehret, C (2014). Bean's World: (Mine) crafting affective atmospheres for gameplay, learning, and care in a children's hospital. *New Media and Society.* Doi 1461444814535192

Holquist, M. (1990). *Dialogism: Bakhtin and his world* (2nd ed.). New York: Routledge. doi:10.4324/9780203330340

Honan, M. (2013, December 30). I, Glasshole: My year with Google Glass. *Wired.* Retrieved from http://www.wired.com/2013/12/glasshole/

Honey, S., & Milnes, K. (2013). The augmented reality America's cup: Augmented reality is making sailboat racing a thrilling spectator sport. *IEEE Spectrum.* Retrieved from http://spectrum.ieee.org/consumer-electronics/audiovideo/the-augmented-reality-americas-cup

Hookway, N. (2008). "Entering the blogosphere": Some strategies for using blogs in social research. *Qualitative Research, 8*(1), 91–113. doi:10.1177/1468794107085298

Hou, C. I. (2012). Gendered avatars: Representation of gender differences between cartoons and simulated online role playing games in Taiwan. *China Media Research, 8*(3), 81–91.

Howard, P. N., Duffy, A., Freelon, D., Hussain, M., Mari, W., & Mazaid, M. (2011). Opening closed regimes: What was the role of social media during the Arab Spring? *Project on Information Technology Political Islam,* 1-30.

Howard, P. N. (2010). *The Digital Origins of Dictatorship and Democracy: Information Technology and Political Islam.* Oxford, UK: Oxford University Press.

Howard, P. N., Duffy, A., Freelon, D., Hussain, M., Mari, W., & Mazaid, M. (2011). *Opening closed regimes: What was the role of social media during the Arab Spring?* Academic Press.

Howard, P., & Hussain, M. M. (2011). The upheavals in Egypt and Tunisia: The role of digital media. *Journal of Democracy, 22*(3), 35–48. doi:10.1353/jod.2011.0041

Howe, J. (2008). *Crowdsourcing: How the power of the crowd is driving the future of business.* Great Britain: Business Books.

Howland, K., & Good, J. (2015). Learning to communicate computationally with Flip: A bi-modal programming language for game creation. *Computers & Education, 80,* 224–240. doi:10.1016/j.compedu.2014.08.014

Hrastinski, S., & Stenbom, S. (2013). Student–student online coaching: Conceptualizing an emerging learning activity. *The Internet and Higher Education, 16,* 66–69. doi:10.1016/j.iheduc.2012.02.003

Hsu, J.-L., & Shih, Y.-J. (2013). Developing computer adventure education games on mobile devices for conducting cooperative problem-solving activities. *International Journal of Mobile Learning Organisation, 7*(2), 81–98. doi:10.1504/IJMLO.2013.055616

Hu, W. (2011). *Math that moves: Schools embrace the iPad.* Retrieved from http://www.nytimes.com/2011/01/05/education/05tablets.html?pagewanted=all&_r=0

Huang, C. (2011). Facebook and Twitter key to Arab Spring uprisings: Report. *The National UAE.* Retrieved from http://www.thenational.ae/news/uae-news/facebook-and-twitter-key-to-arab-spring-uprisings-report#ixzz3GMtr6Mwa

Huang, W-H., & Nakazawa, K. (2010). An empirical analysis on how learners interact in wiki in a graduate level online course. *Interactive Learning Environments, 18*(3), 233-244. doi: 10.1080/10494820.2010.500520

Huang, Y.-M., Lin, Y.-T., & Cheng, S.-C. (2010). Effectiveness of a mobile plant learning system in a science curriculum in Taiwanese elementary education. *Computers & Education, 54*(1), 47–58. doi:10.1016/j.compedu.2009.07.006

Hughes, A. L., & Palen, L. (2009). Twitter adoption and use in mass convergence and emergency events. *International Journal of Emergency Management, 6*(3), 248–260. doi:10.1504/IJEM.2009.031564

Hughes, J., & Lang, K. R. (2003). If I had a song: The culture of digital community networks and its impact on the music industry. *International Journal on Media Management, 5*(3), 180–189. doi:10.1080/14241270309390033

Hull, G. A., & Stornaiulo, A. (2010). Literate arts in a global world: Reframing social networking as a cosmopolitan practice. *Journal of Adolescent & Adult Literacy, 54*(2), 85-97.

Hull, G. A., & Stornaiulo, A. (2014). Cosmopolitan literacies, social networks, and "proper distance": Striving to understand in a global world. *Curriculum Inquiry, 44*(1), 15–44. doi:10.1111/curi.12035

Hull, G., & Katz, M.-L. (2006). Crafting and agentive self: Case studies of digital storytelling. *Research in the Teaching of English, 41*, 43–81.

Hull, G., & Nelson, M. (2005). Locating the semiotic power of multimodality. *Written Communication, 22*(2), 224–261. doi:10.1177/0741088304274170

Hull, G., & Schultz, K. (2002). Connecting school with out-of-school worlds. In G. Hull & K. Schultz (Eds.), *School's out! Bridging out of school literacies with classroom practice* (pp. 32–60). New York: Teachers Coillege Press.

Hull, G., Stornaiuolo, A., & Sterpont, L. (2013). Imagined readers and hospitable texts: Global youths connect online. In D. E. Alvermann, N. J. Unrau, & R. B. Ruddell (Eds.), *Theoretical models and processes of reading* (6th ed.; pp. 1208–1240). Newark, DE: International Reading Association. doi:10.1598/0710.44

Hundley, M., & Holbrook, T. (2013). Set in stone or set in motion? Multimodal and digital writing with pre-service English teachers. *Journal of Adolescent & Adult Literacy, 56*(6), 492–501. doi:10.1002/JAAL.171

Hundley, M., & Parsons, L. (in press). Reading with blurred boundaries: Digital & visual culture influence on young adult literature. In J. Hayn & J. Kaplan (Eds.), *Adolescent Literature Today*. New York: Rowman & Littlefield.

Hundley, M., Smith, B., & Holbrook, T. (2013). Re-Imagine Writing: Multimodal Literary Analysis in English Education. In K. Pytash & R. Ferdig (Eds.), *Exploring technology for writing and writing instruction*. Hershey, PA: IGI Global.

Hurdle, P. (2011). *Hello iPad. Goodbye textbooks?* Retrieved from http://www.mmaglobal.org/publications/ProceedingsArchive/2011_FALL_MMA.pdf#page=51

Husbye, N. E., Buchholz, B., Coggin, L., Powell, C. W., & Wohlwend, K. E. (2012). Critical lessons and playful literacies: Digital media in PK–2 classrooms. *Language Arts, 90*(2), 82–92.

Hutchison, A., & Beschorner, B. (2014). Using the iPad as a tool to support literacy instruction. *Technology, Pedagogy and Education.* doi:10.1080/1475939X.2014.918561

Hutchison, A., & Reinking, D. (2011). Teachers' perceptions of integrating information and communication technologies into literacy instruction: A national survey in the United States. *Reading Research Quarterly, 46*(4), 312–333.

Hutchison, A., & Woodward, L. (2013). A planning cycle for integrating digital technology into literacy instruction. *The Reading Teacher, 67*(6), 455–464. doi:10.1002/trtr.1225

Hwang, G. J., & Chang, H. F. (2011). A formative assessment-based mobile learning approach to improving the learning attitudes and achievements of students. *Computers & Education, 56*(4), 1023–1031. doi:10.1016/j.compedu.2010.12.002

Hwang, G. J., Chu, H. C., Lin, Y. S., & Tsai, C. C. (2011). A knowledge acquisition approach to developing Mindtools for organizing and sharing differentiating knowledge in a ubiquitous learning environment. *Computers & Education, 57*(1), 1368–1377. doi:10.1016/j.compedu.2010.12.013

Hwang, G.-J., & Wu, P.-H. (2014). Applications, impacts and trends of mobile technology-enhanced learning: A review of 2008-2012 publications in selected SSCI journals. *International Journal of Mobile Learning Organisation, 8*(2), 83–95. doi:10.1504/IJMLO.2014.062346

IBM. (2012). *The flexible workplace: Unlocking value in the 'bring your own device' era.* Retrieved from http://www-01.ibm.com/common/ssi/cgi-bin/ssialias?infotype=SA&subtype=WH&htmlfid=ENW03010USEN

IBM. (2014). *Big data.* Retrieved from http://www.ibm.com/big-data/us/en/

IGEA. (2014). *Digital Australia.* Retrieved from http://www.igea.net/wp-content/uploads/2013/11/Digital-Australia-2014-DA14.pdf

IGI Global. (2015). *Qhat is E-S-QUAL.* IGI Global. Retrieved from http://www.igi-global.com/dictionary/e-s-qual/8910

Illeris, K. (2014). *Transformative learning and identity.* New York: Routledge.

Institute of Play. (2015a). *Institute of Play*. Retrieved January 15, 2015 from http://www.instituteofplay.org/about/

Institute of Play. (2015b). *Featured work*. Retrieved January 15, 2015 from http://www.instituteofplay.org/work/

Instructables.com & the Editors at MAKE Magazine. (2008). The Best of Instructables Volume I: Do-It-Yourself Projects from the World's Biggest Show & Tell. Authors.

Intel. (2013). *Big data visualization: Turning big data into big insights. The rise of visualization-based data discovery tools*. Retrieved from http://www.intel.com/content/dam/www/public/us/en/documents/white-papers/big-data-visualization-turning-big-data-into-big-insights.pdf

International Reading Association (IRA). (2002). *Integrating literacy and technology in the curriculum: A position statement*. Newark, DE: International Reading Association.

International Society for Technology in Education (ISTE). (2008). *ISTE standards*. Retrieved from http://www.iste.org/standards

International Society for Technology in Education. (2007). *ISTE Standards for students*. Available at: http://www.iste.org

Internet Archive. (n.d.). Retrieved from http://archive.org

In U. S. SMS texting tops mobile phone calling. (2008). Retrieved from http://www.nielsen.com/us/en/insights/news/2008/in-us-text-messaging-tops-mobile-phone-calling.html

Iskander, E. (2011). Connecting the national and the virtual: Can Facebook activism remain relevant after Egypt's January 25 uprising? *International Journal of Communication*, 5, 13–15.

Ismail, I., Azizan, S. N., & Azman, N. (2013). Mobile phone as pedagogical tools: Are teachers ready? *International Education Studies*, *6*(3), 36–47. doi:10.5539/ies.v6n3p36

Israel, M., Marino, M. T., Basham, J. D., & Spivak, W. (2013). Fifth graders as app designers: How diverse learners conceptualize educational apps. *Journal of Research on Technology in Education*, *46*(1), 53–80. doi:10.1080/15391523.2013.10782613

Israelson, M. (2014). *A Study of Teachers' Integration of App Affordances and Early Literacy Best Practices*. (Unpublished doctoral dissertation). University of Minnesota, Minneapolis, MN.

ISTE. (2007). *ISTE standards-students*. Retrieved from http://www.iste.org/standards/standards- for-students

Ito, M., & Daisuke, O. (2003). Mobile phones, Japanese Youth, and the replacement of social contact. In R. Ling (Ed.), *Front Stage - Back Stage: Mobile Communication and the Renegotiation of the Public Sphere*. Grimstad, Norway. Retrieved from http://www.itofisher.com/mito/

Itō, M. (2009). *Hanging out, messing around, and geeking out: Kids living and learning with new*. Cambridge, MA: MIT Press.

Itō, M. (2009). *Living and Learning with New Media: Summary of Findings from the Digital Youth Project*. Cambridge, MA: MIT Press.

Ito, M., & Daisuke, O. (2005). *Personal, portable, pedestrian: Mobile phones in Japanese life*. Cambridge, MA: MIT Press.

Ito, M., Gutiérrez, K., Livingstone, S., Penuel, B., Rhodes, B., Salen, K., & Watkins, S. C. et al. (2013). *Connected Learning: An agenda for research and design*. Irvine, CA: Digital Media and Learning Research Hub.

Ito, M., & Okabe, D. (2010). Intimate connections: Contextualizing Japanese youth and mobile messaging. In R. Harper, L. Palen, & A. Taylor (Eds.), *Inside the text: Social perspectives on SMS in the mobile age* (pp. 127–145). Dordrecht, The Netherlands: Springer.

Ivarsson, J., Linderoth, J., & Säljö, R. (2011). Representations in practices: A socio-cultural approach to multimodality in reasoning. In C. Jewitt (Ed.), *The Routledge handbook of multimodal analysis* (pp. 201–212). New York, NY: Routledge.

Jackson, A. (2014). *Beautiful science: Picturing data, inspiring insight at the British Library*. Retrieved from http://blogs.nature.com/ofschemesandmemes/2014/02/20/beautiful-science-picturing-data-inspiring-insight-at-the-british-library

Jackson, S. (1996). *Patchwork Girl: by Mary/Shelley/and Herself*. [CD-ROM]. Watertown, MA: Eastgate Systems, Inc.

Jackson, L. A., Zhao, Y., Kolenic, A., Fitzgerald, H. E., Harold, R., & Von, E. A. (2008). Race, gender, and information technology use: the new digital divide. *Cyberpsychology & Behavior: The Impact of the Internet, Multimedia, and Virtual Reality on Behavior and Society, 11*(4), 437–442.

Jacobs, G. (2008). We Learn What We Do: Developing a Repertoire of Writing Practices in an Instant Messaging World. *Journal of Adolescent & Adult Literacy, 52*(3), 203–211. Retrieved from papers://8823b2b3-0f26-4eac-b58e-76a95997f0e0/Paper/p1570

Jacobs, G. E. (2004). Complicating contexts: Issues of methodology in researching the language and literacies of instant messaging. *Reading Research Quarterly, 39*(4), 394–406. doi:10.1598/RRQ.39.4.3

Jacobs, G. E. (2006). Fast Times and Digital Literacy : Construction Within Instant Messaging. *Journal of Literacy Research, 38*(2), 171–196. doi:10.1207/s15548430jlr3802_3

Jaffe, S., Lowe, Z., & Tam, T. (2014). *Project LEAP: Libraries, e-reading, activities, partnership baseline report*. Retrieved August 18, 2014 from http://cdn.worldreader.org/wp-content/uploads/2014/08/Project-LEAP-Baseline-Report_2.pdf

Jaffe, E. M. (2013). Imposing a duty in an online world: Holding the web host liable for cyberbullying. *Hastings Communications & Entertainment Law Journal, 35*(2), 277–302.

Jane, E. A. (2014). "Your a ugly, whorish, slut": Understanding e-bile. *Feminist Media Studies, 14*(4), 531–546. doi:10.1080/14680777.2012.741073

Janks, H. (2010). *Literacy and power*. New York: Routledge.

Janks, H. (2014). *Doing critical literacy*. New York: Routledge.

Janowicz, K., & Hitzler, P. (2012): The digital earth as knowledge engine. *Semantic Web Journal, 3*(3), 213-221. Retrieved from http://geog.ucsb.edu/~jano/Semantics_Digital_Earth2012.pdf

Jayson, S. (2014, March 12). Social media research raises privacy and ethics issues. *USA Today*. Retrieved November 7, 2014, from http://www.usatoday.com/story/news/nation/2014/03/08/data-online-behavior-research/5781447/

Jenkins, H. (2006, June 19). *Welcome to Convergence Culture* [Blog post]. Retrieved from http://henryjenkins.org/2006/06/welcome_to_convergence_culture.html

Jenkins, H. (2006b). *Confronting the challenges of participatory culture: media education for the 21st century*. Chicago: MacArthur Foundation. Available at: http://www.pewinternet.org/files/old-media//Files/Reports/2008/PIP_Teens_Games_and_Civics_Report_FINAL.pdf.pdf

Jenkins, H. (2007, March 22). *Transmedia storytelling* [blog post]. Retrieved from http://henryjenkins.org/2007/03/transmedia_storytelling_101.html

Jenkins, H. (2010, October 6). *Perhaps a revolution is not what we need | MIT Center for Civic Media*. Retrieved from https://civic.mit.edu/blog/henry/perhaps-a-revolution-is-not-what-we-need

Jenkins, H. (1992). *Textual poachers: Television fans & participatory culture*. New York, NY: Routledge.

Jenkins, H. (2006). *Convergence culture: Where old and new media collide*. New York: New York University Press.

Jenkins, H. (2014). Fan activism as participatory politics: The case of the Harry Potter Alliance. In M. Ratto & M. Boler (Eds.), *DIY Citizenship: Critical making and social media* (pp. 65–74). Cambridge, MA: MIT Press.

Jenkins, H., & Carpentier, N. (2013). Theorizing participatory intensities: A conversation about participation and politics. *Convergence (London), 19*(3), 265–286. doi:10.1177/1354856513482090

Jenkins, H., Ford, S., & Green, J. (2013). *Spreadable media: Creating value and meaning in a networked culture*. New York: NYU Press.

Jenson, J., Dahya, N., & Fisher, S. (2014a). Power struggles: Knowledge production in a DIY news club. In M. Ratto & M. Boler (Eds.), *DIY citizenship: Critical making and social media* (pp. 169–178). Cambridge, MA: The MIT Press.

Jenson, J., Dahya, N., & Fisher, S. (2014b). Valuing production values: A 'do it yourself' media production club. *Learning, Media and Technology*, *39*(2), 215–228. doi:10.1080/17439884.2013.799486

Jewitt, C. (2011). Introduction: Handbook rationale, scope and structure. In C. Jewitt (Ed.), *The Routledge handbook of multimodal analysis* (pp. 1–7). New York, NY: Routledge.

Jewitt, C. (Ed.). (2009). *The Routledge handbook of multimodal analysis*. New York, NY: Routledge.

Jiang, J., & de Bruijn, O. (2014). Facebook helps: A case study of cross-cultural social networking and social capital. *Information Communication and Society*, *17*(6), 732–749. doi:10.1080/1369118X.2013.830636

Jiang, Y., & Katsamakas, E. (2010). Impact of e-book technology: Ownership and market asymmetries in digital transformation. *Electronic Commerce Research and Applications*, *9*(5), 386–399. doi:10.1016/j.elerap.2010.06.003

Jimenez, R., Smith, P., & Teague, L. (2009). Transnational and community literacies for teachers. *Journal of Adolescent & Adult Literacy*, *53*(1), 16–28. doi:10.1598/JAAL.53.1.2

Jocson, K. M. (2010). Youth writing across media: A note about the what and the how. In S. J. Miller & D. E. Kirkland (Eds.), *Change matters: Critical essays on moving social justice research from theory to policy* (pp. 77–87). New York, NY: Peter Lang.

Jocson, K. M. (2015). New media literacies as social action: The centrality of pedagogy in the politics of knowledge production. *Curriculum Inquiry*, *45*(1), 30–51.

Johnson, L., Adams Becker, S., Estrada, V., & Freeman, A. (2014). NMC Horizon Report: 2014 Higher Education Edition. Austin, TX: The New Media Consortium. Retrieved from http://redarchive.nmc.org/publications/2014-horizon-report-higher-ed

Johnson, L., Adams Becker, S., Estrada, V., & Freeman, A. (2014). NMC Horizon Report: 2014 K-12 Edition. Austin, TX: The New Media Consortium. Retrieved from http://tinyurl.com/k4lp6fn

Johnson, L., Adams Becker, S., Estrada, V., & Martín, S. (2013). Technology outlook for STEM+Education 2013-2018: An NMC Horizon Project Sector Analysis. Austin, TX: The New Media Consortium. Retrieved from http://tinyw.in/ByT0

Johnson-Eilola, J. (1994). Reading and writing in hypertext: Vertigo and euphoria. In C. Selfe & S. Hilligloss (Eds.), *Literacy and computers* (pp. 195–219). New York: Modern Language Association of America.

Johnson, L., Adams Becker, S., Cummins, M., Estrada, V., Freeman, A., & Ludgate, H. (2013). *NMC Horizon Report: 2013 K-12 Edition*. Austin, TX: The New Media Consortium.

Johnson, L., Adams Becker, S., Estrada, V., & Freeman, A. (2014). *NMC horizon report: 2014 K-12 edition*. Austin, TX: The New Media Consortium.

Johnston, N., & Marsh, S. (2014). Using iBooks and iPad apps to embed information literacy into an EFL foundations course. *New Library World*, *115*(1), 51–60. doi:10.1108/NLW-09-2013-0071

Jonassen, D. H. (2014). *Mindtools (Productivity and Learning)*. NY: Springer. doi:10.1007/978-94-007-6165-0_57-1

Jonassen, D. H., Carr, C., & Yueh, S. P. (1998). Computers as Mindtools for engaging learners in critical thinking. *TechTrends*, *43*(2), 24–32. doi:10.1007/BF02818172

Jonassen, D., Howland, J., Marra, R., & Crismond, D. (2008). *Meaningful learning with technology*. Columbus, OH: Pearson.

Jones, B. (2012). *Spontaneous wanderers in the digital metropolis: A case study of the new literacy practices of youth artists learning on a social media platform* (Dissertation). Arizona State University, Tempe, AZ. Retrieved from ASU Digital Repository.

Jones, A. C., Scanlon, E., & Clough, G. (2013). Mobile learning: Two case studies of supporting inquiry learning in informal and semiformal settings. *Computers & Education*, *61*, 21–32. doi:10.1016/j.compedu.2012.08.008

Jones, B. (in press). Collective learning resources: Connecting social-learning practices in deviantART to art education. *Studies in Art Education*.

Jones, R. H. (2011). Technology and sites of display. In C. Jewitt (Ed.), *The Routledge handbook of multimodal analysis* (pp. 114–126). New York, NY: Routledge.

Jones, T. S., Remland, M. S., & Sanford, R. (2007). *Interpersonal communication through the life span*. Boston: Houghton Mifflin.

Jongedijk, L. (2013). Definition and key information on AR. *Trends in EdTech: Augmented Reality*. Retrieved from http://augreality.pbworks.com/w/page/9469035/Definition%20and%20key%20information%20on%20AR

Jörgensen, C., D'Elia, G., Woelfel, J., & Rodger, E. J. (2001). The impact of the internet on the public library: Current status and signs for the future. In *Proceedings of the Annual Conference of CAIS*. Academic Press.

Joyce, M. (1991). Notes toward an unwritten non-linear electronic text, "The Ends of Print Culture" (a work in progress). *Postmodern Culture, 2*(1).

Joyce, M. (1996/1987). *Afternoon, a story*. [CD-ROM]. Watertown, MA: Eastgate Systems. (Originally published 1987)

Joyce, M. (1995). *Of two minds: Hypertext pedagogy and poetics*. Ann Arbor, MI: University of Michigan Press.

Judd, T., Kennedy, G., & Cropper, S. (2010). Using wikis for collaborative learning: Assessing collaboration through contribution. *Australasian Journal of Educational Technology, 26*(3), 341–354.

Jukes, I., McCain, T., & Crockett, L. (2010). Understanding the digital generation. 21st Century Project.

Julian, S. (2013). Reinventing classroom space to re-energise information literacy instruction. *Journal of Information Literacy, 7*(1), 69–82. doi:10.11645/7.1.1720

Junco, R., & Cotten, S. R. (2012). No A 4 U: The relationship between multitasking and academic performance. *Computers & Education, 59*(2), 505–514. doi:10.1016/j.compedu.2011.12.023

Junco, R., Heiberger, G., & Koken, E. (2011). The effect of Twitter on college student engagement and grades. *Journal of Computer Assisted Learning, 27*(2), 119–132. doi:10.1111/j.1365-2729.2010.00387.x

Junco, R., Merson, D., & Salter, D. (2010). The effect of gender, ethnicity, and income on college students' use of communication technologies. *Cyberpsychology, Behavior, and Social Networking, 13*(6), 619–627. doi:10.1089/cyber.2009.0357 PMID:21142986

Jung, I., & Suzuki, Y. (2014). Scaffolding strategies for wiki-based collaboration: Action research in a multicultural Japanese language program. *British Journal of Educational Technology*, 1–10. doi:10.1111/bjet.12175

Jung, J., Chan-Olmsted, S., & Kim, Y. (2013). From access to utilization: Factors affecting smartphone application use and its impacts on social and human capital acquisition in South Korea. *Journalism & Mass Communication Quarterly, 90*(4), 715–735. doi:10.1177/1077699013503163

Juvonen, J., & Graham, S. (2014). Bullying in schools: The power of bullies and the plight of victims. *Annual Review of Psychology, 65*(1), 159–185. doi:10.1146/annurev-psych-010213-115030 PMID:23937767

Kaare, B. H., & Lundby, K. (2008). Mediatized lives: Autobiography and assumed authenticity in digital storytelling. In K. Lundby (Ed.), *Digital storytelling, mediatized lives* (Vol. 52, pp. 105–122). New York: Peter Lang.

Kaestle, C. (1991). *Literacy in the United States: Readers and reading since 1880*. New Haven, CT: Yale University Press.

Kafai, Y. B., & Peppler, K. (2014). Transparency reconsidered: Creative, critical, and connecting making with e-textiles. In M. Ratto. & M. Boler (Eds.), DIY Citizenship: Critical making and social media (pp. 179-188). Cambridge, MA: MIT Press.

Kafai, Y., Lee, E., Searle, K., Fields, D., Kaplan, E., and Lui, D. (2014). A crafts-oriented approach to computing in high school: Introducing computational concepts, practices, and perspectives with electronic textiles. *ACM Transactions on Computing Education, 14*(1). DOI: 10.1145/2576874

Kafai, Y. (2010). World of Whyville: An introduction to tween virtual life. *Games and Culture, 5*(1), 3–22. doi:10.1177/1555412009351264

Kafai, Y. B. (1995). *Minds in Play: Computer game design as a context for children's learning*. New Jersey: Erlbaum.

Kafai, Y. B., & Burke, Q. (2013). The social turn in K-12 programming: Moving from computational thinking to computational participation. *SIGCSE, 2013,*603–608.

Kafai, Y. B., Fields, D. A., & Burke, W. Q. (2010). Entering the clubhouse: Case studies of young programmers joining the online Scratch communities. *Journal of Organizational and End User Computing, 22*(2), 21–35. doi:10.4018/joeuc.2010101906

Kafai, Y. B., Heeter, C., Denner, J., & Sun, J. Y. (Eds.). (2008). *Beyond Barbie and Mortal Kombat: New perspectives on gender and gaming.* Boston: MIT Press.

Kafai, Y. B., & Peppler, K. (2011). Youth, technology, and DIY: Developing participatory competencies in creative media production. *Review of Research in Education, 35*(1), 89–119. doi:10.3102/0091732X10383211

Kafai, Y. B., & Peppler, K. (2012). Developing gaming fluencies with Scratch: Realizing game design as an artistic process. In C. Steinkuehler, K. Squire, & S. Barab (Eds.), *Games, learning, and society: Learning and meaning in the digital age* (pp. 355–380). New York, NY: Cambridge University Press. doi:10.1017/CBO9781139031127.026

Kafai, Y., Fields, D., & Searle, K. (2012). Making technology visible: Connecting the learning of crafts, circuitry, and coding in youth e-textile designs. In *Proceedings of the International Conference of the Learning Sciences (ICLS)*. Sydney, Australia: Academic Press.

Kafai, Y., Fields, D., & Searle, K. (2014). Electronic textiles as disruptive designs: Supporting and challenging maker activities in schools. *Harvard Educational Review, 84*(4), 532–556. doi:10.17763/haer.84.4.46m7372370214783

Kafai, Y., & Peppler, K. (2014). Transparency reconsidered: Creative, critical, and connected making with e-textiles. In M. Boler & M. Ratto (Eds.), *DIY Citizenship* (pp. 179–188). Cambridge, MA: MIT Press.

Kafai, Y., Searle, K., Kaplan, E., Fields, D., Lee, E., & Lui, D. (2013). Cupcake cushions, Scooby Doo shirts, and soft boomboxes: E-textiles in high school to promote computational concepts, practices, and perceptions. In *Proceeding of the 44th ACM Technical Symposium on Computer Science Education*. ACM. Doi:10.1145/2445196.2445291

Kajder, S. B. (2004). Enter here: Personal narrative and digital storytelling. *English Journal, 93*(3), 64–68. doi:10.2307/4128811

Kaku, M. (2014). *The future of the mind.* New York: Doubleday.

Kalantzis, M., & Cope, B. (2005). *Learning by design.* Melbourne: Victorian Schools Innovation Commission and Common Ground Publishing.

Kalantzis, M., & Cope, B. (2012). *Literacies.* New York: Cambridge University Press. doi:10.1017/CBO9781139196581

Kalanztis, M., & Cope, B. (2012). *New learning: Elements of a science of education* (2nd ed.). Melbourne: Cambridge Univesity Press.

Kalathil, S., & Boas, T. C. (2003). *Open networks, closed regimes: The impact of the Internet on authoritarian rule.* Washington, DC: Carnegie Endowment for International Peace.

Kam, M., Kumar, A., Jain, S., Mathur, A., & Canny, J. (2009). Improving literacy in rural India: Cellphone games in an afterschool program. In *Proceedings of IEEE/ACM Conference on Information and Communication Technology and Development* (ICTD 09). Doha, Qatar: IEEE.

Kamarainen, A. M., Metcalf, S., Grotzer, T., Browne, A., Mazzuca, D., Tutwiler, M. S., & Dede, C. (2013). EcoMOBILE: Integrating augmented reality and probeware with environmental education field trips. *Computers & Education, 68*, 545–556. doi:10.1016/j.compedu.2013.02.018

Kant, I. (1972). *Perpetual peace: A philosophical essay, translation M. Campbell Smith.* New York: Garland.

Kapidzic, S., & Herring, S. C. (2011). Gender, communication, and self-presentation in teen chatrooms revisited: Have patterns changed? *Journal of Computer-Mediated Communication, 17*(1), 39–59. doi:10.1111/j.1083-6101.2011.01561.x

Kaplan, A. M., & Haenlein, M. (2010). Users of the world, unite! The challenges and opportunities of Social Media. *Business Horizons, 53*(1), 59–68.

Kapp, K. M. (2012). *The gamification of learning and instruction: Game-based methods and strategies for training and education.* San Francisco, CA: John Wiley & Sons, Inc.

Karkin, N. (2013). Web 2.0 Tools for Public Participation through Government Websites. In Gestion y Politica Publica Electronic, 309-332.

Karlsson, L. (2007). Desperately seeking sameness: The processes and pleasures of identification in women's diary blog reading. *Feminist Media Studies, 7*(2), 137–153. doi:10.1080/14680770701287019

Karlsson, M. (2012). Charting the liquidity of online news moving towards a method for content analysis of online news. *International Communication Gazette, 74*(4), 385–402. doi:10.1177/1748048512439823

Karpov, Y. V. (2005). *The Neo-Vygotskian approach to child development.* New York, NY: Cambridge University Press. doi:10.1017/CBO9781316036532

Kates, A. (2013). Web users should have the right to remain anonymous in cyberspace. *Engineering & Technology, 8*(9), 32–32. doi:10.1049/et.2013.0927

Katz, R. (2010). *The impact of broadband on the economy: research to date and policy issues.* International Telecommunication Union (ITU) GSR 2010 Discussion Paper.

Katz, M. B., & Stern, M. J. (2008). *One nation divisible: What America was and what it is becoming.* New York, NY: Russell Sage Foundation.

Kaufmann, B., & Buechley, L. 2010. Amarino: A toolkit for the rapid prototyping of mobile ubiquitous computing. In Proceedings of Mobile HCI. Lisbon, Portugal: Academic Press. doi:10.1145/1851600.1851652

Kay, A. & Goldberg, A. (1977/2001). Personal dynamic media. *IEEE Computer – COMPUTER, 10*(3), 31-41. DOI: 10.1109/C-M.1977.217672

Kayany, J. M., & Yelsma, P. (2000). Displacement effects of online media in the socio-technical contexts of households. *Journal of Broadcasting & Electronic Media, 44*(2), 215–229. doi:10.1207/s15506878jobem4402_4

Kayaoglu, M., Dag Akbas, R., & Ozturk, Z. (2011). A Small Scale Experimental Study: Using Animations to Learn Vocabulary. *Turkish Online Journal of Educational Technology, 10*(2), 24–30.

Kaye, B. (2005). It's a blog, blog, blog, blog world. *Atlantic Journal of Communication, 13*, 73–95. doi:10.1207/s15456889ajc1302_2

Kazlauskas, A., & Robinson, K. (2012). Podcasts are not for everyone. *British Journal of Educational Technology, 43*(2), 321–330. doi:10.1111/j.1467-8535.2010.01164.x

Kear, K., Chetwynd, F., & Jefferis, H. (2014). Social presence in online learning communities: The role of personal profiles. *Research in Learning Technology, 22*(0). doi:10.3402/rlt.v22.19710

Kearney, M., Burden, K., & Rai, T. (2015). Investigating teachers' adoption of signature mobile pedagogies. *Computers & Education, 80*, 48–57. doi:10.1016/j.compedu.2014.08.009

Kearney, M., Schuck, S., Burden, K., & Aubusson, P. (2012). Viewing mobile learning from a pedagogical perspective. *Research in Learning Technology, 20*(1), 1–17.

Kee, K. F., Sparks, L., Struppa, D. C., & Mannucci, M. (2013). Social groups, social media, and higher dimensional social structures: A simplicial model of social aggregation for computational communication research. *Communication Quarterly, 61*(1), 35–58. doi:10.1080/01463373.2012.719566

Ke, F. (2014). An implementation of design-based learning through creating educational computer games: A case study on mathematics learning during design and computing. *Computers & Education, 73*, 26–39. doi:10.1016/j.compedu.2013.12.010

Keipi, T., & Oksanen, A. (2014). Self-exploration, anonymity and risks in the online setting: Analysis of narratives by 14–18-year olds. *Journal of Youth Studies, 17*(8), 1097–1113. doi:10.1080/13676261.2014.881988

Kelleher, F. (2014, June 17). The literacy injustice: 493 million women still can't read [magazine]. *The Guardian.* Retrieved from http://www.theguardian.com/global-development-professionals-network/2014/jun/17/literacy-women-illiteracy-development

Keller, W. E. (1992). *The wrong side of the bed.* Bel Air, CA: Children's Universe.

Kellner, D. (2008). Critical perspectives on visual imagery in media and cyberculture. *Journal of Visual Literacy, 22*(1), 81–90.

Kellner, D., & Share, J. (2007). Critical media literacy, democracy, and the reconstruction of education. In D. Macedo & S. R. Steinberg (Eds.), *Media literacy: A reader* (pp. 3–23). New York, NY: Peter Lang Publishing, Inc.

Kelly, D. M. (2012). Teaching for social justice: Translating an anti-oppression approach into practice. *Our Schools/Our Selves, 21*(2), 135-154.

Kelly, D. M. (2014). Alternative learning contexts and the goals of democracy in education. In J. A. Vadeboncoeur (Ed.), *Learning in and across contexts: Reimagining education.* New York: Teachers College Press.

Kelly, H. (2013, April 26). *After Boston: The pros and cons of surveillance cameras.* Retrieved from http://www.cnn.com/2013/04/26/tech/innovation/security-cameras-boston-bombings/

Kelly, D. C. (2008). Civic readiness: Preparing toddlers and young children for civic education and sustained engagement. *National Civic Review, 97*(4), 55–59. doi:10.1002/ncr.234

Kelly, D. M. (2010). Media representation and the case for critical media education. In M. C. Courtland & T. Gambell (Eds.), *Literature, media, and multiliteracies in adolescent language arts* (pp. 277–303). Vancouver: Pacific Education Press.

Kelly, D. M., & Brooks, M. (2009). How young is too young? Exploring beginning teachers' assumptions about young children and teaching for social justice. *Equity & Excellence in Education, 42*(2), 202–216. doi:10.1080/10665680902739683

Kelly, D. M., Pomerantz, S., & Currie, D. H. (2006). "No boundaries"? Girls' interactive, online learning about femininities. *Youth & Society, 38*(1), 3–28. doi:10.1177/0044118X05283482

Kemp, N., & Bushnell, C. (2011). Children's text messaging: Abbreviations, input methods and links with literacy. *Journal of Computer Assisted Learning, 27*(1), 18–27. doi:10.1111/j.1365-2729.2010.00400.x

Kemp, N., Wood, C., & Waldron, S. (2014). Do I Know Its Wrong: Children'S and Adults' Use of Unconventional Grammar in Text Messaging. *Reading and Writing, 27*(9), 1585–1602. doi:10.1007/s11145-014-9508-1

Kendall, L. (2008). Beyond media producers and consumers: Online multimedia productions as interpersonal communication. *Information Communication and Society, 11*(2), 207–220. doi:10.1080/13691180801937084

Kenny, C. (2011, December). *Overselling broadband: A critique of the recommendations of the broadband commission for digital development.* Retrieved from http://www.cgdev.org/files/1425798_file_Kenny_overselling_broadband_FINAL.pdf

Kenny, R. (2001). Teaching, learning, and communicating in the digital age. In *Proceedings of Selected research and Development [and] Practice Papers Presented at theNational Convention of the Association for Educational Communications and Technology.* Academic Press.

Kerr, A. (2003). Women just want to have fun: A study of adult female players of digital games. In M. Copier & J. Raessens (Eds.), *Level Up: Digital Games Research Conference* (p. 270-285). Utrecht: University of Utrecht.

Keskin, N. O., & Metcalf, D. (2011). The current perspectives, theories and practices of mobile learning. *Turkish Online Journal of Educational Technology-TOJET, 10*(2), 202–208.

Kessler, G. (2009). Student-initiated attention to form in wiki-based collaborative writing. *Language Learning & Technology, 13*(1), 79–95.

Khaled, R., & Ingram, G. (2012). Tales from the front lines of a large-scale serious game project. In *Proceedings from CHI '12: SIGCHI Conference on Human Factors in Computing Systems* (pp. 69–78). New York, NY: ACM. doi:10.1145/2207676.2207688

Khaleej Times. (2011, March 2). *Social media a catalyst for political reforms.* Retrieved from http://www.khaleejtimes.com/DisplayArticle09.asp?xfile=data/theuae/2011/March/theuae_March27.xml&section=theuae

Khamis, S., & Vaughn, K. (2011). Cyberactivism in the Egyptian revolution: How civic engagement and citizen journalism tilted the balance. *Arab Media and Society, 13*(3).

Khoja, S., Wainwright, C., Brosing, J., & Barlow, J. (2012). Changing girls' attitudes towards computer science. *Journal of Computing Sciences in Colleges*, 28(1), 210–216.

Khondker, H. H. (2011). Role of the new media in the Arab Spring. *Globalizations*, 8(5), 675–679. doi:10.108 0/14747731.2011.621287

Kim, H. M., & Nitecki, D. A. (2014). *A proposed scale for measuring the quality of social media services: An E-S-QUAL approach*. Paper presented at ASIST 2014. Retrieved from https://www.asis.org/asist2014/proceedings/submissions/posters/250poster.pdf

Kim, T.-Y., Park, J., Kim, E., & Hwang, J. (2011). *The faster-accelerating digital economy*. TEMEP Discussion Papers 201173. Seoul National University. Technology Management, Economics, and Policy Program (TEMEP). Retrieved from https://ideas.repec.org/p/snv/dp2009/201173.html

Kimbrough, A. M., Guadagno, R. E., Muscanell, N. L., & Dill, J. (2013). Gender differences in mediated communication: Women connect more than do men. *Computers in Human Behavior*, 29(3), 896–900. doi:10.1016/j.chb.2012.12.005

Kim, D., Rueckert, D., Kim, D.-J., & Seo, D. (2013). Students' perceptions and experiences of mobile learning. *Language Learning & Technology*, 17(3), 52–73.

Kim, H., Lee, M., & Kim, M. (2014). Effects of Mobile Instant Messaging on Collaborative Learning Processes and Outcomes : The Case of South Korea. *Education Technology & Society*, 17(2), 31–42.

Kimmel, S. (2013). Graphic information visualizing STEM with elementary school students. *Knowledge Quest*, 41(3), 36–41.

Kim, S., Lee, J., & Thomas, M. (2012). Between purpose and method: A review of educational research. *Journal of Virtual Worlds Research*, 5(1), 1–8.

Kingsley, K. V., & Boone, R. (2008). Effects of multimedia software on achievement of middle school students in an American history class. *Journal of Research on Technology in Education*, 41(2), 203–221. doi:10.1080/153915 23.2008.10782529

Kirkland, A. (2014, February 4). *10 countries where Facebook has been banned*. Retrieved from http://www.indexoncensorship.org/2014/02/10-countries-facebook-banned/

Kirriemuir, J. (2010). UK university and college technical support for *Second Life* developers and users. *Educational Research*, 52(2), 215–227. doi:10.1080/00131881.2010 .482756

Kirsch, G. E. (2014). Creating vision of reality: A rhetoric of response, engagement, and social action. *Journal of Rhetoric, Culture, &. Politics*, 34(1-2). Retrieved from http://www.jaconlinejournal.com/archives/vol34.1.html

Kirschner, P., Strijbos, J.-W., Krejins, K., & Beers, P. (2004). Designing Electronic Collaborative Learning Environments. *Educational Technology Research and Development*, 52(3), 47–66. doi:10.1007/BF02504675

Kiss, J. (2014). Facebook's 10th birthday: from college dorm to 1.23 billion users. *The Guardian.com* Retrieved from: http://www.theguardian.com/technology/2014/feb/04/facebook-10-years-mark-zuckerberg

Kiss, J. (2014). Twitter is changing how we interact with the world. *The Guardian*. Retrieved from http://www.theguardian.com/technology/pda/2010/aug/02/twitter

Kissinger, J. S. (2013). The social & mobile learning experiences of students using mobile e-books. *Journal of Asynchronous Learning Networks*, 17(1), 155–170.

Kist, W. (2013). Class, get ready to tweet: Social media in the classroom. *Our Children: The National PTA Magazine*, 38(3), 10–11.

Kist, W. (2013). New literacies and the Common Core. *Educational Leadership*, 70(6), 38–43.

Kivunike, F. N., Ekenberg, L., Danielson, M., & Tusubira, F. F. (2009). Investigating perception of the role of ICTs towards the quality of life of people in rural communities in Uganda. In *Proceedings of the 10th International Conference on Social Implications of Computers in Developing Countries*. Dubai School of Government. Retrieved from http://www.ifip.dsg.ae/Docs/FinalPDF/Full%20Papers/ifip_55_%20Kivunike,%20ekenberg%20and%20danielson.pdf

Kleine, D. (2010). ICT4What? Using the choice framework to operationalise the capability approach to development. In *Proceedings of the IEEE/ACM International Conference on Information Technology and Development 2009*. Retrieved from http://ieeexplore.ieee.org/xpl/login.jsp?tp=&arnumber=5426717&url=http%3A%2F%2Fieeexplore.ieee.org%2Fxpls%2Fabs_all.jsp%3Farnumber%3D5426717

Kleman, E. (2007). *Journaling for the world (wide web) to see: A proposed model of self-disclosure intimacy in blogs*. Paper presented at the 93rd National Communication Association Conference, Chicago, IL.

Kline, D., & Burstein, D. (2005). *Blog! How the newest media revolution is changing politics, business and culture*. New York: CDS Books.

Knobel, M., & Lankshear, C. (2003). *New literacies: Changing knowledge and classroom learning*. Philadelphia, PA: Open University Press.

Knobel, M., & Lankshear, C. (2006). Weblog worlds and constructions of effective and powerful writing: Cross with care, and only where signs permit. In K. Pahl & J. Rowsell (Eds.), *Travel Notes from the New Literacy Studies: Instances of Practice* (pp. 72–92). Clevedon, UK: Multilingual Matters.

Knobel, M., & Lankshear, C. (2007). Online memes, affinities and culture production. In M. Knobel & C. Lankshear (Eds.), *A New Literacies Sampler* (Vol. 29, pp. 199–227). New York, NY: Peter Lang.

Knobel, M., & Lankshear, C. (2008). Remix: The art and craft of endless hybridization. *Journal of Adolescent & Adult Literacy, 52*(1), 22–33. doi:10.1598/JAAL.52.1.3

Knobel, M., & Lankshear, C. (2014). Studying New Literacies. *Journal of Adolescent & Adult Literacy, 58*(2), 97–101. doi:10.1002/jaal.314

Koh, K. H., Nickerson, H., Basawapatna, A., & Repenning, A. (2014). Early validation of computational thinking pattern analysis. In *Proceedings from 2014 Conference on Innovation & Technology in Computer Science Education*. New York, NY: ACM. doi:10.1145/2591708.2591724

Koh, K. H., Repenning, A., Nickerson, H., Endo, Y., & Motter, P. (2013). Will It stick?: Exploring the sustainability of computational thinking education through game design. In *Proceedings from The 44th ACM Technical Symposium on Computer Science Education* (pp. 597–602). New York, NY: ACM. doi:10.1145/2445196.2445372

Konnikova, M. (2014, July 16). Being a better online reader. *The New Yorker*. Retrieved from http://tinyurl.com/mm26ahr

Koole, M. (2009). A model for framing mobile learning. In M. Ally (Ed.), *Mobile learning: Transforming the delivery of education and training* (Vol. 1, pp. 25–47). Edmonton, Alberta: Alberta University Press.

Korkey, H. (2014, September 9). *Can students "go deep" with digital reading?* [web log comment]. Retrieved from http://tinyurl.com/m35qkff

Koskela, H. (2004). Webcams, TV shows, and mobile phones. Empowering exhibitionism. *Surveillance & Society, 2*, 199–215.

Kosner, A. W. (2012). *The Appification of everything will transform the world's 360 million web sites*. Retrieved August 22, 2014 from http://www.forbes.com/sites/anthonykosner/2012/12/16/forecast-2013-the-appification-of-everything-will-turn-the-web-into-an-app-o-verse/

Kostelnick, C., & Roberts, D. (2010). *Designing visual language: Strategies for professional communicators* (2nd ed.). Boston, MA: Allyn & Bacon.

Kovic, I., Lulic, I., & Brumini, G. (2008). Examining the medical blogosphere: An online survey of medical bloggers. *Journal of Medical Internet Research, 10*(3), e28. doi:10.2196/jmir.1118 PMID:18812312

Kowalski, R. M., Giumetti, G. W., Schroeder, A. N., & Lattanner, M. R. (2014). Bullying in the digital age: A critical review and meta-analysis of cyberbullying research among youth. *Psychological Bulletin, 140*(4), 1073–1137. doi:10.1037/a0035618 PMID:24512111

Kowalski, R. M., Giumetti, G. W., Schroeder, A. W., & Reese, H. H. (2012). Cyber bullying among college students: Evidence domains of college life. In C. Wankel & L. Wankel (Eds.), *Misbehavior online in higher education* (pp. 293–321). Bingley, UK: Emerald. doi:10.1108/S2044-9968(2012)0000005016

Kowalski, R. M., & Limber, S. P. (2007). Electronic bullying among middle school students. *The Journal of Adolescent Health*, *41*(6), 22–30. doi:10.1016/j.jadohealth.2007.08.017 PMID:18047942

Kow, Y. M., & Nardi, B. (2010). Who owns the mods? *First Monday*, *15*(5). doi:10.5210/fm.v15i5.2971

Kozma, R. (1994a). Will media influence learning: Reframing the debate. *Educational Technology Research and Development*, *42*(2), 7–19. doi:10.1007/BF02299087

Kozma, R. (1994b). A reply: Media and methods. *Educational Technology Research and Development*, *42*(3), 11–14. doi:10.1007/BF02298091

Krasny, K. (2013). *Gender and literacy: A handbook fro educators and parents*. Santa Barbara, CA: Praeger.

Krauskopf, K., Zahn, C., & Hesse, F. W. (2012). Leveraging the affordances of Youtube: The role of pedagogical knowledge and mental models of technology functions for lesson planning with technology. *Computers & Education*, *58*(4), 1194–1206. doi:10.1016/j.compedu.2011.12.010

Kraut, R., Kiesler, S., Mukhopadhyay, T., Scherlis, W., & Patterson, M. (1998). Social Impact of the Internet: What Does It Mean? *Communications of the ACM*, *41*(12), 21–22. doi:10.1145/290133.290140

Kraut, R., Patterson, M., Lundmark, V., Kiesler, S., Mukophadhyay, T., & Scherlis, W. (1998). Internet paradox: A social technology that reduces social involvement and psychological well-being? *The American Psychologist*, *53*(9), 1017–1031. doi:10.1037/0003-066X.53.9.1017 PMID:9841579

Kress, G. (1997). *Literacy, identity and futures. Before writing: Rethinking the paths to literacy* (pp. 1–17). New York, NY: Routledge.

Kress, G. (2003). *Literacy in the new media age*. New York: Routledge. doi:10.4324/9780203164754

Kress, G. (2010). *Multimodality: A social semiotic approach to contemporary communication*. Abingdon, UK: Routledge.

Kress, G. (2011). What is mode? In C. Jewitt (Ed.), *The Routledge handbook of multimodal analysis* (pp. 54–67). New York, NY: Routledge.

Kress, G., & van Leeuwen, T. (2001). *Multimodal discourse: The modes and media of contemporary communication*. Oxford University Press.

Kristeva, J. (1980). *Desire in language: A semiotic approach to literature and art*. New York: Columbia University Press.

Kristof, N. D. (2009, June 18). Tear Down This Cyberwall! *The New York Times*. Retrieved from http://www.nytimes.com/2009/06/18/opinion/18kristof.html

Krueger, N. (2014, July). *3 barriers to innovation education leaders must address*. ISTE. Retrieved from http://www.iste.org/explore/ArticleDetail?articleid=98

Krum, R. (2013). *Cool infographics: Effective communication with data visualization and design*. Indianapolis, IN: Wiley.

Kuby, C. R. (2013). *Critical literacy in the early childhood classroom: Unpacking histories, unlearning privilege*. New York, NY: Teachers College Press.

Kuiper, E., & Volman, M. (2008). The Web as a source of information for students in K–12 education. In J. Coiro, M. Knobel, C. Lankshear, & D. Leu (Eds.), *Handbook of research on new literacies* (pp. 241–246). Mahwah, NJ: Lawrence Erlbaum.

Kulla-Abbott, T., & Polman, J. (2008). Engaging student voice and fulfilling curriculum goals with digital stories. *Technology, Humanities, Education, and Narrative*. Retrieved from http://thenjournal.org/feature/160/

Kumar, K., & Owston, R. (2014). Accessibility evaluation of iOS apps for education. In C. Miller & A. Doering (Eds.), *The new landscape of mobile learning* (pp. 208–224). New York: Routledge.

Kumta, S. M., Tsang, P. L., & Hung, L. K. (2003). Fostering critical thinking skills through a web-based tutorial programme for final year medical student: A randomized control study. *Journal of Educational Multimedia and Hypermedia*, *12*(3), 267–273.

Kurzweil, R. (2005). *The singularity is near: When humans transcend biology*. New York, NY: Viking Adult.

Kushin, M. J., & Yamamoto, M. (2010). Did social media really matter? College students' use of online media and political decision making in the 2008 election. *Mass Communication & Society*, *13*(5), 608–630. doi:10.108 0/15205436.2010.516863

Kuznekoff, J. H., & Rose, L. M. (2012). Communication in multiplayer gaming: Examining Player responses to gender cues. *New Media & Society*, *15*(4), 541–556. doi:10.1177/1461444812458271

Kuznetsov, S., and Paulos, E. (2010). *Rise of the Expert Amateur: DIY Projects, Communities, and Cultures.* Paper presented at ACM NordiCHI, Reykjavík, Iceland.

KZero. (2013). *Universe Chart.* Retrieved from http://www.kzero.co.uk/blog/universe-chart-q4-2011-avg-user-age-10-15/

Labbo, L. D., Eakle, A. J., & Montero, M. K. (2002). Digital language experience approach: Using digital photographs and software as a language experience approach innovation. *Reading Online*, *5*(8), 24–43.

Ladson-Billings, G. (1995). Toward a theory of culturally relevant pedagogy. *American Educational Research Journal*, *32*(3), 465–491. doi:10.3102/00028312032003465

Lai, C.-H. (2014). An integrated approach to untangling mediated connectedness with online and mobile media. *Computers in Human Behavior*, *31*, 20–26. doi:10.1016/j. chb.2013.10.023

Lai, C.-H., Chu, C.-M., Luo, P.-P., & Chen, W.-H. (2013). Learners' acceptance of mobile technology supported collaborative learning. *International Journal of Mobile Learning Organisation*, *7*(3/4), 277–291. doi:10.1504/ IJMLO.2013.057166

Lam, W. S. E. (2000). L2 literacy and the design of the self: A case study of a teenage writing on the Internet. *Teachers of English to Speakers of Other Languages*, *34*(3), 457–482. Retrieved from papers://8823b2b3-0f26-4eac-b58e-76a95997f0e0/Paper/p2147

Lamb, A., & Johnson, L. (2009). Wikis and collaborative inquiry. *School Library Media Activities Monthly*, *8*(April), 48–51.

Lamb, A., & Johnson, L. (2014). Infographics part 1: Invitations to inquiry. *Teacher Librarian*, *42*(4), 54–58.

Lamberson, G. (2014). *The Julian year* [MMG Sidekick version]. Retrieved from itunes.apple.com

Lambert, J. (2006). *Digital storytelling: Capturing lives, creating community.* New York: Routledge.

Lamb, G., Polman, J., Newman, A., & Smith, C. (2014). Science news infographics: Teaching students to gather, interpret, and present information graphically. *Science Teacher (Normal, Ill.)*, 25–30.

Lameman, B. A., Lewis, J. E., & Fragnito, S. (2010). Skins 1.0: A curriculum for designing games with First Nations Youth. Paper presented at FuturePlay 2010, Vancouver, Canada.

Lammers, J. C. (2011). *The hangout was serious business: Exploring literacies and learning in an online Sims fan fiction community* (Doctoral dissertation). Retrieved from ProQuest Dissertations and Theses. (3453240)

Lampe, C., Ellison, N., & Steinfield, C. (2006, November). A Face (book) in the crowd: Social searching vs. social browsing. In *Proceedings of the 2006 20th anniversary conference on Computer supported cooperative work* (pp. 167-170). doi:10.1145/1180875.1180901

Lam, W. S. E. (2009). Multiliteracies on instant messaging in negotiating local, translocal, and transnational affiliations: A case of an adolescent immigrant. *Reading Research Quarterly*, *44*(4), 377–397. doi:10.1598/ RRQ.44.4.5

Landow, G. P. (1997). Hypertext 2.0 (Rev., amplified ed.). Baltimore, MD: The Johns Hopkins University Press.

Landow, G. P. (2006). *Hypertext 3.0: Critical and new media in an era of globalization.* Baltimore, MD: The Johns Hopkins University Press. (Original work published 1992)

Lange, P. (2011). Learning real life lessons from online games. *Games and Culture*, *6*(1), 17–37. doi:10.1177/1555412010377320

Langos, C. (2012). Cyberbullying: The challenge to define. *Cyberpsychology, Behavior, and Social Networking*, *15*(6), 285–289. doi:10.1089/cyber.2011.0588 PMID:22703033

Lanham, R. A. (2001). What's next for text? *Education Communication and Information*, *1*(2). Retrieved from http://www.open.ac.uk/eci/lanham/femoset.html

Lankow, J., Crooks, R., & Ritchie, J. (2012). *Infographics: The power of visual storytelling*. Hoboken: Wiley.

Lankshear, C., & Knobel, M. (2006). *New Literacies: Everyday Practices and Classroom Learning* (2nd ed.). Maidenhead: Open University Press.

Lankshear, C., & Knobel, M. (2008). *Digital literacies: Concepts, practices, and policies* (Vol. 30). Peter Lang.

Lapointe, D. K., & Linder-Vanberschot, J. A. (2012). *International research: Responding to global needs. In Trends and Issues in Distance Education: International Perspectives* (2nd ed.; pp. 5–22). Charlotte, NC: Information Age Publishing.

LaRose, R., Strover, S., Gregg, J., & Straubhaar, J. (2011). The impact of rural broadband development: Lessons from a natural field experiment. *Government Information Quarterly, 28*(1), 91–100. doi:10.1016/j.giq.2009.12.013

Larusson, J., & Alterman, R. (2009). Wikis to support the "collaborative" part of collaborative learning. *Computer-Supported Collaborative Learning, 4,* 371-402. doi: 10.1007/s11412-009-9076-6

Lassila, O., & Hendler, J. (2007). Embracing Web 3.0. *IEEE Internet Computing, 11*(3), 90–93. doi:10.1109/MIC.2007.52

Latour, B. (2007). *Reassembling the social: An introduction to actor-network theory*. Oxford: Oxford University Press.

Lauraneato. (2010, December 16). *The different categories of art theft* [deviantART journal]. Retrieved from http://www.deviantart.com/browse/all/#/journal/The-Different-Categories-of-Art-Theft-214241001?hf=1

Lauricella, S., & Kay, R. (2013). Exploring the use of text and instant messaging in higher education classrooms. *Research in Learning Technology, 21*(0), 1–18. doi:10.3402/rlt.v21i0.19061

Layne, L., Vostral, S., & Boyer, K. (Eds.). (2010). *Feminist Technology*. University of Ilinois Press.

Lazarsfeld, P. F., & Merton, R. K. (2000). Mass communication, popular taste and organized social action. *Media Studies Reading (Sunderland)*, 22–23.

Leach, J. (2005). *Deep impact: An investigation of the use of information and communication technologies* [Report]. London: The Department for International Development.

Leadbeater, C., & Miller, P. (2004). *The pro-am revolution: How enthusiasts are changing our economy and society*. London, UK: Demos.

Leander, K. (2009). Composing with old and new media: toward a parallel pedagogy. In V. Carrington & M. Robinson (Eds.), Digital literacies: Social learning and classroom practices (pp. 147-162). Los Angeles, CA: Sage. doi:10.4135/9781446288238.n10

Leander, K., & Hollett, T. (2013). Designing new spaces for literacy learning. In P. Dunston, S. K. Fullerton, C. C. Bates, P. M. Stecker, M. W. Cole, A. H. Hall, et al. (Eds.), 62nd yearbook of the Literacy Research Association (pp. 29-42). Altamonte Springs, FL: Literacy Research Association.

Leander, K. M., & McKim, K. K. (2003). Tracing the everyday 'sitings' of adolescents on the internet: A strategic adaptation of ethnography across online and offline spaces. *Education Communication and Information, 3*(2), 211–240. doi:10.1080/14636310303140

Leander, K., & Boldt, G. (2013). Rereading "A pedagogy of multiliteracies" bodies, texts, and emergence. *Journal of Literacy Research, 45*(1), 22–46. doi:10.1177/1086296X12468587

Learning, R. (2014). *Why badges?* Retrieved from http://www.reconnectlearning.org/#whybadges

Ledbetter, A. M., & Mazer, J. P. (2014). Do online communication attitudes mitigate the association between Facebook use and relational interdependence? An extension of media multiplexity theory. *New Media & Society, 16*(5), 806–822. doi:10.1177/1461444813495159

Lee, B. S., & Webb, L. M. (2014). Mommy bloggers: Who they are, what they write about, and how they are shaping motherhood in the 21st century. In A. R. Martinez & L. J. Miller (Eds.), Gender in a transitional era: Changes and challenges (pp. 41-57). Lanham, MD: Lexington.

Lee, Y. (2012). *Learning and literacy in an online gaming community: Examples of participatory practices in a Sims affinity space* (Doctoral dissertation). Retrieved from ProQuest Dissertations and Theses. (3505612)

Lee, B. D., & Webb, L. M. (2012). The ICC (identity, content, community) theory of blog participation. In R. A. Lind (Ed.), *Producing theory: The intersection of audiences and production in a digital world* (pp. 177–193). New York: Peter Lang Publishers.

Lee, E., & Miller, L. (2014). Entry point: Parfticipatory media-making with queer and trans refugees: Social locations, agendas, and thinking structurally. In H. M. Pleasants & D. E. Salter (Eds.), *Community-based multiliteracies and digital edia projects: Questioning assumptions and exploring realities* (Vol. 63, pp. 45–64). New York: Peter Lang.

Lee, J. (2009). Contesting the digital economy and culture: Digital technologies and the transformation of popular music in Korea. *Inter-Asia Cultural Studies, 10*(4), 489–506. doi:10.1080/14649370903166143

Lee, M. (2014). Bringing the best of two worlds together for social capital research in education Social network analysis and symbolic interactionism. *Educational Researcher, 43*(9), 454–464. doi:10.3102/0013189X14557889

Lefebvre, H. (1992). *The production of space*. New York, NY: Wiley-Blackwell.

Leggio, J. (2008, November 28). *Mumbai attack coverage demonstrates (good and bad) maturation point of social media*. Retrieved January 25, 2015, from http://www.zd-net.com/article/mumbai-attack-coverage-demonstrates-good-and-bad-maturation-point-of-social-media/

Lehr, W. H., & Osorio, C. A. (2005, December). Measuring broadband's economic impact. *Broadband Properties*, 12-24. Retrieved from http://www.broadbandproperties.com/2005issues/dec05issues/Measuring%20Broadband%20Eco%20Impact,%20Lehr,%20Gilett,%20Sirbu.pdf

Lele, S., & Norgaard, R. B. (2005). Practicing interdisciplinarity. *Bioscience, 55*(11), 967–975. doi:10.1641/0006-3568(2005)055[0967:PI]2.0.CO;2

Lemke, J. (2010). Lessons from *Whyville*: A hermeneutics of our mixed reality. *Games and Culture, 6*(1), 149–157. doi:10.1177/1555412010361944

Lemke, J. (2011). Mulimodality, identity, and time. In C. Jewitt (Ed.), *The Routledge handbook of multimodal analysis* (pp. 140–150). New York, NY: Routledge.

Lemphane, P., & Prinsloo, M. (2013). *Children's digital literacy practices in unequal South African settings*. Tilburg, Netherlands: University of Tilburg, Tilburg Papers in Cultural Studies #60. Retrieved from http://tinyurl.com/q5uxzov

Lenhardt, A. (2012). Teens and online video. *Pew Internet and American Life Project*. Retrieved from http://www.pewinternet.org/Reports/2012/Teens-and-online-video.aspx

Lenhart, A. (2012a). *Communication Choices*. Retrieved from http://www.pewinternet.org/2012/03/19/communication-choices/

Lenhart, A. (2012b). Teens, Smartphones & Texting. Washington, DC: Pew Internet and American Life Project. Retrieved from http://pewinternet.org/Reports/2012/Teens-and-smartphones.aspx

Lenhart, A., & Madden, M. (2005). Teen content creators and consumers. *Pew Internet & American Life Project*. Retrieved from http://www.pewinternet.org/~/media//Files/Reports/2005/PIP_Teens_Content_Cr eation.pdf.pdf

Lenhart, A., & Madden, M. (2007). Teens, privacy & online social networks: How teens manage their online identities and personal information in the age of MySpace. *Pew Internet Research Project*. Retrieved from http://www.pewinternet.org/2007/04/18/teens-privacy-and-online-social-networks/

Lenhart, A., Arafeh, S., Smith, A., & Macgill, A. R. (2008). *Writing, technology and teens, 83*. Retrieved from papers://8823b2b3-0f26-4eac-b58e-76a95997f0e0/Paper/p59

Lenhart, A., Jones, S., & MacGill, A. (2008). Adults and video games. Washington, DC: Pew Research Center. Retrieved from http://www.pewinternet.org/2008/12/07/adults-and-video-games/

Lenhart, A., Kahne, J., Middaugh, E., Macgill, A., Evans, C., & Vitak, J. (2008). *Teens, Video Games, and Civics*. Washington, DC: Pew Internet & American Life Project. Retrieved from http://www.pewinternet.org/files/old-media/Files/Reports/2008/PIP_Teens_Games_and_Civics_Report_FINAL.pdf.pdf

Lenhart, A., Madden, M., Smith, A., Purcell, K., Zichuhr, K., & Raine, L. 2011. *Teens, kindness and cruelty on social network sites.* Pew Research Internet Project. Retrieved from http://www.pewinternet.org/2011/11/09/teens-kindness-and-cruelty-on-social-network-sites/

Lenhart, A., Purcell, K., Smith, A., & Zickuhr, K. (2010). Social media and young adults. *Pew Internet & American Life Project.* Retrieved from http://www.pewinternet.org/Reports/2010/Social-Media-and-Young-Adults.aspx

Lenhart, A., Madden, M., Smith, A., Purcell, K., Zickuhr, K., & Rainie, L. (2011). *Teens, kindness and cruelty on social network sites: How American teens navigate the new world of "digital citizenship".* Washington, DC: Pew Research Center.

Lennon, R. G. (2012). Bring your own device (BYOD) with cloud 4 education. In *Proceedings of the 3rd annual conference on Systems, programming, and applications: software for humanity* (pp. 171-180). ACM. doi:10.1145/2384716.2384771

Leonard, J., Brooks, W., Barnes-Johnson, J., & Berry, R. Q. (2010). The nuances and complexities of teaching mathematics for cultural relevance and social justice. *Journal of Teacher Education, 61*(3), 261–270. doi:10.1177/0022487109359927

Lepi, K. (2014). 10 ways to use mobile devices in the classroom. *Edudemic.* Retrieved from http://www.edudemic.com/mobile-devices-in-the-classroom-2/

Lesley, M. (2012). *Invisible girls: At risk adolescent girls' writing within and beyond school.* New York, NY: Peter Lang.

Lessig, L. (2004). *Free culture: How big media uses technology and the law to lock down culture and control creativity.* New York, NY: Penguin.

Lessig, L. (2008). *Remix: Making art and commerce thrive in the hybrid economy.* New York, NY: Penguin. doi:10.5040/9781849662505

Lester, P. (2013). *Visual communication: Images with messages.* Independence, KY: Cengage Learning.

Leu, D. J., Jr. (2000). Literacy and technology: Deictic consequences for literacy education in an Information Age. In M. L. Kamil, P. Mosenthal, P. D. Pearson, & R. Barr (Eds.), Handbook of Reading Research (Vol. 3). Mahway, NJ: Erlbaum. Retrieved from http://www.sp.uconn.edu/~djleu/Handbook.html

Leu, D. J., Jr. (2002). The new literacies: Research on reading instruction with the Internet. In A. E. AFarnstrup & S. J. Samules (Eds.), Handbook of reading research (Vol. 3, pp. 743-770). Mahwah, NJ: Erlbaum.

Leu, D., J., O'Bryne, I., Zawilinski, L., McVerry, G., & Everett-Cacopardo, H. (2009). Expanding the new literacies conversation. *Educational Researcher, 38*(4), .264-269.

Leu, D., Kinzer, C. K., Coiro, J., & Cammack, D. (2009). Reading Online - New Literacies_ Toward a Theory of New Literacies. *Theoretical Models and Processes of Reading*, 41. Retrieved from papers://8823b2b3-0f26-4eac-b58e-76a95997f0e0/Paper/p761

Leu, D. J., Forzani, E., Rhoads, C., Maykel, C., Kennedy, C., & Timbrell, N. (in press). The new literacies of online research and comprehension: Rethinking the reading achievement gap. *Reading Research Quarterly.*

Leu, D. J. Jr. (2000). Literacy and technology: Deictic consequences for literacy education in an information age. In M. L. Kamil, P. B. Mosenthal, P. D. Pearson, & R. Barr (Eds.), *Handbook of reading research* (Vol. 3, pp. 310–336). Newark, DE: International Reading Association.

Leu, D. J. Jr, & Kinzer, C. K. (2000). The convergence of literacy instruction and networked technologies for information and communication. *Reading Research Quarterly, 35*(1), 108–127. doi:10.1598/RRQ.35.1.8

Leu, D. J. Jr, Kinzer, C. K., Coiro, J., & Cammack, D. (2004). Toward a theory of new literacies emerging from the Internet and other ICT. In R. B. Ruddell & N. Unrau (Eds.), *Theoretical Models and Processes of Reading* (5th ed.; pp. 1568–1611). Newark, DE: International Reading Association.

Leu, D. J., & Kinzer, C. K. (2003). Toward a theoretical framework of new literacies on the Internet: Central principles. In J. C. Richards & M. C. McKenna (Eds.), *Integrating multiple literacies in K-8 classrooms: Cases, commentaries, and practical applications* (pp. 18–37). Mahwah, NJ: Lawrence Erlbaum Associates, Publishers.

Leu, D. J., Kinzer, C. K., Coiro, J., Castek, J., & Henry, L. A. (2013). New literacies: A dual-level theory of the changing nature of literacy, instruction, and assessment. In D. E. Alvermann, N. J. Unrau, & R. B. Ruddell (Eds.), *Theoretical models and processes of reading* (6th ed.; pp. 1150–1181). Newark, DE: International Reading Association. doi:10.1598/0710.42

Levine, F., & Heimerl, C. (2008). *Handmade Nation: The Rise of DIY, Art, Craft, and Design.* New York: Princeton Architectural Press.

Levine, J. (2004). Faculty adoption of instructional technologies: Organizational and personal perspectives. In C. Crawford et al. (Eds.), *Proceedings of Society for Information Technology and Teacher Education International Conference 2004* (pp. 1595-1598). Chesapeake, VA: AACE.

Levin, H. (2003). Making history come alive. *Learning and Leading with Technology, 5,* 175–185.

Lévy, P., & Bononno, R. (1998). *Becoming virtual: reality in the digital age.* Da Capo Press, Incorporated.

Levy, R. (2008). "Third Spaces" are interesting places: Applying "Third Space Theory" to nursery-aged children's constructions of themselves as Readers. *Journal of Early Childhood Literacy, 8*(1), 43–66. doi:10.1177/1468798407087161

Lewin, T. (2011). Digital storytelling. *Participatory Learning and Action, 63,* 54-62.

Lewin, K. (1946). Action research and minority problems. *The Journal of Social Issues, 2*(4), 34–46. doi:10.1111/j.1540-4560.1946.tb02295.x

Lewis, B. (2005, June). Freedom and Justice in the Modern Middle East. *Foreign Affairs.* Retrieved from http://www.foreignaffairs.com/articles/60796/bernard-lewis/freedom-and-justice-in-the-modern-middle-east

Lewis, K. (2013). Infographics: All the rage, but a must-do for your business? *Forbes.* Retrieved from http://www.forbes.com/sites/kernlewis/2013/08/30/infographics-all-the-rage-but-a-must-do-for-your-business/

Lewis, A., & Lin, F. (2008). *SwitchCraft: Battery-Powered Crafts to make and Sew.* New York: Crown Publishing Group.

Lewis, C. (2001). *Literacy practices as social acts: Power, status, and cultural norms in the classroom.* New York, NY: Routledge.

Lewis, C., & Fabos, B. (2000). But will it work in the heartland? A response and illustration. *Journal of Adolescent & Adult Literacy, 43,* 462–469.

Lewis, C., & Fabos, B. (2005). Instant messaging, literacies, and social identities. *Reading Research Quarterly, 40*(4), 470–501. doi:10.1598/RRQ.40.4.5

Lewis, T. L., Burnett, B., Tunstall, R. G., & Abrahams, P. H. (2014). Complementing anatomy education using three-dimensional. *Clinical Anatomy (New York, N.Y.), 27*(3), 313–320. doi:10.1002/ca.22256 PMID:23661327

Leys, C. (2006). The rise and fall of development theory. In M. Edelman & A. Haugerud (Eds.), *The anthropology of development and globalization: From classical political economy to contemporary neoliberalism* (pp. 109–125). Blackwell Anthologies in Social and Cultural Anthropology.

Li, D. (2007). *Why do you blog: A uses-and-gratifications inquiry into bloggers' motivations.* Paper presented at the International Communication Association Convention, San Francisco, CA.

Liao, Y.-K. C. (1999). Effects of hypermedia on students' achievement: A meta-analysis. *Journal of Educational Multimedia and Hypermedia, 8*(3), 255–277.

Liarokapis, F., & Anderson, E. F. (2010). Using augmented reality as a medium to assist teaching in higher education. In *Proceedings of the 31st Annual Conference of the European Association for Computer Graphics* (Eurographics 2010). Eurographics Association.

Library Journal. (2012). *Public library marketing: Methods and best practices.* Retrieved from: https://s3.amazonaws.com/WebVault/PublicLibraryMarketingRpt2013.pdf

Licoppe, C. (2004). 'Connected' presence. The emergence of a new repertoire for managing social relationships in a changing communication technoscape. *Environment and Planning. D, Society & Space*, *22*(1), 135–156. doi:10.1068/d323t

Limacher, L., & Wright, L. (2006). Exploring the therapeutic family intervention of commendations. *Journal of Family Nursing*, *12*(3), 307–331. doi:10.1177/1074840706291696 PMID:16837697

Lim, M. (2013). Many Clicks but Little Sticks: Social Media Activism in Indonesia. *Journal of Contemporary Asia*, *43*(4), 636–657. doi:10.1080/00472336.2013.769386

Lim, S. S., & Clark, L. S. (2010). Virtual worlds as a site of convergence for children's play. *Journal for Virtual Worlds*, *3*(2), 3–19.

Lim, S. S., Nekmat, E., & Nahar, S. N. (2011). The implications of multimodality For media literacy. In K. L. O'Halloran & B. A. Smith (Eds.), *Multimodal studies: Exploring issues and domains* (pp. 167–183). New York: Routledge.

Lin, C.-C. (2014). Learning English reading in a mobile-assisted extensive reading program. *Computers & Education*, *78*, 48–59. doi:10.1016/j.compedu.2014.05.004

Lind, R. A. (2012). Produsing theory in a digital world: Illustrating *homo irretitus*. In R. A. Lind (Ed.), *Produsing theory: The intersection of audiences and production in a digital world* (pp. 1–14). New York: Peter Lang Publishers.

Lindsay, E. (2013). The space between us: Electronic music + modern dance + e-textiles. In L. Buechley, K. Peppler, M. Eisenberg, & Y. Kafai (Eds.), *Textile Messages: Dispatches from the World of E-Textiles and Education*.

Ling, R. (2008). Should we be concerned that the elderly don't text? *The Information Society*, *24*(5), 334–341. doi:10.1080/01972240802356125

Ling, R. (2010). Texting as a life phase medium. *Journal of Computer-Mediated Communication*, *15*(2), 277–292. doi:10.1111/j.1083-6101.2010.01520.x

Ling, R., & Baron, N. S. (2013). Mobile phone communication. In S. Herring, D. Stein, & T. Virtanen (Eds.), *Pragmatics of Computer Mediated Communication* (pp. 192–215). Berlin, Germany: De Gruyter. doi:10.1515/9783110214468.191

Ling, R., Bertel, T. F., & Sundsoy, P. R. (2012). The socio-demographics of texting: An analysis of traffic data. *New Media & Society*, *14*(2), 281–298. doi:10.1177/1461444811412711

LinkedIn. (n.d.). *Has anyone been Linked to a fake profile?* Retrieved September 26, 2014, from http://www.linkedin.com/groups/Has-anyone-been-Linked-fake-4812009.S.211395951

Li, Q. (2010). Digital game building: Learning in a participatory culture. *Educational Research*, *52*(4), 427–443. doi:10.1080/00131881.2010.524752

Liss-Schultz, N. (2014). This woman was threatened with rape after calling out sexist video games - and then something inspiring happened. *Mother Jones*. Available from http://www.motherjones.com/media/2014/05/pop-culture-anita-sarkeesian-video-games-sexism-tropes-online-harassment-feminist

Litan, R., & Rivlin, A. M. (2001). Projecting the economic impact of the Internet. *The American Economic Review*, *91*(2), 313–317. doi:10.1257/aer.91.2.313

Litt, E. (2012). *Knock, knock*. Who's there? The imagined audience. *Journal of Broadcasting & Electronic Media*, *56*(3), 330–345. doi:10.1080/08838151.2012.705195

Livingston, G. (2010). *Latinos and digital technology, 2010*. Washington, DC: Pew Research Hispanic Trends Project. Retrieved May 31, 2014 from http://www.pewhispanic.org/2011/02/09/latinos-and-digital-technology-2010/

Livingston, G., Parker, K., & Fox, S. (2009). *Latinos online, 2006-2008: Narrowing the gap*. Washington, DC: Pew Research Hispanic Trends Project. Retrieved May 31, 2014 from http://www.pewhispanic.org/2009/12/22/latinos-online-2006-2008- narrowing-the-gap/

Livingston, A. A. (2004). Smartphones and other mobile devices: The Swiss Army Knives of the 21st Century. *EDUCAUSE Quarterly*, 2746–2752.

Livingstone, S., Haddon, L., Gorzig, A., & Olafsson, K. (2011). *EU Kids Online*. Retrieved from http://www.lse.ac.uk/media%40lse/research/EUKidsOnline/EU%20Kids%20II%20(2009-11)/EUKidsOnlineIIReports/Final%20report.pdf

Livingstone, S. (2008). Taking risky opportunities in youthful content creation: Teenagers' use of social networking sites for intimacy, privacy, and self-expression. *New Media & Society, 10*(3), 393–411. doi:10.1177/1461444808089415

Livingstone, S. (2009). *Children and the Internet: Great expectations, challenging realities.* Cambridge: Polity Press.

Livingstone, S. (2010). Interactivity and participation on the Internet: young people's response to the civic sphere. In P. Dahlgren (Ed.), *Young citizens and new media: Learning for democratic participation* (pp. 103–124). London, UK: Routledge.

Livingstone, S. M., Haddon, L., & Görzig, A. (Eds.). (2012). *Children, risk and safety on the internet: Research and policy challenges in comparative perspective.* Chicago, IL: Policy Press. doi:10.1332/policypress/9781847428837.001.0001

Livingstone, S., & Helsper, E. J. (2008). Parental mediation of children's internet use. *Journal of Broadcasting & Electronic Media, 52*(4), 581–599. doi:10.1080/08838150802437396

Livingstone, S., Kirwil, L., Ponte, C., & Staksrud, E. (2014). In their own words: What bothers children online? *European Journal of Communication, 29*(3), 271–288. doi:10.1177/0267323114521045

Livingstone, S., & Smith, P. K. (2014). Annual research review: Harms experienced by child users of online and mobile technologies: The nature, prevalence and management of sexual and aggressive risks in the digital age. *Journal of Child Psychology and Psychiatry, and Allied Disciplines, 55*(6), 635–654. doi:10.1111/jcpp.12197 PMID:24438579

Li, X., Chu, S., & Ki, W. W. (2014). The effects of a wiki-based collaborative process writing pedagogy on writing ability and attitudes among upper primary school students in Mainland China. *Computers & Education, 77*, 151–169. doi:10.1016/j.compedu.2014.04.019

Li, Y., Guo, A., Lee, J. A., & Negara, G. P. K. (2013). A platform on the cloud for self-creation of mobile interactive learning trails. *International Journal of Mobile Learning Organisation, 7*(1), 66–80. doi:10.1504/IJMLO.2013.051574

Li, Z., & Hegelheimer, V. (2013). Mobile-assisted grammar exercises: Effects on self-editing in L2 writing. *Language Learning & Technology, 17*(3), 135–156.

Logan, S. (2012). *Rausim! Digital politics in Papua New Guinea.* Academic Press.

London Mobile Learning Group. (2014). *Theory: Mobile learning* [web log comment]. Retrieved from http://www.londonmobilelearning.net/#theory.php

Long, J. (2013). Why your business should be using infographics. *Huffington Post.* Retrieved from http://www.huffingtonpost.com/jonathan-long/why-your-business-should-_b_4192309.html

Long, M. P., & Schonfeld, R. C. (2014). *Ithaka S+R US Library Survey 2013.* Retrieved from http://sr.ithaka.org/research-publications/ithaka-sr-us-library-survey-2013

Looker, D. E., & Thiessen, V. (2003). Beyond the digital divide in Canadian schools: From access to competency in the use of information technology. *Social Science Computer Review, 21*(4), 475–490. doi:10.1177/0894439303256536

Lopez, M. H., Gonzalez-Barrera, A., & Patten, E. (2013). *Closing the digital divide: Latinos and technology adoption.* Washington, DC: Pew Research Hispanic Trends Project. Retrieved May 31, 2014 from http://www.pewhispanic.org/2013/03/07/closing-the-digital-divide-latinos-and-technology-adoption/

Lopez, L. K. (2009). The radical act of "mommy blogging": Redefining motherhood through the blogosphere. *New Media & Society, 11*(5), 729–747. doi:10.1177/1461444809105349

López-Sintas, J., Filimon, N., & García Álvarez, M. E. (2012). A social theory of Internet uses based on consumption scale and linkage needs. *Social Science Computer Review, 30*(1), 108–129. doi:10.1177/0894439310390611

Lorenzo, G., & Ittelson, J. (2005). An overview of ePortfolios. Boulder, CO: EDUCAUSE Learning Initiative. Retrieved from www.educause.edu/ir/library/pdf/ELI3001.pdf

Lortie, D. C. (1975). *Schoolteacher: A sociological study.* Chicago: University of Chicago.

Losen, D. J. (2011). *Discipline policies, successful schools, and racial justice*. Boulder, CO: National Education Policy Center.

Loureiro, S. M. C., & Ribeiro, L. (2014). Virtual atmosphere: The effect of pleasure, arousal, and delight on word-of-mouth. *Journal of Promotion Management*, 20(4), 452–469. doi:10.1080/10496491.2014.930283

Lowenfeld, V., & Brittain, W. (1964). *Creative and Mental Growth*. New York, NY: Macmillan.

Lucey, T., & Shifflet, R. (2013). Wiki resources: Using the Internet as a tool for educational collaboration and professional development. In L. Ngo, S. Goldstein & L. Portugal (Eds.), *E-collaboration in Teaching and Learning* (pp. 56-74): Edulogue. Retrieved from http://www.Edulogue.com

Luckerson, V. (2012). *OMG: Traditional text messaging is on the decline*. Retrieved from http://business.time.com/2012/11/15/omg-traditional-text-messaging-is-on-the-decline/

Luke, A. (2013). *Second wave change*. Available at: www.youtube.com/watch?v-RgciQLj-57k7

Luke, A., & Freebody, P. (1999). *Further notes on the four resources model*. Retrieved from http://www.readingonline.org/research/lukefreebody.html

Luke, A., Iyer, R., & Doherty, C. (2011). Literacy education in the context of globalisation. In D. Lapp & D. Fisher (Eds.), Handbook of Research on Teaching of English Language Arts (3rd ed.). New York: Routledge. Retrieved from http://eprints.qut.edu.au/31587/2/31587.pdf

Luke, A. (2002). Curriculum, Ethics, Metanarrative: Teaching and Learning Beyond the Nation. *Curriculum Perspectives*, 22(1), 49–55.

Luke, A. (2008). Using Bourdieu to make policy: mobilizing community capital and literacy. In J. Albright & A. Luke (Eds.), *Pierre Bourdieu and literacy education*. New York, NY: Taylor & Francis.

Lund, A. (2008). Wikis: A collective approach to language production. *ReCALL*, 20(1), 35–54. doi:10.1017/S0958344008000414

Lundby, K. (2009). The matrices of digital storytelling: Examples from Scandinavia. In J. Harley & K. McWilliam (Eds.), *Story circle: Digital storytelling around the world* (pp. 176–187). Chichester, UK: Wiley-Blackwell. doi:10.1002/9781444310580.ch12

Lundin, R. (2008). Teaching with Wikis: Toward a Networked Pedagogy. *Computers and Composition*, 25(4), 432–448. doi:10.1016/j.compcom.2008.06.001

Luria, A. R. (1976). *Cognitive development, its cultural and social foundations*. Cambridge, MA: Harvard University Press.

Ly, A., & Vaala, A. (2014, August 15). *What's in store today: A snapshot of kids' language & literacy apps, Part 1*. Washington, DC: New America's Ed Policy Program and the Joan Ganz Cooney Center at Sesame Workshop. Retrieved from http://tinyurl.com/nlxs4wu

Lykourentzou, I., Dagka, F., Papadaki, K., Lepouras, G., & Vassilakis, C. (2012). Wikis in enterprise settings: A survey. *Enterprise Information Systems*, 6(1), 1–53. doi:10.1080/17517575.2011.580008

Lynch, D., Altschuler, G. C., & McClure, P. (2002). Professors should embrace technology in courses...and colleges must create technology plans. *The Chronicle of Higher Education*, 48(19), B15.

Mace, M. (2010, March 19). Why e-books failed in 2000, and what it means for 2010. *Business Insider*. Retrieved from www.businessinsider.com/why-ebooks-failed-in-2000-and-what-it-means-for-2010-2010

Mackey, M. (2002). *Literacies Across Media: Playing the text*. Abingdon: Routledge. doi:10.4324/9780203218976

MacKinnon, R. (2011, July 31). *Our Web freedom at the mercy of tech giants*. Retrieved from http://www.cnn.com/2011/OPINION/07/31/mackinnon.tech.freedom/index.html

MacMillan, D. (2013, November 20). *Snapchat CEO: 70% of users are women* [Blog post]. Retrieved from http://blogs.wsj.com/digits/2013/11/20/snapchat-ceo-says-70-of-users-are-women/

Macnamara, J. (2010). Public communication practices in the Web 2.0-3.0 mediascape: The case for PRevolution. *Prism*, 7(3). Retrieved from http://www.prismjournal.org

MacWilliam, A. (2013). The engaged reader. *Publishing Research Quarterly*, *29*(1), 1–11. doi:10.1007/s12109-013-9305-8

Madden, M., Lenhart, A., Duggan, M., Cortesi, S., & Gasser, U. (2013). *Teens and technology 2013*. Retrieved on January 2, 2015 from http://www.pewinternet.org/2013/03/13/teens-and-technology-2013/

Madden, M., Fox, S., Smith, A., & Vitak, J. (2007). *Digital footprints: Online identity management and search in the age of transparency*. Washington, DC: Pew Internet & American Life Project.

Madden, M., Lenhart, A., Cortesi, S., Gasser, U., Duggan, M., Smith, A., & Beaton, M. (2013). *Teens, social media, and privacy*. Washington, DC: Pew Research Center.

Maddox. (2001). Literacy and the Market: The economic uses of literacy among the peasantry in northwest Bangladesh. In B. V. Street (Ed.), *Literacy and development: Ethnographic perspectives*. New York, NY: Psychology.

Madrigal, A. C. (2011, January 24). *The Inside Story of How Facebook Responded to Tunisian Hacks*. Retrieved September 26, 2014, from http://www.theatlantic.com/technology/archive/2011/01/the-inside-story-of-how-facebook-responded-to-tunisian-hacks/70044/2/

Magazine, H. (2014). *Why 'Big Data' is a big deal*. Retrieved from http://harvardmag.com/pdf/2014/03-pdfs/0314-30.pdf

Magee, R. M., Naughton, R., O'Gan, P., Forte, A., & Agosto, D. E. (2012). *Social media practices and support in U.S. public libraries and school library media centers*. Paper presented at ASIST 2012. Retrieved from https://www.asis.org/asist2012/proceedings/Submissions/334.pdf

Maggiolino, M., Montagnini, M. L., & Nuccio, M. (2014). Cultural content in the digital arena: toward the hybridization of legal and business models. *Organizational Aesthetics*, *3*(1), 42-64. Retrieved from http://digitalcommons.wpi.edu/oa/vol3/iss1/6/

Maghrabi, R., & Salam, A. F. (2011). *Social Media, Social Movement and Political Change: The Case of 2011 Cairo Revolt*. Academic Press.

Magley, G. (2011, October 3). *Grade 8 mobile one-to-one with iPads: Component of the Millis schools personalized learning initiative*. Millisp, MA: Millisp Public Schools. Retrieved from http://tinyurl.com/k7jfato

Mahmood, K., & Richardson, J. V. Jr. (2011). Impact of web 2.0 technologies on academic libraries: A survey of ARL libraries. *The Electronic Library*, *31*(4), 508–520. doi:10.1108/EL-04-2011-0068

Mainardi, C. (2013). Foreword. In B. Bilbao-Osorio, S. Dutta, & B. Lanvin (Eds.), The global information technology report 2013: Growth and jobs in a hyperconnected world (p. vii). Geneva, Switzerland: World Economic Forum. Retrieved from http://www.gov.mu/portal/sites/indicators/files/WEF_GITR_Report_2013.pdf

Mainwaring, S. (2011). *Egypt: Social Media as a Life or Death Proposition*. Retrieved September 27, 2014, from http://www.fastcompany.com/1724837/egypt-social-media-life-or-death-proposition

Maiye, A., & McGrath, K. (2010). ICTs and sustainable development: A capability perspective. *AMCIS 2010 Proceedings, 541*. Retrieved from http://aisel.aisnet.org/amcis2010/541

Mak, B., & Coniam, D. (2008). Using wikis to enhance and develop writing skills among secondary school students in Hong Kong. *System*, *36*(3), 437–455. doi:10.1016/j.system.2008.02.004

Malaga, R. (2010). Choosing a wiki platform for student projects - Lessons learned. *Contemporary Issues In Education Research*, *3*(2), 49–54.

Malin. (2014). *Youth civic development and education*. Retrieved on July 26, 2014 from https://coa.stanford.edu/sites/default/files/Civic%20Education%20report.pdf

Malloy, J. (1986). *Uncle Roger*. Retrieved from http://www.well.com/user/jmalloy/uncleroger/partytop.html

Malloy, J. (1993). Its name was Penelope. Watertown, MA: Eastgate Systems, Inc. (Original exhibition version 1989)

Malone, T. W., & Bernstein, M. S. (in press). Introduction. In *Collective intelligence handbook*. Boston: MIT Press. Retrieved from https://docs.google.com/document/d/1CRVN8uxa_g8i3oLRfVxhsltWNZ_ZM-woI-pl5IosG9VU/edit?pli=1

Maloney, J., Peppler, K., Kafai, Y. B., Resnick, M., & Rusk, N. (2008). *Programming by choice: Urban youth learning programming with scratch. Published in the.* Portland, OR: Proceedings by the ACM Special Interest Group on Computer Science Education. doi:10.1145/1352135.1352260

Manago, A. M., Graham, M., Greenfield, P. M., & Salimkhan, G. (2008). Self-presentation and gender on MySpace. *Journal of Applied Developmental Psychology*, *29*(6), 446–458. doi:10.1016/j.appdev.2008.07.001

Mancusi, M. (2010). *Gamer girl.* New York.

Mancuso, D. S., Chlup, D. T., & McWhorter, R. R. (2010). A study of adult learning in a virtual world. *Advances in Developing Human Resources*, *12*(6), 681–699. doi:10.1177/1523422310395368

Mangen, A., Robinet, P., Olivier, G., & Velay, J.-L. (2014, July 21-25). *Mystery story reading in pocket print book and on Kindle: Possible impact on chronological events memory.* Paper presented at The International Society for the Empirical Study of Literature and Media, Turin, Italy. Retrieved from http://tinyurl.com/llvaeav

Manion, C., & Selfe, R. (2012). Sharing an Assessment Ecology: Digital Media, Wikis, and the Social Work of Knowledge. *Technical Communication Quarterly*, *21*(1), 25–45. doi:10.1080/10572252.2012.626756

Mann, H. (1848). *Annual report of the Board of Education together with the annual report of the Secretary of the Board* (Vol. 12). Boston, MA: Massachusetts Board of Education.

Manovich, L. (n.d.). *Visualization methods for media studies.* Retrieved July 22, 2014, from https://www.academia.edu/2800483/Visualization_Methods_for_Media_Studies

Mansell, R. (2001). Digital opportunities and the missing link for developing countries. *Oxford Review of Economic Policy*, *17*(2), 282–295. doi:10.1093/oxrep/17.2.282

Mansson, D. H., & Myers, S. A. (2011). An initial examination of college students' expressions of affection through Facebook. *The Southern Communication Journal*, *76*(2), 155–168. doi:10.1080/10417940903317710

Mantilla, K. (2013). Gendertrolling: Misogyny adapts to new media. *Feminist Studies*, *39*(2), 563–570.

Mao, J. (2014). Social media for learning: A mixed methods study on high school students' technology affordances and perspectives. *Computers in Human Behavior*, *33*, 213–223. doi:10.1016/j.chb.2014.01.002

Marcu, G., Kaufman, S. J., Lee, J. K., Black, R. W., Dourish, P., Hayes, G. R., & Richardson, D. J. (2010, March). Design and evaluation of a computer science and engineering course for middle school girls. In *Proceedings of the 41st ACM technical symposium on computer science education* (pp. 234–238). New York, NY: ACM. doi:10.1145/1734263.1734344

Marculescu, D., Marculescu, R., Zamora, N., Stanley-Marbell, P., Kholsa, P., Park, S., ... (2003). Electronic textiles: A platform for pervasive computing. *Proceedings of the IEEE.* citeseer.ist.psu.edu/marculescu03electronic.html

Marcum, J. W. (2002). Beyond visual culture: The challenge of visual ecology. *Libraries and the Academy*, *2*(2), 189–206. doi:10.1353/pla.2002.0038

Margolis, J., & Fisher, A. (2001). *Unlocking the Clubhouse: Women in Computing.* Boston, MA: MIT press.

Markoff, J. (2006). Entrepreneurs see a web guided by common sense. *New York Times, 12.*

Markoff, J. (2006, November 12). Entrepreneurs see a web guided by common sense. *New York Times.* Retrieved from http://www.nytimes.com/2006/11/12/business/12web.html?pagewanted=all&_r=0

Marques, D., Costello, R., & Azevedo, J. (2013). *Augmented reality facilitating visual literacy for engagement with science in museums.* Paper presented at Electronic Visualisation and the Arts (EVA 2013), London, UK.

Marra, R. (2013). Mindtools in online education enabling meaningful learning. In Learning, Problem Solving, and Mind Tools: Essays in Honor of David H. Jonassen (pp. 260-277). Routledge.

Marsh, J. (2007). Digital childhoods, digital classrooms: The teaching and learning of literacy in a new media age. In B. Dwyer, G. Shiel, Reading Association of Ireland, & Conference (Eds.), Literacy at the crossroads: Moving forward, looking back (pp. 36–50). Dublin, Ireland: Reading Association of Ireland.

Marsh, J. (1999). Batman and Batwoman go to school: Popular culture in the literacy curriculum. *International Journal of Early Years Education*, *7*(2), 117–131. doi:10.1080/0966976990070201

Marsh, J. (2005). *Popular culture, new media and digital literacy in early childhood*. New York, NY: Routledge Falmer. doi:10.4324/9780203420324

Marsh, J. (2006). Emergent media literacy: Digital animation in early childhood. *Language and Education*, *20*(6), 493–506. doi:10.2167/le660.0

Marsh, J. (2010). Young children's play in online virtual worlds. *Journal of Early Childhood Research*, *8*(1), 23–39. doi:10.1177/1476718X09345406

Marsh, J. (2011). Young children's literacy practices in a virtual world: Establishing an online interaction order. *Reading Research Quarterly*, *46*(2), 101–118. doi:10.1598/RRQ.46.2.1

Marsh, J. (2013). Countering Chaos in *Club Penguin*. In G. Merchant, J. Gillen, J. Marsh, & J. Davies (Eds.), *Virtual Literacies: interactive spaces for children and young people* (pp. 73–88). Abingdon: Routledge.

Marsh, J. (2014). Purposes for literacy in children's use of the online virtual world Club Penguin: Literacy purposes in virtual worlds. *Journal of Research in Reading*, *37*(2), 179–195. doi:10.1111/j.1467-9817.2012.01530.x

Martey, R. M., & Consalvo, M. (2011). Performing the looking-glass self: Avatar appearance and group identity in *Second Life*. *Popular Communication*, *9*(3), 165–180. doi:10.1080/15405702.2011.583830

Martey, R. M., Stromer-Galley, J., Banks, J., Wu, J., & Consalvo, M. (2014). The strategic female: Gender-switching and player behavior in online games. *Information. Technology & Society*, *17*, 286–300.

Martin, F., & Ertzberger, J. (2013). Here and now mobile learning: An experimental study on the use of mobile technology. *Computers & Education*, *68*, 76–85. doi:10.1016/j.compedu.2013.04.021

Marvin, C. (1990). *When Old Technologies Were New: Thinking About Electric Communication in the Late Nineteenth Century*. New York: Oxford University Press.

Marzilli, C., Delello, J. A., Marmion, S., McWhorter, R. R., Brown, P., & Marzilli, T. S. (2014). Faculty attitudes towards integrating technology and innovation. *International Journal on Integrating Technology in Education*, *3*(1), 1–20. doi:10.5121/ijite.2014.3101

Mashable. (2013). *Data visualization*. Retrieved from http://mashable.com/category/data-visualization

Masten, D., & Plowman, T. M. P. (2003). *Digital ethnography: the next wave in understanding the consumer experience*. Retrieved from http://www.dmi.org/dmi/html/interests/research/03142MAS75.pdf

Mathews, J. M. (2010). Using a studio-based pedagogy to engage students in the design of mobile-based media. *English Teaching*, *9*(1), 87–102.

Mattelart, A., & Mattelart, M. (1998). *Theories of Communication: A Short Introduction*. London: SAGE Publications Ltd.

Matthews-DeNatale, G. (2008). *Digital storytelling: Tips and resources* Retrieved from https://net.educause.edu/ir/library/pdf/ELI08167B.pdf

Maull, R., Godsiff, P., & Mulligan, C. E. (2014). The impact of datafication on service systems. *47th Hawaii International Conference on System Sciences (HICSS)*. Retrieved from http://www.computer.org/csdl/proceedings/hicss/2014/2504/00/2504b193-abs.html

Mavrommati, I., & Fotaris, P. (2012). Teaching design from a distance: The deviantArt case of Virtual Design Studio. *IEEE Learning Technology Newsletter*, *14*(2), 24–25.

May, P. (2013). *Apps for helping autistic kids socially and academically*. San Jose Mercury News. Retrieved from http://www.aurasma.com/education/aurasma-listed-among-apps-for-helping-autistic-kids-socially-and-academically/

Mayer, R. E., & Moreno, R. (1998a). *A cognitive theory of multimedia learning: Implications for design principles*. Retrieved from http://www.unm.edu/~moreno/PDFS/chi.pdf

Mayer, R. E. (2001). *Multi-media learning*. Cambridge, MA: Cambridge University Press. doi:10.1017/CBO9781139164603

Mayer, R. E. (2005a). Cognitive theory of multimedia learning. In R. E. Mayer (Ed.), *The Cambridge handbook of multimedia learning* (pp. 31–48). New York, NY: Cambridge University Press. doi:10.1017/CBO9780511816819.004

Mayer, R. E. (2005b). Introduction to multimedia learning. In R. E. Mayer (Ed.), *The Cambridge handbook of multimedia learning* (pp. 1–18). New York, NY: Cambridge University Press. doi:10.1017/CBO9780511816819.002

Mayer, R. E. (2008). Multimedia literacy. In J. Coiro, M. Knobel, C. Lankshear, & D. J. Leu (Eds.), *Handbook of research on new literacies* (pp. 359–376). New York: Taylor and Francis Group.

Mayer, R. E., & Moreno, R. (1998b). A split-attention effect in multimedia learning: Evidence for dual processing systems in working memory. *Educational Psychology, 90*(2), 312–320. doi:10.1037/0022-0663.90.2.312

Mayer, R. E., & Moreno, R. (2003). Nine ways to reduce cognitive load in multimedia learning. *Educational Psychologist, 38*(1), 43–52. doi:10.1207/S15326985EP3801_6

Mazoue, J. G. (2013). Five myths about MOOCs. *Educause Review Online*. Retrieved from http://www.educause.edu/ero/article/five-myths-about-moocs

McAuley, A., Stewart, B., Siemens, G., & Cormier, D. (2010). *The MOOC model for digital practice*. Retrieved from https://oerknowledgecloud.org/sites/oerknowledgecloud.org/files/MOOC_Final_0.pdf

McCaskell, T. (2012). The politics of *common cause*: Using "values framing" to understand the battle over bullying in our schools. *Our Schools/Our Selves, 21*(4), 45-78.

McChesney, R. W. (2013). *Digital disconnect: How capitalism is turning the Internet against democracy*. New York: New Press.

McClean, C. (2010). A space called home: An immigrant adolescent's digital literacy practices. *Journal of Adolescent & Adult Literacy, 54*(1), 13–22. doi:10.1598/JAAL.54.1.2

McClean, C. (2013). Literacies, identities, and gender: Reframing girls in digital Worlds. In B. J. Guzzetti & T. W. Bean (Eds.), *Adolescent literacies and the gendered self: (Re)constructing identities through multimodal literacy practices* (pp. 64–73). New York: Routledge.

McClenaghan, D., & Doecke, B. (2010). Resources for meaning-making in the secondary English classroom. In D. R. Cole & D. L. Pullen (Eds.), *Multiliteracies in motion: Current theory and practice* (pp. 224–238). New York, NY: Routledge.

McCoy, B. (2013). Digital distraction in the classroom: Student classroom use of digital devices for non-class-related purposes. *Journal of Media Education*. Retrieved from http://en.calameo.com/read/000091789af53ca4e647f

McDermott, R., & Archibald, D. (2010, March). Harnessing Your Staff's Informal Networks. *Harvard Business Review, 88*(3), 82–89. PMID:20402051

McElroy, B. D. (2009, June 16). *Twitter maintained service during Iranian elections after US State Dept request*. Retrieved from http://www.telegraph.co.uk/technology/twitter/5552733/Twitter-maintained-service-during-Iranian-elections-after-US-State-Dept-request.html

McEneaney, J. E. (2011). Web 3.0, litbots, and TPWS-GWTAU. *Journal of Adolescent & Adult Literacy, 54*(5), 376–378. doi:10.1598/JAAL.54.5.8

McGaw, J. (2003/1996). Reconceiving technology: Why feminine technologies matter. *Gender and Archaeology*, 52–75.

McGonigal, J. (2011). *Reality is broken: Why games make us better and how they can change the world*. New York: The Penguin Press.

McKenzie, B. A. (2014). Teaching Twitter: Re-enacting the Paris commune and the Battle of Stalingrad. *The History Teacher, 47*(3), 355–372.

McKenzie, M. (2012). Education for y'all: Global neoliberalism and the case for a politics of scale in sustainability education policy. *Policy Futures in Education, 10*(2), 165–177. doi:10.2304/pfie.2012.10.2.165

McKinsey & Co. (2009). *Mobile broadband for the masses: Regulatory levers to make it happen.* Ney York, NY: McKinsey & Co.

McLain, B. (2014). Delineation of evaluation criteria for educational apps in STEM education. In C. Miller & A. Doering (Eds.), *The new landscape of mobile learning* (pp. 192–207). New York: Routledge.

McLean, K., Pasupathi, M., & Pals, J. (2007). Selves creating stories creating selves: A process model of self development. *Personality and Social Psychology Review*, *11*(3), 262–278. doi:10.1177/1088868307301034 PMID:18453464

McLuhan, M. (1960, May 18). *The global village* [Video file]. Retrieved from http://www.cbc.ca/archives/categories/arts-entertainment/media/marshall-mcluhan-the-man-and-his-message/world-is-a-global-village.html

McLuhan, M. (1994). *Understanding media: The extensions of man* (T. Gordon, Ed.). Berkeley, CA: Gingko Press. (Original work published 1964)

McLuhan, M. (2001). *The Medium is the Massage* (9th ed.). Corte Madera, CA: Gingko Press.

McPake, J., Plowman, L., & Stephen, C. (2013). Preschool children creating and communicating with digital technologies in the home. *British Journal of Educational Technology*, *44*(3), 421–431. doi:10.1111/j.1467-8535.2012.01323.x

McPherson, C. (2012). *Using a wiki to facilitate student collaboration in an upper elementary art project: A case study.* Academic Press.

McPherson, M., Smith-Lovin, L., & Brashears, M. E. (2006). Social isolation in America: Changes in core discussion networks over two decades. *American Sociological Review*, *71*(3), 353–375. doi:10.1177/000312240607100301

McQuivey, J. (2013). *Digital disruption: Unleashing the next wave of innovation.* New York, NY: Amazon.

McWhorter, R. R. (2012). *Augmented reality for virtual HRD.* Retrieved from http://virtualhrd.wordpress.com/2012/01/18/augmented-reality-for-virtual-hrd/

McWhorter, R. R., & Bennett, E. E. (2012). *Facilitating transition from higher education to the workforce: A literature review of ePortfolios as virtual human resource development.* Paper presented at the Academy of Human Resource Development International Conference, Denver, CO.

McWhorter, R. R. (2010). Exploring the emergence of virtual human resource development. *Advances in Developing Human Resources*, *12*(6), 623–631. doi:10.1177/1523422310395367

McWhorter, R. R., Delello, J. A., Roberts, P. B., Raisor, C. M., & Fowler, D. A. (2013). A cross-case analysis of the use of web-based eportfolios in higher education. *Journal of Information Technology Education: Innovations in Practice*, *12*, 253–286. Retrieved from http://www.jite.org/documents/Vol12/JITEv12IIPp253-286McWhorter1238.pdf

McWilliam, K. (2009). The global diffusion of a community media practice: Digital storytelling online. In J. Harley & K. McWilliam (Eds.), *Story circle* (pp. 37–76). Chichester, UK: Wiley-Blackwell. doi:10.1002/9781444310580.ch3

Meadows, D., & Kidd, J. (2009). "Capture Wales": The BBC digital storytelling project. In J. Hartley & K. McWilliam (Eds.), *Story circle: Digital storytelling around the world* (pp. 91–117). Malden, MA: Wiley & Sons. doi:10.1002/9781444310580.ch5

Medina, J. (2014). *Brain rules: 12 principles for surviving and thriving at work, home, and school.* Seattle, WA: Pear Press.

Meehan, E. R. (2002). Gendering the commodity audience: Critical media research, feminism, and political economy. In E. R. Meehan & E. Riordan (Eds.), *Sex and money: Feminism and political economy in the media* (pp. 209–222). Minneapolis, MN: University of Minnesota Press.

Mehari, K. R., Farrell, A. D., & Le, A.-T. H. (2014). Cyberbullying among adolescents: Measures in search of a construct. *Psychology of Violence.* doi: 10.1037/a0037521.supp

Meister, J. (2014). The wearable era is here: Implications for the future workplace. *Forbes.* Retrieved from http://www.forbes.com/sites/jeannemeister/2014/06/16/the-wearable-era-is-here-implications-for-the-future-workplace/

Mejova, Y., Srinivasan, P., & Boynton, B. (2013). GOP Primary Season on Twitter: "Popular" Political Sentiment in Social Media. In *Proceedings of the Sixth ACM International Conference on Web Search and Data Mining* (pp. 517–526). New York, NY: ACM. doi:10.1145/2433396.2433463

meme. (2012). In *Merriam-Webster.com.* Retrieved from http://www.merriam-webster.com/dictionary/meme

Menard-Warwick, J. (2007). "My little sister had a disaster, she had a baby": Gendered performance, relational identities, and dialogic voicing. *Narrative Inquiry, 17*(2), 279–297. doi:10.1075/ni.17.2.07men

Menesini, E. (2012). Cyberbullying: The right value of the phenomenon. Comments on the paper "Cyberbullying: An overrated phenomenon?". *European Journal of Developmental Psychology, 9*(5), 544–552. doi:10.1080/17405629.2012.706449

Menesini, E., Nocentini, A., & Palladino, B. E. (2012). Empowering students against bullying and cyberbullying: Evaluation of an Italian peer-led model. *International Journal of Conflict and Violence, 6*(2), 314–320.

Menesini, E., Nocentini, A., Palladino, B. E., Frisén, A., Berne, S., Ortega-Ruiz, R., & Smith, P. K. et al. (2012). Cyberbullying definition among adolescents: A comparison across six European countries. *Cyberpsychology, Behavior, and Social Networking, 15*(9), 455–462. doi:10.1089/cyber.2012.0040 PMID:22817693

Mercado, C. I., & Reyes, L. O. (2010). Latino community activism in the twenty-first century. In E. Murillo Jr et al. (Eds.), *Handbook of Latinos and Education: Theory, research, and practice* (pp. 250–261). New York, NY: Routledge.

Merchant, G. (2003). E-mail me your thoughts: Digital communication and narrative writing. *Reading, 37*(3), 104–110.

Merchant, G. (2007). Writing the future in the digital age. *Literacy, 41*(3), 118–128. doi:10.1111/j.1467-9345.2007.00469.x

Merchant, G. (2009). Literacy in Virtual Worlds. *Journal of Research in Reading, 32*(1), 38–56. doi:10.1111/j.1467-9817.2008.01380.x

Merchant, G. (2010). 3D Virtual worlds as environments for literacy teaching. *Education Research, 52*(2), 135–150. doi:10.1080/00131881.2010.482739

Merchant, G. (2011). Unravelling the social network: Theory and research. *Learning, Media and Technology, 37*, 1, 4–19.

Merchant, G. (2012). Mobile practices in everyday life: Popular digital technologies and schooling revisited: Mobile practices in everyday life. *British Journal of Educational Technology, 43*(5), 770–782. doi:10.1111/j.1467-8535.2012.01352.x

Merchant, G. (2014). The Trashmaster: Literacy and new media. *Language and Education, 27*(2), 144–160. doi:10.1080/09500782.2012.760586

Merchant, G., Gillen, J., Marsh, J., & Davies, J. (Eds.). (2014). *Virtual Literacies: interactive spaces for children and young people.* Abingdon: Routledge.

Merriam-Webster. (2014). *Portfolio.* Retrieved from http://www.merriam-webster.com/dictionary/portfolio

Mesch, G. S., Talmud, I., & Quan-Haase, A. (2012). Instant messaging social networks: Individual, relational, and cultural characteristics. *Journal of Social and Personal Relationships, 29*(6), 736–759. doi:10.1177/0265407512448263

Mesko, B. (2013). *Augmented reality in operating rooms soon! Science roll.* Retrieved from http://scienceroll.com/2013/08/22/augmented-reality-in-operating-rooms-soon/

Metros, S. E., & Woolsey, K. (2006, May/June). Visual literacy: An institutional imperative. *EDUCAUSE Review, 41*(3), 80–81.

Metz, R. (2013). Now you see it, now you don't: Disappearing messages are everywhere. *MIT Technology Review*. Retrieved from http://www.technologyreview.com/news/513006/now-you-see-it-now-you-dont-disappearing-messages-are-everywhere/

Metz, S. (2014). New tools-new possibilities. *Science Teacher (Normal, Ill.)*, (3): 10.

Meyer, L. (2013, June 27). Report: Professional development for mobile learning improves student engagement and interest in STEM subjects. *THE Journal*. Retrieved from http://tinyurl.com/jwg27vv

Mezirow, J. (2000). *Learning as transformation*. New York: Jossey Bass.

Middleton, C. (2013). *Certificates, badges, and portfolios: International education and micro-credentialing*. UT Global Initiative, The University of Texas at Austin. Retrieved from http://sites.utexas.edu/utgi/2013/11/certificates-badges-and-portfolios-international-education-and-mico-credentialing/

Mikulecky, L. (2010). An examination of workplace literacy research from new literacies and sociocultural perspectives. In E. A. Baker (Ed.), *The new literacies: Multiple perspectives on research and practice* (pp. 217–241). New York: Guilford Press.

Milberry, K. (2014). (Re)making the Internet: Free software and the social factory hack. In M. Ratto & M. Boler (Eds.), *DIY Citizenship: Critical making and social media* (pp. 53–63). Cambridge, MA: MIT Press.

Miller, J. D., & Hufstedler, S. M. (2009, Jun 28). *Cyberbullying knows no borders*. Paper presented at the Annual Conference of the Australian Teacher Education Association, Albury.

Miller, C. R. (1984). Genre as social action. *The Quarterly Journal of Speech*, *70*(2), 151–176. doi:10.1080/00335638409383686

Miller, C., & Doering, A. (Eds.), *The new landscape of mobile learning*. New York: Routledge.

Miller, L., Luchs, M., & Jalea, G. D. (2012). *Mapping memories: Participatory media, place-based stories, and refugee youth*. Montreal: Concordia University Press.

Miller, M. (2013). *Sams teach yourself Vine in 10 minutes*. Indianapolis, IN: Sams.

Miller, R. E., Vogh, B. S., & Jennings, E. J. (2013). Library in an app: Testing the usability of Boopsie as a mobile library application. *Journal of Web Librarianship*, *7*(2), 142–153. doi:10.1080/19322909.2013.779526

Miller, S. M. (2013). A research metasynthesis on digital video composing in classrooms: An evidence-based framework toward a pedagogy for embodied learning. *Journal of Literacy Research*, *45*(4), 386–430. doi:10.1177/1086296X13504867

Miller, S. M., & McVee, M. B. (2012). Multimodal composing: The essential 21st Century literacy. In S. M. Miller & M. B. McVee (Eds.), *Multimodal composing in classrooms: Learning and teaching for the digital world* (pp. 1–12). New York: Routledge.

Miller, V. (2008). New media, networking and phatic culture. *Convergence (London)*, *14*(4), 387–400. doi:10.1177/1354856508094659

Millner, V. (2008). Internet infidelity: A case of intimacy with detachment. *The Family Journal (Alexandria, Va.)*, *16*(1), 78–82. doi:10.1177/1066480707308918

Mills, K. A., & Exley, B. (2014). Time, space, and text in the elementary school digital writing classroom. *Written Communication*, 1–35.

Mirzoeff, N. (1998). What is visual culture? In N. Mirzoeff (Ed.), *The visual culture reader* (pp. 3–13). London: Routledge.

Mishna, F., Khoury-Kassabri, M., Gadalla, T., & Daciuk, J. (2012). Risk factors for involvement in cyber bullying: Victims, bullies and bully–victims. *Children and Youth Services Review*, *34*(1), 63–70. doi:10.1016/j.childyouth.2011.08.032

Mishra, P., & Koehler, M. J. (2006). Technological pedagogical content knowledge: A Framework for teacher knowledge. *Teachers College Record*, *108*(6), 1017–1054. doi:10.1111/j.1467-9620.2006.00684.x

Miskec, J. (2007). YA by Generation Y: New writers for new readers. *ALAN Review*, *35*(3), 7–14.

Misuraca, G., Broster, D., Centeno, C., Punie, Y., Lampathaki, F., Charalabidis, Y., & Bicking, M. (2010). *Envisioning digital Europe 2030: Scenarios for ICT in future governance and policy modelling*. Luxembourg: Publications Office. doi:10.1145/1930321.1930392

Mitchell, A. (2014, March 26) *State of the news media 2014*. Retrieved from www.journalism.org/packages/state-of-the-news-media-2014

Mitchell, C., Pascarella, De Lange, N., & Stuart, J. (2010). We wanted other people to learn from us: Girls blogging in rural South Africa in the age of AIDS. In S. Mazzarella (Ed.), Girl Wide Web 2.0: Revisiting girls, the internet, and the negotiation of identity (pp. 161-182). New York, NY: Peter Lang.

Mitchell, A., & Savill-Smith, C. (2004). *The use of computer and video games for learning: a review of the literature*. London: Learning and Skills Development Agency.

Mitchell, C. (2008). Getting the picture and changing the picture: Visual methodologies and educational research in South Africa. *South African Journal of Education*, 28, 365–383.

Mitchell, K. J., Finkelhor, D., Wolak, J., Ybarra, M. L., & Turner, H. (2010). Youth Internet victimization in a broader victimization context. *The Journal of Adolescent Health*, 48(2), 128–134. doi:10.1016/j.jadohealth.2010.06.009 PMID:21257110

Mitra, S. (2007). *Kids can teach themselves*. Retrieved August 22 from http://www.ted.com/talks/sugata_mitra_shows_how_kids_teach_themselves

Mitra, S. (2013). Beyond the hole in the wall: A Q&A with 2013 TED Prize Winner. *TED Blog*. Retrieved January 15, 2015 from http://blog.ted.com/2013/03/04/before-the-hole-in-the-wall-a-qa-with-2013-ted-prize-winner-sugata-mitra/

Mitra, S. (2009). Case study: The hole in the wall, or minimally invasive education representations and imagery in learning. In P. T. H. Unwin (Ed.), *ICT4D: Information and communication technology for development* (p. 390). New York, NY: Cambridge University Press.

Mitra, S., & Dangwal, R. (2010). Limits to self-organising systems of learning—the Kalikuppam experiment. *British Journal of Educational Technology*, 41(5), 672–688. doi:10.1111/j.1467-8535.2010.01077.x

Moe, H., & Van den Bulck, H. (2014). *Some Snowden, a lettuce bikini and grumpy cat? Searching for public service media outside the boundaries of the institution*. Retrieved from Paper for the 2014 RIPE Conference website: http://ripeat.org/wp-content/uploads/tdomf/3693/Moe%20&%20Van%20den%20Bulck%20RIPE%20paper%202014.pdf

Mohamed, N., & Ahmad, I. H. (2012). Information privacy concerns, antecedents and privacy measure use in social networking sites: Evidence from Malaysia. *Computers in Human Behavior*, 28(6), 2366–2375. doi:10.1016/j.chb.2012.07.008

Moje, E. B., Ciechanowski, K. M. I., Kramer, K., Ellis, L., Carrillo, R., & Collazo, T. (2004). Working toward third space in content area literacy: An examination of everyday funds of knowledge and discourse. *Reading Research Quarterly*, 39(1), 38–70. doi:10.1598/RRQ.39.1.4

Moje, E. B., Stockdill, D., Kim, K., & Kim, H.-j. (2011). *The role of text in disciplinary learning The Handbook of Reading Research* (Vol. 4, pp. 453–486). New York: Routledge.

Moline, S. (2011). I see what you mean: Visual Literacy K-8 (2nd ed.). Portland, ME: Stenhouse Publishers

Moll, L., Amanti, C., Neff, D., & Gonzalez, N. (1992). Funds of knowledge for teaching: Using a qualitative approach to Connect homes and classrooms. *Theory into Practice*, 3(2), 132–141. doi:10.1080/00405849209543534

Molyneaux, H., O'Donnell, S., & Gibson, K. (2009). YouTube vlogs: An analysis of the gender divide. *Media Report to Women*, 37, 6–11.

Monteiro, B. (2008). Blogs and female expression in the Middle East. *Media Development*, 55, 47–53.

Montgomery, S. E. (2014). Critical Democracy Through Digital Media Production in a Third-Grade Classroom. *Theory and Research in Social Education*, 42(2), 197–227. doi:10.1080/00933104.2014.908755

Moran, M., Seaman, J., & Tinti-Kane, H. (2011). *Teaching, learning, and sharing: How today's higher education faculty use social media*. Boston, MA: Pearson Learning Solutions.

Moravec, M. (Ed.). (2011). *Motherhood online: How online communities shape modern motherhood*. Newcastle upon Tyne, UK: Cambridge Scholars Publishing.

Moreno, M. A., Egan, K. G., Bare, K., Young, H. N., & Cox, E. D. (2013). Internet safety education for youth: Stakeholder perspectives. *BMC Public Health*, *13*(1), 1–6. doi:10.1186/1471-2458-13-543 PMID:23738647

Morgan, B., & Smith, R. (2008). A wiki for classroom writing. *The Reading Teacher*, *62*(1), 80–82. doi:10.1598/RT.62.1.10

Moritz, D. (2014). *5 brands shaking up visual content strategy with Hyperlapse*. Retrieved from http://sociallysorted.com.au/visual-content-strategy-hyperlapse/

Morningstar, C., & Farmer, F. R. (2008). The lessons of Lucasfilm's *Habitat*. *Journal of Virtual Worlds Research*, *1*(1), 1–20.

Morozov, E. (2012). *The Net Delusion: The Dark Side of Internet Freedom (Reprint edition.)*. New York: Public Affairs.

Morrell, E. (2002). Toward a critical pedagogy of popular culture: Literacy development among urban youth. *Journal of Adolescent & Adult Literacy*, 72–77.

Morrell, E., Duenas, R., Garcia, V., & Lopez, J. (2013). *Critical media pedagogy: Teaching for achievement in city schools*. New York: Teachers College Press.

Morris, C. (2013). *The sexiest job of the 21st century: Data analyst*. Retrieved from http://www.cnbc.com/id/100792215# Mourshed

Morris, R. C. (1995). All made up: Performance theory and the new anthropology of sex and gender. *Annual Review of Anthropology*, *24*(1), 567–592. doi:10.1146/annurev.an.24.100195.003031

Morris, R. D. (2011). Web 3.0: Implications for Online Learning. *Techtrends: Linking Research & Practice To Improve Learning*, *55*(1), 42–46. doi:10.1007/s11528-011-0469-9

Mossberger, K., Tolbert, C. J., & Franko, W. W. (2013). *Digital cities: The Internet and the geography of opportunity*. Academic Press.

Mossberger, K., Tolbert, C. J., & Stansbury, M. (2003). *Virtual inequality: Beyond the digital divide*. Washington, DC: Georgetown University Press.

Motschenbacher, H. (2009). Speaking of the gendered body: The performative construction of commercial femininities and masculinities via body-part vocabulary. *Language in Society*, *38*(01), 1–22. doi:10.1017/S0047404508090015

Mott, P. (2012, August 6). *Freedom of Speech Doesn't Mean a Thing to Twitter -- Or Does It?* Retrieved September 26, 2014, from http://www.huffingtonpost.com/patrick-mott/freedom-of-speech-doesnt-_b_1739207.html

Moulthrop, S. (1991). The politics of hypertext. In G. Hawisher & C. Selfe (Eds.), *Evolving perspectives on computers and composition studies* (pp. 253–271). Urbana, IL: NCTE.

Moulthrop, S. (1991). *Victory garden*. Watertown, MA: Eastgate Systems, Inc.

Moulthrop, S. (1994). Rhizome and resistance: Hypertext and the dreams of a new culture. In G. P. Landow (Ed.), *Hyper/text/theory* (pp. 299–319). Baltimore, MD: The John Hopkins University Press.

Mounajjed, N., Peng, C., & Walker, S. (2007). Ethnographic interventions: A strategy and experiments in mapping sociospatial practice. *Human Technology*, *3*(1), 68–97. doi:10.17011/ht/urn.200771

Mourtada, R., & Salem, F. (2011). Civil movements: The impact of Facebook and Twitter. *Arab Social Media Report*, *1*(2), 1–30.

Moy, L. C. (2008). Disrupting "bully" talk: Progressive practices and transformative spaces for anti-violence work in schools (doctoral dissertation). Vancouver: University of British Columbia; Retrieved from http://hdl.handle.net/2429/5739

Mozilla. (2014). *Open badges*. Retrieved from http://openbadges.org/display/

Mun-cho, K., & Jong-Kil, K. (2001). Digital divide: conceptual discussions and prospect. In W. Kim, T. Wang Ling, Y.J. Lee & S.S. Park (Eds.), *The human society and the Internet: Internet related socio-economic Issues, First International Conference, Seoul, Korea: Proceedings.* New York, NY: Springer.

Mundie, J., & Hooper, S. (2014). The potential of connected mobile learning. In C. Miller & A. Doering (Eds.), *The new landscape of mobile learning* (pp. 8–18). New York: Routledge.

Mungiu-Pippidi, A., & Munteanu, I. (2009). Moldova's "Twitter Revolution". *Journal of Democracy, 20*(3), 136–142. doi:10.1353/jod.0.0102

Murphy, M. E. (2014, August). Why some schools are selling their iPads. *The Atlantic.* Accessed Oct 15, 2014 from http://www.theatlantic.com/education/archive/2014/08/whats-the-best-device-for-interactive-learning/375567/

Mutula, S. M. (2005). Bridging the digital divide through e-governance: A proposal for Africa's libraries and information centres. *The Electronic Library, 23*(5), 592–602. doi:10.1108/02640470510631308

Myracle, L. (2004). ttyl. New York: Amulet.

Naim, H. (2011, May 17). *Social media creating social awareness in the Arab world by Hani Naim - Common Ground News Service.* Retrieved September 27, 2014, from http://www.commongroundnews.org/article.php?id=29759&lan=en&sp=0

Nardi, B. (2010). *My Life as a Night Elf Priest: An Anthropological Account of World of Warcraft.* Michigan: University of Michigan Press.

NASA.gov. (2013). *Curiosity – 7 minutes of terror.* NASA Jet Propulsion Laboratory. Retrieved from http://www.jpl.nasa.gov/infographics/infographic.view.php?id=10776

Nash, R. (2014). What is the business of literature? *The Virginia Quarterly Review, 90*(4). Retrieved from http://www.vqronline.org/articles/what-business-literature

Nastu, J. (2012, October 29). *How "collaborative learning" is transforming higher education* [web log comment]. Retrieved from http://tinyurl.com/owyg9ao

National Conference of State Legislatures. (2014). *Cyberbullying enacted legislation: 2006-2010.* Washington, DC: Retrieved from http://www.ncsl.org/research/education/cyberbullying.aspx

National Council for the Teaching of English (NCTE). (2008). *The NCTE definition of 21st century literacies.* Retrieved from http://www.ncte.org/positions/statements/21stcentdefinition

National Endowment for the Arts. (2007). *To read or not to read: A question of national consequence.* Retrieved from http://arts.gov/sites/default/files/ToRead.pdf

National Governors Association Center for Best Practices & Council of Chief State School Officers. (2010). Common Core State Standards for English language arts and literacy in history/social studies, science, and technical subjects. Washington, DC: Author.

National Research Council of the National Academies. (2011). *A Framework for K-12 science education: Practices, crosscutting concepts, and core ideas.* Washington, DC: National Academies Press.

National Telecommunications and Information Administration. (n.d.). *Broadband USA: Connecting America's Communities.* Retrieved from http://www2.ntia.doc.gov/

Navarro, J. N., & Jasinski, J. L. (2013). Why girls? Using routine activities theory to predict cyberbullying experiences between girls and boys. *Women & Criminal Justice, 23*(4), 286–303. doi:10.1080/08974454.2013.784225

Neff, J. (2008). P&G relies on power of mommy bloggers. *Advertising Age, 79,* 4–24.

Neilson. (2010, June 15). *Social Networks Blogs Now Account for One in Every Four and a Half Minutes Online.* Retrieved September 27, 2014, from http://www.nielsen.com/us/en/insights/news/2010/social-media-accounts-for-22-percent-of-time-online.html

Nelson, T. H. (1981). *Literary machines.* Swatchmore, PA: Theodor H. Nelson.

Neumayer, C., & Stald, G. (2014). The mobile phone in street protest: Texting, tweeting, tracking, and tracing. *Mobile Media & Communication, 2*(2), 117–133. doi:10.1177/2050157913513255

New London Group. (2000). A Pedagogy of Multiliteracies: Designing Social Futures. In B. Cope & M. Kalantzis (Eds.), *Multiliteracies: LIteracy Learning and Design Social Futures* (pp. 9–37). Melbourne: Macmillan.

New Study: 55% of YA Books Bought by Adults. (2012, September 13). Retrieved from http://www.publishersweekly.com/pw/by-topic/childrens/childrens-industry-news/article/53937-new-study-55-of-ya-books-bought-by-adults.html

Ngai, G., Chan, S., & Ng, V. (2013). Designing i*CATch: A multipurpose, education-friendly construction kit for physical and wearable computing. AC Trans. *Computers & Education, 13*(2). doi:10.1145/2483710.2483712

Ngai, G., Chan, S., Ng, V., Cheung, J., Choy, S., Lau, W., & Tse, J. (2010) I*CATch: A scalable plug-n-play wearable computing framework for novices and children. In *Proceedings of the 28th International Conference on Human Factors in Computing Systems* (pp. 443-452). Atlanta, GA: ACM.

Nguyen, D. T., & Fussell, S. R. (2014). Lexical Cues of Interaction Involvement in Dyadic Instant Messaging Conversations. *Discourse Processes, 51*(5-6), 468–493. doi:10.1080/0163853X.2014.912544

Nicholas, D, Watkinson, A., Rowlands, I., & Jubb, M. (2011). Social media, academic research and the role of university libraries. *Journal of Academic Librarianship, 27*(5), 373-375. doi: 10.1.1016/j.acalib.2011.06.023

Nicol, J., & Valiquet, D. (2013). *Legislative summary of Bill C-13: An Act to amend the Criminal Code, the Canada Evidence Act, the Competition Act and the Mutual Legal Assistance in Criminal Matters Act.* Retrieved from Library of Parliament website: http://www.parl.gc.ca/Content/LOP/LegislativeSummaries/41/2/c13-e.pdf

Nielsen, L., & Webb, W. (2011). *Teaching generation text: Using cell phones to enhance learning.* New York: John Wiley.

Nilsson, B. (2014). *Digital badges are clearing the final hurdles for disruption. Extreme networks viewpoints.* Retrieved from http://www.extremenetworks.com/digital-badges-are-clearing-the-final-hurdles-for-disruption/

NOAA.gov. (2014). *Timeline of recovery from the Exxon Valdez oil spill.* Retrieved from http://response.restoration.noaa.gov/oil-and-chemical-spills/significant-incidents/exxon-valdez-oil-spill/timeline-ecological-recovery-infographic.html

No, C. L. B. (2002). (NCLB) Act of 2001, Pub. L. No. 107-110, § 115. *Stat*, 1425.

Nocentini, A., Calmaestra, J., Schultze-Krumbholz, A., Scheithauer, H., Ortega, R., & Menesini, E. (2010). Cyberbullying: Labels, behaviours and definition in three European countries. *Australian Journal of Guidance & Counselling, 20*(2), 129–142. doi:10.1375/ajgc.20.2.129

Noelle-Neumann, E. (1974). The spiral of silence: A theory of public opinion. *Journal of Communication, 24*(2), 43–51. doi:10.1111/j.1460-2466.1974.tb00367.x

Noelle-Neumann, E. (1993). *The Spiral of Silence: Public Opinion - Our Social Skin.* Chicago, IL: University of Chicago Press.

Nokia. (n.d.). *Text 2 Teach.* Retrieved from http/:www.text2teach.org.ph:%3Fpage_id=2

Norman, D. (2013). The paradox of wearable technologies. *MIT Technology Review.* Retrieved from http://www.technologyreview.com/news/517346/the-paradox-of-wearable-technologies/

Norris, K. O. (2004). Gender stereotypes, aggression, and computer games: An online survey of women. *Cyberpsychology & Behavior, 7*(6), 714–727. doi:10.1089/cpb.2004.7.714 PMID:15687807

Norris, S. (2008). *Something to blog about.* New York: Amulet.

Norton, B., & Williams, C. (2012). Digital identities, student investments and eGranary as placed resources. *Language and Education, 26*(4), 315–329. doi:10.1080/09500782.2012.691514

NRK. (2007, February 26). *Medieval helpdesk with English subtitles* [Video file]. Retrieved from http://www.youtube.com/watch?v=pQHX-SjbQvQ. (Originally broadcast in 2001.)

Nucera, D. J., & Lee, J. (2014). I transform myself, I transform the world around me. In H. M. Pleasants & D. E. Salter (Eds.), *Community-based multiliteracies and digital media projects* (pp. 181–202). New York: Peter Lang.

NYC Department of Education. (2014). *Universal design for learning*. Retrieved August 15 from http://schools.nyc.gov/Academics/CommonCoreLibrary/Professional-Learning/UDL/default.htm

O'Brien, D., Ortmann, L., & Rummel, A. (2014). *Disciplinary Literacies: Beyond the Print-Centric Era*. Paper presented at the Annual Meeting, Literacy Research Association, Marco Island, FL.

O'Brien, D., & Scharber, C. (2008). Digital literacies go to school: Potholes and possibilities. *Journal of Adolescent & Adult Literacy*, *52*(1), 66–68. doi:10.1598/JAAL.52.1.7

O'Brien, D., & Torres, A. M. (2012). Social networking and online privacy: Facebook users' perceptions. *Irish Journal of Management*, *31*(2), 63–97.

O'Brien, D., & Voss, S. (2011). Reading multimodally: What is afforded? *Journal of Adolescent & Adult Literacy*, *55*(1), 75–78. doi:10.1598/JAAL.55.1.9

O'Byrne, W. I., & McVerry, J. G. (in press). Online Research and Media Skills: An instructional model to support students as they search and sift online informational text. In T. Rasinsky, K. Pytash, & R. Ferdig (Eds.), Comprehension of informational texts. Academic Press.

O'Byrne, C. (2011). Get the girls online: Why Wales needs a gendered strategy to tackle digital exclusion. *Women in Society*, *1*, 61–66.

O'Byrne, W. I. (2014). Empowering learners in the reader/writer nature of digital information space. *Journal of Adolescent & Adult Literacy*, *58*(2), 102–104. doi:10.1002/jaal.337

O'Donnell, C. (2013). Wither Mario Factory? The role of tools in constructing (co)creative possibilities on video game consoles. *Games and Culture*, *8*(3), 161–180. doi:10.1177/1555412013493132

O'Halloran, K. L., & Smith, B. A. (2011). Multimodal studies. In K. L. O'Halloran & B. A. Smith (Eds.), *Multimodal studies: Exploring issues and domains* (pp. 1–13). New York: Routledge.

O'Mara, J., & Laidlaw, L. (2011). Living in the iWorld: Two literacy researchers reflect on the changing texts and literacy practices of childhood. *English Teaching*, *10*(4), 149–159.

O'Reilly, T. (2005). *What is Web 2.0: Design patterns and business models for the next generation of software*. Academic Press.

Ochs, E., & Capps, L. (1996). Narrating the self. *Annual Review of Anthropology*, *29*(1), 19–43. doi:10.1146/annurev.anthro.25.1.19

Ochsner, A., & Martin, C. (2013). Learning and cultural participation in *Mass Effect* and *Elder Scrolls* affinity spaces. In W. Kaminski & M. Lorber (Eds.), *Gamebased Learning: Clash of Realities 2012* (pp. 97–106). Munich: Kopäd Verlag.

Ochwa-Echel, J. (2011). Exploring the Gender Gap in Computer Science Education in Uganda. *International Journal Of Gender, Science, Technology (Elmsford, N.Y.)*, *3*(2). Retrieved from http://genderandset.open.ac.uk/index.php/genderandset/article/view/119

Ofcom. (2013). *Children and Parents: Media Use and Attitudes Report*. Retrieved from http://stakeholders.ofcom.org.uk/binaries/research/media-literacy/october-2013/research07Oct2013.pdf

Office of Career, Technical, and Adult Education: Workforce Innovation and Opportunities Act. (2014). Retrieved from http://www2.ed.gov/about/offices/list/ovae/pi/AdultEd/wioa-reauthorization.html

Ogletree, S. M., & Drake, R. (2007). College students video game participation and perceptions: Gender differences and implications. *Sex Roles*, *56*(7-8), 537–542. doi:10.1007/s11199-007-9193-5

Ogunsola, L. A. (2005). Information and communication technologies and the effects of globalization: twenty-first century "digital slavery" for developing countries-- myth or reality? *Electronic Journal of Academic and Special Librarianship, 6*(1-2). Retrieved from http://southernlibrarianship.icaap.org/content/v06n01/ogunsola_l01.htm

Oh, M., & Larson, J. F. (2011). *Digital development in Korea: Building an information society*. London, UK: Routledge.

Okutsu, M., DeLaurentis, D., Brophy, S., & Lambert, J. (2013). Teaching an aerospace engineering design course via virtual worlds: A comparative assessment of learning outcomes. *Computers & Education, 60*(1), 288–298. doi:10.1016/j.compedu.2012.07.012

Okuyama, Y. (2013). A case study of US deaf teens' text messaging: Their innovations and adoption of texisms. *New Media & Society, 15*(8), 1224–1240. doi:10.1177/1461444813480014

Oladokun, O. (2014). The information environment of distance learners: A literature review. *Creative Education, 5*(5), 303-317. Retrieved from http://search.proquest.com/docview/1518671480?accountid=45950

Olmstead, K., Mitchell, A., & Rosenstiel, T. (2011). *Audio: By the numbers* [Report]. Retrieved from http://stateofthemedia.org/2011/audio-essay/data-page/

Olweus, D. (1993). *Bullying at school: What we know and what we can do.* Oxford: Blackwell Publishers.

Olweus, D. (2012a). Cyberbullying: An overrated phenomenon? *European Journal of Developmental Psychology, 9*(5), 520–538. doi:10.1080/17405629.2012.682358

Olweus, D. (2012b). Comments on cyberbullying article: A rejoinder. *European Journal of Developmental Psychology, 9*(5), 559–568. doi:10.1080/17405629.2012.705086

Omand, D., Bartlett, J., & Miller, C. (2012). Introducing social media intelligence (SOCMINT). *Intelligence and National Security, 27*(6), 801–823. doi:10.1080/02684527.2012.716965

Ongun, E., & Demirag, A. (2014). An evaluation of Facebook users' blocking tendencies regarding their privacy and security settings. *Global Media Journal, 5*, 263–280.

Ong, W. J. (1982). *Orality and literacy: The technologizing of the word.* New York: Routledge. doi:10.4324/9780203328064

OpenArab.Net. (n.d.). *Arabic Blogs: An Embodiment of Freedom of Expression.* Retrieved September 27, 2014, from http://old.openarab.net/en/node/366

O'Reilly, T. (2006). *Web 2.0 compact definition: Trying again.* Retrieved from http://radar.oreilly.com/2006/12/web-20-compact-definition-tryi.html

Orfield, G. (2014). Tenth annual *Brown* lecture in education research: A new civil rights agenda for American education. *Educational Researcher, 43*(6), 273–292. doi:10.3102/0013189X14547874

Orkwis, R., & McLane, K. (1998). *A curriculum every student can use: Design principles for student access. ERIC/OSEP Topical Brief No. ED423654.* Reston, VA: ERIC/OSEP Special Project.

Orth, M. (2013). Adventures in electronic textiles. In L. Buechley, K. Peppler, M. Eisenberg, & Y. Kafai (Eds.), Textile Messages: Dispatches from the World of E-Textiles and Education. Academic Press.

Orth, M., Post, R., & Cooper, E. (1998). Fabric computing interfaces. In Proceedings of CHI 98 Conference Summary on Human Factors in Computing Systems (pp. 331-332). New York: ACM. doi:10.1145/286498.286800

Orvis, P. (2006). *A 'hole in the wall' helps educate India.* Retrieved August 24 from http://www.csmonitor.com/2006/0601/p13s02-legn.html

Osborne, R., Tasker, R., & Schollum, B. (1981). *Video: Electric current,* working paper no. 51, *Learning in Science Projects.* Hamilton, New Zealand: SERA, University of Waikato.

Osborne, R. (1981). Children's ideas about electric current. *New Zealand Science Teacher, 29*, 12–19.

Osborne, R. (1983). Towards modifying children's ideas about electric current. *Research in Science & Technological Education, 1*(1), 73–82. doi:10.1080/0263514830010108

Oschner, A., & Martin, C. (2013, 23 - 25 May 2012). *Learning and cultural participation in Mass Effect and Elder Scrolls affinity spaces.* Paper presented at the Clash of Realities 4th International Computer Game Conference, Cologne, Germany.

O'Shaughnessy, L. (2011). *Digital badges could significantly impact higher education.* Retrieved from http://www.usnews.com/education/blogs/the-college-solution/2011/10/04/digital-badges-could-significantly-impact-higher-education

Otañez, M. (2011). Ethical consumption and academic production. *Anthropology News, 56*, 26–42. doi:10.1111/j.1556-3502.2011.52426.x

Ottalini, D. (2010). Students Addicted to Social Media-New UM Study. *University of Maryland Newsdesk.* Retrieved from http://www.newsdesk.umd.edu/undergradexp/release.cfm

Owens, T. (2012, September 17). *Sharing, theft, and creativity: deviantART's share wars and how an online arts community thinks about their work.* Retrieved from http://blogs.loc.gov/digitalpreservation/2012/09/sharing-theft-and-creativity-deviantarts-share-wars-and-how-an-online-arts-community-thinks-about-their-work/

Owens, T. (2010). Modding the history of science: Values at play in modder discussions of Sid Meier's *Civilization. Simulation & Gaming, 42*(4), 481–495. doi:10.1177/1046878110366277

Owens, T. (2011). Social videogame creation: Lessons from RPG Maker. *On the Horizon, 19*(1), 52–61. doi:10.1108/10748121111107708

OXFAM. (2012, March 7). *Using pink phones to empower women and girls in Cambodia.* Retrieved from http://policy-practice.oxfam.org.uk/blog/2012/03/pink-telephones-in-cambodia

Oxford Analytica. (2011, February 9). *Middle East: Social media outwit authoritarianism* [Text]. Retrieved September 27, 2014, from https://www.oxan.com/display.aspx?ItemID=DB166066

Pacelli, M., Loriga, G., Taccini, N., & Paradiso, R. (2006). Sensing fabrics for monitoring physiological and biomechanical variables: E-textile solutions. In *Proceedings of the 3rd IEEE EMBS Intl Summer School and Symposium on Medical Devices and Biosensors.* Boston, MA: ACM. doi:10.1109/ISSMDBS.2006.360082

Pachler, N., Seipold, J., & Bachmair, B. (2012). Mobile Learning. Some theoretical and practical considerations. In K. Friedrich, M. Ranieri, N., Pachler, N., & P. de Theux (Eds.), *The "my mobile" handbook: Guidelines and scenarios for mobile learning in adult education* (pp. 11-16). Retrieved from http://www.mymobile-project.eu/IMG/pdf/Handbook_print.pdf

Pachler, N., Bachmair, B., & Cook, J. (2010). *Mobile learning: Structures, agency, practices.* New York: Springer. doi:10.1007/978-1-4419-0585-7

Paechter, C. (2003). Masculinities and femininities as communities of practice. *Women's Studies International Forum, 26*(1), 69–77. doi:10.1016/S0277-5395(02)00356-4

Pahl, K., & Rowsell, J. (2010). *Artifactual literacies.* New York: Teachers College Press.

Pakhchyan, S. (2008). *Fashioning Technology: A DIY Intro to Smart Crafting.* Cambridge, MA: O'Reilly Media.

Pakistan Bureau of Statistics. (2013). *2012-2013 Literacy rates.* Retrieved from http://www.pbs.gov.pk/sites/default/files/pslm/publications/pslm_prov_dist_2012-13/education/2.14b.pdf

Palen, L., & Liu, S. B. (2007). Citizen communications in crisis: anticipating a future of ICT-supported public participation. In *Proceedings of the SIGCHI conference on Human factors in computing systems* (pp. 727–736). ACM. doi:10.1145/1240624.1240736

Palfrey, J., Etling, B., & Faris, R. (2009, June 21). Reading Twitter in Tehran? Why the Real Revolution is on the Streets – and Offline. *Washington Post.*

Pallotta, T. (2011, June 6). *Walkthrough.* Retrieved from http://www.submarinechannel.com/transmedia/collapsus-walkthrough-with-tommy-pallotta/

Palmaers, D. (2014). *Playing a Serious Game to Enhance Financial Literacy: a case study of Skillville.* (Unpublished dissertation). Sheffield Hallam University, Sheffield, UK.

Palmen, M., & Kouri, P. (2012). Maternity clinic going online: Mothers' experiences of social media and online health information for parental support in Finland. *Journal of Communication in Health Care, 5*(3), 190–198. doi:10.1179/1753807612Y.0000000013

Palmer, S. (2006). *Toxic Childhood: how modern life is damaging our children and what we can do about it.* London: Orion.

Pamela Rutledge. (2013, January 25). *How Obama Won the Social Media Battle in the 2012 Presidential Campaign.* Retrieved from http://mprcenter.org/blog/2013/01/how-obama-won-the-social-media-battle-in-the-2012-presidential-campaign/

Pandya, J. Z., & Auckerman, M. (2014). A four resources analysis of technology in the CCSS. *Language Arts, 91*(6), 429–435.

Papadopoulos, D. (2007). Wearable technologies, portable architectures and the vicissitudes of the space between. *Architectural Design*, *77*(4), 62–67. doi:10.1002/ad.488

Papaioannou, T. (2013). Media and civic engagement: The role of Web 2.0 technologies in fostering youth participation. In D. Lemish (Ed.), *The Routledge International Handbook of Children, Adolescents, and Media* (pp. 351–358). London: Routledge.

Papert, S. (1981). *Mindstorms: Children, computers, and powerful ideas*. New York, NY: Basic Books.

Papert, S., & Harel, I. (1991). Situating constructionism. In I. Harel & S. Papert (Eds.), *Constructionism* (pp. 1–11). Norwood, NJ: Ablex Publishing Corporation.

Papic, M., & Noonan, S. (2011, February 3). *Social Media as a Tool for Protest*. Retrieved September 27, 2014, from http://www.stratfor.com/weekly/20110202-social-media-tool-protest

Parker, K. R., & Chao, J. T. (2007). Wiki as a teaching tool. *Interdisciplinary Journal of Knowledge and Learning Objects*, *3*, 57–72.

Park, S., & Burford, S. (2013). A longitudinal study on the uses of mobile tablet devices and changes in digital media literacy of young adults. *Educational Media International*, *50*(4), 266–280. doi:10.1080/09523987.2013.862365

Partnership for 21st Century Skills. (2011). *Framework for 21st century learning*. Retrieved 24.09.2014, 2014, from http://www.p21.org/our-work/p21-framework

Pasupathi, M., & Hoyt, T. (2009). The development of narrative identity in late adolescence and emergent adulthood: The continued importance of listeners. *Developmental Psychology*, *45*(2), 558–574. doi:10.1037/a0014431 PMID:19271839

Patchin, J., & Hinduja, S. (2014). *Cyberbullying facts*. Retrieved from http://cyberbullying.us/facts/

Patel, K. (2013). Incremental journey for world wide web: Introduced with web 1.0 to recent web 5.0 - A survey paper. *International Journal of Advanced Research in Computer Science and Software Engineering*, *3*(10), 410–417.

Patriquin, M. (2014, November 7). Don't overreact, Canada. *New York Times*. Retrieved from http://www.nytimes.com/2014/11/08/opinion/dont-overreact-canada.html?emc=eta1&_r=0

Patton, D., Eschmann, R., & Butler, D. (2013). Internet banging: New trends in social media, gang violence, masculinity and hip hop. *Computers in Human Behavior*, *29*(5), A54–A59. doi:10.1016/j.chb.2012.12.035

Paul, J. A., Baker, H. M., & Cochran, J. D. (2012). Effect of online social networking on student academic performance. *Computers in Human Behavior*, *28*(6), 2117–2127. doi:10.1016/j.chb.2012.06.016

Payton, L. (2014, November 20). Cyberbullying bill raises alarm for privacy commissioner. *CBC News*. Retrieved from http://www.cbc.ca/news/politics/cyberbullying-bill-raises-alarm-for-privacy-commissioner-1.2842034

Peake, L., & De Souza, K. (2010). Feminist academic and activist praxis in service of the transnational. In A. Swarr & R. Nagar (Eds.), *Critical transnational feminist praxis* (pp. 105–123). Albany, NY: State University of New York Press.

Pearce, C. & Artemesia. (2010). *Communities of Play: Emergent Cultures in Multiplayer Games and Virtual Worlds*. Cambridge, MA: MIT Press.

Pearson. (2014, May 9). *Pearson student mobile device survey: National report: Students in grades 4-12*. Author. Retrieved from http://tinyw.in/GJul

Pedersen, S., & Macafee, C. (2007). Gender differences in British blogging. *Journal of Computer-Mediated Communication*, *12*(4), 1472–1492. doi:10.1111/j.1083-6101.2007.00382.x

Pegrum, M., Oakley, G., & Faulkner, R. (2013). Schools going mobile: A study of the adoption of mobile handheld technologies in Western Australian independent schools. *Australasian Journal of Educational Technology*, *29*(1), 66–81.

Peirce, C. S. (1991). *Peirce on signs: Writings on semiotic*. Chapel Hill, NC: University of North Carolina Press.

Pelletier, C. (2007). *Making games: Developing games authoring software for educational and creative use: Full research report* (ESRC End of Award Report No. RES-328-25-0001). Swindon: ESRC.

Pelletier, C., Burn, A., & Buckingham, D. (2010). Game design as textual poaching: Media literacy, creativity and game-making. *E-Learning and Digital Media, 7*(1), 90–107. doi:10.2304/elea.2010.7.1.90

Pelletier, J., Reeve, R., & Halewood, C. (2006). Young children's knowledge building and literacy development through Knowledge Forum®. *Early Education and Development, 17*(3), 323–346. doi:10.1207/s15566935eed1703_2

Pellicone, A., & Ahn, J. (2010). *Construction and community: Investigating interaction in a Minecraft affinity space.* Retrieved from http://ahnjune.com/wp-content/uploads/2014/05/Pellicone-Ahn-GLS-Final.pdf

Peppler, K. (2010). The new fundamentals: Introducing computation into arts education. In E. Clapp & M. J. Bellino (Eds.), 20Under40: Reinventing the Arts and Arts Education for the 21st Century. Bloomington, IN: AuthorHouse.

Peppler, K. (2013). *New opportunities for interest-driven arts learning in a digital age.* New York: The Wallace Foundation. Retrieved from http://www.wallacefoundation.org/knowledge-center/arts-education/key-research/Pages/New-Opportunities-for-Interest-Driven-Arts-Learning-in-a-Digital-Age.aspx

Peppler, K. A., & Kafai, Y. B. (2007). *What videogame making can teach us about literacy and learning: Alternative pathways into participatory culture.* Paper presented at the 2007 Meeting of Digital Games Research Association, Tokyo, Japan.

Peppler, K., Tan, V., Thompson, N., & Bender, S. (2015). *New tools for circuitry learning: evaluating the efficacy of circuitry construction kits.* Paper Presentation at the 2015 American Educational Research Association Conference.

Peppler, K. (2013). STEAM-powered computing education: Using e-textiles to integrate the arts and STEM. *IEEE Computer, 46*(9), 38–43. doi:10.1109/MC.2013.257

Peppler, K. (2014). *New Creativity Paradigms: Arts Learning in the Digital Age.* New York, NY: Peter Lang Publishing.

Peppler, K. A., & Kafai, Y. B. (2010). Gaming fluencies: Pathways into participatory culture in a community design studio. *International Journal of Learning and Media, 1*, 45–58. doi:10.1162/ijlm_a_00032

Peppler, K., & Bender, S. (2013). Maker movement spreads innovation one project at a time. *Phi Delta Kappan, 95*(3), 22–27. doi:10.1177/003172171309500306

Peppler, K., & Danish, J. (2013). E-textiles for educators: Participatory simulations with e-puppetry. In L. Buechley, K. Peppler, M. Eisenberg, & Y. Kafai (Eds.), *Textile Messages: Dispatches from the World of E-Textiles and Education* (pp. 133–141). New York, NY: Peter Lang Publishing.

Peppler, K., & Glosson, D. (2013a). Stitching circuits: Learning about circuitry through e-textile materials. *Journal of Science Education and Technology, 22*(5), 751–763. doi:10.1007/s10956-012-9428-2

Peppler, K., & Glosson, D. (2013b). Learning about circuitry with e-textiles. In M. Knobel & C. Lankshear (Eds.), *The New Literacies Reader.* New York, NY: Peter Lang Publishing.

Peppler, K., Gresalfi, M., Salen Tekinbaş, K., & Santo, R. (2014). *Soft Circuits: Crafting E-Fashion with DIY Electronics.* Cambridge, MA: MIT Press.

Peppler, K., Sharpe, L., & Glosson, D. (2013). E-textiles and the new fundamentals of fine arts. In L. Buechley, K. Peppler, M. Eisenberg, & Y. Kafai (Eds.), *Textile Messages: Dispatches from the World of E-Textiles and Education* (pp. 107–117). New York, NY: Peter Lang Publishing.

Peppler, K., Warschauer, M., & Diazgranados, A. (2010). Game critics: Exploring the role of critique in game-design literacies. *E-Learning and Digital Media, 7*(1), 35–48. doi:10.2304/elea.2010.7.1.35

Perey, C. (2011). Print and publishing and the future of augmented reality. *Information Services & Use, 31*(1/2), 31–38. doi:10.3233/ISU-2011-0625

Perez, S. (2009). Hot, hot, hot! A Twitter augmented reality app for iPhone. *Readwrite*. Retrieved from http://readwrite.com/2009/07/08/a_twitter_augmented_reality_app_for_iphone

Perez, S. (2014). *iTunes App Store now has 1.2 Million apps, has 75 billion downloads to date*. Retrieved on October 10, 2014 from http://techcrunch.com/2014/06/02/itunes-app-store-now-has-1-2-million-apps-has-seen-75-billion-downloads-to-date/

Pérez-López, D., & Contero, M. (2013). Delivering educational multimedia contents through an augmented reality application: A case study on its impact on knowledge acquisition and retention. *Turkish Online Journal of Educational Technology*, *12*(4), 19–28.

Perkel, D. (2011). *Making art, creating infrastructure: deviantART and the production of the Web* (Dissertation). University of California, Berkeley. Retrieved from eScholarship UC. (6fg9f99202)

Perkins, C. (2013). How school principals understand and respond to homophobia: A study of one B.C. public school district using ethnodrama (doctoral dissertation). Vancouver, Canada: University of British Columbia; Retrieved from http://hdl.handle.net/2429/43383

Perner-Wilson, H., & Buechley, L. (2013). Handcrafting textile sensors. In L. Buechley, K. Peppler, M. Eisenberg, & Y. Kafai (Eds.), *Textile Messages: Dispatches from the World of E-Textiles and Education*.

Perren, S., Corcoran, L., Cowie, H., Dehue, F., Garcia, D. J., McGuckin, C., & Völlink, T. et al. (2012). Tackling cyberbullying: Review of empirical evidence regarding successful responses by students, parents, and schools. *International Journal of Conflict and Violence*, *6*(2), 283–292.

Perrone, C., Repenning, A., & Clark, D. (1996). WebQuest: Using WWW and interactive simulation games in the classroom. *First Monday*, *1*(5). doi:10.5210/fm.v1i5.493

Peter, J., & Valkenburg, P. M. (2006). Adolescents' exposure to sexually explicit online material and recreational attitudes toward sex. *Journal of Communication*, *56*(4), 639–660. doi:10.1111/j.1460-2466.2006.00313.x

Petronzio, M. (2012). *A brief history of instant messaging*. Retrieved from http://mashable.com/2012/10/25/instant-messaging-history/

Petronzio, M. (2013). 10 fascinating data visualization projects. *Mashable*. Retrieved from Retrieved from http://mashable.com/2013/03/05/data-visualization-projects/

Pettigrew, J. (2014). Text messaging and connectedness within close interpersonal relationships. *Marriage & Family Review*, *45*(6-8), 697–716. doi:10.1080/01494920903224269

Pew Internet and American Life Project. (2000, May). *Tracking online life: How women use the Internet to cultivate relationships with family and friends*. Retrieved from Pew Internet and American Life website: http://www.pewinternet.org

Pew Internet Research Project. (2014a). *Mobile technology fact sheet*. Washington, DC: Author. Retrieved from http://www.pewinternet.org/fact-sheets/mobile-technology-fact-sheet/

Pew Internet Research Project. (2014b). *Couples and texting*. Washington, DC: Author. Retrieved from http://www.pewinternet.org/2014/02/11/couples-the-internet-and-social-media/pi_14-02-11_techrelationships_435/

Pew Research Center. (2014, August). *Digital life in 2025: AI, robotics, and the future of jobs*. Available: http://www.pewinternet.org/2014/08/06/futureofjobs/

Pew Research Center's Journalism Project Staff. (2012, July 16). YouTube and news: A new kind of visual news. *Pew Research Journalism Project*. Retrieved from http://www.journalism.org/2012/07/16/youtube-news/

Pew Research Internet Project. (2013). *Internet and American Life Teen-Parent Survey*. Retrieved from http://www.pewinternet.org/2013/05/21/part-1-teens-and-social-media-use/

Pidaparthy, U. (2011). *How colleges use, misuse social media to reach students*. Retrieved from: http://www.cnn.com/2011/10/20/tech/social-media/universities-social-media/

Pieschl, S., Porsch, T., Kahl, T., & Klockenbusch, R. (2013). Relevant dimensions of cyberbullying—Results from two experimental studies. *Journal of Applied Developmental Psychology*, *34*(5), 241–252. doi:10.1016/j.appdev.2013.04.002

Piesing, M. (2012). Despite promise, transmedia publishing still mostly a mess. *Publishing Perspectives*. Retrieved from http://publishingperspectives.com/2012/12/despite-promise-transmedia- publishing-still-mostly-a-mess/

Pifarre, M., & Fisher, R. (2011). Breaking up the writing process: How wikis can support understanding the composition and revision strategies of young writers. *Language and Education*, *25*(5), 451–466. doi:10.1080/09500782.2011.585240

Pink, D. (2004). The MFA is the new MBA. *Harvard Business Review*, *82*(2), 21–22.

Pinkett, R. (2000). *Bridging the digital divide: Sociocultural constructionism and an asset-based approach to community technology and community building*. Paper presented at the 81st Annual Meeting of the American Educational Research Association, New Orleans, LA.

Plante, R. F. (2006). Sexual spanking, the self, and the construction of deviance. *Journal of Homosexuality*, *50*(2/3), 59–79. doi:10.1300/J082v50n02_04 PMID:16803759

Plass, J. L., Moreno, R., & Brünken, R. (Eds.). (2010). *Cognitive load theory*. Cambridge University Press. doi:10.1017/CBO9780511844744

Plester, B., Lerkkanen, M.-K., Linjama, L. J., Rasku-Puttonen, H., & Littleton, K. (2011). Finnish and UK English pre-teen children's text message language and its relationship with their literacy skills. *Journal of Computer Assisted Learning*, *27*(1), 37–48. doi:10.1111/j.1365-2729.2010.00402.x

Plowman, L., McPake, J., & Stephen, C. (2010). The technologisation of childhood? Young children and technology in the home. *Children & Society*, *24*(1), 63–74. doi:10.1111/j.1099-0860.2008.00180.x

Plowman, L., & Stephen, C. (2007). Guided interaction in pre-school settings. *Journal of Computer Assisted Learning*, *23*(1), 14–26. doi:10.1111/j.1365-2729.2007.00194.x

Plowman, L., Stevenson, O., Stephen, C., & McPake, J. (2012). Preschool children's learning with technology at home. *Computers & Education*, *59*(1), 30–37. doi:10.1016/j.compedu.2011.11.014

Podcast. (n.d.). In *Merriam-Webster.com*. Retrieved from http://www.merriam-webster.com/dictionary/podcasts

Podlas, K. (2000). Mistresses of their domain: How female entrepreneurs in cyberporn are initiating a gender power shift. *Cyberpsychology & Behavior*, *3*(5), 847–854. doi:10.1089/10949310050191827

Pollock, M. (2011). Research day: Exploring the potential of texting for student-teacher communication. Somerville, MA: The OneVille Project. Retrieved from http://wiki.oneville.org/main/The_OneVille_Project

Pooley, J. (2014, February). Interview with Nick Couldry. *New books in media & communication*. Retrieved from http://newbooksincommunications.com/2013/02/04/nick-couldry-media-society-world-social-theory-and-digital-media-practice-polity-press-2012/

Poor, N. (2014). Computer game modders' motivations and sense of community: A mixed-methods approach. *New Media & Society*, *16*(8), 1249–1267. doi:10.1177/1461444813504266

Porath, S. (2011). Text Messaging and Teenagers: A Review of the Literature. *Journal of the Research Center for Educational Technology*, *7*, 86–99.

Postigo, H. (2007). Of mods and modders: Chasing down the value of fan-based digital game modifications. *Games and Culture*, *2*(4), 300–313. doi:10.1177/1555412007307955

Post, R., & Orth, M. (1997). Smart fabric, or "wearable clothing." In *Proceedings of the IEEE International Symposium on Wearable Computers (ISWC)* (pp. 167-168). IEEE.

Post, R., Orth, M., Russo, P., & Gershenfeld, N. (2000). E-broidery: Design and fabrication of textile-based computing. *IBM Systems Journal*, *39*(3-4), 840–860. doi:10.1147/sj.393.0840

Powell, D., & Dixon, M. (2011). Does SMS text messaging help or harm adults' knowledge of standard spelling? *Journal of Computer Assisted Learning*, *27*(1), 58–66. doi:10.1111/j.1365-2729.2010.00403.x

PR Newswire. (2013, July 31). Wroclaw University Library turns to IBM big data solution to preserve European heritage, open digital archives to the world. *PR Newswire US*. Retrieved from http://www.prnewswire.com/news-releases/wroclaw-university-library-turns-to-ibm-big-data-solution-to-preserve-european-heritage-open-digital-archives-to-the-world-217739731.html

Prensky, M. (2001). Digital natives, digital immigrants part 1. *On the Horizon, 9*(5), 1–6. doi:10.1108/10748120110424816

Prensky, M. (2011). Digital wisdom and homo sapiens digital. In M. Thomas (Ed.), *Deconstructing digital natives* (pp. 15–29). New York: Routledge.

Price, D., Green, D., Spears, B., Scrimgeour, M., Barnes, A., Geer, R., & Johnson, B. (2014). A qualitative exploration of cyber-bystanders and moral engagement. *Australian Journal of Guidance & Counselling, 24*(1), 1–17. doi:10.1017/jgc.2013.18

Prinsloo, M., & Rowsell, J. (2012). Digital literacies and placed resources in the globalised periphery. *Language and Education, 26*(4), 271-277.

Prinsloo, M. (2005). The new literacies as placed resources. *Perspectives in Education, 23*(4), 87–98.

Prinsloo, M., & Rowsell, J. (2012). Introduction to special issue on Digital literacies as placed resources in the globalised periphery. *Language and Education, 26*(4), 271–277. doi:10.1080/09500782.2012.691511

Pritchard, R., & O'Hara, S. (2009). Vocabulary development in the science classroom: Using hypermedia authoring to support English learners. *The Tapestry Journal, 1*, 15–29.

Privacy Rights Clearinghouse. (2012). *Fact sheet 35: Social Networking Privacy: How to be Safe, Secure and Social*. Retrieved from https://www.privacyrights.org/social-networking-privacy-how-be-safe-secure-and-social

Proctor, C. P., Dalton, B., & Grisham, D. L. (2007). Scaffolding English language learners and struggling readers in a universal literacy environments with embedded strategy instruction and vocabulary support. *Journal of Literacy Research, 39*(1), 71–93.

Production. (n.d.). In *Merriam-Webster.com*. Retrieved from http://www.merriam-webster.com/dictionary/production

Project Overview. (n.d.). *Europeana Space Project*. Retrieved from http://www.europeana-space.eu

Prpick, S., & Redel, D. (Interviewer) & Grafton, A. (Interviewee). (2011). *Closing the book*. [Interview audio file]. Retrieved from CBC Ideas Web site: http://www.cbc.ca/ideas/episodes/2011/01/31/closing-the-book/

Public. (n.d.). In *Merriam-Webster.com*. Retrieved from http://www.merriam-webster.com/dictionary/public

Puentedura, R. R. (2011). *A matrix model for designing and assessing network-enhanced courses*. Retrieved from http://www.hippasus.com

Pullinger, K., & Joseph, C. (2011). *Inanimate Alice*. Retrieved from http://www.inanimatealice.com/

Purcell, K. (2013, October 10). Online video 2013. *Pew Internet Research Project*. Retrieved from www.pewinternet.org/2013/10/10/online-video-2013

Purcell, K., Heaps, A., Buchanan, J., & Friedrich, L. (2013). How teachers are using technology at home and in their classrooms. Washington, DC: Pew Research Center Internet Project. Retrieved from http://tinyurl.com/laqo2kb

Purcell, K., Rainie, L., Heaps, A., Buchanan, J., Friedrich, L., Jacklin, A., & Zickuhr, K. (2012). *How teens do research in the digital world*. Pew Research Center's Internet & American Life Project.

Purdue University. (2014). *Nursing faculty and students implement Passport badges to measure learning, achievement*. Retrieved from http://www.itap.purdue.edu/newsroom/news/140417_passport_nursing.html

Putnam, R. D., & Feldstein, L. (2004). *Better together: Restoring the American community*. New York: Simon & Schuster.

Pyzalski, J. (2012). From cyberbullying to electronic aggression: Typology of the phenomenon. *Emotional & Behavioural Difficulties, 17*(3-4), 305–317. doi:10.1080/13632752.2012.704319

Quan-Haase, A., & Young, A. L. (2010). Uses and Gratifications of Social Media: A Comparison of Facebook and Instant Messaging. *Bulletin of Science, Technology & Society, 30*(5), 350–361. doi:10.1177/0270467610380009

Quinn, B. (2010). Reducing psychological resistance to digital repositories. *Information Technology and Libraries, 29*(2), 67-75. Retrieved from http://search.proquest.com/docview/325047755?accountid=45950

Radicati, S. (2013). Email statistics report, 2009-2013. The Radicati Group, Inc.

Rafalow, M., & Tekinbas, K. (2014). Welcome to Sackboy Planet: Connected learning among LittleBigPlanet 2 players. Irvine, CA: Digital Media and Learning Research Hub. Retrieved from www.dmlhub.net/publications

Rainie, L., & Tancer, B. (2007, April 24). Wikipedia users. *Pew Internet Research Project*. Retrieved from http://www.pewinternet.org/2007/04/24/wikipedia-users/

Rainie, L., Kiesler, S., Kang, R., Madden, M., Duggan, M., Brown, S., & Dabbish, L. (2013). Anonymity, privacy, and security online. *Pew Internet Research Project*. Retrieved from http://www.pewinternet.org/2013/09/05/anonymity-privacy-and-security-online/

Rainie, L., Purcell, K., & Smith, A. (2011). *The Social Side of the Internet*. Retrieved from http://www.pewinternet.org/2011/01/18/the-social-side-of-the-internet/

Rambe, P. (2012). Constructive disruptions for effective collaborative learning: Navigating the affordances of social media for meaningful engagement. *The Electronic Journal of e-Learning, 10*(1), 132-146.

Rambe, P., & Bere, A. (2013). Using mobile instant messaging to leverage learner participation and transform pedagogy at a South African University of Technology. *British Journal of Educational Technology, 44*(4), 544–561. doi:10.1111/bjet.12057

Ramirez, M. L. (2011). Whose role is it anyway? A library practitioner's appraisal of the digital data deluge. *Bulletin of the American Society for Information Science and Technology, 37*(5), 21–23. doi:10.1002/bult.2011.1720370508

Ramos, R., & Devers, D. (2014). iPad-enabled experiments in an undergraduate physics laboratory. In C. Miller & A. Doering (Eds.), The new landscape of mobile learning (pp. 334-352). New York: Routledge.

Ramsey & Vecchione. (n.d.). Retrieved from http://scholarworks.boisestate.edu/cgi/viewcontent.cgi?article=1101&context=lib_facpubs

Rand, A. C. (2010). Mediating at the student-Wikipedia intersection. *Journal of Literacy Administration, 507*(7-8), 923–932. doi:10.1080/01930826.2010.488994

Ratto, M., & Boler, M. (Eds.). (2014). *DIY Citizenship: Critical making and social media*. Cambridge, MA: MIT Press.

Raynes-Goldie, K., & Walker, L. (2008). Our space: Online civic engagement tools for youth. In W. L. Bennett (Ed.), *Civic life online: Learning how digital media can engage youth* (pp. 161–188). Cambridge, MA: MIT Press.

ReadWrite. (2009, July 25). *Evolution of a Revolution: Visualizing Millions of Iran Tweets*. Retrieved September 26, 2014, from http://readwrite.com/2009/07/25/evolution_revolution_visualizing_millions_iran_tweets

Real, B., Bertot, J. C., & Jaeger, P. T. (2014). Rural public libraries and digital inclusion: Issues and challenges. *Information Technology and Libraries, 33*(1), 6-24. Retrieved from http://search.proquest.com/docview/1512388143?accountid=45950

Reason, P., & Bradbury, H. (2008). Introduction. In P. Reason & H. Bradbury (Eds.), *The SAGE handbook of action research: Participant inquiry and practice* (pp. 5–10). Los Angeles, CA: SAGE. doi:10.4135/9781848607934

Redsell, S. A., Collier, J. J., Garrud, P. P., Evans, J. C., & Cawood, C. C. (2003). Multimedia versus written information for nocturnal enuresis education: A cluster randomized controlled trial. *Child: Care, Health and Development, 29*(2), 121–129. doi:10.1046/j.1365-2214.2003.00321.x PMID:12603357

Reena, N. R., Singh, R., & Surbala. (2010). Still playing with fire: Intersectionality, activism and NGOized feminisim. In A. Swarr & R. Nagar (Eds.), Critical transnational feminist praxis (pp. 124-143). Albany, NY: State University of New York Press.

Rees, J. (2013). The MOOC racket: Widespread online-only higher ed will be disastrous for students—and most professors. *Slate*. Retrieved from http://www.slate.com/articles/technology/future_tense/2013/07/moocs_could_be_disastrous_for_students_and_professors.html

Regazzi, J. The shifting sands of open access publishing, a publisher's view. *Serials Review, 30*(4), 275-280. doi:.10.1016/j.serrev.2004.09.010

Reichel, M., Schel, H., and Gruter, T. (2006). Smart fashion and learning about digital culture. *Current Developments in Technology-Assisted Education*, 1-5.

Reich, J., Murnane, R., & Willett, J. (2012). The state of wiki usage in U.S. K-12 schools: Leveraging Web 2.0 data warehouses to assess quality and equity in online learning environments. *Educational Researcher, 41*(7), 7–15. doi:10.3102/0013189X11427083

Reich, R. (1992). *The work of nations*. New York, NY: Vintage Books.

Reinking, D. (1998). Synthesizing technological transformations of literacy in a post typographic world. In D. Reinking, M. C. McKenna, L. D. Labbo, & R. Kieffer (Eds.), *Handbook of literacy and technology: Technological transformations in a post-typographic world* (pp. xi–xxx). Mahwah, NJ: Erlbaum.

Remington, A. (2009).Gender-bending gamers dress for success. In *The book of odds: The odds of everyday life*. Retrieved from http://www.bookofodds.com/Daily-Life-Activities/Entertainment-Media/Articles/A0008-Gender-Bending-Gamers-Dress-for-Success

Rennie, J., & Patterson, A. (2010). Young Australians reading in a digital world. In D. R. Cole & D. L. Pullen (Eds.), *Multiliteracies in motion: Current theory and practice* (pp. 207–223). New York, NY: Routledge.

Repenning, A., & Ioannidou, A. (2008). Broadening participation through scalable game design. In *Proceedings of the 39th SIGCSE Technical Symposium on Computer Science Education* (pp. 305–309). New York, NY: ACM. doi:10.1145/1352135.1352242

Repenning, A., Webb, D. C., Brand, C., Gluck, F., Grover, R., Miller, S., & Song, M. (2014). Beyond Minecraft: Facilitating computational thinking through modeling and programming in 3D. *IEEE Computer Graphics and Applications, 34*(3), 68–71. doi:10.1109/MCG.2014.46 PMID:24808170

Repenning, A., Webb, D., & Ioannidou, A. (2010). Scalable game design and the development of a checklist for getting computational thinking into public schools. In *Proceedings of the 41st ACM technical symposium on computer science education* (pp. 265–269). New York: ACM Press. doi:10.1145/1734263.1734357

Resnick, M., & Silverman, B. (2005). *Some reflections on designing construction kits for kids*. Paper presented at the International Conference for Interaction Design and Children, Boulder, CO. doi:10.1145/1109540.1109556

Resnick, M., Maloney, J., Monroy-Hernández, A., Rusk, N., Eastmond, E., Brennan, K., & Kafai, Y. et al. (2009). Scratch: Programming for all. *Communications of the ACM, 52*(11), 60–67. doi:10.1145/1592761.1592779

Rettberg, S. (2009). Communitizing electronic literature. *Digital Humanities Quarterly, 3*(2). Retrieved from http://www.digitalhumanities.org/dhq/vol/3/2/000046/000046.html

Retter, S., Anderson, C., & Kieran, L. (2013). IPad use for accelerating gains in reading skills of secondary students with learning disabilities. *Journal of Educational Multimedia and Hypermedia, 22*(4), 443–463.

Reuter, O. J., & Szakonyi, D. (2013). Online Social Media and Political Awareness in Authoritarian Regimes. *British Journal of Political Science, FirstView*, 1–23. doi:10.1017/S0007123413000203

Review, H. B. (2010). *The New Conversation: Taking Social Media from Talk to Action*. Retrieved from: http://www.sas.com/resources/whitepaper/wp_23348.pdf

Reynolds, R. (2010). Changes in middle school students' six contemporary learning abilities (6-CLAs) through project-based design of web-games and social media use. In A. Grove (Ed.), *Proceedings of the American Society for Information Science and Technology (Vol. 47)*. Academic Press.

Reynolds, R., & Caperton, I. H. (2009). *The emergence of six contemporary learning abilities (6-CLAs) in middle school, high school and community college students as they design web-games and use project-based social media in Globaloria*. Paper presented at the Annual Conference of the American Educational Research Association, San Diego, CA. Retrieved from http://worldwideworkshop.org/pdfs/Globaloria-EmergencofSixCLAs.pdf

Reznik, M. (2012). Identity theft on social networking sites: Developing issues of Internet impersonation. *Touro Law Review, 29*, 455.

Rheingold, H. (2007). *Smart mobs: The next social revolution.* Basic books.

Ricardo, G. (2014). When you do not have a computer: Public-access computing in developing countries. *Information Technology for Development, 20*(3), 274-291, doi:10.1080/02681102.2012.751573

Rich, F. (2011, February 5). Wallflowers at the Revolution. *The New York Times.* Retrieved from http://www.nytimes.com/2011/02/06/opinion/06rich.html

Rich, M. (2008). *Literacy debate: Online, RU really reading?* The New York Times Online. Retrieved from http://www.nytimes.com/2008/07/27/books/27reading.html

Rideout, V. J., Vandewater, E. A., & Wartella, E. A. (2003). Zero to Six: Electronic media in the lives of infants, toddlers, and preschoolers. Menlo Park, CA: Henry J. Kaiser Family Foundation. Retrieved from http://www.kff.org/entmedia/3378.cfm

Riegert, K., & Ramsey, G. (2013). Activists, individualists, and comics: The counter-publicness of Lebanese blogs. *Television & New Media, 14*(4), 286–303. doi:10.1177/1527476412463447

Riesland, E. (2010). Visual literacy and the classroom. *New Horizons for Learning.* Retrieved from http://education.jhu.edu/PD/newhorizons/strategies/topics/literacy/articles/visual-literacy-and-the-classroom

Riley, D. (2005). The Blog Herald blog count October 2005: Over 100 million blogs created. *Blog Herald.* Retrieved from http://www.blogherald.com/2005/10/10/the-blog-herald-blog-count-october-2005/

Riley, S. (2011, Oct 31). Social media one key to the arab spring IT-savvy population it played bigger role in Tunisia, Egypt than in Libya, Yemen, some say. *Investor's Business Daily,* p. A06. Retrieved from http://proxy.consortiumlibrary.org/docview/915383384?accountid=14473

Rinck, M. (2008). The interaction of verbal and pictoral information in comprehension and memory. In J.-F. Rouet, R. Lowe, & W. Schnotz (Eds.), *Understanding multimedia documents* (pp. 185–202). New York, NY: Springer. doi:10.1007/978-0-387-73337-1_10

Ringrose, J. (2010). Sluts, whores, fat slags, and Playboy bunnies: Teen girls' negotiation of "sexy" on social networking sites and at school. In C. Jackson, C. Paechter, & E. Renold (Eds.), Girls and education 3-16: Continuing concerns, new agendas (pp. 170-182). New York, NY: McGraw Hill Open University Press.

Riordan, M. A., Markman, K. M., & Stewart, C. O. (2012). Communication Accommodation in Instant Messaging: An Examination of Temporal Convergence. *Journal of Language and Social Psychology, 32*(1), 84–95. doi:10.1177/0261927X12462695

Riordan, R. (2005). *The lightning thief.* New York: Scholastic.

Ritchie, A., & Barker, M. (2006). "There aren't words for what we do or how we feel so we have to make them up": Constructing polyamorous languages in a culture of compulsory monogamy. *Sexualities, 9*(5), 584–601. doi:10.1177/1363460706069987

Rivers, I., & Noret, N. (2010). "I h8 u": findings from a five-year study of text and email bullying. *British Educational Research Journal, 36*(4), 643–671. doi:10.1080/01411920903071918

Robert Mackey. (2011, April 11). *Blogger Jailed for Insulting Egypt's Military.* Retrieved from http://thelede.blogs.nytimes.com/2011/04/11/blogger-jailed-for-insulting-egypts-military-is-pro-israel/

Robin, B. (2008). The effective uses of digital storytelling as a teaching and learning tool. In J. Flood, S. B. Heath, & D. Lapp (Eds.), *Handbook of research on teaching literacy through the communicative and visual arts* (Vol. 2, pp. 429–440). New York: Lawrence Erlbaum Associates.

Robinson, K. (2009). *The element: How finding your passion changes everything.* New York, NY: Penguin.

Robinson, K., & Diaz, C. J. (2005). *Diversity and difference in early childhood education: Issues for theory and practice.* Columbus, OH: Open University Press.

Robinson, T., Callister, M., Clark, B., & Phillips, J. (2008). Violence, sexuality, and gender stereotyping: A content analysis of official video game web sites. *Web Journal of Mass Communication Research, 13*, 1–17.

Roblyer, M. D., McDaniel, M., Webb, M., Herman, J., & Witty, J. V. (2010). Findings on Facebook in higher education: A comparison of college faculty and student uses and perceptions of social networking sites. *The Internet and Higher Education*, *13*(3), 134–140. doi:10.1016/j.iheduc.2010.03.002

Rodriguez, J. (2014). *Stop fighting constitutional school funding*. Retrieved September 2 from http://krwg.org/post/rodriguez-stop-fighting-constitutional-school-funding

Rodzvilla, J. (Ed.). (2002). *We've got blog: How weblogs are changing our culture*. Cambridge, MA: Perseus Books Group.

Rogerson, S., & Rogerson, A. (2007). ETHIcol. *IMIS Journal*, *17*(5), 1-3. Retrieved from http://www.ccsr.cse.dmu.ac.uk/resources/general/ethicol/Ecv17no5.pdf

Romero, A., Cammarota, J., Dominguez, K., Valdez, J., Ramirez, G., & Hernandez, L. (2008). "The opportunity if not the right to see" The Social Justice Education Project. In J. Cammarota & M. Fine (Eds.), *Revolutionizing Education: Youth participatory action research in motion* (pp. 131–151). New York, NY: Routledge.

Romero, N. L. (2011). ROI. measuring the social media return on investment in a library. *The Bottom Line*, *24*(2), 145–151. doi:10.1108/08880451111169223

Rose, D., Fisch, K., & McLeod, S. (2011). *Did you know: Shift happens*. Retrieved from https://www.youtube.com/watch?v=F9WDtQ4Ujn8

Rose, J. (2011). How social media is having a positive impact on culture. *Mashable*. Retrieved from http://mashable.com/2011/02/23/social-media-culture/

Rose, M. (2014). *Public education under siege*. Retrieved from http://mikerosebooks.com/Public-Education-Under-S.html

Rose, J., Mackey-Kallis, S., Shyles, L., Barry, K., Biagini, D., Hart, C., & Jack, L. (2012). Face it: The impact of gender on social media images. *Communication Quarterly*, *60*(5), 588–607. doi:10.1080/01463373.2012.725005

Rosen, L. (2011). *Social Networking's Good and Bad Impact on Kids*. American Psychological Association. Retrieved from http://www.apa.org/news/press/releases/2011/08/social-kids.aspx

Rosenberg, T. (2011, July 12). *Friends in Revolution*. Retrieved September 26, 2014, from http://opinionator.blogs.nytimes.com/2011/07/12/friends-in-revolution/

Rosenberg, S. (2009). *Say everything: How blogging began, what it's becoming, and why it matters*. New York: Crown Publishers.

Rosenheck, L. (2011). Beetles, beasties and bunnies: Ubiquitous games for biology prototyping language–based locative gameplay. In S. Dikkers, J. Martin, & B. Coutler (Eds.), *Mobile media learning: Amazing uses of mobile devices for learning* (pp. 77–96). Pittsburgh, PA: ETC Press.

Rosen, L. D., Mark Carrier, L., & Cheever, N. A. (2013). Facebook and texting made me do it: Media-induced task-switching while studying. *Computers in Human Behavior*, *29*(3), 948–958. doi:10.1016/j.chb.2012.12.001

Rosenwald, M. (2014). *Serious reading takes a hit from online scanning and skimming, researchers say*. Retrieved September 1 from http://www.washingtonpost.com/local/serious-reading-takes-a-hit-from-online-scanning-and-skimming-researchers-say/2014/04/06/088028d2-b5d2-11e3-b899-20667de76985_story.html

Rossi, C. (2013, September 18). High school gets social media 101 course: Disturbing Twitter trend prompted lesson. *Vancouver Sun*. Retrieved from http://www.vancouversun.com/technology/High+school+gets+social+media+course/8925397/story.html

Rossi, C. (2014, February 27). School creates digital code. *Vancouver Courier*. Retrieved from http://www.vancourier.com/news/school-creates-digital-code-1.869932

Rothman, R. A. (1993). *Inequity and stratification: Class, color, and gender*. Englewood Cliffs, NJ: Prentice Hall.

Rouet, J.-F., Lowe, R., & Schnotz, W. (2008). *Understanding multimedia documents*. New York, Springer. doi:10.1007/978-0-387-73337-1

Roussos, M., Johnson, A., Moher, T., Leigh, J., Vasilakis, C., & Barnes, C. (1999). Learning and building together in an immersive virtual world. *Presence (Cambridge, Mass.)*, *8*(3), 247–263. doi:10.1162/105474699566215

Rowling, J. K. (1999). *Harry Potter and the sorcerer's stone*. New York: Scholastic, Inc.

Rowling, J. K. (2012). *The casual vacancy*. New York: Little, Brown and Company.

Rowsell, J. (2014). Toward a phenomenology of contemporary reading. *Australian Journal of Language & Literacy, 37*(2), 117–127.

Rowsell, J., & Harwood, D. (in press). Let it Go. In *Exploring the image of the child as a producer, consumer, and inventor* (Special Edition). Theory into Practice Journal.

Royal, C. (2005). A meta-analysis of journal articles intersecting issues of Internet and gender. *Journal of Technical Writing and Communication, 35*(4), 403–429. doi:10.2190/3RBM-XKEQ-TRAF-E8GN

Royse, P., Lee, J., Undrahbuyan, B., Hopson, M., & Consalvo, M. (2007). Women and games: Technologies of the gendered self. *New Media & Society, 9*(4), 555–576. doi:10.1177/1461444807080322

Ruane, B., Kavanagh, A., & Waldron, F. (2010). *Young children's engagement with issues of global justice: A report by the Centre for Human Rights and Citizenship Education*. Retrieved from http://www.spd.dcu.ie/site/chrce/documents/TrocaireCHCREreport.pdf

Rubinstein- Ávila, E. (2007). In their words, sounds and images: After-school literacy programs for urban youth. In B. Guzzetti (Ed.), Literacy for a new millennium: Adolescent literacy. Greenwood Publishers.

Rubinstein- Ávila, E. (2011). Exploring (public) Internet use among low-income youth in Brazil, Argentina, and Chile. In D. Alvermann & K. Hinchman (Eds.), Reconceptualizing the literacies in adolescents' lives: Bridging the everyday/academic divide (3rd ed.; pp. 49-63). Routledge.

Rudkin, J., & Davis, A. (2007). Photography as a tool for understanding youth connections to their neighborhoods. *Community, Youth, and Environments, 17*, 107–123.

Rudnick, E. (2010). *Tweet Heart*. New York: Disney/Hyperion.

Rudnicki, A., Cozart, A., Ganesh, A., Markello, C., Marsh, S., McNeil, S., . . . Robin, B. (2006). *The buzz continues: The diffusion of digital storytelling across disciplines and colleges at the University of Houston*. Paper presented at the International Conference of the Society for Information Technology and Teacher Education.

Ruiz, J. (2013, December 14). *The cloud and the crowd: Distributed cognition and collective intelligence.* [Blog Post]. Retrieved from https://blogs.commons.georgetown.edu/cctp-797-fall2013/archives/699

Runions, K. C. (2013). Toward a conceptual model of motive and self-control in cyber-aggression: Rage, revenge, reward, and recreation. *Journal of Youth and Adolescence, 42*(5), 751–771. doi:10.1007/s10964-013-9936-2 PMID:23526207

Rushkoff, D. (1994). *Media virus!: Hidden agendas in popular culture*. New York: Ballantine Books.

Rushkoff, D. (2014). *Present shock*. New York, NY: Penguin Group.

Russell, G., & Hughes, J. (2014). iTeach and iLearn with iPads in secondary English language arts. In C. Miller & A. Doering (Eds.), The new landscape of mobile learning (pp. 292-307). New York: Routledge.

Ruth, A., & Houghton, L. (2009). The wiki way of learning. *Australasian Journal of Educational Technology, 25*(2), 135–152.

Rutkin, A. (2014, August 14). *Digital textbooks adapt to your level as you learn* [web log comment]. Retrieved from http://tinyurl.com/pl225a9

Rutsch, H. (2003). Literacy as freedom. *UN Chronicle, 40*(2). Retrieved from https://www.questia.com/magazine/1G1-105657543/literacy-as-freedom

Ryan, M., Emerson, L., Robertson, B. J., & Ebrary, I. (2014). *The Johns Hopkins Guide to Digital Media*. Baltimore, MD: The John Hopkins University Press.

Ryan, S., & Grieshaber, S. (2005). *Practical transformations and transformational practices: Globalization, postmodernism, and early childhood education*. Oxford, UK: Elsevier JAI.

Sabella, R. A., Patchin, J. W., & Hinduja, S. (2013). Cyberbullying myths and realities. *Computers in Human Behavior, 29*(6), 2703–2711. doi:10.1016/j.chb.2013.06.040

Sacco, D. F., & Ismail, M. M. (2014). Social belongingness satisfaction as a function of interaction medium: Face-to-face interactions facilitate greater social belonging and interaction enjoyment compared to instant messaging. *Computers in Human Behavior, 36*, 359–364. doi:10.1016/j.chb.2014.04.004

Sadoski, M., & Paivio, A. (2001). *Imagery and text: A dual coding theory of reading and writing*. Mahwah, NJ: Lawrence Erlbaum Associates.

Saettler, P. (2004). *The evolution of American educational technology*. Greenwich, CT: Information Age.

Salah, A. (2010, July 5). *The online potential of art creation and dissemination: deviantART as the next art venue*. Presented at the Electronic Visualization and the arts. Retrieved from http://www.bcs.org/upload/pdf/ewic_ev10_s1paper3.pdf

Salah, A. (2013). Flow of innovation in deviantArt: Following artists on an online social network site. *Mind & Society, 12*(1), 137–149. doi:10.1007/s11299-013-0113-9

Salah, A., Salah, A. A., Buter, B., Dijkshoorn, N., Modolo, D., Nguyen, Q., & van de Poel, B. et al. (2012). DeviantArt in spotlight: A network of artists. *Leonardo, 45*(5), 486–487. doi:10.1162/LEON_a_00454

Salazar, L. (2010). *Taking IT mobile: Youth, mobile phones, and social change*. Retrieved on September 26, 2014 from http://www.tigweb.org/resources/toolkits/view.html?ToolkitID=2937

Salem, F., & Mourtada, R. (2011). Civil movements: The impact of Facebook and Twitter. *The Arab Social Media Report, 1*(2), 1.

Salen Tekinbaş, K., Torres, R., Wolozin, L., Rufo-Tepper, R., & Shapiro, A. (2010). *Quest to Learn: Developing the school for digital kids*. Cambridge, MA: MIT Press.

Salen, K. (2007). Gaming literacies: A game design study in action. *Journal of Educational Multimedia and Hypermedia, 16*, 301–322.

Salmon, C. T., Fernandez, L., & Post, L. A. (2010). Mobilizing public will across borders: Roles and functions of communication processes and technologies. *Journal of Borderland Studies, 25*(3-4), 159–170. doi:10.1080/08865655.2010.9695778

Salz. (2014). The Importance of "Push" in the App Age. *eContent Magazine*. Accessed Jan 25, 2015 at http://www.econtentmag.com/Articles/Column/Agile-Minds/The-Importance-of-Push-in-the-App-Age-99018.htm

Samp, J. A., Wittenberg, E. M., & Gillett, D. L. (2003). Presenting and monitoring a gender-defined self on the Internet. *Communication Research Reports, 20*(1), 1–12. doi:10.1080/08824090309388794

Sánchez Abril, P., Levin, A., & Del Riego, A. (2012). Blurred boundaries: Social media privacy and the twenty firstcentury employee. *American Business Law Journal, 49*(1), 63–124. doi:10.1111/j.1744-1714.2011.01127.x

Sandelowski, M., & Barroso, J. (2007). *Handbook for synthesizing qualitative research*. New York, NY: Springer.

Sanou, B. (2014). ICT facts and figures. *WORLD (Oakland, Calif.), 2014*.

Savas, P. (2011). A case study of contextual and individual factors that shape linguistic variation in synchronous text-based computer-mediated communication. *Journal of Pragmatics, 43*(1), 298–313. doi:10.1016/j.pragma.2010.07.018

Sawers, P. (2011). *Augmented reality: The past, present and future*. Retrieved from http://thenextweb.com/insider/2011/07/03/augmented-reality-the-past-present-and-future/

Scardamalia, M., & Bereiter, C. (1994). Computer support for knowledge-building communities. *Journal of the Learning Sciences, 3*(3), 265–283. doi:10.1207/s15327809jls0303_3

Schachter, J., & Kasper, J. (2014). Finding voice: Building literacies and communities inside and outside the classroom. In H. M. Pleasants & D. E. Salter (Eds.), *Community-based multiliteracies and digital media projects* (Vol. 63, pp. 181–202). New York: Peter Lang.

Schaffhauser, D. (2011). *Is the iPad ready to replace the printed textbook?* Retrieved from http://campustechnology.com/articles/2011/06/15/is-the-ipad-ready-to-replace-the-printed-textbook.aspx

Schecter, D. (2009). They blog, I blog, we all blog. *Nieman Reports, 63*, 93–95.

Scheer, P. (2014, December 17). EU bureaucrats want to dictate what content Americans can view on U.S.-based websites. *Huffington Post*. Retrieved from http://www.huffingtonpost.com/peter-scheer/eu-bureaucrats-want-to-di_b_6342762.html

Schelhowe, H., Katterfeldt, E. S., Dittert, N., & Reichel, M. (2013). EduWear: E-textiles in youth sports and theater. In L. Buechley, K. Peppler, M. Eisenberg, & Y. Kafai (Eds.), Textile Messages: Dispatches from the World of E-Textiles and Education. Academic Press.

Schimmel, J. (2009). Development as Happiness: The Subjective Perception of Happiness and UNDP Analysis of Poverty, Wealth and Development. *Journal of Happiness Studies*, *10*(1), 93–111. doi:10.1007/s10902-007-9063-4

Schlosberg, M., & Ozer, N. (2007, August 1). *Under the watchful eye: The proliferation of video surveillance systems in California*. Retrieved from http://www.aclunc.org/publications/under-watchful-eye-proliferation-video-surveillance-systems-california

Schmarzo, B. (2013). *Big data: Understanding how data powers big business*. Hoboken: Wiley.

Schmidt, K. D., Sennyey, P., & Carstens, T. V. (2005). New roles for a changing environment: Implications of open access for libraries. *College & Research Libraries*, *66*(5), 407–416. doi:10.5860/crl.66.5.407

Schmier, S. (2014). Popular culture in a digital media studies classroom. *Literacy*, *48*(1), 4–39. doi:10.1111/lit.12025

Schneps, M. H., Ruel, J., Sonnert, G., Dussault, M., Griffin, M., & Sadler, P. M. (2014). Conceptualizing astronomical scale: Virtual simulations on handheld tablet computers reverse misconceptions. *Computers & Education*, *70*, 269–280. doi:10.1016/j.compedu.2013.09.001

Schneps, M. H., Thomson, J. M., Chen, C., Sonnert, G., & Pomplun, M. (2013). E-Readers are more effective than paper for some with dyslexia. *PLoS ONE*, *8*(9), e75634. doi:10.1371/journal.pone.0075634 PMID:24058697

Schnotz, W., & Bannert, M. (2003). Construction and interface in learning from multiple representation. *Learning and Instruction*, *13*(2), 141–156. doi:10.1016/S0959-4752(02)00017-8

Schott, G., & Kambouri, M. (2003). Moving between the spectral and the material plane. *Convergence*, *9*(3), 41–55.

Schott, G., & Kambouri, M. (2006). Social play and learning. In D. Carr, D. Buckingham, A. Burn, & G. Schott (Eds.), *Computer Games: text, narrative and play* (pp. 119–132). Cambridge, MA: Polity Press.

Schugar, H. R., & Schugar, J. T. (2014). Reading in the post-PC era: Students' comprehension of interactive e-books. Paper presented as the American Educational Research Association, Philadelphia, PA.

Schultze-Krumbholz, A., Hoher, J., Fiebig, J., & Scheithauer, H. (2014). How do adolescents in Germany define cyberbullying? A focus-group study of adolescents from a German major city. *Praxis der Kinderpsychologie und Kinderpsychiatrie*, *63*(5), 361–378. PMID:24877777

Schwartz, D. L., & Heiser, J. (2006). Spatial representations and imagery in learning. In R. K. Sawyer (Ed.), *The Cambridge handbook of the learning sciences* (pp. 283–298). New York, NY: Cambridge University Press.

Schweidler, C., & Costanza-Chock, S. (in press). Common cause: Global resistance to intellectual property rights. In D. Kidd, C. Rodriguez, & L. Stein (Eds.), Making our media: Mapping global initiatives toward a democratic public sphere. Creskill, NJ: Hampton Press. Retrieved from https://www.academia.edu/8297101/COMMON_CAUSE_GLOBAL_RESISTANCE_TO_INTELLEC-TUAL_PROPERTY_RIGHTS

Scivicque, C. (2013). *Why you (yes, you) need a professional portfolio*. Retrieved from https://www.themuse.com/advice/why-you-yes-you-need-a-professional-portfolio

Scollon, R. (2001). *Mediated Discourse: The Nexus of Practice*. London: Routledge. doi:10.4324/9780203420065

Scott-Dixon, K. (2002). Turbo chicks: Talkin' 'bout my generation. *Herizons*, 16-19.

Seaman, J., & Tinti-Kane, H. (2013). *Social Media for Teaching and Learning*. Boston, Ma: Pearson Learning Solutions and Babson Survey Research Group.

Seel, N. M. (2008). Empirical perspectives on memory and motivation. In J. M. Spector, M. D. Merrill, J. van Merrienboer, & M. P. Driscoll (Eds.), *Handbook of research on educational communications and technology* (pp. 39–54). New York, NY: Routledge.

Segal, B. (1995). *A short history of internet protocols at CERN*. Retrieved August 15 from http://ben.home.cern.ch/ben/TCPHIST.html

Selfe, C. (2007). *Multimodal composition: Resources for teachers*. Cresskill, NJ: Hampton Press.

Selfe, C. L. (1999). *Technology and literacy in the twenty-first century: The importance of paying attention*. Carbondale, IL: Southern Illinois University Press.

Selwyn, N. (2004). Reconsidering political and popular understandings of the digital divide. *New Media & Society*, *6*(3), 341–362. doi:10.1177/1461444804042519

Senft, T. M. (2008). *Camgirls: Celebrity and community in the age of social networks*. New York, NY: Peter Lang.

Serin, O. (2011). The effects of computer based-instruction on the achievement and problem-solving skills of science and technology students. *TOJET: The Turkish Online Journal of Educational Technology*, *10*(1), 183–202.

Serin, O., Bulut Serin, N., & Sayg, G. (2010). Developing problem solving inventory for children at the level of primary education (PSIC). *Elementary Education Online*, *9*(2), 446–458.

Serra, M. J., & Dunlosky, J. (2010). Metacomprehension judgments reflect the belief that diagrams improve learning from text. *Memory (Hove, England)*, *18*(7), 698–711. doi:10.1080/09658211.2010.506441 PMID:20730677

ShakeUpLearning.com. (2014). *5 awesome resources for badges in the classroom*. Retrieved from http://www.shakeuplearning.com/blog/5-awesome-resources-for-badges-in-the-classroom#sthash.2b9wVKTI.ZEgy8y1v.dpbs

Shalaby, A. A., Ali, R. R., & Gad, A. (2012). Urban sprawl impact assessment on the agricultural land in Egypt using remote sensing and GIS: A case study, Qalubiya Governorate. *Journal of Land Use Science*, *7*(3), 261–273. doi:10.1080/1747423X.2011.562928

Shapiro, A., & Meyer, D. (2014, November 28). A closer look at EU Parliament's vote to break up Google. In NPR (Producer), *All Things Considered*. Retrieved from http://www.npr.org/2014/11/28/367244283/a-closer-look-at-eu-parliaments-vote-to-break-up-google

Shapka, J. D., & Law, D. M. (2013). Does one size fit all? Ethnic differences in parenting behaviors and motivations for adolescent engagement in cyberbullying. *Journal of Youth and Adolescence*, *42*(5), 723–738. doi:10.1007/s10964-013-9928-2 PMID:23479327

Shariff, S. (2013). Review of *Cyberbullying prevention and response: Expert perspectives. New Media & Society*, *15*(1), 154–156. doi:10.1177/1461444812459453c

Sharp, D. L. M., Bransford, J. D., Goldman, S. R., Risko, V. J., Kinzer, C. K., & Vye, N. J. (1995). Dynamic visual support for story comprehension and mental model building by young, at-risk children. *Educational Technology Research and Development*, *43*(4), 25–40. doi:10.1007/BF02300489

Sheedy, C. S. (2011). *Social media for social change: A case study of social media use in the 2011 Egyptian revolution*. A Capstone Project Presented to the Faculty of the School of Communication, American University.

Shegar, C., & Weninger, C. (2010). Intertextuality in preschoolers' engagement with popular culture: Implications for literacy development. *Language & Education: An International Journal*, *24*(5), 431–447. doi:10.1080/09500782.2010.486861

Sheldon, D. A., & DeNardo, G. (2004). Comparing prospective freshman and pre-service music education majors' observations of music interactions. *Journal of Music Teacher Education*, *14*(1), 39–44. doi:10.1177/10570837040140010108

Sheldon, D. A., & DeNardo, G. (2005). Comparisons of higher-order thinking skills among prospective freshmen and upper-level preservice music education majors. *Journal of Research in Music Education*, *53*(1), 40–50. doi:10.1177/002242940505300104

Sheldon, K. M., Abad, N., & Hinsch, C. (2011). A two-process view of Facebook use and relatedness need-satisfaction: Disconnection drives use, and connection rewards it. *Journal of Personality and Social Psychology*, *100*(4), 766–775. doi:10.1037/a0022407 PMID:21280967

Sheldon, P. (2009). Maintain or develop new relationships? *Rocky Mountain Communication Review*, *6*, 51–56.

Shepardson, D. P., & Moje, E. B. (1994). The nature of fourth graders' understandings of electric circuits. *Science Education, 78*(5), 489–514. doi:10.1002/sce.3730780505

Sherer, P., & Shea, T. (2011). Using online video to support student learning and engagement. *College Teaching, 59*(2), 56–59. doi:10.1080/87567555.2010.511313

Sheridan, M., & Rowsell, J. (2010). *Design Literacies: Learning and Innovation in the Digital Age. Abungdon.* Routledge.

Sherman, C. (2014). What's the big deal about big data? *Online Searcher, 38*(2), 10–16.

Sherrod, L., Torney-Purta, J., & Flanagan, C. (2010). *Handbook of research on civic engagement in youth.* Hoboken, NJ: Wiley. doi:10.1002/9780470767603

Shin, D. H. (2010). The effects of trust, security and privacy in social networking: A security-based approach to understand the pattern of adoption. *Interacting with Computers, 22*(5), 428–438. doi:10.1016/j.intcom.2010.05.001

Shipstone, D. (1984). A study of children's understanding of electricity in simple DC circuits. *European Journal of Science Education, 6*(2), 185–198. doi:10.1080/0140528840060208

Shirky, C. (2011, February). The Political Power of Social Media. *Foreign Affairs.* Retrieved from http://www.foreignaffairs.com/articles/67038/clay-shirky/the-political-power-of-social-media

Shirky, C. (2009). *Here comes everybody: The power of organizing without organizations.* Penguin.

Shi, Z., Rui, H., & Whinston, A. B. (2014). Content sharing in a social broadcasting environment: Evidence from twitter. *Management Information Systems Quarterly, 38*(1), 123–142.

Shotter, J. (1990). The social construction of forgetting and remembering. In D. Middleton & D. Edwards (Eds.), *Collective memory* (pp. 120–138). London: SAGE.

Shrock, S. (1994). The media influence debate: Read the fine print, but don't lose sight of the big picture. *Educational Technology Research and Development, 42*(2), 49–53. doi:10.1007/BF02299092

Shui, E., & Lenhart, A. (2004). How Americans use instant messaging. Washington, DC: Pew Internet & American Life Project. Retrieved from http://www.pewinternet.org/Reports/2004/How-Americans-Use-Instant-Messaging.aspx

Shuler, C. (2009). *Pockets of Potential: Using Mobile Technologies to Promote Children's Learning.* New York: The Joan Ganz Cooney Center at Sesame Workshop.

Shute, V. J., Ventura, M., & Torres, R. (2013). Formative evaluation of students at Quest to Learn. *International Journal of Learning and Media, 4*(1), 55–69. doi:10.1162/IJLM_a_00087

Shu, W., & Yu-Hao, C. (2011). The behavior of wiki users. *Social Behavior and Personality, 39*(6), 851–864. doi:10.2224/sbp.2011.39.6.851

Sidelinger, R. J., Ayash, G., & Tibbles, D. (2008). Couples go online: Relational maintenance behaviors and relational characteristics use in dating relationships. *Human Communication, 11*, 341–356.

Siebler, F., Sabelus, S., & Bohner, G. (2008). A refined computer harassment paradigm: Validation, and test of hypotheses about target characteristics. *Psychology of Women Quarterly, 32*(1), 22–35. doi:10.1111/j.1471-6402.2007.00404.x

Siemens, G. (2006). *Knowing knowledge.* Lulu.com.

Siemens, G. (2008, January 29). ELI podcast: Connectivism. *Educause Connect.*

Simondson, H. (2009). Digital storytelling at the Australian Centre for the Moving Image. In J. Hartley & K. McWilliam (Eds.), *Story circle: Digital storytelling around the world* (pp. 118–123). Chichester, UK: Wiley-Blackwell. doi:10.1002/9781444310580.ch6

Simon, H. (1996). *The sciences of the artificial* (3rd ed.). Cambridge, MA: MIT Press.

Simpson, A., Walsh, M., & Rowsell, J. (2013). The digital reading path: Researching modes and multidirectionality with iPads. *Literacy, 47*(3), 123–130. doi:10.1111/lit.12009

Sims, C. (2014). From differentiated use to differentiating practices: Negotiating legitimate participation and the production of privileged identities. *Information Communication and Society*, *17*(6), 670–682. doi:10.1080/1369118X.2013.808363

Simsek, E., & Simsek, A. (2013). New literacies and digital citizenship. *Contemporary Educational Technology*, *4*(2), 126–137.

Singapore, I. (2014, September 3). *Experience the power of a bookbook* [Video file]. Retrieved from https://www.youtube.com/watch?v=MOXQo7nURs0

Singer, D. G., & Singer, J. L. (2005). *Imagination and play in the electronic age*. Cambridge, MA: Harvard University Press. doi:10.4159/9780674043695

Singh-Joseph, R. (2014). Technology: The good, the bad & the ugly. *Darpan: Reflecting South Asian Lifestyle*. Retrieved from http://www.darpanmagazine.com/lifestyle/tech/technology-the-good-the-bad-the-ugly/

Sinyor, M., Schaffer, A., & Cheung, A. H. (2014). An observational study of bullying as a contributing factor in youth suicide in Toronto. *Canadian Journal of Psychiatry*, *59*(12), 632–638. PMID:25702362

Sitzenfrei, R., Kleidorfer, M., Meister, M., Burger, G., Urich, C., Mair, M., & Rauch, W. (2014). Scientific computing in urban water management. In G. Hofstetter (Ed.), *Computational engineering* (pp. 173–193). Switzerland: Springer International Publishing.

Siu-Runyan, Y. (2011). *Public and school libraries in decline: When we need them*. Retrieved August 17 from http://www.ncte.org/library/NCTEFiles/Resources/Journals/CC/0211-sep2011/CC0211Presidents.pdf

Skerrett, A. (2012). Language and literacies in translocation: Experiences and perspectives of a transnational youth. *Journal of Literacy Research*, *44*(4), 364–395. doi:10.1177/1086296X12459511

Skinner, E. N., & Hagood, M. C. (2008). Developing literate identities with English language learners through digital storytelling. *The Reading Matrix*, *8*(2), 12–38. Retrieved from http://www.readingmatrix.com/articles/skinner_hagood/article.pdf

Slane, A. (2013). Sexting and the law in Canada. *The Canadian Journal of Human Sexuality*, *22*(3), 117–122. doi:10.3138/cjhs.22.3.C01

Slater, D., & Miller, D. (2000). *The Internet: An ethnographic approach*. Oxford, NY: Berg.

Slonje, R., Smith, P. K., & Frisen, A. (2013). The nature of cyberbullying, and strategies for prevention. *Computers in Human Behavior*, *29*(1), 26–32. doi:10.1016/j.chb.2012.05.024

Smiciklas, M. (2012). *The power of infographics: Using pictures to communicate and connect with your audience*. Indianapolis, IN: Pearson Education, Inc.

Smith, A. (2013). *Smartphone Ownership 2013*. Washington, DC: Pew Research Internet Project. Retrieved June 24, 2014 from http://www.pewinternet.org/2013/06/05/smartphone-ownership-2013/

Smith, A. (2014). *African Americans and technology use*. Washington, DC: Pew Research Internet Project. Retrieved May 31, 2014 from http://www.pewinternet.org/2014/01/06/african-americans-and-technology-use/

Smith, A. (2014). Older adults and technology. Washington, DC: Pew Internet and American Life Project. Retrieved from http://www.pewinternet.org/2014/04/03/older-adults-and-technology-use/

Smith, C. (2013, Dec. 13). Tumblr Offers Advertisers A Major Advantage: Young Users, Who Spend Tons Of Time On The Site. *Business Insider*. Retrieved from http://www.businessinsider.com/tumblr-and-social-media-demographics-2013- 12#ixzz3I8FQlCOH

Smith, C. (2014a, October 7). By the numbers: 140 amazing Pinterest statistics. *Digital Marketing Ramblings*. Retrieved from http://expandedramblings.com/index.php/pinterest-stats/5/

Smith, C. (2014b, July 24). *Newsflash: Pinterest is very popular on phones (new and updated stats)* (Rep.). *Digital Marketing Ramblings*. Retrieved from http://expandedramblings.com/index.php/new-updated-pinterest-stats-2/

Smith, C. (2014c, October 1). By the numbers: 60 amazing YouTube statistics. *Digital Marketing Ramblings*. Retrieved from http://expandedramblings.com/index.php/youtube-statistics/

Smith, C. (2014d, October 6). How much time do users spend on Facebook each day? (New and updated Facebook stats). *Digital Marketing Ramblings*. Retrieved from http://expandedramblings.com/index.php/much-time-users-spend-facebook-day-new-updated-facebook-stats/

Smith, J. G. (2012). *Screen-capture instructional technology: A cognitive tool for blended learning.* (Doctoral dissertation). Saint Mary's College of California.

Smith, R. (2013). *What is Digital Media?* Retrieved December 13, 2014 from http://thecdm.ca/news/faculty-news/2013/10/15/what-is-digital-media

Smith, P. (1968). *Body Covering. Museum of Contemporary Crafts.* New York: The American Craft Council.

Smith, P. K. (2012). Cyberbullying: Challenges and opportunities for a research program—A response to Olweus (2012). *European Journal of Developmental Psychology*, *9*(5), 553–558. doi:10.1080/17405629.2012.689821

Smith, P. K., Mahdavi, J., Carvalho, M., Fisher, S., Russell, S., & Tippett, N. (2008). Cyberbullying: Its nature and impact in secondary school pupils. *Journal of Child Psychology and Psychiatry, and Allied Disciplines*, *49*(4), 376–385. doi:10.1111/j.1469-7610.2007.01846.x PMID:18363945

Smythe, D. W. (2006). On the audience commodity and its work. In M. G. Durham & D. M. Kellner (Eds.), *Media and culture: Key works* (revised edition; pp. 230–256). Oxford, UK: Blackwell Publishers.

Snyder, I. (1996). *Hypertext: the electronic labyrinth.* Carlton South, Australia: Melbourne University Press.

Snyder, I., & Prinsloo, M. (2007). Young peoples engagement with digital literacies in marginal contexts in a globalised world. *Language and Education*, *21*(3), 171–179. doi:10.2167/le745.0

Soep, L. (2014, February 21). *Youth productions in digital-age civics.* Paper presented at the University of Minnesota Learning Technologies Media Lab. Retrieved from http://tinyurl.com/oys39ar

Soep, E. (2011). Youth media goes mobile. *National Civic Review*, *100*(3), 8–11. doi:10.1002/ncr.20073

Soep, E. (2015). Phones aren't smart until you tell them what to do. In E. Middaugh & B. Kirshner (Eds.), *youthaction: Becoming political in the digital age* (pp. 25–41). Charlotte, NC: Information Age Publishing.

Soep, E., & Chávez, V. (2010). *Drop that knowledge: Youth Radio stories.* Berkeley, CA: University of California Press.

Sollisch, J. (2012). *On the death of Encyclopaedia Britannica: All authoritarian regimes eventually fall.* Retrieved August 16 from http://www.csmonitor.com/Commentary/Opinion/2012/0322/On-the-death-of-Encyclopaedia-Britannica-All-authoritarian-regimes-eventually-fall

Solow, R. (1987, July 12). We'd better watch out. *New York Times Book Review*, p. 36. Retrieved from http://www.standupeconomist.com/pdf/misc/solow-computer-productivity.pdf

Song, Y. (2014). "Bring Your Own Device (BYOD)" for seamless science inquiry in a primary school. *Computers & Education*, *74*, 50–60. doi:10.1016/j.compedu.2014.01.005

Soni, J. (2013). The reason HuffPost is ending anonymous accounts. *The Huffington Post*. Retrieved from http://www.huffingtonpost.com/jimmy-soni/why-is-huffpost-ending-an_b_3817979.html

Sontag, S. (2004, May 22). Regarding the torture of others. *New York Times*. Retrieved from http://www.nytimes.com/2004/05/23/magazine/regarding-the-torture-of-others.html

Sorrells, K. (2013). *Intercultural communication: Globalization and social justice.* Thousand Oaks, CA: SAGE.

Sosa, T. (2009). Visual literacy: The missing piece of your technology integration course. *TechTrends*, *53*(2), 55–58. doi:10.1007/s11528-009-0270-1

Sotamaa, O. (2010). When the game is not enough: Motivations and practices among computer game modding culture. *Games and Culture*, *5*(3), 239–255. doi:10.1177/1555412009359765

Sotira, A. (2009, August 11). *Update: Quick post on art theft and share tools* [deviantART journal]. Retrieved from http://hq.deviantart.com/journal/Update-Quick-Post-on-Art-Theft-and-Share-Tools-230838615

Sotira, A. (2014, August 8). *The deviantART community turns 14* [deviantART journal]. Retrieved from http://spyed.deviantart.com/journal/The-DeviantArt-Community-Turns-14-473124195

Soukup, P. A. (2014). Looking at, with, and through YouTube. *Communication Research Trends, 33*(3), 3–34.

Speak Up Report. (2014). *Trends in Digital Learning: Students' views on Innovative Classroom Models.* Retrieved from: http://www.tomorrow.org/speakup/2014_Online-LearningReport.html

Spence, E. (2014). 2014 will be the year of wearable technology. *Forbes.* Retrieved from http://www.forbes.com/sites/ewanspence/2013/11/02/2014-will-be-the-year-of-wearable-technology/

Spires, H. A., Lee, J. K., Turner, K. A., & Johnson, J. (2008). Having our say: Middle grade student perspectives on school, technologies, and academic engagement. *Journal of Research on Technology in Education, 40*(4), 497–515. doi:10.1080/15391523.2008.10782518

Spodek B, National Association for the Education of Young Children. (1977). *Teaching practices: Reexamining assumptions* [e-book]. Available from: ERIC, Ipswich, MA. Accessed December 10, 2014.

Squire, K. (2005). Changing the Game: What Happens When Video Games Enter the Classroom? *Innovate: Journal of Online Education, 1*(6). Retrieved from http://www.editlib.org/j/ISSN-1552-3233/v/1/n/6/

Squire, K. (2011). Designed cultures. In C. SteinKuehler, K. Squire & S. Barab (Eds.), Games, learning, and society learning and meaning in the digital age (pp. 10-31). New York: Cambridge University Press.

Squire, K. (2012). *Video games and learning: Teaching and participatory culture in the digital age.* New York: Teachers College Press.

Squire, K., & Dikkers, S. (2012). Amplifications of learning: Use of mobile media devices among youth. *Convergence (London), 18*(4), 445–464. doi:10.1177/1354856511429646

Srinivasan, R. (2010, September 28). *Say You Want To Tweet a Revolution?* Retrieved from http://rameshsrinivasan.org/say-you-want-to-tweet-a-revolution/

Srinivasan, R. (2014). What Tahrir Square Has Done for Social Media: A 2012 Snapshot in the Struggle for Political Power in Egypt. *The Information Society, 30*(1), 71–80. doi:10.1080/01972243.2013.856363

Srisawasdi, N., & Sornkhatha, P. (2014). The effect of simulation-based inquiry on students' conceptual learning and its potential applications in mobile learning. *International Journal of Mobile Learning Organisation, 8*(1), 28–49. doi:10.1504/IJMLO.2014.059996

Stabile, C. (2014). "I will own you": Accountability in massively multiplayer online games. *Television & New Media, 15*(1), 43–57. doi:10.1177/1527476413488457

Stack, M. (2012, February 26). Who are the real bullies? *The Mark.* http://pioneers.themarknews.com/articles/8209-who-are-the-real-bullies/#.VF0IxPnF98E

Stack, M. (2015 in press). "Vomitorium of venom": Framing culpable youth, bewildered adults and the death of Amanda Todd. In D. S. Coombs & S. Collister (Eds.), *Debates for the digital age: The good, the bad, and the ugly of our online world* (Vol. 2). Santa Barbara, CA: Praeger.

Standing, C., & Kiniti, S. (2011). How can organizations use wikis for innovation? *Technovation, 31*(7), 287–295. doi:10.1016/j.technovation.2011.02.005

Starbek, P. P., Erjavec, M., & Peklaj, C. C. (2010). Teaching genetics with multimedia results in better acquisition of knowledge and improvement in comprehension. *Journal of Computer Assisted Learning, 26*(3), 214–224. doi:10.1111/j.1365-2729.2009.00344.x

Starner, T. (2002). Wearable computers: No longer science fiction. *IEEE Pervasive Computing / IEEE Computer Society [and] IEEE Communications Society, 1*(1), 86–88. doi:10.1109/MPRV.2002.993148

Star, S. L., & Griesemer, J. R. (1989). Institutional Ecology, `Translations' and Boundary Objects: Amateurs and Professionals in Berkeley's Museum of Vertebrate Zoology. *Social Studies of Science, 19*(3), 387–420. doi:10.1177/030631289019003001

Statista. (2014). *Number of smartphone users in the US from 2010 to 2018.* Retrieved October 22, 2014 from http://www.statista.com/statistics/201182/forecast-of-smartphone-users-in-the-us/

Statista. (2014). *Number of World of Warcarft subscribers from 1ˢᵗ quarter of 2005 to 2ⁿᵈ quarter of 2014*. Retrieved from http://www.statista.com/statistics/276601/number-of-world-of-warcraft-subscribers-by-quarter/

Stavrositu, C., & Sundar, S. S. (2008). Can blogs empower women? Designing agency-enhancing and community-building interfaces. In *CHI 2008 Proceedings of the Conference on Human Factors in Computing Systems: Works in progress* (pp. 2781–2786). Retrieved from http://delivery.acm.org/10.1145/1360000/1358761/p2781-stavrositu.pdf?key1=1358761&key2=5505519621&coll=GUIDE&dl=GUIDE&CFID=80978056&CFTOKEN=37792974

Stebbins, M. (n.d.). *Expanding public access to the results of federally funded research*. Retrieved from http://www.whitehouse.gov/blog/2013/02/22/expanding-public-access-results-federally-funded-research

Steeves, V. (2012). *Young Canadians in a wired world*. Retrieved on August 28, 2014 from http://mediasmarts.ca/sites/default/files/pdfs/publication-report/full/YCWWIII-youth-parents.pdf

Steeves, V. (2014a). *Young Canadians in a wired world, phase III: Cyberbullying: Dealing with online meanness, cruelty and threats*. Ottawa, Canada: MediaSmarts.

Stein, A., Mitgutsch, K., & Consalvo, M. (2012). Who are sports gamers? A large scale study of sports videogame players. *Convergence*, *19*(3), 345–353.

Steinkuehler, C. (2006). Massively multiplayer online gaming as participation in a discourse. *Mind, Culture, and Activity*, *13*(1), 38–52. doi:10.1207/s15327884mca1301_4

Steinkuehler, C. (2007). Massively multiplayer online gaming as a constellation of literacy practices. *E-learning*, *4*(3), 297–318. doi:10.2304/elea.2007.4.3.297

Steinkuehler, C. A. (2011). Video games and digital literacies. *Journal of Adolescent & Adult Literacy*, *54*(1), 61–63. doi:10.1598/JAAL.54.1.7

Steinkuehler, C., & Johnson, B. Z. (2009). Computational literacy in online games: The social life of a mod. *International Journal of Gaming and Computer-Mediated Simulations*, *1*(1), 53–65. doi:10.4018/jgcms.2009010104

Stein, P. (2008). Multimodal instructional practices. In J. Coiro, M. Knobel, C. Lankshear, & D. J. Leu (Eds.), *Handbook of research on new literacies* (pp. 871–898). New York: Taylor and Francis Group.

Stepulevage, L. (2001). Gender/technology relations: Complicating the gender binary. *Gender and Education*, *13*(3), 325–338. doi:10.1080/09540250120082525

Sterne, J., Morris, J., Baker, M. B., & Freire, A. M. (2008). The politics of podcasting. *The Fibreculture Journal, 13*.

Stevens, L. P., & Bean, T. W. (2007). *Critical literacy: Context, research, and practice in the K-12 classroom*. Thousand Oaks, CA: SAGE.

Stewart, B. (2013). Massiveness + openness = new literacies of participation? *MERLOT Journal of Online Learning and Teaching*, *9*(2), 228–238.

Steyaert, J. (2002). Inequality and the digital divide: myths and realities. *Advocacy, Activism and the Internet*, 199–211.

Sticca, F., & Perren, S. (2013). Is cyberbullying worse than traditional bullying? Examining the differential roles of medium, publicity, and anonymity for the perceived severity of bullying. *Journal of Youth and Adolescence*, *42*(5), 739–750. doi:10.1007/s10964-012-9867-3 PMID:23184483

Stieglitz, S., & Dang-Xuan, L. (2013). Social media and political communication: A social media analytics framework. *Social Network Analysis and Mining*, *3*(4), 1277–1291. doi:10.1007/s13278-012-0079-3

Still, J., & Worton, M. (1990). Introduction. In M. Worton & J. Still (Eds.), *Intertextuality: Theories and Practice* (pp. 1–44). Manchester, UK: Manchester University Press.

Stock-By-Crystal. (2011, March 12). *How to report art theft on dA* [deviantART post]. Retrieved from http://stock-by-crystal.deviantart.com/art/How-to-report-art-theft-on-dA-200713154

Stocker, A., Richter, A., Hoefler, P., & Tochtermann, K. (2012). Exploring appropriation of enterprise wikis: A multiple case study. *Computer Supported Cooperative Work*, *21*(2-3), 317–356. doi:10.1007/s10606-012-9159-1

Stone, B. (2011, January 28). *The Tweets Must Flow.* Retrieved September 26, 2014, from https://blog.twitter.com/2011/tweets-must-flow

Stoney, S., & Oliver, R. (1999). Can higher order thinking and cognitive engagement be enhanced with multimedia? *Interactive Multimedia Electronic Journal of Computer-Enhanced Learning, 1*(2). Retrieved from http://imej.wfu.edu/articles/1999/2/07/index.asp

Stoney, S., & Oliver, R. (1998). Interactive multimedia for adult learners: Can learning be fun? *Journal of Interactive Learning Research, 9*(1), 55–82.

Storck, M. (2011). *The role of social media in political mobilisation: a case study of the January 2011 Egyptian uprising.* University of St Andrews.

Strandberg, K. (2013). A social media revolution or just a case of history repeating itself? The use of social media in the 2011 Finnish parliamentary elections. *New Media & Society, 15*(8), 1329–1347. doi:10.1177/1461444812470612

Strangelove, M. (2010). *Watching YouTube: Extraordinary videos by ordinary people.* Toronto: University of Toronto Press.

Strano, M. (2008). User descriptions and interpretations of self-presentation through Facebook profile images. *Cyberpsychology:Journal of Psychological Research in Cyberspace, 2*(2).

Strasser, T. (2009). *Wish you were dead.* New York: Egmont.

Strasser, T. (2011). *Kill you last.* New York: Egmont.

Street, B. V. (1984). *Literacy in theory and practice.* Cambridge, UK: Cambridge University Press.

Street, B. V. (1993). *Cross-cultural approaches to literacy.* Cambridge, UK: Cambridge University Press.

Stritzke, W. G. K., Nguyen, A., & Durkin, K. (2004). Shyness and computer-mediated communication: A self-presentational theory perspective. *Media Psychology, 6*(1), 1–22. doi:10.1207/s1532785xmep0601_1

Strömbäck, J., & Aelst, P. V. (2013). Why political parties adapt to the media Exploring the fourth dimension of mediatization. *International Communication Gazette, 75*(4), 341–358. doi:10.1177/1748048513482266

Strydom, P. (2002). *Risk, environment and society: Ongoing debates, current issues, and future prospects.* Buckingham, UK: Open University Press.

Stuckey, E. (1990). *The violence of literacy.* New York, NY: Heinemann.

StudyBlue. (2011). *StudyBlue study report* [web log comment]. Retrieved from http://tinyurl.com/7l9vp8b

Sullivan-Mann, J., Perron, C. A., & Fellner, A. N. (2009). The effects of simulation on nursing students' critical thinking scores: A quantitative study. *Journal of Nurse Midwifery and Women's Health, 9*(2), 111–116.

Sung, E., & Mayer, R. E. (2013). Online multimedia learning with mobile devices and desktop computers: An experimental test of Clark's methods-not-media hypothesis. *Computers in Human Behavior, 29*(3), 639–647. doi:10.1016/j.chb.2012.10.022

Support. (n.d.). In *Snapchat.com.* Retrieved from https://support.snapchat.com/ca/snaps

Surbramaniam, V., & Whalen, J. (2014, December 4). Dutch man suspected of tormenting Amanda Todd had 75 other victims, Facebook report says. *CBC.* Retrieved from http://www.cbc.ca/news/canada/dutch-man-suspected-of-tormenting-amanda-todd-had-75-other-victims-facebook-report-says-1.2857281

Susono, H., Ikawa, T., & Kagami, A. (2011). *Digital storytelling workshop for Japanese inservice teachers.* Paper presented at the Global Learn Asia Pacific.

Sutherland-Smith, W., Snyder, I., & Angus, L. (2003). The digital divide: Differences in computer use between home and school in low socio-economic households. *Educational Studies in Language and Literature, 3*(1/2), 5–19. doi:10.1023/A:1024523503078

Suthersanen, U. (2007). Creative commons – The other way? *Learned Publishing, 20*(1), 59–68. doi:10.1087/095315107779490616

Swarr, A. L., & Nagar, R. (Eds.). (2010). *Introduction: Theorizing treansnational feminist praxis. In Critical transnational feminist praxis* (pp. 1–20). Albany, NY: State University of New York Press.

Sweeney, S. M. (2010). Writing for the instant messaging and text messaging generation: Using new literacies to support writing instruction. *Journal of Adolescent & Adult Literacy, 54*(2), 121–130. doi:10.1598/JAAL.54.2.4

Sweller, J. (2011). Cognitive load theory. *The Psychology of Learning and Motivation: Cognition in Education, 55*, 37-76.

Sweller, J. (1999). *Instructional design in technical areas.* ACER Press.

Swigger, N. (2013). The Online Citizen: Is Social Media Changing Citizens' Beliefs About Democratic Values? *Political Behavior, 35*(3), 589–603. doi:10.1007/s11109-012-9208-y

Sylvester, R., & Greenidge, W. (2009). Digital storytelling: Extending the potential for struggling writers. *The Reading Teacher, 4*(4), 284–295. doi:10.1598/RT.63.4.3

Tagliamonte, S. A., & Denis, D. (2008). Linguistic ruin? LOL! Instant messaging and teen language. *American Speech, 83*(1), 3–34. doi:10.1215/00031283-2008-001

Talbert, R. (2013). *Khan Academy Redux.* Retrieved from http://chronicle.com/blognetwork/castingout-nines/2013/02/05/khan-academy-redux/

Talwar, V., Gomez-Garibello, C., & Shariff, S. (2014). Adolescents' moral evaluations and ratings of cyberbullying: The effect of veracity and intentionality behind the event. *Computers in Human Behavior, 36*, 122–128. doi:10.1016/j.chb.2014.03.046

Tannen, D. (1990). *You just don't understand: Women and men in conversation.* New York: William Morrow.

Tannen, D. (2013). The medium is the metamessage: Conversational style in new media interaction. In D. Tannen & A. M. Trester (Eds.), *Discourse 2.0: Language and New Media* (pp. 99–117). Washington, DC: Georgetown University Press.

Taraszow, T., Aristodemou, E., Shitta, G., Laouris, Y., & Arsoy, A. (2010). Disclosure of personal and contact information by young people in social networking sites: An analysis using Facebook profiles as an example. *International Journal of Media and Cultural Politics, 6*(1), 81–102. doi:10.1386/macp.6.1.81/1

Tay, E., & Allen, M. (2011). Designing social media into university learning: Technology of collaboration or collaboration for technology. *Educational Media International, 48*(3), 151–163. doi:10.1080/09523987.2011.607319

Taylor, R. (2004, May 11). Is blog a masculine noun? *The Guardian.* Retrieved from http://politics.guardian.co.uk/comment/story/0,9115,1214393,00.html

Tekinbaş, K. S., Gresalfi, M., Peppler, K. A., & Santo, R. (2014). *Gaming the system: Designing with Gamestar Mechanic.* Cambridge, MA: MIT Press.

Temple, J. R., & Choi, H. (2014). Longitudinal association between teen sexting and sexual behavior. *Pediatrics, 134*(5), e1287–e1292. doi:10.1542/peds.2014-1974 PMID:25287459

Temple, J. R., Paul, J. A., van den Berg, P., Le, V. D., McElhany, A., & Temple, B. W. (2012). Teen sexting and its association with sexual behaviors. *Archives of Pediatrics & Adolescent Medicine, 166*(9). doi:10.1001/archpediatrics.2012.835 PMID:22751805

Templeton, R., & Dohrn, B. (2010). Activist interventions: Community organizing against "zero tolerance" policies. In J. A. Sandlin, B. D. Schultz, & J. Burdick (Eds.), *Handbook of public pedagogy: Education and learning beyond schooling* (pp. 420–433). New York: Routledge.

Teoh, B. S., & Neo, T.-K. (2007). Interactive multimedia learning: Students' attitudes and learning impact in an animation course. *The Turkish Online Journal of Educational Technology, 6*(4), 28–37.

Terranova, T. (2012). Attention, economy and the brain. *Culture Machine, 13*, 1-19. http://www.culturemachine.net/index.php/cm/article/view/465/484

Terranova, T. (2000). Free labor: Producing culture for the digital economy. *Social Text, 18*(2), 33–58. doi:10.1215/01642472-18-2_63-33

The Fair Go Project (Ed.). (2006). *School is for me:Pathways to student engagement.* Sydney: NSW Department of Education and Training.

The Pioneer Woman. (2010, September 15). *Crying my eyes out* [Web log post]. Retrieved from http://thepioneer-woman.com/blog/2010/09/crying-my-eyes-out/

The Turner Channel. (2010, February 9). *Infertility...* [Web log post]. Retrieved from http://mattandjuleeturner.blogspot.com/2010/02/infertility.html

The United Nations Foundation website. (n.d.). Retrieved from www.unfoundation.org/faq.html

Thiberghien, A., & Delacote, G. (1976). Manipulations et representations de circuits electriques simples chez des enfants de 7 a 12 ans. *Revue Française de Pédagogie, 34*(1), 32–44. doi:10.3406/rfp.1976.1613

Thierer, A. D., Crews, C. W., Jr., & Pearson, T. (2002, October). *Birth of the digital New Deal: An inventory of high-tech pork-barrel spending.* Retrieved from http://www.cato.org/publications/policy-analysis/birth-digital-new-deal-inventory-hightech-porkbarrel-spending

Thoman, E., & Jolls, T. (2004). Media literacy: A national priority for a changing world. *The American Behavioral Scientist, 48*(1), 18–29. doi:10.1177/0002764204267246

Thomas, D. (2014). Augmented reality gives physical world a virtual dimension. *BBC News.* Retrieved from http://www.bbc.com/news/business-28399343

Thomas, J., Coppola, J., & Thomas, B. (2001). The effect of technology integration and critical thinking skills in a graduate introductory information systems course. In *Proceedings of the Information Systems Education (ISECON) Conference.* Chicago: AITP Foundation for Information Technology Education.

Thomas, A. (2007). Blurring and breaking through the boundaries of narrative, literacy, and identity in adolescent fan fiction. In M. Knobel & C. Lankshear (Eds.), *A new literacies sampler* (pp. 137–166). NY: Peter Lang.

Thomas, A. (2007). *Youth online: Identity and literacy in the digital age.* New York, NY: Peter Lang.

Thomas, H. J., Connor, J. P., & Scott, J. G. (2014). Integrating traditional bullying and cyberbullying: Challenges of definition and measurement in adolescents – A review. *Educational Psychology Review*, 1–18.

Thomas, K. M., O'Bannon, B. W., & Bolton, N. (2013). Cell phones in the classroom: Teachers' perspectives of inclusion, benefits, and barriers. *Computers in the Schools: Interdisciplinary Journal of Practice, Theory, and Applied Research, 30*(4), 295–308. doi:10.1080/07380569.2013.844637

Thomas, S. (2013). What's in a Wiki for me? How a Wiki can be used to enhance a language learning classroom and student collaboration. *The Journal of Teachers Helping Teachers, 1*(1), 11–32.

Thompson, C. (2011). *How Khan Academy is changing the rules of education.* Retrieved from http://southasiainstitute.harvard.edu/website/wp-content/uploads/2012/08/Wired_2011-8-HowKhanAcademyIsChangingtheRulesofEducation.pdf

Thompson, J. B. (2013). *Media and Modernity: A Social Theory of the Media.* John Wiley & Sons.

Thompson, S. (2007). Mommy blogs: A marketer's dream. *Advertising Age, 78*, 6–11.

Thomson, R. (2006). The effect of topic of discussion on gendered language in computer-mediated communication discussion. *Journal of Language and Social Psychology, 25*(2), 167–178. doi:10.1177/0261927X06286452

Thorhague, A. (2013). The rules of the game – the rules of the player. *Games and Culture, 8*(6), 371–391. doi:10.1177/1555412013493497

Thornham, H. (2008). Gaming, gender, and geeks. *Feminist Media Studies, 8*(2), 127–142. doi:10.1080/14680770801980505

Thornton, J. (2013). The 4E wiki writing model. *Curriculum and Teaching Dialogue, 15*(1 & 2), 49–62.

Thumin, N. (2008). It's good for them to know my story: Cultural mediation as tension. In K. Lundby (Ed.), *Digital storytelling, mediatized stories* (pp. 85–104). New York: Peter Lange.

Thumin, N. (2009). Exploring self-representations in Wales and London: Tension in the text. In J. Hartley & K. McWilliam (Eds.), *Story circle: Digital storytelling around the world* (pp. 205–218). Chichester, UK: Wiley-Blackwell. doi:10.1002/9781444310580.ch14

Thurlow, C. (2006). From statistical panic to moral panic: The metadiscursive construction and popular exaggeration of new media language in the print media. *Journal of Computer-Mediated Communication, 11*(3), 1–39. doi:10.1111/j.1083-6101.2006.00031.x

Thurlow, C., & Poff, M. (2011). Text messaging. In S. C. Herring, D. Stein, & T. Virtanen (Eds.), *Handbook of the pragmatics of CMC* (pp. 163–189). Berlin, Germany: Mouton de Gruyter.

Time Magazine. (2011, February 22). Meet the Man Tweeting Egypt's Voices to the World. *Time*. Retrieved from http://content.time.com/time/specials/packages/article/0,28804,2045328_2045333_2045489,00.html

Tohidi, N. (2005, May). *Transnational feminism: A range of disciplinary perspectives*. Paper presented at Symposium conducted at the University of California, Los Angeles, Los Angeles, CA. Retrieved from http://www.humnet.ucla.edu/humnet/cmcs/#index.html

Tokunaga, R. S. (2010). Following you home from school: A critical review and synthesis of research on cyberbullying victimization. *Computers in Human Behavior*, *26*(3), 277–287. doi:10.1016/j.chb.2009.11.014

Toma, C. L., & Hancock, J. T. (2011). A new twist on love's labor: Self-presentation in online dating profiles. In K. B. Wright & L. M. Webb (Eds.), *Computer mediated communication in personal relationships* (pp. 41–55). New York: Peter Lang Publishers.

Tomasevski, K. (2003). *Education denied*. London: Zed Books.

Torres, R. J. (2009). *Learning on a 21st century platform: Gamestar Mechanic as a means to game design and systems-thinking skills within a nodal ecology* (Doctoral dissertation). Retrieved from ProQuest Dissertations and Theses. (3361988)

Totemyer, G. (1994). Challenges for democracy: Decentralization and empowerment in Africa. *Regional Development Dialogue*, *15*, 49–61.

Toth, C. (2013). Revisiting a genre: Teaching infographics in business and professional communication courses. *Business Communication Quarterly*, *76*(4), 446–457. doi:10.1177/1080569913506253

Tran, T. (2011, March 8). *China blogger angered over losing Facebook account*. Retrieved January 25, 2015, from http://www.washingtontimes.com/news/2011/mar/8/china-blogger-angered-over-losing-facebook-account/

Transitory. (n.d.). In *Merriam-Webster.com*. Retrieved from http://www.merriam-webster.com/dictionary/transitory

Traxler, J. (2014). Mobile learning in international development. In A. Tsinakos & M. Ally (Eds.) *Global Mobile Learning Issues and Trends*. Retrieved from http://www.meducationalliance.org/content/global-mobile-learning-implementations-and-trends

Traxler, J., & Crompton, H., (in press). *Research in Mobile Learning*. United Nations Educational, Scientific, and Cultural Organization (UNESCO).

Traxler, J. (2013). mLearning: Solutions for international development - rethinking the thinking. *Digital Culture & Education*, *5*(2), 74–85.

Trepanier, L. (2011). The postmodern condition of cosmopolitanism. In L. Trepanier & K. M. Habib (Eds.), *Cosmopolitanism in the age of globalization: citizens without states* (pp. 211–227). Lexington, KY: The University of Kentucky Press.

Trepanier, L., & Habib, K. M. (2011). Introduction. In L. Trepanier & K. M. Habib (Eds.), *Cosmopolitanism in the age of globalization: citizens without states* (pp. 1–10). Lexington, KY: The University of Kentucky Press.

Trigger, B. (1976). *Nubia under the pharaohs*. London, UK: Thames and Hudson.

Tripp, L. M. (2011). "The computer is not for you to be looking around, it is for Schoolwork": Challenges for digital inclusion as Latino immigrant families negotiate children's access to the internet. *New Media & Society*, *13*(4), 552–567. doi:10.1177/1461444810375293

Tripp, L. M., & Herr-Stephenson, R. (2009). Making access meaningful: Latino young people using digital media at home and at school. *Journal of Computer-Mediated Communication*, *14*(4), 1190–1207. doi:10.1111/j.1083-6101.2009.01486.x

Tsakonas, G., & Papatheodorou, C. (2007). Exploring usefulness and usability in the evaluation of open access digital libraries. *Information Processing and Management: An International Journal*, *44*(2), 1234–1250.

Tsou, W., & Tzeng, Y. (2006). Applying a multimedia storytelling website in foreign language learning. *Computers & Education, 47*(1), 17–28. doi:10.1016/j.compedu.2004.08.013

Tuck, E., & Wang, K. W. (2013). *Youth resistance research and theories of change*. New York, NY: Routledge.

Tucker, J. S. (2009). Foreward. In M. Friedman & S. Calixte (Eds.), *Mothering and blogging: The radical act of the mommyblog* (pp. 1–20). Toronto, Canada: Demeter Press.

Tufekci, Z. (2008a). Can you see me now? Audience and disclosure regulation in online social network sites. *Bulletin of Science, Technology & Society, 28*(1), 20–36. doi:10.1177/0270467607311484

Tufekci, Z. (2008b). Grooming, gossip, Facebook and Myspace: What can we learn about these sites from those who won't assimilate? *Information Communication and Society, 11*(4), 544–564. doi:10.1080/13691180801999050

Tufte, E. (2001). *Visual display of quantitative information*. Cheshire, CT: Graphics Press.

Turkle, S., & Papert, S. (1992).Epistemological pluralism and the revaluation of the concrete. *The Journal of Mathematical Behavior, 11*(1), 3–33.

Turner, K. C. N. (2012). Multimodal Hip Hop Productions as Media Literacies. *The Educational Forum, 76*(4), 497–509. doi:10.1080/00131725.2012.708617

Turner, K. H., Abrams, S. S., Katic, E., & Donovan, M. J. (2014). Demystifying digitalk: The what and why of the language teens use in digital writing. *Journal of Literacy Research, 46*(2), 157–193. doi:10.1177/1086296X14534061

Tuukkanen, T., Iqbal, A., & Kankaanranta, M. (2010). A framework for children's participation in virtual worlds. *Journal of Virtual Worlds Research, 3*(2), 4–26.

Tyner, K. (2014). *Literacy in a digital world: Teaching and learning in the age of information*. NY: Routledge.

U.S. Census Bureau. (2012). *Computer and internet access in the United States*. Retrieved from https://www.census.gov/hhes/computer/publications/2012.html

U.S. Department of Commerce. (2002). *A nation online: How Americans are expanding their use of the Internet*. Retrieved from http://www.ntia.doc.gov/legacy/ntiahome/dn/anationonline2.pdf

U.S. Department of Commerce. (2004). *A nation online: Entering the broadband age*. Retrieved from http://www.ntia.doc.gov/reports/anol/NationOnlineBroadband04.htm

U.S. Department of Labor Employment and Training Administration. (2014) *Workforce Innovation and Opportunity Act*. Washington, DC: Author. Retrieved from http://www.doleta.gov/wioa/pdf/WIOA-Overview.pdf

Uluyol, C., & Agca, R. K. (2012). Integrating mobile multimedia into textbooks: 2D barcodes. *Computers & Education, 59*(4), 1192–1198. doi:10.1016/j.compedu.2012.05.018

Umberson, D., Chen, M. D., House, J. S., Hopkins, K., & Slaten, E. (1996). The effect of social relationships on psychological well-being: Are men and women really so different? *American Sociological Review, 61*(5), 837–857. doi:10.2307/2096456

UNCTAD. (2010). *Information economy report 2010: ICTs, Enterprises and Poverty Alleviation*. Technical Report. United Nations Conference on Trade and Development (UNCTAD). Retrieved from http://unctad.org/en/docs/ier2010_embargo2010_en.pdf

UNDP. (2010). *Human Development Report 2010—20th Anniversary Edition: The Real Wealth of Nations: Pathways to Human Development*. Technical report. United Nations Development Programme (UNDP). Retrieved from http://hdr.undp.org/sites/default/files/reports/270/hdr_2010_en_complete_reprint.pdf

UNESCO. (2013). *Adult and Youth Literacy* [Fact sheet]. UNESCO Institute for Statistics.

UNESCO/UNICEF. (2007). *A human rights-based approach to education: A framework for the realization of children's right to education and rights in education. United Nations Educational, Scientific and Cultural Organization. United Nations Children's Fund*. London: United Nation's Children's Fund.

Unger, A. (2012). Modding as part of game culture. In J. Fromme & A. Unger (Eds.), *Computer games and new media cultures* (pp. 509–523). Doetinchem, Netherlands: Springer Netherlands. doi:10.1007/978-94-007-2777-9_32

UNICEF South Africa. (2013). *Supporting pregnant women's journey to motherhood.* Retrieved from http://www.unicef.org/southafrica/media_14102.html

UNICEF. (2012). *Moms Connect.* Retrieved from: http://www.unicef.org/southafrica/media_14102.html)

United States Department of Justice. (n.d.). *Cyber crime.* Retrieved http://www.justice.gov/usao/briefing_room/cc/

University of Canterbury. (2012). *New technology brings children's drawings alive.* Retrieved from http://www.comsdev.canterbury.ac.nz/rss/news/index.php?feed=news&articleId=455

University of Illinois. (2014). *Badges at Illinois.* Retrieved from http://news.badges.illinois.edu/

University of Texas Libraries. (n.d.). *Digital repository.* Retrieved from http://repositories.lib.utexas.edu/

Unwin, P. T. (2009). *ICT4D: Information and communication technology for development.* Cambridge, UK: Cambridge University Press.

US Chamber of Commerce Foundation. (n.d.). *Center for education and workforce.* Retrieved from http://www.uschamberfoundation.org/center-education-and-workforce

usability.gov. (n.d.). Retrieved from http://www.usability.gov/what-and-why/glossary/u/index.html

USAID. (2012). *Infrastructure.* Retrieved from http://www.usaid.gov/what-we-do/economic-growth-and-trade/infrastructure

USAID. (2012). *iREAD Ghana study: final evaluation report* [Report]. Retrieved from http://www.worldreader.org/uploads/Worldreader%20ILC%20USAID%20iREAD%20Final%20Report%20Jan-2012.pdf

USDE. (2011). *Digital badges for learning.* Retrieved from http://www.ed.gov/news/speeches/digital-badges-learning

Ushioda, E. (2013). Motivation matters in mobile language learning: A brief commentary. *Language Learning & Technology, 17*(3), 1–5. Retrieved from http://llt.msu.edu/issues/october2013/commentary.pdf

Vaccari, C., Valeriani, A., Barberá, P., Bonneau, R., Jost, J. T., Nagler, J., & Tucker, J. (2013). Social media and political communication: A survey of Twitter users during the 2013 Italian general election. *Rivista Italiana Di Scienza Politica*, (3). doi:10.1426/75245

Vah Seliskar, H. (2014). *Using badges in the classroom to motivate learning.* Retrieved from http://www.facultyfocus.com/articles/teaching-with-technology-articles/using-badges-classroom-motivate-learning/

Vaidhyanathan, S. (2012). *The Googlization of everything:(and why we should worry).* Univ of California Press.

Vakil, S. (2014). A critical pedagogy approach for engaging urban youth in mobile app development in an after-school program. *Equity & Excellence in Education, 47*(1), 31–45. doi:10.1080/10665684.2014.866869

Valenza, J. (2008, April 1). Fair use and transformativeness: It may shake your world. *School Library Journal.* Retrieved from http://blogs.slj.com/neverending-search/2008/04/01/fair-use-and-transformativeness-it-may-shake-your-world/

Valmont, W. J., & Wepner, S. B. (2000). Using technology to support literacy learning. In S. B. Wepner, W. J. Valmont, & R. Thurlwo (Eds.), *Linking literacy and technology: A guide for K-8 classrooms* (pp. 2–18). Newark, DE: International Reading Association.

Van Cleave, J. & Bridges-Rhoads, S. (in press). Rewriting the Common Core State Standards for Tomorrow's Literacies. *English Journal, 104*(2), 41-47.

van den Berg, B. (2014). Colouring inside the lines: Using technology to regulate children's behaviour online. In S. van der Hof, B. van den Berg, & B. Schermer (Eds.), *Minding minors wandering the web: Regulating online child safety* (pp. 67–87). The Hague: Springer. doi:10.1007/978-94-6265-005-3_4

van Dijck, J. (2013). 'You have one identity': Performing the self on Facebook and LinkedIn. *Media Culture & Society, 35*(2), 199–215. doi:10.1177/0163443712468605 van Dijk, J. A. (2006). Digital divide research, achievements and shortcomings. *Poetics*, *34*(4-5), 221–235. doi:10.1016/j.poetic.2006.05.004

van Doorn, N., van Zoonen, L., & Wyatt, S. (2007). Writing from experience: Presentations of gender identity on weblogs. *European Journal of Women's Studies*, *14*(2), 143–159. doi:10.1177/1350506807075819

Van Dusen, G. C. (2014). Digital Dilemma: Issues of Access, Cost, and Quality in Media-Enhanced and Distance Education. ASHE-ERIC Higher Education Report, 27(5).

Van House, N. A., & Davis, M. (2005). The social life of cameraphone images. In *Proceedings of the Pervasive Image Capture and Sharing: New Social Practices and Implications for Technology Workshop (PICS 2005) at the Seventh International Conference on Ubiquitous Computing (UbiComp 2005)*. Retrieved from http://web.mit.edu

van Laer, T. (2014). The means to justify the end: Combating cyber harassment in social media. *Journal of Business Ethics*, *3123*(1), 85–98. doi:10.1007/s10551-013-1806-z

van Meter, P. N., & Firetto, C. (2008). Intertextuality and the study of new literacies. In J. Coiro, M. Knobel, C. Lankshear, & D. J. Leu (Eds.), *Handbook of Research on New Literacies* (pp. 1079–1092). New York: Lawrence Erlbaum.

Van Royen, K., Poels, K., Daelemans, W., & Vandebosch, H. (2015). Automatic monitoring of cyberbullying on social networking sites: From technological feasibility to desirability. *Telematics and Informatics*, *32*(1), 89–97. doi:10.1016/j.tele.2014.04.002

Van Wart, S., Vakil, S., & Parikh, T. S. (2014). Apps for social justice: Motivating computer science learning with design and real-world problem solving. Paper presented at ITiCSE '14, Uppsala, Sweden.

Vandebosch, H. (2014). Addressing cyberbullying using a multi-stakeholder approach: The Flemish case. In S. van der Hof, B. van den Berg, & B. Schermer (Eds.), *Minding minors wandering the web: Regulating online child safety* (pp. 245–262). The Hague: Springer. doi:10.1007/978-94-6265-005-3_14

Vander Veer, E. A. (2008). *Facebook: The missing manual*. Sebastopol, CA: O'Reilly Media.

Varian, H. R. (2006). A plug for the unplugged $100 laptop computer for developing nations. *New York Times: Business*. Retrieved from http://www.nytimes.com/2006/02/09/business/09scene.html

Varis, P., & Blommaert, J. (2015). Conviviality and collectives on social media: Virality, memes and new social structures. (Paper #108). Blommaert & Varis. Retrieved from http://www.tilburguniversity.edu/upload/83490ca9-659d-49a0-97db-ff1f8978062b_TPCS_108_Varis-Blommaert.pdf

Varnhagen, C. K., McFall, P. P., Pugh, N., Routledge, L., Sumida-MacDonald, H., & Kwong, T. E. (2010). Lol: New language and spelling in instant messaging. *Reading and Writing*, *23*(6), 719–733. doi:10.1007/s11145-009-9181-y

Vasquez, V. (2010). *Getting beyond "I like the book": Creating space for critical literacy in K–6 classrooms* (2nd ed.). Newark, DE: International Reading Association.

Vasudevan, L., Schultz, K., & Bateman, J. (2010). Through multimodal storytelling rethinking composing in a digital age: Athoring literate identities. *Written Communication*, *27*, 442–465. doi:10.1177/0741088310378217

Vaughan, D. (2011). The importance of capabilities in the sustainability of information and communications technology programs: The case of remote Indigenous Australian communities. *Ethics and Information Technology*, *13*(2), 131–150. doi:10.1007/s10676-011-9269-3

Velghe, R. (2014). "I wanna go in the phone": Literacy acquisition, informal learning processes, "voice" and mobile phone appropriation in a South African. *Ethnography and Education*, *9*(1), 111–126. doi:10.1080/17457823.2013.836456

Venable, M. (2013). *The power of the online career portfolio*. Retrieved from http://www.onlinecollege.org/2013/08/05/the-power-of-a-career-portfolio/

Verdugo, D. R., & Belmonte, I. (2007). Using digital stories to improve listening comprehension with Spanish young learners of English. *Language Learning & Technology*, *11*, 87–101.

Vickery, J. R. (2010). Blogrings as virtual communities for adolescent girls. In S. R. Mazzarella (Ed.), *Girl wide Web 2.0: Revisiting girls, the Internet, and the negotiation of identity* (pp. 183–200). New York, NY: Peter Lang.

Vickery, J. R. (2014). The role of after-school digital media clubs in closing participation gaps and expanding social networks. *Equity & Excellence in Education, 47*(1), 78–95. doi:10.1080/10665684.2013.866870

Vine. (2014). *Embed vine posts.* [Web log comment]. Retrieved from http://blog.vine.co/page/6

Vinge, V. (1993). *The coming technological singularity: How to survive in the post-human era.* Retrieved from http://www.aleph.se/Trans/Global/Singularity/sing.html

Vision, V. (2012, March). *Broadband as a green strategy: Promising best practices to achieve positive environmental and economic benefits through accelerated broadband deployment and adoption.* Retrieved from http://valleyvision.org/sites/files/pdf/bbgreen_policy_brief_final_printer_withdate.pdf

Voida, A., Newstetter, W. C., & Mynatt, E. D. (2002). *When conventions collide: The tensions of instant messaging attributed.* Paper presented at the CHI Conference, Minneapolis, MN.

Voithofer, R. (2005). Designing new media education research: The materiality of data, representation, and dissemination. *Educational Researcher, 34*(9), 3–14. doi:10.3102/0013189X034009003

Vollman, A., Abraham, L., & Mörn, M. P. (2014). *Women on the web: How women are shaping the internet.* Available from http://www.comscore.com/Press_Events/Presentations_Whitepapers/2010/Women_on_the_Web_How_Women_are_Shaping_the_Internet

Von Braun, J. (2010). ICT for the poor at large scale: Innovative connections to markets and services. In A. Picot & J. Lorenz (Eds.), *ICT for the next five billion people: Information and communication for sustainable development* (pp. 3–14). Heidelberg, Germany: Springer. doi:10.1007/978-3-642-12225-5_2

Vos, N., van der Meijden, H., & Denessen, E. (2011). Effects of constructing versus playing an educational game on student motivation and deep learning strategy use. *Computers & Education, 56*(1), 127–137. doi:10.1016/j.compedu.2010.08.013

Vossen, G., & Hagemann, S. (2007). *From Version 1.0 to Version 2.0: A brief history of the web,* No 4, ERCIS Working Papers. Westfälsche Wilhelms-Universität Münster (WWU) - European Research Center for Information Systems (ERCIS). Retrieved from http://EconPapers.repec.org/RePEc:zbw:ercisw:4

Vu, K. M. (2011). ICT as a source of economic growth in the information age: Empirical evidence from the 1996–2005 period. *Telecommunications Policy, 35*(4), 357–372. doi:10.1016/j.telpol.2011.02.008

Vygotsky, L. S. (1987). The collected works of L. S. Vygotsky:Problems of general psychology (vol. 1; R. W. Rieber & A. S. Carton Eds., N. Minick, Trans.). New York: Plenum Press.

Vygotsky, L. S. (1934/1978). *Mind in society.* Cambridge, MA: Harvard University Press.

Vygotsky, L. S., & Cole, M. (1978). *Mind in society: The development of higher psychological processes.* Cambridge, MA: Harvard University Press.

Vygotsky, Walther, J. D. (1996). Computer-mediated communication: Impersonal, interpersonal, and hyperpersonal interaction. *Communication Research, 25*(1), 3–43.

Waddell, T. F., Ivory, J. D., Conde, R., Long, C., & McDonnell, R. (2014). White man's virtual world: A systemic content analysis of gender and race in massively multiplayer online games. *Journal of Virtual Worlds Research, 7*(2), 1–14.

Wade, S. E., & Moje, E. B. (2000). The role of text in classroom learning. In M. L. Kamil, P. B. Mosenthal, P. D. Pearson, & R. Barr (Eds.), *Handbook of reading research* (Vol. 3, pp. 609–627). Mahwah, NJ: Lawrence Erlbaum.

Waelbroeck, P. (2013). Digital music: Economic perspectives. In R. Towse & C. Handke (Eds.), *Handbook of the digital creative economy.* Retrieved from http://papers.ssrn.com/sol3/papers.cfm?abstract_id=2249690

Waelde, C., & MacQueen, H. L. (2007). *Intellectual property: The many faces of the public domain.* Cheltenham, UK: Edward Elgar. doi:10.4337/9781847205582

Wagler, M., & Mathews, J. (2011). Up river: Place, ethnography, and design in the St. Louis River estuary. In S. Dikkers, J. Martin, & B. Coutler (Eds.), *Mobile media learning: Amazing uses of mobile devices for learning* (pp. 39–60). Pittsburgh, PA: ETC Press.

Wagoner, T., Schwalbe, A., Hoover, S., & Ernst, D. (2012). CEHD iPad Initiative: Year two report. Minneapolis, MN: College of Education and Human Development, University of Minnesota. Retrieved from http://www.cehd.umn.edu/Mobile/About.html

Wahlster, W., & Dengel, A. (2006). Web 3.0: Convergence of web 2.0 and the semantic web. In Technology radar (Vol. 2). German Research Center for Artificial Intelligence (DFKI).

Waldman, A. E. (2012). Hostile educational environments. *Maryland Law Review (Baltimore, Md.)*, *71*(3), 705–771.

Waldron, F. (2010). Introduction. In F. Waldron & B. Ruane (Eds.), *Human rights education: Reflections on theory and practice* (pp. 1–14). Dublin, Ireland: The Liffey Press.

Walker, H. (2011). Evaluating the effectiveness of apps for mobile devices. *Journal of Special Education Technology*, *26*(4), 59–63.

Wallis, S. (2008). *Triple crunch: Joined-up solutions to financial chaos, oil decline and climate change to transform the economy.* Retrieved from new economics foundation website: http://b.3cdn.net/nefoundation/91cd89d66b0d556628_stm6bqsxi.pdf

Walrave, M., & Heirman, W. (2011). Cyberbullying: Predicting victimization and perpetration. *Children & Society*, *25*(1), 59–72. doi:10.1111/j.1099-0860.2009.00260.x

Walsh, M. (2008). Worlds have collided and modes have merged: Classroom evidence of changed literacy practices. *Literacy*, *42*(2), 101–108. doi:10.1111/j.1741-4369.2008.00495.x

Walters, S. (2011). Everyday life, Everyday death. *Feminist Media Studies*, *11*(3), 363–378. doi:10.1080/14680777.2010.542341

Walther, J. B., & D'Addario, K. P. (2001). The Impacts of Emoticons on Message Interpretation in Computer-Mediated Communication. *Social Science Computer Review*, *19*(3), 324–347. doi:10.1177/089443930101900307

Walther, J. B., van der Heide, B., Kim, S., Westerman, D., & Tong, S. (2008). The role of friends' appearance and behavior on evaluations of individuals on Facebook: Are we known by the company we keep? *Human Communication Research*, *34*(1), 28–49. doi:10.1111/j.1468-2958.2007.00312.x

Walton, K., Golick, J., & Golick, S. (Producers). (2010-2012). *Ruby Skye, P.I.* [Webisode series]. Retrieved from http://rubyskyepi.com

Walton, M. (2010). *Mobile literacies & South African teens: Leisure reading, writing, and MXit chatting for teens in Langa and Gugulethu.* Durbanville, South Africa: Shuttleworth Foundation m4Lit Project. Retrieved from http://tinyw.in/lJmr

Wang, J. (2011). *Innovator: DeviantART's Angelo Sotira* [Electronic magazine]. Retrieved June 26, 2014, from http://www.entrepreneur.com/article/217859

Wang, Y. (2013, March 25). *More people have cell phones than toilets, U.N. study shows.* Retrieved from http://newsfeed.time.com/2013/03/25/more-people-have-cell-phones-than-toilets-u-n-study-shows/

Wang, C., & Burris, M. A. (1992). Empowerment through photo novella: Portraits of participation. *Health Education & Behavior*, *21*(2), 171–186. doi:10.1177/109019819402100204 PMID:8021146

Wang, S. S., Moon, S. I., Kwon, K. H., Evans, C. A., & Stefanone, M. A. (2010). Face off: Implications of visual cues on initiating friendship on Facebook. *Computers in Human Behavior*, *26*(2), 226–234. doi:10.1016/j.chb.2009.10.001

Warner, J. (2014). *Networked, social, and multimodal: Adolescents composing across spaces.* (Unpublished doctoral dissertation), Teachers College, Columbia University, New York.

Warnick, B. (2002). *Critical literacy in a digital era: Technology, rhetoric, and the public interest.* Mahwah, NJ: Lawrence Erlbaum Associates.

Warschauer, M. (2003). *Technology and Social Inclusion: Rethinking the Digital Divide.* Cambridge, MA: The MIT Press.

Warschauer, M., & Matuchniak, T. (2010). New technology and digital worlds: Analyzing evidence of equity in access, use, and outcomes. *Review of Research in Education, 34*(1), 179–225. doi:10.3102/0091732X09349791

Wasike, J. (2013). Social media ethical issues: Role of a librarian. *Library Hi Tech News, 30*(1), 8–16. doi:10.1108/07419051311320922

Waters, J. K. (2013). Digital badges. *The Journal, 40*(5), 14.

Waters, S., & Ackerman, J. (2011). Exploring privacy management on Facebook: Motivations and perceived consequences of voluntary disclosure. *Journal of Computer-Mediated Communication, 17*(1), 101–115. doi:10.1111/j.1083-6101.2011.01559.x

Weaver, A. C. A., & Prey, J. C. (2013).Fostering gender diversity in computing. *Computer, 46*(3), 22–23.

Webb, J. (2012). The iPad as a tool for education: a case study. Nottingham, UK: Naace. Retrieved from http://www.naace.co.uk/publications/longfieldipadresearch

Webb, L. M., Wilson, M. L., Hodges, M., Smith, P. A., & Zakeri, M. (2012). Facebook: How college students work it. In H. S. Noor Al-Deen & J. A. Hendricks (Eds.), Social media: Usage and impact (p. 3-22). Lanham: MD: Lexington.

Webb, D. C., Repenning, A., & Koh, K. H. (2012). Toward an emergent theory of broadening participation in computer science education. In *Proceedings of the ACM Special Interest Group on Computer Science Education Conference* (pp. 173–178). New York: ACM. doi:10.1145/2157136.2157191

Webb, L. M., & Lee, B. S. (2011). Mommy blogs: The centrality of community in the performance of online maternity. In M. Moravec (Ed.), *Motherhood online: How online communities shape modern motherhood* (pp. 244–257). Newcastle upon Tyne, UK: Cambridge Scholars.

Wei, K. K., Teo, H. H., Chan, H. C., & Tan, B. C. Y. (2011). Conceptualizing and testing a social cognitive model of the digital divide. *Information Systems Research, 22*(1), 170–187. doi:10.1287/isre.1090.0273

Wei, L. (2009). Filter blogs vs. personal journals: Understanding the knowledge production gap on the Internet. *Journal of Computer-Mediated Communication, 14*(3), 532–558. doi:10.1111/j.1083-6101.2009.01452.x

Weinberger, C. J. (2004). Just ask! Why surveyed women did not pursue IT courses or careers. *Technology and Society Magazine, IEEE, 23*(2), 28–35. doi:10.1109/MTAS.2004.1304399

Weis, L., & Fine, M. (Eds.). (1993). *Beyond silenced voices: Class, race, and gender in United States schools.* SUNY Press.

Weiss, A. (2005). The power of collective intelligence. *Networker, 9*(3), 16–23. doi:10.1145/1086762.1086763

Wenger, E. (1998). *Communities of practice: learning, meaning, and identity.* New York, NY: Cambridge University Press. doi:10.1017/CBO9780511803932

Wenger, E. (1999). *Communities of practice: Learning, meaning and identity.* Cambridge, UK: Cambridge University Press.

Werner, L., Denner, J., & Campe, S. (2014). Children programming games: A strategy for measuring computational learning. *ACM Transactions on Computing Education, 14*(4), 24. doi:10.1145/2677091

Wertsch, J. V. (1998). Mediated action. In W. Bechtel & G. Graham (Eds.), *Companion to cognitive science* (pp. 518–525). Malden, MA: Blackwell.

Wertsch, J. V. (1998). *Mind as action.* Oxford, UK: Oxford University Press.

West Coast, L. E. A. F. (2014). *Cybermisogyny: Using and strengthening Canadian legal responses to gendered hate and harassment online.* Vancouver, BC: West Coast LEAF.

West, M., & Chew, H. E. (2014). Reading in the Mobile Era: A study of mobile reading in developing countries. Paris: United Nations Educational, Scientific, and Cultural Organization; Retrieved from http://tinyw.in/qdSw

Weston, D. C. (2014). *The memory machine* [ibook]. Retrieved from itunes.apple.com

WGBH. (1998). *A science odyssey: The Internet gives rise to the World Wide Web 1992.* PBS. Retrieved from http://www.pbs.org/wgbh/aso/databank/entries/dt92ww.html

Wheeler, W. (2003). Youth leadership for development: Civic activism as a component of youth development programming and a strategy for strengthening civil society. In F. Jacobs, D. Werlieb, & R. M. Lerner (Eds.), Handbook of Applied Developmental Science (2nd ed.; pp. 491–505). Academic Press.

Wheeler, S., Yeomans, P., & Wheeler, D. (2008). The good, the bad and the wiki: Evaluating student generated content for collaborative learning. *British Journal of Educational Technology*, *39*(6), 987–995. doi:10.1111/j.1467-8535.2007.00799.x

Whitacre, B., Gallardo, R., & Strover, S. (2014). Does rural broadband impact jobs and income? Evidence from spatial and first-differenced regressions. *The Annals of Regional Science*, *53*(3), 649–670. doi:10.1007/s00168-014-0637-x

White House. (2013). *Four years of broadband growth*. Washington, DC: Office of Science and Technology Policy & The National Economic Council.

White, D., & Le Cornu, A. (2010). Eventedness and disjuncture in virtual worlds. *Educational Research*, *52*(2), 183–196. doi:10.1080/00131881.2010.482755

White, M. (2003). Too close to see: Men, women and webcams. *New Media & Society*, *5*(1), 105–121. doi:10.1177/1461444803005001901

Whittaker, E., & Kowalski, R. M. (2014). Cyberbullying Via Social Media. *Journal of School Violence*, *14*(1), 11–29. doi:10.1080/15388220.2014.949377

Whitty, M. (2007). Introduction. In M. T. Whitty, A. J. Baker, & J. A. Inman (Eds.), *Online Matchmaking* (pp. 1–14). New York, NY: Palgrave Macmillan. doi:10.1057/9780230206182

Whitty, P., & Iannacci, L. (Eds.). (2009). *Early childhood curricula: Reconceptualist perspectives*. Calgary, AB: Detselig.

Whyte, W. F. E. (1991). *Participatory action research*. Sage Publications, Inc.

Wikipedia About. (n.d.). In *Wikipedia.org*. Retrieved November 7, 2014 fromhttp://en.wikipedia.org/wiki/Wikipedia:About

WikiWikiWeb. (n.d.). In *Wikipedia.org*. Retrieved November 3, 2014 fromhttp://en.wikipedia.org/wiki/WikiWikiWeb

Wilcox, W. (2009). Digital storytelling: A comparative case study in three nothern California communities (MA Thesis). Davis, CA: University of California Davis. Retrieved from http://www.escholarship.org/uc/item/71w6n7qd

Wiley, D. (2013). *On quality and OER*. Retrieved from http://opencontent.org/blog/archives/2947

Willard, N. (2012). Cyberbullying and the law. In J. Patchin & S. Hinduja (Eds.), *Cyberbullying prevention and response: Expert perspectives* (pp. 36–56). New York: Routledge.

Willett, R., Burn, A. C., Bishop, J., Richards, C., & Marsh, J. (2013). *Children, media and playground cultures: Ethnographic studies of school playtimes*. New York, NY: Palgrave Macmillan. doi:10.1057/9781137318077

Willett, R., Robinson, M., & Marsh, J. (Eds.). (2008). *Play, Creativity and Digital Cultures*. London: Routledge.

Williams, S. (2013). *Fiber broadband: A foundation for social and economic growth*. Retrieved from http://www3.weforum.org/docs/GITR/2013/GITR_Chapter1.5_2013.pdf

Williams, D. (2010). The speaking brain. In D. A. Sousa (Ed.), *Mind, brain, and education* (pp. 85–112). Bloomington, IN: Solution Tree Press.

Williams, D., Caplan, S., & Xiong, L. (2007). Can you hear me now? The impact of voice in an online gaming community. *Human Communication Research*, *33*(4), 427–449. doi:10.1111/j.1468-2958.2007.00306.x

Williams, D., Consalvo, M., Caplan, S., & Yee, N. (2009). Looking for gender: Gender roles and behaviors among online gamers. *Journal of Communication*, *59*(4), 700–725. doi:10.1111/j.1460-2466.2009.01453.x

Williamson, B. (2013). *The future of the curriculum: School knowledge in the digital age*. Cambridge, MA: The MIT Press.

Willis, P. E. (1977). *Learning to labor: How working class kids get working class jobs*. New York: Columbia University Press.

Wingate, V. S., Minney, J. A., & Guadagno, R. E. (2013). Sticks and stones may break your bones, but words will always hurt you: A review of cyberbullying. *Social Influence*, *8*(2-3), 87–106. doi:10.1080/15534510.2012.730491

Wirman, H. (2014). Gender and identity in game-modifying communities. *Simulation & Gaming*, *45*(1), 70–92. doi:10.1177/1046878113519572

Witney, D., & Smallbone, T. (2011). Wiki work: Can using wikis enhance student collaboration for group assignment tasks? *Innovations in Education and Teaching International*, *48*(1), 101–110. doi:10.1080/14703297.2010.543765

Wohlwend, K. (2008). Play as a literacy of possibilities: Expanding meanings in practices, materials, and spaces. *Language Arts*, *86*(2), 127–136.

Wohlwend, K. (in press). Making, remaking, and reimagining the everyday: Play, creativity and popular media. In J. Rowsell & K. Pahl (Eds.), *The Routledge Handbook of Literacy Studies*. London, UK: Routledge.

Wohlwend, K. E. (2007). Friendship meeting or blocking circle? Identities in the laminated spaces of a playground conflict. *Contemporary Issues in Early Childhood*, *8*(1), 73–88. doi:10.2304/ciec.2007.8.1.73

Wohlwend, K. E. (2009). Early adopters: Playing new literacies and pretending new technologies in print-centric classrooms. *Journal of Early Childhood Literacy*, *9*(2), 117–140. doi:10.1177/1468798409105583

Wolf, M. (2014, January 3). Four predictions about podcasting for 2014. *Forbes*. Retrieved from http://www.forbes.com/sites/michaelwolf/2014/01/03/4-predictions-about-podcasting-for-2014/

Wolf, M. (2014). *Proust and the squid: The story and science of the reading brain*. HarperCollins.

Wolfsfeld, G. (2014). *Making Sense of Media and Politics: Five Principles in Political Communication*. Taylor & Francis.

Wolfsfeld, G., Segev, E., & Sheafer, T. (2013). Social Media and the Arab Spring Politics Comes First. *The International Journal of Press/Politics*, *18*(2), 115–137. doi:10.1177/1940161212471716

Wolfson, E. (2014, August 15). *How Lessons From Trayvon Helped Make Ferguson News*. Retrieved January 24, 2015, from http://www.newsweek.com/how-lessons-trayvon-helped-make-ferguson-news-264942

Wong, K. (2014, October 22). Why marketers should put Snapchat on their home screen. *Forbes*. Retrieved from http://www.forbes.com/sites/kylewong/2014/10/22/why-marketers-should-put-snapchat-on-their-homescreen/

Wong-Lo, M., & Bullock, L. M. (2011). Digital aggression: Cyberworld meets school bullies. *Preventing School Failure*, *55*(2), 64–70. doi:10.1080/1045988X.2011.539429

Wong-Lo, M., & Bullock, L. M. (2014). Digital metamorphosis: Examination of the bystander culture in cyberbullying. *Aggression and Violent Behavior*, *19*(4), 418–422. doi:10.1016/j.avb.2014.06.007

Wood, C., Jackson, E., Hart, L., Plester, B., & Wilde, L. (2011). The effect of text messaging on 9- and 10-year-old children's reading, spelling and phonological processing skills. *Journal of Computer Assisted Learning*, *27*(1), 28–36. doi:10.1111/j.1365-2729.2010.00398.x

Wood, C., Kemp, N., & Plester, B. (2013). *Text messaging and literacy: The evidence*. New York: Routledge.

Wood, J. (2009). *Gendered lives: Communication, gender, and culture*. Boston: Wadsworth.

Woods, J. (2005). Digital influencers: Business communicators dare overlook the power of blogs? *Communication World*, *22*, 26-30. Retrieved from http://www.iabc.com/cw/

Wooley, A. W., Chabris, C. F., Pentland, A., Hashmi, N., & Malone, T. W. (2010). Evidence for a collective intelligence factor in the performance of human groups. *Science*, *330*(6004), 686–688. doi:10.1126/science.1193147 PMID:20929725

Woollaston, V., & Prigg, M. (2014). Rise of the #selfielapse: Instagram adds a new feature to its Hyperlapse app that lets users film themselves more easily. *MailOne*. Retrieved from http://www.dailymail.co.uk/sciencetech/article-2770554/Rise-selfielapse-Instagram-adds-new-feature-Hyperlapse-app-lets-users-film-easily.html

Woo, M. M., Chu, S., & Li, X. (2013). Peer-feedback and revision process in a wiki mediated collaborative writing. *Educational Technology Research and Development*, *61*(2), 279–309. doi:10.1007/s11423-012-9285-y

Workshop, W. (n.d.). *The results are in: Globaloria improves teaching and learning across the country.* Retrieved from http://globaloria.com/docs/Globaloria_Research_Overview.pdf

Wright, M. F. (2013). The relationship between young adults' beliefs about anonymity and subsequent cyber aggression. *Cyberpsychology, Behavior, and Social Networking*, *16*(12), 858–862. doi:10.1089/cyber.2013.0009 PMID:23849002

Wright, S., & Parchoma, G. (2011). Technologies for learning? An actor-network theory critique of "affordances" in research on mobile learning. *Research in Learning Technology*, *19*(3), 247–258. doi:10.1080/21567069.2011.624168

Wright, V. H., & Burnham, J. J. (2012). Cyberbullying prevention: The development of virtual scenarios for counselors in middle schools. *Professional Counselor: Research & Practice*, *2*(2), 169–177. doi:10.15241/vhw.2.2.169

Wu, M. L., & Richards, K. (2011). Facilitating computational thinking through game design. In M. Chang, W.-Y. Hwang, M.-P. Chen, & W. Müller (Eds.), *Edutainment technologies. Educational games and virtual reality/augmented reality applications* (pp. 220–227). New York: Springer Berlin Heidelberg.

Wu, W. H., Wu, Y. C. J., Chen, C. Y., Kao, H. Y., Lin, C. H., & Huang, S. H. (2012). Review of trends from mobile learning studies: A meta-analysis. *Computers & Education*, *59*(2), 817–827. doi:10.1016/j.compedu.2012.03.016

Wyatt-Smith, C., & Elkins, J. (2008). Multimodal reading and comprehension in online environments. In J. Coiro, M. Knobel, C. Lankshear, & D. J. Leu (Eds.), *Handbook of research on new literacies* (pp. 899–940). New York: Taylor and Francis Group.

Wyld, D. C. (2007). *The blogging revolution: Government in the age of Web 2.0.* IBM Center for the Business of Government.

Wysocki, A. & Lynch. (2012). *Design, compose, advocate.* New York: Longman.

Xu, H., Oh, L., & Teo, H. (2009). Perceived effectiveness of text vs. multimedia location-based advertising messaging. *International Journal of Mobile Communications*, *7*(2), 154–177. doi:10.1504/IJMC.2009.022440

Yang, G., Chen, N.-S., Erkki Sutinen, K., Anderson, T., & Wen, D. (2013). The effectiveness of automatic text summarization in mobile learning contexts. *Computers & Education*, *68*, 233–243. doi:10.1016/j.compedu.2013.05.012

Yang, Y.-T., & Wu, W.-C. (2012). Digital storytelling for enhancing student academic achievement, critical thinking, and learning motivation: A year-long experimental study. *Computers & Education*, *59*(2), 339–352. doi:10.1016/j.compedu.2011.12.012

Yates, D., Wagner, C., & Majchrzak, A. (2010). Factors affecting shapers of organizationsl wikis. *Journal of the American Society for Information Science and Technology*, *61*(3), 543–554. doi:10.1002/asi.21266

Yates, S., & Littleton, K. (2001). Understanding computer game cultures: A situated approach. In E. Green & A. Adam (Eds.), *Virtual gender: Technology, consumption, and identity* (pp. 103–123). London: Routledge.

Ybarra, M. L., Boyd, D., Korchmaros, J. D., & Oppenheim, J. K. (2012). Defining and measuring cyberbullying within the larger context of bullying victimization. *The Journal of Adolescent Health*, *51*(1), 53–58. doi:10.1016/j.jadohealth.2011.12.031 PMID:22727077

Ybarra, M. L., Espelage, D. L., & Mitchell, K. J. (2014). Differentiating youth who are bullied from other victims of peer-aggression: The importance of differential power and repetition. *The Journal of Adolescent Health*, *55*(2), 293–300. doi:10.1016/j.jadohealth.2014.02.009 PMID:24726463

Ybarra, M. L., Mitchell, K. J., & Espelage, D. (2012). Comparisons of bully and unwanted sexual experiences online and offline among a national sample of youth. In Ö. Özdemir (Ed.), *Complementary pediatrics* (pp. 203–216). Rijeka, Croatia: InTech.

Yee, A. (2011, March 14). *Where does the west stand on global freedom of expression?* Retrieved September 26, 2014, from https://www.opendemocracy.net/andy-yee/where-does-west-stand-on-global-freedom-of-expression

Yee, N. (2004). *Daedalus Gateway: The Psychology of MMORPGs.* Retrieved October, 27, 2009 from http://www.nickyee.com/daedalus/gateway_genderbend.html

Yee, N. (2006). The demographics, motivations and derived experiences of users of massively-multiuser online graphical environments. *Presence (Cambridge, Mass.), 15*(3), 309–329. doi:10.1162/pres.15.3.309

Yodle. (2013). *Yodle's First Annual Small Business Sentiment Survey.* Retrieved from http://www.yodle.net/files/smb-sentiment-report.pdf

yokom. (2005, January 16). *Angelo Sotira, interviewed* [deviantART blog post]. Retrieved from http://yokom.deviantart.com/art/Angelo-Sotira-Interviewed-14204533

York, J. (2010, April 8). *On Facebook Deactivations.* Retrieved from http://jilliancyork.com/2010/04/08/on-facebook-deactivations/

Young, A. L., & Quan-Haase, A. (2009). *Information revelation and internet privacy concerns on social network sites: A case study of Facebook.* Retrieved March 5, 2011, from http://www.iisi.de/fileadmin/IISI/upload/2009/p265.pdf

Young, K. (2008). Internet sex addiction: Risk factors, stages of development, and treatment. *The American Behavioral Scientist, 52*(1), 21–37. doi:10.1177/0002764208321339

Young, K., Griffin-Shelley, E., Cooper, A., O'Mara, J., & Buchanan, J. (2000). Online infidelity: A new dimension in couple relationships with implications for evaluation and treatment. *Sexual Addiction & Compulsivity, 7*(1-2), 59–74. doi:10.1080/10720160008400207

YouTube & News. (2012, July 16) Retrieved from http://www.journalism.org/2012/07/16/youtube-news/

YouTube Statistics. (n.d.). Retrieved from http://www.youtube.com/t/press_statistics

YouTube. (n.d.). *Statistics.* Retrieved October 29, 2014 from https://www.youtube.com/yt/press/statistics.html

Yu, P. K. (2002). *Terrorism and the global digital divide: Why bridging the divide is even more important after September 11.* Retrieved from http://writ.news.findlaw.com/commentary/20020211_yu.html

Yu, C., Lee, S. J., & Ewing, C. (2015). Mobile learning: Trends, issues, and challenges in teaching and learning. In J. Keengwe & M. Maxfield (Eds.), *Advancing higher education with mobile learning technologies: Cases, trends, and inquiry-based methods* (pp. 60–87). Hershey, PA: Information Science Reference; doi:10.4018/978-1-4666-6284-1.ch004

Yuen, S., Yaoyuneyong, G., & Johnson, E. (2011). Augmented reality: An overview and five directions for AR in education. *Journal of Educational Technology Development and Exchange, 4*(1), 119–140.

Zacharias, U., & Arthurs, J. (2008). The new architectures of intimacy? Social networking sites and genders. *Feminist Media Studies, 8*, 197–202. doi:10.1080/14680770801980612

Zambelich, A. (2014). Evernote's savvy plan to join the wearables race. *Wired.* Retrieved from http://www.wired.com/2014/07/evernotes-savvy-plan-to-join-the-wearables-race/

Zammit, K. (2008). *Under construction: A world without walls.* Paper presented at the ASLA Online III Virtual Conference - Digital literacy strand – Keynote paper. Retrieved from http://www.asla.org.au/pd/online2008/program.htm

Zammit, K. (2010b). *Working with wikis: Collaborative writing in the 21st Century.* Paper presented at the Key Competencies in the Knowledge Society: IFIP Advances in Information and Communication Technology, Brisbane, Australia.

Zammit, K. (2010a). New Learning Environments Framework: Integrating multiliteracies into the curriculum. *Pedagogies, 5*(4), 325–337. doi:10.1080/1554480X.2010.509479

Zammit, K. (2011). Connecting multiliteracies and engagement of students from low socio-economic backgrounds: Using Bernstein's pedagogic discourse as a bridge. *Language and Education, 25*(3), 203–220. doi:10.1080/09500782.2011.560945

Zammit, K. (2015). Extending students' semiotic understandings: Learning about and creating multimodal texts. In P. Trifonas (Ed.), *International Handbook of Semiotics*. London: Springer. doi:10.1007/978-94-017-9404-6_62

Zelezny-Green. (2013, February13). Boosting mobile learning potential for women and girls: Lingering considerations. *E-learning Africa*. Retrieved from http://www.elearning-africa.com/eLA_Newsportal/boosting-mobile-learning-potential-for-women-and-girls-in-africa-lingering-considerations/

Zetlin, M. (2014). Five things to consider when creating a wearables policy. *CIO*. Retrieved from http://www.cio.com/article/2369944/consumer-technology/five-things-to-consider-when-creating-a-wearables-policy.html

Zhao, S. Y., Grasmucks, S., & Martina, J. (2008). Identity construction of Facebook: Digital empowerment in anchored relationships. *Computers in Human Behavior*, *24*(5), 1816–1836. doi:10.1016/j.chb.2008.02.012

Zhu, E., Hadadgar, A., Masiello, I., & Zary, N. (2014). *Augmented reality in healthcare education: An integrative review. PeerJ.* doi:10.7717/peerj.469

Zickuhr, K. (2010, December 16). Generations 2010. *Pew Internet Research Project*. Retrieved from http://www.pewinternet.org/~/media//Files/Reports/2010/PIP_Generations_and_Tech10

Zickuhr, K. (2013). Who's not online and why. Washington, DC: Pew Internet and American Life Project. Retrieved from http://www.pewinternet.org/2013/09/25/whos-not-online-and-why/

Zickuhr, K., & Smith, A. (2012). *Digital differences*. Washington, DC: Pew Research Internet Project. Retrieved May 31, 2014 from http://www.pewinternet.org/2012/04/13/digital-differences/

Ziliani, C., & Bellini, S. (2003). From loyalty cards to micro-marketing strategies: Where is Europe's retail industry heading? *Journal of Targeting, Measurement and Analysis for Marketing, 12*(3), 281-289. Retrieved from http://www.palgrave-journals.com/jt/journal/v12/n3/pdf/5740115a.pdf

Zimmerman, E. (2009). Game design as a model for literacy in the twenty-first century. In B. Perron & M. J. P. Wolf (Eds.), *The video game theory reader 2* (pp. 23–32). New York, NY: Taylor & Francis.

Zuckerman, E. (2014), New media, new civics? *Policy & Internet, 6*(2), 151–168. Retrieved from http://onlinelibrary.wiley.com/doi/10.1002/1944-2866.POI360/abstract

Zuckerman, E. (2013). *Rewire*. New York: W. W. Norton & Company.

Zweig, J. M., Lachman, P., Yahner, J., & Dank, M. (2013). Correlates of cyber dating abuse among teens. *Journal of Youth and Adolescence, 43*(8), 1306–1321. doi:10.1007/s10964-013-0047-x PMID:24198083

Zysman, J., Feldman, S., Murray, J., Nielsen, N. C., & Kushida, K. E. (2010). Services with everything: The ICT-enabled digital transformation of services. *BRIE Working Paper, 187a*. Retrieved from http://brie.berkeley.edu/publications/WP_187a%20Services...%20revised%206.16.11.pdf

About the Contributors

Barbara J. Guzzetti is a Professor at Arizona State University in the New College of Interdisciplinary Arts and Sciences, Humanities Arts & Cultural Studies, English Department. She is also an Affiliated Faculty member in the Mary Lou Fulton Teachers College, Educational Leadership and Innovation, and an Affiliated Faculty member in the School for Social Transformation, Women's and Gender Studies. Her research and teaching focus on new media, particularly participatory or Do-It-Yourself (DIY) media, and youth culture and gender issues in new media. She is co-author of the Teachers College Press book, *DIY Media in the Classroom: New Literacies across Content Areas*. Her publications on new media have appeared in journals such as *E-Learning and Digital Media*; the *Reading Research Quarterly*, *Research in in the Teaching of English* and the *Journal of Adolescent and Adult Literacy*.

Mellinee Lesley is a professor in the Language, Diversity & Literacy Studies program in the Department of Curriculum & Instruction at Texas Tech University and the Associate Dean for Graduate Education and Research in the College of Education. Her research is focused on the literacy practices of marginalized adolescent and adult learners, adolescents' use of new media, and applications of new media for content area literacy instruction. Her research on these topics has appeared in journals such as *Literacy Research and Instruction* and *The Journal of Adolescent & Adult Literacy* as well as her book *Invisible Girls: At-Risk Adolescent Girls' Writing Within and Beyond School*.

* * *

Arwa Alfayez is a Ph.D. student in Literacy Education at the University of Missouri. She earned her Bachelor degree in English Education from University of Hail, Saudi Arabia. In 2010, she moved with her husband to the US to continue her studies. She earned her masters degree in Reading Education from University of Missouri. She is interested in reading comprehension, visual literacy and multicultural literature. She plans to become a literacy educator for Saudi college students and influence literacy policies in Saudi Arabia that address curriculum and reading problems.

Donna E. Alvermann is a professor in language and literacy education at The University of Georgia. She studies young people's digital literacies and uses of popular media both in- and out-of-school. Join her and Crystal Beach at www.becoming3lectric.com to see how their interests merge.

Chrissie Arnold is an MA Candidate in the Department of Educational Studies at the University of British Columbia. Her research is focused on critical approaches to global citizenship education and human rights. She is also the Education Manager at West Coast LEAF in Vancouver, an organization that works to advance women's equality through the law. Through this role, she has worked extensively on the issue of cyber misogyny, attending to the ways women are disproportionately subject to violence in online spaces.

Elizabeth (Betsy) Baker is a professor of Literacy Studies at the University of Missouri where she specializes in the integration of literacy and technology and new literacies from sociocultural and sociocognitive perspectives. Her research is published in an array of journals and books. She has served as Editor of The New Literacies: Multiple Perspectives on Research and Practice, Co-editor of Literacy Research: Theory, Method, and Practice, and Executive Producer and Host of the podcast Voice of Literacy (voiceofliteracy.org). Before becoming a professor, Dr. Baker was an elementary teacher in South Carolina.

Crystal L. Beach is a current high school English teacher and a language and literacy education doctoral student at The University of Georgia. She has presented numerous times at national and local conferences on new literacies, multimodalities, and technologies in the English classroom.

Richard Beach is Professor Emeritus of English Education at the University of Minnesota. He is author or co-author of 20 books, including Understanding and Creating Digital Texts: An Activity-Based Approach (http://digitalwriting.pbworks.com) and Using Apps for Learning Across the Curriculum: A Literacy-Based Framework and Guide (http://usingipads.pbworks.com). He has published articles in Journal of Adolescent & Adult Literacy, Journal of Research in Educational Computing, Reading Research Quarterly, and Educational Researcher. He served as organizing editor for the annual Annotated Bibliography of Research for Research in the Teaching of English from 2003-2012 and as President of the Literacy Research Association in 2013. He received the 2009 Computers in Reading Research Award from The Technology in Literacy Education Special Interest Group of the International Reading Association.

Thomas W. Bean, Ph.D., is a Professor of Literacy and Reading Graduate Program Director in the Teaching and Learning Department, Darden College of Education, at Old Dominion University in Norfolk, Virginia. Tom earned his Ph.D. at Arizona State University and is considered a leading scholar in content area literacy and the infusion of multicultural and global young adult literature in the classroom. His work has been published in the ALAN Review, Reading Research Quarterly, and the Journal of Adolescent & Adult Literacy. Along with Co-Author Dr. Judith Dunkerly-Bean, he served as Co-Editor of the International Reading Association's Journal of Adolescent & Adult Literacy. Tom is senior author of the widely used text, Content Area Literacy: An Integrated Approach (10th ed.).

George L. Boggs is an assistant professor of English education at Florida State University. His research focuses on the economic, political, and social importance of literacies. A recent exploration of these issues is "Where everything I am came from: George Boggs at TEDxFSU," https://www.youtube.com/watch?v=9EZ3yeRYMCA.

Jill Castek is the Director of the Literacy, Language, and Technology Research Group at Portland State University. She is the principal investigator on two Institute for Museum and Library Services (IMLS) grants. One is focused on digital literacy acquisition among vulnerable adult learners and the second addresses digital equity in libraries by examining patrons' problem solving in technology rich environments. Jill's work also appears in the Journal of Adolescent and Adult Literacy (JAAL), Educational Forum, The Journal of Education, The Reading Teacher, and Reading and Writing Quarterly, among other journals. Castek received a PhD from the University of Connecticut and was a Neag fellow with the New Literacies Research Lab. She is a founding member and regular contributor to the Literacy Beat blog.

Terry Cottrell is Chief Information Officer at the University of St. Francis in Joliet, Illinois. Dr. Cottrell has served on the Board of Directors for the Reaching Across Illinois Library System, the Consortium of Research and Academic Libraries in Illinois, the Illinois Library Association and the Plainfield, IL Public Library District. His most recent publications and presentations cover: library leadership and finance, hands-free augmented reality tools, copyright, instructional technology history, senior citizen access to academic libraries, mobile device deployment and management, effective use of library space with small budgets, academic library influence in surrounding communities, and entry-level job skills for new librarians. Dr. Cottrell holds Ed. D., M.S. and M.B.A. degrees, and currently teaches research methods and writing at the University of St. Francis. He has taught various management and business courses at Colorado State University-Global Campus based in Greenwood Village, Colorado, and Computers for Educators and Google for Education at Northern Illinois University.

Helen Crompton is an Assistant Professor of Instructional Technology at Old Dominion University. She works with graduate students teaching about the effective incorporation of technology in the educational setting. Her research involves the implementation of mobile learning initiatives in K-12 curriculum with a particular connection to Science, Technology, Engineering, and Mathematics (STEM). This connected interest comes from holding a PhD in Educational Technology and Mathematics.

Alan Davis is a Professor of Urban Ecologies and Research Methodology in the School of Human Development at the University of Colorado Denver. His research focuses on the relationship of adolescents and schooling, especially marginalized youth, and includes social uses of technology, identity development, development of aspirations and goals, and high school dropout.

Julie Delello is a Faculty Fellow for Teaching Excellence and an Assistant Professor in the School of Education at The University of Texas at Tyler. She received her PhD in Curriculum and Instruction with a specialization in science and technology from Texas A&M University. Julie has worked in K-12 education for over 20 years as a teacher and as an administrator. Julie has authored a number of articles on the use of technologies in higher education. Her areas of focus include new visual media, virtual science museums, social media platforms, and ePortfolios for authentic learning. She helped to design virtual science museums in conjunction with The Computer Network Information Center in Beijing, China. In addition, she has won several grants and teaching awards including a National Science Foundation Grant for The East Asia and Pacific Summer Institutes, the Golden Apple Educator Award, the 2012 University of Texas at Tyler-Kappa Delta Pi Teacher of the Year award, and the 2014 Jack and Dorothy Fay White Fellowship for Teaching Excellence.

Jill Denner is a Senior Research Scientist at Education, Training, Research, a non-profit organization in California. Her research focuses on increasing diversity in computing fields. She has a PhD in Developmental Psychology.

Patricia Dickenson is Lead Faculty of Teacher Education at National University in San Jose. She completed her doctoral work at the University of Southern California in Educational Psychology. Her research focuses on the sociocultural aspects of motivation, engagement, and instruction, within mathematics, technology and standard-based teaching practices of Latino English learners. Dr. Dickenson began teaching for the Los Angeles Unified School District. She has taught elementary, middle and high school. In addition to classroom teaching Dr. Dickenson was a Mathematics Coach. She believes strongly in the use of alternative assessments such as performance based tasks, project-based learning and authentic assessment to measure students knowledge and skills. Dr. Dickenson has worked as a teacher trainer and consultant for Princeton Review and Harcourt Publishing. She has taught courses in Teacher Education at University of California Santa Cruz, University of Southern California and University of Phoenix. Dr. Dickenson Website: www.doctorofed.com Twitter: @TeacherTechPrep.

Dane Marco Di Cesare (PhD, 2015, University at Buffalo) is an adjunct professor at Brock University and the University at Buffalo. His research interests involve students with disabilities and digital technology. His most recent research examined multimodal authoring practices for secondary students with high incidence disabilities.

Judith Dunkerly-Bean, Ph.D., is an Assistant Professor of Literacy and Graduate Program Director for PK-6 Education in the Department of Teaching and Learning at Old Dominion University. Her work has been published in the Journal of Adolescent and Adult Literacy, Comparative Issues in Education and Language and Literacy, as well as in several edited volumes. Along with Dr. Tom Bean, she is the co-author of Teaching Young Adult Literature: Developing Students as World Citizens. Judith's research utilizes transnational feminist and cosmopolitan theory to explore the intersection of critical literacy, social justice and human rights especially for women and girls.

Leslie Foley is an instructor in the College of Education at Grand Canyon University. Her research focuses on the influence of new literacies practices on elementary students' identity, motivation, and literacy skills.

Elisabeth R. Gee is the Delbert & Jewell Lewis Chair in Reading & Literacy and Associate Director in the Center for Games & Impact at Mary Lou Fulton Teachers College, Arizona State University.

Martin H. Hall is Lecturer in Educational Psychology at Charles Sturt University in Australia, a Chartered Member of the British Psychological Society, and a member of Division 15 of the American Psychological Association (APA) (Educational Psychology). Dr Hall is also a member of the Research Institute for Professional Practice, Learning and Education (RIPPLE). His research interests include cognitive and sociological variables that affect academic achievement in both online and face-to-face environments, and past performance as predictors of future performance and as a mediator of academic outcomes.

Debra Harwood is an Associate Professor at Brock University's Faculty of Education where she is the program advisor for the Bachelor of Early Childhood Education program. She has written several articles focused on varied aspects of early childhood education curriculum and pedagogy. Her current research interests include children's digital play, professionalism in ECE, and inquiry based pedagogies.

Teri Holbrook, Ph.D., is an associate professor of literacy and language arts in the Department of Early Childhood and Elementary Education at Georgia State University. Her work focuses on the effects of arts-infused multimodal affordances of digital technology on dominant notions of qualitative inquiry, academic and literary writing, and literacy education. She is co-editor of the journal Language Arts and the book New Methods of Literacy Research. Her work has appeared in Children's Literature in Education, Visual Arts Research, Qualitative Inquiry, Frontiers, Journal of Adolescent and Adult Literacy, and LRA Yearbook.

Melanie Hundley, Ph. D., is an associate professor of the practice of Literacy, Language, and Culture in the Department of Teaching and Learning at Vanderbilt University's Peabody College of Education and Human Development. Her work focuses on the digital and multimodal composing practices of preservice teachers, transmedia storytelling, digital and multimodal young adult literature. Her work has appeared in the Journal of Adolescent and Adult Literacy, The ALAN Review, and The English Record.

Gloria E. Jacobs is a research associate with the Literacy, Language and Technology Group at Portland State University in Portland, Oregon. She earned her doctorate at the University of Rochester, New York. She researches digital technologies and digital literacy practices among youth and vulnerable adults.

Brian Jones is an artist, scholar, and art educator. He holds a PhD in curriculum and instruction specializing in art education from Arizona State University. He researches and writes on topics relating to youth artists and social technologies including the use of sandbox virtual worlds in art education and the social media platform deviantART.com. His interdisciplinary work draws from New Literacies Studies and contemporary art education theories. Brian has over twenty years of k-12 and post-secondary teaching experience. He lives in the Sonora Desert in Arizona with his beloved K-9 companion – Java.

Deirdre M. Kelly is Professor in the Department of Educational Studies at the University of British Columbia. She is the author of Last Chance High: How Girls and Boys Drop In and Out of Alternative Schools (Yale University Press) and Pregnant with Meaning: Teen Mothers and the Politics of Inclusive Schooling (Peter Lang) and the co-author of "Girl Power": Girls Reinventing Girlhood (Peter Lang, with Dawn Currie & Shauna Pomerantz). Her research interests include teaching for social justice and democracy, gender and youth studies, critical social literacy, and news and entertainment media as public policy pedagogy.

Amir Manzoor, Bahria University, Management Sciences (LUMS), and an MBA from Bangor University, United Kingdom. He has many years of diverse professional and teaching experience working at many renowned national and internal organizations and higher education institutions. His research interests include electronic commerce and technology applications in business. He is a member of Chartered Banker Institute of UK and Project Management Institute, USA.

Jacob Martinez is the founder and executive director of the Digital NEST, a high-tech space for youth.

Renee Smith McInnish is a doctoral student in Learning, Teaching, and Curriculum at the University of Missouri. She earned her Bachelor of Science degree in Family and Consumer Sciences Education from the University of Montevallo in 1994. She earned her Master of Education as a Reading Specialist in 2002 from Auburn University of Montgomery. Renee has been passionate about education for over twenty years. She loves to help others become life-long readers and writers. Her research focus is helping military families help their children to be successful in literacy. Renee is especially interested in dialogic reading and how that helps children to develop their vocabularies and comprehension of text. She also enjoys helping children and adolescents to develop their craft of writing. Since 1994, Renee has worked with hundreds of children ages two to 18.

Rochell R. McWhorter is an Assistant Professor of Human Resource Development in the College of Business and Technology at The University of Texas at Tyler. She received her Ph.D. degree in Human Resource Development from Texas A&M University. She has over 20 years' experience in industry and K-12 education. Rochell has edited and authored a number of journal articles and scholarly resources on technology-facilitated learning in higher education. Her scholarly publications include topics such as ePortfolios as facilitators of learning and professional branding, virtual human resource development, visual social media, scenario planning for leadership development, and virtual learning environments for real-time collaboration. She has been a recipient of numerous teaching awards including the Silvius-Wolansky Outstanding Young Teacher Educator Award from the Association for Career and Technical Education.

Guy Merchant, Sheffield Hallam University, Professor of Literacy in Education at the Sheffield Institute of Education (UK).

Jessica Olin is the Director of the Robert H. Parker Library at Wesley College. Her professional interests include incorporating popular reading materials into traditional academic library collections, building communities at liberal arts college libraries, and bridging the gap between library science graduate programs and professional practice. In her limited spare time, she likes to cross-stitch, watch Doctor Who, spend time with her geriatric cat, and read lots of comic books.

Kylie Peppler is an associate professor of learning sciences in the School of Education at Indiana University Bloomington. An artist by training, she engages in research that focuses on the intersection of arts, new media, computation, and informal learning. She is coeditor of The Computer Clubhouse: Constructionism and Creativity in Youth Communities (Teachers College Press, 2009) and Textile Messages: Dispatches from the World of E-Textiles and Education (Peter Lang Publishing, 2013). Peppler received a PhD in education from the University of California, Los Angeles.

Jennifer Rowsell is Professor and Canada Research Chair in Multiliteracies at Brock University's Faculty of Education where she directs the Centre for Multiliteracies and the Brock University Learning Lab. She has co-written and written several books in the areas of New Literacy Studies, multimodality, and multiliteracies. Her current research interests include children's digital and immersive worlds; adopting and applying multimodal epistemologies with adolescents and teenagers; and ecological work in communities examining everyday literacy practices.

Eliane Rubinstein-Avila is a professor in the Language, Reading & Culture Program, in the department of Teaching, Learning and Sociocultural Studies, University of Arizona. She teaches courses on bilingualism and the acquisition of English as an additional language (undergraduate level), and qualitative approaches to research in education (at the doctoral level). She has published extensively in a variety of academic journals. Dr. R-A, as she is addressed locally, is multilingual and has a passion for travel.

Aurora Sartori is a doctoral student and Paul D. Coverdell Peace Corps Fellow in the Department of Teaching, Learning and Sociocultural Studies, College of Education, University of Arizona. Ms. Sartori's Peace Corps service in northern Namibia at a rural school inspired her research interests, which include educational policy, social justice, and new literacies.

Nicholas Temple (PhD, 2011, North Carolina State University) serves as Instructor in Communication, Central Washington University. His research examines online rhetoric surrounding the U. S. environmental movement as well as additional online messages. He teaches a slate of courses that includes Environmental Communication, Communication Ethics, Persuasion, and Rhetorical Theory.

Kelly Tran is a doctoral student in the Learning, Literacies, and Technologies program at Mary Lou Fulton Teachers College, Arizona State University.

Megan McDonald Van Deventer is a graduate student in Literacy Education at the University of Minnesota, Twin Cites, with an interest in Children's and Young Adult Literature and adolescent literacy.

Lynne M. Webb (PhD, University of Oregon, 1980) is Professor of Communication Arts, Florida International University. Her work on interpersonal communication and social media has appeared in numerous national and international journals including Computers in Human Behavior and the International Journal of Social Research and Methodology as well as in prestigious edited volumes including Producing Theory: The Intersection of Audiences and Production in a Digital World (Peter Lang, 2012) and Advancing Research Methods with New Technologies (IGI Global, 2013). She co-edited Computer-Mediated Communication in Personal Relationships (Peter Lang Publishing, 2011).

Katina Zammit is Director of Academic Program (Primary) and a Senior Lecturer in the School of Education at Western Sydney University. Her research interests revolve around pedagogies and leadership for social justice and change. Katina, specifically, focuses on engagement of students in learning multiple literacies mediated through the use of information and communication technology. Katina has been a co-chief investigator on a number of projects, including The New Learning Environments Curriculum and Pedagogy Framework, Engaging Rural Boys in the Middle Years of Schools, and Teaching and Leading for Australian Schools: A Review of the Literature. She recently completed a project to enhance the experience of students from refugee backgrounds at university.

Index

Printed in the United States
By Bookmasters